D1116963

3 0700 10922 9947

China and the
Global Business
Revolution

Also by Peter Nolan

China's Economic Reforms in the 1980s: The Costs and Benefits of Incrementalism (editor with Fan Qimiao)

Growth Processes and Distributional Change in a South Chinese Province: The Case of Guangdong

Inequality: India and China Compared, 1950–1970 (with T. J. Byres)

Market Forces in China: Competition and Small Business – The Wenzhou Debate (editor with Dong Fureng)

Re-Thinking Socialist Economics (editor with Suzy Paine)

State and Market in the Chinese Economy

The Chinese Economy and its Future (editor with Dong Fureng)

The Political Economy of Collective Farms: An Analysis of China's Post-Mao Rural Economic Reforms

The Transformation of the Communist Economies (editor with Ha-Joon Chang)

Indigenous Large Firms in China's Economic Reforms: The Case of Shougang Iron and Steel Corporation

Coca-Cola and the Global Business Revolution: A Study with Special Reference to the EU

Strategic Restructuring (Zhanlue Chongzu) (with Wang Xiaoqiang)

China and the Global Economy

China and the Global Business Revolution

Peter Nolan

Sinyi Professor of Chinese Management
The Judge Institute of Management Studies
University of Cambridge, and
Fellow, Jesus College, University of Cambridge

palgrave

First published 2001 by
PALGRAVE
Houndmills, Basingstoke, Hampshire RG21 6XS and
175 Fifth Avenue, New York, N. Y. 10010
Companies and representatives throughout the world

PALGRAVE is the new global academic imprint of
St. Martin's Press LLC Scholarly and Reference Division and
Palgrave Publishers Ltd (formerly Macmillan Press Ltd).

ISBN 0–333–80119–9

This book is printed on paper suitable for recycling and
made from fully managed and sustained forest sources.

A catalogue record for this book is available
from the British Library.

Library of Congress Cataloging-in-Publication Data

Nolan, Peter, 1949–
        China and the global business revolution/Peter Nolan.
        p. cm.
        Includes bibliographical references and index.
        ISBN 0–333–80119–9
        1. Business enterprises–China. 2. Industries–China. I. Title.
        HD4318 .N65 2001
        338.0951–dc21

10   9   8   7   6   5   4   3
10 09 08 07 06 05 04 03

Printed and bound in Great Britain by
Antony Rowe Ltd, Chippenham, Wiltshire

In memory of my mother and father
Barbara and Charles

The Chinese have always been a great courageous and industrious nation;
it is only in modern times that they have fallen behind. And that was
entirely due to oppression and exploitation by foreign imperialism and
domestic reactionary governments ... Ours will no longer be a nation
subject to insult and humiliation. We have stood up.
(Mao Zedong, 1949)

(Speech on the founding of the People's Republic of China:
The Chinese people have stood up)

Contents

List of Figures   *xii*

List of Tables   *xiii*

Foreword by Wang Xiaoqiang   *xxi*

Preface   *xxiii*

List of Abbreviations and Acronyms   *xxvii*

1 Large Firms and Economic Development   *1*

Introduction *2* • Competition, Small Firms and Economic
Development: The Neo-Classical View *2* • Large Firms and
Economic Development: The Unorthodox View *8* •
Conclusion *24*

2 The Challenge of the Global Business Revolution   *27*

Introduction *27* • Drivers of the Big Business Revolution *28* •
Competitive Advantage *33* • Industrial Concentration *37* • The
External Firm: An Ever-Larger Sphere of Co-ordination and
Planning? *39* • Inequality in the Regional Distribution of Firms
that Lead the Global Big Business Revolution *46* • Revolutionary
Change in Business Systems Outside the USA *51* • Conclusion *61*

3 Policies to Build National Champions: China's 'National
Team' of Enterprise Groups   *67*
Dylan Sutherland

Introduction *67* • Strategy and Policy: 'Grasp the Large' *69* •
Origins of the National Team's Development *72* • The National
Team *76* • Pillar Industries and an Evolving Industrial
Policy *83* • Policies Promoting Institutional Change in the Trial
Business Groups *87* • Implementing the Policies *91* • Direct Support
Measures *95* • Conclusion *98* • Appendices *100*

4 Aerospace   *141*

International Trends in the Aerospace Industry *141* • China's
Aviation Industry *184* • Conclusion *231*

5 Pharmaceuticals   *241*

Introduction *241* • Changes in the Global Pharmaceutical
Industry *242* • Commercialization of the PLA *271* • Growth
of the Chinese Pharmaceutical Industry *277* • Sanjiu *289* •
Conclusion *320*

6 Power Equipment   *327*

Introduction *327* • Main features of the Power Equipment
Industry World-Wide *328* • The Power Generating Equipment
Industry in China *339* • Harbin Power Equipment Company: The
Competitive Struggle *363* • Conclusion *392*

7 Oil and Petrochemicals   *401*

The Global Setting *401* • The Revolution in the Chinese
Oil and Gas Sector *428* • Conclusion *491*

8 Autos and Auto Components   *501*

Introduction *501* • The Global Context *502* • China's
Automobile and Vehicle Components Industry *536* •
Yuchai *548* • Conclusion *582*

9 Steel   587

Introduction *587* • The Global Iron and Steel Industry *588*
• China's Iron and Steel Industry *622* • Shougang under the
Contract System *643* • Shougang since the Contract
System *683* • Prospects *693*

10 Coal   *695*

The Global View *695* • The Chinese Coal Industry *713*
• Shenhua *734* • Conclusion *756*

11 The Third Technological Revolution   *761*

Introduction *762* • Obstacles for Firms Based in Developing
Countries *763* • The Battle for the Chinese Market *790* •
Conclusion *810*

12 The Challenges Facing China's Financial Services Industry 813
Wu Qing

Introduction *813* • New Trends in Financial Services *814* •
Challenges for China's Banks after WTO Entry *825* •
Conclusion *837*

13 The Response 839

Introduction *839* • Key Issues in the Construction of Large,
Internationally Competitive Firms in China *840* •
Strengthening China's Industrial Policy? *857* • China Joins the
WTO: Abandoning Industrial Policy? *864* • Can Large Chinese
Firms Compete on the Global Level Playing Field? *876* •
Conclusion (i): China Observes the Agreement *892* •
Conclusion (ii): Implications for International Relations of
China's Failure to Observe the Agreement *895*

14 The Long-Term View 897

The Past *898* • China Enters the WTO: The Shock of
Defeat? *916* • China Enters the WTO: An Alternative
Outcome? *925*

Afterword   *935*

Notes   *937*

Bibliography   *959*

Index   *976*

List of Figures

4-1	Structure of AVIC, 1997	*185*
4-2	Long-term investment by Chengdu Aero-engine Company in subsidiary companies	*223*
4-3	The business structure of CATIC Shenzhen	*224*
4-4	The multi-tiered business structure of AVIC	*225*
5-1	China's military–industrial commercial complex	*273*
5-2	The organizational structure of Sanjiu Enterprise Group	*317*
6-1	The organizational structure of the State Power Corporation of China	*344*
6-2	The ownership structure of Harbin Power Equipment Company, October 1994	*366*
7-1	China's petroleum capabilities: Sinopec Group, 1998	*469*
7-2	China's petroleum capabilities: CNPC Group, 1998	*470*
7-3	Provisional structure of CNPC prior to flotation	*475*
8-1	The ownership structure of China Yuchai International Ltd, immediately following the initial public offering in New York, 1994	*574*
9-1	The corporate structure of Shougang Group, 1998	*647*
10-1	Map of the location of the main communication links of the Shenua Coal Company	*732*

List of Tables

1-1   Net share of manufacturing output of the top 100 firms, 1909–63   *14*

1-2   Large firms from the Four Little Tigers, 1999   *21*

2-1   Relative growth of national output and international trade, 1980–98   *29*

2-2   FDI inflows, 1984–98   *30*

2-3   Share of foreign production in total production of manufacturing firms in Japan, Germany and the USA, 1986 and 1995   *31*

2-4   Sustainability of competitive edge of different branded consumer goods companies   *35*

2-5   R & D expenditure in the USA, 1994   *36*

2-6   Global oligopoly in the business revolution   *40*

2-7   Dominance of firms based in high-income countries of the global big business revolution, 1997   *47*

2-8   Top 300 companies, by R & D expenditure, 1997   *48*

2-9   R & D expenditure of the top 300 companies world-wide, 1995 and 1998   *49*

2-10   *Fortune* Global 500, 1997   *50*

2-11   Competitive-edge companies, 1997–8   *50*

2-12   Major industrial diversification of Samsung under Chairman Lee Byung-Chul, 1938–87   *52*

2-13   Major diversification of Hyundai Group under Chairman Chung Ju-Yung, 1938–87   *53*

2-14   The Fuyo *keiretsu*'s structure, 1997   *55*

2-15   Average sustainability of MSDW stocks, by sector   *63*

3-1   Various economic indicators of the national team, 1995   *78*

3-2   Provincial distribution of China's preferred large-scale enterprises and groups, 1997   *82*

3-3   Industrial sectors of the first and second trial group batches, 1991 and 1997   *84*

3-4   Evolution of policies and their implementation within the centrally approved enterprise groups, 1987–99   *88*

3-5	Description of China's national team players	*101*
4-1	Size structure of civil global airliner stock, 1997 and 2017	*142*
4-2	R & D spending, by leading aircraft and component manufacturers, 1997	*143*
4-3	International arms sales, 1987–98	*151*
4-4	International arms deliveries, 1987 and 1988	*151*
4-5	International arms deliveries within East Asia, 1987 and 1998	*151*
4-6	Principal mergers and acquisitions in US defence industry, 1994–8	*153*
4-7	US Defense Department equipment purchase contracts, 1997	*154*
4-8	US and NATO Europe government defence budgets, 1999	*156*
4-9	Relative size of US and EU aerospace and defence companies, 1998	*166*
4-10	Share of R & D spending financed by government, 1970 and 1990	*175*
4-11	Russian defence output and exports, 1990 and 1997	*179*
4-12	Estimated production of military aircraft in China, selected years	*189*
4-13	Non-aviation products as a share of total AVIC revenue, 1997	*198*
4-14	Sales, assets and pre-tax profits of China's leading aerospace companies, early/mid-1990s	*200*
4-15	Growth of China's passenger airliner fleet, 1985–96	*202*
4-16	Main international sub-contracts at XAC and CAC since the late 1980s	*209*
4-17	Relative size of selected aerospace companies, 1997	*228*
4-18	Relative market capitalization of leading US- and European-based aerospace and defence companies, 1997–9	*236*
5-1	Public health expenditure at different levels of income, 1990–7	*243*
5-2	The top 10 and the top 20 drug corporations, by R & D expenditure, 1994–7	*248*
5-3	Top 10 drugs world-wide, 1998	*250*
5-4	Number of products that sell over $500 million per annum, 1998	*250*
5-5	The major M & A deals in the pharmaceutical industry since the late 1980s	*254*
5-6	Market share of the world's top 10 pharmaceutical firms, 1994–9	*267*
5-7	Glaxo Wellcome/SmithKline Beecham, estimated global market share, 1999	*268*
5-8	*Per capita* pharmaceutical consumption in China and other selected countries, 1991 and 1995	*278*
5-9	Chinese pharmaceutical production, 1980–96	*279*
5-10	Selected data on China's pharmaceutical industry, by gross output value, 1996	*280*

5-11   The top 10 and the top 20 pharmaceutical corporations in
        China, by market share, 1996   284
5-12   Structure of China's pharmaceutical industry, 1996   287
5-13   Selected data on China's pharmaceutical industry, 1996   288
5-14   Principal financial indicators for Nanfang Pharmaceutical
        Factory and Sanjiu Enterprise Group, 1987–98   292
5-15   Structure of output and profits in the Sanjiu Enterprise
        Group, 1992–7   301
5-16   Information about cadres at Nanfang Pharmaceutical
        Factory, 1995   305
5-17   Information about ordinary workers at Nanfang
        Pharmaceutical Factory, 1991   305
5-18   Principal businesses within the Sanjiu Group, mid-1990s   308
6-1   Size of HPEC and leading firms in the world's power
        equipment industry, late 1990s   330
6-2   Projected world demand for power equipment: power plant
        capacity by region, 1980–2010   334
6-3   Power plant capacity by type, 1980–2010   335
6-4   Share of world electricity generation, 1995 and 2015   335
6-5   Global power equipment market share, 1993–8   337
6-6   Growth of China's energy output and national product,
        1980 and 1990   340
6-7   *Per capita* energy use, 1994   341
6-8   Output of electricity, coal and oil in China and in the world,
        1980 and 1998   341
6-9   China's electricity industry: increase in installed capacity,
        electricity output and output of power generating equipment,
        1980–2010   342
6-10   Cheung Kong infrastructure's equity interest in mainland
        power stations, 1997   352
6-11   Share of China's energy produced from different inputs,
        1980 and 1996   354
6-12   Structure of electricity output in China, 1980–2010   354
6-13   Increase in installed capacity relative to output of China's
        domestic power equipment industry, 1991–7   359
6-14   Beijing Datang Power Generation Company, origins of
        major pieces of equipment   360
6-15   Main plants producing components for power stations in
        Liaoning and Helongjiang Provinces, 1992   364
6-16   Turnover, profits, dividends, taxation and welfare payments
        at HPEC, 1995   367
6-17   Growth of output at HPEC, 1959–98   374
6-18   Profits and taxation at HPEC, 1991–8   375
6-19   Major technical achievements of HPEC, 1959–91   376
6-20   Valuation of plant and equipment at HPEC, 1994   379

6-21   Main exports from HPEC   *388*
6-22   Share of different manufacturers in China's domestic power
       plant equipment production, 1991–6   *389*
6-23   Turnover of HPEC, 1996   *394*
7-1   World primary energy consumption, 1987 and 1997   *402*
7-2   World primary energy consumption, by energy source,
       1987 and 1997   *402*
7-3   Distribution of world reserves and production of oil, 1997   *403*
7-4   Natural gas production and reserves, 1997   *404*
7-5   Oil production, by region, 1987–97   *405*
7-6   US oil production, consumption and imports, 1948–97   *406*
7-7   Relationship of world reserves of coal, oil and natural
       gas in relation to population   *406*
7-8   Top 15 oil companies, 1996   *409*
7-9   Major oil and gas deals since 1997   *413*
7-10   Top 10 global oil companies, measured by revenues, 1997   *418*
7-11   Selected statistics of the Big Three, 1998   *419*
7-12   Transport growth in China, 1978–97   *432*
7-13   Growth of output of China's main petrochemical
       products, 1980–97   *433*
7-14   Balance of China's oil production and consumption, 1987–97   *434*
7-15   Sources of China's imported crude oil, 1995–7   *434*
7-16   Output, sales and pre-tax profit in CNPC, 1996   *442*
7-17   Profits and assets value of main production enterprises
       under Sinopec, 1995   *446*
7-18   Ethylene output at Sinopec's main subordinate plants, 1995   *447*
7-19   Oil refining at Sinopec's main subordinate refineries, 1997   *447*
7-20   Growth of Sinopec's production, 1989–98   *450*
7-21   World production of ethylene, selected countries, 1989–96   *451*
7-22   Synthetic fibre production capacity, selected countries, 1989–96 *451*
7-23   World production of plastics, selected countries, 1989–96   *451*
7-24   Changes in governmental organizations, March 1998   *467*
7-25   New Sinopec and new CNPC compared   *471*
7-26   Refineries under the new CNPC   *477*
7-27   Financial indicators for CNPC and Sinopec compared to
       the world's leading oil and petrochemical companies
       quoted on the stock market   *480*
7-28   CNPC and Sinopec compared to the global giants   *481*
7-29   Refineries under the new Sinopec   *482*
8-1   Minimum efficient scale in different parts of the auto industry *503*
8-2   Projected growth of world automobile markets, 1995–2001   *507*
8-3   Global production and sales of automobiles, 1998   *508*
8-4   World truck sales, 1995 and 2005   *509*
8-5   Internationalization of world's largest automobile
       companies, 1997   *509*

8-6	World top nine truck makers, 1995–2005	*518*
8-7	Leading global auto components companies, 1998	*522*
8-8	World largest automobile companies, 1998	*533*
8-9	Chinese automobile production, 1978–98	*536*
8-10	Plant-size distribution of China's vehicle assembly plants, 1995	*539*
8-11	China's saloon vehicle production, 1998	*540*
8-12	Main heavy-duty truck producers in China, 1998	*541*
8-13	Main medium-duty truck producers in China, 1998	*542*
8-14	Comparative size of Chinese and selected global truck companies, 1998	*542*
8-15	Size distribution of Chinese component makers, 1995	*543*
8-16	Consolidated profit and loss account at Guangxi Yuchai Machinery Company Ltd, 1991–5	*549*
8-17	Growth of Yuchai, 1975–98	*550*
8-18	Output of trucks in China, 1995 and 1998	*551*
8-19	Main producers of light trucks in China, 1998	*554*
8-20	Share of Yuchai's sales to its three leading customers, 1993	*554*
8-21	Distribution of Yuchai's sales, 1995	*555*
8-22	Selected statistics for China's leading auto producers, 1998	*556*
8-23	China's main diesel engine producers, 1998	*559*
8-24	Structure of China's leading enterprise groups, 1995	*560*
8-25	Comparative size of leading Chinese and global automobile firms, 1998	*561*
8-26	Main vehicle diesel engine producers in China, 1995	*562*
8-27	Dongfeng Automobile Group's structure of ownership and capital, 1992	*564*
8-28	Sales and profits at Yuchai, 1970–93	*570*
8-29	National output of trucks and output of medium-duty diesel engines at Yuchai, 1988–91	*571*
8-30	World leading independent diesel engine companies compared with Yuchai, 1998	*584*
9-1	World crude steel production by regions, 1991–7	*589*
9-2	Long-term changes in regional distribution of world steel output, 1974–96	*593*
9-3	Different production methods of crude steel output and continuous-casting ratios, selected countries, 1997	*597*
9-4	The top 10 and top 20 global crude steel producing companies, 1996–7	*602*
9-5	The top 10 and top 20 in world crude steel production, by countries, 1991–8	*616*
9-6	Tariffs on steel products in selected countries, 1997	*619*
9-7	Iron ore costs in selected countries' steel industries, 1997	*619*
9-8	Labour costs per ton in integrated steel companies, selected countries and Nucor (USA), 1997	*620*

9-9   China's consumption of selected flat steel products, 1996
        and predicted for 2000 and 2005   *624*
9-10   Apparent consumption, imports and exports of Chinese
        iron and steel, 1957–97   *626*
9-11   China's domestic output, imports and exports as a proportion
        of consumption for selected flat steel products, 1996   *627*
9-12   Selected statistics for the Chinese iron and steel industry,
        1980–97   *630*
9-13   Industrial concentration in China's iron and steel
        industry, 1991   *632*
9-14   Distribution of China's steel output between keypoint
        and other enterprises, 1980 and 1997   *632*
9-15   The top 10 and top 20 crude steel producers in China, 1997   *634*
9-16   Structure of principal steel products at major Chinese
        steel plants, 1997   *636*
9-17   Remuneration and labour productivity, selected countries
        and plants, 1994–7   *641*
9-18   Selected statistics of Shougang, 1978–97   *644*
9-19   Steel production facilities at Shougang, 1993   *645*
9-20   Output structure of steel at the eight largest
        Chinese plants, 1997   *646*
9-21   Distribution of profits in Shougang Corporation, 1978–92   *649*
9-22   Average price of iron, steel and rolled bar in China, 1980–93   *655*
9-23   Returns on investment in eight largest steel complexes in
        China, 1980–85 and 1985–90   *660*
9-24   Wage grades at Shougang, 1986   *666*
9-25   Employment structure at Shougang, 1998   *672*
10-1   Change in primary energy consumption, 1986–96   *696*
10-2   Share of global installed capacity for electricity generation,
        1990–2010   *696*
10-3   Distribution of global electricity generation capacity as %,
        1990–2010   *697*
10-4   Primary energy consumption, 1996   *697*
10-5   World coal consumption, 1986–96   *698*
10-6   Coal output, selected countries, 1980–95   *699*
10-7   Structure of output in relation to energy use: China, Japan
        and the USA, 1992–5   *700*
10-8   Coal sector employment in selected countries, 1980
        and 1995   *707*
10-9   Labour productivity and labour costs across different
        countries, 1996   *711*
10-10   Working days lost per 1000 employees in various Australian
        industries   *712*
10-11   Adopting best-practice technology could reduce China's
        coal consumption by 20%   *716*

10-12 China's energy reserves compared to the global average
       and to the USA, 1997   *716*
10-13 Coal output and consumption in different regions
       of China, 1996   *719*
10-14 Transport costs for China's main coal producers, 1997   *720*
10-15 Changes in the institutional distribution of the output in
       the Chinese coal industry, 1979 and 1995   *721*
10-16 Size distribution of output in the Chinese coal industry, 1997   *721*
10-17 Cost structure of different Chinese coal producers, 1995   *722*
10-18 Relative safety of different types of coal mine in China,
       1995–6   *725*
10-19 Size structure of the Chinese coal mining industry, 1991   *727*
10-20 Comparison of thermal coal prices between Australian and
       Chinese coastal cities, July 1997   *729*
10-21 Output, reserves and mine depths at selected Chinese large
       coal mines, 1996   *736*
10-22 Relative quality of raw (unwashed) coal from Shenhua
       and selected large Chinese state-owned coal companies.   *737*
10-23 Capital construction investment of Shenhua Project,
       1985–97   *743*
10-24 Shenhua Coal Group's mining facilities, 1998   *744*
10-25 Source of funds for Shenhua's investment, 1985–97   *744*
10-26 The 'Five Western District Mines' merged with Shenhua,
       October 1998   *754*
11-1   IT companies in the *FT* top 100 global companies,
       4 January 2000   *764*
11-2   R & D expenditure of the top 300 companies world-wide,
       1995 and 1998   *766*
11-3   MSDW competitive-edge companies in IT sectors, 2000   *767*
11-4   Global market share of top 10 companies in knowledge-
       intensive industries, 1998   *768*
11-5   Total value of mergers and acquisitions in knowledge-
       intensive industries, 1988 and 1998   *769*
11-6   Selected indicators of information and telecommunications
       development, by country level, 1997   *789*
11-7   China's leading IT hardware firms in international
       comparison, 1998   *794*
11-8   Growth of China's telecommunications industry, 1997–9   *798*
11-9   Major Chinese telecommunications players in each sector,
       2000   *798*
11-10 China Telecom, China Telecom (Hong Kong) and China
       Unicom compared to other leading telecom firms,
       December 1999   *800*
11-11 Shareholding structure of China Unicom, 1999   *809*
11-12 A partial list of China Unicom's CCF partners, 1999   *810*

12-1	Global banking institution mergers and acquisitions, 1989–99	*816*
12-2	Bank restructuring: number of institutions and size concentration, 1980–97	*820*
12-3	World-wide completed M & A advisers: top five firms	*823*
12-4	International equities bookrunners: top five firms	*823*
12-5	All international convertibles: top five firms	*823*
12-6	Syndicated credit arrangers: top five firms	*824*
12-7	Top four foreign and domestic commercial banks, 1999	*827*
12-8	Top three foreign and domestic insurance companies, 1998	*828*
12-9	Top four foreign and domestic investment banks, 1998	*829*
13-1	Regional differences in economic growth, 1980–98	*851*
13-2	Selected indicators of the competitive capability of leading Chinese companies compared with the global giants: aerospace, 1997	*877*
13-3	Selected indicators of the competitive capability of leading Chinese companies compared with the global giants: pharmaceuticals, 1997	*879*
13-4	Selected indicators of the competitive capability of leading Chinese companies compared with the global giants: power equipment, 1998	*882*
13-5	Selected indicators of the competitive capability of leading Chinese companies compared with the global giants: oil and petrochemicals, 1997–8	*884*
13-6	Selected indicators of the competitive capability of leading Chinese companies compared with the global giants: auto components, 1998	*886*
13-7	Selected indicators of the competitive capability of leading Chinese companies compared with the global giants: autos, 1998	*887*
13-8	Selected indicators of the competitive capability of leading Chinese companies compared with the global giants: steel, 1998	*888*
14-1	Share of world manufacturing output, 1750–1998	*900*
14-2	Growth of the Chinese economy, 1980–97	*913*
14-3	China's world ranking in the production of selected products, 1949–98	*913*
14-4	China's national output compared to the USA and the world, 1998	*913*
14-5	Comparison of China's energy intensity, using two different methods of calculation, 1998	*914*
14-6	Changes in the welfare of Chinese people, 1980 and 1997	*914*
14-7	China's employment structure, 1998	*919*
14-8	Stock-market development in China and other countries/regions, 1998	*932*

Foreword

This book started life in December 1994. I was honoured to join in this work. Together with Peter Nolan, I visited almost all of the cases analyzed in this book.

I can remember each of them with great clarity. The first large firm we visited was Shougang (Capital Iron and Steel Corporation), which was famous in China for its great size, its incredible growth and its successful experiences of reform. When we sat down in the office, the leaders of each of the different departments said to us: 'Any questions? There are already three books written about us. You can check those books first. We are extremely busy.' Then Peter started to ask questions. The discussion grew warmer and warmer. In the end we always ran out of time, and we were often invited to have lunch or dinner with them to continue the discussion.

China is working hard in the so-called 'transition' process. In general usage, 'transition' means to transform the economic system from central planning to a market economy. Numerous Western scholars are busy teaching the transitional countries how to transform their economies into market economies. They come from Western, real, standard market economies. They are used to answering questions, correcting misunderstandings, criticising wrong ideas. They have all the right answers. They do not need to listen or ask questions. Peter is a rare exception.

In the course of our research we stayed in those enterprises. We lived in Shougang's 'hotel' for seven days. Under Shougang's heavy pollution, the sky is always dark, the air is always dirty. When we walked around Shougang, we saw the real daily lives of thousands of people. Two or three generations spent their entire lives in these factories. They struggled hard for survival, for a better life, for development, day after day, year after year, generation after generation. They know much better than anyone else how to make things work in their factory. If you want to make things better, you must first listen and discuss with these people.

Peter's attitude changes him from being viewed as a foreign outsider in the beginning to 'one of us' at the end of the interviews. This enables his book to provide a deeper understanding of China's institutional evolution than any written by a foreign scholar. It constitutes a unique record of change in China's large enterprises at a crucial period in my country's history.

WANG XIAOQIANG
2001

Preface

The research for this book has its origins in the intense policy debates that began in China in the early 1980s and are continuing to this day. Since the earliest days of China's reforms there has been a struggle between the neo-classical, free market position and the experimental, developmental position. Supporters of the former view have consistently argued for rapid reform and opening up, including a rapid reduction in the role of the state. They have argued for the benefits to be derived from fast and deep integration with the global economy. They have emphasized the potential gains from large-scale 'breakthroughs' in policy and the potential damage from incremental change. Supporters of the latter view have consistently argued for the need for caution and experimentation. They have argued for the need to pursue a 'strategic' integration with the world economy that preserves strong elements of policy control in the hands of the Chinese state. They have emphasized the intense nature of China's political and economic struggle with the advanced economies. They have argued for the primacy of socio–political stability in China above all other considerations.

Under the influence of neo-classical thinking, in the mid-1980s China came close to a 'big bang' of comprehensive price and ownership reform. In the late 1980s, China came even closer to comprehensive system change. In the early and mid-1990s, following the collapse of the former USSR, the advocates of comprehensive, high-speed system change were silenced. Later in the 1990s, as the Chinese economy continued to grow rapidly and absorb large amounts of foreign direct investment (FDI), the fears of the earlier period were left increasingly behind. Once again the neo-classical position became stronger. More and more voices were heard arguing for the need to change the system rapidly towards a US-style political democracy and a fully fledged market economy. In 1999 the Chinese government signed the historic agreement with the USA on the conditions under which it would enter the WTO. These amounted to voluntarily dismantling the industrial policy of the previous two decades. The decision was of great importance not only for China, but also for developing countries as a whole, and, indeed, for the entire structure of world political economy in the early years of the twenty-first century.

A central part of this intense, ongoing struggle concerned policies towards the large-scale, former state-owned sector. This in turn involved the relationship between this sector and the global giant corporations that are deeply interested in penetrating the Chinese market, with its vast potential. In 1994, I began a research programme with Dr Wang Xiaoqiang, to investigate the reform of the large-scale state-owned enterprises. In the late 1980s and early 1990s, Dr Wang was a member of the Rural Development Group and from 1985 to 1988 he was Deputy Director of the System Reform Institute under the State Council's System Reform Commission. Our research was based around in-depth case studies of China's 'national team'. It rapidly became obvious to us that alongside the attempt to transform China's leading state-owned enterprises into competitive modern corporations, a revolution in business systems was under way in the advanced economies. We shifted the focus of our research. We attempted to combine our analysis of the evolution of large Chinese firms with an analysis of the simultaneous revolutionary 'restructuring' of capitalist big businesses headquartered in the advanced economies.

The incredible speed and depth of the global business revolution presented a massive challenge to China's attempt to 'catch-up' at the level of the large firm. It became clear to us that China faced a far greater challenge than had faced any previous 'late-comer' country, including Japan, owing to the explosive nature of change in the global business system and associated revolutionary change in technology. The theme of this book is the interaction between China's internal system restructuring in its large enterprises and the global business revolution.

The fieldwork on which this book is based was conducted jointly by myself and Dr Wang between 1994 and 1999. Although this book was written by me (except for Chapters 3 and 12), the ideas in it were the product of innumerable discussions between us over the course of these years. Dr Wang has published numerous papers and books in Chinese that have stemmed from this research.[1]

The research would not have been possible without the support of Dr Liu Yan, Senior Research Fellow of the Chinese System Reform Institute. Dr Liu made a major contribution to the intellectual life of our project. She was invaluable also in the practical administration of our research. Without her immense talent in interacting with people, much of our research would not have taken place. Time and again she was responsible for a breakthrough that enabled us to gain access to a particular company, plant or person. She smoothed the path for us in our fieldwork, keeping everyone around us happy and interested in our project when our own spirits flagged. Repeatedly, she read between the lines of a given statement to make us reflect more deeply on the meaning hidden beneath the words. Working with us over such a long period was not an easy task. We are deeply grateful to her for her contribution to our research programme.

We were also helped at different points in our research by numerous other people. Among those we are especially indebted to are Wang Xuejia and Yang Ying (Jenny). Wang Xuejia accompanied us for most of our research. As well as being a member of our research team, she was invaluable in assisting us in translation of the different specialist vocabularies of the many different industries in which we worked. Jenny Yang provided us with invaluable support in collecting research materials and making innumerable practical arrangements both for our research and for the meetings of the China Big Business Programme. We were extremely fortunate to have research assistance at key points from Dr Godfrey Yeung and Ms Zhang Jin. I am most grateful to Dylan Sutherland for writing Chapter 3 and to Wu Qing for writing Chapter 12.

In 1997, Dr Wang and I had the good fortune to meet Mr Liu Xingli, then head of the research department at the China National Non-Ferrous Metals Corporation. He raised the possibility that I might try to involve leading UK-based companies to support a continuation of our programme of research on large Chinese enterprises. He suggested that these could be used as the basis for a series of interactive meetings with the Chinese firms' Western counterparts, as well as other learning activities, notably 'learning journeys' around the UK-based large corporations. These might enable China's reforming large state-owned enterprises to obtain a better understanding of the way in which they could raise their competitive capability relative to the global giant corporations. Through the meetings the global corporations might gain a deeper understanding of the process of change in China's large corporations. In our attempt to devise and undertake this Programme, we were given invaluable support by Professor Zhang Xinchuan, Professor at the Chinese Ferrous Metals Research Institute, and Mr Lu Yansun, formerly Deputy Minister of the Ministry of Machine Building.

In the UK, the Programme was able to come into being only thanks to the unstinting support and deep involvement of Mr Matthew Bullock, formerly a Director of Barclays Capital, and now Head of the Norwich and Peterborough Building Society. Together we devised the China Big Business Programme (CBBP), for which he acted as the Chairperson. The Programme ran from 1997 to 1999. It involved continuing and deepening the research into large Chinese companies that Dr Wang and I had already begun. Based on this research I wrote a series of case studies that form the basis of this book. These studies formed the basis for a series of twelve meetings held over the course of two and a half years, from 1997 to 1999. The entire Programme was able to operate thanks to the generous support of the following participating companies and organizations: British Aerospace (now BAe Systems), Rolls-Royce, Shell, BP Amoco, Rio Tinto, Barclays Capital, SBC Warburg, The Foreign and Commonwealth Office (UK), and the Department of Trade and Industry (UK). I am most grateful to these companies for funding the research programme. Without their support this research would have been impossible. Moreover, I am extremely grateful to the participating companies for allowing myself, Dr Wang Xiaoqiang and senior strategists from the participating Chinese companies to conduct in-depth research within these organizations.

I am deeply grateful to the participating Chinese large enterprises for allowing Dr Wang and myself to undertake in-depth research in their companies at a time of tremendous change and challenge for them.

The meetings of the CBBP were attended by senior managers from the participating Western, mainly UK-based, large firms. In addition, there were representatives from the Department of Trade Industry and the Foreign and Commonwealth Office. From the Chinese side, the meetings were attended by senior officials of the particular firms being studied, and by senior officials from the relevant ministry, as well as by other senior policy makers. The main activity of these meetings was to debate the significance of the research conclusions of the case studies. Apart from the final meeting, each one focused on a particular sector.

Ten of the meetings took place in the Judge Institute of Management Studies in Cambridge. Two of the meetings took place in China. The first of these meetings was held in Shanghai in 1998, and focused on the aerospace industry. We are most grateful to the Chief Executive of BAe, Mr John Weston, for attending this meeting. His speech made a major contribution to the debate on the development of the Chinese aerospace industry. The final meeting of the Programme was held in Beijing in late 1999. At this meeting there were representatives from all the sectors studied. There was intense debate about the conclusions reached in the papers presented over the course of the Programme. This meeting coincided with the historic Sino–US Agreement on the terms of China's entry to the WTO.

I am deeply grateful to Dr Simon Jiang, Chief Executive of Cyber City, Shenzhen, for his constant support throughout the Programme, including participation in almost all of the meetings. I am most grateful also to both Mr Qin Xiao, President of CITIC, and to Mr Kang Dian, CEO of Guangdong Capital, for their unstinting support.

The organization of the CBBP meetings was extremely complex. This task was performed with the greatest skill and kindness by Felicity Pugh. Her professionalism made a great contribution to the success of the CBBP meetings.

The practical details of organization surrounding the Programme were immense, including preparation and editing of the case studies, as well as innumerable interpersonal interactions with the British and Chinese participants. This work was undertaken throughout by Elizabeth Briggs. She has also edited the resulting book. She performed these demanding tasks with the highest level of professional skill, unflagging enthusiasm and good humour.

PETER NOLAN
2001

List of Abbreviations and Acronyms

AD	Anti-dumping (measures)
ASSM	Anti-ship missile system
AVIC	Aviation Industries of China
AWAC	Airborne warning and control
BHC	Bank holding company
BIS	Bank for International Settlements
BOT	Build–Operate–Transfer
CAAC	Civilian Aviation Administration of China
CAD	Computer-aided design
CASS	Chinese Academy of Social Sciences
CATIC	China Aviation Technology Company for Import and Export of Aviation Products
CBBP	China Big Business Programme
CCB	China Construction Bank
CCP	Chinese Communist Party
CDBW	*China Daily: Business Weekly*
CICC	China International Capital Corporation
CIF	Cost, insurance and freight
CITIC	China International Trust and Investment Corporation
CNNMBG	Chinese New Buildings Material Group
CNOOC	China National Offshore Oil Corporation
CNPC	China National Petroleum Corporation
COFCO	China National Cereals, Oils and Foodstuff Import and Export Corporation
COSCO	China Ocean Shipping Corporation
COSTIND	Commission on Science, Technology and Industry for National Defence
CRES	Commission for the Reform of the Economic System
CSCEC	China State Construction Engineering Corporation

CSFB	Crédit Suisse First Boston
CSRC	Chinese Securities Regulation Commission
DRC	Development Research Centre of the State Council of China
DTI	Department of Trade and Industry (UK)
EADC	European Aerospace and Defence Company
EADS	European Aircraft, Defence and Space Company
EAEC	East Asian Economic Caucus
EBRD	European Bank for Reconstruction and Development
EPA	Environmental Protection Agency (USA)
ETC	State Economics and Trade Commission
EU	European Union
FAA	Federal Aviation Authority (USA)
FDA	Food and Drugs Administration (USA)
FDI	Foreign direct investment
FHC	Financial holding company
FMCG	Fast-moving consumer goods
FT	*Financial Times*
GATT	General Agreement on Tariffs and Trade (now WTO)
GDP	Gross domestic product
GLD	General Logistics Department (PLA)
GMP	Good manufacturing procedures
GNP	Gross national product
GPD	General Political Department
GSD	General Staff Department
HCIC	Hebei Construction and Investment Company
HIE	High-income economy
ICBC	Industrial and Commercial Bank of China
ICBM	Inter-continental ballistic missile
IHT	*International Herald Tribune*
IISI	International Iron and Steel Institute
IISS	International Institute for Strategic Studies
IMF	International Monetary Fund
IPO	Initial Public Offering
IPP	Independent power producer
ISIC	Iron and Steel Industry of China
IT	Information technology
ITC	Industrial and investment trust
JAA	Joint Aviation Authority (Europe)
JV	Joint venture
JSF	Joint Strike Fighter
KMT	Kuomintang
LME	Large and medium enterprise
L/MIE	Low-/middle-income economy
M & A	Merger and acquisition
MITI	Ministry of International Trade and Industry (Japan)

MMB	Ministry of Machine Building Industries
MMI	Ministry of Metallurgy Industry
MNC	Multinational corporation
MOU	Memorandum on market access (USA–China)
MPK	Million passenger kilometres
MSDW	Morgan Stanley Dean Witter
NAFTA	North American Free Trade Agreement
NATO	North Atlantic Treaty Organization
NIC	Newly industrialized country
NTB	Non-tariff barrier
OECD	Organization for Economic Co-operation and Development
OTC	Over-the-counter
PAP	People's Armed Police
PBC	People's Bank of China
PLA	People's Liberation Army
PLC	Programmable logical control system
R & D	Research and development
ROA	Return on assets
ROE	Return on equity
ROK	Republic of Korea
SAM	Surface-to-air missile
SCDRC	State Council Development Research Centre
SCMP	*South China Morning Post*
SDB	State Development Bank
SEG	Sanjiu Enterprise Group
SETC	State Economic and Trade Commission
SEZ	Special Economic Zone
SME	Small and medium-sized enterprise
SOE	State-owned enterprise
SP	State Power Corporation
SPC	Shanghai Petrochemical Company
SSB	State Statistical Bureau
TNC	Trans-national corporation
TRIMs	Trade-Related Investment Measures (agreement)
TRIPs	Trade-Related Intellectual Property Rights (agreement)
TVE	Township and village enterprise
UAV	Unarmed aerial vehicle
UNCTAD	United Nations Conference on Trade and Development
UNDP	United Nations Development Programme
USDA	United States Development Agency
WTO	World Trade Organization
XAC	Xian Aircraft Corporation

1

Large Firms and Economic Development

In the midst of all the exactions of government, this capital has been silently and gradually accumulated by the private frugality and good conduct of individuals, by their universal, continual and uninterrupted effort to better their own condition. It is this effort, protected by law, and allowed by liberty to exert itself in the manner that is most advantageous, which has maintained the progress of England towards opulence and improvement.
(Adam Smith, 1776)

Most countries which ignored their comparative advantage to adopt the leap forward strategy did not realize their intended goals ... Some developing countries and regions, however, did not adopt the leap forward strategy. They relied instead on the function of the market. Market-determined prices reflected their relative scarcities or factor endowments. With the guidance of relative prices, they developed the sectors that could exploit their comparative advantage. These economies achieved unexpectedly rapid economic growth and became the rising stars of economic development.
(Lin Yifu, 1996)

The battle between the large firm and the small is not one which is ever fought to a definite finish, or waged with similar fortune in all parts of the industrial field. But on the whole in the modern world the race is to the swift, and the battle to the strong.
(Robertson, 1923)

Since the beginning of the Industrial Revolution there has been a tendency for the representative firm to increase in size from the workshop to the

1

*factory and to the national corporation to the multi-divisional corporation
and now to the multinational corporation. This growth has been qualitative
as well as quantitative. With each step, business enterprise acquired a more
and more complex administrative structure to co-ordinate its activities
and a larger brain to plan for its survival and growth.*
(Hymer, 1975)

INTRODUCTION

From the late 1970s to the late 1990s, the Chinese government used a wide array
of industrial policies to support the growth of a 'national team' of large firms that
could to compete with the world's leading corporations (see Chapter 3). The foundations of this effort were the large industrial plants inherited from the former
command economy. This approach to economic policy directly challenged the
prevailing trend of globalization and liberalization. It was radically different from
that advocated by the free market orthodoxy of mainstream economics and from
the policies advocated by the international institutions of the 'Washington
Consensus', notably the IMF and the World Bank. It differed comprehensively
from the industrial reform policies pursued in the former Soviet Union and in
Eastern Europe (Nolan, 1995). The attempt raised deep issues about the role of the
state in promoting national economic development and about the nature of capitalism itself. It involved fundamental questions concerning China's international
relations in the early twenty-first century, namely the terms under which it interacted with the high-income countries in general, and, in particular, with the global
super-power, the USA. This chapter examines some of the key theoretical and
empirical issues that underlay the internal debates over China's industrial policies.

COMPETITION, SMALL FIRMS AND ECONOMIC
DEVELOPMENT: THE NEO-CLASSICAL VIEW

SMALL FIRMS IN TRANSITIONAL ECONOMIES

The debate about the transition from the Communist system of political economy
has been intense.[1] Industrial reform was at the centre of this debate. The approach
adopted by the mainstream 'Washington Consensus' was built around the notion
that large enterprises should mostly be closed down and replaced with a sea of new,
small and medium-scale enterprises. In one of the classic statements of the 'transition orthodoxy' of the Washington Consensus, Blanchard and his associates argued:

> For the most part, Eastern Europe's production sector is composed of large, inef-
> ficient firms. Many if not most of them will have to close, and others will need
> to shed labour on a large scale. Growth will come largely from the rest of the
> economy, which exists today in embryonic form. Badly needed are small to
> medium-scale firms, high-tech manufacturing, and most forms of services ... The
> challenge of restructuring will be to efficiently close much of the old structure
> and allow for rapid expansion of a new one. (Blanchard *et al.*, 1993: 64–5)

Throughout the literature on the 'transition' in the industrial sector, attention was focused on the privatization of individual plants. In many industrial sectors under Communist planning, China and the former USSR each had a small number of relatively large plants. This was the case for example in the auto, steel, farm equipment, chemical, power equipment and aerospace industries. The Washington Consensus gave no attention at all to the desirability of merging these plants within any given sector, in order to produce large, globally competitive multi-plant firms. 'Industrial policy' focused simply on ways of privatizing individual plants. In its interpretation of China's economic success since the 1970s, the World Bank has placed great emphasis on the growth of small and medium-sized enterprises (SMEs) as the 'foundation for recent economic growth' (World Bank, 1997b: 21).

It is certainly the case that small firms were neglected within the traditional planned economies (Nolan, 1995: 127–31). It was to be expected that the growth of market forces would lead to a greatly increased role for small firms. Many of these would emerge from the de-merger of segments of large vertically integrated state enterprises. However, this does not mean that large indigenous firms could have no significant role to play in the transition from Communist planning. The approach toward industrial reform that was adopted in the former USSR and Eastern Europe was guided by the powerful influence of the mainstream traditions of neo-classical economic theory. It had a highly idealized view of the workings of advanced capitalism, which greatly emphasized the contribution of small firms and downplayed the contribution of large firms.

SMALL FIRMS IN NEO-CLASSICAL THEORY

Views which emphasize the importance of small firms over large firms have a long tradition in neo-classical economics. The mainstream approach has viewed with suspicion departures from perfect competition, under which there are large numbers of anonymous firms, none of which can exert any influence on the market. Of course, perfect competition rarely, if ever, exists in practice, but it is the desirable state towards which the mainstream of neo-classical economics believes the economy should tend. The neo-classical approach emphasizes the importance of competition among small firms as the explanation for the prosperity of the advanced economies, especially the USA. Milton Friedman, for example, states: 'As I have studied economic activities in the United States, I have become increasingly impressed with how wide is the range of problems and industries that can be treated as if it were competitive' (Friedman, 1962: 120).

This view regards perfect competition as both economically and politically desirable. Under perfect competition, with all the necessary assumptions, price will be equated with marginal cost. This yields the well-known 'Pareto optimal' solution, in the sense that it will be impossible to make anyone better off without making someone else worse off. By contrast, if an industry is monopolized by a single firm, then the neo-classical approach predicts that the price will rise and the quantity produced will fall. By extension, the mainstream neo-classical view believes that the higher the degree of monopoly, the greater the tendency to restrict output and for price to depart from marginal cost.

In addition to the economic arguments for perfect competition, the perfectly competitive model 'has a great appeal to the liberal who is frightened by the exercise of power either by private organizations or by the state' (Lipsey, 1963: 377). Despite the numerous assumptions necessary for the perfectly competitive model to operate, the influence of the model remains deeply embedded in the minds of mainstream economists: 'For one who believes in the individual and hates all power groups, the perfectly competitive model is almost too good to be true' (Lipsey, 1963: 377). Consequently, in this view, a central task for economists is to regulate and prevent a high degree of industrial concentration.

China's neo-classical economists have become increasingly influential in policy debates within the country, strongly supported by the institutions of the Washington Consensus. Their view of advanced capitalism in both their writings and public discussion places great emphasis on the competitive characteristics of the capitalist system. A good example of this view is the book, on China's economic reforms, entitled *The China Miracle* written by Justin Yifu Lin and his associates (Lin *et al.*, 1996). Lin is Director of the World Bank/Ford Foundation-funded Centre for Economic Research at Beijing University. This influential book, funded by the Milton Friedman Foundation, is peppered with references to advanced capitalism as a 'competitive market system' in which there are no 'distortions' introduced by government intervention, as though this were the reality of advanced capitalism. The book makes no reference to the rise and persistence of oligopoly in the USA or other advanced capitalist countries. No reference is made to the central role of the state in the rise of industry in the USA or other advanced economies, through such measures as protection, support for R & D and government procurement. No reference is made to the central role of large corporations in furthering technical progress. It is, by implication, as if these countries grew prosperous through perfect competition.

SMALL FIRMS AND COMPARATIVE ADVANTAGE

A key aspect of the neo-classical view of the roles of small and large firms in the development process is the relationship with international trade and the international economy. These views assume special importance in view of the fact that, in late 1999, China agreed to join the WTO through high-speed integration, faster than that of any other country on joining the institution. This involved comprehensive dismantling of the array of protectionist measures, and associated industrial policies, used by the Chinese government during the reform period.

The neo-classical view of the 'East Asian miracle' regards the reason for their success as the fact that they allegedly conformed to the principle of comparative advantage and were guided by free trade in resource allocation:

> South Korea, Singapore, Hong Kong and Taiwan are examples of economies which have achieved fast and stable economic growth through exploiting

their resources' comparative advantages ... They relied on the function of the market. Market-determined relative prices reflected their relative scarcities or factor endowments. With the guidance of relative prices, they developed the sectors that could exploit their comparative advantages. These economies achieved unexpectedly rapid economic growth and became the rising stars of economic development. (Lin *et al.*, 1996: 93)

From this perspective China's high-speed entry to the WTO is to be warmly applauded since it provides close integration with the world economy and sends the right 'undistorted' price signals to enterprises which will enable maximum efficiency in resource use. The argument is identical to that which Adam Smith made in his passionate criticism of protection in Britain in the late eighteenth century (Smith, 1776). It also underpinned Smith's famous proposition that the USA would be much poorer under a protectionist regime than with free trade:

It has been the principal cause of the rapid progress of our American colonies towards wealth and greatness, that almost the whole of their capitals have hitherto been employed in agriculture ... Were the Americans, either by combination or by any other sort of violence, to stop the importation of European manufactures, and by thus giving a monopoly to such of their own countrymen as could manufacture the like goods, divert any considerable part of their capital into this employment, they would retard instead of accelerating the further increase in the value of their annual produce, and would obstruct instead of promoting the progress of their country towards real wealth and greatness. (Smith, 1776: 388)

A similar logic underlay the confident proposition of British commentators in the early nineteenth century that India would prosper under free trade:

The vast peninsula of India has for centuries been harassed by wars and devastation, rendering property very insecure; but if it becomes open to free trade, under one mild, liberal and effective government, that could protect the property, laws, lives and liberties of the subjects, what a sudden change might we not anticipate? (Lester, W., *The happy era of one hundred millions of the human race, or the merchant, manufacturer, and the Englishman's recognised right to an unlimited trade with India*, London, 1813, quoted in Stokes, 1959: 38–9)

There is a close connection between the neo-classical economists' perspective on international trade and their view of industrial structure. In simplistic neo-classical theory, developing countries are argued to be capital-scarce and labour-abundant. Developing countries are argued to have a comparative advantage in labour-intensive goods but not in capital-intensive ones:

The utilization of comparative advantage in an economy is a process of selecting the economy's industrial structure. Because different goods require different combinations of factor inputs, each country should choose the most

advantageous industrial structure based on its resource endowment ... At the
early stage of a country's development, capital in general is extremely scarce
and is a bottleneck for development; *therefore, the country must develop the
clothing industry instead of the automobile industry.* (Lin *et al.*, 1996: 102,
emphasis added)

Those who advocate state support for capital-intensive industries are argued to
erroneously believe that 'economic development could be accelerated by bypass-
ing the labour-intensive and/or resource-intensive stage of development'
(Lin *et al.*, 1996: 105). In the neo-classical approach, an idealized view of the
Four Little Tigers is presented as the model for China to follow. The Four Little
Tigers were argued to have 'formed relatively labour-intensive production and
export structures to fully utilize their abundant labour resources' (Lin *et al.*,
1996: 95). Taiwan is held up as the best example for China to follow:

Taiwan can be used as an example to illustrate how an economy can rely
on its resources' comparative advantage to achieve the goal of economic
development ... Taiwan relied on the development of labour-intensive and low-
technology industries to push forward the industrialization of the whole economy ... Taiwan's rate of economic development was not hampered by its
initial choice of labour-intensive light industry as the key sector. On the contrary, because its industrial structure reflected the comparative advantage of its
resource endowment, Taiwan's economy was very competitive in the world
economy. (Lin *et al.*, 1996: 107)

The view is widely propounded among neo-classical participants in the Chinese
policy debate that developing countries should go through a 'normal' sequence
of development of their industrial structure. In the early stages of their development, which China is argued still to be in, they argue that China's growth should
be based on small-scale, labour-intensive light industries, rather than using
industrial policy to support the growth of large-scale, capital-intensive and technology-intensive industries. The key to understanding China's rapid growth
during the reform years is argued as being the movement of China towards an
industrial structure that reflects its comparative advantage. The most dynamic
element in this growth is argued to be the small and medium-sized enterprises
(SMEs), especially the so-called township and village enterprises (TVEs). A
great deal of neo-classical literature on the Chinese reforms has for this reason
focused on the growth of TVEs: 'The TVEs' important role can be explained by
the fact that they are well-placed to exploit the comparative advantages of relatively abundant labour resources ... TVEs are concentrated in low capital-intensive industries' (Lin *et al.*, 1996: 180–1).

LIMITS TO THE SIZE AND STABILITY OF THE LARGE FIRM

The mainstream of the neo-classical tradition views the individual large firm as a
temporary phenomenon, which will eventually be cut down to size by competition

from new entrants, which in their own turn grow and decline. This view greatly emphasizes the constant flux among large corporations, arguing that no individual large firm remains large for long. It emphasizes the possibilities for individual firms to 'catch-up' with the industry leaders, and overtake them. These views were classically expressed in Marshall's *Principles of Economics* (1920), first published in 1890:

> [H]ere we may read a lesson from the young trees of the forest as they struggle upwards through the benumbing shade of their older rivals. Many succumb on the way, and a few only survive: those few become stronger with every year, they get a larger share of light and air with every increase of their height, and at last in their turn they tower above their neighbours, and seem as though they would grow on for ever and for ever become stronger as they grow. But they do not. One tree will last longer in full vigour and attain a greater size than another; but sooner or later age tells on them all. Though the taller ones have a better access to light and air than their rivals, they gradually lose vitality; and one after another they give place to others, which though of less material strength, have on their side the vigour of youth ... [I]n almost every trade there is a constant rise and fall of large businesses, at any one moment some firm being in the ascending phase and others in the descending. (Marshall, 1920: 315–16).

OUTSOURCING: DISINTEGRATION OF THE LARGE FIRM?

In his classic article on the nature of the firm, Coase (1937) investigates the determinants of producing goods and services within the firm as opposed to purchasing them through market transactions. Outside the firm, 'price movements direct production, which is co-ordinated through a series of exchange transactions on the market' (Coase, 1937: 35). However, within the firm, 'these market transactions are eliminated, and in place of the complicated market structure with exchange transactions is substituted *the entrepreneur co-ordinator who directs production*' (Coase, 1937: 35, emphasis added). Within the firm there is an 'island of unconscious power'. For Coase, 'the distinguishing mark of the firm is the *supersession of the price mechanism*' (Coase, 1937: 36, emphasis added). Coase quotes, approvingly, Maurice Dobb: '[The entrepreneur] busies himself with the division of labour inside each firm and *he plans and organises consciously*, but he is related to the much larger economic specialization, of which he himself is merely one specialized unit. Here he plays his part as a single cell in a larger organism, mainly unconscious of the wider role he fulfills' (quoted in Coase, 1937: 36–7, emphasis added). Coase conceives of the size of the firm as tending towards an equilibrium position: 'At the margin, the costs of organizing within the firm will be equal to the costs of organizing in another firm or to the cost involved in leaving the transaction to be "organized" by the price mechanism' (Coase, 1937: 55).

The epoch of the global business revolution has brought drastic changes in the range of activities that firms wish to undertake within the firm as opposed to purchase through the market. Several tendencies have converged to drive this process at high speed. First, has been the process of separating core from non-core business. Secondly, there has been the increasing pressure from institutional shareholders to provide strong performance through increase in profits and share price. The relative importance of professional institutional shareholders has markedly increased, subjecting firms to greatly increased pressure to perform. Thirdly, there have been extraordinary developments in information technology. These have drastically reduced the costs involved in undertaking transactions with other firms.

Since the early 1980s, large firms have, on a widespread basis, outsourced service functions such as catering, billing and property management. Extensive outsourcing of components' production has taken place throughout the manufacturing sector. Increasingly, 'outsourcing' has extended to R & D activities and to manufacturing large sub-units of complex products. Systems integrators are less and less involved in the direct manufacture of goods.

For many analysts, the large corporation has become less and less important. The current trends are seen to mark the end of the large corporation, and herald the beginning of a world of virtual corporations based around small firms, even perhaps the end of the firm in conventional terms: 'While big companies control ever larger flows of cash, they are exerting less and less direct control over business activity. They are, you might say, growing hollow' (Malone and Laubacher, 1998: 147). Many researchers argued that these changes heralded a new epoch of production systems based around a greatly increased role for small and medium firms (the so-called 'meso' level of business activity) relative to large corporations:

> Examples of such meso level approaches have been the perspectives on the firm as a nexus of treaties (Aoki et al., 1990), as an actor searching for complementary network partners (Hakanson, 1989), as part of an industrial district (Marshall, 1920; Piore and Sabel, 1984), or as part of a cluster of firms cooperating and competing at the same time (Porter, 1990). Several researchers even speculated that this resurgence of the small firm and of new patterns of inter-firm relationship constituted the outline of a new production paradigm beyond Fordism (Piore and Sabel, 1984). (Ruigrok and van Tulder, 1995: 25–6).

LARGE FIRMS AND ECONOMIC DEVELOPMENT:
THE UNORTHODOX VIEW

The advocates of industrial policy in China have drawn their inspiration from non-mainstream economic theory, and from empirical evidence about the policies pursued in late-industrializing countries as well as from considerations of national pride and power.

The Tendency to Concentration

From the earliest stages in the development of modern capitalism, there were economists who recognized the tendency towards concentration of industrial power. Marx, in *Capital*, Vol. 1, published in 1867, argued that there was a 'law of centralisation of capital' or the 'attraction of capital by capital'. The driving force of concentration was competition itself, which pressured firms to cheapen the cost of production by investing ever-larger amounts of capital in new means of production and in 'the technological application of science', which in turn creates barriers to entry:

> The battle of competition is fought by cheapening commodities. The cheapness of commodities depends, *ceteris paribus*, on the productiveness of labour, and this again on the scale of production. Therefore the larger capital beats the smaller ... Everywhere the increased scale of industrial establishments is the starting-point for a more comprehensive organization of the collective work of many, for a wider development of their material motive force – in other words, for the progressive transformation of isolated processes of production, carried on by customary methods, into processes of production socially combined and scientifically arranged. (Marx, 1867: 626–7).

Alfred Marshall was quite explicit about the forces which led to the emergence of large firms. He provided a detailed set of reasons as to why large firms should tend to emerge and dominate large parts of the economy: '[T]here are a great many advantages which a large factory or indeed a large business of almost any kind, nearly always has over a small one' (Marshall, 1920: 282). These included economies in procurement and transport costs: 'A large business buys in great quantities and therefore cheaply; it pays low freight and saves on carriages in many ways' (Marshall, 1920: 282). It benefits from economies in marketing, branding and distribution: 'It often sells in large quantities, and thus saves itself trouble; and yet at the same time it gets a good price, because it offers conveniences to the customer by having a large stock from which he can select and at once fill up a varied order; while its reputation gives him confidence. It can spend large sums on advertising by commercial travellers and in other ways' (Marshall, 1920: 282). It benefits from superior knowledge: '[I]ts agents give it trustworthy information on trade and personal matters in distant places, and its own goods advertise one another' (Marshall, 1920: 282). It benefits from being able to attract the best human resources: 'The large manufacturer has a better chance than the small one has of getting hold of men of exceptional natural abilities, to do the most difficult part of his work, that on which the reputation of his establishment chiefly depends' (Marshall, 1920: 283). Marshall identifies the 'chief advantage of the modern organisation of industry' as the 'subdivision of the work of business management' (Marshall, 1920: 283). The large firm can employ a group of specialist managers, liberating the chief executives to focus on strategic issues: 'The head of a large business can reserve all his strength for the broadest and most fundamental problems of his trade' (Marshall, 1920: 284).

STABILITY OF THE LARGE FIRM

Having provided a thoroughly coherent set of reasons for the emergence of a group of powerful large firms in most areas of economic activity, Marshall provides a thoroughly unconvincing account of why the large firm should lose its dominant position. He argued that the private firm is likely to atrophy because 'after a while the guidance of the business falls into the hands of people with less energy and less creative genius ... than its original founders' (Marshall, 1920: 316). Marshall argues that as the joint stock company grows in size, it reaches a point at which 'it is likely to have lost so much of its elasticity and progressive force, that the advantages are no longer on its side in its competition with younger and smaller rivals' (Marshall, 1920: 316). He provides no empirical evidence or logical reason for this statement.

In her path-breaking book, *The Theory of the Growth of the Firm* (first published in 1959, and re-issued in 1995), Edith Penrose addresses directly the issue of possible limits to the growth of the firm. Like Marshall, she identifies a number of potential advantages that can be enjoyed by the large firm. Some of these are technological economies of scale at the plant level (Penrose, 1995: 89–92). However, the most significant are those advantages that accrue to the large multi-plant firm. These advantages are known as 'managerial economies':

> Managerial economies are held to result when a larger firm can take advantage of an increased division of managerial labour and of the closely allied mechanization of certain administrative processes; make more intensive use of existing managerial resources by the 'spreading' of overheads; obtain economies from buying and selling on a larger scale; use reserves more economically; acquire capital on cheaper terms; and support large-scale research. (Penrose, 1995: 92)

Penrose investigates in detail the ways in which a large, growing firm can use its resource advantages to generate further growth: 'Economies attributable to the size of firms may, up to a point, not only be responsible for lower costs of production and distribution of the existing products of larger firms, but also for lower costs and competitive advantages enabling larger firms to expand in certain directions' (Penrose, 1995: 98). Crucial to this process are the firm's research activities, enabling the development of new products, and the ability to 'generate the resources to introduce them' (Penrose, 1995: 97). Far from management being a fixed factor of production, with diminishing returns, Penrose argues that large firms can adapt their management structures to growth. Managerial resources become a key part of the large firm's ability to expand further:

> Once a substantial increment of growth is completed, the managerial services devoted to it become available for further expansion ... Furthermore, the growing experience of management, its knowledge of the other resources of the firm and of the potential for using them in different ways, creates incentives for

further expansion as the firm searches for ways of using its own resources more profitably. (Penrose, 1995: xii)

Penrose reaches the important conclusion that there are no theoretical limits to the size of the firm:

We have found nothing to prevent the indefinite expansion of firms as time passes, and clearly if some of the economies of size are economies of expansion, there is no reason to assume that a firm would ever reach a size in which it has taken full advantage of all these economies. (Penrose, 1995: 99)

LARGE FIRMS AND TECHNICAL PROGRESS

Technical progress is the most essential characteristic of economic growth: 'If there had been no technical progress, the whole process of accumulation would have been much more modest' (Maddison, 1994: 53). The research of Alfred Chandler has demonstrated the central role of the large, oligopolistic firm in technical progress. This was, in its turn, central to the whole growth dynamic of modern capitalism. In the late nineteenth century, especially in the USA, the first-mover large firms 'established themselves as dominant oligopolistic players' and became 'the fertile learning ground for technological, managerial, and organizational knowledge for an entire economy' (Chandler *et al.*, 1997: 25). These were primarily in the manufacturing sector that constituted the Second Industrial Revolution, including especially such capital-intensive activities as primary metals, petroleum refining, chemicals, electrical products and transport equipment. In these oligopolistic industries, there took place a switch from price to non-price competition:

[O]ligopolistic firms competed even more effectively through functional and particularly strategic effectiveness: that is, by carrying out processes of production and distribution more capably; by improving both product and process through systematic research and development; by identifying more suitable sources of supply; by providing more effective marketing services; by product differentiation (in branded packaged products primarily through the advertising); and by moving more quickly into expanding markets and out of declining ones. (Chandler and Hikino, 1997: 31)

In this climate of oligopolistic competition, 'market share and profits changed constantly, which kept oligopolies from becoming stagnant and monopolistic' (Chandler and Hikino, 1997: 31).

Technological advances achieved by large firms in these industries had powerful beneficial effects on the rest of the economy. They contributed to improved productivity in a wide range of other industries, including transport, communication and financial services (Chandler and Hikino, 1997: 25): 'These enterprises became a rich spring of managerial and organizational information as well as technological knowledge, all of which spilled over into the wider spheres of domestic and international economies by means of networks, spin-offs and even ordinary market transactions' (Chandler and Hikino, 1997: 25).

Chandler has shown the way in which the Third Industrial Revolution during and after the Second World also was 'dominated by large enterprises'. This revolution involved new technologies in chemicals, pharmaceuticals, aerospace, and electronics. Indeed, with the exception of electronic data-processing technologies, 'the new technologies were commercialized by large, well-established enterprises rather than start-ups' (Chandler and Hikino, 1997: 33). The modern industrial enterprise 'played a central role in creating the most technologically advanced, fastest growing industries of their day'. These industries, in turn, were 'the pace-setters of the industrial sector of their economies'. They provided an underlying dynamic in the development of modern industrial capitalism (Chandler, 1990: 593).

LARGE FIRMS, THE STATE AND TRADE POLICY

In the late 1830s and early 1840s, the German economist Friedrich List provided a comprehensive critique of the notion that free trade is the best path to rapid economic development. His writings formed the foundation for much subsequent thinking on industrial policy in developing countries, and was deeply influential in East Asia. Far from such ideas being overturned by modern economic theory, there is a powerful body of thought, in the shape of 'strategic trade theory' which also casts great doubt on the narrow neo-classical view of international trade and economic growth. The leading light of this approach, Paul Krugman, argued that trade is 'no longer very much like the kind of exchange envisaged in classical trade theory and still taught in textbooks' (Krugman, 1987: 6). A large part of modern trade has come to consist of exchanges that cannot be attributed so easily to underlying advantages of the countries that export particular goods: 'Instead, trade seems to reflect arbitrary or temporary advantages resulting from economies of scale or shifting leads in close technological races' (Krugman, 1987: 7). Krugman argues that the reasons for trade in products in which 'countries have no underlying comparative advantage' are not hard to find:

> They lie in the advantages of large-scale production, which lead to an essentially random division of labour among countries, in the cumulative advantages of experience which sometimes perpetuates accidental initial advantages, in the temporary advantages conveyed by innovation. What is important is that the conventional economic analysis of trade policy is based on a theory of trade that does not allow for these kinds of motives for international specialization. Firms in this situation are described by economists as being in 'imperfectly' competitive markets ... What it means is that what can happen in these markets is different from, and more complicated than, what is captured by the simple concepts of supply and demand. (Krugman, 1987: 8)

A crucial issue for the 'New Trade Theory' developed in the 1980s, was the increasingly central role of technology. In many industries, competitive advantage seems to be determined not by 'national characteristics', nor by 'the static advantages of large-scale production', but rather by 'the knowledge generated by firms through R & D and experience' (Krugman, 1987: 8). Technological innovation is an activity that 'may well generate important spillovers into the rest of the economy'. Its growing importance in international trade 'reinforces the need for a re-thinking of the analytical basis for trade policy' (Krugman, 1987: 8). In industries where the advantages of cumulative experience and the transitory advantages resulting from innovation are important, 'we are not going to see the kind of atomistic competition between many small firms that is necessary for "perfect" competition to be a good description of the world' (Krugman, 1987: 9). Major USA exporters such as Boeing or Caterpillar, 'face few identifiable rivals', they have 'some direct ability to affect prices', and they 'make strategic moves designed to affect their rivals' actions' (Krugman, 1987: 9). Krugman argues that there are certain 'strategic' sectors, which possess powerful external economies, so that producers are not paid in full for the social value of production. Once it is granted that certain sectors can have special strategic value in the form of strong external economies, derived from economies of scale, learning effects and the spread of new technical knowledge, then 'the extreme free trade position has become untenable' (Krugman, 1987: 15). Krugman's ideas were directed towards USA trade policy, but their logic applies equally to developing countries.

DOMINANT POSITION OF THE LARGE FIRM IN ADVANCED CAPITALISM

The Chicago economist George Stigler concluded that as much as 85 per cent of the USA economy in the mid-twentieth century was 'competitive' (quoted in Friedman, 1962: 122). Friedman himself thought that there was 'a general bias and tendency to overemphasize the importance of the big versus the small' (Friedman, 1962: 122–3). Friedman's lecture tours of China in the 1990s were received with great enthusiasm by Chinese audiences anxious to learn about the real nature of advanced capitalism and to understand the sources of the USA's prosperity.

The reality of business history has been quite different from the textbook. Instead of being an occasional deviation from the textbook picture, the normal path of capitalist development has been oligopoly, barriers to entry and imperfect competition. Capitalism's innate tendency to concentration of economic power became manifest almost as soon as the First Industrial Revolution got under way. The earliest forms of the modern industrial enterprise were found in the railways of the USA and Europe in the mid-nineteenth century. These quickly developed into the world's largest business institutions, often with tens of thousands of employees.[2] Such vast organizations quickly developed hierarchical professional bureaucracies, and associated impersonal procedures for co-ordinating and monitoring the large numbers of employees. The railways mobilized vast sums of investment funds from an increasingly widespread body of shareholders

TABLE 1-1 **Net Share of Manufacturing Output of the Top 100 Firms, 1909–63 (per cent)**

Country	1909	1929	1935	1963
United States	22	25	26	33
Britain	16	26	23	38
France	12	16	—	26

SOURCE: Schmitz (1993: 35)

(especially in the USA where government investment in railways played a much smaller role than in Europe). The railways developed the first significant body of salaried professional managers (Schmitz, 1993: 20–1).

These characteristic features of the modern industrial enterprise quickly spread to other parts of the economy in which large businesses emerged. These were industries characterized by greater economies of scale, greater potential gains from vertical integration, greater speed and co-ordination of production flows, as well as greater gains from high-volume marketing. These were notably the food, chemicals, primary metals and transportation equipment sectors (Schmitz, 1993: 23). By the 1930s, the 100 largest firms accounted for around one-quarter of total manufacturing output in Britain and the USA (Table 1-1).

There is intense and unresolved debate as to whether the degree of dominance of large corporations increased over time within each of the advanced economies. What is beyond dispute is that in the late twentieth century, these corporations occupied immensely powerful positions within each of the advanced economies, quite at odds with the views expressed by economists such as Stigler and Friedman. The evidence presented by Schmitz (1993) (Table 1-1) suggests an increase in the degree of dominance of large firms over time. Chandler and Hikino show that in 1947, the largest 200 firms in the USA accounted for 30 per cent of total value-added in manufacturing. By 1987, the share had risen to over 43 per cent (Chandler and Hikino, 1997: 47). In 1987, they accounted for 31 per cent of employment, 40 per cent of total payroll and over 46 per cent of new capital expenditure (Chandler and Hikino, 1997: 47). In 1960, just four firms accounted for 22 per cent of total USA industrial R & D expenditure (Galbraith, 1967: 84). Three hundred and eighty-four firms each employing more than 5000 workers accounted for 85 per cent of total expenditure, while 260 000 firms each employing fewer than 1000 accounted for only 7 per cent (Galbraith, 1967: 84).

THE STATE AND LARGE FIRMS IN THE 'CATCH-UP' PROCESS (i): THE WEST

Far from arising spontaneously through the free play of market forces, even the rise of big business in the West was strongly influenced by the state: 'Virtually all of the world's largest core firms have experienced a decisive influence from government policies and/or trade barriers on their strategy and competitive position.

History matters! There has never been a "level playing field" in international competition, and it is doubtful whether there ever will be one' (Ruigrok and van Tulder, 1995: 221).

Britain. The business revolution in Britain's Industrial Revolution was enormously shaped by state intervention. By the 1840s Britain had become the home of free trade, imposing the doctrine of *laissez-faire* upon its vast colonial territories. However, Britain's own business revolution took place under an explicitly Mercantilist philosophy of high protection and export promotion, not to speak of massive territorial conquest largely in pursuit of economic benefit. Its infant industries were heavily protected, denying the massive textile industries of China and India access to the British market (World Bank, 1991: 97; Li Bozhong, 1998; Xu Dixin and Wu Chengming, 2000; Smith, 1776, Vol. 1, Book iv, Ch. 2; Frank, 1998). Both the importation and wearing of silk and calicoes from these countries were banned in the seventeenth century. These restrictions gave Britain's infant textile industries the chance to mature and modernize through reinvested profits from heavily protected markets. Britain still had an average tariff on manufactures of 50 per cent in 1820. Moreover, while Britain's authoritarian state had no laws to prohibit capitalists from combining to lower the price of labour, it had 'many [laws] against [workmen] combining to raise it' (Smith, Vol. 1: 74–5). By the mid-nineteenth century Britain's 'big business' (compared to the rest of the world) was able to prosper with free trade. It is questionable whether Britain rather than China would indeed have been the 'First Industrial Nation' without extensive state intervention.

Between 1919 and 1945, more than 75 per cent of the increase in market share of 600 leading firms was accounted for by mergers (Schmitz, 1993: 48). In the post-1945 period, in many sectors the state directly organized mergers and acquisitions. Most notably, it combined several medium-sized companies into large state-owned corporations in the search for the requisite scale to compete with the global leaders. These included the formation of British Steel, the British Aircraft Corporation and the British Motor Corporation.

Nineteenth-century USA. The USA in the nineteenth century unashamedly industrialized behind high protectionist barriers, 'free riding on free trade' (Lake, 1988: Ch. 3). As early as 1791, Alexander Hamilton argued for USA industrialization behind tariff barriers (Ruigrok and van Tulder, 1995: 211). From 1820 through to the 1930s, USA tariffs on imported manufactures were never below 25 per cent and mostly were far higher, sometimes reaching as high as 50 per cent (World Bank, 1991: 97; Ruigrok and van Tulder, 1995: 211–12). They were typically twice as high as tariffs in Western Europe. Despite the passage of anti-trust laws, huge oligopolistic firms were allowed to grow. By the inter-war period, USA firms dominated big business globally, with around two-thirds of the world's top 50 companies (Schmitz, 1993: 31). Government military procurement spending was a strong influence on USA big business over many decades. This has had an especially powerful effect in the most technologically advanced sectors, including in recent times the aircraft, computer, semiconductor and electronics industries (Ruigrok and van Tulder, 1995: 221), which in turn strongly affect the civilian capability of the firms involved in military procurement.

Despite extensive public discussion and academic analysis of big business, there is little evidence that anti-trust law in the USA did much to hinder the rise of large USA firms. Indeed, it has even been argued that the key piece of American anti-trust legislation, the Sherman Act of 1890, actually promoted the growth of big business. It is argued that it encouraged the abandonment of cartels in favour of large, integrated firms (Schmitz, 1993: 55). The USA merger mania of the 1890s provided the underpinnings for the business structure of the USA economy for decades thereafter: 'The conversion of 71 important oligopolistic or near-competitive industries into monopolies by merger between 1890 and 1914 left an imprint on the structure of the American economy that 50 years has not yet erased' (Markham, 1955: 180). Sixty-three of the 100 largest USA firms in 1955 had experienced their main spurt of growth as a result of merger activity, including 20 in the 1895–1904 merger wave (Schmitz, 1993: 47–8). The USA turn-of-the-century merger movement was of 'prime importance in shaping many leading American firms' (Schmitz, 1993: 48).

During the First World War and much of the Depression of the 1930s, Federal Government effectively ignored anti-trust law, in order 'to stimulate the economy' (Schmitz, 1993: 50). There has throughout been a tension in the USA between alleged microeconomic inefficiency of big business and its dynamic, growth-inducing characteristics. The perceived anti-consumer tendencies inherent in big business stood in an uneasy relationship with the notion that possessing powerful big businesses was beneficial for the USA economy in international competition.

Having established powerful firms behind protectionist barriers, both Britain and the USA became converts to free trade, allowing their powerful businesses free access to the markets of less developed economies with weaker business structures.

THE STATE AND LARGE FIRMS IN THE 'CATCH-UP' PROCESS (ii): JAPAN

In Japan the catch-up process after the Second World War was facilitated by the Japanese government, MITI in particular, through a wide array of trade and industrial policies that went counter to mainstream economic theory (Johnson, 1982). As one of the key bureaucrats in MITI said: '[W]e did the opposite of what the American economists told USA to do. We violated all the normal concepts' (quoted in Ruigrok and van Tulder, 1995: 214). It was in this environment of close indirect support from the state that the giant Japanese firms, that today lie at the heart of the Japanese economy, developed.

In the early post-war period, the USA occupying forces imposed American anti-trust laws upon Japan. Initially these were strictly applied (Amsden and Singh, 1994). They led to the dismantling of the leading pre-war *zaibatsu*, the large industrial groups which had dominated the inter-war Japanese economy. However, under pressure of the cold war, there occurred a rapid erosion of the competition laws, both *de facto* and *de jure* (Amsden and Singh, 1994). The government encouraged the reconstruction of the *zaibatsu*, albeit in a somewhat looser form, known as *keiretsu*. The goal of the Japanese government was explicitly to create oligopolistic competition:

> [T]he Japanese government takes a more pragmatic approach to anti-trust enforcement, one that makes allowances for national goals such as industrial catch-up. It takes into account other collective values and extenuating circumstances in weighing enforcement decisions against the letter and spirit of anti-trust laws. Included here are such considerations as economies of scale, enhanced efficiency, heightened productivity, business cycle stabilization, industrial orderliness, price stabilization and economic security. (Okimoto, 1989: 12–13, quoted in Amsden and Singh, 1994: 943–4)

MITI, the key planning body, actively encouraged mergers between leading firms in key industries. It was only able to allow competitive large firms to develop through 'draconian import controls' (Amsden and Singh, 1994: 946). However, the government was acutely aware of the need to avoid monopoly and encourage oligopolistic rivalry. It closely monitored market shares and prevented any single investment from being 'so large as to destabilize the market' (Amsden and Singh, 1994: 945). International competitiveness was powerfully encouraged through the use of exports and international market share as the performance goals with which to evaluate the extent of government support for big businesses through different policies:

> Protection, together with restrictions on domestic competition, provided the Japanese companies with a captive home market leading to high profits which enabled them to undertake high rates of investment, to improve the quality of their products, and also to capture market abroad. (Amsden and Singh, 1994: 946)

In post-1945 Japan, the system of cross-ownership provided a powerful mechanism through which the large Japanese corporation was able to grow at high speed and catch-up with the world leaders. Most large companies were members of a small number of industrial groups, the *keiretsu*. A *keiretsu* usually owned less than 2 per cent of any other member firm, but it typically had a stake of that size in every firm in the group, so that between 30 per cent and 90 per cent of a firm was owned by other group members. Japanese corporations have about 70 per cent of their shares held by other corporations (Aoki, 1994: 21). Through the cross-holding process, Japanese managers effectively hired friendly owners: 'The seemingly crisp categories of principal and agent become fuzzy as the managers of one firm become the owners of another, and in turn are held by managers of that firm. It is less that management has been separated from control, therefore, than that control had been merged into management' (Gerlach, 1992: 238). The system was a kind of 'collective defence to maintain the control by management over ownership' (Suzuki, 1991: 78–9).

Under this system there was only a low level of merger and acquisition. From the managers' point of view, to be taken over by others was to surrender to their enemies. Externally hired managers were rare, reflecting the fact that in Japan competition was viewed as a war with no prisoners taken, with a good chance managers in the firm that was taken over would lose jobs after the take-over. This life-and-death battle forced Japanese managers to build an alliance with their employees, building long-term programmes such as housing, training, lifetime employment, and the seniority system. Managers and workers 'agree[d] to trade wage increases for job security or better opportunities for promotion made possible by the growth of the firm' (Aoki, 1987: 273). Hence, the level of strikes in Japan was low. Instead, Japanese labour unions and their members were very interested in having a voice in management (Koike, 1987). Workers in large Japanese firms often endured hardship in order to enable their firm to survive and grow (Hashimoto and Raisian, 1985; Mincer and Higuchi, 1988).

The removal of ownership control meant that the unconstrained Japanese managers could afford to ill-treat owners with impunity. In 1990, the total dividend payout of all public corporations in Japan was 30 per cent of profits compared with 50 per cent in Germany, 54 per cent in the USA, and 66 per cent in the UK. Managers in Japan spent more on corporate entertaining than they paid out in dividends (Aoki, 1987: 622). Without ownership control, internally oriented and immobile managers tended to re-invest profits rather than distribute them (Boltho, 1975; Lichtenberg and Pushner 1992: 7). Depreciation and corporate savings together amounted to as much as half of total domestic savings, underpinning Japan's high investment rates. Japanese firms acted as if they had 'investment hunger', and often 'over-invested' (Wang Xiaoqiang, 1998: 96). Japanese managers could ignore short-term profitability as a measure of their performance and concentrate instead on 'Schumpeterian' competition, such as foreign market penetration, quality control and long-term product development. 'Share price increase' was their least important target (Wang Xigaqiang, 1998: 95–6), and 'market domination' their most important one (Best, 1990: 10). Outside Japan it was a common criticism that Japanese companies owed their success to government assistance and the restriction of foreign business in Japan. Within Japan business leaders considered that the real source of their success was 'fierce domestic competition' (Kanter, 1991: 155).

Alongside rapid growth of national output, Japan's large firms grew at high speed. In 1962 Japan had just 31 of the *Fortune* 500 companies, fewer than either Germany or the UK, and only marginally more than France. By 1993 the number of Japanese firms in the *Fortune* 500 had risen to 135. Not only had the number of large Japanese firms risen at high speed, but their contribution to technical progress in the Japanese economy had also dramatically risen. By 1993 Japan had 49 out of the world's top 200 companies by R & D spending (DTI, 1995: 64–5). By 1995 Japan had 18 of the world's top 100 TNCs (ranked by foreign assets) (UNCTAD, 1997: 29–31) and in 1996 it had 110 of the world's top 500 companies, ranked by market capitalization (*FT*, 22 January 1998).

Despite the numerous difficulties of the 1990s, the core of Japan's large business structure remains immensely strong, with global leaders such as Sony,

Toyota, Fujitsu, Nippon Steel, Matsushita, Bridgestone, Fuji Film, Denso, Hitachi, Honda, Canon and NEC. These firms were still world leaders in terms of R & D expenditure and technological capability, as well as in terms of global brand and distribution systems. In the year 2000, Japan still had no fewer than 107 firms in the *Fortune* 500 (ranked by sales revenue) (*Fortune*, 24 July 2000) and 77 firms in the *FT* 500 (ranked by market capitalization) (*FT*, 4 May 2000). In 1999 it had 79 of the top 300 firms by R & D spending (DTI, 1999).

THE STATE AND LARGE FIRMS IN THE 'CATCH-UP' PROCESS (iii): THE FOUR LITTLE TIGERS

The evidence from the Four Little Tigers is far more complex than is presented by the populist neo-classical view such as that provided in Lin *et al.* (1996). The role of the state in the growth of the Four Little Tigers was much greater than the neo-classical position allows. For example, Ronald Findlay, in his balanced evaluation of the debate, has acknowledged that, with the exception of Hong Kong, the Asian NICs were characterized by 'very far-reaching and pervasive intervention and control by the state in almost all segments of the economy' (Findlay, 1988: 90). In Taiwan and South Korea the state went far beyond influencing the environment within which big business operated. In both cases the state played an important role in the construction of large-scale business through the direct operation of upstream, heavy industry which the private sector was unable or unwilling to undertake. Despite a quite limited role in direct ownership, both Hong Kong and Singapore had a central role for the state in developing human capital and maintaining social stability through high levels of expenditure on education, health and housing. In Taiwan, Korea and Singapore the state in each case had an extremely active industrial policy. In the populist neo-classical view of the Four Little Tigers, their rapid catch-up was reliant on small firms and perfect competition. In fact, large firms played an important role in the economic development of each of the Four Little Tigers.

Both Hong Kong and Singapore throughout their catch-up practised basically free trade regimes. As tiny city states they had little option. However, for both Taiwan and Korea, trade policy was central to their catch-up strategy. Both of them massively protected their economy through high tariff barriers in the early period of development. In Taiwan, after tariffs began to fall in the 1970s, there remained for many years a wide array of non-tariff barriers (NTBs) (Wade, 1990: Ch. 5). The Taiwan government used a variety of measures to actively promote exports. Korea remained heavily protected right up until the 1990s, using both tariff and non-tariff barriers. For example, even in the late 1990s, it was almost impossible for foreign auto makers to sell their vehicles in Korea. In Findlay's (1988) view an interventionist trade policy was an important part of the catch-up strategy in both Taiwan and Korea. He cautions that protection is 'not sufficient for successful industrialization in more technologically complex and capital intensive industries', but the argument that it is not necessary 'seems to be largely an *a priori* one, in view of the fact that most historical examples from Germany and the United States to Japan have involved protection' (Findlay, 1988: 92). He comments: 'Brazil today exports over $3 billion worth of cars and trucks, and low wages and an extensive network of parts and components suppliers give it very strong potential comparative advantage in this field for decades to come. Yet this base would not exist in its present form were it not for the legacy of some very costly episodes of import substitution' (Findlay, 1988: 92).

Taiwan. One of the most eloquent statements on the importance of the state in promoting economic development in the Far East is to be found in the writings of Chiang Kaishek, the leader of the Kuomintang. In 1947, in the midst of his party's struggle with the Chinese Communist Party he wrote:

> China cannot compete with the advanced industrial nations. She must therefore adopt a protectionist policy with regard to foreign trade, and a policy of economic planning with respect to her industrial development. *Private capital alone will not be sufficient to operate on a large scale, or to compete with the trusts and government operated enterprises of foreign nations.* This is the great weakness of laissez-faire economic theory and makes it unsuitable for China. (Chiang Kaishek, 1947: 279, emphasis added)

In the 1950s and 1960s, the state's industrial policy focused on import substitution and export promotion in labour-intensive light industry (Chiang, 1999: 9). However, in the 1970s, 'government policies called for a gradual shift to basic and heavy industries' and 'as part of a backward integration process, intermediate goods industries were established' (Chiang, 1999: 11). This included extensive state ownership of the 'commanding heights' of heavy industry, including steel, shipbuilding, oil refining, chemicals, and electricity generation (Wade, 1990). Even in sectors where public enterprises did not dominate, such as plastics and textiles, the state 'aggressively led private producers in the early years' (Wade, 1990: 110). Through its extensive ownership and operation of vital upstream industries, as well as numerous other measures, such as import controls, tariffs, entry requirements, domestic content requirements and concessional credit, the Taiwanese state strongly influenced the operation of the private sector (Wade, 1990).

By the early 1980s, three-quarters of Taiwan's exports consisted of high and mid-tech products and 51 per cent consisted of technology-intensive products (CEPD, 1998: 206). Subsequently, policy shifted to indirect support, and eventually widespread privatization. However, there was still a strong objective of consciously transforming the economic structure towards higher value-added activities more rapidly than the free market would have produced. For example, the government established the immensely influential Hsinchu Science Park, provided tax benefits for investment in high-technology industries (Chiang, 1999: 12) and in the mid-1980s, it accounted for 60 per cent of total R & D expenditure in Taiwan (CEPD, 1998: 121). By the late 1990s, over 80 per cent of Taiwan's exports were of technology-intensive products (CEPD, 1998: 206). The stylized picture of Taiwan provided by neo-classical economists is of an economy dominated by

TABLE 1-2 **Large Firms from the Four Little Tigers, 1999**

Country	No. of firms among the 50 largest TNCs based in developing countries (ranked by overseas assets)	No. of firms among the 100 largest firms in the non-Japan Asia–Pacific Region (ranked by market capitalization)
Hong Kong	9	20
Taiwan	2	26
Korea	6	11
Singapore	3	10
Sub-total	20	67
Brazil	5	—
Mexico	3	—
India	1	7
Indonesia	0	2
Malaysia	1	4

SOURCE: UNCTAD (1999: 86–7) *FT* (4 May 2000)

small firms. Taiwan does have a vibrant small-scale sector. However, it also has a very strong and dynamic large-scale sector. Taiwan's large firms benefit from economies of scale and scope enabling them to compete on world markets and provide intermediate inputs in an efficient way for Taiwan's other exporters. The Taiwanese government itself describes its industrial structure as a mutually inter-active relationship between large and small firms: 'The close relationship and divi-sion of labour between SMEs and large-scale enterprises make for a very solid "pyramid" or "cluster" economy in terms of industrial structure, which allows the realization of operational efficiencies' (Chiang, 1999: 40).

In the 1970s, Taiwan's large firms, with more than 500 employees, accounted for 58 per cent of manufacturing value-added, compared with 53 per cent in Korea and 49 per cent in the USA (Wade, 1990: 68). In 1979, the top 100 firms account-ed for 44 per cent of total private manufacturing assets (Wade, 1990: 68). In the 1990s, Taiwan's rapid growth of high-technology exports was spearheaded by rel-atively large firms such as Acer Computer (1999 revenue $5.6 billion), Taiwan Semi-Conductor (1999 revenue $1.7 billion) and Quanta Company (1999 revenue $1.7 billion) (*FT*, 4 May 2000). Relatively large heavy industrial enterprises, often former state-owned enterprises, such as China Steel (1999 revenue $3.3 billion), Formosa Chemicals (1999 revenue $1.3 billion), Formosa Plastics (1999 revenue $1.4 billion) and Nanya Plastics (1999 revenue $4.1 billion) (*FT*, 4 May 2000), still form the backbone of the economy. Taiwan has 26 of the top 100 firms in the non-Japan Asia–Pacific region, ranked by market capitalization (Table 1-2).

South Korea. The South Korean government believed strongly in the central role of big business in the catch-up process. President Park Chung Hee wrote as follows:

One of the essential characteristics of a modern economy is its strong tendency towards centralization. Mammoth enterprise – considered indispensable, at the

moment, to our country – plays not only a decisive role in the economic development and elevation of living standards, but further brings about changes
in the structure of society and economy … Therefore the key eco-nomic
problems facing a free economic policy are co-ordination and supervisory
guidance, by the state, of mammoth economic strength. (quoted in Amsden
and Singh, 1994: 949)

The government actively encouraged the growth of powerful, large-scale private
businesses, the *chaebols*, by providing them with a protected domestic market, and
supplying them with tightly controlled, but low interest credit from the state-owned
banking system (Chang, 1994). The South Korean state used pre-existing powerful business families as the foundation for the *chaebol* structure. Korea's large
firms remained predominantly family-owned throughout its catch-up process.
Like the Japanese state, South Korea was acutely aware of the importance of
maintaining competition among its large oligopolistic firms. It went out of its
way to ensure that big business did not collude, by allocating subsidies only in
exchange for strict performance standards (Amsden and Singh, 1994: 948).
Industrial policy focused initially on import substitution, with massive protection
from import competition for a long period while its big businesses were nurtured,
absorbing advanced technologies from abroad, and benefiting from economies of
scale and scope (Amsden, 1989). The state was prepared to provide long-term
support until the businesses became internationally competitive, enabling firms
to have long time-horizons for their investment plans (Amsden and Singh, 1994:
949). Once they were established, a key condition for continued state support
was success in export markets.

The South Korean 'entrepreneurial state' instigated 'every major industrial
diversification of the decades of the 1960s and 1970s' (Amsden, 1989: 80):

The state masterminded the early import-substituting projects … The transformation from light to heavy industry came at the state's behest … The
government played the part of visionary in the case of Korea's first colossal
shipyard … and it was responsible for the Big Push into heavy machinery and
chemicals in the late 1970s. It also laid the groundwork for the new wave of
import substitution that followed heavy industrialization and that carried the
electronics and automobile industry beyond the simple stage of assembly. The
government enacted the automobile protection law as far back as 1962, as part
of its five-year economic development plan. In conjunction with this decision,
it promoted the oil-refining industry. (Amsden, 1989: 80–1)

Korea's *chaebols* were the core of the country's economic development. By the
mid-1980s, the top 10 *chaebols* accounted for over two-thirds of national product
(Amsden, 1989: 116). The large-scale heavy industry sectors, dominated by the
chaebols were at the heart of Korea's dynamic export performance in the 1970s and
1980s (Amsden, 1989: 58; Chang, 1994: 105–6). By 1985, South Korea had 35 of
the top 200 largest industrial enterprises in developing countries, including 11 of
the 29 top 'high-tech' companies and 13 of the top 'mid-tech' companies within

this group (Hikino and Amsden, 1994: 302). By 1995 it had three of the top ten TNCs based in developing countries (Daewoo, L Electronics, and Sunkyong Group) (UNCTAD, 1997: 32). Uniquely among developing countries, by 1993, South Korea had no fewer than four companies in the *Fortune* 100 list of the world's largest companies, namely Samsung, Daewoo, Sangyong and Sunkyong) (Ruigrok and van Tulder, 1995: Table 9A). Even in the wake of the East Asian crisis, it still had 11 of the top 100 Asia-Pacific companies ranked by market capitalization (Table 1-2) and 12 firms in the *Fortune* 500 (*Fortune*, 24 July 2000). In the mid-1990s Samsung and Daewoo were each implementing a plan to expand massively their production capabilities abroad, especially in Europe.

Singapore. Singapore's state had little confidence in the capability of indigenous entrepreneurs to create globally powerful firms. Instead it actively induced multinationals to establish production facilities in Singapore in selected industries: 'Singapore's leaders took great care in selecting the foreign companies whose investment they approved. They sought out stable corporations that had advanced technology and were prepared to invest for the long-term' (Vogel, 1991: 78). It is no surprise that Singapore's industrial structure is dominated by multinational firms. However, alongside these firms, it has also developed a strong group of large indigenous firms. Singapore's bureaucrats over time developed a group of state-run enterprises in telecommunications, banking and transport, that began to establish a serious internationally competitive capability, including Singapore Telecoms, Development Bank of Singapore and Singapore Airlines. However, Singapore also is the home to several powerful private sector regional banking, infrastructure and property development companies. By 1999/2000, Singapore, a tiny city state, had as many firms among the largest multinationals based in developing countries as did Mexico, and more firms among the 100 largest in East Asia (by market capitalization) than India and Indonesia combined (Table 1-2).

Hong Kong. In the neo-classical view Hong Kong is the prime example of development through free markets and small competitive firms. Hong Kong has an outstanding location. It has a powerful entrepreneurial tradition, particularly due to the migration of a group of powerful entrepreneurs from Shanghai after 1949. It obtained enormous benefits from trade with, and investment in, the mainland. The combination of these factors stimulated the growth of numerous powerful firms that were among the largest in non-Japan East Asia. In 2000, there were seven Hong Kong-based firms among the top 15 firms, and 20 firms among the top 100 firms in non-Japan Asia, ranked by market capitalization (*FT*, 4 May 2000). Despite the rise of IT-based Indian firms, such as Wipro and Infosys, India still has only seven firms among the largest in the non-Japan Asia–Pacific region, far fewer than the tiny city state of Hong Kong. In 1995, nine of the 50 largest firms based in developing countries were from Hong Kong (UNCTAD, 1999: 87). Hong Kong was the base for a larger number of firms than any other country among the 50 largest TNCs from developing countries (Table 1-2). The sales revenues of the top 5 Hong Kong companies are equivalent to over 10 per cent of

Hong Kong's GDP. Hong Kong's relatively large companies account for a major share of the total market capitalization of the Hong Kong stock market. The political life of Hong Kong is strongly influenced by a small number of large firms.

Overall. The total population of the Four Little Tigers is just 77 million, the same size as a medium-sized Chinese province such as Jiangsu (72 million) or Guangdong (71 million). The Four Little Tigers were able to grow rapidly, owing to a variety of state actions, both direct and indirect, the advantage of good location, and outward-oriented policies at a time when other countries, such as India and China, were inward-looking. By the late 1990s they had between them 20 of the 50 largest TNCs in developing countries, and 67 of the 100 largest firms in the non-Japan Asia–Pacific region (Table 1-2). As we have seen, large firms played an important role in the development of each of these economies, including even Hong Kong. The facts of the relationship between the state and industrial development, and the role of large firms during the take-off phase in these countries, are far removed from the populist neo-classical view. The occasional neo-classical economist has directly addressed these issues. They have typically argued that without protection, export promotion, a core of large firms and an active industrial policy, Korea, Taiwan, Hong Kong and Singapore would have grown even more rapidly than they did. However, with average annual growth rates of GDP of 7–10 per cent in the 1980s and 5–8 per cent in the 1990s, far above the average for upper-middle-income countries (2.7 per cent and 3.9 per cent, respectively), it is hard to imagine how they could have grown faster under any alternative policy regimes (World Bank, 2000: 250–1).

CONCLUSION

China's policy makers after the 1970s were deeply influenced by the industrial policy experience of the advanced capitalist countries in Europe and in the USA during their 'catch-up' phase of development. Even more influential was the more recent experience of its East Asian neighbours. Among these, by far the most impressive for them was the way in which the Japanese state was able to mastermind the high-speed growth of large corporations. These were entities that came to challenge the global giants of Europe and the USA within their own markets. They developed high levels of business capability, built global brands from nothing and constructed massive R & D capabilities. During the first decade or so of China's post-Mao industrial policy, Japan's large firms were viewed in the West as providing a massive challenge to the existing large corporations. By far the most influential trend in business philosophy in the West was to learn from Japanese large corporations. As we shall see in Chapter 3, the key philosophy of the Chinese leadership's policies towards large-scale industry throughout this period was the attempt to emulate the East Asian 'latecomer' countries, and by means of state support to gradually build globally powerful large corporations. This policy was in the sharpest contrast with that pursued by the former USSR.

As we shall see in the separate chapters of this book, from the 1970s onwards there was great progress in the business capabilities of China's large enterprises. However, there were also innumerable problems encountered within China in the attempt to build large competitive modern corporations. Many of these were specific to the particular Chinese environment, and were not encountered by the other East Asian countries during their comparable period of development. However, even more importantly, the international business environment in which Chinese industrial policy was being implemented changed dramatically in the 1990s. This period saw the most dramatic changes in the global business system that have ever taken place. This was nothing less than a revolution. This provided a severe challenge to the philosophy underlying Chinese industrial policy. As the forces of globalization advanced, and the big business revolution accelerated, so the influence of mainstream neo-classical ideas in Chinese policy making grew. There was an increasing input from international institutions and from Chinese trained in Western, especially USA, universities in mainstream neoclassical economics. The policy debates intensified. They reached a crescendo as China concluded its historic agreement with the USA on its terms of entry to the WTO in late 1999.

2

The Challenge of the Global Business Revolution

Suppose giant multinational corporations (say 300 from the US and 200
from Europe and Japan) succeed in establishing themselves as the dominant
form of international enterprise and come to control a significant share of
industry (especially modern industry) in each country. The world economy
will resemble more and more the United States economy, where each of the
large corporations tends to spread over the entire continent,
and to penetrate almost every nook and cranny.
(Hymer, 1975)

My job is to create oligopoly.
(Investment banker, anon.)

I'd like to build the world a home and furnish it with love,
Grow apple trees and honey bees and snow white turtle doves,
I'd like to teach the world to sing in perfect harmony,
I'd like to hold it in my arms and keep it company,
I'd like to see the world for once all standing hand in hand,
And hear them echo through the hills for peace throughout the land.

INTRODUCTION

Since the late 1970s, China has pursued an industrial policy which has the explicit objective of creating large firms that can challenge the global giant corporations of the advanced economies. China faces a special challenge which did not confront other countries that successfully built globally powerful large firms through industrial policy: China is attempting to catch-up at the level of the large

27

firm in the midst of the most profound revolution in business systems that the world has ever seen. This revolution presents a fundamental challenge not only for China's industrial policy, but for industrial policy in developing countries as a whole. The challenge is made especially severe by the fact that in November 1999 China and the USA agreed the terms under which China would enter the WTO. These terms amounted to a voluntary dismantling by China of all the key features of industrial policy that almost all the successful 'latecomer' countries had used to support large indigenous firms. Through the Agreement, China has agreed to place its indigenous large firms on the 'global level playing field', in direct competition with the world's most powerful corporations. As we shall see in this chapter, the global business revolution has produced an unprecedented concentration of business power in large corporations headquartered in the high-income countries. It is a highly significant paradox that the influence of main-stream neo-classical ideas which emphasize small firms and competitive markets, has increased radically within Chinese policy making circles in precisely the epoch of unprecedented concentration of global business power.

DRIVERS OF THE BIG BUSINESS REVOLUTION

Several forces interacted to drive forward the global big business revolution in the 1990s.

TRADE LIBERALIZATION

Despite slow long-term liberalization under the GATT, the average tariffs on manufactures in developing countries still stood at 34 per cent in 1987, reaching as high as 81 per cent in South Asia (World Bank, 1991: 98). Moreover, there was a wide array of non-tariff barriers (NTBs), covering 27 per cent of manu-factured imports. Tariff protection in the advanced economies fell from moderate levels in the early 1950s to low levels in the late 1980s, when they averaged only around 6 per cent (World Bank, 1991: 97). A major factor offsetting the impact of tariff reductions was the sharp rise in NTBs. By the late 1980s, 21 per cent of developed countries' imports from developing countries were covered by various forms of NTBs (World Bank, 1991: 105). Despite extensive tariff liberalization in developing countries, tariff barriers in the late 1980s were much higher than in the advanced economies. In 1987 they averaged more than 30 per cent (World Bank, 1991: 98). In addition, NTBs covered 28 per cent of all imports to devel-oping countries (World Bank, 1991: 98).

After the mid-1980s, the pace of trade liberalization accelerated. The Uruguay Round of the GATT began in 1985 and was completed in 1993. However, even before the conclusion of the Uruguay Round, many developing countries had put into place large reductions in their import duties (World Bank, 2000: 56). The Uruguay Round resulted in even further reductions in developed country tariffs,

TABLE 2-1 **Relative Growth of National Output and International Trade, 1980–98**

Type of economy	Growth of GDP (% p.a.)		Growth of exports of goods and services (% p.a.)	
	(1980–90)	(1990–8)	(1980–90)	(1990–8)
Low income	6.6	7.3	5.9	11.1
Middle income	2.6	1.9	6.1	7.5
High income	3.1	2.1	6.1	8.4
World	3.2w	2.4w	5.1w	6.1w

SOURCE: World Bank (2000: 250–1, 254–5)

NOTE: w = weighted

and large reductions in developing country tariffs. Although there was an overall reduction in many types of NTBs, the period saw a substantial rise in the use of anti-dumping (AD) measures, 'diluting market access and the gains from trade liberalization' (World Bank, 2000: 58). The period saw a significant widening of the scope of trade liberalization measures, including trade and foreign investment in services. By the late 1990s, 47 per cent of service sectors in industrialized countries and 16 per cent in developing countries had been liberalized (World Bank, 2000: 65). The membership of the GATT and, subsequently, the WTO, has widened greatly. By 1999 it included not only the 24 core members in the OECD, but also 110 members from outside the OECD (World Bank, 2000: 34).

The progressive liberalization of world trade has stimulated long-term growth of international trade. Over several decades the rate of growth of world trade has powerfully outdistanced that of national output. However, the disparity between output growth and trade growth increased sharply in the 1990s (Table 2-1). In the 1980s, world trade grew 60 per cent faster than world output but in the 1990s, trade grew at almost twice the pace of world output. A major part of the rapid growth in exports from developing countries has been associated with the process of 'slicing up the value chain' in different countries, locating different parts of the process in the lowest cost location. It has been loosely estimated that by the mid-1990s almost one-third of all world trade took place within global production networks (World Bank, 2000: 65).

LIBERALIZATION OF CAPITAL FLOWS

Accelerated international flows of long-term capital have been at the heart of the global business revolution. Foreign direct investment (FDI) rose enormously from the early 1980s to the late 1990s (Table 2-2): average annual inflows in 1981–5 stood at $48 billion, rising to $168 billion in 1986–90, and $186 billion in 1991–3 (UNCTAD, 1994: 12), reaching $644 billion in 1998 (UNCTAD, 1999: 477). Inflows of FDI into developing countries accelerated from an annual average of around $22 billion in 1984–9 to $166 billion in 1998 (UNCTAD, 1999: 477).

TABLE 2-2 FDI Inflows, 1984–98 ($ billion, % in brackets)

	1984–9 (annual average)	1990	1991	1992	1993	1994	1995	1996	1997	1998
Total inflow	115.4	203.8	157.8	168.1	207.9	225.7	314.9	358.9	464.3	643.9
	(100)	(100)	(100)	(100)	(100)	(100)	(100)	(100)	(100)	(100)
Developed countries	93.1	169.8	114.0	114.0	129.3	132.8	203.2	211.1	273.3	460.4
	(80.7)	(83.6)	(72.2)	(67.8)	(62.2)	(58.8)	(64.5)	(58.8)	(58.9)	(71.5)
Developing countries	22.2	33.7	41.3	50.4	73.1	87.0	99.7	135.3	172.5	165.9
	(19.2)	(16.5)	(26.2)	(30.0)	(35.2)	(38.5)	(31.7)	(37.7)	(37.2)	(25.8)
Central and Eastern Europe	Neg.	0.3	2.4	3.7	5.5	5.9	12.1	12.4	18.5	17.5
		(0.1)	(1.5)	(2.2)	(2.6)	(2.8)	(3.8)	(3.5)	(4.0)	(2.7)
Developing countries minus China	19.9	30.2	37.0	39.2	45.6	53.2	62.2	95.1	131.3	120.4
	(17.2)	(14.8)	(23.4)	(23.3)	(21.9)	(23.6)	(19.8)	(26.5)	(28.3)	(18.7)
Asia	11.5	22.1	22.7	29.1	50.0	56.3	68.1	82.0	95.5	84.9
	(10.0)	(10.8)	(14.4)	(17.3)	(24.1)	(24.9)	(21.6)	(22.9)	(20.6)	(13.1)
within which: China	2.3	3.5	4.4	11.2	27.5	33.8	37.5	40.2	44.2	45.5
	(2.0)	(1.7)	(2.8)	(6.7)	(13.2)	(15.0)	(11.9)	(11.2)	(9.5)	(7.1)

SOURCE: UNCTAD (1996: 227–31); UNCTAD (1999: 477–81)

NOTE: Neg. = Negligible

The share going to developing countries sharply increased, from under 20 per cent in 1984–9, to 40 per cent in 1994 (UNCTAD, 1996: 227–31), falling back some-what, to 26 per cent in 1998 (UNCTAD, 1999: 477). The inflows were concentrated heavily in a relatively small number of countries. The three largest, Brazil, Mexico and China, together accounted for 30 per cent of FDI inflows into developing countries in 1987–92 and 51 per cent in 1998 (UNCTAD, 1999: 477–81).

Despite the large rise in capital flows to developing countries, the vast bulk of FDI flows were between the advanced economies. The developed countries have consistently accounted for over 90 per cent of outflows of world FDI (93 per cent in 1987–92, and 92 per cent in 1998) and their share of inflows is typically around three-quarters of the world total (UNCTAD, 1999: 477–87). The USA has been much the largest recipient of FDI inflows, accounting for 30 per cent of the world total in 1998 (UNCTAD, 1999: 478).

Over the long run, the post-war world boom was 'export-driven', in the sense that the growth of trade was much faster than the growth of output. However, in the 1990s, the growth of FDI has been faster even than that of trade (Hirst and Thompson, 1995: 5). From 1988 to 1998, FDI grew by 15 per cent per annum (UNCTAD, 1994: 409, 1999: 477) compared to 8 per cent per annum for annual growth of world merchandize exports (World Bank, 1990: 205, 2000: 259). By the 1990s, a large and rising share of total manufacturing production of firms based in advanced capitalist economies was located abroad (Table 2-3). The foreign operations of US-owned corporations in the early 1990s amounted to more than 1 trillion dollars, roughly four times the value of US exports of goods manufactured in the USA (Reich, 1995: 173).

Since the 1980s there has been a progressive liberalization of international short-term capital flows. Across both the developed and the developing world, it has become progressively easier to move short-term capital from one location to another. In the advanced economies, financial markets have 'melded into a global financial system' (World Bank, 2000: 70). Rapid improvements in the technologies for collecting, analyzing and disseminating information have stimulated financial innovation, and created a multi-billion dollar pool of internationally mobile capital. The growth of international trade, and especially the acceleration of international capital flows, has created a massive rise in foreign exchange transactions: in 1998, the daily total stood at around $1.5 trillion, an amount equal to one-sixth of the annual output of the US economy (World Bank, 2000: 71).

TABLE 2-3 **Share of Foreign Production in Total Production of Manufacturing Firms in Japan, Germany and the USA, 1986 and 1995**

Country	1986	1995
USA	20	25 (1993)
Germany	15	20
Japan	4	10

SOURCE: UNCTAD (1996: 48)

A major driver of the growth of international short-term capital flows has been the rise of institutional investors in the advanced economies, with a large fraction of the funds allocated to equity investments. In 1995, these investors controlled $20 trillion, around one-fifth of it invested abroad (World Bank, 2000: 71).

PRIVATIZATION

Only a decade or so ago, a vast swathe of economic activity in the advanced capitalist economies was directly owned and controlled by the state. The extent of privatization has been enormous, opening up huge areas of the economy to private capital. It has included large parts of Europe, the former Communist countries and developing countries. Privatization has included telecoms, airlines, post services, power (generation, transmission and sale), aerospace, defence equipment, automobiles, coal, steel, public transport, oil and petrochemicals. Privatization of formerly state-owned services such as airlines, telecoms, power generation and transmission, has had a cascading effect on sectors that supply these sectors with complex equipment, forcing intense competition upon them.

COLLAPSE OF COMMUNISM

More than two-fifths of the world's population in the late 1970s lived in countries ruled by Communist parties. Global capital was drastically limited in its access to these potentially vast markets. By the early 1990s, almost the whole of this area was opened up to global capital. The opening-up process radically enhanced the growth prospects of capitalist firms. Large areas of the world had become potential purchasers of Western products, recipients of Western capital, and potential locations for extending their global production base. This provided an important stimulus to the 'animal spirits' of Western investors and production enterprises.

INFORMATION TECHNOLOGY

I shall discuss later the dramatic changes in information technology (IT) since the 1980s (see, especially, Chapter 11). At this juncture it is necessary to emphasize how central this phenomenon has been to many key aspects of institutional change in the epoch of the big business revolution. For example, it has facilitated the revolution in global capital markets, in the management of a global supply chain, in the development of global brand names and in the design and maintenance of complex equipment.

MIGRATION

Migration constituted a major exception to the general pattern of liberalization. In the late nineteenth and early twentieth century, international migration played a substantial role in the international economy. Around 60 million people left Europe for the Americas, Oceania, and South and East Africa (Hirst and Thompson, 1995: 23). In the inter-war period, international migration drastically declined. Although numbers increased subsequently, with increased flows from poor to rich countries, the level of migration has never recaptured that of pre-1914. In the 1990s, each year around 2–3 million people migrate internationally. The total number of migrants living outside their home country is only around 2–3 per cent of the world population (World Bank, 2000: 38). There are significant opportunities for women to migrate as temporary domestic workers, and there is a relatively large international criminal traffic in women for prostitution. However, apart from these special categories, long-term migration of unskilled people from poor to rich countries is very limited: 'A world market for labour just does not exist in the same way as it does for goods and services. Most labour markets continue to be nationally regulated and accessible only marginally to outsiders, whether legal or illegal migrants or professional manpower. Moving goods and services is infinitely easier than moving labour' (Hirst and Thompson, 1995: 29).

A substantial proportion of permanent migrants are relatively highly skilled. Instead of capital migrating to developing countries to employ relatively low-priced local skilled employees, a significant number of highly skilled people migrate relatively easily to take up these occupations in developed countries. A key feature of the global business revolution is the great excess demand within the advanced economies for highly skilled labour, especially in the industries of the Third Technological Revolution (see Chapter 11). A significant proportion of the most highly skilled workers in developing countries has migrated to work in the knowledge-intensive industries of the high-income countries. A highly important issue in attempting to understand the changing nature of inequality between rich and poor countries in the course of the business revolution is the dearth of serious empirical research on the degree to which capital and labour flows back to the countries from which the emigration of highly skilled knowledge workers has taken place.

COMPETITIVE ADVANTAGE

In the epoch of the global big business revolution, successful firms have secured their competitive advantage through a number of inter-related mechanisms.

Core Business   After the 1970s, the extent of the market was dramatically widened by the liberalization of wide swathes of the world that had formerly been closed to international capitalism. This created a strong incentive for large firms to narrow their scope of business activity but still become fast-growing corporations within that narrowed range of business activity. The global business revolution witnessed a widespread narrowing of the range of business activity undertaken by the individual large firm. There took place a massive restructuring of assets, with firms extensively selling off 'non-core businesses' in order to develop their 'core businesses'. The goal for most large capitalist firms became the maintenance or establishment of their position as one of the top two or three companies in the global market-place. This position was to be achieved through sharply focusing R & D and marketing resources upon a narrower range of products in order to develop and enhance competitive advantage in the chosen areas of core competence. This period saw significant increases in R & D and marketing spending by leading corporations, but the range of activities upon which this expenditure was concentrated became much narrower for any given firm. The mantra for globally successful business became: 'If you're not number one, two or three in the world, you shouldn't stay in the business.'

Brand   The epoch of the global big business revolution has seen for the first time the emergence of truly global brands. Their penetration of consumers' consciousness across the world has been facilitated not only by the spread of production centres across the world, but also by the explosion of global culture through the globalized mass media. Successful brands spend billions of dollars on marketing. This includes not only the obvious forms of brand-building, notably advertising, but also less obvious forms, such as building a global network of marketing machinery, such as freezers, coolers and dispensing machines, to distribute branded goods in close proximity to customers. It includes constant promotion of new forms of packaging. The first-movers in the great race for the global market-place of branded consumer goods are able to shape the consumption habits of the world's population for a long period to come. They possess powerful, sustainable competitive advantage (Table 2-4).

In their search for ever-more effective brand-building, some of the world's most successful branded goods companies are sharply narrowing their range of products to obtain greater impact from their marketing outlays. Companies such as Diageo, Unilever and Procter and Gamble find that only a small number of 'core brands' account for the lion's share of their revenue and profits. Niall Fitzgerald, co-chairman of Unilever commented: 'You need to get through the clutter of communication with consumers, and if you spread your budget over all your brands it doesn't get through. We will swing all our resources behind a smaller number to achieve higher growth rates for them' (quoted in *FT*, 29 October 1999).

R & D   Spending on R & D by the world's leading firms rose at high speed alongside the acceleration in mergers and acquisitions. From a plateau of around $160–170 billion in the early 1990s, R & D spending by the world's top 300 firms accelerated to over $240 billion in 1998 (DTI, 1996, 1999), growing at 13 per cent per annum from 1995 to 1998. The technical capability of the world's

TABLE 2-4 **Sustainability of Competitive Edge of Different Branded Consumer Goods Companies**

Company	Sustainability (years)*	Company	Sustainability (years)
Coca-Cola	20+	Kellogg	10–15
Gillette	20+	Cadbury Schweppes	10–15
McDonalds'	20+	LVMH	10–15
Philip Morris	20+	Coca-Cola Enterprizes	10
Procter and Gamble	20+	Mattel	10
Eastman Kodak	20	Sara Lee	10
Heineken	15–20	Unilever	10
PepsiCo	15–20	Avon Products	10
Nestlé	15	Colgate Palmolive	10
Bestfoods	10–15	H. J. Heinz	10
L'Oréal	10–15	Fuji	10
Diageo	10–15	Gruma	5–10

SOURCE: MSDW (1998a: 105)

NOTE: *Defined as the number of years it would take an aggressive and well-financed competitor to establish a similar business

leading firms advanced at high speed in this epoch. Moreover, these data fail to capture the full extent of the real increase. A large fraction of the increased expenditure was on IT hardware to facilitate R & D that was dramatically falling in price in terms of the functional capability being purchased for a given investment. Large MNCs are the chief repositories of the world's stock of economically useful knowledge and skills: 'All the screaming in the world will not change this' (Martin Wolf in *FT*, 17 November 1999).

We have seen already that in the 1960s, there was a very high degree of concentration in R & D expenditure in the advanced economies. In the mid-1990s, the picture looked little different. Just five firms accounted for 21 per cent of total US industrial R & D expenditure (Table 2-5). Twenty firms accounted for 41 per cent and 123 firms accounted for 68 per cent of total US industrial R & D expenditure. The key to the technical progress and economic advance of the US economy in the private sector lies in the hands of a small number of giant oligopolistic firms. As far as the overall technical progress of the US economy is concerned, the role of the state is also crucially important. Thirty-six per cent of total US expenditure on R & D is funded by the Federal Government. For fiscal year 2001, 51 per cent ($44 billion) of Federal Government outlays on R & D will be allocated to the civilian sector and 49 per cent ($42 billion) to the military sector (The White House web site). A large fraction of this funding for R & D is channelled to the giant corporations that dominate private R & D spending.

TABLE 2-5 R & D Expenditure in the USA, 1994

Expenditure	$ billion	%
Total	172.6	100
Federal government	62.2	36
Industry	102.1	59
of which:		% of industry R & D
Top 5 firms	21.7	21.3
Top 20 firms	41.8	40.9
Top 123 firms	69.6	68.2

SOURCE: DTI (1996); National Science Foundation website

IT Expenditure   The period of the big business revolution saw a massive increase in expenditure by the world's leading firms on IT hardware, software and services. Data transmission within and between firms grew at an explosive rate, facilitated by the technological revolution. Despite a dramatic advance in the functional capability that can be purchased for a given investment, a major source of competitive advantage for globally successful firms is their ability to undertake larger investment in IT systems. Such investment facilitates numerous competitive advantages. These include deeper and more effective interactions with suppliers and consumers, centralized global procurement, downsizing of the number of employees, more effective interactions between remaining employees, deeper research using data that can be analyzed by new IT systems, better and more effective R & D programmes and better monitoring of performance of complex equipment installed by customers.

No matter what sector one examines, from soft drinks through to complex aerospace machinery, a striking common characteristic of competitive advantage for the world's leading corporations is their ability to use IT to integrate the entire value chain. The world's most successful corporations are, increasingly, systems integrators that bind together whole swathes of business activity within their sphere of influence. This is a modern form of planning, guided by the market and the pursuit of profit, and facilitated by technical progress in IT.

Financial Resources   The big business revolution has coincided with the largest and most prolonged boom ever seen in Western, and, especially US, stock markets. This process has been fed by, and in turn has fed, the explosion in mergers and acquisitions. Investors, especially the fast-rising institutional investors, have increasingly shifted their portfolios to the world's leading companies, with high global market share, global brands, high R & D and core business focus that enable the businesses to be transparently analyzed. The lift in share values has facilitated further mergers by enabling mergers to take place by offering shares in the dominant partner's company. Companies with global competitive edge are able to support their growth through bank borrowing at lower rates of interest than are available to smaller competitors and through large-scale corporate bond issuance.

INDUSTRIAL CONCENTRATION

There are endless debates about the extent of and changes in concentration at the firm level in advanced capitalism. Over the long run it is quite possible that the epoch of greatest concentration of market power in the hands of large corporations was the period immediately after the Second World War. By the 1930s, most analysts agree that the USA was highly concentrated. However, the effect of the Second World War was to destroy vast swathes of production within the former USSR and in Eastern Europe, in large parts of Western Europe and in Japan. In the ensuing forty years or so, output grew rapidly in Japan and Europe as well as within the former Soviet bloc. Within both Europe and Japan, large indigenous corporations emerged to challenge the dominance of US large firms, often with powerful direct and indirect state support. Despite great arguments about the data, it is plausible that the degree of concentration at a global level declined between the late 1940s and the mid-1980s.

By the late 1990s, there was a very high degree of firm-level concentration on a global scale in a wide range of sectors. It is highly likely that the extent of firm-level concentration increased significantly after the mid-1980s. The process of concentration was most visible at the level of the global system integrators. A powerful trend increase in the extent of firm-level concentration of global market share could be observed in industries as diverse as aerospace and defence, pharmaceuticals, automobiles, trucks, power equipment, farm equipment, oil and petrochemicals, mining, pulp and paper, brewing, banking, insurance, advertising and mass media.

However, it quickly became apparent that a powerful associated process of firm-level concentration was at work. As we have seen, associated with the fast-growing concentration of market share among global systems integrators there was taking place a process of intensified pressure on the surrounding network of suppliers. In sector after sector, leading firms, with powerful technologies and marketing capabilities, were actively selecting the most capable among their numerous suppliers, in a form of 'industrial planning' to select 'aligned suppliers' who could work with them across the world. Only those suppliers that were able to undertake the requisite R & D and investment in IT were able to qualify as long-term business partners for the global giants. Thus, across a wide range of activities a 'cascade effect' began to work in which intense pressures developed for first-tier suppliers of goods and services to the global giants to themselves merge and acquire, and develop leading global positions. These, in their turn, passed on intense pressure upon their own supplier networks. The result was a fast-developing process of concentration at a global level in numerous industries supplying goods and services to the systems integrators. The process was most visible in the auto components industry, but was taking place in numerous sectors that supplied the systems integrators, including such diverse activities as metal cans, high value-added steel, aerospace components, and print machinery.

Across a wide range of business activity, instead of competition between anonymous firms, competition had become oligopolistic at a global level, not only among the systems integrators, but, increasingly, among the first tier suppliers. Leading firms at a global level increasingly competed with the clearly identified firms that occupied the commanding heights in a wide range of business activities.

Merger Frenzy   We have seen that mergers played a central role in the growth of the large capitalist corporation. Merger activity has typically intensified in the final phase of a bull market on the stock exchange, as firms use their increased stock market 'wealth' to finance take-overs (Schmitz, 1993: 47). The speed of transnational merger and acquisition in the 1990s increased at an extraordinary rate. From $156 billion in transactions in 1992, the global total nearly doubled to $290 billion in 1994, and then soared to $1100 billion in 1997 (MSDW, 1998a: 4). Eight of the world's 10 largest mergers took place in 1998, with a total value of $563 billion. The total value of mergers and acquisitions in 1998 was over $2000 billion (*Fortune*, 11 January 1999). In 1999, the total value of mergers and acquisitions was over $3300 billion.

The merger explosion of the 1990s is likely to leave a deep and long-lasting imprint, not just on the USA economy, but on the entire world's business structure in the epoch of globalization. As we shall see, US big business is at the heart of this structure. The merger and acquisition explosion of the 1990s will shape the fundamental features of the global business structure for well into the twenty-first century.

Market Share   In sector after sector, the 1990s saw a sharp increase in the global market share of leading companies. The process was inexorable, permeating almost every sector. Middle-sized firms were squeezed out remorselessly. Hardly a sector has not seen this process. The 1990s witnessed a massive process of asset reorganization within large capitalist firms. Following the extensive diversification of the 1980s, the 1990s saw a dramatic change in big business philosophy and practice. Firm after firm shed non-core business in order to focus on the areas in which the firm could compete globally. This sharp focus enabled firms to develop vast global businesses within a much narrower range of competence than previously. Moreover, the sharpening of focus meant that large businesses could now devote much greater resources to their chosen activities. In sector after sector a small number of firms accounted for over one-half of global sales (Table 2-6).

Simply examining market share in different sectors greatly underestimates the role of globalizing large firms in the modern economy. The relative cost of purchasing inputs through the market, as opposed to production within the firm, has fallen radically in recent years. Core globalizing businesses are putting intense pressure on first-tier supplier businesses to meet their global needs. These in turn are concentrating in order to be able to provide high-quality supply of goods and services across the world. In their turn these place pressure on second-tier suppliers. The process of concentration through simultaneous demerger of non-core businesses and merger of core businesses is cascading across the value chain at high speed. In industries as diverse as soft drinks, aerospace and automobiles, manufacturers are selecting a greatly reduced number of 'aligned' suppliers to establish global supply systems. The companies that are successful in this 'industrial policy' organized by big business, are able to use their success to acquire other suppliers and establish leading positions in their respective sectors. Each of them is able to benefit from high levels of R & D, global procurement systems and enhanced resources to spend on information technology, mimicking the development of globalizing core businesses. The process has already begun to cascade down to include second- and third-tier suppliers.

Not only do the world's top two aerospace companies account for 100 per cent of world commercial aircraft sales of planes with over 100 seats, but three engine makers account for 100 per cent of the engines that power these planes. Not only do six firms account for 68 per cent of world auto sales, but two firms alone account for over one-half of total world brake systems sales and three firms account for over one-half of total global sales of tyres. Not only do the top two carbonated soft drinks firms account for as much as three-quarters of world sales, but the top two suppliers of aluminium, a key packaging material, account for around two-fifths of global aluminium supplies. One firm alone accounts for over one-half of the world total of plastic bottle machinery.

THE EXTERNAL FIRM: AN EVER-LARGER SPHERE OF CO-ORDINATION AND PLANNING?

If we define the firm not by the entity which is the legal owner, but, rather, by the sphere over which conscious co-ordination of resource allocation takes place, then, far from becoming 'hollowed out' and much smaller in scope, the large firm can be seen to have enormously increased in size during the global business revolution. As the large firm has 'disintegrated', so has the extent of conscious co-ordination over the surrounding value chain increased. In a wide range of business

TABLE 2-6 **Global Oligopoly in the Business Revolution**

Company name	Sector	Global market share (%)	Source
Aerospace			
Boeing	Commercial aircraft orders over 100 seats	70	MSDW (1998)
Airbus	Commercial aircraft orders over 100 seats	30	MSDW (1998)
Rolls-Royce	Aero-engine orders	34	*FT* (6 Mar. 1998)
GE	Aero-engine orders	53	*FT* (6 Mar. 1998)
Pratt & Whitney	Aero-engine orders	13	*FT* (6 Mar. 1998)
IT			
Lucent	Internet and telecoms equipment	17	*FT* (27 Oct. 1999)
Intel	Micro-processors	85	MSDW (1998)
Microsoft	PC operating systems	85	*FT* (29 Apr. 2000)
Microsoft	Business desktop computer applications	90	*FT* (29 Apr. 2000)
Cisco	Computer routers:	66	MSDW (1998)
	high-end routers	80	
Corning	optical fibres	50	*FT* (15 Nov. 1999)
Hyundai Electronics	DRAMS	21	*FT* (15 Oct. 1999)
Samsung Electronics	DRAMS	20	*FT* (15 Oct. 1999)
Sony	Electronic games	67	*FT* (29 Mar. 2000)
Nintendo	Electronic games	29	*FT* (29 Mar. 2000)
Ericsson	Mobile phones	15	*FT* (8 Feb. 1999)
Nokia	Mobile phones	23	*FT* (8 Feb. 1999)
Motorola	Mobile phones	20	*FT* (8 Feb. 1999)
Pharmaceuticals			
Glaxo Wellcome/	Prescription drugs:	7	*FT* (18 Jan. 2000)
SKB	central nervous system	12	Glaxo Wellcome,
	anti-infection	17	(*Annual Report*, 1999)
	respiratory	17	
	anti-asthma	31	
	anti-herpes	49	
Merck	Prescription drugs:	5	*FT* (18 Jan. 2000)
	statin anti-cholesterol	40	Merck (*Annual*
	angiotension converting enzyme inhibitors	30	*Report, 1998*)
Medtronic	Implantable/interventional therapy technologie:*	45	MSDW (1998)
	pacemakers	50+	MSDW (1998)
Autos			
Ford/Mazda/Volvo	Automobiles	16	MSDW (1999)
GM	Automobiles	15	MSDW (1999)

TABLE **2-6** (*Continued*)

Company name	Sector	Global market share (%)	Source
Daimler–Chrysler	Automobiles	10	MSDW (1999)
VW	Automobiles	9	MSDW (1999)
Toyota	Automobiles	9	MSDW (1999)
Renault/Nissan	Automobiles	9	MSDW (1999)
Auto Components			
Pilkington	Auto glass	25	*FT* (21 May 1996)
GKN	Constant velocity joints	40	*FT* (22 July 1996)
Tenneco	Shock absorbers/car exhaust systems	25	*FT* (28 Oct. 1996)
Lucas	Brake systems	25	*FT* (8 May 1996)
Bosch	Brake systems	31	*FT* (8 May 1996)
Bridgestone	Tyres	19	*FT* (19 Jan. 1996)
Michelin	Tyres	18	*FT* (19 Jan. 1996)
Goodyear	Tyres	14	*FT* (19 Jan. 1996)
Petrochemicals			
BP Amoco	PTA	37	BP Amoco (*Annual Report, 1998*)
	acetic acid (technology licences)	70	
	Acrylonite(technology licences)	90	
Complex Equipment			
Invensys	Control/automation equipment	11	*FT* (24 Nov. 1998)
Siemens	Control/automation equipment	10	*FT* (24 Nov. 1998)
ABB	Control/automation equipment	9	*FT* (24 Nov. 1998)
Emerson	Control/automation equipment	8	*FT* (24 Nov. 1998)
Fanuc	Machine tool controls	45	*FT* (11 Sept. 1996)
Schindler	Lifts	25	*FT* (30 Mar. 1999)
Otis	Lifts	18	*FT* (30 Mar. 1999)
Mitsubishi	Lifts	13	*FT* (30 Mar. 1999)
Kone	Lifts	9	*FT* (30 Mar. 1999)
Fast-Moving Consumer Goods			
Coca-Cola	Carbonated soft drinks	51	Coca-Cola (*Annual Report, 1998*)
Procter and Gamble	Tampons	48	MSDW (1998)
Gillette	Razors	70	MSDW (1998)

TABLE **2-6** (*Continued*)

Company name	Sector	Global market share (%)	Source
Fuji Film	Camera films	35	MSDW (1998)
Chupa Chups	Lollipops	34	*FT* (31 Mar. 2000)
Nike	Sneakers	36	MSDW (1998)
Packaging			
Toray	Polyester film	60	*FT* (15 May 1998)
Sidel	PET plastic packaging machines	55	Sidel (*Annual Report, 1998*)
Alcoa/Reynolds**	Aluminium	24	*FT* (27 Oct. 1999)
Alcan/Pechiney/ Alsuisse**	Aluminium	16	*FT* (27 Oct. 1999)
Power Equipment			
GE	Gas turbines (1993–8)	34	*FT* (24 Mar. 1999)
Siemens/Westinghouse	Gas turbines (1993–8)	32	*FT* (24 Mar. 1999)
ABB–Alstom	Gas turbines (1993–8)	21	*FT* (24 Mar. 1999)

NOTES: * Including pacemakers, implantable defibrillators, leads, programmers for treatment of patients with irregular heart-beats

      ** Mergers pending

activities, the organization of the value chain has developed into a comprehensively planned and co-ordinated activity. At its centre is the *core systems integrator*. This firm typically possesses some combination of a number of key attributes. These include the capability to raise finance for large new projects and the resources necessary to fund a high level of R & D spending to sustain techno-logical leadership, to develop a global brand, to invest in state-of-the-art informa-tion technology and to attract the best human resources. Across a wide range of business types, from fast-moving consumer goods (FMCG) to aircraft manufac-ture, the core systems integrator interacts in the deepest, most intimate fashion with the major segments of the value chain, both upstream and downstream.

The relationship of the core systems integrator with the upstream first-tier sup-pliers extends far beyond the price relationship. Increasingly, leading first-tier suppliers across a wide range of industries have established long-term 'partner' or 'aligned supplier' relationships with the core systems integrators. Key systems integrators play an active role in 'industrial planning' through their selection of those suppliers that are to be their trusted partners and with whom they agree to establish a long-term relationship. Trust is an important ingredient in these rela-tionships. In some cases, the most fundamental aspects of the relationship are not even defined through written contracts. In recent years, systems integrators have widely established global procurement offices. This reflects an enormous increase in the central planning function of systems integrators. Leading first-tier suppliers use their close relationship with systems integrators as evidence of their long-term business viability in order to support and enhance their business position. Some key aspects of the intimate relationship between systems integrators and upstream firms include the following:

- Leading first-tier suppliers plan in minute detail the location of their plants in relation to the location of the core systems integrator. This can apply as much to a leading auto component maker as to a leading packaging supplier to a fast-moving consumer goods firm. It is not uncommon to find the aligned supplier literally supplying key products through a hole in the wall to the systems integrator.

- It is increasingly the case that the aligned supplier produces goods within the systems integrator itself. It is common for leading suppliers of services, such as data systems or even travel agents, physically to work within the premises of the systems integrator. Sometimes there is a large number of employees, perhaps a thousand or more from a given firm, physically within the systems integrator undertaking such specialist functions.

- Leading first-tier suppliers plan their R & D in close consultation with the projected needs of the core systems integrator. An increasing part of R & D is contracted out to small and medium-sized firms (SMEs). This is typically under the close control of the systems integrator.

- Product development is intimately co-ordinated with the systems integrator. This can apply as much to the development of a new packaging design for a fast-moving consumer goods firm, such as a new design of plastic bottle or can, as to the design of an aircraft engine for a huge airliner.

- Precise product specifications are instantaneously communicated to the leading suppliers through newly developed information technology (IT). The production and supply schedules of leading first-tier suppliers are comprehensively co-ordinated with the systems integrator to ensure that the required inputs arrive exactly when they are needed and the inventory of the systems integrator is kept to a minimum.

The systems integrator penetrates everywhere in the value chain in order to provide information to minimize costs across the value chain. It has a powerful incentive to ensure that knowledge is shared in order to reduce systems costs across the whole value chain.

Planning by systems integrators extends downstream also. Manufacturers of complex capital goods, from aircraft and power stations to autos and earth-moving equipment, are increasingly interested in the revenue stream to be derived from maintaining their products over the course of their lifetime. New IT is increasingly being used to monitor the performance of complex products in use, with continuous feedback to the systems integrator in order to construct optimum servicing schedules. Through this pervasive process, systems integrators deeply penetrate a wide range of firms that use their products. However, penetration of the downstream network of firms is not confined to complex capital goods. Systems integrators in the FMCG sector increasingly co-ordinate the distribution process with specialist logistics firms in order to minimize distribution costs. They work closely with grocery chains and other selling outlets, such as theme parks, movie theatres, oil companies (petrol stations have become major locations for retailing non-petrol products), and quick-service restaurants, to raise the technical efficiency in the organization of the selling process. The FMCG systems integrators often have their own experts working within the retail chain.

Through the hugely increased planning function undertaken by systems integrators, facilitated by recent developments in IT, the boundaries of the large corporation have become significantly blurred. The core systems integrators across a wide range of sectors have become the co-ordinators of a vast array of business activity outside the boundaries of the legal entity in terms of ownership. The relationship extends far beyond the price relationship. In order to develop and maintain their competitive advantage, the systems integrators deeply penetrate the value chain both upstream and downstream, becoming closely involved in business activities that range from long-term planning to meticulous control of day-day-day production and delivery schedules. Competitive advantage for the systems integrator requires that it must consider the interests of the whole value chain in order to minimize costs across the whole system.

In the old vertically integrated large firm, employment frequently totalled many hundreds of thousands of people. For example, in 1990, the world's largest capitalist firm by number of employees, General Motors, employed 750 000 people. Among the world's 100 largest international firms (by overseas assets), 51 had more than 100 000 employees (Ruigrok and van Tulder, 1995: 170–3). It is widely thought that the average size of large corporations has sharply declined since the late 1980s owing to the impact of downsizing and the relentless pursuit of cost reduction. However, this is far from clear. In 1998, among the *Fortune* 500 companies (ranked by value of sales), the median firm size was 55 000 employees. There were 5 firms with over 500 000 employees, 27 with 200 000–500 000 employees and 88 with 100 000–200 000 employees (*Fortune*, 2 August 1999: F-14). What appears to have happened is that the impact of mergers and acquisitions has frequently stimulated an increase in the total number of employees within the entire merged company, alongside considerable corporate downsizing within each of the merged entities. The functions of the core systems integrator have changed radically away from direct manufacturing towards 'brain' functions of planning the global development of the firm. The proportion of employees working outside the home market has sharply increased. However, the world's leading firms remain very large entities, not only in terms of their revenues, but also in terms of direct employment. Employment remains large, but slow-growing or even declining somewhat alongside rapid acceleration of revenues.[1]

Within the old 'Fordist', vertically integrated large corporation, the different departments had considerable autonomy and the problem of monitoring performance of subordinate units was a serious and widely discussed issue. Even more difficult were the problems involved in monitoring performance in foreign branches of multinational companies. National branches of major multinational corporations typically developed a high degree of operational autonomy. Leading multinational firms often likened their structure to a feudal system, within which the local chiefs had high degrees of independence. New IT has drastically increased the possibilities for close monitoring of performance within the firm, even across the entire globe. The 'business unit' structure adopted by many firms typically involves constant monitoring of performance in a way that was quite impossible even a few years ago.

As was discussed above, the revolution in the global business system in recent years has meant that a high level of conscious planning of business activity is now undertaken by systems integrators across the whole value chain. A large corporation may have a total procurement bill of many tens of millions of dollars. The total procurement could involve purchases from firms that employ a much larger number of full-time equivalent employees 'working for' the systems integrator than are employed within the core firm itself. In addition, there is typically a large sphere of downstream business activity that is co-ordinated by the systems integrator. A leading systems integrator with 100 000–200 000 employees could easily have the full-time equivalent of a further 400 000–500 000 employees 'working for' the systems integrator, in the sense that their work is co-ordinated in important ways by the core firm. In this sense, we may speak of an 'external firm' of co-ordinated business activity that surrounds the modern global corporation and is co-ordinated by it.

The realm of planning and conscious co-ordination extends beyond the individual large systems integrator. Co-ordination with leading first-tier suppliers and downstream processes, such as logistics, involves systems integrators from totally different sectors co-ordinating their business activities with the same firms. For example, a leading FMCG firm may work closely with leading aluminium or steel can makers. At the same time, the same aluminium makers may work in close co-oordination with the world's systems integrators in aircraft and autos. In the steel industry, a leading high-value-added steel maker may work in close co-ordination with, one the one hand, a leading FMCG firm in the supply of high-quality steel cans, and on the other hand it may work in close co-ordination with a leading global auto assembler.

An even more dramatic expansion of the realm of planning and co-ordination by the systems integrators has been the establishment of a wide range of on-line procurement networks by groups of the most powerful firms within given sectors. The first sector to announce such a process was the auto industry. In early 2000, GM, Ford and Daimler–Chrysler announced that they were going to establish the world's largest electronic market-place to purchase components. Between them they purchase directly several hundred million dollars' worth of components. This announcement was closely followed by many others, including the aerospace, energy and even the steel industry. The implications of these developments were enormous, not least for the competition authorities. They signalled a massive extension of the realm of planning and conscious co-ordination over business activity.

INEQUALITY IN THE REGIONAL DISTRIBUTION OF FIRMS THAT LEAD THE GLOBAL BIG BUSINESS REVOLUTION

This section examines the enormous regional inequality in the distribution of firms that dominate the global big business revolution. This massive disparity in the regional base of the world's leading firms is a deeply sensitive issue in international relations. Failure to recognize this disparity and the way in which in many respects it has become wider makes international economic agreements between developing and advanced economies more difficult to negotiate and implement.

DOMINANCE OF FIRMS BASED IN ADVANCED ECONOMIES

Regions containing a small fraction of the world's population have massively dominated the global big business revolution. The high-income economies contain just 16 per cent of the world's total population. In 1997 they accounted for 91 per cent of the world's total stock market capitalization, 95 per cent of the *Fortune* 500 list of companies which ranks companies by value of sales, 97 per cent of the *FT* 500 which ranks companies by value of stock market capitalization and 99 per cent of the world's top 300 companies by value of R & D spending (Table 2-7).

As the world moves into the new millennium, developing countries are massively disadvantaged in the race to compete on the global level playing field of international big business. The starting points in the race to dominate global markets could not be more uneven. The whole of the developing world, containing 84 per cent of the world's population, contains just 26 *Fortune* 500 companies (ranked by sales revenue), 16 *FT* 500 companies (ranked by market capitalization) and 15 'competitive edge' companies (MSDW, 1999: 18–9).

US LEADERSHIP OF THE GLOBAL BUSINESS REVOLUTION

Not only is there a massive imbalance between the 'starting points' in the great globalization race on the global level playing field, but there is also a deeply uneven distribution of business power within the advanced capitalist economies in the big business revolution. The large firms of the USA are dominant in this process.

The global business revolution of the 1990s saw a sharp change in the relative economic fortunes of large firms in different parts of the advanced capitalist system. In the 1980s and early 1990s a large part of business economics was concerned with explaining the relative success of East Asian 'latecomers'. There was a large literature on the apparent disadvantages of the Anglo–Saxon business structure. The capitalist stock-market-based system was argued to be disadvantageous for long-term growth and competitiveness. The 1990s has seen a dramatic turnaround in relative economic performance, with a sharp improvement in the relative performance of US firms: 'The US has the lion's share of those corporations equipped to exploit global markets. It also supplies the bulk of the

TABLE 2-7 Dominance of Firms Based in High-Income Countries of the Global Big Business Revolution, 1997

	Population		GNP, 1997[a]		GNP, 1997[b]		Fortune 500 companies (1998)[c]		FT 500 companies (1998)[d]		Top 300 companies by R & D spend (1997)		Stock market capitalization (1997)	
	(billion)	(%)	($ billion)	(%)	($ billion)	(%)	(No.)	(%)	(No.)	(%)	(No.)	(%)	($ billion)	(%)
HIEs	926	16	23 802	80	21 091	57	474	95	484	97	298	99	18 452	91
L/MIEs	4 903	84	6 123	20	15 861	43	26[e]	5	16[f]	3	2	1	1 725	9

SOURCE: *FT* (28 January 1999); World Bank (1998: 190–1, 220–1); *Fortune* (2 August 1999); DTI (1998: 70–80)

NOTES: *a* at prevailing rate of exchange
  b at PPP dollars
  c ranked by sales revenue
  d ranked by market capitalization
  e of which: Korea = 9, China = 6, Brazil = 4, Taiwan = 2, Venezuela = 1, Russia = 1, India = 1, Mexico = 1, Malaysia = 1
  f of which: Hong Kong = 7, Brazil = 2, Taiwan = 2, Singapore = 1, Mexico = 1, India = 1, Korea = 1, Argentina = 1
  HIEs = High Income Economies
  L/MIEs = Low/Middle Income Economies

TABLE 2-8 Top 300 Companies, by R & D Expenditure, 1997

Region	No. of companies	% of companies
North America	135	45
Europe	93	31
Japan	69	23
Developing countries	3	1
Total	300	100

SOURCE: DTI (1998: 70–80)

technology that knits those markets together' (*FT*, 14 June 1997). The 1990s' business revolution showed that the stock market can be perfectly compatible with long-term perspectives. Indeed, it may even be argued that the extraordinary surge in stock market valuations for globalizing, downsizing, big businesses has demonstrated an irrational excess of optimism about the long-term growth prospects for big businesses in the epoch of globalization.

US-based big businesses have absorbed many of the lessons of the East Asian model, especially those of Toyotist outsourcing. However, they have applied those lessons on a global scale. Moreover, they have been able to apply the outsourced, lean-production structure to the whole value chain, using the technological revolution in IT that took place in the 1990s: 'Throughout the 1990s corporate America, which grew lazy in the 1970s and early 1980s, has been in the throes of a far-reaching restructuring – much of it learned from Japan. Displaying remarkable flexibility, many US industries have regained their competitive edge ... and this has helped power an extraordinary bull market in equities' (*FT*, 24 January 1997).

The leading US-based companies have led the way in the resurgence of big business investment in R & D. In 1997 no less than 135 of the top 300 companies by R & D spending in 1998 were based in North America (Table 2-8). The pace of growth of US companies' investment in R & D was much faster than across the rest of the world, rising by 15 per cent in 1997 and 19 per cent in 1998 (*FT*, 25 June 1999). Moreover, the USA dramatically dominated the high-technology sectors. The IT hardware sector is much the most important single category of R & D expenditure (Table 2-9), with no fewer than 57 of the top 300 companies by R & D spending in 1998 (*FT*, 25 June 1999). Of these, 37 are US-based companies. The *FT* comments: 'This reflects the astonishing turn-around in confidence among American high-tech companies during the late 1990s. Five years ago they were trembling before the onrushing Asian tigers. Now the US appears to be extending its technological lead over both Europe and Asia in many fields of electronics, engineering, information technology and the life sciences' (*FT*, 25 June 1999).

A large proportion of the accelerated flow of foreign direct investment (FDI) was accounted for by a small number of countries and firms. US-based companies have been at the forefront of the acceleration of foreign direct investment since the mid-1980s. The USA was much the most important single source of outflows of FDI, the total climbing rapidly in the early 1990s, as American

TABLE 2-9 R & D Expenditure of the Top 300 Companies World-wide, 1995 and 1998

Sector	No. of companies (1998)	1995 ($ billion)	1998 ($ billion)	% increase/ decrease in R & D expenditure
Total	300	176.6	253.7	44
of which:				
IT hardware	57	41.8	70.0	68
Software/IT services	17	3.3	7.5	127
Telecoms services	9	9.0	9.8	9
Autos	25	31.2	43.3	39
Pharmaceuticals	35	22.4	33.1	48
Electronic/electricals	28	22.3	26.6	19
Chemicals	31	14.5	20.7	43
Aerospace/defence	11	5.7	6.9	21
Engineering/machinery	21	4.8	6.5	35
Oil/gas	12	4.0	5.1	28
Steel/metals	9	1.2	1.1	(-) 7

SOURCE: *FT* (25 June 1999)

companies powerfully moved towards globalization. American FDI outflows rose from an annual average of $25 billion in 1986–91 to $115 billion in 1997 (UNCTAD, 1998: 367), and the USA's share of total world FDI outflows rose from 14 per cent in 1986–91 to 27 per cent in 1997 (UNCTAD, 1998: 367). Moreover, the process had a powerful element of cumulative causation, with successful investment generating further investment: around 60 per cent of US 'outflows' of FDI in 1994–5 was financed out of reinvested profits (UNCTAD, 1996: 44). In the period 1986–91, Japan's outflows of FDI were 28 per cent greater than those of the USA, but by 1997, the outflows of direct FDI from Japan had declined to only 23 per cent of those of the USA (UNCTAD, 1998: 367).

In 1996, the USA had 28 of the top 100 companies ranked by value of overseas assets (UNCTAD, 1998: 36–8). By 1998, North American firms accounted for 37 per cent of the *Fortune* 500 ranking of the world's leading firms, ranked by sales value (Table 2-10). US dominance of the big business revolution is reflected also in the *Competitive Edge* studies published by Morgan Stanley Dean Witter (MSDW, 1997, 1998a, 1999, 2000). These studies ranked companies by their capacity to have a sustainable 'competitive edge' in the global economy. Morgan Stanley's objective was to 'identify companies with a meaningful advantage in their global sectors'. Their aim was to assemble 'a comprehensive view of the competitive landscape, country by country, and industry by industry' (MSDW, 1998a: Introduction). They ranked large quoted companies in terms of their competitive advantage in their respective sector. A key issue was global market share, which strongly influences the capability of new entrants to catch-up: the higher the share, the more sustainable was the firm's leadership judged to be. In 1998 they identified a total of 238 companies that were

TABLE 2-10 *Fortune* Global 500 (by Value of Sales):
Distribution by Region, 1997 (% in brackets)

Total	500 *(100)*
North America	183 (37)
Europe	170 (34)
of which:	
Germany	42
France	39
UK	35
Japan	112 (22)
Developing countries	27 (5)
of which:	
South Korea	12
Brazil	5
Others	8 (2)

SOURCE: *Fortune* (3 August 1998: F-30-40)

TABLE 2-11 Competitive-Edge Companies, 1997–8

	'Competitive-edge' companies (1997)		Share of world market capitalization (1997) (%)	Share of world GDP (1995) (%)
	Number of companies	*%*		
North America	134	56.3	48.8	23.3
Europe	64	26.9	30.0	20.6
Japan	18	7.6	8.8	8.3
Non-Japan Asia	17	7.1	5.5	22.3
Emerging markets	5	2.1	6.9	25.5
World	238	100.0	100.0	100.0

SOURCE: MSDW (1998: 25)

NOTE: Shares are based on 1995 purchasing power parity (PPP) data

'world leaders' (Table 2-11). Of these 134 were North American. Japan had just 18 companies that were identified as 'world leaders'.

In the *FT*'s ranking of the world's top 500 companies, ranked by market capitalization, North America had 254 companies in 1998, in other words it accounted for more than one-half of the total (*FT*, 28 January 1999). The USA's dominance of world stock market capitalization is crucially important in the epoch of explosive concentration through merger and acquisition. In a virtuous circle of growth and concentration, firms with high stock market capitalization can more easily take over and merge with those with lower stock market capitalizations. Well-focused mergers further enhance stock market capitalizations, paving the way for further expansion through merger and acquisition. Even the largest European companies have often found it hard to match the merger and acquisition capability this provides for leading US firms.

For Japanese companies, to be seriously lagging in stock market capitalization in this period of explosive restructuring of international big business is a deep disadvantage for the long-term positioning of large Japanese firms in the global economy in the twenty-first century. For the vast majority of firms from developing countries, with trivial market capitalizations compared to the global giants (Table 2-7), it is inconceivable that they can participate in the global merger explosion in a serious fashion. They are almost entirely passive observers of the revolutionary re-shaping of the world's big businesses.

In recent years in both the USA and the UK, globally successful large firms have tended to outperform the average for the whole stock market, reflecting investor perceptions of the gains that large, well-positioned companies can make from globalization and from 'the exploitation of technologies in which the US at present has unique strength': 'Argument rages about the causes of the US bull market, and whether it is sustainable, but to some extent it must reflect the remarkable US dominance of many cutting edge high technology sectors' (*FT*, 24 January 1997).

REVOLUTIONARY CHANGE IN BUSINESS SYSTEMS OUTSIDE THE USA

CRISIS FOR THE EAST ASIAN MODEL

An important part of the global business revolution has consisted of lessons learned from East Asia by US and European companies, notably in the organization of outsourced supplier networks. However, the global business revolution of the 1990s went far beyond this concept. In the face of this revolution, the East Asian catch-up strategy for big business faced serious shortcomings. East Asia is now itself in the throes of a deep strategic re-thinking, fundamentally reorganizing its business structures in the face of the intense competitive threat posed by rejuvenated, giant US and European businesses and the refusal of the advanced economies to continue to allow them to maintain protectionist barriers for international trade and investment. The epoch of 'free riding on free trade' is over.

In the 1970s and 1980s, large European and US businesses typically pursued diversification as a strategy for growth in mature, and often relatively protected, markets. As we shall see, a key aspect of the big business revolution has been the opening up of global markets, enabling the growth of huge focused, global businesses. East Asian businesses have continued to be highly diversified, and now face severe competition from the restructured global giants of the USA and, latterly, Europe.

Diversification has been a key part of the growth strategy of large East Asian privately-owned businesses. In the absence of a core technology or brand name firms in late-industrializing countries have typically entered a wide range of unrelated industries. Of the 35 largest private industrial enterprises in developing countries in 1987, only five were specialized companies. The rest were all diversified conglomerates. In the diversified conglomerate group in developing countries, diversification has been 'a defensive tactic for growth'. Large firms have typically grown behind high protectionist barriers with close links to the government in order to maintain such protection (Hikino and Amsden, 1994: 303). Such firms are at a large competitive disadvantage on the global level playing field.

A business revolution is being forced upon formerly distinctive business structures. To be successful on the 'global level field' requires focus on core business and a global capability. The frame of reference for competitive success has become the world's leading-edge firms, instead of national or regional leading firms. The global business revolution, in tandem with the Asian crisis, has forced drastic restructuring of East Asian businesses along Anglo–Saxon lines.

South Korea. Each of the major South Korean *chaebols* was a diversified family-owned conglomerate. With strong state support and encouragement, the leading *chaebols* developed powerful exporting capabilities in items such as

TABLE 2-12 **Major Industrial Diversification of Samsung under Chairman Lee Byung-Chul, 1938–87**

Year	Sector
1938	Overseas trading
1953	Sugar refining
1954	Woollen textile manufacturing
1963	Broadcasting
	(Life insurance)*
	(Department store)
1965	Newspaper publishing
	Entertainment
1966	Hospital administration
1967	(Paper manufacturing)
1969	Electronics
1974	Petrochemicals
	Shipbuilding and engineering/machinery
	Overseas general trading
1976	Real estate
1977	(Semiconductors)
	Precision machinery
1978	Telecommunications
	Construction
1982	Sports entertainment
1983	Watchmaking
1984	Medical equipment supplies
1985	Data processing
1987	Aerospace

SOURCE: Amsden and Hikino (1994: 128)

NOTE: *Brackets indicate acquisitions

TABLE 2-13 **Major Diversification of Hyundai Group under Chairman Chung Ju-Yung, 1938–87**

Year	Sector
1940	Automobile repair
1947	Construction
1955	Marine and fire insurance
1962	Securities dealing
1967	Automobile assembly (later production)*
1968	Real estate
1972	Shipbuilding
1974	Automobile sales
	Engineering
1975	Steel structures and pipes
	Ship repair
	Construction materials
1976	Overseas commercial banking
	Overseas general trading
	Ocean shipping
1977	Precision machinery
1978	(Iron and steel making)
	Electrical engineering
	(Aluminium refining)
	Wooden products and furniture
1983	Electronics
1984	Elevator manufacture
1986	Housing and industrial development

SOURCE: Amsden and Hikino (1994: 127)

NOTE: *Brackets indicate acquisitions

autos, ships, steel, semiconductors and consumer electronics. However, behind high protectionist barriers and with credit from state banks, the *chaebols* also developed highly diversified businesses, often with low levels of technology and low economies of scale. Samsung is typical of the path of development. It began life in the 1930s as an overseas trading company (Table 2-12). In the 1950s it moved into sugar refining and woollen textile manufacturing. In the 1960s it branched into broadcasting, entertainment, hospital administration and paper manufacturing. In the late 1960s it entered electronics, and in the early 1970s established petrochemical and shipbuilding businesses. It subsequently entered real estate, semiconductors, precision machinery, telecommunications, construction, sports entertainment, watchmaking, medical equipment and supplies, data processing and aerospace (Amsden and Hikino, 1994: 128). (For a similar diversification process at Hyundai see Table 2-13.) The diversification path was driven partly by market imperfections and the unavailability of necessary inputs, but also by 'the lure of profits in unmodernized industries' (Amsden and Hikino, 1994: 129). Both these possibilities were accentuated by the operation of a highly protected economy.

In 1998, in the midst of the Asian crisis, South Korea's top five *chaebols*, Hyundai, Samsung, LG, Daewoo and Sk, were forced to agree to a government-orchestrated restructuring. Having re-nationalized the big banks, the government was able to use credit control as an instrument to impose restructuring upon the *chaebols*. They agreed to halve their total number of subsidiaries and participate in a comprehensive asset-swapping exercise that would give a much firmer focus on core business, to gain benefits from economies of scale. The goal was to reduce the number of Korean competitors to just two in critical export industries. After the asset swaps, Hyundai and Daewoo were to be the only car manufacturers, Samsung and LG/Hyundai the only semiconductor manufacturers and Samsung and LG the only consumer electronics groups (*FT*, 8 December 1998). Samsung was to merge its petrochemicals and aerospace divisions with other *chaebols*. Hyundai was to merge its petrochemicals, power generation and railway rolling stock operations with rival *chaebols*. By mid-1999, Daewoo, Korea's second largest *chaebol*, was facing bankruptcy, with debts of $50 billion (*FT*, 13 August 1999). Daewoo was to be comprehensively dismantled. It was to sell its securities, consumer electronics, telecommunications equipment, construction and shipbuilding businesses. After the restructuring, Daewoo was to be left with only its car manufacturing and distribution businesses. Even these were in negotiation to be sold to Ford.

Japan. Pre-1945 Japanese *zaibatsu* typically followed the diversified conglomerate pattern. For example, the Nissan *zaibatsu* in 1937 operated in mining, automobiles, chemicals, fishing, electronics, agriculture and other sectors (Hikino and Amsden, 1994: 305). In the post-war period immensely powerful export-oriented firms grew up with government support. However, these leading companies in terms of world markets functioned within the *keiretsu* structure of cross-holdings. Within a single *keiretsu*, there were typically a wide range of mutually supportive businesses. For example, the Fuyo *keiretsu* contained businesses in trading, chemicals, pulp and paper, petroleum, cement, fibres and textiles, iron and steel, construction, electrical machinery, transportation, property and food (Table 2-14). The Fuyo *keiretsu* contains a core of businesses that are globally competitive. However, it also has a whole set of businesses that are simply too small to compete on the global level playing field. They are protected by formal international protection, by controls over domestic distribution channels and by access to credit from within the *keiretsu*. The *keiretsu*'s core companies are disadvantaged to the extent that they source their inputs from small-scale companies within the *keiretsu* rather than from the least-cost global supplier.

The *keiretsu* system allowed allocation of capital within the group with little regard to returns achieved. An analysis by Goldman Sachs shows that Japanese non-financial groups in the Nikkei 300 collectively failed to achieve a return above their cost of capital after 1990; 'Since that date they have destroyed value of Y3000 billion a year, a cumulative Y21 000 billion, by investing in project and plants that generated negative returns' (quoted in *FT*, 8 December 1998).

TABLE 2-14 **The Fuyo *keiretsu's* Structure, 1997**

Company	Sales ($ billion)	Company	Sales ($ billion)
Finance		Electrical/Machinery	
Fuji Bank	23.4	Nissan Motors	54.7
Yasuda Fire and Marine	7.9	Hitachi	70.1
Yasuda Mutual Life	n.a.	Canon	23.0
Trading		Yokogawa Electric	2.5
Marubeni	113.7	Oki Electric	6.4
Chemicals		NSK	4.1
Showa Denko	6.7	Kubota	8.6
NOF	1.2	Transportation	
Kureha Chemical	1.0	Tobu Railway	3.0
Pulp and paper		Keihin Elec. Express Railway	2.4
Nippon Paper	3.3	Showa Line	0.6
Petroleum		Property	
Tonen	5.7	Tokyo Tatemono	0.7
Cement		Food	
Nihon Cement	2.8	Nichirei	5.0
Iron and steel		Sapporo	5.5
NKK	16.1	Nisshin Flour Milling	3.0
Construction			
Taizel	15.3		

SOURCE: *FT* (28 October 1998)

As long as the Japanese economy prospered, they could be supported by bank loans, from within the group. Once the economy began to falter, the source of capital dried up, and by the late 1990s, the ability of the leading members to support weaker *keiretsu* members was in sharp decline.

Large core companies in Japan typically also are highly diversified. Mitsubishi Electric, the 25th largest Japanese corporation in 1997 (*Fortune*, 3 August 1998), is a vast electrical equipment conglomerate. It produces audio-visual equipment, information systems, semiconductors, communications infrastructure (for example, fibre optic cables, satellite communications, mass communications systems, wireless telephony equipment), energy systems operations, building systems, home electronics, automotive electronics, industrial and factory automation, elevators, escalators and air conditioning equipment (*FT*, 1 April 1999).

Japan's leading companies face great difficulties in open competition with revitalized US and European companies in a world of fast-declining barriers to trade and investment: 'The mergers of Daimler and Chrysler, Sandoz and Ciba, Mobil and Exxon, Amoco and BP...have left Japanese companies looking parochial and underscale' (*FT*, 4 February 1999). The global business revolution saw a dramatic turnaround in the fortunes of Japan's leading companies. In 1990, six of the world's top 10 companies by market capitalization were Japanese.

By 1998, there were none. In 1998, Japan had just 46 companies in the *FT*'s Global 500 list, and only two in the Global 100 (*FT*, 28 January 1999). In 1990, Japan's share of the world's stock market value was 41.5 per cent. By 1998 this had fallen to a mere 10.5 per cent (*FT*, 8 December 1998). In 1998, Japan still had 18 of the world's top 50 corporations by value of sales, but had only one company in the top 50 by total profits (*Fortune*, 3 August 1998).

The poor stock market performance of Japan's leading corporations is a major worry for them, since it drastically weakens their capability to undertake stock-market-based mergers with leading overseas companies. While leading US and European companies merge across boundaries and with each other, at high speed, Japan's corporations are being left behind in the whirlwind of large-scale corporate mergers and acquisitions. For example, despite an improvement in its share price in early 1999, Sony's market capitalization in mid-1999 stood at $38 billion, far behind its US competitors, making it difficult to use its stock to pay for deals in North America (*FT*, 17 May 1999).

There are serious fears in Japan that its high investment and R & D expenditure has been disproportionately channelled into industries of the Second Industrial Revolution: 'Japan leads the way in capital-intensive industries, including shipbuilding, steel, paper and pulp, and heavy chemicals. But it lags behind the USA in the high technology and life science industries' (Katsunosuke Maeda, vice-chairman of Keidanren, quoted in *FT*, 2 June 1999).

Downsizing had once been thought of as impossible in Japan's leading corporations, with guarantees of lifetime employment within a firm that functioned as a 'large family'. In 1999 there were signs that radical restructuring had begun to take hold among Japan's leading corporations. Company after company among Japan's corporate elite announced major downsizing programmes. Hitachi announced that it was cutting its workforce by 10 per cent (that is 6500 workers) and selling off unprofitable businesses (*IHT*, 2 April 1999). Mitsubishi Electric announced that it was cutting 10 per cent of the workforce (that is 14 500 employees) and would sell off or shut down those parts of the business that it 'deemed difficult or impossible to return to profitability' (*FT*, 1 April 1999). Later in the year, Asahi Glass, NKK, Japan Airlines, Toyo Tyre and Rubber, NEC, Mitsubishi Chemical, and Daimaru, all announced large cuts in staff (*FT*, 2 June 1999).

Revolutionary changes in the Japanese banking system precipitated major changes in the *keiretsu* system. In 1999, a series of large-scale mergers took place in the Japanese banking system, viewed as essential if Japan's banks were to compete following the revolutionary mergers in the European and US banking systems. Three huge banking mergers transformed the relationship of the core banks with the *keiretsu* in which they were located. For example, the core bank of the Fuyo *keiretsu*, Fuji Bank, merged with Industrial Bank of Japan and Dai-Ichi Kangyo. Fuji Bank then announced that it was inappropriate for it to continue as leader of the Fuyo *keiretsu*. It made it clear that henceforth it would seek to maximize its return on capital: 'Now our lending criteria are based on rational criteria. We are trying to maximize profits' (Mr Yamamoto, Fuji Bank, quoted in

FT, 9 November 1999). Constituent companies within the Fuyo *keiretsu* have responded by turning away from the banks towards the bond and equity markets.

A revolutionary process of international acquisition of Japanese companies had begun. Merrill Lynch has bought the branch network of Yamaichi Securities. GE Capital has acquired the leasing operations of Japan Leasing, Japan's second biggest company in this sector. Travelers is buying Nikko Securities. Goodyear (US) has, effectively, taken over Sumitomo Rubber, Japan's third biggest tyre company. Renault has taken a controlling stake in Nissan Motors. Some Japanese industry officials see the 'surrender into the arms of Renault' as symbolic of 'a fall from grace for Nissan and the entire automotive industry' (*FT*, 23 March 1999). One former official from the Ministry of International Trade and Industry called the Renault–Nissan alliance a 'national disgrace' (quoted in *FT*, 23 March 1999).

The consequences of take-over by major multinational companies have been profound. None has been more significant for the transformation in Japanese corporate culture than Renault's purchase of a controlling share of Nissan. It is highly symbolic because it signifies a fundamental change in the way the Japanese auto industry is organized. No sector has been more important for Japan's industrial rise than the auto industry. It was the auto industry that pioneered the methods of industrial organization that were later to be replicated by large parts of the US and European industry.

In November 1999, Carlos Ghosn, CEO of Nissan, appointed by Renault announced a drastic transformation of the loss-making company. The plan shocked Japan. The vertical *keiretsu* system resulted in the core firms investing heavily in a wide network of supplier companies. For example, Nissan invested in no fewer than 1394 suppliers. Ghosn bluntly identified Nissan's vertically integrated *keiretsu* system as a fundamental problem for Nissan: 'About 60 per cent of your costs are in the suppliers. You have to have suppliers who are innovative. You want suppliers offering products to many customers so there is a flow of information about best standards. That won't happen with *keiretsu* companies' (quoted in *FT*, 9 November 1999). Ghosn announced that he intends Nissan to cut its supplier base from over almost 1400 to just 600.

While the larger suppliers are thought likely to survive, 'many fear the restructuring will wipe out second- and third-tier parts suppliers that depend heavily on Nissan' (*FT*, 2 November 1999). Only a handful of Nissan's suppliers are considered by industry experts to be internationally competitive (*FT*, 7 April 1999). The close personal relationships between Nissan and its surrounding companies will be decimated at a stroke. The Japanese supplier industry is likely to consolidate rapidly as weaker suppliers are weeded out in the new competitive environment. Giant multinational supplier firms are quickly increasing their role in Japan, including Robert Bosch, Valeo and Visteon. Japanese car makers purchased $13.3 billion worth of components from US suppliers in the first half of 1999 (*FT*, 7 April 1999). In order to survive and compete Japanese car makers will have to establish networks of global suppliers from the world's leading component companies.

Nissan will close five factories. When Ghosn made the announcement to an invited audience, 'a shocked gasp went through the crowd' (*FT*, 19 October

1999). Global employment in Nissan is to be cut by 21 000, or 14 per cent, of which 16 500 will be in Japan. Nissan's dealer network will be consolidated with 20 per cent of its dealer affiliates 'eliminated' and 10 per cent of sales outlets closed. Nissan will adopt a performance-oriented compensation scheme, including stock options and bonuses based on achievement.

Taken together, these changes amount to a radical change in the *keiretsu* system. The process of dismantling the *keiretsu* system is far from complete. However, many analysts feel that Japan is in the midst of a fundamental change in its corporate culture, moving from a corporate world based on relationships to one based on the free allocation of capital: 'We are at an historic moment. We are seeing the unravelling of 50 years of history' (Mr Sheard, of Barings, quoted in *FT*, 9 November 1999).

CONTINENTAL EUROPE

The impact of the rise to dominance of the Anglo–Saxon business system is not confined to Asia. The global business revolution has forced dramatic changes also on the business system of Continental Europe, from the Nordic countries through to France, Germany and Italy. By the late 1990s, most large European industrial corporations had wholeheartedly embraced the philosophy of globalization, shareholder value, cost-cutting and focus on core business.

National Champions. A wave of mergers swept through northwestern Europe to produce large-scale 'national champions' to compete in the epoch of globalization and big business. The process was typically supported by national governments, often with a significant shareholding interest, including a golden share, in the companies concerned. Within Italy, France, Germany, Spain and the Nordic countries, a succession of large-scale banking mergers took place within national boundaries in the late 1990s. The extent of cross-boundary mergers was still quite limited. Few observers doubted that the process would rapidly spill over onto the international stage. In other sectors many highly significant intra-national mergers took place. These included, in Italy, Telecom Italia's merger with Olivetti rather than Deutsche Telekom, after an epic battle in which the Italian government played an important role. In France, the French government strongly supported the merger of Aerospatiale with Matra, to follow the 'French–French' path to building large firms. In the retail sector, Carrefour's merger with Promodes also helped build a 'French' national champion that could compete in the global arena. In oil and petrochemicals, PetroFina's merger with Elf Aquitaine also produced an essentially 'French–French' solution to the search for global scale. In Switzerland, the merger of Ciba–Geigy with Sandoz, to form Novartis, was widely applauded as a 'Swiss–Swiss' solution to the achievement of global scale. In Britain, the merge of BAe with GEC Marconi's defence arm was similarly applauded by many observers. In Germany, the merger of Krupps and Thyssen produced a 'national champion'. In Sweden, Volvo and Saab merged their truck businesses to create a firm with focused global scale.

European Champions. However, the capability of a purely national solution to the problem of scale in the midst of the global big business revolution appeared increasingly anachronistic and inadequate to solve the fundamental problem of achieving the scale necessary for survival on the global level playing field. Alongside the group of national champions being created in the late 1990s, a far more powerful trend was for cross-boundary mergers, which often involved the very firms that had been initially created as national champions. The pan-European merger movement has caused intense debate within Europe on the significance of nationally-based companies in the epoch of globalization and international consolidation. For example, Sweden was arguably the most successful of the smaller European countries in being home to a group of globally powerful corporations. The rollcall of great international companies included Volvo and Saab in autos, Astra in pharmaceuticals, Electrolux in household appliances, and Ericsson in telecommunications. In 1998–9 a revolutionary change took place among Sweden's mighty corporations: 'Sweden's big companies are no longer quite big enough to survive alone in a globalizing economy. In the past year, the search for economies of scale has prompted a wave of mergers and acquisitions that has caused near panic among those Swedes that cherish national industrial champions ... The Swedish media has reacted with barely concealed hysteria, bemoaning the exodus of national talent' (*FT*, 17 May 1999).

In industry after industry former 'national champions' are merging across borders to create what are increasingly being referred to as 'European champions'. The epoch has seen the gradual emergence of companies that are truly 'European' champions. In *power equipment* in the late 1980s, Asea and Brown Boveri merged to form the Swiss–Swedish engineering giant ABB, and GEC (UK) and Alcatel (France) merged their power equipment interests to form Alstom. Even these mighty companies were too small to compete with the global leaders. In 1999, ABB and Alstom merged their power equipment divisions to form a 'European champion' in the power equipment sector (ABB Alstom). In *steel*, Usinor (France) merged with Cockerill Sambrell (Belgium), and British Steel merged with Hoogovens (The Netherlands), to each create a global giant company. In *pharmaceuticals*, Sweden's 'national champion' Astra merged with Britain's Zeneca, which had been de-merged from ICI. Hoechst, the once-mighty engine of the German chemical industry, abandoned chemicals and transformed itself into a focused life sciences company. France's national champion, Rhône–Poulenc followed a similar path. In 1998 they went even further and announced a merger, to form a huge new 'life science' company, able to compete on the global market-place. The new entity, to be named Aventis, was to be a true 'European champion'. In *aerospace*, the Aerospatiale–Matra merger proved to be only the prelude to an even more significant merger, namely that with Dasa, to create a global giant company, called the European Aircraft, Defence and Space Company (EADS).

Transatlantic Giants. A powerful group of focused European businesses have aggressively transformed themselves through transatlantic mergers. In the early

1990s, Daimler–Benz dismantled its high-technology empire to focus on automobiles. The huge reorganization was capped by the merger with Chrysler in 1998. In the German financial sector the transformation of Deutsche Bank has also been highly symbolic of the business revolution in that country. Deutsche Bank, the biggest in Europe, has shifted from a mainly domestic orientation, with extensive holdings in the German industrial sector, to a bank that is mainly concerned to compete internationally. In 1990, Deutsche Bank still sat on the supervisory boards of more than 400 companies across the spectrum of German industry. In 1998 it acquired Bankers Trust, the eighth largest US bank, to transform itself into a fundamentally different kind of bank, with its main focus upon international competition. BP underwent huge transformation in the 1990s. The transformation culminated in the merger with US oil and petrochemical giant, Amoco. Vodafone exemplified the rapid rise to global power of firms in the fast-consolidating and liberalized telecoms sector. Its acquisition of US-based Air Touch turned Vodafone into one of a small group of giant mobile phone companies.

The most dramatic mergers may yet take place in the aerospace sector. The possibility of BAe–GEC Marconi and EADS each merging with one of the USA giant companies is being widely discussed. Nothing would more powerfully signal the end of the epoch of 'national champions' in 'strategic industries'. No industry is more 'strategic' than aerospace.

These developments were radically transforming the traditional ideas of national industrial policy. What point was there in a national government supporting a particular indigenous 'national champion' if at some point in the future it might be merged with a firm based in another European country, or even in the USA or Japan?

REINVIGORATED BIG BUSINESS IN JAPAN AND EUROPE?

Successful reform of business systems outside the USA and UK could lead to a renewed surge of oligopolistic competition between firms based in different regions in the Triad group of countries (Japan, Western Europe and North America). However, the task of reforming business structures in already highly developed economies is very different from framing industrial policy in a still poor country, such as Indonesia, the Philippines or Mainland China. There is a real possibility of business renewal in Japan and Continental Europe, producing large globally competitive firms that provide a strong challenge to those of the USA. The possibility of mounting such a challenge would be much greater if the USA stock market crashed. However, the tasks facing policy makers in developing countries are quite different, facing a vastly weaker domestic business structure. Whatever their respective weaknesses, Continental Europe does possess 135 of the world's *Fortune* 500 corporations and 76 of the world's top 300 companies by R & D spend, while Japan possesses 112 of the *Fortune* 500 companies and 69 of the world's top 300 companies by R & D spend (Tables 2-8 and 2-10).

CONCLUSION

BIG BUSINESS HAS BEEN, AND STILL IS, CENTRAL TO THE DEVELOPMENT OF CAPITALISM

The normal path of development in advanced capitalist countries has been for oligopolistic business organizations to stand at the centre of the system. Big businesses have played a central role in generating high rates of investment and in stimulating technical progress. Oligopolistic competition can be at least as intense as small-scale competition. The top three or four firms in sector after sector are now engaged in competition of unprecedented intensity. They are investing ever-increasing amounts in R & D, IT and marketing systems, and procuring ever-increasing quantities of inputs across the global economy. In sector after sector, from aircraft to coal, ferocious price-cutting battles are taking place. Firms are fighting intensely to improve product quality and lower system costs across the whole value chain, including the entire supplier network.

Since the 1980s there has occurred a big business revolution. Under the impact of increasingly important institutional investment, large capitalist firms have drastically reorganized. They have downsized employment, focused on core business, selling off large segments of assets not relevant to the core activities. They have globalized at high speed, even though large parts of the developing world have received relatively small amounts of FDI. The degree of concentration by sector has risen dramatically. If we examine sub-categories of markets, then it becomes clear that the level of global concentration has risen drastically. This fast-moving change cannot be captured by aggregate data for individual capitalist countries. To understand the true extent of dominance of advanced capitalism by big business, it is necessary to examine global market share by sub-categories of markets (see Table 2-6).

The role played by big business is even more important now than it was at any previous point in the history of capitalism. Large capitalist firms now stand at the centre of a vast network of outsourced businesses which are highly dependent on the core big businesses for their survival. Using new IT, the core firm links together on a global scale a large number of related businesses. However, the core business is in the dominant position, since it is the possessor of the technology and/or brand name which indirectly provides sales to the supplier firms. It is therefore able to ensure that it obtains the lion's share of the profits from the transactions between the two sets of firms. The 'external firm' is typically substantially larger in terms of employment than the core firm.

BENEFITS OF GLOBALIZATION AND BIG BUSINESS

The growth of global big businesses alongside the liberalization of global markets has brought many gains. Globalizing large firms are typically linked closely to an 'external firm' composed of a group of powerful, globalizing first-tier suppliers.

These are, in turn, closely linked to a group of local small and medium-sized enterprises dispersed across the world. Intense pressure cascades down from the core globalizing companies through the first-tier suppliers to the myriads of small and medium-sized local businesses that supply the first-tier components and sub-systems suppliers. This process drives forward technical progress, product quality, and management skills across the value chain. Across the world, individual consumers and firms can have access to lower cost and higher quality products, benefiting from the massive investment in research and development by the global oligopolists and their increasingly powerful first-tier suppliers. They can benefit from the ferocious price competition and pressure to provide high quality products that has developed among the leading companies across the world. Not only the price of primary products has fallen, but also the price of a wide range of complex manufactured goods and services. The real price of IT goods and services is falling at high speed, producing enormous developmental benefits.

THE GAP BETWEEN BIG BUSINESS IN THE ADVANCED ECONOMIES AND THE BUSINESSES OF DEVELOPING COUNTRIES

It is much harder today for a developing country to establish a business that can compete with the most advanced capitalist big businesses than was the case only a decade ago. In the new world of global oligopoly, for a long period ahead, the 'distribution of the gains' will be highly uneven in terms of the geographical distribution of the core big businesses and powerful second-tier suppliers, that are emerging as the global winners. The world of the 'global level playing field' is likely to result in competitive success for those large firms that already have a head-start in the global competition. It has been suggested that the 'global level playing field' is the 'protectionism of the strong'. There is little doubt in the minds of the proponents of the global level playing field that the main beneficiaries among large firms will be those that are based in the advanced economies. Their shareholders are mainly from the advanced economies as are their owners. As late as the early 1990s the senior managers of the world's leading multinationals still came preponderantly from the company's home country (Ruigrok and van Tulder, 1995: 170–3).

We have seen that in terms of several different criteria, developing large firms from developing countries are almost insignificant within the global business revolution. Table 2-7 showed that large firms from developing countries, which contain 84 per cent of the world's population, account for just 5 per cent of *Fortune* 500 companies, 3 per cent of *FT* 500 companies, and a mere 1 per cent of the world's top 300 firms by R & D expenditure.

In terms of competitive capability in the global market-place, the Morgan Stanley list (Table 2-11) provides the most comprehensive evaluation available. Morgan Stanley's selection of 250 'competitive-edge' companies includes 133 from North America, 77 from Europe, and 21 from Japan. It includes just 19 from the whole of the 'emerging market' world. Of these there are six from the whole of

Latin America, three of which are from Brazil and three from Mexico. The whole of the rest of Latin America has none. The entire area of South Asia has just one representative. The whole of non-Japan Asia has 12. There are none from Eastern Europe, the former Soviet Union, the Middle East or Africa (MSDW, 1998a: 16). In other words, in the view of the most brutally honest evaluation available, almost the entire developing world has virtually no representation in the list of the world's most competitive companies. The race for position in the coming struggle for the world's global market-place begins with the runners in a most uneven position.

SUSTAINABILITY OF THE GAP

Barriers to entry are different in different sectors (Table 2-15). It is hardest to catch-up in the most technically complex sectors, and the ones with high R & D outlays. Such sectors in which catch-up is especially difficult include pharmaceutical products, defence and aerospace, and complex machinery, such as power

TABLE 2-15 Average Sustainability of MSDW Stocks, by Sector*

Sector	Average sustainability (years)
Aerospace/defence	23
Capital goods (complex machinery)	16
Consumer goods	14
Paper and packaging	12
Pharmaceutical and medical products	11
Building products	10
Banking and financial services	9
Electric utilities	9
Energy	9
Mining	8
Media	8
Chemicals	7
Lodging	7
Retail	7
Transportation	7
Automotive	6
Insurance	6
Steel	6
Tyres	5
Technology	4
Apparel and footwear	2
Telecommunications	2

SOURCE: MSDW (1998a: 6)

NOTE: *Defined as the number of years it would take an aggressive and well-financed competitor to establish a similar business

equipment, construction machinery, large machine tools, farm machinery and aircraft engines. Morgan Stanley estimate that it will take well over 20 years for an 'aggressive and well-financed competitor' to establish a similar business to the global leaders in the aerospace and defence industry. They believe that it would take an average of 14 years in the heavy machinery sector and 11 years in the pharmaceutical and medical products sector (Table 2-15). However, there are also wide gaps in firm capability in the consumer goods sector. The barriers to entry are especially high in the branded consumer goods sector. The catch-up possibility is especially small as the firms that establish first-mover advantage in the early phase of the epoch of high globalization will be in an extraordinarily strong position to shape the habits of consumption for a long period ahead.

The possibilities appear to be easiest in 'mid-tech' industries rather than low-tech consumer goods or high-tech products. Industries such as steel, chemicals, automobiles and transport equipment appear to offer the best opportunities for emerging big businesses in developing countries to catch-up. However within these sectors, there are big differences in catch-up possibilities. The sub-sectors in which it is easiest to catch-up are basic 'commoditized' goods in which the basic technology is relatively old and non-proprietary, and in which margins and value-added are low. These include products such as coal, low grade tyres, construction steel, chlorine, ethylene, aspirin, vitamin C and nylon.

Even within these sectors in which there is on average a lower degree of sustainability for leading-edge companies, there are still huge and growing barriers to entry in the high value-added, high R & D sub-sectors. These include such products as speciality chemicals, stainless steel and high-carbon steel. Moreover, even within 'traditional', commoditized sectors there are massive technical advances in process technology, which greatly reduce costs of production and increase profitability. High value-added creates high margin pricing, which creates high profitability, which allows further enhancement of competitive advantage through investment in R & D.

Big businesses have been at the centre of the advanced capitalist economies since the late nineteenth century (Chandler, 1990). The 1990s have seen a revolution in the nature of big business in the advanced capitalist economies. As a result of this, their influence on the advanced economies is greater than at any time in the past, despite huge downsizing in direct employment. Globalizing Western companies have entered a virtuous circle of enhanced stock market prices arising in part owing to firms achieving leading positions in the global market-place. This in turn is used as a lever for take-over and merger which is able to further enhance the firm's market position. The revolution in business structure enormously increases the barriers to entry, which is one of the main explicit purposes of the revolution.

THE POLICY CHALLENGE

The challenge for policy makers in developing countries is to determine the degree to which it is desirable to attempt to construct indigenously-owned businesses, which can challenge the global giants.

The global business revolution has thrown up a series of deep questions about industrial policy in developing countries. Given that capital has no nationality, is there any point in attempting to construct one's own 'national big business'? If a given country, even a huge one such as China, attempts to do so, what are the costs that might be involved in the attempt, in terms of sheltering inefficient industries? In the long run, will globalizing big business possess any 'nationality'? Will the ownership and the core of operations naturally gravitate in the long term towards the main locations of the market and global income? As the global shift of income and markets occurs will this not naturally be the Far East, with China at its centre? Is it conceivable that within a relatively short period of time, quintessential 'American' companies, such as Coca-Cola, or 'British' companies, such as British Petroleum (now plain 'BP'), may become more and more Asian, as East Asia's share of the global market and global stock ownership steadily rises? Why fight the process? Is the epoch of active government intervention to support the growth of powerful big businesses in 'latecomer' countries over? Is it a time to follow the advice of Sun Wu: 'Take action only when it is useful to do so. Otherwise do nothing' (Sun Wu, 1996)?

In sum, does the global business revolution signal the end of state-led industrial policy to construct large, globally competitive firms?

We shall see in the following chapters that China's industrial policies since the early 1980s have attempted to build on the experience of industrial policy in other countries, in order to challenge the hegemony of the giant global corporations based in the advanced economies. However, China has been trying to build its own 'national champions' at the time of the most explosive change in the history of the large corporation that has ever been witnessed. China's vast size and the administrative capability of the government institutions provided many advantages for this process, but also provided some unique difficulties compared with other such attempts by 'latecomer' industrializing countries. The interaction of these two processes, one internal to China and one global in scale, is the central theme of this book.

Can China find a way in this new environment to build its own indigenous large, globally competitive corporations? What will be the consequences for China and for international political economy if it fails to do so?

3

Policies to Build National Champions: China's 'National Team' of Enterprise Groups

Dylan Sutherland

The Judge Institute of Management Studies, Cambridge

To quickly enter the Fortune 500 we can't pull
the saplings upward in the hope they will grow.
(Ma and Ma, 1998)

China's economy could be described as a dry prairie,
parched by years of planning,
awaiting the first sprinklings of market reform.
(World Bank, 1997)

INTRODUCTION

By all accounts China has made outstanding economic progress since the 1980s. If China's provinces were each considered individual nations, the twenty fastest-growing nations in the world from 1978–1995 would all be Chinese (World Bank, 1997: 2). It is sometimes argued that China's rapid industrial development, the motor behind growth in this period, has been primarily as a result of the speedy proliferation of small enterprises. The powerful imagery of the healthy young shoots of small private enterprises pushing their way upwards in response to 'sprinklings of market reform' is an image that many observers hold dear. This interpretation considers China's small enterprises the 'foundation for recent growth' (World Bank, 1997: 21). More recently, however, this view has been challenged by those who point out that although small enterprises have played a very important role in China's recent industrial development, the large-scale sector, predominantly state-owned, has also been critical (Lo, 1997, 1999; Nolan, 1996; Nolan and Wang, 1998). Among other things they show that the number of large and medium enterprises (LMEs) and their share of industrial output has increased significantly during the reforms. Furthermore, LMEs are found predominantly in key upstream pillar industries, often supplying smaller-scale enterprises with basic producer goods, or in industries with significant linkages. As well as this, despite being 'parched by years of planning', empirical evidence now also suggests LME productivity and financial performance has bettered that of the small-scale sector (Lo, 1999). In short, there is a growing weight of evidence suggesting the role of the large-scale state sector has been of far greater importance in China's reform than has previously been recognized. Yet relatively little is actually known about it. Many theoretical approaches bracket and analyze enterprises by ownership, not scale, often overlooking the role the state has played in facilitating the institutional transformation of China's largest enterprises. The large enterprise in China, as it was at one time in Japan and South Korea, to a great extent remains an unopened 'black box', and the state considered 'overweening' or 'dismissed as merely supportive, without anyone's ever analyzing the matter' (Johnson, 1982: 7). Yet not unlike Japan in the 1950s and 1960s, and South Korea in the 1970s and 1980s, policy makers and business leaders in China have made great efforts to nurture the 'saplings' of big business, particularly large enterprise groups.

This chapter specifically looks at 120 of China's largest emerging enterprise groups and related policy trials initiated by China's State Council, China's highest decision-making body. These groups are collectively known as the 'national team' and are considered the 'generals' or 'key few' in the current 'large company and enterprise group strategy'. Integral to this strategy is a number of other significant inter-related trial measures, all closely related to enterprise reform in the large-scale sector. Though these trials are looked at in less detail here, many of the enterprises in the 120 trial enterprise groups are also involved in them, highlighting the centrality of the national team of enterprise groups in current reform efforts. These trials include the introduction of modern corporate systems in 100 LMEs. At least 20 of these LMEs are also core or close members of the 120 trial enterprise groups (*Qiye Guanli*, 1 January 1995).[1] In addition, by 1997, direct preferential support measures overseen by the State Economic and Trade Commission (SETC) had been extended to 512 key LMEs, expanded from an initial 300 (Zhou, 1997: 66).[2] At least 74 of these LMEs were also close members of the 120 trial business groups (SSB, 1999: 325–33).[3] Related to the structuring of the large-scale sector, reforms in a number of trial cities promoting enterprise restructuring were also broadened to cover 111 cities and trials with three huge national holding companies, two of which are also members of the national team, are also ongoing.[4] These various official experiments in enterprise reform, backed at the highest level by central policy making bodies, have also been complemented with a number of direct financial support measures directed towards large enterprises and groups. Capital injections to help with technological upgrading, for example, have been provided and the state banking sector has also thrown its support behind the large-scale state sector.[5] Preferential stock market listings have also been given to these large groups and industrial policies have also been formulated across many of the key industries in which these large enterprises are found. Provincial and city-level governments have also intervened with their own packages of measures to help bolster large enterprises and groups.

These measures collectively constitute an ambitious raft of policies aimed at building internationally competitive large-scale multi-plant industrial enterprises from the remnants of the old state sector. The case studies presented in this book provide detailed descriptions of some of the national team members and the particular characteristics and challenges of the different industrial sectors in which they are found. Complementing these studies, this chapter provides a broader overview of attempts by policy makers, transcending boundaries of specific sectors, to build large modern industrial corporations, particularly large enterprise groups. First, by way of introduction, the general strategic intentions of the enterprise group policy are explained. Secondly, the origins and concept of the Chinese business group are briefly explored. As mentioned, not only are there many large-scale groups in China's key industries, such as the national team players, there are now also many smaller groups. Thirdly, a description of the national team is made based upon some of the available aggregate statistics as well as research into each of the individual 120 trial-group members.[6] A summary of each individual group can be found in Table 3-5 in Appendix 1. Fourthly, the main policies of two State Council directives, issued in 1991 and 1997, most important in the history of China's attempts to build large modern enterprises, are described and examined and the selection process related to the trial business groups looked at in more detail.[7] The fifth and sixth sections describe some of the measures that have been taken to help speed the development of the national team of enterprise groups. The conclusion points out that the development of large enterprise groups, though of great interest at present with entry to WTO approaching, has in fact been a long-term objective of leading policy makers in China for some time.

STRATEGY AND POLICY: 'GRASP THE LARGE'

One of the slogans state enterprise reform has now adopted is 'grasp the large, let go of the small'. The latter element, letting go of the small, is itself an important and interesting subject. By the end of 1996 up to 70 per cent of small state-owned enterprises (SOEs) had already been privatized in pioneering provinces and about a half in many other provinces. This was referred to as a 'quiet revolution from below' (Cao, Qian and Weingast, 1999: 105). Equally revolutionary measures, however, have also been undertaken in the large-scale sector. Of particular relevance to this debate are two policy directives, officially issued in December 1991 and April 1997 in which successively 55 and 63 enterprise groups were selected to undergo influential trial reforms.[8] Among the reform measures introduced were the development of internal group finance companies, the systematic introduction of stock-market listings, the promotion of preferential planning within the groups giving them greater autonomy in basic decision making, granting of import and export rights, the empowerment of the group's core with special rights to incorporate state assets into the group and the creation of research and technology centres. Extensive financial support from the banking sector and shelter from international competition by a wall of protective tariffs, not mentioned in these directives, have also been provided. By the end of 1996 the 120 groups had swelled: alone they were accountable for more than 50 per cent of profits and approximately 25 per cent of tax, total assets and total sales of state-owned industrial enterprises in the independent accounting sector (SCDRC, ZJN, 1997: 677). Thousands of member enterprises had been incorporated within the business groups of the national team players, as well as many thousands more in preferred province level teams of business groups. Many of China's LMEs, the large-scale sector, are now incorporated in the 2302 enterprise groups registered at the national or provincial level (Yin, Yuan and Zang, 1999: 132).[9] In 1997 these groups accounted for just 1.27 per cent of the total number of independent accounting enterprises but 51.1 per cent of all assets and 45.5 per cent of all sales (Yin, Yuan, and Zang, 1999). An approximate calculation suggests that these groups produced over 10 per cent of China's GDP (SSB, ZTN, 1998: 56, 431, 444).[10] The significance of policies instituted in the national team lies not only in the impact on the 120 team players but also, perhaps even more importantly, the great influence they have had and continue to exert as role models on the development of provincial and lower-level enterprise groups. Most provincial as well as hundreds more city and lower-level governments are nurturing their own teams of preferred enterprise groups.[11] As a result it is probable that the scale and reach of central and local government industrial policy, if not its effectiveness, far exceeds that which nations such as South Korea or Japan exercised during their most impressive growth periods.

To a great extent the development of the national team of business groups has adopted the traditional Chinese method of reform, using incremental steps, the 'groping for stones' approach as opposed to 'shock therapy'. However, unlike many of the previous incremental reform measures, those related to the trial business groups have over time developed explicitly stated objectives as well as implicitly accepted time horizons. With WTO entry approaching, it is considered 'imperative to develop a number of large enterprise groups to make up the backbone of the national economy and the country's main force to participate in international competition'.[12] Although by the mid-1990s most accounts agreed that China had already succeeded in 'growing out of the plan' there was still a great gulf between Chinese and foreign multinationals. By 1999 there were still only six Chinese enterprises in the Global *Fortune* 500 listings, of which one was from Hong Kong, one a bank and two trade companies (*Fortune*, 2 August 1999).[13] Tariff barriers remained high, sheltering a number of strategic industries. President Jiang Zemin at the 15th Party Conference in late 1997 summarized how efforts were to be made to distil the state sector into key 'pillar' or 'life-blood' industries of the national economy using strategic adjustments to create 'highly competitive large enterprise groups':

> The leading role of the state-owned sectors should manifest itself mainly in its control power. We should make a strategic readjustment of the state-owned sector of the economy. The state-owned sector must be in a dominant position in major industries and key areas that concern the life-blood of the national economy ... we shall effectuate a strategic reorganization of state-owned enterprises by managing well large enterprises while adopting a flexible policy toward small ones. By using capital as the bonds and relying on market forces, China will establish highly competitive large enterprise groups with trans-regional, inter-trade, cross-ownership and trans-national operations. (New Star Press, 1997: 22)

Since the end of the Party Conference in 1997 the implementation of the strategy of developing highly competitive large groups has reached a new level of intensity. After the conference Zhu Rongji launched a radical campaign to turn around the loss-making state enterprises by the year 2000, now seen as 'the decisive year' according to the SETC. The introduction of asset management companies and the writing-off of debts, an increased financial discipline, downsizing of work forces and forced consolidation within certain industrial sectors has ensued.[14] Although this has increased the attention paid to the largest enterprise groups their establishment and development has in fact been envisaged as a key long-term strategy for many years. Even as early as 1987 policy makers were issuing directives claiming 'the development of business groups is of profound long-term importance to the development of production capabilities and deepening the reform of the economic system' (CRES, ZJTGN, 1988: 9–17). The goal of 'grasping a batch of large enterprise groups, using capital ties to link and promote enterprise restructuring, creating economies of scale and thoroughly giving play to their backbone role' more recently has also been included as part of long-term development plans up to the year 2010 (CRES, ZJTGN, 1997: 243). This sentiment, even in the wake of the Asian financial crisis, appears to have remained unchanged. The centrality the CCP leadership attach to large enterprise groups in China's opening to trade is aptly summarized in a speech by vice-premier Wu Bangguo:

> In reality, international economic confrontations show that if a country has several large companies or groups it will be assured of maintaining a certain market share and a position in the international economic order. America, for example, relies on General Motors, Boeing, Du Pont and a batch of other multinational companies. Japan relies on six large enterprise groups and Korea relies on 10 large commercial groupings. In the same way now and in the next century our nation's position in the international economic order will be to a large extent determined by the position of our nation's large enterprises and groups. (*Jingji Ribao*, 1 August 1998)

There is a strong consensus in China that large groups are vitally needed if it is to attain a cherished goal of becoming a leading nation in the international economic order. Debate, however, still surrounds the best way of nurturing groups and this has intensified with the recent Asian financial crisis and moves for WTO entry. Some argue that 'China's situation is quite different from South Korea' because of a huge domestic market and abundant natural resources making the development of business groups 'an inexorable trend' (*CDBW*, 8 December 1998). Others look to the South Korean experience as a lesson: '[it] has told us that in the process of establishing large enterprise groups we must pay attention to the asset and liability ratio' (*FT*, 11 March 1998). The failing conglomerates of Asia have also led to a focus on productivity, not just size: 'size of an enterprise does matter, but it is more important for domestic enterprises to put emphasis on improving efficiency, innovative capability and competitiveness' (*CDBW*, 11 January 2000). In the quest to create large groups 'learning from the top 500 global companies' and looking to successful East Asian models has been encouraged. The rest of this chapter now goes on to look in more detail at the national team, its establishment and some of the policies that have been used to help it develop.

ORIGINS OF THE NATIONAL TEAM'S DEVELOPMENT

There were a number of factors at the beginning of reforms in the early 1980s which increased the potential political and economic gains of forming business groups. Of particular importance was the need to increase the average scale of operations. The centrally planned economy had fostered an excessive degree of vertical integration within the enterprise.[15] This led to a lack of specialization, with relatively small-scale operations, many of which were dispersed, often deliberately located in inaccessible regions. The problem of excessive integration is frequently referred to in China as the '*da er quan, xiao er quan*' problem, literally translated as 'large and complete, small and complete'. Cutting away excessive vertical ties while at the same time building horizontal linkages between producers of similar products was necessary for greater specialization in production which in turn could foster economies of scale. For this rationalization to take place, however, a huge redistribution of capital was required. In the face of unclear property rights and undeveloped capital markets this posed a serious challenge.[16] The development of supra-departmental enterprise groups was one way of breaking through these regional and departmental barriers to enterprise reorganization. Enterprise groups, at the same time as promoting scale, have also been seen as a means of maintaining employment and social stability. By coercing or offering incentives for profitable enterprises to take over less profitable enterprises it has been possible to smooth the transition from the planned economy. The practice of attempting to 'make good' state industry in this way is not unprecedented. It has been noted that enterprise failures were 'handled as the failure of one division of "China Incorporated" ... [and that] the means of arranging take-overs of failing firms is quite reminiscent of the practice used within large Japanese enterprise groups' (Naughton, 1995: 240). Although the motives and means for developing business groups have evolved since the early 1980s, increasing scale and 'making good the entire state industry' by incorporating loss-making enterprises into larger more successful groups still remain important.

The origins of the large business groups in the national team are closely related to the emergence of inter-enterprise production agreements. As early as 1979 in the initial throes of state enterprise reform over 4200 enterprises were empowered to carry out business outside the plan. This rose to 6600 in 1980, or 16 per cent of in budget enterprises producing 60 per cent of industrial output and 70 per cent of all profits (Shao, 1997: 87). In July 1980 the first policy document recognizing the existence of growing inter-enterprise production agreements was published, 'The State Council on pushing forward rules relating to economic links between enterprises'. By April of 1981 Erqi, a large auto producer, and arguably the leading pioneer in the trials with enterprise groups, had become one of the first emergent enterprises to expand from predominantly plant-based operations to a regionally and operationally diversified group of enterprises. At this time it established the Dongfeng Joint Management Company, which attempted to move from a position in which 'the factories jointly manage', to one in which the 'company manages the factories' (CRES, ZJTGN, 1990: 192). While in the early 1980s reform slowed or even regressed, by 1984 reforms again started to gather pace in urban areas and many large enterprises were also devolved to city and provincial governments. As a result of growing autonomy and competitive pressures a new impetus to the formation of economic linkages started and continued to develop throughout the mid- and late 1980s. From a level of 3400 in 1980, by 1986 the number of what were termed 'co-operation agreements' between enterprises is reported to have mushroomed to 50 000. Among these 50 000 agreements 32 000 gained the somewhat vague status of 'economic unions'. Approximately 1000 were also already being labelled as enterprise groups (Chai, 1997: 42).Other reports suggest that by 1987 there were 34 518 'close' links between enterprises, and some 11 785 'semi-close' concerns (CRES Research Group, 1998: 28). Regardless of the exact types of links that were forming, the operations of what were originally plant-based concerns run by industrial departments had started the metamorphosis towards becoming enterprise groups. Of the 45 000 or so links a total of 19.1 per cent were exclusively between state-owned enterprises, 36.3 per cent between collectives, and 34.4 per cent between state and collective industry (CRES Research Group, 1998). Thus even at this early stage in reform the original basis of the state-owned economy had evolved considerably, with a mass of ad hoc linkages taking place between the newly empowered economic units. The origins of business groups date back to these early reforms. Not unsurprisingly this early period is now being labelled as the 'gestation' period of business group development (CRES, ZJTGN, 1998: 270). By December 1987 the publication of 'Some opinions on arranging and developing business groups' marked the first policy document setting out the aims and means of developing enterprise groups. It also heralded what now has become known as the 'developmental stage' of business group development.[17]

A number of trials with several large auto groups, however, actually preceded and gave rise to the publication of the December 1987 document which marked the 'developmental' stage of business group development. With the proliferation of economic linkages between enterprises in the early and mid-1980s it was not long before policy advisers started to realize the potential of further promoting some pioneering groups, particularly those in industries which could benefit from economies of scale. By 1986 influential Chinese economists and policy makers, including Ma Hong, head of the influential State Council Development Research Centre (SCDRC), began to look at policies specifically aimed at the promotion of very large business groups based around former state plants (Chen, 1998).[18] It was in fact these plants, such as Erqi, which had been some of the most influential in co-ordinating economic links between firms in their attempts to improve operative efficiency and increase market share and profits. The SCDRC, led by Ma Hong, undertook a survey of the problems faced at Erqi in March 1986 (later to become Dongfeng Group). By this time these enterprises had already incorporated a number of separate enterprises into joint management companies, the prototype of the business groups that were to later emerge. Ma Hong's discussions with the emerging group were subsequently presented to the State Planning Commission in the form of a report. This report pointed out that the basic problems enterprises such as Dongfeng faced were systemic. Although new types of business organizations were developing they remained controlled by the institutions of the planning mechanism. The State Council Development Research Centre therefore made four recommendations: that Erqi be made a trial group; that this be given the status of a top level planning unit; that support for the development of a financial institution within the group be provided and that governmental departments continue to devolve power to the group (Chen, 1992: 63). By the following month, April 1986, the State Council agreed on the principles of this report and ordered the State Planning Commission and CRES to examine their proposals in more detail. By July, after two months of enquiries and research at Erqi the State Council approved the policy which resulted from this research, 'On Dongfeng Joint Management Company undertaking preferential planning status'. Several months later this new policy was extended to include two more auto groups, Jiefang (Liberation) and Heavy Vehicle Group. Another policy document, 'Notice on Jiefang, Dongfeng and Heavy Vehicle Group joint management companies undertaking preferential planning status' was issued and the trial was expanded (see chronology in Appendix 2 for list of important policies related to the development of large business groups). The following year the policy continued to evolve and by December 1987 the first landmark policy document was published.

The research and policies undertaken at the three large auto groups now stand out as historically significant landmarks. As later sections show, they represented the first cautious steps in what was later to become a greatly expanded and sophisticated long-term industrial development strategy. They ushered in a period, continuing today, in which innovative policies were introduced and cautiously widened to other enterprises in other industries throughout China's regions. Nascent business groups exchanged views with top policy makers in the search for the institutions governing the scope of their activities. From 1988 onwards to the batch of three pioneering groups four enterprises from the electric generating equipment, three from electronics, two from the construction materials and one from the agricultural equipment industries were added (Chen, 1998: 18). The lone policy of the preferential planning was thus expanded in number to 13 groups. On top of these centrally controlled groups another 13 provinces and cities also promoted some 50 or so groups to separate planning status. The inclusion of provincial and city level groups in the trials also marked another important element of the trial policies, namely their quick adoption and implementation at lower levels. Ten years later the batch of trial groups had increased from just a single group, Dongfeng, to over 200 state-level groups and over 2000 province level groups, as well as thousands more lower-level groups based upon a range of policy measures. The investigations in 1986 of the SCDRC, led by Ma Hong, and subsequent directives of the State Planning Commission in 1987, reaffirmed a commitment to the enterprise above the plan, and in particular to promoting large-scale enterprise groups as microeconomic engines of growth. They constituted the very first steps in the policy, yet to be fully conceived, of 'grasping the large and letting go of the small'.

WHAT IS AN ENTERPRISE GROUP?

A defining characteristic of the trial enterprise groups is the existence of a large powerful 'mother' or 'core' company, otherwise known as a 'group company', surrounded by other 'son' companies in which the mother holds a controlling share. This is known as the 'close' layer of the group. Enterprises in which the mother has minority share ownership are known as 'semi-close' members. Often close or semi-close member enterprises also own stakes in other enterprises which in turn become 'grandsons' of the mother. In this way the member enterprises of enterprise groups have expanded quickly. According to an early official definition firms engaging in economic linkages were only recognized as groups if 'the firm at the centre of the group had secure ownership or control over (such as majority ownership in) three or more firms' (Marukawa, 1995: 332). By 1995 this number had increased to five enterprises (either stock controlled or wholly-owned), though in practice the largest groups such as those undergoing trial had many more members. Groups such as Huaneng, Dongfeng, Xinjiang Construction Group and China State Construction Engineering Group, for example, had many hundreds of member enterprises (See Table 3-5 in Appendix 1). On top of the multi-layered structure, it was also necessary that the group's mother company be classified as either a large-scale enterprise or have registered capital exceeding 100 million yuan.[19] Most of the groups are also based around leading products with strong brand names, referred to as 'dragon head' products. According to a recent market research study six of China's top 10 domestic and foreign brands are associated with national team members (*ChinaOnline*,

6 May 2000). Within the trial groups the presence of internal finance companies has also become a defining feature and with the issuing of foreign trade rights trade companies have emerged. Such groups usually have at least one listed enterprise within the group.

Although the true spirit of the Chinese business group is embodied by those based upon large state plants, such as those in the trial groups, the condition stating only 100 million yuan in capital is needed to form a group has also given rise to a large number of small business groups. As a result the actual number of groups registered at all government levels has grown very rapidly. By 1998 one estimate placed this at 20 000. However, it is suggested only 5 per cent were 'cohesive groups' (*ningjuli jituan*) at this time, in which son companies were closely co-ordinated by the mother and the capital ties were close. As early as 1988 there were reported to be 1630 large groups, though only 280 were considered 'closely knit', meeting official definitions (CRES, ZJTGN, 1989: 94). By 1991 this had risen to 431 satisfying CRES's criteria (CRES, ZJTGN, 1992: 306).[20] In 1992 there was a jump in the total number of recorded groups to 7538, rising over fourfold from 1988. The rapid increase in this period is somewhat illusory, however, as it was plagued by the practice of what has been called 'hanging signs' (*gua paizi*), referring to the renaming of industrial departments as groups in the absence of any real structural change. Nonetheless, the development of business groups, particularly evident in the early 1990s, has been very rapid.

THE NATIONAL TEAM

Before returning to describe the evolution of the policies that have shaped the members of the national team, as well as their selection, this section describes in more detail some of the basic characteristics of the 120 national team members. These 120 groups have come to hold a pre-eminent position within the national economy not only because of their scale but also because they are closely integrated with the 'grasping the large' campaign. Many of the 512 trial LMEs and 100 trial LMEs introducing the modern corporate system, as mentioned, are also members of these 120 business groups. The national team, therefore, can be considered the 'generals' at the vanguard of the current policy to develop the large-scale sector.

SCALE

The 120 trial groups eventually chosen by the State Council most vividly embody the spirit of the Chinese business group both for their size and complexity. This is unsurprising as a key goal of 'grasping the large' is to create enterprises capable of reaping economies of scale and scope. Invariably they were leaders in their industries, including automobiles, auto components, agricultural equipment, electronics, power generation, power equipment, aerospace, coal mining, ferrous and non-ferrous metals, building materials, glass, ceramics, pharmaceuticals, civil and freight transportation, forestry and chemicals (Table 3-5 in Appendix 1). The six trial groups in electricity generation and supply, for example, produced over half of China's electricity. The eight metallurgy groups produced 40 per cent of the nation's iron and steel and the six approved auto makers manufactured 57 per cent of the total volume of China's auto industry. The three civilian airlines controlled over 55 per cent of the domestic market (CRES, ZJTGN, 1997: 244).[21] The groups were based upon large-scale enterprises which were the 'core members of the group' with the 'capability to act as investment centres' (CRES, ZJTGN, 1992: 160). These core members were invariably listed among the top 10 in their sectors both in terms of assets and sales (Table 3-5 in Appendix 1). In 1995, the only year for which aggregate statistics can be found (Table 3-1), the 120 trial groups combined workforce stood at approximately 7 million, averaging about 60 000 workers per group and equalling 1.1 per cent of the national workforce and 6.2 per cent of the state sector workforce (CASS, ZGFB, 1998: 121; SSB, ZTN, 1998: 92–102). The workforce of large industrial enterprises stood at a peak of over 24 million in this year so the 120 enterprise groups total employment was approximately equal to a quarter that of the large-scale sector (Liu, Jiang and Shang, 1999: 119).[22] Within the state-owned industrial sector, as mentioned earlier, by 1997 the groups were reported to make over 50 per cent of profits, pay 25 per cent of taxes and make over 25 per cent of all sales. Of the 120 groups it is reported that less than 10 were loss-makers at the end of 1995 (CRES, ZJTGN,1997: 243). The process of '*jituanhua*', the transformation of enterprises into extended groups of enterprises, had also began to subsume much of the large-scale sector. The sales value of these 120 groups was equivalent to approximately one-third of the total output value of the whole large and medium-scale enterprise sector, consisting of nearly 24 000 enterprises (CASS, ZGFB, 1998: 121; SSB, ZDZQN, 1996: 2). State industry, under the aegis of the policy of 'grasp the large, let go of the small', has gradually become distilled in a small number of large enterprise groups.

Within the national team, as Table 3-1 indicates, there were some large size disparities, both in terms of average sales, capital and employment between the enterprise groups. Sectors such as iron and steel, energy (mainly concentrated in electricity generation), autos and construction were on average larger than the other groups and also paid more taxes. These sectors averaged about half a billion dollars in total assets and $350 million in sales, considerably larger than machinery, electronics and pharmaceuticals, for example. In terms of employment some were massive, such as the construction companies, employing millions of people. Others, such as the ceramics producers, were much smaller, employing only around 30 000 people. Size disparities between enterprises within the same sector also existed. Within the auto sector, for example, Heavy Vehicle Group had total sales of $650 millon and a workforce of 84 000 whereas FAW's exceeded $4 billion and 170 000 workers. Similarly in steel, Baoshan Group had assets exceeding those of Chongqing Steel Group by approximately

TABLE 3-1 Various Economic Indicators of the National Team, 1995

Indicator Industry	Assets ($ billion)		Net Assets ($ billion)	Sales ($ billion)		Taxes ($ million)		Exports ($ million)
	(Total)	(Average)	(Total)	(Total)	(Average)	(Total)	(Average)	(Total)
Metallurgy (8)	4.3	0.54	2.3	2.1	0.26	300	37.5	228
Energy (11)	5.0	0.45	2.5	1.8	0.16	200	18.2	31
Chemicals (7)	0.92	0.13	0.35	0.42	0.06	58	8.3	26
Autos (6)	3.2	0.53	1.1	2.6	0.43	290	48.3	42
Machinery (14)	0.52	0.03	0.16	0.29	0.02	29	2.1	26
Electronics (10)	0.52	0.05	0.18	0.52	0.05	43	4.3	103
Transport (8)	2.8	0.35	1	1.2	0.15	73	9.13	256
Pharmaceuticals (5)	0.47	0.09	0.16	0.29	0.06	37	7.4	31
Construction (3)	1.9	0.63	0.38	1.3	0.4	64	21.3	48
Foreign trade (8)	1.4	0.18	0.27	1.6	0.18	37	4.6	765
TVEs	0.75	0.25	0.42	0.7	0.23	85	28	10
120 Total	193.5		78.5	11.2		10.2		1700
120 Average	1.6	0.65	0.65	0.93		86		12

SOURCE: CASS, ZGFB (1995: 122)

tenfold. In mining the Datong Group's workforce of 170 000 was more than double Yanzhou Group, which employed 80 000 (Table 3-5 in Appendix 1).

By comparison with the largest transnational corporations, however, the national team still remained small. Although the largest transnational corporations sometimes employ a global workforce of comparable size to some of their Chinese counterparts, they have vastly superior sales and assets. In 1997 the world's three largest transnational corporations (Ford, GE, Shell) employed on average approximately 250 000 people globally and had sales approaching $400 billion and assets of over $600 billion (UNCTAD, 1999, Ch. 3. 2). While their workforces on average were only about four times larger than the Chinese groups, their sales and assets were over 100 times greater. It has been calculated that in 1998 the average total assets and average sales of China's top 500 enterprises were $712 million and $398 million, respectively. This corresponded to a mere 0.88 per cent of the average assets of the top 500 global companies and 1.74 per cent of their average sales (*CDBW*, 11 January 2000). By comparison with the largest transnational corporations based in developing countries China's largest groups still remained small. These have average assets of $9 billion and sales of $6 billion, exceeding most of China's national team players (UNCTAD, 1999, Ch. 3, p. 12). In terms of employment, however, they were smaller, employing only 35 000 people on average. China's largest enterprises still remain small-scale and bloated with large work forces in comparison to both large Western corporations and the largest transnational corporations based in developing countries.

GROUP EXPANSION AND DIVERSIFICATION

By 1997 the original 57 trial business groups had incorporated over 1800 stock controlled enterprises and over 1300 enterprises in which they held minority share positions (Yu, 1997: 5). On average therefore each mother company had 54 stock controlled or stock participating companies within its group, of which 31 were fully stock controlled companies and 23 linked via minority stock holdings. If the periphery of these groups, the large numbers of 'co-operating' enterprises involved in stable business relationships with the core of the group are also included, the actual number of enterprises involved with the groups was much larger. Among the largest enterprise groups are three experimenting with the introduction of a national holding company system, Aviation Industries China (AVIC, now split into two), China National Non-metallic Minerals Enterprise Group (CNMEG) and Sinopec. These possess hundreds of close and semi-close stock controlled companies involving hundreds of thousands of workers. Other smaller groups, such as China Textile Machinery Group, for example, are still quite large, consisting of over 20 LMEs scattered across over 11 provinces (See fifth column, Table 3-5 in Appendix 1 for details of the number of members in the trial enterprise groups).

Group diversification is closely related to merger and take-over activity, the earliest examples of which date from 1984. Though such activity initially was restricted in number and size, by the end of 1988 over 27 provinces and cities were involved in this type of restructuring. It is reported that a total of 2856 enterprises had taken over or merged with 3424 other enterprises. However, only a quarter of these were reported to be profitable and four per cent of these considered 'comparatively profitable'(Shao, 1997: 90). This reflected, as already mentioned, the role business groups undertook in incorporating and 'making good' poorly performing enterprises. This early period, which is considered China's first 'merger wave', as already noted, also corresponds to what has been labelled the 'developmental' stage of Chinese business groups. The development of groups and such restructuring have progressed together. Large groups such as Yiqi, Dongfeng, Shougang and Jilin Chemical Fibre Group, for example, were groups which incorporated dozens of member enterprises during this period. Interestingly, however, up to the end of 1988 there were still only 220 cross-provincial transactions reported, 6.5 per cent of the total.[23] In contrast 33 per cent of these were trans-industrial (Shao, 1997: 90). It appears, therefore, many groups diversified even earlier on in their development, though they found it harder to spread their operations geographically. According to one 1994 study of the close members of 42 large enterprise groups, 33 produced between two and seven different products and six produced more than 10 different product types. It deemed that 40 of the 42 groups were trans-industrial. Of these 40 there were 36 groups that spanned 2–5 industries, and 4 groups which operated in more than six industries (SCDRC, ZJN, 1994: 659).

The logic driving the development of business groups, and the national team in particular, more recently appears to have turned from salvaging small-scale industry to pushing forward the development of large internationally competitive groups by promoting strong/strong mergers between groups in the same sectors. Attempts to force consolidation are being made across most sectors. In autos, for example, 'China's top 20 auto makers will reshuffle into three or four enterprise groups' (*CDBW*, March 1997). In steel, consolidation is seen not only as the 'key way to bail out loss-making companies' but also of driving economies of scale. The target is for four large groups to produce 40 per cent of production by the end of 2000 (*CDBW*, 16 January 1998). Recently, for example, Shougang has merged with Tangshan Steel with the aim of forming a large northern group spanning Tianjin, Beijing and Hebei, and Baogang in the Shanghai area has also been involved in mergers. In pharmaceuticals, still highly dispersed, there were only 72 enterprises with assets exceeding $12 million in 1998. Consolidation is being promoted. In chemicals and petrochemicals restructuring has been ongoing, with the formation of a number of super-groups such as Donglian and Petrochina, the floated arm of CNPC. In the airline industry, using 'Air China, China Eastern and China Southern as the backbone, China will voluntarily merge and restructure the other 31 airlines to form three big groups' (*ChinaOnline*, 1 April 2000). In the building materials industries small-scale producers are being closed down or taken over in order to 'speed the development of large enterprise groups' (*CDBW*, 30 May 2000). In electronics, the plan is to 'turn the canoes into bamboo rafts and warships', by promoting mergers (*CDBW*, 8 April 1998). In coal mining, thousands of local small-scale producers are being shut down and investment funds are being directed towards key large-scale groups. In power generation Huaneng has cemented its position as one of the largest power generators in a landmark move, taking over another large power group in a share deal. Even trade companies have attempted to consolidate, with CNTIC, one of the largest trade companies, taking over two large groups (see Table 3-5 in Appendix 1 for more details on consolidation).

Unsurprisingly the rate and size of mergers and acquisitions has increased in recent years: 'in terms of the number of enterprises and the volume of state-owned assets involved, enterprise mergers in 1997 far exceeded those of previous years'. In 1997 it is reported there were 3000 state enterprises merged, totalling $1.8 billion (*CDBW*, 1 June 1998). However, even though this is reported as a record year of activity in China, it was tiny in international comparison. The United States in 1998, for example, itself also experienced a record year, with merger and acquisition activity exceeding $1.3 trillion in value (*Global Finance*, February 1999). This was approximately 700 times the value of China's 1997 record year. There appears to be a growing awareness in China of the rapid pace of international restructuring, particularly the trend of the largest global corporations to consolidate amongst themselves across core activities. It is felt that large enterprises and groups must now join forces to have any chance of success in the international market place:

> If we use our strong large-scale enterprises and groups and they all fight alone, everyone will still find it difficult in the ever intensifying domestic and international competition to compete on equal terms with large international companies. We must therefore unite and rise together, develop economies of scale and scope and nurture a 'national team' capable of entering the world's top 500. (Wu Bangguo, quoted in the *Jingji Ribao*, 8 January 1998)

However, by the late 1990s mergers between large enterprises were still a virtually unknown phenomena, and those that did take place usually relied upon state intervention: 'few large State-owned enterprises have realized substantial expansion through market oriented mergers' (*CDBW*, 1 June 1998). Although the prevailing view is that enterprise groups should be free to merge with partners of their choice and that coercion 'is definitely a bad way of doing things', in practice it appears the only way to create mergers between large-scale enterprises.[24] Although China's largest enterprise groups are still small in comparison to large global corporations, perhaps more worrying is the continued lack of a suitable mechanism and the conditions to facilitate rapid restructuring, vitally required if China's national team is to have any chance at all of competing with international rivals.

GEOGRAPHICAL LOCATION OF THE NATIONAL TEAM MEMBERS

Although many of the national team business groups are trans-provincial and some trans-national, making it difficult to generalize about the location of their

TABLE **3-2** **Provincial Distribution of China's Preferred Large-Scale Enterprises and Groups, 1997**

Province	(a)	(b)	(c)	(d)	(e)	(f)	(g)	(h)
Beijing	215	27	32	13	12.6	27.4	9.2	...
Tianjin	277	10	2	2	3.6	4.3	1.9	...
Hebei	328	31	3	3	9.5	10.4	5.3	29
Shanxi	130	14	2	2	10.8	12.3	2.5	...
Inner Mongolia	82	8	2	1	9.8	12.2	1.6	...
Liaoning	489	38	6	5	7.8	9.0	6.9	10
Jilin	168	13	4	2	7.7	10.1	2.7	15
Heilongjiang	277	19	5	2	6.9	8.7	3.8	...
Shanghai	587	47	11	4	8.0	9.9	9.1	50
Jiangsu	552	29	6	5	5.3	6.3	5.5	40+
Zhejiang	332	11	2	0	3.3	3.9	2.0	...
Anhui	191	12	2	2	6.3	7.3	2.2	...
Fujian	93	11	0	0	11.8	11.8	1.7	40
Jiangxi	103	9	0	0	8.7	8.7	1.4	...
Shandong	738	41	6	4	5.6	6.4	7.4	136
Henan	323	22	5	4	6.8	8.4	4.2	...
Hubei	298	22	7	5	7.4	9.7	4.5	...
Hunan	209	16	0	0	7.7	7.7	2.5	...
Guangdong	655	44	8	8	6.7	7.9	8.1	66
Guangxi	152	12	1	1	7.9	8.6	2.0	20
Hainan	24	1	0	0	4.2	4.2	0.2	...
Sichuan	383	28	8	7	9.4	11.5	6.9	...
Guizhou	98	7	3	1	7.1	10.2	1.6	...
Yunnan	91	12	0	0	13.2	13.2	1.9	...
Shaanxi	203	7	3	3	3.4	4.9	1.6	...
Gansu	93	9	0	0	9.7	9.7	1.4	12
Qinghai	31	2	0	0	6.5	6.5	0.3	15
Ningxia	28	4	0	0	14.3	14.3	0.6	...
Xinjiang	49	5	2	0	10.2	14.3	1.1	50
Total	7199	512	120	74	46	n.a	100	...

SOURCES: Column (a), SSB, ZTN (1998: 438); columns (b) and (c), State Economic Trade Commission web site

NOTES: Column (a) The number of large-scale enterprises, 1997
　　　　Column (b) The number of 512 preferred LMEs, 1997
　　　　Column (c) The number of 120 trial enterprise groups
　　　　Column (d) The number of 512 LMEs which are also members of 120 trial groups
　　　　Column (e) (b)/(a), preferred LMEs expressed as a percentage of each provinces LMEs
　　　　Column (f) (b+c)/(a), the percentage share of LMEs which are preferred (either preferred LME or preferred group), by province
　　　　Column (g) The percentage share of national total of preferred business groups and LMEs, by province
　　　　Column (h) The number of groups in provincial-level teams

operations, investigation of the 120 preferred business groups as well as the 512 preferred LMEs, not yet looked at in detail, gives an indication of where these groups originate from. A large number, 33 per cent in total, originate from either Beijing, Shanghai, Shandong or Guangdong. Of all the preferred groups and enterprises 9 per cent originated from Beijing alone, reflecting its proximity to policy makers, and the top six provinces alone were responsible for 47 per cent (see Table 3-2, column g). Preferred enterprise groups and LMEs, therefore, are still concentrated in a small number of provinces and cities, predominantly coastal regions. This has been so throughout their development. Even as early as 1991 of the 431 province and state level enterprise groups recognized at the time 47 per cent originated from Shandong, Guangdong, Shanghai and Jiangsu (CRES, ZJTGN, 1992: 307). These provinces have therefore led and maintained their leadership in the development of large enterprise groups.

It should be noted, however, that although in terms of total numbers the preferred groups and enterprises are biased to certain provinces, if they are considered as a proportion of the total number of large-scale enterprises in each province, the picture appears to change. Even the more backward regions fared just as well in this respect. In Shanghai, Guangdong and Shandong, for example, the preferred groups constituted from between 6 per cent to 9 per cent of the total number of enterprises in the LME sector. In Guangxi, Guizhou, Gansu, Yunnan and Xinjiang, by comparison, 8 per cent to 13 per cent of LMEs were selected among the centrally approved groups and LMEs, exceeding the proportion in more developed regions.

An important feature of business group development, already noted though not explored in detail, has been the rapid progression of policy down to lower levels of government. If preferred provincial-level teams of business groups are also included it can be seen that the true extent of the 'grasping the large' policy is greatly expanded. Certain provincial governments such as Guangdong and Shandong were arguably the pioneers in developing 'provincial teams' of groups via preferential policies. Similar tactics have been adopted by the likes of Liaoning (10 big groups), Jilin (15), Shanghai, Jiangsu (3–5 super-large groups and 40 to 50 smaller ones) and Fujian, to name a few. At the city level extensive efforts have also been undertaken. The provincial and city level focus on 'grasping the large' via provincial and city level teams is one of the remarkable features of business group expansion and one that warrants much more research. Although the 120 groups of the national team are industry leaders and stand out as important examples, in terms of actual numbers and overall impact on the Chinese economy, provincial and lower level supported groups are probably of even greater importance. There are already over 2000 provincial level enterprise groups registered.

PILLAR INDUSTRIES AND AN EVOLVING INDUSTRIAL POLICY

The 120 enterprise groups in China's national team are large, often diversified groups with geographically dispersed operational units, though often with links to the most prosperous eastern provinces of China. To add to these features the national team enterprise groups are also found predominantly within a particular subset of industries. There are two interesting and important points to note as regards the particular industries in which the groups are found. The first relates to the actual industrial sectors and the second the differences between the industries from which the first and second batch of groups were chosen. Regarding the first point it is clear that many of the groups are found in the capital intensive industries that the economic historian Chandler has identified as being bastions of big business (Chandler, 1990). Of the 120 trial groups, energy supply (11), electronics (10), iron and steel (8), autos (6), machinery (14), pharmaceuticals (5), construction (3), aviation and aerospace (6) and chemicals (7) were some of the most important (Table 3-3).

Most of these industries benefit considerably from economies of scale and scope. It is therefore common in advanced economies for these industries to harbour what Chandler has labelled the 'the large modern industrial corporation'.

TABLE 3-3 **Industrial Sectors of the First and Second Trial Group Batches, 1991 and 1997**

Industry	First Batch (1991)	Second Batch (1997)	Total
Electricity generation	8	0	8
Coal mining	1	2	3
Automobiles	3	3	6
Other machinery	10	4	14
Electronics	3	7	10
Iron and steel	4	4	8
Transportation	2	3	5
Civil Aviation	3	0	3
Chemicals	4	3	7
Construction materials	4	1	5
Construction	0	3	3
Textiles	1	3	4
Forestry	4	0	4
Aviation and aerospace	6	0	6
Foreign trade	2	6	8
Domestic trade/services	0	6	6
Pharmaceuticals	2	3	5
Agriculture	0	5	5
Light industry	0	3	3
TVEs	0	3	3
Other	0	4	4
Total	57	63	120

SOURCE: SCDRC, ZJL (1998: 704); CASS, ZGFB (1998: 121); SSB, ZTN (1996: 232); Table 3-5 Appendix 1

These enterprises 'are most crucial to the strength, continued growth, and defence of a modern, urban, industrial and technologically advanced society'(Chandler, 1990: 257). Chinese policy makers refer to them as the 'pillar', 'life-blood' and 'backbone' industries of the national economy. Other industrial sectors, those in which large enterprises are now not so important, have not received the same level of support. Recently a minister responsible for light industry, for example, commented that 'to develop State sectors is critical to the economy but not to light industry because light industry isn't influential enough to national security and the economy' (CDBW, 20–27 March 1997). As a result only a small number of groups have been chosen from what could be considered light industries and these were added in the second batch (Table 3-3). This was mainly to standardize the trials across a wider range of industrial sectors.

THE FIRST BATCH OF TRIAL GROUPS

The first batch of 57 groups selected in December 1991 was clearly biased towards utilities, large construction projects and areas which acted as either the mainstays of economic development or were crucial to national security.[25] Among these 57 groups, for example, were five large power generation groups and five power generation equipment groups. Ten of the first 57 groups were therefore related directly to the generation of electric power, evidently a 'pillar' industry crucial to the 'strength' and 'continued growth' of the economy. Six aviation groups, important in guaranteeing national defence, were also included in the first batch. The four forestry groups also added again highlighted the fundamental nature of these groups to the national economy. Three major national construction and technology projects were also included, all related to power generation. The Shenhua Group involved in coal mining, transportation and power generation, Guangdong Nuclear Power Group involved in developing nuclear power plants and Gezhouba Group, involved in hydroelectric dam construction, were all of great national importance. Three national airlines were also added. In the second batch of groups in 1997 no further additions were made to the sectors from which these 26 groups originated. The selection of these groups was indicative of the particular goals of early policy, which though ostensibly aimed at creating large modern industrial enterprises was also well aware of the practical necessities of providing the most basic inputs to the fast growing Chinese economy. At this time, therefore, the development of the national team appears to have clung to traditional planning concepts, which prioritized the development of basic industries and projects of significance to the continued growth of the national economy.

THE SECOND BATCH OF TRIAL GROUPS

Especially symbolic in the second batch was the inclusion of three TVEs, claimed to be a 'great breakthrough, illustrating that the standardization of the trials had broken through the traditional concepts of state enterprise system' (SCDRC, ZJN, 1998: 704). In the second batch no additions to the power generation groups, power equipment makers, defence groups or major construction projects were made. Instead the remaining 20 groups in steel, autos, chemicals, electronics and machinery industries were expanded. The steel groups were increased from four to eight, autos from three to six, chemicals from four to seven, electronics from three to ten (Table 3-3). This in part was an attempt to promote oligopolistic competition between group members, following principles used by industrial policies in South Korea and Japan, for which many policy makers have an open admiration.[26] As well as this, the selection recognized these were industries with high income elasticity of demand and great export market potential. Electronics, recently the fastest growing industrial sector and of growing significance to the trade balance, is a particularly good example (Lo and Chan, 1998). The number of groups was expanded from three to ten by the second batch, more than any other sector. Also to these ends three more pharmaceutical groups, two mining groups and three construction groups were added. The second batch also included six trade groups, expanding the two groups already approved in 1991, highlighting the growing importance of the trade balance and foreign exchange constraint to China's overall progress. Although there was also far greater emphasis on pushing forward the creation of the 'enterprise' and the legal institutions necessary for its development, the enterprise law having been published several years earlier, policy makers still maintained an element of their pragmatic streak. What claims to be one of China's largest business groups, for example, the Xinjiang Construction Group, which employs several million people and is important in the development of a relatively backward province, was also added to the second batch. A number of other groups from the poorer inland regions, such as Xinjiang Textile Group and Guangxi Guitang Group (sugar production) were also included. This marked a recognition of the need to boost the development of poorer regions as well as to experiment with the business group policy across China's regions. Other new entrants among the second batch of groups included a number of regional development and investment groups, including one of China's earliest groups, the Shenzhen Special Economic Zone Development Group and Changjiang United Economic Development Group.

The particular industries from which the groups have been selected as well as the timing of their selection is indicative of an evolution in policy objectives, as well as a structural change in Chinese industry towards new types of consumer goods. The most noticeable trend is the movement from support of the most basic backbone industries, such as power, defence and construction projects, to those which held greater growth potential as incomes increased and export markets have developed. Autos, electronics, machinery, pharmaceuticals, chemicals and steel stand out as examples. As a result of this expansion the number of groups within these sectors has also increased intensifying competition between the largest groups in these key growth industries.

POLICIES PROMOTING INSTITUTIONAL CHANGE IN THE TRIAL BUSINESS GROUPS

The previous sections have examined some of the features of the national team, including the industries and provinces from which they developed, their origins and the origins of policies aimed at promoting their development, the size of the groups and their strategic importance to the Chinese economy. The next sections go on to look in more detail at policies introduced to the national team trial groups in two important policy directives, central to understanding the current 'grasp the large, let go of the small policy', issued in 1991 and 1997.[27] Although the emergence of trials with groups can be dated back to 1986, these two influential State Council policy directives, in which formal selection of the trial groups was made, are still regarded as a 'a great leap forward' in the development of business groups (Chen Qiaosheng, 1998: 704). As already described, even before the first batch of trial groups was officially chosen in 1991 five years of experimentation, consideration and preparation concerned with the direction of business group policy had taken place. Dongfeng, one of the very first trial enterprise groups, after several months was expanded to include two more auto producers. Shortly after this, by April 1987 the number of trial groups had unofficially expanded to 13 and the preferential planning policy was complemented with the promotion of internal group finance companies. Over the years a number of new policies were introduced and spread to the trial business groups, including foreign trade rights, standardization of the mother/son company system, clarification of property rights within the core enterprises and promotion of technology centres. Table 3-4 illustrates the various measures, the timing of their introduction to the trial groups and the way in which they gradually broadened their coverage. By 1999 the three trial groups had increased to 120 and at least seven major policy measures had been introduced.

Before considering in more detail the policies listed in Table 3-4 the next two sections discuss the general objectives and nature of the two State Council directives of 1991 and 1997.

THE FIRST STATE COUNCIL DIRECTIVE, DECEMBER 1991

The first directive laid out the objectives, principles of experimentation with groups and necessary conditions for choosing the trial groups. Broadly speaking the policies introduced attempted to free the enterprise groups from some of the constraints of the old planning system. This was partly achieved by using the market mechanism to exploit their full potential but also by the introduction of new rules and laws to promote necessary institutions and greater 'cohesion' within the groups. In total five interrelated goals for the national team enterprise groups are listed in this directive. Firstly, and unsurprisingly, a priority was to encourage specialization and redress the historical legacy of geographically dispersed small-scale industry and the 'inability of achieving economies of scale'.

TABLE **3-4** **Evolution of Policies and their Implementation within the Centrally Approved Enterprise Groups, 1987–99**

Policy	1987	1991	1994	1995	1996	1997	1999
Number of groups undergoing trials	13	55	56	57	57	...	120
Single track planning	12	14	34	40	40	57	120
Foreign trade rights	...	...	54	57	...	57[28]	108
Access to foreign finance		...	...	...	...	...	38
Foreign commercial affairs	...	...	46	49	...	51	...
Unified taxation of groups	...	...	...	23	...	...	...
Empowered with state property rights	...	3	7	7	7	...	...
Technology centres	...	...	26	...	...	...	71
Finance companies	13		33	39	35	38	44
Involved in State Council trials with introduction of modern enterprise system	...	...	...	...	15	...	30+
Number of focal 512 LMEs in groups	...	...	...	...	...	...	74
Stock-market listings	...	...	30	...	32[29]	43	66

SOURCE: SCDRC, ZJN (1998: 704–9, 1996: 706, 1995: 601); CRES, ZJTGN (1997: 244); Ying (1999: 34); *Beijing Review* (11–17 January 1999)

Secondly, the groups were seen as a means of breaking through the existing regional and departmental barriers which constrained the natural growth of large-scale enterprise groups. This remains a problem today: 'enterprise mergers are still hindered by regional and departmental barriers. The government should guide the development of large enterprises by industrial policy but not administrative intervention' (*CDBW*, 8 December 1998). Thirdly, they were to give play to the leading role of large enterprises in concentrating and directing investment funds in the hope of reducing replication. Fourthly, even by 1991 it was hoped that international competitiveness could be improved so the groups could become 'major forces' in international markets.

The fifth and final objective was related to the domestic economy. This was to improve what are referred to as 'macroeconomic adjustment capabilities'. This objective highlights the official endorsement groups were given in absorbing enterprises in the small-scale state sector and loss-makers in general, a role they have assumed from early on in reforms. This policy clearly states that ' by reforming a set of large enterprises as the core of the business groups it will be possible to lead more efficiently the economic activities of a large number of medium and small sized enterprises'. In the 1994–7 period alone it is reported, for example, that profitable large groups saved about 2000 loss-making enterprises (*China Business Review*, May–June 1999). The history of enterprise groups, as already noted, is closely associated with that of merger and take-over, a process which in China has usually involved loss-making enterprises. The groups, therefore, have explicitly been given a dual role, one with inherent contradictions. They have been earmarked to lead the large-scale sector into international markets but also to absorb large numbers of poorly performing small enterprises. This dual function of enterprise groups continues to make them an appealing and natural policy for the reform of state industry though it also brings into question whether they will be able to succeed in achieving international levels of competitiveness.

The State Council envisaged several criteria the groups would need to fulfil in order to achieve the foreseen goals. Firstly, a 'strong core member' was needed, hence usually the agglomeration of the groups around successful large state-owned enterprises. Secondly, a 'multi-layered structure' was a prerequisite for a large group company with the ability to lead smaller enterprises, increase scale and become trans-regional. Thirdly, an 'integrated management system' was needed, based around 'capital ties' between enterprises. Furthermore, the selection of groups was to 'correspond to national economic development strategies and industrial policies'. Trans-regional and departmental groups were also encouraged as was their separation from governmental responsibilities. A key feature of this policy were efforts to force the often disparate members of the enterprise groups together into a cohesive organic whole by advocating the unification of the group led by the mother company. To this end the policy of 'six unifications' within the close layer of enterprises of the group was promoted. This foresaw unifying the planning departments of the core members and developing greater contractual relations within core enterprises. Unification of loans needed for large infrastructure and technology projects, of imports and exports, integration of the main management teams (giving responsibility of hiring and firing to the mother company) were other elements of the 'six unifications' policy. Eventual unification in the ownership of core members, to be supervised by the State Capital Management Bureau, was also put forward and this led to the creation of a policy which empowered groups with rights to manage state capital. The 1991 directive also gave details of the single track which were expanded and clarified. To an extent this measure also contributed to unification within the groups. Preferential planning only included 'the core enterprise and the close layer of members but not semi-close and dispersed members'. This created an incentive for enterprises to enter the close layer of the groups. The development of finance companies promoting the 'internal circulation of funds', and export and import rights allowing 'independent export and import management', were also included in this directive.

The first State Council directive in 1991 outlined the reasons for forming business groups and some of the policies that were to be used. It also chose the groups to be included in the trials. It marked an important step in the development of an industrial strategy which had not yet fully crystallized. This involved adopting measures to promote the institutional transformation of large-scale industry in key industries while at the same time giving up control of the small-scale state industry.

THE SECOND STATE COUNCIL DIRECTIVE, APRIL 1997

After a gap of about five years on 29 April 1997 the second State Council directive was published and the additional batch of 63 trial groups was added to the initial 57 groups. It deemed that the initial batch had 'basically achieved the stated goals' but stressed that a 'new phase' had been entered. The new policy, although pushing forward and recognizing many of the reforms initiated in the earlier document, noted that two important changes had taken place. First, the growth pattern had 'transformed from extensive growth to concentrated growth', referring to the need to further focus development in certain key areas of the economy. Secondly, it also stressed the implications of further integration with the international economy: 'as opening to the outside continues enterprises will face more severe domestic and international competition'. Accordingly it was argued that a 'crucial stage' in reform had been entered in which 'two basic transformations', from extensive development to intensive concentrated development within key industries, and from national to international markets, were to be made. To achieve this, it concludes, 'deepening the trial work with large enterprise groups is a vital necessity'.

The five goals laid out in the later document are in many ways quite similar to those given in the 1991 document, though there are two noticeable differences. First, an important position is given to the establishment of the modern corporate system so that the groups and their members could become 'defined legal entities'. To this end it is noted that 'the direction of state enterprise reform is the establishment of the modern corporate system', based upon China's company law, newly established in 1994. Greater emphasis is also placed upon the separation of enterprise and governmental activities and the transformation of government departments, making the groups responsible for their debts as well as granting them rights to retain profits. Secondly, although the role of groups in promoting 'macroeconomic stability' and directing a large number of small enterprises is not omitted entirely as a goal in this later document, it is only briefly mentioned in passing. This signified the intention to move away from direct state intervention in the creation of 'forced marriages'. The second policy continued to attempt to concentrate greater powers within the mother company. This was so they could 'formulate strategies' for the groups and become the leading providers of capital and technology, as well as co-ordinators of foreign investment and technological exchanges within the groups. To this end the investment function of the mother company was expanded, giving it greater freedom in co-ordinating new investment projects as well as utilizing foreign capital for new projects below $30 million dollars. Domestic and international stock market listings were also to be encouraged among the mother companies, as well as corporate bond issues. Trade rights were also expanded to other members of the enterprise groups, creating incentives for them to join. The creation of technology and research centres within the groups to help promote their product development capabilities and hopes of being successful in the international market place were also advanced.

The second State Council directive issued in 1997 recognized China's increasing international economic integration and the need to further develop the framework within which large enterprises operated. It recognized the need to further concentrate industry in certain sectors by creating larger economic units more akin to large modern industrial corporations in developed nations. It expanded the number of enterprises and the industries and regions they covered, it recognized also that large enterprises could also be privately run, by including three TVEs. There were, therefore, a number of important changes in the focus of policy in the second directive as well as the means by which the goals could be achieved.

IMPLEMENTING THE POLICIES

Many of the policies introduced to the trial enterprise groups in the 1991 and 1997 State Council directives were strongly oriented towards the introduction and promotion of new institutions which could operate around the legal framework also being created. These allowed the groups to break away from the traditional planning system and facilitated the transformation from lone plant-based operations to multi-plant trans-regional enterprise groups. This section considers in more detail some of the measures introduced in the 1991 and 1997 directives that helped to shape the institutions now common to China's large business groups. A distinguishing feature of these was their greater reliance upon the use of the market mechanism. The promotion of the national team has relied on both institutional reforms as well as direct measures to help revitalize large-scale state enterprises.

PREFERENTIAL PLANNING STATUS

The single track preferential planning policy was the first and perhaps single most important measure introduced within the trial business groups. It enabled the emergence of the groups from within the planning system and the beginning of their evolution into units more akin to enterprises. For the first time it gave enterprises real autonomy in the most basic of decisions concerning areas such as product output volume, basic construction and investment, foreign technology use, science and education, salary and financial decisions. First introduced in 1986 at Dongfeng and two other auto producers, the system was quickly expanded to other groups, reaching 13 by 1989 (Table 3-4). By the end of 1991 all of the trial groups were using the single track system. Of all the policies directed at the trial groups this one appears to have spread very quickly and at the time was also highly influential. Symbolically this policy elevated the core enterprise to the same level as the planning authorities. Instead of receiving planning orders, the groups were able to make requests directly to the state planning department and other necessary organs, informing them directly of their plans and requirements. By 1991 the right to participate in relevant meetings with the Planning Commission and other related departments was granted. The Planning Commission's role evolved to providing macroeconomic information to the groups to help them better adjust in unpredictable market conditions. The policy also raised the status of managing directors to vice-ministerial level, though significantly their salaries were not raised in line with their new political status. The elevation of the status of the business leaders reflected the growing importance attached to the trial groups in political circles as well as the evolving and emerging ties between business and state leaders.

Although preferential planning was basically phased out as the plan's importance diminished, it had played an important role in stimulating the early development of the enterprise groups. As early as 1986 it recognized the need to clear away the restraints of the planning system and represented the first coherent measure aimed at promoting business groups by empowering enterprises with the most basic of production decisions. It was also the first step in the movement towards a more co-ordinated business group strategy.

INTERNAL FINANCE COMPANIES

In July 1987 the first internal finance company was established, again at Dongfeng. This corresponded to a time when relations between close members of the groups, concerning both production and management, were growing ever closer. Exchanges of products and services had increased quickly. At Dongfeng, for example, by 1987 a third of the groups total sales were made between member enterprises (Chen, 1998). This in turn helped break down not only the regional and departmental ownership structures between close members of the group, it also led to the question of how better internal channels for distributing funds could be developed. A logical step was to establish an organ that could productively harness funds, moving them from enterprises making excess profits to those short of capital. The policy caught on and by 1994 there were 33 such finance companies (Table 3-4). Recent empirical work, among the few studies in Western academia on Chinese business groups, has found strong evidence to show that finance companies have improved the financial and productivity performance among some of China's largest business groups (Keister, 1998). The example of the finance company, therefore, stands out as an innovative measure which, via the development of internal markets for credit, helped stimulate the development of the groups.

The finance companies were restricted to activity within their groups. They tended also to be established using group personnel. As a result this gave the finance companies unique insights into their groups capabilities and longer-term development strategies but sometimes financial expertise was lacking. The problem with the traditional banking system was that it was not capable of undertaking loans of sufficient size nor could it allocate them across the various provincial and departmental boundaries that the business groups often spanned. Finance companies therefore provided indispensable services. Among these were the provision of timely short-term credits to tide over member enterprises in emergency situations and innovative measures, such as the introduction of hire-purchase schemes. The banking system did not offer the kind of flexibility, dedication or innovation needed to promote the interests of the trial groups. Among the problems with the finance companies, however, has been their uneven distribution and lack of standardization. By July 1995 the Bank of China had approved the creation of a total of 53 finance companies, of which 35 belonged to the trial business groups. The 53 finance companies had total assets of 6.6 billion yuan which at this time was equivalent to about one per cent of the entire financial sector's assets (Chen, 1998: 21). By 1997 this had increased to 1.6 per cent, and a further 16 finance companies had been created, increasing the number to 69. However, within the trial groups some finance companies remained very small with less than 100 million yuan in assets while others exceeded 7–8 times this amount. The size disparities of the finance companies was in practice greatly dependent upon the actual size of the group. Another problem with the finance companies in some cases has been that the groups have been unaware of the potential roles such finance companies could play. As a result they have not had a great impact on the groups. Nonetheless, the development of internal finance companies has been an innovative and beneficial measure overall, with very strong evidence to suggest that they have improved the financial and productivity performance of the groups.

EMPOWERING BUSINESS GROUPS WITH THE RIGHTS
TO MANAGE STATE CAPITAL

This policy was introduced more slowly, but by 1997 renewed commitment was shown in efforts to reform the rights to manage state property, a key element in clarifying the ownership relations between the large numbers of group members. Again, Dongfeng was the first group to introduce this policy under the guidance of the newly established State Capital Management Office in 1990. Later in 1990, a small trial among three groups was run, including Dongfeng, Heavy Vehicle Group and Dongfang Group. By 1992 official policy expanded the number undergoing the trial to seven groups. From February 1993 onwards more of the trial groups were given these rights. Provincial and city level governments also started to introduce the policy, quickly widening its impact.

In the five years from 1982 to 1987 Dongfeng had grown from a group of just eight enterprises spanning eight provinces to 118 enterprises spanning 21 provinces. However, as a leading group representative commented, 'this amounted in reality to the linking of industrial departments', not enterprises (Chen, 1992: 64). It became very difficult for Dongfeng to control group members, which, though nominally linked to Dongfeng, were still in large part under local government control. In extreme cases, for example, local authorities simply repossessed enterprises that Dongfeng had turned back into profit. Closely related to this problem was the policy of the 'three no changes' (*san bu bian*) which during the 1980s stated that departmental relations, financial relations and ownership rights within enterprises should not change. Under these conditions the expansion of groups became seriously threatened. To combat this in September 1992 the State Capital Management Office published 'On how to implement the empowerment of trial business groups with state capital management rights' clarifying issues related to the new policy. This specified that it gave '*the rights to run the close members of the group to the core enterprise ... Establishing between the core enterprise and its close members ownership ties, concentrating the group's power, making the close members of the group become the core's wholly invested son companies or stock controlled companies and giving play to the overall advantages of the group*' (SCMB, ZGZN, 1993: 334, emphasis added). This measure, therefore, was designed to give the mother company ownership and hence management control over the close members of the group. The mother company came to supersede the previous regional and provincial controllers in place under the policy of 'three no changes'. By passing the rights to manage the close members of the group on to the 'core' of the group the policy of 'six unifications' put forward in 1991, attempting to promote 'cohesion', was logically extended. It delineated the responsibility for the management of state capital, placing a firm responsibility with the group's core. This policy therefore stood out as another strong endorsement of the positive function of the enterprise group.

TECHNOLOGY CENTRES

Introduced in the 1997 directive, this has involved the annexation of existing scientific research institutions to the business groups as well as the creation of new centres. By 1997 within the 120 business groups 71 state level research institutes had been created or annexed. Measures had also been taken to force all large and medium enterprises to create their own research institutions or face disciplinary measures, such as losing bank loans and also preferential access to material supplies (*CDBW*, 3 April 1999). The central government has been busy in promoting ties between research institutions and state enterprises, keenly aware that if Chinese enterprises are to be successful, especially in the longer term, they must develop research capabilities. By the end of 1998 there were 203 state-level and 500 provincial and city-level R & D centres and 120 000 reported co-operative efforts between universities, research institutions and state enterprises. Of the 203 state-level institutes 100 were affiliated to the national team players and 512 preferred enterprises (*CDBW*, 3 April 1999). This reflected the wish of the State Council to push the groups from technology-acquiring late-industrializing enterprises to modern corporations capable of innovating themselves. Under the centrally planned system research was carried out in institutes well removed from the activities of the plant, and much of the scientific progress was based upon imports from the Soviet Union. It is unsurprising, therefore, that many enterprises still lack adequate research capabilities. Even in 1997 about 80 per cent of all research was undertaken by the state research bodies and 20 per cent by enterprises. In the US enterprises were responsible for half national R & D expenditure and in Japan and Germany over 60 per cent (Li, 1999: 141). It is estimated that the top 500 global companies investment in R & D is about 5 to 10 per cent of their total sales whereas in China LMEs have invested no more than 1.5 per cent of sales in technical innovation since 1990 (*CDBW*, 17 January 2000). Given the great disparities in the average sales of China's largest enterprises and her global competitors, already noted to be less than 2 per cent of the global *Fortune* 500 enterprises for China's top 500 enterprises, it is evident that annual research expenditures of global corporations vastly exceed those of China's largest groups.

By the eve of the reforms not only was China still quite technologically backward, there were also relatively few resources contributed to research and development within enterprises. The incorporation of research institutions into the trial groups represents another strategic step in pushing forward the development of modern corporations in China and reflects the long-term vision and hope of creating internationally competitive groups. It also highlights most clearly the huge gap between China's large modern corporations and those of advanced capitalist nations.

DIRECT SUPPORT MEASURES

The State Council directives issued in 1991 and 1997 were aimed for the most part at the institutional transformation of the groups in the hope of creating enterprises capable of functioning in a market economy. In many respects they conformed to a project of institution building supported by the basic principles of orthodox economic theory. The introduction of finance companies to reallocate capital, for example, and clarification of ownership rights via the introduction of new rights to manage state capital, should be seen as progressive market-oriented measures. The two State Council directives issued at this time, however, made little or no reference to the other direct measures that have also been used to promote the continued growth in scale of the trial groups. This in reality appears to have involved a balance between bolstering groups in the awareness that with 'one mouthful you can't put on weight' but also being aware of the dangers of 'pulling the saplings upward in the hope they will grow'. As noted earlier, a key aim of the groups has become that of reaching internationally competitive levels. It is believed that this can only be achieved if compressed growth of scale, as well as a telescoped institutional transformation, is realized. Stock market listings and financial support from the banking sector, as well as various other measures, such as special loans for technology acquisition, have been heavily biased towards large enterprises and groups. Such measures now stand out as being of most significance in the further promotion of their scale.

STOCK MARKET LISTINGS

The stock market has been used in an unconventional way to foster the development of trial business groups and the large-scale sector of the state economy as a
whole. Stock markets are usually associated with private ownership. In China,
however, firms have been listed while the state has remained the major shareholder in them, diversifying the ownership structure but not taking the crucial
step towards full privatization. By the end of 1998 only about a third of all shares
of listed companies could be traded. This has left the umbilical cord between the
state and enterprise uncut, a practice widely criticized (World Bank, 1997). The
stock market has basically been used as an important tool for industrial policy. Of
the three vital functions stock markets serve in other economies, the raising of
capital, its allocation to the most profitable projects and subsequent monitoring,
only the first, raising capital, has been fully exploited. It has provided the state
with what, at present, seems an inexpensive method of raising greatly needed
capital funds. This in turn 'consolidates the leading role of the state sector', in
particular large state groups, a goal set by Jiang Zemin at the 15th Party
Conference in 1997. Remarkably 78 per cent of listed companies are reported to
be among the largest top ten companies in their respective industry sectors (Liu,
Song and Romilly, 1998: 129). Given that many of the national team members
are also industry leaders it is unsurprising to find many of them are listed. By
1998, 36 per cent of the 512 supported LMEs were listed and 42 per cent of the
120 trial business groups had one of their core enterprises listed. Of the 100 enterprises and groups experimenting with the modern corporate system 48 per cent
were listed (CASS, ZGFB, 1998: 4).[30]

Although the stock market has not yet played an important role in resource
allocation, the trend has actually increased dramatically in recent years. From
September 1993 to May 1995 there were a total of 24 mergers or take-overs
reported on Chinese stock markets. By 1997, however, there was a wave of activity, with in total 202 such mergers or take-overs, which was remarkable as it
involved about one third of China's listed companies (CRES, GQGG, 1998: 26).
In 2000 the takeover of Shandong Huaneng Power by Huaneng Power
International marked the biggest ever merger between two listed Chinese companies. The stock market is becoming a more important means of economic
restructuring although one of its main function so far has been its role in boosting the scale of preferred state enterprises and groups.

SUPPORT FROM THE BANKING SECTOR

The provision of credit by the banking system has historically been of greater
importance than the stock market. It is also heavily biased towards the state sector. The four large state banks, Industrial and Commercial Bank of China
(ICBC), Agricultural Bank of China, Bank of China and the China Construction
Bank (CCB) all take an active part in supporting the development of enterprise

groups and the 512 preferred large state enterprises. This has been referred to at the province level as the 'bank sponsoring system' and one slogan it has adopted is the 'bank and enterprise walk hand in hand'. The ICBC has taken a lead role in this process in which 'banks concentrate limited funds on key state businesses, which can help the country to implement its industrial policies' (*CDBW*, 11 May 1997). Because much of the working capital of state firms comes from bank loans, 80 per cent in 1997, and banks already have large outstanding loans, they have strong incentives to improve the performance of enterprises (*CDBW*, 24 February 97). According to the ICBC vice-president, 'supporting large state enterprises is not only our duty but also a key strategy for our expansion'. In 1997, for example, it acted as the sponsor for 90 per cent of the 512 preferred LMEs, an increase from 272 in 1996. In 1998 it planned to loan 80 per cent of a $4.8 billion loan allocation to trial groups such as Yizheng, Changhong, and First Auto Works, all members of the national team (*CDBW*, 13–19 July 1997). The banking sector has also been encouraged to play a key role in industry rationalization by promoting mergers and bankruptcies, important in the formation of groups, which also as a result have brought it closer ties to the business groups.

The China Construction Bank, one of the first to initiate a bank sponsoring policy in 1995, claims that 'by focusing on large conglomerates and giving up small firms with poor performances, our banks achieved good returns' (*CDBW*, 13 July 1997). It has developed a simplified loan procedure for these groups and claims about 95 per cent of loans are collected on time and problem loans account for less than 1 per cent of the total. The CCB has 500 professional branches based in the large enterprises giving advice as well as providing easier access to capital markets for the groups. At the end of 1997 the bank chose from among the enterprises encouraged by the State Council or else companies already listed which, as already noted, tend to be large-scale state-owned enterprises. The bank's stated policy of supporting 287 'prime clients' is deliberately intended to 'fuel the fostering of international industrial giants', making it one of leading supporters of the national team (*CDBW*, 20 October 1997). The Bank of China has also been active in making loans to large-scale industry. In 1997, for example, it undertook an agreement to supply Konka, a leading electronics firm, with one of the largest ever loans to a manufacturing company (totalling half a billion dollars). The Export-Import Bank of China has also given export credit guarantees to large firms in sectors such as electronics, shipbuilding and high-tech machinery sectors. It financed $4.27 billion worth of electronics and machinery exports to 50 countries in 1996 (*CDBW*, 3 February 1997).

Support from the banking system and capital injections raised via share issues, though not elaborated in detail in the policy documents related to the national team, have nonetheless become a very important means of support and development. The banking sector, because of the large volume of loans provided to preferred groups and LMEs, has become closely involved with the interests of large-scale industry. This has also seen its role expand from not only lender of funds but also mediator in merger and acquisition activity. The stock market, as with the banking system, is also oriented towards preferred large-scale industry. These measures have been implemented with the particular aim of increasing the investment funds of large groups so as to upgrade technology and expand scale and scope. While China's policies to build national champions have appreciated the need for institutional reform, they have also placed an emphasis on increasing the average scale of operations.

CONCLUSION

A vital element of the Chinese policy of 'grasping the large and letting go of the small' has been the development of a small number of large enterprise groups. From among some 20 000 groups that have developed nation-wide only 120 of the largest in key industries have been chosen by the State Council to pioneer important enterprise reforms. By the end of 1996 these 120 groups were reported to account for 50 per cent of profits and 25 per cent of tax and total assets of state-owned industrial enterprises in the independent accounting sector (SCDRC, ZJN, 1997: 677). The national team members, for the most part based around the large state-owned plants of the former planned economy, have incorporated thousands of other enterprises over the reform years. They account for an ever growing share of the state sector's total sales and assets. Following the example of the State Council many more provincial level teams of large enterprise groups have also been established by local governments.

The origins of business group development in fact date from the beginning of reforms in the early 1980s as enterprises expanded scale and market coverage in the face of growing market pressures. Many groups formed naturally as a result of liberalization. However, as early as 1986 policy makers and economists came to realize the far greater long-term strategic potential and significance of a small set of large groups clustered in pillar industries. The first measures aimed at shaping the institutions of the group company were introduced to a small number of elite pioneering groups at this time. By the end of 1991 the State Council had officially chosen a much larger batch of groups to undergo further reform and these trials were expanded in 1997. Although the rationale behind the promotion of the national team has evolved over the years, a number of important reasons has underpinned its expansion and that of large business groups in general. These include the expansion of scale and scope in pillar industries whilst at the same time maintaining economic and social stability via the incorporation of other, often loss-making enterprises. Industrial sectors with a high income elasticity of demand, large export market potential, backward and forward linkages, and important in promoting technological change have also been specifically selected. Methods such as single-track preferential planning, development of internal finance companies and empowerment with the management rights of the close members of the groups, have all helped in their gradual institutional evolution. These policies have encouraged their latent potential via the removal of traditional constraints and the promotion of the use of the market mechanism and market-like institutions. The single-track, for example, empowered the emerging groups for the first time to behave as autonomous decision-making enterprises, allowing them to make basic decisions concerning such things as investment plans and production levels. The development of finance companies allowed the groups to grow organically by developing internal financial markets that not only could act as a substitute for an underdeveloped financial sector but which also led to the more efficient allocation of funds within the group. The handing over of management rights to the mother company also marked an important step in clearly delineating the property and management rights within the group. It might be expected that stock market listings, by encouraging a diversification of ownership and ushering in new ways of overseeing enterprises, would have promoted institutional change. However, in China public offerings have been used as an important tool in boosting the scale of the trial enterprise groups by providing large amounts of capital on an unconditional basis. This has provided a disproportionately smaller impetus to internal change than that which might have been expected. The banking sector has also become heavily involved in the promotion of large enterprise groups. A wide range of support measures have been used, some directing financial support, others promoting institutional change. There is an awareness of the danger of 'pulling saplings upward in the hope they will grow', yet it is also realized that the time horizon within which groups may be nurtured is, by comparison to the many decades in which global leaders have emerged, very short.

Much work on China's recent industrialization considers that it is small-scale private enterprise which has been the 'foundation for China's recent growth'. However, new evidence suggests large enterprises and groups have actually performed far better than previously realized, even outperforming other sectors of the economy, such as the small-scale sector. In some ways, particularly as they are found in important pillar industries, it is more accurate to describe the large-scale sector as the foundation of China's recent growth. The ongoing efforts to create a national team of large enterprise groups are remarkably similar in spirit to the efforts of Japan and South Korea. The current and past performance of these nations also illustrates the close link between large enterprise groups and economic growth. China's bold efforts to catch up, of 'grasping the large and letting go of the small', are becoming ever more closely linked to the performance of a small number of large-scale enterprise groups. As these continue to grow and international integration becomes ever closer, it seems probable, for better or worse, that the national team members and large-scale industry in general will become ever more prominent. The following chapters now go on to look at some of these key groups in greater detail.

APPENDICES

APPENDIX 1   LIST AND DESCRIPTION OF THE TRIAL BUSINESS GROUPS

Notes. The names and descriptions of individual members of the national team of enterprise groups are given in Table 3-5. The first column gives the name of the group. The second and third columns, except where otherwise stated, record the sales and assets positions and their value in millions of dollars (using an exchange rate of 8.3 yuan) of the largest known enterprise in the group. This is taken from the *Chinese Large and Medium-Sized Enterprises Yearbook, 1997* (SSB, ZDQN). This is not the same as the value for the entire group, which consists of many legally independent enterprises and is therefore larger. The fourth column shows whether the group was selected in the first batch of trial groups in December 1991 or the second in April 1997. The fifth column lists the approximate total number of enterprises within the enterprise group as well as the number of 'close' member enterprises, listed beneath the former. The sixth column states whether the group has a listed enterprise among its member enterprises. Often the listed enterprise is the mother or one of the core enterprises of the group. The final column provides a brief description of the enterprise group. Columns five and six are based on information supplied in post-1994 *China Economic Reform Yearbooks* ('pillar enterprise' sections) and the *Almanac of China's Economy* (1996, 1997 and 1998) and the official web sites of the trial groups.

SOURCES: CRES, ZJTGN (1995–8); SSB, ZDQN (1997); www.setc.gov.cn.

TABLE 3-5 Description of China's National Team Players

	Sales Sector	Assets	1st or 2nd	Group Memb.	Listed Arm	Brief Description of the Group
Automobile Manufacturing						
First Automobile Works Group *Zhongguo diyi qiche jituan*	2nd $2615	1st $3386	1st	273 21	Yes	FAW produces a range of vehicles, including modern passenger cars in joint venture with VW. The group has 13 core members but over 500 member enterprises in total when semi-close and dispersed members are included. Based in Changchun, Jilin province, it became a trans-regional group early in its development with members as far afield as Yunnan. FAW is one of the largest enterprise groups in China and considered a role model. It was selected as one of the first three trial groups to implement the single track in 1987. It is being primed as one of several groups to lead the restructuring of the Chinese auto industry: 'China's top 20 auto makers will reshuffle into three or four enterprise groups by the turn of the century to meet overseas competition. The US Big Three – GM, Ford and Chrysler – evolved from as many as 140 auto plants in 1900…116 car makers are registered with the Ministry of Machine Building Industry. The urgency to develop competitive groups is mounting as China begins new negotiations to enter the WTO … The Chinese Government plans to adopt policies to accelerate the process … With three or four auto giants as its backbone by 2000, the country's motor industry has a future. Otherwise, it would be hopeless.' (*CDBW*, 1997: 2). The entire group's sales value approached $4 billion in 1997 with a workforce of 170000 (MMB, ZQGN, 1998: 110). As with other Chinese auto groups, it remains far behind international rivals in nearly every aspect. Even with three or four groups as its backbone the Chinese auto industry faces great challenges.

TABLE 3-5 *(Continued)*

	Sales Sector	Assets	1st or 2nd	Group Memb.	Listed Arm	Brief Description of the Group
Dongfeng Group (Aeoleus) *Dongfeng qiche gongsi*	3rd $1 206	2nd $2 616	1st	550 21	Yes	Dongfeng, like FAW, is a pioneering business group. It was particularly influential in working with central government policy makers to initiate the first experimental trials with business groups, such as the single track and finance companies. It produces a similar range of vehicles to FAW and is similar also in size. Both traditionally have relied on sales of medium-duty trucks though in the past few years both have turned to passenger car production which has the greatest long-term growth potential. Dongfeng produces passenger vehicles in a joint venture with Citroen. The assembly line in Wuhan is one of only seven super-large plants in the Chinese auto industry. These plants are shared among the national team members. An auto industrial policy to support this pillar industry was introduced in 1994. There is still a high degree of fragmentation in the industry though and indigenous groups are heavily dependent upon their foreign partners.
Heavy Vehicle Group (HVG) *Zhongguo zhongxing qiche jituan gongsi*	32nd $181	9th $703	1st	50+ 19	...	HVG specializes in heavy-duty trucks and special vehicles. It has 19 core members and 34 stock-controlled enterprises. The core members are spread across China. It has a total workforce of 84 000 but a relatively low group output value of $650 million (MMB, ZQGN: 110). Attempts to force the core members into a more closely knit group failed in the mid-1990s, highlighting the difficulty of uniting core members into cohesive groups when group members have divergent aspirations.

Company							Description
Shanghai Auto Industrial Corporation *Shanghai qiche jituan*	1st $2 928	3rd $1 386	2nd	38 ...		Yes	SAIC is the most successful auto manufacturer in China. It is closely knit, with most of its members based in or around Shanghai. It also relies heavily on foreign partners, with over 40 joint ventures. It employs a relatively small workforce of just 60 000 though it has a sales output value of over $2 billion and over half of the passenger car market in China. SAIC was added to the second batch of business groups in 1997. It has one of most advanced assembly and engine plants in China, producing Buicks and people carriers in partnership with GM.
Tianjin Auto Industrial Corporation *Tianjin qiche gongye jituan*	5th $607	18th $411	2nd	60 ...		Yes	Like Shanghai, the Tianjin based group has a large number of joint ventures (23 in total) in close proximity to its main assembly providing it with a strong component supply base. It also has a relatively small labour force of about 60 000. Its main foreign partner is Daihatsu, now part of Toyota. Like SAIC, both groups have strong provincial relations and were added to the second batch of trial groups only in 1997. This increased the number of large vehicle assembly groups within the national team from three to six, fostering greater competition.
China Auto Industrial Corporation (CAIC) *Zhongqi jituan*	6th $567	7th $859	2nd	...	14	Yes	This group is based around Yuejin which has a large joint venture with Iveco of Italy. It has 14 core members with a workforce of 40 000. The group output value was $700 million in 1997 (MMB, QZGN: 110).
Jialing Motorbikes *Zhongguo jialing gongye (jituan) gufen youxian gongsi*	... ...	... ...	1st	...	...	...	Jialing Group is based upon former military operations. It was included in the first batch of trial groups and has become a leading motorbike producer.

TABLE 3-5 (Continued)

	Sales Sector	Assets	1st or 2nd	Group Memb.	Listed Arm	Brief Description of the Group
Special Purpose Equipment						
First Tractor and Construction Machinery Group	1st	1st	1st	…	…	The four groups in this sector are ranked 1st, 3rd, 5th and 10th in terms of total assets within their sector and have similar sales positions. They were all included in the first batch of trial groups. The First Tractor works is China's largest agricultural machinery production facility and was established in 1955. Its product range has expanded from a single type of agricultural machinery to eight different product ranges, including high-pressure equipment, bicycles, diesel engines and tractors. It had four foreign invested companies in 1995.
Zhongguo diyi tuolaji gongcheng jixie gongsi	$515	$537		…		
First Heavy Machinery Group	8th	3rd	1st	…	…	Harbin-based group.
Zhongguo diyi zhongxing jixie jituan gongsi	$108	309		…		
Second Heavy Machinery Group	9th	5th	1st	…	…	Sichuan-based group.
Zhongguo dier zhongxing jixie jituan gongsi	$97	$255		…		
China Textile Machinery Group Company (CTMC)	89th	10th	2nd	20+	…	CTMC, officially established as an enterprise group in 1988, is also included as one of China's 512 preferred key enterprises. There are over 20 state-owned LMEs within the group which employs over 50 000 people. It has production facilities covering 11 provinces and makes machinery for spinning and weaving and chemical fibre manufacture as well as dying and printing equipment. Currently the group is attempting to split into three specialist production units to prepare for greater domestic competition with WTO entry.
Zhongguo fangzhi jixie jituan	$27	$172		…		

Ordinary Machinery

| Xuzhou Construction Machinery Group *Xuzhou gongcheng jixie jituan* | 4th $242 | 1st $455 | 2nd | 25 + 3 | Yes |
| Luoyang Bearing Group *Luoyang jituan* | 20th $96 | 12th $262 | 2nd | 16 + ... | ... |

Among Jiangsu's 10 largest enterprise groups it employs over 20 000 people and has assets of over $400 million. It is involved in 18 equity joint ventures with leading multinationals such as Rockwell and Caterpillar (*China Business Review*, May–June 1999). As with many of the other trial groups it is also among the 100 trial enterprises experimenting with the modern corporate system. It is reported to have undergone a three stage development. From 1989 to 1993 three core enterprises were merged as a single legal entity with eight independent subsidiaries. From 1993 to 1995 the municipal government empowered the group with greater autonomy which led to a third stage from 1995 in which steps to introduce the modern enterprise system were undertaken. This involved clearer lineation of property rights and the use of the newly created company law.

Luoyang Bearing Group is a large-scale bearing manufacturer based around the Luoyang Bearing Factory founded in 1954. The group has fixed assets of 605 million yuan and annual sales of over 1.3 billion yuan. It has 16 fully-owned subsidiaries and over 25 000 employees including 4 300 technicians. It has imported over 4 000 sets of advanced equipment and has an annual output of 60 million bearings covering nine different product groups. Following national policies it has established a technology and product development centre which claims to be able to develop various bearing products to meet the diverse requirements of its clients. It has established its own import and export corporation and markets products to over 70 countries.

TABLE 3-5 (*Continued*)

	Sales Sector	Assets	1st or 2nd	Group Memb.	Listed Arm	Brief Description of the Group
Fabricated Metal Goods						
Monkey King *Houwang jituan*	8th $71	2nd $163	2nd	…	…	Monkey King has quickly expanded by taking over other enterprises and incorporating them within its group. It claims this is more efficient than developing its own subsidiaries. In the early 1990s it took over 26 loss making enterprises which it claims to have reinvigorated by introducing market-oriented behaviour.
Electronics						
China Zhenhua Electronics Group *Zhongguo zhenhua dianzi jituan gongsi*	…	…	1st	… …	…	By 1999 China's top 10 electronics producers accounted for 33 per cent of the sector's sales (*CDBW*, 3 April 1999). Five of these top 10 were national team members. China's electronics industry was ranked seventh in the world in 1998 and it is predicted it will enter the world's top five in 2000, becoming the largest industrial sector in China, accounting for 8 per cent of China's gross value of industrial output. Electronics have become increasingly important to China's trade balance, reflecting a shift towards higher-value-added products as it attempts to move away from a comparative advantage in labour intensive products. Its status as key industrial sector is reflected by the addition of seven groups in 1997 to the original three national team members. Zhenhua was included as one of the three groups in the first batch.
Great Wall Group *Zhongguo changcheng jisuanji jituan gongsi*	57th $67	57th $94	1st	… …	…	Great Wall was the leading PC producer in 1990 but has been outshone since. By the end of 1998 it had become the sixth largest producer. Like the other electronics groups, it has developed extensive foreign partnerships. It has three joint ventures with IBM and a video conferencing venture with Intel.

Company						Notes
Changjiang Computer Group *Changjiang jisuanji (jituan) lianhe gongsi*	...	...	1st	...	...	Changjiang, another PC maker, like Great Wall, has been eclipsed by the success of Legend.
Legend *Lianxiang jituan*	33rd $168	58th $94	2nd	...	Yes	Legend has been one of China's most dynamic companies. It was founded in 1984 with a $24 000 loan. By 1999 it was the largest electronics goods producer in China and fifth in Asia. Its main product is personal computers but it has diversified rapidly into system integration, motherboard manufacturing as well as investments in other industries. It has strengthened research and development by merging with the Computing Institute of the Chinese Academy of Sciences as well as taking a 30 per cent share in Kingsun, a software company. It hopes to develop not only hardware but the software to run on its machines. The Ministry of Electronics has encouraged consolidation within the sector, advising that 'domestic companies should not rely solely on expanding investment and their self-development, but should turn the canoes into bamboo rafts and warships' (*CDBW*, 8 April 1998). It has close ties with Bank of China, receiving a total of about half a billion dollars in 65 separate loans in the period from 1990 to 1997. In early 1998 the largest-ever financing package to a Chinese IT company was made by the bank, totalling $120 million. It plans to raise another half billion dollars by 2000 through banks and the stock market (*CDBW*, 28 May 1998).
Caihong Group *Caihong jituan*	6th $477	7th $500	2nd	22 3	...	Caihong's main products are colour television tubes and television parts. It has also diversified into systems control, computers, communications equipment, chemicals and property. Based in Shaanxi the group was China's first television tube

TABLE 3-5 (Continued)

	Sales Sector	Assets	1st or 2nd	Group Memb.	Listed Arm	Brief Description of the Group
						manufacturer, beginning production in the early 1980s using imported Japanese plant. It has a 30 per cent share of the domestic market and exports about a third of its total output (*CDBW*, 10 December 1998). It is not only a trial business group but has also been chosen as one of the 512 focal LMEs by the SETC. In 1997 it had assets of 7.6 billion yuan (net assets of 3.2 billion) and was the 76th largest industrial enterprise in China.
Founder Group *Beida fangzheng jituan*	...	...	2nd	...	Yes	As well as being a member of the national team in 1998 Founder was also one of six companies chosen by the central government to be groomed for entry to the *Fortune* 500, granting it special funds for technology acquisition. The group initially produced Chinese-language software but diversified into PCs in late 1995 where it has rapidly built up a strong position. By the end of 1998 it was the 8th largest electronics group in China.
Panda Group *Xiongmao dianzi jituan*	7th $470	5th	2nd	...	...	Panda is one of China's largest TV producers. It also produces other types of electrical and electronic products, such as DVDs, water heaters and products for farm use. It is based upon the Changsha Electrical Equipment Manufacturing Plant, production dating back to 1936. It claims to have one of the strongest R & D capabilities in Chinese industry, with five state level technical centres employing over 3 500. It also has nine joint ventures (JVs).

							Description
Changhong Group *Changhong jituan*	2nd $1282	1st $1442	2nd	...	...		Changhong dropped to 2nd spot in terms of sales by the end of 1998, though remained the most profitable electronics company ($260 million). It had been number one for the previous three years. It took over two television producers in 1997 in Jiangsu and Jilin provinces and a controlling stake in a battery plant in Sichuan. Like Founder Group, it has been selected as one of six groups which will be given additional support in attempts to enter *Fortune*'s listings.
China Hualu Group *Zhongguo hualu jituan*	48th $87	22nd $219	2nd	...	...		...
Shanghai General Electronics Group (SGEG) *Shanghai guangdian jituan*	10th $274	4th	2nd	70+	...		Shanghai General Electronics Group was the third largest electronics group in China in 1998 (*CDBW*, 3 April 1999). It had registered capital of over 2 billion yuan. Total profits in 1998 were 700 million yuan, with exports valued at $660 million. SGEG has in total 32 fully-funded enterprises, 40 JV enterprises and four overseas enterprises.
Power Generation							Power generation and generation equipment form the backbone, along with aerospace, steel and autos, of the first batch of 57 trial business groups. Regional power generation groups were established in efforts to eventually bring together an integrated national grid. The groups are under the jurisdiction of the State Power Corporation of China, formed in 1997 as a state holding company. Huaneng Power was set up in 1985 to finance power station construction and operation. It is part of Huaneng Group which has 12 main subsidiaries, two of which are listed. It is reported to be the largest enterprise group among the national team in terms of total assets, which exceed 90 billion yuan (CASS, ZGFB, 1998: 122).
Huaneng Group *Zhongguo huaneng jituan gongsi*	8th $1 296	3rd $6 434	1st	524	...	Yes ...	

TABLE 3-5 (Continued)

	Sales Sector	Assets	1st or 2nd	Group Memb.	Listed Arm	Brief Description of the Group
North China Power Group Zhongguo huabei dianli jituan gongsi	4th $2 296	2nd $6 605	1st	132 ...	Yes	North China Power Group consists of various regional owners and operators of power plants, including Beijing Datang Power and Shanxi, Hebei and Inner Mongolia Power Companies. It is China's second largest enterprise group in terms of assets (over 100 billion yuan) reaching a population of about 140 million. It has 132 members. Its operations also involve design, construction and repair of power plants.
China Eastern Power Group Zhongguo dongbei dianli jituan gongsi	27th $307	29th $798	1st	... ...	...	Based on Shanghai, Jiangsu, Anhui and Zhejiang Electric Power Companies. All of these regional producers, as well as the others included in the other three regional groups are ranked in the top 20 power suppliers.
Central China Electric Power Group Zhongguo huazhong dianli jituan gongsi	52nd $42	31st $797	1st	15 + 5	...	Central China Power Group is based around Hubei, Henan, Hunan and Jiangxi Electric Power Companies. It has 10 stock-controlled companies in its close layer and a finance company which services the group. In 1998 its assets were 120 billion yuan.
China North Western Electric Zhongguo xibei dianli jituan gongsi	17th $720	17th $1698	1st	... ...	...	Based on Gansu, Qinghai, Ningxia and Xinjiang Electric Power Companies.
Guangdong Nuclear Electric Group Zhongguo Guangdong hedian jituan gongsi	16th $734	6th $4 032	1st	... ...	...	...

Power Generation Equipment

Company					
Harbin Power Equipment Company	44th	14th	1st	70+	Yes
Zhongguo Haerbin dianzhan shebei jituan gongsi	$77	$232		3	
Dongfang Electric Power Group	43rd	7th	1st	...	...
Zhongguo dongfang dianqi jituan gongsi	$77	$321		...	
Shanghai Electric Power Group	...	...	1st	...	...
Shanghai dianqi (jituan) zong gongsi				...	
Xian Power Generation Machinery Manufacturing Group	6th	2nd	1st	...	...
Xian dianli jixie zhizao gongsi	$283	$515		...	

There were five power equipment manufacturers listed in the first batch of trial groups. Harbin, Dongfang and Shanghai are the largest power equipment producers in China. Harbin, the 'city of power generation equipment', is home to a group which after recent restructuring had 26 000 employees and 70 plus member enterprises. In 1987 a large trans-regional group was proposed integrating some of neighbouring Liaoning's power equipment producers. One of the Liaoning plants, however (based in Shenyang), disagreed with this project and split away to create Northeast Power Equipment Group (Dongbei Group). Harbin Group subsequently grew around firms based in or near Harbin, with three large enterprises at its core.

Along with Harbin Dongfang was the only domestic large-scale producer of hydroelectric power plant. It is also a leading supplier of other power equipment.

...

TABLE 3-5 (*Continued*)

	Sales Sector	Assets	1st or 2nd	Group Memb.	Listed Arm	Brief Description of the Group
Northeast Electric Transmission and Transformation Equipment Group *Dongbei zhuanbiandian shebei jituan gongsi*	22nd $116	9th $285	1st	...	Yes	Based on the Shenyang Transformer Plant and other plants in neighbouring Liaoning. It is the 34th largest industrial group in China.
Aviation and Aerospace						
Xian Aircraft Group *Zhongguo Xian feiji gongye jituan gongsi*	12th $508		1st	200+	Yes	All six groups were included in the first batch of trial groups. Experiments with AVIC, one large holding company controlling the whole industry as an 'ultra-large industrial group', have subsequently given rise to AVIC 1 and AVIC 2. The industry faces great problems as entry to WTO approaches. Although the Xian group was only the 12th largest transportation equipment manufacturer in China it was the largest single maker of aircraft (by assets). It has not been very successful in its diversification strategies, unlike some of the other aviation groups. From its 200 or so child companies an aluminium and bus manufacturing company have been most successful. The mother company employs 20 000.
Nanjing Aero Motive Machinery Group *Zhongguo Nanjing hangtian gongye jituan gongsi*	...	...	1st	...	...	...
Shanghai Aero Industry Group	...	...	1st	...	...	...

Company								Notes
Zhongguo Shanghai hangkong gongye jituan	⋮		⋮		⋮			⋮
Guizhou Aero Industry Group *Zhongguo Guizhou hangkong gongye jituan gongsi*	⋮		⋮		1st			⋮
Nanjing Air Industry Group *Zhongguo jiangnan hangtian gongye jituan gongsi*	⋮		⋮		1st			⋮
Sanjiang Air Industry Group *Zhongguo sanjiang hangtian gongye jituan gongsi*	⋮		⋮		1st			⋮
Textiles								All of the textile groups belong to the second batch of trial groups, reflecting the broadening of the business group strategy in the 1990s characterized by a movement away from basic upstream industries to fast-growing consumer goods industries. It is also noticeable that the textile producers are from relatively poor inland regions of China, reflecting efforts at counteracting growing regional inequalities.
Xinjiang Textiles Group *Xinjiang fanzhi gongye jituan*	13th $2.5	6th $169	2nd	⋮	⋮			⋮
Inner Mongolia Cashmere Group *Neimenggu eerduosi yangrong jituan*	9th $118	3rd $194	2nd	⋮	⋮			⋮
China Shenma Group *Zhongguo shenma jituan*	6th $145	6th $319	2nd	⋮	Yes			Based in Henan province this group is China's largest maker of cord fabric, producing approximately 55 000 tons per year. The sectoral ranking given here is for the chemical

TABLE 3-5 (Continued)

	Sales Sector	Assets	1st or 2nd	Group Memb.	Listed Arm	Brief Description of the Group
						fibre manufacturing sector. Shenma, as with a number of the other trial groups, has issued corporate bonds to raise much-needed capital.
Iron and Steel						
Panzihua Steel Group *Pangang jituan*	5th $1064	10th $1850	1st	72 …	Yes	At the beginning of 1998 there were 47 money-losing state steel producers with debts of $337 million (*CDBW*, 16 January 1998). According to the minister responsible for the steel industry creating industrial conglomerates was a 'key way to bail out the loss making companies'. As with other sectors consolidation is ongoing. The target is for the largest four groups to produce 40 per cent or more of national output by 2000. Panzihua is one of four steel groups among the first batch of 57 groups approved in 1991. All of the steel groups are large, being in the top 10 in terms of sales and assets. Panzihua has made progress in improving the cohesion within the group. By the end of 1994, 25 of the 30 close members in the group were wholly-owned subsidiaries or else stock-controlled. The group has continued to experiment with the modern corporate system and the mother/son enterprise group system.
Wuhan Steel Group *Wugang jituan*	4th $1867	3rd $4953	1st	…	Yes	Wugang is set to take part in the consolidation sweeping China's steel industry. It will be encouraged to merge with surrounding steel mills. Policy makers have also touted the idea of merging it with Baogang to form a giant steel producer.

Group								Fortune 500	
Anshan Steel Group *Angang jituan*	2nd	$2 378	2nd	$5 935	1st		…	Yes	Based in China's northern Liaoning province near Shenyang the group employs over 100 000. It has been suggested that it should merge with another Liaoning-based national team group member, Benxi.
Baoshan Steel Group *Baogang jituan*	1st	$2 850	1st	$9 080	1st	69	…	Yes	Based in Shanghai Baoshan is one of China's leading enterprises. It is one of the youngest and most profitable in the steel sector, specializing in relatively high-value products with a small workforce of 20 000. It exports 15–20 per cent of its total output. In 1997 sales topped $4 billion and after recent mergers involving Shanghai Meishan and Shanghai Metallurgical, other large Shanghai-based steel groups, it accounted for about 15 per cent of China's total steel output. The group aims to become multinational, relying mainly on steel but also integrating finance and trade operations as well. It has also taken over a major software producer believing China's IT sector to be of great potential. It has been suggested it may merge with Wugang Group some time in the near future to create China's only world-class steel producer. It is among the six enterprises being given special support for technological upgrading in a bid to push it into the *Fortune 500*.
Capital Iron and Steel Group *Shougang jituan*	3rd	$2 061	4th	$4 394	2nd	360	28	Yes	The Beijing-based iron and steel group is based around the Capital Iron and Steel Corp. The latter has been doing business for over 70 years. The group has set itself the task of establishing clearer boundaries between the parent company and its subsidiaries which have been accused of swallowing profits. The parent company has about 60 000 staff, a quarter of the group's total (*FT*, 11 March 1998). The number of group member enterprises stretches into the hundreds and over 300 of these have reached international

TABLE 3-5 (Continued)

	Sales Sector	Assets	1st or 2nd	Group Memb.	Listed Arm	Brief Description of the Group
						quality standards. It has diversified into shipping, construction, electronics, and machinery manufacturing. Shougang Group is a member of the 100 centrally supported trial enterprises attempting to introduce modern corporate systems as well as being one of 512 centrally supported LMEs selected for preferential treatment.
Benxi Group *Bengang jituan*	7th $901	6th $2 497	2nd	68 7	...	Lioaning province's Benxi Steel Group is among the top 10 in China. It has 46 member enterprises within the group and has been tipped to join forces with Anshan Group as part of the ongoing restructuring of the steel industry.
Chongqing Steel Group *Chonggang jituan*	17th $423	14th $829	2nd	72 30	...	Chongqing is a specialist iron and steel producer, one of the smaller among the national team steel groups. In 1997 it exported $160 million worth of steel. The inclusion of this group in the trials supports Chongqing's regional devolution and growth as well as broadening the geographical coverage of the trial enterprise groups.
Taiyuan Steel Group *Taigang jituan*	8th $843	8th $2 017	2nd	... ...	Yes	Based in Shanxi the Taiyuan Group is among the top 10 Chinese iron and steel producers. Included in the second batch of trial groups it obtained a stock-market listing in 1998.

Chemicals

Name								Notes
Donglian Petrochemical Group *Donglian jituan*	...	...	...	...		...	...	Based on the merger of four large enterprises, Yizheng Chemical Fibre Co., Nanjing Chemical Fibre Co., Jinling Petrochemicals and Yangzi Petrochemicals, this has become China's largest chemicals group. The former two, Yizheng and Nanjing, were members of the first batch of trial business groups. The creation of Donglian in late 1997, involving $6.5 billion of state-owned assets, was the largest restructuring of state-owned assets since 1949 and is considered of symbolic importance in the reform of large SOEs and the development of business groups. By 1998 record year-end figures were reported of $5.3 billion in sales and $0.4 billion in profits.
Yizheng Group *Zhongguo yizheng huaxian gongye lianhe gongsi*	2nd	$763	2nd	$1 631	1st	23	Yes	Yizheng was China's leading chemical fibre group with 23 members, 16 of which were considered 'close'. It was a member of the first batch of trial business groups.
Tianjin Bohai *Zhongguo tianjin bohai huagong jituan gongsi*	18th	$146	22nd	$236	1st	7	...	This group is based on one of China's 123 super-large enterprises. It has a number of large state-owned LMEs participating in the group and 100 plus close and semi-close members.
Nanjing Chemical Group *Zhongguo nanjing huaxue gongye (jituan) gongsi*	...	...	...	...	1st	...	...	...
China Jilin Chemical Industry Co *Zhongguo jilin huazue gongye gongsi*	1st	$1270	1st	$3900	1st	...	...	...
Shanghai Tianyuan Group *Shanghai tianyuan jituan*	...	...	...	...	2nd	16	...	In 1996 the Shanghai municipal government merged Shanghai Chemical Industrial Group with Shanghai Pharmaceutical Administration and some other subordinate enterprises. This

TABLE 3-5 (*Continued*)

	Sales Sector	Assets	1st or 2nd	Group Memb.	Listed Arm	Brief Description of the Group
						formed Huayi Group. The group consists of Shanghai Pharmaceutical Group, Shanghai Tyre and Rubber Group, Shanghai Pacific Chemical Group and also Shanghai Tianyuan, the group picked to enter the second batch of trial business groups. Huayi Group had sales of $2.8 billion in 1998, about 65 per cent being in the chemical sector. The group has bought out 17 enterprises and absorbed 14 000 staff in recent years. It has more than 100 joint ventures with chemical and pharmaceutical giants such as Du Pont and BASF. Total foreign investment has reached $1.4 billion (*CDBW*, 2 April 1998).
Zhejiang Juhua Group *Juhua jituan*	...	...	2nd	...	Yes	A conglomerate with businesses covering pharmaceuticals, thermal power, metallurgy, building materials, chemical fibres, textiles and machine building.
Shandong Haiyanghua Group *Shandong haiyang huagong jituan*	...	...	2nd	...	...	Also known as Haihua Group, it absorbed 17 enterprises in 1997 alone and has been active in the restructuring of the Chinese chemical industry (*China Business Review*, May–June 1999). It is also one of eight backbone groups being nurtured by Shandong's provincial government.
Mining						
Datong Mine Group *Datong mekuang jituan*	2nd $563	1st $1488	2nd	26	Yes	Shanxi's coal mining group has 15 mines, four construction companies, five affiliated factories, a research centre, four hospitals and 84 schools. Employees total 170 000. It is a leading mining group.

						Description
Yankuang Group *Yanzhou kuangye jituan*	1st $600	2nd $991	2nd	...	...	Yes	Established as a group in early 1996 by the administrative bureau responsible for running the mines in Yanzhou in Shandong. It is also one of the 100 enterprises selected to experiment with the modern corporate system as well as being among one of first 300 preferred LMEs, later expanded to 512, to receive special government support (*CDBW*, 6 September 1998). It has 80 000 staff and produced 17 million tons of coal in 1997 with profits of $107 million. It has assets of over 11 billion yuan and is the leading coal supplier in East China. It is one of China's largest coal exporters, shipping a third of its output to Japan accounting for about 15 per cent of China's total volume of coal exports (*CDBW*, 24 March 1998). The coal fields are rich in high-quality coal. It also has interests in construction, chemicals, electric power generation, machinery and light industry. The mining operations have won national prizes for technical excellence. As with the other national team members, the group also has aspirations to eventually enter the *Fortune* 500. The proceeds of its recent flotation are to be used to buy Shandong's Jining coal field as well as for investments in machinery and equipment.
Shenhua Group *Zhongguo shenhua jituan*	...	...	1st	10	...	Yes	The group is based on developing the massive Shenhua Project, China's first major energy project to co-ordinate coal mines, railways, a port and a power station in an integrated power project. It is wholly state-owned and managed by the State Planning Commission. It has a registered capital of over $300 million. It claims to be 'an industrial conglomerate based on energy and communications, being diversified in operation and featuring trans-regional, multi-industrial and transnational

TABLE 3-5 (Continued)

	Sales Sector	Assets	1st or 2nd	Group Memb.	Listed Arm	Brief Description of the Group
						development', some of the characteristics the State Council has advocated for the national team. Its 10 subsidiaries are in coal mining, trading, construction, power generation and port management, all important elements in carrying out the Shenhua Project.
China National Non-metallic Minerals Enterprise Group (CNMEG) *Zhongguo feijin shukuang gongye zong gongsi*	...	...	1st	200+ ...	Yes	CNMEG is a state agency belonging to the State Bureau of Building Materials Industry. In the past 40 years it has developed over 1 000 mines supplying non-ferrous metals, minerals and building materials. In 1995 over a third of China's non-ferrous metals were produced by enterprises under CNMEG (*CDBW*, 24 December 1996). It was established in 1983 by the then State Economic Commission and was given preferential planning status in 1987 and trade rights in 1988 as were a small number of other pioneering groups. The group has over 200 members including seven listed companies which have raised close to half a billion dollars. It also has 11 scientific research centres and universities. Presently its capital is valued at over 5 billion yuan with 45 000 workers and annual sales of over 1.5 billion yuan. It is one of three groups participating in the trials to develop national holding companies.
Regional Groups						
Shenzhen Special Economic Zone Development Group *Shenzhen jingji tequ fazhan jituan*	... $602	... $467	2nd	... ...	Yes	This group claims to be among the first enterprise groups in China, its origins dating to October 1981 when it was established by the provincial government of Guangdong. By 1995 the group had net assets of 3.88 billion yuan and

					Description
China Xinjiang Construction Group *Xinjiang jiantou jituan*	…	2nd	500+	Yes	This group claims to be the largest in China, encompassing a huge workforce of 2.4 million people. It is based on the Xinjiang Production and Construction Corps which was established in 1954 to promote the development of Xinjiang and guarantee regional security. The group has 172 giant farms, 344 industrial enterprises, 200 hospitals, 500 schools and 46 research institutes. The group plans to list 30 of its enterprises and is keen to import new machinery to improve its agricultural output and efficiency (*Economist*, 19 June 1999).
Changjiang United Economic Development Group *Changjiang jingji lianhe fazhan jituan*	…	2nd	…	…	…
Transport COSCO (China Ocean Shipping Corporation) *Zhongguo yuanyang yunshu*	1st	1st	310+	Yes	COSCO is China's largest shipping firm as well as being the second largest bulk fleet and fourth largest container fleet in the world (*Economist*, 28 November 1998). It has 80 000 staff and over 700 vessels that constitute about 74 per cent of China's total tonnage (*CDBW*, 2 July 1999). Its assets stand at about $13 billion although its debt asset ratio stands at approximately 60 per cent. By 1997 it had 360 foreign offices and carried over half of China's exports to more than 150 countries. The group had expanded its investments to include overseas

specialized in five main areas: tourism, commerce, trade, finance and property. It had a total workforce of 14 000. Sales had reached over 5 billion yuan, projected to more than double by the year 2000. It was among 18 groups sponsored by Shenzhen city, another two of which were also among the trial enterprise groups.

TABLE 3-5 (Continued)

	Sales Sector	Assets	1st or 2nd	Group Memb.	Listed Arm	Brief Description of the Group
						property, stocks, leisure and port management businesses. COSCO has attempted bold reforms. It claims to have hired the first-ever Western executive to work in its headquarters and in late 1998 severed ties with the Ministry of Communications, its state patron. It has also followed guidelines on the establishment of the modern corporate system, including an independent board of directors. Bond issues have been made and by the end of 1999 it had raised $235 million through foreign institutions. The listed arm runs a third of the fleet and holds 62 per cent of COSCO Pacific which leases containers and operates shipping terminals.
China National Foreign Trade Transportation Group (Sinotrans) *Zhongguo waiyun jituan*	...	...	2nd	... ...	...	Also known as Sinotrans, the group claims to have 52 subsidiaries, 508 independently managed enterprises and 238 joint ventures in China, as well as nine representative offices and 67 enterprises abroad. It has 67 000 staff and employees and the total assets of the whole group are 22 billion yuan. It provides air, sea and road transport services.
China Southern Airlines *Zhongguo nanfang hangkong (jituan) gongsi*	1st	...	1st	... ...	Yes	The country's largest passenger carrier carrying 15 million people in 1999 employing 99 aircraft. In recent years it has started international routing. The group is expected to lead consolidation of the airline industry. During 1999 rumours emerged of a merger with Air China. China's largest international provider. The proposed merger, discussed at a State Council meeting on 20 June 1999, is part of plans to rationalize the industry's 34 enterprises.

According to a senior manager (and Party Secretary) at China Eastern Airlines: 'taking Air China, China Eastern Airlines and China Southern Airlines as the backbone, China will voluntarily merge and restructure the other 31 airlines to form three big groups' (*ChinaOnline*, 1 April 2000). The three members of the national team, as with trial groups in other sectors, are positioned to lead consolidation. A merger of CSA and Air China would see the new entity with 38 per cent of China's fleet. Air China, unlike the other two members listed in 1997, has yet to be listed owing to its high debt and lack of corporate structure.

China Eastern carried 2.4 million international and 4.5 million domestic passengers in 1998. It is the second largest passenger airline. It has 57 aircraft and has taken part in consolidation of the airline industry by taking over China General Purpose Airline Co. in 1997. It may also make a move for China Northern (4.4 million passengers and 42 aircraft) in reaction to the likely merger of Air China and China Southern. China Eastern is considered something of a pioneer in the industry. It was the first to take over another airline as well as the first to issue share capital at home and abroad (it is listed in Hong Kong, New York and Shanghai).

Air China, based in Beijing with close ties to the central government, carried 1.7 million international passengers and 6.4 million in total in 1998. With 60 aircraft it is smaller than both China Southern and China Eastern. New bilateral services accords with the USA have forced the group into merger talks with China Southern, whose management is likely to take

China Eastern Airlines	2nd	...	1st	...	Yes
Zhongguo dongfang hangkong gongsi					
Air China	3rd	...	1st	...	...
Zhongguo guoji hangkong (jituan) gongsi					

TABLE 3-5 *Continued*

	Sales Sector	Assets	1st or 2nd	Group Memb.	Listed Arm	Brief Description of the Group
						control of the new group. 1998 has seen record losses for Chinese airlines, with Air China's losses probably exceeding the $65 million loss of China Southern Airlines. Slack demand in Asia owing to the financial crisis and heavy discounting of tickets between the major carriers have been major contributory factors.
Changjiang Shipping Group *Zhongguo changjiang lunchuan zong gongsi*	...	...	1st	22 ...	Yes	Changjiang Group is the largest passenger and freight carrier on China's huge inland waterways. In 1997 it had a turnover of over 5 billion yuan. The group has 22 son companies spread across six provinces. By the end of 1997 it had total assets of 12.5 billion yuan, including over 2 500 ships. Its strategy is to develop its shipping business steadily while at the same time developing interests in property, tourism, trade and finance.
Guangzhou Rail Group *Guangzhou tielu jituan*	...	...	2nd	20+ 4	...	China's largest railway operator and the first business group created in this sector. It is responsible for the operation of networks in Guangdong, Hunan and Hainan covering over 4 000 km of rail network. It has 166 000 employees and total assets of over 42.2 billion yuan (debts of 8.7 billion yuan). It is one of the 512 key enterprises selected by the SETC as well as being one of the 120 trial business groups. The group is based around four fully-owned transportation subsidiaries and four stock controlled companies.

Pharmaceuticals

Sanjiu Group *Sanjiu qiye jituan*	5th $170	2nd $291	2nd	...	...	Yes
Tongrentang Group *Zhongguo beijing tongrentang jituan*	2nd $191	5th $216	2nd	...	...

The Chinese pharmaceutical industry is still dispersed: of China's 3 000 plus enterprises half are state-owned and only 72 of these have assets greater than $12 million (*CDBW*, 1 January 1998) . It faces extreme pressures as entry to WTO will bring stricter intellectual property regulations. Currently many successful Western drugs are copied in China. Of China's 512 preferred key state enterprises 15 are pharmaceutical producers. There are five large trial business groups in pharmaceuticals. Sanjiu is one of the largest, it is also a diversified conglomerate, originating from southern China's Guangdong.

Tongrentang specializes in Chinese medicines which are seen as an area of potential growth in international markets. It claims to have first traded in 1669, migrating from Zhejiang to serve the imperial court of the Qing Dynasty in Beijing. Held back during central planning since reform, the group, formed officially with the approval of the Beijing Municipal Government in 1992, has transformed itself into a successful conglomerate aimed at achieving scale and facilitating co-operation among group members in production and distribution. During its development there was uncertainty about whether scale or agility were more important; scale won and this was partly because of the need to develop a strong brand name which could only be achieved if they 'clung together'. Tongrentang's experience has taught them that 'total company strength is the key factor in market competition'. Like other successful groups it has imported advanced Western equipment to boost production.

TABLE 3-5 (Continued)

	Sales Sector	Assets	1st or 2nd	Group Memb.	Listed Arm	Brief Description of the Group
Harbin Pharmaceutical Group *Haerbin yiyue jituan*	9th $113	17th $103	2nd	…	…	…
Northern Pharmaceutical Group *Zhongguo huabei zhiyue jituan gongsi*	10th $109	4th $267	1st	…	…	This pharmaceutical group is one of the six groups selected for preferential treatment with regard to increasing investment funds aimed at promoting technology acquisition in the hope of pushing it into the *Fortune* 500 listings.
China Northeastern Pharmaceutical Group *Zhongguo dongbei zhiyue jituan gongsi*	…	…	1st	…	…	…
Construction						
Shanghai Construction Group *Shanghai jiangong jituan*	…	…	2nd	… …	…	…
Beijing Construction Group *Beijing chengjian jituan*	…	…	2nd	…	…	…
China State Construction Engineering Corporation (CSCEC) *Zhong jian jituan*	…	…	2nd	… …	…	CSCEC describes itself as a large state-run multidisciplinary enterprise. It employs 1.5 million workers throughout its various provincial operations. It has taken advantage of China's construction boom, engaging in surveying, design and construction of all types of projects including chemical plants, hotels, railway stations, power stations, schools, airports and bridges to name a few areas of construction in which it is involved.

Gezhouba Water Resources and Hydropower Engineering Corp	3rd	1st	1st	14+
Zhongguo gezhouba shuili shuidaing gongcheng jituan	$213	$471	...	...
Construction Materials				
China National New Building Materials Group (CNNBMG)	...	...	1st	...
Zhongguo xinxing jianzhu cailiao (jituan) gongsi	...	...	...	...

This group is based around construction of hydro-electric facilities. It has over 14 subsidiaries employing over 50 000 manual workers and 8 000 engineers and technicians. The group was officially added as the 56th member of the national team in December 1994.

China's building materials sector is still fragmented with many small factories using outdated technology, high energy use and low productivity causing serious pollution. Authorities are attempting to 'encourage large factories ... [and] annex or purchase small plants', particularly in cement, where factories producing under 50 million tons will be closed, and also in glass. The aim is to 'speed the development of large enterprise groups' (*CDBW*, 30 May 2000). Industrial policy has identified 26 key enterprises in this sector, which incorporate the national team players. The mother company and 'kernel' of the CNNMBG is the China National New Building Materials Corporation, established in 1984 on approval of the State Council. In 1987, along with the pioneering group, Dongfeng, it was listed separately in the state plan and was one of the first pilot enterprise groups. In 1994 it entered China's top 500 enterprises. It is based upon construction materials production but has also diversified into other fields such as real estate development, tourist services and consultancy. It has eight series of products: new type wall materials, insulation materials, waterproof and sealing materials, architectural ceramics, chemical building materials and gypsum,

TABLE 3-5 (Continued)

	Sales Sector	Assets	1st or 2nd	Group Memb.	Listed Arm	Brief Description of the Group
						glass fibre, building machinery and metal products. It has 40 per cent of the Chinese paperliner gypsum board, asphalting roll and glass fibre markets. The group has aspirations to become a 'well known transnational group' by 2010.
Anhui Hailuo Group *Anhui hailuo jituan*	...	...	2nd	...	...	Hailuo Group has been given key support by the State Administration of Building Materials to annex and purchase other companies. The China Construction Bank (CCB), which has established a cement sector restructuring team, has also played an active part in restructuring the cement industry. From 1997 to 1999 approximately 24 merger projects were supported by the CCB, involving close to half a billion dollars.
China Yaohua Glass Group *Zhongguo yaohua boli jituan gongsi*	...	...	1st	32 +	Yes	The origins of Yaohua Glass Group date back to 1922. It is classified as a super-large integrated glass producer with 10 subsidiaries, eight wholly owned companies, 10 stock-controlled companies and four companies in which it holds minor stakes. Its net fixed assets are close to 6 billion yuan.
Luoyang Floating Glass Group *Luoyang fufa boli jituan gongsi*	...	...	1st	...	...	...

Trade Groups	Trade volume.					
Sinochem *Zhongguo huagong jinchukou zong gongsi*	1st	...	1st	...	$8 529	Yes	The initial batch of groups contained only two trade groups, Sinochem and China Minmetal Group. Subsequently, in 1997, another six groups were added, highlighting the growing importance of trade to the national economy. Consolidation has taken place and the eight trial groups have quickly expanded. Sinochem, among other activities, is involved in chemical import and exports. The listed arm is Sinochem International, founded in late 1998. The listing is an important step as it gives the group access to capital markets. All of Sinochem International's subsidiaries are reportedly profit making.
China National Technology Import and Export Group (CNTIC) *Zhongguo ji jituan*	3rd	...	2nd	...	$3 422	Yes	This group is focused on technology, high-tech plant equipment, machinery and electronic products. It has more than 30 overseas branches world-wide. In 1998 it merged with China Machinery and China Instruments Import and Export Corporations, as well as China National Corporation for Overseas Economic Co-operation (a provider of overseas labour). The merger involved CNTIC, itself the third largest trade group, with the 7th and 26th largest. The new super import-export corporation known as China General Technology (Group) Holding Ltd has an annual trade volume of over $7 billion. It is hoped this will combine overlapping functions and benefit from less intrusive government oversight.
China National Minerals and Metals Import and Export Corp (China Minmetals) *Zhongguo wujin kuangchan jinchukou zong gongsi*	10th	...	1st	...	$1 875	Yes	Minmetals Development, the listed arm of China Minmetals Group, became only the second and largest listed trade company in mid-1997. China Minmetals, the mother company, is based upon the old centrally planned era government trade monopoly. The listing of Minmetals Development raised $72 million which was to be used to expand its shipping fleet, although

TABLE 3-5 (Continued)

	Sales Sector	Assets	1st or 2nd	Group Memb.	Listed Arm	Brief Description of the Group
						investments in property, such as Beijing's Shangri La Hotel, have reportedly been made. Minmetals Development has total assets of $125 million and an average turnover of $5 billion which ranked it among the top five trade groups in China during the mid-1990s.
China National Textiles Import and Export Corp (Chinatex) *Zhongfang jituan*	8th $2 250	...	2nd	... ...	...	China's largest textile trading house, generating $1.54 billion from exports in 1997. One of six companies originally allowed to issue commercial bonds (including COSCO noted earlier) it has been able to exploit the US capital market. In 1998 it raised $100 million by issuing one year commercial bonds.
(COFCO) *Zhongliang jituan*	2nd $3 429	...	2nd	... ...	...	COFCO, China National Cereals, Oils and Foodstuff Import and Export Corporation is one of China's few *Fortune 500* members, ranked in 362nd position. As with Chinatex it has raised funds via bond issues on foreign capital markets. COFCO Capital Corporation raised $200 million in 1998.
China National Crafts Import and Export Corp. *Zhongyi jinchukou jituan*	16th $1 495	...	2nd	... ...	...	A large trade group with 63 affiliated companies in China and 19 overseas enterprises. It has established 170 manufacturing facilities producing various kinds of art and craft commodities, including jewellery, woven products of grass, wicker and rattan, pottery and porcelain, and toys and light industrial products.
Dongfang International Group *Dongfang guoji jituan*	6th $2 608	...	2nd			...

Light Industry

Guangdong Ceramics Group *Guangdong fotao jituan*	...	2nd	...	10	...	This Guangdong ceramics group, founded in 1956, specializes in several main ceramic product areas, including those for the construction industry, bathroom ceramics and ceramic machinery. It is the largest stock-controlled enterprise in China's ceramic industry. Today the group is based around 10 enterprises and a technology centre. It entered China's largest 500 enterprises in 1995 and is included amongst the 100 enterprises experimenting with the modern corporate system. In 1996 it was also included in the first batch of 512 focal LMEs.
Tangshan Ceramics Group *Tangshan taoci jituan*	...	2nd	...	...	...	Based on the North China Plain in Tangshan, the 'pottery city of the north', supplied by nearby high-quality clay deposits, the company's origins reportedly date back to 1403. Today it claims to be the only large-scale pottery making enterprise in China, employing over 30 000 workers and with total assets approaching 4 billion yuan and annual exports of over 50 million dollars. It is also included in the list of 512 centrally preferred LMEs, entering the first batch of 300 in 1996. It has an approved technology centre and is also implementing trials with the modern enterprise system.
Guangxi Guitang Group *Guangxi guitang jituan*	...	2nd	...	...	...	The only trial business group from inland Guangxi province, which also is home to only 11 of the 512 state-preferred LMEs. The group specializes in sugar production.

Others

China Lucky Film Group *Zhongguo lekai zhaopian jituan gongsi*	...	1st	...	5	...	China Lucky Film was established in 1958. It produces over 100 different kinds of films and is China's market leader. The group is based around five core enterprises and a research centre. In the mid-1990s it had about 60 per cent of China's film market but this has fallen quickly owing to

TABLE 3-5 (*Continued*)

	Sales Sector	Assets	1st or 2nd	Group Memb.	Listed Arm	Brief Description of the Group
						competition from foreign joint ventures (Kodak) and rampant smuggling. It now has a domestic share of less than 25 per cent.
Luoyang Chundu Group *Luoyand chundu jituan*	...	...	2nd	6	...	The group specializes in food processing. Based in Luoyang it has six core members and is one of China's leading food processing groups.
Shanghai Hualian Group *Shanghai hualian jituan*	...	...	2nd	...	...	The group consists of two joint stock companies and six subsidiaries and was officially recognized in 1995 as an enterprise group. Its main business is in retailing and it has a number of department and other stores, mainly in Shanghai. The formation of the group has allowed the parent to gain greater control of the subsidiaries as well as providing financial help to them. It has established a strategy to develop four kinds of chains in department, supermarket, convenience and franchise stores. It has over 100 supermarkets and has a Japanese joint venture with plans to establish over 500 convenience stores in Shanghai alone. A network of franchised stores has been established in large department stores throughout China dedicated to home appliances and garments. It also has interests in distribution.
Zhejiang Goods and Materials Group *Zhejiang wuchan jituan*	...	...	2nd	...	...	...

China State Development and Investment Corporation (SDIC) *Guojia kaifa touzi gongsi*	...	2nd	60	...	Based upon part of the state planning apparatus, the State Goods and Materials Department. In 1988 the State Council established it as a large general investment company and in 1995 it was turned into an experimental group. Its original finance capital came from the state budget special projects fund. It follows state industrial policy and describes itself as a 'governmental investment body'. It has over 60 members and total assets of 46.7 billion yuan ($5.6). Up to 1998 it had invested 47 billion yuan ($5.6 billion) in electricity generation, coal mining, bridge construction, pharmaceuticals, auto parts, chemical fertilizers, building materials and electronics. Of this 95 per cent was invested in large-and medium-scale policy-oriented projects and over 80 per cent was invested in the western and central areas of China (*CDBW*, 17 February 1998). SDIC, by investing in large-scale projects in key industries, often in western regions, follows industrial policies of the central government.
China Ports Construction Group *Zhongguo gangwan jianshe jituan*	...	2nd	...	...	...
TVEs					
Wanjie Group *Wanjie jituan*	...	...	...	...	In terms of sales and total assets the three TVEs equal their state-owned counterparts. They also appear to have less debt (Table 3-1). Wanjie Group is the largest group among the three TVEs. In 1995 it had total assets worth $365 million, net assets of $213 million, sales of $403 million and exports of $22 million.
Hongdou Group (Red Bean Group) *Hongdou jituan*	...	...	...	...	Hongdou Group, a clothing manufacture, is the smallest of the TVEs. It had assets worth $62 million, net assets of $26 million, sales of $110 million and exports of $15 million in 1995.

TABLE 3-5 (*Continued*)

	Sales Sector	Assets	1st or 2nd	Group Memb.	Listed Arm	Brief Description of the Group
Wanxiang Group *Wanxiang jituan*	39th $149	47th $188	2nd	... ...	Yes	Wanxiang is one of only three TVEs in the national team. It started business in 1969 as a cycle repair shop with capital of only several hundred dollars in Hangzhou, Zhejiang. By 1996 the assets had shot to $604 million. In 1999 it spent $80 million on building an R & D centre in Shanghai's Pudong area. This might also later be used to house their headquarters. Wanxiang produces high-quality components and has won orders to 34 countries. In 1988 the group addressed its vague property rights structure by buying out local state interests, to which some of its success is attributed. The strength of the company is based also upon its strong management. It was the largest exporter amongst the TVE groups, totalling $46 million.
Forestry						
Jilin Senlin Group *Jilin senlin jituan*	...	...	1st	69 + 13	...	All of the four forestry groups were included in the first batch of trial groups in 1991. They are all based in China's northern regions and are based upon the administrative departments once responsible for the large forests of this region. Of the 17 close members of Jilin Senlin Group 12 are state-owned LMEs. The group also has over 70 member enterprises, including 13 close members. It is involved in all aspects of forestry and has industrial capital of over 1.2 billion yuan and a workforce of 135 000.

Heilongjiang Anling Forestry Group *Heilongjiang anling jituan*	⋮	1st	⋮	⋮	⋮	⋮	⋮	⋮
Inner Mongolia Forest Industry Group *Nei menggu senlin jituan*	⋮	1st	⋮	⋮	⋮	⋮	⋮	⋮
Heilongjiang Forest Industry Group *Heilongjiang senlin jituan*	⋮	1st	⋮	⋮				
Agricultural Groups								
Zhongshui Group *Zhongshui jituan*	⋮	2nd	⋮	⋮	⋮	⋮	⋮	⋮
China State Farms Agribusiness Group *Zhongken jituan*	⋮	2nd	⋮	⋮	Founded in 1994 as a group, it has 22 internal branch companies and 16 overseas enterprises. Its main businesses include agricultural production and processing and agricultural trade as well as a number of services, such as management of wholesale agricultural markets.			
Zhongmu Group *Zhongmu jituan*	⋮	2nd	⋮	⋮	⋮	⋮		
Shanghai Agricultural, Industrial and Commercial Group *Shanghai nong gongshang jituan*	⋮	2nd	⋮	⋮	⋮	⋮		
Jilin Province Development Group *Jilin sheng jifa jituan*	⋮	2nd	⋮	⋮	⋮	⋮		

APPENDIX 2   CHRONOLOGY OF EVENTS RELATED TO FORMATION
OF CHINA'S BUSINESS GROUPS

1980
'The State Council's provisional regulations on pushing forward economic link-
ages'. The first policy responding to developing inter-firm linkages.
1981
April
Erqi leads the way in establishment of enterprise group by forming 'Dongfeng
Joint Management Company'. Using the Second Automobile Manufacturing
Factory as its base a joint management company is formed with eight other companies. Layers within the group subsequently developed.
1984
Enterprise autonomy widened as large enterprises are handed down from central
government control to provincial and city level authorities. This leads to the early
development of economic linkages between emerging economic units more akin
to enterprises.
1986
March
'Rules on pushing forward problems concerning horizontal economic linkages'.
Basis for early formation of groups. From 1979 to the publication of this document has commonly been referred to as the 'gestation period' in the formation of
business groups.
March
The State Council Development Research Centre, led by economist Ma Hong,
undertakes a survey of Erqi. Makes four recommendations to the State Council,
including starting to experiment with business groups. By April 4th the trial at
Erqi is approved.
April
'On Dongfeng Joint Management Company undertaking preferential planning
status', the first trial policy measure resulting from the research at Dongfeng, is
endorsed by the State Council.
June
'The National Enterprise Contracting Meeting' led by CRES takes place at
Shougang, and discusses enterprise restructuring, including merger and contracting. In September another meeting is held, entitled 'Enterprise merger, turning
around debt and increasing profit'. These two meetings along with an earlier one
in March push forward enterprise merger reforms. Shougang, like Erqi, develops
as a pioneer group in reforms.
6 October
'Notice on Jiefang, Dongfeng and Heavy Vehicle Group linked management
enterprises carrying out single-track planning'. The work at Erqi was expanded
and experimentation in the development of large enterprise groups widened to
three groups.

1987
April
'Temporary regulations of large industrial joint management companies carrying out the single track in the national plan'. Subsequently 12 groups are elevated to separate planning in the national plan and 13 establish finance companies.
December
'Some opinions on constructing and developing business groups' published by CRES and the then State Economic Commission. It consists of 18 points and was the first high level document to spell out the business group strategy. From the March 1986 document until this time is considered the 'developmental stage' (*chuangjian jieduan*) of business group development (CRES, ZJTGN, 1989: 93).
1988
Enterprise contracting and merger and the development of stock systems appear which start to break through the policy of 'three no changes' (*san bu bian*), restricting the ownership of enterprises, administrative subordination and the handing over of public finances. The enterprise groups are now entering their 'growth' stage as important barriers to their expansion are removed.
March
CRES and Hebei provincial government hold a meeting in Baoding, a pioneering city in merger and take-over activity, to discuss 'consolidation'. Later in May CRES holds 'The National Meeting of Enterprise Groups' in Luoyang. Delegates of groups exchange views and forward suggestions to the State Council.
August
A group from the Central Committee for Economics and Finance listen to a report given by CRES and in response decide to choose a small number of focal enterprise groups to undergo more trials involving the enlargement of their economic rights. The concept of developing a larger batch of trial groups starts to emerge more clearly.
1989
Establishment of National State Capital Management Office. Dongfeng discusses property rights problems and proposes some solutions, to which the newly established office agrees. It empowers Dongfeng with independent state capital management rights, pushing forward the core of the enterprise group and development of the modern corporation. Dongfeng leads the way in this trial.
December
State Commission for System Reform holds enterprise group organization and management meeting in Shenzhen. State Planning Commission and SETC along with various industrial departments and banks attend the meeting. Efforts are made at finding ways of promoting the emergent 'national team'. Discussions on implementation of the 'six unifications' policy, later published in the 1991 landmark document, are undertaken.

1991
December
'Notice on choosing a batch of large enterprise groups to undergo trials' is published (policy number 71), 55 groups are included in the national team and trials are proposed. Many of the team members, including Yiqi and Erqi, have been involved in pioneering the reforms over several years.

1992
September
The 'National Exchange Meeting' takes place in Guizhou Province. The State Planning Commission, CRES and State Council Economic and Trade Office attend, along with 130 delegates from the 55 trial groups. The groups complain of excessive local government and departmental interference. The main difficulties arise over profit sharing agreements and the 'core' enterprise or mother companies complain they still lack the funds to pull core enterprises closer. The trial group members suggest national investment policies be inclined towards the groups, finance companies be further promoted and in particular that they be allowed stock market listings.

September
'On the method of implementing the empowerment of trial business groups with state capital management rights'. Empowers the mother company to take control of close members of the group. The 'mother' company system begins to take shape.

November
Document on establishing finance companies published. Until now only 17 finance companies have been established.

1993
November
14th Party congress calls for clear property rights and the use of capital ties to unite business groups. This is part of a broader message in which the use of the modern enterprise system is promoted as the basis of state enterprise reform.

1994
Trials with three national holding companies are started.

1 January
China's enterprise law published which was to be the basis for the modern corporate system as well as the legal basis on which enterprise groups could be standardized.

February
Policy on measures for dealing with the group's tax problems published. Another similar document published later in 1995. These moved towards unification of the taxes so that the group's mother company was responsible for paying the taxes of the close layer which it owned.

18 April   Officially established 'Association for the Promotion of China's Group Companies' with a total of 74 members (later expanded to 110) including all 56 centrally chosen trial groups as well as members which joined in the later 1997 batch.

November

Selection of 100 enterprises to undergo trials with the modern corporate system.

1996

September

'Opinions of business groups being empowered with state capital management rights'. Further clarifies the earlier 1992 policy that passed on close members of the group to the core enterprise and establishes the 'mother' company system. Policy on finance companies is also issued. Restricts finance companies' activities to members of the group who have at least one quarter of their stock held by the mother of the group.

1997

Preferred LMEs chosen by SETC are increased from 300 to 512. At least 74 of these are members of the trial business groups.

April

'Opinions on Deepening the Trial Work on Large Enterprise Groups' is published, 63 groups are added to the national team and the direction of policy is changed to focus on the use of the modern corporate system and corporate law. Three TVEs are included in the groups.

1998

June

'National Enterprise Group Convention' is convened to discuss ways of implementing the 1997 document.

4

Aerospace

*Henceforth, China's domestic airlines should
use only domestically-produced airplanes.*
(Deng Xiaoping, December 1981)

*The development of the US aerospace industry was largely government-
funded. As late as 1986, close to 80 per cent of all R & D in this industry was
Federally-supported. Today this industry is a large employer (480 000 in
1994) and one of the largest exporters ($30 billion per year in 1980–94)
in the nation.*
(White House, 'Supporting R&D to promote economic growth', 2000)

INTERNATIONAL TRENDS IN THE AEROSPACE INDUSTRY

DRIVERS OF INDUSTRY CHANGE

The aerospace industry has special characteristics tending to push the industry towards large firm size and high levels of concentration. Moreover, the forces pushing in this direction have accelerated sharply since the 1980s. By the late 1990s, it had become one of the most concentrated of all industries. In civil aircraft, there was an effective global duopoly, and in aero-engines a triopoly. In the defence sector, a mere four firms now dominated in the USA. In Europe, the entire industry was in the throes of explosive concentration. It is possible that within a short time there will be one massive European aerospace company spanning the production of both civil and military aircraft. The barriers to entry for developing country aircraft and engine manufacturers have grown drastically in recent years, making the possibility of any developing country building a powerful indigenous industry much less than a decade or two ago.

141

Supply. The aerospace industry has very long (10–15 year) cycles. It has experienced sharp and chaotic transition periods usually caused by political events (notably the beginning of wars) and dramatic technological break-throughs, notably the invention of jet engines and the computer. These develop-ments have powerfully influenced the industry's institutional development. Size has always been important. Morgan Stanley Dean Witter's (MSDW) evaluation of competitive advantage in the world aerospace industry concluded: 'Some things never change. We believe success in the aerospace and defence industries boils down to scale, scale, scale' (MSDW, 1999: 89).

There are several respects in which size has become increasingly important in the aerospace industry.

Large-sale investment in technical progress. Technology has changed at high speed, providing the impetus to further concentration in order to be able to com-pete. The shift to large jet airliners fundamentally transformed the institutional structure of the world's aircraft manufacturing business. In 1997, small jet air-liners, with 75–100 seats, accounted for just 12 per cent of the total civil airliner market (Table 4-1). By 2017, their share will have shrunk even further, while the share of the largest size category of aircraft, with over 400 seats, will have risen to over one-fifth of the total number of seats.

R & D expenditures by globally successful aerospace companies in the 1990s, are vastly greater (in real terms) than those of leading aerospace companies fif-teen or twenty years ago. After its merger with McDonnell–Douglas, Boeing's annual R & D spend was well over $2 billion. Aérospatiale's R & D spend in 1997 was $1.3 billion (Table 4-2). Not only are the aerospace companies spend-ing vast amounts on R & D, but so also are the leading suppliers of components. Rolls-Royce and SNECMA each spend $300 million or more on R & D, while United Technologies, which produces Pratt and Whitney engines, spends around $1.2 billion annually (Table 4-2).

TABLE **4-1 Size Structure of Civil Global Airliner Stock, 1997 and 2017 (Aircraft of 70 or more Seats)**

No of seats	Share of no. of aircraft (%)		Share of no. of seats (%)	
	(1997)	*(2017)*	*(1997)*	*(2017)*
70, 85 and 100	12	6	6	5
125, 150 and 175	59	48	48	30
210 and 250	12	15	15	18
300, 350 and 400	16	30	30	26
>400	<1	<1	<1	21
Total no. of aircraft/seats	9 677 aircraft	17 920 aircraft	1.73 million seats	4.07 million seats

SOURCE: *FT* (3 September 1998)

TABLE **4-2 R & D Spending, by Leading Aircraft and
Component Manufacturers, 1997**

Company	R & D spend ($ million)	% of sales
Boeing	1905	4.2
McDonnell-Douglas	352	2.6
Aérospatiale	1286	13.9
Lockheed Martin	781	2.8
British Aerospace	491	3.5
General Electric	747	7.0
United Technologies	1175	4.8
Rockwell International	654	8.5
Rolls-Royce	352	2.6
SNECMA	297	9.6

SOURCE: DTI (1998: 60–2)

Ever-expanding development costs. As technology advances rapidly, the size
of aircraft rises, and demands of airlines intensify for low-cost highly reliable
products, so the costs of new development have risen remorselessly. The development costs of the Airbus A3XX, a mooted super-large aircraft, to seat between
550 and 650 people, are estimated to be around $16 billion (*FT*, 14 March 2000).
The USA Air Force's F-22, which has a delivery date of 2006, has estimated
development costs of $19 billion (IISS, 1998: 18). The USA Army's RAH-66
helicopter, also with a delivery date of 2006, has an estimated $5.4 billion in
development costs (IISS, 1998: 18). Larger volumes of deliveries make the huge
development costs worthwhile, as the costs can be spread over a large number of
aircraft. As we shall see, so large have the development costs of new aircraft and
aircraft engines become, that even the world's leading manufacturers are keen to
involve other firms, such as sub-system suppliers, to participate in the development of new products, sharing the risks and the profits.

Economies of scale in assembly. The industry has always gained from
economies of scale in assembly, in which there are close analogies with automobile manufacturing. The main economies to be achieved by large outputs of one
type of aircraft are obtained by 'spreading launch costs, the costs of designing,
planning and development, and cost of special jigs and tools' (Pratten, 1971:
151). In addition, there are economies achieved through the learning effects
obtained in the course of producing more units of a given model, especially in
the early phase of its production (Pratten, 1971: 152).

As in the car industry, powerful economies of scale are increasingly operating
with the use of common platforms across different types of products. A 'full product line' is increasingly regarded as an important aspect of competitive advantage. It enables the manufacturer to apply given R & D outlays over a wide range
of products, and to obtain economies of scale in procurement of components.

However, the advantages of producing a 'family' of products that share common features go beyond manufacturing economies of scale. They include also powerful operational economies. For example, the Airbus A330/340 aircraft not only share a common fuselage and wing. They also have similar avionics systems, which help reduce crew training and operating costs through 'cross-crew qualification' (MSDW, 1999: 91).

By December 1995 Boeing had delivered around 8,000 modern jet aircraft, including 1010 B-707/720s, 1831 B-727s, 2764 B-737s, 1071 B-747s, 694 B-757s, 595 B-767s, and 13 B-777s (*FT*, 30 August 1996). Whereas Boeing has built over 1000 B-747s, its super-large aircraft, Lockheed built only 250 of its large airliner, the Tristar, and McDonnell–Douglas built 446 of its largest airliner, the DC-10. Boeing had built over 7000 conventional airliners by 1995, whereas its closest competitor, McDonnell–Douglas, had built a total of around 2000 DC-9s/MD-80s. Even the large aerospace industry in the former USSR did not come close to the numbers of aircraft built by Boeing. Tupolev's principal aircraft were the twin-engined Tu-134 and Tu-154, the staple aircraft of airlines in the former Soviet bloc. Tupolev built around 700 Tu-134s and 1000 Tu-154s.

Lockheed Martin has sold more than 4000 of its F-16 fighter planes. Recent versions of the F-16 cost $80–90 million if fully equipped. As we shall see, the United States' JSF (Joint Strike Fighter), which will sell for around $40 million per unit, has initial orders for over 3000. The world's most expensive plane is the F-22, which will cost around $187 million for just one unit. The Pentagon plans to purchase over 330 of these planes over the next two decades (*IHT*, 14 July 1999).

It is unimaginable that any new entrant can compete with such massive economies of scale in either civil or military aircraft production. As we shall see, even the world's most advanced production base outside the USA, namely Europe, is likely to find it difficult to generate sufficiently large sales to benefit from the economies of scale that are available to the USA giants. From a standing start, Airbus was able to increase its cumulative sales to over 1000 by 1992, enabling substantial benefits from economies of scale, but its cumulative sales are still far below those of Boeing.

Integrating the supply chain. Organizing supply networks has become an increasingly important part of the modern aerospace industry. For example, around one-half of the total value of the BAe 146 (Regional Jet) is now bought from suppliers. This consists mainly of engines, avionics, and electronics. Thus, even a relatively uncomplicated jet plane must rely for a large part of its complex components on external suppliers, which may frequently be located in a foreign country.[1] This has affected even guided weapons systems. Under intense pressure to reduce costs, even the European leader, Matra BAe Dynamics, purchases around 60 per cent of the cost base from outside the company, compared to 'well under 50 per cent in the 1980s'. Although constantly monitored for security implications, it is now the case that even key sub-systems are outsourced. Rolls-Royce purchases around 70 per cent of the value of the final product from outside the company, with a total of around 1500 suppliers. Rolls-Royce has around

20 000 people in its aerospace division in the UK, and estimates that around 40 000 people work full-time to supply the company with goods and services.

Airbus Industrie has more than 1500 suppliers in 27 countries. Its system of suppliers is truly global, including over 500 USA companies, and suppliers in Singapore, India, Australia, Indonesia, Korea, Japan and China. Large firms have important benefits stemming from economies of scale in purchasing components. Components purchase from outsourced supply networks has necessitated large investments in IT systems to integrate the supplier networks tightly with the core design and assembly location, and involves increasingly detailed, instantaneous exchange of information. 'Lean production' techniques are essential to cost reduction and control.

Modern aircraft and engines have become so complex, that a major aspect of competitive advantage has been the ability to integrate the whole system of supply to produce the final product. The intensity of inter-action between components and sub-system suppliers, and the assemblers, has grown at high speed alongside the revolution in information technology. The industry is in the midst of a profound transformation of its working methods, involving constant, meticulously detailed, exchange of information between the different links in the supply chain. The surrounding system of suppliers today constitutes a veritable 'external firm', whose activities are closely co-ordinated and planned by the core systems integrators who design and assemble the civilian aircraft or are the prime contractors for defence industry contracts. The consequences have been dramatic for the effectiveness with which the industry operates.

For example Rolls-Royce believes that dramatically intensified inter-actions between the core company and the network of over 1500 first-tier suppliers are the main factors behind the sharp improvements in system performance. It used to take the company 12 weeks to make a compressor disc. It now takes just four weeks. The lead time for manufacturing shafts has been cut from 104 days in 1996 to 48 days in 1999. Drastic changes in supply chain management has helped BAe to cut the lead time for the production of its Regional Jet (formerly the BAe 146) from 29 weeks in 1991 to just 10 weeks in 1998, with the man-hours necessary falling from 31.0 in 1991 to just 12.5 in 1998.

The size of the 'external firm' can greatly exceed that of the core companies. For example, 'Boeing stands at the centre of an extended *keiretsu* of world-wide subcontractors', employing about 230 000 workers directly and perhaps three times that many through its related companies' (*Fortune*, 4 March 1999). In other words, Boeing's 'external firm' employs around three-quarters of a million people across the world, including, as we shall see, sub-contractors in China.

Even the world's largest aircraft company, Boeing, encountered major problems with delivery due to the logistical problems involved in synchronizing suppliers in order to meet the fast increase in aircraft demand. This was a major factor behind their losses incurred in 1997. Boeing was in the middle of a comprehensive reorganization of the supply structure when demand surged. Under its old system, Boeing kept track of its parts through no fewer than 400 computer systems. It is investing $1 billion in a programme that will put all its parts on a single computer system, radically changing the way it organizes components supply and its relationship with its suppliers (*FT*, 3 September 1998).

However, so fast is the nature of the firm changing in this sector, that even the information technology systems that are at the heart of systems integration can be 'outsourced'. For example, Rolls-Royce used to organize its IT operations in-house. However, it realized that it was falling behind the best-practice in the IT industry. In 1995 Rolls-Royce signed a 10-year contract with EDS to undertake the entire IT operations for Rolls-Royce (*FT*, 20 October 1998). Under the contract, almost 1000 Rolls-Royce staff moved into EDS, making a total of 1400 people at EDS that worked permanently on the Rolls-Royce account, including 100 A. T. Kearney management consultants.

In order to meet intense pressure from global systems integrators, the component supply industry has itself been undergoing rapid change. In order to meet the demands of the systems integrators, the major components suppliers have themselves needed to invest heavily in R & D and to grow in order to benefit from cost reduction through economies of scale. A powerful merger movement is taking place among second tier suppliers to the systems integrators: 'More mergers among the smaller sub-scale components and sub-systems manufacturers seem inevitable as the supplier base responds to the pressure being applied by the prime contractors such as BAe, or original equipment manufacturers, such as Boeing' (MSDW, 1999: 87).

For example, in 1998, GEC acquired Tracor (for $1.4 billion), the US-based company, in order to strengthen its position in USA defence systems and services. Through this purchase, GEC–Marconi became the world's sixth largest defence electronics contractor (*FT*, 10 January 1999).

Already, in 1997, two of the world's top five aerospace companies (by value of sales), namely United Technologies and Allied Signal, were principally aerospace components suppliers to the major systems integrators (*Fortune*, 3 August 1998: F-15). In 1999, Allied Signal strengthened its already powerful position still further when it announced that it was to merge with Honeywell (*FT*, 7 June 1999). The merger will create 'a global technology powerhouse with revenues of $25 billion in 1999, staff of 120 000 in 95 countries, and a *Fortune* 50 company with a combined market capitalization of more than $45 billion'. The combined R & D expenditure of the two companies is almost $800 million (DTI, 1998: 60, 63). The new company's largest single business will be aerospace, with about $10.5 billion in annual revenues, 'bringing together Honeywell's focus on sophisticated avionics with Allied Signal's in-flight safety products and systems' (*FT*, 7 June 1999).

The new Allied Signal–Honeywell company will have 'a strong position in everything from manufacturing cockpit controls to handling aircraft service and maintenance' (*FT*, 8 June 1999). The new company's aerospace sales alone will be roughly the same size as the combined aerospace and non-aerospace revenues of each of Aérospatiale, Northrop–Grumman or British Aerospace. The annual cost savings from the merger are estimated to be in the region of $500 million (*FT*, 7 June 1999). Honeywell explicitly points to the consolidation of customers as a major reason for the merger (*FT*, 11 June 1999). Larger customers are likely to drive a harder bargain on prices, and technical progress by suppliers. Only through merger and cost-cutting can companies like Honeywell compete and establish long-run strategic partnerships with the giant customers like Boeing, Lockheed Martin and the new BAe.

The trend towards concentration is affecting smaller companies within the industry also. For example, in June 1999, Meggitt acquired Whittaker Corporation for $380 million. The company supplies valves, ground fuelling products and fire and smoke detectors to 'virtually every aircraft maker in the West' (*FT*, 10 June 1999). The merger was explicitly driven by the assemblers' push to reduce the number of parts suppliers. Without the necessary scale the two companies felt they would no longer be competitive. Mike Stacey, Meggitt's chief executive commented: 'We are very conscious that bigger suppliers is what it's all about' (quoted in *FT*, 10 June 1999).

Building Internal Systems Integration Capabilities. Alongside the trend towards concentration among component and sub-system suppliers, the leading systems integrators are themselves tending to become more vertically integrated. This enables them to perform the increasingly complicated tasks involved in integrating complex sub-systems with multiple interfaces (MSDW, 1999: 85).

For example, in the 1990s, Lockheed bought a succession of aerospace companies, including General Dynamic's military aircraft business (in 1993 for $1.5 billion), Martin Marietta (in 1995 for $10 billion), and Loral (for $9 billion in 1996). Its purchase of Loral gave it access to Loral's extensive defence electronics capability. In 1998 it announced its intention to purchase Northrop Grumman (for $5.3 billion). Had the Pentagon allowed the purchase to proceed, Lockheed would have been able to build almost a whole aircraft-airframe, electronics and weapons – without inviting others to compete for important sub-contracts. Although the Pentagon blocked the take-over, Lockheed Martin remains a strongly vertically integrated company.

Raytheon also bought a succession of defence businesses in the 1990s, including the defence electronics company, E-Systems (in 1995 for $2.3 billion), the defence systems and electronics business of Texas Instruments (in 1997 for $2.95 billion), and the Hughes defence electronics business from General Motors (in.1997 for $9.5 billion). By the late 1990s, Raytheon had become a huge company with a $20 billion annual turnover, and a wide range of systems integration capabilities in missiles and torpedoes. Through the purchase of Hughes, it established a 'near monopoly in USA air combat weapons' (*FT*, 13 January 1997). Its capabilities included metal fabrication, cables, optics, microelectronics, printed wiring board fabrication, sensors and electronic systems, command control and communications systems, intelligence, information and aircraft integration systems (*FT*, 7 May 1998).

In 1997 BAe acquired the Siemens Plessey business, in order to strengthen their in-house capability in information technology, central to electronics systems integration. In 1999, BAe merged with GEC, bringing a major prime contractor in defence equipment together with a major aerospace electronics company, to create the world's third largest aerospace company, by value of sales. A major motive for the merger was to even further enhance BAe's capability as a prime contractor and systems integrator. GEC–Marconi will become the core of BAe's electronics business. It has capabilities in avionics, radar, air defence systems, electro-optics, infra-red sensors and communications systems (*FT*, 20 January 1999). The acquisition dramatically enhances BAe's ability to develop its systems integration capabilities and compete as a prime contractor for the largest defence programmes, including aircraft carriers and combat aircraft.

Benefits of a large installed base. A large installed base provides a long-term source of revenue from spare parts and servicing contracts. A single aircraft engine programme can run for as long as 30–40 years. A modern airliner can operate for several decades.[2] It also provides a strong incentive to continue to buy further products from the same source due to economies in maintenance and operations. In both the civilian and the military sides of the business, a large installed base means that customers can enlarge their fleets without the need to undertake large additional investments in training systems and support infrastructure. As aircraft become more technologically complex, such software and systems investments become more expensive and more difficult to displace (MSDW, 1999: 90).

These factors provide an incumbent, successful manufacturer with large advantages compared with smaller firms and potential new entrants. Product reliability is more important in the aircraft industry than in almost any other industry, with the possible exception of nuclear power equipment. The best demonstration of product reliability is a large installed base. Hence, new entrants to the aircraft and aero-engine business confront a serious 'Catch-22' problem. They can only gain market share by proving the reliability of their product, but the only way to prove the reliability of their product is by selling large numbers that operate reliably.

Shareholder preference for large aerospace firms. Shareholders are strongly driving the concentration process. Large institutional investors and investment advisors have favoured large firms with demonstrated capability to sustain their 'competitive edge' over the long-term. Morgan Stanley summed up its investment philosophy in the aerospace sector as follows: 'We are looking for the largest, most dominant global player. We seek companies with substantial financial resources that can be committed to winning contracts/campaigns throughout the world and can sustain long investment periods. We are interested in competitors with broad product lines that can survive the cancellation of programmes or the loss of a campaign. We search for companies with the cash flows to sustain healthy R & D investments and satisfy shareholders' (MSDW 1998a: 33). It entitled its section on the evaluation of 'competitive edge' in the world aerospace industry: 'big is beautiful' (MSDW, 1998a: 33).

Virtuous circle of concentration and competition. As the industry has become more concentrated, far from the intensity of competition declining, it has become much greater. The weight of resources that can be brought into play by each player in the battle for the global market has greatly risen: 'Competition in the commercial industry remains as ferocious as ever, even though it is now a duopoly following the merger of Boeing and McDonnell–Douglas' (MSDW, 1998a: 33). The battle between Boeing and Airbus in the 1990s has been one of the most dramatic pieces of modern business history, far removed from the textbook world of small business and perfect competition, but with an extraordinarily high degree of competition. Huge forces have been brought to bear by each side in the struggle. As we shall see, the battle between the decreasing number of global players in the defence industry is fast intensifying alongside the civilian aircraft battle.

Demand. The prize for the 'winners' in the global aerospace battle is the vast market that exists today and which will grow much larger in the years ahead.

Civilian aircraft. Airbus forecasts that over the next two decades, the worldwide airline fleet will increase from the 1998 level of 9700 to 17 900 (Table 4-1). Airlines are predicted to buy 13 600 new and replacement aircraft over that period with a total value of $1200 billion (*FT*, 3 September 1998). The predicted market for aero-engines (including original sales and sales of spare parts) is estimated to be around $500 billion in the next two decades.

Although there is the prospect of powerful growth of demand for civil aircraft, the nature of the market has altered sharply. In the former Soviet bloc, the growth of a huge civil aircraft industry was built around a completely protected internal market. In Europe, government purchases were typically used to support domestic aircraft manufacturers by means of purchases made by the domestic government-owned national airlines. This situation has been drastically transformed in recent years. Most of the formerly nationalized airlines in Europe either have been, or are soon about to be, privatized. Privatized airlines have placed great pressure on the aircraft suppliers to lower prices. Price rivalry between Boeing and Airbus in the 1990s reached great levels of intensity as Airbus struggled to wrest market share from Boeing to win orders from highly competitive privatized airlines.

Fierce inter-airline competition in the wake of privatization and substantial deregulation, has driven down airline prices and profits. Airlines are frequently restricted by national government regulations on foreign ownership. The USA government has a 29 per cent limit on foreign ownership of voting stock, and in Europe, the foreign ownership is restricted to 49.9 per cent (*FT*, 23 June 1999). Privatized airlines, like the privatized telecoms companies, are responding to pressure on margins and the opportunity to benefit from economies of scale, by rapidly developing international alliances. Star Alliance includes United Airlines (USA), Lufthansa (Germany), Thai Airways, Scandinavian Airlines System, Air Canada, Ansett Australia, Air New Zealand, Varig and All Nippon Airways (from October 1999). Wings includes Northwest Airlines (USA), KLM (Netherlands), Alitalia and Continental. Delta includes Delta (USA), Swissair, Austrian Airlines, Air France and Sabena (Belgium). Oneworld includes British Airways, Cathay Pacific, American Airlines, Canadian Airlines, Qantas (Australia), Finnair, Lan Chile and Iberia (*FT*, 23 June 1999).

A major reason for forming alliances is to reduce costs through common aircraft purchase and maintenance. This further adds to the pressure upon aircraft manufacturers which emerged in the wake of airline privatization. Indeed, it was reported in September 1998, that Boeing and Airbus had agreed finally to end their ferocious price war. In interviews at the Farnborough Air Show, Harry Stonecipher, Boeing's president, and Noel Forgeard, Airbus' managing director, said they would 'no longer undercut one another on price, but would concentrate on achieving a satisfactory rate of profit on every sale' (quoted in *FT*, 8 September 1998).

Military aerospace. The global military aircraft market has changed radically, and is in the course of changing even more. The period since the Cold War has seen a drastic reduction in defence spending in both the USA and Europe. In the USA, total defence expenditure fell from a peak of $390 billion in 1986 to $253 billion in 1999, and in Europe (NATO) the total budget fell from a peak of $191 billion in 1990 to $135 billion in 1999 (IISS, 1999: 37). The International Institute for Strategic Studies estimates that the USA National Defense Budget will rise from $268 billion in 1998 to $297 billion in 2003 (IISS, 1998: 15). It is possible that the NATO action in former Yugoslavia might lead to a rethinking of defence needs in the EU and a consequent rise in defence expenditure.

The government is the main purchaser of military aircraft in both the USA and Europe, which makes the market a special one compared to that for most products:

> In order to understand the economic operation of the USA defense industry, it is absolutely essential to recognize that there is no free market at work in this area and that there likely cannot be one because of the role played by the government. The combination of a single buyer, a few very large firms in each segment of the industry, and a small number of extremely expensive programmes constitutes a unique structure for doing business. (Jacques Gansler, Head of Procurement at the Pentagon, quoted in *FT*, 3 September 1998)

Not only has the total budget fallen, but the nature of procurement has changed substantially. Procurement techniques are rapidly moving towards those of the civil world as governments push contractors to lower costs. Government procurement agencies are pushing defence contractors to use 'off-the-shelf' products from the civilian sphere, instead of imposing costly military specifications, making contractors more responsible for spare parts and logistic support for the equipment they supply, shortening the development time and delivery cycle of new products, encouraging the use of common production lines for both bespoke military and high volume commercial items, and the development of advanced products with common technological bases (*FT*, 3 September 1998).

Alongside the decline in defence procurement in the USA and Europe, has gone a dramatic widening of the extent of the military aircraft market. Large parts of the world that were excluded from arms sales during the Cold War are now included in the market to which European and USA military aircraft manufacturers can sell. Although the total value of arms deliveries fell by 37 per cent

TABLE 4-3 International Arms Sales, 1987–98 (constant 1997 US$)

	Total		USSR/Russia		USA		Western Europe		Others	
	($ billion)	(%)	($ billion)	(%)	($ billion)	(%)	($ billion)	(%)	($ billion)	(%)
1987	88.9	100.0	31.2	35.1	24.0	27.0	22.1	24.9	11.6	13.0
1998	55.8	100.0	2.9	5.2	26.5	47.5	22.4	40.1	4.0	7.2

SOURCE: IISS (1999: 281)

TABLE 4-4 International Arms Deliveries, 1987 and 1998

	Total		NATO/ Western Europe		Middle East/ N. Africa		East Asia		Others	
	($ billion)	(%)	($ billion)	(%)	($ billion)	(%)	($ billion)	(%)	($ billion)	(%)
1987	88.9	100.0	16.9	19.0	33.0	37.1	9.9	11.2	29.1	32.7
1998	55.8	100.0	18.3	32.9	16.8	30.0	13.2	23.7	7.5	13.4

SOURCE: IISS (1999: 281–3)

TABLE 4-5 International Arms Deliveries within East Asia, 1987 and 1998 (million of constant 1997 US$)

	Total	China	Japan	Taiwan	ROK	Thailand	Malaysia	Singapore	Indonesia
1987	9 926	877	1 512	1 408	1 012	581	95	418	351
1998	13 236	469	2 086	6 258	1 366	313	334	887	365

SOURCE: IISS (1999: 283)

from 1987 to 1998 (Table 4-3), this was largely accounted for by the dramatic decline in the exports of the former USSR, especially to Eastern Europe, and the Middle East. USSR/Russia's share of world arms exports plummeted from 35 per cent in 1987 to just 5 per cent in 1998 (Table 4-3). For the arms manufacturers of the USA and Western Europe, total export sales remained almost unaltered in real terms between the late 1980s and the late 1990s. Arms sales still are an extremely important source of export earnings for the advanced capitalist economies. The price of a single fully equipped F-16 is around $80–90 million, and the price of the basic version of the US-produced Joint Strike Fighter is estimated to be around $40 million per plane. USA arms sales in 1998 totalled $26.5 billion compared with $22.4 billion from Western Europe. Between them they accounted for 89 per cent of the world total of arms exports (Table 4-3). The fastest growing market for Western arms sales was the Far East, to which arms deliveries increased by one-third in real terms from 1987 to 1998 (Table 4-4). The countries around China increased their arms purchases from $9.1 billion in 1987 to $12.8 billion in 1998, compared with China's purchases of $0.9 billion and $0.5 billion in the same years (Table 4-5). Taiwan alone increased its purchases from $1.4 billion in 1987 to $6.3 billion in 1998 (Table 4-5).

The Process of Aerospace Consolidation

We have seen that powerful forces were at work in the 1990s driving forward consolidation of the aircraft industry in both Europe and the USA. This resulted in one of the most dramatic epochs in business history that the world has seen. The process is far from over, and the outcome is far from certain.

Consolidation in the USA

Military aircraft. In the 1990s, the USA has seen one of the most remarkable epochs of merger and acquisition in business history. The initiative came from the Pentagon. In 1993, Les Aspin, the then USA Defense Secretary, invited the chief executives of the biggest American defence and aerospace companies to dinner. He told them that times were tough. He said that there were too many players in the industry to enable full benefits from economies of scale and to undertake necessary R & D to keep the industry advancing at the desired pace. The event was known as the 'Last Supper'. With the green light from the government, a colossal game of 'musical chairs' followed in the mid-1990s, with over $62 billion-worth of mergers and acquisitions occurring between 1994 and 1998 (Table 4-6). At the conclusion of this process, just two front-line aircraft manufacturers were left, namely Boeing and Lockheed Martin. Northrop Grumman did still manufacture aircraft, but its main activities in the aircraft industry involved working as sub-contractor for the two giants.

The most significant event in this process was the merger of Boeing with McDonnell–Douglas. By any conventional criteria used in competition policy, permitting this degree of industrial concentration was unthinkable. Far from

TABLE **4-6 Principal Mergers and Acquisitions in US Defence Industry, 1994–8** (deals of over $500 million only)

Acquirer	Acquiree	Value ($ million)	Date
Loral	IBM Federal Systems	1 575	March 1994
Northrop	Grumman	2 100	April 1994
Lockheed*	Martin Marietta*	>9 000	March 1995
Rolls-Royce	Allison Gas Turbine	525	March 1995
Loral	Unisys Defense Operation	862	May 1995
E-Systems*	Raytheon*	2 300	June 1995
Northrop–Grumman	Westinghouse Electronic System	3 600	March 1996
Lockheed Martin	Loral	9 500	April 1996
Boeing	Rockwell Aerospace and Defense	3 025	December 1996
Boeing*	McDonnell–Douglas*	13 300	1997
Raytheon	Texas Instruments Defense Business	2 950	1997
GM Hughes Defense Business*	Raytheon*	9 500	1997
GEC	Tracor	1 400	1998

SOURCE: *FT* (3 September 1998)

NOTE: * For mergers, acquiring and acquired company are shown in alphabetical order

being opposed to the merger, the move received 'strong support from the USA administration' (*FT*, 23 September 1997). As soon as it was announced in December 1996, European aerospace executives assumed it would be allowed to proceed 'because the White House and the Pentagon wanted it to' (*FT*, 23 September 1997). After the Boeing–McDonnell–Douglas merger, Boeing and Lockheed Martin between them accounted for close to one-half of USA Defense Department contracts (Table 4-7), and almost completely dominated military aircraft sales to the USA government.

There are only two firms that have the capability to bid for the USA government's massive Joint Strike Fighter (JSF) programme, namely Boeing and Lockheed Martin. This is far and away the biggest programme in prospect for the USA and the world's military aircraft sector. Initial orders were estimated at over 3000, with a total revenue of well over $100 billion (*FT*, 3 September 1998), and will eventually rise well above this figure. The explicit goal of both the Pentagon and the USA manufacturers is to make the JSF 'the world's standard combat jet aircraft in the first half of the twenty-first century' (*FT*, 3 September 1998). The programme is so important that 'neither company can contemplate losing it' (*FT*, 3 September 1998). It is widely thought that whoever wins the final contract, the loser will be awarded extensive amounts of work on the resulting enormous programme: 'The

TABLE 4-7 US Defense Department Equipment
Purchase Contracts (fiscal year 1997)

Company	$ billion
Lockheed Martin	18.8
Boeing	15.5
Northrop–Grumman	5.7
General Dynamics	4.9
Raytheon	4.7
General Motors	4.5
United Technologies	2.9
Litton Industries	2.6
Textron Inc	2.3
Others	18.1
Total	80.0

SOURCE: *FT* (3 September 1998)

Pentagon's commitment to competition is such that it could not allow either Boeing or Lockheed to suffer a grievous blow to its business' (*FT*, 3 September 1998).

Civil airliners. Boeing's early development into a multinational company was powerfully affected by the Second World War. The consolidation of several smaller companies into the Boeing company was itself strongly influenced by the prospect of large war-time orders. During the Second World War, Boeing grew tremendously, making a huge number of bombers for the USA Air Force. The USA government invested heavily in the company in order to ensure that the war effort was adequately supported. Lindberg and Campbell (1991) conclude that the ending of the Second World War had a powerful impact upon the growth of leading USA companies that were to emerge onto the world stage with renewed strength after the conclusion of hostilities:

In the post-World War II demobilization, the Federal government sold its vast military facilities to war contractors at very low prices. Using profits earned from sales to the military, the largest firms were able to purchase the most efficient industrial plants in the country, reinforcing their dominant positions in both core and peripheral sectors. In conjunction with the Federal government's earlier procurement subsidies, these sales were the culmination of a massive double subsidy that helped transform the organizational terrain of several important sectors by reinforcing oligopolies ... Continued heavy spending by the much expanded Pentagon bureaucracy in the post-War years led to a quasi permanent link between a new and powerful state actor and dependent sectors or industries, further generalizing the economy-wide trend towards scale and concentration. (Lindberg and Campbell, 1991: 365)

Boeing was a major beneficiary of this process. Up until the mid-1950s, it was primarily a military aircraft maker. Its main product in the early 1950s consisted of large numbers of the heavy bomber, the B-52. This enabled Boeing to develop the resources and skills to produce the B-707, which went into service in 1958, and became the world's most successful commercial jet. Indeed, Boeing used the same government-owned production facilities to make both planes. Moreover, the B-707 started life as the KC135, a military tanker. The B-707 constituted the key product in establishing Boeing's lead in the breakthrough to the epoch of large jet airliners, greatly assisted by the disastrous accidents that befell the De Havilland Comet, which entered service as early as 1952.[3] By the 1960s Boeing had established a substantial lead over other manufacturers.

In the epoch of the leap into larger scale airliners, Boeing's size was critical in enabling it to pull away from its main domestic competitors. Moreover, its crucial lead in the introduction of the new generation of super-large aircraft, the B-747, was greatly facilitated by the fact that it was far advanced in designing a heavy-lift transporter for the USAF, from which the B-747 was spun off. In the early 1960s there were still three other relatively large USA jet aircraft makers – McDonnell, Douglas, and Lockheed. Douglas and McDonnell merged in 1967. Neither Lockheed nor McDonnell–Douglas was able to catch up with Boeing in the ensuing race.

The first-mover advantage was crucial in enabling Boeing to maintain its lead. Boeing was able to watch while first Lockheed left the field of commercial airliners, then a steadily weakening McDonnell–Douglas finally gave up and agreed to merge with Boeing. By 1997, the remarkable situation had been reached that in the country with the world's largest airline market by far, there was only one producer, Boeing. After the merger with McDonnell–Douglas, Boeing accounted for no less than 84 per cent of the world's total aircraft in service (*FT*, 23 September 1997). The merger left Boeing with a complete monopoly on large civil aircraft: Boeing is the only company in the world that produces aircraft able to carry more than 400 passengers. Moreover, unlike Lockheed Martin, Boeing was now a colossus that spanned both the military and civilian spheres of aerospace production.

After the merger with McDonnell–Douglas, Ron Woodard, then Boeing's chief of commercial aircraft, announced that Boeing would now 'bury' Airbus. Following the merger and Ron Woodard's aggressive statement, Jean Peirson, managing director of Airbus Industrie, said that he believed Boeing's goal was to 'financially throttle' Airbus: 'Recent statements by the management of Boeing leave no doubt of a long-lasting strategy implemented with McDonnell–Douglas' active complicity: to limit Airbus Industrie's role to that of a niche player with a long-term view to eliminate it' (quoted in *FT*, 16 June 1997).

The Pentagon plans to reduce even further the number of USA defence industry companies. The Pentagon's chief of procurement, Jacques Gansler has said that he wants to encourage consolidations in the industry, 'where they don't affect the nature of the business': 'so if there are three or four people in a sector, fine, we can consolidate down to two or three. When there's only two or three, you have to look at each one separately and make the decision. How critical is it?' (quoted in *FT*, 3 September 1998). Given the vast size of the USA defence budget compared to those of Europe, it will be able to preserve oligopolistic competition while still having companies that are larger than their European counterparts. The current plan is to reduce the total number of USA manufacturers of bombers from the current three to just one, manufacturers of fighters are scheduled to fall from five to two, and helicopter makers, from the current four to just two.

Consolidation in Europe
Military aircraft
Problems. The European defence industry faces serious difficulties. The contrast with the USA was strong even before the USA merger explosion in the 1990s. It is now even more dramatic. By the late 1990s, the defence industry had become much more concentrated in the USA than in Europe. The USA had just four shipyards, compared to fourteen in Europe; two tank and armoured personnel carrier manufacturers, compared to ten in Europe; three missile companies, compared with 10 in Europe; and five helicopter and aircraft companies compared with nine in Europe.

The level of government procurement in the USA is far above that in Europe. In 1999, the total USA defence budget amounted to $252 billion, compared with only around one-half of that amount for the whole of NATO Europe (Table 4-8). In 1999, the whole of NATO Europe spent $27 billion on equipment, compared to USA spending of $47 billion. NATO Europe spent just $9 billion on R & D for the defence sector, while the USA spent $35 billion: 'This disparity in R & D effort has existed for some time, and the gap shows no sign of closing, nor is there any significant reduction in the duplication and fragmentation of effort that remains a feature of NATO Europe's R & D activities' (IISS, 1998: 33).

Not only is the EU total procurement much lower than that of the USA, but also a large fraction of Europe's procurement spending is still conducted by individual countries: 'There have been few new European cooperative development

TABLE **4-8 US and NATO Europe* Government Defence Budgets (1999, $ billion)**

Country/entity	Defence budget	R & D	Equipment procurement
USA	252	35.3	47.1
NATO Europe*	135	8.9	27.2
of which:			
UK	33	3.9	8.3
France	28	3.1	5.2
Germany	24	1.3	3.7
Italy	16	0.3	1.9

SOURCE: IISS (1999): 37

NOTE: * Includes the 13 Western European NATO countries and Turkey

programmes for major conventional weapon systems since the Cold War, and a marked absence of substantial cooperative commitments in a number of increasingly relevant areas such as ballistic missile defence, unmanned aerial vehicles (UAVs) and command and control systems' (IISS, 1998: 34). National procurement allocations of even the largest European country are very small compared to those of the USA. In 1999 government defence expenditure amounted to just $33 billion in the UK, $29 billion in France, and $24 billion in Germany. For smaller European countries, the total procurement outlay was minuscule compared to the USA (in 1999 Sweden spent $4.4 billion and Spain spent $5.5 billion) (IISS, 1999: 37). This hugely restricts the scope for economies of scale, and hence limits the competitiveness of European defence industry contractors. This constitutes a major source of competitive advantage for USA firms relative to their European competitors. USA government procurement from the leading USA companies was much larger than the total equipment purchases by individual European countries (Table 4-7). It is still far from certain whether a single Europe-wide competitive procurement process is politically feasible. Attempts to establish a Europe-wide procurement process still retain a form of the *juste retour* principle. Under Occar, an embryonic common procurement programme, a rough balance between purchases and work is still be maintained over all the programme that Occar manages (*FT*, 14 June 1999).

The contrast in the size of the respective air forces' fighter fleets is dramatic (IISS, 1998). The USA Air Force has a fleet of over 1900 F-15s and F-16s. The combined Tornado fleets of the air forces of Germany, Italy and the UK, amount to only 600 aircraft. Moreover, under present arrangements, the fleets are substantially operated as separate entities, with consequent large increases in operating costs. France's has 345 Mirage fighters, while Sweden's air force has a fleet of just 151 Saab fighters. The implications for the relative development of the military aircraft industry in Europe and the USA are obvious. John Hamre, the USA Deputy Defense Secretary expressed the dilemma as follows: 'You can't have a defense industrial base if you don't buy anything' (quoted in *FT*, 3 June 1999).

Until recently, the scope for international competition in large-scale defence procurement contracts was very limited. The leading USA defence programme, the JSF, still is a purely domestic competition, between Boeing and Lockheed Martin, with European involvement only as sub-contractors. The USA has been very reluctant to award large procurement contracts to non-USA companies. Hardly a single defence contract has been awarded by the Pentagon in which a European-based company is a prime contractor. However, many NATO countries have long relied on large-scale purchases from USA defence companies, often able to offer superior equipment at lower prices. For example, the Anglo–Italian EH-101 helicopter had a unit cost of $126 million, but similar US-built helicopters, benefiting from economies of scale in sales to the USA armed forces cost only $35 million–$66 million (for the AH-64D and CH-47D respectively) (IISS, 1998: 34).

The balance of trade on military exports between the USA and Europe is massively in favour of the USA. In 1998 the USA imported just $1.1 billion worth of arms, mainly from Europe, while Europe imported $7.7 billion worth of arms, mainly from the USA (IISS, 1999: 282). Between 1990 and 1997, the USA sold a total of over 420 F-16s and over 1100 AMRAAM missiles to seven NATO countries (Belgium, Denmark, Greece, Italy, Netherlands, Norway and Turkey) (IISS, 1998). The British navy is considering buying the carrier-borne version of the JSF. The UK is contributing $200 million to the development costs of the aircraft, and 'will consider the JSF as its Harrier replacement for its Future Carrier-Borne Aircraft to go into service in about 14 years' time' (*FT*, 3 September 1998). The potential advantages of the USA giants in open international competition are enormous. If there were to be a truly 'global level playing field' in defence procurement, it is hard to imagine that the USA giants would not win the lion's share of the orders.

The leading European countries have long realized their disadvantage compared to the USA. If they had each produced their own separate fighter in the 1980s and 1990s, the domestic market would have been only around 200–300 in Germany and the UK. In recognition of this, a three-nation consortium was formed in 1970 to produce the Tornado, a multi-role combat aircraft to form the heart of the German, British and Italian fighter force. As we have seen above, around 600 of these have been supplied to the combined air forces of Germany, the UK and Italy. The first aircraft were delivered in 1980. Each of the participating countries' companies[4] was to be responsible for a specific section of the aircraft. BAe was given responsibility for the manufacture of the forward and rear sections of the fuselage, fin and tail, and for final assembly of those aircraft to be delivered to the RAF. This formula for work-sharing was adopted in order to protect the respective national aircraft industries. It greatly reduced the extent of competition in supply of the sub-systems, and lowered potential economies of scale obtainable during assembly. Consequently, costs were much higher than if purely commercial considerations had governed these choices. The problems were to be replicated in other areas of European aerospace co-operation.

The key programme for the future of the European aircraft defence industry is the Eurofighter. The project began in 1983, with the participating nations producing a common fighter design for deployment in the late 1990s. Its history illustrates vividly the difficulties the European aerospace industry faces. It has taken no fewer than 18 years for the project to come to fruition, 'as the controversial project waded its way through a mire of European bureaucracy' (*Sunday Telegraph*, 28 December 1997). The project was halted in 1992 when Germany insisted that a proposal for a cheaper aircraft be studied. Then the whole project was re-launched. There are even doubts about the relevance of a plane designed during the Cold War to the new conditions it will have to meet in warfare in the early twenty-first century. A USA official commented that the Europeans seem stuck in 'already obsolete aircraft like the Eurofighter, that are really job programmes, not modernization for realistic contingencies' (quoted in *IHT*, 12 June 1999).

Instead of being produced by a single company, it is produced by a consortium, composed of British Aerospace, Daimler–Benz Aerospace (Dasa, of Germany), Alenia (Italy) and Casa (Spain). France initially participated in the programme, but left it in 1985, preferring instead to support the 'Rafale' fighter produced by Dassault (France). Sweden also is buying a domestically produced fighter, the 'Gripen' produced by Saab. Thus, Europe's relatively small market, compared to the US, has three competing fighters coming on stream. Even the largest of these, the Eurofighter, is likely to have total sales which are only a fraction of the United States' JSF. The efficiency gains for the USA producers of the JSF will be enormous compared with those of their competitors in Europe.

Instead of work for the Eurofighter being divided through sub-contracting to the best contractor based on purely commercial criteria, work for the fighter is to be divided among the consortium partners in accordance with the orders placed by the respective national governments. Britain is ordering 232, and is taking 37 per cent of the work. Germany is buying 180 aircraft and will take 30 per cent of the work. Italy is buying 121 aircraft, and will take 19 per cent of the work. Spain is buying 87 and will take 14 per cent of the work. Each of the four main companies will have its own separate final assembly plant. Thus, the Eurofighters for the Royal Air Force will be assembled in Lancashire while those for the Luftwaffe will have their final assembly in Munich. In the same fashion as for the Tornado and the Airbus, each of the participating countries will have responsibility for a different portion of the aircraft: BAe, for example, will make the front fuselage, the canards, and the first stage of the after fuselage, while Dasa will make the central fuselage (*FT*, 3 September 1998).

The contrast between the JSF and the Eurofighter is sharp. The JSF has initial orders of around 3000. The Eurofighter has initial orders of around 500 (*FT*, 3 September 1998). The JSF will be produced by a single company, which will source components and sub-systems from wherever is regarded as most advantageous from a purely business perspective. The Eurofighter will be produced by a consortium of four companies, which must divide up the work in proportion to the size of the orders taken by the participating countries (*FT*, 3 September 1998).

Reviewing the current state of the development of the industry in Europe and the USA, the *Financial Times* painted the following brutally frank assessment of the prospects for the European industry: 'The writing on the wall could hardly be larger: the European aerospace and defence industry must consolidate to achieve economies of scale in a shrinking market. If it does not, European defence procurement agencies will inevitably find themselves forced for budgetary reasons to order American equipment' (*FT*, 3 September 1998).

The attempted solution: EADC. The European military aerospace industry must unify or perish before the challenge of the two USA giants. The companies themselves have known this for some time. The military leaders know that they face an increasingly stark choice. Either they agree to the merger of European defence interests into a single company that can produce advanced weaponry at a price that is acceptable to European taxpayers, or they will end up buying US-made weaponry. The governments of France, Britain and Germany belatedly called upon the key companies to produce a concrete plan for merger.

BAe, Aérospatiale and Dasa reported a plan in March 1998 declaring their intention to unify into a single company, with a single management structure, quoted on the stock market (*FT*, 3 September, 1998). The proposal was supported by the respective governments. The intention is to create a single merged company, the European Aérospace and Defence Company (EADC), which incorporates the leading aerospace companies across Europe into a quoted company with a publicly distributed shareholder base. The proposed company would incorporate at least the following: Aérospatiale and Dassault (France), Dasa (Germany), Alenia (Italy), Casa (Spain), Saab (Sweden) and BAe (UK). It is intended that it will incorporate all sectors of the European aerospace industry, including combat aircraft, military transport, guided weapons, large civil aircraft (including a restructured Airbus) helicopters, space and defence electronics.

There still was a large obstacle in the way of the proposal. The French government is keen, as a buyer of defence equipment, to support the formation of a single, more efficient company. It recognizes too the mighty capabilities of the USA giants. However, until 1999, Aérospatiale was a state-owned company. BAe and Dasa were concerned that a state-owned partner would require non-commercial interests to take precedence over purely commercial interest. Manfred Bischoff, chief executive of Dasa commented: 'The agenda of a government is different – with good reason. They don't want you to lay off people, they don't want to close factories' (quoted in *FT*, 10 September 1998). In July 1998, the French government announced that Aérospatiale would be merged with Matra, the defence arm of Lagardère, and that the state would cut its stake to below 50 per cent. Aérospatiale–Matra came into existence in June 1999, with the French state owning 47.7 per cent and Lagardère owning 33 per cent, and 17 per cent was floated in an IPO (*FT*, 4 June 1999). Aérospatiale–Matra had now risen from the world's seventh largest aerospace company by revenue (*Fortune*, 3 August 1998, F-15) to the world's fourth largest, with a revenue of $14.4 billion (*FT*, 4 June 1999). For BAe and Dasa this was still not enough. The prospect of merging with a company in which the state still held a strong ownership position was unacceptable. The two companies 'made it clear that they wanted the company with which they would merge to have no state holding at all' (*FT*, 3 September 1998).

In late 1998 BAe was reported to 'stand on the brink of a merger with Daimler–Chrysler of Germany' (*FT*, 29 December 1998). It was thought that the merger would produce substantial savings, for example in producing the Euro-fighter. However, the merger was 'constructed with politics very much in mind', and it was thought that the new company would form the core of the EADC, to be joined eventually by Aérospatiale after its privatization. However, the merger talks were extremely protracted. One of the main problems was the fact that Dasa's aerospace revenue ($8.5 billion) is only around two-thirds the size of BAe's ($13.7 billion). The German government was acutely sensitive to the possibility of a *de jure* 'merger' that was a *de facto* 'take-over' by BAe of the heart of the German aerospace industry.

The prolonged negotiations between BAe and Dasa were accompanied by intense discussions between GEC–Marconi and a variety of other electronics and aerospace companies. BAe's 'nightmare' was that a USA company such as Lockheed or Raytheon would step in to buy Marconi. This would enable the new company to compete with BAe for UK Ministry of Defence contracts 'wrapped up in the Union Jack' (*FT*, 20 January 1999). The two sets of negotiations were called to an abrupt halt with the announcement of the merger of BAe with GEC–Marconi in January 1999. This move has created the world's third largest aerospace company by total turnover (re-named BAe Systems), with $20.4 billion in 1998, compared to $26.3 billion for Lockheed Martin and $56.2 billion for Boeing (*FT*, 4 June 1999). In terms purely of defence revenues, the new company will be the world's second largest, with sales of $15.8 billion, compared with $18.5 billion for Lockheed Martin, and $13.8 billion for the next largest, Boeing (*FT*, 20 January 1999). The move was widely regarded as seriously setting back the cause of European aerospace integration. Not the least of the problems was that the new BAe was now almost twice the size of Dasa, so that a BAe–Dasa merger would have been even more difficult to structure other than as a take-over of Dasa by BAe.

In June 1999, the transformation of the European aerospace industry took a further turn when the Spanish government privatized the Spanish aerospace manufacturer, Casa. After an intense battle with both Aérospatiale and BAe, Daimler–Chrysler's bid for the company (£1.3 billion) was successful. Daimler–Chrysler is to form a new company which combines its aerospace company, Dasa, with Casa. The new Spanish–German company will have a workforce of 53 000 and annual sales of around $10.9 billion, ranking sixth among the world's largest aerospace companies. The move would increase Dasa's ownership share in Airbus and the Eurofighter to 42 per cent and 43 per cent respectively (*FT*, 12 June 1999).

Hardly had the deal between Dasa and Daimler–Chrysler been concluded than Dasa announced that it was merging with Aérospatiale–Matra. In October 1999 the two entities announced that they would be merging into a new giant company called the European Aircraft, Defence and Space Company or EADS (*FT*, 15 October 1999). The new company would be 60 per cent owned by a holding company split 50/50 between French and German interests. Stock-market investors would be able to buy the remaining 40 per cent of the company. The German interests in the holding company were to be held entirely by Daimler–Chrysler. The French interests were to be held 50 per cent by the French government, 37 per cent by Lagardère, and 13 per cent by French financial institutions. The French government agreed to sell more shares in the partially privatized Aérospatiale to bring its holdings in the new company eventually down to 15 per cent. The new company will have proforma revenues of around $22 billion. The new company will have extensive duplication of functions from the highest level downwards in order to satisfy the national aspirations of France and Germany: 'This sharing of power will make it hard to take the tough decisions on plant closures and job losses. They will be vital if over-capacity in Europe is to be cut, so that the industry becomes sufficiently profitable and can afford long-term investment' (*FT*, 15 October 1999).

However, it was far from certain that the formation of EADS would be followed by the formation of EADC, including BAe Systems. Despite the damage done to the cause of European aerospace integration by BAe's merger with GEC–Marconi, there remains a possibility that EADC will take off. The European governments are all committed to the emergence of a single giant aerospace company which can compete with the USA giants. BAe Systems is still publicly strongly supportive of the EADC, of which it was the originator. It remains deeply embedded in Europe outside the UK. BAe Systems owns a 35 per cent stake in Saab of Sweden and has a joint venture with Matra of France to produce missiles (BAe-Matra Dynamics). Through the merger with GEC–Marconi, it inherited Marconi's own joint ventures, namely Alenia Marconi Systems, Thomson Marconi Sonar, and Matra Marconi Space (*FT*, 20 January 1999). The formation of EADS creates a new company that closely matches the size of BAe Systems. Moreover, the take-over reduces the number of partners involved in the Airbus and Eurofighter programmes, which should simplify discussions about further institutional change.

However, even if Europe is successful in creating the EADC, many new problems will be created by the new entity. In its bid to match the scale of the USA giants, Europe would be attempting to create a potential monopolist within Europe. This creates international political problems, with a 'fortress Europe' confronting a 'fortress America'. It also creates serious economic problems, especially for Europe. The difficulties that would result for regulation policy are enormous. The USA defence budget is so large that it can support two or three huge companies in each product area that can compete with each other. Moreover, the vast domestic platform creates the possibility for a powerful international sales capability in a virtuous circle of competitive advantage for huge USA aerospace companies. It will be a triumph of regulatory ingenuity if the single giant European aerospace company can be induced to operate in a competitive fashion in selling to European governments.

However, there is another route that the global industry could follow.

The alternative: the trans-Atlantic option. As we have seen, it is far from certain that Europe will successfully construct a single giant aerospace company. Strong pressures are pulling in a different direction. Privatized European companies have a strong incentive to globalize. They are seeking to pull away from 'national' allegiances, which drastically restrict the size of their market. Governments face intense pressure to keep defence budgets under control, and obtain better results for their outlays. The Gulf War and the war in former Yugoslavia both demonstrate that much future warfare will be in the form of coalition operations: 'Whether keeping the peace or fighting, their effectiveness depends on their ability to communicate, share information and intelligence' (*FT*, 28 January 1999). However, there is still a dramatic contrast between the high level of integration of the USA armed forces and the lack of centrally-controlled design, purchase and operations in the EU defence forces. The EU not only spends substantially less than the USA but gets far less for its money in terms of systems capability. The Pentagon has a strong military incentive to push the EU towards using common types of defence equipment.

The possibility of military collaboration between the USA and Europe is being undermined by the growing technological gap between leading European and leading USA companies. The war in former Yugoslavia had revealed sharply the nature of that gap: 'European leaders lamented their countries' yawning techno-logical gap with the USA, revealed by the Kosovo war. Europe contributed only a fifth of the warplanes and very little intelligence to the bombing campaign, while mustering even a peacekeeping force showed up deficiencies in logistics' (*FT* Editorial, 20 July 1999). The allied governments were supportive of the war effort, but were unable to conduct high level bombing raids at night due to their inferior technology. Precision-guided munitions were almost monopolized by USA warplanes. Only France and Britain had laser-guided bombs. Even these comparatively advanced European allies remain ill-equipped for what is termed the 'revolution in military affairs' (*IHT*, 14 June 1999). European governments fear a situation in which 'the USA provides the high-technology aerial surveil-lance and smart weapons and it provides the foot soldiers' (*FT*, 1 July 1999).

Privatized EU-based companies are pushing hard to develop their multina-tional characteristics in order to enhance their market beyond the restricted domestic base. The vastly greater 'national' market in the USA allowed large firms to develop at an earlier stage than in the EU. In pursuit of wider markets beyond the home base, both Rolls-Royce and BAe Systems are actively seeking to remove government restrictions on foreign ownership. In each case, the restrictions are now far less than they once were, and there is every likelihood that they will be removed entirely. For example, BAe (then the British Aircraft Corporation) was a state-owned company in 1977, a traditional 'national cham-pion', of great strategic significance due to the importance of the company's mil-itary production. In 1981, 49 per cent of the company was floated, the remainder being floated in 1985, but there was a strict limitation on foreign ownership. By 1998 around 30 per cent of the share ownership was in foreign hands. The British government has permitted the limit on foreign ownership to be lifted to 49 per cent. If the formation of the EADC goes ahead, then the restriction on foreign ownership will fall by the wayside.

Similarly, Rolls-Royce on privatization in 1987 had a limit of 15 per cent on non-UK ownership because of the company's strategic significance, since Rolls-Royce makes almost all the engines used in military aircraft in the UK. However, Rolls-Royce has lobbied steadily to have the figure increased. After earlier allow-ing the limit to rise to 25 per cent, in 1998 the government allowed it to rise to 49 per cent. Rolls-Royce would much prefer that the limit were lifted altogether, since it would give the company access to much wider sources of capital, and it is 'very likely' that this will happen relatively soon.

The USA has the world's largest defence market by far. Leading European aero-space companies are actively seeking work as sub-contractors and risk-sharing partners for the USA giants. They are trying to be both 'European' and 'trans-Atlantic' simultaneously. BAe already has substantial involvement with Boeing, partnering it in the Harrier programme, the T-45 (Hawk) and the Nimrod 2000. It is partnering Lockheed Martin in its development of the carrier-borne version of the JSF, which uses BAe's experience in vertical take-off and landing developed during the Harrier programme. It is also partnering Lockheed in its TRACER land system integration system. BAe and Lockheed Martin are teamed as prime contractors for this programme to supply both the USA and British armed forces with an advanced battlefield reconnaissance system. BAe will have a large role in the development of a possible European Future Large Aircraft for military transport, through its role in Airbus. However, it is simultaneously contemplating co-operating with Boeing as substantial sub-contractor in the supply of the Boeing C-17 globemaster transport aircraft (*FT*, 8 September 1998). Matra BAe Dynamics is co-operating with Hughes in production of the ASRAAM missile.

Rolls-Royce is involved in the USA JSF programme, working with General Electric to develop the F120 engine, one of the two proposed power plants for the JSF. It is working also with Boeing and Lockheed on the short take-off and vertical landing technology to be incorporated into one of the versions of the JSF. It has contracts worth a total of around $500 million to supply engines for the US' C-130J transport aircraft and Kiowa Warrior helicopters as a result of its purchase of Alison (for $530 million) in 1995, which is the sole supplier of engines for the C-130J (Rolls-Royce, 1997: 11).

European aerospace companies are not only trying to expand their role as sub-contractors to the USA giants. According to a senior executive in the British aerospace industry, if the European aircraft industry is, indeed, successfully restructured along the lines of the EADC, then 'in a few years time we could buy one of the USA giants' (quoted in *FT*, 12 October 1998). Indeed, in late 1998 GEC and Lockheed Martin were reported to be considering merging. Despite its immensely powerful position in manufacturing fighter aircraft Lockheed Martin's market capitalization was only around £11 billion, compared to £14.5 billion for GEC (*Sunday Telegraph*, 27 December 1998). Having permitted over $60 billion worth of mergers inside four years, the USA competition authorities chose to veto the merger of Lockheed Martin with Northrop–Grumman. This is a tempting asset for one of the leading European companies, such as BAe or GEC–Marconi, to merge with or take over. In late 1998, GEC was reported to be in discussion about a possible take-over of Northrop Grumman (*FT*, 19 December 1998). In June 1999, it was rumoured that Manfred Bischoff, Head of Dasa, was in discussion with Northrop Grumman about a possible merger (reported in *IHT*, 14 June 1999). Such a take-over would radically change the nature of the Euro–USA defence industry relationship and have a strong impact on the possible formation of the mooted EADC.

The current conjuncture is highly institutionally unstable. One recent expert opinion suggested that the future of the industry would not be with 'one inefficient merged European firm versus the Americans'. He believed that the result would be 'US firms that became European firms and European firms that became American firms, within and across product lines, enhancing competition and efficiency in a broader trans-Atlantic market' (Gordon Adams, Deputy Director, Institute of Strategic Studies, London, quoted in *FT*, 28 January 1999). This perspective was echoed by John Hamre, USA Deputy Defense Secretary. He envisions 'two transatlantic megaconsortiums competing for contracts in both the United States and Europe' (quoted in *IHT*, 14 June 1999). The *FT*'s 1999 survey of world aerospace concluded soberly: 'For the moment Mr Weston's [BAe's Chief Executive] hopes of wider European restructuring remain just hopes. It could be that Europe's largest defence companies look across the Atlantic for their partners instead' (*FT*, 14 June 1999).

The possibilities for a 'transatlantic solution' seemed to be growing stronger in 1999. The USA government is 'intent on educating the public on the need for globalization even in the defense industry' (*IHT*, 14 June 1999). It is moving towards relaxing its controls on foreign investment in the industry and greater technology sharing with European-based defence firms. In July, Jacques Gansler, (Head of Procurement, Pentagon) announced that the Pentagon was willing to allow European or Asian companies to buy major USA defence companies under certain conditions. He predicted a wave of trans-Atlantic mergers over the coming months (*IHT*, 8 July 1999). He believed that such mergers would create 'a huge new defense market' and would make it easier for allies who are likely to fight together in future wars to co-operate on developing common weapons (*IHT*, 8 July 1999). Mr Gansler predicted that the merger process would 'begin within months rather than within years' (quoted in *IHT*, 8 July 1999). He added that the Pentagon was willing to consider take-overs of USA defence corporations like General Dynamics and Northrop Grumman by European firms, but would protect American technology secrets. Mr Gansler said that a condition for allowing such take-overs and mergers was that other countries must reciprocate, allowing similar access to their own markets (*IHT*, 8 July 1999). He confirmed that the Pentagon had discussed the issue with a number of European governments as well as with executives of big defence companies, including British Aerospace, Aérospatiale–Matra, Thompson CSF and the aerospace division of Daimler-Chrysler (*IHT*, 8 July 1999).

It is quite possible that companies that formerly were predominantly defence producers, such as Lockheed Martin or British Aerospace, or predominantly commercial producers, notably, Airbus, might eventually become part of giant trans-Atlantic aerospace companies that include both powerful commercial and defence aerospace divisions.

Implications. If the mooted trans-Atlantic mergers go ahead, the much greater size of the US-based companies make it likely that the new entities will be controlled from the USA. In 1998 the top 6 defence aerospace companies by value of sales were all US-based (Table 4-9). Their combined R & D expenditure, £3.5 billion, greatly exceeded that of the leading companies in the EU. The domestic market is substantially greater than that of the entire EU, and vastly greater than the fragmented markets of individual EU countries. There may be a compelling business case for leading EU-based aerospace companies to merge with the leading USA companies in defence aerospace. This process may also make it much easier for the EU and the USA to fight together in future, since they will have even more common equipment than today. The degree of co-ordination over the world defence aerospace industry that this will provide for the Pentagon will be greatly increased. Moreover, unlike in the past, the countervailing force of the USSR/Russian Federation has dramatically declined.

TABLE **4-9 Relative size of US and EU Aerospace and Defence Companies, 1998 (£ billion)**

Company	Sales	R & D	Profits
Boeing (USA)	33.8	1.14	1.14
Lockheed Martin (USA)	15.8	0.66	1.52
United Technologies (USA)	15.4	0.79	1.30
Raytheon (USA)	11.7	0.35	1.33
Allied Signal (USA)	9.1	0.24	1.28
TRW (USA)	7.1	0.31	0.52
British Aerospace (UK)	7.0	0.43	1.10
Aérospatiale (France)	6.1	0.84	0.25
Northrop–Grumman (USA)	5.4	0.12	0.33
Rolls-Royce (UK)	4.5	0.17	0.38

SOURCE: DTI (1998: 51)

The world defence aerospace industry is entering the new millennium in a dramatically different institutional shape from that of only 10 years ago. The emerging degree of centralization at a global level is unprecedented. This provides a serious challenge to policy-makers across the world. It provides a deep challenge for policy makers in China. Instead of a multi-polar world of numerous defence aerospace producers within different power blocks, a tiny number of giant producers is emerging, with a real possibility that as few as two (perhaps even one) giant trans-Atlantic systems integrators totally dominates the world market for military aircraft. Each of these may be a US-based company with a close relationship to the Pentagon. The possibility for playing off one segment of the global industry against the other in order to acquire new technologies is receding fast.

Civilian aircraft. In the 1950s, each of the main Western European countries had at least one manufacturer of civilian jet aircraft. At that time, Britain alone had eleven aircraft manufacturing companies. Three large jet engine civil airliners were produced in Britain: the De Havilland Comet, the Vickers VC 10, and the Hawker Siddeley Trident. In the 1970s, the diverse aircraft manufacturing capabilities in the UK were mostly unified into a single company, British Aerospace. However, British Aerospace and its counterparts in Continental Europe were still far too small to compete effectively with the might of Boeing. Europe had failed to produce a super-large airliner to compete with the B-747, or even the smaller Lockheed Tristar and McDonnell-Douglas DC-10. The USA aircraft companies, and especially Boeing, were establishing overwhelming dominance in the epoch of rapidly expanding jet travel.

The Airbus partners took the historic decision to attempt to compete head-on with the USA manufacturers before it was too late. Airbus was born in 1970. It began life as a Franco-German joint venture. It was joined by Spain in 1971 and Britain in 1979. There is little dispute that Airbus would not have been able to grow successfully and compete with Boeing without large-scale state aid from the respective governments. The total amount of aid provided is the source of endless debate. However, the British participant in the project, BAe, alone received a loan of around $400 million from the British government to support its wing development programme (*FT*, 14 March 2000). In early 2000 the British government announced that it would contribute a loan of around $860 million to BAe Systems to support development of the wing programme for the A3XX (*FT*, 14 March 2000).

The corporate structure adopted by Airbus reflected the desire to combine economies of scale and scope with the maintenance of national sovereignty and 'national champions' in the aerospace industry within each of the partner countries. Airbus is not a company in the usual sense. It is an 'Association for developing commercial interests' (*Groupement d'intérêt économique*). This is a uniquely French legal construct, which publishes no detailed accounts and makes no profits and losses in its own right. All the profits go directly to the four partners in proportion to their shareholdings. Aérospatiale and Dasa each owns 37.9 per cent, BAe has 20 per cent and Casa 4.2 per cent. Decisions on whether to develop new aircraft require the unanimous consent of the shareholders. While there have been 'years of discussion about how profits should be divided, there have never been any problems in deciding new projects'.

The partners carry out most of the Airbus manufacturing according to the principle of *juste retour*, under which they receive work in proportion to their shareholdings. Aérospatiale makes the cockpits, Dasa the fuselage, BAe the wings and Casa the tail parts. Final assembly is carried out by Aérospatiale at Toulouse for all models except the narrow-bodied A-319 and A-321 which are assembled by Dasa in Hamburg. The structure has ensured that each of the four partner countries has retained a substantial presence in aircraft manufacturing. They have avoided also potentially destructive intra-European rivalry. An important advantage of the Airbus structure is that each of the partners has a specialist focus on a single area of competence, leaving the Airbus company to deal with marketing the product.

The first Airbus aircraft was delivered in 1974, with 100 delivered by 1980, 500 by 1989, and 1000 in 1993. The 2000th Airbus was delivered in 1999, just six years after the 1000th. It is predicted that the 3000th will be delivered in less than three years (*FT*, 14 June 1999).

In recent years Airbus has consistently won around one-third of the world civil aircraft market, while Lockheed and McDonnell–Douglas have gone out of business in civil airliner production. In 1994, Airbus won marginally more orders than Boeing, the first time that Boeing had been toppled from the number one slot since the advent of the jet age. However, Boeing quickly regained the lead in terms of new orders, winning more orders than Airbus between 1995 and 1998. In 1999, Airbus once more overtook Boeing, with orders for around 490 aircraft compared with 390 for Boeing (*FT*, 14 January 2000). During the five years from 1995 to 1999, Boeing won orders for around 2800 aircraft compared with around 1900 for Airbus (*FT*, 14 January 2000). Moreover, in early 2000, Airbus announced that it intended to proceed with plans to build the super-large aircraft, the A3XX.

Despite Airbus' success in capturing market share, it remains a much smaller company than Boeing, with a total turnover in 1998 of just $13 billion compared to $42 billion for Boeing's commercial aircraft division, and a total turnover of $51 billion (*IHT*, 10 July 1999 and *Fortune*, 2 August 1999). In 1998, Boeing delivered 563 aircraft compared to 229 for Airbus. The advantage of scale is still decisively with Boeing. Boeing's production arrangements are old-fashioned compared with those of Airbus: 'Most Boeing production facilities are based on techniques that date from the days of building bombers for World War Two. The boys in Seattle are fixing wings to the fuselage with rivet guns. At Airbus it's all done by computers and robots' (Chris Avery, aviation analyst at Banque Paribas, quoted in *Observer*, 6 September 1998). The sub-sections of each Airbus plane are produced by the partners, and then shipped to the location of final assembly, where they are 'snapped together' by small crews. In sharp contrast with Boeing, which employed 227 000 people in 1998 (*Fortune*, 26 April 1999), Airbus employs just 3000 people (*IHT*, 10 July 1999). A total of around 37 000 people are estimated to be employed producing Airbus aircraft within the constituent companies (*Fortune*, 2 August 1999). Airbus is responsible only for design, sales, marketing and flight testing. In this sense, Airbus is the ultimate in a lean, 'outsourced', and 'systems integrator' company.

Shocked by the production difficulties in 1997 and the accompanying losses, Boeing is already drastically overhauling its production arrangements. There is huge scope to increase efficiency: 'A company as powerful as Boeing will not stay down for long, and it will come back gunning for Airbus' (*Observer*, 6 September 1998). Noel Forgeard, Airbus' chief executive warns: 'Our competitor is not the Boeing of today. It is the Boeing that will be, that is to say, probably a more streamlined, rejuvenated Boeing. That is what we have to prepare ourselves for' (quoted in *IHT*, 10 July 1999). Boeing's restructuring is now in full swing, having absorbed McDonnell-Douglas. It can turn its full attention to the battle with Airbus. Airbus' restructuring has hardly started.

The Airbus structure has deep in-built difficulties that inhibit the long-run competitiveness of Airbus in the battle with Boeing. For a long period, the partners refused even to disclose their profits to each other, for fear that the price paid by the central management would be reduced if the declared profits were considered to be too high. Consequently, the central management had no idea of how much it cost to make the aircraft. A purely commercial company should be able to place orders with the lowest cost source, not bound by sourcing tied to one of the partners for each section of the aircraft. This approach was only accepted by the partners in principle in 1996, and will take time to implement. There are large vested interests in favour of maintaining the *juste retour* principle.

In 1996 Airbus began the attempt to transform itself from a '*Groupement d' intérêt économique*' into a limited company floated on the stock market. Airbus's restructuring and the associated restructuring of the European defence industry has hardly begun. The operation is so complex that it is hard to imagine that it will not to some degree adversely influence the industry's performance during the turbulence that will inevitably accompany the restructuring. If Airbus does succeed in becoming a limited company with all the Airbus factories placed within the company, then there will be large arguments over which should be shut down, as the new entity seeks to reduce costs in its bid to compete with Boeing.

The constituent companies are at very different stages of internal restructuring. In 1992 BAe incurred 'the largest loss in British commercial history', following its extensive diversification in the late 1980s. This took BAe 'close to bankruptcy'. It was followed by a dramatic change in the company's operating methods, including drastic downsizing, shrinking the total numbers employed by around 55 per cent. This was a 'painful process'. Alongside this, the company drastically reorganized its management methods in a drive to reduce costs and focus remorselessly on customers and profits. The company shed unprofitable subsidiaries, or ones which deflected attention and resources from the core business of aerospace. Although BAe had only been a state-owned enterprise from 1977 to 1981 (it was not fully privatized until 1985), the management system was close to that of a traditional state-owned enterprise, with multiple layers of management and extensive restrictive practices. After 1991 it comprehensively changed the former 'bureaucratic' approach to managing the company. The cost base in the defence business fell by around 40 per cent in just three years.

In the new pan-European company BAe's management style would have to connect with the very different approach of the still partially French state-owned company, Aérospatiale–Matra as well as with that of the largest single shareholder in the new EADS, namely Daimler-Chrysler. It would be a huge managerial achievement if the cultural differences between the German, French and British entities could be successfully merged into a common business culture. At the very least, it is likely, that if the new entity were indeed formed, a great deal of management energy would have to be expended on developing a common culture and resolving the necessary issues of downsizing and location of key common sites. If this was not done, the resulting duplication of functions might impose serious cost burdens on the newly-formed company. The signs from EADS were not promising in this regard. The comprehensive duplication of functions among the French and British parties seen at BAe–Matra were replicated on a larger scale at EADS: 'EADS will have two chairmen (Manfred Bischoff of Dasa and Jean-Luc Lagardère of Aérospatiale–Matra), two chief executives, two headquarters. It will operate in three cultures, with four languages (including the official language – English)' (FT, 3 January 2000).

It would be a complex political task for the BAe approach to be adopted by Aérospatiale–Matra, probably involving substantial job losses, factory closures and changes in working practices. These might be perceived as Anglo–Saxon impositions upon the 'French' approach to running Aérospatiale–Matra. The changes in working practices and employment levels may be perceived as being non-symmetrical, since the bulk of the adjustment may be on the French side, the 'adjustments' having already been made in BAe. Moreover, the largest single owner within EADS will be Daimler–Chrysler.

The European aerospace industry has been preoccupied with the intense struggle over defence industry restructuring. It was planned that Airbus would have been turned into a single company in 1999. However, the talks on restructuring Airbus made little progress. Aérospatiale was concerned at the possibility of Dasa and BAe merging, which would squeeze Aérospatiale. Then Dasa was surprised by BAe's merger with GEC–Marconi. This was followed in short order by Dasa's announcement of a merger with Casa, Aérospatiale's partial privatization and merger with Matra, and then by Dasa's merger with the new Aérospatiale–Matra. The way ahead now seemed clearer for turning Airbus into a single company, with only two owners, one of which had a dominant ownership stake in the entity. Following the merger of Dasa and Aérospatiale–Matra, EADS–Casa will hold 80 per cent of Airbus, compared with just 20 per cent for BAe Systems. This should make it much easier to turn Airbus into a single company.

However, the final shape of the European aerospace industry is far from certain. There is reported to be a deep legacy of distrust between Dasa and BAe as a result of the BAe/GEC–Marconi merger. The final shape of the relationship between the defence and civilian aerospace industry in the USA and Europe is far from resolved. In the background lurks the perennial possibility of any of the main players moving into a deeper relationship with the USA aerospace industry. The head of Aérospatiale Matra believes that it is 'far from inevitable' that Airbus will become a single company: 'I think, frankly speaking, one of the reasons the Airbus discussion failed in the past is that all the partners had, and still have, other fields in which they are either competing or co-operating... If you don't address the global picture, it is very difficult to solve a partial problem because of the complexity of the relationships' (quoted in *FT*, 14 June 1999).

In sum, the future for Airbus is uncertain.

General Difficulties for Europe. 'Europe' is still very far from being a single country. In the USA, the government has powerfully supported the development of global giants in the aerospace industry, to the extent that Boeing is a 'giant' in both defence and civil aircraft. However, Europe still faces considerable difficulties compared to the USA in achieving restructuring. The USA aerospace and defence companies are all subject to the same legal system, speak the same language, have similar business cultures and have the USA government as their biggest defence customer. The difficulties involved in full European aerospace integration were revealed in the Matra–BAe Dynamics joint venture. The 'French' approach is 'Cartesian' – decide the best solution in theory and then put it into practice, whereas the 'British' approach is pragmatic – test it and if it doesn't work, change it. Moreover, the simple difficulties resulting from the absence of a common language were underestimated. It may prove easier to build a 'global' company, or a Euro–American company, based on the English language, than it does to create a truly integrated European company.

The European governments are all in principle in favour of consolidation. However, there is still a reluctance to buy defence equipment from neighbouring countries' manufacturers, as we have seen from the example of the Eurofighter. The fact that the national governments were the main customers for defence industry products presents major problems for European companies compared with their US-based competitors. These were frankly recognized by Manfred Bischoff on the formation of EADS. He acknowledged that attention to national concerns is necessary to satisfy customers and win orders, and that this some-times means doing things that are sub-optimal from a business point of view: 'We have to live with ambiguity. We will have to be a national and a transnational company ... As long as Europe is not the United States of Europe, with one pro-curement office, we will need national representation ... But there is nothing new in a company having to do ambiguous things and managing conflicts of interest' (quoted in *FT*, 3 January 2000).

European governments are still unwilling to allow their national aerospace and defence companies to disappear into a pan-European group: 'People don't get excited by national feelings over who owns a dishwasher company. But they do get excited over who owns their missiles company, who owns Airbus, who owns Ariane' (Manfred Bischoff, Chief Executive of Dasa, quoted in *FT*, 3 January 2000). For example, although Matra–BAe Dynamics is an independent joint ven-ture between a French and a British-based company, there are still agreed key aspects of technology that are not allowed to cross domestic 'firewalls' into the other country. Moreover, assembly, integration and testing is carried on at two separate sites, in order to satisfy national security requirements in Britain and France. This is deeply deleterious to cost reduction in the face of the competition from USA companies such as Raytheon which face a single huge national market.

Although big steps forward have been taken with the Airbus restructuring, there will still be a significant period of time during which the respective national governments' share ownership will continue unchanged. It is still unclear how far and for how long work-sharing arrangements among partner countries will per-sist from the original Airbus arrangement.

The difficulties for European aerospace restructuring will not end with the formation of a single aerospace company. There are severe difficulties with cross-cultural management. The cross-national companies that have already been formed in different branches of European aerospace have encountered consider-able problems. In some cases, the newly formed entities have come very close to breaking up altogether.

Aero-engines. The barriers to entry are at least as great in aero-engines as in aircraft design and manufacture. Extremely advanced skills of system integration are required to manufacture modern engines to power modern large jets safely and economically. In the early days of jet aircraft manufacture there was a large number of aero-engine manufacturers. Indeed, aircraft manufacturers frequently manufactured their own engines. However, the shift to large-scale modern jets radically transformed the picture, causing a step change in technical require-ments. Engines for large-scale commercial jets require massive testing facilities and highly demanding system integration skills. The pressure for reducing sys-tem costs and increasing quality has been passed right down through the value chain from the final consumers through the airlines, the aircraft makers, the engine makers and the components and sub-systems suppliers.

The development costs have increased steadily as the demands from aircraft makers have risen in response to the demands from airlines for cheaper and more reliable aircraft. The development costs for Rolls-Royce's crucial Trent series engine are reported to be over $800 million. Pratt and Whitney spent $800 million developing its PW400 engines series, while GE spent $1.5 billion creating its GE-90 engine for the B-777 (*FT*, 24 November 1995). The huge cost of developing new engines is forcing the top three manufacturers to think increasingly about collaboration among themselves to make new engine types, and to work with risk-sharing partners on particular engines. Rolls-Royce and Pratt and Whitney are partners in International Aero Engines, a consortium which produces the V2500 engine for the Airbus family. GE and Pratt and Whitney have agreed to collaborate in order to produce the engines for a 600-seat airliner should either Boeing or Airbus decide to produce it. GE and SNECMA have a long-standing partnership. Moreover, as we have seen, there is a web of alliances connecting the key system integrators with smaller engine companies, with whom they risk-share or simply sub-contract work. While Rolls-Royce, Pratt and Whitney, and GE between them produce almost all large aero-engines, there are around a dozen manufacturers who each produce more than $100 million worth of aero-engine components and sub-systems for the global leaders.

A key part of the competitiveness of aero-engine makers is the build up of their stock of engines on aircraft. These need to be extensively serviced over a typically long life, and are then often replaced with up-dated versions of the engine. An entire engine programme for a particular aircraft typically lasts 30 or 40 years. This provides a powerful source of long-term income, termed 'embedded value'. A large 'embedded value' enables established players to out-compete new entrants on price, and provides them with a source of revenue to support technical progress and withstand competitive pressure better than new entrants.

There are now only three engine makers left that have the capability to produce large modern jet aircraft engines. Rolls-Royce has greatly increased its market share since the 1980s. In 1997 it occupied around 34 per cent of civil aero-engine orders by value, compared to around 53 per cent won by GE and 13 per cent by Pratt and Whitney, which has fallen to the position once occupied by Rolls-Royce (*FT*, 6 March 1998). Some industry analysts consider that even three players may be one too many. Unlike Pratt and Whitney, which is part of United Technologies, or GE engines, which is a part of GE, the world's largest company by market capitalization, Rolls-Royce is a much smaller company, which is primarily involved in the manufacture of aircraft engines. It is much more vulnerable than either Pratt and Whitney or GE. If the aircraft cycle dips, Rolls-Royce has far smaller alternative businesses to fall back on. Once the limit on foreign ownership is lifted, it is possible that Rolls-Royce could become the object of a take-over bid from either Pratt and Whitney or GE. Equally, Rolls-Royce might be able to take over Pratt and Whitney, which has experienced sharply declining performance in recent years.

Not only has the aero-engine market become a tri-opoly, but the market is fairly segmented. GE is strongly dominant in the market for low and medium-thrust engines for planes such as the B-737 and A-320, while Rolls-Royce is the main player in the high-thrust market. Rolls-Royce has around 40 per cent of the global market for 'high-thrust' engines of over 65 000 lb thrust to power wide-bodied high capacity aircraft such as the B-747. Moreover, it is increasingly the case that only one engine maker supplies a particular aircraft. For example, CFM, a joint venture between SNECMA and GE, is the sole supplier for the Boeing B-737 and Airbus A-340. Rolls-Royce is the sole supplier for the Airbus A-340-600.

The extent of the barriers to entry can be gauged by the fact that even large companies with high levels of technology already cannot directly produce large modern aircraft engines. In the 1980s, BMW wished to re-enter the aero-engine market. It realized that it could not do this directly, so it established a joint venture with Rolls-Royce to jointly produce small regional jet aircraft engines. Mitsubishi Heavy Industries concluded that the only way to upgrade its aero-engine capability was through joint ventures (JVs). It established joint ventures with both Rolls-Royce and General Electric as sub-system manufacturer and risk-sharing partner.

The linkage between military and civilian applications is especially strong in engine manufacture. Almost every one of the USA's vast fleet of military aircraft uses either Pratt and Whitney or GE engines. It is impossible to imagine that the civilian side of the respective businesses does not derive great commercial gain from having a colossal production base, wholly protected from international competition, powerfully supported by government R & D in order to ensure the defence of the USA.

In the 1960s 70 per cent of Rolls-Royce's sales came from the military, and technology acquired in manufacturing military planes was important in helping Rolls-Royce rapidly boost its share of the civilian aircraft market from 4 per cent in the early 1980s to 34 per cent in 1997. It was not 'privatization' *per se* that accounted for the transformation in Rolls-Royce's fortunes in the civilian aircraft market, but its high technical capabilities arising from being a huge maker of military aircraft engines. Hitherto these capabilities had been only weakly applied to profit-making in the civilian sector. By 1997, military sales had declined to only one-third of Rolls-Royce's total sales. The much smaller number of military planes produced in Europe than in the USA has been a severe barrier to Rolls-Royce's capacity to grow in the military sector. Not only is the total number of planes smaller, but substantial sections of the market are reserved for 'national' manufacturers. Most of Sweden's fighter planes are powered by Volvo engines and France's are almost entirely powered by SNECMA engines.

STRATEGIC CHOICES FOR DEVELOPING COUNTRIES

Barriers to Entry. Barriers to entry are of different types and levels in different industries. Morgan Stanley estimate that Boeing and Lockheed Martin have

sustainable competitive advantage of no fewer than 20 to 25 years (MSDW, 1998a:
33). However, this evaluation is in respect of well-funded sophisticated competitors
in the advanced economies. Rolls-Royce believes that it is impossible that a new
entrant could catch up with the three leading players. As the following analysis will
suggest, if one considers catch-up in developing countries, then it is hard to put a
figure on the length of time it would take even a strongly supported domestic firm
to 'catch-up' in aerospace. The gap in this sector is now so wide that it is hard to
conceive of any length of time during which it might be feasible for an aerospace
company in any developing country to catch-up other than in niche sectors.

Military procurement. Military procurement in both the USA and Europe is
vast compared with the rest of the world. Defence purchases by USA and
European governments account for around 60 per cent of the world total, and a
small number of Middle Eastern countries accounts for a large fraction of the
remainder. Developing countries have no way to support indigenous military aircraft manufacturers through procurement in the way that the USA and Europe are
able to do. We have already noted the huge disparity in the size of key government procurement programmes between the USA and Europe.

Many important civilian aerospace products, including aeroplanes, engines
and avionics, had their origins in military programmes. Often, products have a
dual use, such as civilian aircraft used as military transport planes. Even after the
recent changes in procurement practices, it is often the case that the margins are
higher on military products, especially as the product is typically bespoke without competitors. Military programmes work in different cycles from civilian, so
that large military procurement provides stability to the earnings of aerospace
companies which produce both military and civilian products.

Export credit guarantees. These play a vital role in promoting aircraft exports
by European and USA manufacturers. Developing countries have no way to
match such expenditure by the government, which forms very large effective
subsidies from the taxpayers to the exporters. The American Eximbank is popu-
larly called the 'Boeing Bank' after its largest client (Ruigrok and van Tulder,
1995: 50). In 1997 BAe earned 89 per cent of its revenue from overseas sales.
BAe 'would not be in business without export credit guarantees'. A developing
country that seeks to support the development of an indigenous aircraft industry
cannot contemplate providing export credits on anything remotely approaching
the scale provided by the European governments, let alone the USA.

Co-finance of industrial development. This has been an important part of
aerospace industry development in some of the advanced economies, notably
Britain. For example, by 1997 BAe had repaid £316 million in government launch
aid that had been provided after the early 1980s to support the A-320 programme.
Rolls-Royce's Trent series engines have been crucial to the company's long-term
development and present prospects. The Trent series engines grew out of the
RB-211 programme which was developed to power the Lockheed Tristar. The

British government's launch aid support was important in the RB-211's development. In 1998 Rolls-Royce obtained a further £200 million in government launch aid for the Trent 500 and 600 series engines, and BAe was awarded £123 million in launch aid for the development of the A-340-500/600 wing. Launch aid constitutes a risk-sharing, long-term loan, to be repaid at an agreed rate when sales pass a certain point, with the government joining the firm as a risk-sharing partner, but non-repayable if the project fails. These are very large amounts of government support compared to the amounts that developing country governments would have available to support an emerging aircraft industry.

R & D spending by the aerospace companies. As we shall see, the annual R & D spend of AVIC in 1997 cannot be more than $70 million (assuming 10 per cent of aerospace sales is spent on R & D), and is probably considerably below this figure. This compares with over $2 billion for Boeing (after the merger with McDonnell–Douglas), $1.3 billion for Aérospatiale, $800 million for Lockheed Martin, $700 million for GE and Rockwell, $500 million for BAe and $400 million for Rolls-Royce (Table 4-2). This is a vast disproportion, which dramatically influences the catch-up capabilities of developing countries' aircraft industries. China has certainly the largest aerospace industry among developing countries, (if one excludes the former USSR from the ranks of 'developing countries'), yet the roughly estimated total R & D budget for the whole Chinese industry, including aircraft, engines and airborne equipment is pathetic compared to that of the global giants. As we shall see, China is technically able to build aircraft, including large civilian jets, military aircraft, engines and avionics. However, given the disparity of R & D spend, the catch-up possibilities are negligible if it relies purely on domestic R & D.

R & D support from government. All of the advanced economies have large government outlays to support R & D. In 1970, 65 per cent of total national R & D expenditure in France came from the government, compared to 58 per cent in the USA and 45 per cent in Germany (Table 4-10). These are very large fractions indeed, and provided a powerful boost to the competitive advantage of high-technology Western businesses, helping them to attain their pre-eminence in the

TABLE **4-10 Share of R & D Spending Financed by Government, 1970 and 1990 (%)**

Country	*Share of R & D financed by government*		*Share of R & D financed by government, excluding defence-related expenditures*	
	1970	*1990*	*1970*	*1990*
France	65	49	54	34
USA	58	46	40	26
Germany	45	33	38	30
Japan	28	19	28	18

SOURCE: Fransman (1995: 107)

epoch of high globalization in the 1990s. The aerospace industry has consistently been one of the main recipients of government support for R & D. Even in 1990, the share of total R & D that was funded by the government stood at 54 per cent in France, 40 per cent in the USA and 38 per cent in Germany.

The share of defence spending in total government support for R & D has consistently been very large in the USA, accounting for 39 per cent in 1970 and 43 per cent in 1990 (derived from Table 4-10). The main avenue of USA government financial support for the aircraft industry is not through launch aid, but through support for R & D. There is enormous debate about the extent of this, and the degree to which support for military R & D spins off into the commercial sector of the respective companies. It is almost impossible to estimate this. The sums involved in the USA government's support of R & D for military and space industry usage are large. For example, McDonnell–Douglas (now Boeing) received $160 million in contracts from NASA under the advanced composite materials programme to build and test full-scale transport aircraft structures in composite materials to use in air transport wings. Boeing has 250 people working on airframe technology under a $440 million contract from NASA, linked to its high-speed transport programme. One estimate suggests that for every dollar that it spends on military procurement, the USA government spends an additional 83 cents on R & D for future equipment. In Europe, the figure is estimated to be only 34 cents (*FT*, 15 November 1997).

Developing countries' aircraft businesses cannot remotely hope to receive the enormous support that leading aerospace businesses in the West, and especially in the USA, have received from their national governments.

The Example of Japan. The barriers to entry analyzed above raise profound questions about the possibility of developing countries catching-up through the construction of their own indigenous large aircraft firms. This in turn has deep implications for the conduct of international relations. In the past, 'catch-up' in some of the most successful 'latecomer' countries, notably Japan and South Korea, was thought of as not just raising the level of industrialization and income. It was thought of also as constructing indigenously owned firms that could compete with the world's leading companies. Japan and South Korea both set out specifically to re-create the oligopolistic structure of advanced capitalism (Amsden and Singh, 1994).

With government support and protection Japan and South Korea created world-beating large firms in automobiles, steel, heavy engineering and consumer electronics, such as Toyota, Nissan, Toshiba, New Japan Steel, Sony, Mitsubishi Heavy Electrical, Hyundai, Posco, and Samsung. For example, in the early 1950s the Japanese automobile industry, was massively dominated by Ford and General Motors. By the late 1960s, with the support of government industrial policies, Japan had developed its own indigenous giants, able to challenge the supremacy of the global leaders (Nester, 1991).

Japan independently developed a huge capability to manufacture military aircraft in the 1930s and 1940s. We have seen that in the USA, the massive expansion of the USA's technical and institutional base in the Second World War provided the springboard for the rise of the indigenous aerospace industry to world dominance by the late 1960s. In the sharpest contrast, Japan's aerospace industry was dismantled after the defeat of 1945. Once it was permitted to do so, Japan tried hard to develop an independent aircraft industry: 'In recent years, Japan's aerospace industry has been one long crusade to develop a home grown aircraft, including engines, that could compete in the fierce world market... The industry has long been nurtured by the government in the hope that Japan might some day boast a Boeing or a Rolls-Royce' (*FT*, 10 January 1997).

From the late 1950s to the early 1970s Mitsubishi Heavy Industries, Japan's largest aerospace company, developed the 60-seat YS-11, a part state, part private venture. This was to be Japan's first indigenous civil airliner. It was propeller-driven and sold 184 units. Just as it was coming into full production, the world moved on to jet airliners. The industry and the government recognized that the project was commercially infeasible and 'swallowing their pride, terminated the project in 1973' (*FT*, 10 January 1997). The government and Japanese industry gradually was forced to abandon the hope of building an indigenous aircraft industry: 'It became apparent that the project had to be large-scale to be commercially successful' (*FT*, 10 January 1997). As aerospace development has become increasingly costly, and dominated by big players, 'the chance of Japanese companies making a commercial aircraft or engine on their own has receded' (*FT*, 10 January 1997). Even Japanese industry admits that it is difficult to develop something new or different that might help it to compete with the offerings of the established players: 'While Japanese companies probably do have the technology to make a civil aircraft on their own, but, as the YS-11 showed, without proven reliability of companies like Boeing or Airbus and with no marketing expertise, it is unlikely that such an aircraft would be commercially viable' (*FT*, 19 January 1997).

Japan has not formally given up hope of the objective of building an indigenous airliner. The government continues feasibility studies on a 100-seater jet airliner, the YS-X. It hopes to sell not just within Japan but believes 'there is tremendous demand... particularly in emerging economies such as China' (*FT*, 10 January 1997). However, after three years of studying the commercial viability of the project, the YS-X project had failed to progress beyond the feasibility stage.

In practice, Japan's jet aerospace development has been confined entirely to sub-contracting and partnerships with the global giants of the industry. Increasingly, Japanese aerospace companies regard the way forward as collaboration rather than building indigenous capability to manufacture the entire engine or aeroplane. 'It is impossible for Japanese companies to do it on their own. This is the best way, in terms of technology and costs, to participate in global engine projects' (Kawasaki official, quoted in *FT*, 10 January 1997). Kawasaki Heavy Industries, one of Japan's leading aerospace companies, has taken a 6 per cent stake in Rolls-Royce's Trent 900 programme, in order to sustain its capability in the aerospace field. Japanese manufacturers are involved also in the development of GE's CF34-8C engine (*FT*, 10 January 1997). Japan's major aero-engine manufacturers have risk-sharing partnerships with each of the world's leading companies, Pratt and Whitney, GE and Rolls-Royce, with total annual revenues from engine sub-systems alone of around $1.5 billion.

Japan's leading manufacturers took part in the development of the Boeing B-767, with a 15 per cent stake, their first major collaboration in aircraft manufacture, and have taken a 22 per cent stake in the B-777. By participating as stakeholders, Japanese aerospace manufacturers are becoming risk-sharing partners, and can participate in the profits that the engines and aircraft will eventually bring.

The Example of the USSR. As we have seen, the USSR had a very large aircraft industry. It produced a wide range of advanced military aircraft, including bombers from Tupolev, and fighters from MiG (Mikoyan– Gurevich) and Sukhoi. Despite the Soviet collapse, Russia still produces some of the world's most advanced fighter aircraft, notably the Su-27 'Flanker', which entered service in 1984. It is a high-performance fighter of the 'relaxed-stability' type with a fly-by-wire control system. It was the USSR's first 'look-down/shoot-down' fighter. The Su-27 has been radically updated into the Su-35 'Flanker' which used an advanced 'thrust vector control' system. It was supposed to go into service in 1996, but its introduction was delayed due to Russia's intense financial problems. In addition, by the early 1990s Russia was producing the Su-30, which is considered to be 'among the best [fighter aircraft] in the world' (*FT*, 5 December 1996).

Although Russia still possesses a reservoir of immense skill and technical capability in its military aircraft sector, the industry is declining seriously due to the collapse in domestic government procurement and negligible ability of the state to support technical development in aerospace. The level of state procurement has fallen far more severely than in the West. It is estimated that orders from Russia's armed forces have fallen by more than two-thirds since the late 1980s. This has seriously affected the industry's development.

The industry's export capabilities have slumped. The Russian state now has a drastically reduced capability to invest in R & D. Unlike the leading Western arms exporters, Russian arms exporters have little or no support from export credit agencies. These formerly helped support Russian arms exports to countries such as Syria, Libya, North Korea, Cuba and Vietnam. The former captive markets in Eastern Europe have largely disappeared. As these countries attempt to enter NATO, they have mostly turned towards the West's arms manufacturers for upgrading old equipment and for producing new generations of equipment. Often this has been accompanies by local joint venture investment by the Western manufacturer. The Russian industry has remained predominantly under state ownership with little modernization of management practices.

In the mid-1980s, the USSR exported arms worth over $31 billion (at 1997 prices), and accounted for over 35 per cent of the world total of international arms sales (Table 4-11). Its exports were one-third greater than even those of the USA. By 1997, Russia's arms exports had shrunk to less than one-tenth of the level of the USSR in 1987. Its share of the world total had fallen to under 6 per cent. Alongside Russia's collapse, the USA had almost sustained the real value

TABLE **4-11** **Russian Defence Output (Selected Items) and Exports, 1990 and 1997**

Item	1990*	1997
Output of:		
Bombers	40	0
Fighters/Ground attack planes	430	35
Transport aircraft	120	0
Helicopters**	450	70
Exports ($ billion)	16.3	2.5

SOURCE: IISS (1998: 106); *FT* (5 December 1996)

NOTES: * Former USSR
** Including civilian production

of its arms exports, and its share of international arms sales had risen from 27 per cent in 1987, to 45 per cent in 1997.

The combination of a collapse in both domestic procurement and international arms sales had almost destroyed Russia's arms production base. Between 1990 and 1997 Russia's production of fighters fell from 430 to 35, production of bombers fell from 40 to 0, and production of transport aircraft fell from 120 to 0 (Table 4-11).

The former USSR also had a very large civilian aircraft industry. As we have seen, it built over 700 Tu-134s, loosely based on the McDonnell–Douglas DC-9 series, and over 1000 Tu-154s, loosely based on the Boeing B-727. However, production has virtually ceased, and their reputation has been damaged by a series of crashes and poor publicity surrounding planes built in the former USSR. There is no sign of them being up-dated with new versions such as Boeing is doing with the B-717/MD-95. The production costs appear to be beyond the financial capabilities of Russian industry and the market in which they would be competing is the most intensely competitive in the world. In the late 1990s Tupolev was reportedly building a twin-engine plane (the Tu-204) loosely based on the Airbus A-320 series. It uses Rolls-Royce RB211-535 engines. The avionics are from Rockwell-Collins, Honeywell and other Western manufacturers. It was flight-tested in 1992 and certified by Russian aviation authorities in 1995. A small number of the Tu-204 has been produced and entered service within Russia, but the plane has not entered full production. The plane has only so far won a single international commercial order, from Sirocco, an Egyptian leasing company, which agreed to buy fifteen of the aircraft for leasing to airlines (*FT*, 24 August 1999).

Ilyushin produced two versions of a four-engined plane loosely based on the Airbus A-340. The Il-86 was the first wide-bodied plane built in the Soviet Union. It seats 350 passengers. It entered service in 1980. It was handicapped by the fact that its 'turbofans were antique by world standards, and the plane never met its range targets' (*Jane*'s, 1996: 69). A total of only 100 Il-86s was built, and 'many of these were inoperable' (*Jane*'s, 1996: 69). They are used 'only on Russia's fragmented post-Aeroflot airlines, such as Vnukovo and Sibavia'

(*Jane's*, 1996: 69). However, the plane is being up-dated with the co-operation of General Electric and SNECMA, in order to improve the performance of the engines: 'If they are successful, the Il-86 fleet could be given a second chance, with greater range and a Stage 3 noise rating' (*Jane's*, 1996: 69).

The Ilyushin Il-96 is a development of the Il-86, also based on the A-340. It entered service in 1992, but 'due to financial problems only a handful of Il-96s has been built', and they have all been delivered to domestic airlines. The planes are being 'Westernized' with the co-operation of USA manufacturers. The latest variant of the aircraft uses Pratt and Whitney engines and Rockwell–Collins avionics. However, the aircraft has only won a handful of orders, and virtually none in the international market.

The Tu-204 and Il-96 are the strongest attempts in the world today to build serious competitors to the established giants in the field of large commercial aircraft. However, even these only have the slightest chance of commercial success due to the fact that they use engines and avionics purchased from the established giants. Compared to developing countries, the former USSR possessed a very advanced aerospace industry. However, orders for the Tu-204 and Il-96 still appear to be very limited at best and there is no sign of them penetrating markets outside Russia. It will be extremely difficult for them to establish a convincing operating record, and this will drastically limit their sales and revenue for future development. The Russian state is totally incapable of providing financial support for their development. Their best hope lies in limited domestic markets among airlines searching for low priced planes to replace aged fleets bought in the Soviet era. However, it is not certain if the price of these aircraft would indeed match those of the Western giants.

The Example of Brazil. Alone among developing countries, Brazil may be on the verge of building a successful national aerospace industry, though it is still too early to record a final verdict on the endeavour. In 1969, as part of its import-substitution-based industrial policy, the Brazilian government founded a state-owned national aerospace corporation. The company manufactured several thousand small aircraft, including some military aircraft and small civilian turbo-prop planes. The company employed several thousand people, but its total revenues were minute in international terms. In 1994, as part of the privatization drive in Brazil, the company was auctioned. It was bought by three principal shareholders, who between them owned 89 per cent of the company's shares. They were all domestic entities: Bozano Simonson, a powerful conglomerate, SISTEL, and PREVI, the country's largest and second-largest pension funds, respectively. The Brazilian state still retained a 7 per cent holding in the company.

Embraer's development after privatization followed closely the path blazed by Bombardier (Canada). Bombardier was the first company to supply small regional jets. Its first 50-seater jet plane was delivered in 1992. The launch of the jet coincided with a boom in demand stemming from several factors. The first was the deregulation of the North American airline industry, leading to rapid growth in regional airlines. The second was the shift in passenger preference for jets over turbo props, due to comfort, noise levels and perceived safety. A third factor was the advances in technology that made it possible for regional jets to compete on cost with turbo props. Moreover, the long-term prospects for demand in developing countries are thought to be extremely positive, due to the need for planes that can land on short runways with unsophisticated infrastructure, and can meet passenger needs for journeys of several hundred kilometres in areas of poorly developed rail and road systems.

Bombardier developed rapidly from a small-scale aerospace firm into the world's number three commercial aircraft producer in a short space of time. Its aerospace revenues rose from $1.8 billion in 1994 to $4.4 billion in 1999 (predicted) (*FT*, 11 June 1999). Its aerospace division reported pre-tax profits of 9.8 per cent of gross earnings in 1998. Bombardier rapidly developed the skills of systems integration needed to build a modern jet aircraft. It finances, designs, markets and assembles planes using components from a group of the world's leading suppliers. Its supplier network includes its subsidiary Shorts (Northern Ireland) for wings, General Electric (USA) for engines, Rockwell (USA) for avionics, Mitsubishi (Japan) for fuselage parts and Intertechnique (France) for the fuel system (*FT*, 12 June 1997). Bombardier's aerospace revenues grew from $3.4 billion in 1995 to $6.4 billion in 1999 (predicted) (*FT*, 11 June 1999). Bombardier's Canadair RJ-500 (50-seat plane) has captured a large share of the regional jet market (an estimated 46 per cent of the world's 20–90 seat regional jet market (*FT*, 11 June 1999). By 1999 it had a total of over 500 firm orders for the Canadair RJ-500. In 1999, Bombardier launched its new 70-seater jet, for which it announced orders of 236. It is considering producing a new 90–110-seater jet. The development cost of the new aircraft is estimated to be over $1 billion (*FT*, 14 June 1999).

Embraer's rapid expansion after privatization followed closely in the footsteps of Bombardier. It produced its first commercial jet aircraft in 1996, the ERJ-135, with 37 seats. This was soon followed by the ERJ-145, with 50 seats. The aircraft quickly obtained civil aviation certificates in 27 countries, including the USA, the UK, Germany, France, The Netherlands and Spain. Like Bombardier, Embraer targeted North America as its main market, selling to fast-emerging regional airlines, notably Continental Express and American Eagle. Through these successful programmes, Embraer was able rapidly to develop a reputation for supplying low-cost, modern, reliable planes.

Like Bombardier, Embraer rapidly developed the systems integration skills necessary to assemble a modern airliner. It purchased all the key components from outside suppliers, including the avionics, flight controls, engines, wings, tail units and fuselage segments. Its main suppliers included Allied Signal, Honeywell, Lucas Aerospace, Alison, Rolls-Royce's USA subsidiary, and Vickers. By the end of April 1999, Embraer had achieved 373 firm orders for the ERJ-135 and ERJ-145, and 390 options for the planes. In other words, Embraer is quickly catching-up with Bombardier. Indeed, the two companies have waged a fierce battle in the WTO over alleged government support for the respective companies. Bombardier alleges that Embraer's exports have been subsidized by Brazilian government export credits, Proex, which it is alleged amounts to a 3.5 per cent point interest rate subsidy (*FT*, 29 May 1998). Embraer claims that Bombardier benefits from Canadian government defence technology support as well as export financing 'worth 17–25 per cent of the aircraft's value' (*FT*, 29 May 1998).

Embraer grew rapidly from a small regional manufacturer into a significant global player in only a few years after privatization. Its turnover rose from $222 million in 1996 to $1315 million in 1998. It had become the second largest Brazilian exporter, with exports to the value of $1.2 billion. In 1994 Embraer made a loss of $30 million. Thereafter, its operating methods were radically transformed, enabling an increase in revenues per employee from $24 000 in 1994 to $201 000 in 1998. The company invested more than $500 million in product and productivity improvements between 1994 and 1998. In 1998 Embraer reported gross profits of 25.2 per cent on gross earnings (Embraer website). By 1999 Embraer had expanded into a company with over 7000 direct employees, and it estimated that in Brazil alone a further 3000 employees worked in supplier industries.

In 1999 Embraer made a further radical advance in its strategy. It announced the launch of a new family of commercial jets, the ERJ-170 (70 seats) and the ERJ-190-200 (90 seats). The launch order was placed by Crossair of Switzerland, a subsidiary of Swissair. The order, announced in June 1999, was the largest order ever placed for regional aircraft. It was for a total of 200 aircraft with a total value of $4.9 billion. Of these, firm orders alone amounted to a total of 30 each of the ERJ-170 and ERJ-190-200, with a total value of $2 billion, as well as options for a further 100 aircraft in these categories, as well as a further 70 orders for smaller aircraft. The first deliveries are planned for the year 2002. At the Paris Air Show in June 1999 Embraer announced that the French airline, Regional Airlines, had agreed a firm order for 10 ERJ-170s and an option to purchase a further 10, with a total purchase cost of $350 million (Embraer website).

The success in winning such a large order from a leading European airline is highly significant for an aerospace manufacturer based in the Third World. Embraer defeated potential competition from BAe (Avro-RJ), Boeing, Airbus and Bombardier. In order to win the order, Embraer had to satisfy Crossair that it could deliver on a number of fronts other than just price (Crossair website). Crossair set high standards for energy consumption and the environmental compatibility of the new aircraft. This included an insistence that the aircraft meet stringent conditions for noise and harmful emissions. In particular, nitrogen dioxide emissions should be about 50 per cent below current limits.

The dangers for both Bombardier and Embraer in expanding into the 90–110 seat market are obvious. The executive vice-president of Bombardier's regional jet division observed: 'You go over 90 seats and you are up against Boeing and Airbus' (quoted in *FT*, 27 February 1996). As we shall see, there is estimated to be a market of around 2000 planes in the 70–120 seat category from 1998 to 2020, worth over $100 billion. The established giants of the industry do not wish to cede this huge market to new entrants. Nor do they wish to see a potential competitor in larger aircraft use the 100-seater as the platform for a possible future challenge in larger aircraft. Boeing and Airbus already produced highly competitive planes, the smallest versions of the B-737 and A-319 both seating just over 100 passengers.

Moreover, as we have seen Boeing has developed at high speed a 100-seater aircraft, the B-717, based on the MD-95. This flew for the first time in September 1998, and entered service in the summer of 1999 (*FT*, 3 September 1998). As we shall see later, Airbus also plans to build a 100-seater aircraft. In other words, Bombardier, Embraer, Boeing and Airbus will collide in this sector of the market.

The risks for both Embraer and Bombardier in their attempt to penetrate the 100-seater market are very high. Boeing and Airbus have vast resources with which to compete with Embraer. These include the advantages of applying common technology developed in other areas, huge procurement volumes that enable lower costs for common components, a vast marketing network, and the application of common IT systems to assist in design and procurement organization. They include also the benefits from operating a large fleet purchased from a single source. The development cost of the planned Bombardier 90-seater aircraft is estimated to be over $1 billion (*FT*, 14 June 1999). Embraer estimates the development costs of the ERJ-170 and EJ-190 programmes will be around $750 million. These are very large sums for companies each of which has an aerospace sales revenue of a few billion dollars. The example of Fokker demonstrates how difficult it is to make a profit in this sector. The BAe-146 has made a loss for almost the whole of its existence.

It is highly unlikely that Bombardier and Embraer will be able in the long-term to successfully defeat the multinational giants in this sector. There is no reason to imagine that the giants will be content to allow two substantial niche players to operate in direct competition with them. A more likely response is to defeat the smaller players and force them out of this sector altogether. It is quite possible that one or other of the major players in world aerospace will attempt to take over Embraer. In 1999, Embraer was reported to be in deep discussion with more than one international aerospace company about the possibility of selling to them a significant minority stake in the company. Mauricio Botelho, the president of Embraer was reported to be discussing the sale of a 29 per cent stake in the company to a leading multinational who would work with Embraer as a strategic partner. He says that Embraer lacks the skills and resources to venture into an unknown market such as China: 'China will be the largest regional jet market in the world in ten year's time but I have not the slightest understanding of this market. Entering it requires an investment of competence. Not just money' (quoted in *FT*, 14 September 1999).

Options Facing Developing Countries. Developing countries cannot hope to compete with the giants of the USA and Europe in open competition to design and assemble entire large civilian aircraft, advanced military aircraft and engines. The rise of Embraer demonstrates that it is technically possible even for a firm based in a developing country to develop rapidly the technical skills necessary to design and assemble a modern airliner that meets the highest standards of safety, comfort and environmental demands. A large part of the aircraft's most demanding technology is embedded in the complex of components that compose the finished product. The skills required to design and assemble are relatively easily transferable. The rise of Embraer is a highly significant event.

However, technical ability to design and assemble a modern aircraft for a niche market is very different from commercial success. The most that can be expected of a developing country new entrant is to develop a capability to compete in a market niche, such as the smaller regional jet airliners. It is highly uncertain whether Bombardier and Embraer's attempts to compete in the smaller size segment of the 90–110-seater will be successful. They may well be forced out of this business and return to a true niche market of smaller regional jets and business jets. It is almost impossible to imagine that Embraer can hope seriously to compete with the established giants in aircraft above 100 seats, which is where the vastly dominant share of the world aircraft market is located. Even in the 100-seater segment, the future for Embraer is highly uncertain.

Powerful aerospace companies such as Lockheed and McDonnell–Douglas were forced out of the large airliner business. Even Airbus found it very difficult to catch up with Boeing. In the end it may be defeated. Boeing still has a huge scale advantage and the advantage of a large military aircraft production and technology base. The costs to developing countries of trying to build a mainly domestic aircraft industry have risen drastically since the 1950s, when it might have been possible to conceive of a large developing country 'catching-up'. The development costs of a 100-seater aircraft are around $1 billion. As we shall see, this amount is greater than the entire annual aerospace revenues of AVIC, China's 'national champion' in aerospace. The costs of attempting but failing to catch-up are very high, and rising sharply, in both the civilian and the military sectors.

Developing countries have little alternative except to become components or sub-systems suppliers. They have the advantage of lower costs of production. They may then gradually develop capabilities to work their way up the chain of complexity from simple sub-contracts to increasingly complex sub-systems. Moreover, as their financial resources increase, they may be able to participate in more substantial risk-sharing arrangements. Larger developing countries with large aircraft markets may be able to bargain for larger shares of sub-contracting work to be allocated to them, and for assistance to work their way more rapidly up the chain of complexity.

The harsh reality is that the room for manoeuvre for even the strongest developing country has been drastically reduced by the enormous increase in recent years in the institutional, financial and technical gap between their own industries and the world leaders of Europe and the USA.

CHINA'S AVIATION INDUSTRY

WHAT IS AVIC?

From the early 1950s through to the 1990s, the Ministry of Aviation Industry ran China's aviation industry.[5] The Ministry included all the design institutes, air frame assemblers and engine makers as well the components manufacturers. The Aviation Ministry was a self-sufficient entity. In 1993, Aviation Industries of

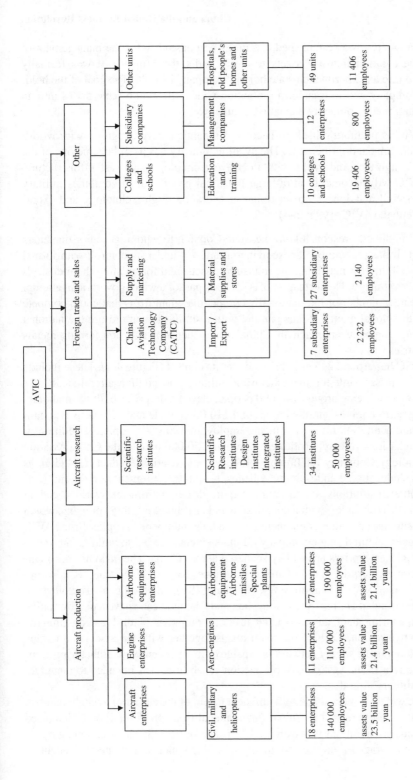

FIGURE 4.1 Structure of AVIC, 1997

China (AVIC), was established, assuming responsibility for the management of all the aviation industry assets formerly under the Ministry. It was formally turned into an experimental state holding company in 1996. The goal of the holding company was to transform the nation-wide collection of enterprises into an internationally competitive aviation company:

> AVIC is promoting itself to become a gigantic enterprise group with world-wide fame and influence ... The aviation industry has itself become one of the key high-tech industries with intensive technology and vast infrastructure. AVIC will become an ultra-large industrial group, which combines military and civil aviation, is transnational in operation, high technology and export oriented. (AVIC, 1998: 2–4)

AVIC is directly responsible to the State Council, to whom its senior managers report. It has the entire Chinese aviation industry under its control, with formal responsibility for managing the industry's assets, and formulating the industry's business strategy. The formation of AVIC was part of a wider government attempt to create a number of internationally competitive giant firms that could compete with the global giants. It runs parallel with a similar attempt to use the national holding company approach in China's petrochemical and non-ferrous metals industries.

AVIC has around 245 enterprises under its control (Figure 4-1). These include 18 enterprises built for manufacturing military and civilian aircraft and helicopters, employing around 140 000 people, eleven enterprises built for manufacturing aero- engines, employing around 110 000 people and 77 enterprises built to manufacture airborne equipment, employing 190 000 people. In addition, it has under it 34 research institutes, employing 50 000 people, the China Aviation Technology Company for Import and Export of Aviation Products (CATIC), as well as educational and training colleges, hospitals, retirement homes, and various other institutions. Its structure is quite different from the world's leading aerospace companies, with a core design and airframe assembly company, which buys engines and other components from a huge number of supplier firms. AVIC embraces within a single company all the elements needed to build an aircraft.

AVIC's enterprises are widely scattered across China. The main aircraft manufacturing enterprises are in Guizhou province (SW), at Shenyang (NE), Harbin (NE), Xian (NW), Chengdu (SW), Nanchang (SE), and Shanghai. The plants in Guizhou, and at Harbin, Shenyang, Xian and Chengdu each have a nearby engine manufacturing plant, and associated airborne equipment plants located within the respective region. Each of the main plants together with the associated engine and components supply network is capable of independently manufacturing complete aircraft. The vast bulk of production capabilities was intended to manufacture military aircraft.

The widely dispersed and self-sufficient nature of the cluster of aviation industry plants is closely related to China's international isolation. After 1960 China faced a serious possibility of war with the USSR and/or the US. This frightening possibility encouraged a drastic re-thinking of China's industrial strategy (Naughton,

1988: 353). Between 1964 and 1971 China undertook a huge programme of capital construction in inland provinces, know as the 'Third Front' (Naughton, 1988). During this period, no less than two-thirds of Chinese industrial investment was allocated to the Third Front. The wide dispersion of the plants, often in remote areas was primarily to protect the industries from military attack: '[I]ndividual Third Front factories were intentionally located in particularly remote sites. Large factories predominated in Third Front projects, but these factories – and sometimes individual workshops – were scattered across thousands of square miles of mountainous terrain ... The dispersal of productive activity capacity reflected the military orientation of the programme, and was designed to minimize the damage from air attack' (Naughton, 1988: 354–5). Self-evidently, protection from air attack was especially critical in the case of aircraft factories. Around three-fifths of the enterprises within AVIC were established as part of the 'Third Front' campaign. When economic reform began in the late 1970s, there were basically no aerospace factories in the coastal areas.

Military Aircraft

Declining Military Orders. The main function of the Chinese aviation industry was to produce warplanes to defend China. At the end of the Maoist period, a large fraction of the Chinese aviation industry produced military aircraft. At that point, non-aviation products accounted for a small fraction of the sector's output and employment, and the civilian aviation sector was weakly developed. Changes in the size of government allocations to military aircraft were of great importance to the development of the sector after the 1970s. Moreover, as we have seen in the first part of this paper, in the global economy, there is a close relationship between the development of military and civilian aviation. It is reasonable to believe that in China also, their development is closely inter-twined.

In the 1950s, China received large-scale technology transfer from the USSR in military as well as non-military industries. Essentially, the USSR transferred 'an entire military industrial base to China, as well as the initial requirements for a military technology base' (Godwin, 1997: 40). After the Sino–Soviet split, China was forced into a prolonged period of technological self-sufficiency. During this time, the attempt to produce nuclear weapons and ballistic missile delivery systems, 'absorbed most of the country's technological resources to the neglect of the conventional forces' (Godwin, 1997: 40). Moreover, in the latter half of China's long isolation, the Cultural Revolution wrought havoc with China's research capabilities: 'Programmes which should have produced prototypes in the mid-1960s did not bear fruit until the early 1980s. Moreover, capacity to absorb new technology was destroyed' (Friedman, 1997: 65).

By the death of Mao Zedong in 1976, China's military technology was 'at least two or three decades behind that of advanced industrial countries' and the nuclear weapons and their delivery systems were 'crude by the standards of other nuclear powers' (Godwin, 1997: 40). The military industrial base was 'incapable of producing modern arms' and the armed forces, including China's large military aircraft fleet, were equipped with 'obsolete equipment copied from Soviet models' (Godwin, 1997: 40).

China's whole military strategy was drastically overhauled at the end of the Maoist period. Deng Xiaoping's 1977 speech to the CCP's Central Military Commission set out the new policy (Deng Xiaoping, 1977). The speech is published in Deng (1984). Deng told the PLA leaders that priority must be given to economic modernization:

> The improvement of our army's equipment must be speeded up. But we must take note of one condition, namely that we must proceed from actual possibilities. The state budget is limited, and moreover, the amount of our military expenditure has to be decided with a view to the overall balance. Our national defence can be modernized only on the basis of the industrial and agricultural development of the country as a whole. (Deng Xiaoping, 1977: 94)

Only after that had been achieved would China be able to achieve rapid growth of its military aircraft capability. Indeed, Deng is reported to have told China's senior military leaders at that time: 'Take from me now only a word "patience" until the year 2000 when I can give you billions of dollars to buy foreign advanced fighters' (quoted in Hua Di, 1997: 34). Deng recognized that China's task of catching up in the military sphere was extremely difficult:

> Even if we gain 10 or 20 years [of peace] in which to modernize our army's equipment, it will still be inferior to the enemy's. For the enemy won't be sleeping while we are advancing. Therefore, if and when war breaks out, we will still have to triumph over superior forces with our inferior equipment. (Deng Xiaoping, 1977: 93)

After the late 1970s, there was a serious fall in the government's real outlays on domestically manufactured military aircraft, which had large consequences for the development path of the entire aerospace industry. There is much debate about the real size of the Chinese military budget. Official figures show that, within the national budget, 'expenditure on national defence' hardly altered in real terms from the late 1970s to the mid-1990s: deflated by the index of industrial prices, expenditure fell by around 2 per cent in total from 1980 to 1995 (SSB, ZTN, 1997: 243 and 282). The relative importance of defence expenditure within the national budget fell considerably, from 19.1 per cent of the national budget in 1971–5 to under 10 per cent in 1986–95.[6] Official budgetary outlays do not include all of the Chinese government's expenditure on the military. Official figures reportedly do not include outlays on military research and development, weapons procurement, and military-industrial construction and maintenance (Gurtov, 1993: 227). Nor do they reportedly include additional off-budget revenues available to the PLA and defence industries, such as income from civilian activity (see below), and budgeted expenses of other ministries used for military purposes.

A major problem for the production of military aircraft and engines has been the failure to reform the pricing policy used for procurement. Military producers complain that the profit rate for military aviation sector sales is fixed at around 5 per cent. Moreover, it appears that the contract price is fixed for three years, using a profit rate fixed at the start of the contract. The contract price is not typically adjusted for inflation in input prices over the course of the contract: 'A profit rate of 5 per cent at the start of the contract can often turn out to be zero by the time the project is finished.'

Although the absolute size of the budget is larger than officially reported, there is broad agreement that the trend of domestic military spending roughly follows the official figures (for example Arnett, 1997: 246; Frankenstein and Gill, 1996: 411–12; Gurtov, 1993: 227). Frankenstein and Gill's study concludes: 'Production of military goods and weapons has been in decline or remained stagnant in China for more than a decade ... Chinese military production is "downsizing" and probably radically so' (Frankenstein and Gill, 1996: 411–12). Arnett estimates that output of Chinese military aviation products fell from 11 billion yuan in 1983 to 3.3 billion yuan in 1992 (both at 1992 prices) (Arnett, 1997: 246). In 1996, they stood at only around 2.4 billion yuan (at current prices), a substantial real drop even from 1992. In other words, the real value of Chinese military aviation output in 1992 is estimated to have stood at just 30 per cent of that in 1983, and in 1996 may have been only one-fifth or even less of the figure in the early 1980s.[7] *China Daily: Business Weekly* noted in 1997: 'Funding constraints, lack of matching equipment and materials are crimping defence production, making it harder to meet airforce demand ... during the new era' (*CDBW*, 4 October 1997).

Western estimates of China's production of military aircraft show a severe decline in the number of domestically produced military aeroplanes. In 1974 China is estimated to have produced around 540 military aircraft, the number declining to around 200 in the early 1980s, falling to around 80 in the mid-1990s (Table 4-12). Frankenstein and Gill gave the following evaluation of Chinese

TABLE **4-12 Estimated Production of Military Aircraft in China, Selected Years**

Aircraft type	1974	1983	1990	1994
J-7 fighter	—	50	50	50
J-8 fighter	—	10	20–4	20–4
H-5 bomber	—	20–5	0	0
H-6 bomber	—	5	5–6	0
JJ-5 trainer	—	50	0	0
JJ-6 trainer	—	50	0	0
JJ-7 trainer	—	0	0	2
HJ-5 trainer	—	12	0	0
Q-5 attack	—	10–12	8–10	5
Total	540	207–14	83–90	77–81

SOURCE: Arnett (1997)

production of military aircraft in the mid-1990s:

> Chinese production of fighters, bombers and trainers has dropped consider-
> ably ... Chinese combat aircraft production has fallen by more than half from
> the levels of the early 1980s ... Currently, China produces approximately
> 70–80 aircraft per year, comprising 20 to 24 J-8I and J-8II aircraft, about
> 50 J-7 and a few JJ-7 combat trainers and Q-5 aircraft (the Q-5 is produced
> mostly for export). These are the only major military contracts the manufac-
> turers of these aircraft have, and in some cases military production at these
> plants is expected to be cut even further ... Production of Chinese military air-
> craft is likely to remain at low levels for the next ten to fifteen years.
> (Frankenstein and Gill, 1996: 412)

There is no doubt that the level of spending on domestic military aircraft fell heavily
under the strategy put into place by Deng Xiaoping. Western expert assessments
concluded that, while the rest of the world was 'racing ahead at a remarkable rate',
China's armed forces in the mid-1990s 'still relied very heavily on obsolete equipment': 'The Chinese airforce relies heavily on aircraft directly descended from
Soviet prototypes of the early- and mid-1950s' (Friedman, 1997: 65, 72).

The role of imports. For a relatively brief period, beginning in the 1980s while
the USSR still existed as the USA's principal adversary, China was allowed
increased access to Western military technology. Under the so-called 'Peace
Programme', Washington approved a $550 million cost-plus contract to sell
avionics equipment, including fighter control systems and navigational technology, to upgrade its fighters. However, this was still tightly controlled. It was limited mainly to the purchase of components rather than complete sub-systems or
entire aircraft. Occasional larger scale transfers occurred, such as the 1976 contract to produce the Rolls-Royce Spey under licence at the Xian Aero-engine
Company. The Spey engine was patented in the 1970s and was intended for use
in China to power the F-4 fighter plane. The complete production line was transferred to the Xian Aircraft Corporation. However, much tighter restrictions on
military technology transfers were imposed by the Western powers after China's
crushing of the student protests in Tiananmen, and the collapse of the USSR.

In the early 1990s, an important new development took place. The former
USSR collapsed economically. As we have seen, Russia's outlays on military aircraft procurement declined dramatically, and the defence industry contracted
drastically. However, the technical level of the former USSR's military aircraft
industry is very high, far ahead of China's, with world class design capability.
The Soviet defence industry was very keen indeed to earn hard currency by selling to China. The post-Soviet Russian leadership was anxious to develop better
relations with China, and the leadership was increasingly impressed by the contrast between the Chinese economic rise and Russian economic collapse.

On the Chinese side, the Gulf War had a big impact on Chinese military thinking. China's military leaders realized that the country lagged badly in its defence
capability, and that urgent measures were needed to deal with its backwardness.

The West would not sell advanced military aircraft to China, and the Russians were able to sell advanced equipment at relatively low prices. The total size of the deals concluded between 1992 and 1994 alone is thought to have been around $4–5 billion (Hua Di, 1997: 35). Over the whole period from 1991 to 1996, it is estimated that China purchased around $6 billion worth of arms from Russia (*FT*, 10 June 1999). In Russia, during the war in Kosovo, *Izvestiya* carried the headline 'Brothers Forever-2'.[8] It argued that in the new world situation, China and Russia could re-create the close economic co-operation of the 1950s. The article said that the combination of Chinese money and Russian military technology could create a powerful force on the world stage. Indeed, the article spoke of the possibility of the return to a bipolar world in international relations.

In 1992, China placed an order for 50 Su-27s, which were delivered in 1993 (IISS, 1998: 171). This was a move of great symbolism, since there had been no arms sales from Russia to China since the 1950s. In 1997, they placed a further order for 150 Su-27s, to be built under licence in China. These were designated the J-11 (IISS, 1998: 171). These are truly advanced fighters, far beyond the level that China itself can produce. If the Su-27s had come fully equipped and not downgraded, PLA pilots would have had 'a helmet-mounted sight with the superb radar and infra-red capabilities built into the aircraft itself' (Godwin, 1997: 48). China's Su-27 purchases came with the most advanced Anti Aircraft Missiles (AAMs), the AA-10 Archer and AA-11 Alamo missiles: 'The combination of AA-10 and AA-11s together with the electronics and avionics suite of the Su-27 make this aircraft one of the world's best interceptors' (Godwin, 1997: 48). In fact, it is thought unlikely that the Russians agreed to supply China with the most advanced forms of the Su-27, which would have caused considerable disquiet in the US, but, instead supplied less sophisticated versions. It is rumoured that Israel is helping to upgrade the aircraft's control systems.

By the late 1990s, the Su-27s had become the core of China's fighter aircraft fleet: 'Of the 5000 fixed-wing combat aircraft, more than 90 per cent are obsolete. Only the Su-27s are truly modern' (Godwin, 1997: 46). One account of the Chinese import of Russian Su-27s concluded:

> The decision to import Russian fighters ... suggests an acceptance that indigenous designs are inadequate as front-line aircraft. China's decision to import a second batch of Su-27s in quantity implies a judgment that the process of copying the first batch – avionics, engines and missiles – would not be practicable even if manufacturing skills are improving. (Friedman, 1997: 82)

Not only is the Su-27 the only modern combat aircraft that China possesses, but it also does not possess an aircraft carrier force. The earliest predicted date for building an aircraft carrier is 2010, with 2020 thought more likely (Godwin, 1997: 50). Moreover, China possesses neither an airborne warning and control (AWAC) system[9] nor an aerial refueling capability: 'Even the technologies available in the West since the 1960s are not yet available to the PLA ... [China] would have great difficulty in conducting air combat operations much beyond 300 miles' (Godwin, 1997: 46, 49). The Su-27s now play a vital part in China's defence: 'If the PLA remains unable to protect its ground and naval forces from air attack, China's ability to project military force will remain negligible ... [W]ithout adequate air power effective maritime defence against a well equipped and determine adversary is not possible' (Godwin, 1997: 46).

The expanded Russian military connection with China since 1992 goes beyond combat aircraft. It includes also, purchase of 4 Kilo class 636 diesel electric attack submarines, the S-300-PMU-1 surface-to-air missile (SAM) system for air defence, the Il-76 troop transport (Hua Di, 1997: 35), two Sovremenny destroyers, (to be delivered in 2000), the SS-N-22 anti-ship missile system (ASSM) (delivery in 2000), 35 Mi-17 helicopters (delivered in 1997), 8 Ka-28 helicopters, and licensed production of the Shmel helicopter (IISS, 1998: 171). Further discussions were reported on the purchase of a wide array of military equipment, including the Su-30 fighter plane, anti-radar missiles, laser-guided bombs and a variety of radar systems (Hua Di, 1997: 38). It was reported in 1999 that China was considering buying from Russia not only more Su-27s, and ordering Su-30 fighter aircraft, but also buying anti-aircraft equipment, intermediate and long-range missiles, more Kilo class 636 attack submarines, and Sovremenny-class destroyers (*FT*, 27 May 1999).

The Sino–Russian connection is of great strategic importance, especially taken in conjunction with a growing Chinese relationship with Russia in the production and shipment of oil and natural gas to China. The enhanced military relationship has raised sensitivities in East Asia and in the West. Moreover, there are warning voices within Russia that caution against the development of too close a military relationship with the former enemy, China, and voices in China that warn that Russia is an unreliable ally.

By the mid-1990s, Western expert opinion noted: 'China's arms industries have no experience in [designing and building] modern aircraft, nor have they experience in building and operating advanced avionics suites ... China's total lack of experience in constructing modern power plants constitutes yet another hurdle to jump' (Godwin, 1997: 49). The strategy that China has adopted since the late 1970s leaves it highly reliant on imported equipment and technology for its national defence. Since the 1970s, military technology outside China has advanced at high speed. A major goal of the USA defence re-structuring and the proposed EU defence restructuring is to provide the institutional base for continued high-speed development of Western military technology through the concentration of large amounts of R & D resources in the hands of a small number of giant companies that are able to generate revenue from large global sales.

A key aspect of the Gulf War was 'command and control' systems. Western experts consider that China 'has lagged badly in this area' (Friedman, 1997: 70). China has tried 'at least three times to buy modern avionics, first from the United States (terminated in 1989) and then from Israel and Russia' (Friedman, 1997: 69). The Israeli programme was reportedly cut back, 'due to inability to manufacture the technology provided' (Friedman, 1997: 69).

The extent of Western involvement in upgrading China's arms capability is of the highest political sensitivity. This was vividly illustrated by the furore in the

USA over the Cox Report on alleged leaking of secrets to China for its nuclear weapons programme. However, there is no doubt of the commercial interests of Western arms manufacturers in selling to China. It was reported that Israel was helping China build its F-10 fighter (IISS, 1998: 169), with avionics and radar from the cancelled Israeli Lavi programme. This programme incorporated American technology and was 'substantially funded by the US' (*FT*, 19 February 1999). The plane is expected to enter service in 2001, with operational capability from 2005 (IISS, 1998: 169). European defence contractors are 'eager to sell equipment to the Chinese military' (*FT*, 19 February 1999): 'Western European sales of military sub-systems and licensed technology are growing' (IISS, 1998: 168). Despite the growth of Western sales to China, there are still severe government restrictions. However, much of the Western military technology which is available for sale to China's Asian neighbours, is not permitted to be sold to China, greatly increasing the country's sense of vulnerability: 'China's military leadership cannot take comfort in the knowledge that advanced technology battlefield sensors, target acquisition systems and command and control systems are available on the open market to add to the complexity of the military environment surrounding China' (Godwin, 1997: 57). One accounts notes soberly: 'Command control issues will probably decide what happens in the event of war over the Spratly Islands ... [N]early all China's rivals in the South China Seas (as well as Taiwan) possess sufficiently modern capabilities and most have a better understanding [than China] of command and control' (Friedman, 1997: 70).

These considerations are especially important in view of Taiwan's purchase in the 1990s of Grumman E-2 Hawkeye AWACs to complement its purchase of 150 F-16s and 60 Mirage-2000s (Godwin, 1997: 47). Western arms manufacturers have signalled openly their determination to sell with renewed vigour to developing countries. In the USA, policy was set by Presidential Directive, signed by President Clinton in 1995. It says that international weapons sales are 'a legitimate instrument of USA foreign policy' (quoted in *IHT*, 1998). The policy 'makes it clear that increasing sales and market share of USA arms manufacturers is a goal of Washington's foreign policy' (*IHT*, 1998). For example, Taiwan is the world's second biggest arms buyer outside the OECD, with more than $9 billion-worth of purchases from 1994 to 1997 (*IHT*, 5 August 1998). In 1997 alone, Taiwan purchased $9.3 billion-worth of weapons compared to $11 billion purchased by Saudi Arabia: these two countries 'were by a tenfold factor the largest buyers among the developing nations, far outstripping their nearest competitors, Egypt, Iran and Kuwait' (*IHT*, 5 August 1998).

Other countries in Northeast Asia have large modern fleets of military aircraft. South Korea's Air Force has a fleet of 488 modern combat aircraft. This includes 88 F-16s, with a further 72 under delivery, 130 F-4s (McDonnell–Douglas) and 195 F-5s (IISS, 1998: 188). Japan's Air Force has 329 combat aircraft, including 50 F-1s, 70 F-4s, and 180 F-15s (IISS, 1998: 185). Moreover, the USA has large military forces in the region, including a fleet of 108 F-16s and 54 F-15s stationed in Japan and South Korea (IISS, 1998: 28).

China's military leaders spoke bluntly of the country's technological backwardness in military affairs. In a key speech in 1993, General Liu Huaqing, then the most senior officer in the PLA, said bluntly: '[The PLA] fails to meet the needs of modern warfare and this is the principal problem with army-building' (quoted in Godwin, 1997: 43). He made it clear that the budget cuts were a serious obstacle to modernizing the armed forces: '[U]nder current conditions of inadequate military expenditures, the contradiction between living expenses and the expenses on equipment is very acute, and indeed, hard to handle' (quoted in Godwin, 1997: 43). In the 1990s, there has been a spate of articles and seminars that express concern over the degree to which China was falling behind the West: 'The tone of these essays and seminars fully reflects the inability of China's armed forces to contemplate any early integration of advanced technologies into their military operations' (Godwin, 1997: 43). A primary concern is 'the simple fact that the Revolution in Military Affairs [in the West] is under way at a time when the PLA has yet to integrate into its operations technologies that have been in wide use since the 1960s and 1970s' (Godwin, 1997: 43).

The impact on Chinese military thinking of the war in Yugoslavia has been at least as great as that of the Gulf War. China's budget for military expenditure is still strictly limited by China's low level of economic development, by the central government's budgetary weakness, and by the pressing need for developmental outlays over military ones. Nevertheless, the war in Yugoslavia, together with the disaster of the bombing of the Chinese embassy in Belgrade, have deeply affected Chinese military thinking. It is viewed as greatly increasing the threat that the USA poses to China's national security. Moreover, the developments in Yugoslavia occurred alongside the continued development of the Theatre Missile Defence System in the Far East, continuing hostilities with China's neighbours over the Spratly Islands, and the release of the Cox Report in the USA. There is a gathering perception in Beijing that USA policy towards China is shifting fundamentally, from 'constructive engagement' towards 'containment'. Kosovo has 'shaken the very foundations of China's world view': 'NATO's eastwards expansion, coupled with a new precedent to strike within sovereign borders on behalf of an oppressed minority has been watched with foreboding by a country containing 55 racial minorities some of which claim to be the victims of human rights abuses and cultural chauvinism' (*FT*, 10 June 1999).

It is hard to imagine that these factors will not lead to a shift in the balance of government expenditure between military and civilian purposes. General Wang Zuxun, Head of the People's Liberation Army military science academy has concluded that there is 'an urgent desire' for China to purchase advanced military equipment as soon as possible' (quoted in *FT*, 27 May 1999). The obvious source from which to make such large-scale purchases is Russia.

Even after China has substantially upgraded its defence capability with imports from Russia, production of Russian planes under licence and assistance through technology transfer from European countries, it will still be drastically weaker in conventional weapons than the USA in Asia, let alone on a global scale. It is worth remembering that even after China has completed its current round of imports from Russia, it will have a fleet of only around 200 genuinely modern fighter aircraft. The USA Navy alone has a fleet of almost 800 F-18s, while the USA Air Force has a fleet of over 700 F-15s and almost 1300 F-16s (IISS, 1998: 24–6). A recent survey of China's expansion of its armed forces concluded: 'It will probably be decades before [China] can challenge the USA as Asia's dominant military power' (*FT*, 19 February 1999). It is not surprising that Deng Xiaoping said: 'We should not fight a war for 50 years. We have to concentrate on economic construction'.

Nuclear weapons. China's principal form of defence against the perceived threat from the USA lies in its nuclear capability. It is expected that the 8000 km Dongfeng-31 ICBM (Inter-Continental Ballistic Missile) will enter service in 1999, with a total of around 10 to 20 missiles deployed. The 12 000 km Dongfeng-41 may enter service in around 2002–5 (IISS, 1998: 18). Whatever the strength of the USA's defensive shield, the risk of even one Chinese nuclear device reaching the USA acts as a powerful bargaining tool for China in its international relations.

Barriers to Entry and Catch-up in Military Aircraft. By the end of the Maoist period, the Chinese possessed a large aircraft manufacturing industry. However, it was far behind the West in almost all key aspects of technology. It was fundamentally producing variants of old Soviet aircraft. Alongside the dramatic advances in the institutional structure of Western defence manufacturers in the 1990s, has gone a period of unprecedented acceleration in military aircraft technology in the West. As we have seen alongside the rapid technological progress in the West and increased intensity of sales efforts to developing countries, there has occurred a rapid decline in the country's domestic production capability. Unquestionably, the gap in military technology with the West has widened at high speed. China is very far indeed from being able to compete on the 'global level playing field' with the global giants in military aviation. Western experts consider that it will be very difficult for China to overcome its deficiencies in military technology. One careful study concluded:

The simple fact that all the PLA's advanced weapon platforms depend on imported technologies for their power plants, weapons and electronics is a clear indication that China's research centres have yet to make adequate headway in these critical areas. Its military R & D has not generated technologies in common use since the 1970s, and its arms industry is yet to produce weapon platforms based on indigenous technology that match those the advanced industrial states were manufacturing in the 1970s. For such a military technology and industrial base, advancing technologies required for the 21st century is a daunting task … Nor does it appear likely that over the next decade China's arms industries will overcome the endemic weaknesses that prevent them from putting advanced weaponry into production … It seems unlikely that without

massive investment [China] will be able realize even the mid-term modernization goals of its military leadership. (Godwin, 1997: 59)

The question of barriers to entry catch-up capabilities is much more important in
the military sphere than in any other. It is clear that China's arms manufacturing
technology is far behind that of the West. However, even fighting limited wars
within the East Asia region would present major challenges due to the fact that
potential enemies possess advanced weapons bought from the West. A national
military strategy built around the possibility of limited local wars along China's
borders and relating to its maritime claims, alongside the competing claims from
the domestic nuclear industry, has 'created requirements for technologies which
the military technology base cannot develop and the industrial base cannot yet
produce' (Godwin, 1997: 59).

NON-AVIATION PRODUCTION

Policy Change. We have seen above how China developed a large aircraft
manufacturing industry from the early 1950s through to the late 1970s. We have
noted also that in the late 1970s China faced a crossroads in its aerospace development. Deng Xiaoping initiated a deep re-thinking of the strategy. There were
several factors to take into consideration. The first was the brutally realistic
appraisal of China's technical capabilities. Unlike the USSR at the time of its
massive system reform, China's technological level was extremely low. In the
aerospace sector, we have seen that the vast bulk of the planes it produced were
for the military, based on Soviet designs of the 1950s. Deng Xiaoping noted
soberly: 'Because of our low starting point, China is still one of the world's poor
countries. Our scientific and technological forces are far from adequate.
Generally speaking we are 20 to 30 years behind the advanced countries in the
development of science and technology' (Deng Xiaoping, 1977: 171).

Deng Xiaoping decided that the first priority for the impoverished country
that he led was to raise the people's standard of living. In the late 1970s, China's
standard of living was extremely low, with around 300 million people who were
'absolutely poor' by international standards. Deng decided that military modernization must take second place to economic modernization. Consequently, as
we have seen, after the late 1970s the level of government spending on procurement of domestic military aeroplanes fell substantially. This had major consequences for the wide array of enterprises under the control of the Ministry
of Aviation Industry. In the early 1980s, the Ministry had under its control well
over 100 production enterprises and numerous design and research institutes,
as well as support units in health, education and other social functions, employing around 700 000 people. Moreover, as we have seen, a large proportion of
these were located in remote areas away from the relatively prosperous east
coast. As well as the workers themselves, there were at least a further one million other family members dependent on the aerospace industry for their survival.

Therefore, the sharp decline in government procurement for military aircraft had major implications for the maintenance of large communities scattered across China.

Not only did AVIC face the problem of a serious decline in military aircraft orders, but it also encountered great difficulties in trying to develop its civilian aerospace industry. As we shall see, it met with major problems in attempting to become a manufacturer of large civilian airliners, leading to failure to generate revenue and employment from aerospace in anything like the hoped-for amounts.

Growth of Non-Aviation Production

Changing structure of output and sales. Alongside the severe decline in military aircraft procurement went the slow expansion of civilian aviation production (see below), including both the production of civilian aircraft, notably the Yun-7, and the expansion of sub-contract arrangements with the multinational companies. A very rough estimate suggests that from the late 1970s to the late 1990s the total real value of Chinese aerospace production fell by at least 15 per cent.[10] Moreover, a rapidly growing proportion of this output consisted of sub-contracting for the multinational aerospace companies (see below).

In response to the emerging crisis for China's aircraft industry, the central government, through the Ministry of Aviation, and latterly through AVIC, instituted the policy of conversion of military into civilian (*jun zhuan min*). In the early 1980s, the market economy was only in its early stages of development, and the extent of conversion was limited to a small range of products with a close relationship to aerospace. In the second phase, spanning the late 1980s and early 1990s, the market economy developed more powerfully, and the aircraft enterprises began more extensive development of non-aviation products, beginning to produce on a large scale products such as autos, motorcycles, textile machinery, refrigerators and air conditioners. In the third phase, from the early 1990s onwards, the scale of non-aviation production grew rapidly. Moreover, new institutional forms of business grew fast, including Sino–foreign joint ventures with branches of the aerospace industry and stock market flotation at home and abroad. The period after the early 1990s saw the most rapid expansion of the growth of non-aerospace production.

In 1979, the share of non-aerospace sales stood at just 7.5 per cent of total sales of the Ministry of Aviation Industry. By 1997, their share had risen to more than 80 per cent. In real terms,[11] the sales of non-aerospace products rose by around 23 per cent per annum from 1979 to 1997.

The shift to civilian production brought about a dramatic transformation of China's military enterprises. For example, the Guizhou Aero-Industry Group was an important base of China's Third Front military aircraft industry producing high-speed fighters and trainers. Today its products include 'Skylark' brand minivans and engines, 'Flying Horse' brand buses, dustbin vans, tricycle motors, '830 kinds of auto parts', food processing equipment, medical apparatus and instruments, machinery for processing tobacco, engineering hydraulic components, marble machining equipment, and high quality plated cooking ware. It was a dramatic transformation from being an elite company producing military aircraft for national defence, selling to the government procurement agency, to being a producer of everyday household products.

By the late 1990s several of the companies under AVIC had become relatively large-scale producers of non-aviation products. In 1997, the leading company for the production of non-aerospace products, Jincheng in Shanghai, accounted for one-quarter of AVIC's total sales value of non-aerospace products in 1997, and the top four[12] accounted for 50 per cent of AVIC's total sales value of non-aerospace products.

Structure of non-aviation output. Automobiles, auto components and motorcycles together are the most important sectors within AVIC's non-aviation sales, accounting for 62 per cent of the total value of AVIC's revenue in 1997 (Table 4-13). It was relatively easy to turn large stocks of machine tools to producing auto industry products. However, AVIC produces a wide array of products in addition to these, including environmental protection equipment, medical machinery, industrial gas turbines, construction materials, textile machinery, hydraulic equipment, foodstuff packaging machinery and a wide variety of other products. By 1997, AVIC had become China's second largest manufacturer of textile machinery. It had become an important manufacturer of electronic products, medical and pharmaceutical machinery, food processing and packaging machinery, refrigeration equipment, air conditioners, washing machines, bicycles, household appliances, clocks and watches, machine tools, precision tools and hydraulic systems. By 1997, AVIC had developed and manufactured more than 5000 types of non-aviation products.

Motorcycles. Until recently 13 of AVIC's subsidiaries produced motorcycles. However, the market has become intensely competitive, and five of them have

TABLE **4-13 Non-Aviation Products as a Share of
Total AVIC Revenue (1997)**

Product	% (approx.)
Motorcycles	25
Automobiles	27
Automobile and motorcycle components	10
Environmental protection equipment	4
Medical machinery	4
Industrial gas turbines	6
Construction material	4
Textile machinery	6
Hydraulic equipment and tools	4
Foodstuff packaging machinery	4
Other	6

SOURCE: Authors' research notes

dropped out of the market. In 1997, AVIC produced a total of 997 000 motorcycles, occupying 13 per cent of the total Chinese market for motorcycles. The largest of AVIC's motorcycle subsidiaries, Shanghai Jincheng Group, has a capacity to produce 1 million motorcycles annually, and in 1997 produced 600 000 units. It has become the fourth largest producer in China. It is China's most profitable motorcycle producer by value of sales per worker.

AVIC's Nanfang Aero-engine Company (Dongli) subsidiary has become the eighth largest motorcycle producer in China by value of output, with an annual capacity of 600 000 units and an output of 300 000 in 1997. This was originally one of the six major aerospace plants set up in the 1950s. In 1954 it produced China's first aero-engine and Chairman Mao wrote a personal letter of congratulation to the plant. It also produced China's first air-to-air missile.

Auto and motorcycle components. In 1997, around 80 of AVIC's subsidiaries produced autos and auto components. They produced around 820 million yuan (around $100 million) in sales revenue, accounting for one-third of the total value of sales generated by AVIC as a whole. In 1997 AVIC had the capacity to produce 180 000 vehicles annually, with actual production totalling 127 000 vehicles, making it the sixth largest auto producer in China. The two main categories of vehicles that it produces are micro-vans and buses. It also produces rural vehicle jeeps and specialist vehicles.

Micro-vans. AVIC has four plants producing micro vans. Harbin Aircraft Corporation is the largest producer, making the *Songhuajiang* brand. Its capacity is 100 000 and in 1997 it produced 50 000 vehicles. The second largest is the Changhe (Jingdezhen) Aircraft Industry Company, with a capacity of 60 000 units and an output of 50 000 in 1997. Hanjiang (Hangzhong) has the capacity to manufacture 30 000 units, but in 1997 it produced only around 8000–10 000 units. None of the micro-van plants is sufficiently large to benefit from economies of scale. It is thought that an annual output of around 300–400 000 units is the optimum plant size for the production of micro-vans, and none of AVIC's plants is close to this level of output.

Buses. Buses are the third major category of AVIC non-aviation products. There are two AVIC subsidiaries producing buses, the main ones being Shenyang and Xian. Shenyang is known as the 'Cradle of China's jet fighter industry'. It has developed and produced thousands of fighters. It is where China's first jet fighter, first supersonic jet fighter and first high-altitude, high-speed jet fighter were developed. With demand for its fighters languishing, it has become a substantial producer of buses, with a capacity of 1500, though its output in 1997 was only 600–800 units owing to the fall-off in market conditions.

Xian Aircraft Corporation. Xian Aircraft Corporation (XAC), located in Northwest China, is the largest single aircraft maker in China by value of assets (Table 4-14). It has around 20 000 employees. It is one of the group of 55 enterprises

TABLE **4-14 Sales, Assets and Pre-Tax Profits of China's Leading Aerospace Companies, Early/Mid-1990s (million yuan)**

Company	Year	Sales	Assets	Pre-tax profits
Xian Aircraft Corp.	1992	423	313	42
	1995	1104	3058	71
	1996	1597	4218	86
Shenyang Aircraft Corp.	1992	786	237	39
	1995	1253	1963	42
	1996	1349	2695	43
Chengdu Aircraft Corp.	1992	869	264	31
	1995	1287	1687	60
	1996	1028	2334	43
	1997	1200	—	—
Harbin Aircraft Corp.	1992	551	208	41
	1995	2040	2876	—
	1996	2105	3546	145
Changhe Aircraft Co.				
(Jingdezhen)	1992	390	143	42
	1995	—	1501	—
	1996	1735	1934	245
Nanchang Aircraft Co.	1992	439	201	12
	1995	810	1524	—
	1996	830	2139	—
Shengang Liming				
Aero-engine Corp.	1992	423	207	17
	1995	511	1360	—
	1996	673	1904	—
Harbin Dongan Engine Corp.	1992	330	206	19
	1995	1064	1639	137
	1996	1210	2388	113
Shaanxi Aircraft Corp.	1992	262	213	9
	1995	—	—	34
Qingan Aerospace				
Equipment Corp.	1992	256	78	33
Xian Aero-engine Corp.	1992	191	474	15
	1995	—	1295	—
	1996	480	1729	—
Guizhou Shuangyang				
Aircraft and Plane	1992	190	70	2
China Southern				
Aero-equipment Co.	1995	1269	2022	130
	1996	2176	3336	—
Chengdu Aero-engine Co.	1995	494	1450	—

SOURCES: SSB, ZDQN (1996: 161–63, 1997: 205–8); DRC (1993: 137–8)

selected by the Chinese government to form the core of China's modern enterprise system. Its principle military aircraft is the B-6 bomber. This plane was first manufactured in the 1960s, based on a Soviet 1950s design. It is a 'middle-sized, middle-range' bomber, of a type that is now virtually obsolete in the West. Procurement demand from the Chinese government 'fell drastically' in the 1990s, and there seems to be little prospect of export markets. XAC also produces the Y-7, China's domestic small passenger plane. However, production of the Y-7 has not compensated for the steep fall in military aircraft orders. It produced a total of 130 Y-7s up to 1996, but by 1997 it had no orders at all, other than a small number of the military transport version of the plane to be sold to the PLA (see below).

XAC has struggled to find successful non-aviation products with which to support its large staff. XAC or its 'children' have invested in over 200 companies. Its subordinate companies now produce machinery, electronic products, automobiles and components, chemical products, and construction materials. Out of these have emerged a small number of large-scale businesses that benefit from economies of scale. The two outstanding examples are XAC Aluminium Company and Xian Volvo Bus Company. Each is fast-growing and reinvesting at high speed.

XAC Aluminium Company is 64 per cent owned by XAC. Its turnover grew rapidly from 108 million yuan in 1994 to 300 million yuan in 1997. It employs 350 people and made pre-tax profits of 30 million yuan in 1997. It manufactures long extruded aluminium h-shapes for use in construction. XAC has invested relatively heavily in developing this company, regarding it as one of XAC's 'little dragons'. However, despite heavy investment, XAC is the sixteenth largest producer of aluminium construction materials in China, and even for aluminium h-shapes has only a 5 per cent national market share. It is a highly competitive, relatively low-technology industry, with over 1300 producers across the whole of China. The main source of competition is from township and village enterprises. The management and technical skills required are far removed from those involved in aircraft design and manufacture.

The second main plank of XAC's survival strategy is a joint venture with Volvo (Sweden) to manufacture high quality tourist buses. This is a 50/50 joint venture in which XAC invested $3.5 million. Output reached 290 vehicles in 1997 and will achieve 400 in 1998, with a sales revenue of 500 million yuan and 700 million yuan respectively. The enterprise is tightly managed by Volvo, which appoints the chief executive officer. Volvo's tightness of control is visible in the pace and quality of work, the fact that the company insists that all key parts (including engine, brake system and electrical control system) are imported, and Volvo's refusal to allow XAC to float the company in order to raise capital. Xian Volvo (Silver bus), occupies around two-fifths of China's fast-growing domestic market for luxury tourist buses. The plan is to expand production to around 1500 vehicles annually within 'a few years'.

It seems likely that by 1997, as much as one-half of the total revenue of XAC was generated simply by XAC's two most successful non-aviation projects, namely the Volvo joint venture and XAC Aluminium Company. Neither product is closely related to the aerospace industry. In the case of the Volvo joint venture,

XAC's role is primarily that of a passive investor rather than a manager of the company, since control is firmly in Volvo's hands. In the case of the XAC Aluminium Company, XAC is entering an entirely different form of competition, in which the competitor companies are predominantly small-scale, labour-intensive businesses, with highly fragmented and competitive markets.

CIVILIAN AIRCRAFT

Market Prospects. The Chinese civilian aircraft market is one of the largest and fastest-growing in the world. From 1990 to 1996, China's total air traffic grew from 11 700 million passenger kilometres (mpk) to 75 000 mpk (SSB, ZTN, 1997: 531), an average annual growth rate of around 22 per cent per annum. Future prospects hinge critically on the growth rate that the Chinese economy is able to achieve. Prior to the 1997–8 global crisis, it was predicted that China would purchase around 240 civilian airliners in the period 1996–2000 (*CDBW*, 3 August 1997). The pre-crisis predicted growth rate of China's commercial airliner fleet was over 11 per cent per annum for the period 1995–2015, more than twice the rate of increase for the global industry (*FT*, 20 August 1996). The pre-crisis predicted increase in China's total commercial airline fleet from 1996 to

TABLE 4-15 Growth of China's Passenger Airliner Fleet, 1985–96

Aircraft	1985	1990	1996	2014
Total	404	421	750	1300[a]
of which:				
Boeing 747	6	11	16	
Boeing 737	15	21	130	
Boeing 707	10	9	0	
Boeing 767	2	6	17	
Boeing 757	0	9	45	
MD 11	—	—	5[b]	
MD 82	5	25	39	
Fokker 100	—	—	10[b]	
Airbus A310	2	2	3	
Airbus A300-600	—	—	10[b]	
Tupolov 154	2	20	32	
Antonov 12	2	2	2	
Antonov 24	28	23	3	
Yun 7	13	45	64	
BAe 146	0	10	14	
Short 360	7	7	0	

SOURCES: SSB, ZTN (1997: 531); Morgan Stanley Asia (1997a: 45)

NOTES: a Predicted (*CDBW*, 5 January 1997)
         b China Eastern only

2014 was 500–600 aircraft (Table 4-15). Airbus Industrie forecast that China would acquire 1320 aircraft between 1996 and 2014, worth a total of $100 billion (*FT*, 12 April 1996). This would account for 35 per cent of predicted sales for the entire Asia–Pacific region. Up until 1997, Boeing had comprehensively dominated the Chinese commercial aircraft market, selling over 240 aircraft to China compared with just 35 from Airbus (*CDBW*, 30 June 1996). The Chinese market is important for Boeing, accounting for around 10 per cent of its total global sales in 1990–6 (*CDBW*, 30 June 1996).

However, after 1996, the market situation altered greatly. In China, as in other parts of the world, Airbus sharply increased its orders at the expense of market share for Boeing. In both 1997 and 1998 China ordered 19 aircraft from Airbus, amounting to around 10 per cent of Airbus' annual output in those years. Although China ordered 50 aircraft from Boeing in 1998, its share of the China market was being substantially eroded.

A key issue in assessing the development prospects of the Chinese civilian aviation industry is the nature of the aircraft purchasers and their relationship to the aircraft manufacturers. An important aspect of the growth of Airbus in its early years was the preparedness of the then state-owned airlines of France and Germany to buy planes from Airbus. Equally, the failure of British Airways to buy Airbus planes until the historic decision in 1998, was a factor which held back Airbus' growth of market share. The Chinese aviation industry is subject to a high degree of regulation by the Civil Aviation Administration of China (CAAC), which is directly responsible to the State Council. This includes the right to approve the purchase of planes. Indeed, all civil aircraft purchases must be conducted through CAAC's subsidiary, CASC (the Civil Aviation Supply Company). This provides CAAC with a great deal of influence over the structure of China's civil aircraft fleet, and provides a potentially powerful instrument for industrial policy should the government choose to use it. It also provides a potentially powerful lever for influencing international relations. Under China's economic reforms CAAC has been reluctant to buy any planes other than from the leading European and USA companies.

Yun-10 (Y-10). In 1970, the central government decided that China should build its own domestic large jet airliner, the Y-10, at almost the same time that France, Germany and the UK decided to attempt to break the dominance of Boeing with Airbus. The decision to start the Y-10 programme appears to have been initiated by Premier Zhou Enlai. He apparently recommended the plan to Chairman Mao, who gave it his support, and then the scheme got under way. The Y-10 programme was launched in August 1970, and hence was termed 708 (August 1970). The Y-10 programme was initiated along with three other major central government large-scale programmes:

- **701 (January 1970)**: this was a programme to construct a rocket vehicle for China's satellite programme. Today's successful Chinese rocket programme has its origins in the 701 scheme.

- **718 (August 1971)**: this was a programme to develop a seaborne telecom-munications monitoring capability.
- **729 (September 1972)**: this was a programme to develop China's nuclear power capability. Today's nuclear power capability stems from this programme.

The decision was taken to build the Y-10 in Shanghai for a variety of reasons, but in part it seems to have been due to the fact that the 'Gang of Four' had their power base in Shanghai. Shanghai Aircraft Manufacturing Factory was chosen as the central location from which the project was co-ordinated and at which the plane was to be assembled. Prior to the Y-10 project it was China's largest military aircraft repair plant. A total of 450 million yuan was invested in the development of the Y-10. The Ministry of Aviation dispatched several hundred technicians from all over China to Shanghai to work on the project. The atmos-phere during the project was highly patriotic. The design of the aircraft was com-pleted in 1978 and the first test flight took place in 1980. Between 1980 and 1985 it made 130 test flights, totalling 170 hours of flying time. It demonstrated an ability to fly in any type of weather condition, and to make landings at a variety of different altitudes, including seven landings at Lhasa in Tibet.

The Y-10 was modelled on the Boeing 707, with a variety of modifications. The engines were based on the Pratt and Whitney JT3D, but also had substantial 'developments' of the imported engines. The entire airframe was manufactured within China. 'Most' of the avionics were manufactured in China, but 'around 20' important pieces of avionics equipment were imported. The vast bulk of domestically manufactured components were produced in different enterprises in Shanghai, with a total of 263 different work units involved. Altogether two Y-10s were assembled and the components for a third aircraft were ready for assembly, but the assembly was not undertaken due to termination of the programme. One aircraft was 'tested to destruction' in ground tests, and the other was used for the test flights, and still stands parked on the airfield at the Shanghai Aircraft Manufacturing Plant.

The Y-10 programme was halted in 1985. It is unclear why this happened. One common explanation is that it was halted for 'political reasons' after 1978, because it was associated with the Gang of Four. Others observe that the Y-10's safety record was unproven and that it would have required a great deal more investment to ensure that it met even the CAAC's safety requirements, let alone those of the FAA. In the face of an uncertain market, with proven international aircraft available on attractive terms, the purely commercial justification for the Y-10 did not exist. It would have required substantial government protection in the form of a guaranteed domestic market in order to provide the initial sales needed to launch the programme commercially. Apparently, the CAAC was unwilling to make such a commitment. The story is, clearly, very complex: 'You could write a novel about the discontinuation of the Y-10 programme.'

For the Chinese aircraft industry the Y-10 provides an important symbol of China's capability to build a large civil airliner independently. Its successful development is seen by many people within the industry as having closed the technological gap between China and the West, as it enabled China to develop valuable skills in building a complete airliner. Since then the central government has never again provided such strong support for the development of a large domestic airliner capability. Design and assembly of the Y-10 in Shanghai also helped rapidly push the Shanghai Aircraft Manufacturing Plant from being a purely aircraft repair into a major assembly company. This in turn helped decide that the assembly of McDonnell–Douglas aircraft (see below) would take place at the site.

Yun-7 (Y-7). In the 1960s the Chinese government decided to support the development of an indigenous domestic feeder, turbo-prop plane, the Y-7. Design work began in 1966, and the first Y-7 flew in 1970. Xian Aircraft Corporation (XAC) was chosen as the location. The Y-7 was successfully developed and batch-produced. This demonstrated that China had one of the developing world's most sophisticated aircraft manufacturing sectors, and was a leading producer among developing countries.

Up until 1996, XAC had produced over 130 Y-7s, in a variety of versions. Earlier versions were designed entirely for the domestic market. The initial Y-7s (Y-7 and Y-7-100) were for 48–52 passengers or cargo, and used entirely domestic components, including engines and avionics (from Harbin Aero-engine Company). Up until the late 1990s, the Y-7 was almost entirely sold to the domestic market, with CAAC its largest customer, purchasing 70 of the planes. However, if XAC wished the Y-7 to break into the international market, it needed to improve the Y-7's performance. The Y-7-200 series was developed, using imported Pratt and Whitney engines, Hamilton (USA) propellers, and key imported avionics from Rockwell and Honeywell. The Y-200 series went into commercial service in 1986. However, these raised the cost of the Y-7. The Y-7's capacity was increased to 60 seats. Still in the late 1970s, the Y-7 had made only limited headway in international sales, with purchases by Laos national airline and three planes sold to different African countries. By 1997–8 XAC had zero orders for Y-7s, a disastrous situation leaving expensive equipment standing idle.

There were a variety of reasons for its disappointing sales. The Y-7 did not apply for an airworthiness certificate from either the JAA (Europe's Joint Aviation Authority) or from the FAA (the USA Federal Aviation Authority). The plane has an excellent safety record but to go through the full process of certification is a very expensive process, costing 'several hundreds of million of yuan', and only worthwhile if the potential market is large enough to warrant the investment. However, there are severe constraints on the potential market for the Y-7, as evidenced by the current absence of orders.

First, there is already intense international competition in the 50–70-seat turbo-prop feeder aircraft market. In 1996 there were reported to be no fewer than 17 manufacturers of regional aircraft across the world (*FT*, 23 January 1996). Strong market positions are already held by the ATR 42 (produced by Aérospatiale and Alenia), the Dash 8 (produced by Bombardier), and the Saab 2000 as well as the Russian-built An-24 in former Soviet states. A powerful player in this market,

Fokker, with the F-50 turbo-prop, went out of business. China has even begun to import ATR 42's, in direct competition with the Y-7. By 1998 five were in operation. Almost 600 ATR aircraft had been sold world-wide by 1998, enabling the company to benefit from economies of scale in a way that the Y-7 has been unable to do. Secondly, the whole future of turbo-prop feeder planes is in doubt. In the developed countries, competition for small, local feeder aircraft has grown from high-speed trains. Moreover, there has been a marked shift in airline preference towards jet-engine feeder aircraft. Jet aircraft are preferred for safety, reliability and customer preference.

The Y-7 programme provided China's aviation industry with the capability to batch-produce a modern aircraft. However, the long-run market for such an aircraft is very limited, both domestically and internationally. The uncertainty surrounding China's turbo-prop production is such that XAC is in deep discussion with ATR (Alenia/Aérospatiale) about the possibility of more comprehensive co-operation, including even the possibility of assembling the ATR-42 at XAC. Indeed, it was confirmed in early 1999 that XAC would become the location for the assembly of ATR72-500 regional aircraft within China (*CDBW*, 31 January 1999). However, China cannot base its strategy around the turbo-prop market if it wishes to become a world force in aircraft manufacture. To achieve this, it must develop the capability to build modern jet aircraft.

Building a Modern Jet Airliner.   After the conclusion of the Y-10 programme, China's aerospace industry re-organized its strategy. China had huge resources within the aerospace industry, despite its technical backwardness. There was a strong feeling within the industry in such a huge country as China, employing almost three-quarters of a million people within the aircraft industry, 'the goal should be to build a large commercial airliner'. The Ministry of Aviation devised a 'three-step take-off plan', with the goal of building a 180-seater plane by 2010. This was highly ambitious, but China was stimulated by the way in which Airbus Industrie had grown from nothing to challenge Boeing's global dominance. The plan was to start with the assembly of the McDonnell–Douglas 80/90 series of planes, which would provide China with an understanding of the skills needed to assemble a large modern aircraft. The second phase involved the intention to co-operate with a leading manufacturer, in order to jointly design and manufacture a state-of-the-art 100-seater plane, to go into service around 2005. The intention was for China to have around 50 per cent of the total work on the plane including wing production, main fuselage manufacture and final aircraft assembly. The final phase involved self-design and manufacture of 180-seater aircraft. One by one each of these objectives fell by the wayside. By the autumn of 1998, the whole strategy needed to be re-thought.

MD-80 assembly.   Co-operation with McDonnell–Douglas (MD) began as early as 1975, when MD first put forward the proposition that MD planes might be assembled in China. Two agreements to assemble MD-80 series planes were signed. The first was in 1985, for 25 planes and the second, in 1989 was for ten planes. For MD the move was clearly intended to facilitate its sales to the fast-growing China market. It was acutely aware of its weakness relative to Boeing, and intended to use the China market as a major weapon in its struggle with Boeing. Consequently, MD was willing to allow China to assemble the MD-82/83, whereas it appears Boeing was unwilling to allow assembly of its aircraft to take place in China. Boeing was at that stage only willing to discuss sub-contracting arrangements with China (see below). The degree of importance that MD attached to the China market is indicated by the fact that the Chinese production line was the only one that MD constructed outside its Long Beach production line in the USA.

MD was willing to provide Shanghai Aircraft Manufacturing Corporation (SAMC) 'free of charge' with the drawings necessary to conduct the aircraft assembly. The drawings weighed 50–60 tons in total and had a market value of an estimated $60 million. In addition, MD provided China Eastern (which operates out of Shanghai) with a flight simulator 'free of charge'. The simulator had an estimated market value of $30 million. As part of the agreement, MD sub-contracted the manufacture of the horizontal stabilizers, inboard flap support, and six different doors to SAMC,[13] accounting for an estimated 10 per cent of the value of the fuselage.

SAMC was chosen as the site for the assembly to take place. This was partly due to SAMC's experience in manufacturing the Y-10, but a more important factor was probably MD's preference for Shanghai as an advanced location technologically and in relation to the business advantages of operating from China's most commercially advanced city. From the Chinese side, the Shanghai leaders lobbied hard with the central authorities to allow the production line to be located in Shanghai. The assembly of aircraft was highly symbolic for Shanghai's leadership, which wished to be viewed as a commercially and technologically advanced city. SAMC made large investments in the necessary machine tools and production line.

From 1986 to 1993 SAMC assembled 34 MD 82/83 aircraft. In 1992 SAMC made the first of five deliveries of the aircraft to the USA and the planes obtained their FAA certificate of airworthiness. From MD's perspective, the programme succeeded in enabling them to expand their sales to China, since 29 of the aircraft produced went into service with Chinese domestic airlines. The number of MD 82/83 aircraft in service in China rose from five in 1985 to 39 in 1996 (Table 4-15). Twenty of the planes were sold to China Northern and 10 to China Eastern.

Although there was no large-scale transfer of technology, there were clearly identifiable gains for SAMC from the assembly contract. It almost certainly made a profit from the assembly work, including unanticipated benefits from the devaluation of the yuan over the course of the contract. The promised income from the contract enabled SAMC to invest in large-scale purchase of advanced machine tools and other advanced equipment, and large-scale transfer of knowledge from MD workers to the Chinese side. SAMC gained important understanding about the complex process of organizing the assembly and testing of a large modern aircraft. SAMC's quality standards were forced upwards in order to obtain FAA approval for the MD 80 series assembly line and the sub-contracted components production. MD assisted the Shanghai Aviation Research Institute to advance its design skills as part of the programme.

Broadly speaking the first phase of MD's co-operation was successful for both sides. The contracted number of planes was manufactured. MD made some significant gains in market share in China, though not as great as it might have initially hoped. SAMC made significant gains in understanding the complex process of assembling a modern aircraft. It was positioning itself to become the core plant in any restructuring of the Chinese aviation industry, since it is the aircraft assembler that sits at the centre of the process of aircraft production in the West.

MD-90 joint production. In the early 1990s MD phased out the MD-80 series and replaced it with the MD-90. Although derived from the MD-80 series, it was a substantially different plane, requiring large-scale re-tooling for the assembler. The plane was 1.6 metres longer than the MD-80 series. It was significantly wider, with an extra two rows of seats. The plane used a new engine (the V2500, jointly produced by a consortium of five companies), which was significantly quieter and had greater thrust. Its avionics were more advanced. The aircraft was more reliable and had lower operating costs.

Despite a broadly successful outcome of the MD-80 series assembly programme, MD was still losing out heavily to Boeing in the race for the Chinese aircraft market. By 1996 there were still only 39 MD-82s (See Table 4-16) aircraft in service in China. The number of Boeing 737s and 757s rose from 15 in 1985 to 175 in 1996. Moreover, Airbus had now appeared on the scene as a potentially formidable competitor. In order to try to capture market share from its rivals, MD agreed to build MD-90 aircraft in China, using designs supplied by MD, with a substantial proportion of domestically-manufactured components.

The plan involved XAC (Xian) producing the wing box, wing flaps and main fuselage (involving around two-thirds of the total value of manufacturing work undertaken within China), Shenyang Aircraft Corporation (SAC) producing the tail, and Chengdu Aircraft Corporation (CAC) producing the nose section. Final assembly would be carried out at SAMC, which would also produce 34 items of components. Domestically produced components would account for around 80 per cent of the value of the airframe. The engines, most of the avionics, auxiliary engine, and landing gear were to be imported, so that considerably below 80 per cent of the total value of the aircraft would be domestically produced. Nevertheless, the agreement in principle was a major breakthrough for the Chinese aviation industry. It marked a potentially significant step on the road towards designing and building a modern airliner within China. Moreover, SAMC felt that it had achieved a leading position in restructuring the Chinese civil aircraft industry, since it was the 'main manufacturer', with XAC, SAC, and CAC as the 'suppliers' of major components.

In the initial discussion in 1992, it was suggested that MD would build 150 MD-90s in China, with the Shanghai assembly line forming one of only two that MD would have across the world, the other being Long Beach. At that point the international aircraft market was growing fast, and the vista for AVIC was of

TABLE **4-16 Main International Sub-Contracts at XAC and CAC Since the Late 1980s ($ million)**

Company	Item	No. of items	Value of contract
XAC			
Boeing	B-737-700 vertical fins	1500	262
Boeing	B-737-300 vertical fins	600	78
Boeing	B-737-300 horizontal		
	stabilisers	300	32
Aérospatiale	ATR-42 wing box	150	25
Alenia	ATR-72 fuselage, section 16	100	23
Other companies/			
items	—	—	34
Sub-total			454
CAC			
McDonnell–	MD-80, MD-90	200*	90**
Douglas	nose sections		
		(126)*	(57)**
Boeing	B-737-200 vertical fin,		
	horizontal stabilisers		
	rear fuselage, section 49	174	140
Airbus	A-320, A-321, A-319		
	Rear access door	n.a.	n.a.
Sub-total			200 (approx.)

NOTES: * Only 126 actually supplied
     ** Approximate estimate, based on a reported figure of $450 000 per nose

exports as well as supplies to the domestic market. The promised co-operation appeared to offer great prospects for the second stage in the development of China's civil aircraft capability. Domestic newspaper reports of the co-operation were glowing in their evaluation of the prospects for the relationship.

When the contract was finally signed in 1993, MD's situation had changed significantly. The final agreement was signed against a background of a deteriorating situation for MD in its competition with Boeing, and it was feeling the growing force of competition with Airbus. More importantly, AVIC was unable to guarantee MD the sales to domestic aircraft companies that MD had hoped for. Indeed, Boeing's sales to China increased rapidly at the very time when MD was negotiating the agreement to produce MD-90s within China. MD's main goal was not to export, but to sell into China. As a result, the final contract in 1993 stipulated that a drastically reduced number of aircraft would be manufactured within China. Instead of 150, the contract stipulated only 40. Moreover, the contract was further revised in July 1995, when it was agreed that only 20 would be manufactured in China and the remaining 20 to be sold within China would be manufactured at Long Beach. The Chinese aviation industry was bitterly disappointed that CAAC was unable to place a larger order for a plane that would be made within China, and could form the springboard for the industry's long-term development.

Production was scheduled to begin in April 1998. The main participating Chinese factories (XAC, SAC, CAC and SAMC) invested heavily in setting up manufacturing facilities and sub-assembly and final assembly lines. While they were setting up the production lines the situation at MD continued to deteriorate (see above), culminating in the merger of Boeing with MD, put into effect in 1997. Only a few months after the merger, in November 1997, Boeing announced that it was going to discontinue production of the MD-90 in 1999 (*FT*, 4 November 1997) and close the MD-90 assembly line at SAMC. In the end CAAC committed itself to buying just two of the MD-90s produced in China. It was said to be unwilling to invest in a plane the production of which was shortly to cease. CAAC's decision not to buy more than two MD-90s was critical for the programme. Indeed, had China bought significant quantities then export markets might even have developed. AVIC even applied to start its own airline which would have used domestically produced MD-90s, but this proposal was vetoed by CAAC. Boeing publicly presented the decision to produce only two rather than the originally scheduled number, 20, as entirely due to the lack of domestic demand from CAAC: 'It's their decision. It's based on low market demand for these aircraft in China. It's a smart decision for them to make and it demonstrates that they are making their decision based on an economic basis' (Boeing spokesman, quoted in *FT*, 5 August 1998).

Instead of producing 20 domestically manufactured MD-90s, the final number was reduced to three in July 1998. In August, even that number was revised down to just two. The termination of the programme involves large losses for the Chinese aircraft makers. Their investments in plant, equipment and stocks were all made on the assumption that at least twenty aircraft would be built. SAMC is the most seriously affected of the Chinese aircraft manufacturers, since it is almost entirely dependent on assembly of civil aircraft. It does not make military aircraft and has limited sub-contracting compared to the other major companies in the sector. By 1998 it was reduced to negotiating with the Shanghai Automobile Company to become a partner in a bus-manufacturing joint venture and abandoning any serious pretence to become an aircraft maker. The Y-10 stands as a forlorn symbol of the aspirations it once held to compete with the global giants.

Jointly designed and built jet aircraft. In the early and mid-1990s, the Chinese civilian aircraft industry was confident of its strategy and prospects for becoming a major aircraft manufacturer. The successful programme to assemble MD-80 series planes had been completed, the next step, to produce a large number of MD-90s with the major share of the manufacturing work being undertaken within China was apparently well advanced. The next stage on the 'flight plan' was to co-design and build a substantial part of a small jet airliner, and thereafter to proceed to independently design and build a large airliner, albeit initially using imports of key components, such as engines and part, at least, of the avionics.

We have already seen that there is a fast-growing world market for jet aircraft of around 100 seats. Airbus' global market forecast for 1998 predicts that there will be a market of around 2000 planes of 70–125 seats between 1998 and 2017, while Boeing estimates that there will be a market of 2500 in the 80–100-seater jet aircraft category over the next 20 years (*FT*, 3 September 1998). The market is worth over $100 billion. It is predicted that the market for 100-seat airliners alone will be around 1300 in the next 20 years (*FT*, 27 April 1999). Asia is the main focus for sales of regional jet aircraft. Some estimates suggest that as many as 2000 regional jets could be sold in the region over the next 20 years (*FT*, 12 June 1997). China is thought likely to constitute a large share of this market.

However, this is an extremely competitive segment of the world aircraft market. Two important makers of 100-seaters jets have either drastically reduced their production or left the business altogether. In the late 1970s British Aerospace gave up producing the BAC 1-11 which seated between 65–119 people. Around 230 of the aircraft were produced. In the 1980s, BAe started to produce the four-engined BAe-146 (re-named the Avro RJ), seating 75–110 passengers. The BAe-146 was loss-making for over 11 years after its launch. It made a profit for the first time only in 1997–8, following intense efforts to improve productivity and lower costs. BAe only produces around 20–22 of the aircraft per year. BAe discussed the possibility of establishing a joint venture with Taiwan to manufacture the BAe-146, but the project 'failed the test of financial viability'. Fokker is the world's oldest aircraft maker. By the mid-1990s it had made over 200 F-28s (70–90 seats) and over 250 F-100s (100–110 seats). However, the firm went bankrupt in 1996 (*FT*, 23 January 1996).

We have seen that Bombardier (Canada) plans to produce a 90-seat regional jet aircraft, expanding on its existing smaller aircraft. We have seen also that Embraer (Brazil) has also built itself into a fully-fledged regional jet aircraft maker, with the first of its 70–108-seater planes planned for delivery in 2002. Boeing and Airbus already produce highly competitive planes, the smallest versions of the B-737 and A-319 both seating just over 100 passengers. Moreover, as we have seen, Boeing has developed at high speed a 100-seater aircraft, the B-717, based on the MD-95. This flew for the first time in September 1998, and entered service in the summer of 1999 (*FT*, 3 September 1998). As we shall see later, Airbus also plans to build a 100-seater aircraft. In other words, Bombardier, Embraer, Boeing and Airbus will collide in this sector of the market. The former two are expanding into larger aircraft, while the latter two are moving down into smaller aircraft.

In the early 1990s, AVIC entered intense negotiations with McDonnell–Douglas, Boeing and Airbus to establish a venture to jointly design and produce a 100-seater aircraft. The stated intention was to produce in China a total of 1000 planes to be sold to both the domestic and the international market, principally regional Asian carriers (*CDBW*, 30 June 1996). The MD proposal quickly fell by the wayside. A protracted period of negotiation took place with Airbus and Boeing over several years, with many different proposals under discussion.[14] In the end AVIC decided to proceed with the Europeans rather than Boeing as their partners in the development of a 100-seater aircraft. It was widely believed that politics had a substantial role to play in the final decision. The agreement received wide publicity and was generally perceived as having a substantial political element. Philip Condit, head of Boeing, 'acknowledged that politics and business could not be separated' and 'hinted that soured Sino–USA relations had affected Boeing's chances in the competition' (*CDBW*, 30 June 1996).

The planned aircraft was called the Air Express 100 (AE-100). The initial agreement to proceed with the scheme was signed in April 1996. The agreement to proceed was signed in Paris by Zhu Yuli, head of AVIC, and Louis Gallon, chairman of Aérospatiale on behalf of the European partners. The agreement was signed at the Elysée Palace, in front of Li Peng, China's Prime Minister, and Jacques Chirac, President of France. The partners in the project were Airbus, AVIC and Singapore Technologies. The co-operative venture was hailed as a prelude to even wider co-operation, with AVIC joining Airbus as a future partner in the A3XX, Airbus' planned 'super jumbo' aircraft (*FT*, 11 June 1996). Enterprises within AVIC were planned to take 51 per cent of the total work involved in the AE-100, including production of the wings, fuselage and final assembly. XAC was intended to be the core plant in the production of the AE-100, as it had been intended to be for the MD-90. The agreement was hailed in the Western press as 'a significant step towards the development of an indigenous [Chinese] aircraft industry' (*FT*, 30 August 1996). It was a major boost for the Chinese aviation industry, which felt that it was now firmly on the road to developing an indigenous modern aircraft industry.

The intention of the agreement was that the AE-100 would be ready to go into service in 2005. The length of time required to design and produce a new aircraft from scratch presented genuine commercial difficulties. The B-717 was ready to go into service in the summer of 1999, and Airbus itself could rapidly develop its own 100-seater aircraft using an existing larger aircraft as the basis (see below). Thus, the main competitors would be very well established in the market before the AE-100 would even have been test-flown. Despite much optimism, the market for the 100-seater planes, as opposed to the smaller versions of existing larger planes (B-737 and A-320), was uncertain. Only half a year before it was due to go into service, the B-717 had firm orders for just 50 aircraft (*FT*, 3 September 1998), and by the summer of 1999 Boeing still had only 115 firm orders for the B-717 (*Fortune*, 2 August 1999). One reason for the lack of interest in the B-717 is that it saved on development costs only by using the existing design inherited from McDonnell-Douglas. This means that the plane is old-fashioned compared to its potential competitors. Fokker had gone bankrupt mainly due to its failure in precisely this market. A key problem for the development of the AE-100 was that CAAC refused to place any advance orders for the plane, causing intense disappointment in the Chinese aviation industry.

Rumours circulated for many months that the AE-100 scheme was in jeopardy. At the Farnborough Airshow in September 1998, it was formally announced that the proposed joint venture had been scrapped. Airbus head Noel Forgeard said 'all three parties have decided it would be too expensive to develop a completely new aircraft' (quoted in *FT*, 8 September 1998). The announcement was coupled with the statement that Airbus intended to develop its own 100-seater aircraft, the A-318, which would be an adaptation of the existing A-320 family. It was announced that it could be developed for 'less than $500 million', and be put into service by 2002 (*FT*, 8 September 1998, 6 October 1998). The plane could be flown by the same pilots and maintained by the same engineers as the A-320 family of planes.

By April 1999, Airbus announced that it had attracted 109 firm orders for the plane. Customers included TWA, International Lease Finance Corporation, Air France and Egyptair. Most interestingly, it was announced that Airbus was 'close to an agreement with Lufthansa and Air China' (*FT*, 27 April 1999). In other words, Air China was unwilling to buy the AE-100, which would have enabled the domestic industry to take off, but was willing to buy the Airbus' comparable plane.

By September 1998 China's 100-seater programme was scrapped and the planned MD-90 programme was finished. A year earlier, neither Airbus nor Boeing produced a 100-seater plane, and China had hoped to produce one by 2005. Now Boeing would have a 100-seater aircraft in service by 1999, and Airbus would have one in service by 2002. China would have nothing.

The double blows of the termination of the MD-90 programme and the AE-100 programme were perceived outside China to 'deal a severe blow to China's nascent aviation industry' and 'throw into doubt its plans to become a substantial aircraft manufacturer' (*FT*, 5 August 1998 and 6 October 1998). Large investments had been made in the MD-90 programme. A great deal of energy had been put into the AE-100 project. Both programmes had substantially raised the industry's hopes. The double blow of the end of both the programmes left the industry reeling. Its development strategy of 'three-stage take-off' was in tatters. The coincidence of the double blow was remarkable. Many people in the Chinese aircraft industry felt that it had been let down not only by Boeing and Airbus, but also by CAAC, which had refused to order either the MD-90 or the planned AE-100. In late summer 1998, it was difficult to discuss the issues with people in the industry, since the experience was so painful for them. Great industry hopes had been pinned on these programmes, and deep re-thinking was now necessary.

The question towards which the Chinese aviation industry had now to turn was: could the industry be rescued through the mechanism of sub-contracts and sub-system joint ventures?

Sub-contract/Sub-system Joint Ventures

Growth of international joint ventures and sub-contracts. Since the late 1970s, international sub-contracts and sub-system joint ventures (JVs) have grown rapidly in China. By 1995, AVIC had signed contracts for a cumulative total of $1.5 billion worth of sub-contracting work. The principal contracts were with Boeing, for the manufacture of vertical fins, horizontal stabilizers and rear fuselage, for the B-737-300, B-737-700 and B-757, and with McDonnell–Douglas for the manufacture of the nose section and horizontal stabilizers, for the MD-82 and MD-90. In addition there was a wide array of smaller contracts, for aircraft doors, wing sections, turbine disks, blades, bores, rings, atmosphere instruments, meteorological radar, general radar instruments, pumps and valves. AVIC had progressed from purely compensation trade to becoming a competitive global supplier of components, including being the sole suppliers of some items (B-747 wing rear ribs, B-737 maintenance doors, BAe 146 doors, Dash-8 cargo doors and LM2500 turbine disks). The role of sole supplier binds the Chinese supplier and global manufacturer tightly together in a relationship of mutual interdependence.

Many of AVIC's plants had international aviation sub-contract arrangements. However, a small number of plants received a large fraction of the total contracts. The two most important locations were Xian Aircraft Company (XAC) and Chengdu Aircraft Company (CAC).

Following the collapse of the proposed joint production plans for the AE-100 and the MD-90, BAe and Boeing both responded with offers of considerably enhanced participation by AVIC in the production of sub-systems. Boeing offered to make China the second supplier of the wing for the B-717, alongside the current supplier, Hyundai. BAe offered to make AVIC a supplier of the wing for the A320. Almost 300 aircraft in the A320 will be produced in 1999 (*Flight International*, 7 October 1998).

Xian Aircraft Company. XAC began sub-contracting in 1980, with a contract for Canadair. Its first major contract was in 1984, sub-contracting with Boeing to produce perpendicular empennage (vertical fin) for the B-737-300. At that point this was the biggest overseas contract that Boeing had made (*International Business (Beijing)*, 1998, No. 7). In 1989 this was followed by a further contract to manufacture horizontal stabilizers for Boeing, again for the B-737-300. In 1995 another contract was signed for the manufacture of the perpendicular empennage for the B-737-700 to supply 1,500 units of the vertical fin. In each case the contracts amounted to around one-half of Boeing's total global supply of the particular item produced at XAC, thereby closely tying the two companies together. In addition, XAC has substantial contracts to supply wing boxes to Aérospatiale for the ATR-42, and section 16 of the fuselage to Alenia. It has a variety of other smaller sub-contracts.

In order to fulfill these sub-contract arrangements, XAC has made substantial investments in advanced equipment, including CNC machine tools, computer-aided design (CAD), manufacturing technologies, such as metal bonding techniques, synthetic materials processing, testing equipment and technologies. Moreover, in order to successfully fulfill the contract, XAC made important advances in 'the organization and management level of production' (*International Business (Beijing)*, 1998, No. 7). In 1997, XAC combined the resources of the Aluminum Company and the sub-contracting part of the company into XAC International, which was floated on the stock market in Shenzhen. In 1996, XAC International's total sales were composed of $22 million from the Xian Aluminium Company and $19 million from XAC's international sub-contracting.

In the early days of sub-contracting at XAC, the sub-contracts were essentially 'offset' arrangements negotiated by CAAC and CATIC for China's purchase of aircraft, mainly from Boeing. Increasingly, XAC has become a competitive supplier of sub-contract capabilities, able to win contracts in open international competition. It has become an important supplier to the global Boeing system, exporting relatively large numbers of some important items. The most significant examples of this are XAC's contracts to supply one-half of the total global supply of vertical fins for Boeing's B-737-700 and B-737-300, and a similar proportion of the horizontal stabilizers for the B-737-300 (Table 4-16). These contracts tie XAC closely to Boeing. Indeed, given the sharp decline in XAC's military sales, and the dearth of orders for the Y-7, it is likely that a large fraction of its aviation revenue is generated by the sub-contract with Boeing.

At one point in the late 1990s, it seemed likely that XAC would soon be manufacturing a large fraction of the value of the Chinese-produced MD-90 and by 2002 would be the main manufacturer of components for the AE-100. It would then truly 'take aircraft as the main thing' (*yi hang wei ben*), with the bulk of its revenue generated by aviation industry products. It could view these as the stepping-stone to becoming the core manufacturing plant within an independent Chinese aviation industry. The period of rapid growth in non-aviation products might then be perceived as a transitional phenomenon to keep the company alive in difficult times.

Instead, by 1998, XAC's aircraft business had been reduced essentially to being a sub-system contractor to Boeing, dependent for the bulk of its aviation sector earning upon sales of vertical fins and horizontal stabilizers for two models of Boeing aircraft. Boeing trains XAC personnel in the production technologies needed to produce the components to a high standard. XAC has paid for around 300 of its personnel to travel to the USA to receive free training at Boeing's headquarters. However, the relationship is one of 'customer and supplier' without transfer of technology and patents. The margins on sub-contract sales to Boeing are, of course, the subject of tough bargaining. Even within China, Boeing is able to use inter-company competition to obtain better terms. For example, CAC beat XAC to the contract for the rear section of the B-757-200 (see below), despite the fact that AVIC wanted the contract to go to XAC, in order to preserve its special capability in the rear sections of the aircraft.

Initially, XAC was the passive recipient of contracts allocated from CAAC and CATIC. Increasingly, XAC has seen a steady accumulation of its rights as an independent 'legal person'. This includes an increase in its rights to retain earnings from sub-contract arrangements, which now remain entirely with XAC, except for 'negotiation fees' in the case where the contract occurs through the efforts of CATIC. XAC now actively seeks out partners for sub-contract work, although the project must be approved by CATIC if it exceeds $1 million. As the constituent companies of AVIC have gradually increased their effective property rights, so their incentive to compete with each other to obtain international sub-contracts has risen. Not only do the constituent companies face severe international competition, but they also face growing domestic competition in winning contracts.

The relatively small size of AVIC's constituent companies, such as XAC, limits their capability to establish individually a global network of offices, whereas

CATIC does possess such a network, and so remains important in identifying partners for XAC. As the military procurement of aircraft has declined, and the hoped-for programmes to build large civil aircraft have failed to materialize (see below), so the struggle to secure sub-contracts has become dramatically more important for AVIC's constituent companies, such as XAC, in their struggle to keep alive their aviation manufacturing capabilities.

Chengdu Aircraft Corporation. Whereas XAC's main sub-contracting partner was Boeing, CAC's main sub-contracting partner initially was McDonnell–Douglas. As part of its bid to gain greater market share in China, MD sub-contracted production of the nose section of the MD-80 and, later, of the MD-90 to CAC. The programme began in 1988. The original contract with MD-80 and MD-90 was for the supply of a total of 200 nose sections, with a total contract price of around $90 million (*CDBW*, 30 June 1996). In fact, as we have seen, following the Boeing take-over of MD, the MD-90 programme was terminated prematurely, and the total number of nose sections supplied to MD (subsequently Boeing) was only 130 for both the MD-80 and MD-90 over the whole life of the contract (1988–98). The rough price of a single nose section is around $0.45 million, so that the total sub-contract for 1988–98 will have been worth around $60 million, or an annual revenue of around $6 million (*CDBW*, 30 June 1996). This formed the vast bulk of CAC's civil aviation sector revenue.

CAC's hope was that these contracts would become the foretaste of large-scale expansion of supplies of nose sections to the domestically assembled MD-90 programme and to the AE-100. Instead, both the domestic and the global production of the MD-90 were axed after the merger of MD and Boeing, and the AE-100 programme was terminated. These developments dealt savage blows to CAC's civil aircraft development strategy.

Alongside the collapse of the contract with McDonnell–Douglas, CAC struggled to develop its sub-contracting relationship with Airbus and Boeing. By 1997 it had begun to produce rear access doors for the A-320, A-321 and A-319. More significantly, in 1998 it began a contract with Boeing to produce the entire empennage, including vertical fin, horizontal stabilizer and number 49 section (extreme rear) of the fuselage for the B-757-200. This was 'very challenging technically', and made CAC the 'most advanced plant in China' in terms of complete sub-system manufacture for the global giants. The contract was for the supply of 174 sets over the period 1998–2008, with a total value of $140 million. Like XAC, CAC is planning to separate the sub-contracting portion of the company in the hope of establishing a separate company under AVIC, with a view to possible flotation.

Aero-engine joint ventures. China's aero-engine companies have developed many sub-contracting and some joint venture arrangements with the global industry leaders. Each of the big three engine makers has become involved in the Chinese engine industry. However, the arrangements are all still relatively small scale. Chengdu Aero-engine Company (CEC) is China's largest, and was a key supplier of engines for China's fighter force. It has been exceptionally active in seeking out international partners, and established sub-contracting arrangements with each of the three global giants. Its largest contracts are with Pratt and Whitney, with whom it began co-operating in 1984. It produces several components, both for the JT8D aero-engine and the FT8 gas turbine non-aviation engine. However, the total value of the export earnings from this contract was only $8 million in 1998, amounting to just 2 per cent of the gross value of output at CEC. In 1997 it established sub-contracting arrangements with Rolls-Royce, and is negotiating with GE to sub-contract engine parts. However, neither of these promises to be as large even as the contract with Pratt and Whitney.

Xian Aero-engine Company (XAEC) has probably the largest international aero-engine partnerships of any Chinese engine company. It has accepted that it cannot independently produce engines for a modern commercial airliner, and has actively sought out international partners for sub-contracts and joint ventures. In the 1970s it was selected as the location for the manufacture of Spey engines under licence from Rolls-Royce. In 1997 it started a relatively large-scale joint venture to manufacture turbine blades for Rolls-Royce. When at full production in the early 21st century it will be producing around $30 million in annual output value (*CDBW*, 11 October 1998). It also has a joint venture with BTI (Israel) and Pratt and Whitney to make turbine blades. The project's total investment is around $30 million. It has sub-contract arrangements with both SNECMA and Pratt and Whitney to make a variety of parts, such as turbine blades and compressor disks for their aero-engines.

Significance of Joint Ventures and Sub-contracts for China's Aircraft Industry

Large relative size of sub-contracts. We have seen that international sub-contracts have come to play an important role in the development of China's civilian aircraft business. It was once thought that sub-contracts would be a temporary phenomenon, as part of the transition towards creating an independent aircraft manufacturing industry. Increasingly, they have become the core of AVIC's civilian aircraft development. By 1997 international sub-contracts accounted for at least one-third of AVIC's total civilian aircraft sector revenue, and the proportion was growing.[15] Moreover, with the substantial decline in military aircraft procurement, their role in the total output of AVIC's aircraft business has risen significantly.

Small size of contracts. Despite their substantial growth, China's sub-contracts with the global giants are small-scale in many important respects. For example, in 1997 sub-contracts were still a less important source of revenue for XAC than either the production of aluminium h-shapes for the construction industry or the manufacture of Volvo buses. In 1996, XAC's revenue from sub-contracts was $19 million, and it was predicted that this would rise to $43 million by the year 2000 (*International Business (Beijing)*, 1998, No. 7). This compares with 1997 sales of $36 million by the Xian Aluminium Company and $60 million by the Xian Volvo bus joint venture. It is likely that these three activities were accounting for over three-quarters of the total sales of XAC. Moreover, they were both increasing fast. At CAC, the annual sub-contract sales value was around $20 million in 1998, forming only around 15 per cent of CAC's total revenue in 1997.

China's sub-contractors are still very small-scale compared to Japan, South Korea or Israel (the latter mainly for military aircraft). Japan is the world's leading sub-contracting country, with an annual value of aviation industry sub-contracts of around $9–10 billion. Daewoo Aviation Manufacturing Industry, one of South Korea's leading aircraft sub-contractors, on its own has an annual revenue of $600 million from international sub-contracting. AVIC's total annual sub-contract value in 1998 was well under $100 million. Between 1998 and 2010, China will probably import around 1000 aircraft from Boeing and Airbus, worth around $50 billion. However, the currently agreed value of sub-contracts with Boeing and Airbus for this entire period is only $600 million for the two leading companies, CAC and XAC. As we have seen, the total annual value of sub-contract sales for the whole of AVIC is only a tiny fraction of the prospective total value of multinational aircraft sales in China.

Fragmented, internally competitive market for sub-contracting. The system of aircraft purchase in China limits the industry's success in obtaining sub-contracts proportionate to the size of the aircraft purchase. CAAC is the body that organizes the purchase of aircraft. Moreover, the decisions to buy aircraft are often made with a view to international economic and political relations rather than viewed by the central authorities as the potential instruments of industrial policy. The central leadership plays a key role in deciding aircraft purchase policy. They must take into consideration not only the development of the national aircraft industry, but also China's international economic and political relations. International aircraft purchases are a mechanism of balancing the interests of the USA and Europe. They are a highly symbolic means of meeting USA and European demands to offset China's exports to them with these regions' exports to China. China's imports of aircraft facilitates China's exports of other products to these regions and helps to combat protectionist pressures from within the USA and Europe. The indirect employment effects of the aviation industry are very large, so this effect is especially politically significant. Sales of advanced military equipment to China by the USA or Europe would be highly significant in terms of symbolizing the transformation of international relations from hostility to friendship.

AVIC has overall responsibility for the development of the domestic aircraft industry, and doesn't participate in the purchase of the aircraft, which limits its ability to place leverage on the global aircraft makers to sub-contract within China. Moreover, the main Chinese aircraft manufacturers are competing with each other to obtain sub-contract work, which weakens the overall industry's bargaining power in obtaining sub-contracts, and in settling the terms for the sub-contracts. Instead of a centrally co-ordinated simultaneous purchase and negotiation of sub-contracts, the system is fragmented and much less effective than it could be, given the large size of China's aircraft purchases. The competition between XAC and CAC for the tail section of the B-757-200 is an illustration of this problem.

Severe international competition for sub-contracting. China has a high level of technical capability in sub-contracting and large surplus stocks of advanced equipment installed for programmes that have been abandoned. As a sub-contractor (as opposed to designer) it can produce the most difficult parts of the fuselage, including the nose, horizontal stabilizer, and most of the wing apart from the main spar. China's leading sub-contractors face not only serious domestic competition but also intense international competition. Israel is a strong competitor for military sub-contracts. In civil sub-contracting, South Korea and Japan are the strongest competitors. Indeed, it has been suggested that Boeing encouraged South Korea's development as a sub-contractor in order to increase competition in the sector. The nose section for the B-717 (MD-95) has been sub-contracted with South Korea rather than China. The severity of competition in the sub-contract business is indicated by the fact that CAC's contracted price of a nose section for the MD-80 and MD-90 was reported to have been $450 000. This compares with a price of approximately three times as much if the nose had been produced in the USA. Bargaining was 'hard', including even the threat of sub-contracting from the former USSR.

A key limitation for China's sub-contractors is their inability to co-finance on a large scale. China's sub-contractors are generally only able to contract for 'Level 3' contracts. These are contracts for which the sub-contractor itself purchases the materials and equipment, but have no design or finance function. 'Level 4' sub-contracts involve risk-sharing, but without a design function for the sub-contractor. 'Level 5' involves risk-sharing and co-design. Japan and South Korea are able to sub-contract at Levels 4–5.

Mechanism for developing capability independently to manufacture large aircraft? Sub-contracting provides one mechanism for modernizing the Chinese aircraft industry. The contracts provide a means to purchase new plant and equipment, to train managers and lower level employees in new techniques, and to gain a closer understanding of international markets.

Some people in the industry hope that through enhancing China's capabilities to manufacture different parts of the aircraft, it may be possible for the Chinese civil aircraft industry to develop the ability to manufacture independently a complete modern large jet airliner. Even a single domestic company, such as XAC, harbours hopes to be able to build a complete large modern aircraft: 'The experience gathered from the sub-contracting deals will play an important role in enabling the [Xian Aircraft] Corporation to make sophisticated planes on its own' (*International Business* (*Beijing*), 1998, No. 7). Under AVIC's scheme for sub-contracting, a division of labour was to take place between different plants. Shenyang (SAC) would specialize in sub-contracts for the tail section, XAC for the main body of the fuselage including the wings, CAC in the nose section and SAMC in the final assembly. In fact, AVIC's scheme for specialization of sub-contracting skills by plant proved difficult to carry out, due both to the opportunism of the subordinate companies and the wishes of Boeing to have autonomy in their selection of plant for sub-contracting.

Some people in the Chinese industry are sceptical that the multinational giants will permit the growth of sub-contracting capability to allow China to develop the capability independently to manufacture competitive large aircraft. The global giants are extremely skilful at dealing with sub-contractors, and none has yet grown into a fully-fledged manufacturer to challenge the established industry giants. Sub-contracting for components or sub-systems is a very different level of capability from designing the whole system, whether for the engine, avionics or airframe, or entire aircraft. Moreover, as we have seen, overcoming the technical challenges involved in complete sub-system or system design is a very different proposition from selling the product successfully in the global marketplace. This requires financial support, and the development of market-place trust in the quality of the product, which is of paramount importance in aviation.

Japan demonstrates that even with a highly developed sub-contracting business, and strong government support, it is very difficult to make the transition from sub-contractor to aircraft manufacturer. Many voices in the Chinese aircraft industry are highly sceptical about the possibility of China building a commercially viable large airliner on its own, even with substantial growth of sub-contracting capabilities in different parts of the aircraft.

Mechanism for aircraft industry survival?   The growth of sub-contracting can be viewed as a recognition that China will not in the foreseeable future be able independently to design and manufacture commercially viable large jet aircraft. The year 1998 could be viewed as a watershed in the world aircraft industry. It may be viewed as marking the end of an era in which 'catch-up' in this sector was regarded as feasible. As we have seen, the main European aircraft manufacturers decided in the 1970s to pool their efforts in an attempt to challenge the global dominance of the leading USA producers. Its successful catch-up was achieved with intense efforts, and it was not obvious until the late 1990s that the effort would finally be successful. As we have seen, even in the late 1990s, Airbus still faced important difficulties in its continuing rivalry with Boeing. Japan had long wished to build an independent aircraft manufacturing capability to rival the global giants. By the mid-1990s, as we have seen, Japan had recognized that this goal was no longer feasible, and decided that its development path should be through sub-contracting and joint ventures with the multinational giants of aircraft design and assembly, avionics and engine design and manufacture.

The Chinese aircraft industry's strategic goal may have become one of simply survival through sub-contracting. This keeps alive technical skills and provides the means through which to ensure substantial investments in machinery and management skills can be undertaken. Moreover, it provides a means through which to retain highly qualified people within the aircraft industry, helping to stem the haemorrhage of such people out of the industry. A major problem with downsizing an industry in decline is that the best people often leave the industry.

The Chinese aircraft industry is experiencing a serious loss of skilled young people, with the losses especially acute in technically sophisticated areas such as computer software, which are vital for the future development of the industry. The annual salary at one of AVIC's plants for a skilled computer software engineer is only around $1500. In Shenzhen the same person could command around $5000–6000 per year, and in the USA many times this figure.

Mechanism for strong aircraft industry growth in China? In 1998, China's sub-contracting relationship with the multinational giants appeared to have potentially taken a further step forward. Following the collapse of the planned MD-90 programme and the collapse of the planned AE-100 programme, both Boeing and Airbus were involved in intense discussions with AVIC about collaboration in wing production. The motive for both Boeing and Airbus is, clearly, to link the production of wings with the sale of aircraft to China.

It was reported in October 1998 that both Boeing and Airbus were in discussions about sub-contracting the manufacture of entire wings within AVIC. Boeing reportedly offered to sub-contract production of the B-717 wing to AVIC in order to supplement its existing relationship with Hyundai (*Flight International*, 7 October 1998). Simultaneously, it was reported that Airbus was in discussion with AVIC about the possibility of establishing a second A-320 wing line in China, to supplement the existing line at BAe in the UK (*Flight International*, 7 October 1998). The plan did not appear to incorporate large-scale design transfer. An Airbus source commented: 'it's one thing getting them to manufacture the wing, it's quite another to get them to design it' (*Flight International*, 7 October 1998). Each of these suggestions would involve heavy transport and logistics problems in shipping the assembled wing to Boeing and Airbus respectively. Although heavy investments in the new lines would be required, much of the advanced machine tooling and other equipment needed might be transferable from that left idle by termination of the MD-80 programme and the failure of the MD-90 programme. If either or both of the wing programmes came to fruition they could signal an important new stage in the relationship between China and the global aircraft giants.

INSTITUTIONAL CHANGE

Children and Grandchildren. Under the commercialization programme, AVIC's subordinate enterprises became substantially responsible for their own development, a dramatic transformation in their method of business operation compared to the 'planned economy' epoch. AVIC has 116 subordinate plants grouped under 56 'children' (*erzi*) enterprises. They construct their own business plans, subject only to quite limited supervision from the centre in Beijing.

AVIC has no rights over the income from the companies established by the 'grandchildren' (*sunzi*) companies. The establishment of new 'grandchildren' companies is formally approved by the AVIC headquarters, but the newly established 'grandchildren' report to the 'child' company, not to AVIC headquarters. The policy of AVIC headquarters is *'fangshui, yangyu'*, or 'allow plenty of water in order for the fish to grow'. AVIC's 'children' companies are supposed to hand over only around 2 per cent of net profits to the AVIC headquarters as a 'management fee', but the requirement appears to be fairly flexible, since there is 'no penalty for refusing to do so'. The profits remaining with the 'children' companies are regarded as re-investment in state assets. AVIC's main control over the 'children' companies is the right to approve the appointment of the child company's general manager and Party secretary. AVIC formally has control over the total wages fund for each 'child' enterprise. However, the 'child' has control over the way in which the wage fund is distributed and control over the size and nature of bonuses: 'Even if AVIC wished to control the bonuses for child companies, it couldn't do so.'

The data on AVIC in this paper all relate to the enterprises directly under the control of AVIC, or the so-called 'second-tier', 'children' companies. However, as the market economy has developed and child enterprises have been encouraged to become more market-oriented and non-aviation oriented in order to survive, and provide jobs and income for their members and their huge number of dependent families, so their business structure has rapidly become more complex. AVIC headquarters has no idea of the total employment and income generated by the offspring of its own child enterprises. There are formally around 540 companies set up by the child companies in which the child companies are controlling owners. However, AVIC's child companies also have extensive investment in companies in which they are only minority owners. Moreover, the 'children of AVIC's children' also set up companies, and/or invest in other companies.

Chengdu Aero-engine Company (CEC) is a representative example of the institutional path through which non-aviation production has developed in AVIC's subordinate enterprises. CEC is China's biggest engine plant, having around 20 000 employees in the early 1990s. It has produced around 12 000 aero-engines over its life, and has the capacity to produce 2000 aero-engines per annum. However, demand for its engines fell 'abruptly', and is likely to fall even further. Its employees 'need to eat', and so CEC adopted three main strategies for survival. Each of these was based on forms of business co-operation:

- *'lao xiang'*– co-operation with the *xiangzhen qiye* (township and village enterprises or TVEs);
- *'lao wai'* – co-operation through joint ventures with foreign companies;
- *'lao da'* – co-operation with large domestic enterprises.

Like other companies within AVIC, non-aerospace products accounted for 70–80 per cent of total sales value by 1997–8. Like other companies of similar size it developed a complex web of investments in 'child' and 'connected' enterprises. By 1997, it had invested 329 million yuan ($40 million) in 104 companies (see Figure 4-2). Of these, it had invested 143 million yuan in 65 'child' companies, 56 of which were wholly-owned, and 9 of which were majority-owned by CEC. In addition, it had invested 186 million yuan in 39 'related' companies, in

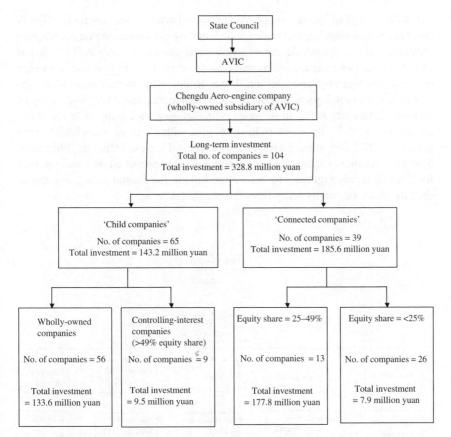

FIGURE **4-2 Long-term Investment by Chengdu Aero-engine Company in Subsidiary Companies**

which CEC had minority ownership positions. Its most important investments were in activities only loosely related to aerospace.

CEC's largest single investment, accounting for around 46 per cent of its total long-term investment was in a minority joint venture with Erqi (Dongfeng), one of China's top three auto manufacturers. CEC held a 46 per cent stake in a joint venture with Dongfeng to produce diesel engines. In return for its investment CEC was able to produce an important part of the components for the plant. Its second large-scale investment outside aerospace is in a joint venture with Kelong, a township and village enterprise that has become one of the largest refrigerator producers in China. As with the investment in the joint venture with Dongfeng, CEC is able to use the investment as a means to ensure a market for its products, supplying Kelong with components. One of CEC's workshops has been wholly turned over to producing components for Kelong. A condition of the joint ventures is that CEC accepted Kelong's requirements for 'flexible' manning levels and wage rates.

CATIC is one of the largest of AVIC's subsidiaries. It was set up in 1979 in order to oversee international trade and technology collaboration in the aerospace industry, and has a high degree of operational autonomy from AVIC.[16] It has grown into a large organization, with assets of over $1 billion and a foreign exchange income of over $6 billion. It has 16 domestic directly controlled subsidiaries, with a total group income of $300 million, and has a very wide array of interests. Like other AVIC subsidiaries it has set up a wide array of 'child' companies (Figure 4-3). They in turn have set up a wide range of 'grandchild' companies. CATIC has subsidiaries in major coastal cities, including Shenzhen, Shanghai, Xiamen, Guangzhou, and Beijing. This is part of a conscious strategy for China's aviation industry to 'gain a foothold in the coastal areas', in order to shift its centre of gravity away from remote inland areas.

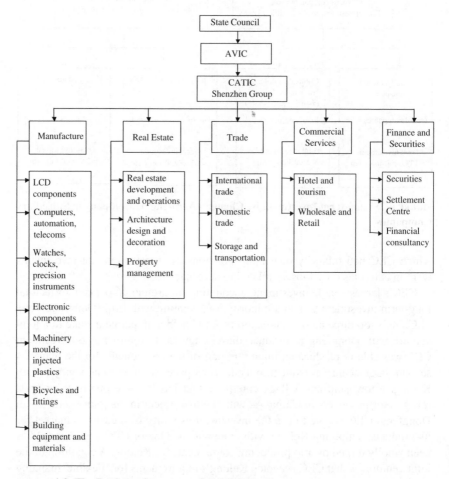

FIGURE 4-3 The Business Structure of CATIC Shenhzen

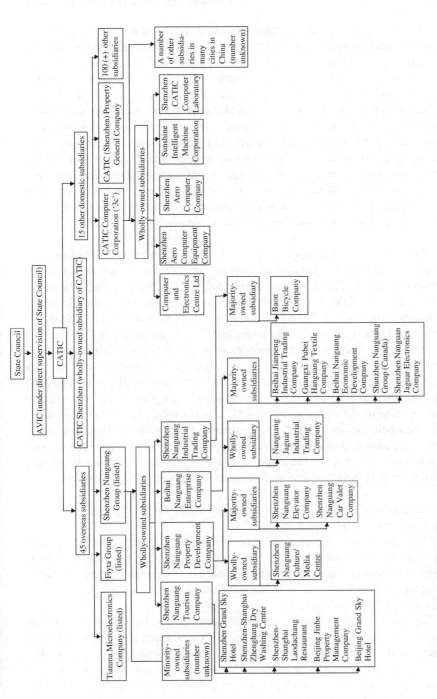

FIGURE 4-4 The Multi-tiered Business Structure of AVIC

The level of complexity that has developed within AVIC's business structure can be seen from Figure 4-4. CATIC is technically a subsidiary of AVIC. Beneath CATIC is CATIC Shenzhen, itself a 'child' company of CATIC. CATIC Shenzhen has over 100 'child' companies, including three listed companies: Shenzhen Tianma and Shenzhen Nanguang are both listed in Shanghai (A shares), and Shenzhen FIYTA is listed in Shenzhen (A and B shares). Shenzhen Nanguang in turn has 35 subsidiaries (its 'children'). A single one of these, Shenzhen Nanguang Industrial Trading Company, itself has six wholly or majority-owned subsidiaries. There is a cascade of businesses each with investments in subordinate companies, from 'children', through 'grandchildren', 'great grandchildren', 'great-great-grandchildren' and 'great-great-great-great grandchildren'. The result is a typical East Asian diversified conglomerate, investing in any activity that brings some short-term profit, but without a common focus.

Flotation. The institutional structure of AVIC has gradually changed since the mid-1990s through the flotation of different parts of the Company. By 1998, four subsidiaries of CATIC had floated, including CATIC Shenzhen in Hong Kong, and Shenzhen FIYTA Group, Nanguang Group and Shenzhen Tianma in Shenzhen. In addition, Liuyuan Hydraulic Company had floated in Shanghai, Nanfang Motor Company in Shenzhen, and XAC International in Shenzhen.

The typical flotation is of a minority share in the floated company, with the majority shareholding still held by AVIC through its subsidiary company. For example, in the case of XAC International, XAC held 64.71 per cent of XAC International. A variety of domestic institutions held less than 1 per cent each and 34 per cent of the equity value of XAC was floated in June 1997 as A shares in Shenzhen, raising 357 million yuan (around $43 million). The assets of the company consisted of the XAC Aluminium Company and the international sub-contracting part of XAC. These accounted for around 54 per cent and 46 per cent, respectively of XAC International's revenue in the year prior to flotation.

Institutional Re-Structuring: The End of the Holding Company Experiment

The issue of size. In terms of employment AVIC is a global giant. It employs a total of 560 000 people, and in the 1980s, the number was around 700 000. The only quoted companies in Europe and the USA with a larger number of employees are Wal-Mart, with 825 000 and General Motors, with 608 000 (*Fortune*, 27 August 1998).

In terms of value of assets, it is a smaller company, but still of considerable size, roughly the size of BAe, with around $7 billion worth of assets. No complete audit of the company's assets is available. While there is evidence in leading enterprises within AVIC of much up-to-date equipment, including many advanced computer numerically-controlled machine tools, it must be questioned whether the figure for the value of assets can truly be compared with that for a modern Western company. The usual procedure adopted by Western accountants auditing Chinese companies for joint ventures or flotation is to estimate item by item the cost of reproducing or replacing in new condition the assets being appraised in accordance with the current market prices of similar assets. Careful consideration is then given to depreciation of plant and machinery arising from condition, utility, age, wear and tear, functional and economic obsolescence, taking into consideration past and present maintenance policy and rebuilding history. A rigorous audit using Western accountancy procedures of the entire stock of AVIC's hugely dispersed assets would be a huge undertaking. Moreover, ascribing a 'fair market value' to assets located for military reasons in remote areas would not be easy.

If AVIC were to be broken up into independent companies with specialisations such as exist in the West (that is the core assembler/designer purchases the bulk of inputs from innumerable supplier companies), then, naturally, the assets value of each of the newly independent companies would be very small compared to leading Western aerospace firms.

If one turns from assets to look at AVIC's total sales and profits, then the company appears in a very different light. Instead of being a 'global giant', it appears very small indeed. Its total sales are less than half of those of Rolls-Royce, one-third of those of BAe and Northrop–Grumman, one-tenth of Lockheed Martin, and around one-twentieth of those of Boeing (Table 4-17). In order to generate much smaller amounts of total revenue, AVIC employs more than twice as many people as Boeing and Lockheed Martin, eight times as many as Raytheon, and 13 times as many as Northrop–Grumman, BAe and Rolls-Royce. Its total sales are close to those of a company such as Airtours (UK), which had sales of $2.8 billion in 1997. Unlike AVIC, which employs 560 000 people, Airtours employs just 12 000 people.

If one considers simply the aerospace component of AVIC, then the company shrinks even more dramatically in relation to the world's aerospace giants. As we have seen, the vast bulk of AVIC's sales in the late 1990s was generated by non-aerospace products. In 1997, the value of AVIC's aerospace revenue was just $650 million. This amounted to less than one-half the sales value of Vickers (UK), a very small player indeed in the world's military industry, with around 10 000 employees (Table 4-17). If AVIC's aerospace division adopted Western manning levels, such as those at Vickers, then the entire aerospace division would employ only around 5000 people. Moreover, even this small total aerospace revenue generated by AVIC is produced by over 100 production enterprises in all branches of aerospace activity (excluding extra-atmospheric rockets). We may assume that the value of the aerospace product sales of the aircraft manufacture, airborne equipment and engine divisions of AVIC in each case are no more than $250 million, with the aircraft division somewhat larger than the other two.[17] Seen in this perspective, AVIC becomes simply a minnow on the world stage. Its engine division produces no more than 2 per cent of the sales value of Rolls-Royce, and its aircraft design and assembly division generates no more than 0.5 per cent of the sales value of Boeing. If AVIC's entire engine division were a separate company, and adopted Rolls-Royce's manning levels, it would employ only around 1200 people.

What direction will restructuring take at AVIC? As we have seen, the rapid expansion of AVIC's non-aviation business in the 1990s created a company which

TABLE 4-17 Relative Size of Selected Aerospace Companies, 1997

Company	Assets ($ billion)	Sales ($ billion)	Post-tax profits ($ million)	Profits/ revenues	Profits/ assets	Sales/ assets	Employees (000s)
Boeing	38.0	45.8	(178)	(0.4)	(0.5)	120	239
Lockheed Martin	28.4	28.1	1300	4.6	4.6	99	190
Raytheon	28.1	13.7	523	3.8	1.9	49	75
Northrop–Grumman	9.7	9.2	407	4.4	4.2	95	47
BAe	7.2	10.4	681	6.5	9.5	144	44
Rolls-Royce	3.8	6.9	(45)	(0.7)	(1.2)	182	43
Vickers	0.5	1.2	83	6.9	17.7	255	10
AVIC	7.1	3.1	72	2.3	1.0	44	560
of which: aviation	—	0.7	—	—	—	—	—

SOURCES: *Fortune* (27 April 1998); *FT* (22 January 1998); authors' research

NOTE: Losses in brackets

consists of a relatively small aircraft firm, by all measures other than size of work-force, within the shell of a vast diversified conglomerate. No-one within the industry believed this was a viable structure upon which to build either a successful aviation business or to construct a successful non-aviation business. From almost the time it was formed, intense discussion went on within AVIC over how to restructure it in the light of its own internal problems and the explosive changes going on in the world industry outside. This culminated in a proposal to the State Council made in the Spring of 1999 to re-shape AVIC fundamentally. The re-shaping of AVIC caused, unsurprisingly, intense debate within the industry. By a curious piece of timing, China's debate over the institutional structure of its aircraft industry took place alongside the similarly intense debate within the European aero-space industry. Like the debate within Europe, the outcome is still far from clear. Even the apparently simplest move to re-structure contains many complexities.

The simplest proposition was to separate the aviation from the non-aviation business. However, even this 'simple' action is far from being as simple as it appears. A large part of AVIC's non-aviation business is not conducted by inde-pendent companies, but is conducted by using the plant, equipment and employ-ees of the aviation companies, within a physical site that combines civilian, military and non-aviation production. At XAC for example, one part of the plant is engaged in the production of military bombers, another part is producing the civilian Y-7, another part is producing Volvo buses, and another part is producing aluminium h-shapes for construction. The employees all live in housing provided by XAC and benefit from social welfare provided by the company. Simply dis-entangling the non-aviation from the aviation business will be immensely com-plex. Workers in the aviation branches of the business fear that cutting away the profitable non-aviation businesses will threaten their social welfare provision. Restructuring the vast non-aviation conglomerate will also be a colossal task, but that is not the concern of this study.

Even if AVIC were successfully to have separated aviation and non-aviation into two separate companies, there would still remain complex choices in rela-tion to the shape of the aviation industry company. It has over 100 production enterprises under its umbrella. Should the new entity combine all the different aspects of aerospace within a single company, including both military and civil-ian, aircraft design, aircraft assembly, engine manufacture, and avionics? If the Chinese industry followed the pattern emerging in the West, it would separate engine production from aircraft design and manufacture. It would also de-merge the extensive production of components that currently takes place within AVIC. As we have seen, in the West, a large fraction of components for both engines and aircraft is sub-contracted to a network of independent suppliers.

If China had followed this path successfully, it would have been left with an air-craft design and assembly company, and an aero-engine company that were both extremely small in international terms (see above). Moreover, the company would still have looked very odd in international comparison. Within AVIC, there are no fewer than five principal aircraft assemblers and four principal aero-engine manufacturers, each with the potential to manufacture complete sets of their respective products. In this respect, the industry is not too dissimilar to that in Europe in the recent past. A major task of restructuring would be to develop specialization and benefit from economies of scale within each of these companies. As in the European restructuring, there would be intense struggles over which company was to be the dominant force in the unified company that finally emerged from the process. Each of the principal aircraft design and assembly companies would feel that it should be the 'Seattle' of the emerging industry, probably supported in this ambition by the regional government.

Moreover, the relationship between military and civilian aircraft production needs to be resolved, not necessarily in favour of a single unified company. Europe is moving towards a single giant integrated military and civilian aerospace company, but it may be unsuccessful in its attempt to construct such a company. Boeing is now a massive, integrated defence and civilian company, but Lockheed Martin and Raytheon are both mainly defence producers. It remains to be seen whether the new AVIC structure involves separation of military aircraft from the civilian side of the business.

There remains the complex issue of the relationship between the new structure of the aerospace industry and the global giants. If China is, indeed, to become more and more deeply involved in sub-contracting to the multinationals, careful thought needs to be given to the company structure that is most to China's advantage in dealing with the multinational giants. Might it be better to attempt to mimic the current Airbus structure in which one company specializes in one part of the aircraft and another company in another part? Such a specialized approach might be a better way for Chinese companies to become internationally powerful sub-contractors, than to develop an aerospace company that attempts to produce all the main parts of the plane or, indeed, the engine.

In the event, it appears that the Chinese government has taken the line of least resistance. Instead of breaking the civilian away from the military aircraft, or any other of the more radical proposals that were considered, in early 1999 it decided simply to split the entire entity of AVIC into two integrated parts, AVIC 1 and AVIC 2. Each group contains the full range of production and sale of military and civilian aircraft, airborne equipment as well as non-aeronautical products. AVIC 1 includes Xian Aircraft Corporation, Shenyang Aircraft Corporation, and Chengdu Aircraft Corporation. AVIC 2 includes Harbin Aircraft Corporation, Shaanxi Aircraft Corporation, China Southern Aero-equipment Corporation, Chengdu Aero-engine Corporation and Harbin Dongan Aero-engine Corporation.

The stated goal of the reform is the 'break up of monopoly and the fostering of fair market economy mechanism' (*CDBW*, 31 January 1999). Zhu Yuli, AVIC president said: 'The two groups will both compete and co-operate' (quoted in *FT*, 2 February 1999). While the world's leading aerospace corporations are in the midst of an unprecedented epoch of merger and acquisition, the Chinese aerospace industry is being divided into smaller components. Compared to the global giants, each of China's 'competing aerospace companies' is now even more of a minnow than before the restructuring, each with aerospace revenues of no more than $400 million, and each surrounded by a sea of unrelated businesses.

Not only did the State Council decided to split AVIC into two, it simultane-
ously decided to split into two the other main branches of national defence industries, under the Commission on Science, Technology and Industry for National
Defence (COSTIND). Thus, the China National Nuclear Industries General
Company, the China National Aero-space Industries General Company, the China
National Shipbuilding General Company, and the China National Armaments
General Company, were each split into two segments in order to 'foster competition'. Instead of five aerospace and defence industry companies, China's 'restructuring' has established ten much smaller companies. China's 'restructuring' of its
defence industries is moving in the opposite direction from the global trends. In
the interests of increased domestic competition, China's national defence industries appear to have become much weaker in relation to the global giants.

CONCLUSION

WHAT SHOULD CHINA LEARN FROM THE USA?

The USA has the world's largest aerospace companies. Not only does the USA
possess the world's largest aircraft makers in Boeing (revenues $46 billion in
1997) and Lockheed Martin ($28 billion in revenues), but it also has colossal
aerospace component, sub-system and specialist weapons companies, including
General Electric ($91 billion in revenues), United Technologies ($25 billion in
revenues), Allied Signal ($15 billion in revenues), Raytheon ($14 billion in revenues), Rockwell ($12 billion in revenues), Textron ($11 billion in revenues),
Northrop Grumman ($9 billion in revenues) and General Dynamics ($4 billion in
revenues). In the aerospace industry size matters greatly. It is difficult for any
other advanced economy's companies to catch-up with those of the US. It is still
far from certain that Airbus will finally succeed in the battle with Boeing, or that
Europe will succeed in building an indigenous unified aerospace and defence
corporation to challenge the USA dominance. Indeed, the USA's dominance of
the world aerospace industry may become even greater in the period ahead
through its possible dominance of the fast-emerging trans-Atlantic partnerships.

For firms based in developing countries to 'catch-up' is almost unthinkable. It
is hard to imagine that in the epoch of large jet aircraft any firm based in a developing country, no matter what its size, could overtake the USA's superiority in
technology and systems integration skills, or in the advantages of an established
reputation and a huge stock of 'embedded value' in existing aeroplanes, engines
and other components. China has to face the harsh reality that for a long period
ahead the Chinese aerospace industry will lag far behind that of the USA.

The success of the leading USA aerospace companies is intimately related to
the USA's role as by far the world's leading spender on arms procurement.
Throughout the history of USA aerospace development there has been a close
relationship between the military and civilian aircraft industry's development.
Military considerations have led to government encouragement of a high degree

of concentration in the aerospace industry in the interests of national security. Military procurement has provided a massive revenue base for the USA's leading aerospace companies. It has provided a huge source of support for R & D throughout the aerospace industry. China cannot hope remotely to match the defence spending of the USA which has underpinned the growth of it's aerospace industry. However, there are many ways in which it can use military procurement and military development spending to support the development of the civilian part of the aerospace industry.

The essence of USA aerospace restructuring in recent years has been the dramatic concentration of business power into a drastically reduced number of giant firms, both in the core design, assembly and systems integration, as well as in the supplier companies. The USA government has actively supported the explosive development of giant oligopolistic business structures in this, the most strategically important of all industries. In the restructuring of its own industry, China's policy makers need to be extremely cautious of applying models based on perfect competition and a large number of producers and consumers.

WHAT SHOULD CHINA LEARN FROM EUROPE?

Thirty years ago, several European countries each had strong civil aircraft industries based within the respective countries. France, Germany, the UK, Holland, Sweden, and Italy each had powerful aerospace companies producing entire aircraft. These were 'national champions' nurtured by national governments in the belief that their own country should possess its indigenously-owned industry in this, the most 'strategic' of all industries. By the late 1960s, it was obvious that individually, the European 'national champions' would be unable to challenge Boeing in large civil aircraft. In order to create a large civil aircraft competitor, the individual countries had to give up the idea of a 'national champion', and construct a multi-country company, Airbus Industrie.

At the time that the first discussions to form Airbus took place, the Second World War had only been concluded 20 or so years previously. There was a long tradition of cultural difference among the main partners, and tremendous mutual suspicion. The only way to marry the interest of national governments for 'national champions' with the reality of the urgent necessity to benefit from economies of scale and scope, was through the *'Groupement d'intérêt économique'*. However, as the USA industry becomes even more concentrated, even this form must now be changed if Airbus is to remain competitive. The current transformation of Airbus into a truly independent company, with all the assets pooled into a single company, signals an important new stage in the transition from a 'national' to a truly 'international' company, far removed from the situation of 'national champions' and 'national industry'.

Can China replicate Airbus? Does the Airbus experience suggest that with powerful government 'industrial policy' support, a latecomer country can 'catch-up' in aerospace? China's industrial planners derived great comfort from the fact that

Europe had, indeed, been able to co-operate and, with strong government support, catch-up with the global leader, Boeing. The lesson for China from Airbus may, in fact, be very different.

AVIC is starting from a very different base. The world aerospace industry has changed drastically since Airbus was established. It is much more difficult to contemplate independent catch-up today. The real level of government support required to develop the equivalent of Airbus today is vastly larger than was the case in the 1970s and 1980s. Moreover, even with the huge financial and technological resources of some of the world's most advanced countries behind it, Airbus had a colossal struggle to succeed. In the end, it may even fail. Its rise in market share has been won through ferocious price competition. The attempt to transform Airbus into a fully integrated company is far from complete. Even if the attempt were completed, the task of blending a truly integrated company out of diverse cultural traditions would still remain a daunting one. Moreover, as we shall see below, the attempt to join the civil aerospace interests of Airbus with restructuring the entire European defence industry may prove to be too complex a task. Failure to link military and civilian aviation would damage the prospects of the EADC. In sum, the example of Airbus demonstrates the enormous difficulty of establishing a competitive international aircraft maker in the face of the enormous power of the long-established market leader, Boeing. This applies even to an entity that has large-scale government support.

For a long time after the formation of Airbus, the military aerospace business in Europe remained firmly located within nationally-based companies, each a 'national champion'. Gradually, the industry began to develop increasing cross-border co-operation for individual projects, with a single prime contractor using components and sub-systems from other countries. Like Airbus itself this was a compromise between the desire to retain 'national champions' in the most sensitive of all sectors and the need to benefit from economies of scale and scope. As we have seen, by the 1990s this became increasingly incompatible with the need to reduce defence budgets and control defence spending. By 1997–8, the European industry had moved rapidly towards a grand plan for Europe-wide consolidation into a single military aerospace company. If it is successful, the interests of 'national sovereignty' will again have given way to the imperative of the logic of the economies of scale and scope.

China might conclude from the European experience with the EADC that even in the military sector, international co-operation is the only feasible path to the development of a high technical production capability at reasonable cost. Such co-operation might even be with countries that were formerly enemies. For example, the Tornado fighter was conceived in the late 1960s, involving the UK and Germany, which had been enemies only twenty years previously. Japan has developed its domestically-produced fighter, the Mitsubishi FS-X, in close collaboration with the former enemy, the USA. This plane is essentially a derivative of the US-produced F-16. Such international co-operation is already under way between China and Russia, and is developing cautiously with both the EU and the USA, despite high levels of sensitivity in both cases.

As we have seen, the final stage of the transformation of the European aerospace industry is intended to involve folding together military and civilian aerospace interests into a super-large company that will stand alongside the two giants of the USA industry. If it is successful, the once conflict-ridden European continent will have succeeded in leaving behind the epoch of 'national industrial policy', and entered the realm of truly multinational companies, even in this, the most sensitive of all areas of economic activity. Age-old national rivalries will have given way before the logic of the world of oligopolistic competition. The price of the industry's survival will have been the loss of intra-European national sovereignty in the most crucial area of all, defence. The EADC may only become a true 'European champion' if Europe develops into a single political entity.

However, the attempt to cling on to national sovereignty too long may yet destroy the possibility of survival of European-based companies as large-scale aircraft makers. Indeed, the possibility of failure for the attempt to create the EADC is high. The idea that the epoch of the nation state is finished is belied by the still intense struggle to construct a single European aerospace entity in the face of the massive challenge from USA restructuring. If Europe cannot unite in the face of the dramatic transformation in the USA aerospace industry, involving a deep commercial and military challenge for Europe, then how can it be believed that the epoch of the nation state is over?

China is far closer to the USA than to Europe, in the sense that it is not driven by national rivalries in the way that Europe is. Like the USA, China is a vast united territory. Its population is several times larger than that of either Europe or the USA. It is able to act with a coherence that Europe has failed to achieve in its search for a united aerospace company. Indeed, ultimately, China is likely to be a nation that is far larger than either the USA or Europe. At some point it is likely that the Chinese aerospace market will exceed that of either Europe or even the USA. A lesson that China may draw from Europe's possible failure to establish a single unified aerospace company, is that there is only one serious challenger in the long-term, namely the USA. It may only be the USA that is able to construct an industrial policy that integrates the national interest in military production with that in the civilian sphere. One possible strategy for China is to link itself closely with the European aerospace industry, in order to join forces to challenge the USA hegemony. It may be thought that Europe's relative weakness would form the basis for a close long-term relationship with China. It may be concluded that the European aerospace industry is more prepared than that of the USA giants to transfer technology due precisely to its weakness compared to the USA giants. However, if China really believes that the European restructuring is likely to fail, then there may be dangers in allying itself with the EU.

What should China Learn from Euro–American Relations in Aerospace?

Even before the discussions over the formation of the EADC, EU-based aerospace companies were developing deeper relationships with US-based firms.

The pace of technical change, escalation of development costs for modern aerospace products combined with intense pressure from government procurement agencies, were already pushing forward trans-Atlantic partnerships in an unprecedented fashion. These included important alliances in military aerospace that would have been unthinkable a short time ago. However, the revolution in the USA aerospace structure since the early 1990s combined with the attempt to form the EADC to challenge USA hegemony in this sector has made the current period an exceptionally dynamic one in terms of trans-Atlantic relationships.

The USA consolidation in the defence sector is more or less complete. Boeing has completed its absorption of McDonnell–Douglas and is working hard to transform its operational methods. We have seen that the attempt to turn Airbus into a single company is far from completion and the prospect is still uncertain. The effort to construct the EADC faces deep obstacles. Many experts believe that the single unified aerospace and defence company will not come to fruition. If the attempt to construct the EADC fails, then the emerging powerful European defence companies, such as the enlarged BAe/GEC–Marconi, Dasa–Casa and Aérospatiale–Matra, will develop in a different direction. The USA government and the leading USA aerospace and defence companies are working hard to prevent the EADC from coming into existence. The EADC would present a serious challenge to US-based firms. The USA government and firms are trying to extend trans-Atlantic integration, offering a greatly enlarged role for the European aerospace industry in USA defence procurement. Equally, the EU countries have reciprocated with some opening of the procurement process to trans-Atlantic competition. It is quite possible that two or three powerful trans-Atlantic giants will emerge. This drastically reduces China's room for manouevre.

Therefore, when China evaluates its strategy in this sector, it must consider the possibility that it will not be able to balance EU-based aerospace companies against US-based companies. It may be unable to leverage the competition between 'US' and 'EU' companies in negotiating the terms of sub-contracting arrangements, joint ventures, risk-sharing partnerships and technology transfer agreements, in either the civilian or the military sector. Moreover, under the emerging structure, it seems likely that US-based firms will comprehensively dominate world aerospace. It is possible that the USA giants will incorporate even formerly powerful EU-based companies as junior partners. EU-based companies are still anxious lest they end up being dominated by the USA giants in an enhanced trans-Atlantic relationship.

However, the intra-EU mergers of the past year, combined with the sharp difference in performance of USA and EU aerospace sector share prices, has produced an important change in the relative size of leading European and US-based companies in this sector (Table 4-18). The new BAe, after it has absorbed GEC–Marconi will have a sales revenue that is larger than Raytheon and close to that of Lockheed Martin. At least as important is the fact that the new BAe will have a market capitalization that is substantially greater than that of either of these companies. Even the newly formed Aérospatiale–Matra will have a sales revenue that is not far short of Raytheon, and its market capitalization may even be above Raytheon's.

TABLE 4-18 Relative Market Capitalization of Leading US- and European-Based Aerospace and Defence Companies ($ billion) 1997–9

Company	Total revenue (1997)	Defence revenue (1997)	Market capitalization (Jan 1999)	% change in market capitalization, (Jan 1998–Jan 1999)
Boeing	56.2	13.8	35.8	−27
Lockheed Martin	26.3	18.5	15.6	−18
BAe/GEC–Marconi	20.4	13.7	24.5 (GEC)	+35
			14.7 (BAe)	+18
Raytheon	19.5	6.3	18.5	+9
Aérospatiale–Matra	14.4	—	—	—

SOURCE: *FT* (15 December 1998, 12 January 1999, 4 June 1999)

Following the announcement of the merger with GEC–Marconi, BAe observed that it felt it was now big enough to seek a US-alliance without having to be swallowed up in so doing. BAe's chief executive, John Weston commented: 'We are moving into a new phase in the company's existence. We will be well-placed to put a bridge between the European and American markets' (quoted in *FT*, 14 June 1999). Under this new circumstance it is possible that the emerging trans-Atlantic relationship is more balanced in terms of company control.

WHAT SHOULD CHINA LEARN FROM JAPAN?

In the early phase of China's economic reforms there was great interest in the possible relevance of the industrial policies through which Japan and South Korea attempted to catch up with the 'West'. Using protection and powerful government support, the two countries 'caught up' in a succession of industries, including steel, shipbuilding, automobiles, and consumer electronics. They intentionally created large, internationally competitive oligopolies, mimicking the institutional structure of the advanced economies. Japan attempted to follow the same path in the aerospace sector, wishing to support domestic firms that would become systems integrators, able to compete eventually with the global giants. However, despite intense efforts, it has effectively abandoned this goal.

Will China now follow the 'Japanese', and accept that it is impossible to become a systems integrator in the foreseeable future? Will it instead, like Japan (and South Korea), see its role to be that of an international sub-contractor, gradually 'climbing the ladder' of capability as skill and capital increase? This would mean giving up its ambitions for the foreseeable future to be able independently to manufacture either military or large civilian aircraft. This would involve a recognition that the difficulties of 'catching-up' in the aerospace industry have become too great for any developing country to surmount, whatever its size. These difficulties reflect the rapid changes in both technology and business institutions.

There are, however, several important differences between China on the one hand, and Japan and South Korea on the other. China still lacks the financial resources to become a full risk-sharing partner in large partnerships with the multinationals. We have seen that these are still mainly very small scale and low-level compared to those of South Korea and Japan. Other things being equal, China is more likely to be able only to function as a sub-contractor with limited investment and technical transfer.

However, 'other things' are not equal. A number of factors provide China with the opportunity to rise up the 'learning curve' of sub-contracting faster than its capital resources would normally permit.

China is a vast country, with great significance in world political economy. Its market for both civilian and military aircraft is very large, and potentially enormous, eventually dwarfing even Japan's. If CAAC had chosen to support the nascent Chinese aircraft industry by agreeing to order large quantities of the MD-80, MD-90 and AE-100, then the Chinese industry would have stood a much greater chance of taking off than did the Japanese aerospace industry. Access to the Chinese civil airliner market is already very important, accounting for around one-tenth of Boeing's and Airbus's revenue. If EU and USA restrictions on sales of military aerospace products were lifted, it could become a vast source of revenue for the global giants. If the USA and EU were willing to pursue this course of action, the logical path would be to involve China in extensive sub-contracting and risk-sharing arrangements. It would also be a deeply significant expansion of China's integration into the international political system. If the West is unwilling to pursue this path, the logical path for China is to rapidly deepen its relationship with the Russia.

WHAT SHOULD CHINA LEARN FROM THE FORMER USSR?

The former USSR had a huge and technically sophisticated military aircraft industry that was in direct competition with the USA. Despite technical inadequacies owing to the absence of consumer pressure, the civilian aircraft industry was very advanced, with large numbers of aircraft produced. There was a high possibility for both the military and commercial sectors to become internationally competitive with suitable policies. Russia's military aircraft industry has experienced great difficulties, and is failing to capitalize on its relatively high starting point. The civilian aircraft business has virtually disappeared. Even access to modern Western engines and avionics does not seem likely to overcome the disadvantages of initially negligible levels of sales in international markets.

The Russian example demonstrates how difficult it is for even initially well-placed industries to catch-up with the global leaders in this sector. The Russian aerospace industry needs powerful state support in order to invest in R & D and in order to gain international certification for its new civilian aircraft. It needs government support in order to ensure that domestic airlines purchase domestically-built planes. It needs government support to provide export credits in order to begin to penetrate international markets and government procurement of large numbers of advanced military aircraft. Each of these things depends on having a strong and effective state and a growing economy. Russia has neither of these things. Even with these pre-conditions, and the advantages of a huge initial aerospace industry, catch-up with the global giants of Europe and the USA would have been difficult. The Russian experience since the fall of the USSR confirms the difficulty in this sector of catch-up through the market alone.

In view of these difficulties, China has a potentially important role to play in the development of the Russian aerospace industry. China has a huge and fast-growing market for both civilian and military aerospace products. It could provide a crucial market for the resurgence of the Russian civilian aircraft industry, using Western components for key parts of the aeroplane, especially avionics and engines. Some form of deeper business collaboration, possibly involving a comprehensive joint venture is a logical possibility, though there is no evidence yet of such a development.

On the military front, we have seen that China has already become a large market for the export of advanced Russian fighter planes. Indeed, China appears to be Russia's largest single market. It is possible that this relationship will deepen considerably. We have already seen that China is manufacturing significant numbers of advanced Russian fighters under licence. The deeper is the resistance of the EU and, especially, the USA, to selling advanced aircraft to China, the more deeply will China be forced to develop its relationship with the Russian industry. This path carries strategic dangers for both the EU and the USA, apart from the loss of potentially large commercial opportunities for US- and EU-based aerospace companies.

However, the Russian aerospace industry is also fast-increasing its business relationships with the global giants. As we have seen, this includes the supply of Western engines and avionics for Russian civilian airliners. It is uncertain how the Western governments and businesses would respond to intensification of China's aerospace relationships with Russia. It is unimaginable that from either a commercial or an international relations perspective the USA and the EU would simply watch the process with dispassionate interest. It may be in China's national interest to explore deeper relations with the former USSR as a bargaining weapon to stimulate re-thinking of the level of military aerospace co-operation with China that is permitted by the EU and the USA government.

What should China Learn from Brazil?

A major reason for CAAC not to purchase the AE-100 was a belief that it is technically impossible for a developing country to rapidly develop the skills necessary to design and assemble an advanced modern airliner. The rapid rise of Embraer into a competitive international commercial aircraft maker demonstrates that it is technically possible for China to independently produce a modern commercial airliner that meets the most advanced requirements of the international airline industry for safety, comfort and environmental controls. It demonstrates that the skills needed to design and assemble a modern commercial aircraft are relatively easily transferable.

The most rapid path to developing an independent capability to build a modern airliner is to purchase the bulk of the components from existing world leaders. This is what both Embraer and Bombardier have done. There is no reason to believe that the world's leading companies in the field, such as Allied Signal, Honeywell, Lucas Aerospace, Rockwell, United Technologies, Rolls-Royce, or GE, would be unwilling to supply components for such a venture. China has already demonstrated with the Y-10, the Y-7 and numerous military aircraft that it has the design and systems integration skills needed to manufacture a modern airliner. A repeated theme in discussion with officials within AVIC is that China is able from a purely technical standpoint to build a modern commercial airliner. There is considerable scepticism from within the Chinese government, and especially, from CAAC. The rise of Embraer, from much weaker technical foundations than AVIC, lends support to the more optimistic view expressed within AVIC. China's planners may conclude from the examples of Embraer (and Bombardier) that it does not need close co-operation with multinational giants of airliner design and assembly in order to build a successful modern airliner. There is little sign of policies to support such an endeavour today. However, it is conceivable that in the future, China's aerospace industry planners may draw great comfort from the experience of Embraer, which is located in a developing country, and has had far less government support than the Chinese government might be able to provide for AVIC.

Not one 'latecomer' country has succeeded in challenging the aerospace giants of the developed countries. Embraer represents the highest achievements so far for developing countries in the field of commercial aerospace. However, it is far from certain that it will be able to compete successfully with the established giants in even this restricted part of the market, let alone in the market for larger aircraft. Embraer has demonstrated the technical possibilities for designing and building a modern commercial airliner, even in a company based in a developing country. However, it seems very unlikely that it will seriously challenge the dominance of Boeing and Airbus. Indeed, the attempt to challenge them in the 100-seater market, could cause them serious commercial difficulties. China cannot conclude from this experience that it is relatively straightforward to compete with the aerospace giants.

However, there is a big difference between Embraer and AVIC. China has a potentially vast domestic market with potential sales of up to 300–500 100-seater aircraft over the coming 20 years. If the Chinese government chose to support a domestically manufactured 100-seater aircraft, such as the Embraer ERJ-190, it might form the basis for a rapidly-growing commercial aircraft industry, with the capability even to challenge the established giants. Through economies of scale and revenue generation from large domestic sales, a virtuous circle of growth, such as Embraer's, but on a much larger scale, might become possible.

The growth of an indigenous aircraft assembly industry, based initially around 100-seaters, could in turn form the basis for the development of an indigenous components industry, which might eventually compete with the established giants of the USA and Europe. If the industry was commercially successful, there is no reason to believe that international risk-sharing partners might not participate in the growth of the industry, in the way they are doing with Embraer and Bombardier.

DOES IT MATTER IF CHINA DOES NOT HAVE AN 'INDIGENOUS'
AIRCRAFT INDUSTRY?

The explosive process of concentration in recent years among the global giants has been accompanied by intense oligopolistic competition. This has resulted in the concentration of colossal financial and technical resources to produce an epoch of unprecedented progress in both military and civilian aircraft, with large declines in the real cost to the consumer of both types of aircraft. It is highly unlikely that competition among a large number of smaller firms could have produced such rapid progress to meet the demands of consumers – including airlines, passengers and governments (as arms purchasers).

The costs of a failed attempt by a developing country such as China to catch-up have never been greater. The resources need to support such a 'catch-up' are enormous. The opportunity cost of the resources devoted to catch-up is very high. Resources devoted to supporting a failed 'national champion' could have been used instead to build dams, roads and schools, or to support the growth of 'infant industries' which stand a good chance of becoming competitive 'adults' in international competition. A country whose airlines are forced to purchase inferior products produced by 'national champions' that are globally uncompetitive will experience commercial difficulties, let alone the possible increased levels of danger to which its passengers may be exposed. If a country is defended by out-of-date products produced by 'national champions' it may be greatly weakened in its international bargaining power, and even find its very existence as an independent state is threatened by its choice of industrial policy.

5

Pharmaceuticals

China has done little to demonstrate that it is backing away from heavy-handed industrial policies ... whereby the Chinese government provides preferential policies to firms to turn them into 'national champions'. Not surprisingly, China's trade partners take exception to this intervention, regardless of the bail-out, infant industry, or national-champion justification. US trade officials routinely express their displeasure with the pillar- or infant-industry-promotion strategy of the Chinese government, which 'indicates the strong hand of industrial policy in actually skewing the market'.
(Groomridge and Barfield, 1999)

The highest of all military principles is to overcome the enemy by strategy ... Skilful military leaders conquer the enemy without fighting battles, capture cities without attacking them and overcome states without protracted warfare. They strive for supremacy without stationing troops long abroad, yet they win complete victory over their enemies.
(Sun Wu, 1996)

INTRODUCTION

This chapter analyzes the growth from scratch of one of the most powerful firms in the Chinese pharmaceutical industry, the Sanjiu Group. Analysis of this firm is interesting for several reasons. First, it sheds light on the importance of existing powerful institutions in shaping the emergence of big businesses in China's reforming economy. Most of China's emerging powerful large businesses are based on the 'commanding heights', 'keypoint' firms of the old planned economy. Unlike these firms, Sanjiu is a 'new entrant'. However, it is a 'new entrant' with a difference, since the owners of the firm until the late 1990s were one of the most powerful institutions in China (some would say, the most powerful), namely the People's Liberation Army (PLA). Until 1998 Sanjiu was owned by the General Logistics Department (GLD) of the PLA. In 1998, the central government announced that it intended to divorce the military from the commercial activities of the PLA. If fully implemented, this move would have major consequences for the institutional structure of wide areas of the Chinese economy.

Secondly, the path through which Sanjiu chose to grow within pharmaceuticals, namely Chinese traditional pharmaceuticals, raises important issues concerning the capability of Chinese indigenous firms to compete directly with the global giants of the industry. These have themselves undergone a business revolution during the period of Sanjiu's growth. Pharmaceuticals are at the leading edge of the capitalist revolution of the 1990s. They have undergone massive reconstruction, a refocus on core business and merger frenzy. They are now far more powerful adversaries than when Sanjiu began life.

Thirdly, Sanjiu's rapid diversification into activities other than pharmaceuticals raises questions concerning the global competitiveness of large Chinese diversified groups based on family relationships or other non-commercial ties of loyalty which are found widely in East Asia. This study sheds light on the capability of this business form to compete with the focused, globalizing big businesses that are fast emerging in the capitalist business revolution of the 1990s. This aspect assumes particular importance in the light of the late 1990s crisis in Asian political-economy. A key issue in the crisis is the degree to which the diversified conglomerate form, characteristic of much big business in East Asia, is viable in open competition with the resurgent capitalist big business of the late 1990s in the OECD countries.

Finally, Sanjiu's rapid growth sheds light on the nature and importance of entrepreneurship in the emergence of big businesses in China's reforming economy. Many firms in the Chinese reforming economy began with Sanjiu's advantages but few matched its successful construction of a powerful modern business.

CHANGES IN THE GLOBAL PHARMACEUTICAL INDUSTRY

DRIVERS OF CHANGE (i): DEMAND

There is a vast and fast-growing global market for patented medicines. Global sales revenue in the sector more than doubled in the 1990s from around $150 billion to over $350 billion (*FT*, 15 March 1999). In the developed countries there is a high income-elasticity of demand for pharmaceutical products causing a strong increase in demand for products that are perceived to improve health and well being. A major aspect of the strong demand for health expenditure is the level of public expenditure on health services. As we will see in Chapter 11, not only are the absolute levels much higher in the advanced economies, but also the proportion of the much higher levels of national product spent on health rises

TABLE 5–1 **Public Health Expenditure at Different Levels of Income, 1990–7**

Country group	Public expenditure on health		Population		Expenditure per capita (1997, $)
	(% GDP 1990–5)	($ billion 1997, approx.)	(billion)	(%)	
Low-income	0.9	7	2.05	35.1	3
Lower-middle-income	2.5	71	2.29	39.2	31
Upper-middle-income	3.3	85	0.57	9.7	149
High-income	6.9	1 642	0.93	16.0	1 766
World total	—	1 805	5.83	100.0	310

SOURCE: World Bank (1998: 190–1, 202–3)

alongside the increase in incomes. The advanced economies account for over 80 per cent of the total patented medicine market (*FT*, 15 July 1999).

Despite the overwhelming dominance of the developed countries, in terms of future market growth, the developing countries are extremely important for the drugs companies based in the advanced economies, despite their low current levels of expenditure on patented drugs. There are strong prospects for market growth in developing countries as incomes rise. Low income countries today spend less than one per cent of GDP on health compared with almost 7 per cent in the advanced economies (Table 5-1). The expenditure on health *per capita* is just $3 in low income countries, rising to $70 in lower-middle-income, $85 in upper-middle-income countries, and reaching over $1600 in high-income countries (Table 5-1). Given the huge populations located in these regions, they are of crucial importance to the long-term growth prospects of Western-based pharmaceutical firms in the twenty-first century. The East Asian market (excluding Japan) alone is predicted to increase from around $20 billion (just 8 per cent of the global total) to $50 billion by 2005 (*FT*, 15 July 1999). Even in developing countries with strong traditional medicine sectors, there is fast-growing demand for patented prescription medicines, especially among the growing numbers of better-off people.

A key issue in the enlargement of the global market for patented medicines has been the rapid increase in the number of former Communist and developing countries that recognize intellectual property rights of companies based in the advanced economies. A truly global market for patented drugs is forming, which offers unprecedented growth opportunities for firms in this sector. This is an especially important issue for pharmaceutical companies, since the incentive to invest in R & D is strongly influenced by the ability to enforce premium pricing through property rights protection. The widening global market for these high-margin products is a strong incentive encouraging growth of traditional pharmaceutical companies, and stimulating traditional diversified chemical companies to focus on this segment of their business and move out of traditional chemicals.

We have seen already that a crucial part of the policy of the advanced economies' policy makers is to establish a 'global level playing field' in products of the 'life sciences' through the TRIPs (Trade-Related Intellectual Property Rights) Agreement. International enforcement of common standards in patent laws is regarded as crucial to the incentive to invest and the ability to earn profits from that investment. It is regarded as a key part of 'fairness' in international economic relations. For example, the Merck Annual Report notes: 'Merck is committed to working ... to create the best and fairest global environment possible ... Strong patent laws allow companies to generate the profits required to finance future R & D while providing investors with a competitive return on their capital' (Merck, *Annual Report*, 1998: 5).

Strong enforcement of this agreement among developing countries is a key part of the attempt by the developed country pharmaceutical firms to obtain maximum returns from their huge investment in patented medicines. We have seen already that a key part of the strategy of the advanced economy pharmaceutical firms is to enforce with increasing strictness the requirement that developing country firms acknowledge and enforce intellectual property rights in medicines. In the past, many developing countries established significant pharmaceutical businesses by replicating without payment patented medicines from the portfolio of the advanced countries' drugs companies. A crucial part of the 1994 Trade-Related Intellectual Property Rights (TRIPs) agreement drawn up by the WTO was the wish to impose far stricter controls over this process, applying common international rules over technology transfer embodied in intellectual property, of which pharmaceuticals constitutes a key area. Developing countries as a whole within the WTO were given only until the year 2000 to adjust their national laws in line with the TRIPs agreement, and the least developed were given only until the year 2005.

The effect of the rigorous implementation of the TRIPs agreement on the pharmaceutical industry of developing countries is likely to be large. For example, India virtually scrapped its patent laws in the early 1970s. A large number of pharmaceutical companies started production in India's protected domestic market, many of them simply reproducing patented Western drugs. By the 1990s there were reported to be around 20 000 pharmaceutical firms 'busily copying Western medicines' (*FT*, 15 July 1999). The fierce competition reduced margins to levels much below those for the same products in the West. However, as a low income developing country member of the WTO India has pledged to bring its patents regime into line with international practice by the year 2005. Foreign pharmaceutical firms that left India in the 1970s and 1980s are thought to be certain to return. A large fraction of local firms are likely to go out of business. The main indigenous survivors are likely to be those local firms that have already attained considerable scale in out-of-patent generic drugs. However, these products are low margin, and provide little capability for the Indian firms to undertake R & D on a sufficient scale to mount a challenge to the global giant corporations in the field of patented medicines for the foreseeable future (*FT*, 15 July 1999). The amounts that leading Indian pharmaceutical firms have available to spend on R & D are 'almost laughable by international standards' (*FT*, 15 July 1999). For example, one of the leading firms, Dr Reddy's Laboratories, based in Hyderabad, has an annual budget of 'a few million dollars, compared with \$2 billion-plus spent by the biggest international companies' (*FT*, 15 July 1999).

DRIVERS OF CHANGE (ii): HIGH AND RISING R & D COSTS

The pharmaceutical industry is knowledge-based. In the patented medicine sector profits are based on earning high margins during the lifetime of the patent in order to recover the high development expenses. In 1998 the profit margins on sales revenue for pharmaceutical firms in the *Fortune* 500 averaged 18.4 per cent, far above the overall average of 2.8 per cent, and well above even the second highest sector, telecommunications, at 10.2 per cent (*Fortune*, 2 August 1999). In 1996 world-wide sales of pharmaceuticals totalled around \$143 billion, of which over 70–80 per cent consisted of sales of patented medicines (*CDBW*, 14 December 1997).

Pharmaceutical R & D expenditure is among the highest of any sector, accounting for 34 of the world's top 300 firms ranked by R & D expenditure in 1998 (DTI, 1999: 59–60). In addition, a further 21 'life science' firms in the chemicals, personal care and health sector were included in the list of the top 300 firms by R & D expenditure. Their R & D expenditure in 1998 totalled over \$51 billion, or almost 1 billion dollars per firm. The 55 firms together increased their spending on R & D by 51 per cent between 1995 and 1998 (DTI, 1999: 56–9). This high level and strong growth of R & D expenditure was caused by many factors. These include the lure of high margins associated with strong long-term prospects for demand in the advanced economies as incomes continue to rise, fast growth of the global market as developing country and former Communist countries liberalize, and recognition of intellectual property rights across an increasing number of countries, especially through the impact of the TRIPs agreement. In addition, as we shall see, pharmaceutical R & D is entering increasingly complex areas of scientific research that demand higher outlays. Competition is intensifying as the industry moves towards global oligopoly through the merger frenzy of the 1990s, and R & D constitutes a major mechanism for establishing competitive advantage. Large outlays are required in order to discover new drugs and bring them rapidly to market. The development stage is especially expensive: typically, over 70 per cent of companies' R & D budget is spent on drug development, including clinical trials and dealing with regulatory authorities Only one out of every 5000 compounds discovered will become a prescription drug. Even the one successful compound will require 10–15 years of work to get it to the market. The established giant companies possess the resources required to take potentially successful drugs through the long and expensive process of clinical trials, through extensive regulatory reviews, to sell the products through large marketing systems using their established brand name, and to withstand potential failures once the products are on the market.

A major development in the sector, paralleling that in IT, is the increasingly close relationship between the leading pharmaceutical firms and the large number of small and medium-sized biotechnology firms. In the same fashion as in the IT industry, leading industry players increasingly generate new technology through investing in small and medium-sized firms, establishing joint ventures with them, and, frequently, simply buying them out if they establish potentially successful products. Around one-third of the drugs launched in the 1990s by the leading pharmaceutical firms came from initial discoveries by smaller outside companies (*FT*, 15 July 1999). In the late 1990s, it was very common for leading pharmaceutical firms to acquire new technology through acquisition of successful start-up companies. Up to one-third of the R & D budgets of the major companies are now thought to be spent on alliances with biotechnology companies offering compounds, projects or drug-discovery tools. In addition, a significant portion of drug development is undertaken under contract by specialist contract research operations. However, there are limits to the degree that the leading pharmaceutical firms undertake outsourcing. The head of Pharmacia and Upjohn, Fred Hassan, commented: 'Certain know-how is better protected inside the company than outside. The more one goes outside, the more one risks losing some of the knowledge forever' (*FT*, 15 July 1999).

In its pursuit of profits, medical research is entering increasingly complex areas of scientific research, such as those associated with organ transplants, Aids, and chemotherapy for cancer. It is stimulating the development of fundamental new areas of research, such as combinatorial chemistry (automated and miniaturized chemical synthesis to create diversity of compounds for testing as drug candidates), genomics (genetic research on diseases) and bioinformatics (application of information technology to genetic and biological data). New robotic technologies have dramatically changed the nature of research in the industry. As recently as 10 years ago, scientists, using hand-held equipment, could test at the most 30 compounds a day. Today, using robotic assembly lines they can run thousands of tests every few hours. R & D expenditure in this sector is notoriously risky, with only a fraction of R & D efforts producing commercially useful results. These developments are driving up the cost of R & D. Moreover, many people in the industry believe that there are strong economies of scope in many new areas of research. Technologies such as combinatorial chemistry, genomics and bioinformatics, are thought to have a wide range of commercially useful applications in both agricultural science and drugs for humans.

In the late 1990s, the development cost of a new drug is estimated to be about $500–600 million. Moreover, there are often powerful benefits to the development of a portfolio of related products. A major driver of the merger wave in this sector is the possibility of economies of scope from merging R & D across a range of products in a number of related treatment areas. R & D expenditure in a given area of treatment is more likely to produce successful results over a number of products within that given area than if it is scattered across a wide range of treatment areas. There are often marketing economies in selling several products within a given area. The company may also develop brand image and product trust as a key player in a particular sector. In other words, as in many sectors, leading firms within the industry broadly-defined are developing global leading positions within specific sub-branches of the sector, establishing even greater barriers to entry and levels of sectoral dominance than at first sight appears to be the case.

The estimated minimum level of R & D investment necessary for a drug company to remain competitive ranges between $1.5–2 billion per annum. The time taken to develop a new drug from synthesis to marketing is estimated to be a full year shorter for the top 15 companies than it is for their smaller competitors.[1] There is a close link between aggregate R & D expenditure and global position in the industry: 17 out of the top 20 pharmaceutical corporations by prescription drug market share in 1997 were also among the top 20 drug companies by R & D expenditure (Table 5-2). MSDW's evaluation of the industry argues for the powerful competitive advantage conferred in this sector by greater R & D intensity (R & D as a percentage of sales revenue) (MSDW, 1998a: 128). There is a high concentration of R & D investment among the world's leading companies: in 1996, the top 20 drugs companies accounted for 49 per cent of the global pharmaceutical R & D expenditure, and the top 35 drug companies account for 85 per cent (*FT*, 21 April 1998).

There are huge potential profits from successful patented drugs. A single success can have a major impact upon the fortunes of the company that develops it. Examples of such multi-billion dollar 'blockbuster drugs' include Zantac (Glaxo), Vasotec (Merck), Prozac (Eli–Lilly), Seroxat/Paxil (SKB), Lipitor (Warner–Lambert), Flixotide (Glaxo Wellcome), Celebrex, an anti-arthritis drug (Monsanto), Premarin (American Home Products), and Viagra (Pfizer). It is estimated that Viagra, a 'lifestyle drug' for curing impotence, may produce as much as $10 billion annual revenue for Pfizer, greater even than its current total annual sales (*IHT*, 4–5 July 1998). Lipitor, an anti-cholesterol drug, earned Warner–Lambert $3.7 billion revenue in 1999. This was a major reason for the hostile takeover by Pfizer. AHP earned $2 billion from its sales of Premarin in 1999, amounting to around 15 per cent of the company's total sales revenue. Vasotec earned Merck $2.4 billion in sales revenue in 1998. Seroxat/Paxil earned SKB $1.8 billion in sales revenue in 1998, while Flixotide earned Glaxo Wellcome over $1 billion in sales revenue in 1999.

A relatively small portfolio of key drugs can form the basis for a large part of a major pharmaceutical company's revenue. The world's top 10 best-selling drugs each has sales of over $1.2 billion (Table 5-3) and there is a total of almost 50 drugs that sell over $500 million per annum (Table 5-4). These drugs account for a large fraction of the total sales of the world's leading pharmaceutical firms. For some of the world's leading drugs firms just three or four drugs can count for more than one-half of total sales (Table 5-4).

There are large risks attached to investment in new drugs. A substantial failure (in the worst case scenario, one that is thought widely to damage health) can

TABLE 5-2 The Top 10 and the Top 20 Drug Corporations, by R & D Expenditure, 1994–7

World rank				Pharmaceutical Corporations	Corporation Nationality	R & D expenditure (£ billion)				Average annual change (%)	1997 R & D intensity (%)
1994	1995	1996	1997			1994	1995	1996	1997		
9	15	1	1	Novartis	Switzerland	0.68	0.64	1.52	1.54	44.14	11.84
2	2	2	2	Hoechst	Germany	1.14	1.18	1.31	1.35	5.88	7.66
3	3	3	3	Bayer	Germany	1.07	1.10	1.22	1.34	7.72	7.21
5	4	5	4	Johnson & Johnson	USA	0.78	0.99	1.16	1.30	18.93	9.46
4	5	7	5	Roche	Switzerland	0.97	0.95	1.02	1.21	7.90	15.47
8	6	6	6	Pfizer	USA	0.69	0.88	1.02	1.17	19.28	15.82
1	1	4	7	Glaxo Wellcome	UK	1.20	1.20	1.16	1.15	-1.58	14.39
6	8	8	8	Merck & Co.	USA	0.75	0.81	0.90	1.02	11.04	7.12
19	19	19	9	Monsanto	USA	0.37	0.40	0.44	0.99	47.21	21.60
17	7	9	10	American Home Products	USA	0.50	0.82	0.87	0.95	26.77	10.97
				Top 10		8.15	9.42	11.00	12.01	18.73	10.56
10	11	10	11	Rhône–Poulenc	France	0.67	0.71	0.81	0.86	8.65	9.50

			Company	Country						
12	12	12	BASF	Germany	0.65	0.71	0.77	0.86	9.98	4.57
11	10	13	Bristol–Myers Squibb	USA	0.67	0.73	0.78	0.84	7.73	8.29
13	13	14	SmithKline Beecham	UK	0.64	0.65	0.76	0.84	9.81	10.79
16	16	15	Eli-Lilly	USA	0.51	0.63	0.72	0.84	18.19	16.22
14	14	16	Abbott	USA	0.59	0.65	0.73	0.79	10.58	10.96
7	9	17	Pharmacia & Upjohn	USA	0.71	0.76	0.77	0.74	1.64	18.48
20	18	18	Astra	Sweden	0.30	0.44	0.54	0.67	31.04	19.47
15	17	19	Zeneca	UK	0.52	0.55	0.60	0.65	8.04	12.57
18	20	20	Schering–Plough	USA	0.38	0.40	0.44	0.51	11.06	12.50
			Top 20		13.78	15.22	17.56	19.63	11.67	10.40
			World-wide pharmaceutical R & D expenditure (in $ billion)			32.2	35.4			

SOURCES: *FT* (16 March 1998, 25 June 1998); Centre for Medicines Research International (1998)

NOTE: Apart from Glaxo Wellcome, the R & D expenditure in other corporations incorporates the budget spends on divisions other than pharmaceuticals for example, agriculture, health care and food ingredients

TABLE 5-3 Top 10 Drugs World-Wide, 1998

Product	Therapy class	Company	Sales ($ billion)
Losec	Ulcers	Astra	3.63
Zocor	Cholesterol	Merck & Co.	2.55
Prozac	Anti-depressant	Eli–Lilly	2.27
Novasc	Blood pressure	Pfizer	1.94
Lipitor	Cholesterol	Warner–Lambert	1.66
Renitec	Blood pressure	Merck & Co.	1.56
Seroxat	Anti-depressant	SmithKline Beecham	1.41
Zoloft	Anti-depressant	Pfizer	1.36
Claritin	Antihistamine	Schering–Plough	1.28
Augmentin	Broad spectrum penicillin	SmithKline Beecham	1.15

SOURCE: *FT* (5 February 1999)

TABLE 5-4 Number of Products that Sell Over $500 million per annum, 1998

Company	Number of products	% of sales
Merck & Co.	9	80
Pfizer	6	78
AstraZeneca	7	68
Glaxo Wellcome	10	66
Eli–Lilly	4	65
SmithKline Beecham	3	50
Abbott	3	50
Novartis	3	30
Roche	1	15
Aventis	1	10

SOURCE: *FT* (10 December 1998)

seriously affect a company's performance. Thalidomide is the most notorious example of a drugs disaster, but drug companies live in constant fear of unanticipated side-effects of drugs. It has been suggested that the liability claims resulting from the re-call of two of American Home Product's anti-obesity drugs Redux and Pondimin, due to alleged association of the drug with heart valve defects, may be as high as $4 billion (*FT*, 2 February 1998, 2 June 1998).

Moreover, a large part of R & D outlays produces no commercially useful results. Failure to meet the increasingly stringent requirements of health authorities, especially the crucially important USA Food and Drugs Administration (FDA), is a major cause of R & D failure. For example, Merck (USA) invested large amounts to develop an anti-obesity drug, Xenical, for which the largest market by far is in the USA. However, the drug may not be approved by the FDA due to fears that it might cause breast cancer (*FT*, 23 March 1998). Part of the reason for failure to produce good results from R & D is simply the fact that drugs research is often hit-and-miss by its very nature. Sometimes, major drugs successes are unintended by-products of other research. For example, the discovery of Viagra was an unintended spin-off from Pfizer's research on drugs for the treatment of angina. Large size enables a pharmaceutical company to withstand better the impact of drugs failures and to sustain the inevitable R & D failures. Small R & D companies can experience huge swings in stock market fortune depending on the performance of the small range of products on which they conduct R & D.

Andersen Consulting estimates that, in order to sustain the average 10 per cent growth per annum in the industry, the top 10 pharmaceutical companies will each have to launch five important new drugs a year with annual sales of $350 million for each product. However, the 10 leading companies were each able to launch an average of only 0.45 new drugs per annum between 1990 and 1994 and only 8 per cent of those new products had sales value of $350 million (*FT*, 16 March 1998). This places tremendous pressure on pharmaceutical firms to engage in mergers and acquisitions (M & A) in order to remain competitive through increased R & D spending.

DRIVERS OF CHANGE (iii): BRAND AND MARKETING

Leading pharmaceutical firms increasingly need to enhance their competitive edge through marketing skills and brand development. The world's top five pharmaceutical firms after the spate of mergers at the end of the 1990s had sales forces in the USA alone of between 5000 and 9000 (*FT*, 16 February 2000). An important reason given for the merger of Glaxo Wellcome with SKB in 2000 was the benefits for Glaxo Wellcome to be derived from drawing on SKB's skills in consumer marketing. The importance of advertising has increased greatly due to a 1997 US regulation which allows prescription medicines to be advertised on TV. In 1998 pharmaceutical companies spent more than $1 billion on direct-to-consumer advertising in addition to 'billions more spent on convincing doctors to prescribe their products' (*FT*, 8 November 1999). Leading pharmaceutical firms spend more on marketing than they do on R & D. In 1998, Merck allocated $4.5 billion to 'marketing and administrative expenses' compared with $2.8 billion to R & D (Merck, *Annual Report*, 1998: 54). Glaxo Wellcome spent $4.8 billion on sales and marketing compared with $2 billion on R & D (Glaxo Wellcome, *Annual Report*, 1999).

DRIVERS OF CHANGE (iv): STOCK MARKET PRESSURE

The large change in the nature of stock market pressure on firms in advanced capitalist countries since the mid-1980s has powerfully affected the pharmaceutical industry. It has had two particularly important consequences for the institutional structure of the pharmaceutical industry. The first has been a drastic push towards rewarding companies that are focused on core businesses and penalizing those that are diversified conglomerates. The traditional chemical companies contained a pharmaceutical component within the diversified structure that typically included a wide range of chemical products. The 1990s saw a revolutionary change in the nature of the world's leading chemical companies. One by one the leading companies decided to de-merge their low-margin chemical businesses and focus on what are perceived as high-margin, high growth 'life sciences', with pharmaceuticals at their core. This massive change in business structure was powerfully promoted by the view taken by the stock markets in the advanced capitalist countries.

The second consequence has been the provision of a powerful stimulus to pharmaceutical companies that successfully cut costs. This has been strongly associated with the changes accompanying mergers and acquisitions. The main source of such savings has been through downsizing employment, often facilitated by the perceived benefits from economies of scale and scope. These have included savings from sharing R & D facilities and from using common marketing systems.

RESPONSE (i): FRENZY OF DE-MERGERS AND MERGERS

Pressures from the stock market, high and rising R & D costs, and the need to cut costs through benefiting from common marketing systems and R & D facilities, combined to produce a unique epoch of simultaneous de-merger alongside explosive merger and acquisition after the mid-1980s. The resulting business reorganization itself stimulated rising stock market prices, which in turn facilitated further acquisitions.

Stimulated by the new developments, several of the world's leading traditional pharmaceutical companies entered a period of unprecedented expansion, in which merger and acquisition played a central role. The traditional diversified chemical conglomerates spanned all aspects of the business from upstream oil exploration and production, through mid-stream ethylene and chlorine production to downstream synthetic fibres, plastics, agro-chemicals, and pharmaceuticals. The 1990s saw a revolution in these businesses, with most of the world's leading firms espousing the break-up of the traditional chemical firm to focus instead on the 'life sciences' with pharmaceuticals at their core. Finally, some companies moved into the life sciences, despite limited previous activity in this sector.

In the first round of restructuring, the emerging new giants of the life sciences industry focused sharply on a narrow range of core competencies in which they became global leaders. In the second round of restructuring, mergers tended to take place increasingly between firms with their main activities in several areas of the life sciences, in each of which the merged firm was a global leader. By the late 1990s a small group of 'life science' giants was emerging, with a portfolio of global leadership positions in several areas, benefiting from powerful economies of scale and scope, particularly in R & D and marketing.

The brief chronology of the main episodes of merger and acquisition from the late 1980s to the late 1990s (Table 5-5) shows how a succession of multi-billion mergers and acquisitions transformed the industry. During the late 1990s the leading players in the industry were constantly discussing the possibility of joining forces in order to benefit from scale economies, especially in R & D and marketing. The merger frenzy reached a peak in 1998–2000. From early 1998 until early 2000 no fewer than one-half of the world's top pharmaceutical firms announced mergers. The value of mergers in 1999 totalled $133 billion (*FT*, 17 January 2000).

RESPONSE (ii): GROWTH OF TRADITIONAL PHARMACEUTICAL COMPANIES

Several of the former leading traditional, focused pharmaceutical companies have grown rapidly since the mid-1980s, with merger and acquisition typically playing a major role, frequently involving cross-country activity (Table 5-5).

Glaxo Wellcome/SmithKline Beecham

By early 2000, the formerly independent pharmaceutical companies Glaxo, Wellcome, SmithKline Beckman (itself the product of several mergers) and Beecham had joined together into a single giant company, to form the largest pharmaceutical company in the world.

SKB. The first stage in the consolidation process was the formation of SmithKline Beecham in 1989, through a $7.8 billion merger of SmithKline Beckman (USA) and Beecham (UK). This was arguably the merger that set in motion the whole subsequent merger frenzy in the pharmaceutical industry. In 1994 SKB purchased Diversified Pharmaceutical Services (USA) for $2.3 billion mainly to use its distribution capability. By 1998 it had a total revenue of $12.9 billion and an R & D spend of $1.5 billion (DTI, 1999: 60). SKB's particular strengths in pharmaceuticals are in anti-infectives and neurosciences, including both anti-depressants and anti-nausea drugs. However, it remains a strong producer of a wide range of consumer healthcare products, including oral care, 'nutritional drinks', over-the-counter gastrointestinal medicines and analgesics. These gave SKB a particular strength in consumer marketing.

Glaxo Wellcome. By the mid-1990s, the separate companies, Glaxo and Wellcome, had each recognized that size had become increasingly important for competitive advantage. In 1995, with the agreement of the Wellcome Trust (which owned 39.5 per cent of Wellcome's shares), Glaxo launched a successful hostile bid for Wellcome, paying $14.8 billion for the company. On its formation it had 62 000 employees, with manufacturing, marketing and sales operations in 120 countries (*FT*, 9 April 1996). Substantial cost-cutting was achieved through a 7000 reduction in the company's workforce by 1998, by some sharing of R & D facilities, and using a common marketing network. The two companies had complementary rather than overlapping product ranges, reducing each company's vulnerability to high dependence on a small range of drugs. The new company invested heavily in robotics and automation, including the acquisition in 1995 of

TABLE 5-5 **The Major M & A Deals in the Pharmaceutical Industry Since the Late 1980s**

Date	Acquirer	Target	Deal value ($ billion)	Remarks
1989	SmithKline Beckman, US merges with Beecham, UK		7.8	SmithKline Beecham formed
1989	Bristol–Myers, USA merges with Squibb, USA		12.0	Bristol–Myers Squibb formed
1989	Merrell Dow, USA	Marion Labs, USA	7.7	Marion Merrell Dow formed
1990	Roche, Switzerland	Genentech, USA	2.1	Bought 60%, biotech firm
1990	Rhône–Poulenc, France merges with Rorer, USA		3.2	Rhône–Poulenc Rorer formed
1993	Merck, USA	Medco Containment Services, USA	6.6	Distribution
1994	Roche, Switzerland	Syntex, USA	5.3	R & D, manufacturing, marketing
1994	SmithKline Beecham, UK	Diversified Pharmaceuticals Services (DPS), USA	2.3	PBM, Distribution
1994	Sandoz, Switzerland	Gerber, USA	3.7	Nutrition (baby food)
1994	Sanofi, France	Sterling Health, USA	1.7	Acquired prescription drug unit
1994	Eli–Lilly, USA	PCS, USA	4.1	PBM, Distribution
1994	American Home Products, USA	American Cyanamid, USA	9.7	R & D, manufacturing, marketing, animal health, crop protection
1994	SmithKline Beecham, UK	Sterling Health, USA	2.9	Acquired over-the-counter (OTC) unit, resold US section for $1 billion to Bayer
1994	Ciba, Switzerland	Chiron, USA	2.1	Bought 50% of Chiron, Biotechnology R & D
1994	Pfizer, USA	SmithKline Beecham, UK	1.45	Acquired animal health division

Year	Acquirer	Target	Value	Description
1995	Colgate, USA	American Home Products (Kolynos)	1.04	Acquired oral healthcare division
1995	Glaxo, USA	Wellcome, UK	14.8	R & D, manufacturing, marketing, formed Glaxo Wellcome
1995	Glaxo, USA	Affymax, USA	0.533	R & D (combinatorial chemistry)
1995	Hoechst, Germany	Marion Merrell Dow, USA	7.14	R & D, manufacturing, marketing, formed Hoechst Marion Roussel
1995	BASF, Germany	Boots Pharmaceuticals, UK	1.3	R & D, manufacturing, marketing
1995	Clariant	Sandoz, Switzerland	2	Acquired chemicals division
1995	Pharmacia, Sweden merges with Upjohn, USA		21	R & D, manufacturing, marketing
1995	Rhône–Poulenc Rorer, USA	Fisons Pharmaceuticals, UK	2.7	R & D, manufacturing, marketing
1995	Johnson & Johnson, USA	Cordis	1.8	Medical technology
1995	Warner–Lambert, USA	Warner–Wellcome, USA	1	Acquired OTC JV from Glaxo Wellcome
1996	Sandoz, Switzerland merges with Ciba-Geigy, Switzerland to form Novartis		27.5	R & D, manufacturing, marketing
1996	Hoechst, Germany	Roussel Uclaf, France	3.5	Bought 43.5% of the remaining share
1997	Roche, Switzerland	Boehringer Mannheim, Germany	10.2	Boehringer Mannheim, a private diagnostics company
Dec. 97	Zeneca, UK	Mogen, The Netherlands	1.1	Biotechnology
1997	Amersham, UK	Nycomed		
1997	Rhône–Poulenc, France	Rhône–Poulenc Rorer, USA	4.2	Acquired the remaining 31.7% of Rorer
1998	Astra announces merger with Zeneca			

TABLE 5-5 (Continued)

Date	Acquirer	Target	Deal value ($ billion)	Remarks
1998	Hoechst announces merger with Rhône–Poulenc to form Aventis			Aborted in January 1998
1998	American Home Products, USA	SmithKline Beecham, UK	180	The deal - Glaxo to own 59.5% and SmithKline to own 40.5% – aborted 3 weeks later
1998	Glaxo Wellcome, UK announces merger with SmithKline Beecham, UK			
1998	United Healthcare, USA	Humana, USA	5.5	Healthcare provider
1998	Du Pont, USA	Merck, USA	2.6	Acquired Merck's 50% stake in the drug's JV
1998	Monsanto, USA	Delta & Pine	1.75	Agricultural genetics
1998	Monsanto, USA	DeKalb Genetics USA	2.5	$2.5 billion to acquire the remaining 55%, agricultural genetics
1998	Monsanto, USA	Cargill Inc., USA	1.2	Seeds
1998	Astra, Sweden	Merck, USA	10	Acquired the remaining 50% of the US JV to market Losec, an anti-ulcer drug

Year	Company	Target	Value	Notes
1998	Johnson & Johnson, USA	DePuy Inc.	3.5	Acquired the spinal implant maker from Roche Holding AG (it focuses on drugs & diagnostics)
1999	Abbott, USA	Alza	7.3	Biotechnology
1999	Pharmacia and Upjohn	Sugen	0.65	Biotechnology
1999	Monsanto, USA announces merger with Pharmacia and Upjohn		23	
1999	Sanofi, France	Synthelabo, France		
2000	Pfizer, USA	Warner–Lambert, USA	90	Successful hostile takeover
2000	Glaxo Wellcome,UK agrees merger with SmithKline Beecham, UK		114	
2000	Healtheon	OnHealth Network	0.31	On-line health supplies
2000	Healtheon/WebMD	Medical Manager Corp	7.6	On-line health supplies
2000	Medical Logic	Medscape and Total eMed	1.4	On-line health supplies

SOURCES: MSDW (1998a:131); *Observer* (8 February 1998); *FT* (21 August 1995, 25 March 1996, 9 April 1996, 24 April 1997, 14 May 1997, 27 June 1997, 24 September 1997, 18 December 1997, 8 February 1998, 25 February 1998, 16 March 1998, 11 May 1998, 29 May 1998, 2 June 1998, 26 June 1998, 16 July 1998, 15 July 1999, 23 February 2000); *IHT* (22 July 1998: 13)

NOTE: Glaxo Wellcome: 1997 sales £7.98 billion (100 per cent pharmaceuticals, prescription drugs) SmithKline Beecham: 1997 sales: £7.8 billion (£4.57 in pharmaceuticals, £2.38 in clinical laboratories, £0.85 in consumer healthcare) *FT* (25 February 1998)

Affymax (USA) which specialized in combinatorial chemistry. Its target was to introduce three new drugs per year from 2000, compared to one per year in the combined companies prior to the merger (*FT*, 9 November 1995). In 1998 Glaxo Wellcome had a sales revenue of $12.8 billion and an R & D spend of $1.9 billion (DTI, 1999: 59).

Glaxo Wellcome/SKB. Despite their great increase in size due to the respective mergers and acquisitions, neither Glaxo Wellcome nor SKB felt that they possessed the necessary scale to compete in the new world of giant pharmaceutical companies. In February 1998, the two companies announced that they were merging. At that point it was 'by far the biggest deal in corporate history'. The new company would have been the third largest in the world by market capitalization. Its global sales would have been around $20 billion, 50 per cent greater than their closest rival, Merck, and would have accounted for about 8 per cent of the global market for pharmaceuticals. The motives for the merger included benefits from massive combined R & D power of over $3 billion, and broadening of the product base. The new company would have been the world leader in the fast-growing, potentially inter-related fields of combinatorial chemistry, genomics and bioinformatics (*FT*, 2 February 1998). The deal was aborted only three weeks after it was announced, with great acrimony between the chief executives of the two companies. However, it was widely thought to show the path along which the industry was likely to move.

Indeed, after 'two years of fraught negotiations, punctuated by lulls of tetchy silence', the two companies finally agreed to merge in early 2000, catapulting the new company into the number one position in terms of sales and R & D expenditure. The new company will have 7.5 per cent of the global market for patented pharmaceuticals, half as much again as its nearest rival at the time of the merger, Merck. The principal rationale for the merger was the perceived necessity to combine the R & D strengths of the two companies. The combined R & D expenditure of the two companies now totalled around $3.6 billion, considerably above the former sector leader, Merck, with $2.8 billion in 1998. The new CEO, Jean-Pierre Garnier commented: 'Putting this engine together will produce more drugs. The quality is here, the scale is here...We will be the kings of science' (quoted in *FT*, 22 January 2000). The incentive to merge was powerfully stimulated by the wish to create sufficient scale to take full advantage of the fast-developing research in genetics: it was argued by the CEO of SmithKline Beecham that there was a five-year window of opportunity during which a pharmaceutical company with sufficient resources could exploit the vast outpouring of genetic information from academic and industrial laboratories across the world.

Pfizer/Warner–Lambert

Warner–Lambert. In the 1990s, Warner–Lambert was in the lower end of the top 20 global pharmaceutical firms. Its R & D spend was somewhat below the other leading pharmaceutical firms, amounting to $840 million in 1998, totalling

8.6 per cent of sales revenue (DTI, 1999: 56). However, Warner–Lambert was extremely successful with its anti-cholesterol drug, Lipitor, which earned the company $3.7 billion revenue in 1999, and was a major factor in the company's 'phenomenal growth' in the late 1990s (*FT*, 4 November 1999). The income stream from Lipitor helped to make it an attractive takeover target.

American Home Products (AHP). In the 1990s, AHP moved firmly from being a diversified company with strong interests in pharmaceuticals into a pre-dominantly pharmaceutical firm. In 1994 it paid $9.7 billion to buy American Cyanamid, a world leader in animal health and crop protection. In 1995 it sold its oral healthcare division to Colgate for $1 billion. In 1998 it was one of the top ten pharmaceutical firms with a sales revenue of $13 billion and a $1.6 billion spend on R & D (DTI, 1999: 59). It had a single 'blockbuster drug', Premarin, the hormone replacement therapy, from which it earned $2 billion in 1999. Despite its great size and research capability, like most of the other leading firms in the sector it had decided that it was too small to survive in the competition against the other leading firms in the epoch of merger frenzy. In 1998–9 AHP attempted in succession to merge with SKB and Monsanto. Each of these fell by the wayside. In late 1999 it tried again to merge with another leading industry player, this time with Warner–Lambert. This would have created a front rank company, with pro-forma sales of $23 billion, R & D spending of $2.4 billion and a market capitalization of more than $140 billion. However, Warner–Lambert and AHP had not announced their deal more than a few hours before Pfizer countered with a $90 billion hostile bid, that eventually won out over AHP's merger proposal. Following the failure of their attempted merger, it was widely thought that it would pursue merger talks with one of the leading European pharmaceutical firms (*FT*, 21 January 2000).

Pfizer. Pfizer had been long established as a leading US-based pharmaceutical firm. In 1994 it entered the merger frenzy, buying SmithKline Beecham's animal health division for $1.45 billion. In 1998 it was the world's eighth largest with sales revenue of over $13 billion, with profits of $3.98 billion, making it one of the most profitable firms in the sector, with a profit rate of over 30 per cent on sales revenue. It sustained its position through a high level of R & D. R & D spending amounted to $2.2 billion in 1998, amounting to 17 per cent of profits (DTI, 1999: 59). Until the year 2000 it had stood aside from the merger frenzy, preferring to grow through internal means rather than acquiring major companies in the sector.

In the late 1990s Pfizer developed the best-known of the new generation of so-called 'lifestyle medicines', Viagra. Annual sales are predicted to reach as much as $10 billion revenue per annum. Despite its powerful position, Pfizer wished to enhance its competitive advantage even further, and in early 2000 made a successful hostile bid to buy Warner–Lambert for $90 billion. The new company will be the world's second largest company by sales revenue, with pro-forma sales of $23 billion and an R & D spend of $4.7 billion (*FT*, 8 February 2000). As well as Lipitor, the new company would have no less than six other medicines with annual sales revenue of over one billion dollars (*FT*, 8 February 2000). The two companies have a total of 12,000 scientists. The head of Pfizer, Mr William Steere, stated: '[This merger] will redefine the industry' (quoted in *FT*, 8 February 2000). The *FT* commented: '[Mr Steere's] boast will not surprise competitors. It will certainly frighten them.'

Merck

In 1993 Merck paid $6.6 billion for the pharmaceutical distribution company Medco (USA). Through this important acquisition, Merck developed a global leadership position in the provision of programmes to manage prescription drugs and to manage patient health and drug utilization. It earned over $11 billion from this segment of its business in 1998, accounting for two-fifths of its total revenues (Merck, Annual Report, 1998: 30).

Merck has not made any large acquisition since then. Rather, it moved into first place, with sales ahead of Glaxo Wellcome in 1997, mainly through a series of joint ventures, alliances and new product development. Merck is unusual among the leading pharmaceutical companies in declaring that it does not consider growing through a major merger. It has increased its revenues fivefold in a decade, from $5.9 billion in 1988 to $26.9 in 1998 (Merck, *Annual Report*, 1998: 54). It has achieved this not only through high levels of R & D but also through extremely successful application of that spending, licensing fifteen new drugs in the period 1995–9. It is a world leader in drugs to reduce cholesterol, which had sales of $4.7 billion in 1998, and drugs to reduce hypertension and reduce the risk of heart failure, which had sales of $4.2 billion in 1998 (Merck, *Annual Report*, 1998: 30).

The merger of Glaxo Wellcome and SKB together with the hostile takeover of Warner–Lambert by Pfizer puts great pressure on Merck. It will shortly shift from number one to number three in the industry in terms of sales. At least as important its R & D spending will be substantially smaller than either of its two chief rivals, standing at $2.4 billion compared with around $4 billion each at the new Pfizer and Glaxo Wellcome/SKB. The pressure on Merck is increased by the fact that it has a batch of major products with US sales of $3.5 billion for which the patents are expiring.

RESPONSE (iii): THE SHIFT INTO LIFE SCIENCES

Even more remarkable than the rapid growth of several leading traditional pharmaceutical companies was the revolutionary change in the structure of most of the world's leading chemical companies. Driven by the search for shareholder value, and by the high margins and high global growth prospects for pharmaceuticals, leading chemical companies in the 1990s one after the other shed their traditional chemicals businesses to focus on the 'life sciences', within which pharmaceuticals played a central role. It rapidly became the industry's conventional wisdom to believe that a wide range of 'life sciences', including the health and well-being of humans, animals and plants were linked by common R & D technologies. These were thought to provide extensive opportunities to benefit from 'economies of scope', through common benefits from new technologies such as combinatorial chemistry, genomics and bioinformatics. R & D in these activities was thought to be as relevant to the agricultural as to the human health sector. For shareholders there was the enticing prospect of de-linking what were perceived as being less attractive sides of the businesses, such as heavy chemicals. By the late 1990s, the proponents of the 'life sciences' strategy included such former chemical industry giants as Du Pont, Ciba–Geigy, Sandoz, Hoechst, Bayer, Rhône–Poulenc, ICI and Monsanto.

Novartis

In the 1980s, Ciba–Geigy and Sandoz (both of Switzerland) were two of the world's most powerful chemical companies, each of which was particularly strong in specialty chemicals. Ciba–Geigy was itself the product of a merger between Ciba and Geigy in 1970.

In 1994, Sandoz acquired Gerber (USA), specializing in nutrition, paying $3.7 billion for the company, strengthening its position in life sciences. In 1995, Sandoz demerged Clariant, its specialty chemicals arm, and bought Genetic Therapy, specializing in gene therapy, further signalling its intention to move towards the life sciences. In 1995, Sandoz was the world's fourteenth biggest producer of pharmaceuticals (*FT*, 25 March 1996). In the mid-1990s, Ciba–Geigy was one of the top 100 companies in the world by value of sales. It was the world's eighth largest chemical producer and its pharmaceutical business was the ninth largest globally (*FT*, 25 March 1996). It gave some indication of its move towards the life sciences with the purchase in 1994 of 50 per cent of Chiron (USA), a biotechnology company, for $2.1 billion.

In 1996 Ciba–Geigy and Sandoz radically changed the shape of the pharmaceutical industry through a simultaneous merger and demerger that 'changed the corporate landscape for the world's pharmaceutical and chemicals industries' (*FT*, 8 March 1996). The main businesses of Ciba–Geigy and Sandoz combined in a $27.5 billion merger to form what was then the world's second biggest pharmaceutical company, named Novartis. As part of the transformation, Ciba–Geigy spun off its slow-growing, specialty chemicals divisions into a new company, Ciba Specialty Chemicals, in order to 'enhance shareholder value' in the new company, Novartis.

Ciba–Geigy was the market leader in drugs for arthritis and high blood pressure treatment while Sandoz dominated the market for drugs to prevent transplanted organs from being rejected (it also has products in schizophrenia and fungal infections). Prior to the merger they were ranked 31st and 44th in the 'Global 500' list of companies ranked by market capitalization, leaping into approximately ninth position after the merger (*FT*, 24 January 1997). The new business had a workforce of more than 100 000 and an annual R & D budget of around £1.3 billion, having become a 'giant in an industry of giants' (*FT*, 24 April 1997). The new company's main products were reduced to healthcare (59 per cent), nutrition (14 per cent) and agribusiness (27 per cent).

Share prices 'rose sharply' after the merger 'in anticipation of cost-savings to be achieved by large job losses': planned job losses were 10 per cent of the total workforce, or around 13 000 jobs in total: 'One motive for the merger was to slash high costs in Switzerland.... Financially it's a merger made in heaven' (*FT*, 6 March 1996). The announcement of the fusion of Sandoz and Ciba–Geigy, through the rise in the companies' share prices 'created $15 billion of value for shareholders in a single day' (*FT*, 22 May 1996).

As the merger frenzy has developed, so Novartis' relative size has shrunk. Following the Glaxo Wellcome/SKB merger and Pfizer's takeover of Warner–Lambert, it will have slipped to ninth place in the world ranking of pharmaceutical firms by sales value, with a global market share of around 3.3 per cent of total prescription drugs. In late 1999 it announced that it was to spin off its agribusiness division and merge it with AstraZeneca's to form a new independent company, Syngenta, which will have sales of around $8 billion. This would enable it to focus still more firmly on pharmaceuticals. Speculation was mounting that it would join forces with one of the giant US companies such as AHP, which had been unsuccessful in finding a partner in the merger process of the late 1990s.

Aventis

Hoechst. Hoechst was for decades the world's number one chemicals producer, within which pharmaceuticals were a sub-branch of the business. In the mid-1990s it dramatically re-shaped itself. The transformation was significant not only for the world's chemical and pharmaceutical industry, but also for the fast-changing nature of German capitalism in the epoch of high globalization.

In 1995 it began the transformation by purchasing Marion Merrell Dow (MMD) for $7.1 billion, which had itself been spun off from Dow Chemicals in 1989 and merged with Marion Labs in a $7.7 billion merger. In 1996 Hoechst sold its lossmaking specialty chemicals business to Clariant, retaining 45 per cent ownership of the new company, to form the largest producer of specialty chemicals in the world (*FT*, 11 December 1996). Hoechst also cut adrift other 'difficult' businesses: textile dyes entered a joint venture with Bayer; bulk plastic polyethylene entered a joint venture with BASF; polypropylene with British Petroleum, and polyester textile fibre with an Indonesian partner (*FT*, 11 March 1997 and 27 August 1997). The most dynamic part of the business was identified as the life sciences, with the renamed pharmaceutical company, Hoechst Marion Roussel (HMR), at its core. Hoechst's new strategic aim was to 'refocus on the life sciences' and 'become the world's largest pharmaceutical company' (Hoechst's finance director, quoted in *FT*, 11 December 1996). In late 1996 Hoechst paid $3.5 billion to purchase 44 per cent of Roussel Uclaf, a leading French pharmaceutical company in which Hoechst formerly had a 66 per cent ownership share (*FT*, 24 April 1997). To focus its core activities on life sciences, HMR sold its low margin, generic drugs subsidiary, Rugby Group (bought by MMD in 1993 for $275 million), to California-based Watson Pharmaceuticals (*FT*, 27 August 1997).

Rhône–Poulenc. During the 1990s, Rhône–Poulenc gradually shifted out of bulk chemicals into pharmaceuticals. Its first important move was the acquisition in 1990 for $3.2 billion of a majority stake in Rorer (USA) to form Rhône–Poulenc Rorer, a specialist pharmaceutical company. In the mid-1990s it divested itself of much of its bulk chemicals business, shifting within chemicals into the higher value-added downstream specialty chemicals (*FT*, 10 January 1996). Within the drug sector it made further important acquisitions, including the acquisition in 1995 of 95 per cent of Cooper (a drug distributor) at FFr2.8 billion and the purchase of Fisons (UK) for $2.7 billion (*FT*, 10 January 1996). By taking over Fisons, Rhône–Poulenc became the world's number four asthma and allergy drug company: the asthma/allergy market is worth almost £7 billion per year and growing quickly (*FT*, 19 August 1995).

By 1996 Rhône–Poulenc had taken on the appearance of 'a pharmaceutical company with chemical interests' (*FT*, 10 January 1996). However, the view from the shareholders' perspective was still that Rhône–Poulenc's pharmaceutical business could not be properly valued by the market while 'buried' inside a chemical company 'Huge value for shareholders could be "unlocked" by selling, de-merging and growing the pharmaceutical business' (*FT*, 5 November 1996). Rhône–Poulenc's decision to rule out a demerger of its chemicals and health care business was deemed by investors to be 'antediluvian' (*FT*, 5 November 1996). However, Rhône–Poulenc quickly took a decisive step towards pharmaceuticals with the acquisition in 1997 of the remaining 37 per cent interest in Rhône-Poulenc Rorer for $4.2 billion, to become one of the world's top 20 drugs companies. (*FT*, 27 June 1997). The financial press judged that the merged company would 'benefit from economies of scale in marketing and distribution' and the balance sheet would 'benefit from further downsizing of employment' (*FT*, 19 August 1995).

Aventis. In 1999 Hoechst and Rhône–Poulenc merged to form a giant new 'European champion' in the pharmaceutical industry, called Aventis. Each partner agreed to shed non-core business prior to the merger. Hoechst agreed to dispose of Celanese, which contains several businesses, Messer (industrial gases), Wacker (chemicals), Dystar (industrial dyes) and HR Vet (animal health). Rhône–Poulenc agreed to sell its 68 per cent share in Rhodia, a chemicals business. The merged company was to be owned 50/50 by the two companies. Following the pattern set by Novartis, this was a neutral name, with no special national connotations. The new company had a combined sales revenue (proforma) of over $40 billion and a combined R & D spend of almost $4 billion (DTI, 1999). Its pharmaceutical sales placed it second only to Merck. The formation of the new Franco–German company was of immense significance for the nature of European capitalism within the globalization process. Along with the merger of Astra and Zeneca (see below), ABB and GEC–Alsthom, Usinor and Hoogovens, Vodafone and Mannesmann, and Dasa and Aérospatiale Matra, it signalled the dramatic emergence of a new group of immensely powerful trans-European corporations, that had shaken off their former position as 'national

champions' in industries that had hitherto been regarded as of 'strategic' importance in national industrial strategy.

AstraZeneca

Zeneca. ICI is the most dramatic example of rapidly moving out of low-
margin bulk chemicals altogether. This was the company that was a pioneer in
modern chemical industry technology, 'the company of Nobel, Brunner and
Mond', which was still in the 1990s, the largest employer of chemical engineers
in Britain.[2] Even in the mid-1990s ICI was 'the nation's chief repository of
industrial chemistry' (*FT*, 26 April 1997). In 1993 ICI spun off Zeneca to produce a free-standing pharmaceutical company, ranked number 16 by value of
sales in 1995. This proved highly successful in terms of 'enhancing shareholder
value': 'The separation of Zeneca ended the discounting of a premium stock to
take account of a raft of sluggish and difficult chemicals businesses' (*FT*, 24
April 1997). Zeneca benefited enormously: 'Today, [ICI's] demerged life science
business has one of the strongest R & D pipelines in the business' (*FT*, 24 April
1997). ICI completed its remarkable transformation, with its decision in 1997 to
transform itself from a bulk chemicals into a specialty chemicals producer, by
purchasing the entire specialty chemicals business of Unilever, financing the purchase by selling its bulk chemicals divisions (*FT*, 8 May 1997). Despite successful growth following the de-merger from ICI, by the late 1990s, the company
remained at the bottom end of the top 20 pharmaceutical companies globally in
terms of sales revenue and R & D. It felt increasingly vulnerable in the face of
the merger frenzy movement.

Astra. For many years, Astra was the Swedish national champion in the pharmaceutical industry. It stayed clear of the merger frenzy of the 1990s, but grew
through relatively large-scale investment and some significant acquisitions. In
1995 Astra acquired Fisons' (UK) research centre for $300 million. In 1998 Astra
paid $10 billion to purchase the remaining 50 per cent of its joint venture with
Merck to manufacture Losec, an anti-ulcer drug. However, it remained a middle-
ranking player, with sales of 'only' around $8 billion and R & D of 'only' around
$1 billion in 1997. Surrounded by frantic merger activity, it felt increasingly that
it was falling behind in the race to compete with leading companies in the sector.

Astra/Zeneca merger. The increased sense of vulnerability of the two
medium-sized companies led them to agree to merge. The merger took them into
the top 10 of world pharmaceutical firms, with sales revenues of almost $13 bil-
lion in 1998 (pro-forma), ranking sixth globally, with a market share of 4.2 per
cent (*FT*, 8 November 1999). The combined entities had an R & D spend of more
than $2 billion The combined market capitalization of the two companies was
around $70 billion (*FT*, 9 December 1998). The newly formed entity was head-
quartered in the UK. The shift in the headquarters of Astra from Sweden to the
UK caused great national debate in Sweden, and was soon followed by Ford's
purchase of the saloon vehicle branch of Volvo. These two decisions were

extremely significant in terms of the erosion of the national characteristics of leading firms that were formerly regarded as national champions in 'strategic' industries.

Du Pont

Du Pont remained a traditional chemicals business until late in the transformation of the world's chemical industry. In 1997 chemicals accounted for 9 per cent of total sales, fibres for 17 per cent, polymers for 15 per cent, petroleum for 45 per cent, life sciences for just 6 per cent and diversified business for 6 per cent (MSDW, 1998a: 97–104). Du Pont has global or regional leadership in almost nine-tenths of its operations, and is a dominant global producer of nylon, titanium dioxide and Lycra. It regards these businesses as too strong to give up and concentrate on life sciences (MSDW, 1998a: 100). Du Pont has 'the advantages which stem from scale, global reach and vast material integration' (MSDW, 1998a: 102). In 1997 Du Pont invested over $6 billion in acquisitions that strengthened it in key areas. The purchase of the ICI Titanium Dioxide business in 1997 raised its global market share from 20 per cent (+) to around 35 per cent (MSDW, 1998a: 102). Its chief operating officer commented: 'Our strategy is to take some of our businesses, where we have a strong global position and low cost base, global' (quoted in FT, 25 September 1997).

However, alongside strengthening the company in key areas of chemicals production in which it has global leadership, Du Pont has signalled that it, also, will sharply increase the role of the life sciences within the company's overall portfolio. As part of this strategy in 1997 Du Pont acquired 20 per cent of Pioneer Hi-Bred – an Iowa corn seed company – for $1.7 billion, and in 1998 it paid $2.6 billion to buy out Merck's 50 per cent stake in their pharmaceutical joint venture. To expand further its life sciences businesses, Du Pont plans the radical move of selling off its oil division, Conoco, which accounts for almost half of the total business. Du Pont's chief executive, Chad Holliday, aims to increase the life sciences businesses to 35 per cent of total revenue by 2002 (*FT*, 2 June 1998).

Pharmacia Upjohn/Monsanto

Monsanto. In the 1980s Monsanto was a powerful chemical industry company, with a diversified portfolio. In the 1990s it turned itself into a focused life sciences company with a powerful position in genetically engineered crops. The move was strongly associated with the appointment of Bob Shapiro as chief executive in 1995. In 1997 it spun off its chemicals business unit into an independent company, Solutia, in order to focus on agricultural products, food ingredients and drugs. In May and June of 1998, Monsanto acquired in rapid succession, DeKalb Genetics for $2.5 billion, Delta & Pine (in which they have had collaborative work on genetically engineered products, for example insect-resistant cotton and herbicide-tolerant soya beans) for $1.75 billion, Cargill Inc. for $1.2 billion and Plant Breeding International Cambridge Ltd (cereal seeds) from Unilever plc for $0.6 billion (*FT*, 2 June 1998, 16 July 1998). It was poised to become the world leader in genetically modified seeds and plant-science-based chemicals including pesticides and herbicides.

In 1998 it was announced that Monsanto and AHP were to merge to form a giant 'life sciences' firm that spanned a wide range of medicines and plant science products. However, the deal was called off shortly afterwards. Monsanto continued to pursue the ambition to dominate the plant science segment of the pharmaceutical industry. It advertised aggressively to promote the virtues of GM seeds and associated chemicals. However, a powerful and extremely effective protest movement against these products developed rapidly in Europe and began to spread to the USA. Monsanto's high profile meant that the company became demonized and eventually Shapiro acknowledged that Monsanto had 'irritated and antagonized more people than it had persuaded' (FT, 21 December 1999). In addition, demand for plant science-based products declined sharply with the world downturn in agriculture. Monsanto's profits slumped to just $50 million in 1998 and it had built up heavy debts in accumulating the seed companies. However, the long-term prospects for plant sciences were not fundamentally dented, and it also contained a strong traditional pharmaceutical business, Searle.

Pharmacia Upjohn. In 1995 Pharmacia (Sweden) joined with Upjohn (USA) in a $21 billion merger. The merger was initially a 'disaster' involving a deep and widely publicized culture clash. However, in 1997 the company recruited a new chief executive, Fred Hassan, who earned great respect in the industry for rapidly turning the ailing company around. However, it remained relatively small scale, at around two-fifths the size of Merck and 'with a market capitalization of less than $30 billion, P & U was never more than an also-ran despite its improving performance' (FT, 21 December 1999). With mergers escalating around it, P & U decided to pursue a merger with Monsanto: 'The merger is undoubtedly a gamble, but the need for scale has persuaded Mr Hassan to take it' (FT, 21 December 1999).

P & U/Monsanto. In late 1999, Monsanto and P & U decided to merge. The newly formed company will enter the ranks of the top ten pharmaceutical firms in terms of value of sales, with a combined (pro-forma) total of $15 billion, an R & D budget of $2.8 billion and a market share of almost 5 per cent, leapfrogging the new company into third place in the global league table of pharmaceutical firms by value of sales.

CONSEQUENCES: MARKET SHARE

In the early 1990s the pharmaceutical industry was considered to be 'extraordinarily fragmented compared to other global industries' (FT, 10 November 1995). In 1994 the top 10 companies held 28.0 per cent of the total global market, and the top 20 companies held 45.5 per cent (Table 5-6 and FT, 25 March 1996). To describe as 'extraordinarily fragmented' an industry in which only 20 firms accounted for 46 per cent of the total world market, which is today vastly greater than it was 20 or 30 years ago, is a reflection of the degree to which control of world markets has passed into the hands of a small number of companies, and concentration of economic power is taken to be a fact of life.

TABLE 5-6 **Market Share of the World's Top 10 Pharmaceutical Firms, 1994–9**
(Percentage of Total World Sales of Patented Pharmaceuticals)

1994		1996		1999	
Company	(%)	Company	(%)	Company	(%)
Glaxo	3.6	Novartis	4.4	Glaxo/SmithKline	7.4*
Merck	3.4	Glaxo Wellcome	4.4	Pfizer/Warner Lambert	6.5*
Bristol–Myers	3.2	Merck	4.0	Merck	5.0
Squibb Roche	2.8	Hoechst Marion Roussel	3.3	Aventis	4.5
Johnson & Johnson	2.7	Bristol–Myers Squibb	3.2	AstraZeneca	4.5
Pfizer	2.7	Johnson & Johnson	3.1	Bristol–Myers Squibb	3.3
SmithKline Beecham	2.5	American Home Products	3.1	Novartis	2.8
Ciba	2.5	Pfizer	3.1	Eli-Lilley	2.8
Hoechst	2.3	SmithKline Beecham	2.7	Johnson & Johnson	2.8
American Home Products	2.3	Roche	2.7	Roche	2.7
Total	28.0	Total	34.0	Total	43.4

SOURCE: *FT* (25 March 1996, 24 April 1997, 4 February 2000)
NOTE: *Proforma

By 1999 the 'merger frenzy' had led to a sharp increase in the degree of concentration within this sector: the global market share of the top 10 pharmaceutical companies had risen to over 43 per cent (Table 5-6). Although not as advanced as the world's aircraft industry, aero-engine industry, or tyre industry, this was still a highly significant and fast-growing degree of concentration. In the mid-1990s, the heads of most pharmaceutical firms thought that within 5–10 years the business would be 'dominated by just a dozen or so companies' (*FT*, 22 August 1995). By the year 2000 that vision was already close to realization.

However, the degree of concentration in the industry has become much greater even than appears to be the case from the aggregate industry data. In the 1990s, leading firms concentrated on a relatively small number of selected areas in which to focus their huge R & D budgets. This enabled them to establish rising barriers to entry, and became a powerful source of competitive advantage, making it steadily harder for potential rivals to catch up. As part of this process, alongside the formation of ever-larger pharmaceutical firms, companies were constantly selling off relatively small segments of the business and buying others as they each built up sharply-focused areas of global leadership. Novartis is world leader in drugs for treating arthritis, high blood pressure and in drugs to prevent rejection of transplanted organs. Merck is a world leader in anti-ulcer drugs and

TABLE 5-7 Glaxo Wellcome/SmithKline Beecham, Estimated Global
Market Share, 1999*

Specialization	Rank	Market share (%)
Total world pharmaceutical market	1	7.3
Anti-infectives	1	16.9
of which: anti-herpes	1	49
Central nervous system	2	11.6
Respiratory	1	16.8
of which: asthma	1	31
Alimentary and metabolic	2	7.0
Vaccines	1	n/a

SOURCE: *FT* (18 January 2000); Glaxo Wellcome, *Annual Report*, 1999: 6
NOTE: *Proforma

in drugs to reduce hypertension and cholesterol. AstraZeneca is a world leader in
anti-ulcer drugs. Rhône–Poulenc is a world leader in asthma and anti-allergy
drugs. American Home Products is a world leader in animal health and crop protection. Monsanto is a world leader in genetically engineered crops. Glaxo–SKB
is a world leader in respiratory drugs, anti-infectives and anti-depressants.

The more disaggregated the level of analysis, the higher the degree of market
concentration is revealed to be. For example, the newly merged combination of
Glaxo Wellcome/SKB has around 7.3 per cent of the world market for patented
medicines. However, within different sub-specializations, the new company's
market share is much higher, rising to 17 per cent for anti-infectives and respiratory medicines (Table 5-7). If one looks within sub-categories the market share
of global leaders is even higher. Glaxo Wellcome accounts for 49 per cent of the
total world market for anti-herpes drugs and 31 per cent of the total global market for anti-asthma drugs (Table 5-7). To take another example, Merck has an
estimated 5 per cent of the total world prescription drugs market. However, it
accounts for more than 40 per cent of world sales of the statin group of drugs to
reduce cholesterol and around 30 per cent of the world-wide market for angioten-
sion converting enzyme inhibitors for the treatment of high blood pressure
(Merck, *Annual Report*, 1998: 33).

Having established global leadership in a small range of often closely related
areas, a new round of super-large mergers in the late 1990s and 2000 was combining companies with global leadership positions in a wider range of sectors, in
order to produce a company with a more diversified, less risky portfolio, each of
which is a world leader. It was a motive also for the merger of the pharmaceutical
businesses of Ciba–Geigy and Sandoz to form the giant Novartis in 1996. It was
a major motive also for the giant mergers of Hoechst with Rhône–Poulenc to
form Aventis, Astra with Zeneca, Glaxo Wellcome with SKB, Pharmacia and
Upjohn with Monsanto and for the take-over of AHP by Pfizer. Each of these
marked milestones in the industry.

Growing US Dominance

The USA is the single most important market for prescription drugs, with sales greater than the whole of Western Europe. During the course of the business revolution of the 1990s, the relative position of US-based drugs firms sharply increased compared to the leading European companies in the sector. A powerful group of US-based firms was beginning to pull away from the leading European firms in several significant senses. Former pharmaceutical powerhouses, such as Bayer of Germany, 'are in danger of becoming bit-part players' (*FT*, 13 April 1999). By the end of the decade, of the 13 pharmaceutical firms in the *Fortune* 500, eight were based in the USA (*Fortune*, 2 August 1999). In terms of market capitalization, a 'first division' of 13 firms with market capitalizations of over $60 billion had emerged (*FT*, 13 April 1999). Of these, nine were US-based, the remainder being composed of two Swiss (Novartis and Roche) and two UK-based firms (Glaxo Wellcome and SmithKline Beecham). The 'second division' consisted of 10 firms with market capitalizations of between $10 billion and $39 billion. Of these, just two were US-based and the remainder were all European firms. In terms of MSDW's comprehensive evaluation of 'competitive edge', seven of the top 10 firms in the sector across the world are based in the USA (MSDW, 1999: 144).

The Franco–German merger of Hoechst and Rhône–Poulenc and the all-French merger of Sanofi and Synthelabo, are regarded by their US competitors as 'weak European companies huddling together for comfort' (*FT*, 13 April 1999). For example, after the merger of Hoechst and Rhône–Poulenc's pharmaceutical divisions, the new company, Aventis, will have almost no 'blockbuster' drugs. Instead, it has hundreds of drugs with 'sales of a paltry $1–2 million'. Its top 10 products account for just 27 per cent of the new company's total pharmaceutical sales, compared with 87 per cent for Pfizer and 85 per cent for Lilly' (*FT*, 16 July 1999). Although Aventis was to become the world's second largest pharmaceutical company by sales revenue, it was to be only the world's seventh largest by market capitalization (*FT*, 13 July 1999).

The merger of Glaxo Wellcome and SmithKline Beecham will create an immensely powerful global giant. However, the announcement of the merger was followed by deep discussion of the 'nationality' of the company that would result from the merger. A key aspect of the merger was the announcement that the operational headquarters of the new entity would be in the US, in the area just north of Philadelphia, the USA's pharmaceuticals equivalent of Silicon Valley. The new company's CEO, Jean-Pierre Garnier commented: 'The new company is global, proud of its roots in the UK. But a world-class competitor cannot operate all of its functions from a market that represents only 6 per cent of its existence' (quoted in *FT*, 17 January 2000). M. Garnier confirmed that strategic decisions would now be taken in the USA. The announcement of the shift of the company's headquarters to the USA raised 'the spectre of a gradual drift overseas of Britain's pharmaceutical industry' (*FT*, 17 January 2000). The two firms together account for three-fifths of the UK's total R & D expenditure in pharmaceuticals, and one-fifth of total UK expenditure on R & D (DTI, 1999).

IMPLICATIONS: BARRIERS TO ENTRY FOR DEVELOPING COUNTRY FIRMS

In the past decade there have occurred two simultaneous revolutions in pharmaceuticals. Within advanced capitalism, a drastic reorganization of business structure has occurred, leading to the emergence of vastly more powerful pharmaceutical companies. Within former Communist and developing countries, there has occurred rapid liberalization of rules governing trade and investment, and widespread application of internationally accepted rules governing acknowledgement of intellectual property rights. In other words, alongside the revolution in the business institutions of the pharmaceutical industry in advanced capitalism has gone a simultaneous revolution in the establishment of a global 'level playing field' in this industry The key instrument for this is the WTO's TRIPs agreement.

In the battle on the global 'level playing field', firms based in the advanced countries have a massive start compared to those in developing countries. They already have a portfolio of drugs bringing in a vast income compared to firms in developing countries and former planned economies. In 1999, the top 10 global pharmaceutical firms ranked by value of sales, consisted of six US-based companies and four European-based companies, one of which had announced that its headquarters was to move to the USA (Table 5-6). Not one firm from a developing or former Communist economy occupied a place in the global top 20 companies in this sector.

The large and rising size of the R & D required to develop patented drugs raises profound issues concerning the capability for developing country firms to grow an indigenous drug industry that can compete on the global 'level playing field' with the giants of the industry. Not only does it require huge sums to develop a single successful drug, but there are considerable economies of scope in researching on a number of related drugs. A key ingredient of the 'level playing field' is the sharp increase in the necessity for developing countries to recognize the intellectual property rights of firms based in the developed countries. This means that developing country drug firms will be less and less able to clone patented drugs produced by advanced countries' firms. If they wish to compete on the 'level playing field' in the market for patented medicines pharmaceutical firms from developing countries need to spend the vast sums required for R & D to develop their own patented drugs. This is far beyond the capabilities of even the leading indigenous firms in China or India, let alone other developing countries.

We have seen that marketing and brand development have become an increasingly important instrument for establishing and maintaining competitive edge for the world's leading pharmaceutical firms. Companies like Glaxo Wellcome and Merck allocate several billion dollars each to sales and marketing, exceeding even their huge expenditure on R & D. These sums are vastly greater than even the entire sales revenue of the leading pharmaceutical firms based in developing countries.

The world's leading pharmaceutical companies today are much more firmly. focused on pharmaceuticals. In the 1990s they became specialized in a narrow range of products, in which they and one or two other companies were leading players globally, so that their R & D and marketing efforts were focused on a narrow range of products, enabling far more effective use of available budgets. Moreover, in the late 1990s, a new series of mega-mergers is producing even more powerful giant life science companies. These combine global dominance in several areas, with a diversified portfolio of world-leading drugs, benefiting from economies of scale and scope in R & D and marketing, as well as from a more stable revenue stream and reduced risk consequent upon the diversified portfolio. The sales revenue from a single blockbuster drug now totals billions of dollars, much greater than the entire sales revenue of the leading pharmaceutical firms based in developing countries.

These factors make the world's leading pharmaceutical companies vastly more powerful competitors even than they were a decade ago, and raises sharply the barriers to entry in this sector. The institutional and technological gap between the pharmaceutical firms in developing countries and those in the advanced economies is growing wider at high speed, making it much more difficult for firms in developing countries to compete with those based in the advanced economies. The strength of the participants on the global 'level playing field' is becoming rapidly more unequal. At the very end of the old millennium and the beginning of the new one, the gap was growing at an even faster pace than in the preceding decade, due to an explosive sequence of mergers and acquisitions that were enormously increasing the relative strength of the world's leading firms in the sector compared to the leading firms based in developing countries.

COMMERCIALIZATION OF THE PLA

MOTIVES FOR COMMERCIALIZATION OF THE PLA

The People's Liberation Army (PLA) is a deeply important part of the Chinese national economy. Western military analysts estimate that China's national defence budget is two to three times higher than the official Chinese estimate of $9.7 billion in 1997 ($10.9 billion in 1998). Not only is the defence budget large, but under China's economic reforms, the PLA has become heavily involved in commercial activity.[3] It is estimated that the PLA controls around 15 000–20 000 enterprises, employs around 3 million workers and produces about 10 per cent of China's gross industrial output value (Yeung, 1995: 163–4). Exports from the military sector reached $7 billion in 1997, of which half consisted of civilian products (*IHT*, 24 July 1998: 4). It is estimated that PLA enterprises produce one-tenth of China's pharmaceutical output, one-fifth of its cars and trucks, and one-half of its motorcycles (*IHT*, 24 July 1998). The central government allowed the PLA's commercial involvement to develop for three main reasons: to provide finance for modernization of the military by providing extra-budgetary sources of funding; to provide jobs for retired military personnel, thereby reducing central government pension requirements for retired troops; and to improve overall China's manufacturing efficiency by utilizing the defence industries' surplus capacity by producing civilian products.

There are two main types of PLA involvement in commerce: conversion of military enterprises to civilian production, and the establishment of new businesses under the PLA.

MILITARY ENTERPRISES CONVERTED TO CIVILIAN PRODUCTION

In military–civilian conversion, the military–industrial complex (including the ministerial defence firms) under the State Council has transformed a large number of former military factories into dual-purpose factories producing both military and civilian products (Figure 5-1).[4] Leading examples include China Electronics Industry Corporation (Chinatron), China Shipbuilding Trading Company (CSTC), China North Industries Corporation (NORINCO), China Great Wall Industry Corporation (GWIC) and China Aviation Technology Company for Import and Export (CATIC).

According to Mr Wu Zhao, the chairman of the Association for the Peaceful Use of Military Industrial Technology (formed in 1987 to stimulate defence conversion), in 1994 around three-quarters of the output value of the defence industry was for civilian use (*FT*, 28 November 1994).[5] Other analysts estimate that in the 1990s, only about 10 per cent of defence factories' production capacity is used for defence purposes, the remaining 90 per cent either producing civilian goods or lying idle (Frankenstein and Gill, 1996: 396, *SCMP*, 24 July 1998).[6] Many former defence factories have become leading producers of such civilian products as colour televisions, motorcycles, washing machines and electric fans (*FT*, 28 November 1994). Sichuan Changhong Electric, a former defence electronics firm converted to colour television manufacturer, was included among China's top 100 listed companies selected by the China Shareholding Enterprises Evaluation Centre and the *Financial Times* in 1995 (*SCMP*, 10 August 1995: 6). Sichuan Changhong had 20 billion yuan of sales in 1997, and is the seventh-largest colour television producer in the world. It has also acquired TV components manufacturers to achieve vertical integration and has diversified into consumer appliances, personal computers and telecommunications (*Far Eastern Economic Review*, 21 May 1998: 10–12).

NEW BUSINESSES UNDER THE PLA

A number of businesses with financial and administrative autonomy has been established with funding from the PLA under the general supervision of the Central Military Commission (CMC) (Figure 5-1). Under the General Staff Department (GSD), the most prominent of these are China Poly Group, China Huitong and China Electronic Systems and Engineering Company (CESEC). Under the General Logistics Department (GLD), the most prominent are China Xinxing Corporation and Sanjiu Enterprise Group, the subject of this study. China Poly Group was formed in 1984 to provide competition for China Northern

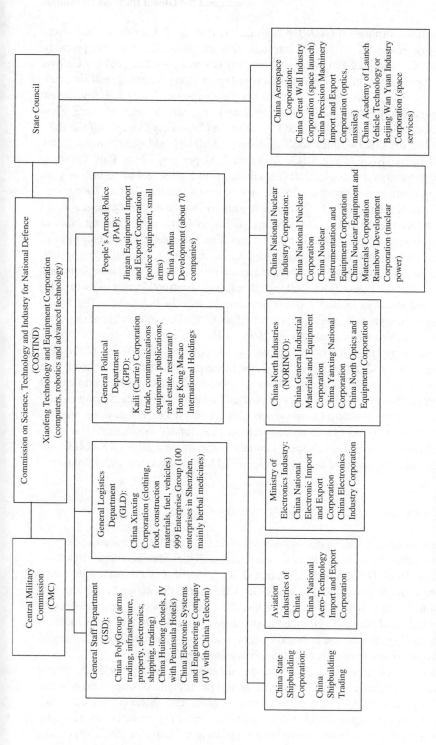

FIGURE 5-1 China's Military–Industrial Commercial Complex

SOURCE: Frankenstein and Gill (1996: 401–2); *FT*; (28 November 1994, 24 July 1998)

Industries Corporation (NORINCO) in arms trading. It later developed into a conglomerate with business interests which included infrastructure, property, electronics, shipping and trading. China Poly Group's president is Major General He Ping, director of the GSD, and son-in-law of Deng Xiaoping, and its chairman is Wang Jun, director of China International Trust and Investment Corporation (CITIC) and son of the late Long March veteran Wang Zhen (Frankenstein and Gill, 1996: 405).[7] Two of the China Poly Group's subsidiaries, Poly Investments Holdings and Continental Mariner (a shipping company), are listed in the Hong Kong Stock Exchange.[8] At present, China Poly Group is thought to incorporate over 100 subsidiaries with total assets of 10 billion yuan and an international revenue of $500 million a year (*SCMP*, 24 July 1998).

China Huitong has a hotel business joint venture with the Peninsula Hotel (owned by the listed Hongkong Shanghai Hotels Group), the five-star hotel in Hong Kong. CESEC is closely allied with China Telecom in the development of China's telecommunications businesses. China Xinxing Corporation was established in 1989. It is thought to include around 100 subsidiaries in Hong Kong and Los Angeles, ranging from clothing, shoes, and construction materials to vehicles, and employs around 200 000 workers (*SCMP*, 24 July 1998). The Sanjiu Group is thought to account for around 10 per cent of the total value of output of PLA-controlled businesses (Yeung, 1995: 164).

One careful general scholarly account of the commercial activities of the PLA (Ding, 1996: 432) reports that PLA-funded enterprises under the PLA work on a variety of profit-sharing arrangements with the central and local departments of the PLA. However, the study acknowledges that these vary greatly from case to case, with little concrete knowledge available to outsiders. For obvious reasons, there is virtually no first-hand research on PLA-funded businesses. The study that forms the basis of this paper is unique in having been allowed access to one of the most important of these (see Figure 5-1) for detailed research purposes.[9]

CONFLICT BETWEEN COMMERCIAL ACTIVITIES AND MILITARY GOALS

There has been extensive discussion both inside and outside China about the possible conflict between the PLA's commercial activities and its military functions (Yeung, 1995: 165–6). These culminated in a series of major reforms announced by the Chinese government in mid-1998. Much of the discussion both inside and outside China is based on rumour rather than hard evidence, often lacks sound economic analysis, and is frequently coloured by hostility to the PLA's function in sustaining the Chinese political system. It also typically conflates a variety of different arguments that benefit from being analyzed separately.

One set of arguments concerns the alleged inability of the PLA to run businesses effectively. This is argued to be due to problems of inappropriate organizational culture, lack of necessary business skills, and absence of a clear structure of property rights (Frankenstein and Gill, 1996). This is said to explain why a large fraction of military-controlled businesses make losses: in 1995, 38 per cent of ordinance firms were reported to be loss-makers, (the 1993 figure was even higher at 50 per cent), while rumours from NORINCO suggest that the true proportion is even higher (Frankenstein and Gill, 1996: 419–20). However, there is little, if any, hard evidence that military officials are systematically less competent 'principals' to manage state enterprises in transition than are civilians. Indeed, the PLA contains many skills associated with the necessity to think long-term, to analyze issues strategically and the requirement to discipline and motivate members of the organization.

Moreover, a large fraction of military factories are located in remote areas where they were established under Mao Zedong as part of the 'Third Front' to protect China in the event of large-scale warfare. In the transition to the market economy, these high-cost enterprises were exposed cruelly to market forces. It would be hard for any form of management to turn them into profitable enterprises. They constitute a long-term social burden for the PLA, as well as a drain on its finances.

A second set of arguments concerns the special possibilities for segments of the PLA to benefit through illegal means from the arbitrage opportunities created by continued state regulation of the economy. Extensive PLA involvement in smuggling was recognized explicitly by Jiang Zemin in his path-breaking speech to military leaders on 22 July 1998 (see below). In the international sphere, continued, albeit declining, state regulation, provides large opportunities for smuggling. Duties for several commodities such as cigarettes, cellular telephones, cars and diesel oil, remained high, making smuggling extremely lucrative. The PLA is in a unique position to benefit from this due to the fact that its vehicles can cross the border free of customs inspection. This problem has been exacerbated by the return of Hong Kong and the great increase in flow of military transport across the border in Shenzhen between Hong Kong and Mainland China. Large-scale smuggling has caused serious loss of tax revenue to the government. According to the General Administration of Customs, rampant smuggling, much of it thought to be associated with the PLA, deprived the central government of 100 billion yuan (*FT*, 23 July 1998). Moreover, large-scale smuggling, often with perceived PLA involvement, provides a big source of income that is widely perceived to be illegitimate.

Domestically, also there are similar arbitrage activities from which the PLA is in a special position to gain, such as local protectionism and continued price control over various commodities. Moreover, the state's attempt to regulate activities deemed to be socially undesirable, such as prostitution, provides opportunities for elements in the PLA to engage in criminal activity to obtain rental incomes, using their political power to escape sanctions from the law. These illegal activities stemming from state regulation of the domestic and international economy undermine the regime's credibility, damage morale within the PLA and undermine its claim to uphold high ethical values in Chinese society.

A third problem is that the extensive involvement in commercial activities, even if it were entirely legal, may seriously erode military professionalism in the army, and endanger the fighting capability of the armed forces. One Western expert on the Chinese military argues that economic involvement 'undermines military modernization', 'interferes with war preparations, impairs specialization, erodes discipline and fosters factionalism' (Ellis Joffe in *IHT*, 10 August, 1998). He argues that 'an army that expects to fight a modern war under high-tech conditions cannot afford this price, whatever the benefits'. Professional army commanders 'have said this for several years, but they made little headway against political leaders and their military allies'.

A fourth problem is the complexity and conflict of interest involved in the way China organized procurement and production of weaponry. The Commission on Science, Technology and Industry for National Defence (COSTIND) was established in 1982, to co-ordinate the PLA's weapons research and to organize PLA procurement from military factories under the State Council and PLA-funded firms under the CMC. COSTIND itself was under the supervision of both the CMC and the State Council, resulting in a complex, cumbersome process of procurement (Frankenstein and Gill, 1996: 404). Moreover, COSTIND was heavily involved in 'commercial activities', both directly through the Xiaofeng Technology and Equipment Corporation (see Figure 5-1), and through its various subsidiaries, including the GLD, GSD and PAP (People's Armed Police), creating a growing complexity and conflict of interest. In 1998, an attempt was made to resolve this problem with the establishment of a separate General Armaments Department, which was to become the sole organization in charge of weapons research, production and procurement (John Pomfret in *IHT*, 23 July 1998), with the tasks of organizing weapons production, procurement and R & D for the PLA, but was not to engage in commercial activities. There still remained the unresolved problem of an organization within the military procuring weaponry from itself.

In recognition of the growing problems being caused by the PLA's involvement in business, the Central Military Commission set up an audit commission to restrain the PLA's business activities in 1992 (*FT*, 28 November 1994). In 1993 the central government banned any local PLA units from running enterprises (*Jiefangjun Bao*, 9 November 1993: 1). In some military regions, the PLA was required to hand over ownership of their enterprises to local governments (*Jiefangjun Bao*, 18 June 1994: 1). Despite the ban and the fact that almost one-third of its business ventures may have closed down or passed out of army ownership, the PLA was still heavily engaged in commercial activities (Ding, 1996: 441–2; *IHT*, 24 July 1998: 4). The continuing problems were highlighted by the high-profile disclosure of a \$120 million fraud investigation into J & A Securities, based in Shenzhen and partly funded by the Guangzhou military region. In early 1998 the government signalled its intention to professionalize the PLA, announcing that the PLA would be reduced from around 3.2 million members to around 2.7 million.

On 22 July 1998 President Jiang Zemin (also chairman of the Central Military Commission) reportedly gave the order: 'The army and armed police forces must earnestly carry out checks on all kinds of commercial companies set up by subsidiary units, and without exception from today must not engage in their operation' (quoted in *FT*, 23 July 1998). It is not clear what this will mean in practice. Some reports suggested that PLA-affiliated companies will be taken over completely by civilian departments at both the central and local level. It is reported that the largest PLA-owned business groups controlled at the military-command level and above, such as the China Poly Group or China Xinxing Corporation, will get a three-year grace period to transfer their ownership to the civilian sector (*SCMP*, 24–25 July 1998). However, 'transition to civilian ownership' could be accomplished in many ways. For example, it could involve leaving the PLA as the principal shareholder in enterprises run by 'civilians' as autonomous businesses. The 'civilians' who manage the transformed PLA enterprises could in principle be former members of the PLA, perhaps even remaining as reservists.

It has been speculated also that the real objective of Jiang Zemin's statement was not intended to signal the transition to civilian ownership of military businesses. Rather, it is suggested that it should be viewed as a threat, which will force the PLA and PAP to take seriously the need to implement anti-smuggling work (*FT*, 24 July 1998; *IHT*, 24 July 1998: 4). Supporters of this view argue that the PLA is such a powerful vested interest group so closely intertwined with the central government that it is impossible successfully to remove it from involvement in commerce. Moreover, they suggest that the government would find it impossible to raise the funds necessary to replace those generated by the military's commercial activities.

GROWTH OF THE CHINESE PHARMACEUTICAL INDUSTRY

Market Size

China is already an important pharmaceutical market (Table 5-8). In 1995, the total value of pharmaceutical sales already accounted for almost one-third of the East Asian market outside Japan. It was the same size as the combined market of Malaysia, the Philippines, Thailand and Indonesia, and was more than double that of India. In the 1980s and 1990s, as incomes rose, demand for medicines rose rapidly. Increased expenditure on medicines was an important factor in the improvements in life expectancy experienced by all age groups other than infants under the economic reforms. From the early 1980s to the mid-1990s, output of both Western and traditional Chinese medicines increased more than fourfold (Table 5-9).

Despite the fast growth of output and consumption, per capita pharmaceutical consumption in China was still small in international terms. In 1996 it was less than $3 per person, compared to $132 in the UK, $334 in the USA and as high as $488 in Japan (Table 5-8). However, it was much smaller also than in neighbouring East Asian developing countries, where the comparable figures were $13 in Malaysia, $16 in the Philippines, $47 in Hong Kong and $75 in Taiwan (Table 5-8). The total size of the Chinese pharmaceutical market was still

TABLE 5-8 *Per capita* Pharmaceutical Consumption in China and Other Selected Countries, 1991 and 1995

	1991					1995					Annual growth 1985–95		
	Population (million)	GDP ($ billion)	Pharma market ($ billion)	Per capita GDP ($)	Per capita pharma cons ($)	Population (million)	GDP ($ billion)	Pharma market ($ billion)	Per capita GDP ($)	Per capita pharma cons($)	Population (million)	GDP (%)	Pharma cons
China	1 170.1	379	2.9	324	2.5	1 221.5	698	3.5	571	2.9	1.1	16.5	4.9
South Korea	43.3	294	2.7	6799	61.8	44.9	456	4.2	10175	93.3	0.9	11.6	11.9
Taiwan	20.6	175	0.9	8516	44.6	21.2	260	1.6	12274	75.2	0.7	10.4	14.8
Singapore	2.8	42	0.1	15318	30.8	3.0	72	0.2	24222	52.5	2.0	14.4	16.6
Hong Kong	5.8	83	0.2	14388	31.3	6.2	140	0.3	22650	47.2	1.9	14.1	12.9
Japan	123.9	3350	33.0	27035	265.9	125.2	5134	61.1	41009	488.2	0.3	11.3	16.7
Malaysia	18.6	47	0.2	2540	8.7	20.7	87	0.3	4221	13.0	2.8	16.7	13.6
Thailand	56.6	98	0.5	1738	9.5	59.4	169	0.9	2840	14.7	1.2	14.4	13.0
Philippines	63.7	45	0.6	711	9.6	70.3	74	1.1	1055	15.9	2.5	13.1	16.4
Indonesia	181.4	116	0.6	639	3.2	193.8	201	1.1	1038	5.4	1.7	14.8	15.7
India	851.7	217	1.3	318	1.6	935.7	339	1.7	362	1.8	2.4	5.8	5.5
Total Asia ex-Japan	2 414.3	1551	10.0	642	4.1	2 576.5	2497	14.7	969	5.7	1.6	12.6	10.2
Developed markets													
USA	252.6	5723	62.4	22652	247.1	263.2	7254	87.9	27563	334.1	1.0	6.1	8.9
France	57.1	1199	12.6	21014	220.3	58.2	1535	18.0	26399	310.2	0.5	6.4	9.5
Germany	80.0	1697	13.7	21215	171.1	81.6	2412	16.4	29550	200.3	0.5	9.2	4.6
UK	57.8	1012	6.1	17500	106.1	58.3	1105	7.7	18969	131.9	0.2	2.2	5.8

SOURCE: MSDW (1998c: 151)

TABLE 5-9 Chinese Pharmaceutical Production, 1980–96 (000 tons)

Year	Chemical pharmaceuticals	Chinese medicines
1980	40	103
1990	221	226
1994	331	379
1995	490	610
1996	430	410
Index (1980 = 100)		

SOURCE: SSB, ZTN (English edn) (1981: 235); SSB, ZTN (1991: 429; 1995: 411
416; 1997: 451)

small compared to that of any of the larger advanced economies. It is widely recognized that in the next century the market will become one of the largest in the
world. The potential for growth of the market is enormous and of great potential
significance for the world's giant companies.

LIBERALIZATION

Domestic Liberalization

Product markets. In the early 1980s, China's pharmaceutical industry was under
tight state control. Plants received instructions from planners, obtained their inputs
through the 'planning' system and supplied products to the material supply system
according to planners' instructions. There were no 'firms' just state administered
plants. In the mid-1980's, the government relaxed state controls over the pharmaceutical industry, allowing competition quickly to develop among suppliers. As
controls were relaxed the industry was able to earn relatively high profits. Even in
the difficult economic circumstances of the late 1990s, net profits amounted to
around 7 per cent of the sector's sales value and over 10 per cent of the value of
fixed assets (Table 5-10). A common saying was: 'If you want to be mayor go for
pharmaceuticals'. Baiyunshan (Guangzhou) was a symbol of the high profits to be
earned in this sector. It was a collective enterprise which quickly grew from nothing to take over the number one position in the pharmaceutical industry, displacing
the old state enterprises, principally by producing traditional Chinese medicines.

However, even in the late 1990s, China's large, old-established state plants
remained quite tightly controlled by the government, with production and sales
'tasks' for its main products. Still in 1997, 'the production costs and profit margins of state-run pharmaceutical producers' were 'strictly controlled by the government' (*CDBW*, 23 November 1997). These plants mainly produce relatively
capital intensive 'upstream' intermediate pharmaceuticals, especially out-
of-patent antibiotics, which are then processed by smaller factories, as well as
producing generic, low-margin final products, such as penicillin and aspirin.
Many of these were on a downward spiral, with old equipment, a high debt–
asset ratio, low salaries and poor housing and research conditions. By contrast,

TABLE 5-10 **Selected Data on China's Pharmaceutical Industry, by Gross Output Value, 1996 (Independent Accounting Enterprises) (% in brackets)**

Gross value of output (yuan)	Sales value	Value-added	Net profits	Fixed assets	Profits/sales (%)	Profits/fixed assets (%)
500 000 and below	78	−175	−70	727	−89.74	−9.63
Chemical pharmaceuticals	38 (49)	−118 (67)	−33 (47)	536 (74)	−86.84	−6.16
Chinese medicines	40 (51)	−57 (33)	−37 (53)	190 (26)	−92.50	−19.47
500 000–1 million:	92	10	−70	273	−76.09	−25.64
Chemical pharmaceuticals	58 (63)	−0.21 (0)	−41 (56)	179 (66)	−70.69	−22.91
Chinese medicines	34 (37)	10 (100)	−29 (41)	93 (34)	−85.29	−31.18
1–5 million	2 183	682	−411	3 901	−18.83	−10.54
Chemical pharmaceuticals	1 455 (67)	413 (61)	−278 (68)	2 756 (71)	−19.11	−10.09
Chinese medicines	728 (33)	269 (39)	−132 (32)	1 145 (29)	−18.13	−11.53
5–10 million	3 504	1 086	−229	4 010	−6.54	−5.71
Chemical pharmaceuticals	2 301 (66)	630 (58)	−185 (81)	2 852 (71)	−8.04	−6.49
Chinese medicines	1 203 (34)	456 (42)	−44 (19)	1 157 (29)	−3.66	−3.80
10–30 million	13 254	4 681	−259	11 305	−1.95	−2.29

Chemical						
pharmaceuticals	9 468 (71)	3 129 (67)	−237 (92)	8 467 (75)	−2.50	−2.80
Chinese medicines	3 786 (29)	1 553 (33)	−22 (8)	2 839 (25)	−0.58	−0.77
30–50 millions	8 597	3 018	119	5 696	1.38	2.09
Chemical						
pharmaceuticals	6 478 (75)	1 997 (66)	59 (50)	4 310 (76)	0.91	1.37
Chinese medicines	2 119 (25)	1 021 (34)	59 (50)	1 387 (24)	2.78	4.25
50–100 millions	15 233	5 019	408	10 090	2.68	4.04
Chemical						
pharmaceuticals	11 349 (75)	3 307 (66)	−11 (3)	8 120 (80)	−0.10	−0.14
Chinese medicines	3 884 (25)	1 712 (34)	419 (103)	1 970 (20)	10.79	21.27
100 million and above:	60 676	21 598	7,308	30 587	12.04	23.89
Chemical						
pharmaceuticals	51 746 (85)	17 039 (79)	5,713 (78)	27 321 (89)	11.04	20.91
Chinese medicines	8 930 (15)	4 558 (21)	1,595 (22)	3 266 (11)	17.86	8.84
Total	103 617	35 920	6,796	66 589	6.56	10.21
Chemical						
pharmaceuticals	82 893 (80)	26 397 (73)	4,987 (73)	54 541 (82)	6.02	9.14
Chinese medicines	20 724 (20)	9 522 (27)	1 809 (27)	12 048 (18)	8.73	15.01

SOURCE: Compiled and calculated from *China Pharmaceutical Yearbook* 1997: 457, 469

manufacturers of traditional Chinese medicines and foreign-funded enterprises enjoyed much greater freedom to set prices.

Despite formal liberalization of the domestic pharmaceutical market, there remained a thicket of *de facto* interventions with the market due to the fact that a large fraction of pharmaceuticals is prescribed by hospitals, mostly run by the state. These are gradually moving towards independent accounting and financial responsibility. The proportion of health care costs, including medicines, that must be financed by the individuals employed in state institutions is rising, providing an incentive to source drugs from the lowest-cost source.

Capital markets. Alongside product market liberalization, the pharmaceutical sector gradually liberalized the structure of ownership, as emerging firms sought capital in the face of declining direct investment sources from the state. An important facet of this was raising funds on the stock market. By the end of 1996, there were 26 pharmaceutical corporations listed in the stock markets in Shenzhen and Hong Kong alone, and several others listed on the Shanghai stock market. Among these were some important examples of capital from international sources. For example, Shandong Xinhua was able to generate 280 million yuan of capital by listing its H-shares on the Hong Kong Stock Exchange in December 1996. Dongbei also listed in the stock market in 1996 (*China Pharmaceutical Yearbook*, 1997: 260). As will be seen below, foreign direct investment also grew fast and changed the industry's ownership structure significantly. Slowly, the industry moved towards diversified ownership, away from monolithic state ownership, driven by the need to raise funds independently for expansion. Moreover, as the 1990s proceeded, it became increasingly possible for one pharmaceutical company to take over another.

International Liberalization

Multinational investment in the Chinese pharmaceutical industry was permitted from early on in the reform process. By the mid-1990s, following the gradual liberalization of the domestic industry, investment had increased to significant levels. By 1997 there was a total of no fewer than 1500 pharmaceutical joint ventures (CDBW, 14 December 1997). All 15 of the world's top pharmaceutical companies had set up joint ventures. By 1997 Novartis had invested $130 million in six joint ventures, including pharmaceutical plants (CDBW, 16 November 1997). Leading examples of multinational joint ventures included four set up by Johnson and Johnson in Shanghai alone, with a total investment of $175 million. Bristol–Myers Squibb's joint venture in Shanghai was set up in the mid-1980s, and by 1996 it claimed to account for 20 per cent of the Chinese vitamin market and no less than 80 per cent of the Chinese multivitamin market (China: Economic Digest, Winter 1996–7: 52). By 1996 SmithKline Beecham's joint venture in Tianjin had become one of China's top six pharmaceutical companies by value of sales (Table 5-11), and a large joint venture with $100 million investment was due to be opened in Shanghai in 1999 (China: Economic Digest, Winter, 1997–8: 67). Jannsen (Belgium) set up a large joint venture in Xian in the mid-1980s which had grown to be the fourth largest pharmaceutical company in China by 1996 (Table 5-11). In the mid-1990s, joint ventures were set up by Schering– Plough in Shanghai, Merck in Hangzhou, Glaxo Wellcome in Chengdu, Eli–Lilley in Suzhou and Da Zhong (Japan) in Tianjin. Glaxo Wellcome's plant in Chengdu had 'several hundred million yuan' in investment, and Merck invested over 200 million yuan in its plant in Hangzhou. Once these plants were completed and production and distribution were under way it was likely that they would enter the ranks of China's top producers. By 1997 it was estimated that 'foreign medicines' accounted for around 60 per cent of the total value of medicines consumed in major cities (CDBW, 14 December 1997).

The multinationals brought technology and new standards of management to the Chinese pharmaceutical industry. They also brought a portfolio of high-margin patented drugs. From 1993 onwards, China basically applied internationally recognized practice in respect to property rights for pharmaceuticals patented in other countries, protecting the company concerned from cloning of the product by local producers. The leading joint ventures, such as Xian Jannsen and Tianjin SmithKline Beecham were able to generate significantly greater total profits than their leading indigenous competitors, and dramatically higher ratios of profits to sales and assets (Table 5-11).

As well as increasing fast to meet domestic needs, the Chinese pharmaceutical industry became rapidly more integrated into international trade in pharmaceuticals. It became an increasingly important low-cost base for pharmaceutical exports, especially of non-patent medicines such as vitamins. By 1995, China's exports of pharmaceuticals reached $43.6 million (compared to imports of just $4.9 million) (SSB, ZTN, 1997: 598–600).

INDUSTRIAL STRUCTURE

Firm-level Concentration. Under the 'planned economy', there were no pharmaceutical firms in the strict sense, only a number of state- and collectively-owned enterprises that received instruction from state planners. Of these much the largest were the traditional state producers of Western medicines, mainly antibiotics. The largest of these were the Huabei plant at Shijiazhuang and the Dongbei plant in Shenyang, with over 7000 employees each.[10]

In the emerging market economy under the economic reforms, as we shall see from the case of Sanjiu, entities with the characteristics of a genuine 'firm' began to take shape. As we have seen, the fast growth of demand for pharmaceuticals and the high profit margins that were to be obtained from this sector, encouraged a rush of capital into the sector. The relatively large profits obtained in the sector led to a wave of new plants being established across the country. By 1987 there were over 2600 independent accounting enterprises producing medical and pharmaceutical products, with almost 700000 employees (SSB, ZGJTN, 1988: 298). By 1990 Guangdong province alone had over 260 pharmaceutical plants and by 1989, Guangzhou city had 68 plants and Shenzhen had 23 plants (SSB, GTN, 1991: 155–7).

TABLE 5-11 The Top 10 and the Top 20 Pharmaceutical Corporations in China, by Market Share, 1996

Pharmaceutical corporations	Sales	Output	Pre-tax profits	Fixed assets	Market share (%)	Sales/output (%)	Profits/sales (%)	Profits/fixed assets (%)
	(million yuan)							
Huabei	2650	2797	471	2482	2.56	94.76	17.76	18.96
Shenzhen Nanfang*	1601	1850	464	593	1.55	86.54	29.01	78.30
Guangzhou Baiyunshan	1562	1301	127	507	1.51	120.11	8.14	25.10
Xian Yangseng (Janssen)	1435	1473	565	217	1.38	97.43	39.35	259.62
Shandong Xinhua	1372	1023	164	785	1.32	134.17	11.96	20.92
Tianjin SmithKline	1180	1163	718	250	1.14	101.42	60.86	286.89
Harbin	942	963	95	472	0.91	97.84	10.13	20.22
Dongbei	910	971	29	640	0.88	93.67	3.22	4.58
Shandong Lukang	785	945	139	553	0.76	83.05	17.65	25.07
Zhuhai Lizhu	770	484	191	534	0.74	159.05	24.86	35.81
Top 10**	13207	13180	3156	7838	12.75	100.20	23.89	40.26
Shijiazhuang	657	605	53	196	0.63	108.64	8.04	26.97
Shanghai Shiguibao								

(Bristol–Myers Squibb)	623	695	89	219	0.60	89.73	14.34	40.80
Jingjiang	609	631	Out of top 500	460	0.59	96.52	n.a.	n.a.
Wuhan Gongtaokai	552	653	179	152	0.53	84.55	32.42	117.86
Shanghai Sanwei	517	622	Out of top 500	153	0.50	83.19	n.a.	n.a.
Hebei	499	565	121	313	0.48	88.33	24.32	38.78
Shanghai Xianfeng	451	464	18	31	0.44	97.26	3.93	57.81
Qilu	451	530	32	227	0.43	85.03	7.05	14.00
Zhumadian	413	422	51	154	0.40	97.86	12.41	33.30
Zhangjiakou Shi	410	484	46	263	0.40	84.68	11.25	17.54
Top 20**	18 390	18 750	4 011	11 158	17.75	98.08	21.81	35.95
China	103 617	110 175	13 247	66 589	100.00	94.05	12.79	19.89

SOURCE: Compiled and calculated from *China Pharmaceutical Yearbook* 1997: 457, 469, 503–30

NOTES: * Leading plant of the Sanjiu Group
** The above top 10/20 ranking of pharmaceutical corporations is based on its market share, if all the top 10/20 figures are based on its market share, the output values were 12 969 and 18 640, pre-tax profits were 2964 and 3553, fixed assets were 7033 and 9200, sales/output ratios were 101.83 per cent and 98.66 per cent, profits/sales ratios were 22.44 per cent and 19.32 per cent, and profits/fixed assets ratios were 42.14 per cent and 38.62 per cent

By 1996, the number of pharmaceutical enterprises in China had risen to no fewer than 3330, an extraordinarily large number for a market of China's size (Table 5-12). There were almost 3000 tiny labour-intensive, handicraft enterprises (Table 5-12), producing under primitive conditions, without benefit from economies of scale or scope. They typically lacked modern technology, brands, marketing systems, or strict quality control. These accounted for over 80 per cent of the total number of enterprises in the Chinese pharmaceutical industry, but for only around one-third of the industry's total output value. A large fraction of these were loss-making by the late 1990s. Indeed, in 1996 each of the enterprise size groups of below 30 million yuan (roughly $3.7 million) per annum made losses (Table 5-12).

The vast bulk of the industry's profits were generated by the largest enterprises, which increasingly benefited from economies of scale and scope, with superior technology, more modern management systems, brand names, growing marketing systems, increasing quality control, and, frequently, access to patented medicines. In 1996, enterprises with annual sales of over 100 million yuan (around $12 million) accounted for around one-half of the pharmaceutical industry's fixed assets, three-fifths of its sales value and two-thirds of the sectors' value-added (Table 5-13).

However, within the largest size group of pharmaceutical firms, the level of firm-level concentration was still low. In 1996 the top 10 firms had a total market share of just 12.8 per cent, and the top 20 firms had a total market share of only 17.8 per cent of the total (Table 5-11). The top 250 firms accounted for over 42 per cent of the sector's total sales (Table 5-12). Sales and profits of the leading firms were tiny compared to the global industry. In 1996, China's top 10 pharmaceutical firms had average annual sales the equivalent of only around $165 million (Table 5-11). The Chinese State Pharmaceutical Administration has committed itself to the policy of encouraging pharmaceutical enterprises 'to form large corporate groups through mergers and acquisitions' (CDBW, 22 March 1998).

A major goal of the attempt to develop bigger pharmaceutical enterprises is in order to pool R & D resources: 'We will thereby achieve a shift in the development mode for the pharmaceutical sector – from imitation to creation' (Zheng Xiaoyu, director general of the State Pharmaceutical Administration quoted in CDBW, 22 March 1998). China's goal is to 'make China one of the world's pharmaceutical giants by the middle of the next century' (CDBW, 14 December 1997). In order to do so, China recognizes that it must develop its own R & D capabilities in order to 'produce patent drugs to compete in the international market'. By 1998 not one Chinese chemical drug had achieved an international patent. From 1985 to 1996 China's pharmaceutical authorities approved 2096 new medicines but of these only 82 were patented medicines and only 59 of these were chemical ('Western') drugs. The central government promised that it would support R & D in the sector through research conducted at the China Administrative Centre for New Drug Research and Development, under the State Pharmaceutical Administration. It would also support the sector's development 'through readjustment of medicine prices in favour of the domestic pharmaceutical industry' (CDBW, 14 December 1997).

TABLE 5-12 Structure of China's Pharmaceutical Industry, 1996 (Independent Accounting Enterprises)

No. of employees	No. of enterprises		Post-tax profits		Fixed assets		Gross value of output	
		(%)	million yuan	(%)	million yuan	(%)	million yuan	(%)
Total	3 326	100	13 247	100	66 589	100	110 175	100
>10 000	2	0.06	505	3.81	3 122	4.69	3 768	3.42
5–10 000	7	0.21	2 340	17.66	2 818	4.23	7 528	6.83
3–5 000	15	0.45	207	1.56	3 951	5.93	4 839	4.39
1–3 000	204	6.13	3 046	22.99	19 872	29.84	30 253	27.46
500–1 000	410	12.33	3 938	29.73	14 281	21.45	27 625	25.07
100–500	1 687	50.72	2 819	21.28	18 857	28.32	30 814	27.97
<100	1 001	30.10	391	2.95	3 689	5.54	5 347	4.85

SOURCE: Compiled and calculated from *China Pharmaceutical Yearbook 1997*: 466–7, 478–9.

TABLE 5-13 Selected Data on China's Pharmaceutical Industry, 1996 (Independent
Accounting Enterprises) (% in brackets)

Selected proxies	Total	Of which: state enterprises	State enterprises as % of total
Number of enterprises:	3 326	1 675	50.36
Chemical pharmaceuticals	2 288 (68.79)	1 114 (66.51)	48.69
Chinese medicines	1 038 (31.21)	561 (33.49)	54.05
Gross value of output			
(million yuan):	110 175	58 566	53.16
Chemical pharmaceuticals	87 570 (79.48)	48 347 (82.55)	55.01
Chinese medicines	22 605 (20.52)	10 219 (17.45)	45.21
Value-added (million yuan):	35 920	16 717	46.54
Chemical pharmaceuticals	26 397 (73.49)	12 684 (75.87)	48.05
Chinese medicines	9 522 (26.51)	4 033 (24.13)	42.35
Fixed assets			
(net value, million yuan):	66 589	41 367	62.12
Chemical pharmaceuticals	54 541 (81.91)	35 159 (84.99)	64.46
Chinese medicines	12 048 (18.09)	6 208 (15.01)	51.53
Sales value (million yuan):	103 617	56 084	54.13
Chemical pharmaceuticals	82 893 (80.00)	46 595 (83.08)	56.21
Chinese medicines	20 724 (20.00)	9 490 (16.92)	45.79
Pre-tax profits (million yuan):	13 247	4 587	34.63
Chemical pharmaceuticals	9 715 (73.34)	3 163 (68.96)	32.56
Chinese medicines	3 532 (26.66)	1 424 (31.04)	40.32
Value-added tax (million yuan):	5 628	2 750	48.86
Chemical pharmaceuticals	4 126 (73.30)	2 046 (74.40)	49.59
Chinese medicines	1 503 (26.70)	704 (25.60)	46.84
Post-tax profits (million yuan):	6 796	1 372	20.19
Chemical pharmaceuticals	4 987 (73.38)	767 (55.90)	15.38
Chinese medicines	1 809 (26.62)	605 (44.10)	33.44

SOURCE: Compiled and calculated from *China Pharmaceutical Yearbook 1997*: 429, 433, 457, 469, 481

Traditional/Western Medicines. Use of traditional medicines has an important place in Chinese culture and daily life. China has a long history of experience in classifying and 'testing' traditional medicines. Unlike Western patented
medicines, the development of the bulk of these products is not attributable to the
R & D of any given company, and cannot be patented under either Chinese or
international law. Their development was attributable mainly to the knowledge
accumulated over centuries by unknown practitioners of traditional Chinese
medicine. By 1996, there over 1000 enterprises producing traditional medicines,
compared to around 2300 producing Western medicines (Table 5-13).

In 1996 China produced around 400 000 tons each of Western and Chinese traditional medicines (Table 5-13). However, the two sectors have very different

economic characteristics. The unit value of Western medicines was far higher than for Chinese medicines. In 1996 Western medicines accounted for around 82 per cent of the pharmaceutical industry's fixed assets, 80 per cent of the sector's total sales value and 73 per cent of its total profits (Table 5-13).

Although traditional Chinese medicines are not mainly patented, their profitability is assisted by generally lower capital costs. There may also be greater scope for product differentiation than in the generic, 'commoditized' pharmaceutical sector. Despite the absence of patents for most products, many of the most successful products are able to command premium prices (see the discussion of Sanjiu below). Also, there is virtually no competition from the multinational giants in this sector (see below). In 1996, Chinese traditional medicine enterprises accounted for only 18 per cent of the sector's fixed assets and 20 per cent of the sector's sales value, but they accounted for 27 per cent of the sector's value-added and net profits (Table 5-13). In the same year, Chinese medicines achieved a ratio of profits to sales of 8.7 per cent compared to 6.0 per cent for Western medicines, and a ratio of profits to fixed assets of over 15 per cent compared to 9.1 per cent for Western medicines (Table 5-10). Within the sector there was enormous disparity in performance between large and small firms. The largest size group of traditional Chinese medicine producers achieved a ratio of profits to sales of 17.9 per cent, and a ratio of profits to fixed assets of 48.8 per cent (Table 5-10). By contrast, enterprises in the smallest size groups made exceptionally large losses in producing traditional medicines (Table 5-10).

SANJIU

INTRODUCTION

The emergence of the fast-growing market economy in China after the late 1970s provided opportunities for existing large plants to grow into more complex big businesses, stimulated especially by booming demand for their 'upstream' products, such as steel and petrochemicals. However, large firms emerged also from among the ranks of new entrants and small producers. The object of this study, the Sanjiu Group, only came into existence in 1986.[11] By the mid-1990s it had risen to become China's largest pharmaceutical firm (by value of output), and was one of the top 100 firms in China (by sales value). Its ambition was to become one of the world's top ten pharmaceutical firms.

In the late 1990s, one of the first sights that greeted the arriving traveller at Beijing International Airport was a huge advertisement for Sanjiu's main product (*Sanjiu Weitai*) stomach medicine, placed prominently on the airport control tower.[12] One of the most prominent advertising sites in Hong Kong has a massive billboard advertising *Sanjiu Weitai*. In 1995 Sanjiu replaced the advertisement for Union Bay Sportswear on a big billboard at the corner of Seventh Avenue and 48th Street in New York.[13] It was the first Chinese firm to advertise in Times Square. Zhao Xinxian, the chief executive officer of Sanjiu was listed in the US publication, *Notable World Figures and their Achievements*. He was reportedly the first person from the Chinese military to be listed in the British *Dictionary of National Biography* (*CDBW*, 22 June 1993).

Sanjiu presents an apparent puzzle. In 1995 Sanjiu still was a 100 per cent state-owned firm based in Shenzhen Special Economic Zone in South China. Not only was it state-owned, but it was administratively controlled from the distant Beijing Headquarters of the General Logistics Department (*Zonghou qinbu*) of the People's Liberation Army. The firm has no private property rights at all. In their absence, it is tempting to explain the growth of Sanjiu in terms of 'nepotism' and 'army connections'.[14]

The apparent puzzle is reinforced by the fact that the sector in which Sanjiu made its initial growth, traditional Chinese medicines, is one that depends greatly on entrepreneurial skills rather than advanced technology, such as is the case in the steel industry, petrochemicals or even Western pharmaceuticals, with their high outlays on drugs research. Management motivation, product choice, quality control, marketing, and brand imagery, rather than scientific skills were the key to Sanjiu's early growth within pharmaceuticals. Moreover, Sanjiu's subsequent growth was increasingly through diversification into a wide variety of other areas, including hotels, real estate, food and drink, construction, and printing, far removed from the core business. In these areas, Sanjiu's headquarters applied the business skills developed in the core business. This was the classic path to growth of the diversified East Asian capitalist conglomerate, in which managerial skills were applied to a variety of business areas in lieu of being able to compete with the most powerful global businesses in proprietary technology (Amsden and Hikino, 1994). Moreover, take-overs and mergers were a critical part of Sanjiu's expansion mechanism. In the execution of these, Sanjiu's leadership operated in a fashion that would be readily recognizable to a capitalist firm, seeking out 'hidden value' to be 'dug out' of the firms it was taking over.

This section attempts to enquire more deeply into the nature and sources of growth at Sanjiu. First it analyzes the relationship between Nanfang (later Sanjiu) and its administrative superiors, the PLA. Secondly it examines the way in which Nanfang's core business, pharmaceuticals, expanded. Thirdly it analyses the transition from a specialized pharmaceutical firm (Nanfang) to a diversified conglomerate (Sanjiu). Fourthly it examines Sanjiu's recent re-evaluation of that strategy in the light of the evolving East Asian crisis. The crisis casts serious doubt on the viability of the traditional East Asian conglomerate business structure as an instrument of international business competition in the new environment of the global capitalist business revolution of the 1990s.

RELATIONSHIP WITH THE PLA

Pre-1998: Autonomy within Constraints. Nanfang was established in 1986 by the Guangzhou Army Hospital. This was the People's Liberation Army's (PLA) No. 1 Medical University, responsible to the PLA's General Logistics Department

(GLD) in Beijing. The decision to set up the firm was strongly influenced by the chance factor of the location of another highly successful business. Baiyunshan was one of the most dynamic new businesses established during the early reform period. It was a collectively-owned pharmaceutical enterprise which grew from nothing to be the largest pharmaceutical manufacturer in China by the late 1980s. In the early 1990s it was in the top 100 Chinese firms (by value of sales) (Development Research Centre of the State Council, 1994: 3).[15] The top two Chinese pharmaceutical firms in 1995 were both firms which began life during the reforms.

Baiyunshan was located opposite the Guangzhou Army Hospital. The Hospital was run by the General Logistics Department of the People's Liberation Army. The Army Hospital had its own laboratories that made traditional Chinese medicines. The leadership of the Hospital was impressed by the explosive growth achieved by Baiyunshan on its own doorstep, producing the type of medicines that it produced itself on a small scale for internal use within the Hospital. The leadership, in consultation with the headquarters in Beijing, decided to establish a factory of its own which made use of its own experience in making pharmaceuticals to enter this fast-growing market. The choice of Shenzhen as the site was strongly influenced by the General Logistics Department's headquarters in Beijing, which already owned many other plants in Shenzhen. The Army's strong presence in Shenzhen had much to do with the fact that there was a great deal of land already occupied by the Army due to the proximity of Shenzhen with Hong Kong. The land on which Nanfang was established had formerly been an area in which the Army Police (*wujing*) had bred dogs.[16]

In the early phase of construction of the plant, Nanfang was under the supervision of a sanatorium in Shenzhen run mainly for overseas Chinese, which was itself subordinate to the Guangzhou Army Hospital. However, the sanatorium ceased operation shortly after the construction of Nanfang was begun, and was later turned into a hotel (see below). From then until 1992 Nanfang was placed directly under the supervision of the Army Hospital.

The Guangzhou Army Hospital reached an agreement with Prof. Zhao Xinxian, a leading researcher in the Hospital. Under the agreement, Zhao selected a small group of co-workers from the Hospital (five in all, apart from Zhao himself), to form the management team of the plant under his command. The group were all 'military intellectuals'. They were to organize the building of the plant, for which the Hospital loaned them five million yuan. Published data (Table 5-14) show that from 1987 to 1991 inclusive, Nanfang handed over 54 million yuan to the Guangzhou Army Hospital, amounting to around one-third of its post-tax profits. Moreover, the relationship was becoming 'more and more tense', with the Army Hospital asking for greater hand-overs from Nanfang as the plant prospered.

The Army Hospital was in the position of the sole shareholder in Nanfang, able to decide the distribution of profits between the plant and itself. The arrangements for hand-overs to the Army Hospital were *ad hoc* and informal. The removal of such a high share of profits was a source of increasing dissatisfaction to Nanfang's leadership. In the early 1990s Nanfang's leaders found a way to increase the plant's autonomy and to retain a higher share of profits.

TABLE 5-14 Principal Financial Indicators for Nanfang Pharmaceutical Factory and Sanjiu Enterprise Group, 1987–98

Year	Gross value of output (million yuan)	Post-tax profits (million yuan)	Post-tax profits % of output value	Taxes (million yuan)	Taxes % of pre-tax profits	Total turned over to superior authorities* (million yuan)	Total turned over to superior authorities* % of post-tax profits	Profits distributed (as bonuses)** (million yuan)
Nanfang Pharmaceutical Plant:								
1987	11	1.65	15.0	0.13	7.3	1.0	60.6	0.29
1988	65	9.75	15.0	4.56	31.9	5.0	51.3	1.46
1989	161	22.50	13.9	5.20	18.8	9.1	40.4	3.38
1990	381	45.60	12.0	18.20	28.5	17.0	37.3	6.84
1991	639	74.20	11.6	24.00	24.4	22.0	29.6	11.13
1992	1011	137.60	13.6	26.20	16.0	50.0	36.3	20.64
1993	1869	254.80	13.6	30.90	10.8	70.0	27.5	—
1994	1809	382.00	21.1	25.10	6.2	80.0	20.9	—
1995								
(Jan.–Oct.)	1124	240.20	21.3	21.60	8.3	—	—	—
1996	—	—	—	—	—			
1997	2055	370.14	18.0	36.19	10.84	—	—	—

	Gross value of output (million yuan)	Pre-tax profits		Taxes		Hand-overs to GLD	
		(million yuan)	% of output value	(million yuan)	% of pre-tax profits	(million yuan)	% of post-tax profits
Sanjiu Enterprise Group:							
1992	1 602	220.12	13.7	48.16	21.9	—	—
1993	2 989	442.92	14.8	49.82	11.2	—	—
1994	3 209	466.42	14.5	40.30	8.6	—	—
1995	4 288	647.89	15.1	147.09	22.7	—	—
1996	4 932	704.32	14.2	149.87	21.3	68§	12.3
1997	5 568	813.83	14.6	222.57	27.3	68§	11.5
1998 (Jan.–Apr.)	—	184.93	—	78.07	42.2	—	—

SOURCES: Nanfang data come from Li Zuokeng and Li Cunhou (1995: 69), except for 1994 figures, which are from interviews at Nanfang. Sanjiu data come from SEG (1997: 20–21, 1998: 2). The 1996–98 data come from the internal documents of the Sanjiu Enterprise Group.

NOTES: * Guangzhou Army Hospital pre-1992, and GLD thereafter
** 15 per cent of post-tax profits were distributed as bonuses
§ Average of total handovers to GLD for 1996 and 1997, which amounted to 136 million in total for the two years

By 1992 the General Logistics Department had set up around 35 enterprises in Shenzhen, many of which were loss-making. In late 1991, Zhao Wangqi, Head of the General Logistics Department in Beijing, visited Shenzhen to try to sort the problem out. A deal was struck with the Nanfang leadership. Nanfang was to cease to answer directly to the Army Hospital in Guangzhou. Instead it was to be placed directly under the supervision of the General Logistics Department. Nanfang would henceforth make its hand-over of post-tax profits to the General Logistics Department, which was the formal owner of the firm.[17] The General Logistics Department made a separate agreement with the Army Hospital in Guangzhou to allocate a proportion of the profits to them. The General Manager of Nanfang was now formally appointed by the Logistics Department, and could be replaced by them if they found his performance unsatisfactory. Zhao Xinxian was reaffirmed in this position. As the General Manager he was Sanjiu's 'legal person' representing the owners.

Nanfang was permitted to put into practice a new wage system, with much enhanced differentials among regular members of the workforce (the 1 : 18 system). The principal way in which the ownership rights of the General Logistics Department was made manifest was through its control of the hand-overs out of Sanjiu's profits. Under the deal there was an agreement that the share of profits handed over would be reduced, and would become more predictable. Moreover, Sanjiu felt that it was now able to bargain more effectively about the share of profits to be handed over to its superior authorities than before the 'deal'.

Under the 'deal' Sanjiu was allowed operational autonomy, subject only to requiring the approval of the General Logistics Department for very large scale investments. Zhao Xinxian, the 'legal person' who had responsibility for the firm, had complete autonomy from the General Logistics Department in the appointment of his management team. Sanjiu did not need to seek permission from the General Logistics Department for the proposed joint venture with Merck (see below). Sanjiu has been praised by the Shenzhen City Government for the clarity with which the line of responsibility is drawn between the enterprise and its superior administrative organ, the General Logistics Department of the PLA. It is regarded as a good example of the 'Modern Enterprise System' in China.

There was strong interest shown in the firm by the General Logistics Department of the PLA and the armed forces in general, with regular visits by senior figures from Beijing.[18] The principles governing hand-over of profits were not formalized, and the hand-overs seem still to have been the subject of 'negotiations'. The data on 'hand-overs' are far from clear. It appears, from fragmentary evidence, that the hand-overs to the GLD were a fairly stable fixed amount, totalling around 70–80 million yuan per annum. Consequently, the proportion of post-tax profits handed over fell from over 20 per cent in the early 1990s, to around 12 per cent in the late 1990s alongside powerful growth in Sanjiu's total profits (Table 5-14). However, the General Logistics Department could still require Sanjiu to make large *ad hoc* 'hand-overs'. For example, in 1995, Sanjiu was required to hand over 23 million yuan, in addition to the agreed 60 million yuan hand-over, to contribute to the building of a new meeting hall for the Department in Beijing.

The second part of the deal was that Nanfang would take over the General Logistics Department's mainly loss-making enterprises in Shenzhen. Nanfang would become the 'core' enterprise in a newly formed 'Sanjiu' (Three Nines) Group. During the years 1992–4 Sanjiu injected around 200 million yuan into these enterprises. Their take-over was to have great significance for the future path of development of Nanfang, helping to push it towards 'conglomerate' form much more rapidly than might (if ever) have happened without the move. Sanjiu controlled and supervised its subordinate companies in the 'second and third tier' ('legal persons' and 'quasi-legal persons', respectively) in the same way as Sanjiu was supervised and controlled by the General Logistics Department (Li Zuokeng and Li Cunhou, 1995: 65). However, whereas Sanjiu itself could be regarded as having become the 'quasi-owner' in place of the General Logistics Department, the 'second- and third-tier' companies within Sanjiu did not possess such independence. Rather the managers of these companies were merely 'managers' (*jingyingzhi*) under Sanjiu (Li Zuokeng and Li Cunhou, 1995: 65). Moreover, upon taking over the second tier firms, Nanfang advertised for new general managers and new department heads. The existing incumbents had to compete openly for their old jobs, though only two or three of them failed to be re-appointed. After their appointment Nanfang monitored the managers' performance closely, practising the system of 'elimination of personnel through selection and competition' (*renyuan taotaizhi*). Existing managers who stayed on in their jobs had to undergo extensive re-training and were dismissed if they didn't pass their exams.

In order to finance its ambitious expansion plans, Sanjiu announced in 1997 that it had been given official permission to issue $200 million worth of H-shares on the Hong Kong market, moving the firm towards a diversified ownership structure. However, in July 1998, it postponed this move in response to the downturn in the Hong Kong stock market. A spokesman said: 'We don't plan to tap the Hong Kong market this year, but we don't rule out the possibility of coming back later.' Simultaneously, Sanjiu also applied for official permission to absorb public capital through the issue of 300 million A shares on the Shenzhen stock market later in 1998 (*SCMP*, 25 July 1998). Even after the flotation, the GLD would still have been the majority owner of Sanjiu.

Second- and third-tier enterprises within the Sanjiu Group could have quite diversified ownership structures, in which Nanfang, the core company in the Group, was only one part of the ownership structure. As we shall see below, Sanjiu undertook an extensive programme of merger and acquisition after the early 1990s. These typically involved Sanjiu, often through second tier companies within the Group, taking majority ownership shares in the acquired firms. However, Sanjiu usually invites local governments to hold 10–20 per cent share of the acquired enterprises. This not only lowers the financial risk in the takeover, but also secures the political support from the local governments (*Sanjiu Jituan Bao*, 25 February 1998: 2).

The 1998 Reforms: Enhanced Autonomy or Complete Independence? Sanjiu's official response to the central government's policy announcement of July 1998 concerning PLA-run businesses, was that this might benefit the Company's long-term development.[19] However, Sanjiu had already obtained a high degree of managerial autonomy under the PLA, including relative independence to appoint 'insider' managers, implement its own remuneration structure, and devise its own business strategy, including an extensive programme of take-overs and mergers. The hand-over of profits by Sanjiu to the PLA was not fundamentally different from the hand-over of dividends by the managers of a capitalist family-owned firm to the family that owns it. It remains to be seen what the nature of the separation of business ties with the GLD will mean in practice.

Sanjiu believes that as one of the largest and most effective PLA-owned business, with a powerful management team, it will be able to take over weaker and smaller competitors in the period ahead. It anticipates that there will be a re-grouping of the PLA's businesses, and it is likely that it will be in a strong position to take over many of the PLA's companies in the near future (*SCMP*, 25 July 1998). As one of the best run of the PLA's businesses, Sanjiu may be allocated an expanded role in managing PLA-owned businesses, though the precise form this may take is not yet clear. Sanjiu may become a major beneficiary of the reforms, allowing it to greatly increase its strength within the Chinese pharmaceutical industry.

GROWTH OF THE CORE BUSINESS: CHINESE MEDICINES

Competition within Pharmaceuticals. Sanjiu's growth path was drastically affected by the nature of the competition within the pharmaceutical sector. Sanjiu could have attempted to establish itself within one or more of the three main areas of pharmaceuticals in China: Western generic medicines, Western patented medicines or traditional Chinese medicines.

The capital costs of becoming a major independent player in generic drugs are relatively high. Also, there were several large-scale established large state-owned enterprises in this sector, which stood a good chance of becoming more effective players as their management improved. This sector offered no chance to develop a high margin business. Even in the advanced economies, 'running a low-margin generics operation successfully has eluded many mainstream drugs companies' (*FT*, 8 March 1996).

In China in the 1980s a common route into generic pharmaceuticals was via the production of Vitamin C in a joint venture with an international company. By the mid-1990s, China was producing about one-quarter of total world output.[20] In the late 1980s when Zhao Xinxian and his colleagues set out to construct Nanfang, they carefully considered taking this route into pharmaceuticals. They decided that they would face stiff competition from the large number of Vitamin C factories. Moreover, the selling price and marketing system of Vitamin C would be tightly controlled by the joint venture partner. This path offered little hope for the development of an autonomous business at Sanjiu.

The second possibility was to attempt to establish itself as an independent producer of patented Western medicines. The possibility of becoming a successful independent producer of Western patented medicines was regarded as negligible. As we have seen, the resources required to develop a new drug were enormous and rising steadily in the 1980s and 1990s. In the period when Sanjiu was considering its strategy, China was liberalizing internationally, with a fast growth of Western pharmaceutical companies in China. Increasingly, Sanjiu would find itself competing with the global giants, such as Glaxo Wellcome and SmithKline Beecham, through their joint ventures in China. The Sino–foreign pharmaceutical joint ventures were backed by the vast resources of the international partner, including especially their huge R & D investment and consequent patented drugs portfolio, as well as their management and marketing expertise.

A third possibility was to establish itself through becoming a joint venture partner producing patented medicines with a multinational. This path was rejected also. Sanjiu's leadership felt that this would prevent them ever becoming a truly independent company. Moreover, it was felt that the intense competition among Chinese enterprises to attract multinational partners meant that their bargaining position was weak, and the terms obtained were unlikely to be favourable to the domestic partner.

The fourth possibility was to attempt to become a successful producer of traditional Chinese medicines. Here, Sanjiu could escape direct competition with the multinationals. The competitors were almost entirely other domestic firms. The sector was highly fragmented, with a large number of new entrants, typically poorly-run, with a large number of loss-makers struggling to survive. Conversely, as we have seen, if the firm was well-run, there were possibilities for high returns in traditional Chinese pharmaceuticals. The sector looked very much like the soft drinks market in its early stage of development in the advanced capitalist economies.

'Getting Close to the Market'. When Zhao Xinxian and his colleagues set up Nanfang none of them had any experience of business. However, they knew instinctively that to be successful they needed to 'get close to the market'.

Product choice. Zhao had developed a strong research base and patient history for traditional Chinese medicines during his years at the Army Hospital. In traditional Chinese medicines there was no direct competition from multinational firms. Zhao and his colleagues tried to select for their main product one with a wide market potential. They were strongly impressed by the fact that Baiyunshan mainly relied on a single product (*Ganmaoqing*), a medicine to treat the common cold.

The Chinese pattern of food consumption leads to widespread stomach acidity due to an excess of glucose arising from high grain consumption. For many years the Guangzhou Army Hospital had produced a stomach medicine, *Sanjiu Weitai* ('Three Nines Stomach Healthy'), designed to cure this condition. Zhao had accumulated over 100 000 patient histories involving treatment with this drug. This type of product was thought by Nanfang's leaders to have a large potential market, but there were many other producers of similar stomach medicines. Finding a good stomach drug was not sufficient for Nanfang to succeed. In 1995 *Sanjiu Weitai* was still Nanfang's best-selling drug, accounting for 60–70 per cent of Sanjiu's total revenue from pharmaceuticals (see below). Sanjiu accounted for around 37 per cent of the total national market for stomach medicines. Its closest competitor in this field was Lizhu (Zhuhai), with around 17–18 per cent national market share.

Sanjiu's other main products were *Ganmaoling*, a medicine for treating colds and *Piyanping*, a skin treatment ointment. The production of *Ganmaoling* was an explicit attempt to capture market share from Baiyunshan in its 'own' product area. *Ganmaoling* was formerly produced by a small pharmaceutical factory from which Sanjiu purchased the prescription for 'several hundred thousand yuan'. Benefiting from Sanjiu's quality control, advertising, brand name and sales system (see below), sales of this product grew from 'a few million yuan' at the time of the purchase of the prescription, to around 200 million yuan in 1995, around 10 per cent of Nanfang's total sales. *Piyanping* was a skin ointment developed by the Army Hospital in Guangzhou. The prescription was sold to a small factory in Shunde (in the Pearl River Delta) but the factory failed to make a success of the product. Nanfang has 'made a success of the product' since they purchased the prescription from the Shunde factory.

A typical new traditional Chinese drug might cost Nanfang around two million yuan (around $200 000) to develop, far less than is required to develop a Western patented drug.

Advertising. Nanfang's location adjacent to Hong Kong had a big impact on the way it used advertising. It quickly became one of the most innovative firms in China in the way in which it used the mass media. Nanfang ran its own advertising campaign and its style has had a substantial impact on the methods of advertising across China. Zhao Xinxian frankly acknowledged: 'like Coca-Cola, Nanfang's products are simple, and our competitors' products are not fundamentally different from ours'. It is relatively easy to identify the chemical composition and the herbs used in making the product although it is almost impossible to identify the sequence in which they are mixed. Nor is the production process especially complex. Consequently, advertising is a centrally important aspect of the growth of the firm.

Nanfang built its own advertising firm, and hired staff from Chinese film studios to make their advertisements. It is illegal in China to use doctors in advertisements to endorse the safety and effectiveness of pharmaceutical products. Nanfang had to search for more subtle ways to convince consumers of the quality and reliability of their brand. They used famous film stars to promote their products. They hired Hou Dejian, a Taiwanese film star, with a huge following in Hong Kong and Taiwan, famous for his 'touching' and sentimental film roles. Their advertising campaign was especially important after the conclusion of the court case (see below) in which Nanfang felt they had been wrongly treated by the Chinese legal system. They hired Li Moran, an actor who was famous for his portrayal of roles in traditional Chinese films in which he was associated with 'justice'. The combination of the publicity given in the press and the effectiveness of their advertising campaign, had a 'huge impact' on Nanfang's sales.

The trademark battle. Subsequent to Nanfang's initial market success with *Sanjiu Weitai*, several firms started to produce *Sanjiu Weitai*, using more or less the same ingredients as Nanfang. In 1989 Nanfang was allowed to register its trademark, *Sanjiu Weitai*, with the National Bureau of Industry and Commerce.[21] The Bureau ruled that Nanfang's competitor factories should cease making the product. However, Nanfang's main competitor, *Haikou Weitai*, produced by the Haikou Pharmaceutical Company, refused to do so. They were supported by the local Hainan government, which intervened on their behalf with the National Ministry of Public Health. They argued that *Sanjiu Weitai* could not be patented, since it was a generic drug, the production of which did not require research and development, and therefore other firms ought not to be prevented from making it. The Ministry of Health upheld their position.

Nanfang took the issue to a national level court investigation. The court ruled that the word *Sanjiu* could be registered as Nanfang's trademark, but not the word *Weitai*. In other words, other firms could legally produce and sell stomach medicines with the same chemical composition as Nanfang's *Sanjiu Weitai*, but they could not market it as *Sanjiu Weitai*. They had to use a different brand name, albeit with the word *Weitai*, appearing in the name. The court ruled also that the rival firms were not allowed to conduct a press campaign against each other, and that each should use their own trademark, *Sanjiu* and *Baodao*. In fact, Haikou continued to produce its own *Sanjiu Weitai*, in defiance of the court ruling, and both firms enormously increased their sales as result of the national level court battle and the associated press coverage.

In 1995 *Sanjiu Weitai* was ranked the most valuable indigenous brand name in China, worth an estimated 3.4 billion yuan (SEG, 1997: 67). In 1997 the 'Sanjiu' ('999') trademark was ranked the sixth most valuable in China, valued at 4.5 billion yuan (SEG, 1998: 8).

Selling methods. Until the late 1980s, all pharmaceutical products, whether imported or domestically manufactured, were sold in China through state-owned wholesale and retail channels. There were three levels of distribution. Level 1 were buyers and sellers directly under the State Pharmaceutical Administration of China. All pharmaceutical products were allocated directly to them, and they in turn sold them to Level 2 distributors. These were buyers and sellers in the different regions, including some large cities. These sold the pharmaceuticals in turn to Level 3 buyers and sellers, who dealt with the county (*xian*) level. From the late 1980s, it became possible for pharmaceutical producers and importers to establish their own distribution network, and sell directly to Level 3 distributors or even to hospitals and retailers. The change is still far from complete. Official state policy is still to restrict selling outside the state supply system. Many of the state distributors are turning themselves into joint-stock companies, and trying through many mechanisms to preserve their monopolistic position. Joint ventures between domestic and foreign firms are not permitted to set up their own distribution system, or to buy shares in the newly marketized state distribution companies.

The changes made so far are large ones. They provide opportunities for larger firms to benefit from the economies of scope involved in constructing effective selling networks. This is a major area of world-wide competition among large Western pharmaceutical producers. Indeed, the benefits to be derived from a common selling network for many different drugs has been a major element in the merger movement in the world pharmaceutical industry in the past few years.

As controls over the distribution system relaxed, Nanfang moved quickly to set up its own sales network, the Sanjiu Trading Company. In 1990 there still were only twenty sales personnel directly employed by Nanfang. By 1995 in Sanjiu there were 62 senior business representatives in charge of the regional markets, and 229 permanent representatives in charge of regional promotion. There were a further 1017 'market information collectors' working on commission for their supervisors. There were branches of the sales network in over 100 cities across the whole of China. This was the largest sales network of any Chinese pharmaceutical company.

To promote further the sales of its medicines, Sanjiu Trading Company purchased majority shares of three large state pharmaceutical trading agencies which were turned into joint stock companies.[22] These were the Ningbo Medical Materials Company, the Changsha Medical Materials Company and the Wuxi Pharmaceutical Company. The total sales of these companies in the mid-1990s was around one billion yuan.

Sanjiu has established 'direct and close relationships with all the large and medium-sized hospitals in these cities'. The members of the sales network maintain 'close business and non-business relationships with pharmacists and doctors in the hospitals'. The company also 'maintains close business relationships with nearly 3000 domestic distributors'. Each local branch 'maintains frequent contact with clinical doctors, and provides technical materials and services to these doctors'. Pharmacies and doctors are 'encouraged to use Sanjiu products'. The marketing staff collect information from the users of the medicines and regularly feedback the results to the headquarters. All those employed in the marketing system are university graduates, 90 per cent of whom are either specialists in pharmacy or doctors. Sanjiu sets strict standards for the appearance of its sales staff. It has an advanced computerized system for information collection and processing, and for assisting decision making. Sanjiu regards the creation of 'an immense sales system' as 'the guarantee of the healthy development of Sanjiu Pharmaceuticals'.

Sanjiu has set up sales offices in a number of foreign countries, including America, Germany, Russia, and South Africa and the Middle East. It has a sales network over most of Southeast Asia, where sales are strong among overseas Chinese who constitute a large potential market for traditional Chinese medicines. It has processing factories in Malaysia and Hong Kong. Sanjiu has serious ambitions to develop international sales of its medicines. Not only is there a large potential market for traditional Chinese medicines among overseas Chinese, who total around 50 million, but also among Western consumers who wish to use Chinese medicines as a complement to, or even as a substitute for, Western medicines. In 1994, the Food and Drugs Administration gave Sanjiu permission to sell its main product, *Sanjiu Weitai*, in the USA.

Like many Chinese firms, Sanjiu also acts as the agent for international firms to sell Western medicines in China and in Asia. It is the agent for Upjohn (USA) for the sale of examethasene, and for Amgen (USA) for the sale of EPO and ENU.

Modernization. Nanfang's profits rose at high speed (Table 5-15). After rising from 96 employees in 1987 when the plant opened, to 1163 in 1990, the number remained at around the same level thereafter. There still were only 1233 employees in 1994. Alongside this had gone a huge growth of output value, with gross value of output per employee rising from 115 000 yuan in 1987 to 328 000 yuan in 1990, reaching 1 468 000 yuan in 1994. This was achieved through ploughing back a large fraction of retained profits into the purchase of new equipment. Indeed, the number of workers on the production line had fallen from 1500 (including temporary workers at peak periods) to just 160 in 1995 (see below).

In order to meet the internationally set 'Good Manufacturing Procedures' (GMP) for the world's pharmaceutical industry, Nanfang needed to have a comprehensively modernized production process. It set about reaching these standards with a two-year comprehensive modernization after 1991. Nanfang was the first firm in China to produce Chinese medicines in a Western fashion. The GMP standards that China follows are those of the US FDA and the equivalent body in

TABLE 5-15 **Structure of Output and Profits in the Sanjiu Enterprise Group, 1992–7**

	Gross value of output		Pre-tax profits		Employees		Fixed assets	
	million yuan	(%)	million yuan	(%)	(no.)	(%)	million yuan	(%)
1992								
Nanfang	1011	63.1	164	82.0	1 369	67.5	124	87.3
Others	591	36.9	36	18.0	659	32.5	18	12.7
Sanjiu	1 602	100.0	200	100.0	2 028	100.0	142	100.0
1994								
Nanfang	1 809	56.4	407	87.3	1 233	53.0	392	78.1
Others	1 400	43.6	59	12.7	1 092	47.0	110	21.9
Sanjiu	3 209	100.0	466	100.0	2 325	100.0	502	100.0
1997								
Nanfang	2 055	36.9	406	49.9	—	—	564	29.6
Others	3 513	63.1	408	50.1	—	—	1 343	70.4
Sanjiu	5 568	100.0	814	100.0	12 731	—	1 907	100.0

SOURCE: Internal documents of the Sanjiu Enterprise Group

Japan, which are the strictest world-wide. The GMP requirements apply to all aspects of the production process, including such matters as quality of raw materials, dust levels and quality of floor and wall tiles.

Meeting the GMP standards also necessitated high worker skill levels. Production workers were each given half a year's training in GMP standards, and if they failed to meet the strict standards set by GMP they were dismissed from the firm. The tightness of the labour market in Shenzhen made dismissal of workers much less of a problem than would be the case elsewhere in China. Failure to meet these standards was a method through which Nanfang was able to legitimize reducing the number of production line workers. Nanfang placed great emphasis on upgrading the technical skills of its permanent employees. In order to have any kind of job at Nanfang in the mid-1990s it was necessary to have a minimum of upper middle school education. Existing cadres were given training courses in GMP methods, and they were removed from the 'front line' if they failed the examinations.

Its core staff of around 500 cadres mostly have university science degrees. They all have been required by company policy to attend training in order to become computer literate, with special training courses to bring the skills of older entrants up to date. Moreover, the cadres were all required to develop proficiency in at least one foreign language by 1998. By 1995 one-third of senior staff had already learned a foreign language. Cadres are strongly encouraged to obtain a post-graduate qualification. Nanfang has a part-time MBA programme in which all its cadres are encouraged to participate. In order to construct a strong image for the company, all new recruits must meet strict physical requirements. Females must be over 1.60 metres and males over 1.75 metres tall. Nanfang's success, good welfare conditions and work conditions has enabled it to attract excellent personnel from elsewhere in China. The Head of the Checking Centre used to be the Head of Changchun City Pharmaceutical Checking Department. Two senior people in the International Finance Department were recruited from Beijing. The Head of the Instruments Room studied at Loughborough University in the UK, and was subsequently Associate Professor at Hubei University. Meeting GMP standards also necessitated the introduction of corresponding management systems. In order to meet the GMP standards, Nanfang in the early 1990s introduced meticulous checking and recording procedures so that if quality problems arose they could be traced back quickly and accurately to their point of origin in the production process.

The high technical and linguistic skills achieved by Nanfang's cadres were most important in enabling Nanfang to select appropriate equipment and use it effectively. The main imported pieces of equipment were made according to Nanfang's engineering specifications.

Modernization of equipment was essential to meeting the strict standards of GMP. Consequently, in the early 1990s Nanfang began a programme of comprehensive upgrading of its equipment, largely through imports. Nanfang was exempt from import duties due to its location in Shenzhen Special Economic Zone. It invested a total of around 70 million yuan, financed entirely from its own funds. There was 'simply no alternative' to such large, self-funded investment if they wished to meet the strict GMP standards. Despite this large investment, the debt–assets ratio at Nanfang Pharmaceutical Plant is just 15 per cent, which is extremely low compared to other Chinese enterprises.[23] For the whole Sanjiu Group the ratio was around 46 per cent. By 1997 the ratio had risen to 41 per cent for Nanfang and 60 per cent for the whole Group, still relatively low compared to other Chinese firms, and well below that in much of East Asia.

By the mid-1990s all the main pieces of production equipment were of 1990s vintage. The main items are as follows:

- **NF-B automatic traditional Chinese medicine extraction line**. This is wholly automated and computerized, and all the components were made within China. The purchase price was 2.4 million yuan. The output capacity is 50 tons per month of extracted product.

- **Automatic packing line for granules**. This was imported at a cost of around 7 million yuan from the Italian Unlogo Company. It packs granules at a speed of one box/minute, with a monthly capacity of 40 000 boxes of *Sanjiu Weitai* granules.

- **Capsule production line**. This uses a Japanese Freund pilling machine, and a German Bosch capsule filling machine. The monthly capacity is 7000 boxes of *Weitai* capsules.

- **Ointment production line**. This is fitted with a Swiss Fryna ointment composer, a German IWKA injector-seamer, and a packing machine. The monthly capacity is 10 000 boxes of *Piyanping* ointment.

- **Plastic container packing line**. This uses a UK made machine supplied by King. It has a monthly capacity of 30 000 boxes of *Zhuang Gu Guan Jie* pills.

- **Tablet production line**. This uses a German Kilian RX55AM tablet-expresser. The production capacity is 500 000 tablets per hour.

- **Quality checking centre.** Over 20 million yuan was spent on imported equipment for the centre, installed in a large new, purpose-built building. The total cost of the centre was around 30 million yuan.

Management. In the early phase of the construction of Nanfang, Zhao Xinxian brought five army colleagues with him. They took a gamble, accepting much lower salaries than they would have received had they stayed in Guangzhou Army Hospital. They earned around 140–150 yuan per month during the two years it took to construct the plant, compared to around 250–300 yuan, including bonuses, at the Hospital. They lived in rough conditions during the years of construction of the plant. Much of their time was spent physically involved in the construction of the plant. Their slogans were: 'production first, life later' (*xian shengchan, hou shenghuo*) and 'hard and arduous struggle' (*jianku fendou*). Zhao considers their army background helped them greatly to sustain their spirit and discipline during this tough and highly uncertain phase of building their business.

During these years a close bond built up among this group, who still remain at the centre of the firm's leading cadres in the late 1990s. These were all young people, recently graduated from university, led by Zhao, who was in early middle age when the endeavour began. Up until 1989, all the management level personnel were members of the People's Liberation Army. Zhao Xinxian is a powerful motivator, who was able to weld together a strong management team and provide a vision and sense of purpose to the firm. His entrepreneurial and leadership abilities (demonstrated dramatically by the subsequent growth of the firm) had been repressed under the command economy and were now given the chance to flourish.

All the leading cadres have subsequently been offered lucrative positions with other pharmaceutical firms, but they have all chosen to stay with Nanfang. This is partially a financial decision. Their income at Nanfang is high by the standards of Chinese state industry (see below), and there are plenty of fringe benefits such as good quality, highly subsidized housing and extensive foreign travel. However, the income available to such highly skilled people in a pharmaceutical joint venture is considerably above even that available at Nanfang. When questioned closely about their reason for staying with the firm, they answered that it is to a considerable degree because of their sense of involvement with an exciting endeavour which they have helped create under Zhao's leadership. His personal influence on the firm is transparent. He is a powerful personality, talking with great clarity about the firm's strategy. All leading cadres speak of him with great respect, recognizing the key role he played in the firm's successful growth and modernization.

The Party still plays an important role in Nanfang. Around one-quarter of Nanfang's cadres are Party members, compared to only around one-eighth of ordinary workers. Zhao Xinxian is Party Secretary of Nanfang. Ninety-five per cent of all department heads and general managers throughout the whole Sanjiu Group are Party members.[24] Political and administrative power in each of the subordinate 'second-level' firms resides in the hands of the Party Secretary. All these have to report regularly to Zhao Xinxian to co-ordinate the work of the different parts of the Group.

The Party plays an important role in ensuring that the institution 'coheres' (*ningju*). Branch meetings occur regularly. The Party plays a central role in implanting and spreading the 'Sanjiu spirit'. This centres around high attention to quality, which is an integral part of success in a modern pharmaceutical firm. The Party is actively involved in the motivational aspects of work quality with precise functions in relation to checking work and ensuring work discipline. The Party still has a role in supervising the work of non-Party cadres. The plant is still emphatically a part of the army, even though the bulk of the workforce are now civilians. The premises are governed by army regulations.

Employment Structure. Alongside the rapid automation of production in Nanfang's core plant in Shenzhen went a large change in its institutional structure. Instead of being a factory with a minority of management staff, and

TABLE **5-16 Information about Cadres at Nanfang Pharmaceutical Factory, 1995**

Category	No. of cadres	%
Total cadres	236	100
MA degree	21	9
BA degree	136	57
College graduates	31	13
Professional high school graduates	48	21
Over 40 years old	5	2.1
Over 30 years old	21	9
Under 30 years old	210	88.9
Average age	26.3	—
Employed before 1991	74	30
Leaving Nanfang	6	2.5
Cadres/total employees	236/1145	20

SOURCE: 'The Sanjiu way under the military flag', in Nanfang Pharmaceutical Factory (1995: 310)

TABLE **5-17 Information about Ordinary Workers at Nanfang Pharmaceutical Factory, 1991**

Category	No. of workers	%
Total	909	100
Temporary workers	846	93
Contract workers	63	7
Number of new entrants	118	13
Number leaving	349	38
Total of new entrants and leavers	467	51

SOURCE: 'The Sanjiu way under the military flag', in Nanfang Pharmaceutical Factory (1995: 311)

a large majority of production line workers, it changed into one that combined a highly automated plant with the headquarters of a large multi-plant, multi-product firm.

The core of the Nanfang business is around 240 managerial cadres, almost all of whom are highly educated (Table 5-16). Within these is an inner group of managers who control the destiny of the business. Of this group, the key members are those half-dozen who founded the business, led by Zhao Xinxian. All of the 900 ordinary workers at the main plant are either temporary or 'contract' workers, with a very high turnover rate, almost 40 per cent per annum (Table 5-17).

The difference between the 'inner' and the 'outer' firm is symbolized by the wage system put into effect after Nanfang shifted to being directly supervised by the headquarters of the General Logistics Department in Beijing. Ordinary workers were now paid according to a regular manual workers' wage scale. In 1995, their monthly wages ranged from 500 yuan[25] to around 1800 yuan. The cadres were remunerated according to 1:18 wage scale for cadres. The greatly enhanced differentials were a key part of the 'deal' won by Zhao Xinxian for Nanfang. In 1995, actual wages paid to cadres ranged from 900 yuan to around 4000 yuan per month for Zhao. Even Zhao's wages were not especially high compare to the average in Shenzhen.[26] The extra income to which cadres were technically entitled was retained in a special interest-bearing fund run by Nanfang, which could be used to buy shares in the firm at a future date should the opportunity arise. Cadres who left the firm were entitled to draw out their savings accumulated in this fund.

In addition to their regular wage income, under the deal with the General Logistics Department, Sanjiu is allowed to allocate as bonuses 15 per cent of the post-tax profits retained by the firm. These are allocated on a much more egalitarian basis than the 1:18 wage scale. The ratio between the top and the bottom bonus is around 1:3. A significant share of Nanfang's retained profits has been ploughed into building high quality housing in the plant's quiet semi-suburban location. All the regular workers at the main Nanfang plant live in company apartments. Rents are nominal, a 'few tens' of yuan per month. Open market rents for equivalent apartments in Shenzhen are around 3000–4000 yuan per month. This amounts to a large addition to the real value of workers' incomes, and constitutes a major incentive to remain in employment at Nanfang. There is little difference in the size or quality of apartments among Nanfang's permanent workers, so the subsidy is a fairly egalitarian one, just as it is in most state-run plants in China.

Expansion of Pharmaceutical Business Outside the Core Plant

Joint venture for the production of Western medicine. In 1993 Sanjiu set up a joint venture, the Sanjiu Pharmaceutical Company. Nanfang accounted for 39 per cent of the share capital, and the remainder was held by seven foreign investors including Chai Tai Company (Thailand), Everbright Group·and Cathay Clement (Hong Kong), Paloma Partners, Citicorp and Tutor Pharmaceutical (USA). Zhao Xinxian is the chairman of the Board of Directors and the General Manager. The firm contained the Jiuxin pharmaceutical plant. This was a modern plant producing Western medicines. The main one was Locekin (Ceftriaxon), which had sales of 22.5 million yuan in 1994, still a small fraction (around 2 per cent) of the value of Nanfang's total sales. It also contained half a dozen of the small pharmaceutical companies that Nanfang had acquired, a domestic genetic engineering laboratory, and the genetic engineering laboratory set up by Nanfang in Singapore (see below). In 1995 the joint venture was the eighth largest in the pharmaceutical sector in China, with a paid-up capital of two billion yuan (*Hong Kong Standard*, 4 May 1996).

This was the vehicle through which Nanfang was to float on the Hong Kong Stock Market. The main goal of the listing was stated to be the expansion of

Nanfang's capacity to produce drugs for the treatment of arthritis and cancer. To consolidate control over the core pharmaceutical business, in 1997 Sanjiu repurchased 60.9 per cent of Nanfang's shares from the seven overseas major shareholders (with a loan) after the State Council's Security Committee approved its application to issue H-shares in Hong Kong. From February 1998 onward, Nanfang was a wholly-owned subsidiary of Sanjiu.

Sanjiu held long discussions with Merck to expand the scope of Sanjiu Pharmaceutical Company in partnership with Merck. Merck required that it owned 75 per cent of the joint venture, that it should choose the General Manager, select the Chairman of the Board of Directors and the Financial Manager, and that only Merck medicines with a Merck trademark should be made in the plant. Sanjiu was very reluctant to produce medicines without its trademark, and the project did not come to fruition. Sanjiu also had 'very lengthy' negotiations with Bayer about a possible joint venture, but nothing emerged.

Biotechnology. Sanjiu has set up a biotechnology research company in Singapore. The Shenzhen City Government put Sanjiu in touch with a group of around ten Chinese post-doctoral scientists in biotechnology. These were at the leading edge of world research, but didn't wish to return to work in China. The Singapore government offers highly advantageous conditions for biotechnology firms, including the use of laboratories at Singapore University. Sanjiu pays the researchers international level salaries. It had invested around 10 million yuan in the firm by 1995. Sanjiu's hope was that it would produce successful products which could be sold through the Sanjiu marketing system.

Pharmaceutical industry mergers and acquisitions. Nanfang took over a dozen smaller pharmaceutical firms across the country, including plants in Hebei province, Shanghai, Jiangxi, Anhui, Sichuan, and Beijing (Table 5-18). Three of these were state owned firms in which Sanjiu acquired the rights to majority share ownership and was given operational autonomy and rights to profits for a contracted period. It could exercise those rights in order to purchase the shares out of future profits if it chose to do so. They each had sales of around 100 million yuan and a total of around 2000–3000 employees. The majority of the newly acquired plants were operated under the administration of different units of the PLA. Nanfang's army connections are likely to have played a role in facilitating the take-over of these plants.

Sanjiu turned around the management systems of the newly acquired plants, re-specialized their production to make Sanjiu products, and sold their products through their own marketing system using the Sanjiu trademark. Nanfang had considered the possibility of a merger with Baiyunshan, but had not had formal negotiations. Sanjiu considers that the fact that Baiyunshan is now listed makes a possible merger 'more complex', since it would not be possible for a less transparent, state-mediated, administrative merger to take place. Sanjiu has considered a merger with a large state enterprise, but thinks the complexities of dealing with so large a workforce (Dongbei, for example, now has around

TABLE 5-18 **Principal Businesses within the Sanjiu Group, mid-1990s**

Core plant
Shenzhen Nanfang Pharmaceutical Plant

Medicine manufacture
Shenzhen Jiuxin Pharmaceutical Co.
Zongcan Hebei Province Taihang Pharmaceutical Plant
Beijing Military District Shijiazhuang Beifang Pharmaceutical Plant
Nanjing Military District Shanghai Jinkang Pharmaceutical Plant
Nanjing Military District Jiuxi Qingyun Pharmaceutical Plant
Nanjing Military District Shangrao Xinxing Pharmaceutical Plant
Guangzhou Military District Luofoushan Baihou Pharmaceutical Plant
Chengdu Military District Jinhua Pharmaceutical Plant
Navy Anhui Chaohu Pharmaceutical Plant
Zonghou Beijing Jiandu Pharmaceutical Plant
Sanjiu Germany Pharmaceutical Co. Ltd.
Sanjiu Pharmaceutical Plant (Malaysia) Co. Ltd.
Hong Kong Sanjiu Xinke Pharmaceutical Plant
Ya'an Pharmaceutical Plant

Health care products
Shenzhen Jiusheng Biotechnology Products Plants
Shenzhen Jintai Household Healthcare Products Plant
Zhuhai Jinyang Natural Healthcare Products Plant

Research institutions
Shenzhen Pharmaceutical Research Institute
Shenyang Pharmaceutical Institute

Real estate
Shenzhen Sanjiu Business Management Co.
Chongqing Real Estate Co.
Chengdu Real Estate Co.
Wuhan Real Estate Co.
Dalian Real Estate Co.
Shanghai Real Estate Co.

Tourism
Shenzhen Sanjiu Tourism Co. Ltd
Sanjiu Hotel Company
Beijing Sanjiu Taxi Rental Co.

Printing
Shenzhen Sanjiu Printing and Packaging Co.
Shenzhen Jiutong Packaging Industry Development Co.

Import–Export
China Xinxing Shenzhen Import–Export Co.

Automobiles
Shenzhen Automobile Trade Co.
Shenzhen Automobile Industry General Co.
Sanjiu Sihui Automobile General Co.

20 000 employees) would be too great. Consequently, the preferred method is to acquire small and medium-sized, non-listed, firms.

In the mid-1990s, Sanjiu began the policy of 'Second Enterprise Establishment' (*erci chuangye*), the goal of which was to establish and acquire enterprises in the remote but resource rich western part of the country, and turn them around through introducing the Sanjiu management system, brand name and marketing network. A leading example of this is the Ya'an Pharmaceutical Plant in Sichuan. This is Sanjiu's largest acquisition within the pharmaceutical sector. It was acquired by Sanjiu in 1995, with Sanjiu taking an 80 per cent ownership share for 17 million yuan. Sanjiu invested heavily in the plant, upgrading its manufacturing facilities substantially. It renamed the enterprise Ya'an Sanjiu Pharmaceutical Co. Ltd. Within a year, the gross value of production in Ya'an increased fourfold to more than 80 million yuan and its post-tax profits increased more than tenfold to 15 million yuan. In 1997 Ya'an's gross value of output of reached 200 million yuan and its post-tax profits reached 64.91 million yuan, which was more than 60 times higher than the best record before the acquisition. Ya'an's 1997 post-tax profits were the second highest registered among pharmaceutical enterprises in Sichuan province (Sanjiu Enterprise Group, 1998: 4–7). It ranked second (Nanfang was first) in the amount of profits turned over to Sanjiu in 1997 (*Sanjiu Jituan Bao*, 8 April 1998: 3, 15 April 1998: 1–3).

NON-CORE BUSINESS: TOWARDS DIVERSIFIED CONGLOMERATE STRUCTURE

Pressures to Become a Diversified Conglomerate

Traditional Chinese pharmaceuticals. In the mid-1990s there were good growth prospects for traditional Chinese pharmaceuticals. Moreover, even though Sanjiu was the leading producer in this sector, its market share even within traditional medicines was still small in the mid-1990s, so it could grow through expanding its market share as well as through overall market growth. Moreover, there were possibilities for expansion by exporting larger amounts of Sanjiu's traditional medicines.

However, there were limits to this strategy and many risks attached to it. Sanjiu was highly dependent on a single, non-patented product, *Sanjiu Weitai*, accounting for around two-fifths of its revenue from pharmaceuticals. We have seen that although its overall share of traditional Chinese pharmaceuticals was low, it had already established a high market share within the specialized market of traditional Chinese stomach acidity medicines, with around two-fifths of the national market. In the absence of patented drugs, it had not been able to establish such a strong market position in other traditional Chinese medicines.

Some serious competitive threats for Sanjiu were on the horizon in the traditional Chinese medicine sector. As we have seen, other institutions, such as local governments are capable of giving support to the growth of their own local 'champion' which might develop a powerful business system such as Sanjiu's. Multi-national investors are starting to develop an interest in the sector.

For example, in the mid-1990s, the Thai investment firm, Zhengda bought several Chinese traditional medicine factories. It approached Nanfang to see if it could buy the firm but was turned down. The product of one of these factories (*Yangwei chongji*) is included in the government's free medicine programme, while Nanfang's main product, *Sanjiu Weitai*, is not. Multinational pharmaceutical firms also are beginning to set up joint ventures in order to produce traditional Chinese medicines.

In the international market, the main possibilities were among overseas Chinese. However, this market is smaller than most Chinese provinces in terms of the total population, and by the mid-1990s, the market was close to saturation. Despite having been approved by the FDA, the prospects for growth of sales of traditional Chinese medicines in the advanced economies among non-Chinese people still were weak. Their consumption remained limited to a small minority of the population. There was still no sign of a major breakthrough in the use of traditional Chinese medicines.

Competition within Western medicines. During its high-speed growth within traditional Chinese medicines after the late 1980s, Sanjiu developed many transferable resources that could be used within the Western patented medicine sector. These included its large R & D capabilities by Chinese standards, including both physical and human skills. It had a large and capable sales force. It had high standards of production quality. It was knowledgeable about the global market-place. It had a small but powerful biotechnology company. However, even after it had become China's leading pharmaceutical firm, it was still far from being able to compete directly with the multinationals within patented Western medicine.

Sales of Merck (USA), the world's leading firm, with which Sanjiu conducted extensive negotiations to establish a joint venture, stood at $11.3 billion, 50 times larger than Sanjiu, one of China's top two companies, and one of the leading pharmaceutical companies in the Third World. Even the sales of the world's twentieth ranked company by value of sales, Takeda (Japan), were $3.5 billion, more than 20 times greater than those at Sanjiu. Even if Sanjiu were to allocate 10 per cent of its annual revenue to R & D, it would produce an R & D spend of only $20 million. In 1997 Merck (USA), had an annual R & D spend of over $1 billion, at least 50 times greater than that of Sanjiu. In a competition on the 'global level playing field' of patented drugs there could be only one winner from such a 'contest'. Even the world's twentieth largest pharmaceutical company by R & D spending in 1997, Schering–Plough, allocated $510 million to R & D, at least 20–30 times greater than that at Sanjiu.

When the opportunity to diversify out of pharmaceuticals presented itself to the management of Sanjiu, it grasped the opportunity firmly. Major reasons for this included the limited growth prospects for traditional Chinese medicines, and especially for Sanjiu's main product, *Sanjiu Weitai*, and the inability of Sanjiu to compete with the multinationals in Western patented medicines. Zhao Xinxian put this bluntly: 'We must diversify, because we simply cannot match the multinationals in proprietary technology' (Zhao Xinxian, Interview, 4 December 1995).

The leadership decided to diversify through venture capital in different activities, in Zhao Xinxian's phrase, 'floating boats on the water' and seeing which of them floated. This repeated the pattern under which Nanfang itself was originally set up.

Non-core Joint Ventures. Sanjiu considered the possibility of entering a wide range of joint ventures with international firms outside pharmaceuticals. These included a leading European furniture-making firm, motor vehicles (Fiat), a real estate firm, and a US department store (J. C. Penny). None of these came to fruition. In the case of the motor vehicles and the department store the problem was government refusal to allow the venture to proceed. There is almost constant discussion with one potential joint venture partner or another.

Sanjiu has set up a modern printing centre (Jiuxing Printing and Packaging) employing print industry technical experts from across the whole of China. This is a joint venture with capital from Germany and Hong Kong. The Centre uses modern imported equipment from Germany (a Mannesmann advanced colour printing machine), Japan (a paper cutting machine) and Hong Kong (a pasting machine). This produces high quality packaging and printing for Nanfang's products, which assists the creation of a high quality brand image. In addition, Jiuxing sells to other domestic firms requiring high quality packaging, such as Nestlé for its Nescafé products.

Non-core Mergers and Take-overs

The 'merger deal'. As we have seen, a key aspect of the 1992 'deal' struck by Zhao Xinxian with the General Logistics Department in Beijing was that Nanfang would merge with the Logistics Department's 35 plants in Shenzhen, many of which were loss-makers. These included firms in construction, clothing, trade, printing and packaging, taxi renting, tourism and a hotel (Table 5-18). At a stroke Nanfang, now renamed Sanjiu Group, had become a highly diversified conglomerate. The output value of the newly absorbed businesses was 37 per cent of that of the whole Sanjiu Group (Table 5-15). These businesses were substantially less profitable than Nanfang. Indeed, many were loss-makers. In 1992 their combined pre-tax profits contributed only 18 per cent of those of the whole Sanjiu Group (Table 5-15).

One of the most successful of these businesses has been the hotel. In 1991, when Nanfang took the business over it was a rest centre for overseas Chinese. It made a loss of 0.4 million yuan. The General Logistics Department also owns a hotel in Guangzhou, administered by the hotel in Shenzhen. Zhao Xinxian selected the manager of this hotel, Huo Shuoping, to run the hotel in Shenzhen. Huo had been running hotels since 1974. As soon as he was appointed, with Zhao's support, he radically changed the management method, and within a year had turned around the hotel's finances, making 8.7 million yuan profit in 1992, rising to 17.9 million yuan in 1993. Huo reduced the number of administrative departments from 11 to six, and dismissed 75 'redundant' workers. His approach was to 'employ the able, frighten off the troublemakers and lazy workers'. Many of those he fired were members of the Army's civilian militia. Sacking them was a very difficult task. Under the old system at the hotel it was impossible to sack workers, while 'cadres were promoted but never demoted'. Huo radically changed this system.

In May 1992 after he had been in the position for a few months, and his capabilities had become apparent, Zhao and Huo had a long discussion about the prospects for the hotel business in China. Huo felt that there was a great opportunity for expansion and profit making given the peculiar conditions of the hotel business in China in the early 1990s (see below). Zhao Xinxian asked Huo: 'If Sanjiu agrees to take no profit out of your business for three years, how long it will it take you to set up a chain of 15–20 hotels across China and make 100 million yuan profit?' Huo was 'dumbfounded', because the hotel had just 300 rooms and no basis for such expansion. Moreover, Zhao said that he would give no financial assistance, just autonomy and the right to plough back profits into expanding the business. Huo rashly promised he could do it within five years. Zhao said he would give him five years to meet the goal and if he failed Huo would lose his job.

Huo's success in 1992 demonstrated the high potential for strong management to turn around the performance of China's large number of loss-making hotels. Huo mapped out a strategy for expansion. He concentrated his expansion plans on middle grade, two-, three- and four-star hotels, since in this sector he could avoid head-on competition with the multinational chains. Moreover, there is a considerable over-supply of five-star hotels, but an under-supply of good quality middle grade hotels for the fast-growing Chinese middle-class and foreign tourists at the lower end of the market. Large numbers of hotels had been built in this category, mainly by various state institutions, but mostly they were run badly, allowing high possibilities for strong management to turn around the businesses. Inland China by and large had hotels that were even worse managed than those in the coastal areas, so Huo began in these areas. His approach was analogous to a military campaign: build first in the rural base areas, encircle the cities and then march on the coastal cities.

In the first half of 1993 Huo sent a team of his employees to tour China in order to investigate hotels for possible take-over. His goal was to find hotels which had 'hidden value' that could be 'dug out' (*wa jue*) through strong manage-ment. Huo's first acquisition was the Zhufeng Hotel in Chengdu. This was a two-star hotel. The superior authority of the hotel was the People's Liberation Army in Tibet, to whom each year the hotel handed over around 0.8 million yuan. The hotel was also under the partial administration of the army authorities in Beijing and Chengdu. Army personnel from any of these regions could come and use the hotel without payment. The general manager at the hotel supported the transfer to Huo, as it gave him a chance to escape from control by the army, and run the hotel as a genuine business. Huo struck a deal with the Army in Tibet. Under the contract he was to manage the hotel for 12 years. He promised to hand over to them each year a fixed sum of 2.88 million yuan, and to provide an initial advance of 0.7 million yuan. Huo gave the existing manager a five-month train-ing course at his own hotel in Shenzhen and then sent him back to be general manager of Zhufeng. Huo commented: 'It's better to brainwash the prisoner than sack him.' A new five-man management team was selected by Huo to work underneath the new general manager.

The number of administrative cadres was reduced from 29 to 13, and the rest either were demoted or had their salary stopped. The latter group were allowed to work outside, but retain their other rights in the enterprise. The new management did sack 'quite a few' workers. Many 'surplus' workers were sent home with a basic minimum wage sufficient for bare livelihood, around 60 yuan per month.[27] The staff were now required to display good manners, obey strict discipline, stand up while working rather than slump in a chair and 'be happy'. Huo makes great use of slogans: 'A hotel without greeting is a forest without birds'; 'A hotel without smiles is a garden without flowers.' Huo says he is building on the Maoist mobilizatory tradition, of which he was a part, since he was in the army from 1970 to 1989. In just one year Zhufeng's profits soared to 7 million yuan, without even any change in decoration. Instead of taking profits out of the hotel, Huo decided to reinvest the profits in redecoration and upgrading the hotel, so that it shifted up from two to three stars. The precise long-term arrangements under which Zhufeng will hand over profits to the headquarters in Shenzhen is still under investigation.

The early success of Zhufeng greatly encouraged him in his plan. He felt that he had simply applied to Zhufeng the same principle that Zhao Xinxian had applied to his own business. He subsequently took over a further 16 hotels, making a total of 18 by December 1995. Each of them was taken over under a basically similar arrangement to that at Zhufeng, with the administrative authority typically being the local government. All the hotels have the 'Sanjiu' (Three Nines) brandname. The 'Sanjiu' chain is already as large as the former dominant player in the Chinese hotel market, Holiday Inn, which took 10 years to build up to 18 hotels. The largest domestic hotel chain is Golden Palace with 12 hotels. In 1996 Huo intended to have expanded to 30 hotels, and Huo's eventual goal is a chain of perhaps 100 or so 'Sanjiu' hotels across the whole of China. Already he has a hotel in most provinces, with a total of around 6000 employees.

Sanjiu's strategy is to quickly gain a central place in the hotel market before other chains can build up a market position as the market economy develops. Huo specifically wants Sanjiu to become the Chinese equivalent of the Holiday Inn in the USA. Indeed, Huo successfully recruited a leading Chinese Holiday Inn manager, Henry Liu. He had managed the Hawaii Holiday Inn for four years and then returned in 1993 to manage the Holiday Inn in Xian. Liu's income with Sanjiu is only around one-fifth of that he received from the Holiday Inn, but he was attracted by the idea of joining such a potentially powerful firm with such a far-sighted strategy. Also he can have a far higher position at Sanjiu than if he remained with the Holiday Inn.

Huo wants to build the chain rapidly until it is several times larger than the closest competitor and 'as close to a monopoly' as he can get. He wants to do this before the potential competitors realize what is happening, and before they are in a position to fight back. Sanjiu has not so far spent much on advertising, as it does not wish to advertise its strategy to competitors before its market position is secure. It plans greatly to expand its advertising once the chain has built a critical mass of around thirty hotels.

Huo's wage is not high by local standards. His monthly income in 1995 was around 3500 yuan, which is close to the average family income for Shenzhen.[28] Moreover, the manager recruited by Huo from Holiday Inn, Henry Liu, was paid around double Huo's salary. However, there are extra-wage elements in his income, such as housing, food and perhaps others, such as travel and use of company vehicles. Huo owns no shares in the company he is building up. He argues that he has no thought of owning the company for himself: 'The company is my undertaking (shiye), my life purpose, my dream.'

Mergers and take-overs initiated by Nanfang. After the Group was set up, Sanjiu acquired further non-core businesses and some of the newly merged businesses grew rapidly. By the mid-1990s Sanjiu had business in around seven different sectors other than pharmaceuticals. There was considerable discussion under way in Sanjiu's headquarters about the group's structure. It was thought to be quite likely that Sanjiu would divest itself of the loss-making businesses in sectors furthest removed from its core business and focus on only around three or four sectors outside pharmaceuticals.

By the mid-1990s Sanjiu was receiving 'many, many' requests from the administrative authorities of loss-making firms to take them over and use their investment capital, management skills, brand name and marketing network to turn the businesses around. The General Logistical Department also asked Sanjiu to take over more of its businesses in addition to those involved in the 1992 'deal'. Sanjiu 'very carefully' investigates requests for merger/take-over, evaluating the possibilities of its being able to effectively manage and turn the firm around. Sanjiu turns down most of these requests, because on investigation they find that the firm has 'negative net worth' and/or cannot be effectively run by Sanjiu.

By and large, it preferred to diversify through taking over firms in the food and drink sector, since it felt that the technical characteristics of firms in these sectors were not too far removed from those of the core business, and it was therefore better able to evaluate their business prospects and to run them effectively. By late 1995, Sanjiu had taken over firms in non-core businesses with a total employment of 'many thousands'. Its take-overs embraced all possible forms, including government administrative merger (jian bing), outright purchase (shougou), mixed share ownership (cangu), and purchase of a controlling share ownership stake (kongzhi gufen). The trend in Sanjiu's take-overs was towards establishing a controlling share-holding in the firms which it acquired.

A good example of its take-overs with a controlling stake is the Shijiazhuang Beer Factory in Shijiazhuang city in Hebei province. This firm was taken over in 1995. It had around 2000–3000 employees. This loss-making firm was administered by the local City government. The take-over deal was as follows. Sanjiu was assigned an option to take a 51 per cent controlling share ownership in the firm, in recognition of Sanjiu's good image, marketing network, trademark and the capital that it would inject into the business. Sanjiu took a five-year contract on the business. If, at the end of the five-year period, the firm was making sufficiently large profits, Sanjiu could exercise the right to use the profits to purchase the shares that had been reserved for this purpose, and could become the majority owner of the business. Sanjiu was given a high degree of autonomy in management. In the case of the Shijiazhuang plant, as in other Sanjiu take-overs, the company head (*yibashou*) was appointed by Sanjiu headquarters. In this case Sanjiu advertised for an expert in the beer industry and replaced the existing manager. Sanjiu cannot simply dismiss 'surplus' workers. It developed the idea of providing surplus workers with the incentive of a lump-sum severance payment (*qiansanfei*). A condition of receiving this was that the worker concerned had to sign a contract formally severing their connection with the factory, though this did not necessarily mean they would forfeit their right to company housing or a pension: 'in all things in China one has to go carefully.' In 1997, Shijiazhuang was able to re-pay the 17 million yuan loans from the Sanjiu Enterprise Group, and turned over 3 million yuan in profits to the mother company (SEG, 1998: 6).

In the mid-1990s Sanjiu took over a biscuit and chocolate manufacturer in Shanghai. This was originally a private business (*getihu*), which had expanded into a small business with several hundred workers. Sanjiu took a controlling share in the firm's ownership and invested around 30 million yuan in modernizing the plant. The firm then was able to use the Sanjiu brandname and have access to the Sanjiu marketing network. Soon afterwards it took over the Great White Shark Fin Restaurant in Shenzhen transforming it from a loss-maker to a profit generator for the Group within two years (SEG, 1998: 5–6).

Non-core New Businesses

Real estate. This is now regarded as a second 'mainstay' branch of activity for Sanjiu. After several years it has grown to a considerable size. Sanjiu has constructed several residential areas, including Liantang and Xiangmihu Zones in Shenzhen, a residential area in Baoan county and an 81-storey building in Shenzhen (Sanjiu Skyscraper).

Construction. At the time that the Sanjiu Group was formed the Group inherited a small construction company. This was rapidly built into a powerful company. It has only around 30 regular employees working from the Group headquarters. However, these organize a huge company with 'several tens of thousands' of contract workers. The largest contract is for construction work on the Three Gorges Dam. Other projects include construction work at the port of Yantian, and the Nanhuan (Southern Orbital) Motorway Project in Shenzhen.

Agricultural technology. Sanjiu has just begun an enterprise to construct an economic development zone in Hebei province. The General Logistics Department has the occupancy rights to a large tract of land in Hebei province in Zhoulu *xian*, a mountainous area within close reach of Beijing.[29] This was formerly used as a state farm by the army. The General Logistics Department has allocated use rights to the land to Sanjiu. The project has the support of the Central Government's Office of Experimental Areas for Agricultural Reform. Sanjiu's goal was to turn the area into a large high-technology agricultural science park. By 1998, it seems that several businesses manufacturing agricultural inputs, including farm vehicles and chemical fertilizers had begun operation.

Vehicles. In the mid-1990s Sanjiu set up the Sanjiu Automobile Company. This incorporated eleven enterprises, which Sanjiu had either taken over or in which they had made direct investments. Between them these enterprises were able to produce, maintain, modify and trade in agricultural, military and civilian vehicles. Sanjiu was in almost constant discussion with different potential international joint venture partners with a view to developing a 'people's car' tailored to the special conditions of the Chinese market (SEG, 1997: 24, 60). From 1994 to 1996, automobiles were even designated as Sanjiu's second 'pillar industry'.

Sanjiu Group's Business Structure in the Mid-1990s. By 1998, Sanjiu had evolved into a very different company from that of the late 1980s and early 1990s. Like most successful East Asian diversified conglomerates, a single chief executive officer has played a central role in the Company's development. Zhao Xinxian was still the most powerful and authoritative person in Sanjiu. He devises and puts into practice all major strategies and decisions. Under his leadership, the Company has developed a Decision Management Committee, which is the 'brain' of the Group in charge of devising major strategic decisions (Figure 5-2). The Strategic Decision 'Think-Tank' Committee, which incorporates a number of Chinese economists and intellectuals, provide numerous suggestions on the development of business strategy. In 1998 the Company had nine major divisions – the General Office, the Enterprise Management Division, the Treasury Division, the International Finance Division, the Human Resource Division, the Communist Party Supervisory Division, the Marketing Division, the Intellectual Property Rights Division and the Communist Party Cadres' Training Centre – which all reported to the General Manager, the founder of Nanfang, Professor Zhao Xinxian.

The Group's business interests were divided under two categories: the general commercial companies and the eight major industries (Figure 5-2). The pharmaceutical sector (pharmaceutical manufacturing and medical health care) was the core (first pillar) business in the Group. After 1996, Sanjiu's second pillar business was the food and beverage sector (which developed to complement the hotel and tourism sectors). The other six major industries of Sanjiu were wine manufacturing (Western and Chinese wines, including beers), agriculture (including the manufacturing of agricultural machinery, chemical fertilizers and cultivation), tourism (including hotels), real estate (including the development of real estate, construction of infrastructure and provision of construction materials), trading (including imports and exports, franchised dealers and shops) and automobiles (including the manufacturing of automobiles and spare parts).

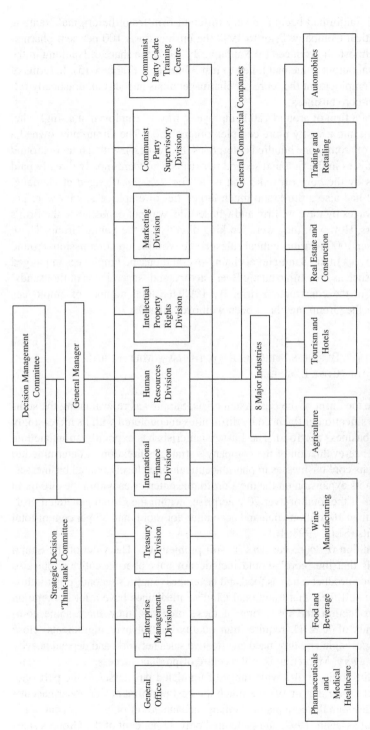

FIGURE 5-2 The Organizational Structure of Sanjiu Enterprise Group

SOURCE: SEG (1997: 18)

By 1995 Sanjiu had become a very different firm from the original Nanfang Pharmaceutical Company. Prior to 1992 the business was 100 per cent pharmaceuticals, almost all produced by Nanfang. By 1997, the share of Nanfang in the Group's total output value had fallen to just 37 per cent (Table 5-15). In terms of assets, and employment the 'core' of pharmaceuticals had shrunk drastically relative to non-core business.

Instead of a firm of around 1200 employees, mostly employed at a single site, it had grown into a vastly more complex organization. The Group now owned a second tier of around one hundred enterprises (*erji gongsi*), with a total of around 3000 employees in the first and second tier firms who were mostly directly paid their wages by the core firm and had their 'file' (*dangan*) lodged at Nanfang. However, it had also a third, and much larger, tier of employees, who were not paid their wages by the core firm and whose 'file' was not deposited at the firm's headquarters. However, they were working directly for the Sanjiu Group. These included over 1000 pharmaceutical salespeople working on commission, around 3000 employees in the Sanjiu hotel chain, several thousand employees in merged businesses such as the Shijiazhuang Beer Factory, and 'several tens of thousands' of workers in the construction firm. By 1998 the total number of employees working for the Group may have been well over 50 000.

RETHINKING THE BUSINESS STRUCTURE FOR THE NEW MILLENNIUM: RETURN TO THE 'CORE BUSINESS'

Even before the onset of the East Asian crisis, Sanjiu was re-evaluating the strategy of diversification, influenced by difficulties encountered with its increasingly diversified business portfolio. The East Asian crisis has explicitly stimulated an even sharper re-evaluation of the company's strategic direction. It determined to re-focus on its core businesses in pharmaceuticals and closely related businesses. It will focus its expansion on the most profitable enterprises within the Group: in 1997 15 out of the total of over 70 enterprises within the Group generated profits of more than 10 million yuan and accounted for more than 85 per cent of total Group profits (SEG, 1998: 16).

The definition of 'core business' is still problematic. The view of the Sanjiu leadership is that the 'core' should include not only pharmaceuticals, but also closely related products such as food and beverages (Sanjiu's second 'pillar industry'). Sanjiu still feels that traditional Chinese medicines have a lot in common with the production and marketing of these products: they share some common elements of R & D, require high quality control over ingredients, close attention to packaging quality, need an effective sales network, and depend heavily on brand imagery. Marketing is at the centre of product success.

Despite the addition of a wide range of unrelated businesses to the portfolio, it was still the case that in 1997–8 much the best performers were pharmaceutical firms. Although the core plant, Nanfang, accounted for only 27 per cent of the Group's total assets in 1997, and generated only 37 per cent of the Group's sales value, it still accounted for one-half of the entire Group pre-tax profits (Table 5-15). Nanfang consistently achieved a profit rate on sales of between 16–22 per cent, while for other businesses, the rate was only around 6–12 per cent (derived from Table 5-15).

Moreover, the two other enterprises apart from Nanfang with pre-tax profits of over 50 million yuan in 1997 also were pharmaceutical firms, and three of the four enterprises with pre-tax profits of 25–50 million yuan in 1997 also were pharmaceutical enterprises (SEG, 1998: 4–5; *Sanjiu Jituan Bao*, 6 May 1998: 3). By 1997, it is possible that the share of non-pharmaceutical businesses in the Group's total assets and sales value may have been as high as 40 per cent, and its share of Group employment even higher. However, pharmaceuticals generated around three-quarters of the Group's total pre-tax profits. In other words, since the take-over 'deal' with the GLD in 1992, Sanjiu had rapidly built up a portfolio of poorly-performing companies in a wide variety of often unrelated businesses. Since 1991, Sanjiu had acquired seventy or more enterprises in twenty provinces, of which around one-half were outside the pharmaceutical sector (SEG, 1998: 3–4). These sapped management efforts, diverted Group capital for low returns, diluted the Company's brand and added little to the Group's profit stream.

In 1997 Sanjiu Group Headquarters devised strict new guidelines to govern the Group's mergers and acquisitions. M & A targets were all to be compatible with the renewed focus on pharmaceuticals and closely related businesses. The first-tier core enterprise (Nanfang) was not be involved directly in any new mergers and acquisitions: all new M & A deals were to be undertaken by the second- or third-tier enterprises. This would reduce the financial risk for Nanfang and lower its debt–assets ratio. M & A targets were to have marketable products and have the potential for further growth. Loss-making enterprises were to be avoided as M & A targets. M & A deals were only to be undertaken if they were financially sound: second-tier enterprises were not to engage in any M & A deals which were beyond their financial capabilities. In 1997, the Sanjiu Group evaluated over 700 potential take-over targets, but, based on these criteria, acquired only about 20 enterprises (SEG, 1998: 3–4).

Sanjiu plans several measures to improve its performance in pharmaceuticals. It plans to raise its in-house R & D investment, and develop co-operative and joint R & D projects with more than 30 medical schools and hospitals in China (for example Shenyang Medical University). At present, Nanfang, the core firm within the Group, is engaged in the development of 16 new drugs, including an anti-AIDS drug and a drug for diabetes (SEG, 1998: 8). Sanjiu plans to build two FDA approved Chinese medicines manufacturing centres, one in Shenzhen and one in Sichuan (*Sanjiu Jituan Bao*, 25 February 1998: 2). It is giving close attention to the importance of intellectual property rights especially including those for Chinese medicines, which is still a grey area of domestic and international law. It will continue to improve the way in which it develops and uses the Sanjiu trademark and its 59 different registered brand names, including the most powerful of them, *Sanjiu Weitai*. It is rapidly developing its information technology sales network to co-ordinate the Sanjiu Trading Company's 3300 sales points across China.

Sanjiu recognizes the great importance of developing human as well as physical capital in order to succeed as a modern pharmaceutical company. Nanfang will continue to invest heavily in the enrichment of human capital, through expanding different forms of training and re-training of employees. It aims shortly to ensure that 100 per cent of its workforce have attained professional high school qualification or above. This will be a powerful instrument of competitive advantage within the Chinese pharmaceutical industry. It is continuing to study and implement ways of raising the company's management skills. (SEG, 1998: 5–9). In 1998, Sanjiu introduced the 'profits-related promotion mechanism' in order to develop a group of talented senior managers.[30] It is attempting to establish and strengthen the responsibility and risk-monitoring mechanism within each affiliated enterprise (SEG, 1998: 17; *Sanjiu Jituan Bao*, 25 February 1998: 2, 22 April 1998: 1). It will introduce a trial experiment with an employees' stock-holding scheme and strengthen the sense of belonging and sense of awareness about the importance of efficiency among Sanjiu employees (SEG, 1998: 19–20).

Under the new policies, Sanjiu abandoned the attempt to make automobiles a 'second pillar industry' and suspended investment in the sector. It closed down or sold off 16 poorly-managed third-tier companies. It integrated and reshuffled the assets of those companies which had recorded losses for two consecutive years or large losses in a single year (12 out of the total of 71 enterprises in the Sanjiu Group were loss-making in 1997) (SEG, 1998: 5–6).

The intention in the recent reforms is to take Sanjiu firmly back to the path of being a focused modern pharmaceutical company, with some related business in the food and drinks sector. As we have noted already, the State Pharmaceutical Administration's goal is to build a small number of domestically-based giant pharmaceutical firms to compete with the multinationals. Sanjiu has been selected by the SPA as one of China's five 'national champions' in the pharmaceutical sector, with the goal of reaching a sales value of 10 billion yuan by the year 2000 (SEG, 1998: 17).

As we have seen, Sanjiu is firmly committed to retain ownership of the Group's core firm, Nanfang, by the PLA, 'its principal', rather than allowing it to pass into the hands of 'outsiders'. However, the reform strategy recognizes the importance of raising funds from the stock market through subsidiaries, and is strongly committed to raising capital and transferring technology through joint international ventures that are consistent with Sanjiu's re-formulated business goals (SEG, 1998: 19).

CONCLUSION

DEBATE OVER THE SOURCES OF NANFANG'S GROWTH

A number of arguments can be advanced to explain Nanfang's exceptional growth and modernization. It enjoyed special advantages consequent upon its location in Shenzhen Special Economic Zone (SEZ), adjacent to Hong Kong. It enjoyed the advantage of starting from scratch without the burdens associated with the reform of a long-established state enterprise, such as those associated with having a large number of retired workers. Most importantly, it enjoyed the advantage of being supported by the Army's General Logistics Department. None of these arguments is wholly convincing.

Like all the businesses in Shenzhen Special Economic Zone, Nanfang certainly derived benefits from its location. Moreover, it is rumoured that its 'automobile' business is heavily involved in smuggling. If this were indeed true, this activity would be assisted by the firm's location in Shenzhen. It was allowed to import capital goods free of import duties due to being in a special economic zone. Also, the close proximity to Hong Kong had a big impact on Nanfang's approach to business, such as in the way it approached advertising. It was also able to dismiss surplus or poorly-performing employees relatively easily due to the tight labour market in Shenzhen. However, location is far from a sufficient explanation for Nanfang's success. Shenzhen contains thousands of firms, but only a few have grown as fast as Nanfang. It took the lead in the way it used Hong Kong style advertising to promote its products. Far from being specially supported by the local government, the Shenzhen municipal government is suspicious of Nanfang due to the fact that its superior authority is the Army rather than the locality. The value of having powerful support from the local government was strongly brought out by the battle with Haikou Pharmaceuticals. In this battle Haikou was resolutely supported by the local Hainan government, whereas the support for Nanfang from the Shenzen government does not appear to have been so strong.

The fact that Nanfang was set up from scratch did mean that it had a small burden in terms of pensions and initially had no workers in company housing. Also it was able to recruit a mainly young, highly skilled workforce for the core permanent jobs. For the non-core jobs it was able to employ mainly temporary workers who could easily be sacked. However, this is not sufficient to explain its growth. Few of the many small businesses begun during the reform years grew in the way that Nanfang did. Moreover, Nanfang quickly reproduced many of the 'problematic' features of long-established state enterprises. For example, within a short period all the permanent staff were allocated company housing. The 500 or so cadres all had secure lifetime employment. The greatest advantage stemming from the fact that Nanfang had to start from scratch may have been that the inner core of those who ran the firm developed a powerful sense of mutual support and trust, derived from together building a highly successful business.

The fact that until 1998 Nanfang was (and still is) owned by the Army's General Logistics Department provided several advantages. The Department provided the start-up capital. It assisted in making available the initial site in Shenzhen. It helped to provide outlets for medicines in the Army's network of hospitals. It probably assisted in the acquisition of new plants and in setting up new businesses, such as the agricultural science park in Hebei province.

However, in some respects it was a disadvantage to have the General Logistics Department as the administrative superior. The Guangzhou Army Hospital provided only a small amount of start-up capital, yet it claimed a large fraction of the profits earned by Nanfang. Nanfang had to fight hard to gain a greater degree of independence through skilful negotiations in order to be released from supervision by the Guangzhou Army Hospital, and directly administered by the headquarters of the General Logistics Department in Beijing. Even after the reorganization, the Beijing General Logistics Department demanded a large share of the profits from Sanjiu. It required also ad hoc hand-overs such as that in 1995 to fund the construction of the General Logistics Department's new meeting hall in Beijing. Moreover, the deal struck with them forced Nanfang to take over many loss-making firms, to inject capital into them, and to diversify into areas that it had no wish to enter. The General Logistics Department owned hundreds of firms across China, but none was as successful as Nanfang. Furthermore, the army 'connections' of the Nanfang leadership were very limited. Indeed when the plant was initially set up Zhao Xinxian was simply a research professor, not a high-ranking general able to pull strings on behalf of his institution. He grew in importance only because the firm he ran grew so successfully.

In sum, none of the above factors is sufficient to explain Nanfang's rapid growth and modernization. The answer instead lies much more in the complex set of factors that helped produce a powerful, modern business organization at Nanfang.

MODERN BUSINESS ORGANIZATION AT NANFANG

Nanfang Pharmaceutical Plant and most of the merged plants in the Sanjiu Group were owned by the Chinese people as a whole. The Army's General Logistics Department was their administrative authority, with rights to use the property under its control. When Sanjiu took over 51 per cent of the ownership of the Shijiazhuang Brewery it was taking over a firm the use of whose assets was supervised by the Shijiazhuang City authorities, which in turn was exercising supervision over the assets on behalf of the Chinese state, which in turn was supervising the use of the assets on behalf of the Chinese people who were the ultimate owners. The firm which was taking over the Shijiazhuang Brewery was itself supervised by the General Logistics Department of the People's Liberation Army. The General Logistics Department was supervising the use of these assets on behalf of the whole Army, which was in turn supervising them on behalf of the Chinese state which was in turn acting on behalf of the ultimate owners, the Chinese people. Technically, the Chinese people were taking over an asset owned by the Chinese people.

Despite the fact that the formal ownership rights to much of the property within the Sanjiu Group resided with the Chinese state representing the Chinese people, Nanfang's struggle for autonomy and the manner of its take-over of other firms demonstrated a clear concept of use rights and rules governing the rights to employ the assets under its control, and to use the income stream derived from the use of those assets. Nanfang's leadership struggled to obtain autonomy first from the Guangzhou Army Hospital, and then from the General Logistics Department in Beijing. The struggle was for autonomy in the way that assets were used, for rights to a larger share of the income stream from the assets and to greater autonomy in the way in which that income stream was used.

Nanfang Pharmaceutical Company used its autonomy to behave in a drastically different fashion from the traditional Chinese plant under the command economy. Nanfang used its autonomy to make a careful selection of product in order to maximize the size of its potential market. It adopted marketing practices familiar to Western pharmaceutical firms. This involved the construction of a large network of salespeople and collectors of feedback from customers. The construction of the marketing system relied also on East Asian patterns of networking, in which Nanfang made strong use of its main institutional support, namely the PLA. Nanfang spent large amounts on advertising.[31] These advertisements were highly effective, and of a standard practised in Hong Kong. It exercised strict quality control in order to be able to convince its customers of the high degree of reliability of its brand of medicine. This involved employing skilled technicians, constructing a strict system of quality control, and investing large amounts of profits in modern equipment. Only in this way could the firm achieve internationally accepted quality controls (the GMP standard). It involved the creation of a strong company ethos among the several hundred core personnel in the firm, building on the army traditions of discipline and using the mobilizatory skills of the Chinese Communist Party. The firm's ethos included meticulous attention to personal appearance, and strong emphasis on the acquisition of human skills such as computer literacy and foreign languages. The coherence and purpose of the inner core of leadership was powerfully affected both by Party and Army values and the bonding experience of building the firm from scratch in both a physical and business sense. Nanfang was the first firm in the Chinese pharmaceutical industry to adopt the full range of practices associated with Western pharmaceutical firms. This gave it the 'first-mover' advantage among domestic firms in China's fast-reforming pharmaceutical sector.

The formal ownership structure at Nanfang and Sanjiu prior to 1998 might appear to be incompatible with effective business behaviour. The firm's assets all were, and still are, owned by the whole Chinese people. Moreover, the intermediary body charged with the exercise of control over those assets, namely the Army's General Logistics Department, is of a type that would appear likely to have little understanding of how to stimulate effective business performance in its subordinate units. The subordinate enterprise, Nanfang and subsequently Sanjiu, paid a substantial share of profits in 'dividends' to the sole shareholder, the General Logistics Department of the Chinese People's Liberation Army, which represented the Chinese state and the Chinese people. However, this apparently unpromising environment was consistent with the construction by the subordinate firm of a highly effective business organization of a kind that would be readily recognizable by a Western pharmaceutical firm or by a diversified East Asian conglomerate. The enterprise management was left with a high degree of operational autonomy, including the right to take over and merge with other businesses. The main reason for Nanfang/Sanjiu's success is not special help from the Army, but rather the fact that its leadership used their autonomy to construct a highly effective business organization.

INSIGHTS INTO THE EAST ASIAN DIVERSIFIED CONGLOMERATE

Subsequently, Nanfang expanded in the fashion typical of capitalist East Asian conglomerates. Unable directly to challenge the multinational firms in patented Western medicines, Sanjiu diversified rapidly into a variety of related areas of business. Initially this was stimulated by the 'deal' to take over the General Logistics Department's Shenzhen businesses, but subsequently it came from Sanjiu's own volition. The acquisitions involved careful consideration of the condition of the firm to be taken over. They involved typically an insistence on establishing majority control for Sanjiu. They involved also the application of Sanjiu's management skills to the newly taken over businesses, the use of its marketing network and its brand name to help turn around the businesses it took over.

However, only a small fraction of these businesses yielded high profit rates, and many of them remained persistently loss-making. Moreover, the core pharmaceutical plant was consistently much the largest profit earner and the other major profit generators were also mainly in the pharmaceutical sector. After several years of attempting to 'float boats on the water', the Company recognized that this strategy had deep flaws. In pursuit of growth, the Company was absorbing businesses that it was unable to run effectively, and was leaking valuable financial and human capital in attempting to turn the businesses around, detracting from its ability to develop the business in which it had the highest competence. Moreover, it was in danger of diluting the valuable brand that it had painstakingly and highly successfully built up in the preceding period. The return to focus on its core competencies in pharmaceuticals marked a radical re-evaluation of its business strategy.

However, the central government's reform proposals announced in 1998 to separate the PLA from commercial activities may lead to pressure on Sanjiu to take over an even more diversified portfolio of PLA businesses as owner and/or manager. This would push Sanjiu firmly back onto the path of a diversified conglomerate, despite the stated intentions of Sanjiu's own internal reforms. There would be a great temptation to use the opportunity of the proposed PLA reforms greatly to increase Sanjiu's size. As an outstanding performer among the PLA's businesses, Sanjiu is in a prime position to absorb a significant segment of the businesses that pass out of the PLA's hands, should this indeed be the outcome of the reforms. In this case, Sanjiu's very success in establishing an effective modern business system would be the cause of its being selected by the PLA to take over many of its businesses. Paradoxically, Sanjiu would be led back to the path of a large typical East Asian conglomerate, despite its best efforts to escape this form.

PROSPECTS

Sanjiu is still firmly anchored within the traditional Chinese pharmaceutical sector. It still cannot provide serious competition for the multinational giants in Western patented medicines. Demand for traditional Chinese medicines seems likely to expand within China at a pace close to or somewhat faster than average incomes. Sanjiu's overall market share is still small, despite being the industry leader. If it is successful in its re-focused strategy upon pharmaceuticals then there is scope for sustained long-term growth based mainly around traditional medicines for the domestic market. The government's intention to separate the PLA's commercial from the military activities may provide an opportunity for Sanjiu to accelerate its position in the Chinese traditional pharmaceutical sector by acquiring more pharmaceutical firms from the PLA. Its main medium-term objective must be to acquire a wider portfolio of market-leading traditional medicines, to match the position it holds in stomach medicines.

In the longer term there is a possibility of a different scenario. The PLA's reforms coincided with the intention announced in 1998 by the State Pharmaceutical Administration to build a small number of powerful domestic pharmaceutical companies through merger and acquisition in order to develop much larger R & D capability. As we have seen, Sanjiu was one of the five firms selected to be part of this group. The acquisition of a substantial segment of the remaining pharmaceutical businesses owned by the PLA might provide a boost to this ambition. With the support of the central government, there is a possibility that Sanjiu will eventually become one of China's emerging groups of powerful producers of patented Western medicines.

China's aspiring global leaders in pharmaceuticals will face a severe struggle on the global level playing field within the WTO. In 1997, Sanjiu's total revenue from pharmaceuticals was the equivalent of less than $700 million. This was less than the annual revenue from a single 'blockbuster drug' from a leading pharmaceutical firm in the USA or Europe. Its total pre-tax profits were less than $100 million, which is less than 2 per cent of the post-tax profits of the world's leading companies in the sector. Its R & D expenditure cannot have been more than around $120–140 million (assuming around one-fifth of sales was allocated to R & D), which is only a tiny fraction of that of the world's leading drugs companies, and would be only a small part of the total required to develop and launch a single successful patented drug.

The key to Sanjiu's potential competitiveness on the global level playing field is the ability to develop a special position within the niche market of Chinese traditional medicines. However, if this market appears likely to grow substantially on a world scale, then there is nothing to prevent the global giants from themselves entering this area of drugs production more actively. They can bring their huge R & D expenditure to bear on these drugs, and use their immense financial resources to put these drugs through all the necessary test procedures. There is nothing to prevent them from sub-contracting to Chinese biotechnology firms and universities to undertake the early-stage research on these products. They are able to use their enormous marketing expenditure to sell the resulting products across the world, including in China. In sum, even traditional Chinese herbal medicines are unlikely to provide Sanjiu with a hiding place from competition with the global giants.

6

Power Equipment

To join the WTO China must unilaterally open its markets and agree to play by the same rules as other WTO members ... China must make all the concessions, and the United States gets the benefit. As a result the United States stands to gain unprecedented access to China's markets, while giving up nothing.
(US–China Trade Council, 'Questions and answers on the
US–China WTO Agreement', 1 December 1999)

China's power industry is facing a serious competitive threat in both foreign and domestic markets. Only through redoubling its efforts will it be able to create space for itself to exist. China wishes to compete as well as co-operate with foreign manufacturers, aiming to create a new situation of common development, in other words, 'I have and you have too.'
(Lu Yansun, Deputy Minister of Machine Building, 1989–94;
Chairman of the Chinese Power Equipment Manufacturers' Association,
Member of the Financial Committee of the National People's Congress)

INTRODUCTION

Power generation equipment is the quintessential capital good. Without electric power, there can be little economic activity. From steel factories to electric hair dryers, electricity is the fundamental source of power. Without a low-cost, low price, reliable power supply, a country's economy is handicapped in international competition.

In China since the late 1970s there has occurred a rapid growth of output from this sector. The manufacture of power generating equipment is an industry characterized by high technology, rapid technical progress and exceptionally strong economies of scale. Only a few firms dominate the industry globally. Within

327

China also, there is only a small number of producers. The current and future projected rapid growth of demand for power generating equipment creates a huge opportunity for China's indigenous power equipment suppliers. Harbin Power Equipment Company (HPEC) grew rapidly and modernized fast after the 1970s, and rapidly changed its operational practice.

HPEC is now at a crossroads in its development. This paper asks the question: Will China's leading power equipment companies be able to compete on the global 'level playing field' with the multinational giants of the power generating equipment industry as full, integrated producers, making turbines, generators and boilers for complete sets of thermal, hydro and nuclear power plants?

This chapter demonstrates that China's leading power equipment manufacturers have made large changes in their operational mechanism and large technical advances. However, despite these advances, even China's leading company, Harbin, is still far behind the leading multinationals in terms of both scale and technology. If China's major power equipment manufacturers are to establish internationally competitive integrated firms, then they need to make a 'second jump' from autonomous plants to large-scale, multi-plant firms benefiting from the economies of scale and scope. If China is to follow this path, then it requires continued substantial assistance from state industrial policy. This involves state orchestration of technological transfer, protection from imports through NTBs, domestic content requirements for joint venture partners and internationally-funded power stations, and, above all, a state-orchestrated merger of the leading power equipment companies. Without a state-led merger of the leading producers, and support from state industrial policy, China will be unable to develop a globally powerful and competitive, integrated power equipment manufacturer. Instead, China's leading firms in this sector will each become a sub-branch of the global giants in the industry.

This chapter demonstrates that it is not a foregone conclusion that this will be the outcome. Powerful forces are working in a different direction. The multinational companies are desperate to become an integral part of the Chinese power equipment industry through establishing sub-branches within China. Powerful domestic forces also are part of the struggle. These include the weakening of China's planning system, changes in ideology within the Chinese government, the interests of China's power generation industry, which urgently needs to buy the lowest-cost equipment and to obtain international funding for power station construction, as well as interests within the power equipment companies themselves that favour becoming subbranches of the multinationals. In sum, the struggle for the Chinese power equipment market is already a complex and tense process, and will become even more so.

MAIN FEATURES OF THE POWER EQUIPMENT INDUSTRY WORLD-WIDE

ECONOMIES OF SCALE AND SCOPE

Power equipment manufacture has large economies of scale and scope. The main elements of power stations, boilers and turbines, are of enormous and steadily increasing size. Competitive advantage in this sector depends on:

- ability to invest in technical progress in the product and maintain technological leadership globally;
- financial strength to withstand technical failures and provide project funding for acquirers of power equipment;
- high level of capability in providing service for power units over the whole of their lifetime;
- ability to lower costs of production through effective internal and external business system integration.

Technical Progress. The average size of a steam turbine in the advanced economies rose rapidly from around 100 MW in the 1950s to around 600 MW in the 1970s, and the maximum size to-day is over 1500 MW. The advance in turbine size has necessitated major advances in such technologies as welding and turbine blade construction.

Technical progress has required that leading firms spend huge amounts on R & D in order to compete. In 1995, the total (that is including all divisions, not just power equipment) R & D spending of Siemens was over $5 billion, while for General Electric it stood at $1.9 billion, ABB $2.6 billion and GEC–Alsthom $444 million (Table 6-1). It took General Electric seven years to develop its F-class gas turbine, which is now being installed in power stations throughout the world. General Electric's research division is so powerful that it has had two Nobel Prize winners. Leading power equipment manufacturers benefited from considerable government support for their R & D efforts. For example, out of GE's total R & D spending of $1.9 billion in 1998, no less than $393 million came from US government funds (GE, *Annual Report, 1998*: 46). Out of Siemens' total R & D spending of $5.5 billion in 1998, $148 million came from grants from the German government (Siemens, *Annual Report, 1998*: 69).

Alongside the rise in the size of the average turbine has gone a large increase in its energy efficiency rate. GE estimates that the average US plant runs at an energy efficiency of 33 per cent (that is only 33 per cent of the energy in the fuels is converted into electricity or by-products for heating systems), whereas state-of-the-art turbines can achieve energy efficiency rates of 58 per cent in combined cycle operations (*FT*, 19 June 1997). Small increases in thermal efficiency can save operators millions of dollars over the course of the life of the plant. For example, General Electric's new H-series combined cycle (gas and steam) turbines run at 55 per cent net thermal efficiency compared to 60 per cent for the F series which they will replace. Each one per cent saving in net thermal efficiency reduces operating costs for a typical combined cycle 400–500 MW plant by $15–20 million over the life of the plant (*FT*, 16 May 1996).

A major advantage for General Electric in establishing its technical lead in turbine technology in recent years has been the spillover from its aero-engine division. A chief executive of GE said: 'The link between power generation and aircraft engines is our hidden unfair competitive advantage' (quoted in *FT*,

TABLE 6-1 Size of HPEC and Leading Firms in the World's Power Equipment Industry, Late 1990s

	Employees	Turnover ($ million)	Assets ($ million)	Net profits ($ million)	R & D ($ million)
HPEC (1995)	27 000	310	934	14	3
(1997)	—	313	1 040	11	3
(1998)	—	346	1 060	9	3
General Electric (1994)	221 000	60 109	—	4 726	1 200
(1996)	239 000	79 179	272 402	7 280	1 400
(1998)	293 000	100 469	355 935	9 296	1 930
of which:					
Power					
Division (1995)	25 000	6 692	6 322 (1996)	782	—
(1998)	—	8 466	7 253	1 306	—
(1999)	—	10 500	—	—	—
Westinghouse (1995)	84 400	8 848	10 398 (1992)	77	—
of which:		—			
Power Division	—	3 000			
Siemens (1995)	376 000	57 948	49 000	990	5 008
(1998)	416 000	68 000	68 000	1 600	5 500
of which:	—		—		
Power division (1997)	28 000	5 700		—	—
(1998)		6 385	2 625	—	—
GEC–Alsthom (1995)	—	11 108	—	—	444
of which:					
Power Division	—	4 000	—	—	—
ABB (1995)	207 557	29 718	24 900 (1994)	1 447	2 589
(1998)		29 700		2 500	2 368
of which:	—	—	—	870	—
Power Division					
ABB–Alstom					
(1998, pro-forma)	—	9 000	—	—	—
(1999)	54 000	11 000	—	—	—

SOURCES: HPEC (1995); *FT* (1 January 1996, 15 May 1996, 27 June 1996, and 24 March 1999); UNCTAD, (1995: 20–1); DRC (1993: 478–9); GE, *Annual Report, 1998*; Siemens, *Annual Report, 1998*; DTI (1996, 1999)

16 May 1995). Subsequently, its rivals constructed alliances with leading aircraft engine manufacturers in order to improve their turbine technology. In 1992 Westinghouse established an alliance with Rolls-Royce,[1] and in 1990 Siemens established an alliance with Pratt and Whitney, allowing Siemens to apply aero-engine technology to its land-based turbines (*FT*, 16 May 1995).[2] By the mid-1990s, three of the leading power equipment manufacturers were closely linked up with each of the world's leading aircraft engine manufacturers, either through an alliance or direct ownership.

Rolls-Royce's decision to enter an alliance with Westinghouse followed its purchase of Northern Electrical Industries shortly after Rolls-Royce's privatization in 1989. Rolls-Royce's objective was to try to break into the large-scale power equipment market, utilizing its aero-engine technology in the same way that GE had done. However, Rolls-Royce found that the nature of the global power equipment industry was fast changing. In the wake of power industry privatization and third world demand growth, there occurred a rapid growth of 'Build–Operate–Transfer' (BOT) power stations. This placed large new demands on the power equipment suppliers. They needed to be able not only to build technically demanding products, but also to be able to finance, operate and service the power station. These requirements introduced a new range of risks for large-scale power equipment suppliers. Northern Electrical Industries was simply too small to form the platform for Rolls-Royce's entry into the new world of power station construction. The alliance with Westinghouse was quickly ended. Rolls-Royce sold Northern Electrical Industries (see below), and turned its back on large-scale power equipment supply. It moved instead to develop small-scale (below 50 MW) power stations using the Trent aircraft engine.[3]

Financial Strength. Leading power equipment companies must make many large strategic decisions, often with substantial elements of risk, as a condition of staying in the industry. For example, all the leading firms in the industry invested hugely in new capacity for gas turbines, assuming that privatization of power plants in advanced countries would produce a surge in demand for gas turbines. In fact, in the 1990s, the anticipated surge in demand did not occur, so that the leading makers all developed large excess capacity in gas turbine making, which helped to push down prices strongly. Another major area of risk is bidding for new projects. This requires the investment of large sums in preparing bids with uncertain outcomes.

R & D investment also involves large elements of risk. Power generation equipment firms must be able to guarantee the quality of their hugely expensive products and have the resources to be able to rectify problems if they arise. Even colossal R & D expenditures cannot guarantee against technical problems. For example, General Electric's F-class turbines developed faults that only became apparent after the first machines had gone into service. Some turbine sections had to be flown back to the USA for repair while GE's roving groups of engineers put others right. The total cost of resolving these problems was at least $100 million (*FT*, 23 July 1996). Only a huge company with corresponding financial resources could withstand such difficulties. If it failed to resolve them, its reputation and its sales would be drastically impeded.

As we have already noted, it is increasingly the case that power equipment makers must be able to provide capital for project construction. A firm such as GE has a huge advantage in winning orders in that it is supported by GE Capital, the financial services division of the parent company. A senior official at GE commented: 'GE Capital has fairly impressive resources ... It participates in funding, owning and even running power plants. The pursuit of opportunities is seamless between us and them' (quoted in *FT*, 16 May 1995). Since the mid-1980s, under CEO Gary Wendt, it has grown rapidly into what has been described as the 'world's largest unregulated bank'. By 1997 it had total assets of $255 billion, a staff of 67 000, and made 300 acquisitions across the world between 1990 and 1997 (*Independent*, 12 April 1998). By 1997 it accounted for 47 per cent of GE's total profits (*FT*, 9 May 1998). Siemens currently has invested in around one-third of the projects it has on its order book : 'If we don't invest, we don't get the business', says a senior officer of Siemens (*FT*, 3 June 1996)

Service Capability. Increasingly, power equipment firms need to have large competitive, service divisions. Equipment sales form a declining share of short term profits for equipment manufacturers. In the past few years GE has expanded its view of the power market to include 'everything from the wellhead to the consumer – a $100 billion addressable power market – with a view to benefiting from utility deregulation and leveraging its valuable brand name' (MSDW, 1998b: 85). It already appears to be winning power equipment orders based on its service capability (MSDW, 1998b: 87).

New entrants face the difficulty that established large producers have built big stocks of 'embedded value' in servicing previously supplied equipment. This applies not only to power equipment, but also to closely related products, such as large aero-engines. A large global installed base is 'like home-court advantage – customers develop an intangible trust in a long time supplier, and to varying degrees, a tangible incentive to stick with one supplier for common and compatible operation and maintenance' (MSDW, 1998b: 88). The nature and importance of servicing has changed dramatically. In the past, public electricity utilities typically bought new equipment and then serviced it themselves with teams of in-house engineers using parts bought from the power equipment companies. Today, power-generating companies have sharply reduced in-house servicing staff and contracted out a large share of servicing activities.

The trend has been reinforced by the rapid growth of power generation in developing countries, which often lack the technical know-how for effective power plant maintenance. Power generators are placing more emphasis than ever on lowering costs through minimizing stoppages. More and more, power plant operators are outsourcing service contracts, and the original supplier of the equipment is in a strong position to win contracts for servicing. Increasingly, long-term service contracts form part of the package provided by the major producers.

The fast growth of computer-based monitoring systems is helping to transform the nature of the servicing of power equipment. The major suppliers are moving towards a situation in which there will exist a global web of computer, voice and video links between each of the plants that a producer has supplied, so that information can be exchanged and engineers benefit from each others' experience. Each of the plants supplied can be linked with remote service centres, so that performance is constantly monitored. Servicing packages are constantly growing in sophistication. Instead of waiting for breakdowns to occur, companies can carry out preventative work in advance. They can also time routine maintenance more accurately, varying the intervals for different plants. Equipment suppliers are using computers to assemble performance information from different sites to build electronic libraries of data which can be shared by all their clients. Taken together, these development have produced a new approach towards servicing: 'Today servicing has taken on a new meaning as customers look to suppliers for innovation offerings and alternative methods for accomplishing missions they have historically done themselves' (Bob Nardell, President, GE Power Systems, quoted in *FT*, 19 June 1997). GE likens its new role in maintaining power equipment maintenance to 'an air traffic controller for electrons' (*FT*, 10 June 1999).

While there are some small independent servicing companies, 'the big companies have the upper hand in high-technology servicing agreements' (*FT*, 19 June 1997). It is in these sectors that the margins are highest. Moreover, the big suppliers are able and willing to share risk with the power generators, signing agreements under which their level of payment will depend on the actual performance of the plants they are maintaining (*FT*, 19 June 1997).

A sharply increasing share of power equipment companies' profits is being generated by after-sales service. In 1998 the share of equipment servicing in total power equipment division revenues totalled nearly half at GE, compared with about one-third at Siemens and ABB-Alstom (*FT*, 10 June 1999). By the late 1990s, GE's power equipment division had around one-half of its employees working in the service and marketing divisions (*FT*, 10 June 1999).

Service activities have further advantages. They generate high returns on little or no incremental capital, with less inherent cyclicality. By the end of 1999 GE, for example, had contracts to operate or maintain over 170 power stations across the world, providing revenues of more than $6 billion per annum stretching out over periods of up to 12 years. Moreover, since the supplier is already very familiar with the customer and product, the operational risk is minimal (MSDW, 1998b: 87). Service provision also enhances the dependence of the customer upon the supplier. The service provider's day-to-day proximity positions it well for future orders. Global and credible service capability is not readily reproducible, and is a 'much more competitive strategy than pricing' (MSDW, 1998b: 87).

Low-cost Supply Base. As in other complex machinery sectors, power equipment producers are more and more outsourcing components. Procurement departments of large companies are able to establish global networks of low-cost suppliers, leveraging their immense purchasing power to obtain lower cost supplies (*FT*, 19 June 1997), and can integrate their buying muscle with large-scale information technology investments. Part of this involves shifting production capacity to low-cost locations outside the home country. ABB, for example, recently took a charge of $850 million to move manufacturing from Western Europe to Southeast Asia in an 'aggressive move to get ahead of the markets' (MSDW, 1998b: 86). We shall see later in this study, that there is a rapid growth of joint ventures within China between global power equipment giants and local manufacturers. The goal is twofold. First, to capture market share for power equipment orders within China, and second, to establish low-cost bases for components supply.

An important part of the integration of the low-cost supplier network, and the network of global sub-branches lies in the management systems that can be put into place. In the late 1980s, GE spent a great deal on introducing the Six Sigma programme of computerized systems management. The system 'measurably improves capacity utilization', producing a 15–20 per cent reduction in GE's capital spending budget during the second half of 1997 despite extra spending on the relocation of plants to low-cost areas (MSDW, 1998b: 31).

DEMAND FOR POWER EQUIPMENT

The underlying prospects for the world's power generating equipment manufacturers is strong. Global electricity consumption grew at around 3.4 per cent per annum from 1980 to 1994. It is predicted that annual orders for power generating equipment world-wide will grow from around 80 gigawatts in the mid-1990s to around 140 gigawatts in 2010 In the period 1985–2005, it is predicted that there will be a 3.5 per cent per annum annual average growth rate of global power equipment orders (Table 6-2), with only a slight fall in the predicted global growth rate consequent upon the Asian crisis (*FT*, 4 June 1998 and Table 6-3). Over the years 1994–2003 it is forecast that total world demand for power generating equipment could be around 820 gigawatts in total: 'Barring disasters, the way ahead looks like being characterized by steady overall growth in the global market for power stations and their components – turbines, generators, and a huge list of supporting parts – for fifteen years or more ... Forecasts about the fundamentals driving the industry paint a rosy picture which would be the envy of many other industrial sectors' (*FT*, 15 May 1995).

TABLE 6-2 **Projected World Demand for Power Equipment: Power Plant Capacity, by Region, 1980–2010 (%)**

Region	1980	1995	2010
Far East/Pacific	17	24	32
Middle East	1	3	4
Africa	2	3	3
Latin America	4	5	6
NAFTA	36	30	27
Eastern Europe	17	15	11
Western Europe	23	20	17
Total capacity (GW)	2070	3150	4380

SOURCE: *FT* (10 June 1999)

TABLE **6-3 Power Plant Capacity, by Type, 1980–2010**

Type	1980	1995	2010
Nuclear	7	12	9
Other renewables	0	<0.5	2
Hydro	23	23	23
Oil	2	2	2
Gas turbine	4	5	6
Combined cycle gas/steam	1	4	12
Steam	63	54	46

SOURCE: *FT* (10 June 1999)

TABLE **6-4 Share of World Electricity Generation, 1995 and 2015 (%)**

Region	1995	2015
North America	31	23
Asia	24	37
W. Europe	19	16
E. Europe and CIS	12	9
Latin America	6	9
Middle East	4	3
Africa	3	3

SOURCE: *FT* (20 May 1996)

The shift in the regional pattern of electricity production is likely to be large, with the share of Asia likely to rise from around 24 per cent in 1995 to a predicted 37 per cent by 2015 (see Table 6-4). Of this total increase in demand, around 50 per cent is expected to come from Asia, around 20 per cent from Europe and the CIS, and around 25 per cent from the Americas.[4] There are strong prospects for the power equipment makers in Latin America. Over the next few years electricity demand is predicted to grow at around 5–7 per cent per annum compared with 1–2 per cent in Europe and North America (*FT*, 10 June 1999). The leading power equipment companies have been forced to become truly global in order to compete. For example, in 1996, 70 per cent of the total value of orders to Siemens' power equipment business came from outside Germany (*FT*, 17 November 1997).[5] Only two-fifths of ABB–Alstom's sales are in Europe. The Americas account for 27 per cent, the Far East and Middle East account for 33 per cent (*FT*, 24 March 1999).

CONCENTRATION OF PRODUCERS

The Epoch of National Champions. Up until the 1980s, the power equipment business was regarded as strategically important, and each country had a national champion, assisted through captive sales to the national electricity industry: 'Relations between public sector utilities and the big power engineers were often coy' (*FT*, 17 November 1997). In the 1960s, the British, French, German and Italian generating authorities bought most of their generating equipment from their national manufacturers (Pratten, 1971: 202). Utilities 'routinely passed on cost increases to customers in the form of higher prices' (*FT*, 19 June 1997).

The First Round of Consolidation. The industry changed rapidly in the epoch of globalization. Electricity generation has been privatized extensively. The privatized electricity companies were much more price-aware than the old state-owned electricity utilities. This radically altered the nature of the market for power equipment, making it far more competitive. Government support for 'national champions' declined, though it remained strong in the nuclear side of the business.[6] Privatization of electricity generation and distribution did not just affect the advanced economies. A combination of privatization of existing facilities and a change in attitude towards establishing new privately-owned power plants, led to a substantial shift in the ownership structure of power generation across the developing world towards the private sector.

As industrialization took off in East Asia, demand for power stations surged, and the prospects for global demand were radically altered. Competition among the main manufacturers for these fast-growing and increasingly open markets intensified. This intensification of competitive pressure stimulated the search for cost-cutting through global economies of scale in manufacturing, research, marketing and after-sales service. As in every sector, increasingly active institutional investors sharply raised the pressure to increase returns from the power equipment business. These developments set the scene for a radical change in the industry's institutional structure after the mid-1980s.

The subsequent decade saw a wave of mergers in the power equipment industry. In 1987 Asea (Sweden) and Brown Boveri (Switzerland) merged to form ABB. In 1989 GEC (UK) and Alcatel (France) combined their energy and transport interests to form GEC–Alsthom. This entity was floated on the stock market in 1998 (renamed Alstom), with GEC and Alcatel together retaining around 42–48 per cent of the total shares (*FT*, 16 April 1998). In addition, Westinghouse and Mitsubishi Heavy Industries arranged a technology and marketing agreement in the supply of steam turbines, and they were joined by Fiat in the supply of gas turbines. By 1995 there were just five main integrated producers of power plants world-wide, General Electric, ABB, Westinghouse, GEC–Alsthom, and Siemens (Table 6-5).

It was widely thought that the already small number of firms would grow even smaller. A 1996 *Financial Times* report on the industry concluded: 'The all-round skills needed to compete simultaneously in building, alliance making, financial investment and servicing gives enormous advantage to the big integrated companies. *The time when this battle of the giants is resolved is fast approaching*' (*FT*, 3 June 1996, emphasis added). In 1996 a leading official of GEC–Alsthom commented : 'The number of players is already low, so future regroupings will be harder to do than before, But *in five years, the industry will be quite different*'

TABLE 6-5 **Global Power Equipment Market Share, 1993–8 (Order Volume, Average) (%)**

Company	Steam turbine	Gas-fired	Hydro-electric	Total (1996)	Total (1998)
General Electric	13	34	12	25	39
Siemens/Westinghouse	14	32	10	18	25
ABB/Alstom	14	21	26	23	—
Mitsubishi	—	—	—	10	—
Others	59	13	52	24	—
Total	100	100	100	100	—
% of world orders	42	45	13	100	—

SOURCE: *FT* (9 June 1998, 24 March 1999)

(quoted in *FT*, 3 June 1996, emphasis added). A sign of the intensity of competition among the main producers was Rolls-Royce's decision in July 1996 to sell its steam turbine business (see above). As one commentator put it: 'If Rolls-Royce can't make a go of it, who can?' (quoted in *FT*, 20 July 1996).[7]

In the mid-1990s there were strong pressures for further consolidation in the industry. There was considerable excess capacity in gas turbine production. Moreover, prices had fallen by no less than 50 per cent from 1992 to 1996, driven by severe competition in emerging markets and privatization in the developed economies (*FT*, 19 June 1997). Leading suppliers were often forced to make a loss on original equipment supply, in the hope of generating profits from servicing the equipment (*FT*, 19 June 1997). Independent power producers (IPPs) accounted for around 30 per cent of the market for new power stations in 1995 compared to just 5 per cent in the mid-1980s (*FT*, 26 June 1996). These developments placed severe pressure on profit margins.

Power equipment companies made great efforts to cut costs in response to these pressures. For example, in the 1990s, Siemens reduced employment in the power equipment sector by almost 6000, from 25000 to 19500 (*FT*, 19 June 1997). Leading companies were fast developing outsourcing components supply, establishing global networks of low-cost suppliers, increasingly located in developing countries, Eastern Europe and the former Soviet Union (*FT*, 19 June 1997). A major new skill required of globally competitive firms in the sector has become quality control over globally dispersed suppliers: 'Maintaining quality is not easy with global sourcing', says Adolf Huttl, President of Siemens power equipment division (quoted in *FT*, 19 June 1997). Despite these efforts, parts of the industry became seriously loss-making. For example, in 1995 and 1996 Westinghouse's power equipment branch made losses of $215 million and $183 million respectively (*FT*, 17 November 1998).

The Second Round of Consolidation. In 1997, the predicted further round of consolidation began with the take-over of Westinghouse's non-nuclear power equipment business by Siemens, paying $1.5 billion to acquire the business (*FT*, 10 June 1999). This move was regarded as 'a big step forward in the consolidation of the power equipment business' (*FT*, 17 November 1997). Even more than the Rolls-Royce decision to leave the large power equipment sector, this decision demonstrated the severity of global oligopolistic competition in this sector. The take-over of Westinghouse is of special significance as it is part of the rapidly developing group of powerful global players that are truly transatlantic corporations in 'strategic industries', including aerospace, pharmaceuticals, and automobiles. The take-over was followed by an announcement of a cut of 1800 in the number of employees in Siemens power equipment division and the establishment of a joint purchasing scheme for the merged businesses to further reduce costs. The purchase of Westinghouse enabled Siemens to benefit from the boom in US power equipment orders after 1997, taking 35 per cent of the market, second only to GE, which took a massive 64 per cent of the market (*FT*, 10 June 1999). Following the take-over, Siemens had four main plants, two in the USA and two in Europe, as well as plants in China (see below) and India. Siemens' restructuring programme following the take-over was planned to result in a reduction of $600 million in annual operating costs within a few years.

Only a few months after the take-over of Westinghouse's power equipment division by Siemens, ABB and GEC–Alsthom announced that they were merging their power generation businesses (*FT*, 24 March 1999). This created a company with annual sales of $11 billion. It was referred to by its new chief executive, Pierre Bilger, as a 'European champion in power engineering' (see, for example *FT*, 24 March 1999). As befits a 'European' company without a national affiliation, the new company's headquarters is in Brussels and it reports in euros. The choice of Brussels was in order to avoid the accusation that the new company was either a Franco–British or Swiss–Swedish take-over. The ownership is carefully structured in order to be a 50/50 joint venture. It employs 54 000 people, around one-third of them working outside Europe. It will spend $700 million per year on R & D. The new company will be the world leader in hydroelectric power stations, with around one-quarter of total world orders, and will be equal first place in steam-turbine power stations, with around 14 per cent of world orders. It has around one-fifth of world orders in gas-fired power stations. It is especially strong in the technologies of fluidized-bed combustion, which enable coal to be used in a way that minimizes pollution. The merger was forecast to produce cost savings of $450 million within three years, owing to 'improvements in efficiency and productivity, and economies of scale'.

GE was a major beneficiary of the deal. In 1990 GE had licensed its technology for the sale of gas turbines to Alsthom in order to gain some revenue from the then highly protected continental European market. As part of the ABB–Alsthom merger, GE was entitled to purchase Alsthom's heavy-duty gas turbine operations for $910 million, based around the technologies involved in the licensing deal. This added 2500 employees to GE's payroll, mainly in Europe, and $818 million-worth of sales of gas-fired equipment, also mainly in Europe. At a stroke this increased GE's share of the European gas-driven market from 9 per cent to around 24 per cent, while its share of the global gas-driven market increased from 30 per cent to 40 per cent (*FT*, 24 March 1999). In North America GE had 64 per cent of the market for gas-driven power stations (*FT*, 10 June 1999), providing it with a massive base for its global sales.

The merger of ABB and Alsthom was the final step in the restructuring of the post-war organization of the world's power equipment industry. The former 'national champions' created to provide national self-sufficiency in this industry that was once thought to have been of crucial national strategic importance, have been swept away to be replaced by large global businesses.

The top three global power equipment companies, Siemens, ABB–Alsthom, and GE, now account for around two-thirds of total global output (Table 6-5). The top four companies (including Mitsubishi Heavy Industries), account for 76 per cent of the 'new build' market for fossil and nuclear-fuelled power station equipment, calculated according to energy output (Table 6-5). The gas-fired power station market is of crucial importance, since it is widely regarded as more environmentally friendly in terms of greenhouse gases than is steam-powered, which principally means coal-driven. The share of the top three companies in this market now amounts to almost ninety per cent of total world orders. These three firms are likely to be major beneficiaries of any substantial switch by developing countries away from coal towards gas-fired electricity generation. In 1990, just 17 per cent of the world's electricity was generated by gas-driven systems, compared with 48 per cent from other fossil fuels. By 1998, 45 per cent of world orders for new power equipment were for gas-powered systems (*FT*, 24 March 1999).

The world's leading power equipment companies were now massively more powerful than the old national champions of the post-war world. The three giants were poised to dominate the world's power station construction in the twenty-first century. They were now far ahead of any developing country's power equipment producers in terms of their size, R & D spending, technical capabilities to provide systems that generate electricity cleanly and safely, business systems skills, capability to organize the 'external firm' of suppliers on a global basis, to earn high quality revenue over a long period from maintenance services, and ability to participate in the financing of power station construction.

THE POWER GENERATING EQUIPMENT
INDUSTRY IN CHINA

CHINA'S ENERGY NEEDS

From 1980 to the mid-1990s, China's economy grew faster than that of any other country, with an average annual growth rate of GDP of well over 10 per cent per annum (World Bank, 1996: 208–9). In order to support such high-speed growth, China needed to generate large amounts of investment resources to support the growth of its energy supply. From 1980 to 1995 China's total output of primary

TABLE 6-6 Growth of China's Energy Output and
National Product, 1980 and 1990 (Index, 1995)

Item	1980 = 100	1990 = 100
GNP*	422	173
Output of primary energy	202	124
Output of electric power	335	162
Energy elasticity**	0.48	0.72
Electricity elasticity§	0.79	0.94

SOURCE: SSB, ZTN (1997: 42, 216–19)

NOTES: * At constant prices
     ** Growth of energy relative to growth of GNP
     § Growth of electricity relative to GNP

energy more than doubled (Table 6-6). Its output of electricity rose even faster, more than tripling over the same period. Despite rapid output growth, China's overall primary energy supply lagged far behind growth of national product, with a total primary energy elasticity of just 0.48 (energy growth relative to GNP growth), and even electricity lagged significantly behind, with an elasticity of 0.79 (Table 6-6). Even in the 1990s, as the relative growth of energy and electricity accelerated, their growth still fell short of the growth of national product. The Ministry of Electric Power estimated that in 1995–6 around 15–20 per cent of demand for electricity could not be satisfied (*FT*, 23 July 1996).

China under Maoist planning was one of the most inefficient countries in the amount of energy used to produce each unit of national product.[8] Although there are large opportunities to raise energy efficiency, these are exhaustible. In the long run it will be necessary for China to increase its output of commercial energy closer to that of output growth, in order to avoid serious barriers to growth from inadequate energy supply (Robinson, 1990). It is rare for economies to be able to sustain long run growth unless energy supplies grow more or less in proportion with growth of national product, that is with an energy elasticity of 1.0 (Robinson, 1990: 243).

Even if China's energy elasticity gives cause for concern, it remains the case that China's energy output is among the fastest growing in the world. Moreover, it is imperative that China find a way to supply the country's energy needs. The limited possibilities for meeting these through economies in energy use mean that in the future it is likely that energy output will grow even faster than in the past, through one means or another. China still has a low level of energy consumption *per capita* (Table 6-7). Despite this, China's huge size means that its total energy consumption already dwarfs that of any other developing country. Indeed, standing at 770 million tons of oil equivalent in 1994, it is substantially greater than the combined energy consumption of India, Brazil, Mexico, Korea and Indonesia, which in 1994 was 680 million tons in the latter countries combined.[9]

TABLE **6-7** *Per capita* **Energy Use (kg of Oil Equivalent), 1994**

Low-income countries	
(excluding India and China)	174
India	243
Indonesia	393
Egypt	608
China	647
Middle-income countries within which:	1593
Mexico	1577
Brazil	691
High-income countries	5168

SOURCE: World Bank (1996: 202–3)

TABLE **6-8 Output of Electricity, Coal and Oil in China and in the World, 1980 and 1998 (million tons)**

	1980	1998	Index, 1995 (1980 = 100)
Electricity (billion kwh)			
China	310	1 136	366
World	8004	13 736	172
China as % of World	3.7	8.3	—
Coal			
China	620	1373	221
World	3736	4764	128
China as % of World	16.6	28.8	—
Crude oil			
China	106	161	152
World	2979	3113	104
China as % of World	3.6	5.2	—

SOURCES: SSB, SYC (1981: 498); SSB, ZTN (1999: 897)

China's demand for energy rose from just 23 per cent of that of the US in 1980, to 37 per cent in 1994 (World Bank, 1996: 202–3), and it is predicted to rise to around 70 per cent by the year 2015 (*FT*, 20 May 1996). The potential significance of the China market is especially great because of the much slower growth rates in energy demand in the advanced economies: while China's electricity output grew by 209 per cent from 1980 to 1994, energy use in the High-income Economies grew by just 17 per cent over the same period (World Bank, 1996: 202–3. China rose from the world's sixth largest electricity producer in 1980 to second largest in 1995, more than doubling its share of world electricity output (Table 6-8).

TABLE 6-9 China's Electricity Industry: Increase in Installed Capacity, Electricity Output and Output of Power Generating Equipment, 1980–2010

Year	Installed capacity (gigawatts)	(Yr/yr %)	Electricity generation (TWh)	(Yr/yr %)	Output of power equipment (gigawatts)	(Yr/yr %)
1980	65.87	—	301	—	4.19	—
1981	69.13	4.95	309	2.89	1.39	−66.8
1982	72.36	4.67	328	5.95	1.65	18.7
1983	76.45	5.65	351	7.23	2.74	66.1
1984	80.12	4.80	377	7.29	4.67	70.4
1985	87.05	8.66	411	8.94	5.63	20.6
1986	93.82	7.77	450	9.47	7.22	28.2
1987	102.90	9.68	497	10.61	9.41	30.3
1988	115.50	12.25	545	9.61	11.09	17.9
1989	126.64	9.65	585	7.26	11.74	5.9
1990	137.89	8.88	621	6.26	12.25	4.3
1991	151.47	9.85	678	9.05	11.64	−5.0
1992	166.53	9.94	754	11.32	12.97	16.9
1993	182.91	9.83	836	10.90	14.72	13.5
1994	199.90	9.29	928	10.94	16.74	13.7
1995	217.22	8.67	1 007	8.51	16.68	−0.4
1996	236.54	8.89	1 079	7.15	16.07	−3.7
1997	250.00	5.69	1 135P	5.19	16.87	5.0
2000E	300.00	—	1 400	—	—	—
2010E	500.00	—	2 500	—	—	—

SOURCES: SSB, SYC (1981: 237); SSB, ZTN (1984: 236, 1986: 302, 1987: 287, 1989: 305, 1991: 430, 1993: 452, 1995: 417, 1997: 452); *Beijing Review* (11 May 1998); Kao (1998)

NOTE: 1 gigawatt = 1000 MW

CHINA'S POWER EQUIPMENT NEEDS

China's role in the future of this industry at a global level is likely to be very large. The Chinese State Planning Commission forecast that China would require an average annual increase of around 9 per cent in electricity generation during the Ninth Five Year Plan (1996–2000). It estimated that this would require around 15 000 to 17 000 MW of additional installed generating capacity per annum (Warburg, 1994: 44), reaching a total of around 300 000 MW by the year 2000, from the present figure of around 200 000 MW (Kao, 1998 and Table 6-9). By 2010 the figure is estimated to rise to around 500 000–550 000 MW (Kao, 1998). Already, China is the world's biggest single market for power generating equipment (*FT*, 16 May 1995). It is anticipated that China will account for about one-half of Asia's expected demand for power generating plant in the next ten years, and about one-quarter of the world's total (*FT*, 26 June 1996). Growth in East Asia in general and in China in particular, is especially important for the world's power generating equipment industry because of the slow growth, or even stagnation, in the demand for power generating equipment in the advanced economies.

A central issue for the world's power equipment manufacturers and for China's power equipment manufacturers, is: who will benefit from China's huge increase in demand for power equipment? Up to the present, the bulk of power equipment orders has been supplied by domestic manufacturers. However, the slowdown in the rate of addition to installed electricity generation capacity after the mid-1990s produced stagnation in the demand for power equipment. At the heart of the slowdown was a decline in the overall rate of economic growth. However, Chinese indigenous manufacturers began to have deep concerns for their market prospects for other reasons as well. These included the rapid change in the nature of finance for power projects, the changing institutional structure of the power generation industry, with an increasing role for multinational finance, the high technical demands for the Three Gorges power equipment and the increasing role being played by multinational power equipment companies within the Chinese power equipment industry through joint ventures. These factors meant that the competitive environment faced by a firm such as Harbin Power Equipment Company (HPEC) was altering sharply.

REGULATING CHINA'S POWER INDUSTRY

Power Generation and Distribution. Up until the early 1990s, power generation and transmission was controlled by the Ministry of Machine Building Industries (MMB). In 1993 the Chinese government set up the Ministry of Electric Power (MOEP) as a separate entity from the MMB. It quickly became obvious that in the transition to the market economy, the interests of these two bodies were in conflict. The MMB wanted to build a powerful Chinese power equipment industry. The MOEP wanted to expand rapidly China's ability to provide cheap electricity for Chinese industry and consumers. The MOEP's function was to set energy policy, prepare industry regulation, plan and co-ordinate the industry's development, and review proposals for new power plants. The whole development of the industry was 'overseen' by the State Planning Commission, whose approval was required for any substantial action within the sector, including construction and finance of power stations.

In 1997–8 the Chinese government radically reorganized the institutional structure of the Chinese power generation industry (Kao, 1998) (Figure 6-1). In line with its policy of separating regulatory from commercial functions in 1997 it set up a new body, the State Power Corporation (SP). This formally assumed ownership of all the power generation assets over around 100 MW (around 80 per cent of China's total power supply) that were owned by the Chinese state.[10] The functions of the SP are to 'plan', 'undertake power station construction', 'dispatch electricity', and 'manage power generation and distribution'. Several wholly-owned regional power groups operate as subsidiaries under it, and they in turn operate the five major regional grids. The internationally listed power generation companies are all subsidiaries of the SP. China Huaneng Group and the growing

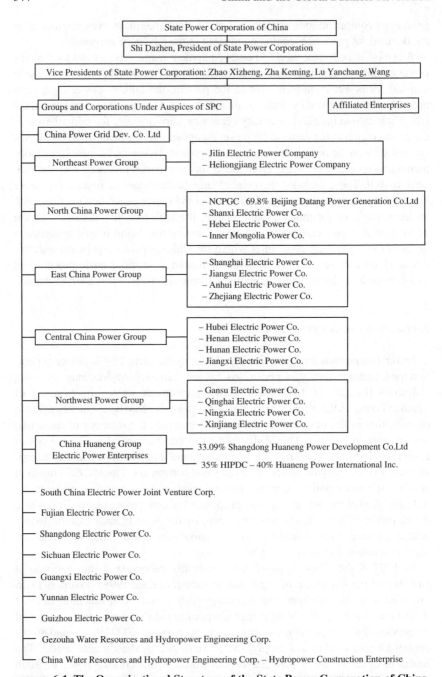

FIGURE 6-1 **The Organizational Structure of the State Power Corporation of China**

SOURCES: Ministry of Electric Power, *Annual Report, 1997*; Morgan Stanley Dean Witter Research

number of independent provincial power companies are also subsidiaries of the SP. It has been argued by some commentators that the creation of the SP was simply the first step in the reforms necessary for the Chinese power industry. They suggest that a further 'separation' is necessary to divorce the functions of offtake and transmission from that of generation, 'in order to introduce fair competition in generation and to eliminate the present unconstrained vertical rivalry within the power sector' (Andrews-Speed and Dow, 1999).

In early 1998, the government drastically reorganized the State Planning Commission and abolished the MOEP. The regulatory functions of these two bodies were assumed by the State Economics and Trade Commission (ETC). A transition period will be required 'before a clear and complete regulatory framework emerges' (Kao, 1998). However, certain aspects of the future shape of the industry were becoming clearer. The central authorities are still intended to undertake general planning and maintain administrative controls over the power generation and transmission industry, including price determination.

The construction and finance of large power stations still requires complex government approval procedures. After the reforms, it appears that the key decision-making body for approval of new power stations will become the ETC. Moreover, as is the case in almost all other countries, the Chinese government exercises tight control over the environment in which power plants operates. These involve virtually all aspects of their operation, including the amount and timing of the plants' scheduled output, setting and adjusting tariffs, performance of scheduled overhaul and maintenance procedures and compliance with grid control procedures.

The SP has been turned into a holding company (*konggu gongsi*) whose subordinate companies operate under a variety of different ownership regimes. These vary from 100 per cent owned by the SP, to minority ownership in a multi-ownership power station, including both domestic and foreign investors, as well as BOT power plants which will revert to ownership and operation by the SP after the specified period of time. Although it owns almost the entire power generation and transmission system for China's electricity, the SP sits at the apex of an immensely complex multi-level structure, with a great deal of operational autonomy at lower levels. China's state power sector has been described as a 'sprawling, heterogeneous and multi-layered organization, with a complex web of relationships between the players' (Andrews-Speed and Dow, 1999).

The SP controls the operation of the electricity grid, which is organized into several regional (Northeast China, Northwest China, Central China, East China and South China) and provincial grids (Shandong, Fujian, Hainan, Sichuan, Tibet and Xinjiang). The goal is to gradually integrate the grid system, with three large grids being established by 2010 and a fully integrated national grid established by 2020 (*CDBW*, 5 October 1997). Gradual unification of the national grid helps to create a unified national market for electricity. The Electric Power Law (1996) aimed to establish a 'unified network, unified quality and unified price' (*tongwang, tongzhi, tongjia*) for electricity.

Government ownership and operation of the electricity grid provides an important mechanism for overall regulation of the industry, since access to the grid is a critical mechanism for influencing decisions taken by the power generators. Foreign investment is explicitly excluded from participation in the construction and management of the electricity network, reflecting the importance that government planners assign to the development of the power sector.

China's electricity tariff structure under the reforming economy was extremely complex. There developed considerable variations in tariffs charged due to a variety of ownership forms, funding sources and considerable *de facto* decentralization of operation, despite formal central control over prices. By 1994, the national average tariff was 245 yuan (around $30) per MWh, which was 'rock-bottom' in international terms (BZW, 1996: 31). However, the tariff varied from a low of 164 yuan in Gansu Province to a high of 463 yuan in Hainan Province (BZW, 1996: 28). The 1996 Electricity Law was intended to centralize control over on-grid electricity tariffs. Electricity prices increased fourfold from the late 1970s to the mid-1990s (BZW, 1996: 33). The Chinese government's long-term goal is to increase prices towards international levels in order to encourage investment in power generation.

During the reform years, there occurred a rapid growth of small local power stations. By 1996, the share of power stations with less than 100 MW stood at 76 million MW, amounting to 32 per cent of the country's total installed capacity. These tended to be older designs, which failed to benefit from more fuel-efficient technologies. A key task for the Ministry of Power (subsequently the SP) was to close down less efficient small plants. (*China: Economic Digest*, Spring, 1998: 14).

Power Equipment. The main power equipment makers in China, Harbin, Dongfang, and Shanghai, were all 100 per cent state owned until the mid-1990s. They were under the jurisdiction of the MMB, which was charged with supporting the growth and modernization of this critical sector. It was also responsible for automobiles, agricultural machinery, basic components, and large and medium-sized machinery (including heavy electrical equipment).

The functions of the MMB changed substantially as the market economy developed. In 1985, under the centrally administered economy, the MMB had 800 employees overall. In the late 1970s it had almost 300 in the electrical machinery branch alone. As the direct control functions atrophied, so the numbers declined. By 1997, the MMB had fallen to around 270 employees altogether. By 1997, the whole 'major equipment bureau', including heavy electrical equipment, heavy petrochemical equipment, heavy mining equipment and the automatic control division, had just 23 employees. The heavy electrical equipment office had just four employees. There was a serious problem with loss of skilled personnel from the MMB as its planning function changed and the Ministry was downgraded in size and importance. In the view of one senior official at the MMB, by 1997 it had 'lost control of the machinery industry'. In 1998 as part of the huge shake-up in the central administration of the Chinese government, the MMB was abolished, and reorganized into the State Administration of Machine-Building Industry. It was placed under the 'management' of the State Economic and Trade Commission (*Beijing Review*, 27 April 1998). The goal of the reforms was to 'give power back to the enterprises' and shift government functions towards macro-control and overall policy guidance, away from detailed intervention in enterprise activities.

Up until the 1990s, the MMB was able to affect directly the choice of equipment adopted by domestic power generators. However, in the 1990s this situation changed. Increasingly strong voices in the central government argued that the 'consumer should decide' the choice of machinery, not the central planners. Industrial policy was fighting against the short-term interest of increasingly commercialized institutions, including those of power generators. The MOEP and its subordinates became increasingly concerned to obtain the cheapest equipment, irrespective of its national origin. More and more finance for power plants came from international sources (see below). Such an 'investment salad' (*pingpang touzi*) increased the incentive to import equipment, since finance often was provided by or through the multinational power equipment companies, precisely in order to promote sales of their products. Moreover, the local governments, often themselves investors in the power plants, were keen to ensure that their own region obtained equipment that could provide the cheapest and most reliable sources of electricity.

The MMB and its successor body, needed increasingly to rely on indirect and more complex means to stimulate the growth and modernization of the power equipment industry. The Chinese government's continuing wish to support the growth of domestic power equipment makers is reflected in the fact that foreign investment in this sector is subject to 'restrictions'. It requires government approval, and can only be undertaken with a Chinese manufacturer as a joint venture. If the foreign and the domestic manufacturer have the same terms and conditions when tendering for a power project, preference must be given to the domestic manufacturer (Lu Yansun, 1997: 8).

In the mid-1990s imports of units of 300 MW and below were prohibited, and in 1998 it was announced that thermal power plants of 600 MW or less could no longer be imported (*Business Weekly*, 31 May 1998). If a foreign power equipment manufacturer contracts for a foreign-financed power project, then a minimum of 30 per cent of the value of the project must be subcontracted to a domestic manufacturer. When importing large power units (600 MW and above) that cannot be supplied from domestic sources, the amount of domestic subcontracting and technology transfer should be clearly specified. Power plants constructed with foreign capital, either jointly or wholly foreign operated, should be 'encouraged to adopt domestically-manufactured equipment' (Lu Yansun, 1997: 8).

This amounted to a powerful set of industrial policies to support the growth of an indigenous power equipment manufacturer. Moreover, we shall see in subsequent sections of this paper the different ways in which the Chinese government bargained with the multinationals to transfer technology to indigenous firms.

Up until 1987 the prices of power plant equipment were controlled by the State Price Control Bureau, with a fixed price for each type of equipment. Price control was relaxed gradually after 1987. By 1990 the prices of power plant equipment had been 'substantially deregulated'. The price of power plant equipment was now 'freely negotiable between the equipment manufacturers and their customers' (Warburg, 1994: 75).

In the early 1990s the Chinese power equipment industry still enjoyed substantial protection. Tariffs were lower than for most products, but still were significant. In 1994 tariffs on imported power generating equipment stood at 6–35 per cent for boilers and turbines, and 15–45 per cent for generators. By 1997, China's tariffs on imported power equipment had fallen even further, and were now close to WTO levels. In the mid-1990s, even after the reduction in tariffs, domestic power equipment still was around 50–60 per cent of the price of international equipment of equivalent installed capacity. Some senior Chinese officials believe that as the power generation industry becomes more commercialized, so the incentive to buy domestic equipment on price grounds will increase. One important advantage of a 'level playing field' in international trade for power equipment is that it would give Chinese power equipment manufacturers access to cheaper imports of raw material and machinery, including machine tools and steel, and might make it easier for them to penetrate many foreign markets.

FINANCING CHINA'S POWER INDUSTRY

Policy Shifts. Up until the early 1990s, as had been the case in most Western countries until the late 1980s, power plant construction was entirely funded by the government. The share of government revenue in China's national product fell from 34.4 per cent of GNP in 1978 to just 14.1 per cent in 1993 (World Bank, 1995: 197). Government expenditure on capital construction fell from 37 per cent of national product in 1978 to 17 per cent in 1993 (World Bank, 1995: 199). The government increasingly focused its expenditure on key large-scale infrastructure investments such as transport and power, leaving enterprises to finance their investment mainly from retained profits and bank loans. However, even with this narrowing of focus, the government found it hard to generate sufficient revenue to fund outlays on infrastructure at the necessary level. By the early 1990s in many areas of China, industries were forced to limit operations to certain hours of the day, or to shut down for part of the week. The MOEP estimated that capacity was 15–20 per cent below demand (CSFB, 1994: 47). Great pressure came from local authorities at provincial, municipality and lower levels for a way to be found to meet the pressing energy needs. From the late 1980s joint investment by central authorities, local authorities and enterprises themselves began to be put into place.

In the early 1990s, the government recognized that the long-term solution to its power plant needs necessitated a radical re-think of its approach. China had one of the world's highest saving rates, but savings were not finding their way into financing power plant construction in sufficient amounts. The Chinese government was forced to consider a number of paths to resolving its desperate need for funds for the energy sector, using diverse sources of domestic capital, and actively pursuing international investment. It attempted to raise foreign funds through direct investment, international loans, flotation on foreign stock markets, and, finally,

'Build–Operate–Transfer' (BOT) arrangements. These changes in power station funding deeply affected the nature of demand for domestic power equipment.

Between 1979 and 1996 China used a total of $13 billion worth of foreign capital in constructing 87 power projects, amounting to 10 per cent of the total investment in the sector (*FT*, 23 September 1997). During the Ninth Five Year Plan (1996–2000) it is estimated that the power industry needs around $83 billion to meet the country's power generation needs. The government hoped that 20 per cent of this would come from overseas, 40 per cent from the central government and the rest from regional sources (*CDBW*, 22 June 1997).[11] It has been estimated that by the late 1990s, less than 5 per cent of funding for power sector investment came from the central government via direct grants. Instead, it is estimated that around one-half came from 'soft loans' from state banks, 20 per cent from provincial and local governments and 17 per cent from foreign institutions and companies (Andrews-Speed and Dow, 1999).

The Battle over the Rate of Return. In the mid-1990s a complex 'game' was played between the Chinese government and potential international investors in power generation. The key factors governing the rate of return are the tariff for the electricity, the price and security of supply of the inputs (mainly coal) and the off-take agreement with the grid system. The Chinese government still is deeply wary about committing itself to potentially inflationary increases in the electricity tariff.[12] Nor is it in the position easily to give cast-iron guarantees of input supplies. For example, part of the coal for coal-fired stations has to be purchased from small coal mines at unpredictable market prices.[13] Moreover, the Chinese government still seems to be unhappy about allowing foreign investors to make a 'high' rate of return from such a basic activity as power generation. Consequently, in the late 1990s there was still great uncertainty among foreign investors about the rate of return that would be allowed to them in the sector over the long run.[14] However, at least BOT agreements, once signed, provided reasonable security in respect to price for power producers, whereas other entities faced the prospect of unpredictable state intervention to influence electricity prices.

Flotation. By the year 2000, four Chinese power companies had been listed on international markets: Shandong Huaneng Power, Huaneng Power International, Beijing Datang and Shandong International Power Development Company. However, this approach could only provide part of the funds needed. For example, the Datang offering was for around $300–350 million. In the late 1970s, construction of a single large power plant of 2000 MW was estimated to cost around $2 billion[15] (*FT*, 23 August 1996). Twenty power plants had listed on the domestic stock market by late 1997, and it was planned that more would follow (*FT*, 23 September 1997).

New Investment Institutions. A major new vehicle, the state-owned Huaneng (China Power) Power Corporation, for financing power station construction and operation was set up as early as 1985 (CSFB, 1994: 19–20). It became a subsidiary of MOEP. Huaneng Power was entrusted with the task of converting existing oil-fired power stations to coal-fired plants, constructing new coal-fired power stations, operating and managing thermal power generating plants, and developing and importing power generating technology. In 1988 it joined an even larger organization, China Huaneng Group, which contained twelve main subsidiaries and had assets worth 45 billion yuan in 1993. The Huaneng Group was one of the 55 large scale enterprise groups designated by the government to play a leading role in their respective industries. These enterprises were given enhanced autonomy compared to other state-owned enterprises. In 1993 Huaneng Power had a total of 10 billion yuan in assets and participated in 32 power plant projects, which would have a total installed capacity of over 11 000 MW when completed, which was greater than the capacity of a single large province, such as Shandong or Guangdong (Peregrine, 1993a: 104). In 1994 the Huaneng Power Corporation set up two new subsidiary companies, Huaneng Power International (HPI) and Shandong Huaneng Power (SHP) for flotation internationally (see above).

The China Yangtze Three Gorges Project Corporation (CYTGPC) is another important new entity in fund-raising for power generation. Under the overall auspices of the MOEP (latterly the SP) it was given considerable operational autonomy. It is the 'proprietor' of the Project (*CDBW*, 2 November 1997), and charged with raising the funds necessary to finance the Project. A central long-term source of revenue will be the fees charged by the Gezhouba hydro power plant itself. Five wholly-owned subsidiaries are under its control. Of these, two are likely to be listed as A shares (Gezhouba Hydropower Plant, and China Yangtze Three Gorges Project Development Corporation Industrial Company). CYTGPC formed the Three Gorges Finance Company, of which it has 49 per cent ownership and Gezhouba Hydropower Plant Company has 45 per cent.[16] CYTGPC itself issued a corporate bond. However, the Three Gorges Finance Company is intended to be the vehicle for the issuance of several rounds of bonds as well as raising finance through a variety of other means, including domestic and foreign commercial loans.

Local Finance. A wide variety of local government institutions participates in financing and running power stations. There is intense interest by local authorities in raising funds to solve their pressing power supply problems, which are a severe brake on local economic growth. For example, in Shandong Province, in the case of Shandong Huaneng Power which was floated in New York in 1994, Huaneng Power owned 31.8 per cent of the share value, Shandong ITIC (International Trust and Investment Corporation) owned 19.1 per cent, Shandong Power Company, the largest provincial power company in China, owned 19.1 per cent (CSFB, 1994: 9), and 30 per cent of the value of the company was floated. Shandong ITIC and Shandong Power are both state-owned institutions.[17]

Equity Participation. In the advanced economies, there has been a rapid growth of Independent Power Producers (IPPs) in recent years. By 1996 they accounted for around 30 per cent of the market for new power plants, compared with less than 5 per cent in the mid-1980s (*FT*, 26 June 1996). Despite great caution at first, the Chinese government gradually liberalized the constraints on foreign equity involvement, inching its way towards full IPP ownership and operation of power plants.

The first foreign participants in constructing and running Chinese power stations involved politically trusted Hong Kong based companies. China Light and Power (CLP), Hong Kong's dominant electricity producer, was a path-breaker in this process. CLP has a monopoly on power supply in Kowloon (Hong Kong), and has close contacts with Beijing. CLP holds a 25 per cent stake in the Daya Bay nuclear power plant in southern China, which began operation in 1993. It was part of a consortium (which included Electricité de France) to which the Chinese government in 1996 gave permission to build a 3200 MW plant in Shandong Province. It was announced in late 1996 that it was about to take a 35 per cent stake in a new power plant to be built in Shenzhen Special Economic Zone, with Kanematsu (Japan) as the other major foreign partner (*FT*, 18 September 1996).

Another important overseas investor in the Chinese power plant industry was Hopewell Holdings, a Hong Kong-based company run by Gordon Wu, with a strong infrastructure construction business in southeast Asia. A subsidiary of Hopewell Holdings, Consolidated Electric Power Asia (CEPA), was allowed to construct Shajiao 'B' and 'C' plants in Guangdong Province, with a 50 per cent and 32 per cent shareholding stake respectively (*FT*, 11 October 1996). Around two-thirds of the construction cost of the two plants came from foreign commercial banks. Part of the finance came from equity injection including that from Hopewell. A portion of the finance also came from suppliers' credits from GEC–Alsthom and Combustion Engineering. Hopewell's policy is to purchase the main equipment from international power equipment suppliers rather than from domestic ones, seeking to gain a discount for bulk purchase by equipping all their projected power plants with matching equipment and to thereby benefit also from economies in training and maintenance costs (Peregrine, 1993b: 47). These are large plants, of 700 MW and 1980 MW respectively, the latter being the largest coal-fired power station in Guangdong Province.

Hopewell Holdings became overstretched, with a debt–equity ratio of more than 92 per cent by late 1996 (*FT*, 11 October 1996), and was forced to dispose of majority ownership of the power plant side of its business. This was purchased by the Atlanta-based Southern Company in late 1996 to create 'the world's largest independent power producer' (*FT*, 11 October 1996). A major reason for the purchase was Southern's hope that Hopewell Holdings would provide the vehicle through which Southern could gain access to the huge China market for power station operation.

Hong Kong's Cheung Kong Infrastructure, a subsidiary of Li Ka-shing's Cheung Kong Holdings, was also heavily involved in investing in China's power generation industry. By 1997 it had interests in four operational power stations and two others were under construction, together with a letter of intent for a seventh (Table 6-10).

TABLE **6-10 Cheung Kong Infrastructure's Equity Interest in Mainland Power Stations, 1997**

Power plant projects	Cheung Kong's equity interest (%)
In operation	
Nanhai Jinagnan Power Plant	36
Shantou Chenghai Power Plant	60
Shantou Chaoyuan Power Plant	60
Shantou Tuopu Power Plant	60
Under construction	
Nanhai Power Plant	30
Zhuhai Power Plant	45
Letters of intent	
Dongguan Power Plant	n.a.

SOURCE: *FT* (7 January 1997)

Many of the world's leading IPPs are keen to take equity positions in the Chinese power industry. For example, Britain's National Power has turned itself into one of the top three international power generation companies, with a capacity of 16 GW in the UK and 10 GW overseas. It intends to increase the overseas share to half of group capacity by 2003. China is one of its main growth targets. In 1998 it concluded two deals to take an equity share in Chinese power stations, investing $180 million in a $700 million project to build a 700 MW power station in Hunan Province, and $66 million to take a 49 per cent stake in a 250 MW plant in Fujian Province (*FT*, 21 May 1998). In 1997 Sithe was the world's seventh largest independent power producer. Marubeni, one of Japan's leading trading companies, purchased a 30 per cent share in the company. Their plan is to build 50 power stations around the world between 1997 and 2002, worth over $2 billion (*FT*, 23 January 1997). The first project will be a joint $175 million power station in Hebei Province.

Other Asian institutions are becoming involved in the ownership of Chinese power stations. For example, a Singapore consortium, including the Singapore Government's Investment Corporation, United Engineers and Singapore Power, took a 49 per cent stake in a $560 million power project in Anhui Province, with 49 per cent of the company held by four Chinese companies (*FT*, 24 June 1997).

However, despite these significant developments, still in 1997/8 the extent of foreign equity involvement in the industry was quite limited relative to the huge funding needs of the sector.

Build–Operate–Transfer (BOT). BOT has provided a powerful instrument to advance power station construction in developing countries. However, the Chinese government was very hesitant about using this method. After a lengthy period of uncertainty, finally in late 1996 it appeared that the Chinese government had found a solution that matched its own interests with those of foreign investors. The Laibin B power plant, a 720 MW station in Guangxi Province in south China was widely regarded as a breakthrough in the Chinese government's approach to foreign funding for power plant construction. The total construction costs of the power station are estimated to be $600 million. The plant will be owned 60 per cent by Electricité de France and 40 per cent by GEC–Alsthom, and handed over to the Guangxi government after 15 years of operation. The bulk of the $300 million worth of equipment will be supplied by GEC–Alsthom and other French suppliers. Finance includes $300 million in export credits from Coface, the French government's credit agency, and $160 million in commercial loans (*FT*, 1 September 1997). The agreed rate of return was said to be 'satisfactory'. However, the consortium 'bid low' in order to win the project: 'Paris, it is said, wants to use Laibin as leverage for other such contracts in China and is, therefore, prepared to consider the project a "loss-leader" ' (*FT*, 4 September 1997).

The Chinese government has used Laibin B as the model for further BOT ventures in China's infrastructure sector. It hoped that with the new pattern set by Laibin, around one-fifth of the funds (estimated in total to be around $83 billion) needed for its energy expansion programme in the Ninth Five Year Plan (1996–2000) would come from abroad (*FT*, 16 September 1996). China's second BOT power plant, located in Changsha (Hunan Province) was due to start construction in 1998. The plant was to be transferred back into Chinese ownership after twenty years. However, at the end of 1999, the contract was still under discussion, and far from the start of construction (Andrews-Speed and Dow, 1999).

The Laibin B contract was clear about the commitment of the Guangxi Provincial Government in respect to purchase of electricity, fuel supply and arbitration procedures (*FT*, 4 September 1997). Moreover, the central government refused to guarantee repayments from the project. The regulatory regime in the Chinese power plant sector in 1997–8 was still highly uncertain. 'Dozens' of power projects have been held up due to disagreements over an appropriate return on investment (*FT*, 4 September 1997 and see above). A large fraction of the numerous schemes which have been discussed with potential foreign investors has not come to fruition, mainly due to this uncertainty.

With such a level of uncertainty, and with so many alternative investment opportunities available in other countries, few private investors have committed themselves to these investments.[18] In 1993, CEPA was involved in discussions for the construction of no fewer than twelve power generating units in six provinces, with a total installed capacity of over 7000 MW, and had signed letters of intent to establish power stations with four of these (Guangxi, Henan, Jiangsu, and Shandong) (Peregrine, 1993a: 73). By late 1996 not one of these projects had come to fruition. Even under the most optimistic view of foreign involvement, around 80 per cent of power station funding would still come from domestic sources in the second half of the 1990s.

Export Credit. Export credit is a major mechanism of Western government support for national companies, and failure to provide this for political reasons can be a major handicap to the international competitiveness even of large companies. For example, in the case of the Three Gorges Project, a major competitive advantage for the successful bidders was the fact that they were able to supply $600 million as export credits with 19–21 year terms (*CDBW*, 31 August 1997).

Commercial Loans. We have seen above that foreign equity participation and BOT often are associated with commercial loans from international financial institutions. Ability to obtain associated loans for given power projects is an important instrument of competitive advantage for large globally successful power equipment companies even where there is no international ownership of the power project. For example, in the case of the Three Gorges Project, French, British, German and Canadian financial institutions were able to provide $500 million in commercial loans[19] (*CDBW*, 31 August 1997).

THE POWER EQUIPMENT MARKETS

Thermal Power Stations. China's main primary energy for generating electricity has been coal. The share of China's total energy production supplied by coal rose from over 69 per cent in 1980 to 75 per cent in 1995 (Table 6-11). The share of crude oil fell from 24 per cent to 17 per cent. China's coal reserves are vast, with estimated reserves of over 5000 billion tons and proven reserves of around 1000 billion tons, sufficient to supply China's needs for well over 200 years (Warburg, 1994: 41). Thermal power stations currently supply around 80 per cent of China's electricity output (Table 6-12). The amount of coal used in electricity generation

TABLE **6-11 Share of China's Energy Produced from Different Inputs, 1980 and 1996 (%)**

Energy	1980	1996
Coal	69.4	74.8
Crude oil	23.8	17.1
Natural gas	3.0	1.9
Hydro-power	3.8	6.2

SOURCE: SSB, ZTN (1997: 215)

TABLE **6-12 Structure of Electricity Output in China, 1980–2010 (% of total in brackets)**

Power	1980	1995	2000	2010
Total output (billion kwh) of which:-	301	1008	1400	2500
hydro power (billion kwh)	58 (19.4)	191 (18.9)	213 (15.2)	400 (16)
thermal power (billion kwh)	242 (80.6)	804 (79.8)	1174 (83.9)	2000 (80)
nuclear power (billion kwh)	negl.	13 (1.3)	13 (0.9)	100 (4)

SOURCES: SSB, ZTN (1997: 219); Lu Yansun (1997: 3–4)

NOTE: negl. = Negligible

rose from 127 million tons in 1980 to 444 million tons in 1995, while the amount of oil used fell from 21 million tons to 14 million tons over the same period (SSB, ZTN, 1997: 217–18). The huge growth in future demand for coal-fired thermal power stations provides China's large producers, such as HPEC, with a big opportunity to grow and develop their technology in this area. Many other developing country markets as well as developed countries are also likely to need coal-fired power station technology.

Average coal consumption per unit of power supply fell from 457 kg/kWh in 1979 to 412 kg/kWh in 1995 due mainly to improvements in the technical level of power equipment (Lu Yansun, 1997: 2). An important contribution to the fall in primary energy consumption per unit of electricity was the growth in average size of power plants. In the 1980s, most installed power units were 100–300 MW. In the 1990s these rose to mainly 300–600MW as the standard size of power generation unit (Lu Yansun, 1997: 2). Imported technology was crucial in raising China's capability to manufacture large size thermal units. However, in the late 1990s the level of primary energy efficiency of China's power industry was still far behind the world's most advanced levels (it is around 350 gm/kWh in OECD countries).

A major impact upon the energy efficiency of electricity production in China was the fact that, in order to simulate local incentives to solve power shortages, the central government allowed small power stations (below 25 MW from 1979 to 1993, and below 50 MW after 1993) to be built without needing central government approval. This led to a proliferation of small power plants, a large fraction of which were relatively poor in terms of energy efficiency and relatively heavily polluting.

In order to raise the level of energy efficiency in China's power generation, the Chinese government instructed that between 1998 and 2001 a total installed capacity of 10 860 MW should be closed down. It instructed also that all newly-built thermal power plants should be of 300 MW or larger. It is intended that the level of coal consumption per unit of power should fall to 340 gm/kWh by the year 2000 (Lu Yansun, 1997: 3). Imported thermal power equipment was especially competitive in terms of operating efficiency and reliability in the larger unit sizes (Lu Yansun, 1997: 2). Indeed, by 1996, for units above 300 MW, imported power equipment accounted for over one-half of total electricity generating capacity (Lu Yansun, 1997: 2). It is necessary also for China to develop its ability to manufacture large size units that use the more efficient supercritical technology.

China is one of the world's largest oil producers, rising from eighth largest in 1978 to fifth largest in 1994, a larger producer than Mexico, Venezuela or Nigeria (SSB, ZTN, 1995: 779). However, China's needs are enormous, since the industry must supply the booming needs of the petrochemical industry as well as attempt to satisfy those of the power generation industry. Moreover, the search for oil has been relatively disappointing, with a rise of 'only' 38 per cent in China's oil output from 1980 to 1995 (Table 6-8). China's coal is mostly in the north of the country. The cost of transporting coal to southeastern China is high.

In the southeast coastal provinces, the price of coal is already close to the international price. It is planned that in these regions, China will gradually increase the role of combined cycle technology using gas turbines fed with natural gas and imported oil (Lu Yansun, 1997: 4). Multinational companies are far ahead of China in the technology of combined cycle gas turbines, so it is essential for there to be a large technology transfer if China is to catch-up in this area.

Hydro Power. The massive Three Gorges Project offers a great opportunity for Chinese hydro power plant makers. It is by far the largest hydroelectric scheme in the world, totalling 18 200 MW when completed. The Three Gorges project will run from 1995 into the next century. In total it will require twenty-six 700 MW hydro units, and involve the purchase of equipment with a total value of close to $30 billion. In the mid-1990s there were only two domestic large-scale manufacturers of hydro power plant units, namely Harbin (HPEC) and Dongfang. Harbin had produced more than one-half of all the hydro power equipment installed in China up to the start of the Three Gorges Project. However, in the early 1990s, Harbin and Dongfang were capable only of manufacturing 300 MW hydro units. A major part of the technological upgrading programme at HPEC involves improving the hydro capabilities so that it is able to participate as a sub-contractor in the first phase of the Three Gorges scheme. By 1996 it had upgraded its hydro power capability to units of 550 MW and was attempting to increase this to the 700 MW level needed to supply complete units to the Three Gorges in the second phase of construction (HPEC, 1997: 3).

The first phase of the Three Gorges programme involves 14 units, all of which will need to be imported owing to the inability of domestic producers to manufacture 700 MW units.[20] A condition of awarding the contracts to the successful international consortia is that they each sub-contract substantial amounts of work to China's two hydro power companies, HPEC and Dongfang. Moreover, they must agree to transfer technology to them also. This is thought likely to play an important part in developing their technical level so that they are able to 'play a significant role in supplying the next twelve units' (Qin Zhongyi, CYTGP Vice-President, quoted in *CDBW*, 31 August 1997). This is a good example of the shift in the Chinese government's strategy towards 'trading market for technology'.

The second tranche of 12 units will be 'earmarked for domestic manufacturers'. A condition of success in the bidding for the first round of the project is that the foreign firms provide 'at least 25 per cent local involvement' in the project and transfer technology to Dongfang and HPEC so that they can be in a position to bid for the second tranche of the project (*FT*, 17 February 1997). A necessary condition for submitting a tender is to have already produced and have in commercial operation, 440 MW hydro power units. However, in the second phase of the project, foreign firms may be allowed to submit tenders through their Chinese joint ventures and use the domestic non-hydro power manufacturer as the sub-contractor even though it cannot independently produce a 700 MW hydro unit. HPEC considers it highly likely that Siemens and Voith will take advantage of this possibility to submit tenders and use Shanghai Electrical Company as the main subcontractor and in this way 'go around' HPEC (and Dongfang). The 'domestic' manufacturers in this case will be a sub-branch of a multinational giant.

China's southwest has abundant hydro power potential. In the near future three large hydro plants are planned for the Yangtze, upstream of the Three Gorges. They will produce a total of over 24 million kilowatts of electricity, greater even than the 18 million that the Three Gorges will produce (*CDBW*, 26 October 1997). By 2010, China's installed hydro power generating capacity is predicted to reach 115 GW, accounting for 22.5 per cent of total installed capacity (Lu Yansun, 1997: 4). This will provide a large market for hydro power equipment.

Nuclear Power. Although still in its infancy, nuclear power is set to expand in China, especially in coastal southeastern China, which lacks both coal and hydro resources. China's first two nuclear power plants were built in the 1990s, at Daya Bay (Guangdong Province) and Qinshan (Zhejiang Province). The installed capacity of nuclear power in China is planned to rise to 9000 MW by 2003 (*CDBW*, 7 December 1997). In the early 21st century, China will build six new nuclear power plants (in Shandong, Fujian, Zhejiang, Guangdong, Jiangxi and Hunan provinces). China's total installed capacity of nuclear power equipment is predicted to rise to 20 GW by 2010 (Lu Yansun, 1997: 4). This will make China much the largest market for nuclear power globally, and therefore, of immense significance to nuclear power manufacturers, who face stagnant markets in the advanced economies. Charles Prior, president of Westinghouse's nuclear division, believes that China will order $50–60 billion worth of nuclear reactors over the next two decades (*FT*, 27 October 1997). The competitive struggle among multinationals was made still more intense by the decision of the US government in 1997 to allow the export of nuclear technology to China.

All three of China's leading power equipment companies are competing to supply nuclear power equipment. No producer in China is able to produce a nuclear core, and China's companies still lag behind in some other aspects of nuclear technology. No domestic supplier was able to produce the 900 MW thermal generator required for the Daya Bay nuclear power station. However, domestic companies did play an important role in China's second nuclear power plant at Qinshan, which was begun in 1994, with substantial involvement of GE (Canada) (*CDBW*, 13 January 1997). Shanghai Electric supplied a 300 MW unit for the first phase of the project, and HPEC was selected as the supplier for the two 650 MW thermal power units for the second phase.

China is still unable to manufacture larger size nuclear power plant units (Lu Yansun, 1997: 6). However, it has chosen to take 1000 MW class power stations as its standard for the future (Lu Yansun, 1997: 6), which means that international technology will continue to be important for the industry's development within China. Among the eight nuclear power units to be constructed in the Ninth Five Year Plan (1996–2000), six will be imported, from Canada,[21] France[22] and the former USSR[23] (*China: Economic Digest*, Summer 1997: 16).

A key consideration in China's selection of partners for its nuclear expansion is their willingness to assist China 'realise localization of nuclear power equipment manufacturing, and self-reliance in designing, operating and managing nuclear power plants' (*China: Economic Digest*, Summer 1997: 16).[24] China's goal is to be able to provide the main components for a 600 MW nuclear power plant by the year 2000 (*China: Economic Digest*, Autumn 1996: 17).

With the intensification of competition due to the arrival of US nuclear manufacturers on the scene, the Chinese government is in an even stronger position to require successful international suppliers to transfer technology to China's power equipment companies. Facing aggressive newcomers, Framatome (France's supplier to the Daya Bay plant) may have to make some changes to its strategy. It is thought likely that it will be forced 'to introduce more advanced technology and do more in China in training local engineers' (*CDBW*, 29 March 1998). US companies are 'vying with each other in promising to transfer their most advanced technology and help China develop its nuclear power sector' (*CDBW*, 29 March 1997). Howard Brusch, vice-president of Westinghouse's science and technology department, has promised to 'help China grow into an exporter of nuclear power' (quoted in *CDBW*, 29 March 1998). Westinghouse estimates that China is currently able to supply only around 40 per cent of the engineering and equipment for a nuclear plant. Michael Jordan, chairman of Westinghouse said 'he hoped to help China raise its capability to 90 per cent' (quoted in *CDBW*, 27 July 1997). ABB has promised to transfer state-of-the-art nuclear technology 'to achieve a high degree of localization in China' (*CDBW*, 7 December 1997).

GROWTH OF MULTINATIONAL GIANTS IN SUPPLYING CHINA'S
POWER EQUIPMENT INDUSTRY

In the mid-1990s, the share in total Chinese installed capacity of imports and joint ventures with multinationals was rising fast (see Table 6-13 on the lag of domestic output behind installed capacity). As we have seen, this was due to a shortage of government funding, a rise in foreign funding, a rise in profit-seeking independent power plant operators, intense price competition, falling tariffs on power equipment, and technical superiority of many types of foreign equipment. In 1994–5 it is estimated that the total share of foreign companies, via imports and domestic joint ventures had climbed to around 30 per cent, of which around one-half was from Westinghouse, much of which was supplied from its joint venture in Shanghai (see below).[25] By 1995, imported power equipment amounted to a total capacity of 40.1 GW (Lu Yansun, 1997: 2), accounting for 18 per cent of total installed capacity in China. The Chinese government anticipates that in the Ninth Five Year Plan around two-fifths of thermal power plant equipment will be supplied by foreign companies. China's explicit strategy is to 'give up part of the domestic market in exchange for technology' (Lu Yansun, 1997: 7). Will the technology transfer be to indigenously owned and controlled Chinese companies, or to local branches of multinational companies lacking the capability to manufacture integrated systems?

As long as the Chinese government directly provided the funds for building and expanding power stations, the contracts were awarded to a domestic producer.

TABLE **6-13** **Increase in Installed Capacity Relative to Output of China's Domestic Power Equipment Industry, 1991–7 (GW)**

Year	Increase in installed electricity generating capacity	Output of China's domestic power equipment industry
1991	13.8	11.6
1992	15.0	13.0
1993	16.4	14.7
1994	17.0	16.7
1995	17.3	16.7
1996	19.3	16.1
1997	13.5	16.7
1991–7	112.3	105.5

SOURCE: see Table 6-8

The competitive struggle for HPEC was then solely with other domestic producers. However, as sources of funding became more diversified, so the pressure for finding the lowest cost supplier of equipment grew. The Ministry of Electric Power (and its successor, the SP) and its subordinate power companies had a strong and growing interest in sourcing power plant equipment from firms that enabled it to produce electricity at the lowest cost. It should be noted that 'cost' from the perspective of the power plant operator must be taken to include not just the original purchasing price of the equipment. It needs also to include the level of operating efficiency, including primary energy consumption per unit of electricity generated, reliability, cost of servicing and manning levels. The power generating authorities must consider the needs of Chinese business and household consumers for low cost electricity.

The examples of two internationally floated companies, Beijing Datang and Shandong Huaneng Power, illustrate the shift in preference of increasingly commercially-driven domestic power producers towards imported power equipment.

Beijing Datang Power Generating Company is a leading example of the new type of power generator that was appearing in China in the late 1990s. It is a subsidiary of the North China Power Generating Group (itself a subsidiary of the SP), which owns 72.4 per cent of Beijing Datang. The Company has investment from other domestic institutions, namely the Beijing International Power Development and Investment Company (BIPDIC), and the Hebei Provincial Investment Company (HPIC), which together own 1.6 per cent of the Company, the other 25 per cent being floated internationally in 1997 (Morgan Stanley Asia, 1997b). The company is seeking international and other domestic financial support for its expansion. Datang is fast-growing, with an installed capacity rising from 3150 MW in 1996, to a planned level of 7650 MW in 2002. It has eight separate plants either operational or planned to come on stream by 2002. Although the company has bought and plans to buy a significant fraction of equipment from domestic manufacturers, it also either has bought or intends to buy much

TABLE 6-14 **Beijing Datang Power Generation Company, Origins of Major Pieces of Equipment**

Name of plant	Ownership share (%)	Installed capacity (MW)	Construction/ first operation	Nature of equipment	Origins
Dou He, Phases 1–4	100	1550	1975–87	2 × 125 MW turbines, generators and boilers	Hitachi
				2 × 250 MW turbines, generators and boilers	Wuhan Hitachi
				4 × 200 MW turbines, generators and boilers	Harbin
Dou He (2), units 1–2	45	1200	2001–2	2 × 600 MW turbines, generators, boilers, control systems	'all from international sources'
Gao Jing	100	600	1960–74	3 units turbines, generators, and boilers	USSR
				3 units turbines, generators and boilers	Harbin
Xin Hua Yuan	100	400	1982–3	2 × 100 MW turbines, generators and boilers	Beijing Heavy Machinery Harbin
			1988	1 × 200 MW turbines and generators boilers	Dongfang Harbin

Xin Hua Yuan Phase 6[a]	70	600	2 × 300 MW turbines, generators and boilers	2001–2	'all domestic'
'Zhang Jia Kou, Phase 1, units 3–4	100	600	boilers, generators and turbines	1994–5	Dongfang
Zhang Jia Kou, Phase 2, units 5–8	55[b]	1200	4 × 300 MW	1998–2001	n.a.
Zhang Jia Kou, Phase 1, units 1–2	0[c]	300	300 MW	1991–2	Dongfang
Tuoketou[d] Phase 1, Plant A	51[e]	1200	2 × 600 MW 'main power generating equipment'	2000–1	'imported'

SOURCE: MSDW (1997b: 52–64)

NOTES: a HPIC will have a 30 per cent share
b HPIC and BIPDIC will hold 30 per cent and 15 per cent, respectively
c Unit 1 is operated on behalf of NCPGC and unit 2 is operated on behalf of Huaneng
d Eventually, it is visualized that Tuotekou will expand to three plants, each with an installed capacity of 3800 MW, so that the final total installed capacity will be 10 800 MW
e Phase 1, Plant A is owned 51 per cent by Beijing Datang, 34 per cent by the Inner Mongolia Electricity Company and 15 per cent by BIPDIC

important equipment from abroad (see Table 6-14), including the entire set of turbines, generators and boilers for the 1200 MW second phase of the Dou He Plant.

Shandong Huaneng Power (SHP) had five power plants in 1996, and was planning to build another three by the year 2000, with a total installed capacity of 6200 MW (BZW, 1996: 93). SHP has used imported equipment for all five of the plants already constructed. They have purchased from GEC–Alsthom, Mitsubishi and GE (USA) (BZW, 1996: 93). A major reason for buying from abroad has been the superior operating efficiency of the plants.[26] However, imported plants are on average around 30–40 per cent more expensive for given installed capacity than domestic plants. As the electricity industry becomes more commercialized, it is not obvious that the lowest operating cost is always achieved through the purchase of imported equipment.

We have seen that, not only did the sources of domestic funding and the nature of operation of Chinese power stations begin to change greatly in the 1990s. At least as important was the fact that multinational investment in power stations also grew fast. Moreover, part of this investment involved multinational power equipment firms themselves investing in Chinese power stations. This increased the ability of these firms to source supplies from their own companies.

The growth of the China market is highly significant for the multinational power equipment giants. By 1996 Siemens was involved in supplying five coal-fired power plants, with a total installed capacity of 5100 MW. In 1994, Siemens established its own private sector investment vehicle, Siemens Power Ventures. Its main purpose is to take ownership stakes in power generating companies in order to ensure that Siemens wins contracts to supply power equipment to those operators (*FT*, 23 September 1997). For example, Siemens took a 12.5 per cent ownership share in the Shandong Rizhao Power Station in Shandong Province. It took the lead in its construction and supplied all the turbines for the project (*FT*, 12 September 1995).[27]

GE, as we have seen, became heavily involved in China's power generation industry. It was greatly advantaged by GE Capital. For example, in 1997 GE Capital took a 30 per cent stake in a project to upgrade a 400 MW gas turbine plant in Shanghai. The Shanghai Power Bureau holds the other 70 per cent stake. GE supplied four turbines for the project (*FT*, 18 December 1997).

ABB has expanded aggressively in China. It plans to have invested around $1 billion in joint ventures by 2000. China already accounted for around 4 per cent of ABB's global turnover by 1996, and the goal was to raise the share to 10 per cent of sales within fifteen years (*FT*, 6 January 1997). Its investments up until 1997 were mostly in manufacturing, with the main focus on power generating equipment. By the late 1990s, ABB was supplying China annually with around 2000 MW of generating equipment, amounting to around 10 per cent of China's total installed capacity. In other words, by 1996–8, the total installed capacity supplied by ABB, had reached around two-thirds of that of China's leading domestic equipment supplier, HPEC. ABB's main focus is on manufacturing rather than investment in infrastructure. However, it was actively considering investing in infrastructure, including power generation. Despite its misgivings about the regulatory environment (see above), it felt that it might be forced to do so 'in order to protect market share from fierce competition' (Goran Lindahl, head of ABB, quoted in *FT*, 6 January 1997).

Many leading policy makers and senior managers in Chinese power equipment companies believe that the multinationals have a clear strategic goal in China. They consider that their ultimate goal is to 'capture the Chinese market', 'put Chinese producers out of business as integrated producers' and turn them into 'branches making sub-systems for the multinational "mother" company'. It was thought that through the joint venture, the Chinese power equipment industry would be 'deprived of independent R & D capability'. It was felt that the Chinese power generating industry might achieve the gains of lower price and perhaps even lower operating costs but at the cost of higher equipment prices in the long-term. At heart, it was thought, 'the multinational joint venture serves the multinational, not the domestic joint venture partner'.

While state regulation of the power equipment industry still is highly significant, the nature and extent of support for indigenous manufacturers has changed greatly. Some domestic critics feel that the level of support is inadequate to the task of building indigenous large businesses in this sector in the face of sharply intensifying international competition, from imports of large equipment and, more importantly, from domestic ventures with multinationals.

HARBIN POWER EQUIPMENT COMPANY:
THE COMPETITIVE STRUGGLE

OWNERSHIP AND CONTROL

The Scope of HPEC. The subject of this study, Harbin Power Equipment Company (HPEC), is located in the city of Harbin in Heilongjiang Province in the extreme northeast of China, close to the Soviet border. Harbin is known as the 'City of Power Generating Equipment'. In the 1950s several large plants and many small ones were set up in or close to Harbin to produce different components of power plant equipment. The main factories were the Harbin Boiler Works (HBW), the Harbin Steam Turbine Plant (HTC), and the Harbin Electrical Generator Plant (HEC). Between them they produced the main parts of thermal power station units. Moreover, there already was a local relay factory, the Acheng Relay Plant (in the suburbs of Harbin), set up before 1949. The three main new plants were regarded from the outset as keypoint large plants: of the 156 major construction projects during the First Five Year Plan which were assisted by the Soviet Union, five related to these three plants.

In the 1950s these plants operated under the control of the MMI. In early 1962–3, China's Premier, Liu Shaoqi, supported the idea of developing some 'big companies', formed administratively from subordinate factories (in the same fashion as the East German 'Kombinat'). These were known as 'trusts' (*tuoluosi*). Harbin's three large plants, HBW, HEC and HTC, together with Acheng Relay

TABLE **6-15 Main Plants Producing Components for Power Stations in Liaoning and Helongjiang Provinces, 1992 (million yuan)**

Plant location name	Sales value	Profits	Net assets
SY Electric Cable Plant	990	92.8	260
SY Transformer Plant	486	37.6	220
SY HV Switch Plant	201	48.4	99
Acheng Relay Plant	144	13.9	58
HB Boiler Plant	433	60.0	261
HB Steam Turbine Plant	324	32.4	215
HB Electric Generator Plant	332	26.3	294
HB Electric Cable Plant	314	38.4	84

SOURCE: DRC (1994: 300–1)

NOTES: SY = Shenyang
HB = Harbin

Plant and the Shenyang Insulation Materials Plant, were administratively amalgamated with the two largest related plants in neighbouring Liaoning Province. These were the Shenyang Transformer Plant, and the Shenyang Electrical Cable Plant (their relative size in 1992 is shown in Table 6-15). The new combination of plants was called the Northeast Power Equipment Trust (*Dongbei Dianli Shebei Tuoluosi – Dongdian* for short).[28] The factories were strongly inter-related in terms of products and technology, since a complete power plant unit requires not only the boiler and main engines, but also a great number of ancillary electrical components. However, the experiment was short-lived, and the 'trust' was wound up in 1967.

In 1980 a new legal entity was established, the Harbin Power Engineering Company (HPEC). The formation of this new legal entity was a reflection of the beginnings of the market economy. Instead of direct instructions from the Ministry of Machine Building to the separate entities involved in building new power plant units, HPEC was to co-ordinate the activities of the separate companies making power equipment in Harbin.[29]

Institutional reform accelerated in the late 1980s. The State Planning Commission, and the State Committee for Restructuring the Economic System, set out the policy of organizing enterprise groups (*qiye jituan*) in order to change China's individual plants into large, multi-plant businesses that could compete in the market economy by taking advantage of economies of scale and scope. In 1987 the governments of Heilongjiang Province and Harbin City responded to the new policy by attempting to construct a 'super company' in the northeast for power plant equipment manufacture. This was one of 55 'enterprise groups' set up in China at that time. This would have been a highly integrated company combining a large part of both the production of the main engines and ancillary equipment within the same 'firm'. In a typical power plant, around 60 per cent of the value of the final product consists of the main engines and boiler, and about 40 per cent of ancillary equipment. In a highly integrated company, such as ABB, General Electric and Mitsubishi, a substantial part of the ancillary equipment is produced in-house, but in a firm such as Westinghouse's power division, almost all ancillary equipment is purchased from suppliers. The proposed super company of the northeast would have taken the new Group firmly down the path of ABB–Alstom and General Electric.

It would have essentially re-constructed the 'trust' structure of 1966–7, but in a new setting of the emerging market economy. The proposal was to combine the main plants in Heilongjiang Province, namely, HBW, HTC, HEC, and Acheng Relay Plant, together with the six main plants in Liaoning Province, namely, Shenyang Electric Cable Plant, Shenyang Transformer Plant, Shenyang High Voltage Switch Plant, Shenyang Low Voltage Switch Plant, Fushun Electromagnetic Plant, and Liaoning Electrical Engineering Plant. The relative size of the main plants is indicated by the data for 1992 shown in Table 6-15. The Liaoning Provincial Government and five of the plants in Liaoning agreed, but the proposal foundered due to opposition from Zhou Zouming, the Head of the Shenyang Transformer Plant (SYT). Zhou's plant was at the core of the production of the ancillary equipment. His ambition was to organize his own enterprise group, with SYT at the core of the six Liaoning plants. Zhou was successful in his goal, subsequently forming the Northeast China Electrical Equipment Company, which was floated on the Hong Kong stock market. By Chinese domestic standards the quality of equipment produced by Northeast Electrical Group is high. When HPEC exports today, it uses their products, but when it produces for the domestic market it uses a much wider chain of lower quality and cheaper suppliers.

Instead of a super-large integrated company, a large new company was formed, that was around one-half the size of that originally proposed.[30] It consisted wholly of firms based in or near to Harbin. The main forces within this were HBW, HEC and HTC. They combined with HPE to form an enterprise group, known as Harbin Power Engineering Group Company (HPEGC). Two smaller companies were also included, namely Harbin Insulating Materials Plant and Acheng Relay Plant. The Harbin Electric Cable Plant wished to join but was excluded because 'the quality of its products was too low'. The formation of HPEGC involved no change in ownership. The main constituent plants remained separate independent legal entities and accounting units. The participating plants were 'linked by products, not by assets'.

The main motive for forming HPEGC was in order to be large enough to be permitted to list overseas. In 1992, the first group of nine Chinese companies was listed on overseas markets. In 1994, HPEGC was selected to be part of the second batch of 22 companies to be listed overseas.

The New Ownership Structure. There were three alternative proposals for restructuring HPEGC. The process of selecting a mode of restructuring involved not just the individual plants, but also the MMB, the System Reform Commission and the State Securities Commission. Under the first proposal, HEC would become a state holding company, HTC would set up a joint venture with an international partner, and HBW would become a joint stock company. Under this path they would remain completely independent companies. However, this would fail to meet the minimum size requirement of the second batch of overseas listings. Two ways of building a larger entity were discussed. The first of these was for the three plants to merge into a single legal entity, losing their individual identities entirely. This was unacceptable to the highly independent constituent plants. Under the third proposal, which was the one finally selected, the 'mother and child' pattern was adopted, which left the three main parties to the restructuring with a higher degree of independence than a straightforward merger. Under this scheme, the 'mother' was the holding company, HPEC, and the 'children' were the constituent plants and the engineering company, which remained independent legal entities owned by HPEC.

Under the restructuring, on 1 October 1994, a newly formed company, Harbin Power Equipment Company Limited (HPEC), took over the entire power plant equipment manufacturing and engineering services previously carried on by HPEGC (Figure 6-2). The production-related businesses of the former HBW, HEC and HTC, were then taken over by the newly-established Harbin Boiler Company, Harbin Turbine Company, and Harbin Electrical Machinery Company, and engineering services were to be provided through the newly established engineering company. HPEGC retained its non-production related business, such as the provision of education, housing, medical facilities, catering services and other investments not directly related to the core business of the Group.

The state holding company (HPEGC) is formally subordinate to the Harbin State Assets Management Bureau. HPEGC owns 62 per cent of the share capital of HPEC (HPEC, 1997: 27 and Figure 6-2). A combination of poor financial performance in 1996–7 (discussed below) and the turbulence on the Hong Kong

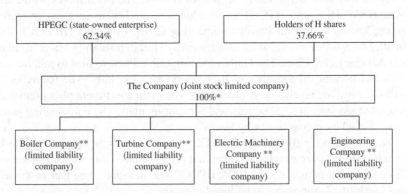

FIGURE 6-2 The Ownership Structure of Harbin Power Equipment Company, October 1994 (Post-Flotation on Hong Kong Stock Market)

NOTES: * Including interests held directly and indirectly through its subsidiaries

** An interest of 1 yuan is held by the Boiler Company in the case of the Electric Machinery Company, by the Electric Machinery Company in the case of the Engineering Company, by the Engineering Company in the case of the Turbine Company, and by the Turbine Company in the case of the Boiler Company

TABLE **6-16** **Turnover, Profits, Dividends, Taxation and Welfare Payments at HPEC, 1995 (million yuan)**

Item	1995
Turnover	2668
Profits before taxation	143.4
Taxes	21.3
Post-tax profits	122.1
Dividends	41.62
of which: dividends accruing to HPEGC	25.8 (approx.)
Payments to pension fund of HPEGC	35.8
Service payments to HPEGC	93.6
Total payments to higher levels	176.5

SOURCE: HPEC (1996)

stock market have together led the Company not to make any further share offerings in Hong Kong, so that the share structure has not altered significantly since the Company was first floated.[31] Dividends from HPEC accrue to it and in turn help to support the life of Harbin City (Table 6-16).[32] Because HPEC is a 'local firm' (*difang qiye*) it pays income tax to the local authorities (VAT goes to the central authorities).[33] Tax payments from HPEC provide around 60 per cent of the total income tax that the City government obtains from industrial revenues. In addition, HPEC pays pension and service fees to HPEGC.[34]

Not only does Harbin City rely heavily upon HPEC for direct financial contributions to its budgetary revenue, but many local firms depend upon HPEC as the main purchaser for their product. Included among the list of major local suppliers to HPEC are Harbin Automatic Control Equipment Company, Harbin Fenghua Machinery Company, Harbin Control Machinery Company, Harbin Heavy Machinery Company, and Harbin Electrical Instrument Company. In addition there are many smaller local suppliers. It is much the most important local firm.[35] In sum, the Harbin City government has a very strong interest in seeing HPEC run successfully, though not necessarily as a short-term profit maximizer, rather in terms of its long-term contribution to the economic life of Harbin City.

In addition to owning 62 per cent of HEPC, HPEGC is the 100 per cent owner of five other subordinate firms[36] and has non-controlling ownership shares (that is below 30 per cent of the share value) in several other companies, most of these companies in closely-related industries.[37] In addition, HPEGC has around 70 'jointly managed' (*lianying*) companies. It has invested in some, but not all, of these. They are principally firms from which HPEC purchases ancillary equipment for making complete power plant units.[38]

HPEC has taken a controlling ownership share in the Waxicun Power Station in Hebei Province using the power equipment supplied to the plant as the investment fund. It intends to continue to expand in the direction of direct ownership of power stations 'if conditions are right', mimicking the behaviour of the multi-national giants.

Integrating the Merged Companies. By the early 1990s, the three main production entities in HPEGC had almost forty years of operation as separate units, albeit under state control.

The plans for **Harbin Boiler Works (HBW)** were laid as early as 1950. The company was founded in 1954. The construction of HBW involved two projects among the 156 large-scale keypoint construction projects within the First Five Year Plan (1953–7). It has its own 'Haguo spirit' (*Harbin guolu jingshen*). People who work for Haguo are *Haguoren*' (Haguo people), a play on the word for the Chinese nation, *Zhongguo*, and Chinese people, *Zhongguoren*. It is not a foregone conclusion that a boiler-making firm must be part of a larger firm. The US company Babcock and Wilcox is a highly successful specialist boiler maker for the power industry, as well as for other industries. Therefore, as the market economy developed in China it was not self-evident that the interests of those who worked at HBW were best served by joining a larger grouping. Prior to the merger, HBW produced boilers also for the petroleum and the chemical industries as well as missile casings for the navy. At that point it was a substantial 'firm', with over 10 000 employees. From 1957 to 1994, HBW sold 543 units of power plant boilers, with a total capacity of 40 900 MW.

Harbin Turbine Company (HTC) was founded in 1956 and was constructed with technical assistance from the Leningrad Electrical Equipment Plant. Its construction involved two of the Soviet-aided projects during the First Five Year Plan, one for hydro power turbines and one for steam turbines. It began production in 1958. Prior to the merger it had around 11 000 employees. Although the bulk of their production consists of turbines for power plants, it also produces axial compressors for the petrochemical industry, and turbines for warships. From its founding until 1994 HTC produced 313 steam turbines for power plants, with a total capacity of 35 812 MW.

Harbin Electrical Generator Company (HEC) was founded in 1951. It was one of the keypoint Soviet-aided projects during the First Five Year Plan. Prior to the merger it had around 10 000 employees. In the 1980s it had set up a substantial sub-factory on the coast in Liaoning Province in order to be able to produce extra-large parts of over 300 tons that could be transported directly by sea. The decision to build this plant was in order to be able to compete more effectively for contracts for the Three Gorges Project. These potentially very large orders would benefit HEC more than the other parts of HPEC. As well as producing steam and hydroelectric generators for the power plant sector, HEC also produces rolling mills for steel plants, as well as alternating- and direct-current engines for use outside the power industry. From its inception until 1994, HEC produced the generators for 114 hydro power stations and 128 thermal power plants, with a total capacity of 48 937 MW.

The relationship between the merged plants was a major issue in the new company. Formerly, they each were 'state administered plants' located in the same city, under the same bureaucratic administration. They frequently contributed to the same final product, a complete power plant unit. However, they had an independent operational status and their independence grew as the market economy developed after the 1970s. They each had a separate identity and spirit. The problems they faced after the merger are similar to those of merged capitalist large firms with a different culture and tradition, and with management of each jealous of their powers.

In the Maoist period, the plants received direct orders from the Ministry of Machine Building. Prior to the restructuring, each of the constituent production companies had one superior authority, the Ministry of Machine Building. They followed the 'small but complete' pattern of the command economy, each having its own forging and casting capability, its own substantial research and development department and transport division. In the 1980s they each increased their operational independence due to the state's policies to expand enterprise autonomy through retention of increasing amounts of profits. The increasing impact of market forces led to a steady widening of the range of activities in respect of which the enterprise needed to take autonomous decisions, such as the purchase of inputs, the organization of suppliers, finding markets for their product, responding to customers' needs for after-sales service. Each of the plants had its own social service facilities. In the 1980s then each engaged in its own separate programme of technical transfer from international firms. Each of them undertook substantial programmes of expansion, involving both the selection and purchase of new equipment as well as the selection, purchase and upgrading of substantial amounts of second hand equipment on the world market. Each of them negotiated their separate joint venture relationship with international companies.

In the wake of the restructuring, the new power relationships between the three main levels, HPEGC (the holding company), HPEC (the joint stock company), and the three main subsidiaries (HBW, HEC and HTC) were still being worked out. Dr Li Genshen, chairman of both HPEC and HPEGC, acknowledged in 1996 that the company was still in the throes of a process of complex 're-engineering'. He recognized frankly the reason that lay behind the form that the restructuring took, with the establishment of four limited liability companies, each with the authority of an 'independent legal person'. This was because the newly established holding company, the 'mother', recognized that with 40 years of history, it would be impossible to fully control the three main individual plants, HBW, HTC, and HEC. HPEC's *Annual Report* (1995) describes HPEC as 'an investment holding company' which 'provides corporate management services to its four subsidiaries' (HPEC, 1995: 6). Chairman Li argued that under the new structure the 'mother' should 'learn to control the children', but 'the children should also learn to listen to the mother'. He considered that in theory 'linking the separate plant by assets' was a good idea, but in practice, the merger came up against 'a powerful historical tradition' in the separate units which could not just be wished away. His own appointment as chairman reflected an attempt to create an authority not rooted in one or other of the 'child' companies.

From the perspective of the subsidiaries, prior to the merger each had just one superior authority, the MMB. In the early 1980s, HPEC, like Dongfang and Shanghai Electric was technically transferred to ownership by the local authority. The State Planning Commission included them in the 'plan list' (*jihua danlie*) which guaranteed that they would receive 'no interference' from the local authority. However, after the merger the branch plants each had three superior authorities instead of one, since they now were responsible to HPEC and to HPEGC as well as to the Ministry. The new firm is a complex multi-layered organization. One analysis of the new structure from within the firm spoke of it as follows: 'There are more than ten levels to the organizational structure. Consequently, it is very difficult for the company to execute its strategies rapidly from the top down to the bottom. The more layers, the slower information feeds back. The multiplicity of layers leads to confusion in management control. Unnecessary layers of management and uncertain job definitions lead to a lack of a motivated enterprise culture' (Wang Weijun, 1996).

Instead of negotiating with the Ministry of Machine Building for new investment funds, or, increasingly in the reform period, making independent investment decisions themselves, the manufacturing companies were now dependent on HPEC for these decisions. In the restructured company investment decisions by the three manufacturing subsidiaries which are in excess of around one million yuan need to be approved by HPEC The most immediate issue of conflict was the allocation of the 1.257 billion yuan raised from the listing in Hong Kong.[39] Up until the middle of 1996, the vast bulk of the money raised, over 1 billion yuan, had been deposited in financial institutions, for which HEPC received 106 million yuan in interest in 1995. Of the total funds received due to the flotation, the three manufacturing subsidiaries had received just 179 million yuan, in order to pay off bank loans and to use for working capital. Around 65 million yuan had been invested in the purchase of new equipment. The subsidiaries could borrow short-term from these funds, but at a 'market' rate of interest.

The decision concerning when and how to allocate the funds raised from the stock market issue is in the hands of the headquarters of HPEC. Theoretically, the profits are a further means of consolidating the power of HPEC's headquarters. The three manufacturing companies were supposed to retain only 20 per cent of the profits generated on account of their separate business activities (10 per cent for the 'public accumulation fund' and 10 per cent as 'surplus profit retention'). As one interviewee from one of the subordinate companies expressed it: 'HPEC collects revenue from us for using *our* assets, and then we have to seek approval from *them* in order to make *our* investments; this is asymmetrical.' In practice it is likely that the subordinate companies have not handed over a large fraction (perhaps none) of their profits to HPEC. The subordinates retain the profits while the headquarters has control over the funds raised from the stock-market issue in Hong Kong.

Not only are there conflicts concerning the allocation of investment funds between the subordinate companies and HPEC, but also among the subordinate companies themselves. For example, it is logical to allocate a disproportionately large share of the funds raised from the stock market issue to expand the hydro capacity of HEC. This would enable HEC to be in a stronger position to bid for the large contracts that are going to emerge from the Three Gorges Project. However, HBW and HTC are concerned that this would greatly enhance the power of HEC within HPEC as a whole, and so oppose this strategy.

The subordinate limited companies are able to set up their own subsidiaries: the 'children' produce 'grandchildren', For example, HEC has set up an AC/DC Motor Plant, allowing a subordinate workshop to become an independent subordinate firm with its own profit and loss account. In 1995 it had an income of 200 million yuan. The firm was established with venture capital from the HPEC headquarters. This was a way to increase the leverage of the headquarters over the subordinate companies, and to provide an avenue for transferring surplus workers out of the core business into other activities, so as to allow 'downsizing without pain'. In mid-1996 HEC completed a joint venture with ABB to produce electricity control systems, in which ABB owns 70 per cent, contributed in the form of a technology transfer and HEC owns 30 per cent, contributed through a cash injection. Each of the other production companies has set up similar 'grandchildren' companies.

In theory, the manager of each of the subsidiary companies is appointed by HPEC headquarters. In practice, the leadership of the subsidiaries has not altered since the restructuring. It is unlikely that the management of the subsidiaries could be easily replaced by HPEC headquarters under the current set of power relations.

HPEC's headquarters is very 'lean', a genuine holding company in terms of size, with around 100 employees. Under this structure there is comprehensive duplication of functions. The separate subsidiaries still are 'small and complete' (*xiao er quan*). Each subordinate company still has its own divisions for R & D, design office, personnel management, accounting, product development, sales and service, quality control, and materials procurement. As well as specialized production departments, each has its own rail and truck transport departments, equipment control department, and even its own casting and forging workshops. This is a costly duplication. The potential savings from rationalizing the structure are especially strong because the subordinate companies are within a stone's throw of each other in the centre of Harbin City.

Control. Operational control of HPEC at flotation was firmly in the hands of those who were then the senior managers of HPEGC and its subordinate plants. The one exception was the chairman, Dr Li Genshen. He was formally appointed chairman of the board of both HPEC and HPEGC. Dr Li was appointed jointly by the Heilongjiang Provincial Government and the MMB. However, the main rights to determine the appointment of the chief executive officers of the company (as at Dongfang and Shanghai Electric) resides with the local government. Dr Li had a long association with the company. He joined Harbin Turbine Works in 1956 as assistant chief designer, after having obtained his PhD in the aerothermodynamics of turbo-machinery the USSR. In 1962 he was transferred to one of the Research Institutes of the State Defence Department, of which he eventually became the director. After 1985 he became successively deputy secretary of the Heilongjiang Provincial Party Committee, First Secretary of Harbin Municipal Party Committee, a member of the Central Committee of the Chinese Communist Party, and Deputy Head of Heilongjiang Provincial People's Congress. He became chairman of the board of directors of HPEGC in March 1994.

Dr Li's appointment as chairman reflects HPEC's national importance both for civilian and for military power equipment. It reflects also the strong provincial and municipal interest in HPEC's success and the fact that managerial control is firmly within the former entities that came together to form HPEC. Li Genshen had a long history of close relations with HPEC's constituent plants, including a substantial period of employment at the Harbin Turbine Works.

The other executive directors are composed entirely of people who were leading managerial staff of the different component parts of the Company prior to its restructuring and flotation. Their appointment reflects the strong continuity of control exercised by the internal management as the Company shifts from traditional SOE to a multi-ownership structure. They all joined HPEGC immediately after graduating and have stayed with the Company ever since. It may be easier for the incumbent managers to maintain managerial control of a large complex machinery company undergoing transition from a traditional SOE, compared to other sorts of businesses, due to the high level of technical expertise required. Almost all of the executive directors had advanced training in engineering.[40] The non-executive directors are drawn from a much wider range of backgrounds. Their appointment reflects a wish on the part of the State Holding Company to appoint people to be non-executive directors who are technically knowledgeable in both engineering and management, and who can help to advance the business prospects of the Company.[41]

Conclusion. Dealing closely with major international companies, such as Combustion Engineering (later ABB), Westinghouse and General Electric (see below), has had a big impact on the way HPEC's senior managers think about their firm. The managers of HPEC have a detailed knowledge of the personnel and the business structure of each of the main multinational firms. These companies constantly appear in discussion as an institutional benchmark against which HPEC evaluates itself. HPEC's leading managers are explicitly striving to 'get close to international standards' in their methods of business organization. ABB is the model which most frequently appears in discussions. However, HPEC is still far from having completed its complex institutional restructuring.

The problems it faces are not unique. Large capitalist companies often face large system re-engineering difficulties after merger or take-over. However, HPEC's institutional difficulties distracted the leaders of the firm at different levels from more important tasks. Moreover, the problems still are unresolved. Yuan Qihong, HPEC's Company Secretary acknowledges that, with the benefit of hindsight it might have been better to recognize the strength of the tradition of independence and list the three manufacturing companies separately. HPEC was pushed towards listing after merging due to the regulations then current for the State Economic System Reform Commission.[42] Instead of creating a much larger, fully integrated company that could benefit from extensive synergies and cost savings, the resulting form is, so far, a hybrid. The participating companies have lost some of the advantages of being independent companies, have not gained the large potential benefits from integration, and are preoccupied with internal power struggles. In time these difficulties may well be overcome, but valuable time and energy will have been lost in the process.

GROWTH AND MODERNIZATION

Growth. Harbin's production capacity grew relatively slowly from the 1950s to the early 1980s (Table 6-17). In the reform period its capacity expanded at high speed. Output more than doubled in physical terms from the early 1980s to the early 1990s, and in the 1990s, total installed capacity rose by no less than 63 per cent from 1991 to 1994 (Table 6-17).

Up until the mid-1980s, the Ministry of Machinery took all significant decisions concerning HPEGC, and funding of most investment of any size came from higher level authorities.[43] Most profits were simply handed over to the Harbin government. Thereafter, the methods of finance and the mechanisms of control shifted greatly. In the Seventh Five Year Plan, state-allocated modernization funds shifted to interest-bearing loans combined with reinvestment out of retained profits. The tightness of the budget constraint on HPEGC hardened in the early 1990s, when repayment of state bank loans shifted from deduction out of pre-tax profits to deduction from post-tax profits.

HPEGC's business environment altered sharply in the mid-1990s. It faced intensified competition from multinational companies, both through imports and through joint ventures with other domestic companies. Also, it faced a serious decline in aggregate growth of demand for power equipment, due to the slowdown in the overall economic growth rate, and government difficulties in financing outlays on power equipment. Orders for power equipment from HPEC amounting to 1100 MW were put on hold in 1996, and in 1997 there continued to be substantial postponements of deliveries of equipment ordered from HPEC (HPEC, 1997: 3).

Although the power equipment market encountered short-run difficulties in 1995–8, the long-run prospects for power equipment demand in China are strong. If Harbin is to maintain or even enlarge its market share, it needs to invest heavily in enlarging its capacity and modernizing technically and institutionally. It faces sharply increased competition from other domestic producers, as well as from international competitors: 'Keen competition from suppliers both domestic and foreign has already been looming over the market. To face the challenge, the Group has to further enhance its competitiveness' (HPEC, 1997: 10).

TABLE 6-17 Growth of Output at HPEC, 1959–98 (output in MW)

Capacity	1959	1991	1992	1993	1994	1995	1996	1997	1998
Total installed capacity of which:	—	2661	4126	3919	4350	3721	2956	3012	3576
hydro power sets	450	566	1151	1003	940	886	926	1442	1616
thermal power generating sets of which:	950	2095	2975	2909	3410	2835	2030		
boiler units	690	1950	3084	2678	3884	2325	1712	1936	2843
steam turbines	600	1955	3122	3460	3335	2585	1700	1996	2138
steam turbine generators	950	2095	2975	2909	3410	2835	2030	1570	1960

SOURCES: Warburg (1994: 46, 77); HPEC (1994, 1995, 1999)

In order to compete successfully, it needs urgently to mobilize investment funds. Immediately before flotation, HPEC was making substantial profits, with pre-tax profits amounting to around 10 per cent of revenue (Table 6-18). However, these were not large in relation to the investment needs of the Company. International flotation provided one path to help resolve these needs. The 1.257 billion yuan thereby raised provides an important source of investment funding. This sum is around 50 per cent larger than the amount that Westinghouse proposed to invest in its Shanghai joint venture in the late 1990s. However, HPEC's investment needs are large. Moreover, pre-tax profits halved from 208 million yuan in 1994 to just 99 million yuan (just $12 million) in 1996 (Table 6-18). HPEC's investment cannot be met from its own profits plus the funds from the flotation.

In order to participate in bidding for the Three Gorges scheme, it needs to invest 0.8–1.0 billion yuan to advance its technical level. This sum is the estimate of what is needed to raise HPEC's annual hydro generation capacity from 800 MW in 1996 to around 2000 MW, so that it can manufacture two 700 MW hydro units annually for the Three Gorges Project, as well as meet its other market needs in hydro power equipment. Moreover, not just capacity expansion is needed. In addition, HPEC needs to enhance its technical ability in hydro power equipment. It must move from the ability to manufacture single unit hydro units of 550 MW in 1996, to the 700 MW unit size necessary to even be considered for competing for the second phase of the Three Gorges Project.

Modernization

First and second phases. In the first phase of expansion, Soviet technology and equipment were central to HPEC's growth. Most of the large-scale equipment came from the Soviet Union.[44] During the 20 years from the late 1950s to the late 1970s HPEC was almost entirely cut off from the technical progress taking place abroad. In the case of HBW, its annual production capacity grew from 690 MW in 1957 to 1200 MW after the completion of the second phase of construction in the 1960s. Relying on it own technical resources, HPEC made

TABLE **6-18 Profits and Taxation at HPEC, 1991–8 (million yuan, current prices)**

Item	1991	1992	1993	1994	1995	1996	1997	1998
Turnover	1 157	1 475	1 533	2 396	2 668	2 403	2 595	2 864
Pre-tax profits	114.7	100.5	107.0	208.5	143.4	98.9	101.8	88.8
Taxes	30.6	28.1	24.3	30.8	21.3	14.4	14.1	13.9
Post-tax profits	84.1	72.4	82.7	177.7	122.1	84.5	87.7	74.9
Pre-tax profits/ turnover (%)	9.9	6.8	7.0	8.7	5.4	4.1	3.9	3.1

SOURCE: HPEC (1995, 1997, 1998)

TABLE **6-19** Major Technical Achievements of HPEC, 1959–91

Thermal power generation equipment		Hydro power generation equipment	
Year of commissioning	Achievement	Year of commissioning	Achievement
1959	First 50 MW high-pressure thermal power generator set in China	1959	First 16 MW Kaplan-type* hydro power generator set in China
1967	First 100 MW high-pressure thermal power generator set in China	1969	First 225 MW Kaplan-type* hydro power generator set in China
1972	First 200 MW power generator set in China	1973	First 300 MW Kaplan-type* hydropower generator set in China
1989	First 600 MW sub-critical pressure thermal power generator set in China	1991	First 302.5 MW Kaplan-type* hydro power generator set in China with runner diameter of over 8 metres

SOURCE: Warburg (1994: 7–8)

NOTE: * In the 'Kaplan'-type turbine the waterflow in the turbine is in an axial direction

some important technical advances during the period of isolation from the world economy.[45] The main highlights of this are shown in Table 6-19.

However, by the end of the Cultural Revolution, HPEC was still technically far behind the world's advanced power equipment producers. In recognition of this, beginning in the late 1970s, the First Ministry of Machine Building produced a programme that it hoped would on completion enable HPEC to build a full range of power plant units from 100 MW through to 600 MW.[46]

As well as trying to advance its own technical levels, during the Maoist years HPEC also contributed substantially to expansion of power equipment capacity elsewhere in China. In 1965, under instructions from the First Ministry of Machine Building, as part of the 'Third Front' movement, HBW dispatched a team to establish the Dongfang Boiler Works in Deyang, Sichuan Province, completed in 1971.[47] HBW had no ownership rights in the new plant, and Dongfang is now a major competitor for HPEC in the emerging market economy.

1980–1990s

Technical transfer programme. HPEC's technical capabilities advanced rapidly after 1980 (Table 6-19). A key part of this was the Fifteen Year (1981–96) Programme for Technical Transfer to the Chinese power equipment industry. This programme was organized by the State Council and the MMB.[48] It was the largest programme of technical transfer to China during this period. The main beneficiaries were HPEC and the Shanghai Electrical Company. In the late 1980s the unit capability for thermal power generation was 125 MW at Shanghai and 200 MW at HPEC. The technical transfer programme raised the unit production capability at

Shanghai to 300 MW and at HPEC to 600 MW. With the aid of a technology transfer agreement with Hitachi, Dongfang also raised its thermal unit capacity to 600 MW, producing its first commercial unit in 1997 (*CDBW*, 31 May 1998).

At HPEC the technical transfer programme involved co-operation with Combustion Engineering (USA) (later merged with ABB) to raise the boiler making capability, and with Westinghouse to raise the steam turbine and electric generator capability. The programme allowed Chinese firms to purchase licences 'very cheaply'. It allowed Chinese technicians to be trained in the foreign firm. Chinese technicians participated in co-design of the (for them) new generation of equipment, and were involved in on-site management of the supply of the new equipment. This was a calculated risk for the multinationals. If they demonstrated goodwill towards the Chinese power equipment industry, then it was possible they might be able to use this as leverage with the Chinese government to gain access to the Chinese market. The co-operating foreign partner insisted that only the company with which they co-operated should be allowed to use the technology.

The first foreign training visits by HPEC technicians were in the early 1980s. The design period for the new power plant equipment was completed in 1983. In the initial stage the equipment used foreign components, but in subsequent units used domestically-produced components. The first machine to result from the programme was produced in 1987, a 600 MW power plant unit. Since then HPEC has built five 600 MW power units. By late 1995, two of the 600 MW units had been in commercial operation for more than three years, which meant that HPEC was then in a position to bid for international projects using this size of unit. In 1996, HPEC remained the only domestic producer able to manufacture a 600 MW thermal power station (Dongfang produced its first commercial 600 MW thermal unit in 1998). HPEC itself developed the imported technology in order to build its first 300 MW thermal power generator set in 1989. By the end of 1996, HPEC had produced and installed 23 units of 300 MW generators (HPEC, 1997: 9). After the completion of the technology transfer programme, HPEC's annual production capacity stood at 3000 MW in thermal power and 600 MW in hydro power generation sets.

For HBW the contract was signed between, on the one hand, the Chinese National Foreign Trade Corporation and the China National Electricity Equipment Company, and, on the other, Combustion Engineering. The contract was for the transfer of technology for 600 MW boiler technology. The contract included (i) a payment of $13.45 million for the purchase of the technology for the electric power station steam production system; (ii) a payment of $22 million for the purchase of components for the boiler; and (iii) a payment of $20 million for air pre-heating technology.

Self-organized technical upgrading. Apart from the main programme of technical upgrading, organized by the Chinese government, HPEC organized its own technical upgrading. In addition to technology transfer in the thermal sector, separate technology agreements were concluded in the 1980s to upgrade HPEC's hydro power capability. HEC co-operated with Kvaerner Brug A/S (Norway),

Hitachi (Japan) and Siemens (Germany) in technology exchanges and in the production of hydro power generating equipment. In 1991 HEC produced a 302.5 MW Kaplan-type hydroelectric power generation set. The turbine diameter was over 8 metres, the largest in China. In the early 1990s, HBW co-operated with Pyropower Corporation, a subsidiary of Ahlstrom Group (USA) to complete a 50 MW circulation fluidized bed boiler, installed in 1995.[49] In 1991 HPEC entered a joint production venture with Cockerill Mechanical Industries (Belgium) for the development of steam-gas combined cycle heat recovery boilers for two power stations in Pakistan. In the early 1990s also HPEC set up a joint venture with Canadian GE to develop hydro power generator sets with a single unit capacity of 550 MW.

In addition to co-operation with foreign manufacturers, HPEC has undertaken its own research and development. Each of the manufacturing subsidiaries has a large number of highly qualified research workers,[50] and its own specialized research institute. In the mid-1990s HPEC as a whole employed over 1500 staff in research and development, of which 24 were high level experts with national recognition, and 1320 were senior engineers. HPEC contains the Harbin Research Institute of Large Electrical Machinery, established in 1958. It employs over 600 staff. It is designated by the PRC government as the authority responsible for the research and development on hydro turbines and large electrical machinery for the whole country. It is the centre responsible for evaluating the technical performance and quality of China's power generating equipment.

The technical transfer from international companies has provided a base from which HPEC's own engineers and scientists can make independent progress. For example, HEC has improved the performance of imported turbine technology in relation to heat loss and improved the cooling techniques in relation to imported technology for generators. In addition, HEC has independently designed and started production of 600 MW and 1000 MW nuclear steam turbines, 800 MW supercritical steam turbines and 25 MW gas turbines for ships. It has undertaken extensive independent studies for the design and construction of 700 MW single unit capacity hydro power generator sets for the Three Gorges Project. HBW has developed boilers particularly suited for use with the different varieties of coal available in different parts of China. It has also completed the design and manufacture of sub-critical controlled cycle and natural cycle boilers with single unit capacity of 300 MW.

Modernization of equipment. In the late 1970s, the vast bulk of HPEC's equipment was either of 1950s Soviet vintage or was supplied from domestic manufacturers. Both of these were far behind the world's most advanced levels. From the late 1970s onwards, HPEC rapidly updated its equipment, while continuing to run older equipment alongside new purchases. HPEC in 1994 had around 6600 pieces of major production equipment, including 1308 pieces of high precision equipment either imported or developed by HPEC itself. In 1994, the total value of plant and equipment was around $96 million (Table 6-20), large in Chinese terms, but pathetically small compared to the global giants.

TABLE 6-20 **Valuation of Plant and Equipment at HPEC, 1994**

Plant	Valuation	
	(million yuan)	*(US$ million)*
Turbine Company	303	35.2
of which:		
Turbine workshop	115	13.3
Dynamic testing workshop	31	3.6
Boiler Company	257	29.8
of which:		
Heavy vessel workshop	74	8.6
Waterwall workshop	39	4.5
Electric Machinery Company	264	30.7
of which:		
Turbogenerator workshop	46	5.3
Hydrogenerator workshop	35	4.1
Welding workshop	35	4.1
Electronic workshop	28	3.3
Research Institute	23	2.7

SOURCE: Warburg (1994: 133–6)

Around one-third of HTC's equipment by number, and 60–70 per cent by value, is imported, with many leading-edge machine tools, especially from Germany.[51] HBW has imported a vast 8000 ton hydraulic press from Mitsubishi Heavy Industries. It has a Linatron 4 Mev linear accelerator for inspecting heavy walls, purchased from the USA. It has many pieces of imported advanced welding equipment, since welding is the key to technical progress in boiler-making.[52] HPEC has begun also to make some large purchases from modernizing domestic machine tool plants.[53]

As well as extensive purchase of new imported equipment, HPEC bought a large amount of second hand equipment in its modernization drive after the late 1970s. For example, HTC's main engine workshops in the 1980s purchased eight large US-made numerically-controlled machine tools from a bankrupt factory, and in the 1990s bought a number of large, numerically-controlled machine tools from bankrupt factories in Russia and Romania. The five or six Romanian machines were originally imported from Scharmann.[54] These machines were of recent vintage (1980s), and would have cost around one million US dollars each to purchase new.[55] HTC has upgraded around one-third of its stock of old machine tools to modern numerical-control systems.[56] In the 1990s HEC also purchased a lot of second hand Russian machinery and upgraded the equipment with its own numerical-control systems.

Modernization Plans. It is projected that the increase in domestic power demand from 1995 to the year 2000 will exceed China's production capacity in

1995 by around 50 per cent. This provides a huge opportunity for HPEC to expand its production base and modernize using the profits generated from meeting this increase in demand. It has large opportunities to develop its technical capabilities to meet a fast growth of demand for coal-fired thermal power stations. With state support and technological transfer, HPEC appears likely to be able to raise its technical level in hydro power equipment, moving from the current limit of 550 MW units to the 700 MW units needed for the Three Gorges. In nuclear power also, China's large potential market provides a channel through which HPEC may be able to rise to international levels using international technological transfer.

In the 1970s HPEC was far behind the technical levels of the world's advanced power equipment makers. By the mid-1990s it had made big advances but there was still substantial leeway in order to catch up fully. Research and development at HPEC in the mid-1990s focused on several main areas of weakness. These include 700 MW hydro units suitable for the Three Gorges Project. For nuclear power generation, HPEC needs to acquire the technology to design and build 1000 MW nuclear power steam turbines and steam turbine generators and 600 MW nuclear power generation equipment for nuclear reactors and related steam turbine generators; it also needs to develop the technology for 600 MW super-critical pressure thermal generator sets.[57]

HPEC believes it would take a very long time to develop independently the technology for the nuclear core or for the steam/gas combined cycle. It does not possess the financial resources to purchase the proprietary technology for these processes. The only feasible way to obtain these capabilities fast is through technical transfer from a multinational firm.

HPEC plans to continue to add to its stock of advanced numerically-controlled machine tools, welding equipment, testing equipment and other equipment, much of which will continue to be imported.[58]

LABOUR ORGANIZATION

Personnel Management Ethos. In the past HPE's managers managed mainly 'by feelings' (*ganqing*). This is shifting to 'management by regulations and laws'. The trend in relation to the provision of social services for staff members is that these should gradually shift 'towards society', away from being the direct responsibility of HPEC. However, in both the above respects, the company is still in the midst of a complex process of transition from one approach to another. The final resting place of the company's structure of personnel organization is unknown.

Restructuring Employment into Core and Non-core. Prior to the restructuring, HPEC's constituent companies had a total of over 40 000 employees. In the standard pattern for flotation of a Chinese state-owned firm, the 'core' production workers were included in the company to be floated, and the rest were transferred to the parent state-owned company. Around 27 000 became employees in the newly formed HPEC, and the remainder were employed by the Group (HPEGC) in a variety of activities. The largest single group, approximately 5500, was transferred to the service companies (*shiye gongsi*), of which there was one for each of the main subordinate limited companies. HPEGC (that is the state) is the 100 per cent owner of each of the service companies.

The separate limited companies still think of themselves as independent 'big families', covering 'their' workers and their families from cradle to grave. Each of them has its own 'services company' (*shiye gongsi*) even after the restructuring. They each take responsibility for employees' children by, for example, using their funds to support the establishment of collective enterprises which provide employment for those of 'their' children who cannot be employed in the main plants.[59] HPEC pays fees to the service companies to provide medical services, hospital charges, education costs, and heating costs.[60] HPEGC has negotiated with the Harbin City government for the City to take over responsibility for social services in return for fee payments by HPEGC to the City.[61] From 1996, payments into the state pension fund will be met according to general state regulations.[62]

Housing. Housing is a highly sensitive issue. Under the old system at HPEC 'there was a book of regulations about how housing should be allocated'. The companies had to provide detailed explanations of the reason for any given decision concerning house allocation. In 1994, as part of the restructuring, the houses of each of the subordinate companies were transferred to the ownership of each of the service companies. Housing reform began prior to this, in 1991–2. HPEC gave its workers the right to buy their apartments (*fangquan*). The price depends upon location and condition, and the local price for such housing. The final purchase price is reduced in proportion to the purchaser's working years at the company and the 'preferential price reduction' (undisclosed) granted by the company to its employees. The purchaser can purchase the ownership rights a fraction at a time if they wish. After purchase, the purchaser is free to let the apartment if they wish. If they wish to sell within five years, then HPEGC has the right of first refusal to buy the apartment back. Mortgages are provided by HPEC's Sanlian Service Company.

Up until the middle of 1996, around 19 000 employees had purchased their houses, with only around 500 having purchased them outright, and the rest having bought a fraction, the rough average being around 60 per cent of the apartment's agreed value. The reason for the enthusiasm to buy is the uncertainty about future house rents and purchase price. In 1996 house rents were around 0.6 yuan per square metre, compared to around 12 yuan per square metre for commercial housing in Harbin. Purchasers felt that both rents at HPEC and the future price offered to purchasers were likely to rise. Almost all of the purchasers are at HTC and HEC. Virtually no-one at HBW has bought their apartment. Its employees still all live in company housing.

Downsizing/Diversification. Employment in HPEC fell at a stroke from over 40 000 to around 27 000 at the time of restructuring. At the end of 1996, the

Company had around 26 000 employees. In 1996, from May to the year-end in December around 1000 workers 'retired', and around 700 were 'sacked' (*jiegu*). Over the whole year, no fewer than 5000 positions within the Company and its subsidiaries were 'streamlined through early retirement and redeployment training schemes' (HPEC, 1997: 9). There are many ways in which the enterprise can achieve downsizing. These included genuine retirements, and 'fake retirement' (early retirement). Another category is 'keeping the post but receiving no wages'*(tingxing linzhi)*. Under this, the worker keeps access to welfare benefits but receives no wages. This can be continued for up to two years and within this time the worker can return to HPEC if they fail to find satisfactory work elsewhere. Straightforward sacking can occur through 'many channels', such as dismissal for failing to report to work for 15 successive days.

The intention to downsize in employment alongside growth of output is explicit. The leadership's goal is to reduce employment in HPEC to only 16 000–18 000 in the year 2000. The clear intention to 'downsize' was strongly influenced by HPEC's feeling for the need to 'benchmark' against the leading global power equipment companies, especially ABB, with which HPEC has a close relationship. A major reason for the felt need to downsize is in order to change the mentality of employees, rather than simply to reduce the wage bill. The stated goal is to produce a firm with higher average incomes and a hard-working ethos among the workforce.

Even by 1996, the character of the employees in the company had already changed greatly. The average age had fallen considerably compared to the old firm (it was around 40 by mid-1996), as older workers retired early or left, and the educational level was rising, as the less well-educated were allowed to leave and better-educated workers were recruited to the company. It was intended that the average age should continue to fall. In the 1980s many workers' children returned from the countryside and HPEC was required to employ them irrespective of their educational level. Even in 1996, not all new recruits were freely selected. For example, HPEC is required by law to accept a certain number of army veterans. Around 70–80 per cent of new recruits are freely selected by the company. For these, HPEC insists on technical school or middle level professional education for ordinary workers. For senior staff, it requires that the new recruit have at least higher level professional education, and frequently education from a good university.

Remuneration. HPEC's international shareholders wished to establish a system of 'international' remuneration for HPEC's directors, with remuneration proportional to profit. However, HPEC refused to do this. The average *annual* remuneration of HPEC's 10 executive directors in 1995 was 27,000 yuan, the equivalent of around (US) $3300 (HPEC, 1995), an income which is a tiny fraction of that of the senior executives of major multinationals with whom HPEC's executive directors do business. Income differentials within the business have only widened to a small degree since the 1970s. There remains a ratio of only around 5 : 1 between the lowest and the highest incomes in the company. The wage structure at HPEC is still controlled by state regulations. In 1995 average wages were around 700 yuan per month, with an additional 50 yuan per month for bonuses, totalling around 9000 yuan for the whole year. In other words, average incomes at HEPC are around one-third of those of the executive directors. The low average income at HPEC, only around $1000 per year, means that despite the large number of workers, wages still amount to well under 20 per cent of total costs of production. Payments to HPEGC for provision of services and pensions, add around 5000 yuan to the annual average income of HPEC's workers, raising the average 'real' wage at the Company to around 14 000 yuan, still the equivalent of only around $1700.

RELATIONSHIP WITH SUPPLIERS

Supplies within the Holding Company. In 1980 as the reforms began to take effect and as HPEC began to attempt to compete on both domestic and world markets, a new entity was set up, the Harbin Power Station Engineering Company (*Harbin dianzhan chengtao gongsi* or HPE). It employs around 200 people and co-ordinates the supplies from the separate HPEC plants involved in the construction of a complete power plant unit. The first 'marketized' export from HPEC took place in 1982. Prior to that point HPEC's exports had been arranged through the planning system largely as a part of China's international aid effort.

The main engines constitute around 50–60 per cent of the total value of the power plant contract. They are always supplied from within HPEC. HPE is the conduit through which market pressure is conveyed to the subordinate companies making the main engines. In order to win contracts against sharpening domestic and international competition, HPE has put increasing pressure on the subordinate companies to lower the price of their supplies. Price is 'constantly negotiated' between HPE and the subordinate companies. In some cases the headquarters of HPEC has had to step in to insist that a given price be set for a power plant unit in order that HPEC wins the contract, even though the subordinate company insisted it couldn't meet the price. In the 1990s since the deregulation of power plant prices and with the growing role of multinational companies, the discussion over price between HPE and the subordinate companies has grown 'more and more intense', giving the head of HPE a 'big headache'.

Suppliers from Outside the Company. Around 40–50 per cent of the value of a complete power plant unit is composed of the ancillary equipment. For equipment sold on the domestic market, the ancillary equipment is supplied from a network of around 200 suppliers, most of which are not specialized in the power industry. A substantial number of its suppliers have joint ventures with international companies, which has enabled them to raise their technical level since the 1970s. For power plant exports HPEC uses a smaller number of higher quality suppliers, particularly from the six Liaoning factories that were formerly a part of *Dongdian*. Other suppliers know that if they wish to participate in this part of HPEC's production, they must raise the quality of their products.

HPE's individual subordinate companies also purchase ancillary equipment, including insulating materials and various electrical/mechanical components for the supply of individual units apart from complete power plants. Both HPE and the individual companies have experienced a steadily increasing pressure of price and quality competition from the marketplace downstream (see below). These have in turn been passed on in the form of pressure on the network of suppliers. One can imagine that many of the 200-odd supplying firms (*lianying qiye*) have become loss-making in recent years in part at least because of the pressure from HPEC to force down the real price of their purchases from them.

Among raw materials, steel is much the most important, accounting for around 50 per cent of HPEC's total raw material costs. Up until the mid-1990s, around 80 per cent of HPEC's steel supplies were supplied mainly through the state plan. Although the proportion of steel allocated through the plan continued to decline sharply in the mid-1990s, the key role of HPEC in China's industrial structure meant that its steel needs continued to be safeguarded by the central government. Around one-fifth of HPEC's steel needs in the early 1990s were imported. These were mainly special steels unavailable or in exceptionally short supply within China. HPEC has long-standing relationships with its main steel suppliers. In 1994 it bought around one-third of its steel from Angang (the nearest to Harbin of the major producers), around one-fifth from Wugang, 16 per cent from Shangang, and 13 per cent from Baogang. Domestic steel suppliers are unable to supply steel in the required dimensions. Therefore the different plants at HPEC need to shape the steel supplies to their precise requirements.

In sum, while the supply network for HPEC is improving, it is much less efficient than that which serves multinational giants, such as ABB or GE.

COMPETITION

The Competitive Mechanism

Market-driven institutional change. In the late 1980s and 1990s, as we have seen, China's power equipment market became increasingly competitive. Initially, the main competitors were domestic enterprises, but increasingly competition came from imports, and following that, it came more and more from the domestic joint ventures of the multinational giants (see below). We have seen already that major changes occurred in the internal organizational mechanism of HPEC as a result of this increasingly intense pressure.

Under growing pressure from the market, HPEC massively restructured, becoming a joint stock company. The attempt to create a single unified company out of the disparate components was itself a major institutional change. The subsequent flotation of part of its share value on the international stock market influenced its culture strongly. It forced greater openness and awareness of share price. In order to compete domestically and internationally HPEC underwent a large process of technological transfer from leading multinational power equipment producers. The consequent close contact between HPEC managers and engineers and those of leading multinationals strongly influenced the internal culture, forcing HPEC to benchmark itself against the global giants. Growing awareness of competition forced the management to become more and more concerned with the supplier network, attempting to improve it as fast as was feasible, towards international standards.

We have seen also how, in order to raise its competitive level, HPEC turned itself towards downsizing and a more youthful and professional structure of employment. In the process of struggling with the market and restructuring, HPEC's management was forced to take an increasing range of autonomous decisions. A sense of corporate identity gradually began to emerge. The pressure of the market mediated itself through the price mechanism and forced the company to develop increasingly a range of skills that had previously been completely absent. Marketing became a key activity, and the pressure to upgrade its technological level became of prime importance. Struggling to win export orders was an especially powerful mechanism for forcing institutional and technological change upon the company.

Prices. Under the command economy, HPEC's constituent plants had no need to concern themselves with the costs of their inputs. However, by the early 1990s costs of production mattered greatly to the firm's capability to grow, since an important part of their investment funds came from self-generated profits. Moreover, the Harbin City government had a strong interest in the firm making profits, since their budgetary income depended so heavily upon the success of HPEC. In the early 1990s steel prices were substantially de-regulated, and then fluctuated greatly,[63] before settling down at close to world market prices. HPEC now had to consider costs of production very carefully in setting the price for its product when tendering for contracts. In the domestic market it was able to work with the State Price Bureau to impose price compensation clauses upon purchasers of its equipment. For HPEC's growing exports this was not possible, so the Company needed to develop new skills in factoring in risk of raw material and other price rises when tendering for international contracts.

Until the early 1990s, there was a substantial price differential between HPEC's price and that of the major international companies in categories of plant for which HPEC was technically able to compete. HPEC could supply similar plant for around 60–80 per cent of that of international competitors (Warburg, 1994: 78). However, the difference had been more or less eroded by the mid 1990s. On the one hand, HPEC's raw material costs had been rising in real terms due to the liberalization of steel prices. On the other hand, in the advanced economies, over-expansion of capacity combined with stagnation in orders for power plants led to ferocious competitive price-cutting, with, as we have already seen, roughly a one-third fall in the real price of power stations in the early 1990s.

We have seen that the scale of the Chinese market has 'encouraged every big manufacturer to bid for business, driving down prices' (*FT*, 26 June 1996): 'Chinese bidding contests have been particularly fierce because all the large integrated groups have seen the country as their top market and have been willing to sacrifice margins for establishing their presence' (*FT*, 16 September, 1996). The head of GE's Power Division considered that the price of power plants in China in the mid-1990s had fallen 'significantly below world levels' (*FT*, 16 May 1996). He commented: 'We see the opportunity to lose a lot of money in China' (quoted in *FT*, 16 May 1996). Each of the big groups blames the others for driving down prices to 'sub-economic' levels (*FT*, 16 September 1996). HPEC was forced to operate in this brutally competitive environment even within the domestic economy.

Marketing. Under the planned economy there was no concept of marketing at HPEC. Output targets, price, method of payment and completion date, were all set by the Ministry of Machinery. Since the late 1980s, all sales have come to depend on HPEC's own marketing efforts. Even within China promoters and operators of power stations have considerable discretion about the choice of supplier from within China. They can also negotiate directly with power equipment suppliers about price and method of payment. From no concept of marketing, HPEC by the mid-1990s had a substantial marketing department, employing around 250 people.

Moreover, as will be seen, the degree of discretion is growing with the granting of access to the Chinese market for international manufacturers and the greatly increased use of the BOT method of power station construction, using international finance. HPEC has had to be highly concerned about marketing both in the domestic and the international sphere. HPEC was set up specifically to compete for power station contracts.

Technical capabilities. We have seen that HPEC made rapid advances in its technical capabilities after the 1970s. These increasingly were self-motivated by the company rather than passive responses to central government instructions. HPEC's technical lead in the production of large-sized power plants gave it a substantial competitive advantage over other domestic producers. In 1998 it was the only Chinese producer capable of producing 600 MW thermal power station units. It is estimated that from 1995 to the year 2000, 80 per cent of total domestic market demand will be for single unit capacities of 300 MW and 600 MW.

Moreover, in order to be allowed to bid independently (that is without a foreign partner) for a 600 MW thermal power plant unit, international practice requires that the manufacturer has produced at least two units which have been in commercial operation for three years. By the end of 1995 HPEC had achieved this position, unique among domestic manufacturers. In tendering for 600 MW units this gave HPEC full discretion in pricing its projects, and the capability to obtain the entire revenue stream from projects for which it tendered successfully.

Exports. Capability to export is a key indication of a firm's competitive strength and a mechanism for driving forward institutional and technological change. HPEC's exports increased sharply in the early 1990s, their share of turnover rising from around 5 per cent in 1991 to 14 per cent in the mid-1990s

($46 million in 1995) (HPEC, 1995). One of the main reasons for establishing HPE was to facilitate HPEC's exports. From 1982 to 1995, HPEC exported seven complete sets of power plant equipment (Table 6-21). In the mid-1990s HPEC was much the largest Chinese power plant equipment exporter, accounting for around 80 per cent of China's total exports of large-scale power plant equipment.

Up until the late 1980s, most of the exports were organized together with the China National Import and Export Commission (CMEC). From the Angat Plant onwards, HPEC itself began to undertake the task of tendering and organizing the contract independently of CMEC. The Angat and Kotri plants were organized entirely by HPEC. The Hiep Phuoc Plant was a joint undertaking between HPEC and the Taiwanese government's Central Trade Development Company (CTDC) (*Zhongyang maoyi kaifa gongsi*). They established a jointly owned company to tender for the project, in which HPEC owned 11 per cent of the share capital and CTDC owned 89 per cent of the shares.

HPEC has made joint tenders with many multinational companies for international projects, including Westinghouse, ABB and GE. The UCH plant (Pakistan) was jointly tendered for by HPEC and GE (USA), with GE as the 'leading partner' in the contract. Of the total contract price of $410 million GE obtained orders worth $270 million and HPEC obtained orders worth $140 million. GE supplied the main engines, including steam turbine, boiler and generator while HPEC supplied BOP (branch of plant) ancillary equipment. In 1996 HPEC was involved in preparing tenders for around 20 international projects, including ones in Vietnam, Malaysia and the Philippines.

Just as export credits are an important part of the armoury of Western power equipment exporters, so too are they gradually becoming part of the Chinese export process. In 1994, the Chinese government set up Eximbank, specifically to provide financial support to Chinese companies setting up branches overseas and contracting for overseas projects. Eximbank gives priority to profitable companies selling machinery and electronic goods (*FT*, 17 March 1998).

The Competitors

Domestic producers. In the early 1990s, the structure of China's domestic power generating industry mirrored the world-wide structure, in that there was only a small number of producers. In 1993, the three principal manufacturers, Harbin, Dongfang and Shanghai, accounted for over two-thirds of total output (Table 6-22).

In the emerging market economy in the 1980s, HPEC began to accustom itself to competition with the major domestic producers, Shanghai and Dongfang. Like HPEC, they became increasingly autonomous. In 1983 the competitive element was increased by the transfer of the property rights for the three plants to the respective provincial/municipal governments. These include rights to appoint managers and receive taxes from the respective companies.

We have seen already that HPEC was the leading producer of power equipment in the Maoist economy. In the reform years it sustained itself in this position, still accounting for around 28–30 per cent of domestic output in 1992 and

TABLE 6-21 **Main Exports from HPEC**

Country	Name of power station and unit no.	Capacity (MW)	Year of contract signing	Year of completion of contract	Contract price ($ million)
Pakistan	Guddu, Unit No. 4	210	1983	1986	56
Pakistan	Jamshoro Units No. 2, 3 and 4	3 × 210	1987	1990–2	230
Philippines	Unit No. 5	18	1990	1992	6
Pakistan	Kotri and Faisalabad Combined cycle plants	2 × 47	1991	1994	83
Pakistan	Muzaffargarh Units No. 5–6	2 × 210	1991	1995	155
Vietnam	Hiep Phuoc Units No. 1, 2 and 3	3 × 125	1993	1997–8	87
Pakistan	UCH	3 × 120; 1 × 180	1995	1999	410
Iran	n.a.	4 × 250	1995	n.a.	n.a.
Pakistan	n.a.	n.a.	1996	n.a.	4940*

NOTE: * Includes also sub-contracting for foreign investment projects within China

1993 (Table 6-22). So long as the Chinese government remained the sole supplier of funds for the construction of power stations, and as long as multinational power plants were not permitted to invest in the Chinese power equipment industry, then the main competitive struggle would have been between HPEC and its domestic rivals. This position was very like that in which the major Western power equipment companies grew to maturity. However, as we shall see, the nature of competition altered sharply from the late 1980s onwards.

Multinational companies: what is an 'indigenous Chinese' company? In the 1990s, the market has become truly global. There is intense interest among Western power equipment producers in the possibility of gaining a share of the potentially vast Chinese market. This can be achieved not only by direct exports, but at least as important, through the establishment of a joint venture with one of the domestic producers. In the 1990s, HPEC's leading domestic competitors, Shanghai Electric and Dongfang each established major joint ventures with multinational companies, approved by the Chinese government. Therefore, competition is no longer simply between 'domestic' and 'foreign' firms. Moreover, for HPEC a major part of its strategy is to succeed in international markets. By the mid-1990s, HPEC's struggle in the domestic market needed to be located within a global context in order to be properly understood.

Shanghai Electrical (Group) Corporation (SEC). Westinghouse was extremely keen to enter the Chinese market. In order to gain entry it was willing to engage in a large-scale technology transfer programme with SEC, involving a wide-ranging licensing agreement, involving technology necessary to produce both 300 MW and 600 MW turbines This programme began in 1981, and it enabled SEC to develop manufacturing capability for 300 MW and 600 MW units. Its first successful 300 MW power station was put into operation in 1987. The co-operation was expanded greatly in 1995, with the conclusion of a full-scale joint venture, sub-divided into four separate agreements with each of SEC's subordinate units. Westinghouse was a minority partner in each of them, with an ownership share of between 30–40 per cent. There was a time limit of 20 years on the duration of the project. Westinghouse's total investment amounted to $82 million. The Chinese

TABLE **6-22 Share of Different Manufacturers in China's Domestic Power Plant Equipment Production 1991–6 (%)**

Plant	1991	1992	1993	1994	1995	1996
Harbin Power Equipment Co.	24.7	32.3	28.4	26.0	22.3	18.4
Dongfang Electric Corporation	19.4	26.6	23.2	n.a.	n.a.	17.5
Shanghai United Electric Corporation	22.2	19.8	21.8	n.a.	n.a.	15.6
Others	33.7	21.3	26.6	n.a.	n.a.	48.5

SOURCES: Warburg (1995: 45), and derived from interviews at MMB (January 1997)

side contributed their existing facilities. Westinghouse committed itself to investing $100 million in modernizing the plants in Shanghai (*FT*, 16 September 1996).
A key part of the joint venture was Westinghouse's commitment to transfer further technologies to the Chinese side. The joint venture agreement specified that
Westinghouse would transfer to the Chinese side all its technical data for steam
turbines and steam turbogenerators. After absorption of the technical data, the
joint ventures 'will have the capacity to design and manufacture 1000 MW thermal power sets with sub-critical and super-critical parameters' (Lu Yansun, 1997).

After Siemens' purchase of Westinghouse's non-nuclear business, Siemens
took over ownership of the joint venture in Shanghai, employing around 8000
people (Siemens, *Annual Report, 1998*). This provides it with a way into the
China market through one of the major domestic players. By 1997 Siemens had
a total of 36 joint ventures in China, with a total investment of around $700
million and sales of $1.38 billion (*CDBW*, 24 August 1997). Its take-over of
Westinghouse's non-nuclear business provides a large addition to its assets in
China, and enables it to add a powerful power equipment joint venture to its
existing stock of assets in China, which are in a variety of electrical and electronics products. Siemens estimated that its orders for power equipment in China
in 1999 would amount to around 1.8 GW (*FT*, 10 June 1999).

SEC's output advanced much more rapidly than that of HPEC during the
mid/late 1990s, at least in part due to the contribution of Westinghouse to its technological progress and through substantial investment in the joint venture.
Between 1990 and 1996, its output of steam turbine increased from 2200 MW to
4700 MW (Shanghai Turbine Company, *Annual Report*, 1998). HPEC's total
installed capacity (including steam and hydro) rose from 2700 MW in 1991 to
3600 MW in 1998, a much slower rate of progress than at SEC. With Siemens as
its joint venture partner instead of Westinghouse, SEC constitutes an even more
formidable competitor for HPEC.

Dongfang Power Equipment Company (Sichuan). Dongfang floated its turbine
generator plant on the Hong Kong stock market in 1994. H share holders (Hong
Kong-listed Mainland Companies) accounted for around 38 per cent of the share
ownership after the flotation. Subsequently, it set up a joint venture between its
hydro generator plant and GE (Canada). The Dongfang plant contributed all its
productive assets from that branch of the business. The Chinese side owns 70 per
cent of the share value of the new joint venture and the foreign partner injected
cash to purchase a 30 per cent ownership share. Dongfang's Jiaxiang (Zhejiang
Province) boiler plant has set up a joint venture with Hitachi. The equity was split
50/50 between Dongfang and Hitachi. A condition of the joint venture was that
Hitachi transfer technology for the manu-facture of sub-critical steam turbines. In
addition, Dongfang had long negotiations with Siemens to set up a joint venture
with its thermal generator plant. However, Siemens' demands in relation to market guarantees and product price were thought to be 'excessive', and the proposed
joint venture failed to come to fruition.

The combination of devolution of asset ownership rights to the local authorities,
international flotation and international joint ventures with different sub-parts of

the business meant that a merger of one or more of China's leading players in this sector, became more difficult.

Not only Dongfang and Shanghai have set up joint ventures with multinational partners. So also have smaller competitors. A Tianjin power equipment company has a joint venture with GEC–Alsthom, making equipment for hydroelectric schemes and another in Suzhou making switchgear. GEC–Alsthom also has a joint production agreement with Beijing Heavy Electrical Generator Company, which makes turbines. Kvaerner (Norway) has a joint venture with a power equipment maker in Chongqing and ABB has one in Hangzhou. The largest independent domestic boiler maker, Beijing Boiler Works (Beiguo), has a joint venture with Babcock and Wilcox (USA). Framatome (France) has a co-production agreement with Eastern China Electric Group in Chengdu (Sichuan) for the manufacture of heavy machine parts, such as steam engines, for Guangdong's No. 2 nuclear power plant. The two sides signed a long-term co-operation contract to develop nuclear plants in China (*FT*, 18 July 1996). In other words, all of HPEC's competitors, large and small, have joint ventures. HPEC considers this to be 'very dangerous'.

Multinational companies are increasingly co-operating with HPEC, using it as a sub-contractor, in tendering for international power plant projects. They have begun also to co-operate with domestic firms in bidding for domestic projects. The largest co-operation of this type for HPEC has been for a power station in Hefei (Anhui Province). HPEC successfully bid for this large project (two 350 MW units) in alliance with ABB.

HPEC: The national champion. From the 1950s onwards HPEGC was China's number one power equipment producer. Right through to the present day it has had a special position as the 'national champion' in this industry.

In 1994, HPEC completed the negotiations with several multinational companies to set up a series of joint ventures. It signed memoranda with each of the companies concerned and the proposal package was approved by the Harbin City government, and by the Ministry of Machinery. However the proposal was turned down by the State Council because they considered that HPEC was 'one of the largest industrial groups in China and should, accordingly, remain in Chinese hands, owned by the state'. This apparent disadvantage also has some advantages. It means that a disproportionate share of government assistance may be channelled towards HPEC, instead of towards the Sino–foreign joint ventures.

HPEC was the first major power plant producer to be established in post-Liberation China. It has been the main producer since the First Five Year Plan. Under the agreement, each of HPEC's subordinate plants was to have set up a joint venture with either GE or ABB, and each was to have two joint ventures, one 'large' and one 'small'. The large joint venture was to have been 70 per cent owned by the Chinese side and 30 per cent by the foreign partner. All the production assets of the subordinate plant were to have been put into the large joint venture. The 'small' joint venture was to have been owned 70 per cent by the foreign partner and 30 per cent by the respective HPEC subordinate plant.

This company was to have had responsibility for transferring technology from the foreign partner to the HPEC plant and responsibility for making international tenders. Equipment for successful tenders was to have been supplied by the 'large' company, and technology purchased from the 'small' company.

In October 1994 Jack Welch, Chief Executive Officer of General Electric, visited China and met with Premier Li Peng. Li Peng told Welch that China wanted HPEC to 'remain in Chinese hands'. He told Welch that HPEC could co-operate with GE in other ways than through a joint venture, such as through co-production, co-tendering and purchase of technology by the Chinese side. While we were researching at HPEC in July 1996, Premier Li Peng visited the company. This was a highly significant visit. He reassured HPEC of their central role in the country's power equipment industry. HPEC's leaders are highly confident that, by whatever channel, HPEC will receive the support it needs to guarantee its leading position.

In July 1996, HPEGC (the state holding company) was one of 300 state-owned enterprises identified by the State Economics and Trade Commission as key enterprises in China's development (HPEC, 1997: 32). In November 1996, the central government identified the first batch of pilot projects that could use foreign exchange reserve loans to purchase domestically manufactured power equipment (HPEC, 1997: 33). This enabled HPEC to sell two sets of 600 MW power units and two sets of 300 MW power units. In 1997, HPEC submitted a detailed plan to the government for its needs in order to upgrade its hydro power technology and production capacity. In August 1997, the State Development Bank agreed to provide two large loans for expanding the Company's capacity to manufacture large-scale hydro power equipment and technological improvements to enable HPEC to compete in supplying hydro equipment for the Three Gorges Project (HPEC, 1997: 5). The loans were for 580 million yuan and 120 million yuan (a total of $84 million), repayable over 13 and nine years, respectively, with rates of interest of 12.42 per cent and 5.94 per cent per annum (HPEC, 1997: 5). A total of around $85 million in policy loans to assist HPEC provided a significant contribution to technical progress at the company, especially in its struggle to upgrade its capability for large-scale hydro projects.

A further advantage for HPEC in remaining independent of the multinational suppliers is that a multinational would be unlikely to subcontract to another multinational competitor's joint venture within China. Already, HPEC has won sub-contracting work from a multinational within China as the multinational does not wish to sub-contract to a competitor's joint venture.

CONCLUSION

FROM STATE FACTORY TO COMPETITIVE FIRM

By the early 1990s HPEC had made a massive transformation from the command economy factory of the Maoist period. It was a much bigger firm. Its technical level had greatly advanced. It was now able independently to compete in the market-place, both domestic and international. It was developing a corporate identity. There were large problems with adjusting to a new institutional form, the holding company, which had been hastily set up in order that the firm could be floated on the Hong Kong stock market. However, in the sharpest contrast to the Maoist period, HPEC was now a 'firm', genuinely competing against other enterprises, attempting independently to find the resources to finance its growth and modernization. Its management was responsible to the Harbin City government. They in turn were anxious for the firm to succeed, and were prepared to back the management in its effort to make the firm more competitive, provided the necessary adjustments were undertaken in a slow and socially manageable fashion.

By 1996 HPEC may not yet have fully developed all the characteristics of Chandler's 'modern industrial corporation' (Chandler, 1990). However, it had moved strongly in that direction, and was far closer to that paradigm than was the state-administered factory of twenty years previously. HPEC had begun to 'compete for market share by improving their product, their processes of production, their marketing, their purchasing', and attempting 'to move into growing markets more rapidly [than their competitors]' (Chandler, 1990: 8). HPEC had 'invested in enlarging and modernizing its production facilities in order to benefit from economies of scale and scope'. It had 'invested in a national and international marketing network so that the volume of sales might keep pace with the volume of production'. It had attempted to 'recruit and train personnel in both production and distribution' in order administer these activities more effectively.

How Big is Chinese 'Big Business'?

Despite the changes in operational methods, technological upgrading and growth in size, in 1996 HPEC was still far from being able to compete directly on the global level playing field with the leading multinational power equipment makers. HPEC, China's 'national champion', remained very small indeed compared to the giants of world power equipment manufacture (Table 6-1). GE has roughly the same size of workforce employed in its power generation equipment division as HPEC, but the division's turnover is 19 times as great as HPEC's. Its profits in 1995 were $1.2 billion and its R & D spending was $1.3 billion. At HPEC the respective figures were a paltry $14 million and $3 million.[64] If the 'playing field' in the power equipment market were made truly 'level', the competitors standing on the field would be of grotesquely unequal size. The battle between a firm such as HPEC and GE is a clash between David and Goliath in which there could only be one possible winner.

HPEC's relatively small size matters not only because of the fact that it is profoundly disadvantaged in its ability to invest in technical progress, and to benefit from economies of scale and scope. It matters also because of the disadvantages its small size offers in relation to bargaining with the multinational giants.

TABLE 6-23 Turnover of HPEC, 1996 (% in brackets)

Item	Million yuan
Main thermal power equipment	1312 (54.6)
Main hydro power equipment	246 (10.3)
Engineering services	320 (13.3)
Ancillary equipment for power stations	253 (10.5)
AC/DC motors and other products	271 (11.3)
Total	2403 (100)

SOURCE: HPEC (1997: 6)

China's three separate leading firms in the power industry compete with each other to attract foreign investment, and are therefore prepared to accept less advantageous conditions of technical transfer than if a single agent were negotiating. The most successful piece of technical transfer to the industry was negotiated by the central government, not by the individual plants. Moreover, each of the separate firms is acutely aware that despite great progress having been made since the 1970s, there is little chance of them being truly competitive with the multinationals. Therefore many people within the companies argue that the firm's best strategy is to accept co-operation as a junior partner with the multinationals, participating in the international division of labour of the vastly larger firm. This 'satisficing' path would produce an easier life for the firm's managers, removing many of the complex decisions from their hands, and enable them to join the international elite, travelling frequently to the headquarters in Europe or the US, and probably to improve their incomes and status. As separate firms there is little hope of any of them individually being able to compete with the global giants.

Compared to its major international competitors, HPEC, like the other main domestic power equipment manufacturers (Table 6-23), has a high degree of concentration on main engine power equipment manufacture, and is, therefore, more likely to suffer from fluctuations in its income. In 1995, only around 13 per cent of the total turnover came from ancillary equipment, and just 8 per cent from engineering services. Had the attempt to reconstruct the Northeast Power Equipment Company been successful then it would have become a much more diversified company within the power equipment branch. It is now slowly moving towards greater diversification into these areas. It still has a very small share of its turnover generated from engineering services. As was seen above, in the power divisions of the multinational companies engineering services now occupy a much large share of turnover and an even larger share of profits. Moreover, for the largest multinationals, such GE, Westinghouse, ABB, Siemens and GEC– Alsthom, the power divisions are just one part of a much more diverse engineering company. A major consequence of the narrow focus of HPEC is that it is highly vulnerable to cyclical changes in demand for power generating equipment.[65]

POLICY CHOICES

In the mid-1990s HPEC was at a cross-roads. It had made the 'first jump' from a state-administered plant to a competitive firm. It had developed institutional and technical capabilities that could form the basis for a further development to challenge the existing multinationals and itself join the ranks of the leading world producers. Moreover, there was a huge domestic demand potential which could underpin this effort. The Chinese domestic power equipment market is the world's largest and fastest growing market. Can HPEC now independently make this 'second jump' to a firm able to compete with the multinational giants as a comprehensive integrated producer of power equipment?

We have seen that the gap between Chinese and global technology and firm size is still large. Alongside China's advances in the reform period has gone one of the most dynamic epochs the world's power equipment industry has witnessed. The institutional and technological gap between HPEC and the world's leaders may now be greater even than before the reforms began.

One possible path is to decide that it will be too wasteful to continue to attempt to build integrated companies that can manufacture the entire power plant unit. Under this scenario, China's leading power equipment makers would all accept that the most efficient path for them and for the whole Chinese economy is to become sub-contractors to the multinational giants within the global division of labour. Attempts to build a 'national champion' would then be abandoned as anachronistic and wasteful. If China decides not to pursue this path, and continues to try to build integrated national power equipment companies that can compete on the level playing field with the multinational giants, what are the ways in which this might be brought about? It is impossible to imagine that this would happen through the spontaneous working of the market. Instead, it would require considerable government involvement in industrial policy to support a 'national champion'.

LESSONS FROM THE ADVANCE ECONOMIES

Each of the world's leading oligopolistic firms in the sector benefited from government support. State procurement contracts for national power stations have played an especially important role in the growth of many of the industry's leading firms. The issue of government procurement for telecommunications, defence, public utilities, and public transportation was put on the agenda at the Uruguay Round of the GATT talks. However, no major breakthrough was achieved and the use of procurement contracts continues to be an important potential weapon in a national government's armoury for supporting the development of national firms (Ruigrok and van Tulder, 1995: 226). Local content regulations are not allowed under WTO. However, they are widely applied in both developing and advanced economies.[66] Moreover, voluntary export restraints are widely used in the advanced economies to limit the extent of market penetration of selected foreign goods.

In the early phase of GE's growth, government procurement contracts were crucial. Throughout its history they have been a major source of demand for the firm's products, providing 'a solid basis for profits and cross-subsidies for the civilian business' (Ruigrok and van Tulder, 1995: 241). Around one-quarter of the funds for GE's famous New York Research and Development Centre, home to two Nobel Prize winners, came from US government funding. In the early 1990s, the Centre's annual budget was around $400 million. Thus, at a very rough estimate, the US government in the early 1990s was contributing around $100 million annually to fund R & D at General Electric (compared with HPEC's *total* annual R & D budget in the mid-1990s of just $3 million) (Table 6-1).

Siemens has benefited hugely from government procurement contracts, and continues to do so. The head of General Electric Power Generating Division commented recently: 'We have not succeeded in selling a turbine in Germany since the Marshal Plan, nor has any other non-German company' (quoted in *FT*, 16 May 1995). In the 1980s, around two-thirds of Siemens' sales were estimated to be in semi-restricted public procurement, which provided a large cross-subsidy for the civilian side of the business. Siemens benefited from large direct subsidies from the German and EC governments for its core technologies (Ruigrok and van Tulder, 1995: 244).

ABB has been treated as a 'national champion' firm in both Sweden and Switzerland. It has probably benefited considerably from cost-plus contracts and cross-subsidies to its civilian business from government procurement contracts in both countries (Ruigrok and van Tulder, 1995: 247). Alcatel Alsthom was nationalized in 1938, and only finally denationalized in 1987. It has throughout been heavily advantaged by government procurement contracts (Ruigrok and van Tulder, 1995: 247). Framatome, Europe's largest nuclear power plant producer has remained in French ownership (mainly owned by the government), due to the government's refusal to allow foreign ownership in France's 'showpiece nuclear industry' (*FT*, 9 October 1996). A major reason for the firm's growth, once attracting 'the cream of engineering talent' and large government research funding, was the large demand from the French government to build and maintain state-owned French power plants. Mitsubishi Electric was greatly stimulated in its early growth in the 1930s by military contracts, and in the post-war period benefited from heavy government protection for the Japanese electronics industry. It is Japan's third largest defence contractor (Ruigrok and van Tulder, 1995: 252).

A commitment on all sides to purely commercial considerations in shaping the development of the global power equipment production would have a profound effect on the global shape of the industry. However, as we can see, this day is still far off, even in the advanced capitalist economies.[67] If China's leading power equipment manufacturers are to continue to catch up, then it is necessary for the Chinese government to continue to protect them through non-tariff barriers, through procurement policy and through domestic content requirement for new power projects.

GOVERNMENT POLICY TO INFLUENCE TECHNOLOGICAL TRANSFER

HPEC cannot compete with multinationals in new technology. It would take a long time for HPEC to develop the most advanced technology itself. Moreover, if China continued to produce electricity with old technology it would impose high costs upon the Chinese power generating industry and a high burden upon Chinese consumers of electricity, both business and private. HPEC has no alternative but to catch up mainly through acquiring technology from the world's leading multinationals.

HPEC cannot afford to purchase the technology. It has, therefore, to be acquired through co-operation with the multinationals. A major advantage for Chinese power equipment firms is that the potential market is so huge that they can bargain for excellent terms for technical transfer. They are assisted in this by the weakness in the power equipment market in the advanced capitalist economies in the 1990s. The difficulties facing the industry's giants have been compounded by the intense competition that has been unleashed among power equipment producers by electricity industry privatization. Moreover, the leading international firms in the power equipment sector are intensely competitive, to the point of tendering 'suicidal' bids for contracts in China. Thus a bargaining agency in China, is in a strong position to play one leading firm off against the other.

The 15-year agreement with Combustion Engineering (CE) and Westinghouse was a good example of the way in which the Chinese power equipment industry can benefit from technology transfer. In the simplest terms, China can 'trade market share for technology transfer'. However, the Chinese government negotiated the CE/Westinghouse deal. It is doubtful if individual Chinese firms could achieve such a desirable outcome for Chinese power equipment manufacturers.

If the planning functions of the central government weaken, then rivalrous individual Chinese producers may be prepared to make themselves more attractive as a joint venture partner by bargaining less hard for technology transfer. Moreover, to the extent that technology is transferred, it is more likely to be for sub-systems rather than for integrated whole system manufacture. Such a competitive struggle among small (by global standards), domestic Chinese power equipment firms, would greatly increase the possibility of the leading Chinese power equipment makers becoming sub-branches within the global division of labour being rapidly established by the giants of the industry. Such firms would be 'domestic' firms, with a large fraction of output locally manufactured. However, they would not be complete system producers able to compete with the multinationals. Continued government involvement in negotiating technology transfer is essential for further catch-up by Chinese power equipment makers.

GOVERNMENT-ORCHESTRATED MERGER

We have seen that there is only a handful of global giants who account for the lion's share of the global production of power equipment. In the advanced economies, even a former industry leader, Westinghouse, cannot compete in non-nuclear power equipment, and has been bought by Siemens. A powerful 'new entrant', Rolls-Royce, quickly realized it was not sufficiently large to be effective in this sector, and moved out of large-scale power equipment only a few years after entering the field. If such powerful players cannot compete in the industry, it is impossible to imagine that a small player in global terms, such as HPEC, could compete on the 'level playing field' of global competition. Even the USA will soon be left with just one integrated power equipment manufacturer. China still has three integrated producers.

In recent years the world's power equipment industry, already highly concentrated, has been going through a process of further consolidation, with little, if any, opposition from anti-monopoly policy.[68] In the power equipment industry in the USA just two firms, GE and Westinghouse, dominate the sector (and in the near future there may just be one). Within France and Britain, GEC–Alsthom is massively larger than any competitor, and within Germany, Siemens has a virtual monopoly. Just three firms, ABB, Siemens, and GEC–Alsthom (Alstom), dominate the European non-nuclear power equipment industry.

Provided that they fulfilled their legal obligations to their joint venture partners, it is inconceivable that international action would be taken against China if the government orchestrated a merger of the leading domestic power equipment firms. Such a merger might logically not only include the principal manufacturers of the main engines, namely HPEC, Shanghai Electric, and Dongfang, but also the main manufacturers of ancillary components, notably the Northeast China Transformer Group, so that the firm might mimic more closely the structure of the leading international firms. It might even contemplate integrating leading aircraft engine enterprises along the lines of GE.

If China wishes to establish itself as a long-run player in integrated manufacturer of power equipment, using its vast domestic market as the base for institutional and technological development, then there is a strong logic supporting a merger of at least the three leading players. There would be powerful economies of scale and scope flowing from this. These would include economies in bidding for international contracts, in centralizing R & D, in unified procurement of components, in bargaining for technological transfer from multinational companies and in specialization of functions between the constituent plants, each of which currently produces the full range of power equipment, with a hugely inefficient duplication of specialized, expensive machinery.

There are many problems with accomplishing such a merger. The ownership structure of the main power equipment companies is now quite complex, including internationally floated portions of the given enterprises, as well as joint ventures with different multinational firms. Many of the senior staff in the different enterprises favour becoming sub-branches of the global giant companies. This offers them an easier and more secure route to improving their personal position. Local authorities too may favour this path as it is less uncertain than attempting to build a global national champion. Harbin Municipality, for example, supported HPEC establishing large-scale international joint ventures. The Ministry of Power (now the SP) opposes a merger, which it considers would strengthen the monopoly power of the domestic power equipment manufacturers.

Although the different ownership structure of the three main Chinese producers would make for difficult practical details, it would be no more complex than many mergers in the advanced economies. Indeed, these have become more and more complex technically as international alliances, joint ventures, joint research and development programmes and joint production agreements have grown apace. Moreover, the fact that the Chinese state was the majority owner of each of the companies makes the merger easier to carry out. In an increasingly internationally competitive market, the construction of a single large Chinese integrated manufacturer would increase, not reduce, competition in power equipment, since it would add a countervailing force to the fast-declining number of players in the global industry. The accomplishment of such a merger would make it clear that China intended seriously to go to the next stage in establishing its own globally competitive giant company. This would provide greatly enhanced opportunities for senior management within each of the constituent companies.

7

Oil and Petrochemicals

The WTO is America's best tool for opening China's markets.
(US–China Trade Council, 1999)

Win the war but do not boast,
Win the war but do not brag,
Win the war but do not show arrogance,
Whatever is in its prime is bound to decline,
For being in the prime is against the Dao,
Whatever goes against the Dao
Will come to an early end.
(Lao Zi, *The book of Dao and De*)

THE GLOBAL SETTING

CENTRALITY OF OIL AND GAS IN THE GLOBAL POLITICAL ECONOMY

Growth of Primary Energy Consumption. Despite enormous advances in energy efficiency since the first oil shock of 1973, world consumption of primary energy continued to rise remorselessly. Between 1972 and 1997, total world primary energy consumption rose by 63 per cent (BP, 1998). Over the decade 1987–97, the growth rate slowed considerably, with an expansion of almost 16 per cent (Table 7-1). However, this slowdown was mainly due to the huge decline in the former Soviet Union, in which a 34 per cent fall in primary energy consumption took place over the decade (BP, 1998). Within Western Europe, significant increases in primary energy consumption took place, with increases of 19.6 per cent in France, 12.0 per cent in Italy, and 8.2 per cent in the UK (BP, 1998). In the USA, consumption rose by 18.6 per cent over the decade, with the

TABLE **7-1 World Primary Energy Consumption, 1987 and 1997
(million tons of oil equivalent) (% in brackets)**

Country/region	1987		1997		% change
World	7352	(100.0)	8509	(100.0)	(+) 15.7
USA	1811	(24.6)	2144	(25.2)	(+) 18.6
Europe	1739	(23.7)	1782	(20.9)	(+) 2.5
Asia Pacific	1494	(20.3)	2376	(27.9)	(+) 59.0
of which:					
Japan	373	(5.0)	506	(5.9)	(+) 35.6
China	587	(8.0)	905	(10.6)	(+) 54.2

SOURCE: BP (1998)

TABLE **7-2 World Primary Energy Consumption, by Energy Source,
1987 and 1997**

Source	1987		1997		% change 1987–97
	mtoe	%	mtoe	%	
Oil	2947	40.1	3395	39.9	(+) 15.2
Natural gas	1581	21.5	1977	23.2	(+) 25.0
Coal	2197	29.9	2293	26.9	(+) 4.4
Nuclear	448	6.1	617	7.3	(+) 37.7
Hydro-electric	180	2.4	226	2.7	(+) 25.6
Total	7353	100.0	8509	100.0	(+) 15.7

SOURCE: BP (1998)

NOTE: mtoe\Million tons of oil equivalent

USA's share of the world total rising from 24.6 per cent to 25.2 per cent. The biggest advance came in the Asia Pacific region, which experienced a growth of 59 per cent over the decade, its share rising from 20.3 per cent in 1987 to 27.9 per cent in 1997.

Central Position of Oil and Gas in Primary Energy Supplies. Following the impact of the first oil crisis of 1973, it was widely thought that the contribution of oil to primary energy consumption would fall significantly as other energy sources replaced it. In fact a combination of both supply and demand-side factors has helped sustain the long-term position of oil in the world's primary energy supplies. On the demand side, significant problems have developed with various potential substitutes. Fears for the safety of nuclear power, fuelled by the accident at Three Mile Island in the USA in 1979 and the disaster at Chernobyl in the USSR in 1986, have dramatically limited the growth of the world-wide nuclear industry. Its share of world primary energy consumption has hardly changed since the 1980s, still standing at only 7.3 per cent (Table 7-2).

TABLE 7-3 Distribution of World Reserves and Production of Oil, 1997

| | Proven reserves | | | | Production | | | |
Source	Oil (billion tons)	(%)	Natural gas (trillion ft³)	(%)	Oil (million tons)	(%)	Natural gas (mtoe)	(%)
World total	140.9	100.0	5112	100.0	3475	100.0	2001	100.0
Middle East	91.6	65.2	1726	33.7	1045	30.1	150.1	7.5
of which:								
Saudi Arabia	35.8	25.2	191	3.7	450	12.9	39.5	2.0
Iran	12.7	9.0	810	15.8	184	5.3	38.7	1.9
Iraq	15.1	10.8	110	2.2	58	1.7	—	—
Kuwait	13.3	9.3	53	1.0	104	3.0	8.5	0.4
Former USSR	9.1	6.4	2003	39.2	363	10.5	561.1	28.1

SOURCE: BP (1998)

NOTE: mtoe\Million tons of oil equivalent

World coal output continues to grow, but its overall share of primary energy is falling (from 29.9 per cent in 1987 to 26.9 per cent in 1997). This has been mainly due to the high costs of reducing its polluting effects and the fact that it is the most highly carbon-intensive of the leading fuel sources, thereby contributing heavily to global warming.

Major new sources of oil supply, such as Alaska and the North Sea, and greatly expanded production in Mexico, as well as increased supply from smaller producers, such as Malaysia, China and Angola, all helped to ease the pressure on prices. Moreover, the incentive to substitute other fuel sources for oil declined as the real price of oil stabilized in the late 1970s, and then fell sharply after the second oil shock of the early 1980s. The net impact of these factors meant that the share of oil, by far the most important single component, in total primary energy supply has remained stable in the past decade at around 40 per cent. Indeed, the share of oil and closely related natural gas taken together actually rose from 61.6 per cent in 1987 to 63.1 per cent, accounting for three-fifths of world primary energy consumption.

Geographical Distribution of World Oil and Gas. The world's oil and natural gas reserves are highly concentrated by geographical region. The exploration, drilling and pipeline technologies for the two products are very closely related. The Middle East accounts for no less than 65 per cent of world proven oil reserves (Table 7-3). The four countries of Saudi Arabia, Iran, Iraq, and Kuwait between them account for over half of total world oil reserves. The former USSR and the Middle East account for 73 per cent of the world's total natural gas reserves (Table 7-4).

Despite the development of important new centres of production, the Middle East has actually increased its relative importance in world oil production. Its share of total world oil output rose from 22 per cent in 1987 to 30 per cent in 1997 (Table 7-5). From 1987 to 1997, Middle Eastern oil output rose by 8.5

TABLE **7-4** **Natural Gas Production and Reserves, 1997**

Area	Production		Reserves		
	(billion metres³)	*(%)*	*(trillion metres³)*	*(%)*	*R/P ratio**
World	2223	100.0	144.8	100.0	64
USA	545	24.5	4.7	3.3	9
South/Central America/Mexico	121	5.4	8.1	5.6	67
Europe	276	12.4	5.6	3.8	20
Former USSR	623	28.1	56.7	39.2	91
Middle East	167	7.5	48.9	33.7	293
Asia Pacific	240	10.8	9.1	6.3	38
Africa	94	4.2	9.9	6.8	105

SOURCE: BP (1998)

NOTE: * Year before reserves are exhausted at current levels of consumption

TABLE **7-5 Oil Production by Region (1987–97: million barrels per day, mmb/d)** (**% in brackets**)

Area	1987	1997	% change	Absolute change (mmb/d)
World	60.7 (100.0)	72.2 (100.0)	(+) 18.9	(+) 11.5
USA	9.9 (16.3)	8.3 (11.5)	(−) 16.2	(−) 1.6
South/Central America/Mexico	6.8 (11.2)	9.9 (13.7)	(+) 45.6	(+) 3.1
Europe	4.6 (7.6)	6.9 (9.6)	(+) 50.0	(+) 2.3
Former USSR	12.7 (20.9)	7.4 (10.2)	(−) 41.7	(−) 5.3
Middle East	13.2 (21.7)	21.7 (30.1)	(+) 64.4	(+) 8.5
Asia Pacific	6.2 (10.2)	7.7 (10.7)	(+) 24.2	(+) 1.5
Africa	5.4 (8.9)	7.8 (10.8)	(+) 44.4	(+) 2.4

SOURCE: BP (1998)

million barrels per day alongside the growth of world output of just 11.5 million barrels per day. However, this greatly understates the central position of the Middle East in the world energy picture, since the vast bulk of Middle Eastern oil is exported. In 1997, the Middle East accounted for over 45 per cent of total world oil exports (BP, 1998). The Far East is especially dependent on supplies from the Middle East, which account for over 78 per cent of the region's total oil imports (BP, 1998: 18).

The significance of the geographical distribution of world oil and gas supplies is of special importance for global political economy, due to the fact that the world's dominant economic power, the USA is increasingly reliant on oil imports. US oil production peaked in 1970, at 11.3 million barrels per day (Yergin, 1991: 567). US oil output has fallen steadily, reaching just 8.3 million barrels per day in 1997 (BP, 1998). The USA's share of world oil output fell from 16.3 per cent in 1987 to 11.5 per cent in 1997. Despite great advances in energy efficiency, US oil consumption rose by 8 per cent from 1972 to 1997. Oil imports rose by 59 per cent from 1987 to 1997, amounting to almost 25 per cent of total world oil imports in 1997 (BP, 1998: 18). By 1997, net oil imports had reached one-half of total US oil consumption (Table 7-6).

Even more alarming from the standpoint of global political economy is the fact that a major part of the USA's increase in primary energy consumption since the first oil crisis has been through a large expansion in the production and use of natural gas and coal, neither of which is sustainable in even the short-term. From 1987 to 1997, the USA increased its (already high) level of natural gas consumption by 27 per cent, by which point it accounted for 29 per cent of total world consumption (BP, 1998). However, the USA's output of natural gas has lagged behind, growing by only 14 per cent in the same period. Already by 1997, the USA accounted for 26 per cent of world natural gas imports, the bulk of its imports coming from Canada (BP, 1998: 29). At current rates of production the USA will run out of natural gas within just nine years (BP, 1998). From 1987 to

TABLE 7-6 US Oil Production, Consumption and Imports, 1948–97

| | | | Net imports | |
Year	Production (mmb/d)	Consumption (mmb/d)	(mmb/d)	(% consumption)
1948	—	5.8*	—	—
1967	—	—	2.2*	19*
1970	11.3*	—	—	—
1972	—	16.4*	—	—
1973	—	—	6.0*	36*
1987	9.9**	16.0**	5.5**	34**
1997	8.3**	17.7**	8.9**	50**

SOURCES: * Yergin (1991: 542, 567)
          ** BP (1998)

NOTE: mmb/d\Million barrels per day

TABLE 7-7 Relationship of World Reserves of Coal, Oil and Natural Gas in Relation to Population

| | Proven reserves of | | | | | | | |
| | Coal | | Natural gas | | Oil | | Population | |
	(billion tons)	(%)	trillion m³	%	(billion tons)	(%)	(billion)	(%)
World	1032	100.0	144.8	100.0	140.9	100.0	5.83	100.0
Asia-Pacific*	311	30.2	9.1	6.3	5.7	4.1	3.04	52.1
of which:								
China	115	11.1	1.2	0.8	3.3	2.3	1.23	21.1

SOURCE: BP (1998), World Bank (1998)

NOTE: *Including South Asia

1997, US coal consumption rose by 16 per cent, accounting for 23 per cent of the world total (BP, 1998: 33). If the USA is serious about reducing its emission of greenhouse gases, then the prospects are for significant declines in the role of coal in the USA's energy portfolio. Given the barriers to increased use of nuclear energy, and slow progress in other forms of renewable energy, current trends in the USA's output of and use of natural gas and coal seem likely to sharply increase the role of oil and natural gas imports in the US economy in the near future.

It would be an understatement to say that the USA has a strong strategic interest in the political economy of the Middle East and the former Soviet Union. Whereas the USA once had huge reserves of oil and large reserves of natural gas, which are now substantially exhausted, the Asia Pacific region (including South Asia) is extremely poorly endowed with both oil and natural gas. The region has only 6.3 per cent of the world's proven natural gas reserves and a mere 4.1 per cent of the world's proven oil reserves (Table 7-7). However, the region has no less than 52 per cent of the world's population. For China especially, the level of endowment with oil and gas appears to be exceptionally difficult. Internationally-accepted data indicate that China has only 2.3 per cent of the world's oil reserves and a mere 0.8 per cent of natural gas reserves, compared to more than 21 per cent of the world's population (Table 7-7). By contrast, the region is relatively well-endowed with coal reserves, containing an estimated 30 per cent of the world's proven reserves (Table 7-7). China's proven coal reserves amount to over 11 per cent of the world's total and even at current high levels of output, China's reserves would last for over 80 years (BP, 1998). However, in so far as the Asia–Pacific region is restricted in the degree to which it can increase or continue to use coal, especially through international pressure to alleviate the emission of greenhouse gases, then it will be pushed even more deeply into importing its primary energy needs. This could only mean even greater imports of oil and natural gas from the Middle East and the former Soviet Union.

It would be an understatement to say that Asian–Pacific countries in general, and China in particular, have a strong strategic interest in the political economy of the Middle East and the former Soviet Union.

THE REVOLUTION IN OIL AND GAS: THE CREATION OF SUPER GIANTS

The 'Disintegration' of the World Oil and Petrochemical Industry. When the Chinese government was considering the first steps in reforming the structure of its oil and petrochemicals industry in the 1980s, the international picture looked very different from today. Powerful state-owned oil companies were a dominant feature of the industry outside the USA. It appeared perfectly reasonable that the state should have a large ownership share in an industry that was of great national strategic importance. Moreover, the close integration of oil production and down-stream processing activities, that had been the foundation of the industry, was fast unravelling.

In Europe, state-owned oil and petrochemical companies dominated the industry within each country. Oil and petrochemicals were considered key strategic industries:

- **UK**. In the UK, one of the world's most successful oil companies, BP, had been under majority state ownership from the beginnings of the First World War. A major reason for the original government holding in the company had been to ensure the supply of oil to Britain from the Middle East, especially during time of war. As late as the 1980s, 31.5 per cent of its shares were still owned by the government, with privatization only taking place in 1987.

- **Italy**. Italy's ENI was founded as a state-owned entity. A major objective of its rapid international expansion in the 1950s had been to ensure Italy's supplies of oil independently of the US giant oil companies (Yergin, 1991: 503). ENI did not begin privatization until 1995, and the whole process was spread out over several years and is still not completed. The vast bulk of ENI's revenue (over 76 per cent) at the start of its privatization came from upstream oil and gas production, with only 26 per cent from refining and petrochemicals (*FT*, 1 November 1995). Under state ownership, ENI was turned from a large loss-maker in the early 1990s into a profitable entity when the privatization began in 1995.

- **France**. In France, as in Italy, the state itself developed the oil industry under a variety of different corporate entities that culminated in the formation of the state-owned national champion, Elf, in 1965. A major goal of the state's activities in the oil and gas sphere had been to develop overseas sources of supply. By 1961, companies owned and controlled by the state were producing oil equivalent to 94 per cent of French national demand (Yergin, 1991: 526). Building on its base in Algeria, Elf launched a global exploration campaign that, like ENI, enabled it to enter the ranks of the world's major oil companies. Elf also, was not privatized until the early 1990s, and then also, in a step-by-step fashion.

- **Spain**. In the 1980s, the Spanish government created a giant state-owned integrated oil and petrochemical company, Repsol. It emerged from 'the remnants of an ungainly public sector monopoly'. It was privatized bit by bit in the 1990s, with the final share offering only taking place in 1997. Following the privatization Repsol embarked on an ambitious international expansion programme. Its most significant acquisition was the newly privatized YPF, the Argentinean national champion, for which Repsol agreed to pay a total of $15 billion in 1999 (*FT*, 4 May 1999). Repsol was predominantly a downstream firm, and YPF was predominantly upstream. Together the two companies will become one of the world's top ten international oil companies.

- **Norway**. Norway's abundant North Sea oil reserves were placed under the control of the state-owned Statoil and (after 1985) State Direct Financial Interest (SDFI). Statoil's performance in developing the country's large oil reserves has been highly successful. In 1999 Statoil made a gross profit (earnings before interest, tax, dividends and amortization) of 36 per cent of its revenue from North Sea oil of Norway (Statoil website). In 1999 there was still intense debate in Norway about whether and to what extent Statoil should be privatized. It remained 100 per cent state-owned in 1999.

Outside Europe and the USA, oil exploration and production in the 1980s was predominantly in the hands of state-owned national champions (Table 7-8). The oil and gas industry in most of the Communist countries was nationalized at the time of the Communist revolution. Outside the Communist countries, widespread nationalization of oil assets took place, becoming the norm for the industry:

- **Middle East**. In 1951, Iran nationalized its enormous oil and gas assets. In the early 1970s, a spate of nationalizations took place, including Iraq in 1972, and Kuwait and Saudi Arabia in 1975. Given the enormous importance of these countries in the world's oil supplies, these developments had a massive impact on the structure of the world's oil industry, and on the behaviour of the giant companies based in the advanced capitalist countries.

TABLE 7-8 Top 15 Oil Companies, 1996
(million barrels per day)

Company	Output
Saudi Aramco	8.6
National Iranian Oil Company	3.8
Petrobas de Venezuela (PDVSA)	2.8
China National Petroleum Corporation (CNPC)	2.8
Pemex	2.7
Royal Dutch/Shell	2.3
Kuwait Petroleum Corporation	2.2
Exxon	1.8
Libya National Oil Company	1.5
Abu Dhabi National Oil Company	1.5
Sonatrach	1.4
BP	1.3
Nigerian National Petroleum Corporation	1.2
Lukoil	1.2
Pertamina	1.1

- **Mexico**. The earliest large-scale nationalization of oil assets and localization of production took place in Mexico in 1943. Pemex emerged as one of the first and most important state-owned companies in the world. Despite substantial privatization of non-oil assets, Pemex still remains a state-owned entity: 'National ownership of Pemex has been almost as sacred as Mexico's patron saint, the Virgin, herself' (*FT*, 17 August 1999). Pemex provides one-third of central government tax revenues.

- **Venezuela**. Venezuela's state-owned oil company, PDVSA, (nationalized in 1972), is one of the largest corporations in Latin America. In the late 1990s, it still had no plans for privatization. In the 1990s it undertook major structural improvements to raise its profitability. The group claims to be the world's most efficient oil company, based on profit to income streams. By 1996 it reported profits of $4.5 billion on sales of $38.5 billion.

- **Argentina**. YPF, the oil and gas giant, is Argentina's largest company, with comprehensive capability both upstream and downstream. It was privatized only in 1993 (see above).

- **Brazil**. Brazil's Petrobras was established as a state-owned monopoly to develop Brazil's national oil reserves. The company claims to be the world's most efficient state-owned oil producer. In 1998 it earned net profits of $1.19 billion on gross sales of $22.3 billion (*FT*, 23 August 199). Despite being a profit-maker, the company's production costs are about $13 a barrel, around 25 per cent above those of the world's lowest-cost producers. The company is undergoing radical overhaul of its operating methods in order to raise profitability. It is possible that around one-third of the company will be floated in the year 2000.

- **Malaysia**. Malaysia's oil resources were developed under the auspices of the state-owned giant, Petronas. With relatively small domestic reserves, Petronas quickly developed into a major actor in the development of overseas oil reserves. Despite great secrecy, Petronas is widely regarded as one of thebest-run of Malaysia's businesses. It is the corporate flagship for the whole country, and is the country's biggest taxpayer (*FT*, 25 October 1996).

In the light of these international developments, it seemed quite reasonable for the Chinese policy makers in the early phase of the economic reforms to emphasize improvements in operational methods rather than change the structure of ownership through privatization. If China had, indeed, pursued privatization as the main policy goal in the 1980s and 1990s, there remains the issue of what entities would have been privatized. As we shall see, the Chinese upstream and downstream sectors each has a large number of 'enterprises', or production units, including oilfields, refining facilities, petrochemical plants and downstream marketing companies. If the privatization had simply sold the component parts of the industry separately there would have been no possibility of building large-scale indigenous oil and petrochemical firms. Moreover, in the surrounding environment of the global industry, the idea that the upstream should operate independently of the downstream did not seem so illogical.

Oil Industry Restructuring in the 1980s and 1990s. A number of factors together stimulated a drastic change in the approach of the major oil companies after the 1970s. These factors included the extensive nationalization of oil assets in the 1970s, the first oil price shock of 1973–4, the second oil price shock of 1978–80, and the long decline in real oil prices from the early 1980s through to the late 1990s. Moreover, the oil majors hoped that they would find a number of new giant oilfields outside the areas in which oil assets had been nationalized. These hopes broadly failed to materialize. Instead, they turned towards comprehensive change in their business systems, aimed at reducing costs and enhancing profitability. A number of important changes took place in the industry:

- **Reduced reliance on internally generated crude oil**. The state-owned oil companies accounted for a larger and larger share of world production after the 1960s. Of the top 15 oil-producing companies in 1996, all but three (Exxon, Shell and BP) were state-owned companies. The growth of oil supply from state-owned companies, especially the massive entities in the Middle East broke down the old system of deep integration of oil production and downstream operations within a single company: 'In the old days, oil had stayed within a company's integrated channels or was swapped among companies. But now state oil companies accounted for larger and larger shares of total production, they had no downstreams of their own, and sold their oil to a wide spectrum of buyers: major oil companies, independent refiners and traders' (Yergin, 1991: 697).

Instead of processing almost all their own internally provided oil, the majors were forced to become much more adept at buying large quantities of oil from outside the company. BP led the way. It had lost 40 per cent of its supply through the upheaval in Iran and the nationalization in Nigeria on top of the nationalizations in Kuwait, Libya and Iraq. It was forced to go out into spot markets and buy oil on a larger and larger scale. This had a profound effect on the whole corporate culture:

> The new BP could shop around for the cheapest crude; it could push efficiency through its operating units; it could beat the competition; it could become more entrepreneurial. The company became much more decentralized, with individuals made responsible for their own profitability. The corporate culture changed from that of the 1970s, dominated by the supply planner, to one dominated by traders and commercial people...BP's new chairman, J.P. Walters, [said]: 'for me there is no strategy that is divorced from profitability' ... Walters became famous for telling managers that 'there are no sacred cows in BP' and 'you tell us which things make economic sense and which do not, and I'll tell you which we keep and which we won't'. (Yergin, 1991: 722–3)

- **Technical progress in exploration and development**. Major investments in the technology of oilfield discovery and development allowed large advances in oil companies' capability to profitably develop oil fields in technically demanding locations, such as in extreme coldness, at extreme depth or in deep sea. New technologies allowed greatly increased recovery rates compared to previous epochs, thereby increasing the returns from existing oil assets. For example, new technology of 'ultra-slim' holes allowed pockets of oil to be reached and exploited that could not formerly be reached. New high-angle, extended reach and horizontal drilling technology allowed oil fields to be developed from fewer drilling sites and with fewer wells. The impact of such developments on costs was substantial. For example, between 1993 and 1997 alone, Exxon's unit operating expenses per barrel of oil (at 1997 prices) fell from $8.3 to $7.70 (Exxon, 1998: 12).

- **Mergers and acquisitions**. From the late 1970s through to the mid-1990s, a steady stream of large-scale mergers took place in the oil industry. These included Shell's purchase of Belridge ($3.6 billion) and its subsequent buy-out of the whole of Shell Oil USA ($5.7 billion), BP's purchase of full ownership of Standard Oil of Ohio (Sohio) ($7.6 billion) and of Britoil, Chevron's purchase of Gulf Oil ($13.2 billion), Du Pont's purchase of Conoco ($7.8 billion) and US Steel's purchase of Marathon ($5.9 billion). A major reason for the mergers and acquisitions was a source of adding to crude oil supplies more cheaply than through exploration and development.

- **Modern IT**. The arrival of modern IT contributed to a large-scale improvement in the ability of the giant companies to integrate the whole global value chain, from exploration through to the petrol pump, in a manner that was impossible only a few years earlier. It also facilitated a revolution in business management within the global giant oil and petrochemical companies. The way in which work was organized, monitored and rewarded changed fundamentally in this period, at least in part due to the massive advances in IT.

- **Internal management systems**. This period saw enormous downsizing in the giant oil and petrochemical companies. This was associated with a fundamental re-shaping of the internal business structure, and enormous changes in the corporate culture. These not only greatly reduced wage costs, but released considerable employee energy that had formerly been untapped. The major oil and petrochemical companies began a revolutionary process of transition from large bureaucracies run along 'feudal' lines, into modern businesses in which autonomy for business units was combined with continual, remorseless scrutiny of their performance.

The Merger Explosion. After going through profound changes from the late 1970s through to the late 1990s, an even more fundamental change swept the industry in the late 1990s. The oil industry had been one of the earliest truly global industries. However, the impact of the merger explosion, which swept through the advanced economies from the early 1990s, hit this industry relatively late.

It is estimated that from March 1997 to mid-1999, about $240 billion-worth of transactions took place in the industry (Table 7-9). A number of factors triggered the frenetic merger activities in the oil and gas industry:

- The costs of producing oil products increased sharply in the 1990s, due to changing consumer preference and the accelerating drive for environmentally friendly products. These pressures stimulated a sustained increase in the production of high-cost, high value-added oil products. Refineries need to be around ten times the size they were in the 1970s in order to benefit from economies of scale and make profits. Moreover, the plants are now so large, that to be economic and overcome the high transport costs for oil products, firms in the industry must be able to sell a large fraction of their output at locations that are reasonably close to the refinery.

- The 1990s saw a powerful fall in the real price of crude oil. The price of Brent crude oil fluctuated at between $15–20 per barrel for most of the period from the late 1980s to the mid-1990s. It then plunged from 1996 through to 1998, when it fell below $10 per barrel, which was highly significant psychologically as well as in business terms. The massive mergers of the late 1990s offered the possibility for wholesale cost-cutting, which might enable the oil companies to make profits at much lower levels of oil and oil product prices than had hitherto been possible. Even the sharp increase in oil prices in 1999 did not stop the merger bandwagon as leading players struggled to find partners before they had all been taken up by other players. However, a major fear of the leading producers is that in the long-term it is impossible

TABLE **7-9 Major Oil and Gas Deals since 1997**

Date announced	Companies		Value ($ billion)
Mar. 1997	ENI third tranche*		7.6
Jul. 1997	Falcon Drilling	Reading and Bates	2.6
Jul. 1997	Burlington Resources	Louisiana Land and Exploration	3.0
Oct. 1997	Occidental Petroleum	Elk Hills Petrol**	3.7
Jan. 1998	Union Pacific Resources	Norcen Energy Resources	3.5
Feb. 1998	Halliburton	Dresser Industries	8.9
Apr. 1998	ENI fourth tranche*		6.6
May 1998	Arco	Union Texas	2.7
May 1998	Baker Hughes	Western Atlas	4.6
Aug. 1998	BP	Amoco	55.0
Oct. 1998	Kerr–McGee	Oryx Energy	3.1
Nov. 1998	Seagull Energy	Ocean Energy	1.1
Dec. 1998	Total	PetroFina	7.0
Dec. 1998	Exxon	Mobil	86.4
Mar. 1999	BP Amoco	Arco	26.8
May 1999	Repsol	YPF	13.4
May 1999	Elf	Saga Petroleum	4.4

SOURCES: *FT* (2 December 1998: 21, 30 March 1999: 23, 4 May 1999, 11 May 1999: 28, 8 June 1999: 28)

NOTES: * Italian privatization, the first two tranches raised $9 billion
    ** US privatization

to sustain the rental element in oil prices. Therefore, the major oil companies have to create business structures that are able to make profits at low long-term prices, whatever fluctuations may occur in the short-term.

- The economic and political turmoil experienced in some substantial oil producing countries, such as Russia and Indonesia, increases the political risks associated with integrated oil companies. Large oil companies are able to spread their assets widely and are thus able to withstand the turmoil in a given country or region.

- Extensive privatization of the oil and petrochemical industry opened up new opportunities for merger and acquisition in both the advanced and developing countries. In Europe in the 1990s, a succession of state-owned oil companies was privatized. In the 1990s, developing countries began to privatize the industry. A crucial new development is the possibility that the state-owned oil companies substantially increase the involvement of the multinationals in their oil exploration and production. Venezuela has already opened its industry to large-scale foreign investment. Iran is reviewing bids for dozens of foreign-financed oil development projects. Kuwait is considering expanding service agreements with Western companies. Iraq has already negotiated detailed contracts with a number of international consortia. Even Saudi Arabia has hinted at possible opening up of the upstream sector to direct foreign investment. According to Mark Moody-Stuart, chairman of Shell, '[T]his is where the big oil companies step in' (quoted in *FT*, 27 November 1998). He expects to see a new relationship developing between the big state oil companies and their Western counterparts. The bargain will be that 'in exchange for capital, technology and management expertise, Western oil companies will get access to vast, low cost oil reserves for long periods of time' (*FT*, 27 November 1998). One investment banker commented: 'Their preferred partners are likely to be those companies that not only have the size and range of expertise to offer comprehensive services but are also viewed by the investment community as dynamic and top financial performers' (quoted in *FT*, 27 November 1998).

- A new epoch of shareholder activism, especially from the institutional investors, forced the oil companies to pay much greater attention to profitability than had hitherto been the case. The cost savings from mergers are potentially very large. BP Amoco estimated that it would make savings of $2 billion per year, and Exxon Mobil believe that the merger would reduce combined costs by as much as $4 billion per year.

- Oil and petrochemical companies benefited from the general inflation of stock market values, especially in the USA. They used the increased stock market values in the same way as was happening in other sectors to take over other large corporations in the sector through predominantly friendly mergers financed through paper deals rather than cash acquisitions. There was a marked increase in the preparedness of investors in one country to accept mergers paid for with shares in a company based abroad. This was especially important for major European companies seeking to merge with US-based companies.

The major mergers that took place in this revolutionary period for the industry were the following:

- **BP/Amoco**. In August 1998, BP initiated the biggest ever merger in the oil industry by combining with the Chicago-based Amoco in a $55 billion stock and debt deal. The combined BP Amoco group is shedding around 6000 jobs out of the total global workforce of 99 000. The combined group had revenues of $68 billion in 1998, ranking it nineteenth in the *Fortune* 500. Its production of oil and gas (oil equivalent) totalled 3.1 million barrels per day (BP, 1998: 68), placing it close behind the world leaders Exxon and Shell. The deal gave BP access to Amoco's lucrative downstream businesses, including Amoco's powerful position in gasoline stations in the Mid-West and Eastern USA, where Amoco is the dominant player. The merger also gave BP a greatly strengthened position in petrochemicals, since Amoco's chemicals division was larger than that of BP. The merger provided the opportunity for large savings in exploration and common procurement. In total, it was estimated that the merger could achieve around $2 billion in initial savings (*FT*, 12 August 1998). The merger is highly significant in that it is one of a series of extremely large-scale transatlantic mergers initiated by European-based companies.

It followed hard on the heels of the massive Daimler-Chrysler merger. BP already had around 20 per cent of its shares held by US citizens and institutions, and the proportion has risen considerably as a result of the merger.

- **Total/Fina**. Total (France's second biggest oil group) acquired PetroFina (one of Belgium's biggest industrial companies) in a $7 billion stock-swap deal and renamed the combined group as TotalFina. In 1997, the combined group had 69 100 employees, 5.71 billion barrels of oil equivalent (boe) in reserves and revenues of $46.56 billion. With a combined market capitalization of $36.11 billion, TotalFina was the fourth largest global oil company in terms of revenues. The take-over of PetroFina enables Total to strengthen its European downstream businesses and enhances its international exploration effort, especially in the North Sea. It is expected that synergies of $352 million per annum within three years will be achieved through combining administrative functions, integrating research and development, improving the refineries' efficiency, rationalizing distributions and centralized purchasing. The significance of this deal is not its value, but the fading of national sensitivity associated with the former state-owned oil companies in Europe (*FT*, 1 December 1998).

- **Exxon/Mobil**. Just three months after the biggest merger in the oil industry, Exxon and Mobil announced their plans to merge in an $86.4 billion deal, the largest merger ever to take place. Exxon is already the world's largest oil and petrochemical producer, with revenues of over $100 billion in 1998. Mobil was the world's number four with revenues of $48 billion. The new company would be the world's third largest by sales revenue, after General Motors and Daimler–Chrysler. The new company's pro-forma profits were almost $12 billion in 1997, and still stood at almost $10 billion in 1998. North America accounts for around 44 per cent of Exxon's production, compared with only one-third for Mobil. The new company will have a much wider global spread of assets. Exxon and Mobil have a sizeable share in some of the most important emerging oil areas, including offshore in West Africa and in the Caspian Sea. Exxon has a total of around 13.8 billion barrels of oil and oil equivalent in gas reserves, while Mobil has around 5.4 billion barrels in total. The merged company will take over from Shell as the world's leading company in terms of oil reserves, outside the OPEC countries. Shell's reserves stand at around 18.2 billion barrels of oil and oil equivalent reserves of gas. The merged Exxon/Mobil will have reserves totalling over 19 billion barrels.

  The combined group will have 33 000 service stations world-wide, of which around 8500 will be in the USA. The lubricants market is fast-growing and profitable. Here there is strong synergy between the two companies. Exxon is the world's top producer of lubricant base stocks, but Mobil is the market leader accounting for 12 per cent of the US lubricant sales. Even though it is a junior partner in the European joint venture with BP, Mobil holds a majority stake in lubricants and it occupies about 18 per cent of the European market. In fact, lubricants generate more than one-third of the downstream profits in Mobil (*FT*, 30 November 1998, 2 December 1998).

In natural gas, both Exxon and Mobil have strong positions in the US and overseas markets. The combined group accounts for 20 per cent of current gas production in the USA and 60 per cent of the proven reserves in Europe, including a big stake in the highly profitable Groeningen field in the Netherlands. The group is also an active explorer and developer of gas fields in the Asia–Pacific region. With a combined sales of 14 billion cubic feet (bcf) per day, Exxon Mobil is well placed to tap the fast growing gas markets in power generation, domestic use and even in advanced fuel-cells installed in pollution-free automobiles. The merger also fills the gap in Exxon's asset portfolio on liquefied natural gas (LNG), where Mobil owns the profitable Arun LNG business in Indonesia (*FT*, 30 November 1998, 2 December 1998). The companies also have complementary assets in polyethylene and paraxylene (used in fibre, film and plastic bottles) (*FT*, 30 November 1998).

- **BP Amoco/Arco**. Only two months after concluding one of the biggest mergers in the energy industry with Amoco, BP Amoco agreed on a $26.8 billion all-stock take-over deal with the Los Angeles-based Atlantic Richfield Company (Arco) in March 1999. The acquisition will increase BP Amoco's oil and gas reserves from 12.9 billion barrels of oil and oil equivalent to 17.5 billion barrels, a very significant expansion. The new company will become the largest producer outside OPEC, with a total of 2.7 million barrels per day. The pro-forma revenues of the combined company in 1998 totalled $82 billion, taking BP up to around the fourteenth largest in the *Fortune* 500. The acquisition will give BP Amoco access to Arco's large chain of petrol stations on the lucrative West coast of the USA, and effectively establish a coast-to-coast network across the country. BP Amoco/Arco will have full operational control of the giant Prudhoe Bay oil and gas fields in Alaska. With 4.5 billion barrels of oil equivalent, the Prudhoe Bay reserves are not only the biggest in the US, but also as big as the proven total reserves of the entire UK. Furthermore, Arco owns 40 per cent of the Tangguh natural gas site in Indonesia, which has over 2.5 billion barrels of oil equivalent in proven gas reserves. Arco also owns gas fields in the Gulf of Mexico, the UK North Sea, the South China Sea, Malaysia, Thailand and Qatar as well as oil fields in Algeria, Venezuela, the Caspian and Russia. BP Amoco's total array of reserves after the merger will rival those of Shell. Moreover, the new company will be especially strong in natural gas, for which global demand is increasing faster than for oil.

- **TotalFina/Elf**. Hard on the heels of the announcement of the merger of PetroFina and Total in late 1998, TotalFina launched a hostile $43 billion bid for Elf Aquitaine. The French government owned a 'golden share' in Elf Aquitaine following its privatization. It gave its support to the merger, widely interpreted as an attempt to create a French 'national champion' The take-over was vigorously resisted by Elf Aquitaine, but after months of protracted negotiation, the two companies finally agreed to a friendly merger in early September 1999. On a pro-forma basis, the new company would have revenues of almost $80 billion, taking it into the *Fortune* 500 top 20 companies by value of sales. It will have around 130 000 employees.

The new company will have reserves of over nine billion barrels of oil and oil equivalent. Its reserves will be widely distributed across the world, with 28 per cent in Africa, 27 per cent in Europe, 25 per cent in the Middle East and 20 per cent across the rest of the world. The new company will produce around 2.8 million barrels of oil and oil equivalent per day, close to that of BP Amoco/Arco. It will be able to focus its refining and marketing activities around six main hubs, providing a 'stronger and more focused platform' and enable better integration of its petrochemicals with its refining. It will have a powerful downstream capability, with strong positions in monomers and polymers, such as polyethylene, polypropylene, and polystyrene.

• **Prospective mergers**. The prospect is for the explosive process of merger and acquisition to continue in the near future. Elf Aquitaine was in discussion with ENI about a possible merger, immediately prior to the hostile offer from TotalFina. Immediately after announcing the successful completion of the agreement to a friendly merger of Elf and TotalFina, the chairman of TotalFina hinted strongly at further mergers: 'Even before the ink on the latest merger document was dry, Mr Desmarest [Chairman of TotalFina] surprised journalists and analysts by dropping broad hints that ENI, the partially privatized Italian oil group which held abortive merger talks with Elf, might be a suitable candidate for inclusion into his growing empire' (*FT*, 20 September 1999). Mr Demarest even suggested a possible name for such a new group, namely 'Euro-Oil'. If Total/Elf were to merge with ENI, it would produce a company that would directly rival the 'three sisters' of the industry's 'super league', Exxon, Shell and BP Amoco. Its revenues would be over $100 billion on a pro-forma basis, taking it into the *Fortune* 500 top 10 companies by revenues. Its oil and gas reserves and production would directly rival those of the 'three sisters'.

In the USA, talks between Chevron and Texaco are reported to have been under way for a long time. They already have extensive co-operation through the 50–50 joint venture known as Caltex, which was set up in 1936. Caltex has leading positions in refining and petrol stations in many countries. It has a refining capacity of 860 000 barrels per day, and runs 8000 petrol stations. If such a merger took place it would catapult the combined company into the *Fortune* 500 top 30 companies by value of sales, and the combined output of oil and gas would be around 2.4 billion barrels of oil and oil equivalent, close to that of the 'three sisters'.

COMPETITIVE CAPABILITY

The revolution in the world's oil and petrochemical industry has made the competitive capability of the players on the global 'level playing field' much more uneven (Tables 7-10 and 7-11). The new super giants of the industry stand in a position of greatly enhanced competitive advantage compared to potential competitors from developing countries.

Size. The mergers of 1998–9 produced a fundamental change in the competitive landscape. It created a group of 'super-majors' that 'could dictate competitive

TABLE 7-10 Top 10 Global Oil Companies, Measured by Revenues 1997

Companies	Revenues	Net profits	Market value	Oil production	Gas production	Number of employees
		($ billion)		(mb/d)	(mcf/d)	(persons)
Exxon Mobil (USA)§	182.36	11.73	139.62	2534	10635	122 700
Royal Dutch/ Shell (Netherlands–UK)	128.14	7.76	113.78	2328	8001	105 000
BP Amoco/Arco§ (UK–USA)	123.30	8.54	111.91	1930	5858	123 901
TotalFina§ (France–Belgium)	46.56	1.92	36.11	680	2060	69 066
Texaco (USA)	45.19	2.66	29.60	833	2177	29 313
Elf Aquitaine (France)	43.57	0.96	42.05	795	1312	83 700
ENI (Italy)	36.96	3.00	49.33	646	375*	80 178
Chevron (USA)	36.38	3.26	35.47	1425	2865	39 362
PDVSA (Venezuela)	34.80	4.77	47.14		5274	56 592
SK (S. Korea)**	33.82	0.13	17.93			30 595
Top 10:	711.08	44.73	622.94			740 407

SOURCES: Compiled from *Fortune* (3 August 1998, 1999); BP Amoco (1999c); Shell (1999a); Exxon (1998); Mobil (1999)

NOTES: The above ranking has already taken the recent mergers into consideration
     * in mboe: thousand barrels oil equivalent
    ** Name changed from Sunkyong from 1 January 1998
    mb/d: Thousand barrels per day
    mcf/d: Thousand cubic feet per day
    § Proforma

TABLE **7-11 Selected Statistics of the Big Three 1998 (31 December)**

Indicators	Exxon Mobil	BP Amoco/Arco	Royal Dutch/ Shell
Financial indicators:			
• Revenues (\$ billion)	171.30	95.27	93.69
• Net income (\$ billion)	8.07	5.44	0.35
• Capital expenditure (\$ billion)	14.79	10.36**	15.74
• Employees (persons)	120 500	115 050	102 000
• Net income–revenues ratio (%)	4.71	5.71	0.37
• Net income per employees (\$)	67 004	47 310	3 431
Upstream – Exploration & Production:			
• Crude oil and NGL production (mmboe/d)	2.50	2.71	2.35
• Gas production (mmboe/d)	1.83	1.36§	1.36§
• Net proven oil reserves (billion barrels)	12.42	12.17	10.03
• Net proven gas reserves (trillion ft³)	57.84	42.56	60.46
• Net proven oil and gas reserves (mmboe)	21 092	19 506	20 445
• Major oil and gas fields	USA, Canada, West Africa, Caspian Sea	USA, UK North Sea	USA, UK, Oman Nigeria
Downstream – Refining & Marketing:			
• Combined oil products sales (mmb/d) *	8.87	9.99	8.94
• Refinery throughput (mmb/d)	6.06	3.16	3.37
• Net refining capacity (mboe/d)	6 088	3 399	4 030
• Service stations (number)	33 000	29 700	47 000
• Leading products:	Petroleum, lubricants, and diesel for cars	Aviation fuels, lubricants and fuels for ship	Petroleum and diesel for cars
Solar:			
• Sales (\$ million)		153±	
• Output of products (megawatts/year)		30	

TABLE 7-11 *(Continued)*

Indicators	Exxon Mobil	BP Amoco/Arco	Royal Dutch/ Shell
• Leading products		Photovoltaic modules, thin film, crystalline silicon	Photovoltaic panels
Chemicals:			
• Sales ($ billion)	14.1	9.7	12.27
• Output (million tonnes/year)		20	19.98
• Leading products	Polyethylene, paraxylene	Acetic acid, polyethylene, acrylonitrile, styrenics, polybutene	Petrochemical building block, major cracker products, large volume polymers

SOURCES: Compiled from BP Amoco (1999b, 1999c); Shell (1999a, 1999b, 1999c); Exxon (1999); Mobil (1999)

NOTES: * Including crude oil
         ** BP Amoco figures only
          § The natural gas production was 7.86 billion cubic feet per day
          ± The $153 million sales figure included the $58 million in Solarex, which was acquired by BP Amoco in 1999
          mmboe\Million barrels oil equivalent
          mmboe/d\Million barrels oil equivalent per day
          mmb/d\Million barrels per day
          mboe/d\Thousand barrels of oil equivalent per day

placement and returns for decades' (MSDW, 1999: 130). In 1997, 10 of the world's top 100 corporations by value of sales were oil and petrochemical producers, and 31 of the top 500. However, there were only two super giants, Shell and Exxon, with revenues of over $128 billion and $122 billion and profits of $7.8 billion and $8.4 billion, respectively (*Fortune*, 3 August 1998: F-23). This situation was radically changed in 1998 and 1999. By the autumn of 1999, two new super giants had been built through merger and acquisition, namely BP Amoco/Arco and TotalFina/Elf Aquitaine, and Exxon had enormously strengthened its position by announcing its intention to merge with Mobil. It seemed very likely that ENI would merge with one of the super giants and that Chevron and Texaco would also merge to produce another super giant.

   Their huge size gave them the potential to construct a portfolio of high quality oil and gas reserves distributed around the world, to invest large amounts in R&D to sustain and extend their technical lead over other companies, to develop integrated global marketing capabilities, to invest in large-scale information technology systems that could better integrate their value chain, to develop their global brand image, and to purchase inputs more cheaply due to the scale of purchases.

The merger frenzy in the world's oil and petrochemical industry between 1997 and 1999 greatly increased the institutional and technical gap between the world's leading companies and challengers from developing countries. MSDW estimates that the super-majors, namely BP Amoco, Exxon Mobil, and Shell have a capability to sustain their competitive edge in the industry for at least 15 years.

A key aspect of this competitive edge relates to the fact that the bulk of world oil and gas reserves is located in countries in which the giants own few or no reserves. The top seven private sector oil companies account for only 60–70 billion barrels of oil and gas reserves, compared to a global total of over 1000 billion barrels of oil (BP, 1998). The oil reserves of Venezuela alone amount to roughly those of the top seven privately owned companies put together. Moreover, the output of the top seven companies accounts for less than 7 per cent of total world crude oil and gas output. A crucial issue for the development of the global industry is that of which entities will have the capital and technology to develop the vast remaining reserves of oil and gas. As the industry liberalizes its controls on foreign ownership and investment those giant companies that have grown even stronger in the late 1990s will be in a relatively strong position financially and technologically to take the lead in this process, which is likely to become increasingly competitive.

Size alone is not sufficient to guarantee the competitive edge of the global giants. As well as being of giant scale, the global leaders also benefit from tangible advantages that enable them to be low cost producers and highly profitable over the long term.

Economies of Scale

Refineries. There are strong economies of scale in refining. Globally, there are over 700 oil refineries, with an average capacity of 5.3 million ton/year. The average refinery capacity in leading European countries and Japan reached 6 million ton/year in the early 1980s (Chen Zhun *et al.*, 1998: 16–17). BP Amoco and Exxon each had an average refinery throughput of 6.1–6.5 million ton/year (BP Amoco, 1999a; Exxon, 1998).

Ethylene crackers. The current world average capacity of ethylene crackers is 330 thousand ton/year and will increase to 628 thousand ton/year by 2000 (Chen Zhun *et al.*, 1998: 17). The average capacity is 413 thousand ton/year in the United States, 327 thousand ton/year in West European countries, and 373 thousand ton/year in Japan (Chen Zhun *et al.*, 1998: 36). In Venezuela, an 830 thousand ton/year ethylene cracker will start to operate in 2000. Brazil is building crackers with capacity ranging from 700 thousand ton/year to 1.1 million ton/year. In Southeast Asian countries such as Thailand, India, Indonesia, and Singapore, crackers with capacity of 700 thousand ton/year are being established.

Integration of Operations

Large integrated sites. Integration of operations and scale are closely related. A powerful trend among the world's leading companies is for an increasing proportion of output to be concentrated at a small number of large integrated sites. Creating a limited network of large integrated sites is a key to lowering costs of production for the global giants. Shell, for example, has announced that its future portfolio of chemical operations will 'focus on major cracker projects, petrochemical building blocks and large-volume polymers' (Shell, 1999a: 35). It emphasises that its chemicals group will focus on businesses that 'share common ingredients for success – leading technologies and the capability to build and operate world-scale plants' (Shell, 1999a: 35). Exxon stresses the central role in reducing costs that will be played by large integrated sites that combine refinery and chemicals operations (Exxon, 1998: 12). A good example of the state-of-the-art large-scale integrated site is BP Amoco's complex in the north east of the UK. The programme to expand the existing large-scale facilities 'demonstrates how the key elements fit together to achieve superior performance': 'The programme is made possible by the availability of feedstock from our upstream and refining operation. This allows an advantaged expansion of the site ethylene cracker capacity, and in turn the growth of key derivatives both at Grangemouth and through our new pipeline link to Hull ... The investments in vinyl acetate monomer, ethanol and ethyl acetate will replace isolated, high-cost plants, with modern integrated low-cost assets' (BP Amoco, 1999c).

Integration of refining and marketing. The integration process within the global giants stretches right through the value chain to the retail side of the business. A key part of the profits of the global giants is their huge distribution network, involving the apparatus of distribution of wholesale products, as well as a vast network of retail outlets, notably the petrol stations. BP Amoco (together with Arco) will have around 30000 petrol station, while Shell has nearly 50000. Moreover, an increasing proportion of these are large scale entities with vastly higher sales per site than only a few years ago. The whole structure of wholesale and retail sales of oil products has been revolutionized by the transformation of supply-chain logistics in recent years.

Centralized Procurement. The global giants of the oil and petrochemical industry make huge annual purchases of goods and services from outside companies. Moreover, a sharply increased proportion of these items is now purchased from third-party-specialist suppliers rather than produced within the company. The development of information technology has permitted hugely increased cost savings for such purchases made by global giant oil companies. The centralization of such functions has been facilitated also by the large changes that have occurred in the nature of the management process. Moreover, the incentive to take advantage of such least-cost solutions has been stimulated by the increased pressure to perform that has developed with the widespread introduction of the business unit system.

The concrete implications of this process can be seen from the example of BP Amoco. In 1996, BP decided that it could save $1 billion per year from its annual purchase of $15 billion spent on outside procurement of goods and services (*FT*, 15 April 1998). The key was information. BP could only make these savings by having an overview of all its spending decisions. Once it had the full picture it was in a position to negotiate better deals with its suppliers. BP built a centralized data warehouse to collate information about who was buying what from whom. Users across the world within the BP system can interrogate the system to find if a potential supplier is doing business elsewhere within the group or if another supplier offers better terms. BP procurement managers can use the information to aggregate purchases and negotiate better terms. Naturally, the vast size of BP's global purchases enables it to strike better deals than were available to smaller competitors. The advantages are not simply through 'using a big stick to beat the suppliers'. A major advance in procurement has been in developing closer interaction with the most effective suppliers. As in many other industries, a powerful process of rationalization of the supplier base is under way. With newly centralized information systems, BP is able to work more closely and interactively with suppliers who can meet BP's global needs.

Product Mix. A major part of the improvement in profitability for the global giants has been the transformation of their production structure towards high value-added products. There has been a pronounced trend to divest assets which produce products in which the company does not have a global leadership position, and focus capital investment, R & D and marketing on those in which it does hold global leadership positions. This has enabled the global giants in both petroleum products and chemicals to concentrate on products in which it can generate high value-added and hold high market share so as to sustain a stronger influence on pricing.

In petroleum products, the global giants have made a great deal of progress in products that are environmentally friendly, such as unleaded fuels. In chemical products, leading companies have sharply narrowed their focus of expertise. For example, BP Amoco's chemicals division has developed leading positions in three important specializations (BP Amoco, 1999d). It is the world leader in PTA and PX (Paraxylene) technology, and has the top position in global sales of these products. In PTA it accounts for 37 per cent of global sales (*FT*, 13 August 1998). It is the global number two in the licensing of polyethylene and polypropylene technology, and the global number two in terms of production of polypropylene. It is the world leader in acetic acid and acrylonite technology, with 70 per cent and 90 per cent, respectively, of world-wide production produced using BP Amoco technology. It is the world's number one producer of these products.

A major reason for the capability of the global giants to develop leading technologies is their high expenditure on R & D compared to the smaller firms in the sector. For example, in 1998 Shell spent $800 million in R & D, while Exxon spent over $500 million and BP Amoco spent $400 million (DTI, 1999: 59). In addition, the global giants were able to spend large sums investing in new plant and equipment to embody the new technologies.

Organizational Structure. Each of the global giants has gone through a similar process of reorganization of its management system in the past decade. The reorganization has involved greatly increased autonomy for subordinate units, alongside enormously increased intensity of performance monitoring that subjects their individual contribution to the company's financial performance to the sharpest scrutiny.

The structure that most of the giant oil and petrochemical companies operated under a decade or so ago involved a matrix reporting hierarchy with innumerable layers of bureaucracy. The system involved a mass of complex procedures, and an absence of simple accountability linking individual and group performance to that of the whole group. This often involved considerable independence for regionally-based branches of the company. One of the most extreme examples was the vast global empire of Shell, consisting of hundreds of operating companies. The company had 'a proliferation of regional baronies, which encouraged too many committees and turf battles' (*FT*, 16 February 1996). The complexity of the lines of command made it difficult to pin responsibility on individuals: 'When things went wrong it was usually someone else's fault.' When Shell began root-and-branch reform of its structure in the late 1990s it faced complex internal political difficulties, since the reformed structures challenged the powerful fiefdoms that the company had developed within itself.

The oil and petrochemical giants have almost all undertaken a drastic restructuring of their management systems since the 1980s, which has many common features. A central part of this reform has been to strip out regional lines of command and replace them with structures based on lines of business. This has included a drastic de-layering of the bureaucracy. At BP Amoco, for example, the size of the headquarters was reduced from over 4000 staff to just 350. The aim is to make each of the business units see themselves as an autonomous profit centre and as a business responsible to internal and/or external customers, rather than as a department or a region. The objective is to make each business unit act in an autonomous way, subject to compliance with the company's policies and accountability for the fulfillment of its contract.

BP Amoco, for example, is divided into 126 business units. Each of them is 'human-sized', averaging around 700–800 people in each. The business units are self-contained entities, each of which is capable of forming an independent accounting unit, whose financial contribution to the overall company can be clearly identified. This is very difficult to achieve if a business unit contains more than one type of business. Therefore, the business units take the form of entities such as an individual oilfield, a refinery, a petrochemical site or a pipeline.

Each unit typically has its own detailed performance contract. For example, at BP Amoco it is a very thorough document that covers all the essential elements of the unit's business activities, including the key financial and operational data. It also embraces some important non-financial targets such as safety and environmental performance. The contract is subject to 'regular monitoring challenge and assessment to ensure that what has been agreed upon is delivered'. These assessments are 'neither cosy nor inconsequential conversations'. They 'have an edge to them'. They are 'not always pleasurable occasions' (BP Amoco, 1999c). Indeed, the performance monitoring is 'done to the point of obsession' and 'in meticulous detail'. Monitoring is undertaken on a monthly basis by peer groups, which each incorporates a small number of business units in the same line of business, such as oil fields or refineries. In addition to the monthly meeting there is a quarterly performance report. Each of the peer groups is part of one of three different business streams, which include 'Oil and gas production', 'Refining and marketing', and 'Chemicals'. Continuous performance monitoring takes place also within the business streams. Remuneration is related to a combination of individual performance, business unit performance and the performance of the peer group.

A crucial part of the way in which the business units' contracts are devised and monitored is through transparency. The potentiality for transparency has been sharply increased by advances in information technology. This in turn depends upon the provision of a 'mass of reliable and credible data which illuminates business unit performance and provides assurance of delivery' (BP Amoco, 1999c). Like other leading oil and chemical companies, BP Amoco has established a common platform for assessing every part of the company in a 'transparent, consistent fashion'. Each of the business units is located within a peer group of business units that face similar technological or operational conditions. They must each 'fight their own corner and justify their own promises to their closest colleagues'. They have to prove that they are deserving of the resources they wish to attract in comparison with their fellow business units.

Capital Control and Asset Reorganization. There are strong central controls over capital allocation in the giant oil and petrochemical companies. For example, at BP Amoco, there is a Company Capital Approvals Committee which meets once per month. Any capital expenditure that exceeds $50 million must be submitted to the Committee for approval. From top to bottom, all new capital expenditures must struggle against competing alternatives in an open struggle to demonstrate against open and transparent procedures that the requested use is more beneficial to the company than the alternatives. The bottom line is simple: 'If an asset can't pay its way we sell it.'

In addition to central control over capital expenditure, the headquarters of the world's giant oil and petrochemical companies wield comprehensive control over crucial issues of reorganization of assets. In the 1990s especially this has become immensely important, as the leading firms have enormously increased their programmes of divesting assets on the one hand, and merging and taking over assets on the other. The leading companies have undertaken a huge programme of divesting themselves of assets that have unacceptably low returns or are non-core businesses. For example, since the 1980s, BP has sold off a sequence of peripheral businesses, including chicken production and marketing, computer manufacture, coal and mineral production, and a travel agency. Almost 15 000 employees left the company from 1990 to 1996 as a result of the sale of these businesses.

However, in addition to selling non-core businesses, the leading oil and petrochemical companies are continuously evaluating the usefulness of their core assets. If a business unit is not contributing sufficiently to the whole company's return on assets, it will be sold off. For example, in 1997 and 1998 BP sold off assets totalling $3 billion and intends to sell a further $10 billion-worth of assets between 1999 and 2001. The objective is to 'high-grade' the assets portfolio by concentrating on the most profitable assets. As one analyst commented: 'If you get rid of the dross and concentrate on the jewels you will automatically improve the return on capital' (John Toaster of SG Securities, quoted in *FT*, 16 July 1999). For example, BP Amoco plans to sell off $3–4 billion worth of assets in the refining division, amounting to 30 per cent of its global refining capacity: 'We wish to be in [refining] only when we can't buy what we need for our marketing activity at competitive prices from anywhere else' (John Browne, Chief Executive of BP Amoco, quoted in *FT*, 2 August 1999).

In 1998, Shell announced that it would reduce the number of chemicals product businesses from 21 to 13, and reduce the capital employed by 40 per cent. It announced: 'the future portfolio will comprise a set of major linked petrochemical businesses in which Group companies possess leading technologies and the proven capability to build and operate world-scale plants' (Shell, 1999a: 35). Finally, vastly important decisions of global merger and acquisition are taken at the apex of the company. They are not discussed in advance with shareholders. Nor are they discussed in depth, if at all, with individual business units. Such decisions can be taken at high speed. They fundamentally re-shape the entire architecture of the company concerned.

Alternative Energy Sources. A major source of competitive advantage for the global giants is that they have the resources to invest in new fuel technologies that may gradually replace oil and gas and/or ensure more effective use of oil and gas. The giant oil and petrochemical companies are in the lead in developing solar technology. For example, in April 1999 BP Amoco acquired the remaining 50 per cent stake in Solarex (the world's leading solar company in the USA) from Enron for $45 million. After the merger with BP Solar, BP–Solarex became the largest solar company in the world with an annual revenue of $153 million. It accounts for about 20 per cent of the global market in solar energy in 1998. The company is equipped with leading-edge solar technology, such as the new generation of thin films (including the world's first large-area, monolithic double-junction amorphous silicon module), and the world's broadest product range in polycrystalline silicon. BP–Solarex produces about 30 megawatts of solar products per year with manufacturing facilities in the USA, Spain, Australia and India. BP Amoco aims to provide cleaner fuels in 40 major cities with pollution problems. BP Amoco believes BP–Solarex's technological edge will enable it to build a $1 billion solar business over the next decade.

Shell has established 'Renewables' as a core business. In 1998 it invested $67 million in its solar energy and biomass energy activities. It is building one of the largest solar-cell manufacturing firms in Gelsenkirchen of Germany, with an annual capacity of 13 million cells (or 25 megawatts). Shell converts sustainable grown wood into energy by combustion or other processes. The first commercial operation was a district heating plant in Norway.

The world's leading oil and automobile companies are working together on fuel cell technology. Exxon Mobil developed the means to use petroleum to generate electricity through fuel-cells, which can double the fuel mileage for automobiles, but with very low emission of pollutants. Shell has developed a process of Catalytic Partial Oxidation to convert liquid fuels into hydrogen-rich gas and is co-operating with DBB Fuel Cell Engines, a subsidiary of Daimler–Benz– Chrysler, to equip the existing service stations for refilling fuel-cell powered cars. Shell (Germany) has established one of the first European Union's hydrogen filling stations in Hamburg.

Human Resources. The world's leading oil companies drastically changed their human relations after the 1980s. A central part of this was a huge reduction in the number of employees. For example, Exxon and Mobil between them shed around 30 000 workers from the early to the late 1990s, 'a blood-letting which has helped them keep ahead of the pack in terms of profitability' (*FT*, 30 November 1998). Following the merger of Exxon and Mobil it is expected that there will be a further 9000–14 000 redundancies out of a total workforce of 123 000 (*FT*, 2 December 1998). ENI cut its workforce by around one-third in the early 1990s, prior to privatization (*FT*, 1 November 1995). BP reduced its staff from 129 000 in the mid-1980s to just 53 000 in the late 1990s. These huge reductions were permitted by a number of factors including the sale of non-core business, the introduction of new information technology and increased work intensity within the companies.

The effect of these developments on the human relations within the globalizing companies was very large. The workers who remained were mostly connected by modern information systems, were on average more highly qualified, younger, and with a greatly reduced proportion of low-qualified manual staff. A large proportion of the staff participated in stock option schemes. The smaller number of employees, the higher average level of education, the relative youth of the employees, linked by modern information technology and the common interest in increasing profits, had a profound positive effect on internal cohesion and energy within the companies. These developments facilitated a 'de-layering' of management structures and enabled decisions to be reached more rapidly. They made it possible to construct business units within each of which there was only a relatively small number of people, further increasing the possibility for cohesion and co-operation among team members.

Global Brand. Developing, sustaining and enhancing a global brand is a complex long-term process. Global oil companies face some common problems with other globalizing firms. A key aspect of competitive edge is the ability to integrate the value chain to ensure that products provided to final consumers are of consistent high quality and reliability. A major advantage of scale is the ability to provide for ubiquitous access to the company's products. Possession of a global chain of well-run petrol stations is a key attribute of brand. However, there are many special features of branding for global oil companies. The nature of the products means that health, safety and the environment are of the highest importance. As we have seen, the global giants are able to invest large sums in developing alternative fuel technologies. They possess the resources to develop effective systems that are able to prevent, control, abate or eliminate releases into the air and water at operating facilities. Shell, for example, estimates that it spent $700 million on such purposes in 1998 (Shell, 1999a: 39). Safe decommissioning and site restoration is a very expensive task. Shell, for example, estimates that in 1998 it spent $2.6 billion on these activities (Shell, 1999a: 40). The global giants are better able to purchase modern, safe, production, transport and sales equipment, than are their potential competitors in developing countries. Moreover, the pressure upon them to do so from lobby groups and shareholders in the advanced economies is intense. The regions in which they operate mean that treatment of indigenous peoples is often a key issue. The global giants have been able to allocate substantial resources to developing special capabilities to cope with the complex issues involved.

THE REVOLUTION IN THE CHINESE OIL AND GAS SECTOR

SUPPLY AND DEMAND FOR OIL AND GAS IN CHINA

Demand for Primary Energy. From the early 1980s to the late 1990s, China had the fastest growth rate of national product of any major country, officially reported to be over 10 per cent per annum (World Bank, 1998: 210–11). China's commercial energy use grew at just over 5 per cent per annum from 1980 to 1997 (World Bank, 1998: 208). This was a relatively low rate compared with the officially reported growth rate of national product. It was, nevertheless, a rapid rate of growth in absolute terms and was significantly faster than the world growth rate of commercial energy consumption. China's share of world energy consumption rose from 6.5 per cent in 1980 to 10.3 per cent in 1995 (World Bank, 1998: 208–9).

There is enormous debate about the prospects for China's over-all energy requirements in the years ahead, with a wide range of legitimate grounds for disagreement. China's *per capita* consumption of commercial energy stands at 707 kilograms, far ahead of the very poorest countries, which average only 198 kilograms (World Bank, 1998: 208–9). For example, India consumes only 260 kilograms *per capita*, far behind China. However, China's level of *per capita* consumption is well behind that of the upper middle income countries, which average around 1600 kilograms *per capita*, and far behind the level of the high income countries, which average 5118 kilograms per capita. As the Chinese economy grows towards the level of richer countries, it is certain that this will generate large increases in energy demands, albeit that the growth may be somewhat slower than in the period since the late 1970s. One recent authoritative survey of China's energy prospects concluded: 'Despite near-term economic uncertainties, China's energy consumption shows incredible potential for growth. Its neighbours to the East – Japan and South Korea – consume over sixteen times more energy than China, on a per capita basis. To the south, Malaysia, Thailand and Indonesia consume approximately eight, four and two times more energy than China, respectively, on a *per capita* basis. As its GDP *per capita* begins to approach comparable levels, we expect similar patterns of consumption in China.

Given this country's sheer size, this translates into an enormous potential for growth on an absolute basis' (Choung and Terreson, 1998: 5).

Structure of Primary Energy Use. China has an abundance of coal, with official international estimates of over 11 per cent of the world's proven reserves (BP, 1998). In reality, China's coal reserves may well be considerably above even these officially accepted figures. Coal has played a central role in China's increased supply of primary energy to fuel the country's industrialization. From 1980 to 1997, China's coal output rose by 753 million tons (SSB, ZDQN, 1998: 221), an increase of 121 per cent. In 1965, China had been the fifth largest producer of coal in the world, but by 1990 it had become the world's largest producer. Coal's share of primary energy consumption fell from its almost complete dominance in the 1950s, but since the early 1970s, its share of national primary energy consumption has remained consistently above 70 per cent, even slightly increasing its long-term contribution to the national total (SSB, ZDQN, 1998: 251). After the 1950s, it was hoped that major new finds of oil and gas would enable the share of coal in China's electricity generation to fall. In the 1980s China turned to a policy of explicitly encouraging the adoption of coal instead of oil for electric power generation ('substituting coal for oil'). The share of coal-fired power stations in China's total electricity generation rose from 60 per cent in 1980 to 68 per cent in 1996 (ABN–AMRO, 1998: 31).

It was long known that China had supplies of natural gas in the south-west of the country. In the 1950s China discovered major onshore supplies of oil at Daqing in the north-east of the country. However, despite intensive exploration, and the discovery of important new supplies, China still remains relatively poorly endowed with reserves of oil and natural gas. Official international estimates of China's proven reserves of oil and natural gas suggest that they are only 2.3 per cent and 0.8 per cent respectively of the world total. Output of oil and gas grew substantially from the 1960s through to the late 1990s, with China's output of oil rising to 4.6 per cent of the world total and its natural gas rising to 1.0 per cent of the world total (BP, 1998). However, for a country of China's size these translated into only a small share of total primary energy output. In 1997, crude oil accounted for only 17.4 per cent of China's total primary energy output and natural gas for just 2.3 per cent (SSB, ZDQN, 1998: 251). The disappointing results in oil and gas exploration were the main reason for the sustained role of coal in China's electricity generation. Between 1980 and 1996, the amount of oil used in electric power generation declined from 21 million tons to 12 million tons, alongside an increase in coal consumption for electric power generation from 126 million tons to 488 million tons (SSB, ZDQN, 1998: 253-4).

However, despite the fundamental supply-side problems that China faces, there are powerful pressures for China to raise the consumption of oil and gas, both absolutely and proportionately:

- **The environment.** A fundamental impact has been the growing seriousness of China's attempt to reduce high levels of pollution resulting from the massive use of coal. China's level of coal consumption rose from 610 million tons in 1980 to 1447 million tons in 1996 (SSB, ZDQN, 1998: 253), by which time China accounted for 29.8 per cent of the world total (BP, 1998: 33). A large fraction of coal used is unwashed and burned with 'minimal or no air pollution controls' (Smil, 1993: 117). Total discharges of particulate matter are officially reported to have reached 15 million tons by 1990s, and are unofficially estimated to have reached 20 million tons (Smil, 1993: 117–18). Even the official figures show China as producing 15 per cent of the global total of 100 million tons, of which around two-thirds is generated by coal combustion (Smil, 1993: 118).

China's leaders recognize the damage that large-scale consumption of coal does to China's environment and to the Chinese people's health. At the 1999 annual session of the Chinese National People's Congress, Premier Zhu Rongji recognized that 'the deterioration of the ecological environment remains a glaring problem', and pledged to 'improve the air quality in the capital and punish polluting enterprises' (quoted in *FT*, 6 March 1999). However, substantial reduction of particulate and sulphurous air pollution in a developing country such as China presents large problems. Effective control of these emissions requires either 'massive conversion to cleaner fuels' or 'an extensive installation of costly techniques'. Sulphur dioxide is especially expensive to control. Until very recently even many rich countries avoided this costly commitment (Smil, 1993: 121). It is estimated that the installation of de-sulphurization facilities could increase the costs of electricity generation in China by 25–30 per cent (Smil, 1993: 235). It is often cheaper to install alternative fuels than to provide expensive measures to control pollution from coal-fired power stations.

In addition to the pressure from within China to control the use of coal, international pressures are fast gathering force. It is now widely accepted that global warming is a consequence of increased release of carbon dioxide. It is generally accepted that the net impact of global warming is highly damaging, most especially through the impact on rising sea levels and on climate change. The 1997 Kyoto Conference on climate change appeared to mark a radical shift in perspective towards global warming. At the conference, the industrialized nations agreed to bring emissions of carbon dioxide down to below 1990 levels by the year 2010. The main thrust of their action will be over fossil fuels, which are the main source of greenhouse gases. Coal is much the most carbon-intensive fossil fuel. If the 1997 Kyoto agreement takes effect, then it is thought likely that its implementation will have a substantial negative effect on demand for coal in the high income countries.

China's level of *per capita* emissions of carbon dioxide is still low, at just 2.7 tons, compared with 20.8 tons in the USA. However, China's huge population means that its absolute size of carbon dioxide emissions is very large. Between 1980 and 1995, China's carbon dioxide emissions rose from 1477 million tons in 1980 to 3195 tons in 1995, and its share of the world total rose from 10.9 per cent to 14.1 per cent (World Bank, 1998: 208–9).

There is strong political pressure in Europe and, especially, in the USA, to support the Kyoto agreement only if the same restrictions apply to large developing countries, especially China. The USA is unwilling to sign an agreement allowing developing countries to voluntarily assume obligations of their own, rather than shoulder the same responsibilities as the advanced economies. It is even possible that the WTO may extend its remit to imposing environmental conditions upon member countries. They could include controls on the emission of 'greenhouse' gases, notably carbon dioxide.

Although there are huge uncertainties surrounding the future use of coal in China, it is undeniable that there do exist large pressures both from within and outside China to reduce the role of coal in the overall energy portfolio.

- **Transport.** With current technology, there are some severe constraints within the transport sector on the substitutability of oil by other forms of primary energy supply, whatever the response of the Chinese government to environmental pressures. Despite the strong desire to substitute coal for oil, in 1996, China's transport sector consumed just 12 million tons of coal, compared with over 29 million tons of various oil products (SSB, ZDQN, 1998: 257). Both China's passenger and freight transport have increased at high speed since the late 1970s, at rates close to those reported for the growth of national product. Rates of growth of road and air transport have been especially rapid, outstripping the rate of expansion of railway transport (Table 7-12). Moreover, China's railway system has switched towards diesel consumption at high speed, with the share of diesel engine operation rising from 14 per cent in 1978 to 54 per cent in 1996 (SSB, ZDQN, 1998: 544). Water transport also has increased at a rapid rate, and remains the most important single form of freight transport if international trade is taken into consideration (Table 7-12). This also places large demands on oil supplies.

- **Chemical industry.** With existing technology, there are only limited possibilities to substitute other materials for oil and natural gas as the main feedstock for the chemicals industry. Coal chemistry is the most promising avenue, but it is still a highly uncertain prospect in terms of providing low-cost, reliable supplies of feedstock for the chemical industry. At the heart of China's industrial revolution since the early 1980s has been an explosive growth of demand for a wide variety of products which ultimately depend on oil and natural gas as the feedstock. China's textile and garment industry has moved rapidly into first place in the world. Much of this has been based on the supply of chemical fibres. In the late 1970s, China was the world's seventh largest producer of chemical fibres. From 1980 to 1997, China's chemical fibre output grew by 15 per cent per annum (Table 7-13), and China had risen to second place in the world (SSB, ZDQN, 1998: 933). China's rapidly-growing plastics goods industries, from plastic bottles to motor car components, required high-speed growth in the supply of a wide range of plastics. Output of plastics rose by 13 per cent per annum from 1980 to 1997 (Table 7-13). China's farm sector also generated a large increase in

TABLE 7-12 **Transport Growth in China, 1978–97**

	Passengers (billion passenger-km) (% in brackets)				Freight (billion ton-km) (% in brackets)			
	Total	Rail	Road	Air	Total	Rail	Road	Water
1978	174 (100)	109 (63)	52 (30)	3 (2)	983 (100)	535 (54)	27 (3)	378 (38)
1997	1002 (100)	355 (35)	554 (55)	77 (8)	3821 (100)	1310 (34)	527 (14)	1924 (50)
Av. annual growth rate 1978–97 (%)	(9.6)	(6.4)	(13.5)	(18.6)	(7.4)	(4.8)	(16.9)	(8.9)

SOURCE: SSB (1980 and 1999)

TABLE 7-13 Growth of Output of China's Main Petrochemical Products 1980–97 (million tons)

	Chemical fibre	Synthetic detergents	Chemical fertilizer	Plastics
1980	0.45	0.39	12.3	0.90
1997	4.72	2.80	28.2	6.86
Average annual growth rate 1980–97 (%)	(14.9)	(12.2)	(5.0)	(12.5)

SOURCE: SSB, ZDQN (1998: 465–471)

demand for products from the chemical industry, stimulating a 5 per cent per annum growth in the output of chemical fertilizers. China rose from being the world's third largest producer in 1978 to the first largest by 1996 (SSB, ZDQN, 1998: 933).

International Trade in Oil. China did produce oil and natural gas before 1949. Indeed, China was the originator of deep-drilling techniques, used to extract brine and natural gas (Zhong Changyuan and Huang Jian, 1997). The first salt wells in China were recorded around 2250 years ago. Historical records indicate that at the beginning of the 3rd century AD salt wells as deep as 138 metres were dug in Sichuan province. Around the year 1750, wells in Sichuan's Zigong area were typically around 300–400 metres deep. In 1815, one of these wells reached a depth of 798 metres, and in 1815 a well of over 1000 metres depth was drilled. Despite these early technical achievements, China's oil industry in the 1950s was still small, with an output of just 75 mb/d in 1959. Domestic production accounted for only around 40 per cent of total demand. In 1959 the Chinese oil industry was transformed by the discovery of the giant Daqing oilfield in north-eastern China. By 1963 approximately 1200 wells had been drilled and production had reached 120 mb/d.

It was at one time thought possible that China might become a significant oil exporter. The share of oil in China's primary energy production rose from under 3 per cent in the early 1950s to 24 per cent at its peak in 1980 (SSB, ZDQN, 1998: 251). In that year, China's oil production was 18 per cent greater than domestic consumption. However, the relatively disappointing results of oil exploration to date have meant that domestic production has grown less rapidly than was at one time thought possible. From 1980 to 1997, crude oil output grew by only 2.5 per cent per annum (SSB, ZDQN, 1998: 251). However, the pace of growth of consumption has been much more rapid, averaging 4.5 per cent per annum from 1980 to 1997 (SSB, ZDQN, 1998: 251), despite the extensive substitution of coal for oil in electricity power generation.

In the early 1990s, the surplus of China's oil production over consumption reduced drastically alongside the accelerated growth of Chinese industrial output, and by 1993 had disappeared altogether (Table 7-14). The 1990s saw a rapid growth in the oil deficit. From 1995 to 1997, China's gross oil imports almost

TABLE **7-14 Balance of China's Oil Production and Consumption 1987–97 (million barrels per day)**

Year	Production	Consumption	Balance
1987	2.69	2.11	(+) 0.58
1988	2.74	2.21	(+) 0.53
1989	2.76	2.26	(+) 0.50
1990	2.78	2.26	(+) 0.52
1991	2.83	2.41	(+) 0.42
1992	2.84	2.66	(+) 0.18
1993	2.89	2.92	(−) 0.03
1994	2.93	3.18	(−) 0.25
1995	2.99	3.43	(−) 0.44
1996	3.17	3.73	(−) 0.55
1997	3.20	4.01	(−) 0.81

SOURCE: BP (1998)

TABLE **7-15 Sources of China's Imported Crude Oil* 1995–7 (thousand barrels of oil/day, mb/d)**

Source	1995	1996	1997	% of 1997 total	CAGR** (%)
Middle East	155	242	336		
North Africa	6	2	—		
West Africa	28	34	104		
Total Middle East/ Africa	189	278	440	36	53
Australasia	2	4	6		
Japan	19	23	52		
Other Asia	383	437	522		
Total Asia	404	464	580	48	20
USA	8	8	22		
South/Central America	—	—	22		
Western Europe	6	—	20		
Former USSR	27	19	83		
Unidentified	10	12	43		
Total Other	51	39	190	16	93
Total China Imports	644	781	1210	100	37

SOURCE: BP (1996, 1997, 1998)

NOTES: * Import numbers represent total imports, as opposed to net imports
　　　** CAGR = Compound Annual Growth Rate

doubled from 644 mb/d to 1210 mb/d (Table 7-15). By 1997, China's gross imports amounted to no less than 30.2 per cent of consumption and net imports totalled 18 per cent of consumption (BP, 1998). China had now become a significant purchaser on international markets, accounting for 3 per cent of world imports (BP, 1998: 18).

Projections of both demand and supply are fraught with great difficulties. If the growth of consumption continued at the rate of the past decade (that is, around 6–7 per cent per annum), then China's oil consumption by the year 2010 would rise to almost 9000 mb/d. Moreover, if China pursued more radical policies to substitute oil and gas for coal, as the environmental lobbyists within and outside China wish, then the growth of oil consumption could be even greater. On the supply side, it is extremely difficult to estimate the probable growth of output. If China's output grows at the rate of the past decade (that is, 1.4 per cent per annum), then output would only reach around 4000 mb/d. This would leave a yawning deficit of 5000 mb/d. This would mean that China's net oil imports might amount to more than one-half of total consumption, around one-half the USA's current level of gross oil imports, or around 12 per cent of today's level of world oil imports. Of course, it is possible that China's oil output grows at a much faster rate than it has over the past decade: 'production could swing dramatically in either direction' (Choung and Terreson, 1998: 11).

One recent expert view predicted that China's net imports of crude oil could rise from their 1997 level of around 700 mb/d to 1.4 mb/d by 2000 and 'more than double this figure five years later' (Choung and Terreson, 1998: 9). This would amount to around one-third of China's projected oil consumption, assuming that consumption grew by the same rate as from 1987 to 1997. Other experts have predicted that China may soon import more than one-half of its oil demand. Semi-official Chinese estimates predict that China will import 40 per cent of its oil needs by 2010 (*China Economic Daily*, 30 April 1999).

The possibility of a rapid increase in China's reliance on oil imports has large implications for international political economy. The fastest-growing source of oil imports for China is the Middle East. By 1997, its share of China's total oil imports had risen to 36 per cent (Table 7-15). The Middle East has the advantage that it possesses vast reserves with only limited domestic needs for oil . Southeast Asia's reserves are much smaller, and the region has large domestic requirements for oil and gas. However, there are fears of the USA's political dominance in the Middle East, exacerbated by the Gulf War and the USA's role in Yugoslavia. The *China Economic Daily* warned: 'We must pay close attention to the fact that the US controls the oil in the Middle East.' It urges China to consider favourably the development of deeper relationships with the former USSR to ensure long-term supplies of oil and gas: 'Russia has many times expressed its wish to jointly develop western Siberia and export natural gas to us. We have reacted positively and have sent teams to conduct feasibility studies' (*China Economic Daily*, 30 April 1999). Some oil experts have warned that 'China may be as robust as the United States in defending its access to oil supplies'. The South China Seas are a major part of the war scenario projected for China by Bernstein and Munro (Bernstein and Munro, 1998: 74–5). A key part of this is China's growing thirst for oil which some people argue may be behind China's assertion of its sovereignty in the South China Seas: The Spratly Islands are located over substantial undersea oil and gas reserves.

INSTITUTIONAL CHANGE IN THE CHINESE OIL AND GAS INDUSTRY
(i): THE PARTIALLY REFORMED STRUCTURE – FROM DIRECT ADMINISTRATIVE
COMMANDS TO HOLDING COMPANIES AND 'QUASI-FIRMS'

General Comments. Across the world, since the 1980s privatizations have been of great importance in the oil and petrochemical sector. However, China's reforms have taken place in a different context from that of most reforms in this sector. China's entire economy was cut off from international markets and capital in the 1970s, and almost the whole of its industrial economy was under administrative planning. China had no stock market that could absorb the mass flotation of state-owned enterprises. The entire oil and petrochemical sector operated as a single enterprise directed from central ministries in Beijing. Domestic prices for all oil-based products were isolated from world market prices. China's chosen path has been to experimentally reform the institutional structure of this enormous sector rather than risk a one-shot solution to improvement of performance of this crucial sector which forms the foundation of the entire economy. The first stage in the institutional reform process involved the formation of two state holding companies, China National Petroleum Corporation (CNPC) and China National Petrochemical Corporation (Sinopec), as well as the smaller China National Offshore Oil Corporation (CNOOC). Many complex problems arose in their relationship with both subordinate units and with each other. Intense debate took place about how best to resolve these problems. This debate took place against the background of revolutionary change in the world's oil and petrochemical industry in the 1990s, which has substantially influenced the thinking of Chinese policy makers about how best to proceed with the reform of this sector.

Upstream: CNPC
CNPC monopoly of onshore oil production. Before the 1980s, China's entire oil and gas exploration and production was controlled by the Ministry of Petroleum Industry (MPI). Investment allocations, output targets, product mix, marketing, and pricing were all tightly controlled from the Ministry. In 1988, the Ministry was reorganized into the China National Petroleum Corporation (CNPC) vested with control over the assets formerly under the MPI. CNPC was transformed from a Ministry into a holding company, with formalized ownership rights over the constituent production enterprises. However, CNPC was to continue with many of the 'Ministerial' functions formerly undertaken by the MPI, including such matters as deciding the policy for environmental regulation. It continued to be the main vehicle for oil exploration and production within China, as well as to be a major vehicle for the development of sources of oil and gas supply outside China. This important function was not purely commercial, but related to the government's desire for energy security for China. In 1997 CNPC produced 89 per cent of China's total oil output.

Upon the establishment of CNPC in 1988, the direction of enterprise reform in the Chinese oil and petrochemical industry was unclear. The broad thrust of

China's enterprise reform was to separate the government bureaucracy from the operation of enterprises. In the late 1980s and early 1990s a series of reforms increased the degree of enterprise autonomy, including the rights to retain profits. Many of these changes were formalized in the 'Company Law of the PRC', which became effective in 1994. Under the Chinese enterprise reform, individual production enterprises within CNPC were wholly or partially owned by the state, through CNPC. However, under the enterprise reform, they were granted the status of incorporated legal persons, able to sign contracts, responsible for their own profits and losses, and able to retain profits. As will be seen below, in the case of the key large-scale enterprises within CNPC, the enhanced autonomy of the reform period built upon already strong traditions of enterprise identity. It was far from clear where the 'enterprise' that constituted the heart of China's 'enterprise' reform would finally be located in the oil and gas sector. Individual large enterprises under CNPC had reason to believe that they might indeed end up as autonomous firms.

The establishment of CNPC signalled an important transition from purely administrative control functions of the Ministry towards a market-oriented method of functioning. However, it was still unclear where the 'firm' would be located. Would CNPC become a truly independent company, owning and managing the subordinate production units under its control, or would it be simply a Ministry with no direct ownership and management rights over the subordinate entities? The period from 1988 until 1998 was essentially one of experimentation, groping towards the correct business structure for the industry. Not until the 1998 restructuring was it finally decided by the central policy makers that CNPC would indeed become a truly integrated company, casting off its old 'ministerial' functions.

A continuing theme of the period pre-1998, was the tension between the ambitions of the large constituent enterprises within CNPC, and the hope of elements within CNPC and within higher-level policy makers, to make CNPC into a truly modern enterprise, with the constituent enterprises as part of a fully integrated company. As we shall see despite the crucially important policy decision taken in 1998, the final shape of the company is still far from certain, and tension between the centre and the largest of the production enterprises is far from over.

Main production units. Despite extensive exploration onshore, and the discovery of many new oil fields, in the 1990s, China's oil production was still heavily concentrated in a small number of fields. The principal oilfields, apart from Daqing (see below), were the following:

- **Shengli Petroleum Administration**. The Shengli oilfield was discovered in 1961, and comprises around a dozen fields in northern Shandong province. Output increased from the early 1960s through until the 1980s, but has begun to decline from its peak of 670 mb/d in 1990. In 1997 production had fallen to 560 mb/d. It is still the second in importance after Daqing, accounting for one-fifth of total CNPC output in 1997. Although it is considerably smaller than Daqing, Shengli is, nevertheless, China's seventh largest 'enterprise' in terms of sales revenue. In 1997 its sales value was $2.5 billion, slightly ahead of the giant Number One Automobile Group. It employs around 200 000 people. Like the other large oilfields, it constitutes a complete social welfare system, with many hundreds of thousands of people dependent on it for their livelihood. Within Shengli, production is scattered over several dozen smaller fields.

- **Liaohe Petroleum Administration**. This field consists of around 25 producing structures of different sizes in the Liaoning Basin in north-east China. It was discovered in 1969. Production started in 1970. By 1997 it had reached 15 million tons, amounting to around 11 per cent of the total output of CNPC. It is somewhat smaller in terms of employment than either Daqing or Shengli, with around 130 000 employees.

- **Xinjiang Petroleum Administration**. The Xinjiang Petroleum Administration (XJPA) manages all the oil fields in the vast Xinjiang Province in the extreme west of China, with the important exception of those in the Tarim Basin and Tu-Ha Basins. The main field under XJPA is the Karamay, in the Jungar Basin. Total crude oil production under XJPA in 1997 totalled around 6 per cent of CNPC's output.

- **Tarim Petroleum Exploration and Development Headquarters**. Recent developments in the Tarim Basin are of immense potential importance for China and for CNPC as a company. The Tarim Basin in Xinjiang has long been thought by Chinese geologists to contain enormous reserves of oil and gas. Oil and gas exploration in the Tarim Basin has been mainly under the direct control of CNPC. A special body, the Tarim Petroleum Exploration and Development Headquarters (TPEDH), was established in 1991 specifically for this purpose. Large-scale exploration only began after this date. The Tarim Basin and the Tu-Ha Basin are now regarded as the major hope for expanding China's onshore oil and gas production capabilities in the next century. The 560 000 square kilometre basin is the world's largest oil-bearing basin yet to be developed.

The potential development of the region as a major oil and gas production base has major strategic significance for China. If it were proven to be the case, it might greatly reduce China's dependence on imports. However, it also means that China has to cope with the high transport costs involved in moving the raw material across China to the eastern seaboard, which would be very expensive. Alternatively, a major new development of industrial production might be supported in the region. This is closely related to mooted large-scale schemes to develop the region through diverting water from other regions of China. The region could then become a major centre for the absorption of China's enormous population growth which will take place over the coming decades, and relieve the pressure on the eastern coastal regions.

The investments required to develop production from the Tarim Basin are enormous. They include not only the high costs of exploration and production in an arduous desert environment. The oil-bearing strata are often at a depth of over 5000 metres below ground level (*CDBW*, 11 October, 1998). Most importantly, the costs of transporting oil and gas out of the region to the east coast would be extremely high. The Chinese government apparently ear-marked $20 billion yuan for oil exploration in 1991–5 alone.

Major breakthroughs were reported in oil and gas exploration in the Tarim Basin in 1997 and 1998 (*CDBW*, 11 October 1998). The reported finds suggested massive reserves. The 'geological reserves' in the basin are now estimated by Chinese geologists to be as large as 10.8 billion tons of oil and 8,400 billion cubic metres of gas. This compares with China's proven reserves of just 3.3 billion tons of oil and 1160 billion cubic metres of gas (BP, 1998). The vice-president of CNPC's Research Institute of Petroleum Exploration and Development commented: 'I am confident that over 1100 billion cubic metres of natural gas will be proven in the basin by 2005' (quoted in the *CDBW*, 11 October 1998).

If these reports are accurate, they have major implications not just for China's oil and gas self-sufficiency, but also for the business structure of CNPC. By ensuring that the main potential source of future domestic expansion for CNPC's supplies of oil and gas is directly under the administration of CNPC headquarters, CNPC has ensured that a large fraction of the possible future domestic growth of the company will be tightly controlled from the corporate headquarters. The THPEDH does not have a large number of employees with cradle-to-grave tenure. It employs 'only' 10 000 permanent employees. The remainder are contract workers.

Financial control. Neither CNPC's Annual Report nor the detailed published documents on CNPC (see especially CNPC, 1998), provides a clear picture of the evolving pattern of financial control within CNPC. Each constituent enterprise constructs its own budget, which is forwarded to the CNPC headquarters for 'inspection' and inclusion in the consolidated budget for the whole company. There are a number of channels through which the financial control of CNPC headquarters can be exercised:

- **Profits**. It is likely that a substantial fraction of CNPC's reported 'company profits' are in fact under the direct control of the constituent enterprises. For example, in 1997, CNPC reported pre-tax profits of 33.2 billion yuan on sales of 167.8 billion yuan. After handing over 22.9 billion yuan in taxes, CNPC was left with post-tax profits of 10.3 billion yuan (CNPC, 1998: 444). CNPC's largest constituent enterprise, Daqing, accounted for 63 per cent of CNPC's post-tax profits (6.5 billion yuan out of a total of 10.3 billion yuan) (CNPC, 1998: 281 and 444). However, it is extremely difficult to know the degree to which the profits of subordinate enterprises were handed over to CNPC headquarters. Data provided to the author at Daqing report that Daqing had sales of 50.6 billion yuan in 1998 from its oil production. It 'handed over' 11.4 billion yuan to the central government's financial bureau, and 10.4 billion yuan to CNPC headquarters (data provided to the author at Daqing). If Daqing's contribution to CNPC's revenues were excluded, then CNPC as a whole would have been a loss-maker in 1998. However, the financial picture at Daqing, as at other large Chinese enterprises, is enormously complicated by the fact that a great deal of revenue comes from 'diversified business' which does not appear in officially published data. If these were included, Daqing's sales revenue would be much larger than the above figures, and so too would be its 'hand-overs' to CNPC headquarters. Intense negotiation surrounds the whole issue of the level of hand-overs with prolonged negotiations each year on the figure to be handed over. In 1999, the relationship between Daqing and CNPC headquarters was still routinely spoken of in terms of a *'baogan'* or contract for hand-overs.

- **Bank loans**. A crucial source of revenue for CNPC is central government budgetary allocations for investment. In 1997, CNPC was allocated 11.4 billion yuan (that is $1.4 billion) in the central government's budget. Of this, 1.2 billion yuan were soft loans from the State Development Bank, 5.2 billion yuan were repayable loans from other banks, and 4.3 billion yuan were loans from the Construction Bank (CNPC, 1998: 208). In 1997 also, for the first time, CNPC issued oil enterprise bonds, raising 5 billion yuan (CNPC, 1998: 208). The degree to which these loans were directly under the control of CNPC headquarters as opposed to the constituent operating units is unknown.

- **Foreign investment in oilfields**. A further important potential source of central financial control is in the absorption of international funds for oilfield exploration and development. CNPC was given exclusive rights to co-operate with multinational companies for onshore oil exploration and production. In marked contrast to CNOOC, it is widely thought that CNPC is much less interested in foreign participation in onshore oil exploration and production. The first formal onshore licensing round did not take place until 1993. CNPC is proud of its technical capability. At this stage, bidding areas offered to foreign companies have been 'limited to areas in which China would have technical and financial difficulties undertaking the operation on its own' (Choung and Terreson, 1998: 15). This is widely referred to as the policy of giving the multinational companies the 'hard bones'. Up until the end of 1998, there was a total of 47 onshore oil contracts, with a total of $1.1 billion in foreign investment. Thirty Sino–foreign contracts were in operation, producing just 2.3 million tons of crude oil, with a total foreign investment of only $558 million (CNPC, *Annual Report, 1998*: 39). One of the main reasons for the 'dismal' response from multinational investors was said to be the 'CNPC head office seems to have limited authority over the regional oil field companies' (Andrews-Speed and Gao Zhiguo, 1996: 176).

CNPC is strongly and increasingly aware of the importance of financial control in order to establish a globally competitive company. However, the degree to which it had succeeded in establishing such controls over constituent entities by 1998 was unclear. Anecdotal evidence suggests that the constituent operating units of CNPC significantly increased their operational autonomy under the reforms and their sense of corporate identity grew stronger. Gradually, the headquarters seems to have grown increasingly aware of the need to establish central financial control. However, by 1998, the constituent operating enterprises still seemed to have a great deal of financial autonomy. A major part of the 1998–99 restructuring (see below) was directed at trying to increase financial control of the CNPC's headquarters.

Overseas investments by CNPC. By the end of 1997, CNPC had made cumulative overseas investments of $808 million (CNPC, 1998: 210). These included investments in Sudan, Venezuela, Kazakhstan and Peru. The total recoverable reserves thereby acquired by CNPC totalled over 400 million tons, equivalent to around 12 per cent of China's total recoverable reserves within its own boundaries. CNPC's share of production from overseas reserves in 1998 totalled only 1.9 million tons, around one per cent of China's domestic output. However, the long-term prospects are for sustained increases in overseas investment by CNPC in order to increase its access to secure sources of oil and gas from abroad. It is, clearly, working closely with the central government in order to contribute to China's energy security. Some experts believe that China may within a few years import as much as one-fifth of it oil imports through the foreign reserves of its domestic companies.

As well as the investments already made, CNPC has signed other large-scale contracts to develop oil supplies from central Asia and the Middle East. It has signed a $1.2 billion contract to develop Iraq's Ahdab field when the UN-imposed sanctions are lifted. Most importantly, in 1997 it signed a total of $9.5 billion worth of agreements with the Kazakhstan government to develop two oil fields in the country. The project involved the construction of a $2.4 billion pipeline, 3277 kilometres in length, from Kazakhstan to Xinjiang in Western China. The project was 'shelved' in July 1999, due to 'uncertainty over the price of oil' and the heavy financial burden that the pipeline would impose on CNPC.

To the degree that CNPC increases its foreign supplies, the relative importance of constituent production enterprises within CNPC will decline. If the Tarim Basin proves to be at all successful, then the balance of oil supply within CNPC will shift radically away from the large, relatively independent east coast oilfields within CNPC, towards sources that are under the direct control of the headquarters.

An important aspect of CNPC's development of foreign sources of supply, is that it will enhance its skills in managing a complex global portfolio of oil resources in the same way that the global giants do.

In one sense, the expansion of its oil and gas portfolio outside China can be viewed as a quasi-governmental function, since a major motive is to enhance China's national energy security. However, in another sense, such a move can be regarded as consistent with the commercial behaviour of the capitalist global giants, which also attempt to create diversified global sources of supply outside their home country. In the case of smaller countries like Britain and the Netherlands, this has always been necessary, but even the largest US-based companies have long sought to internationalize their sources of supply of crude oil and gas.

Daqing: Oilfield or Company? Over a long period, Daqing Petroleum Administration has been much the most important single production unit in the Chinese oil industry. Output at Daqing remained fairly steady at around

TABLE 7-16 Output, Sales and Pre-tax Profit in CNPC, 1996

	Output (1997)*		Sales**		Pre-tax profits§	
	(million tons)	(%)	(billion yuan)	(%)	(million yuan)	(%)
Total	143.2	100.0	145.7	100.0	29.6	100.0
of which:						
Daqing PA	56.0	39.1	43.7	30.0	19.2	64.9
Shengli PA	28.0	19.6	22.0	15.1	3.2	10.8
Liaohe PA	15.0	10.5	13.3	9.1	2.1	7.1
Xinjiang PA	8.7	6.1	13.2	9.1	1.0	3.5

SOURCES: * CNPC, Annual Report (1998: 98–99)
          ** SSB, ZDQN (1997: 277, 289)
          § CNPC (1998: 448)

NOTE: PA = Petroleum Administration

56 million tons (1120 mb/d) over a long period. Daqing is now a relatively old field. It is thought likely that it will sustain output at around this level for at least the next 10 years. However, some industry experts believe that Daqing's production level will fall more sharply, so that it is essentially exhausted within as little as five years. Around 80 per cent of Daqing oil is exported out of Heilongjiang province, in which it is situated. In 1996 Daqing accounted for two-fifths of the physical output of CNPC (Table 7-16), and almost two-thirds of CNPC's pre-tax profits. In other words, Daqing has been for a long period and is likely to continue to be for at least a few years hence, the core of CNPC's oil production.

Daqing has an important place in modern Chinese political life, since Chairman Mao selected it in1964 as the model for Chinese state enterprises. The oilfield was developed in the 1960s under arduous conditions following the Soviet withdrawal. Funds for construction were scarce. China desperately needed to become self-sufficient in oil as fast as possible. Daqing was held up as the model for selfless mass enthusiasm and frugal construction, minimizing costs: 'We must save construction funds for the state and establish the idea of taking pride in plain living among the workers. Promote the "one penny" spirit. That is, we must not waste one drop of oil, one unit of electricity, one tael of coal, one inch of steel or timber. Everybody must practise austerity. Austerity must be practised everywhere, in everything, and at all times.' The rapid development of Daqing helped China achieve oil self-sufficiency by 1963. Daqing feels deeply proud of its enormous long-term contribution to the Chinese economy and to national finances.

Not only is Daqing much the most important enterprise in the oil industry, it is also the largest and most profitable enterprise in China. In 1996, its revenue totalled $5.3 billion, far ahead of even the second-ranked enterprise, the China Northeast Electricity Corporation Group (SSB, ZDQN, 1997: 277). Daqing's pre-tax profits totalled $2.3 billion. This compares, for example, with sales of $2.5 billion and pre-tax profits of $540 million at the highly successful Shanghai Automobile Corporation Group.

Daqing employs around 250 000 people. Around 800 000 people are directly dependent on a member of their family working in Daqing. The total population of Daqing is around two million, the livelihoods of almost all of whom are closely linked to the prosperity of Daqing. Like other SOEs it has a huge welfare system of houses, schools and health facilities. It has provided cradle-to-grave security for the several hundred thousand people who are almost completely dependent on it. The remoteness of a large oilfield increases the sense of community. Like most other large state enterprises in China, Daqing was tightly controlled in respect to increases in the wage income of its employees. Up until 1978, Daqing's pioneering spirit was reflected in relatively spartan living conditions. All the housing, for example, was in the form of '*gandalei*', rough, single-storey mud houses. However, a major consequence of China's post-1978 liberalization was that it became politically legitimate for Daqing to increase its social welfare spending. Since then, the 'social wage' at Daqing has hugely increased. Daqing has extremely high quality public services. Its housing stock has increased rapidly. All of Daqing's employees are provided with generous housing by the standards of Chinese state enterprises, with virtually no rent to pay. Nor are there any heating costs for the individual, a major issue in a region which has temperatures of minus thirty degrees in the winter. Daqing has outstanding educational facilities from crèches through to higher education. For example, it has recently completed the construction of a huge secondary school, whose facilities rival those of any school in East Asia. Education is provided free to Daqing employees.

Daqing has built a high quality medical infrastructure, with a high level of health provision free of charge to the individual. The quality of road maintenance and maintenance of public spaces is extremely high.

It is not too fanciful to speak of Daqing as like 'Norway in the Northeast of China'. The immense revenue provided over the long-term by the Daqing oilfield has been ploughed back into raising the quality of human resources at Daqing. When the oil runs out, which may be in a relatively short period of time, Daqing will be left with a rich legacy of human resources. So remote and self-contained is Daqing that it thinks of itself as almost a 'country', with intense ambitions for 'its people'.

Daqing's ambitions were fuelled strongly by the enterprise reforms after the mid-1980s, which allowed enterprises to retain a significant proportion of their profits. They were given even stronger impetus by the intense discussions and policy experiments to create large enterprise groups in the 1990s. As we have seen, a key part of this process was the beginnings of a process of take-over and merger through which strong individual enterprises became even more powerful. In 1996, under the 'visionary' leadership of Ding Guiming, Daqing developed its own reform plan. The reform plan charted a course for Daqing to develop autonomously into a global giant corporation. Daqing planned to use its abundant accumulated financial reserves to acquire international oil assets, particularly in the former USSR. This is extremely important since it is predicted that at the most Daqing will have another 10 years or so of life left in the Daqing Oilfield. If permitted, Daqing would have taken over other domestic oilfields. A crucial part of the enterprise's strategy was to become a fully integrated oil company with extensive refining and petrochemical operations. Daqing planned a series of large-scale mergers with other strong Chinese companies. Daqing's merger philosophy was to merge with other strong companies. It strongly wished to avoid merging with weak companies. Daqing planned to merge with refineries in the north-east of China so that a close integration could be developed with its oil supply. Even more ambitiously, the plan included a merger with Shanghai Petrochemical Company (SPC) in Shanghai. Exploratory talks were even held with SPC. Daqing already supplied, as we have seen, around one-third of SPC's crude oil supply. In addition, SPC's location would have provided Daqing with a base in the fast-growing coastal area of China, surrounded by a huge and highly dynamic market and low transport costs to other highly developed parts of China. Daqing held talks also with Yanshan (Beijing) with a view to merger, and developing its vertically integrated operations.

Daqing recognized the key importance of developing downstream operations, and planned also to develop a network of petrol stations around high-speed motorways in the coastal areas. It planned to take over or merge with chain stores that would co-operate in the development of high margin retail stores to sell food and other products at petrol stations. It explored the possibility of developing its own tanker fleet. It held talks with Dalian port, through which Daqing's oil is exported, with a view to merger. It held talks with China's largest automobile companies, Yiqi and Erqi, with the objective of establishing joint ventures to co-operate in the development of high quality lubricants.

It planned to spin off gradually the oilfield 'technical service' companies, so as to focus on the core business of integrated oil and petrochemical production. Under suitable conditions, Daqing's schools, hospitals and other social service activities were to be handed over to the care of the local government.

Daqing even contemplated merging with Sinochem, the giant China National Chemicals Import and Export Corporation, in order to provide Daqing with a direct link to international markets.

In sum, by the mid-1990s, Daqing had developed intense ambitions for domestic and international expansion. The goal of the leadership was to make Daqing the core of a new giant integrated oil and petrochemical company, that would lead the Chinese industry in its competition with the global giants of the industry. A key part of the strategy was to focus on the core business of oil, oil products and petrochemicals, integrating upstream and downstream. The emphasis would be on growing by merging with or taking over other strong companies 'through the market', in other words in order to meet the business interests of the two enterprises.

Daqing's ambitious plans were resolutely opposed by the headquarters of CNPC. If Daqing had succeeded in achieving its goals for 'restructuring through the market', it would have meant the death of CNPC. In the words of one industry expert, CNPC would have had to face the question: 'If you are a giant, who am I?' After fierce discussion, the central government supported CNPC headquarters and rejected the Daqing plan. Instead, the central government decided to support the path of reconstruction to build global giant companies through administrative means. The basis for these new companies was to be the old ministries and their quasi-ministerial successors, CNPC and Sinopec. This firmly turned the government's back on the possibility of allowing and encouraging competitive giant firms to emerge as the basis for industrial reform to build competitive giant companies. This was a highly significant decision in the history of China's industrial reform. It decisively set the industrial reform path in a new and different direction in the oil and petrochemical sector, and has profound implications for the whole of China's reform of large-scale industry. Following the defeat of Daqing's plans, its ambitious leaders, such as Ding Guiming, were transferred to other parts of CNPC (Ding Guiming became the Deputy General Manager of CNPC).

For Daqing itself, the rejection of its plans by the central government and by CNPC set the scene for the fierce struggles of restructuring in 1998 and 1999 (see below). Under any kind of institutional reorganization that might take place within the Chinese oil industry, the relationship of Daqing with the central authorities in the oil industry in Beijing was likely to be fraught with difficulties. Sinopec had no subordinate entity of the size of Daqing to deal with in its long march from state administrative organ to a modern large, integrated company.

A further important consequence of the central government's rejection of Daqing's proposal was that it strongly reinforced the tendency to develop 'diversified production'. Over a long period, Daqing was prevented by controls from CNPC and the Chinese state from using its large revenues to develop its oil business beyond a certain point. Its annual output was tightly controlled by government planning targets, and it was impossible to even consider merging with other oil and petrochemical companies. Consequently, Daqing had a strong incentive to use its large annual retentions of profits to build up a portfolio of businesses outside its core business of oil. By the mid-1990s, it had over 1000 subsidiary companies. These included businesses in a wide variety of industries all over China. Around 80 000 people are directly employed in Daqing's subsidiary companies, and a great many more in the various partially owned businesses in which it has invested. In the province of Shandong alone, Daqing has over seven billion yuan in investments. Daqing subsidiaries include a huge range of businesses. They include many property investments, food processing, plastics, garments, textiles, aerospace, and auto components. Many of these companies are joint ventures with multinational companies, especially those from Japan and Korea. One aspect of the huge accumulation of non-core business assets is the intense wish to develop a large portfolio of businesses that enable the 'citizens' of Daqing to survive and prosper after the oil runs out. These investments are the physical counterpart of Daqing's large-scale investment in raising the quality of human capital through investment in housing, education and health. The total income from diversified business may even rival that from the Daqing oilfield.

An important consequence of the government's rejection of Daqing's development plan is to strongly reinforce the tendency to invest in diversified production rather than the core oil business.

Downstream: Sinopec. Sinopec was created in 1983. It was a Ministry-level enterprise under the direct supervision and control of the State Council. Its creation was a very significant step in the reform of the institutional structure of the Chinese petrochemical industry. It brought together within one entity, a set of enterprises with closely related business activities that had formerly been within four different ministries, namely Petroleum, Petrochemicals, Textiles and Light Industry. Moreover, many of these were formerly under local government supervision, but on the creation of Sinopec, they were placed directly under Sinopec.

Sinopec spanned the full range of petrochemical industry production including crude oil refining, oil products, the manufacture of petrochemicals, chemical fertilizers, synthetic resins, fibres and rubbers, and the marketing of these products. The functions of Sinopec were primarily intended to be complementary to those of CNPC, one focusing on the upstream and one on the downstream parts of the oil and petrochemical business.

In the mid-1990s, Sinopec had a total of 36 subordinate production enterprises. Total employment in the mid-1990s was around 650 000. Several of these enterprises were relatively powerful enterprises in their own right, each with powerful traditions and a unique history and culture. Five enterprises stood out for their relative size within Sinopec, namely Shanghai, Qilu, Yangzi, Yanshan and Daqing. Between them these five subordinate enterprises accounted for 30 per cent of Sinopec's total value of fixed assets (Table 7-17). The five enterprises accounted for 87 per cent of Sinopec's total ethylene production in 1995 (Table 7-18). Over one-half of Sinopec oil refining capacity was accounted for by eight large-scale refineries (Table 7-19).

From its inception until the late 1990s, Sinopec played three roles simultaneously. It served as a government organ for overseeing the development of China's

TABLE 7-17 **Profits and Assets Value of Main Production Enterprises under Sinopec, 1995**

	Pre-tax profits (million yuan)	Net value of fixed assets (million yuan)
Sinopec total	2 594	103 401
of which:		
Shanghai	33 958	7 886
Qilu	1 320	7 987
Fushun	1 572	2 082
Yangzi	689	6 167
Gaoqiao	1 176	2 321
Daqing	1 146	5 676
Yanshan	1 007	2 890
Zhenhai	1 107	n.a.
Maoming	1 073	1 535
Liaoyang	263	2 435
Jinling	996	2 086
Tianjin	639	2 259

SOURCE: Sinopec (1998: 525, 601)

NOTE: There was a total of 36 production enterprises under Sinopec in 1994.

TABLE **7-18 Ethylene Output at Sinopec's Main Subordinate Plants, 1995 (million tons)**

Sinopec total	2.03
of which:	
Yanshan	0.47
Daqing	0.31
Qilu	0.31
Yangzi	0.27
Shanghai	0.41

SOURCES: Sinopec (1998: 526) China Chemical Information Centre (1997: 37)

TABLE **7-19 Oil Refining at Sinopec's Main Subordinate Refineries, 1997**

Refinery	Refining capacity (million tons/year)
Sinopec total	
of which:	
Yanshan	9.5
Fushun	9.2
Maoming	8.5
Qilu	8.0
Zhenhai	8.0
Gaoqiao	7.5
Dalian	7.1
Jinling	7.0
Daqing	7.1
Baling	5.5
Lanzhou	5.5
Jinzhou	5.5
Shanghai	5.3
Guangzhou	5.2
Jingmen	5.0
Jinxi	5.0
Laioyan	4.0

SOURCES: Sinopec (1999: 18); Choung and Terreson (1998: 28)

petrochemical industry. It served as an industrial association that strove to help the development of the whole industry. Finally, it served as a holding company that controlled most of China's petrochemical companies. These roles came into serious conflict.

Sinopec as a government organ. As the government organ responsible for developing China's petrochemical industry, Sinopec drew up the petrochemical development plan for the Ninth Five Year Plan and the long-range objectives for the sector. Sinopec's goal was to ensure that by the turn of the century, China's petrochemical industry matched international standards of production and technology. This meant, for example, ensuring that future refineries were designed to produce more than 5 million tons a year and new ethylene projects had a minimum capacity of 450 000 tons per annum. Sinopec was to be the vehicle to ensure that China introduced the latest international technology. Its constituent enterprises all were required to obtain Sinopec's approval for any large project. Sinopec controlled the pricing and distribution of crude oil. It was charged with managing the reform of the price system for crude oil to bring it in line with the international market price.

Sinopec as an industrial association. The concept of industrial association is relatively new in China and its function is hotly debated. With the government's policy to introduce market forces as the principle mechanism for resource allocation, the ministries have been extensively abolished and replaced with 'industrial associations'. In principle, the industrial association of a particular industry will be formed spontaneously by voluntary participation of enterprises in the given industry. In fact, the emergence of industrial association was 'by design' rather by 'evolution'. The main responsibilities for an industrial association include setting technology standards and lobbying the government for preferential treatment or policies for the given sector. Sinopec's role as an industrial association was unclear beyond the general goal of facilitating and enhancing the competitiveness of China's petrochemical industry in the international market.

Sinopec as a holding company. From the outside, it appeared that Sinopec controlled all its subordinate enterprises. However, Sinopec and each of its subsidiaries is a legal identity responsible for maintaining and increasing the assets registered under its name. Sinopec headquarters makes important decisions concerning production, development, science and technology, co-operation with international firms and appointing managers at the subsidiary level. The main production enterprises are autonomous units responsible for organizing and optimizing production, market expansion, facilitating technological progress, paying tax and achieving the profit quotas set by the Sinopec headquarters. Firms at this level are autonomous units competing with each other.

Some of the key aspects of the relationship between Sinopec headquarters and the subordinate enterprises are the following:

- **Selection of managers**. In principle, Sinopec is responsible for appointing all managers at the enterprise level. However the Chairman of large subordinate enterprises, such as SPC, is appointed directly by the State Council and the CCP's Organizations Department. An important result of success in running a subordinate enterprise is promotion to the headquarters.

- **Financial autonomy**. Under the 'two-level legal person' approach, each of Sinopec's subsidiaries is a profit centre and an independent legal entity, responsible for its own financial affairs, just as Sinopec also is a legal person with financial responsibility. They each produce an annual financial report, which is submitted to Sinopec headquarters for inclusion in Sinopec's consolidated annual balance sheet. Sinopec is not permitted to transfer profit from one subordinate enterprise to another. Sinopec's subordinates are supposed to hand over around 25 per cent of post-tax profits to Sinopec headquarters, and retain 75 per cent themselves. In other words, they have a high degree of financial autonomy under the enterprise reforms of the 1980s. In practice, at least until the restructuring of 1998–9, the subordinate enterprises may have retained more than 75 per cent of their post-tax profits. For example, in 1996, Sinopec received around one billion yuan in profits handed over from its subordinate enterprises. This compares with a total 5.5 billion in operating profits for the whole of Sinopec in that year (Sinopec, 1999: 12). It should be emphasized that these are only rough estimates. On the formation of joint stock companies floated on international markets, such companies, notably SPC and Zhenhai Refinery, Sinopec received a stream of revenue from its rights as a majority shareholder in the company concerned.

The use of retained profits by internationally floated companies within Sinopec were said by Sinopec to be 'matters for the floated companies themselves to decide'. However, in practice there was still considerable negotiation between floated companies and the headquarters about the total amount of 'hand-overs', of which dividends were just one element.

Sinopec's subordinate enterprises were entitled to raise capital from the international market, but any big capital investment plan (above 200 million yuan) needed to be approved by the State Planning Commission through Sinopec.

- **Resource and product allocation**. Sinopec controls the crude oil allocations to the subordinate companies. Prior to 1992 Sinopec was the agency through which the state petrochemical plan allocations were made. An important function of Sinopec was to act as the material supply co-ordinator for inter-enterprise allocations within Sinopec. As market economy has penetrated even the petrochemical sector in ever more powerful fashion in the mid/late 1990s, this function increasingly lapsed. Marketing became a seriously important issue for Sinopec's subordinate enterprises.

Refining. At the time it was created in 1983, Sinopec had a virtual monopoly over oil refining in China. At that point it controlled 31 refineries, which accounted for 91 per cent of China's total capacity (Choung and Terreson, 1998: 27). Since then Sinopec's refining capacity has expanded rapidly to meet the booming needs of the Chinese petrochemical industry. Sinopec's refining capacity grew from 1.9 million b/d in 1983 to 3.6 million b/d in 1996. However, alongside Sinopec's growth there had taken place a proliferation of other refiners as the market had consistently been characterized by excess demand with strong market incentives for other enterprises to enter production. As in many sectors,

TABLE 7-20 Growth of Sinopec's Production, 1989–98 (million tons)
(% China total in brackets)

Production	1989	1998	1998 as % of 1989
Refined oil	96.2 (91.4)	118.0 (82.9)	123
Gasoline, kerosene, diesel oil, lubricating oil	47.0 (92.0)	65.5 (82.9)	139
Ethylene	1.27 (91.1)	2.45 (80.7)	193
Plastics	1.20 (58.5)	3.03 (56.0)	253
Synthetic rubber	0.22 (76.6)	0.44 (75.1)	200
Synthetic fibre materials	0.83 (98.6)	1.85 (81.3)	223
Synthetic fibre polymers	0.50 (51.5)	0.68 (17.8)	136
Synthetic fibres	0.38 (29.7)	0.60 (12.0)	158
Synthetic ammonia	3.14 (15.2)	3.68 (12.0)	117
Chemical fertilizers	2.28 (16.0)	2.67 (12.6)	117
Urea	4.85 (46.6)	5.82 (28.2)	120

SOURCE: Sinopec (1998: 526)

a proliferation of small enterprises entered production, often with very small-scale production units. Local governments were very active in setting up small-scale refineries. In addition, CNPC itself began to expand its refining capacity. By 1996, despite rapid absolute growth, and continuing overall dominance, Sinopec's share of total refinery capacity had fallen from over 90 per cent in the late 1980s to 83 per cent in 1996 (Table 7-20).

Alongside its near-monopoly of oil refining, at the time of its establishment, Sinopec also held a near-monopoly over the production of the key oil products, namely gasoline, kerosene, diesel oil and lubricants. In 1989 it accounted for 92 per cent of China's national output of these products. Over the following years, Sinopec's output of these products rose rapidly, increasing by 40 per cent from 1989 to 1996, to meet booming domestic demand (Table 7-20). Although a variety of competitors entered the field, Sinopec still accounted for 83 per cent of domestic production of key oil products in 1996.

Petrochemicals. China's industrialization since the mid-1980s has been accompanied by a huge increase in both the consumption and production of petrochemical products. For example, from 1989 to 1996, China's output of ethylene more than doubled (Table 7-21), its synthetic fibre capacity rose by 46 per cent (Table 7-22), and its output of plastics rose by 64 per cent (Table 7-23). By 996, China had risen to be the world's second largest producer of synthetic fibres, and it is likely that it will surpass USA production within a few years.

However, the base from which China began the modernization and growth of its petrochemical industry in the 1980s was very weak. In the late 1980s China produced less than 10 per cent of the USA's output of ethylene and plastics. Despite rapid rates of growth of key petrochemical products in the 1980s and 1990s, China is still far behind the world's leading petrochemical producers.

TABLE **7-21 World Production of Ethylene, Selected Countries, 1989–96 (million tons)**

Country	1989	1996	Increase 1989–96	(%)
USA	15.9	22.3	6.4	(40)
Japan	5.6	7.2	1.6	(29)
Germany	3.0	3.8	0.8	(27)
Korea	0.7	4.0	3.3	(571)
France	2.5	2.7	0.2	(8)
Canada	2.3	3.2	0.9	(39)
China	1.4	3.0	1.6	(114)

SOURCE: Sinopec (1998: 526, 562)

TABLE **7-22 Synthetic Fibre Production Capacity, Selected Countries, 1989–96 (million tons)**

Country	1989	1996	Increase 1989–96	(%)
World	18.0	24.2	6.2	(34)
USA	3.5	3.7 (1995)	0.2	(6)
Japan	1.8	1.9	0.1	(6)
Korea	1.2	2.0	0.8	(67)
Taiwan	1.7	2.5	0.8	(47)
China	1.3	3.2	1.9	(146)

SOURCE: Sinopec (1998: 569)

TABLE **7-23 World Production of Plastics, Selected Countries, 1989–96 (million tons)**

Country	1989	1996	Increase (1989–96)	(%)
World	95.2	129.4	34.2	(36)
USA	26.5	38.6	12.1	(46)
Japan	11.9	14.7	2.8	(24)
Germany	9.1	10.9	1.8	(20)
Korea	2.5	7.7	5.2	(208)
Taiwan	2.5	4.6	2.1	(84)
The Netherlands	3.3	4.2	0.9	(27)
Belgium	2.8	4.6	1.8	(64)
France	4.3	5.2	0.9	(21)
China	2.2	3.6	1.4	(64)

SOURCE: Sinopec (1998: 526, 565)

In 1996 its output of ethylene was still only 13 per cent of that of the USA and two-fifths of that of Japan. China still produced less ethylene than either Germany or Korea. In plastics production, China produced less than one-tenth of the output of the USA, and only one-quarter of that of Japan. China was ranked only ninth in the world, producing less than one-half of that of Korea, and three-quarters of that of Taiwan. Despite widespread perceptions that the advanced economies are de-industrializing in the products of the 'Second Industrial Revolution', such as steel and chemicals, large absolute increases in the output of many basic chemicals were recorded in some of these countries between the late 1980s and the late 1990s, far exceeding the absolute increase in China. For example, ethylene output in the USA rose by 6.4 million tons from 1989 to 1996, compared with an increase of 1.6 million tons in China. Output of plastics in the USA rose by over 12 million tons in the same period, compared with an increase of only 1.4 million tons in China.

A major aspect of competition in the Chinese petrochemicals industry in the 1990s was the fast growth of imports. By 1998, imports accounted for 31 per cent of domestic consumption in polyester staple fibres and polyester filaments, 44 per cent of domestic consumption of PE and PP, and 80 per cent of domestic consumption of acrylics (SPC, 1999: 17–18).

In contrast to the advanced economies, in which market shares are strictly controlled beyond a certain point, the Chinese government created in Sinopec a massively dominant petrochemical company in the domestic market for petrochemical products. In 1989 Sinopec accounted for 91 per cent of China's ethylene output, 76 per cent of synthetic rubber output, 59 per cent of plastics output and 99 per cent of the output of materials for synthetic fibres. Sinopec's output of its key petrochemical products grew rapidly in the late 1980s and 1990s. Despite some dilution in its dominant position, in the late 1990s, in 1996 Sinopec still accounted for 81 per cent of ethylene output, 75 per cent of synthetic rubber output, 81 per cent of the materials for synthetic rubber and 56 per cent of plastics output.

Production of chemical fertilizers was much more dispersed even in the 1980s, with a large number of small plants making an important contribution to production. This remained the case in the 1990s, with Sinopec's share of total output standing at 16 per cent in 1989 and 13 per cent in 1996. In the output of ammonia, for example, small and medium plants accounted for 78 per cent of national output in 1995 (China Chemical Information Centre, 1997: 29). In downstream chemical fibres, Sinopec sustained strong competition also, especially from large-scale producers within the Ministry of Textiles. Sinopec's share of synthetic fibres fell from 30 per cent in 1989 to 12 per cent in 1996.

Growing Autonomy of Subordinate Enterprises (i): General Issues. Despite the fact that the subordinate companies were wholly or partially owned by the state holding company, Sinopec, the larger ones in particular began to develop ambitions of their own, often with the support of the local governments. As we have seen, the largest refiners and petrochemical plants were big institutions within

Sinopec. This growing autonomy of large subordinate enterprises developed in response to the need to make a much wider range of decisions alongside the expansion of market forces. The subordinate enterprises were able to retain a greatly increased share of profits. They greatly increased their autonomy to make investments. They increasingly borrowed in order to finance expansion with responsibility at the company level for debt repayment. They developed increased autonomy through the issuance of shares to external entities, which reduced the ownership rights of Sinopec over the subordinate enterprises. They organized joint ventures with multinational companies. They increasingly initiated mergers and acquisitions in order to develop strong positions in the production of particular products. In sum, a key feature of the development of Sinopec from its foundation in 1983 until the massive restructuring of 1998, was the tension between the need for centralization within a modern large company, and the growing push for autonomy from the subordinate enterprises, which were increasingly developing a sense of 'corporate identity' distinct from the central holding company. This process accelerated in the 1990s, as the sector liberalized rapidly. The following are some of the channels through which this developed:

- **Growing impact of market forces**. Under China's economic reform policies, China's petrochemical enterprises needed to take an increasing range of decisions themselves. The share of petrochemical products in China that were sold outside the state plan rose from a negligible level in the late 1980s to over 70 per cent by 1996. By the late 1990s, the petrochemicals sector was one of the least protected in China. The level of tariffs on imported petrochemicals fell to around 15 per cent by the end of the 1990s. Moreover, on the upstream side, in the 1990s, crude oil prices rose towards world prices, so that China's petrochemical companies experienced the full force of the great fluctuations in world crude oil prices.

- **Flotations**. Since the early 1990s, important parts of Sinopec have been floated on domestic and international markets. By 1997 a total of 16 subordinate companies had been floated on domestic and international markets. Sinopec's share holdings in the listed subordinate companies amounted to 62 per cent of their total shares (Sinopec, 1999: 13). The total assets of the listed companies amounted to about one-fifth of Sinopec's total assets (Sinopec, 1999: 13). The most important flotations were those of Shanghai Petrochemical Corporation, floated in 1993, and Yanhua, floated in 1997. Both were floated as H-shares in Hong Kong. The flotations produced a sharp change in the ownership structure of the respective companies. Sinopec remained the majority owner of each of the floated companies.

- **Joint ventures**. In the 1980s and 1990s, many Sino–foreign joint ventures were agreed and began functioning. However, in the mid-1990s, a sequence of multi-billion dollar joint ventures was agreed between multinational companies and Sinopec's subordinate production enterprises. Sinopec participated in the negotiations, and had the last word to approve the joint venture, but to some degree they reflected the ambitions of the subordinate enterprise. The centrepiece of several of these joint ventures was a 6–800 000 ton ethylene plant, together with associated facilities. Such agreements were signed between BP and Shanghai Petrochemical Company, BASF and Yangzi Petrochemical Company in Nanjing, Dow Chemical and Tianjin Petrochemical Company, and Phillips Petroleum Corporation and Lanzhou Chemical Company as well as that between Shell and CNOOC at Huizhou (see below). Each of these joint ventures was intended to form an important part of the global business system of the global giants. For example, the Huizhou ethylene and petrochemicals complex is one of five major new chemical plants planned in the near future, the others being planned for the USA, Singapore, India and Australia (Shell, 1999a: 33). One industry expert commented: 'The Chinese petrochemical industry is being cut up piece by piece!'

- **Mergers and acquisitions.** In the mid-1990s, a great deal of discussion began to take place about the inadequate size of China's petrochemical companies for international competition. By 1997, Sinopec had publicly stated that the way forward for the Chinese petrochemical industry was to allow and encourage the creation of a 'a number of large enterprise groups to hone [our] competitiveness in the market' (*CDBW*, 4 January 1998). Sheng Huaren, President of Sinopec commented: 'It is the key way to improve the state economy's control capability and better confront foreign rivals' (quoted in *CDBW*, 4 January 1998). Official policy relaxed and a number of significant mergers took place. In some cases these were organized from the centre, most notably the merger of four petrochemical companies in Nanjing, to form a giant company, called 'Donglian'. However, the resulting mergers often arose from the initiative of the enterprises themselves rather than from Sinopec itself. For example, in 1997, Yanshan Oil refinery merged with Tianjin Hangu Petrochemical Plant, China's largest lubricants producer, to form Yanhua Corporation.

Growing Autonomy of Subordinate Enterprises
(ii): The Case of Shanghai Petrochemical Company

Operational autonomy. We have seen above that Shanghai Petrochemical Company (SPC) was arguably the most important subordinate enterprise within Sinopec, contributing a greater volume of pre-tax profits than any other production unit. It was one of the ten largest enterprises of any kind in China in the mid-1990s. By the early 1990s, SPC had become a formal legal person, with operational and financial autonomy. Although Sinopec was the majority owner of the enterprise, SPC had strong ambitions of its own. SPC has the strong support of the Shanghai municipal government, which is keen to see SPC develop into a world class competitive company, alongside other Shanghai 'giants', notably Baoshan Iron and Steel Corporation and Shanghai Automobile Corporation. The period since the 1970s saw the gradual development of a sense of corporate identity and ambition at SPC. SPC successfully lobbied the central government to allow SPC to be the site for a large (300 000 ton) imported ethylene unit.

It borrowed heavily in order to be able to finance the purchase, much of the loan coming from international markets, repayable in hard currency.

The combined effect of the Asian crisis and a decline in the domestic growth rate hit SPC severely. Its sales revenue slumped from 11.9 billion yuan in 1996 to 10.7 billion yuan in 1998, and pre-tax profits fell from a peak of 2.5 billion yuan in 1994 to just 0.25 million yuan in 1998 (SPC, 1999: 3). Despite the sharp downturn, SPC was still extremely optimistic about its expansion plans: 'Difficult times have not dulled ambitions. Shanghai Petrochemical plans an expansion which will consume more than 20 billion yuan in fresh capital and nearly double capacity in some core businesses. The investment is intended to catapult the company from the top division of China's petrochemical industry into the big league of international producers' (*FT*, 29 April 1998). SPC plans to expand its refining capacity from 5.3 million tons to 10 million tons and ethylene production from 550 000 tons to 800 000–850 000 tons (*FT*, 29 April 1998). The President of SPC, Lu Yiping, commented: 'In order to compete internationally, we need to map out strategic targets in terms of capital expenditure. The most important thing is to increase the scale of production' (quoted in *FT*, 29 April 1998). In the midst of the crisis, SPC announced: 'The Company plans to enlarge its production scale through the capital expenditure programme, joint ventures and mergers and acquisitions' (SPC, 1998).

Ownership change. SPC successfully lobbied the central government to allow it to become the first Chinese company listed on international markets. Through the initial listing, and subsequent share issues, the ownership share of Sinopec fell from 100 per cent in the early 1990s to 56 per cent in 1997. The President of SPC, Wu Yixin, reported that he would be quite happy to see the ownership share of Sinopec fall below 50 per cent, though he thought it unlikely that it would fall below 30 per cent (interview, 1996). Through the flotation and subsequent share issue, SPC raised a total of nearly $380 million. This was intended to repay loans taken out to expand capacity.

International joint ventures. International joint ventures have been a major route for SPC to realize its ambitious expansion plans. Prior to 1996, SPC had already established several joint ventures. These included a joint venture between SPC and Japan's Itochu Corporation for a plastic packaging project and a joint venture with Union Carbide, which both went into operation in 1997. In 1996, the level was sharply stepped up with the announcement of two major projects. The smaller of these was a $100 million project to build a 100 000 ton per annum linear low-density polyethylene plant, in partnership with Phillips Petroleum. The project is 60 per cent owned by SPC, and was completed in 1998. This important project was dwarfed by the announcement later in 1996 of a $2.5 billion joint venture with BP. The core of the joint venture was to be a 650 000 ton ethylene plant. If this plan came to fruition, it would increase SPC's ethylene. capacity from 400 000 tons in 1998 (and a planned capacity of 650 000 tons in 2000, excluding the BP joint venture) to over 1 million tons, making it one of the world's largest ethylene plants.

Mergers and acquisitions. Once the central government announced that it wished to allow the development of a number of large-scale petrochemical companies through merger and acquisition, SPC began to acquire other petrochemical companies. In 1996 SPC acquired the Shanghai Jinjiang Acrylic Fibre Plant. As a result of the merger, SPC's share of China's acrylic fibre production rose from 32 per cent to over 44 per cent. Shortly after this, SPC announced that it was taking over the Zhejiang Acrylic Fibre Plant which would 'enable the Company to increase its market share for acrylic fibre products' (*SPC, 1998*: 13). SPC's share of national acrylic fibre output now surpassed one-half. Moreover, in its drive to create 'Shanghai Champions', the Shanghai government formed the giant Huayi Group in 1996, which produces a wide variety of downstream chemical products, from rubber tyres to pesticides. The Shanghai government closely considered the possibility of encouraging a merger between the Huayi Group and SPC, which would have created a giant company in Chinese terms. The merger overtures were successfully resisted by SPC, as it believed this would dilute the Company's focus and submerge it within a larger entity within which it would lose managerial control.

SPC's strategic goal was to merge with companies with which it had real business synergies. Such synergies, it felt, were best achieved 'through the market' rather than through state administration. SPC's ambitious leadership in the mid-1990s felt strongly that the construction of a national integrated oil and petrochemical giant company would be best accomplished by allowing increasingly autonomous entities such as SPC to merge and take over other companies, including those upstream and downstream of SPC. A key part of SPC's ambitions was to merge with a crude oil supplier: 'Without an integrated crude oil supply we are not a modern oil and petrochemical company'. One obvious possibility for merger was with CNOOC (see below). Another possibility was with Daqing, from which almost one-half of SPC's crude oil was supplied. As we have seen, at one point in the mid-1990s, SPC held serious discussions with Daqing to explore this possibility.

Growth through the market or through administrative means? SPC's leaders in the mid-1990s strongly believed that China should build a small group of integrated oil and petrochemical giant companies, but that this should be done 'through the market'. Their goal was to develop SPC's core business of petrochemicals by investing in new technology, lowering costs of production, changing its production structure towards high value-added products and merging with other strong firms. Under an ambitious chief executive officer, a group of leaders emerged at SPC who fought strongly for the company's independence from the headquarters of Sinopec. They believed that the path through which China would best create a small group of powerful integrated oil and petrochemical giants was 'through the market', not through central government administrative means. SPC was acutely aware of its need to increase scale as well as business capability. A key reflection of its small scale compared to the global giants is the fact that its R & D budget in 1998 was a mere $4 million, compared to many hundreds of millions at the global giant oil and petrochemical companies. A central part of the restructuring process of 1998 and 1999 (see below) was to shift SPC's ambitious leaders out of the company into other tasks within Sinopec, as part of the battle to reassert central leadership and control from the headquarters.

Marketing and Distribution of Oil, Oil Products and Petrochemical Products. A long and tortuous reform of China's crude oil, oil products and petrochemical products' price and distribution system has taken place since the early 1980s, gradually and haltingly moving towards a market system.

Crude oil. Imports of crude oil and oil products have been subject to quotas and restrictions right through to the present day. These rights were for a long period in the hands of the State Planning Commission. In 1997, Sinopec was given independent rights to import crude oil, and in 1998 the restructuring CNPC was also given the right to import oil and oil products.

With relatively minor exceptions, multinational companies have not participated in the refinery business in China. The extreme uncertainty about the kind of price regime and the absence of access to the wholesale distribution channels has greatly deterred foreign investment in this sector. The allocation of both crude oil and oil products, whether domestically produced or imported is entirely under state control, although the allocation went almost entirely through Sinopec, until 1998, and subsequently through Sinopec and CNPC. We have seen that from its inception through to the present day, Sinopec has been vastly the dominant force in refining crude oil within China. Even after the restructuring of 1998, it still remains the most important force in refining. Right through until the late 1990s, one of Sinopec's key functions was to plan the distribution of the vast bulk of China's domestically consumed crude oil. Up until 1992, a three tier price structure was operated by Sinopec in accordance with government policy. The vast bulk of allocations to a typical large refinery were at state-controlled and subsidized prices. In the case of SPC, for example, in 1992, 97.5 per cent of its allocations were at these prices. Refiners were free to buy extra amounts at domestic free market prices or from the world market. However, the state-subsidized price included a 'State Low Price' and a 'State High Price'. In 1992 at SPC for example, 1.72 million tons were allocated at the State Low Price and 2.2 million tons at the State High Price. The price differential was considerable. The State Low Price for Daqing crude oil was 265 yuan per ton (on a CIF basis), compared to 621 yuan per ton (on a CIF basis) for State High Price allocations, and 1000 yuan per ton (on a CIF basis) for open market purchases.

In 1993–4 as part of the general liberalization of prices, the state ceased to sell crude oil at the State Low Price. Moreover, it permitted a growing percentage of crude oil to be sold outside State allocations, and somewhat liberalized the controls on imports of crude oil. This resulted in a chaotic situation which led to further reforms. In 1994 the so-called New Policy was introduced. Under this system Sinopec's control over the distribution of crude oil was made even tighter. However, the prices at which the crude oil was supplied moved significantly closer to the international price. As international prices plummeted in 1997, state-fixed domestic prices rose to around 15 per cent above the international price. This placed great pressure on crude oil users, and strongly encouraged smuggling.

In June 1998, the system was finally switched to one that directly linked domestic crude oil prices to international prices, with prices set once per month in line with changes in the international price.

Oil products. Major oil products, including gasoline, diesel, kerosene, aviation fuel and fuel oil have been subject to import quotas and import licensing right through to the present day. Reforms of the domestic market for oil products paralleled those of crude oil. In the 1990s, a two-tier system was introduced. Refined products produced from low-priced crude oil were required to be sold at the 'in-plan low price', and the remainder at the 'in-plan high price'. In 1993–4 as part of the process of the overall price liberalization, part of the output of refined products could be sold at a market price.

Under the New Policy introduced in 1994, major changes took place also in the allocation and pricing of refined products. The government abolished the two-tier price system and placed almost the entire system of refined products distribution under government control. Major refined products that were controlled in this fashion included gasoline, kerosene, diesel, naphtha, domestic LPG, fuel oil and fertilizer. Prices were standardized for the 35 major cities, and in other areas were controlled by the local authorities. The prices set quickly rose substantially above international prices as the price of these plummeted in 1997–98. This encouraged rampant smuggling and did significant damage to the domestic refining industry.

In June 1998, refined products, as with crude oil, were placed under a new regime that closely linked domestic prices with those on international markets. However, the mark-ups for wholesale at the provincial and local level, as well as at the retail level were legally controlled by the state, administered through CNPC and Sinopec.

Petrochemical products. Prior to 1993 the prices of almost all petrochemical products were subject to government control, and prices of most petrochemical products were significantly below world prices. Beginning in 1993, the government began gradually to lift price controls, permitting an increase in the range of products whose prices were determined by the market. From May 1994, following the guidelines of the New Policy for the petrochemical industry, most products could be sold at market prices. By 1996, state price controls applied to less than one-fifth of petrochemical sales. By the late 1990s, most petrochemical products had been freed from government control.

The level of protection from the international market declined drastically in the 1990s. The average tariff on imported petrochemical products stood at around 30 per cent in 1993, and had fallen to 23 per cent in 1996. In April 1996, the PRC reduced the general level of tariffs from 36 per cent to 23 per cent. The average tariff on petrochemical products fell to around 15 per cent in 1998–2000 within a range of 5–21 per cent for the main products (SPC, 1999: 18).

This was a dramatic change in the market for petrochemicals in a short period of time. It stimulated a large change in the outlook of managers in China's petrochemical industry. The change in outlook was further stimulated by the erratic behaviour of market prices. In the early phase of price liberalization, there was a powerful increase in market prices of most petrochemical industry products. From 1993 through into the middle of 1995 market conditions were strong. Prices rose sharply and allowed a substantial rise in producers' margins. However, thereafter prices began a serious decline, continuing through into 1998. This was a combination of a surge in imports, including extensive smuggling, increased competition among increasingly autonomous Chinese petrochemical companies, and cyclical weakening of domestic demand. For the first time, Chinese petrochemical producers were feeling the impact of the kind of market volatility that is the regular stuff of business for multinational petrochemical companies.

Unlike many integrated multinationals, with production spanning the entire product range from oil and natural gas extraction through to downstream petrochemicals, China's emerging petrochemical industry companies, such as SPC, were entirely reliant on purchasing their crude oil from outside the company. Consequently, they experienced the full impact of the switchback in market prices of crude oil. They benefited from the fall in oil prices from 1992 through to 1994. They then were severely squeezed by the precipitous climb in oil prices from 1994 to early 1997. The result was a precipitous decline in profits in 1996–97. They were to some degree shielded from the decline in final product prices by the collapse of crude oil prices up until late 1998. Thereafter, they felt the full effects of the sharp rise in crude oil prices into 1999. This was a powerful learning experience for China's newly emerging large petrochemical firms such as SPC.

Wholesale and retail. A crucial difference between China and the global giants pre-1998 was not just the separation of 'upstream' and 'downstream', but also the separation of refining from sales and marketing.

Oil products are in two categories. Part of the output of oil products is supplied directly by the refiners to the State's 'designated key users', such as the military, public transport, railways and civil aviation enterprises. All other oil products are required to be sold to provincial and municipal petroleum companies, which then arrange the distribution of oil products to end-users. From 1994 onwards, refiners under the supervision of Sinopec could also supply oil products to city and county petroleum companies and other enterprises. They were still prohibited from selling directly to provincial companies or service stations.

China's retail sector is extraordinarily fragmented. It is open to the Chinese public provided they fulfil safety and management requirements. Huge numbers of retail outlets have been established. As a result of stricter government guidelines, no less than 50 000 retail units were shut down in the late 1990s, and 30 000 were forced to improve their safety and management standards. There are currently around 100 000 gas stations across the country. Prior to the 1998 restructuring, around 14 000 of them were under the control of the provincial and local governments. The others were owned and operated by a wide variety of different 'social' institutions. An important feature of the reform of 1998 was that it placed the local state-run gas stations under the control of CNPC and Sinopec, dividing them up on a regional basis (see below). This attempted to construct truly integrated oil companies from upstream to downstream. It became increasingly clear to China's policy makers just how important this aspect of vertical integration was in international competition.

The retail situation is widely acknowledged to be chaotic. The only legal channel through which gas stations can obtain their petrol and diesel is through CNPC or Sinopec. In practice, the proliferating non-state gas stations obtain a large fraction of their petrol and diesel from the numerous small-scale refineries outside Sinopec (or CNPC). They typically produce low quality, highly polluting products. Local governments have a powerful incentive to allow small, low quality refineries to operate, because they provide much-needed employment and tax revenue. Moreover, as we have seen, the state allocates a substantial fraction of refined products to the special state customers, including the army, railway, aviation industry, shipping and forest departments. These are supplied at special low prices. These entities have a strong economic incentive also to sell their allocations illegally to the small 'social' gas stations.

No foreign companies are allowed to engage in the wholesale or retail of refined products. The only exceptions are some speciality products, and some cases of license being granted by local governments. Were China to enter the WTO and the global giants be allowed to enter wholesale and retail, they would encounter an extraordinarily uncompetitive sector compared to their own organization.

Problems with the Partially Reformed Structure. The structure that was painfully established in the Chinese oil and petrochemicals sector from the early 1980s through to the late 1990s produced a great many unresolved problems. These produced intense debate about how to restructure this vast industry at the heart of the Chinese economy. Moreover, the debate was given dramatically increased intensity by the explosive changes in the world's oil and petrochemical industry in the late 1990s, notably the BP Amoco merger and the merger of Exxon and Mobil. Chinese policy makers openly acknowledged the inadequacies of the industry (see especially Chen Zhun *et al.*, 1998). The two over-arching problems were firstly, the ambiguity of the relationship between the headquarters and the subordinate production units, and secondly, the separation of the upstream and downstream parts of the industry:

- **Ambiguous corporate structure**. The most fundamental problem is the nature of the relationship between the headquarters of CNPC and Sinopec, on the one hand, and their subsidiary enterprises on the other. The problems can be summarized by the question: 'Where is the firm'? Was the 'competitive firm' which was to emerge from reforms in this sector to be the huge central bodies, CNPC and Sinopec, or was it be the small number of giant enterprises that gained increasing autonomy during the course of the reforms? The central policy makers did not provide a clear answer to this question. This was unsurprising, as there was enormous argument about the desirable form of institutional structure for the industry.

In fact, the period saw a hesitant attempt by China's policy makers to create two large-scale state-owned entities, CNPC and Sinopec, broadly following the path of many other developing countries. However, this attempt was combined with the growth of powerful forces from the level of the 'enterprise', or production units, which threatened to gravely weaken the degree of central co-ordination by the headquarters of the newly emerging giant state-owned 'companies'. Many of the subordinate enterprises had been large-scale entities under the planned economy, with their own traditions and ambitions. Their ambitions were fuelled by the overall thrust of the state's policy for enterprise reform which was to strengthen the autonomy of the 'enterprise' relative to the 'state', meaning the central government bureaucracy. 'Enterprises' were allowed greatly increased management autonomy, rights to retain profits, and decide important investment decisions. In its attempt to raise capital and modernize management methods, the central government allowed large, subordinate 'enterprises', or production units to become the main agents for negotiation and signing joint venture contracts with the leading multinational companies. They also allowed a series of international flotations that increased further the financial autonomy of the production units, especially large well-run ones. Over the course of the reform years, subordinate enterprises within the oil and petrochemical sector began to develop a genuine sense of 'corporate identity' and corporate ambitions, distinct from those of the central supervisory authorities.

The tensions resulting from the above forces were seriously undermining the efforts of the central authorities to build large-scale firms that could challenge the global giants. The shortcomings of the Chinese strategy were vividly illuminated by the world-wide merger explosion that rocked the industry in the late 1990s. These dramatic developments made strikingly clear the shortcomings of the Chinese approach. While the global giants were building highly integrated super-giants, the Chinese industry was building corporate entities that were only 'firms' superficially. Within the apparently large 'corporate' entities of CNPC and Sinopec, there were in fact many subordinate quasi firms that were fiercely struggling for autonomy from the central authorities. The central authorities became increasingly aware that if they wished to create true giants that could compete with the global leaders, not only did they have to resolve the division between 'upstream' and 'downstream', but also had to tackle the issue of growing fragmentation of authority and decentralization.

- **Disintegrated industrial structure**. The separation of the upstream and downstream components of the industry within China produced many problems. Most fundamentally, CNPC and Sinopec were close to being domestic monopolists within their part of the value chain, immune from competitive pressure in the still relatively protected international environment.

Rather than working to increase efficiency and profits, they each had a strong incentive to improve financial performance through leveraging their monopoly position to the detriment of the other party. The upstream and downstream companies competed for funding from the government as well as for the right to set prices for crude oil, refined products, and petrochemicals. One party's gain in investment capital from the government was often at the cost of another party's resources for further development. The two segments of the industry had a fundamental conflict of interest. CNPC wanted the price of crude oil to be as high as possible, and Sinopec wanted it to be as low as possible. Sinopec had a strong interest in opening up the supply of crude oil from international markets, to ensure supply from the lowest cost source globally, but CNPC wished to keep the market closed so as to push up the price from its own production. CNPC had every incentive to supply its own refineries with as much of its own crude oil as possible given the low crude oil prices relative to the price of refined products.

It is widely acknowledged among international companies that there are some significant advantages to having a large fraction of feedstock supplied from within the company. It may make it easier to locate refining and petrochemical plants in an optimal fashion relative to crude oil supplies. It may make long-term planning easier by reducing the huge fluctuations in company earnings that affect companies that are solely focused on one part of the value chain.

INSTITUTIONAL CHANGE IN THE CHINESE OIL AND GAS INDUSTRY
(ii): THE REFORMS OF 1988 – FROM HOLDING COMPANIES TO INTEGRATED
OIL AND PETROCHEMICAL COMPANIES?

The Battle for Change
The debate pre-1997. Early on in the Chinese industrial reform process, the view quickly emerged that China needed to establish a group of powerful firms within each sector. The stimulus to do so came from several sources:

- **Big business in the West**. Any realistic study of advanced capitalism in Europe and the US would have to recognize the central role of large-scale enterprises in the growth and dynamism of these economies (Chandler *et al.*, 1997). Chinese policy makers were well aware of this.

- **The examples of Japan and South Korea**. Chinese industrial policy was strongly influenced also by the experience of Japan and South Korea. Behind high protectionist barriers, with strong state support, they built large oligopolistic firms, enjoying powerful economies of scale and scope.

- **The example of the former USSR**. The former USSR contained an immensely powerful group of enterprises in many different sectors, from aerospace to oil and gas, that could have formed the basis for globally powerful indigenous firms if suitable policies had been followed. In fact, the political and economic policies followed in the former USSR led to the destruction of these potentially powerful entities.

- **The influence of nationalism and international relations**. It was simply unacceptable to most senior Chinese policy makers that China should be a land of small businesses and a market for the global giants. It was regarded as a national humiliation that China should have no powerful firms to match those of the advanced economies in general and the USA in particular. For Europe and the USA, 'internationalization' meant to a considerable degree cross-border investment in both directions across the Atlantic by large corporations. In the Chinese perception, 'internationalization' could easily come to mean domination of Chinese markets by inward investment from Europe and the USA. The incentive to build powerful domestic large firms was given enormous impetus by the explosion of global mergers and acquisitions in the 1990s.

- **Lobbying from existing large enterprises within China**. A vast number of people are employed in the 'commanding heights' of the Chinese economy. It is unsurprising that the large enterprises should themselves support policies that attempted to nurture them and turn them into globally successful firms able to compete on the global marketplace.

The attempt to build large firms ran sharply contrary to the policy advice from the international institutions. Moreover, an increasingly powerful group of policy makers in China questioned the usefulness of this goal, arguing that China should simply accept the reality of globalization. They argued that it would be futile and wasteful to try to support large indigenous firms that could not ultimately succeed against international competition. The rapid pace of consolidation amongst the global giants reinforced this view. Furthermore, if China wished to benefit from liberal international trade and the access this gave Chinese exports to the advanced economies, then it needed to give up many of the protectionist weapons that were essential if large, internationally competitive indigenous firms were to develop. Intense argument rages among senior policy makers about the correct path to follow.

Despite intense arguments, the predominant view among senior policy-makers of the way in which to develop the oil and petrochemical sector remained dominated by those who wished to build powerful indigenous firms to challenge the global giants. In this sector as in other key 'strategic' industries, the key policy slogan became 'grasp the large, let go of the small'. The question was: 'What is the "large" entity around which to attempt to build competitive firms?' There was great uncertainty surrounding this issue. All parties were aware of the dangers of establishing firms that were protected from international competition but were allowed a domestic monopoly. Both Japan and South Korea had been careful to establish oligopolistic competition, and studiously avoid monopoly. In the auto industry, policy centred on supporting four key enterprises as the basis for reorganizing the entire, fragmented and disorganized industry. These were Yiqi (Northeast), Erqi (South), Shanghai and Tianjin. In the steel industry, there were three giants that formed the basis of industrial policy for the sector, namely Shougang (Beijing), Angang (Northeast) and Baogang (Shanghai). Each of these undertook extensive modernization, absorbed large-scale foreign investment, and were encouraged and/or allowed to merge with a large number of smaller enterprises in the sector.

Up until 1997, there was considerable ambiguity about the path that the oil and gas sector should take. If the industry followed the example of the steel and automobile sectors, then the 'firm' would be at the level of the large enterprise. Many people in the industry, especially those at the enterprises concerned, were strongly supportive of this strategy. As we have seen, over the whole reform period, but especially in the 1990s, with the acceleration of foreign investment and international flotation, and rapid growth of mergers and acquisitions within the industry, the sense of corporate identity at the level of the large enterprise grew significantly. In the mid-1990s, there was a strong view among the industry's planners that this was the desirable path for the industry to follow. Under this model, the function of Sinopec would gradually atrophy, becoming an increasingly passive holding company, with a less and less active role in managing the subordinate enterprises.

Those who supported this approach believed that there should be half a dozen companies that would expand into large-scale entities and lead the industry away from the planned economy. By the mid-1990s it was already quite widely accepted that an internationally competitive firm in this sector generally needed to incorporate both upstream and downstream assets. Those that were upstream companies would be allowed to expand downstream, and those that were downstream companies would be allowed to take over upstream assets. The probable foundations of the industry were thought to include Shanghai Petrochemical Corporation ('China East'), Yanshan ('China North'), Daqing ('China Northeast'), Donglian (Nanjing, 'China South'), and China National Offshore Oil Corporation.

Critics of this approach pointed out that this path would lead to a replication of one of the key problems of the 'planned' economy, namely the tendency to produce local systems that were 'small and complete' (*xiao er quan*) but highly inefficient in terms of economies of scale.

Sinopec and the Holding Company Experiment. By the mid-1990s, the Chinese policy makers were becoming more and more aware of the ambiguities involved in the path chosen to organize China's oil and petrochemical sector. Indeed, they were aware that similar ambiguities existed in several other key sectors. In January 1997, the State Council formally designated the petrochemical industry as the model industry for others to study in experimenting with the national holding company system. The goal was to create truly independent holding companies that cast off their former 'ministerial' functions, and became genuinely independent business entities.

The State Council appointed Sinopec to manage all state-owned properties within the Sinopec system. Sinopec entered into a contract with the State Council that specified Sinopec's power, responsibility, and interests. As a holding company, Sinopec had the following functions:

- **Management of capital and property**. As the sole agent of the state, Sinopec was responsible for managing all state owned properties within the company. It was entitled to take decisions concerning merging, closing down, increasing/decreasing capital and issuing corporate bonds for those wholly owned subsidiaries. It was to receive dividends, and profit from trading property rights according to its shares in subordinate companies.
- **Decision making and being the centre of investment**. Sinopec was to decide its own development strategy and approve its subsidiaries' (wholly or partly owned) development plan, decide on large investment projects, approve plans for raising capital, decide on profit distribution, make changes in subsidiaries' organization and business structure, organize research and development, and promote international co-operation.
- **Deciding personnel arrangements**. Sinopec was to decide the subsidiaries' management team, and train, appraise and supervise subsidiaries' managerial staff. Sinopec was to recommend members to the board of directors and the supervising committee, and appoint share holder representatives proportionate to the shares it held in those subsidiaries.
- **Engaging directly in business operations**. Through subsidiaries, Sinopec was to take on business operations, including raising funds, domestic and international trade, R & D, engineering projects, and set up specialized groups or affiliated companies to market petrochemicals.
- **Internal auditing and supervision**. Sinopec was to carry out the internal auditing, and supervise subsidiaries' safety and technological development.

Prior to the Holding Company experiment, Sinopec had many 'rights' over subordinate enterprises, including the right to appoint senior managers. However, these were mainly rights to approve actions at lower levels, such as joint ventures, flotations, and large projects, rather than meaningful central control over revenues. Senior officials at Sinopec in early 1997 (interviews at Sinopec headquarters, January 1997) expressed their determination to change an 'administrative' company into an 'economic' company. However, they were well aware of the complexity of the task of centralization of rights in the hands of Sinopec headquarters, given the growth of corporate identity at the large enterprise level, encouraged by ambiguity in central government policy towards the sector. Moreover, the headquarters believed that it was essential to unify upstream and downstream if Sinopec was to truly compete with the multinationals: 'The situation of separation of exploration, processing and sales cannot continue to exist in China, or China will be at a disadvantage compared to the multinational companies' (senior official at Sinopec, January 1997). They believed that turning

Sinopec into a genuine 'economic' entity required vertical integration and genuine centralization of key functions, especially financial control.

The Sinopec Holding Company experiment was hardly put into action before a further frenzy of institutional change overwhelmed the industry.

The Donglian Experiment. The debate intensified in the Autumn of 1997, with the decision to form a giant merged petrochemical company in Nanjing. Nanjing has four large petrochemical enterprises. Yizheng Chemical Fibre is the most important single polyester plant in China accounting for almost one-half of national polyester production. It is the fifth largest producer of polyester in the world. Yangzi Petrochemical, also in Nanjing, is one of China's largest petrochemical plants. In addition to these enterprises, Nanjing also has two other powerful petrochemical industry companies, Nanjing Chemical and Jinling Petro-chemical Company. The four companies fell under three different administrative departments, Sinopec (Jinling and Yangzi), the National Textile Council (Yizheng) and Jiangsu Provincial Government (Nanjing Petrochemical Company). Each of the enterprises is one of the largest (by value of sales) in the country in their respective sector: Jinling is the fourth largest oil processing enterprise. Yangzi and Nanjing are the first and the twelfth largest chemical materials enterprises in China respectively, and Yizheng is the second largest chemical fibre enterprise in China (SSB, ZDQN, 1996).

In the Autumn of 1997, the Chinese State Council decided to launch the merger of the four enterprises into a single new company, Donglian. Li Yizhong, the executive vice-president of Sinopec was charged with the task of executing the merger. The combined sales of the four companies in 1995 totalled 31.77 billion yuan, making the newly formed company the second largest in the whole of China (SSB, ZDQN, 1996: 221), forming 'China's largest petrochemicals, chemical fibres and fertilizers manufacturing base' (*CDBW*, 14 September 1997). The new company was highly integrated vertically. Donglian refined 10 million tons of oil, produced 400 000 tons of ethylene (until the new joint venture with BASF comes on stream), one million tons of chemical fertilizers, 900 000 tons of phthalic acid, 850 000 tons of arene, and 800 000 tons of polyester. Yizheng obtained over three-fifths of its PTA requirement and almost 70 per cent of its MEG requirement from Yangzi Petrochemical Company. Yizheng purchased almost the entire PTA and MEG output of Yangzi Petrochemical Company (Warburg, 1994: 49–50). PTA and MEG are the main raw material used by Yizheng. Jinling supplies Yangzi with naphtha. Yangzi supplies Nanjing Petrochemical with benzene and heavy asphalt. Nanjing Petrochemical supplies Jinling with sulphuric and nitric acid.

Donglian announced its intention to expand its joint venture relationships with the multinational petrochemical giants. It has said that it wished to issue new shares in both domestic and international markets (*CDBW*, 14 September 1997).

The new company commenced operation in early 1998. Its formation provoked intense debate. Critics argued that the central government was misguided to attempt to construct large firms through administrative means in the hope that they could compete globally. Others argued that Donglian was a move in the right direction, but that the new entity was still far too small to compete with the global giants. This view was dramatically reinforced by the announcement of the BP/Amoco merger later in 1998.

The 1998 Restructuring. In June 1998, after years of intense debate and experimentation, China's most senior policy makers decided to undertake a dramatic transformation of the institutional structure of the oil and petrochemical industry, which was far bolder than most industry observers had predicted.

Government restructuring. The restructuring of the oil and petrochemical industry occurred alongside a major reorganization of the central government's organizations. In March 1998, China's Ninth National People's Congress (NPC) approved many major governmental reform measures proposed by the State Council (Table 7-24). The reform measures reduced the number of government ministries and state commissions from 40 to 29. In addition to three newly

TABLE **7-24 Changes in Governmental Organizations, March 1998**

Old organization		*New organization*
State Planning Commission	→	State Development and Planning Commission
State Economic and Trade Commission	→	State Economic and Trade Commission
Ministry of Coal Industry	→	State Bureau of Coal Industry
Ministry of Mechanical Industry	→	State Bureau of Mechanical Industry
Ministry of Metallurgical Industry	→	State Bureau of Metallurgical Industry
Ministry of Domestic Trade	→	State Bureau of Domestic Trade
National Council of Light Industry	→	State Bureau of Light Industry
National Council of Textile Industry	→	State Bureau of Textile Industry
Ministry of Chemical Industry plus government functions of CNPC and Sinopec	→	State Bureau of Petroleum and Chemical Industry
Ministry of Geology and Mineral Resources		
State Land Administration	→	Ministry of Land and Natural Resources
State Oceanography Bureau		
State Bureau of Surveying and Mapping		
Sinopec	→	New Sinopec Group
CNPC	→	New CNPC Group

SOURCE: *Oil and Gas Journal* (10 August 1998)

established ministries and one new state commission, 25 of the original 40 ministries and state commissions were retained. The remaining 15 were restructured and transferred into seven newly created 'state bureaux', which include coal, petroleum and chemicals, metals, machine-building, textile, domestic trade, and light industry. These state bureaux are affiliated to the State Economic and Trade Commission (SETC). For the energy sector, the most notable change is the abolition of the Ministry of Coal Industry, the Ministry of Chemical Industry (MCI), and the Ministry of Power Industry. While the respective state bureaux have been set up for the coal and chemical industries, no corresponding state bureau was created for the power industry.

The State Bureau of Petroleum and Chemical Industry (SBPCI) was established as an administrative body to take over the government function of MCI, of Sinopec and CNPC (See below). In addition, SBPCI administers several other bodies such as the Chemical Overseas Co-operation Centre and the Sub-Council of the Chemical Industry, which act as service institutions facilitating overseas business. It is placed under SETC and headed by Li Yongwu, the former vice-minister of MCI. There are two main responsibilities of SBPCI. One task is to map out overall development strategies for the industry and carry out industrial planning. It also promotes 'the continued restructuring of the 7500 state-owned enterprises under Sinopec and CNPC'. Another main responsibility is to formulate re-employment programmes for workers made redundant as a result of restructuring measures.

The Ministry of Geology and Mineral Resources (MGMR) had its role, although minor, in China's petroleum industry. It conducted limited exploration activities both onshore and offshore. However, for many years before 1997, MGMR turned the fields it discovered over to CNPC for development. At the end of 1996, its exploration functions were split off from the ministry and turned into China's third upstream state oil company, named China National Star Petroleum Corporation (CNSPC), still a minor part of the industry. MGMR now has been merged into the new Ministry of Land and Natural Resources. Thus it disappears from the petroleum industry's organizational structure.

Oil and petrochemical industry restructuring. The restructuring programme for the oil and petrochemical industry, following the elimination of the Ministry of Chemical Industry, created two new giant, vertically integrated oil and petrochemical groups: [New] China National Petrochemical Corporation (Sinopec) and [New] China National Petroleum Corporation (CNPC). Together, they account for 11 per cent of China's industrial output value.

The State Council's stated aim was to establish completely independent companies. Their only aim was to be the pursuit of profits. They were to be given complete operational independence from the State Council. They were to be allowed and encouraged to compete with each other as giant oligopolistic companies.

The assets of Sinopec and CNPC were reorganized along geographical lines, with those located in eastern and southern China coming under the management of Sinopec and those in northern and western China coming under CNPC. Under the reorganization scheme, Sinopec transferred 19 petrochemical enterprises to CNPC, of which 14 are engaged in production and 5 in marketing. The enterprises transferred include Daqing General Petrochemical, Fushun Petrochemical, Dalian Petrochemical, Dalian West Pacific Petrochemical, Lanzhou Chemical Industrial, and Jinzhou Petrochemical. CNPC transferred to Sinopec 12 enterprises of which 11 enterprises were engaged in oil exploration and production and a twelfth enterprise, Zhongyuan Petrochemical. In addition to the assets transfer between CNPC and Sinopec, refineries and olefin plants formerly under the Ministry of Chemical Industry were transferred to either Sinopec or CNPC depending on the location of these refineries.

The new Sinopec now has assets worth 381 billion yuan ($45.9 billion). It is headed by Li Yizhong, the former President of China East United Petrochemical Groups and also the former Executive Vice President of Sinopec. It controls oil and gas fields, oil refineries, and petrochemical companies in 19 provinces, autonomous regions, and municipalities (Figure 7-1). Among the 89 subsidiaries, 25 are petrochemical producers, including China's major petrochemical enterprises such as Shanghai Petrochemical, Beijing Yanshan Petrochemical, Yangzi Petrochemical, Tianjin Petrochemical, and Qilu Petrochemical. It accounts for about 60 per cent of China's total refining capacity and about 30 per cent of the onshore crude production capacity, and well over half of total Chinese output of the main petrochemical products.

Sinopec Group
President: Li Yizhong

Field/Complex/Basin	Pro-forma 1997 output		Major Refineries	Crude Capacity 1 000 metric tons/year
	Oil 1 000 metric tons	Gas million metres³		
			Yanshan Petrochemical Corp	9 500
			Tianjin Petrochemical Corp	6 000
			Gaoqiao Petrochemical Corp	7 500
			Shanghai Petrochemical Corp Ltd	5 300
			Jinling Refinery	7 000
			Yangzi Petrochemical Corp	6 000
			Anqing Petrochemical Corp	2 800
Shengli	28 011.6	1 002.0	Zhenhai Refining & Chemical Co Ltd	8 000
DianQianGui	48.7	97.0	Funjian Refinery	4 000
Jidong	610.9	33.9	Qilu Petrochemical Corp	8 000
Anhui	90.1	—	Jinan Refinery	4 000
Henan	1 850.6	32.0	Luoyang Petrochemical Plant	5 000
Zhongyuan	4 020.7	1 157.0	Jingmen Petrochemical Plant	5 000
Jianghan	820.6	66.0	Baling Petrochemical Corp	5 000
Jiangsu	1 172.3	12.0	Maoming Petrochemical Corp	8 500
			Guangzhou Petrochemical Corp	5 200
Total Sinopec	36 625.5	2 399.0	Dagnag Refinery	3 000
			Total Sinopec	125 240

FIGURE 7-1 China's Petroleum Capabilities: Sinopec Group, 1998

```
                        ┌─────────────────────┐
                        │     CNPC Group      │
                        │ President: Ma Fucai │
                        └─────────────────────┘
```

Pro-forma 1997 output			Major Refineries	Crude Capacity 1 000 metric tons/year
	Oil 1 000 metric tons	Gas million metres³		
			Daqing Petrochemical Corp	6 000
			Fushun Petrochemical Corp	9 200
			Liaoyang Chemical Fiber Corp	4 000
Field/			Jinzhou Petrochemical Corp	5 500
Complex/			Jinxi Petrochemical Corp	5 000
Basin			Dalian Petrochemical Corp	7 100
			Lanzhou Refining & Chemical Corp	5 500
Daqing	56 009.2	2 340.0	Daqing Chemical Synergist Plant	3 500
Xinjiang	8 701.7	1 244.0	Dushanzi Refinery	6 000
Jilin	4 002.7	231.0	Karamay Refinery	3 300
Changqing	3 300.2	166.0	Yumen Refinery	4 000
Yumen	400.2	12.0	Jilin Chemical Industry Group	4 500
Sichuan	232.5	7 509.0		
Yanchang	1 072.7	—	Total CNPC	87 800
Huabei	4 680.7	329.0		
Liaohe	15 040.8	1 551.0		
Tarim	4 203.5	183.0		
Tu-Ha	3 000.8	602.0		
Dagang	4 350.1	389.0		
Qinghai	1 602.0	220.0		
Total CNPC	106 597.3	14 776.0		

FIGURE 7-2 China's Petroleum Capabilities: CNPC Group, 1998

The new CNPC is led by Ma Fucai, former CNPC Vice President and Director of CNPC's Daqing Petroleum Administration, and has assets worth about 470 billion yuan ($57.8 billion). CNPC manages oil, gas, and petrochemical facilities in 12 provinces, regions and municipalities, including oil and gas producing complexes such as Daqing, Liaohe, Xinjiang, Tarim (Talimu), and Sichuan. With its priority of oil and gas exploration and production, the new CNPC accounts for 40 per cent of China's refining capacity and 69 per cent of onshore crude production capacity (Figure 7-2).

Within China they are massively dominant (Table 7-25). The two companies account for around 90 per cent of crude oil production in China, and they are responsible for over 75 per cent of the output of natural gas. Combined oil refining capacity amounts to over 95 per cent of the total in China. The two companies also account for 90 per cent of the ethylene cracking capacity. In the petrochemical sector, Sinopec has 32 petrochemical enterprises, while CNPC controls 35. For capacity in ethylene, polyethylene, polypropylene, and synthetic resin, the proportions between Sinopec and CNPC are, respectively, 57 and 33 per cent, 55 and 34 per cent, 57 and 23 per cent, 39 and 21 per cent (Table 7-25).

All the provincial state-owned petroleum companies and their petrol stations were placed under CNPC and Sinopec. CNPC was allocated the companies in the north and west (including Inner Mongolia, Gansu, Ningxia, Heilongjiang,

TABLE **7-25** **New Sinopec and New CNPC Compared**

Item	New Sinopec	New CNPC
Fixed assets	$30–40 billion	$30–40 billion
Annual sales	$25–30 billion	$25–30 billion
No. of oilfields	7	14
No. of petrochemical plants	32	35
No. of sales companies	19	12
Share of oil output (%)	23	66
Share of natural gas output (%)	11	66
Share of primary oil processing (%)	52	45
Share of residual oil processing (%)	56	42
Share of ethylene capacity (%)	57	33
Share of PE capacity (%)	55	34
Share of PP capacity (%)	57	23
Share of synthetic resin capacity (%)	39	21

SOURCE: _Asian Chemical News_ (7 September 1998)

Liaoning, Jilin, Xinjiang and Sichuan), and Sinopec was allocated the remainder. We have already noted that this was a highly significant move in terms of creating a genuinely integrated modern oil and petrochemical company. Each was encouraged to compete in the other's territory, and there is some evidence that this has already begun.

The two giant companies were empowered by the State Council to make their own investment decisions, including forming joint ventures with foreign companies and raising their own financing. Formerly, all major investment decisions needed the approval of the State Development and Planning Commission and/or the Economic and Trade Commission. Prior to the restructuring, any large-scale borrowing by CNPC and Sinopec also needed approval from the government authorities. The Annual Reports of the restructured companies (CNPC, 1999; Sinopec, 1999) emphasize that each of the companies is 'no longer engaged in government administrative or managerial functions' and is 'an independently operating legal entity that is responsible for its own profits and losses, development and self-discipline'. Prior to restructuring, CNPC and Sinopec each made negotiated 'hand-overs' to the state Ministry of Finance. These ought now to be regularized as purely tax payments according to law.

1999: Restructuring for Flotation. Soon after the initial restructuring involved in the creation of integrated upstream and downstream companies, the central Chinese government announced that the restructured companies were to issue H-shares in Hong Kong. Intense, feverish activity took place in both companies in order to get them ready for flotation as early as possible. A huge outside team of over 1000 people was involved in the valuation of assets and advising on restructuring at CNPC alone. It was widely thought that the flotation of Sinopec would follow that of CNPC. The goal was to produce companies that looked like the global giants in their fundamental business structure.

Sinopec. The listing of Sinopec is technically more complex than that of CNPC, since Sinopec already contains more than ten listed companies. The most important of these were Yanhua, Yizheng, Zhenhai and Shanghai Petrochemical Company (SPC), which are all H-shares, listed in Hong Kong. In addition there is a number of A-share companies, including Yangzi and Qilu. These accounted for over one-quarter of Sinopec's fixed assets before restructuring and around one-fifth of its pre-tax profits.

There is still great uncertainty within the floated companies about whether the new Sinopec has really transformed itself from a government ministry into a genuinely competitive company. As we have seen, the most powerful of the internationally floated companies, such as SPC, have their own corporate ambitions. SPC's strong ambition before the 1998 restructuring was to become one of a small group of powerful Chinese integrated oil and petrochemical companies. SPC wanted to be allowed to 'grow through the market', merging with other Chinese firms to become a national champion for China. Instead, the central government has attempted to construct two giant companies by administrative means. SPC's ambitions have not been dimmed by the impending flotation. Despite the restructuring SPC still retains its status as an independent legal person. SPC's stated goal in mid-1999 was still to establish itself as 'China's pre-eminent petrochemical producer'. Its ambition is still to become a globally strong middle-rank petrochemical producer, such as Phillips Petroleum (USA), with which it has a substantial joint venture. SPC's goal is to have world scale in everything it does, whether that is ethylene, acrylics, or plastics.

SPC still had considerable autonomy to raise capital independently. In 1998 it had a fairly cautious level of debt, with a debt to assets ratio of 42 per cent at the end of the year. Its publicly stated goal is to greatly expand its ethylene capacity, from 550 000 tons to 850 000 tons by the year 2002. It considers this to be the key to its growth strategy in the near term (SPC, 1999: 7). This will enable it significantly to expand its output of downstream products. In order to construct the new ethylene facilities SPC will take on more debt, raising its debt to assets ration to around 70 per cent. If the planned joint venture with BP proceeds, then SPC will add a further 650 000 tons to its ethylene capacity. SPC plans also to expand its refinery capacity from 6.3 million tons to 8–10 million tons by the year 2002.

SPC has its own plans to downsize and upgrade its human resources. When SPC was itself restructured for flotation in 1993, it separated off its 'business development companies' (*shiye gongsi*) from the core business. This reduced the total number of employees from around 60 000 to around 37 000. In 1998, in an effort to further streamline the company, another 11 000 employees were separated off from the main company (*fenliu*), leaving only around 25 000–26 000 employees within the core company. The core company is becoming steadily younger and more professional. More than 60 per cent of staff are under 35 years of age, and most of those who left the company in 1998 were from the lower skill categories. SPC's goal is to reduce costs and establish manning levels comparable with those of its global competitors.

Even after the 1998 restructuring, SPC was still actively pursuing mergers and acquisitions: 'The Company believes that acquisitions will become an increasingly important part of its expansion strategy' (SPC, 1999: 8). SPC believes that if it is to develop into a world force it needs to be allowed to merge with an oil company, so that it can be integrated vertically. It is not clear how this ambition will be realized if Sinopec really does become an integrated company.

Despite its struggle for autonomy, SPC still had many constraints on its business operation in the summer of 1999. Sinopec decides the source and amount of crude oil supplies to SPC. It controls the price of domestic crude oil and charges SPC international prices for imported crude oil. Over 700 'documents' are sent down annually from the Sinopec headquarters to the subordinate units, including a myriad of detailed matters. The authority to appoint the senior officers of the company is firmly in the hands of Sinopec headquarters. SPC's leaders for the past few years, President Wu Yixin and Vice-President Zhou Yinong, were both replaced by Sinopec headquarters during the restructuring. SPC's wage bill and wage policy is still tightly controlled by Sinopec. Consequently, real wages have risen only a little at SPC since the company's flotation and retaining the highest level personnel was causing some problems. SPC must legally hand over 55 per cent of its distributed profits to the Sinopec headquarters according to their shareholding. However, there is still considerable pressure from Sinopec for large subordinate entities such as SPC to also hand over a proportion of retained profits to the headquarters.

We have seen that over the first three years after flotation, the state's share in ownership of SPC fell to just 55 per cent. It was still at that level in 1999. However, despite the impending flotation of Sinopec, SPC plans to issue more H-shares, which could take the share of state ownership in SPC below 50 per cent. It has been suggested that if Sinopec were to create a truly integrated company it would be necessary to swap shares in SPC for those in the new Sinopec. This would be a very complex operation. However, it is not strictly necessary for Sinopec to resume full ownership of SPC's floated shares in order to function as a competitive modern corporation. Most large corporations have equity shares in other companies, which are either consolidated in the balance sheet or not, depending on the extent of ownership by the investing company. Nor is it unusual to have a subsidiary that is floated on the stock market. What is unusual among successful global petrochemical companies is to have a small number of very powerful subsidiaries, each of which is floated on international stock markets, and each of which has its own distinct ambitions. The more powerful and distinct are the interests and ambitions of the subsidiaries, the closer the core company becomes to a pure holding company, with correspondingly reduced ability to control the direction of development of the whole business.

Sinopec may successfully restructure itself and float on international stock markets. Over time it may grow to look more and more like a global oil and petrochemical company. However, its internal structure still has major differences from the global giants. It is still in transition from a government holding company to an integrated and centralized modern enterprise. As long as it contains powerful subordinate enterprises with independent property rights and ambitions, such as SPC, it will still lack the business capability of its major international competitors.

CNPC. It was reported in June 1999 that CNPC intended to sell up to 30 per cent of the company's equity, raising $5–10 billion, which would make it one of the biggest IPO's in Asia, and almost certainly the largest to date from China (*FT*, 29 June 1999). Both CNPC and Sinopec declared their intention to separate core from non-core assets, with the floated company containing only high quality core assets. From the outside this appears a relatively straightforward task. Following the model of other international Chinese flotations, the joint stock company that is to be floated is separated from the 'social' aspects of the business, including pensions, schools, hospitals and 'diversified production' (Figure 7-3). Following the common international model, key 'technical service functions' are to be separated from the joint stock company. These are then intended to compete with one another for business from the joint-stock company as well as on the international marketplace. It is visualized that through the competitive process, the strongest of these will emerge as successful, autonomous companies. Initial indications suggested that around 500 000 workers would be placed in the floated company, and around one million workers would be placed in the different entities that were not included in the floated company.

However, in practice, the process of restructuring CNPC for flotation (the 'second restructuring') has proved exceptionally complex, reflecting the tortuous path that CNPC has to follow in its effort to become a globally competitive company.

The struggle between Daqing and CNPC headquarters. We have seen that under the old CNPC, Daqing accounted for around two-fifths of total crude oil output. Under the new CNPC, Daqing's contribution is even greater, accounting for over one-half. Daqing is crucial to the profitability of the whole of CNPC. Daqing's oil is on average only around 1000 metres below the surface, and it is thought that the costs of production are considerably below those for the Chinese oil industry as a whole. In 1998, Daqing 'handed over' 10.4 billion yuan to the headquarters of CNPC, as well as handing over 11.4 billion yuan to the central government Ministry of Finance. CNPC's operating profit in 1998 was just over 5 billion yuan (CNPC, 1999: 98). It can be seen that Daqing is quite central to the profitability of CNPC. A big issue for CNPC's profitability is the fact that it has taken over many small-scale, often loss-making refineries. Daqing has a very proud history as the pillar of the whole industry. Daqing wished to itself constitute the core of a new giant, internationally competitive company, that would grow organically by taking over other enterprises in the oil and petrochemical industry, possibly including even a merger with SPC.

The first issue of the struggle was the question of which entity should be floated, Daqing or the new CNPC. We have seen that, like SPC, Daqing had intense ambitions to become a vehicle through which the Chinese oil industry established one or two global giants, but these ambitions were thwarted. When the

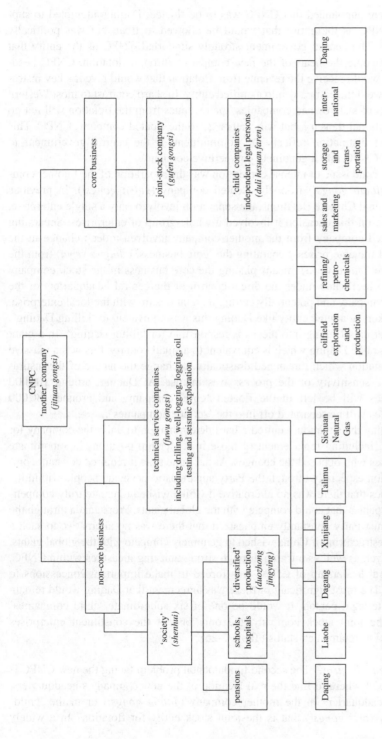

FIGURE 7-3 Provisional Structure of CNPC Prior to Flotation

plans were announced that CNPC was to be floated, Daqing attempted to supplant CNPC as the entity that would be allowed to float, but was politically defeated. The central government strongly supported CNPC as the entity that would become the heart of the new company. Through flotation, CNPC headquarters would receive the revenue from flotation that would give it a key instrument to weld the company into a unified entity. In sharp contrast to most Western flotations of state-owned companies, the revenues from the flotation will not go to the national treasury, but will, rather go to the floated company, CNPC. This important distinction reflects the commitment of the central government to building CNPC into a genuinely competitive company.

The second issue of intense contention was the separation of the 'mother company' (*jituan gongsi*) from the floated company (*gufen gongsi*). In previous international Chinese flotations, the separation involved only a single enterprise. However, on this occasion it involved a whole group of enterprises. Separating the floated company from the mother company involved a deep change in the nature of the enterprises. Separating the 'core business' (*zhugan yewu*) from the 'non-core' (*fuwu yewu*), means placing the core business in the stock company that is to be floated under the direct control of the central headquarters of the floated company and potentially cutting its relationship with the local enterprise. For workers at a huge entity like Daqing this was equivalent to 'killing Daqing': 'Whoever cuts Daqing into pieces is responsible for killing Daqing'. In a giant enterprise like Daqing which is equivalent to a small country, this was a massive transformation which threatened drastically to change the nature of the institution. The sensitivity of the process was intense. At Daqing, around 106 000 employees will be left in the floated 'core' company, and around 180 000 employees will be separated off into the 'service companies'.

Handling the situation required a hard determination to unify the company for flotation, including replacement of those in leadership positions in subordinate enterprises who opposed the changes. At the same time it required constant communication especially through the Party apparatus to persuade people within the enterprises that there was no alternative if China wished to create truly competitive companies that could compete with the global giants. Propaganda through the Communist Party constantly emphasized that there was no alternative to such a drastic restructuring if China wished to genuinely compete with the global giants.

However, as well as pushing through strong unifying measures within CNPC, the central leadership of CNPC was forced to make important concessions to Daqing. The most significant of these was agreement that Daqing would remain a separate legal person. It would be one of six subordinate 'child companies' within the joint stock company, the only one of the constituent enterprises permitted to retain such status (Table 7-26).

Where is the firm? The second fundamental problem facing the new CNPC is the issue of where to find the real location of the new company's headquarters. Is the headquarters in the mother company (*jituan gongsi*) or in the 'child' company (*erzi gongsi*) that is the joint stock entity for flotation? In a widely

TABLE **7-26 Refineries under the New CNPC**

Refinery	Subsidiary name	Capacity (metric tons/year)
Refineries formerly under CNPC	Jilin Refinery	300
	Huhhot Refinery	1000
	Liaohe Oilfield Asphalt Plant	2500
	Daqing Chemical Synergist Plant	3500
	Sichuan Nanchong Refinery	150
	Dushanzi Refinery	6000
	Golmud Refinery	1000
	Karamay Refinery	3300
	Yumen Refinery	4000
	Zepu Refinery	150
	Shaanxi Majiatan Refinery	100
	Shaanxi Majialing Refinery	300
	Yanchang Refinery	100
	Qinghai Refinery	1 350
	Xianyang Refinery	2 500
Refineries from MCI	Mudanjiang Petrochemical Works	350
	Jilin Chemical Industry Group	4 500
	Fuyu Refinery	200
	Tumen Yanbian Petrochemical Works	200
	Nong'an Petrochemical Works	150
	Dandong Petrochemical Works	300
	Shenyang Xinming Wax Chemical Works	100
	Qiqiha'er Chemical Works	350
	Heilongjiang Petrochemical Works	500
	Acheng Petrochemical Works	100

TABLE 7-26 (*Continued*)

Refinery	Subidiary name	Capacity (metric tons/year)
Refineries from Sinopec	Daqing Petrochemical Corp.	6 000
	Linyuan Refinery	2 500
	Harbin Refinery	1 500
	Qianguo Refinery	2 500
	Fushun Petrochemical Corp.	9 200
	Anshan Refinery	2 500
	Liaoyang Chemical Fiber Corp.	4 000
	Jinzhou Petrochemical Corp.	5 500
	Jinxi Petrochemical Corp.	5 000
	Dalian Petrochemical Corp.	7 100
	Lanzhou Refining & Chemical Corp.	5 500
	Urumqi Petrochemical Plant	2 500
CNPC Total Capacity		87 800

SOURCE: *Oil and Gas Journal* (10 August 1998)

publicized article in CNPC's newspaper, *China Oil* (*Zhongguo Shiyou Bao*, 15 September 1999), Ma Fucai, President of CNPC, emphasized that CNPC Group Company (*jituan gongsi*) is the 'mother' (*mugongsi*) that is the controlling company (*konggu gongsi*) of the joint stock company and that the joint stock company for flotation is the 'child' company (*erzi gongsi*). Ma Fucai emphasizes that the mutual interests of the two entities are 'mediated through capital'. He stresses that not only will the floated company expand, but so also should the mother company. In other words, the mother company is not simply a 'shell'.

CNPC's leaders emphasized that the child company is an independent legal person that must struggle autonomously to succeed in both domestic and international markets. However, the autonomy of the child company is not unlimited. CNPC's leaders emphasize that the child company is still subject to important controls from the mother company (*jituan gongsi*). The mother company needs to 'strengthen its function of strategic decision-making, and its co-ordination and control at the macro level' (*China Oil*, 15 September 1999). The mother company is to 'focus on making strategic decisions on large-scale projects and large investments in capital operation, production and business operation'. The mother company is to 'concentrate on "big things", differentiating macro strategic decision-making from micro-management'. In other words, even within the floated company's core business, its operational autonomy is not unlimited.

Through the development of core business in the joint stock company, the further growth and development of non-core business should be promoted within the mother company. A stream of revenue will flow from the floated company to the mother company 'through capital', in other words through the payments of dividends to the majority shareholder in the joint stock company. These resources can be used to develop a wide variety of businesses under the control of the mother company.

Comparison with the Global Giants. Superficially, China's two giant oil and petrochemical corporations now look much like the other global giants. The element of similarity is greatly increased by the impending flotation of both companies as H-shares in Hong Kong. Intense work was under way in late 1999 to ensure that flotation of both companies took place within a few months. To what extent do the newly restructured Chinese giant companies resemble the global giants?

Size

Employment. The Chinese restructuring has created truly global giants in terms of some simple indicators. At a stroke, the Chinese has created the two largest companies in the world in terms of the number of employees. Sinopec already occupies the top position in the 1999 *Fortune Global* 500 list for the number of employees, its 1.2 million outstripping even the fast-growing giant Wal-Mart.

Sales. The value of sales places the two companies firmly among the world's top one hundred companies. In the 1999 *Fortune* 500 list (*Fortune*, 2 August 1999), Sinopec was listed at number 73. If CNPC had also been ranked it would have been listed at number 77. This places the two companies alongside the leading second tier of global oil and petrochemical companies, such as ENI, Texaco and Elf Aquitaine (Table 7-27). However, their sales still fall considerably short of those of the industry leaders, Exxon Mobil, Shell and BP Amoco. Similarly, the value of CNPC and Sinopec's assets exceeds that of all but three of the oil and petrochemical companies quoted on the world's stock markets (Table 7-28).

Output. In terms of output, CNPC is already close to the level of the world's leading companies, with an output of oil and gas together of around 2.4 million barrels of oil and oil equivalent per day (Table 7–29), compared with 2.1 million at TotalFinaElf, 3.0 million at BP Amoco/Arco, 3.8 million at Shell and 4.5 million at Exxon Mobil. Sinopec is much smaller scale, at less than 1 million barrels of oil equivalent per day.

Reserves. The total oil and gas reserves of the whole of China are estimated by BP (BP, 1998) to be around 32 billion barrels of oil and oil equivalent. This

TABLE 7-27 **Financial Indicators for CNPC and Sinopec Compared to the World's Leading Oil and Petrochemical Companies Quoted on the Stock Market**

Company	Revenue ($billion)	Net profits ($million)	Assets ($billion)	Employees	Revenue/worker ($000)	Profits/worker ($)	Profits/turnover (%)	Profits/assets (%)
CNPC	32.6	107	61.2	1 540 000	21	69	0.3	0.2
Sinopec	34.0	194	51.6	1 190 000	29	163	0.6	0.4
Exxon Mobil	148.4	8074	135.4	120 500	1231	67 004	5.4	6.0
Shell	93.6	350	110.1	102 000	918	3431	0.4	0.3
BP Amoco	68.3	3260	84.5	96 650	706	33 713	4.8	3.9
ENI	32.4	2594	48.5	78 906	410	32 877	8.0	5.3
Texaco	31.7	578	28.6	24 628	1289	23 467	1.8	2.0
Elf Aquitaine	35.9	601	43.2	85 000	422	7071	1.7	1.4

SOURCES: *Fortune* (2 August 1999); CNPC (1999); Sinopec (1999)

TABLE 7-28 CNPC and Sinopec Compared to the Global Giants, late 1990s

Company	Oil production (million barrels/day)	Gas production (billion feet³)	Gas production (million barrels of oil equivalent/ day)	Total oil and gas production (million barrels/day)
Exxon Mobil	2.53	10.64	1.92	4.45
Shell	2.33	8.00	1.44	3.77
BP Amoco/Arco	1.93	5.86	1.05	2.98
TotalFina/Elf Aquitaine	1.48	3.37	0.61	2.09
ENI	0.65	0.38	0.07	0.72
Texaco	0.83	2.18	0.39	1.22
Chevron	1.43	2.87	0.52	1.17
CNPC	2.14	1.43	0.26	2.40
Sinopec	0.74	0.23	0.04	0.78

SOURCE: Annual reports

compares with reserves of oil and gas estimated at 19.5 billion barrels of oil equivalent at BP Amoco/Arco, 20.4 billion at Shell and 21.1 billion at Exxon Mobil (Annual Reports). However, the domestic estimates of China's oil and gas output are considerably greater than BP's estimates. CNPC estimates that its reserves of 'recoverable' oil and gas amount to 40 billion barrels of oil equivalent.

There are, however, crucial differences between the reserves and output of China's leading oil companies and those of the global giants. Firstly, the global distribution is strikingly different. CNPC and Sinopec are almost entirely producers within a single country, China. Their attempts to develop global portfolios of reserves have so far been very limited due to both financial and technical constraints. By contrast, BP Amoco has production and exploration activities in 27 countries and Exxon has them in 30 countries. Secondly, the quality of the portfolio of oil and gas assets is very different. The Chinese state has given its national champions the rights to develop domestic oil and gas reserves. However, these face serious problems. As we have seen, the main onshore oil reserves are declining seriously. The main possible future growth areas onshore are in remote parts of the country. The reserves are at great depths and require high cost transport across long distances to the main consuming centres in the east of the country. Moreover, even the quantities of reserves are far from certain. Similarly, the offshore oil and gas reserves are mainly located in areas with high technical difficulties, and high costs of exploration and production. Through their financial and technical resources, the global giants have attempted to construct a portfolio that can make a profit at as low as $10 per barrel of oil. There is little sign of the emerging Chinese giants being able to match this for the foreseeable future.

Financial Performance. There are enormous changes that need to be undertaken if the returns on CNPC and Sinopec's enormous assets are to compare with those of the world's most competitive firms in this sector. Net profits at CNPC

TABLE 7-29 **Refineries under the new Sinopec**

Refinery	Subsidiary name	Capacity (metric tons/year)
Refineries formerly under Sinopec	Yanshan Petrochemical Corp.	9 500
	Tianjin Petrochemical Corp.	6 000
	Shijiazhuang Refinery	2 500
	Cangzhou Refinery	1 500
	Gaoqiao Petrochemical Corp.	7 500
	Shanghai Petrochemical Co. Ltd	5 300
	Jinling Petrochemical Corp.	7 000
	Yangzi Petrochemical Corp.	6 000
	Anqing Petrochemical Plant	2 800
	Jiujiang Refinery	2 500
	Zhenhai Refining & Chemical Co. Ltd	8 000
	Fujian Refinery	4 000
	Qilu Petrochemical Corp.	8 000
	Jinan Refinery	4 000
	Luoyang Petrochemical Plant	5 000
	Luoyang Experimental Plant	200
	Wuhan Petrochemical Plant	2 500
	Jingmen Petrochemical Plant	5 000
	Baling Petrochemical Corp.	5 000
	Maoming Petrochemical Corp.	8 500
	Guangzhou Petrochemical Corp.	5 200
Refineries from CNPC	Refinery of Henan Oilfield	120
	Shengli Heavy oil Plant	2 500

TABLE 7-29 *(Continued)*

Refinery	Subsidiary name	Capacity (metric tons/year)
	Shengli Refinery	150
	Dagang Refinery	3 000
	Huabei Chemical Pharmaceutical Plant	200
	Jianghan Oilfield Refinery	300
	Nanyang Refinery	620
	Zhongyuan Refinery	1 300
	Beihai Refinery	500
Refineries from MCI	Hangzhou Refinery	300
	Baoding Petrochemical Works	500
	Qingdao Petrochemical Works	2 500
	Zhongjie Petrochemical Works	150
	Nandagang Petrochemical Works	100
	Taizhou Petrochemical Works	300
	Wuxi Petrochemical Works	150
	Qingjiang Petrochemical Works	200
	Yangzhou Petrochemical Works	150
	Jianhu Petro chemical Experimental Plant	100
	Yangchen LPG Plant	100
	Binzhou Petrochemical Works	400
	Ji'nan No 2 Petrochemical Works	300
	Kenli Refinery	400
	Linyi Petrochemical Works	200
	Guangrao Petrochemical Works	300
	Shouguang Petrochemical Works	150
	Changyi Petrochemical Works	150

TABLE 7-29 (*Continued*)

Refinery	Subsidiary name	Capacity (metric tons/year)
	Dongming PetroPlant Works	150
	Lijin Refinery	100
	Boxing PetroPlant Works	100
	Boxing Oil & Grease Chemical Works	1 500
	Yan'an Refinery	300
	Yongoing Refinery	150
	Xi'an PetroChemical Works	1 500
Sinopec Total Capacity	Zhanjiang Refinery	125 240

SOURCE: *Oil and Gas Journal* (10 August 1998)

and Sinopec are extremely small compared to the world's leading oil and petro-chemical companies. 1998 was a difficult year for Shell, with profits slumping from $7.8 billion in 1997 to $350 million, but it still achieved profits that were two to three times those of either CNPC or Sinopec. Profits at other similar-sized companies in the sector were many multiples of those at CNPC and Sinopec. For example, on a similar revenue base, ENI achieved net profits that were 13 times those of Sinopec and 24 times those at CNPC (Table 7-28). Revenue and profits per worker at CNPC and Sinopec are minuscule compared to those at the world's leading companies in the sector. More significantly, CNPC and Sinopec achieve a return on assets that is only a small fraction of that at the leading companies in the sector.

If CNPC and Sinopec are to move towards the financial performance of the global giants, then many changes will have to take place. Most of these are fairly obvious from a technical point of view. They include closure of small-scale refineries and petrochemical plants, changing the product mix towards high value-added products, integrating the entire value-chain of production from oil exploration and production through to retail sales, downsizing the vast workforce across almost all parts of the business, and transforming the remuneration and motivation system for the management and workforce. The institutional obstacles in the way of such changes are enormous.

Economies of Scale
Refineries. The 1980s and 1990s saw a proliferation of small-scale refineries in China. By the late 1990s there were no fewer than 220 in total, of which over 160 had less than one million tons capacity. Small refineries with capacity below 0.5 million ton/year account for 62 per cent of the total number of China's oil

refineries (Chen Zhun *et al.*, 1998: 29–30). Many of these were set up as non-state enterprises, such as township and village enterprises. Many of these are polluting and technically unable to produce non-polluting products, such as unleaded petrol. In the late 1990s, the central government was waging a major campaign to close down many of the refineries.

Sinopec and CNPC between them have a total of 93 refineries (Tables 7-26 and 7-29), including not only the refineries formerly under Sinopec, but also many refineries taken over from the former Ministry of Chemical Industry. A lot of these were small-scale, often using outdated technology. The average capacity of CNPC's refineries is just 2.4 million tons and those of Sinopec average 2.2 million tons (Tables 7-26 and 7-29), only around one-third of the global giants. Even within CNPC and Sinopec, the profile of the refinery sector was close to that of the advanced economies in the 1950s. Only 11 of Sinopec's refineries are greater than 5 million tons capacity. Forty-five are of less than 5 million tons capacity, of which no less then 30 are of below 1 million tons. Only seven of CNPC's refineries are over 5 million tons capacity. Thirty refineries are of less than 5 million tons capacity and 15 of these are under 1 million tons (Table 7-26).

A major task ahead for the two companies is to close down small-scale high-cost refineries. However, this is a complex task, as they employ a lot of people. There are typically high costs involved in closing down oil refineries, especially arising from the high costs of making the environment safe. They also often have the support of local governments, since they provide tax revenue as well as employment. Although the products may be polluting and the refineries themselves may be polluting, they may produce a product that is cheaper per unit than the higher quality product, and for which there is local excess demand.

Ethylene crackers. Of the total of 18 ethylene crackers in China, only seven have a capacity above 400 000 ton/year and the other 11 have a capacity of less than 200 000 ton/year (Chen Zhun *et al.*, 1998: 17, 30, 147).

Integration of Operations

Large integrated sites. The assets restructuring between CNPC and Sinopec enormously increased the potential for reducing costs through integration of upstream and downstream operations. It is widely recognized that there are significant advantages to integration of internally generated feedstocks with refining and petrochemical production. The simplest goal for the new Chinese integrated giants is to achieve a more rational structure within each of the new giant companies in terms of the location of crude oil supply in relation to the refining and petrochemical production. It is likely that CNPC will continue to be a much larger producer of crude oil within China than Sinopec for a long time to come. CNPC should be able to benefit by closely linking its main oil production bases in western and northern China with newly acquired refineries and petrochemical capabilities in those regions. For example, within the old structure Daqing was by far the largest oil field in China, run by CNPC. However, the Daqing refinery was in the hands of Sinopec. Sinopec is likely to need to purchase an increasing proportion of its oil supplies from international markets. It will be able to integrate its refining and petrochemical operations more closely with both local onshore crude oil, but also with imported supplies to the east coast refineries and petrochemical complexes. Throughout China, it should in principle prove much easier to integrate oil production, refining and petrochemical operations within two integrated companies. There should be substantial potential cost-savings arising from this source.

Wholesale and retail of petroleum products. CNPC and Sinopec each absorbed the wholesale and retail distribution operations of the local state-owned enterprises. The gas stations systems they have taken over are primitive compared to those of the multinational giants. For example, the Harbin City Petroleum Company, now under the control of CNPC, has a total of around 900 employees for just 40 small gas stations and associated logistics activities. It has a total value of sales of a few million dollars. A single business unit within a global giant is the same size in terms of employees, yet has revenues of many hundreds of millions of dollars. Moreover, the individual local petrol companies purchase and run their own tanker fleets and storage facilities. Harbin, for example, has a 'fleet' of 20 tankers and has 45 000 cubic metres of storage tanks that it built itself. Moreover, neither CNPC nor Sinopec has much experience in these business activities. They will need time to develop the considerable technical expertise involved in running these operations well. Moreover, they still face ferocious competition from a sea of small-scale enterprises. They have a long way to go before they develop the logistics expertise of the global giants or are able to develop a comparable brand name.

On the one hand, there are huge potential cost-savings available to the two companies if they are able to achieve progress on these fronts. On the other hand, the global giants are deeply interested to develop their business in China. CNPC and Sinopec would find it very difficult to compete if the global giants were allowed rapidly to develop their production, wholesale and retail networks for petroleum products in China. One industry expert commented: 'If the wholesale and retail business for petroleum products is opened up, CNPC and Sinopec will be defeated'.

Product Mix. A high proportion of CNPC and Sinopec's petrochemical and oil products are low value-added products. In part this reflects technical weakness, a consequence of investment in technically backward, older and cheaper technologies. This is reflected, for example, in the high energy consumption per unit of final product. In ethylene production, China consumes an average of 9.21 million kcal per ton of ethylene while the world lowest level is 4.2–5.5 million kcal per ton of ethylene (Chen Zhun *et al.*, 1998: 29, 36). Technical weakness is also reflected, for example, in the fact that in the process of ethylene production, only 55 per cent of the chemicals from the cracking process are further processed and utilized (Chen Zhun et al., 1998: 29). Both CNPC and Sinopec have a large number of research scientists, and they have made many important technical advances. However, the levels of R & D expenditure are far below those of the global giants. Moreover, a large fraction of the research staff are located within the separate production units. Both companies are still far behind the global giants in their development of world-leading technologies.

The companies' technical weakness is reflected in the predominantly low-value-added nature of the product mix. Chinese industry experts recognize the wide gap between the Chinese companies and the global giants. In oil products, CNPC and Sinopec need to increase their 'deep processing' capacity, raise the ratio of light oil in oil production, develop 'green' products, increase the production proportion of high-quality lubricants and broaden the product range to include other high value-added products (Chen Zhun et al., 1998: 168). In the petrochemical sector, new synthetic materials such as synthetic fibres and plastics, synthetic rubber and products, and polymeric materials should be developed. There is a huge market demand and excellent prospects for further development of these synthetic materials. The ratio of speciality chemical production in total chemical production is still only one-third. The goal is to raise this to close to one-half within five years or so and from 33 to 45 per cent at the end of this century. Areas targeted for increased supply include food and fodder additives, chemical products for the information and electronics sectors, paints, dyes, biological chemical products, non-toxic pesticides, and high-effectiveness catalysts. A key target for China is the development of environment-friendly chemical products. However, China still needs greatly to expand the supply of ethylene, the most basic raw material for chemical products, thereby allowing renovation of the whole chemical product mix (Chen Zhun et al., 1998: 31–32).

Organizational Structure. CNPC and Sinopec are still far from the management structure of the global giants, especially since the revolution that has occurred in the structure of the latter since the 1980s. However, they are removed also from the pre-reform structure of the global giants as it was in the 1980s. Although the latter had many subordinate operating units, often with their own identity, sometimes loosely termed 'feudal', they did not possess the degree of autonomy that China's powerful subordinate units had acquired by the mid-1990s. By the mid-1990s, the enterprises under CNPC and Sinopec had become independent legal persons. They had developed their own traditions and ambitions. They were often supported and encouraged in these ambitions by local governments. They had floated on international stock markets. They had negotiated and signed major joint ventures with international companies. They had undertaken their own R & D and technical transfer programmes from abroad. They retained a large share of their profits for self-disposal. The capability of the headquarters to monitor the subordinate enterprises was reflected in the small size of the headquarters. Sinopec, for example, had only around 300 employees in its central offices. Its international project co-operation team has less than 20 members, so it cannot possibly monitor in detail the negotiations with many different multinational companies.

The headquarters of CNPC and Sinopec are only too aware of the gap in operational mechanism between themselves and the global giants. There appears to be strong support from central policy makers for the leaders of CNPC and Sinopec, in their bid to turn their respective headquarters into entities that mirror those of the world's leading multinationals. They are fully aware of the complexity of the task that faces them in trying to transform their companies into genuinely competitive companies on the global stage. They face enormous opposition and concern from their subordinate operational units, which have so significantly increased their sense of corporate identity and developed substantial independent corporate ambitions under the reforms.

There are some obvious mechanisms that will increase the degree of central control within CNPC and Sinopec. These include the fact that the potentially large funds arising from international flotation will be in the hands of the headquarters of the respective companies. It was hoped that these would be as much as $10 billion in the case of CNPC and several billion dollars also from the flotation of Sinopec. This would radically change the financial situation of the headquarters of CNPC and Sinopec. For example, prior to the restructuring and flotation, Sinopec's annual income was around $100 million from profits handed over by subordinate enterprises. This was used to pay the salaries of the headquarters staff (around 300 people), to support Sinopec's network of research institutions and colleges, and provide support for subordinate enterprises that were in difficulties. After the flotation it may have several billion dollars at its disposal. However, this is a once-off injection, rather than a change in the structure of internal financial control.

It is likely that for CNPC a fast-increasing share of its oil output will come from internal sources under the direct control of the headquarters, either in western China or in the former Soviet Union. Their intention is in future to have complete control over the negotiations and decisions to establish international joint ventures, with no independent rights for subordinate production enterprises to negotiate and sign contracts as independent legal persons. It is likely that for Sinopec also, an increasing share of crude oil will be imported, unless the prospects for domestic production change dramatically. This must mean that Sinopec, and possibly CNPC, will enhance their control through the development of an international oil trading capability, which will probably become progressively more important for their respective companies. This function is a powerful potential instrument for centralization within the respective companies.

Since the restructuring of 1998, great efforts have gone into attempting to centralize control over subordinate entities within CNPC and Sinopec, including both personnel and financial control. Subordinate enterprises in both companies have felt that weight of a central government-supported attempt to use the restructuring for flotation as a vehicle for greatly increased financial control by the headquarters. This has been an intense 'political' struggle. The process of restructuring for flotation provided a further vehicle through which to centralize control over the ambitious subordinate entities.

It is too soon to say whether these efforts have produced a stable institutional structure within either CNPC or Sinopec. There is no doubt that intense ambitions still remain at the level of the subordinate enterprises, despite the major changes in leadership personnel brought about during the 'restructuring'. However, even if these elements of centralization are successfully accomplished, there is still a large distance between the resulting structure and the type of transparent, intensively monitored business unit structure based on detailed performance contracts that is now the norm within the world's leading oil and petrochemical companies.

In fact, the listing of CNPC (the floated portion of the company was named PetroChina) in the Spring of 2000 was intensely disappointing. Instead of the hoped-for $10 billion, the offer was scaled down to $7 billion, then $3.4 billion, and finally the flotation brought just $2.9 billion (*FT*, 1 April 2000). It was interpreted by the financial press as 'a wake-up call for China': 'The weak response was partly due to problems associated with Chinese state companies: huge workforces, poor management control and debt' (*FT*, 1 April 2000). The *Financial Times* commented: 'The success of the IPO will have a significant bearing on the ability of many Chinese state-owned enterprises to tap the international market for funds as they prepare for the onslaught of foreign competition, following China's accession to the WTO'.

CHINA NATIONAL OFFSHORE OIL CORPORATION (CNOOC)

CNOOC was established in 1982 as a state-owned enterprise designed to lead the exploration and development of China's offshore oil. China faced severe technical challenges in this endeavour, and a major objective of CNOOC was to act as the vehicle for channelling foreign investment into joint exploration and development. The prospect of major new oil finds in the Pacific Ocean off the coast of China was extremely attractive to the multinationals, and much interest was expressed. A total of over 160 contracts had been signed for joint exploration and development with 68 multinational companies by 1998. From 1992 to 1998, multinationals invested a total of $6.0 billion in exploration and development, compared with a total of $5.0 billion invested by CNOOC. Of the CNOOC investments, $2.6 billion was in entirely self-managed projects and $2.4 billion was in jointly managed projects with the multinationals. By the late 1990s, crude oil and gas was being produced in significant amounts, reaching 16 million tons of crude oil and 38 million cubic metres of gas in 1998. This accounted for over 10 per cent of China's total crude oil output and 17 per cent of its gas output.

However, the results were very disappointing from the perspective of the multinational companies. They failed to find the giant fields that had been hoped for and investment did not increase in the way that had originally been hoped.

From 1982 to 1986, multinational investment had averaged over $300 million per annum, but by the years 1994–8 it had fallen to just $160 million per annum. The prospects for CNOOC's oil and gas production are uncertain.

As a much newer company, without the Ministerial background of CNPC and Sinopec, as well as through constant contact with multinational companies, CNOOC has developed a different ethos from CNPC or Sinopec. It has a relatively small workforce. The numbers peaked at just over 30 000 in 1988, but have been allowed to fall to 27 000 in 1998. Of these, 6000 are employed in the oil company, 7700 are employed in the service company (including technology, geology, and offshore engineers), and 12 200 in other activities. It has managed to contain its costs much better than either CNPC or Sinopec, enabling it to enjoy a considerably higher rate of profit on sales revenue.

CNOOC has been allowed to develop considerably its downstream activities, including the massive (800 000 ton) Huizhou ethylene complex agreed as a joint venture with Shell. It also plans to build itself a 450 000 ton synthetic ammonia plant, a 630 000 ton urea plant and at least two LNG projects.

In order to pursue its ambitions further to explore and develop oil and gas, as well as expand its downstream activities, CNOOC had hoped to float the oil company through a dual listing in Hong Kong and New York in the Autumn of 1999. It had hoped to raise about $2.3 billion through the listing (*FT*, 29 September 1999). The specialist service company and other parts of the company were not included in the listing. They are planned to develop gradually as independent entities. In fact, the listing was withdrawn after the roadshow, due to disappointing investor response. This was a severe blow to CNOOC's ambitions. It hoped to return to the market in late 2000 or 2001.

Although the reserves discovered so far are disappointing in relation to the initial hopes, they are still a significant addition to China's production capacity. Moreover, given the disappointing overall growth of oil and gas production in China in the 1990s, CNOOC has accounted for a large fraction of the increments to national output. From 1994 to 1997, it accounted for 69 per cent of China's national increase in oil and gas output. It is possible that large reserves may be found in the future though many of the reserves are located in extremely difficult terrain that new technologies may make feasible and profitable to explore. Even the existing output levels place CNOOC in the ranks of a medium-sized producer, with roughly the same level of annual output as ENI.

Further, CNOOC is developing its own strong business culture and ambitions. With revenues of $1.4 billion in 1998, a successful flotation, and fast-growing downstream production, it is beginning to take the shape of a significant small-medium sized oil and petrochemical company. It would appear in the US rankings of the top 1000 corporations. If one adds to that its ambitions to develop fast in the downstream sector, then the company has the potential to become a very significant part of the Chinese oil and petrochemical structure. There are considerable debates about the most desirable path for CNOOC to take in relation to the rest of the industry.

CONCLUSION

INTERNATIONAL COMPETITION AND RESTRUCTURING

One way or another China must at some point face up to the full weight of international competition in the oil and petrochemical sector. If China joins the WTO sooner rather than later, this will simply accelerate the speed at which China's oil and petrochemical industry needs to become ready to compete with the global leaders. There is every likelihood that the WTO will concern itself increasingly with issues of freedom to invest and compete, as opposed to purely trade matters. Such issues are deeply important in the oil and petrochemical sector. For the global giants, the issue is not simply one of the level of international protection on crude oil, oil products and petrochemical products. For them, the key issues include the freedom to compete for contracts to explore for and develop oil and gas fields, the freedom to source crude oil from wherever is most efficient, the freedom to establish refineries and petrochemical plants in the most efficient location, the freedom to source diesel, petrol and other oil products from the most efficient supplier, the freedom to establish a network of service stations, and the freedom to develop their brand name. In the longer term, leading sector analysts believe that CNPC and Sinopec 'will be operating in a highly competitive domestic and global energy marketplace' (Choung and Terreson, 1998: 38). They believe that both companies will 'need to implement additional restructuring measures if they are to compete effectively among their global peers' (Choung and Terreson, 1998: 38). However, for the time being they are operating in a very different world from the global giants.

The stimulus for restructuring China's oil and petrochemical industry is different from that of the multinational giants. The global giants are emphatically international in their orientation. This affects their exploration activities, the source of their raw materials, the nature of their internal transport systems, the location of their production facilities and markets, and the nature of their staff. The frenetic restructuring of the global giants is driven by the direct impact of ferocious global competition. By contrast, China's oil and petrochemical companies are still mainly oriented towards the domestic economy. China's current relatively closed marketplace means that both CNPC and Sinopec have 'a window of opportunity to prepare themselves for future competition' (Choung and Terreson, 1998: 38). China's restructuring is heavily influenced by study of the surrounding trends in international restructuring, but those who are responsible for policy in the sector are still far from feeling the full direct force of global competition.

There are still great uncertainties about the real extent of China's oil and gas reserves. However, even if the more optimistic forecasts turn out to be correct, these will not shield the Chinese industry from the eventual impact of the full force of global competition. National oil reserves are a very different thing from possessing an internationally competitive oil and petrochemical company.

CAN CHINA COMPETE ON THE GLOBAL LEVEL PLAYING FIELD?

China's institutional reforms in the oil and petrochemical sector have been cautious and experimental. From the start of the reforms the central policy makers have emphasized their strong intention to create globally competitive giant companies in this sector. However, the shape of the industry around them has altered at high speed, so that they have been chasing a moving target. The global giants have entered a period of unprecedented change. In response to the long-term trend of decline in real oil and petrochemical prices, they have undertaken revolutionary transformations of their internal organizational structures, contributing to large falls in the cost of finding and extracting oil and gas, and in processing and marketing the final products. They have been assisted in this by the revolution in information technology, which has gathered pace in the 1990s. In the latter part of the period, the industry has seen a process of massive merger and acquisition that has radically re-shaped the nature of the global leaders in the private sector. It has taken the industry into a new era of super giant corporations that re-defines the scale needed in order to be globally competitive. From being an industry in which there were a large number of powerful state-owned integrated oil and petrochemical companies, the state has retreated from the sector with a wave of privatizations across both the advanced and the developing countries. These have helped also to contribute to even greater fluidity in the global institutional structure and to heightened intensity of competition in the sector as shareholder pressure sharply increased.

By the late 1990s, despite important advances in the Chinese industry, it still remained extremely weak in key respects compared to the global giants:

- the management structure is highly bureaucratic, rule-bound, and cumbersome
- their internal management is still in the early stages of transition from 'feudal decentralization', to a centralized 'command and control' system and intense monitoring of subordinate business units
- their workforce is of a relatively low educational level and has weak financial incentives at all levels
- they are weak in their technical capability to explore and produce low-cost oil and gas
- the Chinese industry is internationally competitive in exploration and development at middle-level technology, but relatively weak in oilfield development that requires the highest levels of technology
- they have a relatively high proportion of high-cost reserves
- their reserves are almost all within China, lacking the regional balance of the portfolios of the global giants
- they lack the economies of scale in refining and petrochemical plants
- they do not possess close integration of the location of refineries and petrochemical operations

- they have a high share of low quality, low-value-added products in their portfolio of oil and petrochemical products

- the marketing network's logistical capability is extremely weak and costs are high

- they have a very limited or no brand name or reputation for customer service and quality.

In sum, if the Chinese oil and petrochemical companies were opened to direct competition with the multinational giants, they would find it hard to survive.

THE CHOICES FACING THE CHINESE POLICY MAKERS

No-one seriously involved with the industry disputes that fundamental 'restructuring' of the industry is necessary. The question is what kind of restructuring and by whom? The core of argument within China concerns the virtues of 'following the dictates of the market' in restructuring as opposed to 'following the administrative path of restructuring'. There are at least two very different interpretations of the phrase 'following the dictates of the market'.

'Following the Guidance of the Market' (i): Privatization and Withdrawal of Direct Government Involvement. Since the mid-1980s, many former 'national champions' in this sector have been privatized and left to survive on their own in the face of intensified international competition. Notable examples include the sale of the British government's stake in BP, and the privatizations of ENI (still with a 36 per cent state ownership share), Elf Aquitaine and Repsol. Each of these has had to confront complex issues of nationality. A major issue in the Elf/PetroFina merger was the French government's apparent refusal to allow a non-French company to make a bid for Elf. However, it was able to do this through its 'golden share'. The legitimacy of such an arrangement is dubious under international law and is most unlikely to remain an internationally acceptable policy instrument for much longer. There is great reluctance in Italy to allow ENI to merge with Elf/PetroFina, since this would amount essentially to a take-over of ENI by the French-based firm, since ENI is much smaller than Elf/PetroFina. Even if the respective governments agree to such an international merger, the resulting firm would still be a 'European champion' rather than a transatlantic entity. However, the commercial pressure for companies such as ENI and Elf/PetroFina to merge across borders are intense and likely to become steadily stronger.

Since the late 1980s, BP has undergone a dramatic process of internationalization. This has culminated in the merger with Amoco and the subsequent merger with Arco. These are of deep significance since they are transatlantic mergers. They emphasize that privatization and allowing the market to drive decisions leads inexorably to cross-border mergers, and, ultimately, even to transatlantic mergers. China is no longer competing with 'national' champions or even 'regional' champions. Rather, its emerging large firms are competing with global super-giants of an increasingly international character.

For oil and petrochemical firms based in developing countries, the choices are even more stark. A striking example is the case of YPF. This is a powerful company that was created in order to be Argentina's 'national champion' under state ownership. This is Argentina's largest company with strong upstream and downstream assets. Following privatization in 1993, a powerful CEO, Roberto Monti, led the company. His goal was to build YPF from a strong regional player, mainly based within Argentina, into a powerful international company: 'These ambitions were clearly demonstrated with its 1995 purchase of US independent exploration and production company Maxus Energy' (*FT*, 13 October 1998). YPF developed a close relationship with Petrobras of Brazil. Its aim is to 'pump natural gas into energy-hungry southern Brazil'. YPF was awarded the right to develop a number of exploration blocs in Brazil in tandem with Petrobas. It also has a joint venture to develop service station chains with Petrobas (*FT*, 12 October 1998).

Following its privatization in the mid/late 1990s, Repsol, the Spanish oil and petrochemical company, began a process of rapid international expansion. This culminated in its hostile, all-cash bid of $13 billion for YPF in 1999. Roberto Monti, chairman of YPF 'made clear his opposition to seeing YPF fall into the control of the Spanish company' (*FT*, 5 May 1999). However, the Argentinean government, which still held 5.3 per cent of the shares in the company, and three provincial governments with smaller stakes, as well as other private investors favoured accepting the offer: '*The deal is done. Everyone just wants their money*' (Christopher Ecclestone, of Buenos Aires Trust, quoted in *FT*, 5 May 1999, emphasis added).

By May 12, the board of YPF had conceded defeat. Having forcefully opposed the offer, Roberto Monti commented: 'The cash offer ensures just and equal treatment for all shareholders. *We have always maintained a business philosophy based on value creation*, and it is the board's view, which I back, that Repsol's bid offers the best alternative for our shareholders in current market conditions' (quoted in *FT*, 12 May 1999, emphasis added). The merged group will become the world's eighth largest oil company. YPF's take-over by Repsol, the largest ever by a Spanish company, underlines the commitment of Repsol to international expansion and its belief that size as well as effective management are crucial for long-term success in this rapidly changing industry. Following the announcement of the offer for YPF, Repsol was 'the star performer on the Madrid stock market as investors reacted enthusiastically to the company's Argentinean bid' (*FT*, 4 May 1999).

If China were to privatize its oil and petrochemical industry and accept the rules of the WTO, it is possible that within a short period, the core of the industry would have followed the logic of 'increasing shareholder value' and been bought by one or other of the global giants. Privatization and liberalization are inseparable from internationalization. Internationalization and liberalization under conditions of enormous inequality in the initial starting points, must mean essentially take-over of the weak by the strong. The results of such a path for China would mean an enormous improvement in the effectiveness with which the industry is run, large-scale investment in modern technology and a drastic change in management methods. It could produce social dislocation due to the speed and dramatic change in the nature of the institutions that might result. There might also be considerable tensions from the perceived 'take-over' of a 'strategic' Chinese industry by multinational giant companies. It is unlikely that such a path will be followed.

'Following the Guidance of the Market' (ii): Allowing Strong Chinese Companies to Grow Through Merger and Acquisition. We have seen that the enterprise reforms of the 1980s and 1990s had the result of fuelling the ambitions of large Chinese oil and petrochemical enterprises. For a long period it seemed that China's reforms in the sector were moving towards progressive fragmentation of the industry. The industry was divided into upstream and downstream segments. A group of powerful enterprises emerged with strong corporate ambitions, encouraged by policy makers' fears of a monopoly within each part of the industry. The corporate ambitions of the subordinate enterprises were fuelled by the confusion over property rights, with legal person status being granted to both the subordinate enterprises and the central holding company. Their ambitions were fuelled also by the enterprises' greatly increased autonomy in retaining profits, in issuing shares on international markets and in identifying and signing contracts with international joint venture partners. China's reforms in the sector had the desired effect of increased competition internally and a growing awareness of the requirements of the market economy. However, the level at which the 'firm' was emerging was relatively small scale.

This process culminated in a wave of mergers and take-overs in the late 1990s during the period of 'merger frenzy'. The most powerful enterprises in the Chinese oil and petrochemical industry, such as Daqing within CNPC and SPC within Sinopec, pursued their own plans for enhancing their independence from the holding companies in Beijing. They each wished to become the nucleus of powerful global giant companies based around their own self-expansion. We have seen that at one point they even discussed the possibility of merging and forming a single huge integrated company.

If China had followed this route, or reverts to it in the future, it has the large advantage that the core of the emerging companies had a powerful, ambitious leadership focused firmly on developing the company's core business. They wished only to merge with strong partners that could improve their performance and help them to face global competition. The core companies, notably Daqing and SPC, possessed a strong and growing sense of corporate identity and ambition. A striking feature of the transformation of the world's oil and petrochemical companies in the 1990s has been the importance of strong leaders with strong ambitions for their companies. These companies were led by ambitious people of this type, such as Ding Guiming at Daqing and Wu Yixin at SPC, and were surrounded by an ambitious management team. In these important senses, significant 'companies' already existed in China by the late 1990s. They had fought hard battles for autonomy and were ready to fight further battles to develop the capabilities of the companies they ran: '*A leader of a corporation such as ours should fight for our rights with Beijing.*'

However, this path also contains potential pitfalls. Without full-scale privatization, such a process of consolidation was likely to be slow and laborious. If rapid privatization of assets were to take place within the industry, then it would probably be accompanied by China joining the WTO. Under such a scenario, it is possible that multinational companies might rapidly increase their ownership of the Chinese industry, rather than domestic companies merging with domestic companies. The logic of shareholder value would make this hard to avoid. Already, six of China's main oil and petrochemical enterprises have negotiated separate major joint ventures with different multinational giants.

On the other hand, if privatization does not happen rapidly, and most assets in the industry remain under some form of public ownership, then it will be very hard for the emerging, ambitious companies like Daqing and SPC to take over major assets in the industry 'through the market', because there is not yet a real capital market in the oil and petrochemical industry. The problem for Daqing and SPC was not just opposition from the respective holding companies, but also the sheer practical difficulties of merging with other state-owned companies, in which a wide play of regional and local political and social interests operated. Time and again in discussing possible mergers with the aspiring giant Chinese oil and petrochemical companies one receives the answer: 'Local political difficulties surrounding the company we wished to merge with, prevented us taking over such-and-such a company that would have fitted closely with our own business.'

The fact is that by the late 1990s, not a single major cross-regional merger had taken place. Instead, the 'core' companies within each region had expanded through a laborious process of merger and acquisition involving a mixture of bureaucratic and market means, often being forced to take over loss-making companies as the only route to growth. In the steel industry, the major companies merged with smaller entities, but the leading players, Shougang, Angang, and Baogang remained independent of each other. In the automobile industry, each of the giant companies, Yiqi, Erqi and Shanghai absorbed a wide range of second tier suppliers, but did not merge with each other. Meanwhile, within the advanced capitalist economies, massive mergers of 'strong with strong' were taking place through the market in these and other sectors.

There is a further major danger with this route. We have seen from the example of Daqing, that in the absence of the possibility to grow rapidly by merging with 'strong' players within the sector, there is instead a strong incentive to grow through the development of 'diversified business' (*duo zhong jing ying*). This still further weakens large Chinese firms in their capability to compete in their core business with the global giants.

China urgently needs to restructure. It cannot afford a strategy that will take a long time if it is to construct competitive firms rapidly. The choices of China's central policy makers in the late 1990s were strongly influenced by the revolution that was taking place around them in the global oil and petrochemical business, as well as by the looming possibility of China joining the WTO.

Building Strong Firms Through Administrative Means

The decisive shift in government policy. We have seen that the Chinese policy makers decisively rejected the attempt by strong individual enterprises to build powerful companies with themselves as the core. The door to such a path appeared to open during the period of 'merger frenzy' that affected the Chinese oil and petrochemicals industry in 1996–97. However, the central government policy makers decisively closed the door with the dramatic restructuring undertaken in 1998. The move is of extreme importance for the whole course of China's enterprise reform. It marks also a deeply important episode in the history of industrial policy in developing countries. The move shows a deep determination by China's policy makers to mould rapidly through administrative means, business institutions that are a serious match for the global giants in terms of their scale and scope. Instead of the multinational giant's large joint ventures being with increasingly autonomous companies, the multinational's Chinese partners have been subsumed within one or two giant entities committed to building unified large state firms. The shape of the multinational's partners appears to have altered drastically.

The struggle to centralize power. It would be naïve to imagine that the decision to restructure the industry in this way, rather than through the development of emerging strong companies such as Daqing and SPC, was unrelated to the interests of the headquarters of CNPC and Sinopec. It would be disingenuous to pretend that the process was not accompanied by intense political struggle. The process is analogous to the centralization of power in the early modern state that broke down the decentralized power of feudal lords. If China wishes to build globally competitive companies through administrative means there is no alternative to such centralization, and all the power struggles that are involved. A decentralized 'feudal' company cannot compete with the global giants.

The restructuring of 1998 and 1999 was accompanied by widespread replacement by the headquarters of key leadership personnel in powerful subordinate companies such as Daqing and SPC. Such struggle is not unique to Chinese companies. Large-scale institutional change in large capitalist companies has also typically involved intense struggles between different management groups. Major international mergers are more often than not accompanied by, or soon followed by, widespread 'blood-letting' at the corporate headquarters. The massive shake-up at the head of Daimler–Chrysler in September 1999 is just the latest example of a widespread phenomenon accompanying the 1990s merger boom. Of the original five-strong senior executive team of Chrysler three had lost their jobs by September 1999 (*FT*, 25 September 1999).

The restructuring was accompanied also by a strong attempt to recentralize financial control in the hands of the headquarters. The most powerful of the subordinate entities are extremely strong institutions, and this process is far from complete. However, the central government appears to have firmly backed this endeavour. There are clear signs from the subordinate enterprises that the degree of headquarters control over key financial matters increased during the period of restructuring. If the headquarters of the new institutions are able successfully to centralize control, the new institutions need then to put into place new mechanisms of restructuring which create business units that can be subject to the intense pressure of scrutiny and monitoring from the corporate headquarters. This will enable the restructured companies to benefit from intense pressure and scrutiny from the headquarters while providing operational autonomy for the business units.

Can 'administrative methods' build successful large firms? The view is widely expressed both inside and outside the oil industry in China that CNPC and Sinopec are still essentially 'government organs', despite the external restructuring and apparent increase in autonomy from the state. Such views typically note the origins of Sinopec and CNPC in the former ministerial structures. In this view, the 1998 restructuring created simply the outward appearance of global giants. In this view the only way in which to build powerful globally competitive companies is 'through the market'.

However, the evidence of history suggests that it is possible to build a competitive company through administrative means. There are important examples of government mediated mergers forming the basis for a subsequently powerful global corporation.

British Aerospace, today a global giant in aerospace, was formed through an Act of Parliament (The Aircraft and Shipbuilding Industries Act, 1977) which brought together the British Aircraft Corporation, Hawker Siddeley Dynamics, and the Scottish Aviation Corporation, to form a nationalized corporation, British Aerospace. British Steel (now Corus) and Usinor, now both global leaders in the steel industry, were each formed by their respective government's wishes to build 'national champions'. Each of them was formed from the merger of several smaller private companies into a single powerful state-owned company. It is questionable if any of these companies, all of which were subsequently privatized, would have even existed without state-led merger and acquisition. A key part of this process of turning these companies into competitive global giants was the state's willingness at a certain point to appoint strong managers to whom genuine operational authority was delegated by the state. For example, British Steel was radically turned around, several years before privatization, under Ian MacGregor. Usinor was dramatically turned around after 1986, a decade before privatization, under the charismatic leadership of Francis Mer.

The formation of the Airbus consortium owed almost everything to government intervention and the wish of the respective national governments to build a 'European champion' in this strategic industry. In this case, the formation of a potential global giant came about from the even more unlikely source of inter-government co-operation to build a completely new institution. From a textbook perspective, the company ought not to work, since Airbus is deeply hamstrung by the commitment to divide work among the partners in proportion to their share of the ownership of the company. Moreover, for part of its life, two of the three main partners were state-owned companies (Aerospatiale and BAe), and one of them is still partially state-owned today (Aerospatiale–Matra). Despite the institutional peculiarities, Airbus has grown from nothing to challenge the world leader, Boeing, in an industry in which catch-up is more difficult than in almost any other.

More recently, in the recent round of European mergers in the oil and petrochemicals industry, various governments have played a key role in deciding the direction of mergers and acquisitions. The French and Italian governments have played, and are still playing, a central role in the process of merger and acquisition. The French government used its right of veto through its 'golden share' in Elf Aquitaine, to ensure that Elf merged with TotalFina rather than a foreign oil company. It was even suggested that the resulting company should be called 'French Oil'. As we have seen, there is a strong possibility that the merged Elf/Fina company may merge with Italy's partially-privatized ENI. The respective governments are heavily involved in the process.

In Norway, the government is likely to play a central role in restructuring the powerful Norwegian oil and gas industry. The government holds 100 per cent of Statoil, held 51 per cent of Hydro and through the State Direct Financial Interest (SDFI), managed by Statoil, owned 40 per cent of Norway's offshore reserves. The Norwegian government dominates the Norwegian oil industry. It is widely accepted in Norway that the industry needs to be privatized and restructured in order to meet the intense competition from the global industry. Rather than just privatize the industry passively, it is likely that the government will merge SDFI with Statoil. This will treble the size of Statoil, creating the world's fourth largest quoted oil company by size of reserves. The merger will 'give the company the critical mass necessary to compete for capital in the increasingly competitive market and pursue an aggressive international exploration strategy ... In addition the combination would create a leading gas supplier to Europe ... giving it the potential to integrate with downstream gas markets' (*FT*, 23 September 1999). Only after the restructuring is it thought possible that the Norwegian government will consider even partial privatization of the company.

In sum, government intervention in large-scale industrial restructuring is not unique to China. Nor have the long-term results of such intervention always been disadvantageous to the creation of globally powerful companies. Indeed, without such intervention, many of the world's most competitive firms would not exist. The mere fact that the restructuring of CNPC and Sinopec has occurred through administrative means rather than through the market does not guarantee that the resulting institutions will be uncompetitive. However, the foregoing analysis demonstrates that a great deal of work remains to be done if these institutions are to truly rival the world's leading companies in their institutional capability.

Flexibility for future restructuring. An important aspect of the method of restructuring that has been chosen is that it leaves open the door for still further restructuring through the state. The government will still be the majority owner of each of the three main oil and petrochemical companies after the flotations of 1999–2000. It is quite possible for the central policy makers to combine the three entities (CNPC, Sinopec and CNOOC) into a single company at a stroke in the same way that the reorganization of 1998–99 has taken place. China would then have a company that would have a larger oil and gas production than any publicly quoted company with the exception of Exxon Mobil (Table 7-28).

WHERE IS CHINESE GOVERNMENT POLICY GOING?

Taken in isolation, the Chinese government's decision to reorganize dramatically most of the country's oil and petrochemical business into two giant integrated companies, would appear to indicate that the central government has made a decisive shift in policy. However, such a view would be incorrect. As we have seen, alongside the massive restructuring of the oil and petrochemical industry has gone an equally dramatic restructuring of the aerospace industry. This restructuring has gone in the opposite direction to that of the oil and petrochemical sector.

The sharply different paths of restructuring in the oil and petrochemical industry on the one hand, and the aerospace industry on the other, suggests that the Chinese government is still groping for a philosophy with which to reorganize its large-scale, mainly state-owned industries. The current restructuring of the world's aerospace industry is still in a highly dynamic phase, with the final institutional shape very far from clear. Similarly, the Chinese oil and petrochemical industry may be far from a structure that is likely to endure for a long time to come. The fact that the industry makes three large-scale IPOs on international markets in no way commits the associated institutional structure to permanence, any more than the flotations of Elf or ENI have done.

8

Autos and Auto Components

Regarding the numerous challenges that China will face on its entry to the WTO, including SOE reform, foreign exchange, banking, information technology, foreign trade, and human rights, China should take this one-shot gamble in relation to these challenges that result from the country's complete opening up to the outside world. No matter what, China must take this gamble.
(Zhang Wuchang, 2000)

People are the foundation;
strive to be number one;
start every day from scratch.
(Wang Jianming, CEO, Yuchai)

Wield one's arm to attack by showing no arm to lift,
Face the enemy by showing no enemy to attack,
Hold weapons by showing no weapon to hold,
No disaster is greater than underestimating the enemy.
(Lao Zi, *The book of Dao and De*)

INTRODUCTION

The main body of China's emerging large indigenous firms in the 1980s and 1990s has come from initially large state-owned enterprises (SOEs), such as Shougang Iron and Steel Company, Shanghai Petrochemical Company, and Harbin Power Equipment Company. However, a small number of large firms has emerged in a different way. These firm have both advantages and disadvantages in relation to the initially large SOEs. This chapter examines one striking case, Yuchai Diesel Engine Company in Yulin City, Guangxi Province. In the mid-1980s Yuchai was a struggling medium-sized SOE, ranked 173rd largest engine maker in China by value of sales. By the mid-1990s, led by a dynamic chief executive officer, Wang Jianming, it had risen to be the largest diesel engine manufacturer in the country. In 1995 Yuchai accounted for around 49 per cent of the total market for engines installed in medium-duty trucks in China. Within two years, Yuchai had encountered severe difficulties and by the summer of 1997 it had no production at all for months on end.

This chapter attempts to discover the factors that accounted for the rapid rise and fall of Yuchai. It concludes that the path to growth chosen by Yuchai left it highly vulnerable in its competitive struggle with large domestic enterprises, typically large former SOEs, which had occupied dominant positions in the old command economy. It also faced fast-growing competition from the emerging multinational giants in the automobile component sector who were rapidly increasing their investment in China, often in the form of joint ventures with large former SOEs. The experience of Yuchai demonstrates the great reservoir of entrepreneurial talent in China, capable of manifesting itself powerfully even in a geographically remote area. It also shows the great difficulty that new entrants in China face in competing with the established giants from the old planning system, who form the heart of China's emerging big business system, and with the rapidly-growing multinational companies.

THE GLOBAL CONTEXT

The object of study in this chapter is a remotely located Chinese diesel engine maker. To reach it one must first take either a long plane ride from Beijing, or a rather shorter one from Guangzhou, to Nanning in Guangxi province, in southwest China. There follows an eight-hour journey across back-breaking roads to Yulin City. This is a deeply impoverished area, with rutted streets and few amenities of modern urban life. Yulin City is essentially a huge, poor village. Yuchai grew up in this location, remote both geographically and culturally from the mainstream of global economic life. However, Yuchai's evolution was powerfully shaped by remote forces, including not only those within the fast-changing Chinese automobile industry, but also, closely connected to the revolution in the world's automobile and components industry. The following section outlines some of the key forces at work in the global economy which affect Yuchai's evolution, and which shed light on the path that China's automobile and components industry may follow as the Chinese industry becomes increasingly integrated with the global economy.

AUTOMOBILES

The Traditional Industry

Economic determinants of industrial structure. The traditional auto industry was characterized by large economies of scale (Table 8-1). Building a new model involves large investment in new dies for body stampings, as well as fixed costs incurred in design, fabrication and extensive testing of prototypes, tooling to produce new engines and other major drive components, and in some cases

TABLE **8-1 Minimum Efficient Scale in Different Parts of the Auto Industry**

Activity	Volume Required to Achieve Minimum Unit Costs
Casting engine blocks	1 million
Casting other parts	100 000–750 000
Power train machining/assembly	600 000
Axle making/assembly	500 000
Pressing various panels	1–2 million
Painting	250 000
Final assembly	250 000
Advertising	1 million
Finance	2–5 million
R & D	5 million

SOURCE: Rhys (1989), quoted in Dicken (1992: 280)

investments in new plants. A major source of such economies is the high initial tooling costs involved in producing a new model. In the 1990s, these considerations still applied. Scherer estimates that the cost per vehicle falls from $7000 at volumes below 100 000 to $1400 at 500 000. Cost per vehicle continues to fall beyond this level, reaching as little as $140 per vehicle at volumes over five million (Scherer, 1996: 293). Scherer notes: 'If total model cycle sales number only the few hundreds of thousands, a severe cost penalty is incurred' (Scherer, 1996: 293). The massive economies in high volume production of stamped parts from a set of extensive dies is so compelling that it forms a major part of the incentive for auto manufacturers today to try to build common body platforms for 'global' vehicles.

There are several other aspects of economies of scale in the auto industry. There are large advantages to having dealerships spread throughout a given market. Such distributional advantages were found in the USA to increase up to annual volumes of two million vehicles (Scherer, 1996: 296). Despite great investment in development programmes, large mistakes can be made in auto design. Large firms are far better able than small ones to withstand such mistakes. Major styling mistakes caused the demise of a number of smaller players in the US auto market (Scherer, 1996: 295).

Automobile companies have long been at the forefront of R & D spending. Large auto companies are able to devote far larger sums to R & D than smaller firms, and are able to achieve considerable benefits by spreading research costs over a greater output (Pratten, 1971: 147). Large companies often derive benefit from greater consumer confidence. For most people, a car purchase is a major decision, and brand reputation and reliability are important factors determining choice. Building brand reputation has always been important for auto firms. Large auto companies are able to spend far larger amounts on marketing, and there is evidence of substantial scale economies in advertising (Scherer, 1996: 294).

Whether auto firms make or buy components there are large benefits from greater volumes. If firms make a given component, then they can often benefit from economies of scale in production. In so far as auto firms have elected to buy in the components that they need, then they typically can make large gains through procurement of larger quantities of any given component, enabling them to obtain a lower price than smaller auto firms.

State intervention and industrial structure. Government intervention played an important role in the evolution of the industry at a global level. Within Europe, the French, German and Italian states each provided extensive support for domestic 'national champions', believing that the industry was a key driver of wider economic progress. Without extensive state support, major parts of the European auto industry would simply not exist, and much of it might have grown much less rapidly, or even been wiped out in open international competition.

Germany's 'national champion', Volkswagen, was established in 1937 by the Hitler government (Ruigrok and van Tulder, 1995). It grew rapidly to meet military needs during the Second World War. After the war it began production of the vehicle that became a symbol of national regeneration, the 'people's car', or Volkswagen 'beetle'. Volkswagen was entirely state-owned until 1960. As late as 1990 it was owned 20 per cent by the Federal government and 20 per cent by the Lower Saxony government. It received substantial state support through a variety of subsidies during its development. Only after Volkswagen had become one of the world's leading auto companies did the process of privatization begin.

Between the First and Second World Wars, Italy's auto industry benefited greatly from tariff protection (Ruigrok and van Tulder, 1995). Fiat benefited greatly from tariff protection between the wars. Domestic production accounted for 80 per cent of all cars sold in Italy in this period. In the post-war period, Italy continued to heavily protect its car industry, with tariffs of around 30 per cent in the 1950s. When the threat of imports from the major Japanese makers appeared, the Italian government imposed a 'strict and low' quota on Japanese imports, totalling just 1800 vehicles per year until 1992. Fiat was a major beneficiary of location subsidies to site plants in southern Italy.

Renault was nationalized under de Gaulle for Nazi collaborations during French occupation by Germany (Ruigrok and van Tulder, 1995). It remained a state-owned firm for most of the period since 1945, receiving extensive state subsidies. It developed in the 1950s behind high tariff barriers. In the 1980s it benefited greatly from government import restrictions that limited Japanese imports to just 3 per cent of the domestic market. A new chief executive officer, Louis Schweitzer, was appointed in 1991. By 1999, he had led a dramatic turnaround in the company's performance, establishing it as one of the lowest-cost producers in the world auto industry. Privatization only began in 1994, and even then the state's share did not fall below 50 per cent until 1996 (*FT*, 20 February 1998). In 1999 the French state still owned 44 per cent of Renault.

Japan's 'catch-up' in automobile production is one of the most dramatic examples of government-led industrial policy in the modern world. It has exerted considerable impact on the thinking of the Chinese government in shaping its ambitions and policy goals, not only in autos, but also in industrial policy generally.

In the 1920s and 1930s car production in Japan was dominated by Ford and General Motors, who occupied around 90 per cent of the total market. Under strong pressure from the army, the government licensed just two domestic firms, Toyota and Nissan, to make automobiles, and simultaneously outlawed car imports and foreign car production in Japan. Toyota and Nissan grew rapidly under the impact of huge government procurement demand. After 1945, under US occupation, import controls were drastically weakened. The domestic car industry faced certain destruction as imports flooded the market in the early 1950s. The government responded by erecting a 'barrage of import barriers', including outright prohibition of most types of car imports and high tariffs. The share of imports fell from 45 per cent in 1951 to just 1 per cent in 1960 (Nester, 1991: 103).

MITI played a key role in upgrading motor industry technology in the 1950s by bargaining with foreign producers to establish short period joint ventures during which technology was transferred over a few years and the joint venture was then terminated (Nester, 1991: 104–5).[1] MITI supported the growth of a small number of oligopolistic 'national champions': by 1970 Toyota and Nissan between them accounted for over 65 per cent of national vehicle sales (Nester, 1991: 107). Huge firms were established, gaining massively from economies of scale, with a comprehensive programme of government indirect support, and based mainly on the domestic market. Only then did Japan's car producers attempt to conquer world markets[2] and were there moves to liberalize imports (Nester, 1991: 113). Right through into the 1990s there was 'a bewildering web of non-tariff barriers' (Nester, 1991: 108). Japan's rise to global power in this industry was remarkable. As late as 1960, it still produced only 165 000 vehicles, and accounted for only 1.3 per cent of the world total output. By 1980 vehicle output had risen to nine million and its share of world vehicle output had risen to 26 per cent (Dicken, 1998: 319).

Following closely the Japanese approach, the South Korean government powerfully supported the growth of a large-scale indigenously-owned auto industry. It specified three main producers, Hyundai, Kia and Daewoo that would form the pillar of the industry. Its 1974 plan had as its objective the achievement of 90 per cent domestic self-sufficiency in components for small passenger cars by the end of the 1970s, and to turn the industry into a major exporter by the early 1980s. The government's measures of industrial policy support included strict protection against imports and limits on foreign investment, approval of expansion plans of the different domestic producers, a promotional plan for the domestic components industry, export targets for the three big producers, and large export subsidies (Dicken, 1998: 348). A major consequence of high levels of protection alongside indigenization, and domestic production that was still relatively small was that Korea's components makers were typically relatively small-scale (FT, 1 March 1999).

The strategy was highly successful in some senses. By 1986, just a decade after the plan was devised, Hyundai was already exporting 300 000 vehicles. By 1994 it had become the world's thirteenth largest auto producer, with an output of 900 000 vehicles. It had established a plant in Canada (producing 120 000 vehicles per year), and was planning to build plants in Turkey, India, Eastern Europe and Vietnam (Dicken, 1998: 349). During the Asian crisis it bought Kia Motors, the third largest Korean car maker. Through the takeover, Hyundai acquired the joint venture that Kia had established in China at Yangchen. Hyundai announced plans to expand capacity at the plant to 150 000 vehicles by 2002 eventually rising to 300 000 vehicles per year (*FT*, 27 January 2000). Its total world-wide output in 2000 is predicted to be around 2.8 million vehicles, with a target of 4 million vehicles by 2010, making Hyundai one of the world's top five car makers (*FT*, 27 January 2000).

Alongside Hyundai, Daewoo also grew at high speed with powerful state support. Daewoo had the ambition to become one of the world's top 10 auto firms (Dicken, 1998: 349). It initially developed as a 50/50 joint venture with GM and was closely integrated into the global GM system. This arrangement did not endure and GM exited from the venture. By 1999 Daewoo had built four major plants within Korea, with a total capacity of 1.4 million vehicles (Daewoo website). Daewoo rapidly built up its overseas operations, acquiring five Eastern European auto makers in the 1990s. They had a total capacity of 650 000 vehicles by 1999, more than the entire Chinese auto industry in the late 1990s. In addition, Daewoo acquired car makers in India, Iran and Egypt. Its overseas operation had a production capacity of 830 000 vehicles by 1999, and its world-wide capacity totalled around 2.2 million vehicles.

By the late 1990s, Korea's total car capacity from plants within Korea and in foreign plants of Korean companies had reached around 4.2 million, around eight times the total capacity of China's auto industry. However, compared with the other major car manufacturing countries, Korea had a substantial weakness in the shape of the relatively small size of the domestic market. Car sales in the peak year of 1996 were only 1.5 million vehicles (*FT*, 25 January 2000).

Institutional structure and change. In the early days of the automobile industry, there were scores of manufacturers each producing a narrow range of vehicles for national markets. In 1920, for example, there were more than 80 automobile manufacturers in the USA, more than 150 in France, 40 in the UK and more than 30 in Italy (Dicken, 1992: 289). However, from early on the industry's structure was strongly affected by the existence of the large economies of scale outlined above. As early as 1921, the Ford Motor Company alone accounted for 56 per cent of US production of passenger cars, though it was later to relinquish this dominant position to General Motors (Chandler, 1990: 205). Moreover, in the inter-war period, rapid concentration of production occurred in each of the leading producing countries. Already, by 1938, the top three firms accounted for 56 per cent of national car output in Britain, 75 per cent in Germany, and 85 per cent in the USA (Prais, 1981: 154). In Japan, the top two firms grew rapidly, with strong government support, and by 1940, Toyota and Nissan accounted for 85 per cent of total output, with Isuzu producing most of the rest (Nester, 1991: 101). The process of concentration continued, so that by the late 1980s, the top four firms accounted for 88–100 per cent of national output in each of the major automobile producing countries (Dicken, 1992: 289). In France and Sweden only two companies produced the entire national output of cars. In Italy one firm alone, Fiat, was totally dominant.

The auto industry has been at the heart of the twentieth century business structure. In the 1990s, the industry directly employed around 3–4 million people world-wide, and a further 9–10 million in the manufacture of materials and components. If one adds the numbers involved in selling and servicing the vehicles, then a total of around 20 million people is employed in this sector. It is a sector with high outlays on R & D. The top twelve firms in the sector each have outlays of over $1 billion, rising to almost $8 billion for the global leader, General Motors (DTI, 1999: 51). The leading firms are giant corporations. By the early 1990s, twelve of the top 50 *Fortune* 500 companies were auto firms.

Autos in the Epoch of the Global Business Revolution
Drivers of industry change
Widening of the scope of the market. The growing scope and impact of the GATT and its successor body, the WTO, progressively reduced the scope for trade protection and limits on international capital flows among the advanced economies. The creation of an integrated European market stimulated trade and capital flows across national boundaries. It also contributed to the erosion of former conceptions of firms that were supported as 'national champions'.

For much of the period since the Second World War, large parts of the world were either excluded from international trade and investment in autos or operated with large restrictions on multinational companies. In the 1990s, this altered sharply. The whole of the former Communist world opened to multinational trade and investment. Large parts of the developing world radically altered rules on foreign investment and liberalized imports. Rapid growth rates in East Asia for much of the 1990s changed perceptions of the future regional balance of the auto marketplace. It was predicted that by 2001, 'emerging markets' would overtake Western Europe, and account for around 30 per cent of total world sales (Table 8-2).

By the late 1990s, developing countries accounted for a significant part of world demand for both trucks and saloon vehicles (Table 8-3). There were prospects for

TABLE 8-2 Projected Growth of World Automobile Markets, 1995–2001

| | 1995 | | 2001 | | % Change |
Market	(million)	(%)	(million)	(%)	(1995–2001)
World	47.7	100	58.5	100	23
North America*	16.0	33.5	18.1	30.9	13
Japan	6.7	14.1	7.0	12.0	4
Western Europe	13.3	27.9	16.1	27.5	21
Emerging Markets	11.7	24.5	17.3	29.6	48

SOURCE: *FT* (13 May 1996)

NOTE: * USA, Canada, and Mexico

TABLE 8-3 **Global Production and Sales of Automobiles, 1998**

Region/Country	Sales		Output	
	(million)	*(%)*	*(million)*	*(%)*
Western Europe	14.4	39.2	15.2	39.2
Eastern Europe	1.9	5.2	2.3	5.9
NAFTA	9.3	25.4	7.9	20.3
of which:				
USA	(8.1)	(22.1)	5.5	(14.2)
Latin America	2.1	5.7	1.7	4.4
of which:				
Brazil	(1.2)	(3.3)	1.2	(3.1)
Asia	6.5	17.7	11.2	28.9
of which:				
Japan	(4.1)	(11.2)	8.1	(2.6)
Korea	(0.6)	(1.6)	1.6	(4.1)
China	(0.5)	(1.4)	0.5	(1.3)
India	(0.5)	(1.4)	0.5	(1.3)
Middle East	0.9	2.5	0.2	0.5
Africa	1.0	2.7	—	—
Oceania/Australia	0.6	1.6	0.3	0.8
World	36.7	100.0	38.8	100.0

SOURCE: *FT* (16 September 1999)

NOTE: Subtotals in brackets

strong demand growth in developing countries (Tables 8-2 and 8-4). In the 1990s, the world's leading firms rapidly increased their investment in production facilities within developing countries. For example, in India, liberalization in the 1990s saw a 'deluge' of foreign vehicle investment. By 1996, Hyundai, Daewoo, Mercedes, Ford, Peugeot, Fiat, General Motors, and Honda had all either established or begun to build plants (mainly joint ventures) to build their vehicles in India (*FT*, 5 March 1996). In Southeast Asia, Thailand is regarded as the region's motor manufacturing hub. By 1997, General Motors, Ford, Mazda, Honda, Mitsubishi and Nissan had each set up plants in Thailand, with an eventual combined capacity of around 1 million vehicles (*FT*, 24 March 1997). Despite the much smaller total market size, Turkey's liberalization in the 1990s saw the entry of Toyota, Renault, Hyundai, Honda, Fiat, and Kia, with Daihatsu also considering setting up a plant (*FT*, 28 October 1997). In Mercosur (Brazil, Argentina, Paraguay and Uruguay). Ford, General Motors and Volkswagen have long been the region's leading car makers, with a secure base in Brazil, much the region's largest market, since the 1950s. In the 1990s, alongside continued expansion by the established global giants, Chrysler, Renault, Fiat, Toyota, and Honda all announced plans to expand production in the region (*FT*, 2 August 1996). After the fall of the Communist regimes in Eastern Europe in 1989, Volkswagen, Fiat, General Motors, Renault,

TABLE 8-4 World Truck Sales, 1995 and 2005 (000 Vehicles)

Region/Country	1995		2005		
	(000)	(%)	(000)	(%)	% Change
NAFTA	421	26.6	508	27.9	20.7
Western Europe	254	16.0	302	16.6	18.9
Asia Pacific	707	44.6	726	39.9	2.7
Eastern Europe	91	5.7	126	6.9	38.5
South America	82	5.2	105	5.8	28.0
Other	30	1.9	53	2.9	76.7
World	1585	100.0	1820	100.0	14.7

SOURCE: *FT* (3 December 1999)

TABLE 8-5 Internationalization of World's Largest Automobile Companies, 1997; Foreign Assets, Sales and Employment as a Percentage of Total

Company	Foreign Assets	Foreign Sales	Foreign Employment
Ford	26.5	31.2	47.8
General Motors	—	28.9	—
Toyota	39.8	56.9	—
Volkswagen	—	65.7	47.9
Daimler–Benz	40.6	66.8	25.0
Fiat	43.0	39.9	39.3
Nissan	45.8	55.9	—
Honda	58.9	69.4	—
BMW	63.8	75.3	44.1
Renault	52.4	52.0	32.6
Peugeot	41.9	51.6	22.9

SOURCE: UNCTAD (1999: 78–9)

and Daewoo all set up wholly-owned or majority-owned joint ventures with former state-owned enterprises in the region (*FT*, 5 March 1996).

In the 1990s, the share of international production in total output of the global auto giants greatly increased. By 1997, the world's leading auto producers had around two-fifths of their assets located abroad, over one-half of their sales abroad and close to one-half of their employment located abroad (Table 8-5).

Impact of global competition on manufacturers' costs. As the marketplace moved to a global scale, so the level of marketing expenditure required to compete effectively grew rapidly. Brands now had to be developed on a truly global scale. Instead of using a national campaign with national advertisers, campaigns needed to be global. Moreover, there are, as we have seen, considerable economies of scale, so massive global vehicle firms not only were able to mobilize greater resources for global campaigns building global brands, but were able to do so more efficiently than smaller auto firms. For example, global car companies are able to advertise on prime time global broadcasts, buying huge 'volumes' of advertising at much lower costs per unit than smaller auto firms.

As global competition deepened and intensified, so the need to develop new vehicles more quickly intensified. Moreover, growing environmental legislation greatly stimulated the need to develop more environmentally friendly vehicles, forcing such processes as lightweighting through new metallurgical technologies. The constant pressure to meet consumer demands for greater safety further spurred on technical developments. Consequently, the development costs of new vehicles rose inexorably. By the late 1990s, R & D outlays of the major auto companies exceeded those of most other industrial categories. In 1998 twenty-five of the world's largest spenders on R & D were auto firms, with an average R & D spend of $1.7 billion (DTI, 1999: 51). The top five auto producers in 1998, GM, Ford, Daimler–Chrysler, Toyota and VW, each spent between $3.4 billion and $7.6 billion. This greatly exceeds that of even high-technology firms such as Boeing, which spent $1.9 billion. The only sector with greater R & D expenditures is IT hardware.

Japanese competition and the global industry. We have seen that the rise of the Japanese auto industry was strongly supported by the state. Behind protectionist barriers, the Japanese industry was able to develop powerful economies of scale producing for the large domestic market, with explicit state support for a small number of oligopolistic firms. However, a further powerful influence on Japanese competitiveness in the auto industry was the distinctive form of business organization developed within this industry. In the 1970s, the competitiveness of Japanese auto firms rapidly moved ahead of European and US auto firms. Japanese auto firms 'used fewer labor hours to assemble vehicles, carried lower (*kanban* or 'just-in-time') inventories, designed new models more quickly, and were unencumbered by much smaller managerial hierarchies' (Scherer, 1996: 322). Japanese auto firms emphasized the 'lean production' philosophy. This included especially, delegating much more responsibility to their workers for ensuring that high quality vehicles rolled off the production line. In the extreme case of the 'just-in-time' system at Toyota, the process was greatly facilitated by the close physical proximity of the network of suppliers in or around a single city, literally 'Toyota City' (Koromo) (Cusumano, 1985).

In both the USA and Europe, Japanese companies started to make large inroads into the market share of domestic firms. The share of foreign production in the total output of Toyota rose from 8 per cent in 1989 to 18 per cent in 1994. That of Nissan rose from 14 per cent to 33 per cent in the same period, while that of Honda rose from 28 per cent to 42 per cent (Dicken, 1998: 336–7). The fast increase in market share was a major reason behind the crisis in the US auto industry in the early 1980s. In the 1980s, each of the big four reported losses and in 1982 Chrysler was on the brink of bankruptcy, saved only by a US government loan guarantee (Scherer, 1996: 313). The response of the auto industry in the USA and Europe was, on the one hand, to lobby successfully the respective government to impose heavy 'voluntary restrictions' on exports from Japan, and on the other hand, they set about drastically altering their production methods in order to learn from the Japanese. The main response from the Japanese firms was greatly to increase their production capabilities within the USA and Europe.

The impact of the rise of the Japanese auto industry was ultimately greatly to intensify the forces of inter-firm competition at the global level.

Globalization of outsourcing. In their search to meet the intensifying global competition, the USA and European auto firms radically reorganized their whole procurement system. They were greatly assisted in this by the revolutionary changes that took place in information technology in the 1990s. Using the new technology, the major auto producers massively reorganized their production processes. Prior to the revolution of the 1990s, leading Western vehicle makers bought in around one-half the total value of total components.[3] In the 1990s, that proportion sharply increased, so that the major auto makers have essentially become the orchestrators of the value chain. Rather than producing a large fraction of components, their function has become one of designing and financing new models, undertaking R & D, in which meeting increasingly severe environmental demands has become more and more important, marketing including crucial activities of brand development, and exercising control of the distribution system. Even the assembly function is undergoing large-scale change, with large segments of car bodies increasingly being assembled by first tier components suppliers. These changes closely parallel those taking place in the aerospace industry. In each case, independent first tier suppliers increasingly assemble major sub-systems. Only final assembly is undertaken by the core global firm. One can speak of a process of globalization of the Japanese auto industry's 'just-in-time', 'lean production' system.

In the USA, Chrysler pioneered this process, setting up a department led by Tom Stallkamp, Chrysler's 'Mr Procurement' (*FT*, 19 January 1998). GM followed suit. In 1992 it replaced 27 separate purchasing units across the world with a single central purchasing department, in order to 'focus its buying power'. This self-styled 'extended enterprise' enabled a reduction in costs through benefits from economies of scale among suppliers. At least as important, it devolved development and manufacturing work to suppliers, which enabled auto assemblers to benefit from shortened product development times and cut the cost of bringing new vehicles to market.

The value chain for globalizing core firms is extremely long, extending down through first, second and third tier suppliers and into the extended system of distribution and retailing. Alongside a sharp compression in the number of first tier suppliers for a typical global corporation, the number of second and third tier suppliers has increased greatly as the process of outsourcing has accelerated. For example, the Ford Motor Company has a direct procurement spend of around $80 billion. However, its extended supply chain involves a total spend of around $300 billion, with a total of over 30 000 suppliers involved in direct and indirect sales to the company (*FT*, 8 November 1999). Ford's vast global supply network is in the process of being linked through an internet trading exchange.

Aligned suppliers. A major development in the 1990s has been the attempt to push down production costs by actively encouraging the growth of a relatively small group of globally 'aligned' first tier suppliers. These are able to meet the needs of globalizing auto firms across the world. They can supply a homogeneous product to a given auto firm's plants in many different locations, creating a form of 'global Toyotism'. These firms are able to benefit from economies of scale, higher R & D expenditure, and are themselves able to organize their own 'external firm' in the form of a surrounding group of first and second tier suppliers. A crucial part of the competitive advantage of globally successful auto companies is the possession of an ability to integrate the global value chain. This requires high quality management skills and massive investment in information technology to link the information flows up and down the value chain.

Extending the value chain beyond car manufacture. It is estimated that the average lifetime spending on a car is around $120 000, of which only around $35 000 is spent on the initial purchase of the vehicle. A major development in the late 1990s was the determination of the world's leading auto makers to begin to penetrate deeper into the value chain in the search for sales revenue. This was symbolized by Ford's purchase of the UK's Kwik-Fit vehicle repair business for $1 billion. Ford intends to transform itself into a 'consumer services company specializing in the automotive sector' (Jacques Nasser, Ford's chief executive officer, quoted in *FT*, 16 September 1999). This means that Ford will benchmark itself against the leading players in all industries, not just the automotive sector. It means that Ford will involve itself deeply in all aspects of sales and after-sales service: 'By going right down into the customer service areas we have a real chance of forging one-on-one relationships with our customers, which can result in long-term loyalty to Ford Group' (Ford spokesman, quoted in *FT*, 16 September 1999).

Industrial Structure: Autos. We have seen that in the 1990s, the world auto industry entered a period of dramatically increased competition on a global scale. More than ever before, competitive advantage required scale, to benefit from economies in product design, speed of product development, economies in large-scale global procurement, world-wide marketing capability, and investment in supply chain management to co-ordinate the 'external firm'. The sharp intensification of pressure resulted in important changes in the industry's institutional structure. The economic logic pointed strongly to the need for large-scale mergers. However, the auto industry is a large-scale employer both directly and indirectly. This meant that national governments were extremely reluctant to support mergers that could lead to cost cutting through capacity reduction. By 1996, capacity utilization in the global industry had fallen to 78 per cent (*FT*, 8 May 1998). Mooted mergers between the largest European firms were fiercely resisted by unions and discouraged by national governments fearful of the socio-economic results.

Alliances. One response to the rising intensity of global competition was to develop alliances to share costs of R & D, vehicle development and to source or produce key components in common. A 'veritable spider's web of strategic alliances' developed, forming 'a web which stretches across the globe' (Dicken, 1992: 291).

All three leading US firms forged collaborative links with Japanese manufacturers. For example, GM has an alliance with Isuzu, taking a 39 per cent ownership share in the company. It established joint ventures with both Toyota and Suzuki to build small cars in North America (Dicken, 1998: 337). In 1996 Ford took its ownership share in Mazda to 33 per cent, sending a 'shudder through the Japanese business community' (*FT*, 4 February 1999). In 1997, Ford and Mazda agreed to 'synchronize production cycles of a large number of vehicles and to share platforms and powertrains (engines and transmissions) ... The measures would allow the two to share design and engineering expertise and free resources to create a variety of products' (*FT*, 18 April 1997). Honda had a long-standing relationship with Rover to produce cars in the UK.

Most of the main European manufacturers established collaborative arrangements. Fiat and Peugeot collaborate on the production of engines and steering components. In 1998 Renault and Fiat merged their bus and coach making activities. The resulting company occupies around 25 per cent of the European bus market, compared with around 33 per cent for Daimler–Chrysler. The move was regarded by the two companies as a way to benefit from economies of scale and meet the intensification of pressure from customers, as large pan-European bus operators began to develop (*FT*, 6 May 1998). State-owned bus companies traditionally ordered from local suppliers, but privatized and consolidating bus companies increasingly sourced buses through open tenders (*FT*, 7 May 1998). The merger was followed by consolidation of the two companies' foundry operations, to create a jointly owned entity with sales of around $2 billion (*FT*, 19 November 1998).

In Latin America, Volkswagen and Ford agreed to establish a joint venture, called Autolina, for producing vehicles in Argentina and Brazil, and another $2.6 billion agreement to produce a 'people's car' in Portugal (*FT*, 7 January 2000). Ford and Honda entered an agreement to co-operate in the development of fuel cell technology. GM and Honda decided to co-operate in an engine supply agreement. Ford and Peugeot agreed to establish a far-reaching partnership to produce diesel engines.

Such collaborative arrangements are notoriously unstable. For example, the Honda–Rover link was broken in 1994, when BMW took over Rover. Volvo and Renault severed a long-term collaborative relationship when a mooted full-scale merger failed to materialize. The Ford-Volkswagen collaboration in Latin America and Portugal was dissolved. Most experts in the auto industry believe the alliances are simply a way of postponing full-scale mergers: 'All they are really doing is buying time. Relationships can be strained, and don't always deliver larger scale at lower cost. For some motor manufacturers, they are simply a way of putting off the inevitable' (Garel Rhys, quoted in *FT*, 7 January 2000). The second half of the 1990s saw a decisive shift forward in the move towards full-scale industry consolidation via mergers and acquisitions.

M & A

Daimler/Chrysler. In 1998, Daimler–Benz and Chrysler took the auto industry into a new era with a mammoth transatlantic merger which 'stunned rivals for its size, scope and audacity' (*FT*, 8 May 1998). The merger brought together companies with combined operating revenues in 1997 of $133 billion and operating profits of $8.2 billion. It employed 440 000 people. Daimler–Benz was already the world's largest truck company and one of the leading bus and coach builders, as well as being the world's leading producer of luxury vehicles. After facing near-bankruptcy on two occasions in the previous two decades, Chrysler had become the model of lean production, with a return on capital employed of almost 20 per cent in 1997, compared with 5.1 per cent for Toyota and just 3.4 per cent for Daimler–Benz (*FT*, 8 May 1998). The merger took the combined firms ahead of Volkswagen with world-wide vehicle sales of over 5 million units, to become the world's third largest auto producer. The merger was made comparatively easy to execute due to the relative lack of overlap in either the geographical scope of markets or the product portfolio.

The two companies estimated that they would make savings of up to $3 billion per annum due to the merger. The savings were to come from a number of sources. A crucial contribution was planned to come from combining the two firm's purchasing power into a single global procurement function. The combined annual purchases total $94 billion in 1998 (Daimler–Chrysler, *Annual Report, 1998*: 3). The companies planned to save costs through more effective deployment of their massive R & D spend. In 1998 Daimler–Chrysler spent $7.9 billion on R & D, employing 36 000 people world-wide on R & D (Daimler–Chrysler, *Annual Report, 1998*: 21). Not only was the new company spending massively on R & D, but also it was actively engaged in integrating its R & D needs with the R & D development of its major suppliers (Daimler–Chrysler, *Annual Report, 1998*: 21). The new company had believed that there would be large savings from sharing manufacturing and engineering: 'We will quickly share components, engines and transmissions' (spokesman for Daimler–Chrysler, quoted in *FT*, 8 May 1998). The two companies announced that they were dedicated to creating a truly global culture, with the official language of the supervisory and executive boards being English.

The merger was of much wider significance than just to the auto industry. It signalled strongly how far German capitalism had been transformed by the pressures of the global market marketplace. Leading German firms now were firmly bound on a course of internationalization of production, ownership, control and managerial styles. Sales in the USA accounted for 49 per cent of the new entity's global revenue, compared with 37 per cent for Europe. Absorbing the leanest and most cost-conscious auto company in the world could not but have a drastic effect on Daimler–Benz's corporate culture.

Daimler–Chrysler's determination to become a truly global leader was further demonstrated by its decision in early 2000 to take a 34 per cent equity share in Mitsubishi Motors. In September 2000, Mitsubishi agreed to allow Daimler–Chrysler the right to raise its stake to 100 per cent within three years.

It replaced Mitsubishi's CEO with one of its own executives (*FT*, 9 September 2000). In June 2000 Daimler–Chrysler acquired a 10 per cent stake in Hyundai, South Korea's largest car maker, with the option of buying another 5 per cent in three years. In addition, Mitsubishi owns a 4.8 per cent shareholding in Hyundai (*FT*, 27 June 2000). Daimler–Chrysler aims to raise its sales in Asia from the current figure of 3.5 per cent to 25 per cent in the medium term (*FT*, 25 May 2000).

Ford/Volvo. Another milestone in the consolidation of the world auto industry took place in 1999, with Ford's acquisition of Volvo's auto business. The possibilities for small niche players to be competitive globally drastically declined with the intensification of global competition, and Ford had already bought the small niche companies Aston Martin and Jaguar. Volvo was the world's fifteenth largest auto manufacturer in 1997, with sales of $24 billion, and an output of around 400 000 units. This is almost as much as the output of saloon cars for the whole of China in the late 1990s (output in 1998 was just over 500 000), and considerably greater than that of China's leading auto producer, Shanghai Auto, which had a output of only 160 000 units in 1995. However, the management of Volvo felt that the returns it was getting from the auto division were simply too low. They felt that there was no way to compete with the massive economies of scale of the leading firms in the sector. The decision to sell to Ford was greeted with howls of anguish from the Swedish press at the sale to a US company of arguably the 'crown jewel' of the Swedish economy. When Volvo's chief executive officer, Leif Johansson, announced the decision, the headline in Sweden's top-selling daily paper simply read: 'How could you Leif?' The sale liberated Volvo to pursue its goal of concentration on a global scale in trucks (see below). Ford believed that they could greatly enhance Volvo's global sales through Ford's vast marketing machinery. They planned radically to cut costs by using common components leveraging Ford's massive global procurement function, and even sharing common platforms with other Ford cars (*FT*, 29 January 1999).

Renault/Nissan. A further installment in the dramatic re-structuring of the global auto industry was announced in March 1999. Japan's second largest auto company, Nissan, had been seriously affected by the deep recession in the Japanese domestic auto industry, and was heavily indebted. In a highly significant move in terms of Japanese industrial restructuring, Renault purchased a 36.8 per cent controlling stake in Nissan. The two companies had highly complementary markets, with Nissan's main sales coming from the domestic market and North America. Renault's main strength is in Europe and Latin America. Despite attempts to internationalize, Renault still had made only 15 per cent of its sales outside Europe. The move raised Renault's share of the global auto market to 8.9 per cent, and moved it into fourth position among the world's largest auto makers. It gave the opportunity for large gains through technology sharing, common procurement, global platforms and common marketing. Renault stood to gain greatly from Nissan's deep reservoir of engineering skills and knowledge.

Nissan stood to gain from Renault's great success in cost-cutting. Only a few years previously, Renault had been written off as a 'basket-case' within the world's auto industry. Moreover, the state still held a 44 per cent share in the company that was now among the leaders of the world industry in terms of both scale and efficiency. Few economists would have believed that such a firm could have become so powerful and effective without complete privatization.

Renault's purchase of a controlling stake in Nissan is of the highest significance for the internationalization of the auto industry in the epoch of high globalization. Some Japanese industry officials see the 'surrender' to Renault as a 'fall from grace for Nissan and for the entire [Japanese] automotive industry' (FT, 23 March 1999). One former official from MITI called the Renault take-over of Nissan 'a national disgrace' (quoted in FT, 23 March 1999). However, other officials argued that there was no alternative. Kaoru Yosano, MITI minister, publicly said he would 'welcome' the deal as part of the globalization of the Japanese industry (quoted in FT, 23 March 1999). Renault's purchase of a controlling share of Nissan is highly symbolic because it signifies a fundamental change in the way the Japanese auto industry is organized. No sector has been more important for Japan's industrial rise than the auto industry. It was the auto industry that pioneered the methods of industrial organization that were later to be replicated by large parts of US and European industry. The full impact of Renault's purchase of a controlling share in Nissan became dramatically apparent in late 1999, when Carlos Ghosn announced wide-ranging changes to Nissan and its relationship with its supplier base.

GM/Daewoo. The Asian financial crisis and sharp downturn in domestic sales, combined with massive overseas expansion during the 1990s left Daewoo Motors in a desperately weak financial position. By the end of 1999 the entire Daewoo group, of which Daewoo Motors is a part, had a total debt of an estimated $73 billion (FT, 5 November 1999). Daewoo had become one of the world's biggest corporate insolvencies. Its foreign debt alone was estimated to be $6.7 billion. The foreign creditors insisted that Daewoo Motors be sold as part of the work-out programme. Many people within the industry inside Korea hoped that Daewoo would be nationalized (FT, 25 January 2000). Yet another hope was that Hyundai would take over Daewoo. However, Hyundai lacked the financial resources to do this, and would have needed to do so in partnership with a multinational. This was unacceptable to Hyundai.

In early 2000 it seemed highly likely that Daewoo would be taken over by either Ford or GM. Korea's chief financial and corporate regulator, Lee Yong-keun said that a foreign owner would be in a better position to improve the potential of the Korean car industry: 'If a domestic car company takes over Daewoo Motor and uses local components it could be said that its chances of survival would be slim' (quoted in the FT, 24 January 2000). Both Ford and General Motors were in close discussion with Daewoo with a view to buying the company, including not only its Korean, but also its Eastern European operations (FT, 17 December 1999). If that happened, then GM or Ford would account for around one-half of

Korea's total global output of autos (*FT*, 25 January 2000). The possibility that GM or Ford might acquire Daewoo provoked fierce debate in Korea.

The Federation of Korean Industries (FKI), the big business association, said that a GM take-over of Daewoo could 'destroy' Hyundai, A senior official in FKI said: 'GM is certain to adopt a low-pricing strategy to drive Hyundai Motor and Kia out of business, even at the risk of [incurring] astronomical losses for several years' (quoted in *FT*, 17 December 1999). Moreover, there were fears that GM or Ford would use the take-over of Daewoo as a platform with which to grow fast in East Asian markets and attack Hyundai in foreign as well as formerly protected domestic markets. Ford and GM have made clear their intention rapidly to build their sales in Asia. It has been suggested that they would use Korea as a platform from which to export to China after its tariffs fall to 25 per cent in 2005 as a result of its membership of the WTO (*FT*, 27 January 2000).

Prospective mergers. It is widely thought that the intense period of mergers and acquisitions will continue. Among the leading possibilities was that of Fiat merging with one of several possible partners. For at least two years it had been expected that Fiat would merge with a major auto maker: 'Apart from Daimler–Chrysler, regarded as the leading candidate, the names of Ford, General Motors and Mitsubishi have regularly been floated as possible merger partners.'

Industrial Structure: Trucks. The 1990s saw a succession of mergers and acquisitions in the truck industry. In the truck industry as in the car industry, the same fundamental forces were at work, driven by ferocious global competition. As in the car industry, the costs of developing new models has greatly increased in recent years. The development costs for new engines escalated as producers struggled to meet rising environmental control requirements across the world. Larger truck companies are able to benefit from developing global brands, and global service networks. They could take advantage of massive global procurement and close relationships with large globally aligned suppliers. The shift to modular production, rising warranty expenses and heavy leasing costs imposed further burdens on smaller truck makers (*FT*, 7 August 1999).

The North American truck company Paccar grew from a strong player into one of the global leaders. Paccar was built through the supply of the Sherman tank to the US Army during the Second World War. In 1945 it bought the Kenworth Truck Company. In 1958 it acquired Peterbilt. In 1981 it became a major player in the European market with the acquisition of Foden (UK). However, as consolidation accelerated it realized that in order to become a global player it had to develop greater international capability. In 1996 it purchased DAF (Holland) and in 1998 it bought Leyland (UK). By 1999 it accounted for over 7 per cent of world truck output (Table 8-6).

The other powerful North American producer, Navistar, underwent a radical business transformation in the 1990s, dramatically changing its management methods, and sharply improving its business performance. It greatly increased its output, from 106000 in 1995 to 155000 in 1999, and now accounted for 10.6 per cent of total global output (Table 8-6).

TABLE 8-6 World Top Nine Truck Makers,* 1995–2005 (000)

Company	1995 (No.)	1995 (%)	1999 (No.)	1999 (%)	2005 (No.)	2005 (%)
Daimler–Chrysler	199	12.3	276	18.9	272	14.5
Navistar	106	6.5	155	10.6	151	8.0
Volvo/Scania	121	7.5	127	8.7	140	7.5
General Motors/Isuzu	133	9.0	123	8.4	150	8.0
Dongfeng (Erqi)	171	10.6	96	6.6	167	8.9
Paccar	77	4.8	106	7.3	105	5.6
FAW (Yiqi)	91	5.6	79	5.4	138	7.3
RVI (Renault)	66	4.1	79	5.4	71	3.8
Iveco (Fiat)	57	3.5	62	4.2	61	3.2
Sub-total	1021	63.9	1103	75.5	1255	66.8
World total	1620	100.0	1460	100.0	1879	100.0

SOURCE: *FT* (3 December 1999)

NOTE: *Over 6 tonnes GVW

In the early 1990s, General Motors was only a medium-sized player in the truck industry. However, it held a significant ownership share in Isuzu, the largest Japanese truck maker. In 1999, GM took advantage of the weakness of Isuzu in the wake of the Asian crisis, by raising its ownership share in Isuzu from 19 per cent to 50 per cent, so that Isuzu essentially became a part of GM. General Motors–Isuzu was now one of the world giants of the truck industry, accounting for 8.4 per cent of total world output in 1999 (Table 8-6).

The Daimler–Chrysler merger further accelerated consolidation in the truck industry. Daimler–Benz had already acquired Freightliner, a leading US truck company. With the merger of Daimler and Chrysler, the company became by far the largest truck and bus maker in the world. In 1999 it produced 276 000 trucks, amounting to 18.9 per cent of total world production. In 1998, Daimler–Chrysler's commercial vehicles division alone had a sales revenue of over $27 billion and an R & D expenditure of $837 million. It invested $976 million in new plant and equipment (Daimler–Chrysler, *Annual Report, 1998*: 37).

In 1999, the sale of Volvo's saloon vehicles division to Ford was followed by the merger of Volvo and Saab's truck divisions. They had each transformed themselves from diversified, niche market auto industry firms into focused heavy truck producers, and now they joined their strengths together to form a giant specialist truck and bus producer with global reach (*FT*, 7 August 1999). The combined Volvo–Scania company had 8.7 per cent of the global total truck output in 1999 (Table 8-6). The chief operating officer of the new company said: 'This is an industry where the players are increasingly becoming not regional, but global. We saw what was happening and decided to make a move' (quoted in *FT*, 7 August 1999). The shake-out of the truck industry has been underway for several years. The number of truck makers is estimated to have fallen from more than 40 in 1975 to less than 20 in the late 1990s (*FT*, 7 August 1999). By 1999, the share of the top five truck-makers had risen to 54 per cent (Table 8-6).

COMPONENTS

The institutional structure of automobile components production has undergone a revolution in the past decade and the transformation appears to be far from finished. Ten years ago a large fraction of components in Europe and the USA was produced within highly integrated 'Fordist' firms. Those components that were purchased from outside typically were supplied by a large number of small firms producing mainly for national vehicle makers, with small international sales. Several large changes have occurred simultaneously in the automobile industry, radically changing the components industry. A common element in the transformation in the global components industry has been relentless pressure from globalizing large auto assemblers to reduce costs through applying pressure to components makers. This has produced a 'cascade' effect that flows down from the auto assemblers to the first tier components makers, with consolidation at the assembler level pushing forward consolidation at the level of the components suppliers. The first tier components makers have only been able to meet this pressure by themselves developing greater and greater scale on a global level. The head of Valeo commented: 'I do not see any signs of a slowdown or let-up in terms of consolidation. Car manufacturers are asking even more of their suppliers and we have to be global[to meet their demands]' (quoted in *FT*, 1 February 2000). The estimated number of auto components makers world-wide has shrunk from around 30 000 in 1990 to around 8000 in 2000. The number is predicted to shrink to just 2000 in six–eight years, with around 30 'mega-suppliers' that dominate the industry (*FT*, 19 June 2000).

The following are some of the factors that have influenced the recent institutional evolution of the auto components industry across the world:

- **Aligned suppliers**. In the mid-1990s Volvo had around 400 'first-tier' suppliers of components. It plans to reduce these to around 100 by 2005: 'We are not satisfied with operating margins at present and cutting the supplier base is one way to reduce operating costs' (Lief Johansson, chief executive of Volvo, quoted in *FT*, 18 May 1998). In early 1998 Peugeot announced that it would nominate a small group of favoured 'supplier partners' with which it would establish a 'fundamental partnership' on a global basis (*FT*, 1 January 1998). Renault simultaneously announced that they, like other large car makers, were cutting their supply base, and would shortly publish a shortened list of favoured 'supplier partners'. Renault declared that it was moving towards Japanese-style long-term relationship with suppliers, with component companies expected to co-operate more closely in product planning and problem-solving (*FT*, 2 January 1998). Renault declared that within two years it would lower costs drastically, with one-half of the cost reduction coming from their suppliers, the rest from internal efficiency improvements. Carlos Ghosn, the executive spearheading the efficiency drive, denied that the savings would be achieved by squeezing component suppliers, but would instead stem from a 'fundamental partnership' (quoted in *FT*, 2 January 1998).

- **Liberalization of global vehicle markets**. Tariffs are still often relatively high for vehicles, but restrictions on foreign investment have loosened dramatically. Indeed, in most developing countries, the vehicle industry is regarded as a 'pillar' industry, with enormous linkage effects to many other sectors, and foreign direct investment typically is strongly encouraged. As we have seen, vehicle production and sales are globalizing at high speed.

- **Outsourcing of components**. The rapid move towards outsourcing in European and US auto firms has mimicked the 'lean production' practice already developed most effectively by Toyota. This has been driven by the need to reduce costs. A major reason for outsourcing has been that components suppliers tend to be less unionized, and can therefore pay much lower wage rates than the core vehicle manufacturer.[4] By purchasing from several suppliers, core vehicle companies were able to bargain hard for low price, and high quality supply. As supplier firms drastically reduced in number, the relationship changed. Vehicle firms often establish exclusive long-term relationships with their largest suppliers. The bargaining power in many cases has begun to shift towards the much reduced number of large suppliers.[5] However, as the number of suppliers has reduced, there still are reasons for continuing to outsource. The growing size of suppliers enables them to benefit from economies of scale, to undertake more and more R & D and to undertake increasing amounts of sub-assembly, leaving the core firm free to concentrate on design, marketing and strategy.

- **Spinning off components makers from vehicle assembly**. In recent years, a large number of components operations has been spun off into independent companies by the vehicle assemblers. The dramatic nature of the changes under way is well illustrated by the recent developments at General Motors and Ford. In 1999 GM spun off its Delphi components making subsidiary with an initial public offering of 17.7 per cent of the company. Delphi immediately leaped into the number one position among components makers, with annual sales of around $29 billion, alongside Robert Bosch, with similar sales. Delphi will probably be included as a top 100 company in the *Fortune* 500 ranking. Ford also appears to be moving in the same direction. In September 1997 it announced that it was turning its components subsidiary into a stand-alone operation, Visteon, which currently has over 78 000 employees in 19 countries, and sales of $6 billion in 1996 (*FT*, 9 September 1997).

- **Accelerated globalization of production**. As the global auto giants increase production in developing countries, they encounter only rudimentary indigenous components industries. However, there are huge cost savings in having suppliers located close to, or even inside, the main assembly plant.[6] This has provided a huge opportunity for leading global components suppliers to establish businesses on the doorstep of globalizing vehicle manufacturers.

The world's leading auto components companies have a network of production facilities across the world. For example, Delphi has 168 production sites in 37 countries across the world, with 201 000 employees. Robert Bosch has 120 production sites world-wide. Valeo has 129 sites in 19 countries, including five in China. Denso has 72 production sites in Japan and 29 in Europe and North America and 30 in developing countries, including five in China.

- **Rapid evolution of 'global' vehicles**. A new species of global vehicle uses common design features. All leading vehicle producers, for example, are reducing sharply the number of 'platforms' on which their model ranges are based. This reduces the cost of design, development and marketing. It requires, however, that components are also 'global', and produced in the immediate vicinity of each global car plant, to ensure 'just-in-time' delivery: 'To ensure reliable and prompt supplies, car-makers are inviting their components suppliers in more advanced economies to follow them into new markets' (*FT*, 28 October 1996).

- **Spiralling R & D costs**. In every area of components production, whether engines, tyres, wheels, fuel injection, lighting, suspension, brakes, exhausts, body technology, windscreens, or seats, there is rapid technical progress. The firm that does not lower costs alongside rapid technical progress in each of these areas will die. Increasingly, vehicle manufacturers have delegated these functions to specialist suppliers in each component sector, taking over many of the risks that were formerly borne by the auto assemblers. In the late 1990s, the world's top ten components suppliers each spent over $300 million on R & D (Table 8-7). The top two firms spent over one billion dollars each. Even ninth ranked Valeo spent almost $400 million and had around 3000 research engineers and scientists. In 1997 Valeo filed 500 patents (Valeo, *Annual Report, 1997*: 14). The big components makers supply more than one customer, 'giving them greater economies of scale than those available even to a mammoth such as GM' (*FT*, 28 October 1996). The ability of leading suppliers to spread their resources and specialist expertise across a number of large car-producing customers has large cost benefits for the vehicle makers.

- **Modularization**. Suppliers of global assembly firms are no longer merely delivering batches of parts to order, but instead are delivering entire and often very complex modules, from complete suspension packages to ready-to-bolt-in driver cockpits: 'Car makers increasingly see their roles as assemblers of such modules, produced by a small and dwindling number of big, usually multi-billion dollar turnover, first-tier suppliers, required to operate globally. Such suppliers have the extensive technological and financial resources needed to design, develop and produce these modules and sometimes even to fund them on a shared-risk basis' (*FT*, 9 September 1997). For example, air conditioners are increasingly provided as complete systems that include heating/air conditioning, control panel, hoses, compressor and condenser. The next step is towards supplying complete cockpit modules direct to the assembly line.

TABLE 8-7 Leading Global Auto Components Companies, 1998

Company	Revenues ($ billion)	Profits ($ million)	R & D ($ million)
Robert Bosch	28.6	446	2071
Delphi*	28.8	—	—
Denso	13.8	461	1384
Michelin	13.3	—	—
Dana	12.8	534	272
Johnson Controls	12.6	338	244
TRW	11.9	477	—
Lear	9.1	116	—
Goodyear	12.5	1114**	417
Valeo	6.0	401**	365
Pioneer	4.9	193**	272
Pirelli	6.8	520**	213
Autoliv	3.5	365**	175
GKN	4.9	1191**	144

SOURCES: *Fortune* (2 August 1999); UNCTAD (1999: 78–80); DTI (1999: 51–2)

NOTES: *IPO completed in May 1999, previously a part of General Motors
**Before interest, tax and dividends

- **Incorporating IT into components systems**. The most dynamic segment of the components industry has become the application information technology and advanced electronics to important parts of the automobile. For example, Denso, one of the world's top four components companies, estimates 13 of its 16 product groups use electronics, and it has established a central 'electronics clearing house' to co-ordinate the purchase and development of electronics control capabilities for the whole company (Denso, *Annual Report, 1999*: 8). Electronics systems have increased their share of the final value of the vehicle to such an extent that it now exceeds the value of steel consumed in making the vehicle (*FT,* 23 February 1998). It has been noted that some mass market cars contain more computing power than was deployed in the moon landings. The future value-added from advanced transport communications technology will be much higher still, as the installation of high-value systems such as satellite navigation, automatic crash location and emergency signal sending, collision-avoidance radar and even on-board internet become widespread (*FT,* 23 February 1999).

- **Procurement capabilities**. We have seen that the core auto assemblers are establishing an 'external firm' of suppliers, and often benefiting from centralized procurement. Similarly, the first tier components suppliers are themselves organizing 'external firms' of suppliers and benefiting from large-scale procurement. For example, Delphi, the world's largest components company, purchases annually around $13 billion worth of components (Delphi website).

- **Relentless pressure on prices**. As the components industry has responded to the above changes, so the competition among the components producers themselves has sharply accelerated, with those producers able to gain competitive advantage, pulling away fast in the competitive struggle: 'The consistent demands by vehicle makers for ever lower prices has weeded out smaller or less efficient manufacturers from bigger rivals offering better economies of scale' (*FT*, 12 June 1997).

In the 1990s in response to these forces a very rapid consolidation of component makers has occurred: 'in the biggest change in its history the once diversified components business is being rationalized as large specialists gobble up the minnows' (*FT*, 28 October 1996). It is widely thought that the number of leading components companies will be reduced from around 150–200 to just 15–20 global groups over the next decade (*FT*, 28 October 1996). The pace of consolidation in the auto components industry is reflected in the fact that the total value of mergers and take-overs in the sector in 1996 alone was reported to be 'comfortably in excess of $15 billion' (*FT*, 12 June 1997). In 1996 alone there were five mergers of over 1 billion dollars.

By the mid-1990s a small group of players with global sales of over $3 billion was emerging, each able to spend large amounts on R & D and each with a global reach. Of the 26 firms in the sector with annual sales of over $3 billion, one-half were American (Table 8-7).

However, 'auto components' is a broad category, containing several sub-markets, each with its own specialist technologies. Within each sub-market consolidation is already well advanced. The chief executive of Tenneco believes that 'the number of suppliers for many key parts will be whittled down to two players, maybe three ' (quoted in the *FT*, 28 October 1996). Indeed, in many branches, the consolidation is already close to this position. The size and growth rate of the global market for specialist automobile components is so large that narrowly focused firms can enjoy global sales much greater in real terms than those of even a relatively large, but nationally based, automobile firm of a decade or so ago. In almost every sector of the world's components industry, there has occurred explosive consolidation in recent years:

- **Seats**. As late as 1984, US car makers made nearly all their own seats, but today they buy in around 70 per cent from outside sources. In car seats there are just two main producers: Johnson Controls and Lear, both of the USA, who between them account for around one-half of the total number of seats fitted to cars in North America and Europe (*FT*, 21 May 1996). Johnson Controls was formerly a manufacturer of non-automotive heating controls and plastic containers. In the 1990s it divested itself of these businesses and rapidly expanded in car seat production through a series of divestments and acquisitions. These included the acquisition of Auto Industry's seat business (1995), Prince (1996) and Becker (1997) as well as numerous smaller acquisitions. By the late 1990s, Johnson had over 140 plants, mainly in Europe and the USA. These were mainly satellite plants close to big car factories, with seats delivered on a 'just-in-time' basis straight to the assembly line (*FT*, 23 September 1998). Lear is Johnson Controls' main competitor. Like Johnson it acquired a string of smaller companies in the 1990s. Its main acquisitions were Delphi's seat business (1997) and Keiner (1998), each for around $0.7 billion.

A key part of their competitive success is the ability to develop new seating technologies. Johnson, for example, employs 1500 seating engineers who pursue improvements in seat safety, comfort, aesthetics, and efficiency of product building. Johnson aims to develop around 80 per cent of its new capabilities as proprietary technologies that can be used to raise revenue in sales to several different auto companies. Both Johnson and its arch-rival Lear are trying to develop a 'total interior service' to auto makers (*FT*, 23 February 1998).

- **Air conditioners**. Denso (Japan) is one of the world's top four components producers. Its largest single division is air conditioners, which account for around one-third of the company's total sales (Denso, *Annual Report, 1999*). The air conditioner and heating division had global sales of $4.6 billion in 1999. It is the largest supplier of air conditioners world-wide, with a market share of around one-quarter. Denso faces fierce competition from its main competitors, such as Valeo, whose own air conditioner sales amount to over $4 billion (Valeo, *Annual Report, 1997*: 26).

- **Exhaust systems and shock absorbers**. Arvin and Tenneco Automotive account for the bulk of exhaust systems and shock absorbers (*FT*, 28 October 1996). Tenneco claims around 25 per cent of the global market for exhaust systems, through its Walker Manufacturing subsidiary, and a similar share of the world market for shock absorbers and ride control systems, through its Monroe Equipment subsidiary (*FT*, 31 January 1996). Tenneco is accelerating its world-wide acquisitions drive 'in the belief that within a decade, each motor components sector will be dominated by one or two fully global groups' (*FT*, 31 January 1996). In 1995–6 it acquired new shock absorber and exhaust businesses in China, the Czech Republic, Germany and Spain. It now has 'the lion's share of the European exhaust systems business' (*FT*, 31 January 1996).

- **Constant velocity joints**. Constant velocity joints transfer power from the engine to the wheels of front-wheel drive vehicles. GKN is much the largest producer, accounting for around 40 per cent of total world output (*FT*, 22 July 1996). Its operations are 'ringed by protective patents and licences' (*FT*, 23 July 1996). It is one of the industry leaders in setting up its plants alongside the businesses of first world car-makers in developing countries. It has, for example, set up two local joint ventures to supply the Shanghai Volkswagen plant.

- **Wheels**. The supply of wheels is also becoming increasingly global and concentrated. In 1996 two of the biggest producers, Hayes Wheels and

Motor Wheels merged to form a company which accounted for around 35 per cent of the North American wheels supply (*FT*, 21 May 1996).

- **Automobile glass**. A technological revolution is under way in this sector, 'almost as far-reaching as that of in-car electronics', including solar-reflecting glass, rain-sensitive windscreens, heated front windscreens, using windscreen glass as a location for an embedded radio reception antenna (*FT*, 21 May 1996). Specialist automobile glass companies are at the forefront of auto glass technology. Pilkington Automotive Division is a world leader in this process. It has expanded fast, 'spreading its tentacles into many markets, mainly through opportunistic acquisitions': it now has 17 auto glass plants in Europe alone (*FT*, 12 June 1997). It has become the world's largest maker of automobile glass, with its glass fitted to around one-quarter of all the world's automobiles (*FT*, 21 May 1996).

- **Car braking systems**. In the mid-1990s, two companies already dominated this sector. In 1995 Lucas and Bosch together accounted for 56 per cent of total sales of brake systems in Europe, North America and Japan, including in-house production (*FT*, 8 May 1996). The top four firms accounted for 87 per cent of global sales in the same regions (*FT*, 8 May 1996).

- **Airbags and seatbelts**. Autoliv, Morton and Breed (which bought Allied Signal's seat belt business for $0.9 billion in early 1997) will dominate airbags and seatbelts (*FT*, 28 October 1996). These have grown into large companies following the consolidation of the components sector. Breed, for example, has 60 plants in 30 countries (*FT*, 9 September 1997).

- **Growth of producers with cross-functional specializations**. The bulk of the recent wave of mergers in auto components has been mainly within functional specializations: wheelmakers have bought wheelmakers, and seat makers have merged with seat makers. However, it is thought likely that the next stage of consolidation will come from cross functional deals (*FT*, 12 June 1997). For example, Tenneco is already making whole 'corners' of vehicles for customers, involving the sub-assembly of an entire unit, including not only shock absorbers and suspension struts but also axles and brakes bought from third parties. It is seeking to expand into the production of brakes and axles through the purchase of major producers in this field (*FT*, 21 June 1996). In 1999, TRW bought Lucas–Varity, changing itself into a massive components business that combined Lucas' capabilities in brakes with TRW's expertise in steering systems and suspension. The combined sales of the new entity were $19 billion (pro-forma) (*FT*, 1 March 1999).

    Even more significant for the industry's development trend was the acquisition by Valeo of ITT's Electrical Systems in 1998. This gave Valeo a comprehensive capability to integrate electronics control capabilities into a wide range of applications: 'The car is going to be 100 per cent electrified and Valeo is going to be a part of it' (Valeo spokesman, quoted in *FT*, 1 March 1999). Valeo has developed into the world's leading manufacturer of clutch

systems and engine cooling systems, and is the European leader in air conditioning, lighting and security systems. Each of these benefits from its
enhanced electronics control system capabilities.

- **Tyres**. Over the long-term, global tyre sales have been growing steadily,
  alongside the growth of automobile production, with predicted unit sales rising by around 19 per cent from 1996 to 2005 (*FT*, 14 March 1997). The
  global tyre market in the late 1990s was estimated to be around $75 billion
  (*FT*, 4 February 1999). However, the pace of growth in different regions is
  predicted to be very different. From 1996 to 2005, North American unit sales
  are predicted to grow by 21 per cent, but Western Europe's are predicted to
  remain unchanged, its share of global sales falling from 30.2 per cent to
  25 per cent. Asia's predicted growth over the same period is 24 per cent,
  with a predicted global market share of 33 per cent in 2005 : 'Tyre makers'
  principal focus of attention [is] the burgeoning vehicle markets of the
  Asia–Pacific region, and the race is on to be in at the start of the motoriza-
  tion of India's 800 m and China's 1bn-plus inhabitants ... Month by month
  the list of joint ventures and capacity investment grows longer' (*FT*, 14
  March 1997). Despite the Asian crisis, the medium-term prospects are still
  for this to be the most dynamic region in the world for car sales. An important part of the globalization of tyre production is the close association of the
  tyre supplier with a given car manufacturer as 'original equipment' supplier
  (as opposed to the supply of replacement tyres) on a global scale.

  This sector has undergone a somewhat longer-term consolidation than
  other auto component sectors, but the process has been remorseless. The drivers of change in the tyre industry have been similar to those in other components sectors. Consolidation among the car assemblers is placing even
  greater pressure on tyre makers in the original equipment part of the market.
  Tyre makers gain competitive advantage by developing global reach to be
  situated close to the major manufacturing centres around the world.
  Marketing and brand development have become increasingly important. For
  example, a major reason for Goodyear's take-over of Sumitomo (see below)
  was the inability of Sumitomo to spend sufficient resources on the Dunlop
  brand. After taking over Sumitomo, Samir Gilbira, the head of Goodyear,
  commented: 'With a clever advertising campaign and a good communications programme, we can make the Dunlop name as powerful as one of the
  two or three best brands in Europe' (quoted in *FT*, 1 March 1999).

  Research and development is exceptionally important for the tyre industry, especially, but not exclusively, in the high quality, high value-added segment of the market. A major advantage enjoyed by the largest firms is their
  large R & D budget, which can be spread over a far larger output than that
  for the smaller firms. The large firms can take advantage of R & D progress
  to increase sales and/or margins even at the lower end of the market for
  replacement tyres. Even before its take-over of Sumitomo, Goodyear spent
  over $400 million on R & D. Pirelli, in the second rank of tyre makers, with

a 4.4 per cent global market share, spends $213 million on R & D, massively ahead of any developing country tyre maker. Michelin, for example, has a 2300-strong R & D department. Technical progress has been of great importance in respect both to product and process.

The R & D spending of the leading companies has produced major advances in tyre-making technologies. Each of the leading firms has developed its own highly automated technology in the past few years, radically reducing production costs. It also allows efficient production of very small batches of different models of tyres. This is being propelled by the changes in the production of vehicles, with a great increase in the number of vehicle types produced by a single manufacturer. Michelin has pioneered the development of the single assembly station (C3M) which can produce at low cost more complex tyres in small batches of just a few thousand or even a few hundred. Goodyear has developed its own parallel technology, called Impact (integrated manufacturing precision assembled cellular technology). It is claimed that Impact reduces cycle times by 70 per cent, material costs by 15 per cent, labour costs by 35 per cent, inventories by one-half, and curing time by 20 per cent. It is estimated that Impact will eliminate one in three jobs in a traditionally highly labour-intensive industry (*FT*, 16 September 1999). The capital costs of the new technology are very high. Moreover, each company is developing its own technology, which it will be hard for other players to have access to. The development of the new technology is 'causing considerable unease among the dozen of smaller companies that share the market – less than 30 per cent – not controlled by the leading manufacturers' (*FT*, 16 September 1999).

As well as dramatic changes in process technology, the huge R & D expenditure by leading tyre makers is causing important advances in products. For example, tyre makers are constantly striving to gain competitive advantage by developing more durable, longer-lasting tyres, and lighter tyres that cause less friction, save fuel and need less energy to manufacture.

The net impact of these developments on the global tyre industry has been radically to increase the extent of global consolidation. The clear industry leaders have emerged as Bridgestone, Goodyear and Michelin:

– Fifteen years ago, **Bridgestone** was a relatively small Japanese producer. Since then it has grown fast as the main supplier to the indigenous motor industry, with around 46 per cent of the domestic market, which formed the basis for its profits. It made a leap into the USA alongside the rapid growth of North American production by Japanese vehicle makers. Its critical move was the purchase of Firestone in 1988. Firestone was an established large producer, with 18 plants. In recent years, Bridgestone has grown rapidly in Asia, with subsidiaries in several countries. A major reason for its outward move has been the decline in domestic vehicle production as Japanese vehicle makers have shifted production overseas. By the mid-1990s, Bridgestone had risen to the position of number one tyre maker globally, in terms of value of sales.

- In the 1950s, **Michelin** was a relatively small firm, based mainly around the French market. Between 1960 and 1990 it opened or bought an average of one new plant every nine months, which culminated in the Uniroyal Goodrich purchase (USA) in 1989. By the early 1990s it had 67 plants and a workforce of 140 000. It had risen to number one position globally in terms of unit sales, and number two in terms of value of sales. Having reached a position at the top of the global tyre making league, Michelin sharply reduced costs in the early 1990s, with a large fall in employment to 117 000 in 1995 (*FT*, 5 October 1995).

- Although it ceased to be the single most important global tyre producer, **Goodyear** remained a powerful force. In the early 1990s, it divested itself of non-core businesses, sharply reduced costs and introduced a 'blitz of new products' (*FT*, 29 January, 1996). In 1999, Goodyear shocked the tyre industry when it took a controlling stake in Sumitomo, Japan's second largest tyre maker: 'At a stroke Goodyear Tyre and Rubber shifted the goal posts for the structure and economics of the global tyre industry as surely as [the 1998s] Daimler–Benz and Chrysler alliance did for the vehicle makers' (*FT*, 3 February 1999). The deal established six joint ventures. Goodyear took a controlling stake (75 per cent in each case) in Sumitomo's EU and US businesses, as well as having a controlling stake in newly established global purchasing and research and development joint ventures. Sumitomo retained majority control of its Japanese businesses. The head of Goodyear estimated that the take-over would result in annual savings of up to $360 billion through more effective purchasing, distribution, research and development, and other synergies (*FT*, 4 February 1999). The new entity is likely to have an R & D spend of over $500 million.

    The Goodyear take-over of Sumitomo enabled it to pull away decisively from Michelin and Bridgestone in terms of sales revenue and global market share. Its global market share now reached 22.5 per cent compared with 18.5 per cent each for Michelin and Bridgestone (*FT*, 16 September 1999). The share of the top three tyre makers had risen to 60 per cent (*FT*, 16 September 1999). There are just two middle-ranking players left in the industry, Pirelli and Continental, both based in Europe. However, they together account for just 11 per cent of the global market, each with total sales only around one-half of those of the 'Big Three'. It is widely thought that these firms face serious difficulties, other than as global 'niche' players. It is thought likely that each of them faces a high chance of being taken over by one of the 'Big Three' of the global industry. A myriad of small companies accounts for the remaining one-quarter of the global market. The vast bulk of the firms are small-scale, producing low quality, labour-intensive, low value-added low margin tyres. For example, in China in 1996, the largest rubber tyre firm, Shanghai Rubber Tyre Company, had a sales revenue of $440 million, with pre-tax profits of $72 million (SSB, 1997: 173–4). The top ten rubber tyre companies firms in China have total sales of $2.5 billion. Thus, even a merger of the entire top ten rubber tyre makers would still result in a firm that was only around one-fifth as large as each of the world's 'Big Three' firms in terms of sales revenue, let alone profits or R & D spending.

- **Vehicle engines**. This sector has lagged behind other branches of automobile components in outsourcing. Most vehicle manufacturers make their own engines. However, it is predicted that even engine making will be widely spun off to independent companies in the next few years: 'Such a reorganization would enable the best engines to be produced in much larger quantities ... At present the production of even an exceptionally good engine, whose development costs can reach $1 billion, may amount to only about 500 000 units a year. ... [A] specialist engine maker would be able to offer engines of improved design at prices between 3 per cent and 7 per cent below competitive suppliers' (*FT*, 28 May 1996). It is predicted that this process will get under way very shortly. Indeed, one study predicts that there will soon be as few as two globally dominant specialist engine makers (*FT*, 28 May 1996).

   Independent engine makers are more prevalent in the diesel than in the petrol engine sector. The major manufacturers tend to consume much smaller numbers of diesel than of petrol engines, so an independent maker selling to several vehicle makers can achieve economies of scale, and develop the specialized technology associated with diesel engines. Diesel engines operate with higher pressure than petrol engines and the pump system is critical to the success of the engine. It is not surprising that the most powerful independent vehicle engine makers today each makes diesel engines. The diesel engine sector has experienced consolidation alongside other components sectors. The dominant players that have emerged from this process are Caterpillar, Cummins, and Detroit Diesel: These three firms now account for over 80 per cent of the market for heavy duty truck engines in the USA (Detroit Diesel, *Annual Report, 1998*: 11):

- **Caterpillar**. Caterpillar is the world's largest producer of diesel engines. Its total diesel engine sales in 1998 were $6.5 billion, of which truck engines totalled around $1.7 billion. The company has around 23 per cent of the North American heavy-duty truck market for diesel engines. Caterpillar acquired a succession of other diesel engine businesses in the 1990s, including twenty in the period 1995–9 alone. Among these were Perkins Diesel Engine (UK) and MaK Motors (Germany). In addition, it formed 20 joint ventures. As well as producing diesel engines, Caterpillar also produces a wide range of large pieces of equipment for use in mining, construction and forestry. By 1998, Caterpillar had established 88 production facilities across the world, of which 43 were in the USA, 26 were in Europe and 16 were in other parts of the world, including four in China. The company spent heavily on developing new capabilities in its engines. Its total R & D spend in 1998 was $838 million.

   Caterpillar has built its brand through developing a reputation for product reliability, quality and high quality service. The company has established a world-wide network of independently owned dealers. There are Caterpillar dealers in almost every country in the world, including 64 in the USA and 131 in other countries. The dealer network employs 82 000 people, constituting a veritable 'external firm', analogous to the bottling network of the Coca-Cola business system (Nolan, 1999). The average tenure of the dealers with Caterpillar is almost 50 years. The dealers must meet stringent quality standards. They have invested millions of dollars in their own operations. The massive global dealer network constitutes a major source of competitive advantage for each of the main divisions of Caterpillar.

– **Cummins**. Cummins is the world's largest producer of diesel engines over 200 hp. Like other leading firms in the sector it acquired a number of other firms in recent years. These included Universal Silencer, Holset, Kuss, Fleetguard and Nelson Industries. Kuss Corporation installs the filters on 60 per cent of US automobiles and 20 per cent of autos in Europe. Holset is a world leader in turbocharge technology. Nelson Industries is North America's largest producer of exhaust systems and its number two supplier of air intake systems for diesel engines. Cummins has built a global production capability, with nine production units in the USA, five in Europe, and eight in developing countries, including three in China. It has a further 15 plants producing components, of which six are in the USA, three are in Europe, and six are in developing countries, three of which are in China.

Cummins manufactures a full range of diesel engines from 135 to 600 hp. There are powerful economies of scope that enable expenditure on R & D, marketing and establishing a global dealer network, to benefit the whole product line. This enables costs to be spread across different products, obtaining greater benefit from a given expenditure.

Cummins invested over $200 million per annum on R & D throughout the second half of the 1990s, rapidly pushing forward its technical capabilities. Like other leading diesel engine firms, a crucial area of technical progress was meeting the increasingly severe emission standards set by the US government. These technical advances mean that Cummins is among the industry leaders in meeting the increasingly stringent emissions requirements of developing countries such as China. Cummins has developed a powerful world-wide network of dealers that specialize in selling and servicing Cummins engines. In all, by 1998 it had 31 North American and 110 international distributors.

For the past 26 years Cummins has been the North American leader in sales of heavy duty truck engines, with a 32 per cent market share in 1998. The North American market is by far the largest in the world, and it provides a huge base from which Cummins is developing its international presence, including China, as we shall see below. Not only is Cummins the world's largest producer of heavy duty truck diesel engines. It is also a major producer of medium duty diesel engines, selling almost 300 000 units in 1998. There are considerable synergies from enjoying a powerful position in both markets. Cummins' sales of heavy duty truck diesel engines in 1998 totalled $1553 million, compared with $1075 million from medium-duty diesel engines. The combined total was twenty times the total sales of Yuchai. Even the medium duty engine sales alone were eight times as large as those of Yuchai, China's leading medium duty diesel engine manufacturer. In 1998, a single customer, Daimler–Chrysler, purchased 93 000 medium duty engines.

– **Detroit Diesel (DDC)**. DDC was originally a part of General Motors. In 1993 GM spun off its heavy duty engine division to form Detroit Diesel. Through a combination of organic growth and acquisitions, DDC grew rapidly, increasing is output from 67 000 units in 1993 to 160 000 unit in 1997. The company increased its share of the North American heavy-duty diesel engine market from under 10 per cent in the late 1980s to 30 per cent in 1997. DDC increased its output of diesel engines from 3000 units in the late 1980s to 160 000 in 1997. It produces a full range of diesel engines, from 10 to 10 000 hp, allowing benefits from economies of scope in R & D spending, marketing and service organization, and procurement. DDC has one major manufacturing plant in the USA, one in Italy and one in Brazil. It has three re-manufacturing plants.

Detroit Diesel invested around $100 million in R & D in 1998 alone and over $420 million over the entire period from 1992 to 1997. A major objective of its R & D investment has been to advance the company's ability to meet rising environmental standards. This is not just a matter of reducing emissions. It is also a matter of reducing the amount of fuel needed to haul a given load through greater engine efficiency. In 1977 a DDC diesel engine of 350 hp in a Class 8 (heavy-duty) truck averaged about 4–5 miles per gallon of fuel hauling a gross vehicle weight of 80 000 pounds. In 1997, the distance accomplished in hauling the same load with a gallon of fuel had risen to around 7 miles. This was achieved through the use of electronic injection and sophisticated combustion chamber design (Detroit Diesel, *Annual Report, 1998*: 19).

Like other leading diesel engine manufacturers, a major source of competitive advantage for DD is its global network of dealers and service centres. It has an international support network of more than 2500 authorized distributors and dealers. Diesel engine manufacturers gain a large share of revenue from providing lifetime service, including components and re-manufacturing their engines. However, even Detroit Diesel proved too small to survive as an independent engine maker in the intensely competitive environment at the end of the twentieth century. In July 2000 it was taken over by Daimler–Chrysler, one of Detroit Diesel's main customers (*FT*, 21 July 2000). The move caused speculation that even Cummins might be taken over.

Even in diesel engine manufacture, there are several powerful firms that manufacture mainly or entirely within the firm, notably those in the heavy duty vehicle sector. Heavy duty trucks almost entirely use diesel engines, and have developed specialized technologies. The world's most powerful heavy truck producers, such as Mercedes, Volvo/Scania, each meets a large fraction of its diesel engine needs from within the firm. Indeed, Volvo makes a point of not selling any of its heavy duty diesel engines outside the Volvo system. The world's largest truck-maker, Daimler–Chrysler, produces a large fraction of its own diesel engines and sells significant amounts of these to third party buyers. The Daimler–Chrysler Powertrain division (which includes transmission units, axles, and steering systems, and petrol engines as well as diesel engines) sold a total of $3.8 billion-worth of goods and services in 1998 (Daimler–Chrysler, *Annual Report, 1998*).

CONCLUSION: BARRIERS TO ENTRY AND CATCH-UP IN THE
AUTO INDUSTRY IN DEVELOPING COUNTRIES

The 1990s has seen a revolution in the automobile industry, involving large-scale changes in the degree of concentration among auto assemblers, fundamental changes in the relationship between the assemblers and the components companies, and large-scale changes within the components industry. We have seen that in the past, in both advanced and developing countries, the state has in almost all cases played a key role in supporting the growth of the indigenous auto industry. In the USA, the industry developed with high levels of state protection. In Europe, the industry grew with high levels of protection, extensive state ownership and large-scale subsidies, often disguised as 'regional aid'. In 'latecomer' countries, the state has also been crucial in those cases of successful 'catch-up' at the firm level in the auto industry. The two most striking examples of this are Japan and South Korea. These examples have been an inspiration for China in developing its policy towards the auto industry. As we shall see, its strategy has been firmly built on the belief that the industry should construct a small number of powerful auto assemblers and components firms that can compete on the 'global level playing field'. However, during the period that China has been trying to build its indigenous industry almost from scratch, the international environment of the auto industry has changed beyond recognition. The task of 'catch-up' at the level of the firm is now vastly harder for potential competitive firms on a world scale than was the case ten years ago.

The 1990s saw a dramatic opening up of world markets to international competition and internationalization of production. The intensity of inter-firm competition increased greatly. Only the lowest-cost manufacturers could survive. Scale became even more important than before in achieving minimum cost. Larger scale, along with effective management, enabled cost reductions per unit in R & D, vehicle development costs, marketing, and procurement. Liberalization of international capital markets combined with much more active institutional investors meant that poorly-performing auto firms were mercilessly penalized by the market, further intensifying the pressure to improve performance through cost reduction. The sharp rise in competitive pressure produced great financial difficulties for even the world's leading firms, including near-bankruptcy for Chrysler and Nissan, and outright bankruptcy for Daewoo. Formerly successful smaller producers, such as Rover, Volvo and Jaguar, found it hard to compete and agreed to be taken over by larger auto firms.

The 1990s saw a sharp acceleration of mergers within the auto assemblers. The most dramatic of these was the Daimler–Chrysler merger. This was highly significant. It illustrated the drastic decline of the concept of the 'national champion' in the auto industry. Moreover, the merger was between two of the world's largest auto makers. If neither of them felt able to compete successfully, what possibility did this hold for vastly smaller new entrants from developing countries such as China? The search for scale and internationalization of production and markets accelerated with the *de facto* take-over of Volvo by Ford and Nissan by Renault. Each of these was of great significance for the concept of the 'national champion' in this industry. Many Japanese policy makers regarded the take-over as an act of national betrayal. In Sweden there was a national outcry at the take-over of one of the nation's industrial 'jewels' by a US corporation. In early 2000 Korea's Daewoo Motor Corporation was on the verge of being taken over by GM or Ford. Heavy rumours circulated about the possible merger of Fiat with another major auto maker. By the year 2000, the top 10 auto makers accounted for two-thirds of global auto output (Table 8-8). The world's leading auto makers, Ford, GM, and Daimler–Chrysler, produced over 5 million vehicles each, and VW, Renault–Nissan and Toyota produced over 4 million each. There was considerable doubt about whether even large auto producers such as Honda, Fiat and Peugeot, with an annual output of 2–3 million vehicles, could remain viable as independent firms.

By comparison with these giants, the attempts by developing countries' indigenous firms to compete on the global stage appeared hopeless. The scale of the

TABLE 8-8 **World Largest Automobile Companies, 1998**

Company	Output (million)	% World Total	Revenues ($ billion)	Profits ($ billion)	R & D Expenditure ($ million)
General Motors	7.55	14.8	161.3	2.96	7834
Ford/Volvo*	7.21	14.1	171.2	23.16	7485
Daimler/Chrysler*	5.08	9.9	154.6	5.66	5788
Volkswagen	4.69	9.2	76.3	1.26	3501
Renault/Nissan*	4.57	8.9	92.9	1.28	1604**
Toyota	4.48	8.8	99.7	2.78	3907
Fiat	2.50	4.9	51.0	0.69	1356
Honda	2.39	4.6	48.7	2.39	2513
Peugeot	2.25	4.4	37.5	0.54	1531
Mitsubishi	1.52	3.0	27.5	0.04	766
Other	8.92	17.4	—	—	—
World	51.16	100.0	—	—	—

SOURCES: MSDW (1999: 45); Fortune (2 August 1999); DTI (1999)

NOTE: *Pro-forma
     **Renault only

international competition had grown vastly beyond that of even a decade previously, let alone 20 years before, when Korea had begun its attempt to catch-up, or 40 years before when Japan had begun its attempt to catch-up in autos. The world's auto industry had grown from just 13 million vehicles (passenger cars only) in 1960 to 39 million in 1998, so that the absolute size of the leading firms had massively risen in terms of unit output and real value of sales. The size of these institutions was now extraordinary. The global sales of GM and Ford were each over $160 billion, around the same size as the GNP of Turkey or Thailand. Thus, behind protective international barriers, the industry could not hope to build up indigenous firms that could remotely match the economies of scale and cost structure of the leading companies. The output of Ford or GM was now 15 times as great as the entire auto output of either India or China. China's leading firms, Yiqi, Dongfeng and Shanghai Auto, were minuscule in comparison with the world's leading firms. Even if the three entities were merged, their sales revenue would still be under $12 billion, the same size as the world's sixteenth ranked auto maker, Suzuki. Moreover, a large fraction of the revenue from the Chinese auto industry, and an even larger share of the industry's profits were generated by Shanghai Auto's joint venture with VW.

Ford's global procurement in 1998 totalled $80 billion, around the same size as the total GNP of Venezuela or Egypt. Such massive global procurement provided huge potentialities for cost reduction by leading car assemblers compared to the potential smaller competitors. The R & D spending of the leading auto firm GM, which reached $7.5 billion in 1998, was greater than the entire national product of most developing countries. Such massive spending provided vast potentialities for improving the nature of the product and developing vehicles faster than potential new entrants to the industry.

The process of concentration and growth of scale was not confined just to the passenger vehicle industry. In the world truck industry the 1990s saw a major round of mergers and acquisitions, These included Paccar's acquisition of DAF and Leyland, GM's *de facto* take-over of Isuzu, the merger of Daimler–Chrysler, the purchase by Daimler–Chrysler truck subsidiary, Freightliner, of Canada's Western Star and the merger of Volvo and Scania. By 1999, the share of the top nine truck makers globally had reached 63 per cent of world unit sales. China's two leading truck firms stood out among developing countries as having sufficient scale to enter the ranks of the world's leading firms in terms of unit sales. If the two leading firms were merged, their total unit sales would place them in the lead globally, overtaking even Daimler–Chrysler (Table 8-6). However, the nature of the product produced by Yiqi and Dongfeng is very different from that of the leading truck companies in terms of vehicle sophistication. The average price of a truck from Paccar or Navistar is $60–100 000, compared to just $20–30 000 from Yiqi or Dongfeng. This reflects, among other things, the fundamentally different levels of R & D and technology incorporated into the respective vehicles. China's trucks have virtually no export sales at all, and rely heavily for their survival on high levels of protection in the Chinese market, including marketing channels as well as tariffs. The level of profits at the leading

Chinese truck makers is extremely low compared to the global leaders. Even pre-tax profits are just a small fraction of those of Navistar or Paccar , not to mention the truck division of the world leader, Daimler–Chrysler.

We have seen also, that the process of sharply increased industrial concentration has affected the components industry as much as the core vehicle assemblers. The pressure to achieve scale and associated cost reductions cascaded down from the vehicle assemblers to the first tier components makers. These in turn needed to achieve scale in order to leverage their own supplier networks of smaller second- and third-tier firms, to invest in R & D, and to develop global supply and service networks. We have seen that a drastic process of consolidation took place in this period in almost every part of the components industry. By the late 1990s, a small group of giant first tier suppliers had emerged, with sales of over $5 billion reaching as much as $29 billion for the industry leaders, Robert Bosch and Delphi. The leading components firms such as Robert Bosch, Delphi and Denso had R & D investments of over $1 billion. In 1998 Bosch's R & D expenditure for example, was greater even than that of Boeing ($2.1 billion compared to $1.8 billion) and Denso's was the same as that of Aerospatiale ($1.3 billion). Even tenth-ranked components firm Valeo, invested $365 million in R & D in 1998.

The level of concentration of market power within sub-categories of components had rapidly progressed to a high level. In seats, the leading makers, Johnson and Lear together accounted for around one-half of the total seats fitted to autos in Europe and the USA. In air conditioners, the top two firms, Denso and Valeo, together accounted for around one-half of the total world consumption of auto air conditioners. In car exhausts, Tenneco accounts for around one-half the world total fitted in the late 1990s. In constant velocity joints, GKN accounted for around two-fifths of the world total. In car braking systems, two firms, Bosch and Lucas, accounted for around three-fifths of total world consumption. In tyres, the top three firms accounted for around three-fifths of total world consumption. In diesel engines, the top three firms accounted for over 80 per cent of the North American market.

The size, global reach, R & D spending, marketing and service capability of the emerging giants of the world's auto components industry dwarfed even the largest firms in developing countries such as China. It was extremely difficult to imagine a strategy that could enable new entrants or existing small and medium firms in China or India to compete on the global level playing field with industry giants such as Delphi, Denso, Bosch, Valeo, Dana, Johnson Controls, TRW, Lear, Goodyear, Bridgestone, Michelin, Caterpillar, or Cummins Diesel Engine. Even the most powerful small and medium businesses in the world, the German Mittelstand engineering firms experienced a merger boom in the late 1990s. A large fraction of these are in the auto components industry. They have recognized that in order to compete they also have to achieve a scale far beyond their current level (*FT*, 8 February 2000).

In sum, the global business revolution in the auto industry has made the prospects for new entrants from developing countries extremely bleak in terms of capability to compete as either auto assemblers or first tier suppliers. Even the second and third tier are in the process of increased concentration to benefit from economies of scale and scope. The best that can be hoped for is to enter the value chain at the 'lower end' and work up to higher levels. Beyond that the only feasible strategy is to hope to attract global players to produce within the economy in order to raise competencies within the industry by employing local people in the industry. At the level of the firm, the business revolution leaves little prospect of competitive success.

CHINA'S AUTOMOBILE AND VEHICLE COMPONENTS INDUSTRY

OUTPUT GROWTH

China's rapid economic growth after the 1970s stimulated a matching increase in demand for motor vehicles. China's demand for automobiles (including trucks and buses) stood at under 150 000 in the late 1970s. By the mid-1990s, demand had risen to over 1.5 million vehicles (Table 8-9). Alongside the Asian crisis and the slowdown in the domestic economic growth rate, the growth of demand for automobiles almost halted, increasing by just 4 per cent from 1995 to 1998 (Table 8-9). In the mid-1980s, growth of demand greatly exceeded domestic production capacity, leading to a massive influx of foreign vehicles, especially saloons. In the peak year, 1985, imports amounted to 44 per cent of total domestic demand (Table 8-9). This shocked the government into more carefully considering its policy towards this hugely important sector.

The government responded by designating the auto industry a 'pillar' sector to be strongly supported. It tightly controlled legal vehicle imports (there was still a large amount of vehicle smuggling, the size of which it is impossible to estimate), and strongly promoting domestic vehicle and component production. Right up to the late 1990s, vehicle imports were subject to strict licensing and high tariffs. Imported components also were subject to import duties. The standard tariff on imported diesel engines in 1994 still stood at 35 per cent (Bear, Stearns, 1994:18). The final level of duties payable on imported components depended on the degree

TABLE 8-9 **Chinese Automobile Production, 1978–98**

Year	Production (000)				Imports	
	Total	Trucks	Saloons	Buses	Units	% Demand
1978	149	96	3	—	—	—
1985	443	237	5	12	354	44.4
1990	509	269	42	23	65	11.3
1995	1453	572	325	247	158	9.8
1998	1629	483	508	367	40	2.4

SOURCE: ZQJYZ, ZQGN (1999: 5, 10)

of domestic content achieved by a given vehicle firm. For example, for the period 1993–7 the Guangzhou Peugeot joint venture was liable to a 32 per cent import tariff on components if the level of domestic content was above 80 per cent, but the tariff rose to 60 per cent if the domestic content fell below 60 per cent (Peregrine, 1993b: 13). Vehicle makers in China were subject to other 'tough' local regulations. For example, Guangzhou Peugeot was required to ensure that the engine, and at least two of the other three main components (rear axle, transmission system, and vehicle body) were domestically sourced (Peregrine, 1993b: 13).

By 1998, officially-recorded imports accounted for less than 3 per cent of China's total vehicle market. The leading vehicle makers had all achieved a high degree of local content, sourcing a large fraction of their components from domestic producers. For example, at Beijing Jeep and Shanghai Volkswagen, the share of local components had risen from under 20 per cent in 1987 to over 80 per cent by 1995 (Lo, 1997: 191).

In the mid-1990s, as part of its effort to enter the WTO, China began cautiously to reduce the level of protection for the automobile industry. The tariff on imported vehicles fell from 180–220 per cent (depending on the engine capacity) in 1992 to 110–50 per cent in 1994 (Lo, 1997: 189). In 1996, tariffs on vehicle imports were further trimmed, to 100–120 per cent (*CDBW*, 15 March 1996). By 1999, tariffs on imported cars and components had fallen to 80 per cent and 50 per cent respectively (*Beijing Revue*, 4 October 1999). After China's entry to the WTO, the rate for the former will fall to 25 per cent, while that for the latter will fall to zero.

The production of *saloons* was minuscule in the late 1970s, a national total of just 3000 but grew rapidly thereafter (Table 8-9). Optimistic estimates in the mid-1990s were forecasting that by 2010 China would produce around 4 million saloons, accounting for around two-thirds of total vehicle output in China. The Chinese automobile market would then have been the fourth largest in the world, after North America, Europe and Japan (*FT*, 25 June 1997). Although these estimates now seem over-optimistic, the long-term prospects for the Chinese saloon vehicle market are enormous, and mean that all the major vehicle manufacturers have had to consider carefully the role that China will play in their global plans.

The role of *commercial vehicles* remains highly important. Despite fast output growth, in 1998 saloons still only accounted for less than two-fifths per cent of China's total automobile output (Table 8-9). *Trucks* accounted for 30 per cent and *buses* for 23 per cent (Table 8-9). The growth rate of truck output in the 1990s was substantially faster than the growth of national product, reflecting the growing intensification of market relationships, and the urgent need for vehicles to transport goods. Bus output was growing as fast as output of saloons: output of both rose more than tenfold from 1990 to 1995 (Table 8-9).

The components industry is growing in tandem with vehicle output growth, spurred by tough local content rules, lower transport costs and the imperative of 'just-in-time' production required by global vehicle makers. One estimate is that the Chinese automotive components market will be worth $45 billion by the year 2005, the largest of any single country (*FT*, 21 May 1996). By the end of 1997 around 60 per cent of saloon components and 80 per cent of truck components were manufactured domestically.

Despite the rapid growth of the Chinese vehicle industry, the small size of the base from which it started meant that at the end of the 1990s, it was still only a small part of the global industry. In 1998, China's national output of saloon vehicles amounted to only 1.3 per cent of total world output, while total automobile output, including commercial vehicles, amounted to less than three per cent of the world total. China's total automobile output, including commercial vehicles, amounted to 1.6 million units in 1998. This was the equivalent of 36 per cent of the total unit output of Toyota, VW or Renault Nissan, and one-fifth of that of Ford or General Motors. Moreover, the value per vehicle was much below that of the world's leading firms, mainly reflecting the much lower level of technology embedded in the vehicle. In 1998 the combined value of output of the three 'giant' corporations within the Chinese industry, Yiqi, Dongfeng, and Shanghai Auto, totalled $12 billion, amounting to only 16 per cent of the sales revenue of VW, 12 per cent of that of Toyota, and under 10 per cent of that of Ford or General Motors. In other words, even if the entire Chinese auto industry was combined into a single company, it would still total a small fraction of the size of the world's leading auto companies in terms of unit production and an even smaller fraction of their total sales revenue, not to speak of profits or R & D.

INSTITUTIONAL STRUCTURE

Vehicles. After the 1970s, China's economic reforms stimulated a rapid growth of demand for vehicles. Alongside high levels of protection, this encouraged a proliferation of vehicle makers. Demand greatly exceeded supply for some years, encouraging new entrants to the industry, often producing on an extremely small scale. The number of automobile assembly plants rose from around 50 in the mid-1970s to over 120 in the early 1990s (MMB, ZQGN, 1996: 68). In 1990 only two of the vehicle manufacturers had an annual output of more than 50000 units. The majority of them produced fewer than 10000 units per annum. Indeed, of the 122 vehicle assembly plants which operated in 1995, 48 of them produced fewer than 1000 vehicles per annum (Table 8-10). In 1990, the top five producers accounted for only 12 per cent of total vehicle output (Lo, 1997: 181). As early as 1987 the Chinese government announced its intention to attempt to concentrate the automobile industry into much larger units which could benefit from economies of scale (Lo, 1997: 181–2).

A key part of this was the way in which the entry of multinational automobile companies was organized. This process was tightly controlled by the Chinese government. It permitted the establishment of five major equity joint ventures and one major licensing agreement in the saloon vehicle sector. The foreign partner in a joint venture in vehicle manufacture was limited to 50 per cent of the total equity value. Three of the joint ventures were with the three 'giants' among the SOEs, namely, *Shanghai Automobile Company* (with Volkswagen, established

TABLE **8-10 Plant-Size Distribution of China's
Vehicle Assembly Plants, 1995**

Annual Vehicle Output	No. of Plants
> 50 000	8
20 000–50 000	7
10 000–20 000	9
1000–10 000	50
< 1000	48

SOURCE: MMB, ZQGN (1996: 69)

in 1985), *Yiqi (First Automotive Works)*, Changchun (also with Volkswagen, established in 1992 and *Dongfeng Automobile Works (Erqi: No. 2 Automobile Works)*, Hubei province (with Citroën, established in 1992). The other major joint ventures were with the Beijing Automotive Industry Corporation (with Chrysler, in 1984), Guangzhou Auto (with Peugeot, in 1985) and Tianjin Auto to produce the Charade mini-car (with Daihatsu, established in 1988 as a licensing agreement, later extended into a joint venture). In 1997 Shanghai Automotive Works was allowed to set up its second major joint venture, with General Motors as its partner. The joint venture entered production in 1999.

In 1994 the Chinese government made a further key policy announcement for the automobile sector. It made even clearer the commitment to concentrating vehicle production in a small number of large firms. These firms were to be the 'national champions', that would be able to withstand the onslaught from international competition when China's protection was reduced. An official government researcher commented:

> For various historical reasons, China's auto industry had long been subject to slow, disorderly and inefficient development. Many experts referred to the situation as a 'sheet of loose sand'. China previously had 126 auto manufacturing plants, more than 600 auto refitting factories and more than 4000 components factories. Most of the factories operated on a small scale, with some having annual output of less than 10 000 units ... In the face of fierce competition, China decided to introduce a strategic reorganization of its auto industry, with the goal of establishing a batch of sizeable pillar enterprises or conglomerates ... *The scattered and disorderly state which long dominated China's auto industry is expected to come to an end in the not-too-distant future (Beijing Review, 6 November 1995, emphasis added).*

The government's aim was now to construct a market structure characterized by 'effective competition', that is *'competition among a small number of big firms'* (Lo, 1997: 185, emphasis added). The government's goal was to reshuffle the top twenty or so auto manufacturers into just three or four enterprise groups by the turn of the century 'in order to meet foreign competition'. The government supported a policy of mergers and acquisitions by the emerging giants in order to achieve this result. Each of the top firms was planned to have an eventual output of at least 400 000 vehicles per year. The government earmarked a large fraction of its funds to support the auto industry to the emerging giants (Huang Wei, 1995).[7]

It was planned that the myriad of small vehicle plants should convert to components suppliers for the giants of the industry (*CDBW*, 7 September 1997). Loss-making firms in the sector were to be declared bankrupt and sell their assets to larger firms or merge with them. The Ministry of Machine Building announced that each year it would withdraw the licences of several small loss-making plants if they continued to make losses or were reluctant to merge with other plants. Promising enterprises were to receive priority for government endorsement in overseas listings and issuing industrial bonds abroad (*China Economic Digest*, Spring 1997: 20). They were to be eligible for tax exemptions and state-approved loans.

The rapid growth of output from the government's targeted keypoint plants produced an explosive process of concentration of market share in saloon vehicle production. By 1996 Shanghai Volkswagen's joint venture with VW accounted for 47 per cent of total domestic saloon vehicle production and the Tianjin Charade joint venture accounted for 20 per cent (Table 8-11). Joint ventures with multinationals accounted for almost the entire output of saloon vehicles. The indigenous partner lacked the capability to independently develop new vehicles. It was bluntly recognized that China had failed comprehensively to catch up with the global giants of the industry:

> Lacking the capacity to develop complete cars, the industry is at a disadvantage in the competition of products. In addition China's auto industry has a low product development capability. Apart from technical disadvantages, a key problem lies in the shortage of funds. It costs at least US$150 million and takes several years to develop a new product. None of the Chinese auto enterprises finds this affordable. The low capacity in the development of new models also reduces the Chinese auto industry's competitiveness (*Beijing Review*, 4 October 1999).

TABLE **8-11 China's Saloon Vehicle Production, 1998**

Producer's Name	000	%
Total	508	100.0
of which:		
Shanghai Auto/Volkswagen JV	236	46.5
Tianjin/Daihatsu JV	100	19.7
Yiqi/Volkswagen JV	66	13.0
Dongfeng/Citroen JV	36	7.1
Beijing Jeep/Daimler–Chrysler JV	8	1.6
Others	62	12.1

SOURCE: ZQJYZ, ZQGN (1999: 5–7)

NOTE: Total number of producers = 19

Thus, rather than the policy of focusing on a few giant firms allowing the creation of a small number of indigenous, globally competitive giant car firms, China's policies allowed the multinational car makers to develop reasonably large branch plants within their global system. In the year 2000 there was no sign that indigenous car makers had progressed at all towards a capability to compete directly with the multinational giants of the industry.

In the bus sector, Mercedes–Benz established a joint venture with Yangzhou Motor (with a 50 per cent ownership stake for Mercedes–Benz). Mercedes–Benz is transferring the technology necessary for Yangzhou to produce international standard tourist buses for use on the newly-developing network of highways (*FT*, 17 September 1996). The head of Mercedes–Benz's vehicle arm commented: 'This project opens a highly promising perspective for us in the largest and most attractive bus and coach market in the world' (*FT*, 17 September 1996). In 1994, Volvo established a joint venture to produce buses with Xian aircraft corporation. By 1999 it had an output capacity of 1500, which enabled it to take around one-half of the market for luxury tourist buses within China, the other major competitor being the Mercedes–Benz joint venture. In other words, the two joint ventures accounted for the lion's share of the high value-added luxury tourist bus market.

The extent of foreign involvement in the heavy and medium duty truck sector was much lower than in the saloon car sector. At the start of the reform process, the truck sector was more advanced than the saloon car industry, and there were already two dominant enterprises, Yiqi and Erqi (Dongfeng). These two entities were strongly supported by central government policy during the reforms, as the pillars of the Chinese truck industry. In 1998, Dongfeng alone accounted for over one-half of total domestic production of heavy duty trucks, while Dongfeng and Yiqi together accounted for 67 per cent of total national output (Table 8-12). In medium duty trucks, Yiqi was the number one producer with 56 per cent of the national market, while Yiqi and Dongfeng together accounted for 91 per cent of national output (Table 8-13).

In terms of units of output, Yiqi and Donfeng were on a truly global scale, since the Chinese truck market is relatively much larger than the saloon vehicle market. In 1998, they together accounted for around 12 per cent of total world

TABLE **8-12 Main Heavy-duty Truck Producers in China, 1998 (000)**

Producer's Name	Output
Dongfeng (Erqi) Vehicle Company	9.5
China Heavy Duty Truck Company	1.1
Yiqi Group Company	6.3
Sichuan Vehicle Plant	0.8

SOURCE: ZQJYZ, ZQGN (1999: 00)

NOTE: Share of output produced by:
    the top producer = 51.1%
    the top four producers = 95.2%
    Total number of producers = 15

output of trucks of over six tonnes. Their combined output was second only to Daimler–Chrysler in terms of units of output (Table 8-14). However, separately, they ranked as middle-level players in terms of units of output. Moreover, in terms of sales revenue, they lagged far behind the world's leading firms in the sector. Even the combined sales of Yiqi and Dongfeng amounted to just one-quarter of those of the world leader, Daimler–Chrysler (Table 8-14). Together they made a pre-tax profit of just $16 million in 1998, compared with over $1 billion for Daimler–Chrysler. The world's leading truck companies were able to spend large sums on R & D to develop their technical capability, on IT to develop their global systems integration with their supplier network, and on service and

TABLE 8-13 Main Medium-duty Truck Producers in China, 1998 (000)

Producer's Name	Output
Yiqi Group Company	72.2
Dongfeng (Erqi) Auto Company	45.7
Dongfeng Liuzhou Auto Company	5.5
Hubei Special Vehicle Company	1.7
Dongfeng Lianying Company	1.5
Dongfeng Hangzhou Auto Company	1.4
Luoyang Auto Company	0.6
Dongfeng Nanjing Auto Company	0.5

SOURCE: ZQJYZ, ZQGN (1999: 340)

NOTE: Share of output produced by:
   the top producer = 55.6%
   the top two producers = 90.8%
   Total number of producers = 13

TABLE 8-14 Comparative Size of Chinese and Selected Global Truck Companies, 1998

Company	Output (000)	Sales Revenue ($ billion)	Profits ($ million)	Employees (000)
Daimler–Chrysler*	234	27.2	1100**	90
Navistar	124	7.9	299**	18
Paccar	78	7.9	417**	23
Yiqi	156	4.4§	21§±	156§
Dongfeng	113	2.6§	−5§±	134§

SOURCES: FT (3 December 1999); Fortune (26 April 1999, 2 August 1999); Daimler-Chrysler (Annual Report, 1998; ZQJYZ, ZQGN (1999: 312–13)

NOTES: * Commercial vehicles
      ** Post-tax profits
      § Including non-truck production
      ± Pre-tax profits

marketing networks to develop product value to the customer. Neither of China's leading truck companies was able to compete with these capabilities. Despite their considerable scale, one could not be optimistic of the capability of even China's large truck companies to compete within the rules of the WTO.

Components

From extreme fragmentation to rapid consolidation. Consolidation of the auto parts industry lagged behind that in vehicle assembly. A large number of vehicle makers produced vehicles in small batches, with low quality and price, using cheap, low quality components manufactured by local firms, typically township and village enterprises, with small entry costs. By the mid-1990s it is estimated that there were around 4800 components manufacturers across the country, most of which were tiny (*FT*, 5 March 1996). Chinese official statistics list over 1600 components makers in 1995 (Table 8-15). In the late 1980s there were at least 200 enterprises manufacturing internal combustion engines (Yuchai was ranked number 174 in the mid-1980s). In the early 1990s, even in the medium-duty truck diesel engine sector there were around 10 main producers (Bear, Stearns, 1994: 14), and several smaller manufacturers.

China's tough local content rules (see above) are 'a boon to the components sector' as Chinese vehicle production rises (*FT*, 21 May 1996). These forces created pressures for the expanding automobile industry to purchase an increasing share of its inputs from local components makers, and placed pressure on them to improve quality, timeliness of delivery and to reduce costs of production. Even in the absence of foreign investment or government policy towards consolidation of the sector, it is likely that the growth of automobile output and the increasing role for market forces would have produced a period of rapid change in institutional structure in China's components industry.

In fact the government's goal in the components sectors, as in vehicle assembly, has increasingly become the creation of a small group of powerful manufacturers. The Ministry of Machine Building released a list of 300 companies in the components sector that it wished to support. These were eligible for policy loans and other preferential policies (*FT*, 5 March 1996). Foreign investment is encouraged

TABLE 8-15 **Size Distribution of Chinese Component Makers, 1995**

Plant size Category	No. of Plants	Value of Vehicle Industry Sales (million yuan)	Sales/Plant (million yuan)
Total	1671	40 213	24.1
Large	156	19 534	125.2
Middle[a]	86	4677	54.3
Middle[b]	250	6782	27.1
Small	1179	9219	7.8

SOURCE: MMB, ZQGN (1996: 66)

NOTE: *a* Large middle
       b Small middle

in these enterprises. By the turn of the century the Chinese government aims to have a network of just five to ten internationally competitive components manufacturers (*FT*, 5 March 1996). A major difference from the vehicle assembly sector is that the foreign partner in the joint venture is permitted to have over 50 per cent of the equity value of the joint venture. Initially, it seemed as if the engine sector might be more restrictive, limiting the foreign ownership share to 50 per cent (*Beijing Revue*, 6 November 1995: 17). However, it seems that even in engine manufacture, the joint venture partner can occupy majority ownership.[8]

In the 'planned economy', vehicle makers were highly vertically integrated. For example, at the start of the 1980s, Erqi, one of China's top three vehicle makers, produced 75 per cent of its components in-house (Marukawa, 1995: 341). The government encouraged giant vehicle makers such as Erqi to reorganize the production of components, so that an increasing proportion were produced by specialist makers, benefiting from economies of scale. The emerging giant vehicle makers increasingly formed close relationships with associated components makers, sometimes through capital investment, sometimes through long-term purchasing arrangements. The 'core' vehicle assemblers stood at the centre of 'industrial groups', and played a key role in advancing specialization and division of labour in the vehicle sector (Marukawa, 1995). The advice of Peregrine, the Hong Kong-based investment bank was that foreign components manufacturers should seek joint ventures with firms that are associated with the emerging large vehicle assembly makers, 'which have a "stranglehold" on the commercial segment' (*FT*, 21 May 1996).

Very rapidly, the Chinese vehicle industry will become one in which a small number of giant vehicle assembly firms will be closely associated with a small number of giant component makers. In China, as across the globe, the dominant vehicle assemblers wish to purchase their components from those component suppliers who dominate the global industry, and can provide a 'global' product that is consistent in design and quality across countries. China's emerging giant vehicle assemblers increasingly have powerful multinational companies as joint venture partners. Components firms which do not have close links with the major auto assemblers, and which do not have joint ventures with multinationals will find it increasingly hard to compete in the fast-changing market structure. Shanghai VW, for example, has around 180 suppliers, and in the mid-1990s the share of joint ventures among these is rising fast (*FT*, 2 May 1995).

Components industry investment companies. One route through which multinational capital enters the Chinese components industry sector has been through specialist components industry investment companies. Two of the most important of these are ITT Automotive Pacific and Asimco. *ITT* already has two component industry joint ventures in Shanghai to manufacture auto electrical systems and anti-locking brake systems respectively. In addition, it plans to raise around $150–200 million to invest in four other joint venture projects in the automobile components sector, including the production of automotive fuel handling systems, sensors, switches and after-sales products.

Asimco is an investment company which specializes in auto components, with a subsidiary interest in brewing. It selected the components industry because this was a high growth sector, and one which the government regarded as a 'pillar' industry. Moreover, it felt that the growth of joint ventures in vehicle manufacturing would provide a ready market for the products of Asimco's joint ventures (Asimco, 1997). Since August 1994 it has set up 13 auto component joint ventures across China (Asimco, 1997).[9] Asimco staff visited over 350 potential partners across China before selecting the 10 initial joint ventures. Far from finding an amorphous sea of enterprises, Asimco was able to identify suitable partners which had 'proven Chinese managements', which are 'aggressive, profit-oriented and have a track record of building their business to a position of industry leadership' (Asimco, 1997).

By mid-1997 Asimco had invested $230 million in its joint ventures in auto components. In all cases, Asimco has majority ownership. Its aim is to build 'the leading auto components business in China', 'capable of competing internationally' and giving access to equity markets outside China. It directs the business planning function of its subsidiary companies from the head office in Beijing and accesses new products through co-investment or licensing agreements with multinationals. Asimco considers that it is in a strong position to benefit from the 'current trend of consolidation', and believes that its joint ventures will have the 'opportunity to dominate their sectors' (Asimco, 1997).

Investments by specialized multinational components companies. Already by 1995 there were over 60 joint ventures in the automobile sector, mostly for the manufacture of components (MMB, ZQGN, 1996: 352–413). In the mid-1990s the pace of foreign investment in components accelerated sharply, with many of the global leaders entering the industry. The following are some of the investment made by leading global auto components companies in China in the 1990s:

- **Delphi**. By 1996 Delphi Automotive Systems, the vast subsidiary of GM (see above) had established seven joint ventures in China (*China: Economic Digest*, Spring 1996). These were large-scale ventures. For example, the joint venture in Hubei Province is scheduled to produce 600 000 automotive generators per year, with technology upgraded by Delphi (*China: Economic Digest*, Spring 1996).

- **Robert Bosch**. By 1998, Bosch had a total of 120 production sites across the world, of which four were in China. It has set up China's largest auto components project (with 50 per cent ownership), a $321 million project with Shanghai's Zhonglian Automotive Electronics Company. It will manufacture EMS (engine management systems) using 'the world's most advanced techniques' introduced by Bosch. The computer-controlled EMS can control precisely the mixture of gasoline and air to ensure complete combustion, and will greatly reduce pollution. The product will be highly sought after when the government introduces a state law limiting exhaust emissions in the near future. In 1997, the plant will have a capacity of 500 000 sets and is planned to reach 1.23 million sets by 1999 (*China: Economic Digest*, Summer 1996). Its other plants in China include a spark plugs plant in Nanjing, with 1000 employees, and a joint venture in Wuxi to manufacture diesel engine fuel injection components.

- **Valeo**. By 1997, Valeo had a total of almost 50 production facilities in developing countries. Of these, six were in China, including clutch production in Nanjing, air conditioning and automobile lighting in Hubei, automotive electrical systems and automotive electrical motors in Shanghai (Valeo, *Annual Report, 1998*). In five of the six joint ventures, Valeo owned over 49 per cent of the equity.

- **Denso**. Between 1994 and 1997 Denso established five plants in China as part of its global network of production facilities. These included two plants (one at Yantai, another at Tianjin) to manufacture automobile air conditioners, one to manufacture alternators and starters (in Tianjin), one to manufacture magnetos, CDI amplifiers and ignition coils (at Chongqing), and one to manufacture automotive electronic control components (at Tianjin). In the two joint ventures established in 1994–5, Denso held a minority share, but in the three established in 1996–7 it held a majority stake (Denso, *Annual Report, 1999*: 40–1). In total the five plants employed more than 1000 people.

Foreign investment in engine making. In the mid-1990s, joint ventures with globally powerful firms in the components sector were a major element in the rapid institutional change in the engine making sector. These were to have major significance for the prospects for specialist engine makers such as Yuchai. Of particular importance is the fact that two of the world's leading independent vehicle diesel engine makers, Lucas–Varity and Cummins, has each set up joint ventures with Yuchai's competitors. The following are some of the leading joint ventures in vehicle engine making:

- **Volkswagen**. By 2001, Volkswagen's joint venture (40 per cent owned by VW) with First Automobile Works (Yiqi, in Changchun) will be able to produce around 500 000 passenger car engines while the Shanghai VW joint venture with Shanghai Automobile Company (50 per cent owned by VW) has a planned capacity of 333 000 per year (*FT*, 2 December 1994).

- **Mercedes–Benz**. Mercedes' joint venture with South China Motor Corporation (45 per cent is owned by Mercedes) is planned to involve the construction of capacity to build 100 000 engines for minibuses (as well as around 60 000 minibuses) annually (IHT, 7 July 1995).

- **Toyota**. In 1996 Toyota was given permission to set up an enginemaking joint venture with Tianjin Auto (each partner with 50 per cent ownership) with designed capacity of 150 000 1.3 litre car engines, mainly intended for use in the Charade mini-passenger vehicle produced by Tianjin Auto under licence from Daihatsu (*China: Economic Digest*, Summer 1996).

- **Hino**. Hino is a truck making affiliate of Toyota, in which Toyota has an 11 per cent ownership share. It has agreed to set up a joint venture with the China National Heavy Duty Truck Corporation to produce truck engines at the Corporation's Hangzhou Automobile Engine Plant (*FT*, 10 July 1996).

- **Mitsubishi**. Mitsubishi has set up a joint venture in Shenyang, with the China Aerospace Automotive Industry Group, and Shenyang Construction Investment to manufacture vehicle engines of 2.0 and 2.4 litre. The company expects to produce 150000 units per year (*FT*, 9 September 1997).

- **Lucas–Varity**. In 1997, Perkins, the diesel engine subsidiary of Lucas–Varity, entered a joint venture with the Tianjin Engine Works. Perkins will own 60 per cent of the joint venture. It is intended to make the joint venture 'one of the country's biggest makers of diesel engines for use in trucks, buses and power-generating equipment', using technology transferred from Perkins (*FT*, 15 May 1997). By 2001 it is planned to produce around 50000 engines per year at the plant. Perkins plans to generate around 30 per cent of its revenue from Asia by the year 2000, and China is considered by the management of the company to be an 'excellent base' from which to expand into southeast Asia (*FT*, 15 May 1997).

- **Cummins**. After several years with a technical transfer arrangement, in the mid-1990s Cummins and Dongfeng (Erqi) finally set up a full joint venture to manufacture truck diesel engines (see below).

Lessons from Brazil. The Brazilian components industry offers an important object lesson for China. The automobile industry is much further advanced than the Chinese, with a total output of vehicles and components that was roughly three times that of the Chinese in the mid-1990s (Mukherjee and Sastry, 1996). Like China it has developed a proliferation of mainly small indigenous components makers, totalling around 1000 in 1997. For decades, indigenous firms were able to 'charge high prices for often low quality products' (*FT*, 9 July 1997).

Alongside the rapid institutional change in the global components industry and fast expansion of international investment by the emerging giants of the industry has gone rapidly accelerating foreign penetration of the Brazilian components industry. In the past three years 'a string of foreign parts makers, including Dana, Echlin and Tenneco, have strengthened their position through mergers, acquisitions and joint ventures' (*FT*, 9 July 1997). Small indigenous makers have found it hard to compete with joint ventures established by the multinational giants: 'The only way to attain the technology, management skills and economies of scale needed to survive is to join forces with the big international groups' (*FT*, 9 July 1997). Within Brazil it is predicted that the total number of component makers will shrink from the present 1000 to only around 200 by the beginning of the next century. The strongest of these will be the subsidiary operations of the global giants: 'Many manufacturers can only hope to survive in the "second-tier", supplying the motor industry's suppliers' (*FT*, 9 July 1997).

YUCHAI

YUCHAI'S HIGH-SPEED GROWTH AND COLLAPSE

Growth. Prior to 1984 Yuchai was a small producer of low-power diesel engines for agricultural machinery (the 2105 engine), ranked number 173 among China's internal combustion engine producers (broadly defined).

Experimental production of the medium-duty truck diesel engine, the 6105 began in 1981, and full production began in 1984. Shortly after this, Wang Jianming was appointed as chief executive officer of the plant, and played a central role in the company's rapid rise. Output accelerated rapidly to over 8000 units in 1989, by which point Yuchai had become one of China's 500 largest enterprises in terms of profitability and tax contribution. By 1991 Yuchai had climbed to be the third largest diesel engine manufacturer. By 1993 output of medium-duty diesel engines had risen to over 38 000 units and Yuchai had become China's largest diesel engine manufacturer by value of sales (Bear, Stearns, 1994: 40). In the early 1990s it rose rapidly from being China's 645th largest enterprise by value of sales (*Management World*, 1993: 9) to 216th in 1995 (SSB, ZDQN, 1996: 225). By 1995, Yuchai was China's fifth largest producer of general machinery (SSB, ZDQN, 1996: 153).

Yuchai's share of China's medium-duty truck engine market climbed sharply from zero in the early 1980s to 17 per cent in 1991 and 33 per cent in 1994, peaking at around 49 per cent in 1995. This was a remarkable story of growth, from nothing to almost one-half of the total market for one of China's most important, fast-growing and technically demanding products. As we shall see later, a key slogan of Wang Jianming was 'start from scratch every day' (*ling qi dian*). This slogan was particularly appropriate for Yuchai since it really had 'started from scratch'. Yuchai was only able to achieve this growth through the application of a complex set of modern business practices that differentiated it from its more slowly-changing competitors among the state-owned enterprises.

In the early and mid-1990s Yuchai entered a period of accelerated expansion (Tables 8-16 and 8-17). An important part of the finance for this expansion was obtained through the establishment of a Sino–foreign joint venture and flotation on the New York Stock Market (see below). In 1993, Yuchai's capacity was around 37 000 medium-duty engines. It planned within two to three years to expand capacity to around 130 000 medium-duty engines.

In addition, Yuchai anticipated that the fastest growth rate for diesel engines in the foreseeable future would be for heavy-duty engines. Accordingly, Wang Jianming decided to purchase a second-hand production line from Ford of Brazil which on completion would have a capacity of 70 000 units per year (Bear, Stearns, 1994: 43). Thus, Yuchai's goal was to have increased capacity from around 12 000 units in 1990 to around 200 000 within less than a decade, and to consolidate its position as China's number one diesel engine manufacturer, with a dominant position in the medium-duty market and a leading position in the heavy-duty market. In the classic fashion analyzed in Chandler (1990) it hoped

TABLE **8-16 Consolidated Profit and Loss Account at Guangxi Yuchai Machinery Company Ltd, 1991–5 (million/yuan)**

Item	1991	1992	1993	1994	1995
Sales	218.4	422.1	968.8	1802.2	1818.2
Operating profit*	5.1	86.6	263.0	529.1	448.5
% of sales value	2.3	20.5	27.1	29.4	24.6
Income tax	4.8	5.3	61.4	—	13.8
Net profit/(loss)**	(22.0)	47.2	198.3	457.7	446.4
% of sales value	(10.1)	11.2	20.4	25.4	24.5

SOURCES: Bear, Stearns (1994: 827); Peat Marwick Huazhen (1995: 4)

NOTES: *Sales value minus sales tax and surcharge, cost of sales, selling expenses, general administrative expenses, and financial expenses

**Operating profit plus non-operating income, plus previous year's profit/(loss) adjustments, minus income tax

to be able to benefit from 'economies of scope' by applying to the heavy-duty diesel engine market the managerial skills developed in rising to a leading position in the medium-duty market.

Collapse. Yuchai's peak year was 1995. In 1995–7 due to the government's credit squeeze, demand for trucks fell substantially in China. National output of trucks fell from a peak of 623 000 units in 1993, falling precipitously to 483 000 units in 1998 (ZQJYZ, ZQGN, 1999: 5). The sharp decline in demand and output caused serious losses among China's truck makers and their suppliers. Yuchai's main customers substantially contracted their purchase of truck engines. Moreover, demand from Yuchai's main customer, Dongfeng (see below) and its subordinate enterprises, fell especially severely. Dongfeng had a 'terrible' year in 1996–7 and gave preference to diesel engine purchases from engine makers within its own group.

By late 1997 Yuchai's situation had become desperate. It had still not produced any commercial output of the new heavy-duty diesel engine (Ford 6112), and output of its main product, the medium-duty 6105 series had fallen severely. Yuchai's production in the first eight months of 1997 was around 25 000 units, much below its peak level with reported sales of just 18 000 units, over the same period. By August there was 'no production at all', and it seemed likely this would be the case for another month or so. In 1997 employees were reported to be working in rotation, being paid for less than one day out of three. By the Autumn of 1997 Yuchai had paid no bonuses 'for some time' and was unable to pay many of its creditors. The outlook was bleak. Output fell from a peak of 79 000 units in 1995 to around 50–55 000 in the years 1996–8 (Table 8-17). The value of output fell from a peak of 2 billion yuan in 1995 to 1.1 billion yuan in 1998. The fall in pre-tax profits was even more severe, from 570 million yuan ($69 million) in 1994 to just 125 million yuan ($15 million) in 1998.

TABLE 8-17 Growth of Yuchai, 1975–98

Item	1975	1980	1985	1990	1991	1992	1993	1994	1995	1996	1998
Output of: agricultural machinery engines (2105)	3 761	1 625	216	2 129	2 022	—	—	—	—	—	—
Diesel engine production capacity (000)	—	—	—	—	—	—	37	—	130	—	190
Output of medium-duty truck engines (000)	—	—	3.0	12.2	14.0	23.3	37.7	65.0	79.2	50.4	53.5*
Yuchai's sales as a % of total medium-duty truck diesel engines installed in China	13	7	—	—	17	20	27	33	49	—	—
Value of sales (million yuan)	—	—	23	188	247	450	1 008	1 804	2 000	1 600 (est.)	1 126
Value of assets (million yuan)	—	—	8 (1984)	—	110	411	506	1 004	—	—	3 290
Net value of fixed assets (million yuan, year-end)	—	—	—	—	—	—	268	417	669	—	—
Profits/taxes (million yuan)	4	1	4	21	27	81	381	570	510	250 (est.)	125
Employees (000)	—	—	2 000	—	—	—	—	—	—	10 000** (est.)	8 900

SOURCES: Fieldnotes and ZQJYZ, ZQGN (1999: 355, 470)

NOTES: * Pre-1998, these were all 6105 medium-duty truck engines; the 1998 figure includes output of the 6108 engine
** An additional 4 000 are employed in the 'labour service' company

MARKETS

Market Growth and Structure. We have seen (above) that China's high-speed growth of national product has been accompanied by a fast growth of vehicle output. Although the share of trucks in total output has fallen alongside the rapid growth of saloon vehicles and buses, trucks still accounted for 42 per cent of vehicle output in 1995 (Table 8-9). Moreover, medium-duty trucks constitute the principle carrier of cargo by road. The use of heavy-duty trucks is limited by the narrowness and poor maintenance of roads which place a premium on manoeuvrability. In 1993 there were over 178 000 medium-duty trucks produced in China, compared to just 10 000 heavy-duty trucks. Medium-duty trucks accounted for 27 per cent of total motor vehicle production (Bear, Stearns, 1994: 40).

The demand for diesel engines for medium-duty trucks rose exceptionally fast in the 1990s as diesel engines were replacing gasoline ones as the choice of truck purchasers. Although diesel engines are more expensive to buy, they are preferred because of their higher power, fuel efficiency and reliability. By 1995, almost all new heavy-duty trucks, over one-half of new medium-duty and over one-third of new light-duty trucks were fitted with diesel engines (Table 8-18).

The above factors contributed to an exceptionally rapid growth of demand for medium-duty diesel engines in the late 1980s and 1990s. Between 1989 and 1993, China's output of medium-duty diesel engines rose from 55 000 to 144 000 (Bear, Stearns, 1994: 41). However, it was to be expected that the rate of growth would fall off, since the change in the structure of demand towards diesel engines was a one-off phenomenon. Moreover, over the long term, as road conditions improve, it was to be expected that the share of large trucks in freight haulage would rise. This influenced Wang Jianming's decision to try to develop Yuchai's heavy-duty diesel engine capability.

The nature of demand altered in the 1990s also in respect of the type of purchaser. Instead of state units, there occurred a rapid growth of individual purchasers due to the rise of private and collective transport companies, and the leasing out of transport units by state-owned enterprises. Consequently, the consumers became much more discriminating, with much closer attention to the purchase price, reliability and operating costs of the engines.

TABLE **8-18 Output of Trucks in China, 1995 and 1998 (000)**

Trucks	Total (1995)	Of which: Diesel	Total (1998)
Total	642.5	260.6	573.8
of which:			
Heavy-duty	23.6	20.6	13.6
Medium-duty	208.8	116.5	129.8
Light	301.1	123.4	280.0
Micro	109.0	0	145.4

SOURCE: MMB, ZQGN (1996: 81)

The demand for trucks is highly cyclical. From 1978 to 1980, truck output rose by 80 per cent, only to plummet by 20 per cent in 1980–1. From 1980 to 1988 output rose by 168 per cent, only to plummet by 26 per cent in 1988–90. From 1988 to 1993 output rose by 71 per cent, only to plummet once more by 22 per cent between 1993 and 1998 (ZQJYZ, ZQGN, 1999: 5). However, over the long-term, if national product continues to rise, demand for freight transport must rise also in reasonable proportion, since growth of freight traffic is a crucial part of the growth of a market economy. Over the long period from the late 1970s to the late 1990s, China's truck making capacity grew from around 80 000 units to over 600 000 units, reflecting the dramatic change in the size and nature of the Chinese economy. Truck output grew more or less in step with the long-term growth of national product at around 11 per cent per annum.

In times of fast-growing demand for medium-duty trucks, Yuchai's profit rate was high. Its engines were in high demand, due to their high quality compared to other domestic manufacturers, Yuchai's wide service network and strong guarantee. Consequently, Yuchai was able to charge a considerable price premium and enjoyed booming demand for its products, which made the company attractive to external investors.

Product Choice and Development. Yuchai's period of explosive growth in the late 1980s–early 1990s was based on the 6105 engine (that is, a six-cylinder engine with a 105 mm bore). This was a more powerful engine than that produced at the time by Yuchai's chief rivals, which mattered greatly in the competitive struggle for the Chinese medium-duty engine market. Most Chinese medium-duty trucks are now operated by individuals and their goal is to load the trucks as much as possible. Hence, there is a significant premium for trucks with a more powerful engine. However, as the 1990s progressed, other domestic producers were quickly catching up. The two diesel engine producers within the Yiqi Group, Dalian and Wuxi, by 1996 could both produce engines of 110 mm bore, achieving greater power than Yuchai's 6105 engine.

Yuchai could foresee these problems, so it attempted three paths to keep it ahead of the competition:

- **Upgrading the 6105 engine**. Yuchai attempted to upgrade the quality of the 6105 to 108mm bore, enabling the engine to generate greater power, and thereby head off the challenge from Dalian and Wuxi. A complete new production facility was constructed to produce the remodelled engine, using almost entirely domestic equipment.[10] Yuchai hired the consultancy services of FEV (Germany) and AVL (Austria), as well as the Shanghai Research Institute for Combustion Engines, to attempt to achieve this. The development of the new engine and associated production facilities cost 500–600 million yuan, using the bulk of the revenue from the New York listing (see below). Unfortunately, development of the engine encountered major technical problems. The engine block was unable to diffuse the heat generated by the higher bore size. Yuchai was unable to produce the 6108 commercially. This was a major setback and a huge waste of resources with large opportunity costs for Yuchai. The whole complex for the 6108 consisted of 13 plants, and the annual capacity was around 70 000 units.

- **Improving the quality of the fuel pump injection for all its engines**. In order to do this, Yuchai invested in a joint venture with Asimco. It purchased 20 per cent of the value of the Nanyue Fuel Pump Company (located in Hengyang, Hunan Province), with Asimco as the majority owner. This was reputedly the best fuel pump maker in China, and Asimco's goal was to upgrade the technical level at the company through licensing from a multi-national producer. A major goal of the joint venture was to produce pumps for the 6108 engine. Nanyue produced thousands of pumps for the 6108, but these were all returned to the company as the engine failed to come to fruition.

- **Development of a heavy-duty truck engine**. Wang Jianming purchased at an exceptionally low price, reportedly just $16 million,[11] a second hand production line from Ford (Brazil) to produce a six cylinder, 112 mm bore engine (the 6112 model). The line had a design capacity of 45 000 engines in Brazil, but it was hoped that the output in Yuchai would be 50 000 units per annum. Unfortunately, although the plant was purchased 'cheaply', the engine is a 'poor performer', and has serious emission problems even in terms of China's lax pollution controls. The engine has been test produced but has 'not found a market' (see below). In 1996–7 the plant was simply lying idle.

Thus the situation in late 1997 was that in the medium-duty truck market, the mainstay of Yuchai's growth, the 6105 was no longer able to command a mass market due to the development of technically superior and attractively priced competitors. The 6108 is a technical failure despite the expenditure of large sums on its development. In the heavy-duty market, the 6112 has failed to find a market due to its technical backwardness. Yuchai has the capacity to produce annually around 70 000 of the 6105 engines, around 70 000 of the 6108 engines and around 50 000 of the 6112 engines. In 1997 it seemed likely Yuchai would sell well under 30 000 units, not even one-half of the capacity of one of the three engines that it is able to produce.

Customers. In 1995 there were around 80 truck producers in China. However, even under the old planning system, production was dominated by a small number of powerful state-owned firms. Moreover, the market power of the large producers has been at least sustained, if not increased, alongside the growth of output after the 1970s. We have seen that Yiqi and Dongfeng comprehensively dominate domestic production of heavy-and medium-duty trucks. The production of light trucks is more fragmented, but even in these, Yiqi and Dongfeng are the leading producers, accounting for around one-third of total domestic output (Table 8-19), and the top five firms account for almost two-thirds of national output.

It is clear from the foregoing that Dongfeng and Yiqi have immense market power in the purchase of automobile components for large and medium trucks. Moreover, government policy is strongly supportive of the maintenance of the dominant position of the top producers in these sectors. As we have seen, a large and growing fraction of truck engines is diesel powered. Without the market of these two leading producers, the future of an independent Chinese medium- and heavy-duty diesel engine maker would be severely constrained.

In 1995 Yuchai sold its engines to 37 factories, but a small number of these were disproportionately important. Over three-fifths of Yuchai's sales were to just four customers, Dongfeng (Yiqi), Hangzhou, Nanjing and Liuzhou (Tables 8-20 and 8-21). However, the degree of reliance on Dongfeng is much greater than at first sight appears to be the case. Liuzhou, Yunnan and Hangzhou is each majority-owned by Dongfeng (Marukawa, 1995: 343) and Nanjing (Special Automobile Plant) also is part of the 'Dongfeng system'. In total, over three-fifths of Yuchai's sales in the mid-1990s were to plants within the Dongfeng 'system'.

Dongfeng (Erqi) was China's third largest automobile firm (by value of sales) in the late-1990s (Table 8-22). Yuchai's relations with Dongfeng have been erratic. The first year in which Yuchai sold engines to Dongfeng was 1993. In that year

TABLE **8-19 Main Producers of Light Trucks in China, 1998 (000)**

Producer's Name	Output
Dongfeng Auto Company	47.3
Yiqi Auto Group Corporation	43.2
Qingling Auto Group Corporation	32.7
Yuejin Auto Group Corporation	32.3
Beijing Light Vehicle Company	21.0

SOURCE: ZQJYZ, ZQGN (1999: 341)

NOTES: Share of output produced by:
        the top producer = 16.9%
        the top two producers = 32.4%
        the top five producers = 63.0%
        Total number of producers = 54

TABLE **8-20 Share of Yuchai's Sales to its Three Leading Customers, 1993**

Sales	Million yuan
Total sales	968.8
of which:	
1 Liuzhou Automobile	388.2
2 Nanjing Dongfeng Special Automobile	108.2
3 Hangzhou Automobile	99.7
Sub-total (1–3)	596.1
% total sales	60.3

SOURCE: Bear, Stearns (1994: F27, F46)

TABLE 8-21 **Distribution of Yuchai's Sales, 1995**

Name of Vehicle Plant	Yuchai Sales	Output of Trucks Compatible with Yuchai's Engines
Total sales	70 000	—
of which:		
Liuzhou	18 000	19 000
Erqi (Dongfeng)	9 000	80 000
Hangzhou	8 000	9 000
Nanjing	8 000	9 000
Hubei	3 000	9 000
Yunnan	1 500	2 000
Yangzhou	800	n.a.

SOURCE: Authors' research notes

it supplied just 1500 units. However, in 1994 Dongfeng stopped buying from Yuchai, and was able to fulfil all its diesel engine needs from its own enterprise, Chaoyang. In 1995 and 1996 it once again started to buy from Yuchai. From negligible production levels in the early 1980s, supplying only a small fraction of the engine needs of the Dongfeng Group, by the mid-1990s, Yuchai had become much the most important supplier of diesel engines to the Group, China's leading truck manufacturer. By 1995, Yuchai was supplying close to one-half of the Group's diesel engines. The Group's strategy seems to have been to supply almost all its diesel engine needs in Erqi itself from the company's core plants, but to rely heavily on purchasing from Yuchai to supply its 'second tier' subsidiaries (for the concepts 'first-' and 'second-' tier firms see below). In 1995, for Dongfeng itself, only around 10 per cent of its diesel engine needs came from Yuchai, but for the latter group of enterprises, close to 90 per cent of its diesel engine needs came from Yuchai.

The rapid growth of Dongfeng's reliance on Yuchai was stimulated by both demand and supply side factors:

- **Faster-than-anticipated growth of demand for medium-duty diesel engines**. Demand for diesel engines for medium-duty trucks grew much more rapidly than had been generally anticipated. As we have seen, the switch to diesel was closely connected with the rise of individual operators who were more discriminating purchasers than institutions. Diesel engines were better able than petrol engines to cope with overloading on bad roads. Dongfeng had not anticipated the rapid growth of demand for diesel engines, and had invested mainly in building up its petrol engine capacity. Both Dongfeng and Yiqi were caught with inadequate internal diesel engine capacity. Each responded by taking over diesel engine makers and bringing them into the respective enterprise groups (see below).

- **Yuchai's strong supply position**. Yuchai developed a strong product, given Chinese conditions at the time (see above). A large number of customers to

TABLE 8-22 Selected Statistics for China's Leading Auto Producers, 1998

Name of Enterprise	Sales ($ billion)	Pre-tax Profits ($ million)	Employees (000)	Output of Vehicles (000): of which:			
				(Total)	(Trucks)	(Saloons)*	(Buses)
Yiqi	4.43	21.2	156	289.5	156.8	81.3	52.4
Dongfeng	2.55	−5.4	134	155.0	113.3	3.9	5.0
Heavy Truck	0.82	−130.6	81	8.9	2.5	1.1	0.6
Beijing	0.80	−31.4	43	81.8	40.6	39.6	1.5
Tianjin	1.32	34.2	53	155.3	11.5	100.0	43.8
Shanghai	4.76	594.3	60	36.4	—	235.0	1.0

SOURCE: ZQJYZ, ZQGN (1999: 312–3)

NOTE: * Including off-road vehicles

the Dongfeng system specifically requested that their vehicles be fitted with Yuchai engines. Yuchai developed a powerful brand image, product guarantee and a pioneering approach to customer service, which reinforced Dongfeng customers' demands to have their Dongfeng trucks fitted with Yuchai engines (see below).

To be so reliant on a single customer proved extremely dangerous for Yuchai. This was especially so since Yuchai's main customers were also its main competitors (see below). This danger was reinforced by the fact that personal relations between Wang Jianming and the heads of Dongfeng and Yiqi deteriorated badly in the mid-1990s. Part of the reason for this deterioration was Yuchai's relentless search for customers. It realized that the shift towards diesel engines was so strong that truck operators could be persuaded to swap their petrol engine for a Yuchai diesel engine. This 'after market' grew rapidly, creating a large market in second-hand petrol engines for medium-duty trucks, further undermining the market for new petrol engines. Yiqi and Dongfeng had 'to bear the ignominy of seeing new trucks having their engines ripped out and replaced by Yuchai engines almost as soon as they left the factory'. The heads of Yiqi and Dongfeng were extremely angry at what they considered to be Yuchai's predatory behaviour, which caused them much embarrassment and loss of face for their companies. They demonstrated their anger by placing a joint advertisement in the national press saying that they would not honour guarantees on their vehicles if the original engines had been replaced.

Marketing. We have seen that Yuchai developed an advanced product in the late 1980s and early 1990s, suitable for the nature of the medium-duty truck market in China. However, a good product is not sufficient to capture markets. The post-reform diesel engine market in China became fiercely competitive. Yuchai was able to capture a fast-growing market share because it developed an advanced system of advertising and service provision. Under the 'planned' economy there was no conception of 'marketing'. By 1993 Yuchai had 280 people employed in the marketing department, and by 1996 the number had expanded to almost 500.

Yuchai was in the vanguard of a revolution in Chinese advertising. In a most unusual move for an engine making company, it put great efforts into TV advertising. From 1990 it began to use China Central TV to make advertisements that were very sophisticated by Chinese standards at that time. In 1994–5 Yuchai sharply increased its advertising activity, spending 40 million yuan in 1995. It targeted peak times, such as immediately after the evening news bulletin, just before the weather forecast. It developed strong brand imagery, with Yuchai championed as the 'king of engines'. In addition to the TV adverts Yuchai had widespread adverts in the newspapers, magazines and on billboards. In Beijing, Shanghai and Guangzhou it had billboards on the prime sites along 'airport roads', paying 3.1 million yuan to advertise on a billboard above the Baiyun Hotel at Guangzhou airport.

Since a large fraction of Yuchai's engines is sold direct to the factory for fitting in new trucks, an important aspect of competition is the ability to liaise with the factory, supplying product in a timely fashion and meeting any installation problems that the factory might encounter. An important part of Yuchai's competitive success was its high attention to promptness of supply compared to other producers, and the high technical skills it required of those working to liaise with the assembly factories. It quickly distinguished itself from traditional Chinese SOE manufacturers, who had much less highly developed concepts of customer service.

Yuchai was the first Chinese engine maker to put into practice the concept of an engine guarantee and to develop a comprehensive, nation-wide service network. Yuchai carefully studied the world's leading diesel engine companies and realized the crucial importance of a service network for establishing competitive advantage in the diesel engine industry. By the end of 1996 Yuchai had established a network of around 450 franchised service stations, with an average of five–six employees in each. These had all to meet strict Yuchai standards for repair quality, personnel capability, space and equipment quality, and staff had to undergo training by Yuchai. Around one-fifth of Yuchai's engines are sold through the service stations, but their main function is repair.

Yuchai pioneered the concept of engine guarantees. An engine can be exchanged within one month from the date of purchase if the customer is dissatisfied with the product. Yuchai steadily raised the guaranteed mileage for its engines, rising from 30 000 km in 1993 to 150 000 km. by 1996. Yuchai provided three guarantees, depending on the nature of the engine failure–repair, replacement or compensation. Yuchai's main competitors, Yiqi and Dongfeng were forced to introduce engine guarantees and raise the mileage involved. By 1996 they each had a 100 000 km guarantee.

Yuchai was able to produce much more cheaply than similar types of imported engines. For example, the Mitsubishi engine is closely comparable to the 6105, and in 1996 it sold for around 48 000 yuan, twice the price of Yuchai's 6105. The Mitsubishi engine is 'better' in terms of pollution, and more economical in its use of fuel, since it is lighter than the Yuchai engine. However, Yuchai has the advantage of a huge service network and a much more robust engine less likely to experience a cracked engine block.

COMPETITORS

Overview of Diesel Engine Production. By the early 1990s, the diesel engine business in China had become highly competitive. In 1995 there was a total of 34 enterprises manufacturing diesel engines for vehicles (MMB, ZQGN, 1996: 426). Around 10 producers, each with an annual output of over 10 000 units (Table 8-23), accounted for 'substantially all' medium duty truck engine sales. However, unlike Yuchai, some of its main competitors were subordinate units of larger automobile producers (see below).

In the West, especially in the USA, there is a large role for independent diesel engine makers. A central issue for Yuchai is the degree to which there is a role in China also for a large independent manufacturer in this sector at this stage in China's economic development. Wang Jianming's explicit goal was to turn Yuchai into a Chinese version of Caterpillar, Cummins Perkins Diesel or Detroit Diesel. He believed that in trying to do this he was swimming with the tide of Chinese policy towards the components sector, namely to construct large firms which would benefit from economies of scale and would be the instruments through which international technology would be transferred to China via joint ventures and technology licensing agreements. Having launched Yuchai into a leading position by the mid-1990s, Wang Jianming was confident that he would be able to take advantage of his first-mover position to remain China's number one diesel engine maker.

As the vehicle industry in China in the 1990s became quickly more concentrated, so the relationship of Yuchai to the emerging giants became crucial to its success. Much the most important producers of heavy- and medium-duty trucks are Yiqi and Dongfeng. One of Yuchai's central problems has been that its main customers were also its main competitors. The most important of these by far are Yiqi and Dongfeng (Erqi), both of which are both large consumers and large manufacturers of truck diesel engines.

Yuchai's growth has also been heavily affected by the large change in the institutional structure of the Chinese truck industry which has taken place since the 1970s, mirroring those in the vehicle industry at large. In order to overcome the

TABLE **8-23 China's Main Diesel Engine Producers, 1998 (000)**

Producer's Name	Output
Dongfeng	141.8
of which:	
Dongfeng Chaoyang	77.7
Dongfeng Auto	52.4
Dongfeng Nanchong	10.5
Dongfeng Sichuan	1.2
Yiqi	92.4
Yuchai	53.5
Yunnan Internal Combustion	46.9
Yangzhou Diesel Engine	44.7
Qingling Auto	28.1
Chengdu Kaiwei Internal Combustion	21.3
Yuejin Auto	20.9
Jiangling Auto	20.0
Nanjing Gear	14.9
Hangzhou Auto	6.0
Hunan Dongli Group	4.9

SOURCE: ZQJYZ, ZQGN (999: 355–6)

NOTES: Share of output produced by:
the top producer = 27.4%
the top two producers = 45.3%
the top five producers = 73.5%
Total number of producers = 31

diseconomies of scale consequent upon a proliferation of small-scale, highly self-sufficient producers, the government encouraged the formation of 'enterprise groups', at the centre of each of which was a single dominant enterprise. In the truck sector, the two outstanding enterprises were Yiqi and Dongfeng (Erqi). Each of these began a process of simultaneous output expansion and extension of their relationship with smaller producers, turning them into specialized producers, either assembling inputs produced elsewhere within the group or supplying components to other group members (Marukawa, 1995).

By the mid-1990s each of China's major automobile producers had developed a 'group' structure with a large 'core' enterprise, which in each case had been a keypoint plant under the old planned economy (Table 8-24). The core enterprise was actively engaged in restructuring the subordinate enterprises (see below).

Yiqi (No. 1 Automobile Plant). Yiqi was the largest automobile plant in China under the command economy. It still is China's largest automobile plant in terms of units produced and the second largest by value of sales, having been overtaken only by Shanghai (Tables 8-25 and 8-22). However, it has a more diversified output structure than its main competitors. It produces a relatively large number of saloon cars, though not as many as Shanghai or Tianjin (Table 8-22). It is China's number one producer of medium-duty trucks, the number two producer of light trucks and the number three producer of heavy trucks (Table 8-19 and Table 8-12).

Yiqi is a potentially very important market for Yuchai. It is also a potentially key competitor. Within the Yiqi 'system' were three major diesel engine producers, Chaoyang, Dalian and Wuxi. Along with several other formerly independent plants these were transferred to the 'control' of Yiqi in the late 1980s as part of the government's policy of forming large automobile 'enterprise groups' with a single giant plant from the old command economy at the centre of each (Marukawa, 1995: 344). Up until the mid-1990s Yiqi had a 'loose' relationship with these plants,[12] buying regularly from them and investing a certain amount of capital in them, but not directly controlling them (Marukawa, 1995: 344–8).

In 1995 *Dalian* and *Wuxi* produced around 65 000 diesel engines (Table 8-26), and the planned output for 1996 was around 80 000. The capacity was thought to be considerably in excess of this amount, probably over 100 000. The combined

TABLE **8-24** **Structure of China's Leading Enterprise Groups, Showing their 'Closely Linked', 'Second-Layer' Enterprises, 1995 (number of enterprises)**

Name of Group	Total	Vehicles	Vehicle Refitting	Motor Cycles	Vehicle Engines	Vehicle Components
Yiqi	21	9	7	0	2	3
Dongfeng	17	6	4	0	2	5
Beijing	27	6	0	0	0	2
Tianjin	59	5	0	0	2	52
Shanghai	26	2	0	1	1	22

SOURCE: MMB, ZQGN (1996: 122)

TABLE **8-25** **Comparative Size of Leading Chinese and Global Automobile Firms, 1998**

Company	Units (million)	Sales ($ billion)	Profits ($ million)	Employees (000)	R & D ($ billion)
Yiqi	0.29	4.4	21*	156	—
Erqi	0.16	2.6	−5*	134	—
Shanghai	0.24	4.8	594*	60	—
Toyota	4.48	99.7	2 780	159 (1997)	3.9
Renault/Nissan	4.54	92.9	1 280	278 (1997)**	1.6
Volkswagen	4.69	76.3	1 260	280 (1997)	3.5
Daimler/Chrysler	5.08	154.6	5 660	300 (1997)§	5.8
Ford/Volvo	7.21	171.2	23 160	364 (1997)**	7.5
General Motors	7.55	161.3	2 960	608 (1997)	7.8

SOURCES: ZQJYZ, ZQGN (1999: 312–13); Fortune (2 August 1999); DTI (1999)

NOTES: * Pre-tax profits
** Pro-forma
§ Daimler–Benz only

capacity of Dalian and Wuxi in medium-duty diesel engine production was around 120 000 units. They were both able to produce 110 mm bore engines (6110 series) able to generate 160 b.h.p., making them more powerful than the main product at Yuchai, the 6105. In interviews at Yuchai, the Company freely acknowledged the high quality (in relation to the Chinese conditions) of Dalian and Wuxi's engines. There was little chance of Yuchai selling to Yiqi, and every chance of Yiqi's subordinate plants competing elsewhere with Yuchai, especially as market conditions worsened and Yiqi had spare capacity.

In 1995, with the support of the central government, following its renewed commitment to create powerful large-scale automobile companies, Yiqi took full control of both Dalian and Wuxi Diesel Plants. As we have noted, before 1995 they were both 'loose' subsidiaries of Yiqi but in 1995 Yiqi turned both Dalian and Wuxi into a wholly owned subsidiaries (wholly-owned 'child companies' *quanzi zigongsi*) (MMB, ZQGN, 1996: 33, and interviews). In order to ensure the agreement of the local governments, the assets became the property of Yiqi, but the taxes remained with the respective local governments. The relationship between Yiqi and Dalian is especially close: Dalian's engine blocks are supplied by Yiqi, and the bulk of Dalian's output is supplied to Yiqi.

The transformation of these two major diesel engine plants into tightly controlled subsidiaries of Yiqi was highly significant for the Chinese diesel engine industry. It took Yiqi down the 'Fordist' path of increasing the degree of vertical integration. In 'Coasian' terms (Coase, 1988), Yiqi had decided that the costs of purchasing its diesel engines through the market were greater than those of producing within the firm. This was at odds with wider developments in the components industry, which mostly were moving towards greater outsourcing and achieving economies of scale within semi-autonomous second-and third-tier firms. Even though Yiqi had never

TABLE 8-26 **Main Vehicle Diesel Engine Producers in China, 1995**

Company Name	Main Product	Output (units)	Profits and Taxes per Employee (yuan)	Profits and Taxes per 100 yuan of Industrial Capital (yuan)
Liuzhou Diesel Plant	4102Q, 495Q	83 350	18 425	12.7
Guangxi Yuchai Joint Stock Company	6105QC, 6108Q	79 244	56 374	38.7
Dongfeng Chaoyang Diesel Company	CY6102, 4102, 6105	51 050	23 681	5.0
Yunnan Engine Plant	4100	41 000	45 412	40.0
Yiqi Group Dalian Diesel Plant	6110	39 094	73 176	27.1
Chengdu Engine Plant	493 490	38 450	10 082	8.3
Yiqi Group Wuxi Diesel Plant	CA6110	25 300	17 573	11.7
Dongfeng (Erqi) Vehicle Company	6BT5, 9, EQ6102	19 505	3 664	2.2
Yuejin Group Company	n.a.	10 309	8 351	4.1
Yuejin Group Nanjing Shandong Engine Plant	NJ4120Q	10 216	6 601	10.1
Hangzhou Engine Plant	X6130, WD615	6 262	−507	−0.4
Hunan Engine Plant	6105Q-1, 6105HD	5 701	3 312	3.6
Luoyang Vehicle Company	LR6100ZQ2	5 055	747	0.4
Weifang Diesel Plant	WD615	5 008	4 195	5.2
Guangxi Liufa Joint Stock Company	6105	4 931	−32 102	−14.0
Caiyang Engine Plant	1041	4 710	—	—
Shandong Mouping Engine Group Company	6102QA, 4102QA	4 662	4 518	8.0
Dongfeng Group Nanchong Engine Plant	6102, 4102	3 812	44	0.0
China Aircraft Industry Company Chengdu Engine Company	493Q	3 137	−902	−0.2
Shanghai Diesel Joint Stock Company	DD680, D6114	2 005	22 856	16.5
Shaoyang Vehicle Engine Plant	SF480, 485	1 927	−5 362	−18.3
Beijing Group Company	912	1 272	6 364	4.2

SOURCE: MMB, ZQGN (1996: 426)

NOTE: In 1995 there was a total of 34 enterprises producing diesel engines.

been a large market for Yuchai, this significant development cast a shadow over Yuchai's long-term strategy. After this move, *ceteris paribus*, a multinational diesel engine investor would have been more inclined to invest in the tightly controlled diesel engine subsidiaries of Yiqi than in an independent supplier such as Yuchai.

Dongfeng (Erqi: No. 2 Automobile Plant). In 1981, with the support of the central government, Erqi, together with eight other vehicle industry enterprises, formed Dongfeng, one of China's earliest 'enterprise groups'.[13] The central government granted greatly enhanced managerial autonomy to Dongfeng: in 1987 it was raised to the status of a Ministry or provincial government in its dealings with the State Planning Commission (Marukawa, 1995: 337). The state transferred to Dongfeng the management of a number of additional enterprises. Dongfeng began a process of investing in enterprises within the group. It undertook also the reorganization of the production structure of enterprises within the group, and organized the transfer of technology to them. From the original nine enterprises, the group had expanded to over 300 enterprises by 1989 (Marukawa, 1995: 337–8). By the early 1990s, the group had evolved into a four layer structure, with the different layers distinguished by the degree of control exercised by the core firm, Erqi. (Table 8-27).

In 1992 the *first layer* consisted of over 40 enterprises directly owned and controlled by the Dongfeng headquarters. These included the *Xiangfan* engine plant.

The *second layer* consisted of 22 enterprises, over which the group headquarters 'maintained a strong grip', and in many of which it had invested capital. These firms mainly produced finished vehicles, using components supplied from other parts of the Dongfeng Group, and the products were typically subject to quality control from the headquarters and used the Group's brand name. These included the *Nanchong*[14] and (after 1994) the *Chaoyang* Diesel Engine Companies, the Liuzhou, Yunnan, Xinjiang, Hangzhou and Wuhan vehicle assembly plants, and various component plants. It typically was a majority or sole owner of the second tier plants.

The *third layer* included 23 enterprises in which the core enterprise had invested smaller amounts. These enterprises mainly produced products for the Group, which had a strong say in appointing their management and supervising their business plans.

The *fourth layer* consists of well over 200 enterprises, in which the headquarters typically had no investment. These enterprises tend to rely heavily on the Group as a market for its products and/or for the supply of inputs for assembly.

The Group headquarters sharply reoriented the structure of production among the Group members. By the early 1990s, the core firm, Erqi, had reduced the level of in-house components production from around 75 per cent to around 50 per cent (Marukawa, 1995: 341). It now relied much more heavily on purchasing from components suppliers within the Group. The main automobile assembly plants within the Group, namely Hangzhou, Liuzhou, Yunnan and Xinjiang, all second layer enterprises, also came to rely much more on components supplied from other enterprises within the Group rather than from internal production: under the guidance of the Group headquarters, a large alteration in the division of labour had occurred within the Group.

TABLE **8-27 Dongfeng Automobile Group's Structure of Ownership and Capital, 1992**

First layer (5 enterprises, 6 institutions)
Dongfeng Group Corporation:
35 directly-controlled factories
3 directly-controlled subsidiaries:
  China Dongfeng Automotive Industry Export and Import Corporation
  Dongfeng Automobile Trade Corporation
  Dongfeng Automobile Industry Finance Company
6 directly-controlled research centres and schools including:
  Hubei Institute of Automotive Industry
  Dongfeng Automotive Industry Engineering Institute
Dongfeng Enterprise Development Corporation

Second layer (22 enterprises)
2 joint ventures with foreign companies:
  Shenlong Automobile Limited (Dongfeng 70%, Citroën 25%)
  Dongfeng–Thomson (Dongfeng 60%, Thomson International 40%)
10 administratively-controlled or majority-controlled enterprises:
  Dongfeng Hangzhou Automobile Corporation
  Liuzhou Automobile Works
  Yunnan Automobile Works
  Xinjiang Automobile Works
  Nanchong Engine Plant
  Dongfeng Hangzhou Heavy Machinery Plant
  and so on
2 joint ventures with Hong Kong firms:
  Xiamen Jinlong United Automotive Industry Ltd
  Changshu Special-Purpose Vehicle Works
8 enterprises with Dongfeng capital participation:
  Yangzhou Passenger Car Works
  Shangrao Passenger Car Works
  Nanjing Dongfeng Special-Purpose Vehicle Works
  Anshan Passenger Car Works
  Heilongjiang Passenger Car Works
  and so on

Third layer
  Guizhou Automobile Works
  Shiyan Axle and Hub Works
  Hubei Automobile Body Works
  and so on

Fourth layer (240 enterprises, 2 organizations)
  Hanyang Special-Purpose Vehicle Works
  Shanghai Xinhua Automobile Works
  and so on

SOURCE: Marukawa (1995)

In the mid-1990s Dongfeng's Xiangfan (Hubei Province) plant produced the 4102 and the 6102 diesel engines. Dongfeng seems from early on to have been keen to develop its own diesel engine production within the Group (Byrd, 1992). Indeed, the objective was to 'develop diesel engine production on a large scale' (Byrd, 1992: 402). In order to enhance its technical capabilities in diesel engine manufacture, in 1986 it concluded a collaboration agreement with Cummins diesel engine company (USA). However, as we have noted, in the mid-1990s this was turned into a full joint venture. Capacity expanded to around 30 000 units in 1996 and is planned to rise quickly to 60 000 units. By 1996, Xiangfan was able to produce 6102 series diesel engines.

Yiqi had for many years bought engines from Chaoyang Diesel (Liaoning Province), and in the 1980s it took the enterprise over wholly. However, in 1993 the enterprise left the Yiqi system, and in 1993 it was taken over by Dongfeng after a vote by the employees in favour of Dongfeng allowing them to choose between being owned by Yiqi or Dongfeng. There were several reasons for the take-over by Dongfeng. Firstly, it was felt that if Chaoyang remained an independent diesel engine maker, it would find the price it was able to charge was forced down by the main purchasers in the vehicle assembly industry. Second, Chaoyang encountered major quality problems with its crankshaft which damaged its reputation. Third, Liaoning Province had two diesel engine makers, Chaoyang and Dalian. Of the two, Dalian's engines were much more suitable for Yiqi's vehicles, and Chaoyang's more suitable for the main vehicles produced by Dongfeng, so the Provincial government was agreeable to the purchase of Chaoyang by Dongfeng, since this would not harm Yiqi.

Around one-half of Chaoyang's output in the mid-1990s was 6102 diesel engines, but it was reported to have developed the capability to manufacture 6105 engines, though these were still low powered compared to the market leaders. In 1996 Chaoyang sold around 20 000 medium-duty diesel engines to Dongfeng.

By 1996–7 neither Chaoyang nor Xiangfan was able to produce engines of as high a power as those from Yuchai, let alone those of Dalian and Wuxi. Both were still confined to the relatively low-powered 4102 or 6102 diesel engine. However, their technology was in the process of being fast transformed by the joint venture with Cummins. Like Yiqi, Dongfeng had taken the highly significant step in the mid-1990s of increasing the diesel engine production facilities under its direct ownership and control. Both the joint venture with Cummins and the transfer of Chaoyang from Yiqi to Dongfeng's ownership were highly significant for Yuchai's long-term prospects. They signalled Dongfeng's wish to produce a large number of diesel engines within the first and second tier companies of the Dongfeng system, and to ensure that the technical level of these developed fast.

In sum, the combination of developments at Yiqi and Dongfeng in the mid-1990s were ominous for Yuchai's aspirations to become a Chinese equivalent of Caterpillar, Cummins or Perkins Diesel.

Heavy-duty Trucks. Yuchai faced special problems in the heavy-duty truck sector. Here the competitive pressure faced by Yuchai was even more intense than in the medium-duty sector. Almost ninety per cent of heavy-duty trucks in China use diesel engines. (MMB, ZQGN, 1996: 81). Although the total output of heavy-duty vehicles is much smaller than for other vehicles, with only around 24 000 produced in 1995 (MMB, ZQGN, 1996: 414), as we have seen, their growth potential is high, especially as the Chinese road system develops.

In the mid-1990s, the output of heavy-duty trucks was very highly concentrated. In 1995 the top producer, Erqi (Dongfeng), accounted for 48 per cent of total output, and the second largest, the specialist China National Heavy Duty Truck Corporation, accounted for 24 per cent, together producing around 72 per cent of China's total output of heavy duty trucks (MMB, ZQGN, 1996: 414). The top four producers in 1995 accounted for 96 per cent of total Chinese heavy duty truck output (MMB, ZQGN, 1996: 414). Each of the main producers in China wishes to be self-sufficient in heavy-duty engines, following the pattern of Volvo and Mercedes. Almost all the engines they use are produced within the firm.

The dominant multinationals are quickly entering this activity. Not only has Erqi established a joint venture with Cummins, which also produces heavy-duty diesel engines, as well as smaller size, but the China Heavy Duty Truck Corporation produces Steyer trucks and engines under licence. In 1997 it concluded a joint venture with Volvo to produce both trucks and engines. Freightliner (the US subsidiary of Mercedes–Benz) has established a joint venture in Shanghai to produce heavy-duty trucks, initially at least, using imported Cummins diesel engines.

Yuchai's gamble with the purchase of the Brazilian heavy-duty engine plant was a complete failure. As we have seen, the plant was simply idle. The fact that the industry was so highly oligopolistic made it especially difficult to break into the heavy-duty diesel engine market against the established producers in alliance with multinational investment and technology. Purchase of the plant was risky. Careful analysis of the global pattern of heavy-duty diesel engine manufacture might have suggested greater caution.

Yuchai's Position in Relation to its Main Competitors

Yuchai's business strategy. The rapid growth of demand for diesel engines (see above) provided the opportunity for a small number of producers to emerge out of the old state system, growing and modernizing faster than other producers and dominating the market for diesel engines. In this environment, Yuchai had thrust itself forward from complete obscurity to become the number one diesel engine maker in China and the number one maker of engines for medium-duty trucks. As we have seen, Wang Jianming hoped that Yuchai would be able to capitalize on its first-mover advantage and from subsequent support from the government, which was eager to create powerful indigenous component manufacturers, to become a Chinese version of Cummins, Detroit Diesel, or Varity–Perkins. Wang Jianming is a visionary entrepreneur who believed that he could take Yuchai from zero into the ranks of the world leaders in the field.

Dongfeng. The prospects for Yuchai's long-term relationship with *Dongfeng* were problematic. We have seen that Dongfeng's long-term ambition was to establish a strong independent diesel engine-making capacity within the

Dongfeng Group. Indeed, the prospectus issued for the flotation on the New York Stock Market warned potential purchasers: 'Any additional funding that [Dongfeng] may obtain [through stock market flotation][15] will enable it to further develop its diesel engine business and thus intensify the competition Yuchai will face in the diesel engine industry' (Bear, Stearns, 1994: 11). Dongfeng's pursuit of this goal involved the technology transfer agreement and subsequent joint venture with Cummins Diesel.

There is a number of reasons why Dongfeng sought to build up its own internal diesel engine making capability, rather than relying on Yuchai for a growing fraction of its diesel engine needs. The profit margin on diesel engines in China is high in international comparison. For example, in 1993–4, during the boom period in Yuchai's development, the total output of diesel engines was vastly below that at Detroit Diesel, one of the world's top diesel producers. However, the absolute level of dollar profits at Yuchai was close to that at Detroit Diesel.[16] Compared with Detroit Diesel, Yuchai's wage costs and R & D expenditure were negligible. In the mid-1990s many customers specifically requested that their Dongfeng truck be fitted with a Yuchai engine, because of the superior quality and service system throughout China. In the early 1990s, Yuchai was able to rapidly raise the price of the standard 6105 engine, from around 19 000 yuan in 1992 to around 25 000 yuan in 1995. Dongfeng wished to capture the supernormal profits being earned by Yuchai. Dongfeng's goal may have been to draw Yuchai into the Yiqi system, by investing in Yuchai and making it a 'second-tier' firm within the Dongfeng Group. If Dongfeng was unable to do this, then its goal was to treat Yuchai as a long-term enemy and 'destroy' it.

Yiqi. We have seen above that *Yiqi* also was very keen to develop its diesel engine production capability from within the Group rather than be dependent on supplies from an independent diesel engine maker. Indeed, after Yuchai's success in selling Yuchai engines to replace petrol engines in Dongfeng and Yiqi's trucks, the head of Yiqi issued an instruction that none of the plants within the Yiqi system was to purchase any engines from Yuchai. Thus, the two major potential consumers of truck diesel engines had made clear their long-run intention to develop a production capability that directly threatened the growth and prosperity of Yuchai as a major independent diesel engine maker.

Evidence from petrol engine production in China. The precedents within the Chinese automobile industry generally were not favourable. Most large Chinese vehicle makers produce the bulk of their petrol engines within the firm, including Shanghai Volkswagen, Yiqi and Tianjin Auto. The exception to this is the Beijing Internal Combustion Engine Company ('Beinei'). This is China's largest engine maker, with an output of over 175 000 petrol engines in 1995 (MMB, ZQGN, 1996: 425). Beinei was the original supplier for jeep engines to Beijing Jeep (BJC), a joint venture with Chrysler (USA). Beinei sold BJC around 40 000 units per annum. However, in 1995–6 BJC decided to produce its own engines for its jeeps. Moreover, the engine for BJC's high quality vehicle, the Cherokee, is made within the firm. Moreover, in analogous fashion to Yuchai, in the early 1990s Beinei bought a second-hand production line 'cheaply' (for a reported figure of

$15 million) from General Motors to produce a 3.2 litre engine, but by 1997 it had still not produced vehicles commercially, due to the absence of a market.

Wang Jianming's lobbying efforts with the central government. Spurred on by the above considerations, in the mid-1990s Wang Jianming intensively lobbied the central government. His goal was for them to agree to support Yuchai as China's flagship diesel maker, to rival the world's leading companies, Cummins, Detroit Diesel and Perkins Varity. A major part of his strategy was to persuade the central authorities (Ministry of Machinery) to encourage and/or instruct Yiqi and Erqi (Dongfeng) to give up producing diesel engines, and allow Yuchai to take over the ownership of their associated diesel engine plants. However, the combined might of Yiqi and Erqi enabled them to persuade the Ministry of Machinery to reject Wang Jianming's proposal.

During the course of the lobbying by Wang Jianming, relationships with Yiqi and Erqi became highly strained. We have seen already that Yiqi and Erqi together took out a full page advertisement in the national press, effectively accusing Wang Jianming of 'unfair practices'. Moreover, there was reported to be strong personal animosity between the head of Dongfeng, Ma Yue, and Wang Jianming. It must be assumed that Yiqi and Erqi were afraid of the market power that a greatly enlarged Yuchai would have. They were highly uneasy about being greatly dependent upon Yuchai for their key component for truck production, the engine.

The joint venture route for Yuchai. Yuchai held extensive discussions with most of the major multinational diesel engine makers. The closest Yuchai came to establishing a joint venture seems to have been with Mercedes–Benz. However, Yuchai was not prepared to give up its own products and become the instrument for producing and marketing exclusively Mercedes–Benz engines. This was the only condition under which Mercedes–Benz was willing to invest in Yuchai. Wang Jianming and HLA, its foreign joint venture partner (see below) appear to have been agreed that this was not the desirable path to follow. HLA believed that such a joint venture would leave open the possibility that Yuchai might be closed as a production centre, with the foreign partner using only Yuchai's network of dealers in order to sell their imported engines.

INSTITUTIONAL CHANGE

Faced with a booming domestic market for medium-duty trucks, and the possibility of even faster growth of heavy-duty trucks, Yuchai embarked on a colossal institutional transformation in the 1990s, led by its dynamic chief executive officer, Wang Jianming. The driving force behind this was the urgent need to obtain capital to finance the company's expansion plans. Guangxi is a poor region,[17] and the provincial government has limited financial means with which to assist local businesses.

Underlying its ability to attract external funding was the high quality of the management, especially Wang Jianming personally, the coherent medium-term business strategy, and the high profit rate that was capable of being generated in the late 1980s and early 1990s by an effective independent diesel engine manufacturer. Yuchai's institutional transformation went through a number of stages, from traditional state plant to market oriented state-owned enterprise, to joint stock company, to Sino–foreign joint venture, to foreign flotation, to 'Big Yuchai'.

In 1993 Yuchai could produce around 40 000 units annually of the 6105 engine. It needed large investment to expand capacity to 70 000 units of the 6105, to upgrade the engine to the 6108 version, and build the new line to manufacture this product, and to purchase and put into place the heavy-duty line from Ford (Brazil).

From Traditional SOE to Market-oriented Firm. Under the traditional planning system, Yuchai had no rights to retain profits. It was directly under the supervision of the Guangxi Province branch of the Ministry of Machine Building. In most years it handed over all its profits to higher levels, and frequently 'handovers' to higher levels technically exceeded realized profits and taxes (Table 8-28). From the early 1980s onwards, following a path common across Chinese industry, Yuchai was allowed to retain a portion of the profits it generated. In 1984 it signed a contract with the Guangxi Ministry of Machine Building under which it would 'hand-over' to the Ministry around 200 000 yuan annually, the amount to be unchanged for five years.[18] From 1980 to 1986, 'handovers' amounted to around 50–70 per cent of profits generated (Table 8-28). For the first time Yuchai began to experience the stimulus of market forces, albeit in a limited way.

In the late 1980s, Yuchai was allowed to retain a much higher fraction of realized profits and taxes. This signalled a substantial break in the state's attitude towards its subordinate enterprise, allowing enhanced autonomy in the hope of better enterprise performance and greater 'hand-overs' to the superior authority. Alongside a sharp rise in profits from 1988 through to the early 1990s, the 'handovers' to superior authorities grew much less rapidly than did realized profits, so that the absolute level of total profits remaining within the firm rose very fast. The 'hand-overs' were subject to negotiation rather than according to strict rules, with 'income tax liabilities … not strictly related to the profitability of the Company' (Bear, Stearns, 1994: F35). Whereas in the 1970s, no profits at all were retained within the enterprise, these rose to significant positive numbers in the early 1980s, around 200 000–300 000 yuan per year. In the mid-1980s retained profits rose to 2–3 million yuan annually, and by the late 1980s/early-1990s, these had risen to 24–50 million yuan. By 1993 a further stage of enhanced autonomy had been reached with profits of over 300 million yuan retained by Yuchai.

In the late 1980s Yuchai's management approach altered sharply. It realized at an early point that there were large possibilities for a rapid advance in medium-duty diesel engine sales if the producer could manufacture a high quality product (in relation to China's particular market needs). Yuchai's success in developing both its products and widening its market is reflected in the vivid contrast between the deep downturn in the Chinese truck industry in 1988–91 alongside explosive growth of output at Yuchai (Table 8-29).

TABLE 8-28 Sales and Profits at Yuchai, 1970–93

Year	Sales (million yuan)	Profits/Taxes		Hand-overs to Higher Levels		Post-tax Profits	
		(million yuan)	(% sales)	(million yuan)	(% of Profits and Taxes)	(million yuan)	(% of Sales)
1970	11.1	4.3	38.8	6.9	161	neg.	0
1975	13.2	4.4	33.3	4.6	105	neg.	0
1980	7.4	1.2	16.2	0.8	67	0.4	5.4
1981	4.3	neg.	neg.	0.4	—	neg.	0
1982	7.0	0.5	7.0	0.2	40	0.3	4.3
1983	5.9	1.0	16.9	0.7	70	0.3	5.1
1984	10.9	0.9	8.3	0.7	78	0.2	1.8
1985	22.8	4.0	17.5	2.4	60	1.6	7.0
1986	30.3	6.1	20.1	2.7	49	2.8	9.2
1987	33.4	2.5	7.5	2.2	100	0	0
1988	63.5	7.5	11.8	1.9	36	3.4	5.4
1989	134.1	30.9	23.0	7.5	24	23.7	17.7
1990	188.3	21.0	11.2	9.4	23	31.0	16.5
1991	247.2	27.0	10.9	12.3	24	38.1	15.4
1992	450.4	80.8	17.9	30.4	37	51.0	11.3
1993	1008.2	380.5	37.7	59.1	16	321.5	31.9

SOURCE: Authors' research notes

NOTE: Yuchai is shorthand for Yulin Diesel Engine Company, and its successor, Guangxi Machinery Company, China Yuchai International (CYI) is the majority owner of Yuchai, produces its own set of accounts and is floated on the New York Stock exchange. neg. = Negligible

TABLE 8-29 **National Output of Trucks and Output of Medium-Duty Diesel Engines at Yuchai, 1988–91 (000)**

Output	1988	1989	1990	1991
All China output of trucks: units	364	343	269	361
: index	100	94	74	99
Yuchai's output of medium-duty				
diesel engines : units	4.2	8.11	2.2	14.0
: index	100	1913	290	333

SOURCES: MMB, ZQGN (1996: 83); Yuchai; firm visit

Yuchai realized that the shift in demand towards diesel engines combined with the powerful growth of a new type of discriminating truck purchaser, created large opportunities for growth at Yuchai if it could expand capacity and produce high quality products suitable for Chinese conditions. However, this was a period of severe retrenchment in government expenditure. Yuchai needed to find routes outside regular state funding if it wished to capitalize on this opportunity. It turned initially towards a joint venture with a foreign partner.

The approach of the Guangxi Provincial Government towards Yuchai changed sharply in the late 1980s as Yuchai commenced its high-speed growth. In order to meet the anticipated growth in demand, Yuchai wanted to buy the Brazilian Ford Production line for the 6112 heavy-duty engine. They had heard in 1992 of its availability for purchase. Long discussions were held between Yuchai and the Guangxi government, including the Ministry of Machine Building to investigate how to help. The provincial government was not able to help with substantial financial support, but it was able to 'support Yuchai with policies'. They quickly gave their support to Yuchai's proposal to establish a Sino–foreign joint venture as a way to raise funds to support Yuchai's expansion. They realized and accepted that this would mean a great dilution of direct state control over the enterprise. A major reason for giving Yuchai such support was that a successful Yuchai was able to make a large financial contribution to the region's prosperity. For example, in 1995 Yuchai was responsible for 80 per cent of the total industrial tax revenue collected by Yulin city.

From Market-Oriented Firm to Sino–foreign Joint Venture. We have seen above that Yuchai turned towards international capital at least in part in order to fund its ambitious expansion plans, since the Guangxi government was unable to provide the necessary funding. This simultaneously greatly changed the nature of government control over Yuchai, and it may be speculated that a further reason for Yuchai pursuing this path was in order to increase its degree of independence from the Guangxi government's administrative control.

In July 1992, with the help of advice from the System Reform Commission under the Chinese State Council, the diesel engine business of Yuchai (formerly Yulin Diesel) became a formally approved joint stock company, the first SOE in

Guangxi to be allowed to do so. The social services connected with the business were transferred to the State Holding Company. The State Holding Company owned 110 million shares and Yuchai also issued 80 million legal person shares to various Chinese institutional investors (Bear, Stearns, 1994: 20). Yuchai raised around 240 million yuan from the share issue, which was almost two and a half times the 100 million yuan that the Guangxi Construction banks had been able to loan to Yuchai in the early 1990s for technical modernization, and almost ten times the sum of 25 million yuan that had been loaned for technical transformation from 1985 to 1990.

In May 1993 Yuchai became a Sino–foreign Joint Stock Company. The Guangxi government gave its approval for a radical dilution of the state's ownership of the firm, and a massive change in its structure. Majority ownership (51.3 per cent of the then-outstanding Yuchai shares) passed into the hands of various foreign share owners, among which much the most important was Hong Leong Holdings, which was the organizer of a number of other lesser overseas investors, including Sun Yuan BVI, Cathay Investment Fund, and GS Capital Partners. The intention of the overseas investors was to organize further financial restructuring in order to list the company on the New York Stock Market. The establishment of the Sino–foreign Joint Stock Company raised a capital injection of $52.3 million into Yuchai, further increasing its ability to finance its ambitious expansion plans.

Hong Leong (HLA) is an overseas Chinese company. It is one of the top five groups in Singapore, which is where it has its headquarters, with gross assets in excess of $16 billion and a world-wide staff of about 30 000 (*FT*, 17 September 1996). It is run by Quek Leng Chan, one of the 'Fujian Five',[19] famous overseas Chinese entrepreneurs from Fujian Province. Hong Leong is strong in hotels. Its intention is to become a big global operator and is 'one of the world's most acquisitive hotel owners, operating 57 hotels in 11 countries' (*FT*, 17 September 1996). However, it also has interests in real estate, manufacturing and finance. It has no special expertise in automobiles.

HLA has many small investments in China, and two large ones. The other large investment apart from Yuchai is Xinfei (Henan), which was the seventh largest consumer electrical goods manufacturer in China in 1995 (MMB, ZQGN, 1996: 169). Hong Leong always establishes a majority ownership position in its joint ventures. Its goal is to find a strong firm and 'allow it to grow'. It is important for HLA's operations in China that its investment in Yuchai is a success. In order to safeguard their investment HLA sent two accountants to work in the central offices of Yuchai, closely monitoring the business' performance.

HLA invested in Yuchai because they believed that Yuchai had the potential to become the dominant diesel engine manufacturer in China. They considered that in a developing country the heart of a truck is the engine. Therefore, they considered that a strong truck engine manufacturer had high long-term growth prospects. They pinned their hopes on the possibility that with their investment and the capital from the New York flotation (see below), Yuchai would be able to upgrade the 6105 into the 6108, maintaining Yuchai's leading position, and become a leading supplier of heavy-duty engines through the 6112 model using the second hand Ford (Brazil) line.

In preparation for the New York listing (see below), Yuchai's accounting procedures shifted to international conventions, and its accounts were re-worked retrospectively to 1991. An important influence on its growth was the tax holiday and tax reduction consequent upon becoming a Sino–foreign joint venture. Yuchai paid no income tax in 1994, and was supposed not to pay any income tax in 1995. It was then to be liable for a greatly reduced rate of income tax for the following six years, paying just 7.5 per cent compared to the standard income tax rate of 24 per cent (Bear, Stearns, 1994: F46). The introduction of value-added tax in 1994 to replace the old sales tax did not seem to have any effect upon the Company, since the tax authorities stipulated that Yuchai should only pay a total of 'VAT' amounting to no more than the amount it had formerly paid in sales tax (Table 8-28).

While the new institutional set-up signalled a big change in the attitude of the state towards the Company, 'hand-overs' to higher levels continued in the form of dividend payments. After the formation of the Joint Stock Company, 40 per cent of the dividends accruing to the State Holding Company were handed over to the Yulin City Asset Management Bureau. Only 20 per cent of dividends were allowed to be freely used by the State Holding Company (Yuchai Group Company), and the remainder of the dividends could be used by the Company only with the payment of interest to the Yulin City Asset Management Bureau. Thus, in 1994, the total dividend accruing to the State Holding Company was approximately 22 million yuan,[20] and the 'hand-overs' to the Yulin City Asset Management Bureau were almost 9 million yuan, with interest accruing to them on 40 per cent of the dividends left with the Company and employed by it.

New York Listing. HLA became a partner in Yuchai with the intention of listing on the New York Stock Market. In November 1994 the company was further restructured prior to the 16 November flotation on the New York Stock Market (Figure 8-1). The state's ownership share in Yuchai Machinery Company was further diluted, falling to 22.1 per cent at the point of flotation. China Yuchai International (CYI) (see below) owned 76.4 per cent of Yuchai and the share of indigenous Chinese institutions fell to 1.5 per cent. Public shareholders purchased 30 per cent of the share value of CYI, raising around $64 million.[21]

CYI is a Bermuda-based holding company whose sole purpose is the ownership of Yuchai. The main shareholder in this company is Diesel Machinery Limited, in which HLA owns 53 per cent and China Everbright Holdings Company, an affiliate of China Everbright ('Guangda'), owns 47 per cent. The latter technically counts as a 'foreign' investment since Guangda is a red chip company, operating independently in Hong Kong.

It is very difficult to identify exactly where power resides in the company. In one sense, Yuchai itself controls the company. Domestic institutions own around 42 per cent of the share value of the company: the State Holding Company owns 22.1 per cent, and Guangda (essentially a Mainland institution) owns around 16 per cent

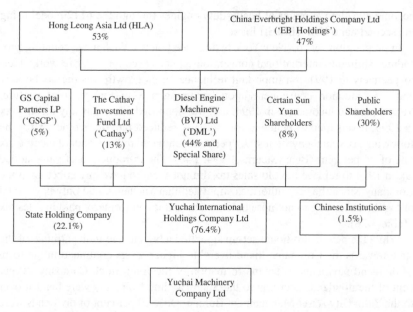

FIGURE **8-1 The Ownership Structure of China Yuchai International Limited, Immediately following Initial Public Offering in New York, 1994**

SOURCE: Bear, Stearns (1994: 10)

NOTE: The State Holding Company was formed, along with Guangxi Yuchai Machinery Company, in the restructuring of Yuchai's predecessor, Yulin Diesel in July 1992; other than the machinery business of Yulin Diesel which was transferred to Guangxi Yuchai Machinery Company, the businesses of Yulin Diesel were transferred to the State Holding Company, including certain social service related operations, assets liabilities and employees (that is, cafeterias, cleaning services, security operations, hotel and department store)

through its 47 per cent share of Diesel Machinery Limited (DML), itself the main shareholder of CYI. Wang Jianming's view is that the domestic institutions can act together so as to enable 'domestic' entities to have effective control of Yuchai.

However, HLA controls 53 per cent of DML, and through this owns around 18 per cent of Yuchai. Moreover, the genuinely foreign investors in total (that is, excluding Guangda) own around 44 per cent of Yuchai. More significantly, HLA has a Special Share. This entitles HLA to designate six of the 11 members of the Board of Directors of CYI. The board appoints the officers of CYI. The Board of Yuchai is agreed to consist of eleven members, nine of whom are designated by CYI. Of these nine, five are designated by HLA by virtue of its Special Share. It is agreed in the Shareholders' Agreement and the By-Laws of the Company that the nine Yuchai Directors will vote in accordance with the majority of the nine directors. Therefore, in fact, it appears that HLA has real control over Yuchai. This control is reflected in the appointment of a member of HLA as the Treasurer of Yuchai in order to monitor the firm's behaviour closely. This person is an accountant who has intimate knowledge of the company and daily access to the other chief executive officers. He sends daily reports to the HLA headquarters.

Wang Jianming. Wang Jianming was crucial to Yuchai's success. He arrived at Yuchai in 1970 as a Red Guard from Shanghai. He quickly rose to become Deputy Head of the Yuchai Revolutionary Committee, but he was then demoted to be head of the casting workshop. In 1983 he won the highest number of votes in a workers' poll, and was appointed deputy manager. However, Wang felt that he deserved to be made head of Yuchai. Shortly afterwards, when the then Director visited Beijing, Wang talked with the Guangxi Provincial Ministry of Machinery (Yuchai's superior body) and won them over to support him. When the director arrived back at Nanning airport, he was dismissed from his post and Wang Jianming appointed in his place.

This proved to be the turning point for Yuchai. When Wang Jianming took over the plant in the mid-1980s it was deeply indebted. From early on Wang Jianming drove Yuchai to 'look towards the market', and change its traditional pattern of behaviour. He was directly responsible for the huge change in Yuchai's institutional structure, for mapping out the course of its becoming a Joint-Stock Company, a Sino–foreign joint venture and its flotation on the New York Stock Market.

Wang was directly responsible for the transformation of the firm's philosophy in marketing its products, and in trying to capture large areas of the truck engine market through raising capital to upgrade its technical level. Wang Jianming's position may be closely analogous to that of the head of a powerful Western family business, such as Michelin or Ikea. There were no serious rivals for Wang's position once the firm started its high-speed growth in the late 1980s, and few people who understood the business like Wang. Like the heads of strong family-run firms, Wang's visionary leadership was strongly growth-oriented, rather than short-term profit-oriented and risk minimizing. Even after its flotation on the New York Stock Market, there is little evidence that Wang Jianming was much concerned about Yuchai's stock market price. His main interest in the flotation had been to raise cash to finance Yuchai's ambitious expansion plans.

In recognition of his key position in the company, CYI appointed him Chief Executive Officer of Yuchai for a six year term from May 1993. Under the terms of appointment, Wang Jianming was paid 3.8 times the average salary at Yuchai. Wang Jianming was to receive an annual incentive bonus equivalent to 2.5 per cent of Yuchai's audited net after tax profit provided Yuchai attained a minimum of 80 per cent of its annual after tax profit as approved in the annual budget of the board of directors. The Company also granted Wang Jianming stock options for up to 1.85 million shares of Common Stock at an exercise price of $7.80 per share, which could be re-sold after a two year period had elapsed.

The Prospectus for the New York flotation warned potential share purchasers of the central role of Wang Jianming: 'The success of Yuchai is substantially dependent upon the expertise and services of Mr. Wang Jianming, Chairman and Chief Executive Officer of Yuchai and Chairman of the Board of the Company, and certain other senior managerial personnel. The loss of the services of Mr Wang and certain other senior management personnel for any reason would have a material adverse effect on Yuchai's business' (Bear, Stearns, 1994: 15). In June 1994, Wang Jianming was granted approximately 68 million yuan (approximately $7 million) as a one-time compensation expense for the stock options granted to him. HLA regarded the stock options as a necessary expense in order to tie Wang Jianming to the company.

Big Yuchai. The problem of the high degree of dependence on sales to Dongfeng and Dongfeng's own interest in developing their diesel engine business, preoccupied Wang Jianming. His goal in the mid-1990s was to extricate Yuchai from this dependence by building a new institutional structure, 'Big Yuchai'. Big Yuchai would create a large integrated firm, including engine production (at Yuchai), light vehicle assembly (Liuzhou Automobile Plant), fuel pump manufacture (including two of Asimco's joint ventures, namely Nanyue and BYC), and a foundry.[22] It was approached in many different forms by Wang Jianming. However, the heart of the scheme had a common goal, namely to create a large integrated company manufacturing substantial numbers of vehicles which could absorb directly a large fraction of Yuchai's engine production, and through a share exchange with Dongfeng would bind Dongfeng and Yuchai together.

A key part of Wang's attempt to create a 'Big Yuchai' was to be a $0.29 billion capital injection from Asimco. The 'price' of Asimco's capital injection is that it would have obtained majority ownership of Yuchai through buying out Hong Leong. When asked how Yuchai could retain control of the new institution, Wang Jianming's answer was: 'you need fuzzy mathematics to understand this'. Some of the capital injection from Asimco would have been used to purchase from Dongfeng part of the value of Liuzhou, China's third largest medium duty truck manufacturer, and invest in its technical modernization.

Another part of the scheme was a 'share exchange' between Yuchai and Dongfeng. In return for allowing Yuchai to obtain partial ownership of three truck manufacturing plants wholly or partially owned by Dongfeng, namely Yunnan, Xinjiang, and Hangzhou, and 100 per cent ownership of Liuzhou, Dongfeng was to obtain partial ownership of Yuchai. Yuchai wished also to be allowed to acquire partial ownership of Dongfeng's light truck manufacturing business, and simultaneously develop its own light diesel engine manufacturing capability. This would then have given 'Big Yuchai' a complete integration of key aspects of the business, including engine casting and fuel pumps, manufacture of light, medium and heavy diesel engines, through to the production of each of the different downstream components of truck assembly, light, medium and heavy.

Wang Jianming's calculation was that the desperate situation in the Chinese truck industry would incline Dongfeng to agree to the proposal. In the first three months of 1996 it is reported that Yiqi made 80 million yuan losses and Dongfeng lost 170 million yuan. Big Yuchai would have had an initial vehicle output of around 60 000 vehicles, to which Yuchai engines could be directly supplied, rising rapidly to around 80 000. Wang Jianming's hope was that Yuchai's diesel engine output would expand to 210 000 by 2001, eventually including light-, medium- and heavy-duty engines.

By late 1997, Wang Jianming's attempts to create a Big Yuchai had still not come to fruition. Dongfeng was highly resistant to the idea, despite its short-term financial difficulties. It, clearly, did not wish over the long-term to allow Yuchai to dominate its diesel engine supply or become a rival in the manufacture of medium-duty trucks. It took half a year to persuade the head of Dongfeng even to discuss the scheme with Wang Jianming. It seems that the only way Dongfeng would have agreed is through pressure applied from the central authorities. Wang Jianming lobbied with great intensity, including discussion with all the relevant central authorities, but the countervailing lobbying power of Dongfeng was too great, and the Big Yuchai scheme was not supported by the central authorities. The level of antagonism developed between Yuchai and Dongfeng is such that, as we have seen, it is rumoured that Dongfeng's leadership wished to 'kill Yuchai'. Potential investors were concerned that the strategy could not succeed without the co-operation of Dongfeng, since Dongfeng was essential to the growth of Yuchai's market.

Yuchai's final hope was to purchase another vehicle maker. It could not independently develop as a vehicle manufacturer, since this required government licensing, and was most unlikely to be granted, especially given the intense opposition from Dongfeng and Yiqi. Another option was to take over an existing small vehicle manufacturer or even to combine several smaller makers. However, this required government mediation, as well as capital both to buy the businesses and to develop their production capability. Several possibilities were considered, including Dadong (big buses), Jinan (small trucks), a heavy truck maker in Shanxi, Nanjing Special Vehicle Company, and Zhengzhou Bus Company. Moreover, the central government had promised that if vehicle producers didn't quickly reach a minimum level of production, they would have their licences to produce revoked, which increased the risks attached to this strategy.

A constant theme of Yuchai's business activities in the mid-1990s was discussion with a joint venture partner. Many discussions were held with the leading diesel engine manufacturers including both the independents and Mercedes-Benz's diesel engine division. However, the potential partner insisted on majority ownership and production of its own products.

LABOUR ORGANIZATION

Yulin is a rough, backward city compared to China's coastal cities. The quality of the local labour force is poor. A major objective of Wang Jianming's management was to build a professional 'modern enterprise system' at Yuchai. Many approaches were employed to achieve this objective.

Ethos. Wang Jianming has attempted to devise a distinctive management philosophy at Yuchai as it has turned to 'face the market'. The 'Yuchai spirit' has three elements. Firstly, at the heart of Wang Jianming's approach towards management is the philosophy that the people are the foundation of business success: 'People are the foundation' (*ren wei ben*). Second is the slogan 'strive to be number one' (*zheng di yi*). The third is the slogan 'start every day from zero' (*ling qi dian*), meaning that your past achievements are nothing. You are only as good as your achievements in the coming day.

Recruitment. By the mid-1990s Yuchai had built up a core of highly qualified technical personnel. In 1995 it had more than 550 engineers, over one-half of whom were devoted to research and development, product enhancement and new designs. It had a staff of approximately 1000 employees in its technology and engineering department. In the early 1990s it head-hunted key personnel from the Shanghai Internal Combustion Engine Research Institute in order to help it upgrade its engines. As the plant has modernized, so the quality of workers required rose steadily. The new production lines require more skilful, computer-literate workers than previously. After 1993, as Yuchai began its accelerated drive for growth and modernization, it recruited high level technical specialists and senior engineers from all over China.

It is more difficult to sack local workers and thereby discipline the workforce. Migrant workers have no extended set of social relationships either within the workplace or outside it. They tend to be more insecure and vulnerable than local workers. For many ordinary categories of worker, Yulin has shifted towards hiring an increasing number of workers from outside Yulin City, with a disproportionately large share of new workers being hired from other parts of the country.

Training. In its struggle to become the number one engine maker in China, Yuchai set great store by upgrading its human resources: 'If you don't have the personnel, then everything is a waste of time.' In the 1990s, Yuchai allocated around 5 per cent of the total wage bill on training, a high proportion for a Chinese company. From the 1980s, it established its own internal training programme to upgrade existing workers' technical skills, especially in computing and internal combustion engine technology.

In 1992 Yuchai instituted special training programmes for its senior staff. Each employee of deputy department head level or above is entitled to enrol in a three year part-time management course at Guangxi Economic Management College. Yuchai has set up a special purpose-built MBA Programme at Beijing Aviation College. This is a sandwich course, with one year resident at the College and then return to Yuchai to complete the course through part work/part study. Each year Yuchai pays for 26 senior managers to participate in this course.

Yuchai has established a regulation that all its technical workers must have 200 hours annual off-the-job training. All technical workers must also sit an annual exam, which is not only a means to ensure that standards are maintained, but also is used as a means of determining promotions.

Yuchai selects many of its ordinary workers from among those who have failed their university entrance exams, who are then given training at Yuchai to upgrade their skills. New entrants from the countryside must undergo at least three months training before starting work. Each year, all lower level employees must sit a technical exam, and if they fail they have to take additional training, receiving only their basic salary during the training until they pass the exam. Only a small fraction (around ten hours in total) of the course is devoted to 'political' study.

Housing. The State Holding Company (Yuchai Group Company) receives dividends from Yuchai, and a major item of expenditure is housebuilding. In 'old Yuchai' around three-quarters of employees lived in company housing, a total of around 40 000 people. However, the housing quality was poor. Since the late 1980s, the State Holding Company has built a large housing complex immediately opposite the main plant, including such amenities as a large modern swimming pool. Altogether, the complex includes 43 high-rise apartment blocks, and it houses around one quarter of Yuchai's families. The high quality of the buildings and the street facilities both literally and metaphorically represent the 'modern enterprise system' at Yuchai. The estate is highly significant culturally. It is an impressive local symbol of modernization in an impoverished, isolated part of China.

Until recently, rents for old apartments were less than one yuan per square metre per month. Such a low rent did not even cover maintenance costs. The local market price for renting apartments is around 15 yuan per square metre. Yuchai is gradually raising rents towards the market price, and recently raised them to 3 yuan per square metre, and plans to raise them to 10 yuan. Alongside this it introduced a subsidy for rents in workers' wages, but the intention is to make workers increasingly aware of the real cost of providing housing. Yuchai has made it possible for workers to buy their apartments if they wish, both old and new, but at a commercial price.

Remuneration. Yuchai rewards its workers relatively well compared to the local standards. The average basic salary and bonus in 1992 stood at 6000 yuan, rising sharply to 11 500 yuan in 1993 (Bear, Stearns, 1994: 51). In 1993 the average annual wage in manufacturing industry in Guangxi was 3400 yuan (SSB, ZTN, 1994: 121), less than one-third of that at Yuchai.

Yuchai was allowed by the Guangxi government to introduce 'revolutionary' changes in the wage system. It radically increased wage differentials. In 1992 their new bonus system caused a 'sensation' in Guangxi province. An annual bonus of up to around the same amount as the basic wage was introduced, its award being dependent upon the achievement of a variety of targets.

Welfare benefits. Yuchai provides its employees with a variety of subsidies. In 1995–6 these totalled around 390 yuan per worker per month, and added around 30 per cent to the wage bill. The main subsidies were provided for medical expenses (80 yuan per month, with variations for length of service), housing (140 yuan per month, with variations for length of service), food (30 yuan per month), schooling (30 yuan per month), and transport (30 yuan per month). Medical subsidies are provided directly to the State Holding Company which administers the medical facilities, but the others are added to workers' take-home pay. In the mid-1990s Yuchai covered 100 per cent of medical expenses, but it intends to move gradually towards a system under which only a proportion of expenses is covered, as the present system 'encourages waste'. It intends to adopt a sliding scale with increasing proportions of expenditure being covered as the cost of the treatment rises.

In addition to the above subsidies, Yuchai pays an amount equal to 21 per cent of its basic wage bill into the local state-run retirement pension scheme. HLA regards these expenditures as a normal part of the cost of doing business in China.

Downsizing. Employment at Yuchai grew rapidly in the mid-1990s up until 1996. However, even before the severe downturn in its fortunes, Yuchai had begun to contemplate employment downsizing. Its workforce grew from around 2000 in 1984 to 6–7000 in 1994, reaching over 10000 at the start of 1996. In mid-1996 it was already planned to reduce the workforce by around 1000 by the year end. Workers were screened to decide whose employment would be terminated. The strong intention was to retain younger, more skilful workers. Already by 1996 the average age of employees was just 35–40 years.

SUPPLIER RELATIONSHIPS

Under the former 'planned economy' inputs were allocated to the enterprise. The supply department had a wholly passive function. As Yuchai turned towards the market, so the function of the supply department became steadily more active. By 1996 it employed 265 people.

Yuchai has outsourced an increasing fraction of its components, with over 90 per cent (by number) bought from outside suppliers. However, some important parts are still predominantly produced within Yuchai. The Company produces around 80 per cent of its engine cases, 70 per cent of its engine blocks, and 50 per cent of its camshafts and crankshafts. It has around 350 component suppliers. It has strict quality standards, which it reportedly has steadily raised over time. Its suppliers are very stable with little change in the main suppliers from year to year. It works closely with its suppliers to help them raise quality. Supplies are placed into different categories: fully qualified, usable but improvable, and below standard. If they don't meet Yuchai's quality standards then various financial penalties are levied on the supplier.

We have already seen that Asimco is a major force transforming the Chinese automobile components industry, and Yuchai has allied itself closely with Asimco. The fuel pump is the crucial component in ensuring reliability of a diesel engine. It was in order to secure a reliable source of supply for this key component that Yuchai entered a joint venture with Asimco (see above). Most of Yuchai's fuel injection systems are purchased from this joint venture (Nanyue). The condenser is another important component which Yuchai sources from an Asimco joint venture, with around 40–50 per cent of its purchases coming from Asimco's joint venture with Langfang.

A second key component is the engine block, which also is critical to the quality of the engine. Yuchai was looking for a foundry that could guarantee a stable long-term supply of the necessary amount of high quality engine blocks, but had still not found one in mid-1996. The New York Stock Exchange prospectus warned: 'Should Yuchai not complete such an agreement, and if no alternative supplier can be found, Yuchai's expansion could be adversely affected' (Bear, Stearns, 1994: 14). No reliable domestic source could be found for the 6112 heavy-duty truck engine, and Yuchai was planning to import these from New Zealand if full production started.

CONCLUSION

Yuchai's Rise

Yuchai's dramatic growth from zero to become China's leading diesel engine producer demonstrates the great reservoir of entrepreneurial talent that exists in China. The fast-growing market economy of the reform period provided large opportunities for well-managed 'first-movers' rapidly to develop their business. Yuchai under Wang Jianming quickly developed a 'modern business system'. It selected its product with careful regard to the market. It invested in developing its product, which was highly suitable to the business environment of the late 1980s and early 1990s. It paid careful attention to recruiting and training a well-educated and well-motivated workforce. It was a pioneer in brand imagery, advertising, product guarantees and after-sales service. It demonstrated a keen awareness of the importance of quality control and timeliness of supply from its own suppliers. It was highly creative in raising capital through a Sino–foreign joint venture and an initial public offering on the New York Stock Market.

Yuchai's growth also owed much to the fact that it was better able to anticipate the fast growth of demand for medium-duty diesel engine production than were the slower-moving large competitors, Dongfeng and Yiqi. It may also be the case that they had not clearly decided their strategy towards the degree to which they wished to incorporate engine production within the respective firms. It was only once Yuchai had catapulted into the position of China's number one diesel engine maker with almost one-half of the market for medium-duty diesel engines that their determination to rely mainly on their own diesel engines may have finally crystallized.

To some degree its main disadvantage, namely its remote location, was also an advantage. The central government monitored Yuchai less closely than it monitored other firms of comparable size. The poverty of the locality made the local government quickly come to rely heavily on Yuchai's success. Therefore it allowed Yuchai more freedom and support in unorthodox methods of financing than might have been the case in a large urban area in which Yuchai was just one of many large businesses vying for support from the local government.

In the final part of its accelerated rise, Yuchai was assisted by highly professional advice from the Hong Leong company. However, too much should not be made of this, since Hong Leong was, essentially, attracted by Yuchai's success rather than being a cause of it. Indeed, it was only shortly after Hong Leong's arrival that Yuchai started to encounter serious problems.[23]

YUCHAI'S FALL

Yuchai's success seems to have been short-lived. It can now perhaps be seen as a function of the opportunities offered by a 'window' in which the components industry was underdeveloped, with limited foreign participation, and in which the existing dominant vehicle producers may have been temporarily uncertain of their strategy in relation to diesel engine production. It looks likely that the dominant diesel engine producers in China in the foreseeable future will not, as at one point seemed possible, be fast-growing independent producers of the Caterpillar, Cummins or Perkins Diesel engine type. Rather, it now seems most likely that the dominant diesel engine makers will be the in-house plants that are owned by the established giants that dominated automobile production under the command economy.

The most important single reason for Yuchai's collapse lies in the decision of the main producers to attempt to become highly self-sufficient in diesel engines. The effect of this decision was exacerbated by the coincidental downturn in demand for diesel engines.

Yuchai's very success in rapidly developing its markets, raising funds and earning substantial profits may have helped make up the minds of the existing giants of the Chinese automobile industry, Yiqi and Dongfeng, to attempt more strongly to develop their own diesel engine capability, in order not to be in the thrall of a large indigenous engine producer. Wang Jianming's ebullient personality may even have played a role in pushing them towards a more integrated approach towards engine-making within the firm. The very speed with which Wang Jianming's business moved may have made them nervous about the possible future power that a single dominant independent diesel engine maker may have held. It is impossible to imagine that the heads of Yiqi and Dongfeng did not discuss these matters among themselves, as their joint national newspaper advertisement demonstrates.

In the 1990s, foreign participation in the Chinese automobile component industry grew rapidly, permitted by the regulations which allowed foreign firms to be majority owners in this sector. As foreign participation grows, the opportunities for Yuchai are likely to shrink even further. There is little reason for multinationals to choose Yuchai as their JV partner unless Yuchai is dominant. They can find literally hundreds of domestic firms in the components industry which can be sleeping partners in the construction of state-of-the art greenfield sites, over which they have complete control, close to the major vehicle makers, and to which they have no need to make a technological transfer. A small bankrupt Chinese SOE in the component sector would be extremely keen to make a joint venture with a multinational, and would be strongly supported in this by the local government, which would have a loss-making enterprise taken off its hands, and a revenue-generator created in the process.

We have seen that in the West there is an important role for large, independent diesel engine manufacturers. However, in China at the present stage of development, it is hard for an independent indigenous diesel maker to compete. The rise and fall of Yuchai demonstrates the great politico-economic power of the emerging giant corporations in the Chinese automobile industry. Through their fast-growing dominance of the different segments of the Chinese vehicle industry they are able to exert great pressure on suppliers. Moreover, the emerging giants were in the position to internalize supernormal profits earned by supplier industries, by developing these from within the enterprise group. While these firms are 'giants' within China, they are relative pygmies on the world stage, in terms of physical units of output, but, more importantly, in terms of procurement, revenue, profits, R & D and global production systems.

We have seen also that in the West the heavy-duty market is unusual in that several of the leading makers all manufacture their own diesel engines within the company. If Yuchai had been successful in developing its heavy-duty truck engine business it would have been contrary to the dominant global pattern. The technical gap between an ageing Ford (Brazil) plant and that of Volvo/Scania and Mercedes is wide. Essentially China's heavy-duty truck makers have either allied themselves with, (via joint ventures), or modelled themselves on, the world's leading heavy-duty truck makers (as integrated producers) rather than ally themselves with Yuchai.

Even after its explosive growth, Yuchai was still a tiny firm in international perspective, despite being the number one diesel engine maker in China (Table 8-30). Its sales value at the peak of Yuchai's success was less than $200 million. Over 50 Western components makers had annual sales at that time of over $2 billion, ten times the size of Yuchai. Yuchai stood little chance of success in open competition with the Western diesel engine giants. Compared with the top three independent diesel engine manufacturers, Yuchai was a minnow, with sales revenue in the late 1980s that was less than 10 per cent of Detroit Diesel, less than 4 per cent of Cummins and less than one per cent of the global leader, Caterpillar. These firms had global procurement systems, R & D spending that was far beyond that of Yuchai, and had built up a comprehensive global supply and service network. It could not possibly compete head on with these firms in the global marketplace. Yuchai's only hope was to use the window of opportunity during which China was protected from the full force of global competition, to build itself up within the domestic market. This required establishing a close, long-term relationship with the leading Chinese truck makers. Yuchai's attempt to do this foundered.

Instead of Yuchai establishing a close relationship with the leading truck makers, it was the multinationals that were able to achieve this, notably Cummins, in its joint venture with Dongfeng. Given the massive dominance of a small number of Chinese automobile producers in their respective sectors, and their apparent preference for self-sufficiency in engine production, the most rational strategy for

TABLE 8-30 World Leading Independent Diesel Engine Companies Compared with Yuchai, 1998

Company	Sales ($ million)	Sales (000 units)	Profits $ million (Pre-tax)	Profits $ million (Post-tax)	Employees (000)	R & D ($ million)
Caterpillar	20 977	—	2 174	1 513	65 824	838
of which:						
engines	6 524	—	—	504	—	—
of which:						
trucks	1 700	—	—	—	—	255
Cummins	6 266	—	(6)*	(21)*	28 300	—
of which:						
engines	3 982	—	—	—	—	—
of which:						
200 HP (+)	—	260	—	—	—	—
50 HP (+)	—	422	—	—	—	—
of which:						
heavy-duty trucks	1 553	106				
medium-duty trucks	1 075	287				
Detroit Diesel (1997)	2 164	160	46	30	6 500	98
of which:						
on-highway	1 210	—	—	—	—	—
of which:						
heavy-duty trucks	—	83				
Yuchai	136	54	15	—	8 900	—

SOURCES: Annual Reports; ZQJYZ, ZQGN (1999: 355, 470)

NOTE: *The losses in 1998 were attributable to special charges for restructuring and a settlement with the US Environmental Protection Agency (EPA); pre-tax profits in 1996 were $214 million and in 1997 were $286 million.

a multinational is to construct a joint venture with a firm that is within the 'tight' circle of core companies of one of the established automobile giants.

Yuchai's rise and fall raises questions about the nature of entrepreneurship in China's reforming economy. Yuchai's success in establishing a joint venture with Hong Leong Holdings and achieving a flotation on the New York Stock Market testify to the firm's determination to break out of the boundaries of the old planning system. Yuchai attempted to create new forms of human resource management and developed a powerful marketing system. This was a form of 'modern business system', as opposed to the network, familistic style of traditional overseas Chinese business organizations (Min Chen, 1995).

However, under Wang Jianming's dynamic leadership, Yuchai took some calculated risks. The most important of these were its purchase of the second-hand Ford heavy-duty engine production line, the attempt to upgrade the 6105 engine, the opportunistic pursuit of the 'after-sales' market for engines which provoked confrontation with Dongfeng, and the failure to accept that Yuchai might need to swallow its pride and be bought out by the much larger Dongfeng (or even Yiqi). Instead of regarding itself as a successful form of venture capital, the main purpose of which was to release shareholder value by selling out to the dominant firm at the right time, Wang Jianming really believed that Yuchai could become a major independent player in diesel engines on the global market. In this sense, Wang Jianming's leadership may be considered to be of a traditional, risk-taking 'entrepreneur' type, rather than practising management of a type found in a large modern business organization, based on systematic rules and risk minimization.

9

Steel

*We have made the fight, the enemy is at our mercy, now do not let us
be foolish enough to throw away the fruits of victory.*
(Andrew Carnegie)

*China's early masterly development of steel-making by advanced methods,
so long before the rest of the world, is an achievement of very great
interest to the history of technology in general.*
(Joseph Needham, 1965)

INTRODUCTION

The world's steel industry is in a process of high-speed change. The regional distribution of production is changing rapidly, with a large shift in world production from the developed to the developing countries. Steel production in the once-mighty USSR has collapsed. Technical progress in steel and new products that can substitute for steel are changing the nature of competition in the industry. In the advanced economies and in many developing countries the industry has been mostly privatized, producing large changes in the way steel firms operate, including massive downsizing in employment. In the advanced economies state support for 'national champions' in the steel industry has virtually disappeared. Foreign direct investment is beginning to increase fast in this industry, which once was immune from such internationalization. Cross-border mergers and acquisitions are beginning to take place. A major international shift in the geographical location of both the production and consumption of steel is taking place.

This chapter examines the rapid transformation of the Chinese steel industry since the 1970s in relation to this international and domestic background. China's rise has, arguably, been the most important change in the global steel industry in the past 20 years. Alongside explosive growth of demand and rapid growth of output, there have occurred important institutional changes in the Chinese steel industry. China has serious ambitions to build a small group of three to four globally competitive giant steel corporations. Shougang, the subject of this chapter, is one of these.

Firstly, the changing patterns of the global and Chinese iron and steel industries are analyzed. Then the case study, Shougang, is presented. There is an analysis of Shougang under the contract system, which operated from the late 1970s to the mid-1990s, under Zhou Guanwu, followed by an analysis of the change in direction that Shougang has pursued since the retirement of Zhou Guanwu and the termination of the contract system, both of which occurred in 1995. Finally, the prospects for the Chinese steel industry are outlined.

THE GLOBAL IRON AND STEEL INDUSTRY

DEMAND

Central Importance of Steel. The world steel industry had an annual output value of $250 billion in the mid-1990s (*FT*, 6 March 1998). Steel is an important business, and is likely to remain so, far into the future. Industrialization and steel have gone hand-in-hand since the nineteenth century. Writing in the midst of the global economic crisis of 1997–8, Lernhard Holschuh, General Secretary of the International Iron and Steel Institute commented: 'Perhaps it's as well to remind ourselves that beyond the immediate uncertainties, steel is an essential component of economic activity, and as countries grow richer they will need more of it' (quoted in *Steel News*, 28 October 1998).

Steel has a key role in such central economic activities as construction, automobiles, packaging, wire manufacture, mechanical engineering and electrical goods. In the EU in 1997, 41 per cent of steel was used for construction and infrastructure, and fixed installations, 24 per cent for mechanical engineering, electrical machinery and electronics products, 17 per cent for automobiles and industrial vehicles, and 18 per cent for other uses, including packaging and domestic appliances (Usinor, 1998: 4).

Long-term Changes in Aggregate Demand. Steel is a highly cyclical industry. World-wide steel output grew from 135 million tons in 1947 to over 700 million tons in 1974. Since then there have been four major cycles. In the mid-1970s, world steel demand slumped, and in 1980 global output had recovered only to a level of 716 million tons (Hogan, 1994: 1–2). In the early 1980s, output slumped severely, falling to 645 million tons in 1982, with a precipitous fall in the US, declining fully 38 per cent from 120 million tons in 1978 to 74 million tons in 1982 (Hogan, 1994: 2). By 1989 global output had grown far beyond the previous record level, reaching 786 million tons. In the early 1990s there was another severe downturn in output, strongly associated with the collapse of the former Communist economies of the Soviet Union and Eastern Europe. World output

TABLE 9-1 World Crude Steel Production by Regions, 1991-7

Regions	Output (million metric tons)/ output share (%) in brackets							1991-7 (% change)	Average annual change
	1991	1992	1993	1994	1995	1996	1997		
Western Europe	161.9 (22)	157.4 (22)	158.2 (22)	166.6 (23)	170.9 (23)	162.8 (22)	176.3 (22)	8.9	1.53
Eastern Europe	33.2 (5)	29.4 (4)	29.8 (4)	32.4 (4)	34.2 (5)	30.9 (4)	33.2 (4)	0.0	0.33
Former USSR	132.8 (18)	118 (16)	98.1 (13)	78.3 (11)	79.1 (11)	77.2 (10)	79.0 (10)	−40.5	−7.87
North America	101.4 (14)	107.5 (15)	113 (16)	116.2 (16)	122.7 (16)	123.6 (17)	130.1 (16)	28.3	4.26
South America	30.9 (4)	32.3 (4)	33.8 (5)	35.0 (5)	34.6 (5)	35.6 (5)	36.9 (5)	19.4	3.02
Africa	14.6 (2)	14.3 (2)	14 (2)	13.5 (2)	13.7 (2)	12.6 (2)	12.7 (2)	−13.0	−2.25
Middle East	4.8 (1)	5.6 (1)	6.9 (1)	7.8 (1)	8.1 (1)	9.1 (1)	9.8 (1)	104.2	12.80
Asia	247.1 (34)	247.7 (34)	265 (36)	266.5 (37)	279.7 (37)	287 (38)	306.9 (39)	24.2	3.71
Australia/ New Zealand	6.9 (1)	7.6 (1)	8.7 (1)	9.2 (1)	9.3 (1)	9.2 (1)	9.5 (1)	37.7	5.61
World	733.6	719.7	727.5	725.3	752.3	748.1	794.5	8.3	1.38

SOURCE: International Iron and Steel Institute (IISI) (1998) (Website)

fell to 714 million tons in 1992 (Hogan, 1994: 3). After 1992, output rapidly recovered, reaching a new record high level of 795 million tons in 1997 (Table 9-1). Following the world economic crisis of 1997, it is estimated that global consumption of steel will slump to around 690 million tons in the years 1998–9, but should recover to around 760–770 million tons in 2005 (*Steel News,* 29 October 1998). The long-term forecasts are that world steel output in the first decades of the twenty-first century will reach around 800-850 million tons (Hogan, 1994: 1).

Underlying these large fluctuations in demand for steel, there has been a slow long-term decline in the growth rate of global steel output. From 1950 to 1960, the average annual growth rate was 6.2 per cent, declining to 5.5 per cent from 1960 to 1970, 1.9 per cent from 1970 to 1980, 0.7 per cent from 1980 to 1990 and 0.4 per cent from 1990 to 1997 (IISI, 1998). However, these long-term declines in growth rate disguise wide regional changes in the distribution of steel production. Moreover, the industry has achieved large technical progress in the nature of both product and process. Owing to the changing composition of steel output, with a steady rise in the amount of high quality, high value-added steel, the growth of real value of global steel output is greater than the growth of physical output.[1] Despite the decline in the global growth rate, the industry faces the probability of substantial global growth of demand over the long-term, and little possibility of serious long-term global decline.

Competition from Other Products. The continuous threat of competition from other materials is a major factor driving technical progress in the world's steel industry. The main sources of such competition have come from plastics, aluminium, cement and ceramics (Hogan, 1994: Chapter 4).

Automobiles. Lightweighting became a central preoccupation of the automobile industry from the early 1980s onwards. The major motives were to reduce fuel consumption and pollution. One response was to reduce the size of vehicles. In the USA this was the main reason behind the drastic reduction in the amount of steel used per vehicle. In 1976 the USA automobile industry produced 11.5 million vehicles, using 21.4 million tons of steel, but in 1988, it needed just 12.6 million tons of steel to produce 11.2 million vehicles (Hogan, 1994: 122).

However, in addition to reduction in average vehicle size, steel faced serious challenges from substitute materials, principally aluminium and plastics. Aluminium has the potential advantage of much lower weight, which enables vehicles to reduce fuel consumption and pollution. It does not require special treatment to resist corrosion. It needs less investment than steel in order to roll, form and shape the metal, thereby eliminating the investment in die costs and heavyweight stamping presses required for steel used in automobiles. The use of aluminium increased only slowly from the 1980s into the 1990s, but the efforts of aluminium producers intensified in the 1990s. By the late 1990s, most leading carmakers had produced aluminium prototypes, and VW had begun to produce a commercially available model, the Audi 80, with an extruded aluminium skeleton and bonded aluminium body (*FT*, 5 March 1998). It saw no reason why 'even the highest volume cars, like the Golf, should not be made of aluminium' (*FT*, 5 March 1998). VW worked closely with Alcoa (Aluminium Company of America) to develop new production processes that would enable high-volume production of automobiles (*FT*, 5 March 1998).

Plastics also present a challenge to steel in the automobile. However, a major limitation on their use up to the late 1990s, was their lower degree of recyclability compared to steel or aluminium. The use of plastics in automobiles was still relatively limited: in the USA their use rose from an average of 195 pounds in 1980 to 243 pounds in 1993 (Hogan, 1994: 123). However, the threat was potentially very serious for steel.

The steel industry responded with important innovations to lightweight vehicle production using steel, with close inter-actions between the steel and the auto industries. Some of the main advances in the lightweighting of vehicles include 'monologuing', new types of ultra-light steels, 'tailored blanks', changes in welding technologies, hydro-forming, and the use of steel 'sandwiches' (Hogan, 1994: 120–8). Monologue construction uses the automobile body itself as a structural member replacing the heavy steel frame that was formerly used. New ultra-thin, but high-strength steels can be used for up to 90 per cent of the car's body. Lightweight steel 'sandwiches' are being formed of thin, but high-strength steels bonded together either side of a composite honeycomb filling. Hydro-forming involves stamping the steel sheet around a mould into water at high pressure. This greatly reduces the number of parts required for a conventional body shell. 'Tailored blanks' are sheets of thin, high-strength steels further reinforced in strategic areas by additional laser-welded panels. These are playing a central role in reducing bodyweight of steel structured automobiles. They enable designers to locate various steels within a structure precisely where the extra strength is most needed. This avoids unnecessary mass that would arise from using steel of uniform thickness in unstressed areas of the vehicle. Continuous laser welding rather than conventional spot welding enables greater strength and lightness.

Construction. In the advanced economies from the 1950s onwards, the concrete industry made heavy inroads into steel's dominant position in the market for construction materials. A great deal of research was undertaken to develop methods of adding strength to concrete. In the USA the share of steel in all types of building construction fell below 40 per cent by 1990. However, the steel industry has fought back with much research into new ways of using steel in construction. In addition the great advances in productivity within the steel industry in the advanced economies reduced the real price of steel more than that of concrete (Hogan, 1994: 129). By 1993, the share of steel used in construction in the USA had risen to 53 per cent (Hogan, 1994: 130).

Containers. The market for containers has been highly competitive between different materials. The first modern change was from glass to tinplate, which is essentially steel with a thin coating of tin. By the 1960s it had become the overwhelmingly dominant material in the field. Increasingly, aluminium began to gain market share from tinplate in the manufacture of containers, principally in the beverage industry. The main reason for this was the drive to lightweight the product, but it was also easier to recycle aluminium than to recycle tinplate beverage cans. Intense research by steel companies, typically in co-operation with the leading beverage companies, produced major advances in the lightweighting of steel for beverage containers, and major improvements in their recyclability. When the first metal beverage cans were introduced in the early 1960s, they weighed 164 pounds per 1000 units. By the early 1990s, the weight had fallen to just 35 pounds per 1000 units, around one-fifth of the original weight. A large part of this decline was attributable to the competitive responses of the steel and aluminium industries to the remorseless demands for lightweighting made by the giants of the beverage industry.

Not only has the industry responded with technical progress to develop lightweighting, but also to enable steel to be used in new ways to make beverage cans. For example, a major development in the late 1990s involved the development of new stamping processes to permit steel to be used in producing shaped beverage cans (mimicking the shape of the contour bottle) in order to shift the steel beverage can away from an 'industrial commodity' image.

By the mid-1990s, steel and aluminium roughly shared the market for beverage cans within Europe, but aluminium was massively dominant in the USA. Steel continued to monopolize the market for cans for food and other uses, such as paints and oil.

Appliances. Until the 1980s, steel had a virtual monopoly in the supply of materials to the domestic appliance industry, which includes products such as refrigerators, ovens, freezers, washing machines, clothes dryers, waste disposers, air conditioners and dishwashers. However, since then there has been intense competition from the plastics industry. Steel responded by developing lighter steels and attempting to compete with the prices offered by the plastics industry. In the USA between 1983 and 1994, these two influences led to a small fall (2 per cent) in the amount of steel used in the appliance industry alongside a significant growth in the industry's output (38 per cent increase in the number of units shipped) (Hogan, 1994: 136).

SUPPLY

Changes in Global Distribution of Production. We have seen in the previous section that despite the intensification of competition for the steel industry, arising from both aluminium and plastics, the material remains centrally important, even in the advanced industrial economies. However, the regional distribution of steel demand and production is shifting fast, and is likely to continue to do so in the foreseeable future.

In the advanced capitalist economies, output fell heavily in the 1970s. Since then, despite the usual cyclical fluctuations to be expected in this industry

TABLE 9-2 **Long-Term Changes in Regional Distribution of World Steel Output, 1974–96 (million tons, % in brackets)**

Country/region	1974	1980	1992	1996
OECD countries:				
USA	137	101	84	95
Japan	119	112	98	99
Germany	53	44	39*	40*
UK	27	11	16	18
France	27	23	18	18
Italy	24	27	25	24
Spain	12	13	12	12
Belgium	16	12	10	11
Canada	14	16	14	15
Sub-total	429 (61)	359 (50)	316 (44)	332 (46)
Selected developing countries:				
China	21	37	80	101
Brazil	8	15	24	25
Taiwan	1	3	11	12
Mexico	5	7	8	13
Turkey	2	3	10	14
India	7	10	18	24
South Korea	2	9	28	39
Sub-total	46 (7)	84 (12)	179 (25)	228 (30)
Former USSR	136 (19)	148 (17)	118 (17)	77 (10)
World	700	716	714	748

SOURCE: Hogan (1994: 9); *Steel News* (28 October 1998); Clarke (1983: 91)

NOTE: *Including the former GDR

(see above), long-term output has more or less stabilized at somewhat above 300 million tons in the leading economies taken as whole (Tables 9-1 and 9-2). Indeed, the USA enjoyed significant growth of output in the early 1990s, albeit that output was still much below the peak levels reached two decades previously.

Environmental pollution regulations are a major influence on the growth of the steel industry in the advanced economies. Coke ovens are the principal source of pollution. The cost of reducing their pollution output to levels currently deemed to be acceptable in the advanced economies is high. For example, in the USA it was estimated that it would require an investment of $4–6 billion to repair or replace existing coke-oven capacity in order to conform with the standards specified in the 1990 Clean Air Act amendments (Hogan, 1994: 145). Such high costs involved in meeting environmental regulations were a major influence on the decision to close down steel capacity in both the USA and Europe after the 1980s.

Two major episodes of catch-up in the twentieth century transformed the global distribution of steel output. In the 1920s, the combined weight of Western

European and US steel production was vastly greater than any other region of the world. Britain, France, Germany and the Benelux countries between them produced an annual output of 39 million tons of steel in the years 1926–9 (Mitchell, 1976: 705) and the USA produced around 50 million tons (Yonekura, 1994: 3). The USSR and Japan each produced around 3–4 million tons (Yonekura, 1994: 3). In the latter countries high-speed industrialization was accompanied by rapid growth in steel production, interrupted in each case by large losses during the Second World War. By the early 1970s, output in both Japan and the USSR had reached around 120 million tons (Yonekura, 1994: 2), overhauling the output in the USA. In the early 1970s, the USSR accounted for around 19 per cent of world output and Japan for around 17 per cent (Table 9-2). The steel industry in both cases grew fast on the basis of a rapid growth of demand for steel-using products, including infrastructure, shipbuilding, automobiles, machinery and consumer electronics. However, Japan increasingly became a powerful steel exporter also. By 1973 it had established itself as the world's largest steel exporting country, with no less than 29 per cent of total world steel exports (Yonekura, 1994: 2).

Alongside the stabilization of long-term output in the advanced economies in the 1990s, two dramatic changes took place in other regions. First, steel output in the former USSR collapsed. Alongside the approximate halving of national product in the former USSR, steel output in the mid-1990s had fallen also to around one-half of the level in the 1980s at its peak. The former USSR's share of total world output fell from 21 per cent in the early 1980s to just 10 per cent in 1996. Excluding the former USSR, world steel output grew by just over 1 per cent per annum from 1980 to 1996 (from Table 9-2).

Matching the drastic decline in output from the former USSR since the late 1980s, there was an explosive process of output growth in selected parts of the developing world. Combined steel output in the seven leading producers in the developing world increased fivefold from 1974 to 1996. Their share of world steel output grew from just 7 per cent to 30 per cent in the same period. The vast bulk of this increase took place in East Asia. China, South Korea and Taiwan increased their combined output from just 24 million tons in 1974 to 153 million tons in 1996. South Korea rose from negligible levels to become the world's sixth largest producer in 1996, and China rose from the world's seventh largest producer in 1974 to become the world's largest producer by the mid-1990s (Table 9-2).

Despite the decline in output in the advanced countries, levels of *per capita* consumption of steel are still far beyond those in the developing countries. In 1997, the approximate levels of *per capita* consumption of finished steel products in the EU and in NAFTA (North American Free Trade Agreement) stood at around 420 kilograms (IISI, 1998). In the former USSR, the level of consumption has fallen from over 400 kilograms in the early 1990s to around 100 kilograms. In Asia and Oceania, the level still stood at around 100 kilograms, in Central and South America, at around 70 kilograms, and in Africa at a mere 20 kilograms or so (IISI, 1998).

It appears very likely that growth of steel output in developing countries will march in step with their continued industrialization. A recent authoritative account of the prospects for the global distribution of the world steel industry concluded:

> In the years ahead the industrialized countries will probably shrink in size by as much as 10 per cent in total crude steel production, whereas the developing countries will grow by probably 25 per cent ... This projected growth on the part of the developing countries and a relatively small shrinkage on the part of the industrialized countries mean that competition between the two will increase considerably, particularly as the developing countries reach out for export markets on a world-wide basis. Competition between the two worlds, the developing world and the industrialized world, will have an effect on total world steel production in terms of where it will be produced and how much will be produced in the various areas. (Hogan, 1994: 184)

Technical Change. Several factors have combined to spur the pace of technical change in the iron and steel industry. First, as we have seen, there have arisen important new substitutes for steel. Secondly, as we shall see below, large changes have occurred in the regulatory and institutional environment. Levels of protection have fallen considerably in the advanced economies. Across the world privatization has swept the industry, radically altering methods of management. It has been accompanied by drastic changes in the nature of employment within the industry, with widespread downsizing of numbers employed in the industry. Government support for 'national champions' has sharply fallen. Controls on international flows of foreign direct investment have fallen drastically. These changes have amounted to nothing less than a revolution in the industry: 'The end of state interference and the creation of a commercially-driven international or even global steel industry are within sight' (*FT*, 22 March 1995). In addition to these changes, the collapse of the former USSR has greatly stimulated steel exports from the countries within the former USSR, and the Asian crisis has added further great impetus to exports from East Asia. These have together intensified international competition in steel markets.

Product Change. It is difficult to separate technical change in products from process, since many of the new products require changes in processes. We have seen that in recent years there has occurred an intensification of pressure on the steel industry due to the rapid growth in the use of materials other than steel to produce goods that formerly used steel. We have seen that the main such materials have been aluminium, concrete and plastics. We have already seen several important examples of product change (and the associated changes in processes) in response to this intense market pressure. These have included lightweighting for vehicles and packages, and new types of steel for use in the construction industry. The steel industry has responded to these pressures with a much closer relationship with its main customers to meet their needs for improved materials at competitive prices.

In the late 1990s, leading steel companies, such as British Steel, Usinor, NKK and Thyssen–Krupp, spent between 0.6 and 1.3 per cent of sales revenue on

R & D (DTI, 1998: 22–62). This was a smaller proportion than sectors such as aerospace or vehicles. However, this still amounted to a total annual spend of around $75–200 million per company (DTI, 1998: 62–3). Usinor, for example, with 'one of the two most extensive R & D operations in the steel industry world-wide' (Usinor, 1998: 17), has around 1500 R & D employees. These work closely 'with technicians and salespeople from the automobile, electronic appliances and packaging industries on projects aimed at developing practical solutions and applications for these industries' (Usinor, 1998: 17).

Process technology. The modern epoch has witnessed continuous evolution in iron and steel technology. In the post-war period the first major development was the basic oxygen furnace (BOF) for converting iron into crude steel. The process was developed in Austria in 1952. The BOF enabled the refining time to be reduced to almost one-tenth of that required under the traditional open hearth method, greatly increasing both the efficiency of the furnace and the construction costs required. It was rapidly adopted in the fast-growing Japanese steel indus-try: by 1965 already over one-half of Japanese steel was produced with the BOF method (Yonekura, 1994: 9). The adoption rate was rather slower in Europe and the USA, but by the late 1970s, three-quarters or more of steel in Japan, the USA and the EU was produced with the BOF method (Yonekura, 1994: 10).

The second major development, which is still being evolved, concerns the attempt to transform the steel making process from a stop-start, batch production approach into a single continuous operation: 'The ideal steel plant would permit a continuous flow of production from start to finish' (Hogan, 1994: 139). The first important step in this process was the introduction of the continuous caster. In comparison with the conventional process, in which refined steel was cooled into ingots and then reheated to make slabs, bloom and billets, the continuous caster reduced energy costs, and increased yields and productivity. By the early 1980s, continuous casting accounted for 21 per cent of steel production in the USA, 45 per cent in the EU and 71 per cent in Japan (Yonekura, 1994: 10). By the mid-1990s, continuous casting accounted for over 90 per cent of crude steel output in Japan, the EU and the USA, though the former USSR stilled lagged far behind, with just 31 per cent (IISI, 1998).

The electric furnace had long been used to produce speciality alloy steel and stainless steel. However, from the 1950s onwards large improvements took place that transformed the electric furnace into a scrap-melting producer of carbon steel. By the late 1990s, the share of the electric furnace in total crude steel pro-duction had risen to 26 per cent in Germany, 33 per cent in Japan, 43 per cent in the USA and South Korea, though the former USSR lagged far behind, with just 12 per cent (Table 9-3). As we shall see below, the developments in electric fur-nace technology were to have important implications for the economic viability of small-scale steel plants.

The entire steel making process involves a complex sequence of operations, from mining of iron ore, coal and limestone, through the preparation of raw materials, iron making, steel making, semi-finished production and various

TABLE 9-3 Different Production Methods of Crude Steel Output and Continuous-casting Ratios, Selected Countries, 1997

Countries/ companies	Open hearth	Oxygen converter	Electric furnace	Total crude steel output*	Continuous-casting**
			(million metric tons, % share in brackets)		
Japan	0.00 (0)	70.22 (67.2)	34.28 (32.8)	104.5 (100)	101.0 (96.6)
South Korea	0.00 (0)	24.18 (56.9)	18.32 (43.1)	42.5 (100)	42.0 (98.7)
USA	0.00 (0)	56.35 (56.8)	42.85 (43.2)	99.2 (100)	92.3 (94.7)
Germany	0.00 (0)	33.12 (73.6)	11.88 (26.4)	45.0 (100)	43.2 (96.0)
Former USSR	29.14 (37.5)	39.08 (50.3)	9.48 (12.2)	77.7 (100)	26.6 (34.2)
World	49.26 (6.2)	476.70 (60.0)	267.75 (33.7)	794.5 (100)	630.2 (79.8)
China	9.70 (8.9)	79.84 (73.29)	19.12 (17.55)	108.94 (100)	66.10 (60.68)
within which:					
Baogang	0.00 (0)	8.49 (98.84)	0.10 (1.16)	8.59 (100)	5.22 (60.76)
Angang	3.35 (40.46)	4.82 (58.21)	0.11 (1.33)	8.28 (100)	3.04 (36.76)
Shougang	0.00 (0)	7.59 (94.88)	0.41 (5.13)	8.00 (100)	6.25 (78.13)
Wugang	1.42 (23.32)	4.61 (75.70)	0.06 (0.99)	6.09 (100)	4.98 (81.75)
Baotou	1.72 (40.76)	2.49 (59.00)	0.01 (0.24)	4.22 (100)	0.01 (0.03)
Magang	0.42 (13.95)	2.50 (83.06)	0.09 (2.99)	3.01 (100)	1.66 (55.18)
Pangang	0.00 (0)	2.88 (98.97)	0.02 (0.69)	2.91 (100)	1.18 (40.65)
Bengang	0.00 (0)	2.35 (89.69)	0.27 (10.31)	2.62 (100)	negl. (negl.)

SOURCE: Compiled from International Iron and Steel Institute (IISI) (1998) Website; CMISI (1997: 5, 34–9)

NOTES: * Percentages do not always sum to 100 because a small amount of steel was produced by 'other methods'

** The figures in continuous-casting are independent of those in open hearth, oxygen converter and open furnace finishing operations. A great increase in efficiency has resulted from the use of computer systems to co-ordinate functions within and across the major stages of production, attempting to eliminate or minimize bottlenecks, and permit flows that are more nearly continuous.

Mini-mills. The traditional integrated mills produced steel from iron ore produced in blast-furnaces and then cast it into steel products. The dominance of integrated mills was sharply challenged after the 1960s by the rise of the mini-mill, especially in the USA. The key technical advance of the mini-mill was the ability to cut out the capital intensive process of making iron ore through the blast furnace route. This was done through the use of scrap steel as the feedstock, which was turned into molten steel in an electric furnace. This avoided the most capital intensive part of the steel making process, namely the production of iron in a blast furnace. It also cut out the need to supply iron ore, coal and coke. It coincidentally avoided much of the pollution associated with the production of coke. The mini-mills were typically non-unionized so that they were able to operate in a much more flexible fashion than the traditional integrated steel plant.

A second path to the attempt to cut out the blast furnace route to the production of iron was through directly reduced iron (DRI). DRI is beginning to be used more widely, and is being driven faster by the rising cost of scrap steel (see below). In early 1998, Ispat claimed to supply its plants with DRI at $94 per ton compared to the scrap steel price of $156 per ton (*FT*, 17 March 1998).[2] Ispat (London) is the world leader in the production of DRI. It operates mini-mills (as well as some larger plants) in several countries. It manufactures over 5 million tons of DRI per annum, which it supplies to several of its mini-mills (*FT*, 24 July 1997).

By the mid-1980s in the USA, and increasingly in other advanced countries, mini-mills had come to dominate the production of 'long steel products'. Flat-rolled products were widely regarded as beyond the capabilities of mini-mills. It was thought that there were significant scale requirements attached to conventional slab-casting and hot-strip-mill operations. However, from the late 1980s onwards, new technologies permitted thin-slab casting to take place competitively in mini-mills. Thin-slab casting allows the production of a semi-finished shape that is much closer to the shape of the final product thereby greatly reducing the need for capital intensive investment in rolling equipment.

Since the 1980s, under the impact of the rise of the mini-mills, the US steel industry has undergone a revolution, and the steel industry in the other advanced countries has been substantially affected also. By the mid-1990s, mini-mills accounted for around one-third of world steel production (*FT*, 22 March 1995).

There is intense dispute about the future role for large integrated plants and large steel companies in the advanced economies. A recent survey of steel industry firms produced conflicting results between North America and Europe (reported in *FT*, 10 January 1996). Steel producers in the USA believe that the steel industry is likely to continue to fragment with 'more companies, more locations and smaller facilities'. European steel producers believe that there the trend is towards consolidation, with 'fewer companies and locations and larger facilities'. While there is considerable dispute about the future role of large plants in the advanced economies, there is little dispute about the future role of large enterprises in developing countries.

Mini-mills have considerably increased their role in developing countries, including China (see below). In South Korea, for example, alongside the continued rapid growth of output at the main company, Posco, mini-mills have increased their share of national output to around one-third (derived from Hogan, 1994: 40–1). However, it is unlikely that they will increase their share of global output to the same degree that they have done in the USA. Most industry prognoses anticipate that integrated steel mills will account for the major part of steel output growth in developing countries for the foreseeable future (MSDW, 1998a: 202). A number of factors supports this conclusion:

- Integrated steel mills are making significant technical progress, to lower costs of production. The application of pulverized coal injection (PCI) into blast furnaces greatly increases the operational efficiency of the traditional integrated iron and steel plant (Hogan, 1994: 151–2). Rapid progress is taking place in computer modelling of blast furnaces, and in their monitoring and automation. It is claimed that application of state-of-the-art methods of blast furnace control can save around $28 billion in reduced raw material costs and energy savings (FT, 29 May 1997).

- Scrap steel, the main feedstock of mini-mills, is much less easily available in developing countries than it is in the developed countries, and even in the advanced economies, there is doubt about the security of supply and price of scrap. For example, in the mid-1990s, the price of scrap surged (FT, 22 March 1995). In the long-term, 'as a growing list of mini-mills tap into the low-residual scrap supply, upward pressure will be exerted on scrap prices, and even more so when scrap is in heavy demand' (Hogan, 1994: 113).

- Part of the advantage of mini-mills in the USA has been their use of non-union labour to negotiate much more flexible working conditions, with greater intensity of labour for the workforce. A new 1 million ton per annum mini-mill might have only around 300 employees (FT, 2 June 1998). Under pressure from the mini-mills, union power in the traditional large-scale integrated sector has been eroded drastically, eliminating the labour cost differential between the two sectors. A major influence on the current wave of mergers in this sector is the capability of merged steel companies to reduce costs through large reductions in the workforce. For example, this was a major path through which the merged steel interests of Thyssen–Krupp intended to make large cost savings after their merger.

- 'Mini-mills' are growing in average size. Many of the new 'mini-mills' are more properly termed 'midi-mills'. For example, several new 'mini-mills' built in the USA in the 1990s have annual capacities of 2–3 million tons (Hogan, 1994: 110). Nucor is the USA's leading 'mini-mill' company and its largest plants have 1.9 and 2.2 million tons capacity respectively

(Hogan, 1994: 110). Moreover, the mini-mill sector has seen considerable consolidation within the USA. Nucor, with a total annual output of over 12 million tons, will shortly have nine plants, (*FT*, 2 June 1998). The fastest-growing international steel company, Ispat, will shortly have a total output of around 19 million tons.[3] This is produced from numerous plants scattered across the globe, including Kazakhstan, Indonesia, the USA, Mexico, Ireland, Trinidad and Tobago, Canada and Germany.

- Mini-mills depend heavily on the use of electricity to power their electric furnaces. Coke provides up to two-thirds of the fuel and reductants needed to sustain a blast furnace. In developing countries with shortages of electric power there may often be advantages in the use of locally available coke rather than the purchase of electricity from the grid which would be necessary for the mini-mill.

A combination of changes in management style associated with privatization of former state-owned firms, technical progress and severe downsizing has enabled some of the traditional integrated steel producers to be highly competitive in the face of mini-mill competition. For example, British Steel owns four integrated mills but it became one of the most profitable and lowest-cost steel producers through productivity improvement and cost cutting (*FT*, 22 March 1995). In developing countries, large integrated steel firm are among the lowest-cost and most competitive steel companies, including such enterprises as Posco (South Korea), China Steel Taiwan, Tata Iron and Steel (TISCO, India) and Usiminas, the privatized large Brazilian, integrated steel firm (MSDW, 1998a: 205).

INSTITUTIONS

Large Firms in the World Steel Industry. The traditional steel industry is well known for the powerful economies of scale at the plant level (Cockerill, 1974, Ch. 7). There are also significant economies of 'scope' associated with multi-plant operation, such as transport cost savings, smoothing cyclical fluctuations, combining plants with best-practice techniques each with different locational and minimum economy of scale requirements, and applying R & D and marketing efforts across many products and plants (Cockerill, 1974: 87–8). Larger firm size enables larger absolute amounts to be spent on R & D, which may permit gains in total sales and/or market share due to cost savings in production and/or developing superior products.[4] Vertical integration into raw material production can make supplies more assured.

The most important examples of 'catch-up' in the steel industry in industrializing countries were each based around large firms. Three key examples were the rise of the US steel industry to compete with and overtake the European industry, and the rise of the Japanese industry and, in recent years, the rise of the South Korean industry. At the centre of each of these processes was a single giant firm, each of which became the world's number one producer in its turn.

Each dominated the industry in their respective countries, made huge investments in plant expansion and drove forward technical progress and efficiency in the industry.

US Steel. US Steel's origins were in the Carnegie Steel Company founded in 1864. Carnegie Steel prospered behind the high US tariff barriers from the mid-nineteenth century onwards (Ruigrok and van Tulder, 1995: 211–12). Only in 1913 was tariff protection substantially removed from the US steel industry.[5] Prior to that date, a large part of US industry had been 'free riding on free trade' with Britain.[6] Carnegie obtained 'first-mover' advantage by becoming the first firm to build from scratch a giant, integrated railmill. It remained for decades the largest steel mill in the world (Chandler, 1990: 128). The blast furnaces were installed just in time for Carnegie to meet the huge demand created by the railway boom of the 1880s. Carnegie used the profits to expand rapidly into the production of construction steel and high quality steel for transport equipment, for which demand was also booming. In the 1890s, in the phase of ferocious competition and rapid concentration of the US steel industry, Andrew Carnegie came close to destroying all his competitors and establishing a monopoly for a single firm: 'We have made the fight, the enemy is at our mercy, now do not let us be foolish enough to throw away the fruits of victory' (quoted in Smythe, 1995: 14).

In 1900, Carnegie merged with Federal Steel to create a 'giant of giants' (Chandler, 1990: 130), US Steel, much the largest steel producer in the world and the world's largest industrial corporation. In 1901 US Steel was a highly integrated company, from iron ore through to wire nails. In that year its share of US output was 66 per cent for crude steel, 60 per cent for steel rails, 62 per cent for heavy structural shapes, 65 per cent for plates and sheets and 78 per cent for wire rod output (Chandler, 1990: 138). Although US Steel's degree of dominance declined, it remained much the largest producer in the USA right through until the 1990s.[7] US Steel was the largest steel firm in the non-Communist world from its founding in 1900, through to the formation of New Japan Steel in 1970 (see below).

Along with other US steel producers US Steel faced huge challenges after the 1960s from emerging low-cost producers, especially from Japan. The US government began a programme of protection with voluntary export restraints agreed with the EU in 1969. These were expanded into other protective measures in the 1980s, most importantly voluntary export restraints agreed with Japan, which greatly stimulated inward Japanese investment into the US (Ruigrok and van Tulder, 1995: 261). US Steel was saved from bankruptcy and given breathing space in which to restructure. It invested heavily in new steel facilities, and set up major joint ventures with both Kobe Steel (Japan) and Posco (South Korea) (Hogan, 1994: 20). In the 1980s US Steel diversified into oil production, with the acquisition of Marathon Oil. Oil and natural gas now accounted for around two-thirds of its turnover. Although a much-changed and more diversified firm, in 1997 it was still the world's eighth largest non-Communist steel producer, with an output of 12 million tons (Table 9-4).

TABLE 9-4 The Top 10 and Top 20 Global Crude Steel Producing Companies, 1996–7

Companies	Output (million metric tons)		Output share (%)		1996–7 % change
	1996	1997	1996	1997	
Nippon Steel (Japan)	26.4	28.1	3.53	3.54	6.44
Posco (S. Korea)	24.3	26.4	3.25	3.32	8.64
Arbed (Luxembourg)*	11.8	18.8	1.58	2.37	59.32
Thyssen–Krupp (Germany)**	17.7	17.4	2.37	2.19	−1.69
British Steel (UK)	16.1	17.0	2.15	2.14	5.59
Usinor (France)	15.0	16.1	2.01	2.03	7.33
Riva (Italy)§	14.1	14.8	1.88	1.86	4.96
USX (USA)	11.3	12.0	1.51	1.51	6.19
NKK (Japan)	11.3	12.0	1.51	1.51	6.19
SAIL (India)	11.0	10.9	1.47	1.37	−0.91
Top 10	159.0	173.5	21.25	21.84	10.21
LMN (UK)	8.4	10.9	1.12	1.37	29.76
Kawasaki (Japan)	10.6	10.9	1.42	1.37	2.83
Sumitomo (Japan)	9.9	10.6	1.32	1.33	7.07
Bethlehem Steel (USA)	8.6	9.6	1.15	1.21	11.63
Cherepovets (Russia)	8.9	8.9	1.19	1.12	0.00
BHP (Australia)	8.4	8.9	1.12	1.12	5.95
Nucor (USA)	7.6	8.8	1.02	1.11	15.79
China Steel (Taiwan)	6.4	8.7	0.86	1.10	35.94
Baogang (China)	7.7	8.6	1.03	1.08	11.69
Angang (China)	8.6	8.3	1.15	1.04	−3.49
Top 20	244.1	267.7	32.63	33.69	11.72
World	748.1	794.5	100	100	10.96

SOURCE: International Iron and Steel Institute (IISI) (1998) (Website)

NOTES: * Includes entire 1997 tonnage of Aristrain, which became part of Aceralia (Arbed Group) in October 1997
** Includes 50% of HKM
§ Includes ILVA LP

New Japan Steel. (Nippon Steel) was the world's biggest steel company in 1997 with an output of over 28 million tons. It had its origins in the Yawata Steelworks, founded in 1896 by the Japanese government. This was Asia's first integrated steel plant, built mainly for military reasons (Yonekura, 1994: 274). It was massively dominant within Japan, producing 62 per cent of Japan's total crude steel output in 1926 (Yonekura, 1994: 97). During the inter-war years, several smaller, non-integrated producers emerged, stimulated by fast-growing domestic demand for steel and steel products. Periodic bouts of price-cutting and market instability appeared. The government responded to the excess capacity which appeared during the sharp decline in steel output during the Showa depression in the early 1930s, by 'rationalizing' the steel industry structure. In 1934, Japan Steel was established, composed of Yawata and several smaller producers. Technically, the new firm was a private company, but the government owned more than 50 per cent of the company's stock, and retained many other rights to intervene in the firm's operations: Japan Steel was 'a semi-public corporation rather than a private one' (Yonekura, 1994: 143). Japan Steel's investment and output expanded fast in the late 1930s and during the Second World War, stimulated especially by demands for the war effort. By 1945 it produced almost 90 per cent of Japan's pig iron output, and over one-half of crude steel output (Yonekura, 1994: 210).

The Allied forces demanded that Japan Steel be split into two companies, Fuji and Yawata, as part of its effort to reduce the concentration of economic power in Japan. The combined market share of the two firms declined slowly, from over 50 per cent of crude steel output to under 40 per cent by 1965 (Yonekura, 1994: 210), under the impact of the aggressive expansion of firms such as NKK and Kawasaki. However, this was consistent with fast absolute growth for Yawata and Fuji, since Japan's total demand for steel was increasing rapidly, with huge advances in output from the construction, shipbuilding, and machinery industries, as well as from the steel industry itself (Yonekura, 1994: 224). The major Japanese steel producers pioneered enormous technical progress as the industry grew in leaps and bounds with massive investments: Japan's crude steel capacity rose from under ten million tons in 1955 to 93 million tons in 1970 (Yonekura, 1994: 222–4). BOF technology was widely introduced, which 'revolutionized the steel making process in both speed and scale'. Other key advances in Japan in this period were the continuous caster and computerized process-control (Yonekura, 1994: 221).

The characteristic method of financing the huge investments was through external borrowing (the 'over-borrowing' growth path).[8] This in turn had the effect of making the break-even point very high. This rendered Japanese steel producers especially vulnerable to the normal vagaries of the steel industry, namely high fixed costs and cyclicality of demand: oversupply was a persistent problem and Japanese steel prices were the 'most unstable in the world' (Yonekura, 1994: 231). The Japanese government responded to the consequent difficulties by attempting various measures of administrative control over prices and production quantities (Yonekura, 1994: 226–2).

When these measures failed to achieve their desired result, the merger of Yawata and Fuji was proposed by these companies' leaders as a way of achieving market stability. In 1970, New Japan Steel (Nippon Steel) was established out of the re-merger of these two companies, reconstituting the firm that had been broken up by the Allied powers in the 1940s. The other principal steel firms supported the merger. Indeed, the President of NKK acknowledged: 'If [New Japan Steel] behaves properly as a leader of the industry in the competition over capacity expansion and sales, we will find a way out of the swamp' (Yonekura, 1994: 235). The new 'Japan Steel' accounted for around two-fifths of total Japanese steel output (Yonekura, 1994: 210). The merger, 'the largest in Japanese industrial history', was also supported by the government and MITI: 'they faced the liberalization of foreign trade and investment in Japan and felt the necessity of fostering world class companies to compete internationally' (Yonekura, 1994: 235).

In the 1980s, faced with growing competition from mini-mills and from developing countries, New Japan Steel diversified into a number of areas, related to steel production. President Takeda said: 'Though Nippon Steel will diversify, it will never give up steel-making, like US Steel did. We'll never buy an oil company. Moreover, we will compete with developing countries and mini-mills in the full range of products, even at the very low end' (quoted in Yonekura, 1994: 262). In 1984 New Japan Steel added production of non-ferro alloy, fine ceramics, chemicals and plant engineering to its articles of incorporation (Yonekura, 1994: 258). It intended to become 'a total basic materials producer', which meant that the company would be a producer of basic chemical products and new materials in technologically related fields as well as of iron and steel. In addition, it used its capabilities in computing and related fields to expand into silicon wafer and semiconductor manufacture.

Posco (South Korea) is widely acknowledged to be the world's most successful steel company. In 1997, its output of crude steel was 26.9 million tons. In the late 1990s it took over from Nippon Steel as the world's number one producer. It was founded by the South Korean government in 1968, as a calculated planning move to enable South Korea to supply domestically the steel it needed for its fast-growing shipbuilding, automobile, electronics and construction industries (Amsden, 1989, Ch. 12). It was hugely assisted in its construction by finance from the Japanese government in compensation for '36 years of hardship under Japanese rule', and even more importantly, by comprehensive technical assistance from Nippon Steel, the world's technical leader (Amsden, 1989: 295). Fast-rising demand 'enabled Posco to undertake capacity expansions in rapid succession, thereby accelerating the acquisition of project execution skills and technological knowledge of the steel-making process' (Amsden, 1989: 317).

Famously, the World Bank advised against building the plant, arguing that it was 'premature' for the country to have a large steel plant (Hogan, 1994: 40). The firm is still owned and controlled by the state.[9] The risk of pressing ahead with a huge integrated steel plant was entirely borne by the state. Foreign exporters have difficulty in competing with Posco in the domestic market due to import tariffs. In addition, the Korean government gave extensive subsidies through the provision of low-cost capital and infrastructure services (Amsden, 1989: 296–7). Moreover, domestic prices do not necessarily move directly with international prices or domestic supply and demand due to government price controls (*FT*, 15 March 1996).

Posco is in the process of expanding its capacity to 28 million tons, which will make it the largest steel producer in the world. Posco has had a near-monopoly within domestic supply. Despite the entry into steel production by other Korean firms, Posco still accounted for 65 per cent of South Korea's steel production in 1997 (MSDW, 1998c: 197). In marked contrast to the *chaebol* investment pattern, with extensive diversification into non-core businesses, Posco has remained sharply focused on steel. In contrast also to them, Posco tightly controlled its level of debt, which amounted to only around half the value of its equity at the height of the Asian crisis in late 1997, compared to four times equity for some of the leading conglomerates (*FT*, 27 December 1997). It drastically downsized employment, reducing total numbers from 25 000 to 19 000 between 1992 and 1997 (*FT*, 27 December 1997). This enabled it to offer generous wages and social benefits, which eliminated labour disputes (*FT*, 27 December 1997). After extensive automation and downsizing, Posco was the highest rated of Korean companies in the eyes of international investors. In May 1998, MSDW evaluated Posco as follows: 'Posco's production costs are the lowest in the world, and its scale and efficient work force should entrench its globally competitive position' (MSDW, 1998c: 197).

For most of its life Posco has been a state-owned enterprise. Despite partial privatization in the late 1980s and early 1990s, Posco remained 33 per cent owned by the Korean government, with tight controls on maximum privately-held shares. In July 1998, the Korean government announced that Posco would be fully privatized, a process which is likely to be completed by the year 2000. Posco's sharp focus on steel, downsizing of employment and high-level of operating efficiency, all achieved under state ownership, is of great interest for the theory of the firm, and for China's steel sector reform.

Privatization and Downsizing. After the Second World War, European governments mostly nationalized their steel industry. Steel was regarded as a key strategic sector, supplying crucial materials for armaments and a wide range of other industries. Steel was regarded as essential for national survival during military struggle. The steel sector received a great deal of government support, and in most of Europe was predominantly state-owned, with over one-half of steel output in the 1980s being produced by state-owned enterprises. Within each of the advanced economies the steel industry was highly concentrated. In 1969, the top 11 firms in the USA accounted for around 82 per cent of total crude steel output. In France the top two firms accounted for over 68 per cent of national output. In Germany the top two producers accounted for 42 per cent of national output. In Italy the largest firm accounted for 58 per cent of national output, and in Japan the top seven firms accounted for over 81 per cent of national output (Cockerill, 1974: Ch. 6). In many developing countries, the steel industry was strongly protected from international competition and a large part of national output was produced by large state-owned firms.

By the late 1990s, a wave of privatizations had transformed the institutional background of the steel industry in Europe and a number of developing countries. National governments had more or less phased out subsidies for the steel industry within their countries. Moreover, the traditional steel companies faced intensified competition from both mini-mills and new materials that could substitute for steel.

Massive downsizing of employment was a major reflection of the change in management practices accompanying privatization. In fact, much of the downsizing preceded privatization as the companies which were to be privatized were 'put into good shape'. In Europe, a wave of privatizations took place from the late 1980s onwards. By 1998 the proportion of steel produced in state-owned firms had fallen to under 5 per cent (MSDW, 1998a: 203). From 1974 to 1996, steel output in the six largest steel producing countries in the EU fell by around 23 per cent, but employment in the same countries' steel industry plummeted by over 70 per cent, from 840 000 to 240 000 (IISI, 1998). A dramatic change in working practices accompanied the downsizing. Output per worker in the steel industry in these countries increased from 190 tons in 1974 to over 500 tons per worker in 1996 (IISI, 1998). Across the EU countries as a whole employment in the steel industry fell from 998 000 in 1974 to 290 000 in 1997 (IISI, 1998).

The wave of privatization not only changed management behaviour. It also signalled the end of the epoch of 'national champions' in steel, which were immune from take-over or merger with steel firms in other countries. Up until the 1990s, it had been impossible for truly global steel firms to emerge, with plants in many different countries. As late as the mid-1990s, in contrast to such industries as chemicals, there were no truly multinational steel companies. Steel could be sold across world markets, but it was still produced and supplied largely by national companies.That situation changed rapidly.

Important privatizations in the steel sector took place also in developing countries. The largest developing country privatization programme took place in Brazil between 1991 and 1993, during which time eight government-owned steel companies, constituting almost the entire integrated steel industry, were sold to the private sector. Privatization was widely opposed: 'Violent scenes at privatization were a symptom of widespread fears over job losses. Those fears were justified' (*FT*, 16 February 1996). The number of employees in the sector fell from 138 000 in 1989 to 75 000 in 1997 (*FT*, 16 February 1996; IISI 1998). Output per worker in the sector rose from 158 tons in 1990 to 330 tons in 1996 (*FT*, 16 February 1996; IISI 1998). Under state ownership the government controlled steel prices and employment levels. The industry was loss-making over many years, and the state provided an estimated total of $26 billion in subsidies to the industry over fifty years (*FT*, 16 February 1996). The sharp fall in costs of production, mainly due to downsizing and changed employment practices, greatly increased the industry's international competitiveness. After making losses consistently in the early 1990s, the sector became profit making in 1994 (*FT*, 16 February 1996). Brazil was a major exporter of steel in the mid-1990s, exporting over 10 million tons in 1996, ahead even of the UK, and on a par with South Korea (IISI, 1998). In 1992 import tariffs were cut from 30 per cent to 10 per cent, but domestic producers were able to retain their market share (MSDW, 1998a: 203). By early 1998 every major steel producer in Latin America had been privatized (MSDW, 1998a: 203).

Increased international competition affected the major East Asian producers as well. In South Korea in the 1990s, alongside fast-growing steel output, employment remained constant, allowing output per worker to increase from 418 tons in 1992 to 591 tons in 1996 (IISI, 1998). In Japan, output remained constant at around 99 million tons, but employment fell from over 300 000 to 240 000, allowing output per worker to rise from 320 tons in 1992 to 413 tons in 1996

(IISI, 1998). Ferocious cost-cutting by the leading Japanese steel makers allowed them to make profits in the 1990s, despite intensification of competition. For example, Nippon Steel cut employment by no less than 53 per cent from 1985 to 1995 (*FT*, 25 May 1996).

International Trade. Levels of protection declined gradually in the 1990s, albeit that there were still important restraints remaining in the form of both tariffs and voluntary export restraints. International trade in steel products grew rapidly as privatized producers sought markets with greatly increased intensity. In the late 1970s, world exports of steel stood at around 120–140 million tons, amounting to around 23–24 per cent of world output. By the mid-1990s, total exports had doubled to around 230–240 million tons, accounting for around 37–38 per cent of world production (IISI, 1998). The pressure to be competitive was dramatically increased.

The new international environment facing the world steel industry was illustrated dramatically by the impact of the Asian economic crisis. In 1997–8, faced with large declines in domestic demand and depreciation of their currencies, major steel producers outside the EU and the USA sharply increased their exports to the advanced economies. By August 1998, it was reported that US steel imports were equal to one-half of national production in that month (*FT*, 23 October 1998). The EU became a net importer for the first time in the first half of 1998 (*FT*, 23 October 1998). Accompanying sharply increased levels of penetration of steel imports went plummeting prices and profits for steel makers in the EU and the USA. In the USA the price of cold-rolled steel decreased from an average $580/ton in March 1995 to $320/ton in October 1998 (*IHT*, 6 November 1998): 'Steel prices are probably falling faster than at any time in recorded history. We really are staring at a black hole at the moment' (a steel analyst at Salomon Smith Barney quoted in *FT*, 17 November 1998).

Calls for increased protection for EU and US steel makers became increasingly urgent. Faced with intense lobbying, the USA's trade representative, Charlene Barshefsky, said the administration was investigating 'seriously and sensibly' the USA's steel makers' demand for trade relief (*FT*, 23 October 1998). Even President Clinton joined the debate, declaring that the US would not tolerate a 'flood of cheap steel' from abroad (*IHT*, 12 November 1998). In 1998, both the EU and the USA steel makers were putting heavy pressure on governments to intensify anti-dumping actions against foreign steel producers. The USA had already filed around 250 cases since 1980 (*Fortune*, 11 January 1999). Anti-dumping enforcement falls within the letter of international law. However, the process is 'often a thin excuse for protectionism': 'The murky formulas calculating what constitutes dumping are skewed in the domestic industry's favour. And if foreign firms don't provide the massive amounts of information needed to mount a defence, the government can rely on information supplied by the companies that initiated the dumping claim' (*Fortune*, 11 January 1999).

The difficulties of the world steel industry are likely to be one of the first big tests of the ability of the world trade system to stand up to the shocks of the world economic crisis. The comments made by the Investor Director at British Steel, Mr John Bowden, highlighted the bitterness being felt among Western steel producers: '*Are we going to bail those countries out via the IMF and let them export their way out of trouble*? That's not just a steel industry question but a general trade question' (*FT*, 7 January 1998, emphasis added). *Fortune* magazine commented: 'If Big Steel wins its cases, watch out for other industries vulnerable to competition – such as chemicals, paper, and machine tools – to join the queue. That could really get a trade war going' (*Fortune*, 11 January 1999).

Consolidation and Globalization. We have seen that major changes shook the world steel industry after the 1970s. Competition from alternative materials intensified. Traditional integrated producers faced competition from mini-mills. Demand collapsed in the former Soviet Union. Support for national champions in Western Europe and in many developing countries disappeared. Levels of protection fell significantly. Privatization was widely put into effect. For the first time, there emerged the possibility of true multinational companies in the steel industry. In response to the dramatic changes in the competitive landscape, in recent years there has been a substantial growth of multinational investment by some leading steel firms. In the 1990s there has been a wave of joint ventures and mergers, increasingly across international borders.

Foreign investment by leading East Asian steel companies. Following the same path as the leading automobile manufacturers, leading Japanese steel firms began to invest abroad in significant amounts in the 1980s. Japanese steel makers found it increasingly difficult to export profitably due to the appreciation of the yen. Their main target, as in autos, was the USA. Their investments include a $1.6 billion investment (50 per cent share) by Kawasaki in a galvanizing line for Armco Steel and a $2.2 billion investment (70 per cent share) by NKK in an integrated steel mill with National Steel (Yonekura, 1994: 267). As one NKK manager explained: '[G]lobalization is a principal strategy NKK has planned for a long time. It isn't *ad hoc* at all. Since globalization has progressed in many fields, why haven't Japanese [steel] businesses become more internationalized? At least until the twenty-first century, steel demand will never disappear, and steel will be the best material in terms of cost, configurability and durability ... It will be impossible for [Japanese] steel firms to compete with developing countries at the lower end for a long time. So, logically speaking, there is no way except to globalize basic production and specialize in the high end in Japan' (quoted in Yonekura, 1994: 272).

As well as investing in the USA, Japanese steel makers started to invest in developing countries. For example, in the early 1990s Nippon Steel set up two joint ventures in Thailand (*FT*, 10 January 1995). In 1997, it formed a 200 million JV with Usiminas (Brazil) in Brazil. The plant, with capacity to produce 400 000 tons of hot-dip coated steel sheets a year, is expected to be in operation in 1999. The high-grade steel is mainly tailored for the automobile manufacturers in South America (*FT*, 15 December 1997).

In the 1990s, Posco rapidly expanded its overseas operations. By late 1998 it had established 21 subsidiary companies in nine countries (Posco Website). Posco's stated goals in international expansion are threefold. The first is to establish major downstream production bases, principally in East and South-East Asia. Its four plants in China produce 410 000 tons of steel products per annum, its Indonesian plant produces one million tons, its three plants in Vietnam produce 276 000 tons, and its Thai plant produces 910 000 tons. In addition, its subsidiary in Pittsburgh (USA), produces 1.44 million tons of downstream steel products. The second goal in Posco's overseas expansion is to move into upstream crude steel production in South-East Asia. Its third goal is to secure raw materials and scrap substitutes, especially to supply its growing portfolio of mini-mills. To this end, it has already established an iron-ore pellet-manufacturing facility in Brazil, producing 4 million tons per annum.

European consolidation. We have seen that from the mid-1980s onwards the vast bulk of the European steel industry was privatized. We have seen also that the international competitive pressures were intensifying, culminating in those emanating from the world economic crisis. A process of consolidation has been gathering speed as the 1990s have progressed. This reached a peak in 1997, which 'will be remembered as the year of merger and rationalization in the European steel industry' (MSDW, 1998a: 202). This activity has included 10 European steel companies with a combined capacity of 43 million tons, or 30 per cent of Western European production. A small number of globally powerful 'European champions' is in the process of emerging from the ranks of the old state-owned 'national champions'. Indeed, analysts began to speak of the emergence of a 'European steel oligopoly', consisting of British Steel, Usinor, Thyssen–Krupp and Arbed. The following are some of the main developments in recent years:

- **British Steel**. The British Steel Corporation (BSC) was formed in 1967, with the nationalization of all steel firms in the UK with an output of over 0.5 million tons. It comprised a total of fourteen steel companies, with an aggregate output of 25 million tons of crude steel, making it the world's second largest producer at that time. The British government's White Paper of 1973 announced a 10-year development plan for an expansion of BSC's output to 36–38 million tons by the early 1980s, most of which would be produced at just five large plants (Cockerill, 1974: 55). In fact, the expansion plans were based on wildly over-optimistic evaluations of the demand for steel. By 1979 BSC was producing just 14 million tons of crude steel, and recorded a loss of £1.78 billion, the largest in British corporate history.

  In 1980, the British government appointed a new chief executive officer to BSC. He was Ian MacGregor. His appointment was highly controversial. MacGregor was given the authority to change radically the way in which BSC was run in order to transform it into a profitable entity. In 1980, BSC employed 166 000 people and produced 14 million tons of steel. By 1983, total employment had fallen to just 71 000. Output remained constant at around 14 million tons, and losses had fallen to £0.26 million. By 1985, BSC had become profitable, and 'one of the most efficient steel companies in the Western world' (*Daily Telegraph*, 14 April 1998). Only after this path-breaking, and highly controversial restructuring was BSC privatized, in 1988–9, almost a decade after the restructuring began.

BSC has continued to produce around 15 million tons of steel annually, and employment fell slowly to around 50 000 in 1997. In the early 1990s, BSC invested heavily in modernizing its production facilities (Hogan, 1994: 28–9), investing more than £1 billion in plant modernization from 1990 to 1995 (*FT*, 16 January 1996) and raised the share of high value-added products in its product portfolio. It also made intense efforts to improve the closeness of its relationship with its customers. By 1996 it had become the lowest-cost steel producer in Western Europe, and made profits of over £1 billion (*Observer*, 2 November 1997). However, in contrast to other leading EU steel companies, BSC was very cautious in its international expansion, with around 90 per cent of its assets still in the UK (*Observer*, 2 November 1997). More than half its output is exported, so that BSC suffered severely from the appreciation in the value of the pound sterling and was damaged by the intense competition from Asian steel producers due to the world economic crisis. By late 1998, BSC was planning to reduce employment by more than 12 000 by the year 2000 in order to further lower costs (*The Times*, 17 November 1998).

In 1999, British Steel responded to the surrounding process of steel industry consolidation with a highly significant merger with Dutch-based steelmaker Hoogovens. The deal creates a company with 70 000 employees, a turnover of $15 billion and a market capitalization of $6.5 billion. The new company will have a steel output of over 23 million tons, making it the world's third-ranking producer on 1998 output figures. The two companies declared that they needed scale because a wave of mergers among their main customers was creating pressure for the broadest possible range of products and geographical presence. A key driver of this is the forecast that the number of car-makers will continue to contract, meaning fewer buyers and encouraging steel-makers to supply car plants anywhere in the world. Some industry experts predict that there will be just five dominant car firms globally within 10 years. The merger is also justified in terms of the need to offer a broad range of products to global customers. The merged company will include both stainless steel (from British Steel's Avesta Sheffield joint venture) and aluminium (from Hoogovens). The expanded firm will use its increased size as a base for acquisitions in the USA and Eastern Europe, as well as China and other emerging markets: 'As a merged group, we are better placed to follow our clients to these regions' (Fokko Van Dyne, Chief Executive of Hoogovens, quoted in *FT*, 8 June 1999).

- **Usinor**. Usinor is the product of a long series of mergers and acquisitions within France. It was formed through mergers pre-1950 and absorbed

Lorraine–Escaut in 1966 (Cockerill, 1974: 43). Subsequently, the French government attempted to build a state-owned 'national champion', merging Usinor with Wendel-Sidelor and their jointly-owned subsidiary Sacilor. In the 1980s it spent 'several billion dollars' on plant and equipment (Hogan, 1994: 34). After the appointment of Francis Mer as chairman in 1986, Usinor began a process of rapid increase in size through acquisitions alongside large-scale downsizing of employment. Usinor reduced employment from 96 000 in 1989 to around 62 000 (*FT*, 8 February 1995). It established itself as the leading supplier of flat rolled steel to the European automobile industry, and Europe's largest stainless steel maker. By 1995 it was ranked the world's third largest steel producer, after Nippon Steel and Posco, though its ranking slipped subsequently due to mergers elsewhere in the industry (*FT*, 8 February 1995). Between 1989 and 1992, Usinor expanded its downstream processing and distribution activities through more than 25 acquisitions and participations, mainly in Europe (France, Germany, Spain, Italy and the UK) (Usinor, 1998: 6). It also expanded in the US, purchasing Jones and Laughlin, the US's largest stainless steel producer in the late 1980s (*FT*, 8 February 1995).

Following its privatization in 1995, Usinor (France) began an ambitious programme of international investment and growth. In 1997–8 it made a number of important overseas acquisitions (Usinor, 1998: 5–6). It became the majority owner of a 400 000-ton cold-rolling mill in Spain, and of a speciality steel producer (springs and torsion bars for the automobile industry) in Argentina, designed to gain access to the Brazilian market. It acquired 40 per cent of Arvedi (Italy). This deal allows Usinor to explore mini-mill technology (*FT*, 1 May 1998). It spent $625 million to acquire a 30 per cent stake in Acesita (Brazil, a speciality steel producer) and a 16 per cent stake in CST (Brazil, a steel slabs producer) (*FT*, 27 May 1998). Usinor is the largest foreign investor in Thainox, a cold-rolling joint venture in Thailand (Usinor, 1998: 9–10). In late 1998 Usinor took over Cockerill–Sambrell (Belgium). This acquisition lifted Usinor's output to around 23 million tons, making it the world's third largest steel producer. In mid-2000 it was strongly rumoured that Usinor was about to take over the steel-making arm of Thyssen–Krupp. If completed this would catapult the new entity into first place in the world steel industry.

- **Thyssen–Krupp**. In the late 1960s, there were 11 firms in Germany that produced over one million tons of steel (Cockerill, 1974: 45). The three largest were Thyssen, Krupp and Hoesch. The seven largest manufacturers each provided a full range of steel products. By the late 1980s, the number of steel companies had been reduced to five (Hogan, 1994: 30). In the early 1990s, Krupp launched the first major hostile take-over in modern Germany with the acquisition of Hoesch. This launched Krupp–Hoesch into the position of the world's largest stainless steel producer, with a 17 per cent share of the world market in the mid-1990s (*FT*, 14 March 1996).[10] Even after the merger,

Thyssen was still the largest steel producer in Germany, with around 10 million tons crude steel output, compared to around 8-9 million tons for the combined Krupp–Hoesch (Hogan, 1994: 31). In 1997, in a milestone merger for the whole of German industry, Krupp–Hoesch launched a massive hostile bid for Thyssen. After intense debate, frequently in public, the two companies were eventually merged to form a giant steel and engineering company with 180 000 employees and a turnover of $33 billion, making it the largest company in Germany (*FT*, 10 January 1998).

In the steel sector, in 1997 Thyssen-Krupp produced over 17 million tons of crude steel, making it the fourth largest steel company in the world. The aim of the merger was to 'forge an operation with the strength and malleability to withstand fierce foreign competition (*FT*, 31 July 1997). Prior to the merger, both companies had downsized heavily: Thyssen laid off 13 000 people in 1993–4 and Krupp–Hoesch laid off 13 000 in 1993 alone (Hogan, 1994: 30–1). The Thyssen–Krupp merger was to be followed by a further reduction in the number of steel sector employees by 7000, leaving a total steel workforce of 17 000 (*FT*, 31 July 1997). A rising share of the companies' employees were working outside Germany. Already by 1997, 40 per cent of Krupp employees were working abroad. The head of Krupp, Gerhard Cromme, explained its strategy as producing 'high value investment goods'. These are 'products which are manufactured in many countries in the world', in markets in which there are 'no monopolies any more' (quoted in *FT*, 6 November 1997). He said: 'We produce for our customers where they want us to produce ... If they demand that we produce in the USA, Mexico, Brazil or in China, then we go there and produce locally' (quoted in *FT*, 6 November 1997).

Thyssen–Krupp intends to expand international joint ventures in downstream, high value-added steel products, such as cold-rolling, coating or tailoring steel plates to customers' requirements (an increasing trend in the automobile industry) (*FT*, 31 July 1997). As we shall see, one of the major international investments recently made by Krupp is a $1.4 billion stainless steel joint venture in Shanghai. The plant will produce 400 000 tons of stainless steel per year, which compares with China's total current demand of around 900 000 tons per annum (*Hong Kong Standard*, 9 October 1998). Thyssen–Krupp and CSN (the largest steel producer in Brazil) have formed a JV, GalvaSud, to manufacture galvanized products for the automobile industry in Brazil. The $250 million JV will have an annual capacity of 350 000 tons and begin operating in 2000 (*FT*, 28 May 1998).

- **Arbed**. In the1970s, Arbed was a medium-sized producer, accounting for 27 per cent of Belgium's national output, with a total production of 5 million tons (Cockerill, 1974: 40). In the early 1990s, it was still only the sixth largest EU producer, with an output of 7.1 million tons (Hogan, 1994: 34). Thereafter, it began a process of rapid expansion through investment and acquisition. In 1995 it bought the steel division of Kloekner Werke (Germany). In 1997 it bought a 35 per cent share in Corporación de la Siderúrgica Integral (CSI, Spain) in a partial privatization by the Spanish government. CSI's privatization followed a dramatic fall in employment in the early 1990s, from 22 000 to 12 000, following which the company made significant profits (*FT*, 30 July 1997). With a combined output of 18.8 million tons in 1997, this acquisition effectively made Arbed the largest producer in Europe, and the third biggest in the world (*FT*, 30 July 1997 and 30 March 1998). Arbed regarded the acquisition as 'a qualitative step forward in the expansion, modernization and global strategy of the group' (*FT*, 30 March 1998).

Consolidation in the USA. In the early 1970s, *Bethlehem Steel* was the second largest US steel producer, with around 20 million tons of crude steel output (Cockerill, 1974: 57). Along with US Steel, it greatly reduced its output in the face of the mini-mill revolution. Crude steel production fell to less than 9 million tons in 1996 (IISI, 1998). In the mid-1990s, pressure on steel prices caused speculation that the US steel industry would see a consolidation process such as that which had already started in Europe. The process began with discussions between US Steel and Inland Steel, though the merger did not come to fruition (*FT*, 8 April 1997). In 1997, Bethlehem Steel (USA) agreed to pay $400 million to acquire its rival Lukens (USA), a specialist manufacturer of steel plates and stainless steel.[11] To cut costs, Bethlehem Steel would shut down one of its steel plate mills and one of the four steel plate mills operated by Lukens after the acquisition.[12]

We shall see below that Ispat has taken over one of the leading US integrated steel companies, Inland Steel. It is widely thought this will give added impetus to the process of US steel consolidation. *US Steel* is a likely candidate to lead this process. It has the 'healthiest balance sheet in the industry', and is in a good position 'to consolidate the US Steel industry through acquisition' (MSDW, 1998a: 202).

Far East. A move of immense potential significance was announced in 1999 in response to the world economic crisis. Posco and Nippon Steel have bought shares in each other as part of a scheme to create 'a mutual anti-takeover alliance' (*FT*, 25 January 1999). Posco and Nippon Steel have a long working relationship. If the share-swap presages an even deeper alliance between the two giants then it will have enormous implications for the institutional structure of the world's steel industry. In the view of Morgan Stanley Dean Witter, if this alliance occurs, 'the race for regional dominance would appear to be over before most producers realized it had begun' (MSDW, 1998c: 51).

The global steel corporation. Ispat is, arguably, the only truly global steel corporation to have developed. Significantly, it began life only in the 1980s, but has rapidly transformed itself into the most global and fast-growing of all steel companies. From 1986 to 1995 it bought a succession of struggling steel makers in different countries, including Canada, Mexico, Ireland, Trinidad and Tobago, the

UK, Germany and Indonesia. It typically downsized employment and invested in modernizing the plant, drastically improving the companies' financial performance. Typical of its purchases was the Sicartsa complex in Mexico. It cost the Mexican government $2.2 billion to build, but the plant was running at only 25 per cent of capacity and its order books were depleted. Ispat paid just $220 million to buy the plant. Even more audacious was its purchase of a mini-mill in Cork for nominal I£1. Most of the plants acquired by Ispat had electric furnaces fed with Ispat's own DRI (see above). A major advantage for the mini-mills that Ispat acquired was the ability to find markets for their products that they were unable to achieve on their own. By 1995 it had a total output of 6.5 million tons of steel, and had entered the ranks of the top thirty world steel producers (*FT*, 8 August 1995).

In 1996 Ispat began even faster expansion. It acquired the Karmet steel plant in Kazakhstan, the second largest in the former USSR. Ispat paid around $450 million for the plant with a commitment to invest around $500 million to modernize the facility (*FT*, 27 February 1996). Karmet employed around 38 000 people at the time Ispat took it over. It planned to downsize the workforce to around 28 000, and link the plant to Ispat's international sales network.

Throughout the 1990s, Ispat invested heavily in modernizing its Mexican subsidiary. Between 1991 and 1997, Ispat Mexicana's output of steel slabs tripled to 2.8 million tons. It had already become Mexico's largest steel exporter and was poised to become Mexico's largest producer. Ispat is spending $175 million to boost its liquid steel production to 4.4 million tons by 1999 (*FT*, 17 March 1998). Ispat Mexicana's goal was to become the first domestic producer to supply the high quality market for automobiles and white goods (*FT*, 17 March 1998). In 1997 Ispat was floated in New York and Amsterdam (*FT*, 24 July 1997), but retained Karmet and its Indonesian steel interests outside the floated company. Its net profits on sales stood at 14.7 per cent (*FT*, 24 July 1997).

In 1998, Ispat acquired Inland Steel (USA) in a landmark take-over, paying $1.43 billion (*FT*, 18 March 1998). Inland Steel was the sixth largest US steel company, with 9400 employees and an output of 5.3 million tons in 1997 (IISI, 1998). Ispat will also acquire Inland's two US JVs with Nippon Steel. The take-over rocked the world's steel industry:

> The deal could herald a new phase in the consolidation of the world steel industry. ... [It] will put pressure on other steel companies to consolidate, particularly in North America, where the biggest companies are noticeably smaller than their East Asian competitors. [Ispat's] advance raises fundamental questions about the industry's structure which for decades has been organized on national lines. (*FT*, 18 and 19 March 1998)

The take-over of Inland Steel makes Ispat the world's eighth largest steel maker, with an annual output of 12.5 million tons from the entities included in the floated company. However, if its interests in Indonesia and the Karmet plant are included, then the group's output is no less than 19 million tons. This makes Ispat the world's third largest steel company, and the only one that is truly global.

Ispat now has major production facilities in Europe, Latin America, the USA and the former Soviet Union. The chairman of Inland Steel (the sixth largest steel-maker in the USA), Mr. Robert Darnell, suggested that this deal provides the merged company 'with an international production capability and global market reach, [and this] will have a major edge over other producers' (*FT*, 18 March 1998). Ispat now has unique experience in the management of a global steel company. It has a network of steel plants that are uniquely positioned to respond to the needs of global customers in the automobile, white goods or packaging industries.

Ispat's expansion continued later in 1998. In May it signed a memorandum of understanding with the outgoing Suharto government to acquire 51 per cent of Krakatau Steel, the largest steel company in Indonesia, for $400 million (*FT*, 4 June 1998). In June it acquired a one-third stake in Germany's Westfälische Drahtindustrie, a large maker of high-value steel wire for such goods as fasteners and ropes (*FT*, 24 June 1998).

Industrial concentration. At first glance, the global industry still appears very fragmented, and it certainly is, in comparison with some, such as soft drinks or aerospace. Despite the recent emergence of substantial cross-border merger activity, the top 10 companies still account for only around 22 per cent of world steel output, and the top 30 for 34 per cent (Table 9-4). None of the world's top 20 steel companies produced more than 4 per cent of global output in 1997. The world's two leading companies, Nippon Steel and Posco each produces only around 3.3–3.5 per cent of the world's total.

However, on closer inspection, the level of concentration is higher than it appears to be. The institutional transformation of the world's steel industry is still at a relatively early stage compared to some other industries. One reason for this is the fact that the world's largest producer, China, still, as we shall see, has experienced only negligible merger and acquisition among its largest producers. Nor have the large production facilities in the former Soviet Union made much movement towards substantial merger and acquisition. The world's top five companies already account for 19.1 per cent of the world's total output excluding China and the former Soviet Union, and world's top 10 account for 31 per cent (from Tables 9-4 and 9-5). Moreover, the trend towards merger and acquisition in 1997–8 makes it likely that the trend towards greater concentration is accelerating.

Moreover, if one analyzes different products, then the level of concentration is even higher than appears to be the case from an aggregate analysis. For example, in stainless steel, we have already seen that two companies, Thyssen–Krupp and Usinor are the world leaders, and may account for as much as 25–30 per cent of total world output between them. In the mid-1990s, Krupp–Hoesch accounted for around 17 per cent of world stainless steel output (see above). In 1997, Usinor accounted for 11 per cent of world output of flat stainless steel products, in which it is the world's second largest producer, and in long stainless steel products it accounted for around 8 per cent, and was the world's leading producer (Usinor, 1998: 11).

TABLE 9-5 The Top 10 and Top 20 in World Crude Steel Production by Countries, 1991–8

Output (million metric tons)/output share (%) in brackets

Countries	(1988)	(1990)	(1992)	(1994)	(1996)	(1997)	(1998 Jan.–Sep.)	1988–97 % change	Average annual change*
China	59.4 (7.6)	66.3 (8.6)	80.9 (11.2)	92.6 (12.8)	101.2 (13.5)	108.94 (13.7)	83.54 (14.5)	83.4	7.02
Japan	105.7 (13.6)	110.3 (14.3)	98.1 (13.6)	98.3 (13.6)	98.8 (13.2)	104.5 (13.2)	70.75 (12.2)	−1.1	−0.03
USA	90.7 (11.6)	89.7 (11.7)	84.3 (11.7)	91.2 (12.6)	94.7 (12.6)	99.2 (12.5)	75.14 (13.0)	9.4	1.13
Russia	n.a.	n.a.	67.0 (9.3)	48.8 (6.7)	49.3 (6.6)	46.9** (5.9)	31.34 (5.4)	−39.2	−7.66
Germany	41.0 (5.3)	38.4 (5.0)	39.7 (5.5)	40.8 (5.6)	39.8 (5.3)	45.0 (5.7)	34.46 (6.0)	9.8	1.30
South Korea	19.1 (2.5)	23.1 (3.0)	28.1 (3.9)	33.7 (4.6)	38.9 (5.2)	42.5 (5.3)	30.07 (5.2)	122.5	9.39
Brazil	24.7 (3.1)	20.6 (2.7)	23.9 (3.3)	25.7 (3.5)	25.2 (3.4)	26.2 (3.3)	19.74 (3.4)	6.1	0.96
Ukraine	56.4 (7.2)	52.6 (6.8)	41.8 (5.8)	24.1 (3.3)	22.3 (3.0)	25.5** (3.2)	18.07 (3.1)	−54.8	−7.73
Italy	23.8 (3.1)	25.5 (3.3)	24.8 (3.4)	26.2 (3.6)	24.3 (3.2)	25.2 (3.2)	19.70 (3.4)	5.9	0.79
India	14.3 (1.8)	15.0 (2.0)	18.1 (2.5)	19.3 (2.7)	23.8 (3.2)	23.8§ (3.0)	17.89 (3.1)	66.4	5.94
Top 10	435.1 (55.8)	441.5 (57.3)	506.7 (70.4)	500.7 (69.0)	518.3 (69.2)	547.7 (68.9)	400.7 (69.3)	125.9	2.73

France	19.1 (2.5)	19.0 (2.5)	18.0 (2.5)	18.0 (2.5)	17.6 (2.3)	19.8 (2.5)	15.32 (2.7)	3.7	0.52
UK	19.0 (2.4)	17.8 (2.3)	16.2 (2.3)	17.3 (2.4)	18.0 (2.4)	18.5 (2.3)	13.52 (2.3)	−2.6	−0.23
Taiwan	n.a.	n.a.	10.7 (1.5)	11.6 (1.6)	12.4 (1.7)	15.9** (2.0)	12.33 (2.1)	44.6	6.87
Canada	n.a.	n.a.	13.9 (1.9)	13.9 (1.9)	14.7 (2.0)	15.4§ (1.9)	12.28 (2.1)	18.5	2.92
Mexico	n.a.	n.a.	8.5 (1.2)	10.3 (1.4)	13.2 (1.8)	14.3** (1.8)	11.03 (1.9)	78.8	10.22
Turkey	n.a.	n.a.	10.3 (1.4)	12.6 (1.7)	13.6 (1.8)	14.2** (1.8)	10.51 (1.8)	51.1	7.17
Spain	n.a.	n.a.	12.3 (1.7)	13.4 (1.8)	12.2 (1.6)	13.8 (1.7)	11.55 (2.0)	7.8	1.56
Belgium	n.a.	n.a.	10.3 (1.4)	11.3 (1.6)	10.8 (1.4)	10.8 (1.4)	8.68 (1.5)	−4.4	−0.55
Australia	n.a.	n.a.	6.8 (0.9)	8.4 (1.2)	8.4 (1.1)	8.7 (1.1)	6.74 (1.2)	42.6	6.26
South Africa	n.a.	n.a.	9.1 (1.3)	8.5 (1.2)	8.0 (1.1)	8.2 (1.0)	5.98 (1.0)	−12.8	−2.18
Top 20	n.a.	n.a.	622.8 (86.5)	626.0 (86.3)	647.2 (86.4)	687.3 (86.5)	508.6 (88.0)	108.9±	1.46±
World	780.0	770.0	719.7	725.3	749.4	794.5	578.0	8.3±	1.37±

SOURCES: *FT* (22 March 1995); International Iron and Steel Institute (IISI) (1998)

NOTES: * Based on 1988–97 data
** Based on 10 months' data
§ Based on 11 months' data
± Based on 1991–7 data

BARRIERS TO ENTRY IN DEVELOPING COUNTRIES

At first glance the steel industry presents very different possibilities for 'catch-up' in developing countries than do high technology industries such as aerospace, industries which have high R & D, such as patented pharmaceuticals, and industries in which massive investments are needed to created a global brand, such as soft drinks. There are a number of reasons to be believe that a group of large indigenous integrated steel firms in developing countries will be able to catch up with and even overtake those in the advanced economies. The reasons include the following:

- The pace of technical progress has been slower in the steel industry than in industries such as aerospace, Steel industry firms have devoted much smaller proportions of their revenue to R & D than most other industries in the advanced economies. In 1997, among the world's 300 largest companies by R & D expenditure, pharmaceuticals spent 12.8 per cent of revenue on R & D, compared to 6.5 per cent in electronics and electricals, 6.3 per cent in chemicals, 4.2 per cent in vehicles, and 4.1 per cent in engineering (DTI, 1998: 56–84). Leading steel companies such as British Steel, Thyssen–Krupp, NKK and Usinor, spent only 0.6–1.3 per cent of revenues on R & D (DTI, 1998: 22, 62). For basic steel making processes, the technology is embodied in equipment that can be purchased relatively easily and operated effectively in a relatively short time (Amsden, 1989: Ch. 12).

- Booming markets for steel provide considerable advantages for local production. We have seen that the trend has been, and is likely to continue to be, that developing countries achieve high growth rates of output of steel, while demand for steel in the advanced economies grows slowly, or even stagnates. If local steel firms in developing countries are able to meet fast growing local demand they may be able to generate rapid increases in revenues with which to reinvest in order to benefit from economies of scale, modernize production facilities and begin to generate technical progress: 'The healthiest steel companies are typically those that sell to rapidly growing domestic markets' (MSDW, 1998a: 198). Although steel is traded in increasing quantities in international markets, it does have relatively high transport costs compared to many other industries. Moreover, in many developing and developed countries, local producers' advantages are reinforced through protection, through both tariff barriers (see Table 9-6) and non-tariff methods of protection.

- Many developing countries enjoy advantages through the local availability of iron ore and coal resources. Both of these have low value-to-weight ratios. Iron ore typically accounts for around 11–13 per cent of total costs of steel produced in integrated steel plants. India and Brazil are especially favoured in this respect (see Table 9-7). Though China does not enjoy significant advantages in access to low cost iron ore compared to leading

TABLE 9-6 Tariffs on Steel Products
in Selected Countries, 1997

Country	Tariff (%)
China	6–40
India	25–35
Indonesia	5–30
Japan	0
Korea	8
Malaysia	0–25
Pakistan	78–83
Philippines	3–20
Taiwan	2.5–14
Thailand	5–13
Vietnam	0–30

SOURCE: MSDW (1998c: 191)

TABLE 9-7 Iron Ore Costs in Selected Countries' Steel Industries, 1997

Country	Cost per ton ($)	Transport costs/ton ($)	Cost per contained ton ($)	Iron ore as % of total costs
Australia	20.5	5.0	40.1	8
Brazil	12.0	7.0	28.0	8
China	20.0	n.a.	38.0	13
Europe	19.0	8.0	40.9	11
India	9.5	n.a.	18.9	5
Japan	21.2	5.0	47.3	12
Korea	17.0	n.a.	32.0	11
Taiwan	19.0	n.a.	46.0	13
USA	32.0	4.5	56.2	12
UK	25.0	n.a.	35.8	7

SOURCE: MSDW (1998a: 201)

producers in the advanced economies, it does have the advantage of vast availability of domestically-produced coal and coke.

- A major source of advantage for mini-mills in the advanced economies lies in the availability of plentiful supplies of cheap scrap steel. However, in developing countries where *per capita* consumption of steel is still far below the advanced economies, such scrap availability does not yet exist, and will not do so for a considerable time ahead. Therefore, at the present stage of development, large integrated steel plants, using established technology, still are a competitive way of producing steel.

- We have noted already the fact that developing countries have less strict environmental regulations, especially in the blast furnace stage of the steel making process in integrated steel plants. A major reason for plant closure in the advanced economies has been the high cost of upgrading blast furnaces to ensure that they pass ever stricter environmental regulations. Such considerations do not limit growth of integrated steel plants in developing countries to anything like the same degree.

- Large integrated steel firms in developing countries enjoy the advantage of vastly lower wage costs. Hourly labour costs are only $1.4 in Indian integrated steel companies, and just $0.5 in China, compared to $8.8 in Mexico and $14–15 in Brazil and Taiwan (Table 9-8). Of course, integrated steel firms in developing countries have much higher manning levels than do firms in advanced economies, and often use more labour-intensive processes, especially in ancillary activities. Moreover, as we have seen, large steel firms in advanced economies have greatly downsized employment in the past 10–15 years. Levels of labour productivity are vastly above those in developing countries. In the USA, Japan and Europe, it requires only around 3–4 man hours to produce a ton of coal, compared to 45–55 in China and India. However, the extremely low labour costs in developing countries more than compensate for the much larger amounts of labour employed to produce a ton of coal. Consequently, in leading coal producing developing countries such as China and India, labour costs per ton of coal are only around $30–70, rising to over $80 in Brazil, and reaching around $155 in Japan and the USA. In China, labour costs amount to less than 10 per cent of total costs, despite the very high manning levels. In the advanced economies labour costs are mostly above 20 per cent, and in the USA and Europe rise to 26–27 per cent of total costs. Overall, costs per ton in

TABLE 9-8 **Labour Costs Per Ton in Integrated Steel Companies, Selected Countries and Nucor (USA), 1997**

Country	Hourly labour costs ($)	Man hours per ton	Labour costs per ton ($)	Labour costs as % of total costs	Total costs per ton ($)
China	0.49	55.2	27.3	8	350
USA	37.2	4.2	155.5	27	529
Brazil	14.9	5.6	83.5	23	292
Mexico	8.8	4.3	38.0	10	380
UK	21.5	5.1	110.0	18	599
Europe	31.3	3.4	106.5	26	405
Japan	40.7	3.8	156.1	23	680
Korea	14.0	2.1	29.4	8	360
India	1.4	46.7	66.9	17	395
Australia	26.0	5.0	130.0	22	588
Taiwan	14.4	3.2	46.5	13	360
Nucor (USA)	34.0	0.8	27.2	9	295

SOURCE: MSDW (1998a: 200)

integrated steel firms in China and India are less than $400 per ton, compared with $500–700 per ton in Japan and the USA (Table 9-8).

- The process of globalization of markets and ownership is far less advanced in the steel industry than in most other sectors. It has only recently gone through large-scale privatization and is still subject to considerable state intervention even in the advanced economies. The absence of a small number of globally dominant firms in the sector provides an easier institutional environment for emerging large firms in developing countries.

Successful 'latecomer' industrializing countries have typically established internationally competitive steel industries and internationally competitive integrated steel companies. In the late nineteenth century, the USA caught-up with Europe mainly through large integrated steel companies, with US Steel pre-eminent among these. After 1945, Japan rapidly caught-up with and eventually overtook both Europe and the USA through their large integrated steel company, and became the world's leading steel exporter. Massive investment in new greenfield factories combined with rapid technical progress enabled Japan's large firms remorselessly to lower their production costs. Two major innovations helped the large Japanese firms to achieve even greater economies of scale than had been achieved previously.[13] These were the Basic Oxygen Furnace (BOF) and the continuous caster (Yonekura, 1994: 9). They also widened their comparative advantage by building larger blast furnaces, and improving rolling equipment and surface detailing in order to maximize the effectiveness of the two major innovations. Moreover, they utilized sophisticated processing technology via computer control for the entire process of steel making. By the 1980s the Japanese iron and steel industry had become the most efficient and cost competitive in the world (Yonekura, 1994: 10–11). More recently, we have seen how South Korea established a powerful, internationally competitive steel industry, with a single mighty company, Posco, at the centre of the catch-up process. Large integrated steel companies have also played an important role in the catch-up process in countries such as Brazil and Taiwan.

Despite the advantages for large integrated steel firms based in developing countries, there are some important issues that affect their competitive capability on global markets. Although technical progress may be slower than in some other industries, there are still important areas, especially high value-added products and processes, such as special steels, in which large technical gaps exist between leading firms in advanced economies and those in developing countries. There have been important advances in recent years in the way in which the world's leading firms based in advanced economies interact with their customers. In the merger and acquisition boom of the 1990s it has been the steel firms within the advanced economies that have taken the lead. Successful advanced economy steel companies have developed a deep understanding of the requirements of globalizing large firms that are large users of steel, such as automobile and beverage companies. In sum, in the highest profit-margin areas of steel production, there is a small group of industry leaders that is emerging to dominate the global market. The industry is fast becoming bifurcated into two sections, one producing low quality, low value-added products, typically for local firms and the other producing high value-added, high profit margin products for global firms. Developing country firms face extremely severe competition in the latter segment of the steel industry.

CHINA'S IRON AND STEEL INDUSTRY

STATE AND MARKET

Administrative Control. Until the late 1980s, the overall development of the Chinese steel industry was under the close control of the Ministry of Metallurgical Industries (MMI). However, even in the 1980s, a large and fast-growing share of output was produced in local plants, often outside the system even of local state ownership. Since the 1980s, even for the large state keypoint plants, the role of market forces has increased strongly. The changed planning environment was reflected in the system reforms of 1998. Under these reforms the old Ministry of Metallurgy was abolished, and replaced by the State Bureau of Metallurgical Industry (SBMI). Many of the functions of the old Ministry of Metallurgy were transferred down to the province level.

Despite the change, the SBMI still retained important planning functions. These included influence over such key policies as the level of protection, the function of small steel plants, environmental regulation, mergers and acquisitions within the steel industry, and the way in which steel industry modernization is to be pursued. Moreover, with the exception of Shougang (which reports directly to the Beijing municipal government), the other largest Chinese steel makers, such as Angang, Baogang and Wugang, all report directly to the SBMI. The SBMI still assigns the managers of the largest steel plants and is responsible for monitoring their performance.

Domestic Liberalization

Prices. Throughout the 1980s, steel prices were controlled by the government, but controls were relaxed substantially in the early 1990s. In 1994, the government freed all steel prices. However, the government continued to fix 'guidance' prices for the main steel products, and steel firms could technically be prosecuted for selling steel at prices outside the specified range. Moreover, in 1998, faced with the sharp decline in steel prices and industry profitability, the government introduced lower limits to steel prices to attempt to support the industry's profits.[14] However, these controls were quickly lifted. A leading official at the State Development Planning Commission commented: 'Our view is that prices should be decided by the market, and by supply and demand. We have just come from the planned economy. How can we go back there?' (quoted in *Business Post* (Hong Kong), 10 November 1998).

Customers. In parallel with the controls on prices, in the 1980s a large fraction of steel from the large integrated producers was sold through the state supply system, without freedom to determine either the product mix or the customer. This system changed rapidly in the 1990s. By 1998, there were few restrictions on the product mix or choice of customer for China's large integrated steel plants.

Protection. In the 1980s, the Chinese steel industry was protected by high tariff barriers. However, in its efforts to gain admission to the WTO, China sharply reduced tariffs on steel imports. Overall import tariffs on iron and steel (raw and finished) fell from 23.8 per cent in 1992 to 12.0 per cent in 1996 (Dickson, 1996: 23). Import tariffs varied from a low of 1.4 per cent for pig iron to a high of 20.3 per cent on stainless steel bars and rods (Dickson, 1996: 23). By 1996 the licensing system was ended. However, shocked by the explosion of steel imports in the early 1990s (see below), powerful new non-tariff barriers (NTBs) to protect the steel industry were erected in the mid-1990s. These included import 'registration', which could be withheld if there was felt to be a 'market need', and 'canalization' of steel imports through selected state importing companies (Dickson, 1996: 98–9). China has strong aspirations to build domestic import-substituting industries, and it has used international protection as a weapon to support this objective:

China's steel industry, despite being a behemoth, is still an *infant industry* ... Pressured by the United States, China has endeavoured to retain administrative control over imports, but in a way which conforms to the 1992 MOU [Memorandum on Market Access between the United States and China]. Instead of binding quota constraints, China seems to have designed a system which is discretionary in nature. The government gives itself the leeway to impose control if necessary, for example, where 'market disruption' is perceived. The threshold for 'disruption' would be anything threatening the viability of domestic iron and steel enterprises, so essentially the motivation is protection of industry. (Dickson, 1996: 20–2)

DEMAND

Fast-growing developing countries typically generate fast growth of demand for steel. During the development stage in which *per capita* GNP jumped from $400 to $2000, that is from 1950 to 1970, Japan's steel output grew at 1.7 times the rate of growth of GDP. At the comparable stage in South Korea's development, namely from 1971 to 1981, steel output grew at over three times the rate of growth of GNP. In the years of recovery from economic crisis in the US and Germany (1933–40 and 1951–60, respectively), the rate of growth of steel output was, respectively, 2.2 and 1.4 times that of GDP.

In China since the 1970s, the rate of growth of GDP has been exceptionally rapid, officially estimated to have been around 10 per cent per annum from 1981 to 1996 (SSB, ZTN, 1997: 25). In the 1980s, steel consumption rose by two-thirds, from 31.7 million tons in 1980 to 53.1 million tons in 1990 (SBMI, 1998), or an annual average rate of 5.3 per cent. In the 1990s, the growth of steel consumption accelerated as China started to increase at high speed the production of steel-using products. Steel consumption rose from 53.1 million tons in 1990 to 103.5 million tons in 1997 (SBMI, 1998), or an annual average rate of 10.0 per cent. No country has witnessed such a massive rise in steel consumption in such a short period of time. One recent forecast predicts that China's steel consumption will reach 115–20 million tons in the year 2000, rising to 140 million tons in 2010 (SBMI, 1998).

China is still a poor country. The main engine of growth in demand for steel has come from lower quality steels. Ordinary steel still accounted for 72 per cent of total Chinese steel output in 1996 (CMISI, 1997: 5). However, demand for high quality steels increased significantly. Output of all high quality steels together rose from 12 million tons in 1984 to 28 million tons in 1996 (CMISI, 1997: 5). Output of ferro-alloy steel rose from negligible levels in the 1980s to 5.0 million tons in 1996 (ISIC, 1997: 89).

As China's economic growth continues, Chinese incomes rise, Chinese people's consumer demands become more discriminating and China penetrates demanding international markets, so the demand for high-quality, high-value-added steel will grow strongly. Sectors such as construction, automobiles, petro-chemicals, beverages, shipbuilding and electrical appliances will all see rapid growth of demand for high quality steel (Table 9-9). For example, the future growth of the construction industry will increase demand for new steel products, such as welded steel, H-shape steel, high-strength reinforced bars, coating sheets, and stainless steel (for decoration) (SBMI, 1998: 2).

TABLE 9-9 China's Consumption of Selected Flat Steel Products, 1996 and Predicted for 2000 and 2005 (1000 tons)

Item	1996	2000	2005
Hot rolled sheets (commercial)	10 040	18 100	19 900
Hot rolled sheets (including for cold rolling)	22 358	28 500	36 000
Cold rolled sheets (including coating)	10 576	14 400	21 150
Car sheets	266	780	1 340
Galvanized sheet	1 499	2 000	2 700
Tin sheet	676	1 000	1 100
Silicon sheet	1 129	1 100	1 300
Shipbuilding plate	1 000	1 400	2 000
Container plate	970	1 050	1 100
Cold rolled stainless plate	216	580	885
Domestic appliances sheet	1 140	1 630	2 110

SOURCE: SBMI (1998)

SUPPLY

Output Growth. We have seen above that China's aggregate steel demands grew rapidly in the 1980s, but surged at even higher speed in the 1990s. To meet the demands generated by this growth, China's steel output tripled from 37 million tons in 1980 to 109 million tons in 1997 (SSB, ZTN, 1998: 469). China rose from the world's fifth largest steel maker in 1980 to become the number one producer in 1996 (SSB, ZTN, 1998: 933), accounting for 14 per cent of total world production (IISI, 1998). Despite this impressive expansion, the growth of steel output from 1980 to 1997 lagged behind growth of national product (6.6 per cent and 10 per cent, respectively). Although the growth halted in 1997–8, long-term predictions suggest that China's steel output in the twenty-first century will peak at over 150 million tons, and may reach considerably higher than this figure, depending on the assumptions used, possibly well over 200 million tons (Tan Chengdong, 1994: 5). This provides a huge opportunity for China's steel makers and the associated industries. It is also, a highly significant market in which the multinational companies would wish to be involved. The size and dynamism of the Chinese steel market contrasts strikingly with the stagnation in steel demand in the advanced capitalist countries.

China's explicit aim is to be substantially self-sufficient in steel production. Over the whole reform period, growth of steel output has lagged slightly behind growth of steel consumption. From 1980 to 1997, consumption grew at 7.2 per cent per annum compared to 6.5 per cent for steel output (SBMI, 1998). From 1980 to 1990 steel output grew at 5.8 per cent per annum and in the 1990s, from 1990 to 1997, the growth rate increased to 7.4 per cent per annum (SBMI, 1998). Large investments have been necessary to sustain China's growth of steel output. For example, in 1995 alone, the Chinese steel industry invested over $7 billion in fixed assets and over the whole period 1990–6 invested almost $23 billion in fixed assets (ISIC, 1997: 89).[15]

The strong and sustained long-term growth of China's steel output has occurred alongside large short-term fluctuations in the pace of growth of steel demand. From 1980 to 1990, crude steel output grew at 5.8 per cent per annum, somewhat faster than steel consumption, which grew at 5.3 per cent per annum (SBMI, 1998). However, in the early 1980s, steel consumption surged, rising by 78 per cent from 1980 to 1985, while output rose by 36 per cent (CMISI, 1998: 83). By 1985, imports accounted for 33 per cent of total consumption. Consumption then stabilized alongside steady growth of steel output, and controls over imports. By 1990, imports had fallen to 7 per cent of consumption (CMISI, 1998: 83). In the early 1990s, consumption again surged ahead of production. We have seen already that steel consumption doubled (from 53 million to 106 million tons) in the space of just three years, from 1990 to 1993, a remarkable episode in the history of the world's steel industry. Imports surged, from 3.7 million tons to 30.3 million tons alongside steadily growing domestic output. In 1993, imports accounted for 29 per cent of domestic consumption (CMISI, 1998: 83). Thereafter, the growth of consumption tailed off, and output grew strongly, so that by 1997, imports had

TABLE **9-10** **Apparent Consumption, Imports and Exports of Chinese Iron and Steel, 1957–97 (in 1000 tons)**

Finished steel products	Consumption*	Production	Imports	Exports	Self-sufficiency ratio** (%)
1957	4 964	4 364	696	96	87.9
1965	9 236	8 949	759	472	96.9
1970	14 685	12 233	2 667	215	83.3
1975	19 814	16 217	4 007	410	81.8
1980	31 764	27 158	5 006	400	85.5
1985	56 378	36 923	19 635	180	65.3
1990	53 125	51 532	3 683	2 090	97.0
1995	97 842	89 798	13 972	5 928	91.8
1996	105 150	93 381	15 984	4 215	88.8
1997	108 470	99 870	13 220	4 620	92.1

Pig iron	Consumption*	Production	Imports	Exports	Self-sufficiency ratio** (%)
1957	5 738	5 936	0	198	103.5
1965	10 265	10 767	16	518	104.9
1970	17 228	17 055	184	11	99.0
1975	25 081	24 490	615	24	97.6
1980	38 290	38 024	353	87	99.3
1985	46 744	43 837	2 911	4	93.8
1990	63 039	62 373	1 215	549	98.9
1995	99 989	105 286	136	5 433	105.3
1996	104 041	107 210	425	3 594	103.0
1997	110 170	115 110	600	5 540	104.5

SOURCE: CMISI (1997: 83)

NOTES: *Consumption is production + imports − exports
   ** Self-sufficiency ratio is production/consumption

fallen to 13 per cent of domestic consumption (Table 9-10 and CMISI, 1998: 83). China intends that by the year 2000, imports will account for just 8 per cent of domestic consumption (SBMI, 1998).

Product Quality and Structure. We have seen that China faces the prospect of a fast growth of demand for higher-quality, higher-value-added products in the years ahead. In lower-quality products, China is substantially self-sufficient. For example, in 1996, China produced 96 per cent of the domestic consumption of

TABLE 9-11 China's Domestic Output, Imports and Exports as a Proportion of
Consumption for Selected Flat Steel Products, 1996 (%)

Item	Domestic	Imports	Exports
Hot rolled sheets (commercial)	78.8	22.7	1.5
Hot rolled sheets (including for cold rolling)	60.2	43.3	3.4
Cold rolled sheets (including coating)	47.1	56.3	3.4
Car sheets	50.0	50.0	0.0
Galvanized sheets	51.8	53.1	4.9
Tin sheets	31.2	70.7	2.0
Silicon sheets	67.8	32.2	0.0
Ship building plates	84.0	16.0	0.0
Container plate	26.8	73.2	0.0
Cold rolled stainless sheet	23.0	81.0	4.4
Domestic appliance sheet	13.2	86.8	0.0

SOURCE: SBMI (1998)

general section steel (by weight), 89 per cent of long products, 98 per cent of welded pipes, 99 per cent of plates and 99 per cent of seamless pipes (SBMI, 1998). However, China's demand for high value-added products greatly exceeded domestic supply capabilities. For example, in 1996, imports accounted for 43 per cent of China's consumption of hot rolled sheets, 50 per cent of car sheets, 56 per cent of cold rolled sheets, 53 per cent of galvanized sheet, 71 per cent of tin sheet, 73 of container plate, 81 per cent of stainless sheet, and 87 per cent of domestic appliance sheet (Table 9-11). A major policy aim in the steel industry is to increase rapidly the domestic supply of high-value-added products, such as sheet for cars, packaging sheets for domestic appliances, cold rolled silicon sheets, cold rolled stainless sheets, galvanized sheets, ship building plate, container plate, hot rolled sheets of less than 2 mm in thickness, and cold rolled sheets of less than 1 mm in thickness (SBMI, 1998). China aims to become 95 per cent self-sufficient in steel products by the year 2000, which means that it must rapidly increase its output of high-quality steel products.

To improve productivity and quality control for high-value-added products, SBMI has initiated a comprehensive quality control programme including raw materials selection, iron making, steel making, finishing, heat treatment, coating and inspection. The old small rolling mills will be replaced by 40–50 sets of continuous or semi-continuous rolling mills. The development of continuous casting will be accelerated: it is intended to increase the continuous-casting ratio from 60 per cent in 1997 to 80 per cent by the year 2000. Large continuous-casting machinery to make big blooms and slabs will be installed in Angang, Shougang, Baogang, Magang and Pangang, while large continuous-casting facilities to make thin slabs will be installed in Baogang and Hangang (SBMI, 1998: 4). In 1996, 31 per cent of total steel industry investment was allocated to improving the variety of products and improving product quality (CMISI, 1997: 133).

Technology. China's steel industry has ancient origins:

One finds a very early appearance of the mastery of cast-iron technology. From the sixth century onwards clear descriptions exist of the making of steel by co-fusion of cast and wrought iron ... [China's] early masterly development of steel-making by advanced methods, so long before the rest of the world, is an achievement of very great interest to the history of technology in general. (Needham, 1970: 112)

Pre-1949, China had a large traditional iron and steel industry (Wagner, 1997). However, it had no large-scale steel firms, and technology was far behind that of the world's most advanced producers. China ranked only number 26 in the world by volume of steel output (SSB, ZTN, 1998: 933). With great assistance from the Soviet Union, China's steel technology made large strides forward in the 1950s. However, in the 1960s and 1970s, China was cut off from both the Soviet Union and the developed capitalist countries. Its steel technology made slow progress, and essentially continued along the technological path that had been established in the 1950s. In many key respects the industry was very backward technologically. In the late 1970s, the ratio of continuously cast steel was only 6 per cent, around 30 per cent of steel was made by the open-hearth method (CMISI, 1997: 4) and output per worker was a mere 15 tons (ISIC, 1997: 92). Production of high quality, high-value-added steels occupied a small fraction of total output. Levels of pollution from the steel industry were high.

During the period of high-speed growth of steel output since the 1970s, large improvements have taken place in Chinese steel industry technology. We have noted already the huge investment made to increase steel output since the 1970s. The proportion of this investment allocated to technical updating and transformation rather than simply building new capacity increased from under 20 per cent in 1966–76 to 55 per cent in 1991–5 (ISIC, 1997: 95). The ratio of steel made by continuous casting increased sharply, rising from just 4 per cent in 1975 to 53 per cent in 1996 (CMISI, 1997: 32). The ratio of rolled steel to crude steel rose from 0.74 in 1975 to 0.92 in 1996 (CMISI, 1997: 32). Open-hearth production fell from 28 per cent of steel production in 1984 to 12 per cent in 1996 (CMISI, 1997: 4). The share of converters rose from 51 per cent in 1984 to 69 per cent in 1996, and the share of electric arc furnaces rose from 9 per cent to 19 per cent in the same years (CMISI, 1997: 4). The improvements in steel industry technology are reflected in the fall in energy consumption per unit of steel produced: specific energy consumed per ton fell from 2.04 tons in 1980 to 1.39 tons in 1996 (ISIC, 1997: 91).

However, despite significant progress, China's steel technology still lags behind the world's leading producers in important respects. For example, it is estimated that the technologies used in top-blown oxygen converters and continuous-casting in China are about 20 years behind that of Japan and Europe and 15 years behind that of South Korea (STD, 1997: 18). As we have seen, China still lags behind the world's leading companies in technical capability in many types of special steel, and significant proportions of high quality steels are still imported. The comprehensive energy consumption in the Chinese steel industry is 30–40 per cent higher than in that of their counterparts in advanced countries (STD, 1997: 9; SBMI, 1998: 5). This means that the level of pollutants arising directly from steel production is still high. Moreover, a great deal of indirect pollution also results from the continued use of large amounts of transport-intensive inputs, notably iron ore, coke and coal.

The Chinese steel industry planners intended to accelerate the process of steel industry modernization through a combination of joint ventures and imported equipment, as well as making use of funds raised through international stock market flotation. The main thrust of China's drive to upgrade steel industry technology and product quality will focus on the four leading steel companies, Angang, Shougang, Baogang and Wugang. Some of the more important projects for technological modernization, apart from Shougang which will be discussed later, include the following:

- **Wuhan Iron and Steel**. Wugang is to receive a large injection of capital from the central government to up-grade the manufacturing equipment. It plans to undertake a $400 million renovation of the silicon steel mill. It intends to invest another $1 billion to build the No. 3 Steel Plant, which will be installed with the start-of-the-art technology from Mannesmann and Westinghouse. After the renovation, Wugang will be the only Chinese steel maker to manufacture international standard cold-rolled silicon steel sheets (*Fortune*, 29 September 1997: 122).

- **Baoshan Iron and Steel**. Baogang is China's most advanced integrated steel producer. It has imported a great deal of advanced foreign equipment, as well as beginning to develop its own R & D capabilities. High technology and high-value-added products account for over 60 per cent of Baogang's total output value. It has put into operation four continuous rolling mills (including the 2050 mm and 1580 mm hot-rolling mills and the 2030 mm and 1420 mm cold-rolling mills) to produce high-value-added quality flat-sheet steels (Baosteel, 1998: 2; SBMI, 1998). The third phase of construction, to be completed in the year 2000 at a cost of around 62 billion yuan (over $7 billion), will further enhance its capabilities in high-value-added steel products. Its joint venture in Ningbo will be completed by the year 2010, and will manufacture steel billets and thin plates, further upgrading its technical level (*CDBW*, 5–11 January 1997).

- **Anshan Iron and Steel**. Since the late 1980s, Angang has imported substantial pieces of equipment from Germany, the USA and Japan to upgrade its technical level in its cold rolling, wire rod and thick plants (ING–Barings, 1997: 68). Apart from imported equipment from Japan and Germany, Angang are also seeking technological transfer through establishing JVs with foreign partners. For instance, the 1780 mm continuous hot-rolling mill was renovated (SBMI, 1998). Subsequently, the ratios of continuous-casting, plate and tube steel in Angang's output increased from 30 per cent to 72 per cent and 57 per cent to 62 per cent, respectively (*Beijing Review*, 28 October–3 November 1996: 12).

- **Shanghai Pudong Iron and Steel**. In 1998 Thyssen–Krupp Stainless Steel (Germany) and Shanghai Pudong Iron and Steel formed a stainless steel JV. The first phase of the JV, a $300 million cold-rolling plant, will be completed by the year 2000. The $1.4 billion project will eventually produce 440 000 tons of stainless steel per annum and employ 1300 workers, which compares with a current annual Chinese consumption level of 900 000 tons (*Hong Kong Standard*, 9 October 1998).

Industrial Concentration

Large number of very small plants. During the Maoist period, a large number of small iron and steel plants was established in order to meet local steel requirements under the policy of local self-reliance. Since the late 1980s, steel demand has regularly exceeded domestic supply. In the slowly forming market economy of the 1980s, local protectionism was still extensive and there were still large market imperfections. Moreover, there is a long gestation period for building a new blast furnace, converter, or rolling mill for a large integrated steel plant. Under these conditions, many further small iron and steel plants were established. By the late 1990s there were reported to be almost 7000 enterprises engaged in smelting and pressing ferrous metals (CMISI, 1998: 336). There were around 1600 iron and steel enterprises that were 'within the system' (Table 9-12).

TABLE **9-12** **Selected Statistics of the Chinese Iron and Steel Industry, 1980–97**

Proxies	1980	1985	1990	1995	1997
No. of enterprises	1332	1318	1589	1570	1570
Annual output:					
<0.5 million tons	1318	1300	1561	1532	1524
0.5–0.99 million tons	2	6	12	17	18
>1 million tons	12	12	16	21	28
Gross output value					
(1980 constant price and					
100 million yuan)	306.44	440.50	1310.33	2593.72	2027.34*
Sales (100 million yuan)	319.59	514.30	1087.19	2920.02	2854.28*
Steel consumption					
per capita (kg)	32.0	51.8	46.9	80.9	87.0
Value-added (current price					
and 100 million yuan)	105.43	175.80	317.89	1 218.70	880.26
Investment in fixed assets					
(100 million yuan):	46.31	78.42	127.46	576.75	445.10
Capital construction	30.08	38.81	63.12	264.83	199.90
Technical transformation	16.23	39.61	64.34	311.92	245.20

TABLE **9-12** (*Continued*)

Proxies	1980	1985	1990	1995	1997
Pre-tax profits					
(in 100 million yuan)	55.50	82.47	66.54	113.52	44.07*
Profits/sales ratio (%)	17.37	16.04	6.12	3.89	1.54
Profits/fixed assets ratio (%)	19.84	105.16	52.20	19.68	7.96*
Number of employees at year					
end (in 10 000 persons)	244.10	268.14	315.23	342.34	376.88
Labour productivity:					
In yuan/man/year	12 860	16 574	42 242	57 331	87 686
In ton steel/man/year	15.28	16.56	22.50	29.40	28.91
Output of major products					
(in 10 000 tons):					
Crude steel	3 712	4 679	6 635	9 536	10 894
Pig iron	3 802	4 384	6 237	10 529	11 511
Finished steel products	2 716	3 692	5 153	8 980	9 987
Iron ore (crude ore)	11 258	13 735	17 934	26 192	26 861
Coke	4 343	4 795	7 327	13 502	13 902
Ferro-alloy	99	149	238	432	404
Carbon products	43	67	91	169	125
Refractory bricks	382	546	675	1755	1565
Annual production capacity					
(in 10 000 tons):					
Iron ore mining	11 852	13 352	17 532	20 737	25 808*
Coking	3 831	3 981	5 087	7 499	6 798*
Iron making	3 972	4 543	6 531	11 073	11 589*
Electric furnace steel making	367	1 130	1 754	3 084	3 075*
Converter steel making	1 496	2 602	3 959	7 038	7 529*
Continuous casting steel	295	657	1 686	5 396	6 192*
Steel rolling	3 000	4 971	7 338	14 581	13 232*
Ferro-alloy	7.8	178	324	555	496*

SOURCES: Compiled from Iron and Steel Industry of China (ISIC), 1997: 87–92; CMISI (1998: 3, 117–18, 235, 261, 282); SBMI (1998: 8)

NOTE: * 1996 data

Of these, 33 were large 'keypoint' enterprises. Another 56 were 'major local' enterprises, roughly corresponding to the western 'mini-mills'. A further 6000-odd plants were truly small scale. These typically had low technical efficiency, used old techniques and were often highly polluting. In 1991 around 3000 very small scale plants accounted for 29 per cent of total employment in the iron and steel industry, 24 per cent of the value of output and 13 per cent of the value of fixed assets. However, they accounted for only 9 per cent of the sector's profits (Table 9-13). In 1996, around 5000-odd small-scale plants reportedly accounted for just 7 per cent of the long-term investment of the iron and steel sector, for

TABLE 9-13 Industrial Concentration in China's Iron and Steel Industry, 1991

Size category (no. of employees)	No. of enterprises		Gross value of output		Pre-tax profits		Value of fixed assets		No. of employees	
	No.	(%)	billion yuan	(%)	billion yuan	(%)	billion yuan	(%)	1000s	(%)
Total	3432	100	153.9	100	20.8	100	131.8	100	3172	100
>10 000	58	1.7	96.1	62.4	17.4	83.6	103.6	78.6	1848	58.2
3000–10 000	82	2.4	20.3	13.2	1.6	7.7	11.1	8.4	411	13.0
<3000	3292	95.9	37.5	24.4	1.8	8.7	17.1	13.0	913	28.8

SOURCE: SSB (ZGJTN) (1993: 379)

TABLE 9-14 Distribution of China's Steel Output between Keypoint and Other Enterprises, 1980 and 1997 (million tons; % in brackets)

Year	Steel output	Keypoint plants	Local plants	'Non-system' plants	Others
1980	37.1 (100)	29.0 (78.2)	5.8 (15.6)	2.2 (5.9)	0.2 (0.3)
1997	108.9 (100)	67.7 (62.2)	34.8 (32.2)	5.9 (5.4)	0.4 (0.2)

SOURCE: CMISI (1994: 6, 1998: 6)

10 per cent of the sector's total fixed assets, and 12 per cent of total sales revenue. The small-scale sector (that is non-keypoint and major local producers) had become loss-making, making an aggregate of 1.61 billion yuan in losses (ISIC, 1997: 154–6).

Mini-mills. By 1996, 56 major local steel enterprises accounted for 28 per cent of China's crude steel output and 25 per cent of China's total output of steel products (ISIC, 1997: 103–4). They were all founded before 1973, and around two-thirds had their origins in the Great Leap Forward of 1958–9 (ISIC, 1997: 142–4). They responded to the market opportunities of the 1980s and 1990s by rapidly increasing their output and improving their technical level. In 1996, 83 per cent of their steel was produced by converters, and 17 per cent by electric furnace (ISIC, 1997: 103). In 1996 'local' and 'non-system' steel enterprises together produced 65 per cent of China's steel from electric furnaces (ISIC, 1997: 103). In 1996, the 56 major local steel enterprises produced an average of 0.38 million tons of steel products (ISIC, 1997: 160). Twelve plants produced over 0.7 million tons of steel products, and the leading enterprises, Handan and Anyang produced 1.5–1.6 million tons of steel products (ISIC, 1997: 160–2). Some of the mini-mills were highly profitable. Even in 1996, a very difficult year for the Chinese steel industry, Handan made a pre-tax profit of 700 million yuan, amounting to 16 per cent of sales revenue and Anyang made 410 million yuan, amounting to 10 per cent of sales revenue (ISIC, 1997: 154–5).

Despite the rapid advance of the major local plants, the sector still had significant weaknesses. In 1996 the aggregate profits for the whole group of 56 major local steel plants amounted to just 1.43 billion yuan, of which Handan and Anyang alone accounted for 1.11 billion, or 78 per cent of the total (ISIC, 1997: 154). Sixteen of the 56 plants were loss-makers, and a further 20 made zero profits (eight enterprises) or negligible profits[16] (nine enterprises) (ISIC, 1997: 154–6).[17] For the major local plants as a whole, aggregate profits were only 31 per cent of those of the keypoint plants. In 1996 the overall ratio of profits to fixed assets was only marginally better than for the keypoint plants (the ratios were 1.9 per cent and 1.8 per cent, respectively), and the ratio of profits to sales was significantly worse (2.0 per cent and 2.5 per cent respectively) (ISIC, 1997: 114–15).

Keypoint enterprises. Despite the rapid advances made by small-scale steel plants, 33 large, 'keypoint' enterprises still make up the core of China's iron and steel industry (Table 9-14). In 1996 they accounted for 71 per cent of fixed assets in the steel industry, 64 per cent of sales revenue and 72 per cent of the sector's long-term investment (ISIC, 1997: 154–6). Keypoint enterprises' total profits were three times the total of the major local enterprises (4.6 billion yuan compared with 1.4 billion yuan). We have already noted that the ratio of profits to sales revenue for keypoint enterprises was significantly above that for the major local enterprises.

Data for 1997 show that the top 20 steel enterprises accounted for 49 per cent of sectoral gross output value, 62 per cent of national steel output and 63 per cent of sectoral value-added (Table 9-15). China's top 10 steel enterprises in 1997

TABLE 9-15 The Top 10 and Top 20 Crude Steel Producers in China, 1997 (% share in brackets)

Companies	Steel output (10 000 tons)	Gross output value** (100 million yuan)	Value-added** (100 million yuan)	Sales** (100 million yuan)	Pre-tax profit**	Profits/ sales (%)	Labour productivity** (yuan/ man/year)	(ton steel/ man/year)
Baoshan Iron & Steel Corp.	859.0 (7.89)	227.24 (6.88)	89.89 (10.21)	258.63	22.00	8.51	1 125 585	529
Anshan Iron & Steel (Group)	828.0 (7.60)	188.10 (5.69)	61.92 (7.03)	173.97	0.82	0.47	66 089	51
Shougang Corp.	800.1 (7.34)	185.19 (5.60)	55.18 (6.27)	179.63	2.09*	1.16	106 766	70*
Wuhan Iron & Steel (Group)	608.8 (5.59)	150.32 (4.55)	52.73 (5.99)	168.31	3.12	1.85	77 804	51
Baotou Iron & Steel	421.7 (3.87)	85.39 (2.58)	40.01 (4.55)	89.14	1.72	1.93	66 132	58
Maanshan Iron & Steel Co. Ltd.	301.2 (2.76)	75.76 (2.29)	25.01 (2.84)	74.74	0.73	0.98	88 819	64
Panzhihua Iron & Steel (Group)	291.0 (2.67)	78.65 (2.38)	31.79 (3.61)	97.35	0.03	0.03	47 923	35
Benxi Iron & Steel (Group)	262.2 (2.41)	61.64 (1.87)	19.22 (2.18)	67.98	0.50	0.74	49 010	38
Handan Iron & Steel	253.5 (2.33)	56.10 (1.70)	23.87 (2.71)	46.19	5.03	10.89	49 753	41
Shanghai No. 1 Iron & Steel	252.1 (2.31)	50.65 (1.53)	7.45 (0.85)	50.20	1.50	2.99	135 797	115
Top 10	4877.60	1159.04	407.07	1206.14	37.54	3.11	181 368	105

Company								
	(44.77)	(35.07)	(46.24)					
Shanghai Pudong	242.1 (2.22)	57.46 (1.74)	2.25 (0.26)	58.54	1.01	1.73	189 513	144
Taiyuan Iron & Steel (Group)	240.4 (2.21)	65.41 (1.98)	22.82 (2.59)	64.52	2.03	3.15	80 547	40
Tangshan Iron & Steel Group	238.4 (2.19)	50.58 (1.53)	21.01 (2.39)	47.66	2.07	4.34	60 656	47
Jinan Iron & Steel Group Co.	236.3 (2.17)	51.53 (1.56)	20.69 (2.35)	52.04	1.75	3.36	105 436	86
Anyang Iron & Steel Group Co.	206.1 (1.89)	43.46 (1.32)	16.89 (1.92)	44.43	3.59	8.08	67 437	51
Kunming Iron & Steel Corp.	172.2 (1.58)	39.25 (1.19)	16.79 (1.91)	36.23	1.52	4.20	65 074	49
Laiwu Iron & Steel	166.4 (1.53)	38.04 (1.15)	13.31 (1.51)	39.35	1.06	2.69	70 979	58
Shanghai Huchang Iron	160.1 (1.47)	49.79 (1.51)	10.23 (1.16)	49.02	0.92	1.88	142 278	85
Jiuquan Iron & Steel Co.	133.0 (1.22)	26.64 (0.81)	7.08§ (0.80)	26.11	0.83	3.18	58 682	49
Chongqing Iron & Steel (Group)	124.2 (1.14)	42.87 (1.30)	16.53§ (1.88)	42.86	5.22	12.18	44 298	27
Top 20	6 796.80 (62.39)	1 624.07 (49.14)	554.67 (63.01)	1666.90	57.54	3.45	134 929	84.40
China	10 894	3 304.76	880.26	n.a.	n.a.	n.a.	63 364	28.91

SOURCE: Compiled from CMISI (1998: 18, 30–1, 261–4, 276–7, 282–4, 284–312).

NOTES: * Shougang's internal document reveals that the pre-tax profits of the Shougang Group were 351 million yuan (in which the Shougang Corporation accounted for 958 million yuan) and the labour productivity reached 156 tons per man year in 1997 (SG, 1998: 3, 7); it is unknown why the differences existed

** Based on the gross output value (current price)

§ 1996 data

TABLE 9-16 **Structure of Principal Steel Products at Major Chinese Steel Plants, 1997**

Company/category of plants		Major products									
	Heavy rail	Large section	Medium section	Small Section	Quality section	Wire rods	Medium plate	Sheet	Strip	Seamless steel tubes	
	10 000 tons (% share in total in brackets)										
Baogang	0.0	0.0	0.0	0.0	0.0	0.0	116.9	415.5	49.5	56.4	
	(0.0)	(0.0)	(0.0)	(0.0)	(0.0)	(0.0)	(9.8)	(31.8)	(9.5)	(15.6)	
Angang	28.2	12.3	44.3	35.0	6.6	64.2	140.5	204.1	56.5	34.5	
	(29.3)	(9.4)	(10.4)	(1.4)	(1.1)	(3.3)	(11.7)	(15.6)	(10.9)	(9.6)	
Shougang	0.0	0.0	17.0	235.9	36.0	269.8	44.4	4.2	31.6	0.0	
	(0.0)	(0.0)	(4.0)	(9.3)	(6.1)	(13.8)	(3.7)	(0.3)	(6.1)	(0.0)	
Wugang	3.6	37.7	9.8	2.0	7.6	40.4	148.9	208.5	3.8	0.3	
	(3.7)	(28.9)	(2.3)	(0.1)	(1.3)	(2.1)	(12.5)	(15.9)	(0.7)	(0.1)	
Baotou	29.2	29.7	0.0	42.8	11.9	64.4	0.0	0.0	56.5	34.5	
	(30.3)	(22.7)	(0.0)	(1.7)	(2.0)	(3.3)	(0.0)	(0.0)	(10.9)	(9.6)	
Maanshan	0.0	0.7	42.0	24.2	0.0	86.7	36.6	0.0	15.2	0.0	
	(0.0)	(0.5)	(9.9)	(1.0)	(0.0)	(4.4)	(3.1)	(0.0)	(2.9)	(0.0)	

Pangang	34.9	33.3	0.4	4.6	1.6	22.1	33.4	36.4	13.0	0.0
	(36.2)	(25.5)	(0.1)	(0.2)	(0.3)	(1.1)	(2.8)	(2.8)	(2.5)	(0.0)
Bengang	0.0	0.0	0.0	0.0	19.1	0.0	21.1	176.7	0.0	0.0
	(0.0)	(0.0)	(0.0)	(0.0)	(3.3)	(0.0)	(1.8)	(13.5)	(0.0)	(0.0)
Key plants	95.9	122.7	157.4	786.4	605.3	921.1	824.7	1 213.5	234.3	243.2
	(99.5)	(94.0)	(37.1)	(31.1)	(103.3)	(47.1)	(69.0)	(92.8)	(45.1)	(67.5)
Local plants	0.4	7.6	179.5	1 131.5	188.3	884.0	396.4	50.3	125.4	64.7
	(0.4)	(5.8)	(42.3)	(44.7)	(32.1)	(45.2)	(33.1)	(3.8)	(24.1)	(17.9)
Non-system	0.0	0.4	87.4	612.7	57.9	148.5	1.8	44.3	96.6	52.6
output	(0.0)	(0.3)	(20.6)	(24.2)	(9.9)	(7.6)	(0.2)	(3.4)	(18.6)	(14.6)
China:	96.4	130.6	424.2	2 530.6	585.7	1 953.6	1 195.9	1 308.1	519.8	360.5
	(100)	(100)	(100)	(100)	(100)	(100)	(100)	(100)	(100)	(100)

SOURCE: Compiled from CMISI (1998: 8–9, 42–4)

accounted for 35 per cent of sectoral output value, 44 per cent of China's steel output and 46 per cent of sectoral value-added. The large gap between the share of gross value and value-added reflects both the different product composition and the different level of technology and business organization in the largest of China's steel enterprises compared to most other steel enterprises. For example, in 1996, China's 'keypoint enterprises' produced 91 per cent of China's quality steel. Within this category, they produced 71 per cent of China's output of alloy steel (ISIC, 1997: 103). The level of concentration is higher than even these data suggest. In lower-value-added products, such as small and medium section steel, small plants dominate, producing 69 per cent and 63 per cent respectively of national output. Around 30 'keypoint' plants account for 99.5 per cent of heavy rail output, 94 per cent of large section steel, 93 per cent of sheet steel 69 per cent of medium plate output and 68 per cent of seamless steel tubes. Within heavy rails and large section steel three plants account for nine-tenths of national output. Within sheet steel, one enterprise alone, Baoshan, accounts for 32 per cent of national output (Table 9-16).

Grasp the large, let go of the small. Within the largest size group of steel enterprises is a group of four super-large integrated steel enterprises, consisting of Angang, Shougang, Baogang (Shanghai) and Wugang. These each had an annual output of over 5 million tons in 1996, and account for 28 per cent of China's total steel output (Table 9-15). Their aggregate pre-tax profits in 1996 amounted to 4.4 billion yuan, equal to the total profits for the entire Chinese steel industry (ISIC, 1997: 83, 134–5).

Despite the leading position of the four largest steel enterprises within the Chinese steel industry, in the mid-1990s they were still not in the front ranks of the world's steel producers. China, the world's largest steel-producing country, has no steel firms in the world's top 10 firms ranked by physical output. China's highest ranking steel enterprise in 1996 was Angang, which ranked fifteenth. Baogang ranked nineteenth and Shougang twentieth (IISI, 1998). Their level of labour productivity is far behind that of the world's leading steel firms, with vast levels of employment compared to the world's leading firms (see below). Apart from Baogang, their level of profitability is low: in 1996, the ratio of profits to sales stood at over 13 per cent at Baogang, compared to 5 per cent at Wugang, and 1–2 per cent at Shougang and Angang (ISIC, 1997: 154–6). Apart from Baogang, product quality is still significantly behind advanced standards: in 1996, the proportion of steel products judged to be at the level of 'advanced world standards' stood at 99 per cent at Baogang, 81 per cent at Wugang, 61 per cent at Angang and just 29 per cent at Shougang (ISIC, 1997: 138). With the exception of Baogang, energy consumption per ton of steel is high compared to the world's most advanced plants: in 1996, the consumption of coal-equivalent per ton of steel was 0.75 at Baogang, compared with 0.90 at Shougang, 0.95 at Wugang and 0.98 at Angang (ISIC, 1997: 124–5).

The Chinese government has determined to develop the four leading steel enterprises in China into world-class companies, rivalling Nippon Steel and

Posco for efficiency and global influence. The strategy for the steel industry is part of the wider industrial policy of 'grasping the large and letting go of the small' (*zhua da, fang xiao*). The Chinese government intends that by the year 2000 the group of four leading steel conglomerates, Baogang, Shougang, Angang, and Wugang, will have increased their share of national steel output to 40 per cent (*SCMP*, 18 November 1998). These enterprises are to form the key-point of China's technical modernization of the steel industry and are to stand at the centre of a process of merger and acquisition that it is anticipated will enable these emerging giant companies to benefit from economies of scale. As part of this policy, the central government has banned any new steel plant construction until at least the end of the year 2000 (*SCMP*, 28 October 1998).

Baogang is the most important enterprise in this process. It is unique among China's leading steel enterprises in that it began production as recently as 1982. This enabled it to establish a much lower manning level than other major plants: it employs only 34 000 people compared to 200 000 or more at Shougang and Angang (ISIC, 1997: 122). Consequently, it has much lower welfare costs, and its workforce was able to establish a different pattern of labour organization than traditional Chinese steel plants. It also was able to use modern imported equipment and from the start a large fraction of its output was of high quality, high value-added steel to meet the booming needs of the East China region for high quality steel (the vast majority of its output consists of steel sheets) (Table 9-16). It is much the most profitable steel enterprise in China. In 1996 its pre-tax profits totalled 3.14 billion yuan, which amounted to 71 per cent of the total profits of the whole Chinese steel industry.

In 1997, it was announced that Baogang would merge simultaneously with Shanghai Metallurgical Holdings and Shanghai Meishan. Shanghai Metallurgical Holdings is a steel producer which itself has more than 30 plants and a workforce of 120 000. Shanghai Meishan has around 26 000 employees, produces around 1.6 million tons of pig iron but only around 0.27 million tons of steel (ISIC, 1997: 128). This deal allows Baogang to expand its market share and sales channels in China (*FT*, 25 November 1997). In 1998, Baosteel's annual production capacity will reach 20 million tons and annual sales of about 100 billion yuan after completing the merger with Shanghai Metallurgical Holding (Group) and Shanghai Meishan (Group). The new group, Shanghai Boashan Iron and Steel Group, will have net assets of 70.5 billion yuan, which amounts to 20 per cent of the entire Chinese steel industry's fixed assets. It is expected that even more mergers will take place around Baogang.

Baogang's central role in the government's plans for the Chinese steel industry can be seen from the large size of the capital construction spending at Baogang. In 1996, total capital construction at Baogang amounted to 15.4 billion yuan ($1.9 billion), which amounted to 52 per cent of the whole capital construction investment for the entire Chinese steel industry in that year (ISIC, 1997: 112, 122).

Baogang has high ambitions to become more than just a globally successful steel company. It is planning to diversify into trading (Baosteel Group

International Trade Corporation), shipping, real estate, tourism, insurance and banking. In 1997, Baogang invested 210 million yuan in the United Security Company. This is the first major step adopted by Baogang to set up a foothold in the Chinese financial sector (Baosteel, 1998: 4): 'By 2010, Baogang aims to have built itself into a large multinational – one of the top 500 enterprises in the world – with steel production at the core, but integrating industry, finance and trade,' (Mr Li Ming, chairman of Baogang, quoted in *FT*, 11 August, 1997). Unlike the other major Chinese steel producers, Baogang does not own its own iron ore mines. In 1998, Baogang began the construction of a one billion yuan port on one of the Zhoushan islands near Shanghai to handle all its imported iron ore shipments. This decision will have tremendous implications on the Ningbo's Beilun Port, which used to handle 8 million tons a year of imported iron ore from Australia, Brazil, South Africa and Peru before being shipped to Baoshan (*SCMP*, 15 October 1998).

Wugang also has an important role in the strategy of building a small group of powerful steel companies. In 1997, Wugang merged with Echeng Iron and Steel and Daye Steel to form a steel group with assets of 52.1 billion yuan and 176 000 workers (*FT*, 26 November 1997). In October 1998, Wugang acquired the Xiangfan Iron and Steel Group (it lost 120 million yuan during the last four years) (*FT*, 28 October 1998: 4). However, unconfirmed reports suggest that Baogang's merger plans may soon involve a merger with Wugang, which would be a truly world class steel company in terms of total steel output (*FT*, 11 March 1998).

International Capital. The amount of foreign direct investment (FDI) in the iron and steel industry is still small. In 1997, total output from foreign-invested enterprises (including joint ventures and wholly-owned foreign enterprises) in the steel enterprises amounted to only 4.4 per cent of the total output value of the steel sector (SSB, ZTN, 1998: 456, 448–51, 452–3). Since 1993, a number of companies in the steel sector has listed on the Hong Kong stock market. The main reason for doing so has been to raise finance for investment. Listings in Hong Kong so far include Maanshan, Chongqing Iron and Steel, and Angang. Both Baogang and Shougang are actively considering listing parts of their respective businesses in the near future.

Employment. We have seen that in the early 1990s in Brazil's large integrated steel plants, large-scale downsizing of employment followed privatization. This was associated with extensive labour unrest. China's steel industry is vastly over-manned by world standards. A single one of China's largest steel plants, such as Shougang or Angang employs around 200 000 people, as many as the whole steel industry of Europe or the US. Employment at the world's leading steel firms, Nippon Steel and Posco, which produce more than three times the annual steel output of Angang or Shougang, is only 20 000–30 000 (Table 9-17). Undoubtedly, downsizing could reduce costs in the Chinese steel industry. The Chinese government has announced plans to reduce employment in the sector by 25 per cent, or around 700 000, by the year 2000 (*FT*, 25 November 1997).

TABLE 9-17 **Remuneration and Labour Productivity, Selected Countries and Plants, 1994–7**

Countries/firms	Year	No. of steel workers	Average weekly wage ($)*	Labour productivity (ton/man/year)
Japan:	1996	2 40 000	1 197.00	655.2
Nippon Steel	1995	27 583		948.9
NKK	1995	17 692		614.8
Kawasaki	1995	13 384		753.5
South Korea:	1996	66 482	453.5	585.2
Posco	1994	22 891		966.1
Taiwan:	1996	22 878	304.6	528.9
China Steel	1995	9 239		666.9
Germany:	1995	n. a.	732.0	412.3
Thyssen	1995	1 26 987		84.3
Krupp	1995	66 740		74.3
France:	1995	39 000	n.a.	462.0
Usinor–Sacilor	1995	58 335		265.7
UK:	1997	36 000	n.a.	
British Steel	1995	40 000		335.0
USA:	1996	167 000	770.78	524.2
USX	1995	20 845		529.3
Bethlehem Steel	1995	19 500		486.1
LTV	1994	15 300		489.3
China:	1997	3 768 860	24.3	28.91
Baogang	1997	34 688	57.7	529.0
Angang	1997	180 519	23.7	51.0
Shougang	1997	218 153	23.5	70.0**
Wugang	1997	119 518	27.8	51.0
Baotou	1997	94 494	22.2	58.0
Magang	1997	46 218	27.0	64.0
Pangang	1997	95 707	25.4	35.0
Bengang	1997	91 541	25.2	38.0

SOURCES: Compiled from ISIC (1997: 122–3; CMISI (1998: 276–80); IISI (1998)

NOTES: * For advanced countries, the wage rates were in 1995 data. For China, the wage rates were in 1996 data

** Shougang's internal document revealed that the labour productivity was 156 tons per man year (SG, 1998: 7). This higher figure may exclude those workers not directly involved in steel production

However, the social problems faced in downsizing are especially acute in China. Also, remuneration is so low that the impact of downsizing on the competitiveness of China's large steel plants will be far less than was the case in advanced economies, or even in Brazil, where hourly wage rates are around 30 times as high as in China (MSDW, 1998a: 200).

The Chinese large state enterprise is a complete society, with comprehensive social responsibilities towards both the employees and their families. For example, Wugang runs 31 schools, two hospitals, six universities and polytechnics, as well as heavily subsidized housing for its 120000 employees and their families, plus another 30000 retirees. As the largest corporate employer in Wuhan city, the steel plant is not permitted by the local government to add more people to the city's unemployed, which is already unacceptably high. Around 250000 people in Wuhan depend directly or indirectly on Wugang. This is why the president of Wugang declared that he 'will not push our people into society' (*Fortune*, 29 September 1997: 122).

An important path to downsizing for steel plants, as for other large state-owned enterprises, has been to develop non-core businesses in order to release workers from the steel sector. For example, in 1996, Angang transformed 17 subsidiaries into independent legal entities with responsibility for their own finances. Another 34 collective factories were 'spun-off' from the main company. As a result, only 74000 workers remained directly engaged in iron and steel production. Other loss-making auxiliary units were required to reverse their losses within three years. Angang's target is to reduce its workforce directly engaged in steel production to 50000, increase its labour productivity by five-fold to reach 200 tons/man/year by the year 2000 (*Beijing Review*, 28 October–3 November 1996: 12–13).[18]

PROFITABILITY

As in most countries, the profitability of the Chinese steel industry is highly cyclical. In the peaks of the economic cycle in the 1980s, with a considerable excess of demand over supply, China's steel industry reported pre-tax profits as high as 16–17 per cent of sales revenue (ISIC, 1997: 90). However, the ratio of pre-tax profits to revenues slumped to only around 6 per cent in 1990, during the slowdown in economic growth alongside an increasingly competitive market. Aggregate industry profits in the 1980s stood at less than 10 billion yuan per year (ISIC, 1997: 83).

In the early 1990s, as we have seen, there occurred an explosive growth of demand far ahead of domestic production capabilities. The ratio of pre-tax profits to revenue for the steel industry rose sharply to over 10 per cent in 1993–4 (ISIC, 1997: 90). Aggregate profits leaped to 29.0 billion yuan in 1993 and 26.3 billion yuan in 1994 (ISIC, 1997: 83).

From 1993 to 1996, the total level of steel consumption in China remained quite stable at around 105–106 million tons per year (CMISI, 1997: 33). In 1997–8 the situation worsened due to further slowdown in China's economic growth and increased competition from East Asian imports, often through smuggling. The large integrated steel companies had borrowed heavily to finance anticipated expansion in demand. By the late 1990s, they were operating well below full capacity, and with an increased ratio of debt to assets. The combination of domestic market weakness and increased imports caused severe difficulties for

China's steel producers. Profits contracted sharply, falling to just 4.4 billion yuan in 1996 (ISIC, 1997: 83). Wugang's net profits tumbled from 751 million yuan in 1996 to 312 million yuan in 1997 (CMISI, 1997–1998). Even the most profitable steel plant in China, Baogang, registered a 36 per cent fall in pre-tax profit to 2 billion yuan in 1997 (Table 9-15 and *Hong Kong Standard*, 30 September 1998). Other big steel enterprises' profits also halved during the first half of 1998: Angang New Steel's fell by 56 per cent, Magang's fell by 44 per cent, and Chongqing Iron and Steel's fell by 53 per cent (SCMP, 28 and 31 August 1998 and *Hong Kong Standard*, 19 August 1998).

The Chinese government responded to the crisis by announcing that it would spend $361 billion on infrastructure investment in 1998 alone, in order to achieve the government's 8 per cent economic growth target. This would in turn provide a large stimulus to steel demand (*Hong Kong Standard*, 10 September 1998). China plans to spend around $1 trillion over the next three years on infrastructure investment (*Hong Kong Standard*, 10 September 1998). In addition, the government tightened up on the control of steel imports, especially steel that was being smuggled into the country. In the first seven months of 1998, steel output reached 94.7 million tons, an increase of 6.1 per cent on the same period in 1997 (*Business Post* (Hong Kong), 28 October 1998). This was a remarkable contrast to the situation in surrounding Asian countries, and principally achieved through domestic demand increases.

SHOUGANG UNDER THE CONTRACT SYSTEM[19]

In 1978, Shougang was a traditional large, integrated iron and steel producer, located at a single site in Beijing. Along with the rest of the commanding heights of Chinese industry, state planners directly administered the plant. It had no significant operational independence. After 1978, Shougang grew at high speed. It is still a state owned plant. Until 1995 it was run by a former army commander and senior figure in the Communist Party. However, it had dramatically changed the nature of its business operation. Indeed, in 1995 the leadership of the old Maoist–Stalinist plant hoped that it would soon be quoted in the *Fortune* 500 index of the world's largest companies.

The source and nature of its growth from 1978 to 1995 is a subject of great controversy. This controversy intensified in February 1995 with the retirement of Zhou Guanwu, the Corporation's chairman and Party Secretary. Zhou's retirement was followed closely by the arrest of his son, Zhou Beifang, who had headed Shougang's operations (Shougang Concord International) in Hong Kong.[20] Zhou Guanwu had planned to build a huge second steel plant at Qilu in Shandong Province. Had Qilu been completed, Shougang's crude steel production capacity would have increased by ten million tons. It would have become one of the world's top three steel firms, following hard on the heels of Posco. These plans were shelved following Zhou's retirement (see below). These events marked the end of an extraordinary epoch in Shougang's history.

GROWTH AT SHOUGANG

Shougang was established before 1949, developing into a large-scale integrated iron and steel plant with Soviet assistance in the 1950s. By the mid-1970s it was China's eighth largest steel plant. After 1979, Shougang experienced 15 years under the 'contract responsibility system', during which time huge changes took place.

Shougang's output of crude steel rose from 1.7 million tons in 1978 to 8.3 million tons in 1994 (Table 9-18), around ten per cent per annum. In 1978, it was only China's seventh largest steel plant. By 1996, it was poised to become China's largest steel producer. It had become one of the 20 largest steel producing firms in the world. Shougang's growth was firmly based on its core business: still in 1992, iron and steel production accounted for 87 per cent of the Company's turnover, and over 89 per cent of its profits (Salomon Brothers, 1994: 9). Growth of output was accompanied by comprehensive modernization and expansion of the plant at the main site in Beijing (Table 9-19) as well as extensive

TABLE **9-18 Selected Statistics of Shougang, 1978–97**

Statistics	*1978*	*1994*	*1997*	*Average annual growth (%)*
Output of crude steel (million tons)	1.79	8.33	8.00	8.16
Output of steel products (million tons)	1.18	5.83	6.43	9.33
Profits and taxes handed over to the state (million yuan)*	294	n.a.	2000**	8.35
Total profits and taxes (million yuan)	299.70	n.a.	208.60§	−1.9
Average employees' income (yuan/month)	61.15	606	845±	15.72
No. of subordinate large and medium-sized enterprises	n.a.	157	n.a.	
No. of joint ventures	0	65	71	
No. of industries involved	2	18		
No. of employees	110 000	260 000	218 153	3.66

SOURCES: Compiled from *Beijing Review* (14–18 August 1992: 14–15); Salomon Brothers (1994: 5, 10); SG (1995); *CDBW* (17 February 1984, 21 March 1993: 2, 17 May 1993: 27); *SCMP* (20 September 1993); ISIC (1997: 134); CMISI (1998: 30, 262, 288); interviews with Shougang officials

NOTES: *Excludes extraordinary taxes and hand-overs
  **Turnover tax: Shougang hands over turnover tax only to the Beijing authorities, it does not hand over any income tax, only turnover tax
  § Shougang's internal figures revealed that the Group profits was 351 million yuan (SG, 1998: 3)
  ± 1996 data

TABLE **9-19 Steel Production Facilities at Shougang, 1993**

Activity/operation	Comments
Iron production:	
4 blast furnaces	7.9 million tons production capacity. 3 furnaces reconstructed during 1992–3; reconstruction of the fourth took place in 1993–4
Steel refining:	
No. 1 steel mill	3 basic oxygen furnaces of 30 metric tons each, with 2.2 million metric tons annual crude steel production capacity; commissioned in 1965
No. 2 steel mill	2 basic oxygen furnaces of 210 metric tons each, with 3 million tons annual crude steel capacity; commissioned in 1987; a third BOF constructed in 1993–4; total capacity of 4.5 million metric tons
No. 3 steel mill	3 basic oxygen furnaces of 60 metric tons each, with 2.5 million metric tons annual production capacity, commissioned in 1992
Special steel mill	17 electric arc furnaces with 800 000 metric tons annual special steel production capacity
Shaping:	8 continuous-casting machines and 17 rolling mills; the annual production capacity of the principal machines is:
Billet casting	300 000 metric tons of billets; commissioned in 1988
Bloom casting	1.2 million metric tons of blooms; commissioned in 1987
Slab casting	800 000 metric tons of slab; commissioned in 1989
17 rolling mills	5.6 million metric tons; all modernized between 1983 and 1993

SOURCE: Salomon Brothers (1994: 10)

merger with smaller domestic ferrous metal producers. By 1997, almost all the steel at Shougang was produced with oxygen converters,[21] and a very high share (78 per cent) of its steel products was produced by the continuous-casting method (Table 9-3).[22] The share of electric furnaces at Shougang was high compared to other large state enterprises.[23] Electric furnaces are typically necessary for the production of high quality and alloy steel (WCFL, 1993: 42), and by the early 1990s, Shougang had become the largest producer of special steels in China (Salomon Brothers, 1994: 10). In 1997, it produced 312 000 tons of alloy steel, the largest producer of such steel product in China (Table 9-20).

Alongside rapid growth and modernization of its core steel business, Shougang expanded rapidly into other activities. By the early 1990s, it owned 158 large and medium-sized plants, had 57 domestic affiliates, 39 JVs and 26 equity JVs or solely-funded enterprises. It had risen to be the fourth largest company in China in terms of total sales value, the fourteenth largest in terms of the net value of assets, and number one in terms of total profits (DRC, 1993: 2–3). Shougang Group had become a conglomerate with business interests ranging from iron and steel, mining, machinery, electronics, construction, shipping, trading and financing (Figure 9-1).

TABLE 9-20 **Output Structure of Steel at the Eight Largest Chinese Plants, 1997 (10 000 tons, % share in brackets)**

Country/ companies	Ordinary steel	High-quality steel		Total crude steel output
			(of which Alloy steel)	
Baosteel	0.0 (0)	859.0 (100)	19.2 (2.24)	859.0
Angang	636.8 (76.91)	191.2 (23.09)	23.7 (2.86)	828.0
Shougang	680.5 (85.05)	119.6 (14.95)	31.2 (3.90)	800.1
Wugang	317.4 (52.14)	291.4 (47.86)	0.6 (0.10)	608.8
Baotou	298.7 (70.83)	123.0 (29.17)	1.2 (0.28)	421.7
Magang	249.2 (82.74)	52.0 (17.26)	3.4 (1.13)	301.2
Pangang	227.1 (78.04)	63.9 (21.96)	6.9 (2.37)	291.0
Bengang	233.1 (88.90)	29.1 (11.10)	14.1 (5.38)	262.2
China	7 869.9 (72.24)	3 021.2 (27.73)	547.3 (5.02)	10 894

SOURCE: Compiled from CMISI (1998: 6, 36–7)

Simultaneously, Shougang rapidly expanded its international operations. By 1994, Shougang had 26 overseas enterprises and offices scattered in 13 countries and regions including America, Europe, Southeast Asia, Hong Kong, the Middle East and the Commonwealth of Independent States (SG, 1995). It had become China's largest manufacturing exporter.

It is widely believed that Shougang's extraordinary growth from the late 1970's to the mid-1990s was mainly attributable to special financial advantages in the contract struck with the government.[24] Shougang's explosive growth was thought to be the consequence of Zhou Guanwu's special relationship with Deng Xiaoping, rather than to possess any economic rationale. After Zhou's retirement and his son's arrest, the *Financial Times* commented: 'Zhou Guanwu was a military commander under Mr. Deng in China's revolutionary war, which ended in 1949. *This long association was the basis for the privileges granted to Shougang*, enabling it to establish companies in Hong Kong and the US, buy an iron mine in Peru, gain a banking licence in China and secure the capital for domestic expansion.' (*FT*, 20 February 1995 emphasis added).

CONTRACT RESPONSIBILITY SYSTEM

Gaining Autonomy. In 1979, the Chinese government began to experiment with the system of enterprise profit retention. Shougang was one of the first pilot enterprises to undertake this reform. From 1979 to 1981, the contract was implemented on an annual basis. The amount of profit to be turned over was fixed each year through negotiations and the above-quota profit was placed at the disposal of the company. It put into effect its famous contract in 1981. The contract was struck with the direct administrative superior of the enterprise, namely the

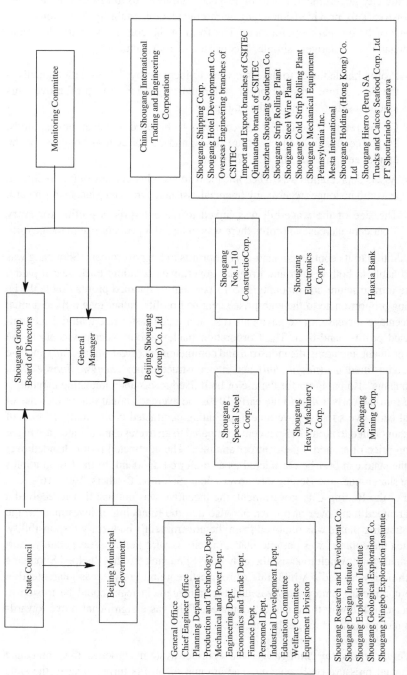

FIGURE 9-1 The Corporate Structure of Shougang Group, 1998

SOURCE: Shougang Group (1998)

Beijing city government. It was of 15 years' duration, to run from 1981 to 1995 inclusive. This provided Shougang with considerable stability in an important aspect of its business environment. The form of the contract system adopted at Shougang was relatively simple. It consisted of four elements:

- Profits handed over to the state were to increase by 7.2 per cent annually – the base figure was the profit submitted in 1981.[25] Any profits over this amount were retained by the enterprise.

- Of the retained profit, 60 per cent was to be used as development funds, 20 per cent as collective welfare funds, and 20 per cent as bonuses for the employees: this was the 6 : 2 : 2 system.

- Assets depreciation was to become the responsibility entirely of the enterprise. It would no longer receive any financial assistance from the state in this regard.

- The size of the wage-bill was linked to the enterprise's profits: for every 1 per cent increase in profits there was to be a 0.8 per cent rise in the payroll.

In addition to its contracted hand-over of profits to the government, Shougang was also liable to both regular and irregular government taxation. Each year it paid a state infrastructure tax, amounting to 15 per cent of retained profits (Table 9-21). Being proportionate to the enterprise's retained profits, rather than a fixed annual percentage increase, these payments rose at a much faster rate than did the contracted profits hand-over. The Corporation made various other payments to the government, including the industrial and commercial tax (*gongshang shui*), income tax, adjustment tax (*tiaojie shui*), and city construction tax (*chengshi jianshe shui*). Shougang also paid fees for the use of both fixed assets and circulating capital.

From the early 1980s to the early 1990s the average annual rate of increase of total hand-overs to the government, including contracted profits and all forms of tax, amounted to around 13 per cent, compared to an average annual increase in the retail price of around 7 per cent per annum.[26] The contracted profits handed over to the state can best be considered as a 'preferred dividend' to the Corporation's sole shareholder, the Beijing city government (Salomon Brothers, 1994: 16).

For the Beijing City government, the incentive was not just that it received a guaranteed hand-over of profits, but also that the financing of investment in the contracting plants was removed from the government's budgetary responsibility. When the contract was put into place, the city government was desperately short of funds with which to assist the growth of Shougang, so they 'helped Shougang with policy instead'. A high rate of reinvestment and growth was guaranteed in the contracting enterprise, provided the management team could be trusted to behave in the way the contract stipulated. This was a significant move towards indirect planning through the market.

Implications for Shougang. The contract system hardened the immediate financial pressure on Shougang. The amount of profits turned over to the state was set to increase by 7.2 per cent per annum irrespective of the level of profits made by Shougang. To fulfil the profits quota, the company needed to improve

TABLE **9-21 Distribution of Profits in Shougang Corporation, 1978–92**

Year	Total profits	Handed-over profits	Retained profits	State infrastructure tax*
		(million yuan % share in brackets)		
1978	300 (100)	294 (98.2)	6 (1.8)	0.8
1979	369 (100)	336 (91.1)	33 (8.9)	4.9
1980	444 (100)	382 (86.0)	62 (14.0)	9.3
1981	445 (100)	380 (85.4)	65 (14.6)	9.7
1982	527 (100)	408 (77.4)	119 (22.6)	17.9
1983	633 (100)	438 (69.2)	195 (30.8)	29.3
1984	778 (100)	469 (60.3)	309 (39.7)	46.3
1985	934 (100)	504 (54.0)	430 (46.0)	64.6
1986	1 121 (100)	540 (48.2)	581 (51.8)	87.2
1987	1 345 (100)	579 (43.0)	766 (57.0)	115.0
1988	1 615 (100)	620 (38.4)	994 (61.5)	149.1
1989	1 893 (100)	665 (35.1)	1 228 (64.9)	184.1
1990	2 092 (100)	713 (32.1)	1 379 (65.9)	207.2
1991	2 361 (100)	964 (40.8)	1 396 (59.1)	194.2
1992	3 202 (100)	830 (25.9)	2 372 (74.1)	323.9
1993–7**	23 101 (100)	16 197 (70.0)	6 904 (30.0)	n.a.
1979–97**	40 903 (100)	24 025 (59.0)	16 878 (41.0)	n.a.

SOURCES: 1978–92, annual data: Salomon Brothers (1994: 16); other data: personal information from Shougang officials

NOTES: * 15% of retained profits

      ** These data were provided separately from the other information in the table; Data for 1993–7 are derived from the other information in the table

its management performance and produce better economic returns. If it made losses, wages and other employee benefits would have had to be reduced. Under the contract system the state was no longer responsible for funds for capital construction, technical transformation, worker welfare, medical care, wage increases and bonuses. All these outgoings had to be met by Shougang itself out of resources left after it had handed over the requisite funds to the state. In order to be able to meet these goals the company set itself the high target of increasing profits at an average 20 per cent per year.

The contract struck by Shougang was risky for the management, especially given the uncertain environment faced in the early 1980s. Indeed, a major reason for the introduction of the Shougang contract system to several large firms was precisely the serious slowdown in Chinese economic growth in the early 1980s.[27] This in turn affected the government's revenue-raising ability. To some degree, the ceding of autonomy to huge enterprises was a way out of the fiscal difficulties facing the government, shifting the financial burden to the enterprise itself. Indeed, the Shougang method was referred to by Beijing government officials as 'the path to follow when there is no other solution' (*meiyou banfa de banfa*).

This form of contract could have been a disaster for Shougang if sales and profits had not performed outstandingly well. The fact that the share of profits retained by the company rose steadily was attributable to massive growth of sales and profits. If gross profits had merely doubled between 1980 and 1990, from 444 million yuan to around 900 million yuan, then under the Shougang contract system the amount of profits retained by Shougang would have been only around 20 per cent of the total. If profits had increased by merely 60 per cent to around 700 million yuan then Shougang would have had zero profits to retain in 1990. Moreover, if the growth of profits had been slow, then a vicious circle would have operated as a lower amount of retained profits for reinvestment would have slowed down the company's expansion.

It was not apparent at the time that the contract was greatly to Shougang's advantage. The prospects for the Chinese economy were uncertain. No-one predicted that the national growth rate would be as high as it turned out to be, with concomitant rapid growth in demand for basic industrial products such as steel. Nor could it have been predicted that the inflation rate would rise as fast as it did.[28] At current prices the contracted profits handed over to the government rose by 182 per cent from 1978 to 1992 (Table 9-21), but deflated by the retail price index, the increase was only around 11 per cent.

Under the Soviet model of highly centralized management, state organizations exercised rigid control and enterprises had no autonomy. The general manager of a large plant such as Shougang needed approval by the next higher level of administration for the purchase of any item above 800 yuan (*Beijing Review*, 3–16 February 1992: 34–5).[29] Under the new contract system, Shougang was granted 'complete autonomy' in the way in which it allocated its resources earmarked for investment, as long as it fulfilled its target for profits hand-over to the state.

In May 1992, Deng Xiaoping visited Shougang. After this visit the State Council decided to allow Shougang enhanced freedom as another step in the effort to make SOEs less confined by the dictates of state commands and more responsive to market forces. Shougang was designated a 'super enterprise'. This was an important signal of the central government's determination to construct a group of super-large companies that could challenge the multinational giants. It was granted autonomy in respect to its own construction projects that were funded by the corporation itself (from its own reserves and from self-financed capital), in respect to foreign trade, overseas projects with less than $10 million of investment, and JVs in China with a total investment of less than $36.4 million. It was permitted to set up its own bank (Hua Xia) (*Beijing Review*, 17–23 August 1992). This provided Shougang with 'the highest level of autonomy of any Chinese industrial enterprise' at that point.

The contract system did not provide large material rewards for Shougang's leadership. The average income of the top leadership of Shougang was only around double that of the ordinary workers, and subject to the same constraints on its increase. In the 1980's, the total income of the Company chairman, Zhou Guanwu, was equivalent to around $150 per month, including various bonuses. The leadership had access to fringe benefits, including the use of company cars, service personnel, and better housing allocations. However, even their housing was not dramatically better than that of ordinary workers. Apart from Zhou, the largest house allocation to any employee was a four room apartment.[30] Unlike the leaders of most TNCs, Shougang's leaders did not possess share options.

The Corporation had no fear of take-over. Even in the early 1990's, it was virtually impossible for one super-large enterprise of the size of Shougang to take over another. It had no share price to worry about. The sole shareholder was the Beijing municipal government, and it was much more interested in the long-term expansion and prosperity of the Corporation than in short-term profit maximization. This was reflected in their encouragement of the growth of Shougang, and in the contract that Beijing had with the Corporation.

AUTONOMY WITHIN CONSTRAINTS: CONTINUING STATE CO-ORDINATION

The managerial autonomy permitted to Shougang after 1978 was much less than that which farmers received under the contract system. State control was only relaxed gradually, and in many respects remained tight even in the mid-1990s.

Controls on Expansion. Under the contract system, Shougang endeavoured rapidly to expand steel output. It did so through investment in new capacity at the main plant in Beijing and through merging with local steel plants. However, its most ambitious plan was to expand through developing new capacity outside Beijing. At Shougang's main plant in Beijing, and at the plants with which it merged in Beijing, there were severe space constraints. This was in sharp contrast to Baogang, in Shanghai. A large part of Shougang's strategy of diversification under the contract system was related to this attempt. The defeat of this attempt had enormous consequences for the Group. In the long-term, Shougang's attempt to diversify away from heavy reliance on steel has been strongly influenced by the combination of physical limitations on expansion in Beijing, together with state limits on its expansion of steel production outside Beijing.

Its external expansion plans were twofold. The first involved an attempt to set up a joint venture, the Liuzhou Steel plant, in Guangxi province. The factory wanted to expand production from 0.5 million tons to 2 million tons. The local government and Shougang were keen for the JV to go ahead as Shougang would provide needed capital, technology and marketing links. However, the central authorities refused permission for the plan to go ahead. The reason given was that the scale proposed was 'too small for a plant of this type' and 'it didn't fit in with the national plans for development of the steel industry'.

The second, and much more important attempt, was Shougang's plan to build a massive new steel plant at Qilu in Shandong province. The plant was intended to produce 10 million tons of steel, and would have catapulted Shougang into the front ranks of world steel production. Shougang needed to obtain approval from the State Planning Commission, the Ministry of Metallurgical Industries (MMI), from the local government as well as from the State Council. It needed also approval from the Ministry of Transport before it could construct the harbour with which the plant would be connected to the rest of China and to the international market. Despite being apparently given approval by the State Council in 1993 (*Metal Bulletin Monday*, 10 May 1993), the highly controversial project was not finally permitted to go ahead. This was to have enormous implications for the whole expansion strategy that Shougang mapped out in the final phase of Zhou Guanwu's period as head of the Group.

Input and Output Co-ordination. The steel industry is a massive consumer of fuel and other raw materials.[31]

Coal. In the mid-1980s, Shougang's steel output was rising fast, but its coal allocations from the state plan remained virtually unchanged from 1984 to 1989 at around three million tons, so that it needed to meet around one-fifth of its annual needs from the free market in the late 1980s. The price and allocation of coal was technically released in the early 1990s. However, in the mid-1990s, the main supplies for large SOEs, such as Shougang, were determined by a massive twice-yearly conference at which the contracts for coal supply were linked directly to the allocation of transport space. The price of coal allocated through this mechanism was still tightly controlled by the state, with 'negotiation permitted only to the extent of a variation of 5 per cent either side of the state's 'guideline price'. Although in the early 1990s, the proportion of Shougang's coal needs obtained outside the planned mechanism of the coal conference still was very small, Shougang attempted to make its supplies secure by taking over a large state coal mine in Northwest China. However, permission for this was refused by the Coal Ministry. Any coal allocated outside the annual conference had to pay much higher prices for transport. In the mid-1990s access to transport by train was still controlled tightly by the Ministry of Transport. There was massive excess demand. Even Shougang had to 'beg for transport space'. Since Shougang had grown so fast, it faced especially large problems in trying to transport both inputs and outputs around the country.

Electricity. Shougang is a major consumer of electricity. It supplies a portion of its electricity from its own power stations, and is endeavouring to expand the extent of self-supply but is still heavily reliant on outside supply (Salomon Brothers, 1994: 14). The planned quota of electricity supply was at prices below those on the free market, once the latter had begun to operate. There was hard bargaining over the price of electricity to be supplied at above plan prices. In electricity as in other input supplies a consequence of Shougang's rapid output growth was that it needed to rely on the free market for its input supplies to a greater degree than more slow-growing large state steel plants.

Coke. Coke is the input in which Shougang had to rely most on the free market. Large steel plants in China traditionally supplied most of their own coke needs. Coke ovens in the traditional steel industry are a major source of pollution. Shougang's cramped size and pollution controls in Beijing, meant that it was unable to meet the large increments in its coke requirements from its own coking facilities.[32] By the early 1990s, there was no state plan for coke sales. The vast bulk of Shougang's coke needs had to be met from purchases on the free market. Most of these were from small native coke plants in Shanxi province using local native mined coal and primitive production methods. The coke all has to be shipped outside the planned transport system. Teams of trucks still bring the bulk of Shougang's coke needs at high cost (compared to the railway) hundreds of kilometres from Shanxi province. One reason for Shougang's desire to build the Qilu Plant in Shandong (see below) was in order to use the Qilu site to produce coke for Shougang's needs, avoiding the need to purchase from distant, high-cost sources.

Iron ore. Shougang was allowed to set up its own iron ore mine (at Qian'an *xian* in Hebei province) in 1960. This enabled it to guarantee supply of acceptable quality iron ore.[33] By the 1990s, it had over 26 000 employees (ISIC, 1997: 166). However, the local government has had protracted negotiations with Shougang over the rights to mine on 'its' land, even the land on which the mines are located is owned by the state. These were only resolved by the late 1990s. The complex negotiations involved the Hebei provincial government as well as the local government and Shougang. Without the support of the provincial government it is unlikely that Shougang would have been able to establish any ownership rights to the mine. Shougang has been forced to pay large, undisclosed natural resource fees (*ziyuanfei*), much of which goes to the local government. In 1997, the Qian'an mines made a loss of 297 million yuan. The large fees paid to the local government for Shougang's right to mine were a major reason for the loss (SG, 1998: 3–4, 39).

Steel output. Throughout the 1980s, steel prices were controlled by the government. As late as 1991 across the whole of China, the prices of 98 per cent of steel products (by tonnage) still were fixed by the government, the proportion falling to around 70 per cent in 1992 (*Metal Bulletin Monday*, 23 November 1992). In 1994, the government freed all steel prices. Shougang, along with the other steel enterprises, was then able to sell 100 per cent of its output at free market prices. Controls over output composition were gradually relaxed for large integrated steel firms over the course of several years, only finally coming to an end in the late 1990s. Shougang set up its own marketing companies in 1993, a sharp change from the behaviour under the planned economy.[34]

The excess demand for steel in the early 1990s meant that there was a considerable disparity between planned and market prices.[35] Under the contract system, Shougang was allowed to sell 15 per cent of planned output (compared to 2 per cent for ordinary enterprises still in 1986–7) and all output above the plan at up to 20 per cent above planned prices (the 20 per cent ceiling was abolished after 1988). Throughout the period 1985–92, the proportion sold by Shougang to the free market was around one-third to one-half of total output.[36] The rights to sell a relatively high proportion of output at market prices is regarded by most analysts as an important privilege, perhaps of even greater benefit to Shougang than the financial retentions, giving a unique stimulus to the Company's development (for example, Hassard *et al.*, 1992). However, much of the output sold to the 'free market' was in fact used to expand Shougang's production of steel products directly within the Corporation.

Administrative Merger. We have seen that the central government has become increasingly explicit about the importance of mergers as a key path to the construction of large, internationally competitive steel companies in China. That sharpness of awareness has been strongly influenced by the merger boom in the international economy. As we have seen, in the 1990s, this process began to penetrate even the global steel industry.

Shougang was in the vanguard of the merger movement within China. It merged with more than 100 large and medium-sized enterprises after 1980. Almost all large and medium enterprises are state-owned. Merger between such enterprises is typically handled by administrative co-ordination, either by a single local government, or between different local governments. Shougang's 14 second-tier companies (*erji gongsi*) were tightly managed by Shougang's headquarters, operating under a strict contract determined by the headquarters and handing over a large share of their profits to the headquarters.[37] Subject to negotiation with the relevant state authorities, Shougang had the right to appoint new management, reorganize the production structure, and shift the enterprises' assets and workers to other locations. It assumed responsibility for the merged enterprises' debts, but had the right to take a specified share of the profits of the merged business should that business be in profit. loss-making enterprises with which Shougang merged were given strict performance targets by the Shougang headquarters. In the last resort, if they failed to meet these targets and remained a loss-making burden to the headquarters, they could simply be returned to their original administrative authority and cast out of the Shougang system. This happened more than once during the contract years.[38]

The most important episodes in Shougang's domestic mergers and acquisitions under the contract system are the following:

- **Steel enterprises**. Under the contract system Shougang's steel output grew through two channels. The first was modernization and expansion at the main site in Beijing (see below). The second path was through mergers. In 1983, Shougang merged with 17 large profit making steel works in the Beijing area, with a total of around 30 000 employees. Shougang had 'long thought of merging with them', but the decision ultimately was an administrative one executed by the city government. Before this merger, all the 17 enterprises as well as Shougang itself were subsidiaries of the Beijing Metallurgical Bureau. After the merger, the Bureau was abolished. In other words, Shougang replaced the Bureau. These factories, together with Shougang itself, form the backbone of the Shougang steel business.

TABLE **9-22** **Average Price of Iron, Steel and Rolled Bar in China, 1980–93**

Item	1980	1988	1990	1993
Iron (yuan/ton)	200	410	750	1 550
Steel (yuan/ton)	572	1323	1887	3 859
Rolled bar (yuan/ton)	4390	6411	7593	13 576
Iron/steel ratio	1 : 2.9	1 : 3.2	1 : 2.5	1 : 2.5
Iron/rolled bar ratio	1 : 22	1 : 16	1 : 11	1 : 8.8

SOURCE: RCMED (1994)

The merged enterprises were all in the steel-processing sector and used to be consumers of Shougang's iron. In the 1980s and early 1990s, the price of iron was set far below that of steel and steel products (Table 9-22). It was much less profitable to produce iron than to produce steel and steel products. Once enterprises such as Shougang were given autonomy, they were unwilling to continue supplying cheap iron to other enterprises for them to make high profits, adding value in the downstream parts of the industry.

Through this strategic move, these plants became the main force in Shougang's expansion of its steel processing capacity. Their equipment was modernized with investment from Shougang. Their output structure was reorganized by Shougang's headquarters. Shougang gained access to the more profitable downstream segment of the iron and steel chain of production. In 1982, iron output in Shougang reached three million tons, but its annual steel processing capacity was only two million tons (Li, Zhai and Liu, 1992: 225). By 1994, after the merger, Shougang produced 6.9 million tons of iron, but 8.2 million tons of steel, 20 per cent more than its iron output (SG, 1995). The large restructuring of production permitted by this move was a major factor behind the steady growth in Shougang's profits. It was estimated to be responsible for roughly 30 per cent of the Corporation's total increased profits (*CDBW*, 22 December 1990).

- **Construction enterprises**. In 1992, Shougang administratively took over two construction companies with a total of 16 000 employees from the China National Non-ferrous Metals Corporation. These were the No. 4 Metallurgical Construction Company in Guixi County, Jiangxi Province, and No. 10 Metallurgical Construction Company in Huayin County, Shanxi Province. The main goal of these take-overs was to assist in the construction of the Qilu plant (*CDBW*, 20 November 1992).

- **Civilian heavy machinery enterprises**. Between April and mid-October 1988, Shougang merged with 33 large enterprises. These included Kaifeng Combine Harvester Plant (one of the largest agricultural machinery makers in China), Qinhuangdao Tractor Component Plant, Jinzhou Electronic Computer Plant, and Zhenjiang Shipbuilding Plant. These enterprises had a total of 59 000 employees in ten provinces and six industries. None of the enterprises was purchased. All of them were administratively merged into Shougang (*CDBW*, 7 November 1988). They signalled Shougang's intentions to diversify away from steel into related activities.

The Universal Machine Works (UMW) is another plant that was administratively merged with Shougang. It was originally called the Beijing Heavy Machinery Factory, and was one of China's eight largest producers of heavy machinery. In 1994, it had a work force of 6942 with 121 sets of ultra-heavy equipment.[39] By the end of March 1992, plant losses amounted to 132 million yuan and the net debt was 182 million yuan. The fiasco of this factory was widely known in Beijing. In March 1992, the entire firm was incorporated into Shougang, and became part of the Shougang Heavy Machinery Corporation.

Shougang employed its managerial skills to transform UMW's operational mechanism. It adopted the contract responsibility system and assumed sole responsibility for its profits and losses. In the second month after the system was altered, the factory made a profit of 109 000 yuan, ending many years of successive financial losses. Profits rose each month thereafter. By March 1993, there was a total profit of 20.24 million yuan. In April 1993, profits reached the highest recorded for the factory since its establishment 35 years previously. Sales revenue increased significantly. It was extremely helpful to Beijing Municipality that Shougang was able to turn around the financial performance of UMW. The main buyer was Shougang itself, purchasing many large pieces of machinery from UMW in order to meet its urgent expansion needs (*Beijing Review*, 26 July–1 August 1993: 21–4).

- **Military enterprises**. Also included in the 33 enterprises merged in 1988 were 13 large military enterprises. They employed a total of 45 000 workers and had 550 million yuan of fixed assets. These were mainly 'Third Front' factories located in remote inland areas such as Gansu province and Ningxia Autonomous Region. They were all loss-making and with old equipment. Although other large enterprises were also involved in the scheme to salvage loss-making military enterprises, Shougang took over far more than any other enterprise. Its enhanced independence compared to many other large enterprises also carried with it special responsibilities to the Chinese state.[40] The suggestion of merging with the military factories originated with the Head of the Ministry of Machinery, who was formerly the head of Military Industries. Shougang took over the assets free of charge and assumed responsibility for the factories' debts and for the employees' livelihoods.

The administrative mergers with the military enterprises put a great financial burden upon Shougang. Unlike the other enterprises that Shougang had acquired, it was not allowed to return them to their previous owners, even though they were losing a great deal of money and unable to fulfil the contracts. Shougang 'begged' the central government to put into place special policies and is negotiating for these 13 firms to be entitled to tax exemption, loan and other privileges for the former 'Third Front' army firms (SG, 1998: 38–9).

Management Appointment and Control. Under the contract system Shougang massively increased its independence in respect of the allocation of retained profits. However, the allocation of retained profits in the proportions 6:2:2 (development funds: collective welfare: employees' bonuses) was specified by the state. Under the contract system elsewhere, it was common for enterprises to allocate a higher proportion of retained profits to workers' collective welfare and to bonuses than was agreed in the contract. There is every evidence that Shougang stuck rigidly to the 6:2:2 condition in the contract. A major reason for the government's willingness to allow such a large measure of independence to Shougang may be that it was able to rely on the Shougang leadership to ensure that the re-investment condition would be adhered to.[41]

Although there was no direct representative of the Beijing city government on the Board of Directors of Shougang, under the contract system Shougang's chief officers were effectively appointed by higher levels. The Shougang Party Committee made nominations for the leading positions. The letters of appointment of the Party Secretary, Factory Head, Deputy-Head and General Manager were issued by the All-China Central Party Organization and the State Council. The Deputy General Manager and other comparable positions were appointed by the Beijing city government. When asked whether Beijing Municipality or the Central government owned the plant, leading cadres answered: 'We don't know'.

Zhou Guanwu's retirement in 1995 was, self-evidently, determined by levels above Shougang itself. Essentially, Zhou was asked to step down by the government.[42] It may be more accurate to describe what Shougang itself calls its 'Board of Directors' (*lishihui*) as the 'management team' or the executive directors. In the mid-1990s, Shougang's real 'Board of Directors', in the sense of the ultimate source of authority, was the Beijing government, to whom the 'preferred dividend' was paid, and who could hire and fire the managers of the company.

Strategic Control. In the 1980s, an important part of investment in the steel industry came from the MMI's budget. In 1993, this still amounted to around one-quarter of the total amount spent on basic construction investment in the industry. However, in addition to this any investment of substantial size needed to be submitted to the Ministry for its approval. Even for Shougang, its rights to decide new investment were incomplete. The central government still played a central role in determining the framework within which all producers in the industry operated through its impact upon the level and nature of protection for the Chinese steel industry. Such fundamental issues as the enterprises' wage structure and the rights to make workers redundant were set by the government. Even in the mid-1990s, it was not feasible for Shougang to attempt to improve performance by making large numbers of workers redundant. Unlike Western steel firms, Shougang was forced to look towards growth rather than redundancy as the main path to solving the problem of surplus employees.

Under the planned economy, the overall pattern of specialization among major producers was heavily influenced by the MMI. Shougang was China's leading producer mainly at the lower end of the chain of sophistication (and unit price) of steel products. It was, and still is, China's number one producer of small sec-tion steel and wire rods (Table 9-16). This was advantageous in the sense that demand for these products boomed in the reform period, since these are espe-cially heavily used in construction. However, a disadvantage stemming from this pattern is that it was in these areas that the competition was strongest from emerging small-scale producers. In 1997, local and 'non-system' (that is, outside the planning framework) plants accounted for 69 per cent of output of small sec-tion steel and 53 per cent of the output of wire rods. These products benefited much less from economies of scale, often required less complex, lumpy equip-ment, and needed less attention to product quality, than was the case for many other steel products. Government control over Shougang's production structure gradually atrophied, only finally disappearing in the late 1990s.

Wage Growth and Structure. The growth of average wages at Shougang was tightly constrained not only by the contract, but also by Party policy. Still in the 1990s, there were only small differentials in average income among leading Chinese steel plants.[43] In 1996 average annual wages (including bonuses and subsidies) in Chinese keypoint steel plants stood at 10 507 yuan, with the figure at Shougang standing at 10 136 yuan, compared to 10 230 yuan at Angang and 12 232 yuan at Wugang (ISIC, 1997: 122). Baogang alone among the large steel plants had substantially higher average wages, standing at 25 000 yuan (ISIC, 1997: 122). Under the contract system, the earnings structure within large state steel firms also was tightly controlled by official policy.

Summary. The contract system gave Shougang a good deal in terms of finan-cial retentions, but, at least as importantly, it provided it with greatly enhanced autonomy.[44] Shougang's greatly increased autonomy was exercised within a framework of continuing state co-ordination both in respect to the organization of input supplies and involvement in the mergers with other enterprises. The state continued to control other important aspects of Shougang's behaviour, including the appointment of top managers, the pattern of product specialization, the wage structure, as well as the terms of the contract. The contract provided the possi-bility for dynamic, growth-oriented management behaviour, but it did not ensure that this was how the Corporation would behave. Indeed, given the advantageous market conditions that Shougang faced during the period of the contract system, with booming demand for its products, the contract provided the opportunity for a relaxed, non-dynamic, satisficing approach by the management. However, the rest of this chapter will suggest the contract system is not sufficient to explain Shougang's exceptionally rapid growth, nor does it explain the manner in which it grew.

MODERNIZATION OF THE CORE STEEL MAKING BUSINESS

Growth Begets Growth. We have seen that demand for steel in China grew at a rapid rate from the late 1970s to the late 1990s, with cyclical surges in which

demand far outstripped domestic supply capabilities. This created a huge opportunity for Chinese steel firms. Shougang's contract system provided it with a
mechanism to fund high-speed expansion. By generating profits from meeting this
high-speed demand growth, it was able to reinvest to fund further expansion to
meet the surging demand. This market environment provided a high incentive to
bring production capacity on-stream as fast as possible.[45] However, Shougang
faced the booming market demand after the late 1970s with such outdated facilities that foreign visitors in the early years of reform called it a 'museum of metallurgical history'.[46] It was imperative to both grow and modernize simultaneously.

Shougang's success in rapidly increasing steel output to meet the surging
demand generated a rapid growth in profits for reinvestment: retained profits
after payment of all taxes and hand-overs to the Beijing Government reportedly
increased by 34 per cent per annum from 1980 to 1992. In the early 1990s, during the 'Golden Years' for the Chinese steel industry, Shougang's profit rate as a
proportion of sales value was estimated at 25–27 per cent (Salomon Brothers,
1994: 14–16). This was much higher than the average international rate at that
time, of under 10 per cent (Zhang, 1994: 30), and almost double the Chinese
average for major steel plants (MMI, 1994: section 9). It was imperative to bring
new production capacity on-stream as fast as possible in order to meet booming
demand.

During the years of the contract system, enormous physical investment took
place at Shougang. From 1980 to 1990, Shougang spent a total of 4.27 billion
yuan (roughly $1.56 billion) for technical renovation and capital construction:
108 key projects and thousands of minor ones were completed (*CDBW*, 28 July
1991). Sixty per cent of these 108 projects earned sufficient profits to recoup
their investment outlays within two years, 30 per cent within half a year, and
10 per cent within two months (Li, Zhai and Lui 1992: 226). In the Sixth and
Seventh Five Year Plan periods (1980–5 and 1986–90), the returns per yuan of
fixed investment at Shougang were the highest of the eight largest steel makers
in China (Table 9-23).

As we shall see, under the contract system, Shougang hugely upgraded its
R & D and design capability and comprehensively automated its main production
processes. After 1978, Shougang comprehensively modernized its blast-furnaces,
and by the early 1990s, nearly all its steel was produced by oxygen converters
(Table 9-3). In 1994, out of 55 leading economic and technical indices, Shougang
came first in more than 30 across the whole country (SG, 1995). By the late
1990s, its output per worker was 50–100 per cent above that at old integrated
steel plants such as Panzihua, Benxi, Baotou, Angang, Wugang and Magang
(Table 9-15). Its costs of production were significantly below these plants: in the
early 1990s, the production costs of wire rods was around 1000 yuan/ton in
Shougang, compared with 1400 yuan/ton at Angang and Magang (Salmon
Brothers, 1994: 13).

Technological Renovation. The contract system meant that higher levels no
longer had responsibility for enterprise expansion. From 1982, state investment in

TABLE 9-23 **Returns on Investment in the Eight Largest Steel Complexes in China, 1980–5 and 1985–90 (million yuan)**

Complex	Increase in total profits (A)	Investment in fixed assets (B)	Returns on investment A/B	Rank
		(in million yuan) 1980–5		
Shougang	201.7	79.0	2.67	1
Wugang	291.1	116.6	2.50	2
Taigang	79.8	39.0	2.05	3
Pangang	71.2	42.0	1.70	4
Magang	71.2	42.4	1.68	5
Baogang	70.6	46.4	1.52	6
Bengang	60.1	74.3	0.81	7
Angang	107.1	230.1	0.47	8
		(in million yuan) 1985–90		
Shougang	564.0	284.8	1.98	1
Wugang	397.9	256.0	1.55	2
Taigang	123.1	89.8	1.37	3
Pangang	77.9	226.6	0.34	8
Magang	91.6	141.3	0.65	5
Baogang	101.8	94.0	1.08	4
Bengang	132.6	249.9	0.53	6
Angang	261.9	589.7	0.44	7

SOURCE: RCMED (1992: 143)

Shougang was reduced to zero (*CDBW*, 10 November 1982).[47] This made Shougang's investment responsibility clear-cut: 'Under the contract system, our complex, not the state, is the investor. So we should make the best use of every cent' (Luo Bingsheng, acting general manager, quoted in *CDBW*, 28 July 1991). For instance, when Shougang built the technologically advanced No. 2 Steel Mill and Wire Rod Plant, the goal was 'to introduce the most advanced foreign equipment at the least possible cost' (*Beijing Review*, 27 January–2 February 1992: 23). As we shall see, Shougang bought much of the equipment from the international second-hand market, and then upgraded the equipment itself. The total cost of the No. 2 Steel Mill was 400 million yuan, only one-third of the estimated cost of a comparable set of new equipment from abroad.

Shougang's approach to modernization under the contract system was to make careful comparisons of the costs of repair and replacement, and not hesitate to combine them if this reduced costs and speeded up improvement with minimum interruption to production. Foreign equipment was only bought if it was suitable, and was combined as far as possible with Shougang's own technology.

Shougang's approach was: 'Shougang first, China second, imports third'. In other words, if any aspect of a piece of technology could be provided from within the firm, it would be sourced from there. Failing that, it would be sourced from within China. Only if Shougang failed to locate a suitable domestic source would it purchase from outside China. From 1980 to 1990 Shougang imported a total of 512 items of advanced technology and equipment at a total cost of $315 million (*CDBW*, 9 October 1990), much of it second-hand or core pieces of equipment which were combined with indigenous technology in order to reduce the overall cost. This was a modest outlay of foreign exchange given the size of the modernization task being undertaken.

This approach is radically different from that of Baogang, for example, which was built on a greenfield site in the 1980s. Moreover, Shougang's approach to its modernization was strongly influenced by the restricted space at the main site in Beijing. As we shall see, the 'military style' of mobilization for modernization was heavily influenced by the need to rely mainly on the reconstruction of existing plant. Since it could not rely on building large new segments of the plant from scratch without halting production, speed of renovation of existing plant was vitally important. The self-financing nature of its investment due to the contract system dictated that it complete each phase of modernization in the minimum amount of time in order to minimize the halt in the flow of income and profits. This process of combining repair and transformation played a powerful role in upgrading Shougang's technical capability through learning by doing.

Compared with many other state-owned enterprises, Shougang relied heavily on upgrading existing equipment rather than purchasing large new pieces of equipment to expand its production. For example, the No. 1 Steel Mill, commissioned in 1965, had three 30-ton steel-smelting furnaces with an original design capacity of 600 000 tons. However, through technical transformation, this was increased 3.5-fold to 2.2 million tons in 1986 (Ai, 1992: 189). One of Shougang's largest rolling mills had an original design capacity of 0.5 million tons, but by 1994, through technical transformation this had been raised to more than 1.9 million tons, four times its original design capacity.

A key path for technological upgrading was the automation of steel production. We shall analyze later Shougang's rapid progress in human capabilities in steel automation. In 1983, Shougang purchased $0.7 million worth of computer hardware from the USA in order to automate production in their sintering plant. The software was all produced by Shougang. Subsequently it began to manufacture its own programmable logical control system (PLC). By the early 1990s, the main production process was entirely automated. The 60 000 workers in the steel branch of the company are almost all employed in activities other than direct production, such as repair, maintenance and R & D. Shougang was able to win internationally competitive contracts for the automation of leading US steel plants in the early 1990s (see below).

Good Luck: The 'Industrial Flea Market'. Unlike either Posco during its early years (Amsden, 1989: 309) or Baogang, Shougang under the contract system did not have access to substantial external funding or technical assistance from a leading international steel maker. Therefore, in order to meet its goal to introduce the most advanced equipment at the lowest cost, Shougang relied heavily on purchasing second-hand equipment. It was fortunate for Shougang that the world steel industry experienced a serious recession during this period. In the 1980s an estimated 70 million tons of steel mill capacity were laid aside in the US and in Europe also there were substantial sales of steel plant. A large amount of second-hand equipment was waiting to be bought, often of relatively recent vintage, typically at less than one-fifth of the original price (Wang, 1993: 94).

By the end of 1992, Shougang had introduced 16 major pieces of imported second-hand equipment. For example, in 1984, Shougang planned to build a new mill to expand steel production capacity. Unable at that stage itself to produce complete steel making equipment, the company asked for help from the Shanghai Heavy-Machinery Plant. It was told that it would take three to four years to design and manufacture the 300 million yuan worth of equipment weighing 21 000 tons. If imported new from abroad, the company would have had to wait four to five years and spend one billion yuan. After considering these options, the Corporation decided to import the equipment second-hand from those Western countries anxious to sell machinery from their own depressed iron and steel industry.

The Seraing Works in Belgium with a design production capacity of 2.5 million tons and a technical level of the 1970s was up for sale. The mill also had three important patented technology items. The equipment and the workshop weighed 50 000 tons. The cost of the mill, 40 million yuan, plus the cost of moving, was one-tenth of the estimated cost for new plant and equipment. Also the construction period would be shortened by two to three years. Shougang shipped them by sea to China in August 1985. The mill was put into operation in August 1987 (*Beijing Review*, 27 January–2 February 1992: 23).

In October 1992, Shougang bought the California Iron and Steel Company's Second Converter Steel Mill (Wang, 1993: 207). When it opened in 1978, the Basic Oxygen Process (BOP) Shop No. 2, at the California Iron Industrial Company, was among the most formidable steel making facilities in the world. The two huge Voest-Alpine furnaces could produce up to 2.8 million tons of high-grade carbon steel annually. It cost $287 million to build. But soon after Kaiser Steel built the plant the company encountered new environmental regulations and rapidly rising union wages, making the mill uncompetitive compared to US mini-mills and overseas producers. Within just five years of its opening, Kaiser had shut the plant down. Shougang paid only $15 million to purchase the plant. Soon after the purchase, 290 engineers and labourers arrived from China. They dismantled their new possession, packed it up and shipped it back to China (*CDBW*, 17 May 1993: 23–4). It was intended to incorporate it into the new Shougang plant at Qilu.

Shougang intentionally purchased equipment that was in good condition but was not highly automated, and itself automated the equipment. Shougang's technically successful purchase of second-hand equipment reflected its relatively high technical skills. The process of purchase and installation also helped to pro-mote those skills, creating a virtuous circle of advance.

A second-hand high-speed wire rod rolling machine was bought from a Belgian firm in 1984 and installed in Shougang's No. 2 Wire Rod Plant. The machine is able to roll a 12-metre-long steel billet into a 5200 m long rod with a diameter of 6.5 mm. In addition to its high speed, its precision is as high as that found in parts used for aircraft and missiles. All spare parts for the machine are made by Harbin and Xian aircraft manufacturing plants. Its automated control system was bought from Germany in July 1983. Shougang bought the rolling machine together with the new control system. This included 26 mainframe com-puters and programmable controllers. The cost of using German technicians to install and debug the machine was prohibitive, so Shougang undertook the work itself. The machine was assembled by Shougang technicians and put into opera-tion in 1989. In the following year, the machine rolled 550 000 tons of wire rods, reputedly an international record (*Beijing Review*, 27 January–2 February 1992: 23–4).[48] Shougang's technicians and workers made more than 100 technical innovations aimed at modernizing the equipment. In 1992, it produced 700 000 tons of wire rods, which exceeded its original design capacity by 250 000 tons (*CDBW*, 21 March 1993).

The high rates of profit that Shougang made under the contract system, pri-marily through being able to meet the fast-growing demands from China's con-struction industry, were substantially reinvested in expanding and modernizing its iron and steel production. By the mid-1990s these processes had been mas-sively transformed. An important part of the process of technical change at Shougang was 'learning by doing' through the purchase of second-hand equip-ment from Europe and the US, dismantling and shipping it, and reassembling and further transforming it on site in China.

MANAGEMENT METHOD: MILITARY-STYLE ORGANIZATION

Technical Renovation as a Series of Battles. Renovation of any single sub-stantial segment of Shougang had large inter-connections with activity in other parts of the enterprise. Limited funds and constraints of space which meant that Shougang had to rely heavily on upgrading existing facilities, impelled them to carry out technological transformation as quickly as possible. Under the contract system, time was money. Everyone working at Shougang knew that in 1993, for example, it would generate 4.5 billion yuan in profits ($775 million), an average of 13 million yuan ($2.2 million) per day (*CDBW*, 21 March 1993). Time spent in renovation meant income foregone from having segments of the plant shut down. It was from this income that the resources for further renovation came. In this sense the contract system imposed the hardest of budget constraints upon Shougang.

From the late 1970s through to the early 1990s, each of the major technolog-ical renovations was treated as a battle, with the Corporation organized like an army. From 1992 to 1995 alone, Shougang carried out more than ten large technological renovation projects. The main items of modernization are shown in Table 9-19. The new No. 3 Blast Furnace with 29 new technologies and totalling $2500\,\text{m}^3$, was put into operation in just three months. The renovation of the No. 2 Blast Furnace involved the investment of 130 million yuan in dismantling 13 000 tons of material and installing 25 000 tons of material. Over 7000 workers were assigned to work day and night in a $100\,\text{m}^3$ area. Financial pressure made them finish the project as quickly as possible: 'The original time limit for the project was 104 days but after a plan was worked out to hoist the entire furnace wall, the schedule was reduced to 58 days. Later, a more detailed plan was put forward by the 17 construction units and it was completed within 55 days. They knew that one day meant 2.95 million yuan in profits' (*Beijing Review*, 13–19 January 1992: 16).

The combination of strict technological inter-linkage between different segments of the plant and the hard financial constraint pressing upon the management to urgently complete each renovation task, tended to push the firm towards a highly centralized military style structure. Success could not be achieved by extensive discussions with independent subordinates sitting round a table bargaining democratically about how to allocate limited funds. The technological and financial imperatives led to each major technological renovation being treated as a battle. This required: (1) a unified command system, in order to plan and act as an integrated entity; (2) strict discipline, in order to meet severe technological requirements; (3) full mobilization, in order to master new and imported technology at all levels; (4) an adequate supporting service, in order to support full mobilization and the 'first front' battle. The four were the necessary conditions for successful military-style organization.

Unified Command System. Shougang was far from being a legal umbrella for many more or less autonomous firms. Because of the long chain of production that is at the heart of integrated steel production, different subordinate units were treated as part of a technologically unified structure. The requirement to treat each renovation task as a strictly unified planned activity was made even more imperative by the fact that Shougang itself carried out the entire technological renovation using its own construction units. As we have seen under the contract system the second-tier companies were managed tightly by Shougang's headquarters, closely integrated into the overall strategy for modernization and growth.

Strict Discipline. The industry's technological characteristics combined with the renovation battles helped produce a highly disciplinarian style of management at Shougang under the contract system. In the same fashion as in an army, a mistake by a single individual in the renovation 'battle' can result in the loss of the whole battle. A single mistake in a large technologically-based firm can lead to large loss of output and/or damage to equipment of high value.

Under the contract system Shougang was famous for its strict discipline. The 'three one hundred per cent system' was introduced in 1980 by Zhou Guanwu.

Under this system, every employee had to obey regulations 'one hundred per cent'. Any violation of the regulations had to be recorded and reported 'one hundred per cent'. Violators were deprived of their bonus 'one hundred per cent', no matter what the financial consequence for the family of the person who had violated the code of discipline (Wang, 1993: 52–88).[49]

The strict disciplinary code caused great debate in a country where workers are nominally the masters (Wang, 1993: 52–88). Shougang periodically operated a seven day week working schedule, especially during big renovation battles, with no time allowed off for Sundays, as in most other Chinese state enterprises. If workers missed work on Sunday once, they lost their monthly bonus. In addition, the worker would be criticized by the Party secretary, making it difficult to get promotion, and lose quarterly bonuses as well. While most Chinese enterprises allow their workers at least four or five days holiday at the Spring Festival, Shougang leaders reportedly did not allow their workers a single day off, instead exhorting them to 'Spend a revolutionary Spring Festival', 'Pass the holiday at work with a fighting spirit', and 'Don't take time to breathe, don't take time to rest' (*SCMP*, 9 February 1993).

The strict discipline did not just apply to workers, but to cadres also. At Shougang in 1983–4 alone, over 200 leading cadres, one half of the total, were removed from their posts (*CDBW*, 18 July 1984). From 1978 to 1990, 678 of Shougang's cadres at and above the level of subordinate plant and division management were either demoted (643) or dismissed entirely (35), amounting to almost 10 per cent of the total (Hao, 1992: 157; Xu and Liu, 1992: 217). This was, almost certainly, the highest ratio in China. The former popular practice of 'no mistake, no demotion' was done away with. If production targets were not fulfilled three months running, the work of senior staff was examined and those considered responsible were removed.

The counterpart of the strict discipline at Shougang is that the average income of employees at the plant was relatively high by Chinese state industry standards. Average total wages (that is, including bonuses and subsidies) per worker at Shougang in 1993 were 5946 yuan, 27 per cent above the average total wages in the manufacturing sector in Beijing (4671 yuan) (SSB, ZTN, 1994: 122, 366–9, 378–83). However, this was not an especially high figure compared to other key-point steel enterprises (Table 9-17). Average wages at Shougang were on a par with those at Angang, and considerably below those at Baogang. However, as will be seen later, an important component of income at Shougang was derived from collective sources, including subsidies for food, housing and welfare. A 1992 survey found that at Shougang remuneration was 'on a par with that of employees of wholly foreign-funded enterprises or Sino–foreign joint ventures but much higher than ordinary workers, college professors, journalists and public functionaries earn' (*Beijing Review*, 27 April–3 May 1992: 20).

The wage structure under the contract system was based on three components. The first was the basic wage, which was responsible for 50 per cent of wage income in 1993. The worker's allocation in the wage scale depended on skill and performance (Table 9-24). There was considerable movement from one

TABLE 9-24 Wage Grades at Shougang, 1986

Cadres				Workers			
Grade	Wages (yuan per month)	No. of people	Proportion (%)	Grade	Wages (yuan per month)	No. of people	Proportion (%)
3	310	1*	—	—	—	—	—
4	285	4	0.10	—	—	—	—
5	260	5	—	—	—	—	—
6	240	9	—	—	—	—	—
7	220	55	0.28	—	—	—	—
8	200	113	0.58	—	—	—	—
9	181	457	2.35	10	181	—	—
10	162	2 215	11.41	9	162	167	0.16
11	144	3 609	18.58	8	144	4 068	3.95
12	126	3 307	17.03	7	126	10 348	10.05
13	110	3 129	15.60	6	110	16 177	15.70
14	94	3 049	15.70	5	94	20 361	19.77
15	80	2 371	12.21	4	80	17 322	16.82
16	68	671	3.46	3	68	14 366	13.95
17	57	387	1.99	2	57	13 342	12.95
18	48	138	0.71	1	48	4 022	3.90
—	—	—	—	Apprentices	30, 35, 40	2 836	2.75
Total	—	19 420	100	—	—	103 009	100

SOURCES: Editorial Commission of *Reform in Shougang*, 1992, 1: 99

NOTES: The data reflect only basic wages, and do not include bonuses, which amount to around 25% of wages.

*This figure is for the wages of Zhou Guanwu, President of Shougang until 1995. Until 1990, Zhou had a total of 495 yuan per month, including 375 yuan basic wages, 70 yuan in bonuses, and 50 yuan benefit related to profit increases (Hao, 1992: 158)

wage grade to another, mainly upwards, but also downwards, in relation to work performance. Around 20–30 per cent of employees changed grade annually. The second element in the wage system was the bonus, which was allocated in relation to the monthly evaluation of the employee's performance. This accounted for around 30 per cent of wage income in 1993. The third element was the year-on-year bonus. This accounted for around 20 per cent of wage income in 1993. All workers shared in this award, which was related to the overall performance of the whole enterprise.

Wage levels were not the same in all other Shougang plants as at the headquarters in Beijing. Strict requirements were placed by the headquarters on newly merged enterprises. Only once they had reached their targets in terms of eliminating losses and meeting the profit targets set by Shougang could they enter the Shougang wages system. By 1994, only around one-third of the merged enterprises had met these requirements.[50]

Full Mobilization. The broad targets of the Corporation (some of which were set by the state) were divided into 20 categories including planning, technical, financial, equipment supply and maintenance, welfare and personnel work. These 20 categories were subdivided into 1325 detailed economic and technical tasks for plants and mines and 23 126 post contract systems (*CDBW*, 6 November 1982, 6 April 1983, Joint Research Group, 1992: 91). These tasks were further divided into 235 684 targets for individual workers, with frequent performance checks (*CDBW*, 11 November 1982). In 1982, a copy of the second edition of the text on the economic responsibility system was distributed to every employee in Shougang (*CDBW*, 16 September 1982).

While the Corporation was responsible to the state, each of its subdivisions and each member of the staff knew their responsibility for the fulfilment of the overall output, profit and other economic and technical tasks. There were numerous contracted targets for each individual in the Corporation. These targets linked each employee's responsibility and reward with Shougang's overall goal. The function of the internal contract system was to mobilize rather than to monitor, as the Taylorist monitoring/reward system does. It owed much more to the mobilizatory tradition of the Chinese Communist Party and the People's Liberation Army than to study of Western management theory.

Under the contract system, training was an important mechanism, not only for advancing the technical level of the workforce, but also for further mobilizing Shougang's employees for the 'battles'. Shougang paid great attention to training its employees. In 1978, only 5 per cent of the total number of employees were educated to above middle professional level engineering. By 1990, the proportion had risen to 47 per cent. From 1978 to 1990, 38 000 young employees graduated to beyond high school level. More than 85 per cent of its staff participated in different training courses. The number of employees who participated in more than twenty annual study hours rose from 17 700 in 1978 to 232 000 in 1990. In 1991, Shougang's leadership decided that 83 per cent (90 per cent in 1995) of all employees in the company were required to participate in different training courses amounting to more than 80 annual study hours.

Special training programmes were set up for leaders at different levels. From 1984 to 1987, 95 per cent of the 11 000 chiefs at workshop level in production, construction, and rear-service systems, participated in full-time out-of-work training for one to two weeks. During the Sixth Five Year Plan (1980–5), 34 000 cadres of subordinate plants and divisions participated five times each per year in different training programmes, and 11 000 workshop level cadres participated four times annually in different training programmes. Moreover, training programmes went far beyond simply improving skills. Training programmes in Shougang had the same function as those in the army, namely raising the employees' fighting spirit for the battle.

Shougang used the slogans, 'The contract is the base' (*chengbao wei ben*) and 'the people are the base' (*renmin wei ben*). Other means of mobilization included meetings and study sessions, frequently out of regular working hours, encouraging employees to make suggestions which might reduce costs, increase quality and efficiency (there were more than 10 000 rationalization suggestions from the workshops over the period of the contract system). Full mobilization was an especially important source of generating increased profits in the early period of the contract system when Shougang had insufficient funds to undertake large technological renovation projects.

Shougang's mobilizatory, highly disciplined management style under the contract system has much in common with that found elsewhere in Asia, including leading steel firms. The analogy with Posco, the world's most efficient, and fastest-growing steel producer, is striking. Posco attaches great importance to employee training, with almost half the workers in any one year attending training courses (Amsden, 1989: 210–11). The use of slogans is also similar: at Posco, the key slogan is 'Resources are limited, but human creativity is unlimited' (Amsden, 1989: 212).

Strong Support from Rear services. Under the contract system, Shougang developed a big internal tertiary sector. The Commission for Managing the Livelihood of Employees was responsible for operating the internal services. It had more than 20 000 employees. Shougang not only provided its employees with heavily subsidized housing, but also cheaper food, daily-use commodities, kindergartens, and martyrs' graves. Under the 6:2:2 system the Commission was allocated 20 per cent of Shougang's retained profits. Typically, 40 per cent of this amount was allotted to house building and repair. The remainder was divided between subsidies to workers' health and for food, and wages of the workers in the Commission.

Shougang's food processing factory provided food for its employees. The factory had 1000 workers and 15 production lines. The food was of high quality and provided to the workers at cost price. In addition, Shougang had nearly 600 purchasing agents who bought food and daily-use goods from all over the country. By taking advantage of economies of scale in purchasing, they were able to sell food to Shougang's employees at 20 per cent below market prices and daily-use commodities at 10 per cent below market prices.[51] In addition to setting up food processing facilities and benefiting from economies of scale in purchasing food, Shougang also set up its own agricultural production bases.

Sufficient staff funds were available to allow Shougang to provide a wide array of internal service systems. In the 1980s Shougang built 1.7 million m^2 of housing for its employees. The Corporation had its own construction company with around 3000 employees. Housing space per employee rose from 2.7 m^2 in 1978 to 7.3 m^2 in 1994.[52] In 1994, the Corporation charged its employees 3.4 yuan per month of rent for an average-sized apartment of 25 m^2. This compared with 5.5 yuan per m^2 for a similar apartment rented by Beijing residents from the city government. This was in turn only a small fraction of the market rent for dwelling space, which is roughly 1000 yuan (approximately $100) for a similar-sized unmodernized apartment. Moreover, Shougang employees paid only one *mao* (one-tenth of one yuan) for a unit of electricity compared to 2 *mao* per unit paid by Beijing residents. The company also distributed gas-ovens, TV cables, and telephones free of charge to its employees.

Shougang had a general hospital with 600 beds. It had over 1000 beds in new clinics built, at a total cost of 30 million yuan, under the contract system. It bought a great deal of advanced medical equipment, enabling it to upgrade the quality of its medical services. Hospital treatment was free of charge for employees and family members paid fees equal to around one-half of the real cost of providing these services. After 1988, Shougang provided a free biannual comprehensive health examination for all employees.[53] Shougang had 51 kindergartens, 25 of which were built after the reform. They cared for around 10 000 children in 1990. Now all employees could leave their children in Shougang's own internal kindergartens. Nurseries were free of charge (except for food) for children from 90 days to 6 years old.

These internal service systems were non-profit-seeking. They played an important function in supporting Shougang's employees in the battles for technological transformation. During these battles, all internal service systems were required to support the collective effort. The food processing, medical care, training programmes, and kindergartens were required to supply high quality services, irrespective of the time of day or whether or not it was officially a holiday. This is analogous to the function of rear supply units in an army.

Even by the end of the contract system, China's social security system had hardly begun to develop. Under these conditions, although the in-house provision of subsidized social services was costly, it played a powerful role in cementing the firm as a big family, which supported the mobilization of the whole plant to fight battles. Like Shougang, Posco also regards itself as a 'big family' with a duty towards the wider livelihoods of all its members (Amsden, 1989: 210).

The Military Approach to Management. The head of Shougang under the contract system, Zhou Guanwu, was the leader of a guerrilla unit in the anti-Japanese struggle. The long-time head of South Korea's most powerful steel firm, Posco, also was from an army background. Not only is an ex-army officer more likely to impose strict discipline within the firm, but he is more likely to be trusted by higher authorities to carry out official policy (for example, to focus on reinvestment and technological transformation rather than short-term profit maximization).

In contrast to the traditional theory of consumer economics and profit maximization, Thurow (1991) has suggested that an alternative way of approaching economic activity is 'producer economics, in which power and conquest are the basic motivation for the firm.' He has argued that in Japan during its rise to global power in the 1980s, competition was treated as warfare rather than a rational process of profit maximization. He believes that 'a content analysis of military metaphors would surely show their much more widespread usage in Japan [than in the West]' (Thurow, 1991: 51). Janelli's detailed account of a large Korean firm speaks of a 'military style of life [that] pervaded the enterprise' (Janelli, 1993: 226). Shougang's management style under the contract system is a variant of the same East Asian tradition.

The notion of competition as analogous to military struggle is not unique to East Asia. Under advanced oligopolistic capitalism, large firms are engaged in a form of warfare. They have clearly identified opponents, in sharp contrast to the world of perfect competition, where thousands of small anonymous firms struggle in a single sector. The language of military struggle deeply imbues the business system of large, globally powerful firms in the 1990s. The capacity to organize the firm's activities in a strategic fashion is a key weapon determining the potential success of a large firm.

Shougang under the contract system had a central goal, to overtake Angang and become China's largest steel producer. However, its ambitions extended beyond that. Zhou Guanwu seriously intended that Shougang would become the number one steel company in the world. Construction of the Qilu plant would have taken the company a long way down this path. Such an ambition is not the unique prerogative of the leader of a 'Communist, state-owned' steel company. A similar ambition drove Andrew Carnegie when he built US Steel. It drove those who mapped out the future for the British Steel Corporation in the 1973 British White Paper. It drove the leaders of Nippon Steel. Today it drives the leaders of Posco. Nor does such ambition appear to be lacking in Lakshmi Mittal, the chief executive officer of Ispat International. It appears also to drive the leaders of Baogang, supported by the Shanghai Municipal government.

The Chinese Communist Party was the main instrument through which the military style of management was put into effect at Shougang. Shougang's leaders spoke of themselves as having been 'catapulted to the forefront of China's industrial captains,' commanders in the industrial battlefront of steel-making. In the transition from the command economy to a market-oriented economy, the military style of traditional Communist culture is a potentially valuable institutional force to assist the struggle to modernize and do battle in the market-place. It can help to avoid the institutional problems of the typical large Western firm, such as principle/agent struggle, free-riding and bureaucratic hierarchy, which arise because the employees are motivated primarily by individual economic interests. Shougang's army-style of organization, fighting not for profit maximization but for victory in the battles of technical modernization and growth, made it an irrational and difficult competitor for the profit-maximizing firm to struggle against.

Shougang's fast modernization occurred under a distinctive system of management. This was mobilizatory, quasi-military and highly disciplined. The emergence of this management style was related to the technological characteristics of the steel industry. This was reinforced by the need to modernize through a sequence of carefully planned battles, which in turn was closely connected to the way in which the modernization process at Shougang was funded under the contract system. It was influenced also by the inherited work style of the Chinese armed forces and of the Chinese Communist Party. Finally, it was related to the background and personal characteristics of Zhou Guanwu. It is a style of management that is more closely related to that of other large East Asian steel firms, such as Nippon Steel or Posco, than it is to that of large Western steel firms today, such as US Steel or British Steel.

MERGER, DIVERSIFICATION, TRANSNATIONALIZATION

It takes time for factor and product markets to emerge in less developed countries in general and in Communist, reforming, less developed countries in particular. A huge number of transactions between firms, which formerly were administered through the command system of material balance planning, now needed to be organized in a different way. This creates pressure for large firms to cut through the uncertainty, delay and absence of legally enforceable contracts to create their own internal supply networks, minimizing the cost of organizing these activities through the still highly imperfect market apparatus. This in turn helps push emerging large firms towards diversification via internal growth, acquisition and merger, over and above the forces that assist the emergence of large firms in many sectors in the developed economies.

The main channel for Shougang's expansion in steel production after 1995 was intended to be through the planned construction of the new ten million ton plant, Qilu Iron and Steel. This would launch Shougang into the ranks of the world's top three steel producers by the end of the century. However, as we have seen, this project was shelved in 1995 by the central government. Much of Shougang's diversification and transnationalization in the later phase of the contract system was related to this goal.

Machine-building Capability. China's machine-building industry for the steel industry is in a process of transition. There is a huge opportunity for China to develop a powerful group of firms producing for the machinery needs of this fast-growing sector. During the period of the contract system, most large equipment was manufactured by plants within the Ministry of Machine Building. These were mainly large diversified manufacturers of equipment, for which the steel industry was just one among many customers. The MMB recognizes that the industry needs to move towards the pattern found commonly in the advanced economies, in which this sector is dominated by firms that are specialized producers for the steel industry. China is still a long way from such a structure. Shougang's expansion into this sector needs to be viewed against the large opportunities that exist in the manufacture of machinery for the steel industry in China and the still undeveloped nature of the business structure in this sector.

We have seen that in 1988, 20 large machinery enterprises and 13 military factories were merged administratively with Shougang. Shougang's leadership considered that the upgrading of China's iron and steel plants would need a great deal of modern steel rolling machinery. After reorganization, the factories it had taken over were linked up to form a single, large machinery engineering company under Shougang's control, the Shougang Heavy Machinery Corporation.

This Corporation was now responsible for the design and manufacture of machinery for the metallurgical and mining industries (*CDBW*, 27 June 1988). As we have also seen, in 1992 Shougang took over the Universal Machine Works in Beijing. This also was incorporated into the Shougang Heavy Machinery Corporation. The Heavy Machinery Corporation was now a large-scale entity with a total of almost 60 000 employees in the late 1990s (Table 9-25). One of its main functions was to build machinery to meet the urgent needs generated by Shougang's growth.

By 1994, Shougang had an annual machinery manufacturing capability of 70 000 tons. It was able to design, manufacture and erect large-sized machinery and equipment. Shougang could design and manufacture a complete set of equipment for steel plants with an annual production capacity of three million tons (*Beijing Review*, 13–19 January 1992: 16). It could manufacture a full set of metallurgical and mining equipment, non-standard machines plus components for the chemical and textile industries, as well as general-purpose equipment. Shougang now had more than 20 machinery plants scattered in eight provinces. It had exported metallurgical equipment, internal combustion engines, large-sized farming machinery, automobile components, hardware and tools, as well as various ships (SG, 1995: 8).

Construction Capacity. By 1985, Shougang had eight construction companies, comprising the Shougang Construction Corporation, with a total of 80 000 employees. They were engaged in the construction, installation and commissioning of blast furnaces, steel-making factories, oxygen plants, power stations, and other heavy auxiliary equipment relating to the steel industry. In 1991, the annual output of steel structures exceeded 10 000 tons, all of which was for Shougang

TABLE **9-25 Employment Structure at Shougang, 1998**

Sections of the Group	No. of employees
Iron and steel	83 311
Core steel mills	46 722
Construction	48 576
Machinery	58 956
Electronics	2 690
Overseas companies	2 927
Others, including mining	21 492
Grand total	217 952

SOURCE: SG (1998: 2)

NOTE: The employees at the Hierro mine in Peru are not included in the employment statistics usually quoted for Shougang, they would be conventionally included in the figures reported for a Western multinational, since the mine is wholly owned by Shougang. It is not clear if the figures for the workers at the Qian'an Mines in Hebei are included in the officially reported figure for total employment at Shougang. Official data record a total of over 26 000 employees in Shougang's iron ore mines within China (ISIC, 1997: 166)

itself (*Beijing Review*, 13–19 January 1992: 16; Salomon Brothers, 1994: 11). In 1992, as we have seen, Shougang took over a further two construction companies, mainly in order to meet the anticipated construction needs of the Qilu plant.

Electronic Control Capability. In 1984, Shougang began to computerize management control systems with a total of only eight specialists in charge of computer hardware development, software design and installation. Over the course of three years' intense effort they automated four converters (Ai, 1992: 190). By 1994, Shougang Electronics Corporation employed 3000 technicians and professionals experienced in electronics design, programming, engineering and manufacturing. In 1990 through Mesta, Shougang's purchase in the USA (see below), ten of Shougang's engineers carried out the design, programming and engineering of two computerized supervisory and process control systems for seven basic oxygen furnaces of USX (formerly US Steel), the leading steelmaker in the USA (Salomon Brothers, 1994: 11), and for the Geneva Steel Works in Switzerland (*Beijing Review*, 27 January 1992: 30).

In 1990, Shougang and NEC (Japan) set up a \$200 million JV designed to produce 50 million integrated circuits a year.[54] Sixty per cent of the capital for the JV was contributed by Shougang. China's capability in micro-electronics was then relatively backward, and the JV was an important aspect of the country's technological modernization. By 1996, Shougang NEC had become China's largest semiconductor manufacturer (*FT*, 24 January 1996). In January 1996, NEC announced that they were investing a further \$114 million in the Shougang JV, in order to start manufacturing advanced memory chips (*FT*, 24 January 1996).[55] The production technology of the JV was significantly upgraded, in order to be able to manufacture 0.5 micron and six-inch IC chips. The expanded JV made NEC Shougang the first firm in China to manufacture value-added semiconductors. Hitherto, all semiconductors had been restricted to assembly, rather than fabrication. The technology is among the most advanced in the world. The price of this expansion has been that NEC's control of the operation was significantly increased, raising its share of the ownership rights from the original 40 per cent to 51 per cent (*China: Economic Digest*, *Spring*, 1996: 52).

This was the first such venture in China. At first sight it appears to be an example of irrational diversification by Shougang into areas far removed from the core business. However, when in the mid-1980s New Japan Steel and other top Japanese integrated steel producers diversified into the production of silicon wafers and semiconductor manufacturing, 'the move astonished the business world, since it seemed unnatural for steel firms to diversify into the high-tech business' (Yonekura, 1994: 258). Shougang's ultimate goal in the JV was not just to produce the integrated circuits, but, more importantly, to develop downstream products using the integrated circuits from the JV (and the steel and machinery from other branches of Shougang). These activities typically have higher profit rates than the direct production of integrated circuits. Within a few years, Shougang planned to start production of computers, fax machines, video recorders, TVs and video cameras.

Design Capability. In 1993, Shougang allocated 320 million yuan to scientific development, equivalent to 2.5 per cent of total sales value and around 10 per cent of total profits in that year. As we have seen, leading Western steel firms typically spend under 2 per cent of their revenue on research and development. Moreover, a major element in Western firms' R & D outlays is the vastly higher wages paid to their researchers. A powerful long-run influence stimulating the future location of research and development activities within the multinational company is the much lower salaries paid in the developing economies to people of equal technical abilities to those in the advanced economies. In 1980 Shougang had a total of around 2500 research personnel. By 1994, Shougang had three design institutes and 72 research institutes, employing a total of around 8000 full-time research personnel. This was an enormous expansion of Shougang's research capability. It constituted a potential source of competitive advantage compared to even the most powerful multinational steel company.

Shougang's research departments were capable of undertaking the engineering design of large and medium-sized ferrous metal mines, iron and steel complexes, industrial and civil construction projects, municipal facilities, and thermal power stations as well as plant design for the chemical, construction material and food industries (SG, 1995). By the early 1990s, Shougang had developed the capability to produce every component for an integrated steel plant with hot-rolling capability for steel flats. In 1991, Shougang manufactured its first complete blast furnace in which all the parts, including the computer control system, were produced within the Corporation.

Shougang's technical capability was greatly extended by its policy on overseas' acquisition. In July 1988, Shougang Corporation purchased 70 per cent of the shares of the Mesta Engineering Company in Pittsburgh for $3.4 million. This famous company was founded in 1888 and was involved in the design and production of rolling mills, continuous casters and their supporting equipment. It has designed more than 600 rolling mills world-wide. More than half of the total working rolling mills in the world have the Mesta trademark. At the time of its purchase by Shougang, Mesta was one of the technological leaders in the world's metallurgy industry. It possessed about 850 design blueprints to make rolling mills and continuous-casting mills, 46 computer software packages, 41 still effective licenced patents and two trademark registrations.

The purpose of this purchase was to combine Mesta's technology with Shougang's own machine-making capability in order to manufacture large continuous-casting and steel rolling equipment for both domestic and overseas clients. For instance, in September 1992, Mesta's technical strength and international reputation enabled Shougang to win the bid to design and manufacture a bolt plate leveller for the Portland Plant of Morgan Steel Mills Inc. (*Beijing Review*, 10–16 October 1988).[56] This gave Shougang a powerful design capability both to assist the growth of its own continuous-casting capability, and to be well-positioned to meet growing domestic and international demand for continuous-casting equipment. The share of continuously cast steel world-wide rose from 49 per cent in 1986 to 70 per cent in the mid-1990s. In the developed economies the share is typically 90 per cent or above (Table 9-3). In China, the share is predicted to rise rapidly from around one-third currently to over 70 per cent by the year 2000 (ECB, 1995: 31).

After the purchase, Shougang installed its own Chinese president at the head of the company (Wang, 1993: 242–50). Then, the company, co-operating with Shougang's engineers, immediately designed a technologically advanced 2060 mm hot-rolling mill for Shougang to upgrade its product quality so that Shougang could supply high quality steel to the motor vehicle industry (Liu, Liu and Gan, 1994). Since China's motor industry began to take off in the 1980s, wide sheets and tubes for the industry have accounted for a large share of China's steel imports: in 1991 they stood at 88 per cent of steel imports (WCFL, 1993: 35). There is a potentially large and fast-growing market for high quality domestic steel supply to the motor vehicle industry.

Mining Capability. China's iron ore is mostly of poor grade, with an iron content of only 30–35 per cent on average. As a result, Chinese-mined iron ore typically requires expensive dressing. Only 3 per cent of its deposits exceed 50 per cent iron content, compared with over 55 per cent iron content for Australian and Brazilian ores. One estimate is that by the year 2010, China will need to import around 100 million tons of iron ore annually, worth $3.2 billion at today's prices (Liu, Liu and Gan, 1994: 46), which is equivalent to one-quarter of the total amount of iron ore traded world-wide today.

The domestic shortage of iron ore has prompted representatives from many large Chinese iron and steel works to look for foreign sources of supply.[57] From the mid-1980s onwards Shougang began to try to open channels for the import of iron ore and for co-operation with overseas mining firms. In November 1992, Shougang purchased the Hierro iron mine in Peru for $120 million. This was the biggest purchase abroad by a Chinese institution (Liu, Liu and Gan, 1994). The reserves were estimated to have a life of around 40 years at an annual rate of production of around 15 million tons. Shougang placed the Hierro Peru mine under the jurisdiction of its own mine, Qian'an. The company sent officials and technicians to Peru, taking over the management of the mine at the beginning of 1993. The Qian'an mine trained hundreds of Chinese employees in Spanish. Output in 1993 was only 5.1 million tons, but Shougang planned to raise the output to 15 million tons within three years.

A major objective of the purchase was to guarantee the supply of raw material for Qilu. It was thought also that it might provide a secure and relatively cheap source of iron ore supply for Shougang in Beijing, as well as supplying other Chinese steel plants. Shougang estimated it would be around $10 per ton cheaper to import iron ore from the Hierro mine than to import it from Australia. The purchase has been the subject of much controversy and is discussed below.

Shipping Capability. Freight charges amounted to around one-third to one-half of the total purchase price of Shougang's purchases of the second-hand equipment (Wang, 1993: 235).[58] The high price of freight led Shougang to set up a shipping

JV with Hong Kong Hongda Shipping Company. In 1990, the JV company merged with Zhenjiang Shipping Company with 84 000 tons capacity in ocean-going transportation, with nearly 2000 employees, to form Shougang Shipping and Ship Construction Company.[59] By 1994, it had a total transportation capacity of 2.4 million tons. Prior to Zhou Guanwu's retirement, Shougang had planned to build a huge new deep-water harbour at Qian'an in Hebei province, close to its mine, using rock from the mine. The harbour was to be used as the basis for entering shipbuilding on a large scale. Shougang planned to construct large ships of 100 000–200 000 tons depending on the state of the world market.

Export Capability. On 23 October 1992, Shougang spent $20 million to purchase 51 per cent of the shares of a steel trading company in Hong Kong, Tung Wing Iron and Steel Ltd. This firm accounted for more than one-third of Hong Kong's steel and iron trade (Wang, 1993: 207; *Metal Bulletin Monday*, 10 May 1993). By using this trading company's network, Shougang greatly enlarged its export capability at a stroke (Liu, Liu and Gan, 1994). Hong Kong's consumption of construction steels is huge. Rebar consumption alone was estimated at about 1 million tons per year in 1991. By 1993, Shougang controlled seven listed companies in Hong Kong, with $1.54 billion worth of assets (*CDBW*, 20 February 1994: 2; *SCMP*, 29 January 1994).[60] In 1995, Shougang Southeast Asia Holdings was registered in Singapore to further facilitate steel exports in Southeast Asia. Its next step was to have been a bid to be listed on the US stock market. Shougang's next goal was to penetrate the European and American steel markets.

Innovation combined with technical renovation raised some of Shougang's design and manufacturing technologies to advanced world levels. A number of patent technologies, such as bell tops for blast furnaces, top burning hot-air induction stoves and pulverized coal injection furnaces, were transferred to some developed countries, including the USA, Japan, Britain and Luxembourg. Shougang's metallurgical and automation technologies gained increasing popularity with foreign enterprises, especially in developing countries. Some of these contracted with Shougang for the provision of technology, design, consulting services and personnel training. For example, Chagra Steel of Indonesia was unable to regulate the automatic control system of the steel-rolling production line it imported from Germany in 1992. It turned to Shougang requesting it to provide a complete set of equipment, as well as spare parts and technology, for the automatic system. Soon afterwards, a contract valued at $1.15 million was agreed between Chagra and Shougang (*Beijing Review*, 4–10 October 1993: 18–19).

Shougang believes there is a large long-run opportunity for the sale of steel making equipment in East and Southeast Asia. The region's steel production is certain to rise fast. Shougang has developed a manufacturing capability in a potentially fast growing market in East and Southeast Asia, namely continuous-casting technology. The equipment from Europe and America is typically too expensive and too modern for developing country consumers in the region. The only serious regional competitors in the supply of steel industry equipment in the early 1990s were South Korea and Japan, but both faced much higher costs of production than Shougang.

In the early 1980s, Shougang exported a mere 15 kinds of roughly processed products such as pig iron, steel billet, castings and cast iron pipes. By the early 1990s, its growth strategy had led it into a steadily strengthening position as an exporter of steel products, machinery and knowledge. By 1993, it was exporting around 260 different products, including construction steel via Hong Kong, complete sets of metallurgical equipment, building materials, chemicals, rare gases, farm machinery, ships, diesel engines, bicycles and body-building equipment. These products had made their way into more than 40 countries and regions in North America, Western Europe and Southeast Asia.

By 1992, Shougang's foreign exchange earnings had reached $350 million. This figure represented 17 per cent of Shougang's total revenue. Exports of machinery and electronic equipment alone reached $94 million, or 27 per cent of its total foreign exchange earnings (*Beijing Review*, 4–10 October 1993: 17–18). By 1993, Shougang had become much the most important single exporting firm in China's manufacturing sector. By 1996, Shougang's exports had risen to $1.03 billion (UNCTAD, 1998: 48), sustaining its position as much the largest manufacturing exporter in China. By 1996, Shougang had entered the ranks of the world's top 30 TNCs from developing countries, ranked twenty-second by value of assets, with a total value of sales close to that of Singapore Airlines and Hutchison Whampoa[61] (UNCTAD, 1998: 48–9). Shougang's foreign sales in 1996 totalled $1.03 billion, accounting for 24 per cent of its total revenue (UNCTAD, 1998: 48). Shougang's share of China's rapidly-growing exports rose from 0.10 per cent in 1990 to 0.68 per cent in 1993, and remained at 0.68 per cent in 1996. This was an exceptionally high share for a single firm. To sustain such a high share during the period of China's explosive export growth was a remarkable performance.

Summary. The main path of Shougang's growth under the contract system was within iron and steel. Its diversification was mainly into closely-related sectors. Its expansion path provides a striking illustration of the impact of economies of scope in a transitional developing economy. The core plant's engineering capabilities, management skills, marketing networks, and investment capital were used to transform domestic merged enterprises. It re-specialized the newly-merged firms so that they were able to meet Shougang's particular technological requirements. Shougang built up the newly merged firms' capabilities through further diversification, transnationalization and exports as specialist producers. A powerful stimulus to technical change in the merged enterprises was produced by the fact that they mostly were supplying the fast-growing needs of the core firm, and were required to meet Shougang's quality and timeliness demands. Its foreign company purchases greatly added to the firm's technical capabilities, assured its raw material supply and much enhanced its export capabilities, both through raising its technical level and by the possession of firms through which Shougang's products could penetrate world markets.

Shougang's expansion outside the core iron and steel business was characterized by the construction of a closely integrated multi-plant firm, with powerful synergies between the component parts. The expanded firm was more powerful than merely the sum of the individual parts. Only a small fraction of Shougang's diversification can be described as pure profit seeking unrelated to steel production. The main examples of this were investments in hotels and apartment blocks. Shougang had held discussions with many firms outside its core business with a view to setting up JVs, including McDonald's, Coca-Cola and PepsiCo, but had decided not to proceed in these directions.

CONCLUSIONS

Shougang under Zhou Guanwu. Analyses of Shougang have focused almost exclusively on the expanded autonomy given to Shougang as the explanation of its exceptional growth under the contract system. This chapter has argued that a relatively high degree of autonomy compared to other state enterprises is not a sufficient explanation. Many other enterprises adopted the 'Shougang system', but few were as successful as Shougang. The most outstanding success story using the 'Shougang' contract system was Erqi, China's number two motor vehicle manufacturer. No one has seriously suggested that the contract system is sufficient to explain Erqi's rapid growth after the early 1980s.[62]

A distinctive feature of Shougang's growth was the central role for industrial entrepreneurship. The government's reforms encouraged entrepreneurship in a general sense, but did not specifically target industrial entrepreneurship. Industrial entrepreneurs played an important role in the rise of big business in the West. People such as Ford and Carnegie who devoted their entire working life to building an empire in one sector of the economy are very different from the classic entrepreneur, for whom the technical characteristics of the entrepreneurial activity are irrelevant. The goal is to switch capital to whatever yields the highest return over a specific period. In a sense, the industrial entrepreneurs of early big business in the West can be thought of as economically irrational. Whereas Carnegie fought for supremacy within steel, its successor, USX, has diversified into oil as the main line of business. Yonekura contrasts the integrated diversification at New Japan Steel with that at the New US Steel: 'Nippon Steel utilized accumulated technology in its diversification moves. This was in sharp contrast to the situation with its American counterparts. US Steel Corporation (now USX), for example, diversified into the oil business ... while National Steel diversified into financial services and food business ... The Americans seemed to utilize only accumulated capital, while technological continuity did not appear so important' (Yonekura, 1994: 259).

In China during the period of the contract system at Shougang there were numerous outlets for investment capital, including many forms of short-term speculation. The rational choice for profit-making enterprises, state-owned and private enterprises alike, often was not to invest in long-gestating industrial projects, such as the Qilu steel plant, with all the complex of investments associated with it. Rather, it was frequently more rational to reinvest profits into speculation, such as property, or deposit funds in financial institutions. Frequently, those Chinese firms which issued shares abroad held on to their inflow of cash, using it for short-term speculative gain rather than the long-term industrial investment, which they informed potential investors was their main aim in going to the stock market. Shougang's firm focus on growth within the steel industry and related businesses is all the more striking in that its period of most rapid technological up-grading was the early 1990s, which coincided with a property speculation boom in which most Chinese firms participated, whether or not they were state-owned. Shougang's ambition was for projects rather than profits, so that it might become the world's number one steel producer. Industrial entrepreneurs like those at Shougang work for growth within their industry rather than for short-term profit maximization.

For an industrial entrepreneur, such as Zhou Guanwu or Nishiyama Yataro of Kawasaki, competition is about battles for growth, modernization and supremacy, with profits as the means for growth rather than the end purpose. In order to be victorious, industrial entrepreneurs may organize their firms as troops fighting a battle rather than as contractual institutions, but in the fight there is no room for democracy and negotiation, nor even a guarantee that everyone will become better off. Rather, there is a unified command system, strict discipline, full mobilization, and well-organized rear-service support. If necessary, part of the army can be sacrificed. To succeed in battle, there can be no free-riding.

From the early 1980s to the mid-1990s, Shougang's behaviour was sharply against the mainstream thinking of neo-classical economics. It raised many doubts in the public perception. There were many criticisms not only from outside, but from inside Shougang also. This was the price of building a fighting unit, rather than one whose goal was profit maximization. Shougang challenged not only the traditional theory of the firm, but also the liberal neo-classical ideology which was battling for supremacy in China.

Integrated Diversification. Shougang's growth in the period of the contract system was unusual among late industrializing giant companies. Lacking the proprietary technology to permit growth mainly through core business activities, such firms typically have grown through diversification into largely unrelated activities (Amsden and Hikino, 1994). In contrast to these firms, Shougang's main growth occurred through massive investment in modernization and capacity expansion in its main line of business, iron and steel production. Its main basis of expansion was the growth of domestic demand in traditional steel products. The huge growth in demand for steel during the reform period helped to cushion the reform process for large-scale enterprises such as Shougang. It is easier to reform a firm if it is confronted by buoyant demand, than if demand is stagnant or falling. The demand-side stimulus enabled Shougang to generate large profits in its core business, namely ordinary steel products, simultaneously generating profits with which to reinvest and rapidly modernize the technological basis of production.

However, it was able simultaneously to use its vast capital resources to expand rapidly into activities outside the core business, but these were almost entirely in spheres closely related to the core business, such as shipbuilding, electronics, heavy machinery manufacturing and mining. A major feature of the expansion of non-core businesses was the stimulus given to the growth of these activities by internal demand from Shougang's expansion in the iron and steel sector. Demand from the core business of iron and steel, especially its rapid modernization, placed pressure on internal supplier units to grow and modernize to meet the needs of the core business. Quality and timeliness of supply from within the Shougang Group were critical to Shougang's overall modernization efforts. The logic pushing towards expansion of the Shougang Group into ownership rights in related supplier activities was especially strong in a poor transitional economy such as China's with weakly developed market systems. Shougang had a flagship role, leading supplier units forward. Unlike the relationship with independent supplier firms, the absorption of many key input suppliers into ownership by the Shougang Group gave Shougang a strong incentive to improve the capabilities of supplier units through the transfer of technology and management capability, since the transfer would result in benefits internalized within the Shougang system.

If an international consultancy firm had sent a mission to Shougang in the mid-1970s, they would probably have recommended that a large proportion of the workforce be fired as they were surplus to requirements. Shougang's experience shows that with sufficiently rapid growth it is possible usefully to re-deploy surplus workers in a state-run plant which initially has substantial surplus labour. The growth in employment opportunities in Shougang came from both expansion in the steel sector as well as diversification into other lines of production. Moreover, this growth occurred with simultaneous rapid advance in the degree of automation and a sharp decline in labour input in the first front of steel production.

Organizational Capabilities in the Pre-reform Communist Institutions. A central proposition of the 'transition orthodoxy' about how to transform Communist economies was that the pre-reform Communist institutions should be destroyed. It was thought by almost everyone outside China's leadership that these institutions were implacably opposed to reform. Their interests were thought to be irreconcilable with the market economy. Their members were thought to be incapable of turning towards the market and competitive behaviour. The experience of Shougang shows that the Chinese Communist Party and the People's Liberation Army possessed a rich legacy of organizational and motivational skills. Even old Party cadres and army officers such as Zhou Guanwu possessed the capability to make the transition to the market economy if given the correct incentive structure. Indeed, their lifetime experience of thinking strategically and mobilizing people in complex institutions was a valuable weapon for the construction of an effective market-oriented business organization.

Institutional First Movers. The Communist planning system intentionally destroyed the competitive firm. Instead, the whole nation, in practice the relevant ministries, became the firm, with the enterprise the passive recipient of instructions from bureaucrats. A central part of the transition from command system to a market-based system was the re-creation of the competitive firm as the basic form of business institution. This can come in different shapes and sizes. The reasons that explain this are complex and often are specific to the firm concerned. When increased operational independence was granted to state-owned enterprises, some responded more quickly than others to construct a competitive institutional structure. Those that were able to do so rapidly improved their market position: Shougang rose from seventh largest to third largest steel manufacturer in China.

A striking feature of large multinational firms has been the relative stability of position once they have achieved large size. Those large firms that are able to take the lead in the Chinese big business race may well be able to maintain their position for a long time, whatever are the short-term fluctuations in government attitudes towards a particular firm. In the process of institutional reorganization discussed in the preceding section, the individual enterprises, which gradually were acquiring firm-like characteristics, were not passive observers. With enhanced enterprise autonomy, they were active agents in the complex institutional reorganization that was taking place alongside the explosive process of growth and modernization.

From State Factory to Modern Corporation? Can large plants in former command economies make substantial changes in their operating mechanism without privatization? This chapter suggest it is, indeed, possible for this to happen, even within the Soviet-assisted core of the command economies' heavy industrial sector.

Under the contract system, Shougang radically altered its method of operation. Instead of blindly carrying out the orders of higher authorities, it responded highly effectively to the opportunities offered by the surging demand for steel and its increased autonomy. Shougang's growth was quite different from that of Baogang, which had huge assistance from the government, received a great deal of foreign technical assistance to build a state-of-the-art integrated steel plant, and began life with vastly lower manning levels than traditional Chinese large steel plants. Shougang's growth came from internal accumulation and complex investment decisions. The goal of these was to produce rapid, low-cost expansions to production capacity, for example through purchasing second-hand equipment and adapting it through its own efforts. This was a classic example of learning-by-doing, initiated by the firm itself, not by the government.

Shougang invested extensively in setting up its own R & D capabilities so that it could itself upgrade the equipment it purchased. It demonstrated sophisticated business acumen in its programme of integrated diversification, at home and abroad. It became acutely aware of the need to compete internationally. It established a powerful system of human motivation though its ideology and organization, summarized by the slogan 'people are the base'. It diversified upstream to assure input supplies in the way that Carnegie and US Steel did in the late nineteenth and early twentieth century, and in order to assist its expansion within the steel sector. It diversified downstream into fabricated steel and other activities in pursuit of higher profits. It diversified into shipping in order to reduce transport costs and assure supplies. It substantially altered its product mix within steel in order to meet the demands of the market. It undertook a complex and enormous programme of merger and acquisition.

This amounted to a comprehensive change in business behaviour compared to the Maoist epoch. After 1978, under the contract system, and Zhou Guanwu's dynamic and highly centralized leadership, Shougang moved fast towards becoming a 'modern corporation'. Its autonomy was granted by the state, but Shougang's leadership exercised that autonomy in a highly effective fashion, albeit still within many constraints set by the government. Through its struggle to grow and modernize, Shougang steadily developed the sense of corporate identity that is a key characteristic separating the modern corporation from a state-administered plant.

Mergers. A large process of mergers developed in China under reform. The example of Shougang demonstrates how rapid growth in firm size can occur in the absence of privatization and a developed stock market, due to state-mediated merger by a state-owned firm. There were three main causes of this process.

First, it was due to the state requiring SOEs to assist the authorities in resolving the problems of loss-making enterprises by re-organizing their business structure, changing management methods and advancing technology. To this extent, it was a top-down process. An example of this in the case of Shougang was its merger with loss-making military enterprises, which seems to have been initiated by higher levels of government.

Secondly, it was due to bottom-up pressure from a successful, emerging large firm, of which Shougang is a prime example. A large part of Shougang's mergers came from its own initiatives, though they always required state mediation and sanction. China is not unique in this. Typically, mergers and take-overs among large capitalist firms are closely involved with the highly political process of obtaining approval from the relevant government anti-monopoly apparatus, both national and international,[63] and may often be brokered by the government.[64] Shougang's mergers used methods familiar under capitalism, whereby some firms acquire other loss-making firms believing that they can dig out hidden value, change their organizational structure and transform them into profitable entities. Bankruptcy is not the only way to resolve the problems of loss-making enterprises.

Merger may be an especially powerful process of advancing business capabilities in a transitional economy, since business and technical skills are not so widely available as in an advanced economy. The merger process led by capable firms such as Shougang with advanced technological and management skills, can have a powerful positive externality effect, spreading business capability more rapidly than would be the case in the absence of merger. Moreover, the pressure for mergers is reinforced in a poor transitional economy such as China. This provides especially large incentives for merger consequent upon the undeveloped state of market institutions, which inhibits the capacity to obtain needed inputs easily and reliably through contracts mediated by the market mechanism.

Thirdly, the merger movement was due to opportunism by large firms such as Shougang. They used their bargaining power with local governments to enhance the number of firms owned by them, in order to be able to increase the size of their business empire as property rights become more formalized and ownership become more tangible. To some degree (unknown),[65] this can be seen as a 'positioning' process, in anticipation of a possible future move towards more concrete private property rights being permitted over former state-owned enterprises. Through merger, a large state firm can acquire potential future assets of great value, including the land on which the firm is located. In principle, a merger between two state enterprises today, could bring considerable personal gain for some groups of people at a future point.

SHOUGANG SINCE THE CONTRACT SYSTEM

FINANCIAL RELATIONSHIPS WITH THE BEIJING CITY GOVERNMENT

We have seen that the contract system served a powerful stimulating function for the development of industrial entrepreneurship at Shougang. However, it was a relatively crude instrument for allocating the income stream from assets operated by the Shougang employees and managers. At the end of the formal date of the Shougang contract, namely December 1995, the contract was discontinued. By that point most other enterprises that had experimented with the same system had stopped using it. After the conclusion of the contract system in 1995, Shougang was technically supposed to hand over to the Beijing government only profits taxes and turnover taxes as laid down by law. However, the end of the contract system in practice seems to have made little difference to the system of 'hand-overs' to the Beijing city government. Indeed, Shougang continued to talk of 'hand-overs' and 'profits left with the company', and to organize financial data around these concepts (Table 9-21). The Beijing government appeared only to be interested in the global figure of hand-overs, not the detailed sub-headings under which they occurred.[66] Under these arrangements, the Beijing government directly reimburses Shougang all of its profits tax, which amounted to around 70 million yuan in 1997 (on pre-tax profits of 351 million yuan). However, Shougang has to pay 10 per cent of its total sales revenue as 'turnover tax' to the Beijing government (around 1.7 billion yuan in 1996 and 1.8 billion yuan in 1997), which is much higher than the profits tax reimbursement, and several times higher than the total retained profits, which were officially recorded as only 180–200 million yuan in 1995 and 1996.

The 'tax' payments from Shougang are vital for the Beijing government's finances, since these still account for around one-fifth of Beijing's total revenues generated from industry. It appears that the 'turnover tax' has replaced the contracted 'hand-overs' of the contract system as the 'preferred dividend' to the sole shareholder, the Beijing City government.

REASSESSMENT OF SHOUGANG'S STRATEGY

Under the contract responsibility system Shougang was able to advance at high speed. However, in the late 1990s, a radical re-assessment of Shougang's strategy took place. It was recognized that the Corporation's development was limited by several factors (SG, 1998). These included the poor products mix: high-value-added products accounted for only 12 per cent of total steel products (SG, 1998: 3), low profitability of second-tier companies, a heavy debt burden, and a large number of surplus workers. In order to finance the ambitious programme diversification in the early 1990s, mainly in order to develop the Qilu plant, Shougang had borrowed heavily. In 1996 Shougang's total debt was 18.4 billion yuan, of which 79 per cent was short-term (ISIC, 1997: 134–7). However, Angang's ratio of short-term to long-term debt was even higher, at 86 per cent. In 1996 the ratio of debt-to-assets stood at 50 per cent at Shougang, compared to 49 per cent at Angang and 66 per cent at Wugang (ISIC, 1997: 134–7). The Corporation recognized frankly the shortcomings of its management system (SG, 1998: 3–4). These included lack of clarity in the rights held by the legal person, overlapping personnel and functions between the Board of Directors and the management group, and lack of clarity in relationships with the subordinate 'child' companies: 'Shougang still has a great deal of work to do if it wishes its enterprise management system to meet the demands of the market economy' (SG, 1998: 4).

In June 1998 Shougang's Board of Directors outlined five development strategies for taking Shougang into the twenty-first century:

- establishing a modern management system;
- extending the integrated development of information technology and electronics industries;
- developing the tertiary sector;
- continued restructuring and technological upgrading of the traditional industries;
- continued overseas businesses development.

ESTABLISHMENT OF A MODERN MANAGEMENT SYSTEM

As we have seen, under the contract system, within the Shougang Group, only the Shougang headquarters was a 'legal person'. The personification of this was the Corporation Head, Zhou Guanwu. Shougang's subsidiaries were all 'entrusted' by the legal person at Shougang headquarters with the right to sign contracts (*weituoren*). Zhou Guanwu alone had the legal right to sign contracts, and to bear the accompanying responsibilities. If the 'entrusted' company failed to carry out the contract, legal recourse was to Zhou Guanwu. Following the termination of the contract responsibility in 1995, Shougang began slowly to transform itself toward a limited company, with clearly defined obligations and responsibilities between the core and second-tier subsidiaries. From 1998 onward, this transformation process will be accelerated. The following are the main features of this transformation:

- The State Council assigned the shareholder's responsibility to the Beijing municipal government. Shougang Corporation (the core company) was renamed as Beijing Shougang (Group) Company Limited, and was re-registered (Figure 9-1). The Beijing government designated Beijing Shougang (Group) Company Limited (BSGCL) as the core company with the authority to enforce its shareholder's rights upon second-tier companies within the Shougang Group (SG, 1998: 17, 31).

- Shougang will separate off seven production units (including the No. 2 Iron Mill, No. 2 Steel Mill, No. 2 and No. 3 Wire Rod Plants) to form the Beijing Shougang Stock Holding Company Limited. This entity will be listed as an A-share company on the Chinese stock market, and it will include around one-third of the total value of Shougang's steel assets.[67] Over time, other steel production lines will be incorporated into the Beijing Shougang Stock Holding Company through periodically issuing new shares. After this round of restructuring, the Beijing Shougang Stock Holding Company Limited will become a second-tier company within the Group (BSGCL). In 1999, some of the second-tier companies were to be restructured into either stock holding limited companies or limited companies, by following the path of Beijing Shougang (SG, 1998: 5–6, 18, 32). Cross-holding of shares between second-tier subsidiaries is to be permitted.

- The obligations and responsibilities between the shareholders and the companies are becoming more clearly defined. The 'child' companies have been turned into 'legal persons', with all the associated rights and responsibilities. They have managerial and financial autonomy. The main shareholder, BSGCL, is not allowed to intervene in their daily operation. Economic transactions between the core and second-tier company (or among second-tier companies) must be based on market principles. For example, transactions between them must take place at market prices.

- A hierarchical managerial system with the Board of Directors, Managers and a Monitoring Committee in the core and second-tier companies has been established (Figure 9-1). The Board of Directors in the core company is assigned by the central government, with a three-year term of office. A worker representative is entitled to sit on the board. The General Managers and members of the Monitoring Committee also are assigned by the government. The Monitoring Committee's task is to supervise the Board of

Directors and the General Managers. None of its members can simultaneously sit on the board of Directors or the General Management Team. The
second-tier company with diversified investment must hold an annual shareholders' meeting (SG, 1998: 19–20).

- Shougang is establishing throughout the Group a system of professionalized
  employment, in terms of recruitment, training and re-training, promotion,
  demotion and redundancy. Employees must undertake routine tests to evaluate their technical skills. Those that fail the tests must receive re-training or
  accept voluntary redundancy (that is, re-assignment to subsidiaries). The
  administrative personnel and cadres are recruited according to their capabilities, using open recruitment tests. The remuneration system is to be based
  on productivity. Each individual constituent company within the Group,
  including both the core company and the second-tier companies, has the
  right to establish its own remuneration system. It is accepted that in order to
  raise productivity, income differentiation within the Group will increase
  (SG, 1998: 28, 30).

In 1997, there was a total of 71 second-tier companies, of which 25 were loss-
makers, with losses totalling 830 million yuan. By 2000, through the managerial
and other complementary reforms (see below), Shougang aims to reduce losses
by 80 per cent, or 664 million yuan, and to eliminate loss-makers entirely by
2005 (SG, 1998: 6).

ELIMINATING ACTUAL OR POTENTIALLY LOSS-MAKING BUSINESSES
FROM THE GROUP

A number of businesses has been sold or substantially restructured since the end
of the contract system and a number of expansion plans has been dropped.
Much of the change of direction stems from the failure of Shougang to obtain
approval from the central government to expand steel production outside Beijing.
Shougang's plans to develop large new steel production facilities outside Beijing,
at Qilu and Liuzhou have been dropped. This immediately had some important
consequences for the Group's business structure.

The plant purchased from Kaiser Steel in California was intended for the Qilu
Steel Plant. The Kaiser Steel Plant has been sold to Baotou Steel Company (Inner
Mongolia). Including the cost of transporting and dismantling the plant, Shougang
made a substantial loss on the whole transaction.

One reason for the take-over of heavy machinery plants was in order to build
new steel making facilities. The Heavy Machinery Corporation is in the process of
being profoundly restructured. The Kaifeng Heavy Machinery Company was
'given' back to Henan Province, for which Shougang had to pay around 30 million
yuan in compensation. However, the Kaifeng Company only employed around
3000 people. This still leaves the Heavy Machinery Corporation with around

50 000 employees, mainly in former military enterprises, which cannot easily be restructured to make profits. The sector is heavily loss-making, and constitutes a large drain on the Group's balance sheet.

If the Qilu plans had gone ahead, Shougang would have needed greatly increased supplies of coal, iron ore and would have needed to ship large quantities of iron ore from abroad. With the collapse of the Qilu project, Shougang's shipping fleet has been placed into a joint venture with P & O. Shougang's plans to enter coal production in Shaanxi and Inner Mongolia have been dropped. As we have seen, Shougang owns a large iron-ore complex at Qian'an. The three main constituent mines employ over 26 000 people and produce around 5.4 million tons of iron ore concentrate annually (ISIC, 1997: 166). An investment of 120 million yuan will be injected into the Mining Corporation in the next three years to reduce its debts and improve the production efficiency (SG, 1998: 5–6, 13–14). However, plans are for production to be substantially scaled back in order to concentrate on raising efficiency.

INTEGRATED DEVELOPMENT OF IT AND ELECTRONIC INDUSTRIES

We have seen above that Shougang's ambitious plans to enter a variety of activities related to steel production have been sharply curtailed since the end of the contract system. The main focus of Shougang's expansion outside steel in the period ahead is to centre on two activities, information technology/electronics and real estate.

By 2000, Shougang aims to develop integrated information technology (IT) and electronics industries and increase the electronic sector's revenues from 1.6 billion yuan to 3.2 billion yuan. To achieve this goal, Shougang has established the Shougang High Technology Development Office to co-ordinate the development of this branch of the Group. In addition, Shougang will inject another one billion yuan to import technology through establishing Sino-foreign JVs, to cultivate domestic R & D capability, and to accelerate the transformation of technological advances into commercially applicable products (SG, 1998: 7–9).

Shougang NEC is the centrepiece in the development of Shougang's electronics capability. Shougang and NEC together will invest a further $150 million in the JV. This will raise the technological manufacturing capability from the present 0.5 micrometers to 0.35 micrometers, increase the production capacity of integrated circuits (IC) from 54 million to 120 million units, and production capacity of chips from 60 000 to 96 000 units. The advances in chip and IC manufacturing capacities in Shougang NEC will assist the development of the newly established robots manufacturing firm ('Motorman' Robotics), a Sino–Japanese JV started in 1997. In 1998 it will sell 70 units, with a value of 27 million yuan, and intends to expand quickly to 800 units with a sales revenue of 400 million yuan. The goal is to sell to both the domestic and the international market.

Shougang hopes these two major projects can act as the catalyst for the development of an integrated IT and electronics industry and generate substantial revenues in the twenty-first century. These form the key part of Shougang's attempt to increase the share of the non-steel sector in total Group revenues. By 2010, Shougang aims to increase the share of non-steel industry to account for more than 50 per cent of total Group revenues, up from 46 per cent in 1997 (SG, 1998: 6, 8).

DEVELOPMENT OF THE TERTIARY SECTOR

Shougang cannot radically downsize employment. This is not possible on social grounds, since the enterprise leaders still treat Shougang as a 'large family' to whom it has ultimate responsibility. Moreover, in the absence of a state-provided social safety net, the consequences of enforced redundancy for families so affected are severe, especially during a period when the economy is growing less rapidly than in previous years. Large-scale lay-offs at Shougang would create a severe social problem for Beijing. The socio–economic environment in China is very different from that in Europe and the USA, with extensive social welfare and large redundancy payments provisions from the company itself to cushion the shock of unemployment. Even middle-income Brazil experienced large-scale social upheaval during the large-scale downsizing that followed the privatizations of the early 1990s. Shougang's alternative strategy has been to re-assign to the newly-developed real estate and service sectors, employees who are redundant in the iron and steel sector. Shougang estimates that roughly one-third of its total employees are redundant (SG, 1998: 34).

Shougang Real Estate Stock Holding Company has been established to expand Shougang's real estate activities. The Company is owned by both the core and the second-tier companies within the Group. Shougang has several advantages in developing its real estate business. It owns about two million square metres of property in the centre of Beijing. Shougang itself spends around 400 million yuan per annum on workers' accommodation. It is China's largest manufacturer of construction steel products. It has a huge construction company employing around 50 000 people. Shougang Real Estate Stock Holding Company has a total targeted capital of 10 billion yuan. Shougang's aim is that the Company generate revenues of 600 million yuan by the year 2000 (SG, 1998: 9–10).

Alongside the development of the real estate sector, the Group has established the Shougang Service Company. Already, around 400 000 Shougang employees and their families live in housing owned by Shougang. Over the next three years, Shougang will build another 2 million square metres of housing (1 million square metres is for workers' accommodation and the other million is for private accommodation). We have already seen that rents are charged at only nominal rates. Gradual commercialization of the management of this huge stock of property will provide an important source of employment and income. By the year 2000, Shougang aims to generate 270 million yuan from the Service Company. Eventually, the Service Company will become an independent business entity.

Other small-scale welfare units within the Group will be allowed to merge, to form joint stock companies, to contract out their services, to re-organize and even to go bankrupt. The ultimate goal is to transform them all into financially self-sufficient companies (SG, 1998: 10–11, 31).

RESTRUCTURING AND TECHNOLOGICAL UPGRADING OF IRON AND STEEL

The Beijing City government has set a limit of around 8 million tons steel making capacity at Shougang, in line with its goal of changing the production structure of Beijing towards knowledge-based, high value-added products with new and high technologies (Luo Bingsheng, 1998). In order to expand the value of its output, Shougang needs to shift towards high value-added steel products. Moreover, it needs to focus on generating increased profits from an output capacity which the Beijing government officially wishes to limit to 8 million tons. Accordingly, Shougang's main objectives in iron and steel are to improve product quality, increase the share of high value-added products, and improve product variety. However, Beijing Municipality still obtains a large fraction of its industrial revenue from Shougang. It is thought that in practice, the City government may have little alternative but to support expanded steel capacity at Shougang. Moreover, although the central government has prohibited the construction of new large steel plants, the government's commitment to build four internationally competitive steel companies is quite consistent with Shougang merging with a major producer outside Beijing.

Shougang plans also to improve still further the application of computers to automate the production process, and improve production efficiency so as to reduce the inputs per unit of finished product and reduce the emission of pollutants. Moreover, as we have seen, the degree of control over the large integrated steel plants' production structure has drastically declined. This was symbolized by the change in 1998 in the Ministry of Metallurgical Industries (*Ye Jin Bu*) into the Bureau of Metallurgical Industries. This means that there are no longer any bureaucratic constraints upon Shougang expanding production of high value-added steel products.

Renovation of the No. 3 Steel Mill was completed in 1998. Upgrading of the No. 2 Steel Mill will soon be completed. A 2160 mm hot-rolled mill will soon be installed, significantly enhancing Shougang's product mix. To enhance further the role of high value-added products, steel products are increasingly to be manufactured into semi-finished or finished form, according to the customers' specifications. The general strategy is to improve the whole production and marketing processes from the selection and preparation of iron ores to the distribution and after-sales services. Shougang aims to raise the share of high value-added steel products from a mere 12 per cent in 1997, to 30 per cent in 2005, and over 60 per cent in 2010 (SG, 1998: 7). By 2000, it intends to raise average annual productivity per employee to more than 209 000 yuan (over $25 000) and 380 tons per year (SG, 1998: 6–7, 11–12).

Shougang aims to control the emission of carbon sulphur, carbon particles and other pollutants. The renovation of No. 2 Coking Plant will lead to an enormous reduction of carbon sulphur and particles contained in the emitted gases. To recover and make use of steel discarded during the production processes, Shougang is investing 50 million yuan to construct a new oxygen converter production line with an annual capacity of 1.2 million tons. This new converter is able to recycle the iron dust from the open-hearth and blast furnaces. Shougang aims to raise the waste water treatment rate to 100 per cent and recycle 95 per cent of waste water by 2005 (SG, 1998: 12–13). The above technological improvements will not only reduce the emission of pollutants, but also reduce the production costs of Shougang through re-cycling of solid wastes and sewage water.

To restructure the Group, the development strategy of the Shougang Special Steel Corporation will be integrated with that of the other steel mills and will cease to duplicate the production of items produced in other Shougang steel mills. Shougang is very keen to establish a JV project with a leading multinational steel company to develop high-value-added steel products. Shougang has identified light construction steel as a key route to enhance its capabilities in high-value-added steels.

FURTHER DEVELOPMENT IN OVERSEAS BUSINESSES

By 1996, Shougang had become one of the leading TNCs from developing countries, ranked twenty-second by value of overseas assets. Shougang's objective is still to build itself into 'a large enterprise group, which is trans-regional, trans-industrial, trans-ownership and trans-national in production and management' (Luo Bingsheng, 1998). In 1996 its foreign employment amounted to only 1600, comprising less than one per cent of its total employment (UNCTAD, 1998: 48). However, its overseas assets were valued at $1.6 billion, amounting to 24 per cent of the Group's total assets[68] and its foreign sales amounted to $1.0 billion, amounting to 24 per cent of its total revenue (UNCTAD, 1998: 48).

Through China Shougang International Trading and Engineering Corporation (CSITEC), Shougang aims to develop further the export markets and generate more revenues in Southeast Asia, South America and Africa (Figure 9-1). The Beijing government strongly supports Shougang's continued efforts to become a major international company. Shougang plans to set up a new company in Lima (Peru), in partnership with the Beijing government, to develop further the South American market, both for its own products and for those of the Beijing municipality.

Shougang intends to develop its capability as an exporter of turnkey steel projects to third world countries, using its design, manufacturing, and installation capabilities. It has already exported steel-making facilities to developing Asian countries, and it is beginning to penetrate the African market. It is completing a blast furnace project in Zimbabwe, and intends to make this a focus for further expansion in Africa. It hopes to win the contract to build further facilities in Zimbabwe, including a converter, continuous caster and rolling facilities.

In Hong Kong, it is intended that Shougang Holdings (Hong Kong) will play an enhanced role in raising capital to restructure and renovate the core and second-tier companies in China. It is intended also to be a vehicle through which Hong Kong and foreign capital can participate in JV projects. In order to modernize and regularize the structure of Shougang Holdings (Hong Kong) it aims to reduce substantially the debt–asset ratio of Shougang Hong Kong, which stood at 32.5 per cent in 1997. Shougang aims to reduce the company's debt from HK$1.17 billion to HK$300 million in 1998. It intends to inject high quality assets from the mainland into the Hong Kong vehicle.

As we have seen, Shougang made a major decision in 1993 to purchase the Hierro Iron Ore Mine in Peru. The decision was much-criticized, and it was widely believed that Shougang had substantially overpaid for the purchase. The Hierro mine covers a large area, totalling 680 square kilometres. The purchase was part of the Peruvian privatization programme. As we have seen, Shougang paid $120 million for the mine. It is not disputed that the mine has large deposits of iron ore. Moreover, the iron ore content of 55 per cent is relatively high, much above the Chinese average of around 30 per cent. However, the iron ore has a relatively high sulphur content, which made it unsuitable for use in countries with advanced anti-pollution regulations. Since completing the purchase, Shougang has invested $150 million in order to process the iron ore at the mine so that it meets pollution regulations in the advanced economies. It has also invested in pelletizing facilities. Iron ore pellets are in especially high demand relative to fines and lumps, because they can be used in the process of making steel through direct reduced iron ore. Pellets command a significant price premium. These investments in upgrading the product quality have enabled the mine to export iron ore to a wide range of countries, including Brazil, the USA, Japan (Nippon Steel), South Korea (Posco), as well as to China. From 1994 to 1996 the mine reportedly made losses, but in 1997 and 1998, made annual pre-tax profits of around $3 million.

As well as iron ore, the Hierro mine has rich copper and nickel resources. These have not yet been fully explored. Shougang is in discussion with multinational companies about the possibility of joint development of the copper and nickel resources. It is planned to restructure the Hierro mine and float the company on the USA and Canadian stock markets.

RELATIONSHIP BETWEEN STEEL AND NON-STEEL PPRODUCTION

If the Chinese economy maintains a reasonable growth rate over the next decade, then large integrated steel firms such as Shougang should be able to maintain and enhance their dominant position in the domestic iron and steel market. However, the political and social constraints on making large numbers of workers redundant have pushed firms such as Shougang towards the path of diversification, alongside powerful growth of the main iron and steel business. The process has been stimulated also by the fact that the core iron and steel industry typically has quite low profit margins, and is subject to great cyclicality in market conditions. Moreover, the iron and steel industry requires large-scale lumpy investments, with long gestation periods. In sharp contrast, the downstream consumer goods markets and service sector activities are often perceived to have higher value-added, higher profit margins and short gestation lags. The drive to diversification has not only been a characteristic of old steel firms with huge numbers of employees. As we have seen, this behavioural characteristic has also been strongly exhibited at Baogang, a state-of-the-art greenfield plant, with relatively low employment. This suggests that the diversification drive is not only stimulated by the desire to re-employ surplus workers.

In fact, there are costs attached to extensive downstream and service sector diversification. A large integrated steel company will have only limited business skills in such activities. It may be unable to generate economies of scale. It may encounter fierce competition from businesses which are larger and more capable in these activities. There is a danger also that these activities may divert investment funds away from the core business of iron and steel. It is striking that the most successful steel company in the world, Posco, under state ownership has studiously avoided the path of conglomerate diversification so characteristic of the *chaebol* business structure of the rest of Korea. Extensive diversification into downstream consumer goods and services would take Shougang, and other leading Chinese integrated steel producers, along the path of the *chaebols* rather than Posco.

There are already warning signs of the difficulties this may pose for Shougang's balance sheet. In 1997, the core iron and steel company made a profit of 958 million yuan, but the Shougang Special Steel Corporation lost 141 million yuan, mining operations lost 297 million yuan and the other non-steel operation lost another 393 million yuan, which offset 87 per cent of the profits generated from the core company (SG, 1998: 3–4). Shougang's international operations made a profit of 212 million yuan (SG, 1998: 4). Thus, the total Group profit of 351 million yuan disguised a very different performance between the separate branches of the Group.

In so far as the path of diversification is pursued in order to avoid severe downsizing of employment, then this method of providing a social safety net may be costly for Shougang. The Corporation is well aware that this is a potential danger. However, like other Chinese large integrated iron and steel plants, Shougang's leaders feel that they have a duty to the Corporation's workers and their families. Moreover they know that the central and local government still have a long way to go before they can establish an effective social safety net which will reduce the costs to individual workers of large-scale downsizing at Shougang. They cannot drastically downsize employment in the way that has occurred in the steel industry in the advanced economies since the 1970s or in the post-privatization Brazilian steel industry. One advantage of setting up diversified subsidiaries with independent accounting, as opposed to leaving the workers under-employed in the steel sector, is that it highlights the financial costs involved in not downsizing in line with international competitors and the leading 'greenfield' competitor, namely Baogang.

PROSPECTS

The steel sector presents very different possibilities for catch-up among firms in developing countries than exist in many other sectors, such as branded consumer goods, aircraft, aircraft engines, pharmaceuticals, heavy electrical equipment, telecommunications equipment, automobiles and auto components. Firms in this sector are less able to establish competitive advantage through brand, technical progress in product or process, and systems integration and high investment in information systems. The contrast in the pace of growth of markets in developing countries with that in the advanced economies is especially strong. The process of globalization of business systems is much less advanced than in other sectors, so that the international large firms are relatively less far advanced compared to those in developing countries.

The Chinese government is seriously committed to attempting to build a group of globally powerful giant firms in the steel sector, as it is also doing in other sectors. China possesses the massive advantage of already being the world's largest consumer of steel. As well as central government support for emerging giant steel firms, there is also powerful support for them from local governments. There are many ways in which local and central governments can support indigenous large firms. Not only is the Chinese overall market fast-growing but there is every prospect that it will continue to grow powerfully over the long-term, albeit with the usual cycles that characterize demand for steel in all economies. Furthermore, Chinese demand is rapidly changing its structure towards high-quality steel as manufacturing output advances, consumer tastes change and Chinese manufactures increasingly penetrate world markets with the associated demands for high quality raw materials.

Shougang is one of the three or four steel companies that have been selected by the Chinese government to constitute the core of the future Chinese steel industry. The contract system at Shougang, which operated from the late 1970s to the mid-1990s unleashed an extraordinary entrepreneurial energy in the formerly traditional state-run steel plant. This chapter has examined the enormous reinvestment and modernization from the late 1970s to the mid-1990s. It involved large-scale purchase and upgrading of second-hand equipment from the advanced capitalist countries, extensive automation of production and upgrading of human resources. The contract system constituted an important transitional step away from the complete absence of entrepreneurial incentives under the command economy.

However, the contract system was a crude instrument for allocating the stream of revenue stemming from the assets that Shougang operated. In the post-contract system, the direct influence of state planners on Shougang has substantially declined. Shougang's range of decision-making independence in respect to the purchase of inputs, its production structure and product marketing has increased substantially compared to the contract system, when the government still controlled many of the key decisions. Shougang is moving towards a new epoch, with the plans to float parts of the steel business on the stock market, perhaps even floating internationally. It wishes to expand both the total volume of steel output and the value of output and per unit profits through increasing the production of high value-added products.

Within the core of the Shougang Group with over 200 000 employees is a profitable steel business: Shougang's mother company employs 47 000 people, with sales of around $2 billion, or $41 000 per employee. In 1997, the core company's profits of $115 million amounted to 6.0 per cent of sales revenue, which compares favourably with leading European steel companies.[69] The whole of the steel-producing component of Shougang employs 83 000 people and produces 8.0 million tons of crude steel. It has a sales revenue of $2400 million and profits of $82 million, or 3.4 per cent of sales revenue. Moreover, Shougang spends a relatively high share of its sales revenue on R & D. Its total R & D spend in the mid-1990s was around $40 million annually, around one-half of British Steel's ($75 million in 1997) and less than one-quarter of Usinor's ($180 million in 1997) (DTI, 1998: 22, 62). However, this purchased a much larger number of research employees than in the advanced capitalist companies (1500 at Usinor compared with more than 8000 at Shougang).

If Shougang is able successfully to divest itself of loss-making non-core business, raise capital on the stock market and slowly downsize employment in the core business, it should be able to generate the resources for continued upgrading of its steel technology and diversifying its product portfolio. Steel industry joint ventures could accelerate the process of raising capital, improving marketing skills and advancing technology in high value-added steel activities. It is possible that at some point, Shougang will be permitted to merge with major steel plants outside Beijing, either through the market or through government mediated administrative merger. Obvious candidates would be those in broadly the same region, such as Tangshan (52 000 employees, 2.1 million tons of crude steel, and pre-tax profits of $30 million), Taiyuan (72 000 employees, 2.4 million tons of crude steel, and 201 million yuan pre-tax profits) and even Baotou (98 000 employees, 4.1 million tons of crude steel and pre-tax profits of $34 million) (ISIC, 1997: 122–35). Such merger(s) would enable Shougang to escape from the constraints that exist due to its location on a relatively small site within China's capital city.[70]

In sum, China will continue gradually to construct a group of giant steel companies that will challenge the established global giants. Shougang will be one of these. Despite the huge size of the Chinese markets, if China is successful in this endeavour, the experience of Japan and South Korea suggests that such firms would not confine themselves to the domestic market. If Chinese firms were able to develop into globally competitive, modern integrated steel companies, then there is every likelihood that they would become formidable international competitors for the established giants.

However, high-speed changes are simultaneously taking place in the steel industry based in the advanced economies. A small group of powerful globalizing firms is emerging. They are merging with each other at high speed. They are rapidly developing their technical and marketing skills, and benefit from large economies of scale. Even in this sector, China faces a severe competitive challenge in the high-value-added segments of the industry.

10

Coal

Ordinary people can't dig for oil, but anyone can dig for coal.
(Shenhua official)

We are in an era of unprecedented consolidation.
(Brian Gilbertson, Chairman, Billiton mining corporation, 6 September 2000)

The best ruler is unknown to his subjects,
next comes the ruler loved and praised,
next comes the ruler being feared,
next comes the ruler disdained.
The best ruler is leisurely and carefree
seldom issuing orders.
When the affairs of state are properly dealt with,
the people all say,
'It should have happened to us like this.'
(Lao Zi, *The book of Dao and De*)

THE GLOBAL VIEW

DEMAND

Energy Demand. Despite great improvements in the technical efficiency with which energy has been used to generate output of goods and services, the world's demand for primary energy has increased sharply since the 1980s. In the decade 1986–96, the world's consumption of primary energy rose by 18 per cent, and excluding the former USSR, it rose by 29 per cent (Table 10-1). Fast-growing developing countries, especially those in East Asia, spearheaded the growth in

TABLE 10-1 Change in Primary Energy Consumption,
1986–96 (million tons of Oil Equivalent)

Country/region	1986	1996	% change
World	7118	8380	17.7
World excl. former USSR	5805	7457	28.5
USA	1743	2130	22.2
Former USSR	1313	923	−29.7
China	566	874	54.4
Japan	365	502	37.5
Germany, France, UK	771	818	6.1

SOURCE: SPC (1997: 147)

TABLE 10-2 Share of Global Installed Capacity for
Electricity Generation, 1990–2010 (% in brackets)

Fuel type	1990	2000	2010
Total (GW)	2830 (100)	3580 (100)	4450 (100)
Nuclear	(12)	(11)	(10)
Gas	(17)	(20)	(22)
Oil	(15)	(14)	(13)
Coal*	(33)	(32)	(32)
Hydro**	(23)	(23)	(23)

SOURCE: FT (9 June 1998)

NOTES: * And other solid fuels
          ** And other regeneratives

energy demand. Most importantly, China's consumption of primary energy rose by no less than 54 per cent from 1986 to 1996. However, large increases took place also in advanced economies. Primary energy consumption in Japan rose by 38 per cent, and in the USA by over 22 per cent. Indeed, the USA's share of global primary energy consumption rose from 24.5 per cent in 1986 to 25.5 per cent in 1996.

Global electricity consumption is predicted to continue to grow rapidly. Current estimates suggest that by 2010, global installed capacity will have risen 57 per cent compared with 1990 (Table 10-2). The world distribution of energy consumption is altering rapidly, with great implications for geo-politics. Siemens estimates that by the years 2003–7, Asia will account for 49 per cent of global orders for power equipment (FT, 9 June 1998). It is estimated that the share of the Asia–Pacific region in global electricity generation will rise from 20 per cent in 1990 to 33 per cent by 2010 (Table 10-3).

Coal and Energy. Coal remains one of the most important sources of primary energy, accounting for 27 per cent of the world's primary energy consumption in 1996. Known reserves are thought likely to last for 250 years at current levels of consumption. By contrast, known oil and gas reserves are thought likely to run out

TABLE 10-3 Distribution of Global Electricity
Generation Capacity as %, 1990–2010

Region	1990	2000	2010
Total	100	100	100
Western Europe	21	19	17
Eastern Europe	16	14	13
Asia–Pacific	20	28	33
Africa/Middle East	6	7	7
North and South America	37	32	30

SOURCE: FT (9 June 1998)

TABLE 10-4 Primary Energy Consumption, 1996 (million tons of Oil Equivalent)

Country/region	Oil	Natural gas	Coal	Nuclear	Hydro	Total
World	3313	1972	2257	620	218	8380
USA	833	569	516	183	29	2130
China	173	16	666	4	16	874
Former USSR	197	474	181	53	19	923
Japan	270	60	88	77	7	502
Germany/France/UK	130	181	149	170	9	818

SOURCE: SPC (1997: 148)

within 50–70 years. In fact, given the rate of discovery of new reserves and improvements in extraction rates, oil and natural gas reserves will last longer than this, but not for as long as coal. Unlike oil and gas, coal reserves are widely distributed, with almost one hundred countries involved in coal production. It is still a highly competitive industry: 'Coal is a plentiful and cheap fuel and productivity gains reaped by the producers seem to have a way of falling to the buyers' benefit in lower prices, rather than the coal producers' gain in higher profitability' (FT, 8 July 1996).

Even in the USA, coal still accounts for over 24 per cent of energy consumption (Table 10-4). The USA accounts for 23 per cent of the world's total coal consumption. However, in many developing countries, coal is even more important. Most notably, in China it accounts for no less than 76 per cent of total primary energy consumption. China accounts for almost 30 per cent of total global coal consumption. Between them, China and the USA account for over 52 per cent of the total amount of coal consumed globally.

Although the real price of both oil and natural gas has fallen over the long-term much more than that of coal,[1] it remained the case in the mid-1990s that coal was a highly competitive source of fuel for electricity generation. For example, in the USA in 1996, the cost of electricity generation was over $55 per MW for wind power, $34 for natural gas, $20 for nuclear power and just $18 for coal (FT, 9 June 1998). The effect of extensive privatization and de-regulation of electricity generation and supply is to reinforce the incentive to consume coal, usually the cheapest source of fuel for electricity generation: 'Deregulated generators will look to produce incremental power from the lowest cost source possible. For many, this source will be coal' (Slater, 1998). Consequently, despite the rise of nuclear fuel, and the increased use of natural gas and hydro power, coal remains much the most important single source of fuel for electricity production. In 1990 it accounted for 33 per cent of the installed capacity of global electricity generation (Table 10-2). The World Coal Institute estimates that in 1996, 37 per cent of world electricity was generated with coal as the fuel, compared with 20 per cent for hydro, 17 per cent for nuclear, 16 per cent for natural gas, and 10 per cent for oil. In China, 75 per cent of electricity is generated by coal, while in Germany and the USA, coal's share is 53 per cent. Across the EU as a whole, 29 per cent of electricity is generated by coal.

Far from declining, as popular consciousness believes to have been the case, the world's coal industry has grown strongly. Global coal output today is around three times as large as it was in the late 1940s, growing from around 1600 million tons to around 4700 million tons (Slater, 1998). Moreover, coal consumption is continuing to grow: global coal consumption rose by around 6 per cent from 1986 to 1996, and by 15 per cent if the former USSR is excluded (Table 10-5). Within that total are marked differences in regional trends. In the former USSR, output collapsed by 45 per cent from 1986 to 1996, and in Europe, output fell heavily, by 28 per cent, in the same period, with extensive substitution of natural gas for coal. For example, in the UK, which had large-scale substitution of North Sea natural gas for coal, coal output declined by 60 per cent from 1980 to 1995 (Table 10-6). In the USA, output grew strongly, increasing by 19 per cent from 1986 to 1996 (Table 10-5).

In the Far East output grew extremely strongly, rising by no less than 46 per cent from 1986 to 1996 (Table 10-5). Asia's share of world coal production rose from 33 per cent in 1986 to 46 per cent in 1996. Within Asia, China is much the most important single actor. Output in 1995 was no less than 2.2 times greater than in 1980 (Table 10-6). China's share of world coal output rose from 17 per cent in 1980 to 29 per cent in 1995. Between them, China and the USA account for no less than 49 per cent of the world's coal output. Between 1980 and 1995, their combined coal output rose by almost one billion tons, and increased by

TABLE 10-5 World Coal Consumption 1986–96
(million tons of Oil Equivalent)

Region	1986	1996	% change
World	2135	2257	5.7
USA	435	516	18.6
Europe	529	380	−28.2
Asia	712	1037	45.6
within which: China	446	666	49.3
Former USSR	330	181	−45.2

SOURCE: SPC (1997: 165)

TABLE 10-6 Coal Output, Selected Countries 1980–95
(million tons)

Country	1980	1995	1995 as % of 1980
USA	763	934	122
Germany*	482	252	53
Poland	230	200	87
India	113	272	241
UK	129	51	40
Former USSR	716	442	62
Australia	107	278	260
South Africa	116	206	178
China	620	1361	220
World	3736	4717	126

SOURCES: MGB, ZMGN (1997: 322); SSB, ZTN (1992: 854, 1998:
69); SSB (1981: 498, in English)

NOTE: * Including East Germany

66 per cent. There is considerable debate about the future growth of the USA coal
output, almost entirely due to uncertainty about the impact of environmental legislation (see below). However, there is little dispute that coal will remain for the
foreseeable future the overwhelmingly dominant fuel for the Chinese power
industry, as it will be for many developing countries. Indeed, China's Ministry of
Power Industry predicts that the share of coal in China's total electricity supply
will actually rise from 70.7 per cent in 1995 to 73.0 per cent in 2010. Chinese
industry experts predict that China's coal output will rise from 1361 million tons
in 1995, to 2100 million tons in 2020, reaching somewhere between 2600 and
3000 million tons in 2050 which amounts to well over one-half of today's global
coal output. Unless there are dramatic changes in technology, energy policy in
China, and world environmental controls (see below), China is destined to be a
hugely important actor in the world's coal industry.

The production structure of developing countries is shifting fast towards highly
energy-intensive activities. The economic structure of the advanced capitalist
economies is shifting fast away from manufacturing towards services. Rapid
industrialization in East Asia in general, and China in particular, has been associated with a powerful relative shift of manufacturing activity out of the advanced
economies towards the fast-growing developing countries: in 1990–7, the average annual growth rate of industrial value-added in the high-income countries
was 0.7 per cent per annum, compared with 14.5 per cent per annum in the East
Asia and Pacific Region (World Bank, 1998: 211). However, industrialization of
countries such as China shifts their structure of production towards relatively
highly energy-using sectors (Table 10-7).

Coal and Environmental Pollution. In the advanced economies, burning coal
on open fires and in old-fashioned power stations was responsible for large

TABLE 10-7 **Structure of Output in Relation to Energy Use: China, Japan and the USA, 1992–5**

Indicator	China (1995)	Japan (1992)	USA (1993)
Total GDP	100	100	100
Agriculture	21	2	2
Industry	48	43	26
Services	31	55	72
Total manufacturing value-added	100	100	100
Energy-intensive industries	35.8	22.9	20.5
Metals and processing	14.2	6.0	4.1
Non-metal mineral products	9.4	4.3	2.6
Chemical materials and products	9.8	10.0	9.0
Paper products	2.4	2.6	4.8
Rest of manufacturing	64.2	77.1	79.5

SOURCE: World Bank (1997a: 48)

amounts of atmospheric pollution through the generation of airborne particulates. These caused large-scale damage to the urban built environment, and high levels of respiratory disease.

Not until the 1950s did serious efforts get under way to improve the quality of the atmosphere consequent upon using coal as a main source of primary energy. Both government legislation and the demands of shareholders forced large changes in the way coal is mined, transported and used. Reclamation and rehabilitation work is now a central part of mine development. Coal is prepared, stockpiled and transported in a much more careful way, including washing coal, spraying stockpiles and covering coal in transport. The use of coal on open domestic fires and in primitive industrial boilers has been reduced drastically. The almost universal use of precipitators and filters means that power stations no longer emit large quantities of black smoke and dust, which were the primary cause of pollution.

However, there still is major concern over the emission of sulphur dioxide and oxides of nitrogen (NOx). These gases react with water vapour in the atmosphere to form weak acids, which fall as acid rain and are thought to cause large-scale damage to forests, lakes and stonework. These problems can be greatly reduced through such measures as the use of lower sulphur coals, the application of flue gas desulphurization, new combustion technologies and the employment of low NOx burners. These can reduce sulphur emissions by up to 95 per cent and NOx emissions by 60 per cent (*FT*, 8 July 1996). Rapid progress is taking place in power station technology to enable further falls in the emission of particulates. These include fluidized bed combustion and its variants, and a number of different gasification and combined cycle systems to enable the removal of 99 per cent of sulphur compounds and permit the reclamation of pure sulphur as a valuable industrial material (*FT*, 7 July 1996).

Despite the impressive progress in technologies to still further reduce pollution, enforcement of the application of these technologies requires government action. Arguably the most advanced legislation is now in place in the USA, in the shape of enhanced standards of control over soot, smog and haze, introduced by the Environmental Protection Agency in 1997–8. Meeting these standards will require high investments. One estimate suggests that meeting these targets would require the US power industry to spend $22 billion between 1998 and 2008 in retro-fitting pollution control technologies. This is thought likely to have a significant effect on the price of electricity.

However, in most developing countries, the ways in which coal is mined, transported and used as a fuel approximate those of the advanced economies before the 1950s. Large quantities of coal are mined and stored with little care for the environmental impact of mining operations. Coal is mostly transported unwashed and uncovered. Large quantities of high sulphur coal are used. Large quantities of coal are burned on open fires and in primitive boilers. China is by far the biggest of developing countries, and has by far the largest total amount of pollution: 'Burdens of air pollution are not surprising in a nation where combustion of one billion tons of coal, largely uncleaned and burned with minimal or no air pollution controls, supplies three-quarters of all primary energy (Smil, 1993: 117). The recommended maximum daily mean total for suspended particulates is no more than 300 micrograms per cubic metre. In fact, in northern China in the early 1990s, the levels were commonly as high as 500–1000 micrograms per cubic metre, and on the worst days reached as high as 2000 (Smil, 1993: 117). Daily means of sulphur dioxide concentration in North America have now fallen to around 20–100 micrograms per cubic metre. In China in the early 1990s, they were commonly between 100–400 micrograms per cubic metre, and regularly surpassed 600 micrograms in the heating season, sometimes reaching as high as 2000 micrograms (Smil, 1993: 117).

Total discharges of particulate matter are officially reported to have reached 15 million tons by 1990s, and are unofficially estimated to have reached 20 million tons (Smil, 1993: 117–118). Even the official figures show China as producing 15 per cent of the global total of 100 million tons, of which around two-thirds is generated by coal combustion (Smil, 1993: 118).

Despite very high levels of sulphur dioxide in the atmosphere, North China has only low levels of acid rain. This is due to the large amounts of calcium, potassium and magnesium compounds in the atmosphere. These neutralize the emitted sulphur dioxide. However, South China has serious problems of acid rain, caused mainly by burning coal with high sulphur content. Much of the sulphur could be eliminated through washing, but only around 10 per cent of China's high-sulphur coal is washed (Smil, 1993: 118).

The substantial reduction of particulate and sulphurous air pollution in a developing country such as China presents large problems. Effective control of these emissions requires either 'massive conversion to cleaner fuels' or 'an extensive installation of costly techniques'. Sulphur dioxide is especially expensive to control: 'Until very recently even many rich countries avoided this costly commitment' (Smil, 1993: 121). Indeed, Smil estimates that the capital costs of installing de-sulphurization facilities increases the cost of electricity by 25–30 per cent, and operating costs 'add a similar mark-up to the electricity generation cost' (Smil, 1993: 235).

China's leaders recognize the damage that large-scale consumption of coal does to China's environment and to the Chinese people's health. At the 1999 annual session of the Chinese National People's Congress, Premier Zhu Rongji recognized that 'the deterioration of the ecological environment remains a glaring problem', and pledged to 'improve the air quality in the capital and punish polluting enterprises' (quoted in *FT*, 6 March 1999). However, there are powerful pressures for continued increases in the consumption of coal.

Coal and Global Warming. The international effects of particulate and sulphurous emissions can be important. However, in large developing countries, their main impact is within the economy concerned. The issue of global warming is entirely different. The effects of carbon dioxide emission from fossil fuel combustion are felt almost entirely at the global level. The issue of global warming and the emission of 'greenhouse gases' is, therefore, a matter of great importance in global international political economy. The two main sources of carbon dioxide generation are de-forestation and coal burning. Global emissions of carbon dioxide have significantly increased, from around 275–280 parts per million (ppm) before the Industrial Revolution to 350 in the 1990s (Smil, 1993: 129). Global carbon dioxide emissions rose from 13.6 billion tons in 1980 to 22.7 billion tons in 1995 (World Bank, 1998: 209). It is now widely accepted that global warming is a consequence of increased release of carbon dioxide. There are many positive consequences of global warming, such as increased crop productivity. However, it is now widely accepted that the net impact of global warming is highly damaging, most especially through the impact on rising sea levels and on climate change.

The high-income countries, containing just 16 per cent of the world's population, account for 49 per cent of the world's carbon dioxide emissions (World Bank, 1998: 209). The USA alone, containing just 4.6 per cent of the world's population, accounts for over 24 per cent of the world's carbon dioxide emissions (World Bank, 1998: 209). The 1997 Kyoto Conference on climate change appeared to mark a radical shift in perspective towards global warming. At the conference, the industrialized nations agreed to bring emissions of carbon dioxide down to below 1990 levels by the year 2010. The main thrust of their action will be over fossil fuels, which are the main source of greenhouse gases. Coal is much the most carbon-intensive fossil fuel. If the 1997 Kyoto agreement takes effect, then it is thought likely that its implementation will have a substantial negative effect on demand for coal in the high income countries.

There are many uncertainties surrounding the agreement. It will have no legal force until it is ratified by countries accounting for over one-half of the world's emissions. It was thought this would take at least two years to complete (*FT*, 16 April 1998). Full implementation of the Kyoto agreement could have a substantial effect on electricity prices in the advanced economies. There are deep fears concerning the impact that implementation of the Kyoto agreement might have on international competitiveness through its effect on electricity prices. One estimate is that it could raise USA wholesale electricity prices by 11 per cent by the year 2010 (*FT*, 9 June 1998).

The most important issue is the fast-growing role of developing countries in the generation of greenhouse gases. These are not signatories to the Kyoto agreement. The share of low and middle income countries in global generation of carbon dioxide rose from 35 per cent in 1980 to 51 per cent in 1995 (World Bank, 1998: 208). Of these, much the most important was China. Its generation of carbon dioxide rose by 116 per cent from 1980 to 1995. Its share of the global total increased from 10.8 per cent to 14.1 per cent. In 1980, China's emissions of carbon dioxide were 33 per cent of those of the USA, but by 1995, they had risen to 58 per cent of those of the USA. By the year 2010, it is predicted that China's emissions of carbon dioxide will overtake those of the USA (*FT*, 28 November 1997). Between them they will account for close to one-half of the global total of greenhouse gases. There is strong political pressure in Europe and, especially, in the USA, to support the Kyoto agreement only if the same restrictions apply to large developing countries, especially China. The USA is unwilling to sign an agreement allowing developing countries voluntarily to assume obligations of their own, rather than shoulder the same responsibilities as the advanced economies.

This is a big political difficulty, since the levels of *per capita* output in developing countries are still tiny compared to those in the advanced economies. For developing countries to restrict the growth of their carbon dioxide emissions to the same degree as the advanced economies would deprive them of the chance to raise their national product through extensive use of cheap coal-generated electricity. In 1995, *per capita* emissions of carbon dioxide stood at just 0.7 tons in low income countries and 3.7 tons in middle income countries, compared to 12.5 tons in the high income countries (World Bank, 1998: 209). In the USA the level is 20.8 tons. In China the level is just 2.7 tons, despite the fact that China's share of the global total of carbon dioxide emissions is so high.

The development pressures on China are immense. It faces the prospect of another 250 million people added to its population during the next generation. Its income level is still very low: 'China cannot be forced to maintain its current carbon dioxide emission levels while trying to accommodate another 250 million people during the next generation: the chasm between these two requirements is unbridgeable' (Smil, 1993: 136). In the absence of external pressure, there is a strong incentive to continue to use coal as the main source of primary energy and the main fuel for electricity generation. As we have seen, China plans very large additions to its coal output over the next few decades. China's problems place in dramatic form the general issue of carbon dioxide emissions from developing countries. John Browne, chief executive of BP, recognized the dilemma posed by the conflict between the developed countries' ambitions to control global warming and the need of poor countries to achieve growth of national product: 'Developing countries cannot be denied heat, light and mobility simply because some people have an opinion that it might not be right for the world' (quoted in *FT*, 28 November 1997).

The policy problems surrounding global warming are extremely complex. Within the advanced economies, efforts to reduce emissions of carbon dioxide from burning fossil fuels will add greatly to costs of generating electricity within these countries. In the USA, it is thought that, if they are fully implemented, the Kyoto agreement and the most recent Environmental Protection Agency (EPA) restrictions on airborne particulates, will lead to a radical change in the structure of fuels for the electricity sector. A report commissioned by Edison Electric concludes that they will result in a 'dramatic shift away from the historic national energy policy that has resulted in a mix including coal, natural gas, oil, nuclear and hydro power' (quoted in *FT*, 9 June 1998). This shift could 'have broad ramifications for the economy'.

Within developing countries, of which China is much the most important, the prospect is for considerable progress in the efficiency with which fuel is used, reducing the amount of coal per unit of electricity. This will come about through the increased application of more modern equipment to generate electricity. As we shall see, China has made considerable progress in this area. However, even with these measures, other things being equal, there will be a very large increase in the use of fossil fuels, notably coal. The resulting global warming would be a problem for the whole global economy and society, not just for China. As we have noted, developing nations are not signatories to the Kyoto agreement on global warming. They argue that their poverty forces them to continue to use the cheapest sources of fuel available, namely fossil fuels in general and coal in particular. Radical reduction in the share of coal in China's fuel mix would require extensive assistance from the advanced economies. Such a programme would provide 'a bonanza for companies in the energy efficiency business' (*FT*, 28 November 1998). A successful attempt to control greenhouse gas emissions in developing countries such as China could result in 'an unprecedented transfer of energy-efficient technology from rich countries, which would allow developing nations to cut emissions while reducing their energy costs' (*FT*, 28 November 1998). Serious attempts to try to reduce absolutely, or substantially cut the rate of growth, of emission of greenhouse gases in China will have large implications for the structure of fuels supply for electricity generation. Increased use of oil and, especially, natural gas as substitutes for coal would tend to reduce carbon dioxide emissions per unit of electricity generated.

More radical reductions in carbon dioxide emissions in developing countries would only be compatible with sustained economic growth if there was an accelerated increase in use of renewable energy sources, hydro power, and, more fundamentally, increased use of nuclear energy. In the view of Bill Wilkinson, chairman of the British Nuclear Industry Forum, 'if European governments are serious in their ambitions to reduce greenhouse gases in line with their international commitments, I cannot see how it can be done without retaining the contribution of nuclear power' (quoted in *FT*, 28 November 1998). There is still deep fear among the international community about the safety of nuclear energy and the dangers of proliferation of nuclear weapons. The 'Brundtland' Report concluded: 'The generation of nuclear power is only justifiable if there are solid solutions to the presently unsolved problems to which it gives rise'. The Kyoto agreement lifted the prospects for the nuclear industry. However, industry experts do not anticipate a major shift in policy-makers' perception of the risks associated with nuclear energy: 'Even if the nuclear industry has a stronger case for its future than 10 years ago, the political climate in which it must make that case is no easier than before' (FT, 16 April 1998). Industry predictions are still that the share of nuclear power in global electricity generation will decline to around 10 per cent in 2010, from around 12 per cent today (FT, 9 June 1998).

Because of its implications for global warming, coal use in China is one of the key issues in international relations in the decades ahead. However, the prospects are highly uncertain: 'These are uncharted territories of national policy making and international co-operation, and only the threat of acute crises would show if a new globalism could succeed' (Smil, 1993: 137). There is not a high probability that large-scale international aid will be forthcoming in the foreseeable future to assist China to make large-scale changes away from coal as its main source of fuel for electricity. Moreover, the long-term trend is for the real price of coal to fall, and for the price of oil and natural gas to fall even further. This further diminishes the incentive to switch from these sources of fuel towards other sources of fuel.

International Coal Trade. International trade in coal has increased at high speed, much exceeding the rate of growth of coal output. In 1973, a mere 19 million tons was traded internationally (FT, 8 July 1996), totalling only around 0.5 per cent of total world output. By 1995, 238 million tons was traded internationally, over 5 per cent of world output. Industry predictions are that by the year 2010, around 520 million tons will be traded internationally, close to 10 per cent of predicted world output. A recent survey of the world coal industry concluded: 'Coal is a commodity for which demand appears to rise inexorably each year. It is now by far the largest bulk commodity traded by sea, well exceeding the former dominant bulk cargoes of grain and iron ore. Although the future of coking coal trade appears fairly static, that for steam coal is a vista of sustained growth as far ahead as any forecasters can see' (FT, 8 July 1996). The rapid growth of internationally traded coal has attracted the interest of several multinational companies.

The main driver of demand has been the growth of steam coal. In Europe, oil and gas have increasingly substituted for coal as a source of primary energy, their share having risen to 42 per cent and 21 per cent respectively by 1996 (MGB, ZMGN, 1997: 317). However, in the Asia Pacific region, over 45 per cent of primary energy consumption still comes from coal (compared to 22 per cent in North America and 16 per cent in the EU) (MGB, ZMGN, 1997: 317–8). Asia accounts for 47 per cent of the world's total international coal demand, and the share is predicted to rise to over 60 per cent by 2010: 'Growth in Asian demand has been astonishing. Largely driven by the construction of modern, efficient, environmentally friendly advanced power stations in Japan, South Korea and Taiwan, the Asian market has expanded at a pace which the producers have barely been able to match' (FT, 8 July 1996). Unlike Europe, there is no easily available source of natural gas. Coal remains a highly competitive fuel source, with falling real prices over the long term. With production distributed among so many countries and producers, coal provides a more secure source of supply than oil and gas. Despite the dramatic recent decline in the oil price, memories of the oil price shock linger, and reinforce the desire to maintain a balanced portfolio of fuel sources.

New sources of international supply are growing rapidly. By 2005 it is predicted that Australia alone will account for 26 per cent of internationally traded coal, South Africa for 16 per cent, and Colombia and Indonesia together, for 19 per cent. The big question mark surrounds the role of China. In 1996, it exported 29 million tons (SSB, ZTN, 1998: 630), less than 3 per cent of total output. However, major uncertainty surrounds China's future exports. A small proportionate change in domestic consumption could result in a large absolute change in China's coal exports, with a consequent large impact upon the international market for coal.

SUPPLY

Reserves. I have noted already that there is great uncertainty about the real level of reserves of exhaustible energy resources. Major uncertainty still surrounds the issue. In China's case, there is still considerable dispute about the full extent of its coal reserves. More importantly, there is great uncertainty about its reserves of oil and natural gas. Although China became a net importer of oil in the mid-1990s, there is large-scale exploration activity both in the South China seas and in Central Asia. Major finds in one or both of these areas would radically re-shape China's entire energy strategy, and have a major impact on the global energy market.

Employment. In the developed countries, a number of influences have combined to cause a drastic decline in the level of employment in the coal industry (Table 10-8). In Europe coal consumption has fallen by almost 30 per cent since 1980. Other influences include privatization of mines in Europe, increased international trade and competition in coal, privatization of electricity generation in Europe, long-term declines in the relative prices of competitive fuels, notably oil and natural gas, changes in European labour laws to weaken trade union bargaining power, increased unemployment in Europe, and internationalization and consolidation among coal-producing companies. These forces combined to encourage coal producers to reduce costs through reducing employment and increasing industry productivity.

Coal sector employment in the USA in 1995 had fallen to 43 per cent of the level in 1980. In Germany the figure was 47 per cent, in Poland, 68 per cent and in the UK, 15 per cent. Output per worker in underground mines rose in the USA from 7 tons in 1980 to over 26 tons in 1995. In Germany it rose from 3.4 tons in 1980 to 5.6 tons in 1995, and in the UK, from 3.0 tons in 1980 to 8.8 tons in 1995 (MGB, ZMGN, 1997: 327–8). The decline in employment was facilitated by large changes in the nature of mining equipment. In open-cast mining especially, there was a significant increase in the level of mechanization, with a large rise in the average size and efficiency of equipment.

TABLE **10-8 Coal Sector Employment in Selected Countries, 1980 and 1995 (000)**

Country	1980	1995	1995 as % of 1980
USA	246	107	43
Former USSR	2200	1500	68
Poland	406	275	68
Germany	205	97	47
UK	294	44 (1993)	15
China	4420 (1985)	5210	118

SOURCES: MGB, ZMGN (1997: 335–6); SSB, ZTN (1995: 376, 1998: 432)

Consolidation. Compared to the institutional changes under way in other industries, such as aerospace, automobiles, oil and natural gas production, the coal industry still lags far behind in terms of global consolidation. However, consolidation is affecting even the coal industry. Following the oil shocks of the 1970s, widespread fears about depletion of exhaustible energy sources led major oil companies to enter the coal industry. However, views on exhaustible energy sources radically shifted. Broadly speaking, oil and natural gas reserves have risen significantly over the past two decades. Additions to reserves are more or less keeping up with depletions. The leading oil companies have returned to a much sharper focus on oil, selling off most of their coal assets. Since the mid-1980s there has been 'a virtual stampede for the exits by virtually all major oil companies with investments in coal' (Slater, 1998). Alongside the re-focusing by major oil companies, focused mining companies grew significantly, mimicking the trend in other sectors. In the late 1990s, mergers and acquisitions grew to record levels in the mining industry, rising from $16.5 billion in 1995 to more than $18 billion in 1997: 'Mergers and acquisitions have become the most favoured way of expansion in the mining industry' (*FT*, 29 May 1998). Mergers and acquisitions in the metals and mining sector reached a new peak of $26 billion in 1998, and 'most factors point to continued high M & A spending' (*FT*, 24 February 1999).

The mining companies also became notably more specialized after the 1980s. In part this was a consequence of liberalization of mining regulations in many developing countries. Many developing countries nationalized mining properties in the 1960s and 1970s. The Communist countries typically prohibited foreign investment in mining. A large number of mines fell into disrepair, and production fell under public ownership. Since the mid-1980s, there has occurred the collapse of the Communist system, extensive privatization and liberalization of regulations on foreign ownership of mining resources. This has made it possible for a specialist mining company to grow into a large global business.

Following the trend in other sectors to concentrate on core business, mining companies also disposed of non-core businesses and acquired businesses in the mining sector. For example, Rio Tinto, the world's biggest listed mining company, sold its real estate, chemical, building and engineering businesses (MSDW, 1998e: 166). In 1995 it merged with CRA to 'provide significant synergies and cost reduction' (MSDW, 1998e: 168).The deal was valued at $4 billion. Rio Tinto acquired a succession of businesses in metals and mining, including major purchases in the coal, copper and gold industries. By 1997, Rio Tinto had become a specialist mining company, producing iron ore, industrial minerals, copper, aluminium, coal, gold and other metals (Rio Tinto, 1998).

Size is an important competitive advantage in the mining industry. It enables the company to make significant acquisitions in times of market weakness. Modern low-cost mines are highly capital-intensive. The way in which open-cast mining takes place has been revolutionized since the 1960s, with the introduction of large surface mining equipment, such as stripping shovels, draglines, and off-highway trucks: 240-ton vehicles have replaced the 50-ton trucks in use 25 years ago; 50-yard shovels have replaced nine-yard shovels. The application of these methods has greatly increased the maximum depth at which open-cast mining can be carried out, from only around 15 metres in the 1940s to over 200 metres today. Open-cast mining using modern technology typically has lower costs of production than underground coal, especially where the location is favourable and the quality of the coal is high.

A large fraction of the growing international investment of coal companies has been directed at large-scale open-cast mining: 'These vast open-cast projects require major capital expenditures, not only on the mines themselves, but also on the associated infrastructure, which may involve the construction of townships, power-lines, roads and railways and, in some cases, even port facilities. This infrastructural expenditure represents a huge fixed cost and requires very high production levels in order to maintain profitability.' The high capital costs involved in a large-scale modern mine mean that profits are not usually made for 7–10 years after the mining operation has begun. The use of large-scale equipment by powerful multinationals has allowed substantial reductions in workforces, with large consequential cost-savings. Large mining companies are able to develop a superior set of skills in the complex task of mine management. These skills can be applied to the entire set of mines within the company: 'Managers must design the optimal mine plan, financial structure, and development schedules to maximize the net present value of a project. This requires technological prowess, scale and financial strength' (MSDW, 1998e: 163).

Large mines often are located in inaccessible areas. Their development often requires integrated construction of large-scale transport and port facilities that are beyond the financial capabilities of small mining companies. For example, Rio Tinto's enormous Hammersley iron ore operation in Australia, with 55 million tons per annum output, operates a company-owned 540 kilometre railway to the coast.

Large mining companies possess the resources and technical skills to undertake the complex, time-consuming and expensive process of identifying the precise extent of resources at a given mining site. Conducting a due diligence study for a large coal mine of 10–20 million tons per annum output might involve the expenditure of $12–15 million, followed by a further $6 million in the exploration phase. Thus a total of over $20 million might need to be spent before the mine even began to be developed.

Despite great advances in the degree of environmental sensitivity of mining operations, large-scale mining is still a controversial issue, with severe criticism from ecological groups. Multinational mining companies are extremely vulnerable to criticism from ecologists. This applies in both developing and developed countries. For example, in the USA, regulations governing the development of mining properties have become much stricter in recent years: 'The process of obtaining environmental permits has become extremely time-consuming and complicated, with the time required to obtain a permit now stretching to 3–6 years for new mines compared with 3–6 months a decade ago' (MSDW, 1998e: 166). This has made the USA 'a much less attractive country in which to invest in mining development' (MSDW, 1998e: 166).

Mining operations often involve sensitive issues of land rights of local people. Native land rights claims are beginning to have a significant impact on the growth of mining in some parts of the world. For example, in both Canada and Australia, the granting of permits to mine has become a much more extended process, due to native land rights claims.

Greater size brings greater public attention. However, it often provides the capability to develop the specialist skills needed to deal with such issues. Effectiveness in dealing with environmental and land rights claims constitutes a source of competitive advantage. A global mining company can make use of its deep well of experience in applying best practice techniques to these issues across the world.

I have already noted the long-run tendency for primary commodity prices to decline. That process accelerated alongside the Asian crisis. The mining industry is still too fragmented for mining companies to influence price. Even the largest companies are essentially price-takers. The global market for mining commodities has become much more competitive as sources of supply have increased and liberalization of markets for mining products has taken place in a large number of countries. The decline in the real price of mining products has placed intense pressure on high-cost producers. Companies at the high end of the cost spectrum are being forced out of the business. Large companies that are focused on core competencies in mining are able to invest in large-scale, capital-intensive mines, conduct expensive survey operations, deal with native land rights claims and environmental issues more effectively, integrate their global mining operations within a single global marketing system, and attract outstanding managers and technicians, and thus are able to force down costs more successfully. MSDW's survey of the mining industry concluded: 'The net result of this focus on core competencies is likely to be more intense competition... Companies which narrow their focus and emphasize their core business ... normally perform better' (MSDW, 1998e: 167). It is the focused, low-cost large-scale firms that are the likely winners in the competition in the global mining industry.

At a global level, the coal industry is still far behind the level of concentration of most other sectors. Even the largest private sector coal company, Peabody (USA) produces only 4.5 per cent of global production. However, the consolidation process has begun to move quite fast. As we have seen, the USA is by far the most important coal mining country outside China, accounting for around one-third of the world's output excluding China. The process of consolidation has proceeded rapidly since the mid-1980s. Shell, BP, Exxon, Mobil, Du Pont, Chevron, Kerr McGee, and ARCO (Atlantic Richfield) are among the leading firms to have left the coal mining business in the USA. Mergers and acquisitions have proceeded at increasing speed. Rio Tinto moved into the USA in 1993. By 1997 it owned seven coal mines and was the fourth largest US producer. In 1998 it acquired the Jacobs Ranch mine from Kerr McGee. It produces low-sulphur coal and is poised to take advantage of the USA's clean air laws. This acquisition increased its annual output from 62 million tons to around 90 million tons. Arch Coal was formed from a merger of Ashland Coal and Arch Mineral Corporation to form the sixth largest US coal company in 1997. It subsequently took over the coal interests of ARCO for $1.14 billion to form the second largest US coal company, with an annual output of 110 million tons (*FT*, 24 March 1998). By 1998 the top five US coal producers (Peabody, Cyprus, Consol, Rio Tinto and Arch Coal) accounted for around 45 per cent of total US coal production.

Not only is the industry consolidating, but truly global coal companies are emerging. The world's largest private sector coal producer, Peabody, is a mainly US operation, but it is owned by the UK's Energy Group. The USA's fourth largest coal company in 1997 was Consol, a joint venture between Du Pont and RWE (Germany), which produces over 70 million tons per annum. In 1998, Du Pont sold its share of the joint venture to RWE. BHP (Australia) is in the top ten private coal producers in the world, with an annual output of almost 70 million tons. It has mines in Australia, Indonesia and New Mexico. Rio Tinto is developing fast in the coal business, and should have a total output of well over 100 million tons in 1999. As well as Kennecott Energy in the USA, which produced 56 million tons in 1997, it has acquired Jacobs Ranch (USA) with an annual output of 24 million tons, and has further coal mining operations in Australia and Indonesia, as well as developments under way in Colombia and Zimbabwe (Rio Tinto, 1998: 23–4).

Multinational companies are able to develop their global operations in low-cost regions, taking advantage of the great differences that exist in productivity between coal operations in different parts of the world. These differences can be due to differences in natural conditions, notably the typically much higher costs associated with underground mining (for example, in most mining operations in the UK and Germany) compared to open-cast mining (for example, most mining operations in Australia, and an increasing proportion of those in the USA). However, a major difference between costs in different parts of the world stems from differences in labour costs. Even in highly mechanized mining operations in Australia and the USA, labour costs account for around 35 per cent of total costs (excluding materials and overheads) (Tasman Asia Pacific, 1993: 26). There are large differences in annual wages of mine workers in different parts of the world (Table 10-9). Annual earnings of mine workers in Germany and Australia are almost $50 000. In South Africa, Colombia and Poland, they are only $10 000–20 000.

TABLE 10-9 Labour Productivity and Labour Costs Across Different Countries, 1996

Country	Productivity (1000/ton/man/year)	Labour costs ($1000/man/year)	Labour costs ($1000/ton)
Australia	7.6	58.4	7.7
Canada (1997)	8.8	40.3	4.6
Colombia (1992)	2.6	17.0	6.5
Germany	0.6	59.3	98.8
Poland	0.5	11.7	23.4
South Africa	3.3	10.9	3.3
UK	2.6	47.5	18.3
USA	9.8	41.4	4.2

SOURCE: International Energy Agency, *Coal Information* (1998)

However, there are also large differences between costs of production in different regions and firms arising from differences in management practices. Some of these arise from technical factors concerned with handling the individual parts of the production process and the integration of the different components of a mining operation. Others relate to the organization of labour. It is striking that despite their relatively high wages, labour costs per ton in the USA and Canada are close to South Africa's and even lower than Colombia's (Table 10-9), due to the high degree of effectiveness with which the North American mine workforce is managed. In sharp contrast, the bulk of coal mining operations in Australia lag far behind their competitors in the USA in terms of labour costs per ton of product. To a high degree this is accounted for by the relative strength of the Australian trade union movement. The Australian coal mining labour force is able to resist management's efforts to raise the intensity of labour through such measures as reducing the number of shifts, reducing idle time, taking breaks on machines rather than in central locations, and reducing manning levels required per machine.

For a variety of reasons, the coal industry tends to be one of the most confrontational in terms of labour relations. In Australia, for example, the coal industry has a vastly greater number of days lost per thousand employees than any other industry (Table 10-10). In the UK, the biggest strike of modern times took place in the mining industry in 1984–5 (following earlier major miners' strikes in 1972–3 and in 1974). In recent years in Russia, the Ukraine and Romania, large-scale protests by miners have seriously threatened political stability.

The emerging multinational companies are intently benchmarking performance of different parts of their global operations. An important part of their management skill is their capability to introduce best practice techniques across the whole global portfolio of coal mining assets.

Although many firms are leaving the coal business, the large, expanding multi-site companies in the field are able to reduce costs and make profits even in difficult times for the industry as a whole. For example, Rio Tinto's coal division

TABLE 10-10 Working Days Lost Per
1000 Employees in Various Australian
Industries (average for 1992–6)

Industry	Days lost
Coal mining	4865
Other mining	581
Construction	241
Metal products	229
Other manufacturing	144
Education, health, etc.	116
Transport and storage	101
Other industries	28
All industries	107

SOURCE: National Institute of Labour Studies
(1997), quoted in Tasman Asia Pacific (1993: 33)

made net profits amounting to 11.7 per cent of sales in its coal division in 1997
(Rio Tinto, 1998).

Catch-up in the Coal Industry in Developing Countries. Leading global
companies in the mining sector do not rely mainly on research and development
for competitive advantage. Their levels of R & D expenditure are low compared
to such sectors as pharmaceuticals, aerospace or automobiles. Unlike leading
consumer goods companies, this sector does not establish competitive advantage
through large outlays on building a global brand name, though reputation as a
high quality reliable supplier is an important source of competitive advantage.

The capital goods necessary to operate large modern coal mines are easily
available from specialist mining equipment companies, without any restriction
on technical transfer. Considerable technical skills are required to operate large,
complex pieces of mining equipment, such as a modern long-wall mining installation. However, these skills are reasonably easily obtainable if operators are
suitably trained.

Although large global coal mining companies are beginning to emerge, the
level of consolidation in the industry appears at first sight to still be very low. The
largest private producer has less than 5 per cent of the global market. The industry is highly competitive. Coal producers are emphatically price takers. There are
still no large competitive private producers from developing countries. However,
in principle, it should be relatively easy for potential global companies from
developing countries to become established in this sector and compete with the
multinationals, compared with sectors that rely on high levels of R & D expenditure, and sectors that rely on high levels of marketing expenditures to construct
a global brand name. A further factor assisting the development of globally
competitive large coal firms from developing countries is the fact that none of
the current international leaders in the coal trade is primarily focused on coal.

The industry leaders mostly have a diversified portfolio of metals and minerals. It may be the case that there are competitive advantages in being a global coal producer whose main focus is simply on coal. As we shall see, the Chinese government intends to produce just such a focused modern giant enterprise in the shape of the Shenhua Group.

However, even in the coal industry there are formidable challenges for potential world leaders based in developing countries. Competitive advantage in the global coal industry lies primarily in size and management skills. Size enables global reach and the construction of a set of low-cost coal mines across the world. This reduces risk, and ensures location within or close to each major market. Successful global firms in this sector have the financial resources to purchase mines, invest in exploration and evaluation of resources, negotiate with governments, deal with complex land rights and environmental issues, and apply best practice across the whole portfolio of mines. They also have some benefits in global procurement and operation of large quantities of expensive mining equipment and through the use of common marketing channels and expertise. A multinational mining company may be in a stronger position to employ cost-minimizing methods of labour organization than is a large local firm, especially if the local firm is state-owned, and occupies a symbolic place in national politics. The knowledge needed to turn around a loss-making coal business may not be complicated. However, implementing those policies may be a highly complex process, with severe constraints placed by national and local politics on the degree to which manning levels and labour organization can be altered.

Although the level of concentration in coal production is small at an overall global level, there is a rapid growth of industrial concentration in the high value-added international coal trade, mainly to meet the needs of large modern power stations. Leading industry commentators have even spoken of the emergence of a global oligopoly in the international trade in coal, as well as in some other bulk commodities, notably iron ore (*FT*, 6 September 2000).

In sum, even in an apparently commoditized and homogeneous product, such as coal, the industry is undergoing rapid consolidation, with substantial competitive advantages available to large, well-managed global corporations.

THE CHINESE COAL INDUSTRY

Coal Demand

Domestic. China's rapid industrialization since the late 1970s has required a matching rapid growth in energy supply. Electricity output has slightly lagged behind GDP growth, with average annual growth rates of 8 per cent and 9 per cent, respectively, since the late 1970s. Due to the time lags involved in building power stations, it is not possible for GDP and electricity supply to match each other precisely. In the first half of the 1990s, there was a large supply/demand imbalance, with various estimates of excess electricity demand, but agreed by all observers to be substantial. However, the slow-down in output growth, especially in heavy industry due to the operation of the 'accelerator' principle upon demand for capital goods, led to the emergence of an electricity supply surplus in the late 1990s. Over the long-term, sustained growth of national output in China will require roughly matching increases in electricity supply.

As we have seen above, coal plays a central role in energy supply in China. Far from declining, we have seen that the importance of coal has actually increased and is predicted to continue to do so, in the absence of a major shift in policy from its present path. Indeed faced with disappointing finds from the oil and natural gas sector, in 1981 the Chinese began an explicit policy of 'substituting coal for oil' (*mei dai you*), in order to ensure that the main source of fuel for power generation came from domestic sources. Since 1993 China has been a net importer of petroleum, and became a net importer of crude oil in 1996. The policy of 'substituting coal for oil' had a clear strategic imperative of intending to minimize China's dependence on imported fuel sources, by making use of domestically produced coal, of which China has abundant supplies. The share of coal-fired power stations in total electricity generation rose from 60 per cent in 1980 to 68 per cent in 1995 (ABN–AMRO, 1998: 31). Coal-fired power stations are planned to account for 80 per cent of planned new capacity, so that the share of coal-fired power stations in electricity generation will rise to 77 per cent by the year 2000 (ABN–AMRO, 1998: 10). As we have seen, it is expected that coal production in China will rise from 1.3 billion tons in 1995, to 2.10 billion tons in 2020. In the absence of fundamental policy shifts it may rise as high as 2.6–3.0 billion tons by 2050. China's share of world coal consumption could rise from its present high level of almost 30 per cent to as high as 40 per cent or even more. We have noted already the enormous importance this could have for world climate change.

China's electricity industry grew at high speed after the 1970s. The total amount of electricity generated rose from 301 TWh in 1980 to 1080 TWh in 1996, and is predicted to rise to as much as 2500 TWh in 2010 (Kao, 1998: 5). In the 1980s most power plants were relatively small scale, with 100–300 MW units as the mainstay. Even in this period, a large number of small power plants of less than 100 MW were installed. In the 1990s, the average size of new power plants increased, and 300–600 MW power units became more common (Lu Yansun, 1997: 11). However, still in 1994, only around 12 per cent of power units were above 300 MW. It was still the case that in 1996, small power units of less than 100 MW accounted for 37 per cent of total installed capacity of thermal power stations (Lu Yansun, 1997: 11). These small-scale power plants typically were much less efficient in converting coal into electricity and have higher emissions of pollutants per unit of electricity (World Bank, 1997a: 55). Smaller, more dispersed power stations provide better opportunities for small-scale local mines to compete with large state-owned mines (see below).

The Chinese government policy is committed to continuing to raise the share of large, modern power plants in new power installations. From the late 1990s onwards the government intends that only power plants of 300 MW or above are built. It is possible that the government may introduce a tax on emissions from power stations and large industrial boilers (World Bank, 1997a: 55). This will further discourage the construction of small power stations.

China also intends to increase the number of large pit-head power plants alongside large coal mines, which will further enhance their competitiveness in relation to small coal mines. This will eliminate high-cost transport of coal by rail, with electricity instead being transported through power lines to the centres of consumption ('coal by wire'). The first large-scale pit-head power project will go into operation in 1999. It is located in Yancheng in Shanxi Province, and will have six 350 MW generators (US Energy Information Agency, 1998). Another 10 large and medium-sized pit-head power plants are planned to go into operation in the near future.

There has been a substantial improvement in the efficiency with which the Chinese economy uses energy. In 1980, China consumed 3.5 tons of coal-equivalent per $1000 of GDP. By 1995 this had fallen to under 2 tons (World Bank, 1997a: 47). This large improvement was achieved due to a number of influences, including the rising real price of coal, oil and electricity, and investment in modern, energy-efficient equipment. Despite the large improvements, China is 'still among the world's most energy-intensive economies' (World Bank, 1997a: 47–8). If current trends continue, China's energy intensity will reach 0.586 tons of coal-equivalent per $1000 of GDP by 2020, three times less than in 1995, but still above the current US level of just 0.5 tons per $1000. 'Thus there is a huge potential for reducing China's energy intensity' (World Bank, 1997a: 48).[2] The World Bank has identified several paths through which China could continue its already considerable achievements in energy-efficiency improvements, by advancing its energy-using technology towards the standards of the advanced economies (Table 10-11). It estimates that at the 1995 level of energy use China could reduce its level of coal consumption by 20 per cent, or around 250 million tons if it adopted best-practice technology already available in the advanced economies (Table 10-11).

Unfortunately, China's capability to substitute other sources of energy for coal is very limited: 'China is an energy-scarce economy, with *per capita* energy endowments far below the world average' (World Bank, 1997a: 48). China's *per capita* reserves of crude oil are just 3 tons, compared to a global average of 28 tons (Table 10-12). Its *per capita* reserves of natural gas are just 1416 cubic metres, compared to a global average of 28 400 cubic metres. China's *per capita* reserves of hydro power are 1603 kilowatt hours per year, compared to a global average of 2909 kilowatt hours. Even China's huge coal reserves amount to just 95 tons *per capita*, compared to a global average of 209 tons. Despite enormous efforts to increase electricity generation through hydro power, its share of overall energy supply has fallen. China's limited domestic oil resources have been used mainly for transportation and the petrochemicals industry. Natural gas still plays an insignificant role in the economy. Nuclear power and renewable energy still play a small role in energy supply: 'China's ambitious nuclear energy programme must deal with high capital costs, inadequate domestic expertise, a potential lack of indigenous uranium reserves, and the uncertain costs and safety of nuclear waste disposal' (World Bank, 1997a: 49).

TABLE 10-11 **Adopting Best-Practice Technology could Reduce China's Coal Consumption by 20%**

Equipment or production process	Share of China's energy consumption	Average efficiency in China	High efficiency in OECD countries	One-time energy savings at 1995 level of energy use
Industrial boilers	30% of coal consumption	65%	>80%	70 million tons of coal
Coal-fired power plants	30% of coal consumption	414 kgs of coal equivalent	<350 grams of coal equivalent per kilowatt hour	60 million tons of coal
Steel making	10% of total energy use	40 gigajoules per ton of steel	20 gigajoules per ton of steel	60 million tons of coal
Cement kilns	7% of coal consumption	170 kgs of coal equivalent per ton of clinker	100 kgs of coal equivalent per ton of clinker	30 million tons of coal
Fans and pumps	30% of electricity use	75%	>85%	30 billion kilowatt hours or 17 million tons of coal
Electric motors	40% of electricity use	87%*	92%	18 billion kilowatt hours or 10 million tons of coal
Total saving				247 million tons of coal

SOURCE: World Bank (1997a: 49)

NOTE: *Average efficiency of mean motor size

TABLE 10-12 **China's Energy Reserves Compared to the Global Average and to the USA, 1997**

Country	Raw coal (tons)	Crude oil (tons)	Natural gas (cubic metres)	Hydropower (kilowatt hours per annum)
China				
Total	115 billion	3.3 billion	1.7 trillion	1 923 billion
Per capita	95	3	1 416	1 603
United States				
Total	241 billion	3.8 billion	4.6 trillion	376 billion
Per capita	962	15	18 400	1 504
World				
Total	1044 billion	141.0 billion	142.0 trillion	14546 billion
Per capita	209	28	28 400	2 909

SOURCE: World Bank (1997a: 49)

A deep strategic issue for China is the degree to which it increases imports of oil, natural gas, and even coal. In 1995, China's net imports of oil and gas totalled around $1.4 billion. However, it is possible that high-income, fast-growing coastal provinces, especially those in the south, could increasingly use imports to substitute for increases in coal consumption from domestic sources, or even to replace some portion of coal consumption in those areas (World Bank, 1997a: 49–50). Policy in this area is in the course of continual evolution. An important recent policy signal was the decision announced in early 1999 to build a large liquefied natural gas (LNG) project in Guangdong Province in Southern China (*FT*, 4 March 1999). This multi-billion dollar project centres around a terminal near Shenzhen, capable of processing some 3 million tons of imported gas annually. The LNG would then be shipped through a 100 kilometre-long pipeline to a power station. Multinationals companies, such as Shell, Total, BP and others are reported to be 'interested in forming a joint venture' to run the project with a Chinese counterpart. The most likely domestic partner is thought to be China National Offshore Oil Corporation, 'which is keen on taking a majority stake'. LNG still accounts for only around 2 per cent of China's annual fuel consumption. The Shenzhen project is thought to reflect 'growing preoccupation with minimizing pollution and emphasizing efficiency in energy consumption' (*FT*, 4 March 1999).

International. The degree of competitiveness of the Chinese coal industry on the 'global level playing field' is a vexed question. In 1995, China's large state-owned coal mines were able to produce coal for an average of around $13 per ton for underground mined coal and $4–8 for open-cast coal (see below). Transport costs from the main coal mining regions in Shanxi/Inner Mongolia to East Coast ports add around 60–90 yuan ($7–11) per ton to pit head costs. Thus, the cost per ton of supplying Chinese coal from Shanxi/Inner Mongolia to the East Coast ports, in the late 1990s could range from $11 to 24 per ton. This compares with an international price for steam coal of $42 per ton in 1996, and $34 in 1998 (*FT*, 10 February 1999). Devaluation of the yuan would, self-evidently, have an impact on the export potentialities of the Chinese coal industry.

In fact, over the medium-term, China's coal exports have grown relatively slowly. Coal exports in 1996 stood at just 29 million tons, amounting to less than 3 per cent of national coal output, and less than one-half of the total supplied to world markets by Australia, the world's leading coal exporter. However, these amounted to around 13 per cent of the total world trade in coal in the late 1990s. It is easy to imagine that emerging large Chinese coal producers could in time become competitive exporters. A large modern coal company based in China would have large proximity advantages due to being close to the main markets for steam coal in Northeast Asia. For much of the reform period there was substantial excess demand for coal to meet China's booming energy needs, but that situation altered sharply in 1997–8. Even a small fraction of China's enormous and fast-growing coal output could constitute a very large fraction of internationally-traded coal. China's coal exports have begun to increase quite rapidly, rising to a predicted level of 40 million tons in 1999 (*FT*, 11 January 1999).

China's main coal export markets are in neighbouring East Asian countries. In 1997, out of a total of 27 million tons of coal exported through the China National Coal Export Company, 12 million tons went to Japan, seven million tons to Korea, five million tons each to Taiwan and Hong Kong. China and Korea have both invested heavily in the coal industry in Australia and Indonesia in order to guarantee supplies. An important strategic issue for China is to decide the degree to which it wishes these countries to deepen their relationship with China through increased investments in the Chinese coal industry. This could provide enhanced prospects for China's coal exports and help to deepen political relationships between China and these countries. China's exports to Japan are thought to be substantially 'government propelled'. South Korea's president, Kim Dae Jung promised during his visit to China that Korea would increase its imports of Chinese coal. Formosa Plastics in Taiwan has established a long-term contract, which currently accounts for 80 per cent of China's coal exports to Taiwan. Taiwan's Asia Cement imports all its coal from Pingshuo.

SUPPLY

China's Coal Resources. It is currently thought that the world has around 1100 billion tons of recoverable coal reserves. Although these are widely distributed across different countries, no less than 57 per cent are concentrated in the USA, the former USSR and China. Current international estimates of China's recoverable reserves indicate that it has around 11 per cent of the world's total, or around 126 billion tons (Bear, Stearns, 1998: 50). However, using a much broader definition of reserves, the China Coal Consultancy estimates that China's 'available reserves' are more than 600 billion tons. Moreover, they estimate that China's total coal reserves within a vertical depth of 1000 metres from the surface amount to no less than 2800 billion tons.

China's coal reserves, especially those in the Northwest and North, are of 'fairly high quality'. About 70 per cent are bituminous, 16 per cent anthracite and 14 per cent lignite. Around 35 per cent are coking coals. The sulphur content is mostly relatively low (Thompson, 1996: 732).

Unfortunately, a large fraction of China's coal reserves is underground. The latest estimates suggest that only around 11 per cent of China's coal reserves are suitable for open-cast mining (China Coal Consultancy, 1998). Currently, only 4 per cent of China's coal output is from open-cast mines. However, the reserves suitable for open-cast mining total 67 billion tons, around 50 times the total current annual output from all Chinese coal mines. China's large absolute reserves of potential open-cast mines means that it could greatly expand open-cast mining beyond the present level. Inner Mongolia has by far the richest potentialities for developing open-cast mining. It accounts for over 50 per cent of total national reserves of coal suitable for open-cast mining. Inner Mongolia's open-cast reserves total 33 billion tons (China Coal Consultancy, 1998).

TABLE 10-13 Coal Output and Consumption in Different Regions
of China (million tons), 1996

Area	Production	Consumption	Balance
Northwest coal base			
Shanxi	350	164	(+) 194
Shaanxi	46	41	(+) 5
Inner Mongolia	73	49	(+) 24
Sub-total	469	244	(+) 225
Northwest and North			
Hebei	74	114	(−) 40
Others	81	120	(−) 39
Sub-total	155	234	(−) 79
Northeast			
Heilongjiang	82	60	(+) 22
Others	86	145	(−) 58
Sub-total	168	204	(−) 36
East			
Shandong	90	100	(−) 11
Jiangsu	26	88	(−) 62
Anhui	46	53	(−) 7
Zhejiang	1	46	(−) 45
Fujian	12	18	(−) 7
Shanghai	-	41	(−) 1
Jiangxi	24	27	(−) 3
Sub-total	199	373	(−) 176
Central/South			
Henan	108	82	(+) 26
Others	88	190	(−) 103
Sub-total	195	273	(−) 79
Southwest			
Sichuan	96	92	(+) 3
Others	92	79	(+) 13
Sub-total	188	171	(+) 17
Grand total	1374	1499	(−) 125

SOURCE: Ministry of Coal Industry, quoted in ABN–AMRO (1998: 26)

China's coal reserves are highly imbalanced in their regional distribution
(Table 10-13). Three provinces/autonomous regions in Northwest China constitute the 'coal base'. They account for one-third of national production. Within
this group, a single province, Shanxi, accounts for fully one-quarter of national
output. The three 'coal base' provinces/ autonomous regions export 225 million
tons of coal, mainly to other parts of China. Southwestern China is more or
less in balance. However, each of the other main regions is in substantial deficit.
Eastern China is the largest consumer of coal, accounting for one-quarter

TABLE 10-14 Transport Costs for China's Main Coal Producers, 1997

Coal producer	Province	Production (million tons, 1996)	Main seaport	Transport cost, 1 July 1997 (yuan/ton)
Datong Mining Bureau	Shanxi	37.1	Qinghuangdao	68.2
Pingdangshan Mining Co.	Henan	20.7	Lianyungang	50.7
Kailuan Mining Bureau	Hebei	18.6	Qinghuangdao	16.4
Xishan Mining Bureau	Shanxi	17.7	Qingdao	58.6
Yanzhou Coal Co.	Shandong	17.2	Rizhao	23.1
Huaibei Mining Bureau	Anhui	16.9	Lianyungang	23.5
Yangquan Mining Bureau	Shanxi	16.2	Qingdao	51.6
Xuzhou Mining Bureau	Jiangsu	12.8	Lianyungang	17.7
Pingshuo Coal Co.	Shanxi	12.6	Qinghuangdao	80.8
Jincheng Mining Bureau	Shanxi	11.5	Rizhao	48.6
Luan Mining Bureau	Shanxi	10.2	Rizhao	54.9
Xinwen Mining Bureau	Shandong	9.0	Rizhao	29.6
Shenhua Coal Group	Inner Mongolia/ Shaanxi	7.8 (1997)	Qinghuangdao	110 (1998)

SOURCES: Ministry of Coal Industry and Ministry of Railways, quoted in ABM–AMRO, (1998: 24); except for data for Shenhua Group

of national consumption. It consumes around 174 million tons more than it produces. Jiangsu, Shanghai and Zhejiang province between them consume 148 million tons more than they produce.

Given that the Chinese government wishes to restrict coal imports to a minimum for reasons of energy security, the coal deficit provinces must essentially meet their coal requirements from domestic sources. A major issue in China's coal and energy development is the long distances involved in shipping coal from the Northwest to the main consuming regions. Transport costs per ton from local mines are a small fraction of those involved in shipping coal from the Northwest to the main seaports. For example, it costs an estimated 16–18 yuan per ton to ship coal from mines in Hebei and Jiangsu provinces to local seaports, compared to 70–80 yuan per ton to ship coal from the more remote coal mines in Northwestern China to the nearest ports (Table 10-14).

Small Local Coal Mines. During the Maoist epoch, before 1978, China encouraged the development of local mines. By the late 1970s, local state and non-state mines together accounted for over two-fifths of China's coal output. However, within the local mines sector, state mines accounted for over three-fifths of total output (Table 10-15). In the late 1970s, the central authorities took the decision to concentrate their investment resources on large-scale state mines. They gave greatly increased autonomy to localities to encourage the development of local mines using local resources. The demand for coal from local markets exploded from the early 1980s onwards alongside the boom in output from the

TABLE **10-15 Changes in the Institutional Distribution of the Output in the Chinese Coal Industry, 1979 and 1997 (million tons, % in brackets)**

Year	Total	Keypoint state mines	Local state mines	Local non-state mines
1979	635 (100)	356 (56)	171 (27)	108 (17)
1997	1372 (100)	535 (39)	220 (16)	617 (45)
Index (1979 = 100)	216	150	129	571
Annual rate of growth of output (%)	(4.4)	(2.3)	(1.4)	(10.1)
No. of mines (1995)	76 121	609*	2593	72 919

SOURCE: Thompson (1996: 730) and China Coal Consultancy (1998)

NOTE: *In 1995 these were organized in 78 'coal mining administrations', 9 corporations and 17 mines directly under the Ministry of Coal Industry.

TABLE **10-16 Size Distribution of Output in the Chinese Coal Industry, 1997**

Category of mine	Output (million tons, % in brackets)
Large (>1.0 million tons)	340 (25.2)
Medium (0.45–0.9 million tons)	130 (9.6)
Small (30 000–300 000 tons)	290 (21.5)
Very small (<30 000 tons)	590 (43.7)
Total	1350 (100)

SOURCE: China Coal Consultancy (1998)

township and village enterprises (TVEs). By the late 1990s, there were over 60 000 TVE coal mines, and an unknown number of small-scale private coal mines. TVEs remained much more important than purely private coal mines. In 1993, TVEs reportedly accounted for around 38 per cent of national coal output compared with 5 per cent from private mines (Thompson, 1996: 731). In the late 1990s, there were around 100 keypoint state coal administrations (under which were around 600 coal mines), and around 1700 local state-owned coal mines (China Coal Consultancy, 1998).

Local non-state owned mines were the main source of growth of coal output after the 1970s. Output from these mines grew by no less than 509 million tons from 1979 to 1997 (Table 10-15), amounting to 69 per cent of the total increased in China's coal output. Local state mines hardly increased their output at all, while keypoint state mines raised their output by almost 180 million tons, or around 50 per cent. By 1997, output from local non-state mines had overtaken that from the keypoint state mines. By the late 1990s, small mines with an annual output of less than 30 000 tons each accounted for 44 per cent of total Chinese coal output (Table 10-16).

TABLE 10-17 Cost Structure of Different Chinese Coal Producers, 1995 (yuan per ton, $ in brackets)

Items	Average cost for major state mines	Costs for some open-cast mines	Cost structure for a TVE mine in Heilongjiang province [a]	Cost structure for a TVE mine in Inner Mongolia [b]
Unit cost of raw coal	107 ($13)	34–63 ($4–8)	41–43[d] 64–66 $8[e]	14[d] 27 $3[e]
of which: materials	23	8–24	8–9	5[h]
Wages	38[c]	5–12	27	1[f]
Electricity	9	5–9	4[f]	—
Depreciation charges and engineering costs	11	5–9	—	—
Major repair funds	6	3–4	—	—
Simple reproduction maintenance funds	7	—	—	7[i]
Other	14	5–24	2–3	13[j]
Local taxes	—	—	23[g]	—

NOTES: a No. 7 mine, Xinxing District, Qitaihe Municipality
b Yaogouxiang Pit, Zhunge'er Banner, Inner Mongolia
c Including welfare funds
d Pit head cost, excluding local taxes
e Pit head cost, including local taxes
f Power
g Including 'development funds', 'simple reproduction maintenance funds', 'moving expenses', 'afforestion funds', 'environmental protection expenses', 'land-occupation expenses', 'rock- stocking expenses', 'resource compensation expenses', 'management expenses of TVEs', 'management expenses of free floating population' and 'land utilization tax'
h Including materials
i Including loading and transporting coal underground and on the surface
j Including 'simple reproduction development expenses', 'production development funds', 'water and soil conservation expenses', 'resource compensation expenses', 'organizing of marketing services', 'management of TVEs' and 'afforestation expenses'.

The costs of producing coal at China's local coal mines can often be highly competitive with large keypoint state mines. Moreover, the quality of their raw coal is not necessarily lower than that of large coal mines.[3] The China Coal Consultancy (CCC) estimates that in 1995 the average cost per ton of raw coal at a typical large state-owned underground mine was 107 yuan per ton, compared to 34–63 yuan per ton for coal from some open-cast mines (Table 10-17). Costs of production in TVE coal mines vary enormously. The CCC gives examples of two TVE coal mines. In one case, pit head cost were 14 yuan per ton, exclusive of local taxes, and 27 yuan per ton including local taxes. In the other case, pit head costs were 41–43 yuan per ton exclusive of local taxes, and around 65 yuan per ton including local taxes (China Coal Consultancy, 1998). Shenhua estimates that its pit head cost of coal is around 90 yuan/ton (exclusive of transport), compared to an average pit head price of around 40 yuan/ton for local TVE coal mines in Inner Mongolia.

To a considerable degree there has been a segmented market in coal in this period. Large keypoint state-owned (SOE) coal mines mainly supply large entities such as major steel plants, and, especially, large power stations. A large fraction of the transport space available for coal on railways is allocated to the large state coal mines. We have seen that small coal mines on average produce at lower pit head costs than the large state mines (China Coal Consultancy, 1998). However, the small mines typically have to truck their produce to a rail-head. Trucking costs average around 25–40 yuan/($3–5) ton for a distance of 70–100 kilometres. Moreover, due to the priority allocation to the large state producers, the low prices charged for rail transport (see below), and the huge excess demand for slow-growing railway freight space, small-scale mines have to pay a large number of 'fees' in order to get their produce on to trains. The China Coal Consultancy lists fourteen 'fees' that small coal mines have to pay in order to get their goods on the railway.[4] These total more than 25 yuan ($3) per ton. These two sets of costs compare with regular railway fees of around 70 yuan/ton to transport coal from Datong to Qinghuangdao. In other words, the small coal mines in Northwest China might have to pay almost double the cost paid by a large local state-owned coal producer in transporting their product to the coast.

Unsurprisingly, local coal mines are much more competitive in local than in long-distance markets. Local industrial enterprises, households and power stations have been mainly supplied by local small-scale non-state coal mines. In Shanxi, 94 per cent of coal for its power applications comes from the local mines. In Inner Mongolia, the proportion is around 65 per cent, and in Shaanxi, about 50 per cent (China Coal Consultancy, 1998). Eighty per cent of the coal produced by local mines is sold in the local province or region (China Coal Consultancy, 1998). We shall see below that small local mines frequently supplant large state mines in supplying large power stations, even though formal letters of intent have been signed with the large coal mines.

The price and allocation of coal sold by large state coal mines was strictly controlled until 1994. However, under the 'dual track' approach to price reform in the 1980s, the price of coal produced by small non-state mines was relatively free of state controls from early in the reform process (Lo, Dic 1997: 68). Not until the mid-1990s did state and TVE coal mines operate on a 'level playing field' as far as price was concerned.

Local governments were keen for local coal mines to develop, since they solved pressing local shortages of energy that emerged as rural industrialization proceeded at high speed. They provided sources of employment and income for under-employed farmers. At least two million people work in TVE mines. Not only was employment provided directly in large numbers in labour-intensive mines, but also there was a large amount of employment and income generated through the labour-intensive transport of coal, mainly in trucks. Moreover, a wide variety of service sector activities sprang up around the production and transport of coal. Given the remote location of much of this activity, people working in this sector are less able to seek protection than those working in more densely-settled areas. There is little academic study of the social conditions of the large number of people employed directly in the TVE mining sector or in the industries that service it. The TVE mines provide local governments with an important source of revenue through a variety of taxes. Local taxes typically add 50–100 per cent to the mine-mouth price of coal from TVE coal mines (see below).

Local coal mines were highly competitive in supplying local energy needs. They were able to capture the lion's share of the fast-growing local market for coal, supplying the myriad of small-scale power stations and factories that developed after the 1980s. Their growth had many positive effects on the local economy. However, their development also resulted in many serious problems.

Although there is a considerable degree of market segmentation between TVE and large state-owned coal mines, the degree of segmentation is far from complete. Although large modern power stations are technically supposed to use only coal of a requisite quality, supplied under contract from large state-owned mines, there is much evidence that TVEs do compete with large mines to supply them. The incentive for TVEs to compete with state mines has greatly increased as market liberalization since 1994 has substantially eliminated the price differential that used to exist between planned and free market coal prices. This does not necessarily mean that large power stations sacrifice quality, since a significant fraction of the coal from TVEs is of high quality, with low sulphur and high calorific value. Moreover, much of the coal even from large state mines is unwashed, and is not superior in this respect. In 1992, only 37 per cent of the coal from large state mines was washed (Thompson, 1996: 733). However, part of the competition with large state-owned mines has taken the form of substitution of cheap, low quality local coal from local non-state mines for contracts that are agreed for the supply of higher quality coal from large state mines. This intensifies the pollution generated by electricity generation and other forms of coal use.

Mining developments in almost all countries need to be approved by governments. However, the explosive development of small local coal mines in China has been accompanied by a great deal of unlicensed mining development. As we have seen there is a strong incentive for local governments to turn a blind eye to coal developments that would be unlikely to receive licences, since coal mines provide many stimuli to the local economy. It was reported that in 1998 there were no fewer than 51 200 coal mines operating in China without official approval, with an annual production capacity of 430 million tons. Even a 'legal' mine is hard to police. A small mine may be given a licence, but it is hard to identify whether the mine has encroached on the resources of a neighbouring large coal mine through underground development.

Equipment limitations mean that small coal mines are typically only able to extract the top metre or so of a coal seam. The seam can be 9 or 10 metres thick. Having taken only the top fraction of the seam, the remainder is typically rendered useless for large-scale mining due to water penetration and gas build-up. The recovery rate for China's local non-state coal mines is only around 10–20 per cent, compared to 30–40 per cent for small state-owned mines and 50 per cent for key-point state-owned mines (Thompson, 1996: 736).

The levels of safety in small local mines are dramatically worse than in state mines. In 1996 in keypoint SOE state mines there were just three large accidents, in which more than 10 people died. In local state mines there were nine such accidents. In local non-state mines there were no less than 61 such accidents. Deaths in large accidents per million tons of coal were 0.3 in keypoint mines, compared with 0.9 in local state mines and no less than 1.8 in local non-state mines (Table 10-18). In 1995 in the UK and USA there were reported to be just 0.04–0.05 deaths per million tons of coal.

In 1998–9, the Chinese government announced drastic measures to control the growth of small local non-state coal mines. The measures were impelled by the long-term problems of illegal coal mining, damage to China's coal resources, competitive pressure on the profit margins of large coal mines, and frequent substitution of low quality coal from local mines for contracted coal of higher quality from large mines. However, the measures were stimulated also by the fact that the Chinese rate of growth slowed down sharply in 1998–9, with a disproportionately large fall in the rate of growth of electricity demand. This reflected the fact that the slow-down disproportionately affected the most energy-using sectors

TABLE 10-18 Relative Safety of Different Types of Coal Mine in China, 1995–6

Category of mine	No. of deaths in mining accidents (1996)	Coal output (1995)	Deaths mining accidents per million tons of coal
UK	—	—	0.04 (1995)
USA	—	—	0.05 (1995)
Poland	—	—	0.25 (1994)
Russia	—	—	0.96 (1993)
China:			
Keypoint state	132*	535	0.3*
Local state	197*	220	0.9*
Local non-state	1086*	617	1.8*

SOURCE: MGB, ZMGN (1997: 131–6, 336–7)

NOTE: *Including only 'large' accidents in which more than 10 people died in heavy industry. In December 1998 the central government announced that it planned to close 25 800 small coal mines, to reduce national coal output by no less than 250 million tons by the end of 1999 (*CDBW*, 13 December 1998). It estimated that the closure would mean the loss of almost one million jobs in the coal industry. The linkage of the closure of small mines with the profitability of large state-owned mines was explicit. Wei Maohe, director of the office for reconstructing local township coal mines, under the State Coal Industry Bureau said that there was no choice but to close small mines in order to reduce coal production and 'help bail out the loss-stricken sector' (quoted in *CDBW*, 13 December 1998). It was thought that the closures could reduce the industry's losses by around one-half (*FT*, 11 January 1999).

It is questionable whether the central authorities will be successful in closing down large numbers of small mines. The pressure of market forces and the pressure from local governments to continue to allow small coal mines to operate is intense.

State-Owned Coal Mines. Despite the rapid rise of small-scale coal mines, large state-owned coal mines are still the mainstay of the industry. Detailed data for the early 1990s show that just 90 large-scale SOE coal mines accounted for 74 per cent of the total fixed assets in the coal mining sector (Table 10-19), and over one-half of the number of employees. However, the large-scale sector accounted for only 60 per cent of the sector's gross output value. Moreover, the large-scale sector was heavily loss-making, accounting for almost the entire losses of the sector. In sharp contrast, taken overall, small-scale mines were profitable. Of course, the small scale sector contained tens of thousands of mines, and the sector undoubtedly conceals a wide variation in levels of profitability. Although the small-scale sector had only one-third of the value of assets per worker of the large-scale sector, it was able to generate an almost identical level of output value per worker. It is impossible to estimate the degree to which this was due to greater efficiency in the use of inputs, as opposed to the fact that the market for coal in the early 1990s was still highly segmented, with the two sectors operating in very different economic environments in terms of control over output allocation and price paid for their products.

Liberalization of Markets. Prior to 1993, coal allocation from state-owned mines was tightly controlled as part of the mandatory planning system. Most coal from state-owned mines was purchased from state-designated suppliers. From 1994, the plan changed from mandatory to guidance status. An annual coal allocation convention implements the state's General Allocation Plan (GAP). Around one half of annual coal supplies are allocated according to letters of intent signed at the state-organized convention. A key function of the conference is to link coal allocation with transport allocation. Typically, contracts entered into at the convention obtain matching state allocations on the rail system. Coal transportation accounts for around 40 per cent of the total volume of railway freight in China. There has typically been an intense transport bottleneck in the reform period. Explosive growth of coal supply has proceeded alongside slow growth of the railway system.

TABLE 10-19 Size Structure of the Chinese Coal Mining Industry, 1991

Category of enterprise (No. of employees)	Gross Value of Output		No. of enterprises	Post-tax profits (billion yuan)	Fixed assets		Per worker (yuan)	No. of employees (million)
	Total (billion yuan)	Per employee (yuan)			Total (billion yuan)	Per enterprise (million yuan)		
Total*	51.88	8600	9682	(−) 5.55	117.95	12.2	19 500	6.04
of which:								
>10 000	30.86	8767	90	(−) 5.77	87.37	970.8	24 800	3.52
1000–10000	9.45	8217	495	(−) 0.50	20.07	40.5	17 500	1.15
<1000 **	11.57	8445	9097	(+) 0.72	10.51	1.2	7700	1.37
TVE coal mines (2)	13.8	8070	21 980	—	—	—	—	1.71
of which:								
Township (xiang)	7.13	7940	7168	—	—	—	—	0.898
Village (cun)	6.77	8021	14 812	—	—	—	—	0.839

SOURCES: SSB, ZGJTN (1993: 373); SSB, ZTN (1993: 441–2)

NOTES: * Enterprises with independent accounting
** There is substantial overlap between these categories, but it is impossible to determine the exact extent of such overlap.

Before 1994 coal prices for China's state coal mines were set by the state at a substantial discount compared to world market prices. Coal prices form the foundation of all other prices, due to the central role of coal in energy supply in China. Up to 1965 the average price of coal was raised only minimally. From 1965 to 1978, despite rising costs of production, there was no increase at all in the state-set price of coal. For much of the period since 1956, 'coal has been sold at half, or even less, of the costs of production' (Thompson, 1996: 744). This placed great pressure on the operating margins of China's coal producers. China's SOE coal mines' losses were propping up the rest of the economy, since 75 per cent of China's electricity is produced with coal.

In the 1980s the government declared its intention to gradually liberalize China's price system. Intense debate took place in the 1980s on the best way to reform the prices of China's energy sector: 'Literally hundreds of articles were written in the newspapers and academic journals on how best to reform energy prices' (Thompson, 1996: 745). In the early 1980s there were several upward adjustments of coal prices. Then, in 1984 the government introduced the famous dual track price system for coal and for a wide range of other products. Coal sold outside the state's planned delivery system could be sold at 'above quota' prices determined by planners or at genuine 'free market' prices. 'Above-quota prices' were initially fixed at a 50 per cent premium on state planned prices, and subsequently this was raised to 70 per cent. However, a large fraction of coal output from state mines continued to be sold at planned prices. This contributed to an artificial inflation of free market prices much beyond the level they would have been at in the absence of the state's planned purchase system. The main beneficiaries of the high free market prices were the (small-scale) non-state coal mines which sold the bulk of their output at free market prices.

In 1993, the price of coal was substantially liberalized, with an end to the dual track pricing system. Liberalization was followed by a substantial rise in domestic coal prices during 1994–7. In Shanghai, the price of number 2 clean coal rose steadily from 260 yuan per ton in January 1994 to 380 yuan per ton in January 1997 (MSDW, 1998a: 16). This period coincided with a substantial rise in world coal prices: the price of internationally traded steam coal sold under contract rose from \$34 per ton in 1994 to over \$40 per ton in 1996–7 (FT, 10 February 1998).[5] By the mid-1990s, domestic coal prices were close to those on the international market (see Table 10-20). In 1995, the price of steam coal was \$1.1–2.0 per kilojoule, compared to \$1.2–1.5 in the USA and around \$1.5 in the spot market (World Bank, 1997a: 53).[6] However, the market for coal was far from perfect. We have already noted the large transport costs from the main coal-producing areas to the main coal-consuming areas. In June 1994, it was reported that the mine-mouth price of mixed coal in Datong (Shanxi province) was 128 yuan per ton, compared with 230 yuan per ton for the same coal in Shanghai, 280 yuan per ton in Guangzhou and 340 yuan in Xiamen (World Bank, 1997: 55).

China still maintains a tariff on imported coal, but this has fallen to very low levels: in 1997 the tariff was 15 per cent (MSDW, 1998a: 10), and in 1998, the tariff on imported steam coal fell to just 6 per cent and 3 per cent for coking coal. Some price ceilings still remained for coal sales to domestic power utilities,

TABLE **10-20** **Comparison of Thermal Coal Prices between**
Australian and Chinese Coastal Cities, July 1997

Region	City	Thermal coal price ($/ton)
Eastern China	Shanghai	31.3
	Ningbo	36.3
	Nanjing	39.8
	Qingdao	40.5
	Xiamen	42.8
Northern China	Tianjin	31.1
	Beijing	31.3
Northeast China	Harbin	29.5
	Dalian	32.5
Southern China	Shenzhen	43.4
	Guangzhou	45.5
Australia		48.2*
		35.0* (Nov. 1998)

SOURCE: MSDW (1998e: 10)

NOTE: *Includes shipping charge of $10.5/ton from Queensland, Australia to
China

with the state intervening to slow the rate of increase of domestic prices towards
world prices. Since 1997, coal prices in world markets have fallen sharply due
to the Asian crisis, from over $40 per ton for steam coal in 1997 back to around
$34 per ton (*FT*, 10 February 1998).

Foreign Investment. Foreign direct investment in the Chinese coal industry
has been extremely limited: 'Substantial capital and infrastructure is generally
required, while profit margins are slim ... The government also remains cautious
in relinquishing control over the strategic sector'. The only substantial joint venture has been between Occidental and the Antaibao mine. The foreign partner in
the venture was Occidental. The mine opened in 1987, 'after years of planning and
negotiations'. At that point it was the largest single joint venture project in China.
The venture encountered many problems. These included problems recruiting the
necessary Chinese personnel and obtaining necessary materials, such as winter
fuel. However, the key problem was the collapse in the international coal price.
Occidental eventually pulled out of the project in 1991 (*Far Eastern Economic
Review*, 7 February 1991).

The only other significant foreign investment in the Chinese mining industry
was a Japanese loan of $0.8 billion on concessionary terms to facilitate develop-
ment of the Zhunge'er Project in Inner Mongolia (see below).

PRICES, PROFITS AND LOSSES

China's coal industry has had chronic financial difficulties throughout the
planned economy period. In 1957 one-half of the state-owned keypoint coal

mines were loss-makers. In the 1980s, almost all keypoint coal mines made losses (Thompson, 1996: 739). The government 'almost routinely bailed out the mines with shortfalls, even those which had been fiscally irresponsible, as opposed to merely incompetent' (Thompson, 1996: 740). In 1992, among the 100 largest coal mining enterprises (by gross value of output), no fewer than 77 were loss-makers (DRC, ZDQP, 1993: 76–7). Of these, 16 made losses of between 100 and 300 million yuan, 22 made losses of between 50 and 100 million yuan, and 39 made losses of less than 50 million yuan. Among the top 500 Chinese enterprises (by gross value of output), there were 42 loss-makers in 1992. Of these no fewer than 21 were coal mining enterprises (DRC, ZDQP, 1993: 2–11). The burden on provinces with highly developed coal mining industries was large. For example, in 1992 in Inner Mongolia, Liaoning, Jilin and Heilongjiang, among the top 100 enterprises within each of these provinces and autonomous regions there was a total of 19 enterprises which made losses of over 50 million yuan. Of these, no fewer than 15 were coal mining enterprises (DRC, ZDQP, 1993: 294–301).

In the 1990s, the industry's financial performance began to turn around alongside the liberalization of prices. Price liberalization was of great benefit to state-owned enterprises, which were now able to enjoy prices that were close to world market prices. Moreover, liberalization took place alongside a period of substantial increases in world coal prices. By 1997 the state-owned coal mining sector as a whole ceased to be loss-making. However, even in 1997, around 60 per cent of coal mines were loss-makers (MSDW, 1998a: 15). A large fraction of small mines was reported to be making losses, for the reasons outlined above.

However, the effect of liberalization was to end the price differential between state planned prices and those in the free market. This tended to produce a fall in the relative price paid for the coal sold by small non-state coal mines. Many small coal mines that had previously been able to earn profits became loss-makers. In addition, the rate of growth of the Chinese economy slowed down substantially in 1997 and 1998. The rate of growth of demand for coal slowed substantially. Large stock piles of coal developed. Moreover, in 1997/98 the Asian crisis placed intense downward pressure on world coal prices. International prices for steam coal fell from $42 per ton in 1996 to $34 in late 1998 (*FT*, 10 February). In 1998, state coal mines once more became loss-makers, with reported losses of 3.75 billion yuan in the first nine months compared to profits of 4.43 billion yuan in the same period in 1997 (*SCMP*, Hong Kong, 13 November 1998). There were reports of widespread difficulties among small non-state coal mines.

Of the 100 or so keypoint state coal mining enterprises, a mere 13 were reported to be making profits in 1998. Thirty were breaking even and the remainder were all loss-makers. There are around 20 'natural loss-making' keypoint coal mines, accounting for only around 10 per cent of the output of keypoint coal mines, but close to 40 per cent of their total losses. These mines have encountered fundamental natural problems, such as exhaustion of reserves or technically insurmountable problems with the exploitation of reserves. The largest of the natural loss-makers, such as Jixi (Heilongjiang), Fuxin and Fushun (both in Liaoning), each has losses of around 1–200 million yuan per annum. There are several 'small loss-makers' with annual losses of 'several tens of millions of yuan'.

The Chinese government has adopted different policies towards different types of keypoint mine. These policies were announced in 1993 but only began to be strictly put into practice in 1996. Profit-makers are to hand-over a proportion of their profits to an industry fund to assist loss-making keypoint mines. Loss-makers with the potential to develop are being given 2–4 years to continue as loss-makers with subsidies, but they must become profit-makers within the time specified. Big 'natural loss-makers' are being given 'some years' to continue as loss-makers with government subsidies. The two categories of loss-makers are each year in the mid/late 1990s receiving over 4 billion yuan (the equivalent of around $0.5 billion) in government subsidies. They are receiving around 1 billion yuan per annum from the Ministry of Finance and around 3 billion yuan from the Industrial and Commercial Bank of China in zero interest rate loans. In addition, they have 4 per cent of the VAT tax on their coal sales returned to them and all their income tax returned to them.

There is no clear government view of what will happen in three to four years if these keypoint coal mines are still loss-making. Up until October 1998 all key-point mines were under the control of the central government's Ministry of Coal Industry. In that month all the keypoint mines were transferred to the control of their respective provinces. Shenhua (see below) was the sole exception to this. It remained under the control of the Ministry of Coal Industry's successor body, the Coal Bureau. The transfer of keypoint coal mines to the authority of local governments assumes large significance in view of the problem of loss-making, which has not disappeared. In the view of the China Coal Consultancy, 'it is up to the local authorities to take the ultimate decision about whether these mines should continue in production'. The problems of closing large loss-making coal mines are well-known. The largest loss-making mines, such as Jixi, have over 100 000 employees and a total dependent population, including miners' families, of 400 000–500 000 people. The Chinese government is acutely aware of the potential for social turbulence if mines such as these are closed down.

Attempts to transfer employees to other local occupations have not typically been successful. The large keypoint mines are typically in remote areas: 'There is no way other than to keep on supporting them'. Since Liberation, the state's pricing policy has, in effect, taken away profits that today's loss-making keypoint mines might have made. The state has had an implicit contract with the keypoint mines that it would support them irrespective of whether they made profits. It has encouraged large numbers of employees to enter the industry, believing that the state would guarantee their future employment prospects.

China's subsidies to the coal industry need to be seen in perspective. The world's most heavily subsidized coal industry is probably that of Germany. Employment in the German coal industry fell from almost 500 000 in 1960 to just under 100 000 in 1995 (*FT*, 13 February 1997), alongside a fall in German coal production from around 470 million tons to 252 million tons in 1995 (Table 10-6). In 1997, German coal production costs were estimated at around $170 per ton,

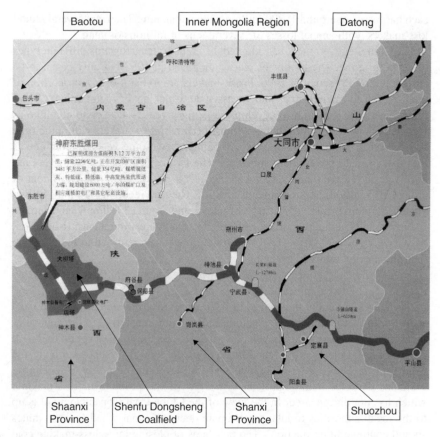

Figure 10-1 Map of the Location of the Main Communication Links of the Shenhua Coal Company

compared to the (then) world price of around $45 per ton (*FT*, 13 February 1997). The German government has decided to provide large subsidies to the coal industry. This is partly for strategic reasons. Germany has few domestic sources of energy. A spokesman for Ruhrkohle commented: 'The most important point is to keep the option of a German coal industry open for future generations' (*FT*, 13 February 1997). Abolishing subsidies 'would lead to a complete shutdown of the industry'. Once the mines were closed, they would be hard to reopen, as they would deteriorate without maintenance and would fill with water. The second objective is to protect a 'living coal industry' in order to provide a local market for Germany's powerful coal equipment industry. Germany accounts for an estimated 40 per cent of coal machinery produced by Western industrialized nations. The difficult conditions of German coal mining have stimulated technical progress in the German coal machinery industry. It is argued that without the substantial home market in which to develop technologies, Germany will miss out on the fast-growing markets of Asia.

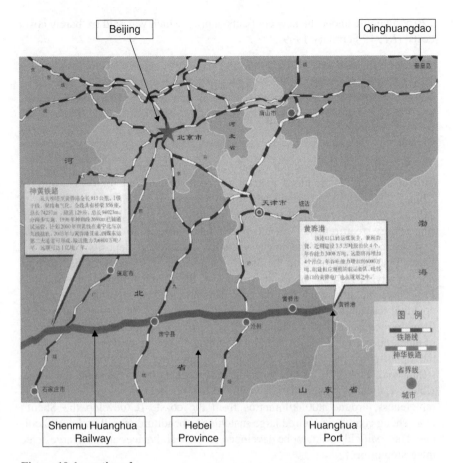

Figure 10-1 continued

In order to sustain the high-cost German industry, in the late 1990s the German government provides annual subsidies of around 10 billion DM per annum, the equivalent of over $6.1 billion, totalling more than $60 000 per worker in the German coal industry. Germany's subsidies to the coal industry amount to the equivalent of no less than one-third of the total gross output value of the entire Chinese coal industry (the equivalent of approximately $18.3 billion in 1997) (SSB, ZTN, 1998: 444). They amount to around twelve times the subsidy that the Chinese government reportedly provides to its loss-making coal mines (see above).

The British coal industry is not directly subsidized by the British government, and the industry has sharply reduced its sales to the British power industry (from 65 million tons in 1991 to 37 million tons in 1997) (*FT*, 19 February 1999). However, there have been large indirect subsidies through the government-enforced contracts signed with the fossil fuel generators before the coal industry was privatized. These contracts ended in 1998. Under the old contracts, the power generators paid a reported 140 p/gigajoule for coal, compared to only

120 p/gigajoule under the new contracts, a price which was said to 'barely cover costs' (*FT*, 19 February 1999).

SHENHUA

THE STRATEGIC ROLE OF THE SHENHUA GROUP IN CHINA'S
ECONOMIC DEVELOPMENT

The Shenhua project grew out of several sets of influences. China's explosive growth after 1978 produced matching growth of demand for coal. Many of China's old-established large-scale mines were facing increasing costs due to exhaustion of easily-worked seams and steadily increasing depth. China's long-run energy requirements meant that China needed to find reliable low-cost sources of coal. The huge, virtually unexploited deposits beneath the Ordos Plateau, that make up the Shenfu Dongsheng coalfield, provided such an opportunity. A further important stimulus to the establishment of the Shenhua Project was the high quality of the coal. This provided an opportunity to provide coal that was suitable for the modern, low-emission power stations that were to form an increasing part of China's energy portfolio. Moreover, the combination of the large size of the deposits and the high quality of the coal provided a potential opportunity for China to develop a competitive international supplier of steam coal, especially to the booming coal markets in surrounding East Asia. However, a major reason that the coalfield had not been developed earlier is its remoteness, around 800 kilometres from the coast. To develop the Shenfu Dongsheng coalfield required large matching expenditure on rail and port facilities. The coalfield could not be developed piecemeal. It necessitated a large-scale integrated project.

The Project began in 1985. The third phase of construction will be completed by the year 2005. By that time the coalfield will be connected by a dedicated rail link to a dedicated port facility. Output is predicted to be around 60 million tons, with a long-run goal of around 100 million tons. The aggregate investment over the 20 year period will be the equivalent of over $9 billion, making it one of the world's largest single projects. Within China it is second in scale only to the Three Gorges Dam. This compares with a figure of $3.2 billion for China's total investment in the coal industry in 1997 (SSB, ZTN, 1998: 194). In 1997, investment in the whole Shenhua project totalled the equivalent of $0.4 billion, compared with a total investment in the Chinese coal industry of $3.2 billion. In other words, the Shenhua project alone accounted for the equivalent of over 12 per cent of the total investment of the Chinese coal industry. The project is designated one of China key construction projects during the Ninth Five Year Plan, and in China's Long-Term Development Plan up to the year 2000.

The high importance that the Chinese government attaches to the project is indicated by the fact that the chairman of Shenhua is Ye Qing. He is appointed by the State Council and took up his position as head of Shenhua in 1998.

Ye Qing was formerly the deputy director of the State Planning Commission, with special responsibility for energy. Ye Qing is acutely aware of the nature of international competition in this industry. His strategy for the company is driven by the knowledge that Shenhua must compete with the global leaders in the mining industry both within China and in global markets. His goal is to turn Shenhua into a globally competitive mining company to rank with the world leaders.[7] One of his first tasks was to simplify the administrative structure of Shenhua, by merging the two separate production companies, Shenfu and Dongsheng into a single entity. In order to ensure that Shenhua's costs are in line with its global competitiors, Ye Qing is trying to ensure that manning levels at Shenhua are comparable with those in the international giant companies. He has tried to instill a market orientation to the company. This has been reflected especially in his drive to increase Shenhua's exports. This in turn meant completing at high speed the new railway link with the coast, which will sharply reduce Shenhua's costs of production (see below). By the year 2000, Shenhua's exports had risen from negligible levels to 10 million tons and Ye Qing's intention was to build Shenhua into a major player in international markets, directly challenging the international giant companies exporting to East Asia. In order to develop markets for Shenhua's coal in domestic markets, Ye Qing has begun to invest in large modern power stations. In order to raise revenue for expansion, he plans that Shenhua will gradually issue shares on international markets, taking Shenhua's best assets and piece by piece floating them. In this way, he will be able to put pressure on the company steadily to improve its management level, since successful further share issues will depend on good financial performance of the existing flotations. Ye Qing believes that Shenhua must replicate the structure of the global mining giants, such as Rio Tinto, by developing mining businesses other than coal.

RESERVES

Size. The Shenfu Dongsheng coalfield is one of the world's largest and richest coalfields. The total coal-bearing area is 31 200 square kilometres. The coalfield has proven reserves of 223.6 billion tons (Shenhua Group, 1998). It is estimated that the total recoverable reserves of the area may be as high as 600 billion tons. These figures compare with an official estimate of only 126 billion tons for 'proven reserves' and 600 billion tons for 'total available reserves' for the whole of China, and 2800 billion tons of coal available across China at a depth of above 1000 metres (see above).

Whatever the precise figures of the reserves at the Shenfu Dongsheng coalfield, it is certain that it is one of the world's largest remaining undeveloped major coalfields. The Shenhua Group has overall responsibility for developing the entire coalfield. This provides the company with secure access to one of the world's largest concentrations of high quality coal. The reserves under the control of Shenhua dwarf those of other coal mining companies in China, and of

TABLE 10-21 Output, Reserves and Mine Depths at Selected Chinese Large Coal
Mines, 1996 (in Brackets: Rank by Physical Output)

Mine Name/Location	Output (1996)	Proven Reserves (MT)	Probable Reserves (MT)	Average Mine Depth (metres)
Shenhua Coal Group/Inner Mongolia–Shaanxi of which:	—	223 600*	600 000*	30–70
Area already opened up for development	6.6	35 400	—	—
Datong MA/Shanxi (1)	37	2 567	—	320
Yanzhou CMC/Shandong (3)	19	850**	1 422	397–1 000
Kailuan MA/Hebei (4)	19	1 663	—	1 000
Xishan/Shanxi (5)	18	3 097	—	350
Yangquan MA/Shanxi (7)	16	1 100	—	380
Pingshuo CC/Shanxi (9)	12	453	—	100–200
Jincheng MA/Shanxi (10)	12	373	—	325

SOURCES: China Coal Consultancy (1998); MSDW (1998e)

NOTES: * Reserves for the whole Shenfu–Dongsheng coalfield
   ** Including Jining III, which is not yet part of the company
   MA = Mining Administration, CMC = Coal Mining Company, CC = Coal
   Company, MT = Million Tons

any of the current leading multinational coal companies, such as Peabody or
Rio Tinto. The reserves are so large that if Shenhua were to produce the equivalent of the entire national Chinese coal output today (that is around 1.3 billion
tons), it would still take over 80 years to exhaust the coalfield's proven reserves
(assuming a 50 per cent extraction rate). Even the relatively small area so
far opened for development, in the western part of the coalfield, encompassing
3481 square kilometres, has proven reserves of 35 400 million tonnes of coal
(Shenhua Group, 1998).

The areas already opened up by Shenhua have reserves that are fourteen times
as large as those of China's largest coal company, Datong. The proven reserves
of the whole coalfield, for which Shenhua has responsibility, amount to no less
than 80–90 times the size of those of Datong (Table 10-21). Datong's reserves
are already substantially depleted. It is thought that at the present rate of production, Datong will be exhausted by 2030. Unlike the older, large state-owned
mines, Shenhua's vast reserves have hardly been touched. Only a small fraction
of the total deposits have been taken by small-scale coal mines, mainly TVEs
using primitive technology.

Depth. Not only does Shenhua have vast reserves under its control, at least as
important is the fact that the average depth of the reserves is shallow, at between
30–70 metres below the surface. Much of the coal is accessible using open-cast
techniques, with a relatively small 'overburden' compared to many open-cast

mines around the world. With present open-cast mining technology, it is thought that in the areas currently being developed, around one-quarter of the coal will be mined using open-cast techniques. Underground mining at Shenhua typically is able to employ the 'incline' method. This means that coal can be shipped out of the mine by means of a conveyor belt, rather than through lifting vertically up a mine-shaft. 'Pit-head' costs of production at Shenhua are very competitive. The average depth of China's coal mines is about 480 metres, and average mining depth is falling by around 8–10 metres per annum (China Coal Consultancy, 1998). Almost all the old, large-scale coal mines in Northeast China are deep mines. Even in Northwest China, the old, large-scale state-owned mines are mainly deep mines. The average mine depth of the large coal mines in Shanxi, Shaanxi, Inner Mongolia and Hebei is 415 metres. Among China's top 10 mining companies, the average mining depth at Pingshuo is 100–200 metres, at Datong, Xishan, Yangquan, and Jincheng it is between 300–400 metres, at Yanzhou, 400–1000 metres, and at Kailuan, 1000 metres (Table 10-21).

Quality. Not only is the Shenfu Dongsheng coalfield of huge size, but the coal is also of high quality. This is a large advantage in an epoch in which coal is increasingly being differentiated by the category and quality of the product. This provides Shenhua with firm long-run market potential in view of the intensifying pressure within and outside China to reduce emissions from power stations and other coal users. The ash content is low, at under 10 per cent for raw, uncleaned coal. This compares with an ash content of 15–45 per cent for many large Chinese state-owned coal mining companies (Table 10-22). The sulphur content is very low, at less than 0.4 per cent for raw coal. This compares with a sulphur content of 0.5–5.0 per cent for many Chinese large state-owned coal mining companies (Table 10-22). These characteristics make Shenhua's coal excellent for use as steam coal, for coal gasification and for coal chemistry applications.

TABLE **10-22 Relative Quality of Raw (Unwashed) Coal from Shenhua and Selected Large Chinese State-Owned Coal Companies (late 1990's)**

Company Name	Ash Content (%)	Sulphur Content (%)
Shenhua	6–10	0.3–0.7
Kailuan	15–30	0.5–2.0
Yanzhou	20.3	0.6
Datong	5–20	0.5–1.9
Pingshuo (Antaibao)	20–45	0.3–4.9
Xishan	14–23	0.5–2.7
Yangquan	13–27	0.4–2.5
Jincheng	15–20	0.2–3.4

SOURCES: China Coal Consultancy (1998); MSDW, (1998e); Shenhua Group (1998)

It means that Shenhua's coal has strong long-term prospects for market growth through the sale of high quality coal to modern power stations, for use in house-holds and industrial boilers in areas that have tight controls over pollution. It is unsuitable for use as coking coal.

TRANSPORT

Rail. The main reason for the lack of development at the Shenfu Dongsheng coalfield has been the long distance from the major centres of coal consumption in China, and to the ports in order to export.

The construction of a dedicated rail link to the coast is central to the Shenhua scheme. The development of the railway is proceeding in tandem with the growth of production at Shenhua. The first stage of the railway development was to build a 172 kilometre link to the north, from Shenmu to Baotou, in order to link with the existing main west-east railway line. This was completed in 1989. A longer section of line to the east, totalling 269 kilometres, links Shenmu with Shuozhou, which in turn can also connect to the north with the existing west-east railway link. This was completed for trial operation in 1997. It is able to ship 32 million tons of coal per annum initially, and eventually to ship 52 million tons annually. The longest piece of rail construction is the final stage of the link between the coalfield and the sea. This is a 588 kilometre railway from Shuozhou to Huanghua port. By the year 2000 it will link with the main Beijing-Kowloon rail-way. The entire railway link will be completed in 2003. The designed capacity will be 69 million tons initially, rising over time to 100 million tons.

When it is completed the rail link from Da Liu Ta in the heart of the Shenfu Dongsheng coalfield, to the port of Huanghua, will total 825 kilometres. The ter-rain through which the railway passes includes large mountains in the first half of the route from Shenhua to the sea. In the latter half, it passes across the North China Plain, with a high risk of flooding. It will encompass 356 bridges, with a total length of 74 kilometres, and 129 tunnels, with a total length of 94 kilome-tres. Some idea of the importance of the Shenhua railway can be gauged by the fact that the average annual addition to China's entire railway network between 1980 and 1997 was just 450 kilometres (SSB, ZTN, 1998: 538). In other words, the Shenhua rail link from the coalfield to the port will be the equivalent of almost twice the average annual addition to China's rail network in the 1980s and 1990s.

China's rail network has grown far more slowly than the national economy. The rail network expanded by only 4200 kilometres between 1980 and 1997 (SSB, ZTN, 1998: 538). The average annual rate of growth of the rail network was just 0.9 per cent from 1980 to 1997, with only a marginally higher growth rate in the 1990s than in the 1980s. As we have noted, around 60 per cent of China's coal output is carried on the railway network, and coal accounts for over 40 per cent of the total volume of rail freight in China (China Coal Consultancy, 1998). There is especially high pressure on the allocation and transport capacity of coal produc-tion bases in Northwest China: 'To tackle the problem of coal transport is to solve the problems of the outward transport of coal from Shanxi Province, Shaanxi Province and Inner Mongolia' (China Coal Consultancy, 1998).

The construction of a dedicated railway for Shenhua provides an enormous competitive advantage. We have seen already that small coal mines face a large competitive disadvantage compared to large mines in gaining access to the rail network. The new rail link will enhance that potential advantage for Shenhua. However, it will provide a large advantage for Shenhua compared to the many state-owned mines that have to ship their produce along the highly congested west–east rail link from Shanxi to the coast.

At present, Shenhua's coal makes a very long and circuitous journey. There are two possible routes to ship Shenhua coal out of the coalfield to the coast. One is to the north through Baotou. The other is to the east initially, and then to the north to link with the Baotou–Beijing railway, running through Datong. In 1996, railway transport costs for shipping coal from Datong to the coast at Qinghuangdao were 68 yuan/ton (Table 10-14). Shenhua is around 400 kilometres from Datong, which is itself around 700 kilometres from Qinghuangdao. The extra distance from Shenhua, adds another 40 (+) yuan/ton to the transport costs.

The completion of the rail link to Huanghua will greatly reduce the distance over which Shenhua coal has to be transported to the coast, since Qinghuangdao is considerably to the Northeast of Huanghua. However, the extent to which Shenhua's transport costs will finally be reduced is uncertain. The Chinese government currently provides a large subsidy for rail transport. The official price for transporting coal on the railway is 0.08 yuan/ton/kilometre. State subsidies are reportedly 0.027 yuan/ton/kilometre. Unsurprisingly there is great excess demand. The cost/ton/kilometre on Shenhua's own rail links to Baotou and Shouzhou is set at 0.15–0.18 yuan/ton/kilometre. The latter figure may be taken as a rough approximation of the market price. After the completion of the rail link to Huanghua port, Shenhua will probably have to repay the large loans to the central government through which the construction of the railway was funded. Shenhua officials doubt that the net effect will be a significant fall in the cost of transport per ton for the Shenhua Group.

The construction of the dedicated rail link to the sea at the newly constructed port of Huanghua will provide Shenhua with a much more direct link with the coast. Instead of shipping its coal through a complicated series of rail links that join several systems together, the link is direct and under Shenhua's immediate control. Instead of having to contest for space with other large scale coal producers and with small scale producers willing to pay large extra fees in order to get their goods on the train, Shenhua will have the entire railway dedicated to the transport of its goods. This will be of great advantage in guaranteeing timely delivery of goods. The railway's capacity can be increased to meet the sales needs of Shenhua. The much-reduced distance over which Shenhua's coal will be transported will considerably reduce Shenhua's transport costs per ton. However, the reduction will be enhanced by the fact that there are considerable economies of scale in moving large quantities of coal along a dedicated rail line. We have already noted that a key to Hammersley Iron's low cost operations in Australia is the fact that it moves almost 60 million tons of iron ore per annum along its own dedicated 540 kilometre rail link to the port.

The degree to which benefits from economies of scale and dedicated route operation offset the costs consequent upon paying back the loans through which the railway was built are uncertain. Moreover, the whole price structure of the Chinese rail system may have altered by early in the new millennium.

Port. Port charges vary greatly around the world. In some cases, such as Queensland, they are 'especially high', and constitute a potential source of competitive disadvantage for mining companies that operate in those locations. China's ports have experienced severe over-crowding as their pace of construction has lagged behind the pace of economic advance. A large fraction of China's coal shipments in North China has been channelled through Qinghuangdao, but the port is subject to severe congestion. A key part of the Shenhua Project has been the construction of a dedicated port alongside the Huanghua railway and coalfield development. The construction of the port is divided into three phases, matching the expansion in coal production. The first phase of the port's construction will enable the handling of an annual capacity of 30 million tons. The second phase will allow the handling of 60 million tons annually, and the third phase, 100 million tons. The construction period will last from 1998 to 2004.

PROPERTY RIGHTS

Origins of Shenhua. The Shenhua project grew out of a scheme developed by the Huaneng Power Company. Huaneng Power was established in 1985. Its mandates from the government were to convert China's oil-fired power plants to coal-fired plants, to construct new coal-fired power plants, to operate and manage thermal power plants and develop and import advanced power generating technology to promote the growth of China's thermal power industry. In 1988, Huaneng Power was subsumed into the China Huaneng Group, one of the government's 55 large-scale enterprise groups set up with the approval of the State Council. By 1993, the China Huaneng Group had total assets of 45 billion yuan (CSFB, 1994: 19). Huaneng Power had assets of 10 billion yuan, and had participated in over 30 power generation projects, with a total capacity of over 11 000 MW.

In 1988, the Chinese government set up the Clean Coal Company to promote the use of high quality coal in order to reduce pollution. It began exploration activities in the Shenfu Dongsheng Coalfield and started to develop coal mines in the coalfield to produce high quality clean coal for modern power stations. In the same year the Clean Coal Company was transferred to Huaneng Power Company. In the same year, the State Council approved the feasibility of a large-scale project to develop the Shenfu Dongsheng Coalfield. Already, the central government was concerned about the variety of negative aspects of the rapid development of small-scale coal mines. Its policy shifted from one of encouraging the spontaneous development of small coal mines, to one of active support for large-scale modern coal mines as the main path to develop the coal industry. However, the State Council decided that Shenhua should become a separate company, completely independent of the Huaneng Power Company. It decided that the Shenhua Project required very large-scale investment. It believed that Huaneng was an electricity generation company, and should focus on electricity, rather than integrate vertically into an entirely different business, coal production. It believed that the Clean Coal Company was unsuitable to develop the Shenfu Dongsheng Coalfield due to its trans-regional nature. Accordingly, it was determined that the Shenhua Project should be an independent company, one of the 55 large enterprise groups approved by the State Council to spearhead China's business development (see above).

Overall Structure. The Shenhua Group Company is 100 per cent owned by the state. The company was established with stockholder rights formally exercised by the State Planning Commission. Its board of directors consists of 14 people. Eight of these are from Shenhua itself. The others are from related state institutions that have a close interest in Shenhua. These include the provinces of Shanxi, Shaanxi, and Hebei, Inner Mongolia Autonomous Region, the Ministry of Railways and the Ministry of Transportation. The Group makes no distribution of profits, as its assets are owned entirely by the state.

Coal Reserves. The Shenhua Group is 'responsible for the overall planning, development and operation of the coal reserves of the Shenfu Dongsheng coalfield' (Shenhua Group, 1998). This coalfield is located partly in Inner Mongolia Autonomous Region (Shenfu) and partly in Shaanxi Province (Dongsheng). These are adjacent administrative regions in Northern China. China's coal reserves are owned by the Chinese state. The National Bureau of Land Resources licenses the opening and operation of mines. Shenhua operates nine mines, which account for a small fraction of the total reserves of the whole Shenfu Dongsheng Coalfield. As the entity with formal responsibility to develop the entire coalfield's vast reserves, it seems very likely that Shenhua would be given licences to develop other parts of the field. The terms on which it does so are a potential source of future negotiation. It is in principle a possibility that the central government may not provide licences in the future to Shenhua, though this seems to be unlikely. Moreover, in the area in the western part of the coalfield which is already opened up for mining, the recoverable reserves are estimated to be 35.4 billion tons. If Shenhua climbs to its intended peak production of 100 million tons early in the next century, then simply by exploiting the small share of the reserves already approved for mining, it would be able to produce for over 150 years (at a 50 per cent rate of extraction).

Railway and Port. As we have seen, the Shenhua railway system consists of three segments: the line from Baotou to Shenmu, in the middle of the coalfield, that from Shenmu to Shuozhou, and that from Shuozhou to Huanghua (see below). The railway alone is one of China's largest current construction projects, amounting to the equivalent of a total of $3.0 billion for the entire system. It forms a key part of the state railway expansion since the 1970s.

The Shenmu to Baotou segment of the railway required an investment of 0.55 billion yuan. This was financed entirely as a capital injection from the central government's 'coal to replace oil' funds. The cost of building the Shenmu to Shouzhou section of the railway system is estimated to be 4 billion yuan, which will need to be financed by an estimated total of 7.6 billion yuan in loans. The finance is from the State Development Bank (SDB) (3.3 billion yuan), the State Construction Bank (2.5 billion yuan), and foreign loans (1.78 billion yuan). This portion of the Shenhua railway system is 'entirely owned by the Shenhua Group'.

The longest section of the rail system is that from Shuozhou to Huanghua. This is being constructed by the Shenhua Railway Company, which is an equity joint venture between the Shenhua Group (45 per cent of the equity), the Ministry of Railways (44 per cent of the equity), and the related local governments of Hebei (10 per cent) and Shanxi (1 per cent) provinces. The cumulative investment in the Shenhua railway system totalled 6580 million yuan by 1997. It is anticipated that it will require an investment of 16.6 billion yuan for the construction of the Shuozhou to Huanghua portion of the railway system by the time it is completed in the year 2002. Of this, 6.4 billion yuan will come from the SDB and 5.1 billion yuan from foreign loans.

Huanghua Port is being built by the Shenhua Huanghua Port Company Limited (see below), of which Shenhua Group is the holding company. The Company has equity contributed by both the Shenhua Group and Hebei Provincial Government. It is a state-owned entity with the status of an independent legal person. It has the responsibility for construction, operation and administration of the port. The total investment to construct the port is predicted to be 5.1 billion yuan ($0.6 billion).

The final status of the property rights of the port and railway is uncertain. Large loans have been made to Shenhua to construct the port and railway as part of the integrated Shenhua project. It is possible that Shenhua may be able to raise revenue by using surplus capacity to charge other entities to use these facilities. This is far from certain. Shenhua officials considered that it was impossible that the port and railway facilities would not ultimately 'belong to society' instead of the Shenhua Group: 'It cannot be imagined that the port and railway will ultimately belong to Shenhua'. This would only be possible if there was a very large change in the surrounding policy environment.

FINANCE

We have noted already that the total size of the project is very large, totalling 80 billion yuan (the equivalent of $9.6 billion) over its 20-year lifetime (see Table 10-23 for details of Shenhua's capital construction costs up to 1997). The vast bulk of the funding for the project is in the form of loans to the Shenhua Group.

TABLE **10-23 Capital Construction Investment of Shenhua Project, 1985–97**

Item	1997		1985–97	
	(million yuan)	*(%)*	*(million yuan)*	*(%)*
Total	2 631	100	15 187	100
of which:				
Coal mines*	1 255	48	8 505	56
Railway	1 306**	50	6 580	43
Port	70	3	152	1

NOTES: * Including power stations, which total 1.0 billion yuan
       ** of which: Shenmu-Shuozhou = 600 million yuan and Shuozhou-
          Huanghua = 706 million yuan

The main reasons for the large size of the investment required to build the company are, firstly, the need to construct large-scale railway and port facilities to make the whole project viable, and secondly, the fact that Shenhua has imported mainly modern mining equipment to equip its mines.

One large portion consists of 'soft' loans' from the Japanese government, which is extremely anxious to help reduce China's level of emissions from its power stations. It provided a total of around $400 million in low interest loans for the construction of Shenhua's Huo Ji Tu Mine (Table 10-24 for a full list of the mines within the Shenhua Group). The terms of the loan are 'soft', with an interest rate of just 2.6 per cent, repayable over 30, with a 10 year grace period. Although this amounts to 27 per cent of the total investment from 1985 to 1997, it amounts to under 5 per cent of the total cost of the project over its entire period of construction.

The state has injected a relatively small amount of capital, only 2 per cent of the total from 1985 to 1997 (Table 10-25). Shenhua is intended to be a model for China's modern enterprise system, with real economic independence. Part of this process is for Shenhua to be responsible for earning profits to repay the loans necessary to build the company. The major source of funding is from domestic loans, totalling 67 per cent of funds for investment in 1997. By 1997, Shenhua's total debts amounted to 16.8 billion yuan (the equivalent of over $2 billion), of which long-term borrowing totalled 14 billion yuan. Shenhua's sales revenue in 1997 was just 1.8 billion yuan. In relation to current revenue, Shenhua's level of indebtedness is extremely high. However, the project is far from completion, and its revenue should build up strongly once the railway and port are completed, and the mines being constructed move towards full capacity.

Shenhua's original plan was to proceed with the simultaneous construction of 20 pits in order to reach the target output of 60 million tons. However, the pressure of debt repayment and the slack market for coal, has forced it to reassess its initial strategy. It has decided to expand output to the level of 50 million tons simply using the nine pits already opened or under construction (Table 10-24).

TABLE **10-24 Shenhua Coal Group's Mining Facilities, 1998**

Mine Name	Devised Capacity (MTA)	Actual Capacity (MTA)	Output in 1997 (MT)	Employment	Reserves (MT)	Comments
Da Liu Ta	6	8	3.6 (1999 = 5.5)	400	1350	
Huo Ji Tu	5	8		270	930	Under construction
Shi Ke Tai	3	—	—	—	670	Under construction
Wu Jia Ta	8–10	—	—	270	329	Open-cast
Bu Lian Ta	3	5	—	—	740	Open-cast, began operation in 1997
Shang Wan	3	6 (predicted)	—	—	540	Open-cast, under construction
Wu Lan Mu Lu	0.3	1.8–3.0 (predicted)	0.6	—	640	
Huo Luo Wan	—	Phase 1 = 3 Phase 2 = 5	1.2	—	390	Open-cast
Ma Jia Ta	0.6	1.8 (predicted)	1.2	—	93	Open-cast
Sub-total		50 (+) (predicted by 2005)	—	2700		

SOURCE: Author's research notes

TABLE **10-25 Source of Funds for Shenhua's Investment, 1985–97 (%)**

Item	1997	1985–97
Self-raised funds	—	2
Capital injection from state	11	2
Foreign capital	22	27
'Coal to replace oil' funds	—	15
Domestic loans	67	54

SOURCE: Author's research notes

This will improve the financial performance, and enable it to pay back its debt more rapidly. In addition, as we have noted, alongside expanding output, Shenhua plans to reduce substantially the level of employment in the company.

The State Development Bank (SDB) is much the most important lender to Shenhua. By year-end 1998, it had lent 11.8 billion yuan (the equivalent of $1.4 billion), amounting to one-sixth of its total loans of 70 billion yuan (over $8 billion) to the entire coal industry. These are all technically 'hard' loans, with an annual interest rate that varies from a low of 8.01 per cent to a high of 15.3 per cent, with different rates for different tranches. The repayment period is 15 years. Interest repayments in 1998 were 0.2 billion yuan, and in 1998 will be 0.4 billion yuan. The peak period for repayments will be around 2005.

When the plans for Shenhua were drawn up, the prospects for coal demand looked much brighter than they are today. Coal demand domestically and internationally seems set to be weak for a considerable period ahead. We have already seen that Shenhua has significantly reorganized its expansion plans in order to cope with the unanticipated change in the medium-term prospects for the coal market. There is a possibility that in the light of these difficulties, the state's loans to Shenhua may be turned into asset injections. Moreover, as we shall see below, Shenhua was hugely restructured in 1998, with the absorption of five major coal producers, and a huge associated labour force. As a group these mines have large problems. The price of their administrative merger with Shenhua may be that a portion of Shenhua's debt to the SDB is turned into state capital injections. Without this, Shenhua's prospects to develop into a globally competitive, modern coal firm will be severely weakened.

Much will depend on the way in which the domestic and international coal markets behave in the years ahead. If the Chinese government is, indeed, successful in closing down large number of TVE coal mines, then the domestic market situation should improve substantially, and the capability for large state coal mines to return to profit will be much improved. This would increase the potentialities for debt repayment by these companies. However, the choices are harsh. The level of debts outstanding to the SDB would decline, but at the expense of great distress in the TVE coal mining sector. It may be politically easier to deal with unemployed mine workers in scattered rural communities than among huge concentrations of coal employees in large coal mines. These have been the source of social turbulence in almost all countries that have large coal industries, from the UK, Australia and the USA, through to the former USSR and Romania.

The government faces very difficult choices. These are not issues merely of 'balance sheets' and a 'hard budget constraint'. They involve complex issues of the political economy of development.

The implications for Shenhua's future cost structure and profitability of the treatment of its domestic debt are enormous. The greater the degree to which the government decides to treat the loans from the SDB as capital injections the greater the profits Shenhua will be able to earn and the more powerful it will be relative to both domestic and international competitors. The issue of the final status of Shenhua's long-term debt to the SDB is far from resolved.

One important route for raising capital is through flotation. China's ambitious plans for flotation have been sharply cut back in the wake of the East Asian crisis, the collapse of the Hong Kong stock market and the sharp decline in international investors' confidence in Chinese business institutions. However, there are clear signs that the worst of the East Asian crisis may be over. There is every chance that more large international flotations may get under way again. Shenhua is actively considering the possibility of floating part of the company. The most likely choice is the Da Liu Ta mine (Table 10-24).

MARKETS

Domestic
Electric power stations. We have seen that after 1980 there took place a rapid growth of small-scale power stations to meet urgent local needs. These provided a rapid short-term solution to the explosive growth of demand for electricity, especially from TVEs. These power stations typically used small generating units of under 200 MW, frequently below 100 MW. These were mainly of indigenous Chinese design. Environmental regulations were not strict. The huge number of small local power stations was designed mainly to use low quality, unwashed coal. These had a serious impact on China's emissions of particulates and tended to slow the pace at which China's energy efficiency was able to advance.

In the 1990s, the electricity generation industry has altered rapidly. The main changes include increasingly stringent anti-pollution regulations, development of the national grid network facilitating inter-regional transmission of electricity, growing commercialization of the production and sale of electricity, expansion of foreign investment, advances in the technical capabilities of domestic power equipment makers and growing imports of power equipment. Taken together, these forces have pushed the industry towards larger-scale, modern, equipment. This is often imported, produced within China in a Sino–foreign joint venture, or makes use of imported technology to supply advanced equipment from domestic manufacturers.

The net effect is that a fast-growing share of the new additions to China's power stations consists of large-scale modern units of 300 MW and above. These units are designed to use cleaner coal for greater efficiency and in order to meet tougher environmental standards. A large modern power station typically will be designed with a particular grade of coal in mind. Such a power station will often establish a long-term relationship with a particular coal supplier.

Shenhua already has letters of intent for the supply of 50 million tons of coal annually to large power stations that will be built in the next few years. However, it believes that in practice the contracted sales will not all materialize, because the power stations will take lower priced coal from other sources, notably TVEs. This has been the case, for example, with the huge Da La Te power station. This power station is 150 kilometres to the north of the Shenfu Dongsheng coalfield. It has a total capacity of 1000 MW (consisting of three 300 MW units). It is planned that Da La Te expands to become the biggest power station in Asia, with a final capacity of 5000 MW. However, in 1998 Shenhua believes that TVEs are able to substantially undercut the price at which they can sell coal to Da La Te. Local TVE mines are able to sell to Da La Te at a figure believed by Shenhua to be only 100 yuan (around $12) per ton, including transport costs. This compares with Shenhua's pithead price of around 100 yuan exclusive of transport costs to the power station. Shenhua anticipates that by 2004, it will be able to sell around 30 million tons to power stations, instead of the contracted figure of 50 million tons.

A major issue in the development of China's electricity system is the degree to which electricity is produced through 'mine-mouth' power stations and transferred to the main electricity-consuming areas, as opposed to transporting the coal to power stations close to the main consuming areas. There is still considerable uncertainty about the long-term pattern that will emerge. A major problem with large-scale production of electricity in the Northwest is the acute shortage of water. At Baotou, in the heart of the region, the Yellow River is now reduced to a mere trickle for most of the year. Large modern power stations typically require large quantities of water. However, China is attempting to develop air-cooled technology for such stations. The successful development of such technology could greatly improve the possibility of developing large centres of electricity generation in the Northwest and transporting the electricity by wire rather than transporting the coal to be converted into electricity elsewhere. There are also longer-term possibilities for the large-scale transfer of water from the water-rich Southwest of China to the Northwest. Developments such as these would have large implications for the business prospects of the Shenhua Group which could find that it had a vastly expanded market for coal close at hand.

Not only does Shenhua wish to sell coal to modern large coal-fired domestic power stations. It also intends to develop a network of power stations along the Huanghua railway. It is possible that these may be partially invested in by Shenhua, and will then provide an assured market for its coal. Shenhua has already developed a significant electric power plant, with two 12 MW units and two 100 MW units. It has established a joint venture with a US electricity partner, which has made a $60 million investment to take a 50 per cent equity share in the joint venture. Shenhua has had 'endless' discussions with multinational power generators. Although they have so far not yielded a great deal, the hope is to build on the existing joint venture and establish a steadily growing capability in power generation through joint venture power plants using Shenhua's coal. Shenhua is also in discussion with the Northwest China Electricity Bureau as a possible domestic joint venture partner, with a view to supplying Shenhua coal to the power stations that might be established. Such a partnership might provide a secure market for the electricity from the joint venture(s).

The target is to build power stations with a capacity of 6000–7000 MW, which provide demand for 10 million tons of Shenhua steam coal, in addition to the 30 million tons that Shenhua hopes to sell to domestic power stations in which it does not have ownership rights. There is some discussion of the possibility of vertical reintegration with the Huaneng Power Corporation, which might provide a further source of assured markets for Shenhua's coal.

We have seen already that Shenhua's coal is of high quality, and super-abundant. Moreover, we have stressed the competitive advantage that Shenhua will soon enjoy through possessing its own dedicated railway system and port. It will not have to tolerate the innumerable delays that affect competitors in ensuring the carriage of goods on the hugely overcrowded railway system, or in avoiding delays in China's overcrowded ports. Shenhua will be insulated from these difficulties. We shall see also that Shenhua enjoys a special position as the only coal company in China that has the right to engage directly in the export market. This constitutes a further source of competitive advantage in relation to its domestic competitors.

Industrial and domestic use of coal. It is not only China's power stations that are shifting to cleaner coals. Direct consumption of coal by industry and house-holds still accounts for over 60 per cent of total coal use in China (SSB, ZTN, 1998: 256). Coal is the major cause of the extremely high levels of suspended particulates in China. Indeed, although households account for only 15 per cent of urban coal use in China, they typically account for 30 per cent of ground level pollution in Chinese cities (World Bank, 1997a: 8). Despite some improvement, urgent measures are needed to improve the quality of urban air. The levels of sus-pended particulates in China's major cities are many times greater than World Health Organization guidelines (World Bank, 1997a: 6).

The possibility of further serious attempts to improve the quality of urban air provides an important potential market for Shenhua's coal, and one in which it has strong competitive advantages. For example, Beijing consumes around 30 million tons of coal annually. The Beijing City government has passed regu-lations that limit coal consumption to that which has less than 10 per cent ash content and 0.5 per cent sulphur content. At the moment much of its coal is sourced from nearby Men Tou Gou, but this has an ash content of over 20 per cent, compared to 6–10 per cent for unwashed coal from Shenhua. Shenhua is already supplying 2 million tons of clean coal to Beijing and hopes that the city's consumption of Shenhua coal will rise to 5 million tons by 2000. If Shanghai, Tianjin and other more economically and culturally advanced cities also pass more stringent regulations governing the quality of coal used, then the market for Shenhua coal will widen still further.

Coal Chemistry. Coal chemistry is a potentially important part of the pro-gramme to replace oil with coal. By the year 2000 it is thought likely that China will import as much as 50 million tons of oil. The process of converting coal into oil was developed during the second world war. It is now well-established. In the wake of the oil crisis of the 1970s, large oil companies became very interested in the possibility of converting coal into oil. However, the long-run fall in oil prices greatly reduced their interest in this route. Prices would have to be far above their current level to make the conversion of coal into oil a profitable activity.

However, China is fearful of excessive dependence on imported oil, and may be willing to subsidize production of oil from coal for strategic reasons. Moreover, research into the technology is ongoing, and it is conceivable that a major technical breakthrough may occur that would reduce costs of conversion. Also, there is still uncertainty about the long-term real price of oil.

Shenhua's coal is especially suitable for conversion into oil. It has become the *de facto* centre of China's efforts to convert coal into oil. The national 'coal into oil' fund may be transferred completely to Shenhua. Since becoming chairman of Shenhua, Ye Qing has started work on the construction of two 'coal into oil' plants. They will have the capability to produce a total of 7–8 million tons of oil which will require around 15–16 million tons of coal. Shenhua is co-operating with the US Hydro-Carbon Corporation to develop 'coal into oil' technology. The US government is providing financial support for the co-operative effort. There are two other plants in China that are involved in 'coal into oil' production.

Competition. In the early 1990s, China's 90 largest state-owned mines had an average of over 39 000 employees each (SSB, ZGJTN, 1993: 373). By 1997, Shenhua had already become one of China's 20 largest coal companies by value of output, with an output of almost 8 million tons in 1997. Early in the next century its output is planned to reach 60 million tons. China's largest coal mining company today, Datong, produces just 37 million tons (Table 10-21). The Shenhua Group (excluding the merged 'Five Western Region' mines discussed below), employs around 9000 people, of whom around 4200 are employed directly in mining. Shenhua's plans are to reduce the total number of employees. It believes that the proportion of non-production workers is too great for an internationally competitive coal company. Output per worker at Shenhua is already around 850 tons. This is far above the industry average of 230 tons for the whole of China. As output expands towards full capacity, output per worker will rise to over 5000 tons early in next century, and may even rise beyond this if employment does, indeed, decline below 9000. Shenhua's position in the coal industry will be analogous to Baogang Iron and Steel Company. Baogang was created from scratch and was able to employ a much smaller number of workers than other traditional iron and steel plants.

Not only are the numbers of employees much smaller, and the output per worker far higher than in traditional state-owned enterprises. A further large source of competitive advantage is the absence of traditional labour attitudes. It is likely that the workforce is much younger and more flexible. Moreover, the company is able to pay significantly higher wages than other coal mines. This should enable it to attract higher quality personnel than traditional mines.

In the weak market situation since the onset of the Asian crisis, the price of coal has fallen significantly and the market is weak both domestically and internationally. We have seen that the coal sector as a whole has once more returned to making losses. If the Chinese government does decide to allow some of the large-scale coal producers to go bankrupt, as well as close down illegal small producers, this can only strengthen Shenhua's competitive position within the domestic industry.

We have seen already that the mining sector stands in sharp contrast with most other sectors in terms of the paucity of joint venture activity. A major problem for potential mining joint ventures is that multinationals cannot commit themselves to large-scale investments unless they are sure of the nature of the reserves in which they are investing. However, even to ascertain the full extent of a particular mine requires large investments. They are not prepared to make such an investment without being confident that the project will proceed if the surveys prove positive. Multinationals believe that the Chinese side is reluctant to commit itself to a relationship with the multinational until they are sure of the extent and nature of the reserves under consideration. Multinationals want to sign a contract before they make any investment. A recent pattern for multinationals is to sign a 'contract of work' even before any investment is made in exploration, which establishes the principles under which the whole operation is conducted from beginning to end. China's mining companies are unwilling to undertake such contracts. In the eyes of multinationals, this is because they are concerned lest they commit themselves to sharing a resource that is far greater than they had anticipated: 'They are afraid the multinationals will find a bonanza'. The Chinese side still appears to be uncertain of what is the appropriate share to be taken by domestic and foreign parties should a major new reserve be found.

Shenhua has held extensive discussions with multinationals about possible joint venture co-operation. It has been in discussion with ARCO since 1995. Shenhua may well prove to be a more hopeful environment for multinational joint venture co-operation than other coal companies. The broad extent of the reserves already seems to be fairly well established. It seems likely that the vast reserves are fairly homogeneous in terms of quality. A joint venture does not need to be constructed for a large fraction of the vast Shenfu Dongsheng coalfield. It can easily proceed incrementally from one mine to another. A multinational could be a majority partner for individual coal mines, but would still own only a small fraction of the total assets of the potentially huge Shenhua company. This means that Shenhua should be far less nervous of the foreign party than other large Chinese coal companies might be.

The institutional background appears more favourable also, because Shenhua has strong central government support as part of China's broad strategic plans to raise the share of high quality clean coal in China's coal production portfolio. Unlike other Chinese coal companies, Shenhua has the huge advantage of a dedicated rail link to the sea, and a dedicated port facility at the coast. It has strong prospects for exports to East Asia, which is particularly attractive to the multinational companies. Shenhua has some strong reasons to participate with multinationals. It needs the expertise of the multinationals to develop its skills in the complex task of integrating the different aspects of mining, from coalface through grading, washing, transporting to the coast and finally to the customer. It needs the skill of multinationals in building up global marketing expertise. It needs multinationals for the capital resources they may bring. Shenhua is heavily indebted due to the huge costs of the construction of the mines, the railway and the port. However, it has so far developed only a tiny fraction of the reserves under its control. With financial resources from the multinationals it could develop even faster into a powerful player in the Chinese and international coal trade.

These advantages mean that Shenhua is in a strong position to develop joint ventures ahead of other Chinese coal companies. Should this prove to be the case, it could provide a further source of competitive advantage for Shenhua in relation to its domestic competitors.

Exports. We have seen that Shenhua currently produces coal for a pit-head price of around 90 yuan ($13)/ton. Its transport costs to the coast are around 100 yuan ($11)/ton. It estimates that the sea transport costs to East Asia are around $5/ton. Sea transport costs from Australia to Northeast Asia are around $8/ton, a significant differential. Shenhua is able to supply coal for export to East Asian markets at around $29/ton. It is possible that on the completion of the rail links with the coast, its transport costs/ton will fall. It is also possible that as output grows it will benefit from economies of scale and its pit-head costs will fall. In sum, it is quite possible that Shenhua will become an internationally competitive producer in terms of its costs of production.

We have seen above that, unlike other large producers in former planned economies, Shenhua has started life from scratch since 1985. This provides Shenhua with the advantage that it begins life with much lower manning levels than most other large state-owned enterprises. Moreover, as we have seen, Shenhua has bought mainly advanced imported equipment. Its output per worker is already far above the industry average in China, even though production is still far from peak capacity. Output per worker is already over 800 tons per annum, which is greater than the level in Poland and Germany. As production grows towards full capacity, it should rise to an output per worker of over 5000 tons early in the next century, which should surpass those achieved in Colombia, the UK and South Africa and begin to approach those of Australia and North America. Shenhua plans to reduce employment to below present levels alongside rising output, attempting to replicate the productivity performance of leading multinational companies. It plans to have only 5000 employees in the company when output reaches 50 million tons. If this were achieved, it would mean that output per worker would be 10000 tons, on a par with productivity in the Australian and North American coal industries.

We have seen that Shenhua has much lower manning levels than most other large-scale state-owned mines. The average wage is significantly higher than the national average for the mining sector. In 1998, Shenhua employees earned an average of over 13000 yuan per annum. This compared with an average annual wage of 7091 yuan for all employees in state-owned mines (SSB, ZTN, 1998: 162). It is roughly comparable to the average wage of non-state sector employees in such activities as scientific research and real estate (13250 yuan and 14400 yuan respectively). It is still well behind the highest-paid non-state sector occupations, such as computer services (average wage of 26000 yuan in 1997) (SSB, ZTN, 1998: 163). However, in international terms this is still a very low wage, amounting to the equivalent of only $1600 per annum. This is still a small fraction of the average earnings of employees in modern coal mines in other parts of the world. It is less than one-twentieth of the wage of employees in the coal industry in Australia, the US or the UK. Moreover, it is less than one-fifth of the wage of coal employees in Poland. This provides a further potential source of international competitive advantage for Shenhua.

Most major international coal companies have several sites across the world. In sharp contrast, Shenhua possesses one of the world's largest high quality coal reserves in a single location. Unlike most of the other large coalfields, the Shenfu Dongsheng field is in its infancy. It will be many decades before Shenhua has to extract higher cost reserves at greater depths or in less easily extractable locations and structures.

The benefits for Shenhua of having a single huge high-quality deposit within China are enormous. Once established, the rail link will serve the company for an indefinite period of time, long after the large initial capital cost has been repaid. Unlike competitor companies, Shenhua will not have to go through the costly process of undertaking surveys of new coalfields. Unlike international competitors, Shenhua will not have to establish from afresh the international reputation of the coal that is supplied from its resources. Unlike international competitors, Shenhua will not have to go through costly processes of negotiating with indigenous peoples and national governments in order to gain access to new resources. Unlike international competitors, Shenhua is unlikely to have to face the possibility of a change in the property rights environment that can follow a change of government in a developing country.

We have seen that Shenhua not only has huge coal deposits but also high quality steam coal. It has a medium to high calorific value, with a low ash and sulphur content. Its products are of the type that, other things being equal, should face attractive market prospects in surrounding East Asian countries, and even further afield. Shenhua's physical closeness to the world's fastest-growing markets for steam coal, which are in East Asia, is a big advantage. This gives it an advantage in terms of sea transport costs over Australian and other more distant suppliers. It also may give Shenhua a competitive edge in terms of cultural and political links that surrounding East Asian countries may wish to build with China over the long term.

Shenhua must establish a reputation for itself as a reliable supplier of competitively-priced high quality produce. Building a reputation is crucial in order to be a competitive international supplier. This process takes times. For example, Hammersley Iron took around 20 years to develop its reputation as a high quality, reliable, low-cost supplier. A major problem in the past was that China's coal exports mainly were channelled through the state-run China National Coal Import and Export Company (CNCIEC). In 1996 Shenhua gained the rights independently to export coal. The only other agency with the right to export coal is Shanxi Province. In 1997, CNCIEC exported 30 million tons of coal, compared with 6 million tons from Shanxi and one million tons from Shenhua. Shenhua's goal is to export around 20 per cent of its total output over the long-term. The advantage of having the right to export is that Shenhua can establish direct long-term relationships with foreign customers. At least as important, it can control the quality of its exports. It now has direct responsibility for ensuring that there is no foreign matter in the coal it supplies and for ensuring timely delivery. Shenhua is acutely aware that this provides it with the opportunity to develop its international reputation as a reliable supplier of high quality coal.

MERGER WITH THE 'FIVE WESTERN DISTRICT MINES'

In August 1998 the nature of Shenhua and its development strategy was sharply altered. Through an administrative decision, taken by the State Council, Shenhua was instructed to take over the 'Five Western District' (*xi wu ju*) mines in Inner Mongolia: Wuda, Haibowan, Baotou, Wanli and Zhunge'er (Table 10-26).

Baotou, Wuda and Haibowan are three old state coal mines in the area around the Shenfu Dongsheng Coalfield. They were constructed mainly to meet local needs for coking coal at the Baotou Iron and Steel Company, a large Soviet-assisted plant established during the 1950s. These are heavily loss-making mines, making an average of over 100 million yuan in losses each in 1997. The three mines receive around 50–60 million yuan each (a total of the equivalent of around $20 million) in subsidies from the state. They have only around 20 years of recoverable reserves left. They are each deep mines, with an average depth of 350–440 metres. The quality of the reserves is below that at Shenhua. For example, the ash content of the coal at Haibowan and Wuda is between 14 and 33 per cent.

They are traditional state-sector mines, with large numbers of employees and low levels of output per worker. The whole of Shenhua had only around 9 000 employees, and as we have seen, it plans to produce an output of 60 million tons with no more than the current number of employees. Wuda, Baotou and Haibowan employ a total of over 70 000 people to produce an output of only 5–6 million tons. Moreover, within this number are included around 20 000 retired personnel. The employees have often not been paid wages for 'several months on end'.

The other two mines included in the administrative merger have very different characteristics. Zhunge'er is around 50–80 kilometres to the East of the Shenfu Dongsheng Coalfield. It is in its early stages of development. It has plentiful reserves that can be mined with low-cost open-cast methods. The coal is of excellent quality, and is suitable for modern power stations, though it does have much higher ash and sulphur content than Shenhua's coal that necessitates washing. Zhunge'er already has letters of intent to supply 20 million tons of coal per annum to nine power stations in the region. In addition, the Ministry of Electricity Industry has approved plans to build two pit-head power stations close to Zhunge'er, with a total of over 2 million kW of generation capacity.

Zhunge'er's development is planned to take place over fifteen years from 1995 to 2010. The development will take place at three pits: Heidaigou Nos 1 and 2, and Haerwusu. Zhunge'er's total planned devised capacity is over 50 million tons.

TABLE 10-26 The 'Five Western District Mines' Merged with Shenhua, October 1998

Mine name	Devised capacity (MTA)	Actual capacity (MTA)	Output in 1997 (MT)	Employment	Comments
Baotou	2	—	<1	20000–30000	
Haibowan	2.8	—	—	—	
Wuda	2	—	<2	20–30 000	
Wanli	15 (predicted)	—	0.8	1000	
Sub-total		15	6	60 000	
Zhunge'er	50 (+)				
of which:					
Heidaigou No. 1	12	15	3	9000	Open-cast, not yet officially in operation
Heidaigou No. 2	15	—	—	—	Constructionn not yet begun
Haerwusu	15	—	—	—	Open-cast, construction not yet begun

The first to be developed is Heidaigou Pit No. 1. This is nearing the end of the construction phase. It is a wholly state-owned pit, that will have a devised capacity of 12 million tons on completion in the year 2000. It already has 9000 employees, and produced 3 million tons of coal in 1997, even though it has not yet officially completed its construction phase. If Heidaigou No. 1 Pit can reach an output of 12 million tons, then it has a good chance of making profits. However, despite the signing of letters of intent to supply coal to power plants in the region, Zhunge'er has faced a dual problem. On the one hand, the power plants have not been established as planned, due to the decline in the growth rate of demand for electricity. On the other hand, the plants that have been established have turned to the more competitive TVE coal mines to buy their coal. Zhunge'er will be forced to officially 'go into operation' in one or two years. At this point it will have to start to repay its state loans. If it cannot raise its sales to 5–6 million tons then it will be loss-making, constituting a further drain on Shenhua's balance sheet.

Construction of Heidaigou No. 2 Pit, with a planned devised capacity of 15 million tons, has not yet begun. Haerwusu will have a devised capacity of 14 million tons on completion in 2010. Before 1995 Zhunge'er had extensive discussions with BHP about a possible joint venture, but nothing resulted from these discussions. It is currently in discussion with another major multinational about the possibility of a joint venture. However, as we have seen, there are still large uncertainties about the environment in which multinationals operate in China. These include the degree to which TVEs will be allowed to win markets from established large producers and the nature of the approvals process for joint ventures, especially the sequencing of expenditure on exploration activity relative to the signing of joint venture contracts. The sudden transfer of Zhunge'er to Shenhua makes the surrounding institutional environment extremely uncertain for multinational investors.

Wanli is the final mine in the group transferred to Shenhua in 1998. Wanli is under construction. It is located around 50 kilometres south of Baotou, and has letters of intent to supply substantial amounts of coal to Da La Te power station. However, like Shenhua, it has found that it has been substantially squeezed out of supplying Da La Te due to the lower price offered by TVE coal mines. It is planned to have four pits, with a final capacity of 15 million tons. However, faced with difficult market conditions in general and severe competition from TVE coal mines, it has chosen to grow in a cautious fashion. So far, it only has two pits in operation. These have a devised capacity of 1.2 million tons. In addition, Wanli has taken over two local coal mines, with a devised capacity totalling 3.1 million tons. As a new mine, growing incrementally in the face of difficult market conditions, Wanli is thought to be the best of the 'Five Western Region Mines' in terms of its current profitability. It has a total of 1200 employees, far below the level that would be employed in a traditional SOE company of this level of output.

The merger of Shenhua with the 'Five Western District Mines' has transformed the company's structure. As we have seen, by 1998, Shenhua was in the midst of the second phase of its construction. It had the rights to mine one of the world's largest, high quality coal deposits. The associated network of railway and ports was well under way. Shenhua had a coherent strategy for expansion that would make it a formidable competitor for other large-scale domestic coal companies and perhaps also for established international coal companies. Immediately before the merger, Shenhua was a company with 9000 employees producing 8 million tons of high quality coal. It would soon be producing 30 million tons, and in the medium-term, it would be producing up to 60 million tons with no increase in the workforce.

Following the merger, Shenhua has become a company with 70 000–80 000 employees producing 18 million tons of coal. Much of the additional coal was low quality. Three of the mines were close to exhaustion and heavily loss-making. The social problems of trying to integrate such a diverse group of mines presents great challenges to the Shenhua leadership. Instead of trying to build a modern mining company, it has to cope simultaneously with the run-down of non-viable mines employing large numbers of workers. Within the 'Five Western District Mines' are two mines that may become viable in the long-term. However, at least one of these, Zhunge'er, has serious short-term problems, and is likely to become a drain on Shenhua's balance-sheet as soon as it officially enters production in the next year or two.

The administrative merger that has transformed Shenhua stands in the starkest contrast to the merger wave that has engulfed the advanced capitalist countries in the last few years. The main characteristic of the Western merger wave has been the merging of 'strong with strong' through the marketplace. Leading international metals and minerals producers have been expanding their portfolio by establishing new mines with high quality reserves and merging with or taking over companies, or parts of companies, with high quality reserves. They have pushed forward with large increases in labour productivity, necessitating fewer and fewer workers to produce a given output. Through these cost-effective expansions, the competitive position of the leading multinationals has increased. In the sharpest contrast, China's emerging big businesses have to fight with one hand behind their backs. The potentially internationally competitive Shenhua coal company has had its competitive advantage greatly weakened. It is still too early to predict the final impact that the merger will have on the shape of the company. The final nature of the relationship with Shenhua is still under discussion. However, it is hard to imagine that it will do anything other than substantially weaken its competitive capability in the foreseeable future.

CONCLUSION

SHENHUA'S COMPETITIVE ADVANTAGES

Shenhua has the potential to become the most powerful coal company within China, and also to become a major player in the international coal industry.

Shenhua has been granted secure property rights to a huge coal reserve in the middle of one of the world's richest remaining undeveloped coal fields. It is likely that it will be allowed to expand further into the huge Shenfu Dongsheng Coalfield, since the government has given Shenhua responsibility for the development of the whole coalfield. Even for leading multinationals, mining property rights are not perfectly secure. They are rendered insecure by the political instability in developing countries, uncertainty about native people's claims on resource ownership, and the potential impact of environmental pressure groups. Shenhua's rights to mine the coal in the Shenfu Dongsheng Coalfield may be more secure than those of multinational mining and mineral companies in many locations. If the reported size of the reserves in the Shenfu Dongsheng Coalfield are accurate, then Shenhua will have a larger base of reserves than any of the multinational companies.

Not only are the reserves that Shenhua is likely to be allowed to develop of vast size. They are also of high quality, with medium to high calorific value, and low ash and sulphur content. In so far as domestic and international markets shift towards high quality, less polluting coals, Shenhua stands to gain steadily expanding markets for its coal. If demand for its coal grows rapidly, Shenhua is in a position to quickly increase output up to around 100 millions tons, with the infrastructure already under construction.

Shenhua has been chosen by the Chinese government as the company that will lead the country's attempt to construct a globally competitive coal company. The central government is providing strong support to enable it to develop and compete. This includes the property rights to extract coal from the Shenfu Dongsheng Coalfield, large-scale financial support to build the necessary infrastructure, including railway and port, and attempting to enforce contracts signed with large power plants to buy Shenhua's high-quality coal. It includes also providing Shenhua with the rights independently to import and export coal. Shenhua is the only Chinese coal company to have been granted such rights. This provides it with the opportunity to build its international reputation as a high-quality, reliable supplier.

Unlike the multinationals, Shenhua has the enormous advantage of the highly concentrated location of its reserves. For the multinational giants, such a concentration of reserves would constitute a political risk. Given that the political risk for Shenhua is so low, the great concentration of reserves is a potential source of powerful competitive advantage, with economies of scale in production, preparation, and transport, in building reputation, undertaking exploration and negotiating new contracts to mine.

Security of supply is crucial to large modern power stations. Unlike many mines, Shenhua has the huge advantage of a dedicated rail system and a dedicated port. Possession of this integrated system provides Shenhua with the opportunity to become a secure supplier both to emerging modern power plants within China and to neighbouring East Asian countries.

Unlike other large Chinese competitors, Shenhua is a young company. It has a low level of employment and a relatively high average wage level. It has the opportunity to build a high productivity company, without the immense burden of a large workforce with low output per worker, work traditions inherited from the era of the planned economy and a large number of retired workers. Shenhua has a unique opportunity among large Chinese coal companies to compete on a 'level playing field' with the multinational giants in terms of manning levels and work practices. It has the ability also to attract the most talented people in the industry through the capability to pay its much smaller staff a significantly higher wage than the industry average.

SHENHUA'S PROBLEMS

Although the central government has chosen to build Shenhua as the industry leader in the coal sector, it is unable to implement industrial policy in the detailed fashion that Japan and South Korea were able to do in their phase of rapid indus- trialization. The central government has a wide array of vested interests playing upon it. China is a vast, complex economy and society. Even in the Maoist epoch, a wide range of decisions was undertaken by the localities. Moreover, the central government has intentionally streamlined the operations of the central bureau- cracy, so that a great deal more detailed decision-making is carried out at lower levels than was the case a few years ago.

Despite the central government's intention to support Shenhua as a globally powerful coal company, the central government's industrial policy operates within many constraints. Central among these are those that stem from China's vast pop- ulation, rural poverty, and surplus labour. These elemental forces of economic development are nowhere observed more dramatically than in the coal industry. The coal industry provides extreme ease of entry for small-scale producers. Workers from poverty-stricken rural families 'voluntarily' go to work in primitive mines in huge numbers, at immense cost to their health and to the environment, but with consequential additions to family income. Such employment brings a vast train of additional employment in its wake, in the shape mainly of primitive and virtually unregulated service facilities in remote areas. The socio–economics of this phenomenon in China has been hardly touched by scholarly study.[8]

We have seen how rapidly the local small-scale sector rose to dominate the production of coal. A large number of small local coal mines is able to compete effectively with large coal companies in supplying local needs. Even Shenhua, one of the lowest-cost producers, finds it difficult to compete on price with local producers in Northwest China. Moreover, there is a strong incentive for those who operate railways to divert space on railways from large-scale producers to small-scale local producers in return for a variety of payments. There is an incen- tive also, for large-scale producers allocated space on railways, themselves to buy from small-scale producers and ship coal as part of their own shipment on the railway. Consequently, even in long-distance trade, the small-scale producers can play a significant role. These powerful underlying pressures have restricted the government's ability to operate an industrial policy that supports the emer- gence of large-scale producers in this sector.

In 1998–9 the central government announced sweeping closure of small-scale 'illegal' mines in order to assist the reduction of losses at large-scale state-owned mines, to reduce damage to China's coal reserves, to reduce damage to miners' health in TVE mines, to reduce the damage to the environment from transport of huge quantities of unprotected coal and from extensive production of coal for local consumption in polluting industrial boilers, homes, and small, old power stations. However, the pressure from local authorities and miners themselves to continue production is immense. It remains to be seen if the central government can successfully implement this dramatic measure in the face of such powerful forces working against the implementation of the policy.

The central government has attempted to ensure that new large-scale power stations contract to buy their coal from large-scale coal mines. Permission to establish new power stations is only given where there is an assured source of coal supply from a large-scale coal company. However, in practice, letters of intent to supply large new power stations bear little relationship to the actual source of supply. Small-scale local coal mines frequently supplant large coal mines as the preferred, low-cost source of supply.

As long as the central government is unable to close down illegal small coal mines in large numbers, then the market prospects for large coal mines remain uncertain. Their markets, at least within China, will be severely contested with small-scale mines.

The second serious constraint upon the central government's industrial policy in the coal sector arises from the severe difficulties faced by the large-scale SOE coal mines. A large fraction of these mines suffered from long years of loss-making due to the state-regulated low price of coal, extensive over-manning, and from exhaustion of reserves. The long-postponed price liberalization was finally accomplished in the mid-1990s. Having briefly achieved overall profits in 1997, the sector was plunged once more into loss-making due to the Asian crisis and the associated slump in world and domestic demand and prices.

One 'solution' to the crisis for the central government was to force profitable enterprises to take over loss-makers. In Shenhua's case, it was forced to merge with the 'Five Western District Mines', three of which were old-style SOE loss-makers. This has drastically altered the character of Shenhua. It will seriously weaken its capability to compete with powerful coal companies at home and abroad. It amounts to a serious dilution of the previous path of industrial policy aimed at creating a powerful internationally competitive coal company at Shenhua. It creates a massive millstone around the neck of the company, sapping the company of profits and confusing the management about the company's objectives.

STRATEGIC CHOICES FOR THE CHINESE COAL INDUSTRY

The Chinese government faces complex choices in the coal industry. Moreover, its capacity to implement choices is constrained by the imperatives of making policy in a vast, impoverished country. The choices it faces in the coal industry crystallize the wider problems it faces in many sectors. Can it really build powerful, internationally competitive companies while simultaneously supporting low-cost, labour-intensive industries? Should it impose upon small-scale producers the full social costs of their production, but at the expense of the growth of employment in these sectors and the incomes of some of the poorest segments of the population? Should it handicap the growth of potentially powerful, internationally competitive businesses by forcing them to merge with old, uncompetitive SOEs? Will short-run solutions to the problems of some loss-making SOEs be achieved at the expense of a dynamic, modern large-scale business sector?

Can the government 'grasp the strong' without 'letting go of the weak'?

11

The Third Technological Revolution

[The World Telecoms Agreement] is a triumph for the American way...
US companies are the most competitive telecommunications providers in the
world; they are in the position to compete and win under this agreement.
(Charlene Barshefsky, US trade representative designate,
quoted in *FT*, 18 February 1997)

The days when telecommunications companies (both incumbents and new
entrants) could focus on a single country are drawing to a close.
(McKinsey Telecoms Group, quoted in *FT*, 24 November 1999)

Knowledge, more than ever before, is power. The one country that can lead
the information revolution will be more powerful than any other. For the
foreseeable future, that country is the United States. America has apparent
strength in military power and economic production. Yet its more subtle
comparative advantage is its ability to collect, process, act upon, and
disseminate information, an edge that will almost certainly grow over the
next decade. This advantage stems from Cold War investments and
America's open society, thanks to which it dominates important
communications and information processing technologies – space-based
surveillance, direct broadcasting, high-speed computers – and has an
unparalleled ability to integrate complex information systems.
(Nye and Owens, 1996)

You don't need 200-odd telco companies around the world. You need
somewhere between five and fifteen, and at least half of those
will be new world players.
(John Chambers, CEO, Cisco Systems, quoted in *FT*, 7 October 1998)

This [WTO] agreement means that we will be dancing with wolves –
hungry wolves.
(Chinese official, quoted in *FT*, 30 November 1999).

INTRODUCTION

We have seen already that the revolution in information technology (IT) is changing massively the structure of business and daily life. Information technology
will be at the heart of the global economy for at least the first few decades of the
new millennium. The revolution is changing everything from the nature of the
firm to the nature of warfare.

It is widely argued that the explosive rise of knowledge-intensive industries provides great possibilities for developing countries to compete effectively. It is
thought that developing countries can 'leapfrog' the advanced economies in these
industries. Because these are relatively new industries, many people believe that
barriers to entry are low, and that small and medium firms based in developing
countries are at a competitive advantage. This possibility is thought to be reinforced
by the sheer force of numbers, since large developing countries such as China and
India contain a vast pool of educated people who are able to use their human capital rapidly to develop knowledge-intensive industries. It is thought that the 'knowledge-intensive' industries require relatively small amounts of capital compared to
the 'old technology' industries, reinforcing the possibility for small and medium
firms to compete effectively. Such views have been fuelled by the rapid growth of
'information technology' exports from certain developing countries. For example,
Indian software exports have risen rapidly in recent years, growing from $1.7 bil-
lion in 1997 to an expected figure of over $4 billion in 1999 (*FT*, 29 June 1999).

This chapter argues that the reality is quite different. It argues that despite its
relative youth, this sector has witnessed in the space of just a few years a process
of explosive concentration that has already established very large barriers to
entry in many sectors. It is firms based in the advanced economies, especially the
USA, that are far ahead in the high-speed race to develop the new technologies
that are pushing the industry forward. It is in this sector more than in any other
that the dominant firms based in the advanced economies are desperate to extend
their market to the vast developing economies such as China and India. This was
revealed vividly in the debates in the USA over China's accession to the WTO.
There are, undoubtedly, massive gains for developing countries through access to
the new technologies. However, through the operation of the free market, the
gains may be highly unevenly distributed between businesses and people in high
and low income countries. Developing countries need to pay careful attention to
the ways in which their own businesses can become a part of the high value-
added 'brain' activities within this revolution.

OBSTACLES FOR FIRMS BASED IN DEVELOPING COUNTRIES

CENTRAL POSITION OF THE KNOWLEDGE-INTENSIVE INDUSTRIES AT THE BEGINNING OF THE TWENTY-FIRST CENTURY

The Third Technological Revolution. In this study, the 'First Technological Revolution' refers to the revolution which began around 8000 BC and 'ground to a halt around 2500 BC' (Lilley, 1973: 188). It involved the development of all the basic agricultural techniques, textiles, pottery and metallurgical industries, the techniques of fermentation, the sailing ship, the wheeled cart, and complex organization of labour, able to build large structures such as the pyramids. The 'Second Technological Revolution' refers to the revolution that began in the Middle Ages in China, Europe and elsewhere, accelerated during the British Industrial Revolution, and continued through different phases right up to the late twentieth century. In this perspective, the whole period since the Middle Ages can be seen as having an essential continuity: 'This Second Technological Revolution has been going on continuously from the early Middle Ages up to our time' (Lilley, 1973: 190). This revolution was based around increasingly intensive use of exhaustible resources. The first great natural resources casualty of this revolution was the widespread destruction of forests across China and Europe (see Ho Ping-ti, 1959; Boserup, 1981). Indeed, Boserup links the technical progress of the Industrial Revolution itself closely with the exhaustion of the most fundamental natural resource of the late Middle Ages, wood: 'With increasing population density in Europe, shortage of wood became a major problem. Many of the technological innovations in the eighteenth century were the result of attempts to develop substitutes for wood as fuel and as raw material for industry and construction' (Boserup, 1981: 106).

The term 'Third Technological Revolution' is used in this context to indicate the revolution in which technology moves from exhaustible to renewable resources. The beginnings of this revolution could already be seen at the end of the twentieth century in the revolution in information technology and biotechnology. In the long-run, it is likely that this revolution will lead to a fundamental change in the pattern of production, employment, consumption and settlement. Deng Yingtao (1991) provides an extended exposition of these issues, especially in relation to China's potential contribution to this revolution. Information technology and the 'life sciences' constituted the core of the early stages of this revolution as the world entered the third millennium. The central importance of these two sectors in this revolution is indicated by the fact that in 1998, the 'life sciences' and information technology companies together accounted for 134 of the top 300 companies in the world by R & D expenditure (DTI, 1999) and their combined R & D expenditure totalled $140 billion (55 per cent) out of a total of $254 billion.

Information Technology. The centrality of information to the global economy in the twenty-first century is reflected vividly in the dramatic rise in importance

TABLE 11-1 **IT Companies (Including IT Hardware, Software, Services, and Content) in the** *FT* **Top 100 Global Companies, 4 January 2000**

Company	Country	Market Capitalization ($ billion)	Sector Code	Sales Revenue ($ billion)
Microsoft	USA	586	977	19.7
NTT Mobile Communications	Japan	366	678	30.2
Cisco Systems	USA	349	938	12.2
Intel	USA	277	936	26.3
NTT	Japan	275	673	94.2
Lucent Technologies	USA	238	938	38.3
Deutsche Telekom	Germany	210	673	35.6
Nokia	Finland	209	938	13.7
IBM	USA	201	932	81.7
AOL	USA	176	974	4.8
AT&T	USA	164	673	53.2
Oracle	USA	152	977	8.8
British Telecommunications	UK	152	673	25.6
SBC Communications	USA	150	673	49.5
Vodafone AirTouch	UK	150	678	5.5
MCIWorldcom	USA	141	673	17.8
France Telecom	France	131	673	25.4
Ericsson	Sweden	130	938	22.0
Nortel Networks	Canada	129	938	18.6
Sun Microsystems	USA	125	932	11.7
Sony	Japan	123	345	65.8
Dell Computer	USA	120	932	18.2
Mannesmann	Germany	117	678	19.7
Yahoo!	USA	117	678	0.2
Qualcomm	USA	115	938	3.9
EMC	USA	110	932	4.0
Softbank	Japan	111	977	5.1
Hewlett–Packard	USA	109	932	42.4
Motorola	USA	98	938	29.4
China Telecom (Hong Kong)	Hong Kong	92	673	3.2
Bell Atlantic	USA	90	673	31.6
Fujitsu	Japan	89	932	56.8
Bell South	USA	84	673	25.2
Telefónica	Spain	81	673	18.0
Time Warner	USA	80	535	14.6
Texas Instruments	USA	80	936	9.5
Siemens	Germany	73	252	62.0
TIM	Italy	71	678	6.3

TABLE 11-1 (*Continued*)

Company	Country	Market Capitalization ($ billion)	Sector Code	Sales Revenue ($ billion)
Telecom Italia	Italy	71	673	24.0
Telstra	Australia	69	673	11.5
AT&T Liberty Media	USA	67	542	1.6
Disney	USA	66	538	23.4
NTT Data	Japan	64	972	6.6
GTE	USA	64	673	25.4
Matsushita Electrical	Japan	58	253	74.0
Hutchison Whampoa	Hong Kong	57	240	6.6
BCE	Canada	55	673	6.8
Hitachi	Japan	55	938	77.2

SOURCE: *FT* (4 May 2000)

NOTES: Sector codes:
240 Diversified industrial
252 Electrical equipment
253 Electronic equipment
345 Household appliances
535 Home entertainment
538 Leisure facilities
542 Broadcasting contractors
673 Fixed-line telecoms
678 Wireless telecoms
932 Computer hardware
936 Semiconductors
938 Telecoms equipment
974 Internet
972 Computer services
977 Software

of the cluster of industries concerned with producing information technology hardware, software, services and content. This sector is the key to the world's socio-economic 'superstructure' of communications and culture. It is the 'brain' of the global firm in the Third Technological Revolution.

No fewer than 48 out of the top 100 global companies by market capitalization in 1998 were primarily in this sector or were rapidly moving into this sector as their main business (for example, Siemens, Hutchison Whampoa, Sony, Mannesmann) (Table 11-1). To some degree the massive rise in stock market value of the firms in these sectors constituted the classic speculative herd instinct at work. However, to a considerable degree, it reflected a real underlying phenomenon, namely, the central role that these technologies are playing, and will increasingly play, in the Third Technological Revolution. By the end of April 2000, the combined stock market capitalization of the top ten IT firms stood at over $2800 billion, more than the combined GNP of the entire group of upper middle income countries in the late 1990s (*FT*, 4 May 2000; World Bank,

2000: 231). On the 'global level playing field' they were able to acquire other firms across the world at a fantastic rate, comprehensively consolidating their position as the first-movers in the construction of the 'brain' of the global business revolution of the early part of the twenty-first century.

In 2000/2001, the speculative 'bubble' in high technology stocks burst. However, beneath the frenzied speculative boom there lay a genuinely revolutionary development in business structure based on the explosive progress in IT, comparable in its impact with the railways in the nineteenth century. The sharp fall in IT share prices was likely to be followed by a period of 'shake-out' of relatively weak firms and intensified industry consolidation. The underlying 'real' nature of the stock market phenomenon can be seen vividly in the large rise in the R & D expenditures in these sectors and their sharply increasing role in the overall pattern of R & D expenditure. By 1998, the world's top 300 companies by R & D expenditure included over eighty from the information technology sectors (Table 11-2). The IT hardware is much the most important single sector in the total R & D spending of advanced capitalist firms. In 1998, the IT hardware sector accounted for 57 of the top 300 firms by R & D spending, much the most important single sector. Total R & D spending by these firms amounted to over $70 billion, two-thirds greater than that of the auto sector, the next largest in total R & D spending and more than double that of the pharmaceutical sector, the third largest (Table 11-2). It accounted for 28 per cent of the total R & D spend of the top 300 global firms. The sales revenue of these 57 leading IT hardware firms

TABLE 11-2 **R & D Expenditure of the Top 300 Companies World-wide, 1995 and 1998 ($ billion)**

Sector	No. of Companies (1998)	of which: USA	1995	1998	% Increase/Decrease in R & D Expenditure (1995–8)
Total	300	129	176.6	253.7	44
of which:					
IT hardware	55	36	41.8	70.0	68
Software/IT services	17	16	3.3	7.5	127
Telecoms services	9	1	9.0	9.8	9
Autos	25	5	31.2	43.3	39
Pharmaceuticals	35	13	22.4	33.1	48
Electronic/electricals	28	7	22.3	26.6	19
Chemicals	31	9	14.5	20.7	43
Aerospace/defence	11	7	5.7	6.9	21
Engineering/ machinery	21	8	4.8	6.5	35
Oil/gas	11	6	4.0	5.1	28
Steel/metals	9	0	1.2	1.1	(−)7

SOURCE: DTI (1999)

TABLE 11-3 **MSDW Competitive-edge Companies in IT Sectors, 2000**

Sector	No. of Firms	Of which: USA
Media	14	8
Computer and business services	4	2
Data networking and telecoms services	7	4
Enterprise hardware and software	18	13
Internet, PC hardware, software, consumer electronics	12	7
Semiconductors, components	18	10
Telecoms services	13	6
Total	86	50

SOURCE: MSDW (2000)

amounted to $790 billion, greater even than Brazil's GNP of $773 billion (1997) (World Bank, 1998: 190). If IT software and services are included, then the IT sector as a whole accounted for over 34 per cent of total outlays of the top 300 firms by R & D spending.

IT figured centrally among MSDW's list of the world's top 250 firms in terms of their 'competitive edge', or their ability to 'sustain global advantage over well-financed competitors' (MSDW, 2000: iii). No fewer than 86 of the top 250 'competitive edge' firms were in the information technology sectors (Table 11-3).

Life Sciences. Alongside the revolution in the information technology industries, there took place a related revolution in another knowledge-intensive sector, the so-called 'life sciences'. The nexus of industries that advance agricultural productivity and human health has been one of the fastest-growing parts of the world economy, and can be expected to continue to grow rapidly as income levels rise in developing countries. The share of GDP spent on health rises sharply as incomes increase. In low income countries a mere 0.9 per cent of GDP is spent on health. The proportion rises to 2.5 per cent in lower-middle-income countries, 3.3 per cent in upper middle income countries and 6.9 per cent in high-income countries (see Table 5-1). The absolute gap in spending *per capita* is vast. In addition, there are sharply increasing private expenditures on health as income levels rise. The great importance of the 'life sciences' in the advanced economies at the turn of the millennium is reflected in the fact that in 1998, 40 out of the *FT* 500 companies (ranked by market capitalization) were in this sector.

In 1998 the 'life science' industries accounted for 51 of the top 300 firms by R & D expenditure (DTI, 1999). In 1998 35 pharmaceuticals companies together spent over $33 billion on R & D, seven chemical/pharmaceutical companies spent over $13 billion and nine health care companies spent $46 billion. Total spending by the combined group of 'life science' companies amounted to over $90 billion.

COMPREHENSIVE DOMINANCE OF THE THIRD TECHNOLOGICAL REVOLUTION BY
OLIGOPOLISTIC FIRMS FROM THE ADVANCED ECONOMIES

Firms from the advanced economies are even more dominant in the knowledge-intensive industries than in the traditional industries of the Second Industrial Revolution. The key to progress in this sector, more than almost any other sector, is investment in R & D and in high quality human resources. The sector is advancing technically at such high speed that only those firms which undertake high and effective R & D investment can compete. Despite the relative youth of these sectors, already an explosive process of business concentration has taken place, making it hard for 'latecomer' firms to catch up with the industry leaders. Across all knowledge-intensive industries a small group of companies, all based in the developed countries, controls an ever-growing share of the global market. In 1998, the top 10 companies accounted for 32 per cent of the $23 billion global market in commercial seeds, 35 per cent of the $297 billion global market in pharmaceuticals, 60 per cent of the $17 billion market in veterinary medicines, 70 per cent of the $334 billion global market in computers, 85 per cent of the $31 billion global market in pesticides and 86 per cent of the of the $262 billion global market in telecommunications (Table 11-4).

In 1998, the top five companies in the information technology sector, IBM, Lucent Technologies, Compaq, Hitachi and Nortel, spent an average of $4.8 billion on R & D, amounting to around 10 per cent of their total revenue. Their combined revenues totalled $240 billion, greater than the GNP of Austria ($226 billion in 1997) (World Bank, 1998: 191). IBM alone has a revenue of $82 billion, greater than the GNP of Chile or Egypt ($73 billion and $71 billion respectively) (World Bank, 1998: 190). In 1998 it spent $5.4 billion on R & D, greater than the GNP of 46 developing countries included in the main tables of the World Bank's annual report (World Bank, 1998: 190–1).

There is no doubt that oligopolistic competition is driving the knowledge-intensive industries forward at incredible speed, bringing huge benefits to the businesses in terms of super-normal profits, to the shareholders in terms of

TABLE 11-4 Global Market Share of Top 10 Companies in
Knowledge-intensive Industries, 1998

Sector	$ billion	Global Market Share (%)
Commercial seeds	7.4	32
Pharmaceuticals	104.0	35
Veterinary medicine	10.2	60
Computers	233.8	70
Pesticides	26.4	85
Telecommunications	225.3	86

SOURCE: UNDP (1999: 67)

'supernormal profits' and 'supernormal' wealth gains, and to the customers who use the new technology. For example, in October 1999, Intel announced the launch of more than a dozen high-performance Pentium III microprocessor chips, 'reclaiming the speed title from rival Advanced Micro Devices (AMD)' (*FT*, 26 October 1999). The new Intel chips outrun their predecessors with a greater than 20 per cent advantage. They also overtake AMD's fastest Athlon chips by about 5 per cent. Intel has achieved new speed ratings of 500 MHz to 733 MHz by shrinking the dimensions of circuit elements to 0.18 microns, down from 0.25 microns. The smaller the dimensions, the more semiconductor manufacturers are able to squeeze on to a single chip of silicon to create more sophisticated devices. The shrink also enables more chips to be manufactured from each silicon wafer, reducing manufacturing costs. The new chips will be used by leading PC manufacturers. A new notebook with 500 MHz Pentium III chips is expected to sell for less than $2000. AMD has already demonstrated samples of its Athlon chips with speeds of up to 800 MHz and plans to offer 1000 MHz chips in the year 2000: 'We're going to be neck-and neck with Intel for the foreseeable future', say AMD (quoted in *FT*, 26 October 1999).

Despite the fact that the industry was relatively new, by the year 2000 consolidation had already progressed very rapidly, telescoping into a few years processes that took decades in other sectors. Firms based in developing countries already face serious barriers to entry and growth. A small group of immensely powerful firms has emerged rapidly to dominate key parts of the new information technology sector. These firms have rapidly established powerful barriers to entry at the level of systems integration. Across the industry, from IT hardware, through software, services, telecoms, and even in the Internet, a relatively small group of firms has established powerful competitive advantage. This derives from their huge expenditure on R & D and large outlays on global brand-building. In the same way as in many other sectors, the leading hardware and software firms, and, increasingly, the content providers, have developed a high capability as 'system integrators'. They have constructed an 'external firm' consisting of a large number of small enterprises that undertake a variety of subcontracting functions for the core systems integrators, including R & D, components manufacturing and local programme-making.

At the end of the 1990s, a series of colossal mergers transformed these sectors (Table 11-5). We have seen that in the *FT*'s year 2000 ranking of the world's top

TABLE 11-5 Total Value of Mergers and Acquisitions in Knowledge-intensive Industries, 1988 and 1998 ($ billion)

Sector	1988	1998
Computers	21.4	246.7
Biotechnology	9.3	172.4
Telecommunications	6.8	265.8

SOURCE: UNDP (1999: 67)

companies by market capitalization, no less than 48 of the top 100 companies were in the information sector (Table 11-1). The massive stock market valuations of information companies enabled them to merge with or take over rivals or complementary companies that enhanced their competitive position. The pace of consolidation was fantastic. The explosion of merger activity was taking place both horizontally and vertically. Processes of industry consolidation that took decades in other sectors are happening at incredible speed in this sector.

By the late 1990s, in sector after sector within the IT industry, from IT hardware through to media, a relatively small number of giant players had emerged to dominate their respective sectors. Moreover, a powerful process of vertical mergers had begun to take place leading to the emergence of super-giant IT companies that spanned more than one area of expertise.

The information technology revolution was comprehensively dominated by firms based in the advanced economies. Only one of the top 48 information technology companies in the *FT* top 100 firms by market capitalization (Table 11-1) is from a developing country. Not one of the top 300 companies by R & D spending in 1998 was from a developing country. Within the MSDW 'competitive edge' firms in the information technology sector, only seven out of 86 firms were from developing countries, and the number falls to just two if Taiwan and Korea are counted as 'developed' countries (MSDW, 2000: 14–15).

Among the oligopolistic firms based in the advanced economies, those based in the USA are especially powerful. Of the 48 information technology firms in the top 100 firms by market capitalization no less than 26 are from North America, compared with just 11 from Europe and eight from Japan (Table 11-1). Among the top 55 information technology firms in the world's leading firms by R & D expenditure, 36 are US firms, and, even more strikingly, among the top 17 IT software firms by R & D expenditure, 16 are US firms, an extraordinary degree of dominance of the 'brain' of the information technology revolution. Within the MSDW list of the world's leading companies in terms of 'competitive edge', no fewer than 50 out of the 86 information technology firms are from the USA (Table 11-3).

IT HARDWARE

IT hardware is at the heart of the global business revolution. Seventeen of the world's top 100 firms by market capitalization are in this sector (Table 11-1). This sector is of central importance within MSDW's list of the top 250 firms in terms of 'competitive edge' (Table 11-3). We have noted already that the IT hardware sector is much the most important in terms of the number of firms among the world's leading companies by R & D spending. The leading firms in the sector now spend almost as much as the entire auto and pharmaceutical industry put together (Table 11-2). Most of the twentieth century saw the telecoms equipment industry grow steadily through sales of infrastructure equipment, corporate and commercial devices to the public, usually state-owned, telecom enterprises. Liberalization, privatization, competition, technological change and globalization over the past decade have profoundly transformed the telecom equipment industry. There has been an explosion of new products. Among the most dramatic of these are in the network equipment industry, which provides everything to enable digital data transmission, and wireless telephony. Ten years ago there was a small group of mainly US-based dominant manufacturers in the data networking industry. New entrants appeared in the 1990s. However, these have in turn established high barriers to entry through huge investment in R & D and now stand alongside the traditional industry giants as the dominant players in the vastly expanded industry.

The leading players in the sector have achieved enormous increases in their market capitalization, as investors have acquired stocks in the firms that they believe will shape the infrastructure of the early twenty-first century. By 1998, Cisco and Lucent between them accounted for no less than 52 per cent of the total world market capitalization of the telecoms hardware sector, with a combined market capitalization of almost $300 billion. By early 2000, five out of the top 10 *FT* 500 companies were from this sector (Table 11-1). Leading firms were able to use their massive market capitalization as an instrument for take-over and acquisition, often as a means to acquire new technology. However, at least as important a motive for acquisitions is the acquisition of scarce human resources. Cisco Systems CEO John Chambers commented: 'We are able to attract the world's best and brightest engineers. Most people don't understand how important that is. I would rather have one of the top 20 engineers in the world than have 100 average engineers because that is where your creative ideas come from, that is where your time-to-market comes from' (quoted in *FT*, 7 October 1998).

The battle to dominate the new information technology infrastructure is intense. A small group of global winners was already emerging in the late 1990s: 'This battle [for Internet Protocol Infrastructure] is going to be over within five years and by then, clear leaders and losers will be determined. At the end of the showdown between the old and new network companies, there will be only three to five significant companies left' (John Chambers, CEO of Cisco Systems, quoted in *FT*, 7 October 1998). The pace of acquisitions was intense. Between January 1999 and April 2000 alone, MSDW recorded the following acquisitions by the leading players (MSDW, 2000: 126):

- *Cisco Systems* committed more than $22 billion to acquire companies in the new high-growth mega-markets, namely optical transport and broadband access, 'in an effort to maintain high margins and displace large revenue streams of future competitors'.

- *Lucent* made significant acquisitions in the data networking, systems integration, and billing systems industries. These totalled more than $35 billion.

- *Nortel Networks* committed around $7 billion to acquire a wide spectrum of technologies ranging from general telecom and data networking equipment to optical networking and e-commerce software producers, with a primary focus on the optical arena.

- *Motorola* announced acquisitions to establish its broadband communications segment and augment its semiconductor business. These developments included the $17 billion purchase of General Instruments, which increased Motorola's capabilities in the broadband area.

The leading players in the sector are predominantly based in the USA. None is from a developing country. The leading players in the industry have immense technological capabilities and are shaping the entire architecture of IT hardware systems during the epoch of the IT revolution. The global leaders have established commanding technical capabilities to enable them to dominate the IT revolution, through colossal R & D expenditure and through extensive merger and acquisition:

- **IBM**. IBM was the leading information technology company prior to the Internet revolution. It remains immensely powerful, arguably still the world's strongest IT company, despite the fact that by the year 2000 its market capitalization had slipped behind that of Cisco, Microsoft, Lucent and even Nokia. Despite its relative decline, IBM's market capitalization in January 2000 still stood at $200 billion, not far short of the value of the entire Chinese stock market at the end of the 1990s. IBM's sales revenue had grown from $64.5 billion in 1992 to $87.5 billion in 1999, a growth of more than one-third during the global business revolution, and an average annual growth rate of 4.5 per cent. IBM's total revenues are as large as those of a substantial-sized developing country like Egypt. IBM's 1999 profits stood at $7.7 billion, almost equal with Microsoft (*Fortune*, 31 July 2000), and comfortably inside the top 10 most profitable companies in the world.

  IBM sits at the centre of the IT revolution. It is the world's second largest software company, with software revenues second only to Microsoft, at $13 billion in 1999, compared with Microsoft's $14 billion, but far ahead of the third-ranked Oracle, with revenues of $7 billion. However, it is also the world's fifth largest IT hardware firm, with hardware revenues of $37 billion. This is substantially behind Hewlett–Packard ($48 billion revenue) and Fujitsu ($47 billion revenues), but alongside those of Lucent and Compaq (both $38 billion revenues) and far ahead of those of Cisco ($12 billion) and Nortel ($21 billion). Even more importantly, IBM is the world's leading provider of strategic outsourcing of computer-related services, including 'end-to-end e-business implementation of offerings like supply chain management, enterprise resource planning and business intelligence'. IBM's revenue from these forms of outsourcing reached $32 billion in 1999, far in excess of the world's largest specialist data services company, EDS, which had revenues of $18 billion in 1999 (*Fortune* 31, July 2000).

  IBM's technological lead is sustained by huge investments in R & D, totaling almost $6 billion in 1999 (IBM, 2000: 44). Like the other leading IT hardware firms, it uses its huge market capitalization to acquire technology through investing in and purchasing large numbers of other companies, as well as itself undertaking huge amounts of R & D. For example, in 1999 alone, IBM acquired seventeen companies, for a total outlay of $1.7 billion (IBM, 2000: 72). IBM sets the standards for large parts of the world's IT industry, with the number of patents issued rising from 1400 in 1992 to almost 2800 in 1999 (IBM, 2000: 44). IBM aims to achieve 'pervasive computing', with 'a mosaic of computing that extends beyond traditional computers and PCs to include an array of small computing devices like hand-held computers and intelligent phone cells, as well as lots of everyday things – from household appliance to clothes and machine tools – all containing a little embedded computing and networking capability' (IBM, 2000: 44).

- **Lucent**. Lucent Technologies was spun off from AT&T in 1996. When it was spun off it was only one quarter the size of AT&T, but by late 1999 its market capitalization was slightly bigger than that of its former parent, as investors piled into the companies that make the hardware that underpins the Internet. Lucent has quickly become one of the leading providers of next-generation network equipment, and 'the clear leader in providing end-to-end communications networks'. Its IT spending in 1998 amounted to almost $5 billion and its sales totalled almost $30 billion (DTI, 1999: 56). New modes of access including cable, xDSL, fibre and wireless, mean that oper-ators are looking for turnkey solutions spanning a range of technologies: 'Lucent is the clear global leader in the ability to respond to these needs' (MSDW, 1999: 264). Around 70 per cent of the world's Internet traffic now travels over Lucent equipment.

  A major advantage for Lucent has been its ability to use its huge and fast-growing market capitalization to buy new technologies to reinforce its leading position in the technologies of the Internet. It is engaged in intense competition with Cisco and Nortel to enhance its leading position through acquisition as well as R & D, in the explosively rapid areas of growth of data networking and telecoms equipment. In 1999 and the first quarter of 2000 alone it made 10 significant acquisitions. These included the purchase of the data network-ing firms, Ascend Communications (for $24 billion) and Ortel (for $3 billion), and the IT professional services firm Excel Switching (for $3.7 billion) (MSDW, 2000: 129). Lucent continued its process of high-speed acquisi-tions with the purchase of Chromatis (Israel) for $4.5 billion in June 2000 (*FT*, 1 June 2000). Chromatis makes equipment that 'promises to increase the capacity of local metropolitan networks at half the cost of other optical networking gear' (*FT*, 1 June 2000).

- **Cisco**. Cisco has grown from nothing to become in only a few years 'by far the biggest player in the data networking market, *with a commanding posi-tion in each of its key product lines*' (MSDW, 1999: 264, emphasis added). Cisco produces 80 per cent of the networks that the Internet runs on and is the third largest public corporation in the world by market capitalization. Cisco made over 40 acquisitions in less than three years at the end of the 1990s. It is 'a master in identifying important technologies, using the high value of its shares to make acquisitions, and quickly integrating those companies into its overall structure' (*FT*, 2 February 2000). In 1999 and the first quarter of 2000 alone, it made 14 significant acquisitions. These included Cerent (for $7 billion) in optical networks, and GeoCorp (for $2 billion) and Pirelli Optical Systems (for $2.2 billion) in data networking (MSDW, 2000: 129).

In the first five months of the year 2000, Cisco completed no fewer than ten acquisitions, and aimed to double this number for the whole year. These acquisitions included the purchase of Arrow Point (for $6 billion) announced in May 2000. Arrow Point makes Internet switching equipment. It has developed a key Internet technology that routes web site content to specific locations ('content switching') (FT, 6 May 2000). In early May 2000, Cisco's market capitalization reached $465 billion, overtaking Microsoft as the world's most valuable company in terms of stock market capitalization (FT, 6 May 2000). Cisco largely managed to weather the storm of the early 2000 downturn in the valuations of technology stocks: 'This is important to Cisco since it relies on the high value of its stocks to execute its business strategy of acquiring smaller companies with cutting edge technologies and products. The strategy provides Cisco with faster time to market, without having to develop products in-house' (FT, 6 May 2000).

- **Nortel**. Nortel is engaged in an intense struggle with Cisco Systems and Lucent for leadership of the hardware for the Internet and broadband revolution. The market for fibre-optic technology is growing at around 50 per cent per year, and is expected to be valued at $35 billion by the year 2001. High-speed technical developments are rapidly cutting the cost of transmitting data over the Internet. In order to keep up in this competition, Nortel needs to invest large amounts in R & D and capacity expansion. In late 1999 it announced that it was investing $400 million to triple production of advanced Internet transmission equipment. In 1999 alone it doubled its production of optical transmission systems and dense wavelength division multiplexing (DWDM) equipment, which is vital to the next generation of high capacity systems (FT, 3 November 1999). In 1999 and the first quarter of 2000, Nortel made seven significant acquisitions. These included the purchases of optical networking firms Qtera (for $3.2 billion) and Clarify (for $2.1 billion) (MSDW, 2000: 129).

- **Nokia, Motorola and Ericsson**. In wireless handsets, Motorola, Ericsson and Nokia are clear global leaders, with around three-fifths of the total world market. Moreover, they are also massively dominant in the associated equipment. Nokia, for example, not only supplies around one-quarter of the world's handsets, it also supplies mobile services switching centres, base stations, and transmission and data communications equipment. Even where domestic telecoms firms (typically with state support and/or ownership) play a large role in the telecoms services, the equipment is typically purchased from the dominant global telecoms equipment firms. They have sales of between $15 billion (Nokia) and $28 billion (Ericsson) and R & D of between $1.5 billion (Nokia) and $3.4 billion (Ericsson) (DTI, 1999: 57), allowing them to continually extend their technical lead in one of the fastest-growing areas of telecoms hardware. A crucial part of their investment is in the development of Third Generation (3G) mobile phones and the associated infrastructure that will be the instrument for broadband, convergence-based communications. Already, by 2000 it appeared that Ericcson had established itself as the global leader in the race to dominate the 3G mobile devices. Ericsson was selected as the supplier for each of the first four 3G licences awarded, in Japan and Finland respectively. In May 2000, Vodafone selected Ericsson as its supplier for 3G mobile infrastructure. It is estimated that as many as 84 3G licences could be awarded in total, 'a massive opportunity which helps explain the recent enthusiasm for Ericsson shares' (*FT*, 17 May 2000).

SOFTWARE AND IT SERVICES

If a firm is to compete in this sector, it needs not only large size and R & D spend, but also a proven track record of high quality investment: 'A repeatable process for innovation and execution is the only real competitive advantage over the long term' (MSDW, 1999: 274). We have already noted that the world's leading software firms are almost entirely US-based. The USA has established an extraordinarily high degree of dominance of the 'mental architecture' of the global business revolution.

Rather than build an 'impenetrable fortress', the leading firms attract a wealth of third party, complementary products around their technology to form a 'sphere of influence'. The sphere of influence extends beyond third party technologies to include consulting, training and education, implementation and outsourcing services: 'The extended ecosystem around a company can be compelling for customers who want choice as well as orderly and planned integration' (MSDW, 1999: 274). Customers are fearful of being responsible for integrating products that weren't designed to work with each other. Successful companies lower the risk of integration by making their products easier to interface with outside technologies, providing consulting services to make the integration happen, and having fewer things that need to be integrated because of the breadth and consistency of the product line. Successful companies not only need to have economies of scale. It is imperative that they continuously invest in improvements in design: 'To make the cut, companies must add more value/functions at a given unit price point to hold average selling prices to more moderate declines' (MSDW, 1999: 275).

A small number of powerful firms based in the advanced countries are creating the global architecture for this part of the IT industry. The firms that initially create competitive advantage are able to pull ahead rapidly, not only through high levels of R & D and investment in human resources, but are able to acquire technologies through merger and acquisition. A crucial way to develop skills across the different boundaries of the industry is to acquire other companies. Even in the newest segments of the industry, a group of dominant players has emerged at high speed: 'While Cisco is the company that is laying the tracks of the Internet, Sun, IBM and EMC are developing the track's width standards and building the railroad cars ... Sun, IBM and EMC are the companies using software to drive standards for a networked world. By controlling the middleware standards these vendors can capture both the applications and the hardware that run the Internet' (MSDW, 1999: 267).

The following are some of the dominant players in the sector:

- **Microsoft**. Microsoft has comprehensively dominated the operating systems for the world's 300 million PCs. Microsoft's revenues have grown to around $14 billion and its market capitalization reached no less than $600 billion, the world's most valuable company, reflecting investors' understanding of the central place the company occupied in the IT revolution. Its R & D expenditure reached $4 billion in 1999 on revenues of almost $20 billion. Not only does Microsoft upgrade its technological capability at high speed, it also has a massive marketing capability, spending almost $3 billion on marketing in 1998. Microsoft is using its huge R & D expenditure to develop an integrated 'platform' for delivering software programmes, information and services via the Internet, including the software and services needed to power the myriad of 'intelligent' devices like pocket PCs and smartphones. Microsoft Windows accounts for 85 per cent of the world total of operating systems installed on personal computers. Microsoft Office accounts for 90 per cent of the world total of business desktop applications (*FT*, 29 April 2000). Even after the anti-trust battles in the USA, Microsoft remains an immensely powerful company, with a market capitalization still standing at $347 billion in April 2000 (*FT*, 4 May 2000).

- **Oracle**. Oracle has become the 'dominant supplier of large database software' (*FT*, 2 February 2000). It has sales of around $7 billion and an R & D spending of almost one billion dollars. The company has positioned itself at the centre of the world-wide business transition towards the Internet. Most *Fortune* 100 companies use Oracle database software.

- **Sun Systems**. Sun was founded in the early 1980s and is now widely acknowledged to be one of the leading Internet technology suppliers. Sun has sales of around $9 billion and R & D expenditure of over $1 billion (DTI, 1999: 57). Its server hardware and Solaris operating system powers the majority of Internet web sites. Its Java programming language has become the world-wide standard, used in everything from supercomputers to smart cards. Sun's Jini intelligent networking technology enables devices to identify and exchange data with each other, and is poised to become an industry standard.

TELECOMS SERVICES

Alongside the revolution in information technology has gone a parallel revolution in the institutional structure of telecoms services. A succession of national monopolies run by the state has been privatized and forced to compete with radically transformed companies that have entered the telecoms services arena. This process has included intense competition in such revolutionary developments as the explosive growth of wireless telephones and the convergence of technologies, such as mobile phones that can also communicate with the Internet. The established giants rapidly changed their behaviour, and all are trying to build a global capability. Newcomers have grown with incredible speed to become giant players against which it will be hard for later new entrants to compete.

The realization that telecoms services were going to form the basis of the new world order of the twenty-first century stimulated a massive boom in stock market valuations of both the established private companies and the newly privatized telecoms firms. By 1998, there were 18 telecoms companies in the top 100 companies ranked by market capitalization. A colossal boom in mergers and acquisitions took place within the sector. By the end of the 1990s, truly global companies were beginning rapidly to emerge. These were much more competitive than the former state monopolies. They built their global capability on providing telecoms services mainly for the huge markets within the advanced economies, but were increasingly serving the global needs of businesses based in the advanced economies. They were distinguished by their ability to understand the profound technology changes that were taking place within the industry. The enormous scale of the new telecoms giants also enabled them to benefit from economies of scale procurement and branding. At least as important, they are able to influence the whole direction of development of the global industry through their position as the major consumers of the products of the hardware and software industry.

The nature of the competition that awaits China's indigenous telecoms companies within the WTO is dramatically different from that of only a few years ago. Two of the most powerful sources of competition are the US telecoms giants and the emerging global players in the European telecoms industry. The strongest challenges to the US giants come from the European mobile phone sector, but this is to a considerable degree due to the relatively slow take-up of mobile telephony in the 1990s. However, wireless phones are now rapidly increasing in the USA, and it is highly likely that US-based giants will quickly develop in this sector of the industry also:

- **US consolidation since 1996**. Following the de-regulation, especially of the local industry, set in motion by the USA's 1996 Telecommunications Act, a wave of mergers swept the US telecoms industry, with large-scale re-consolidation of the formerly fragmented structure which had been created by the break-up of 'Ma Bell'. By 1998, a group of 'super-carriers' had emerged, including Bell Atlantic/GTE, AT&T, SBC/Ameritech, MCI/WorldCom and Bell South. They had revenues in 1997 of between $21 billion and $54 billion. The objective of the emerging giants was clearly global. The head of international operations at one of the US giants commented: 'This industry is going global – our customers are going global. We really believe growth overseas will exceed growth domestically' (quoted in *FT*, 30 September 1998). By the late 1990s, the US giants were poised to become 'the dominant acquirers in the global consolidation game'. 'Domestic corporate activity in the past three years has created four national powerhouses – AT&T, MCIWorldCom, SBC and Bell Atlantic. Their attention will certainly turn to Europe. The stage is set for a frenzied round of merger and acquisition activity over the next several years. No European company is safe from take-over' (Douglas Wight, analyst at Commerzbank, quoted in *FT*, 24 November 1999).

- **Vodafone–Mannesmann**. The example of Vodafone provides a vivid illustration of this changed world of telecoms. It highlights the extent to which this 'new' industry has already produced a small number of incredibly powerful global giants against which China's telecoms firms must compete on the global level playing field after it enters the WTO. Vodafone's merger with AirTouch of the USA was itself a landmark development in the telecoms industry signalling the dramatic breakdown of national barriers to merger and acquisition in this formerly 'strategic' industry. Vodafone's subsequent merger (agreed in early 2000) with German-based Mannesmann was even more symbolic of the pace of change in the world telecoms industry, and illustrative of the high speed with which global giant players were emerging. Despite intense discussion within Germany about the desirability of allowing a 'national champion' to pass out of German hands, the German government did not interfere to oppose the merger, and allowed the creation of a giant trans-European and transatlantic company. The merger will create the world's fourth largest public company, third largest telecoms company and a clear market leader in wireless communications.

The new company, Vodafone AirTouch Mannesmann (VAM) will have mobile operations in 25 countries, a coverage of more than half a billion potential subscribers, of which only about 10 per cent is currently utilized. It will have a total of over 40 million subscribers, rising to 65 million in the year 2000. This compares with a total of 43 million mobile phone subscribers in the whole of China at the end of 1999. VAM already has 11–12 per cent of the world's mobile phone customers. Its market capitalization will be $329 billion, giving it a huge potential to add to its portfolio of telecoms companies through further merger and acquisition. The forecast annual revenues for 2000–1 are more than $37 billion, with a projected average annual growth rate over the next three years of at least 17 per cent, and possibly as much as 31 per cent. Moreover, it has the potential to reach another 500 million customers in the same markets, most of whom are in relatively high-income markets able to afford high-value-added services.

VAM has the resources to place itself at the head of the race to become the world leader in the 'third generation' of mobile phones which will give its subscribers access to all the information on the Internet. The rapid technical progress that drives the convergence of wireless and the Internet will yield increased traffic, higher revenues, lower churn rates (disconnection rates), reduced operating costs and higher returns. VAM plans to launch its 'wireless data platform' in the year 2000. This will provide services including messaging, location-based content and e-commerce in a uniform manner on a global basis.

Not only are the global giants building their capability across the highly developed markets of Europe, Japan and North America. They are already consolidating their market position in large parts of the developing world. In much of East Asia in the late 1990s, the telecoms sector still remained highly protected. In those parts of the developing world in which extensive privatization and liberalization of the rules governing foreign investment had taken place, the global giants used their colossal market capitalization to acquire local firms. In Latin America, full privatization of the industry was followed by a comprehensive take-over by the global giants. By the late 1990s, 18 out of the 20 largest telecoms operators in the region were controlled by international strategic partners.

Among the world's top 16 telecoms companies by market capitalization, excluding two that are based in Hong Kong, none are from developing countries. The largest publicly-quoted developing country telecoms company by sales revenue is Telmex, the former state-owned monopoly in Mexico. Its revenues stood at around $8 billion in 1998. Telmex was able to preserve its competitive position largely due to a protective government regime, which allowed Telmex to charge high connection charges. The US Trade Representative has threatened to take Mexico to an arbitration panel of the WTO if corrective measures are not taken (*FT*, 21 June 2000) to bring Mexico's practice into line with the 1997 World Telecoms Agreement. It is highly likely that this will erode Telmex's competitive position relative to the global giants north of the border.

THE INTERNET

Even the youngest of the telecom service industries has seen a dramatic process of consolidation. Already many aspirant Internet companies have disappeared. The industry first movers are 'taking advantage of their position and the consolidation frenzy has begun' (MSDW, 1999: 280). The massive stock market valuations allowed the successful early movers rapidly to consolidate their position through merger and acquisition (see below). The global leaders benefited from classic scale economies, such as in the purchase of IT equipment and software, attracting the best human resources and negotiating better deals with global advertising firms than smaller companies could hope to achieve. The huge market valuations have allowed a decisive development of global businesses that acquire other businesses internationally, building global markets and global brands. Moreover, the huge market valuations of successful Internet firms have enabled them to acquire information technology companies outside the Internet sector, benefiting from potential economies of scope in linking businesses at different parts of the IT value chain.

A large number of Internet companies has been started up. However, the ferocious process of competition is quickly driving out most of the players. Christmas 1999 was called the 'Internet Christmas' in the USA: 'The competition is enormous. There's a theory that there will only be two or three players in every category and if you are not one of those three players at the end of the holiday season, raising funds and building your company, you may not get a second chance ... Its Pepsi and Coke. There'll be two players in everything. If you're the third or fourth, I think you have to start worrying' (advertising executive quoted in *FT*, 17 November 1999).

A major weapon of competition in the Internet is the ability of firms to spend on advertising to create a global brand. Advertising for Internet services has exploded. In the early days of the Internet, entry costs were low. Almost anyone could start an Internet business with a computer and an Internet connection. With the market leaders sharply raising their advertising expenditure, the barriers to entry are rising rapidly: 'When Yahoo!, Ebay and some other businesses began, it seemed possible to build a brand, or at least to get some tremendous groundswell for $10–15 million. Now these numbers have changed pretty radically. Increasingly, you can't build an Internet brand for less than $100 million from scratch' (industry analyst, quoted in *FT*, 17 November 1999). In late 1998, advertising by Internet companies totalled already $200–250 million at an annual rate (*FT*, 17 November 1999). By late 1999, that figure had shot up to $7.5 billion. A process of brand building that took many years or even decades is happening in a matter of months: 'In all my sixteen years in advertising I've never heard of a company wanting to build a brand in a month. But that's what's happening. The whole process has speeded up, and the only way you can speed up the process is to spend money on it' (advertising executive, quoted in *FT*, 17 November 1999).

Although the size of the market in developing countries is much smaller than in the advanced economies, already the fast-emerging major players are turning their attention to these markets. In Latin America a 'bloody war' between the US giants and the local Internet companies has already begun (*FT*, 17 November 1999). Most Latin American Internet companies are minnows compared to the US giants: 'Juggernauts like AOL and Yahoo! can acquire local services complete with clients and contents ... Local sites just do not have the capital to compete' (industry expert, quoted in *FT*, 17 November 1999).

The leading Internet companies are powerfully driving their businesses into Asia:

- **Yahoo!** At the head of the race into Asia is the global market leader Yahoo! In Japan it has established a joint-venture with Softbank Corp. and has replicated the tremendously successful model it used in America and Europe. Yahoo! is trying to build on its unprecedented strength by continuous acquisitions of local content start-ups. Yahoo! has established itself as the leading site in Japan, and has become the clear market leader also in Korea, with about one third of the total market share and 23 million clicks per day. The notion that local market peculiarities, knowledge of local language and culture will provide a protection against the global Internet giants has been completely exploded by the explosive pace with which the global leader has established its dominance in these formerly highly protected markets and inward-looking cultures. Yahoo! has also launched powerful sites in Taiwan, Hong Kong and Singapore, all in the Chinese language, making it the top Asian site overall (*Business Week*, 17 January 2000).

- **America Online (AOL)**. AOL entered Japan in 1997 with a local version of its product and soon after introduced the Hong Kong version with the intention to use this base in order to be one of the first movers into China. It partnered with a popular Hong Kong-based portal, China.com, which was the first Chinese Internet IPO (*Business Week*, 17 January 2000). In early 2000, AOL was poised to merge with Time Warner. Time Warner, along with Viacom, had already made clear its ambition to use its colossal resources to expand rapidly in China after it enters the WTO. They both see joint ventures with the local cable companies in large east coast cities as the simplest path through which rapidly to develop their businesses in China. For example, it was reported that in 1999, Sumner Redmond, the CEO of Viacom, went to Shanghai to discuss a cable TV deal with Jiang Zemin's son, a local cable operator (reported in *FT*, 2 March 2000). At the same time, Gerald Levin, Time Warner's CEO, hosted a global gathering of CEOs with his 'very good friend' Jiang Zemin (reported in *FT*, 2 March 2000).

MEDIA

The battle for control of the global mass media is of exceptional importance in the shaping of global culture in the epoch of globalization. It is of crucial importance in influencing the nature of political developments in post-Communist societies. In times of intense debate, such as over China's entry to the WTO, the global mass media have a potentially highly influential role.

A small group of clear global leaders emerged at the end of the 1990s. These were Time Warner (revenues $27 billion in 1998), Disney (revenues $23 billion in 1998) and Viacom (revenues $13 billion in 1998). Each of these is a US company. The global leaders possess vast libraries of entertainment, a huge news collection capability, a global brand, global advertising revenues and huge market capitalizations with which to acquire other media companies. Both Time Warner and Disney are in the world's top 100 firms by market capitalization, an indication that investors expect these firms to benefit massively from the liberalization and growth of the mass media across the world, with huge potential markets, as yet hardly tapped, in countries such as China and India.

Not only are the mainstream of entertainment and news provision consolidating, with a small number of oligopolistic firms emerging. In addition, former niche markets are also rapidly consolidating. For example, in music production and distribution, just five companies, BMG, Sony Music, EMI, Time Warner and MCA-Polygram, account for around nine-tenths of total world recorded music sales. In the view of many people in the media industry, music will be a central part of the future global competition in the entertainment industry, as important as sports, education, cinema and games.

In the provision of financial information, just two firms, Reuters and Bloomberg account for around three-fifths of the global market. In the advertising industry, just three giant firms, WPP/Young and Rubicam (merger announced in May 2000), Omnicom and Interpublic together account for around one-half of total global revenues (*FT*, 12 May 2000). Even tenth-ranked Publicis has total billings that are just one-fifth of WPP/Young and Rubicam.

BROADBAND AND CONVERGENCE

In the words of one enthusiastic commentator, broadband will be 'the Internet on steroids', which will 'change forever how we consume broadcast and recorded entertainment'. Broadband consists of the provision of digitally-transmitted information through high-speed, high bandwidth telecommunication communication channels. This allows the provision of multiple, interactive forms of communication. A single channel can provide voice ('telephone'), data, TV/video and music, with innumerable multiple related services, such as home shopping, on-line banking and gambling. Almost all forms of entertainment can be 'repurposed' for the Internet (MSDW, 2000: 34). The given channel can be cable (fibre optic or upgraded copper wires), 3G (Third Generation) wireless phones and, possibly, satellite, though there is considerable debate about the price and feasibility of this channel for inter-active services. It is quite possible that the Direct Digital Device (DDD) combined with a wireless linking technology, such as Bluetooth, will become the dominant mechanism for personal communication. These revolutionary developments have stimulated massive flows of capital across formerly separate industry boundaries, in the pursuit of capturing the massive potential profits from this 'convergence' of technologies:

- **AT&T/TCI/Media One**. In the space of less than two years AT&T transformed itself from a traditional telecoms company, albeit the largest in the US, with around one-half of the long-distance market, into a giant of the broadband age. In June 1998, it announced a $46 billion merger with TCI, the US's biggest cable TV company. Following the acquisition of TCI, AT&T owned more than 600 local cable systems (*FT*, 24 November 1999). The cable systems of TCI and its affiliates are capable of reaching 33 million homes. AT&T plans to reach the other two-thirds by franchising its service to other carriers or through partnerships. The objective was to help AT&T achieve 'the long-sought combination of telecoms and entertainment businesses by delivering voice, data, and video to millions of consumers' (*FT*, 25 June 1998). AT&T believes that cable will become 'the leading distribution choice for consumers and businesses' (quoted in *FT*, 24 November 1999). The move enables AT&T to by-pass completely the networks of traditional telephone companies. In 1999, AT&T extended its strategy even further, when it announced the acquisition of MediaOne Group. The $44 billion merger was completed in June 2000 (*FT*, 21 June 2000).

- **AOL/Time Warner**. AOL was the first to recognize the importance of the convergence between entertainment, information, communications and online services. At the start of 2000 it used its huge market capitalization to announce a merger with the world's best-known publishing and entertainment house, Time Warner. This was not only one of the largest and boldest mergers in the history, with a value of $180 billion at the time of its announcement, but it established the first fully integrated media company for the 21st century. AOL Time Warner is a 'traditional business with big brands, long consumer relationship, strong cash flow' (*Business Week*, 24 January 2000, quote by CEO Pittman). The combination of infrastructure, distribution and content is hard to match – Time Warner's cable pipes will give AOL a smooth entry into the long awaited and strongly demanded broadband. This will in turn enable launching of AOL TV, the service that provides the Internet over TV that is expected to make a boom in the USA when deployed in June 2000. AOL stood to gain hugely from Time Warner's distribution and content, while Time Warner stood to gain access to the world's largest cyber community and vast web infrastructure. The giant merged entity would be well-positioned to dominate the world of media and communications.

- **Sony**. Sony, with total revenues of $66 billion in 1999, has massively reallocated its resources towards the media field. As well as buying Columbia Pictures, Sony has become one of the world's leading music producers and distributors. However, its most significant development has been in the field of broadband. It has invested massively in the development of PlayStation 2 (*FT*, 22 February 2000). This is ostensibly a 'toy', a video game console. In fact, it is the mechanism through which Sony intends to transform itself into a broadband Internet company. One industry analyst commented: 'Sony has positioned PlayStation 2 as a gaming platform that will do more than play games. It will connect via cable and phone lines into Sony's web sites. If the platform is in as many homes as the PlayStation 1, then it will be a major force in the computer and Internet industry' (quoted in *FT*, 22 February 2000). The original PlayStation was in no fewer than 70 million homes. If PlayStation 2 equals this number, which seems highly likely, then Sony would have as many subscribers as AOL. Sony is simultaneously in discussion with GM about 'broad co-operation'. This follows the announcement that GM cars would use a Sony data storage device, know as the Memory Stick, to allow drivers to download data into their cars. The device is compatible with several Sony products, including the Vaieo computer, digital video and still cameras, digital photo printers and voice recorders. The alliance 'underscores the eagerness of both GM and Sony to move beyond traditional manufacturing operations into web-based activities' (*FT*, 22 February 2000). The two companies have a close relationship, and Nobuyuki Idei, Sony's president joined GM's board in October 1999.

- **Vivendi/Seagram**. In addition to its large stable of alcoholic drinks, Canada's Seagram also contained a large music and film entertainment business, accounting for over one-half of its total revenues. In 1998 it acquired Polygram Music to create the Universal Music Group, the largest in the world. It also included Universal Studios. Seagram's music and entertainment divisions had combined sales of $7 billion in 1999 (*FT*, 15 June 2000). In February 2000, the family-owned Seagram decided that 'a movie studio, cable TV networks and even the biggest music business in the world, were no longer enough to compete in the new digital landscape heralded by

AOL's $125 billion take-over of traditional media goliath Time Warner'
(*Observer*, 25 June 2000). It started to cast around for a buyer. In June, it
was announced that Seagram was to merge with Vivendi, the French media,
communications and utilities group. Vivendi's telecommunications and
media activities produced a revenue of around $8 billion in 1999. The expec-
tation was that the drinks business of Seagram and the utilities business of
Vivendi would be spun off from the merged entity, which would form a new
broadband giant, with a market capitalization of around $100 billion. A key
part of the strategy was the joint venture between Vivendi and Vodafone,
announced in early June 2000. Vivendi launched its Internet portal joint venture with Vodafone (Vizzavi). Vizzavi will be 'the default home page for
80 million potential mobile and interactive TV customers. The intention was
that Vivazzi would be a multi-access portal to serve as a gateway for online
information, entertainment and services (*FT*, 15 June 2000). Jean-Marie
Messier, the Head of Vivendi, believes that music is the 'master missing
piece' in his 'drive for interactive supremacy' (*Observer*, 25 June 2000). He
believes that music was born for the Internet' (quoted in *Observer*, 25 June
2000). The merged entity of French and North American business interests
promised to constitute a major player in the broadband age.

- **Murdoch**. Rupert Murdoch's News Corp established a joint venture
between its subsidiary Star TV and Hong Kong Telecom (HKT) to create a
network of high speed Internet access and video-on-demand to almost every
home in Hong Kong, with the specific intention of using this powerful base
to expand into the mainland. Already, News Corp has established a joint
venture with Liu Changle, a Chinese-born businessman, to establish
Phoenix, a Chinese language TV station. It is the only foreign-owned television service with a mass audience in China. It claims to reach 45 million
homes (*FT*, 10 June 2000). His ultimate goal is clearly to provide Internet-
based broadband for the mainland market. Murdoch already has relationships with over 6000 local cable TV networks in East and South Asia,
and he would be deeply interested in penetrating China through this
channel.

- **Pacific Century Cyberworks**. In early 2000, Li Kashing's son, Richard Li,
used the rapidly escalating stock price of his Pacific Century Cyberworks
(PCCW) to launch a successful $35 billion bid for Cable and Wireless's
HKT, Hong Kong's dominant telecoms company. Richard Li's goal is to
build a company with high speed broadband Internet service across Asia via
cable and satellite. It now has a powerful set of assets with which to do this,
including the most advanced broadband network in the world, which reaches
around 80 per cent of Hong Kong's population. PCCW inherits the joint
venture with Murdoch's News Corp. The two companies share the same
goal, of building powerful Internet companies across Asia, developing rapidly
within the Chinese mainland after China enters the WTO.

GLOBAL LEVEL PLAYING FIELD

A key part of the WTO negotiations during the Uruguay Round of the GATT and a central issue for the future development of international economic relations under the WTO is the rules governing competition in knowledge-intensive industries. The issue has been a central one in the intense negotiations between China and the USA about China's entry to the WTO (see below). The world's leading firms based in the advanced capitalist economies have invested vast sums in R & D and systems capability. They are deeply interested in the degree to which they are allowed to compete openly in the fast growing markets of developing countries, of which China is by far the most important. Two landmark agreements already have signalled the future path that firms based in the advanced economies wish to use as the basis for the rules governing future international development of this crucial sector of the world economy. These are the TRIPs (Trade-Related Intellectual Property Rights) Agreement and the World Telecoms Agreement.

TRIPs. We have seen that a small number of companies now accounts for a large segment of global market share in the knowledge-intensive industries. Moreover, we have also seen that they account for a very large share of the top 500 corporations ranked by market capitalization and for a very large share of the top 300 companies by R & D expenditure. Global demand for the products of these sectors is growing at high speed. Their dominant position in the world stock markets is closely related to the high value-added and high profit margins that can be achieved in these sectors. In the *Fortune* Global 500 ranking of corporations by returns on revenues, eight of the top 10 companies are in the information technology, telecommunications and life sciences, and 26 of the top 50 are in these sectors (*Fortune*, 2 August 1999: F-14). Among 31 sectors, the average return on revenues in 1998 was 2.8 per cent. The leading sector was pharmaceuticals with 18.4 per cent and the second highest was telecommunications with 10.2 per cent (*Fortune*, 2 August 1999: F-23). Their high profitability is closely related to their dominant position in R & D. Firms from high income countries account for 97 per cent of all patents held world-wide. In 1995 more than one-half of total global royalty and licensing fees were paid to the USA, mostly from Japan, the UK, France, Germany and the Netherlands. In 1993 firms from just 10 countries accounted for 84 per cent of global research and development, controlled 95 per cent of the US patents of the past two decades and captured more than 90 per cent of cross-border royalties and licensing fees.

In their catch-up process, Japan and first-tier Asian NICs greatly reduced the costs of catch-up by the weak enforcement of intellectual property rights in the region before the mid-1980s. However, in 1994, the WTO drew up the far-reaching TRIPs agreement (UNDP, 1999: 67). This drastically increased the level of international control over technology transfer. The TRIPs agreement affects such diverse areas as computer programming, circuit design, pharmaceuticals and transgenic crops. Although each country administers intellectual property right law at the national level, the TRIPs agreement imposes minimum standards on patents, copyright, trademarks and trade secrets. These standards are derived from the legislation of the advanced economies, applying the form and level of protection of the industrialized world to all WTO members. This is far tighter than the existing legislation in most developing countries. Developing countries in the WTO have been given until 2000 to adjust their laws, and even the least developed have been given only until 2005.

The TRIPs agreement is vital for the world's leading corporations in the knowledge-intensive industries, if they are going to be able to extend the benefits from their technology to markets in developing countries as these expand. They provide a huge legal form of protection for firms based in the advanced economies, that enable their technology truly to constitute a barrier to competition for firms based in developing countries, and ensure that they are able to earn the same profit margins from sales in developing countries as they earn from sales in the advanced economies.

World Telecoms Agreement. In February 1997, the WTO concluded the World Telecoms Agreement. Colossal US government effort over three years of 'gruelling negotiations' was put into brokering this incredibly complex deal. The historic agreement was signed by almost 70 countries, the notable exceptions being China and Russia. It will usher in 'an era of free competition, low prices and cross-border investment' (*FT*, 18 February 1997). Undoubtedly, poor developing countries will benefit from access to capital with which to construct telecommunications facilities, which will in turn have powerful positive externalities in stimulating market development.

However, the gains for a small number of competitive telecommunications companies in the advanced economies are likely to be vast. The telecommunications market is huge. World-wide industry revenue has grown from around $440 billion in 1990, to around $830 billion in 1996, and is predicted to rise to over $1200 billion in 2000 (*FT*, 18 February, 1997). Mr Neil Macmillan, who chaired the negotiations, commented bluntly: 'The developed countries will get the lion's share of this market' (*FT*, 18 February 1997). Charlene Barshevsky, then US trade representative designate commented that this was 'a triumph for the American way … US companies are the most competitive telecommunications providers in the world; they are in the position to compete and win under this agreement' (quoted in *FT*, 18 February 1997). The British and US negotiators 'know that their countries have the advantage of the experience of more than a decade of competition – and are best placed to benefit from liberalization' (*FT*, 18 February 1997).

The principal beneficiaries from the telecoms agreement will be the big carriers with a well-developed international presence, notably AT&T/BT, WorldCom/MCI/Sprint, Vodafone/AirTouch, Mannesmann/Orange, France Telecom, Deutsche Telekom and Olivetti/Telecom Italia. The vast bulk of the equipment that they use will be produced by the leading companies based in the advanced economies, such as Cisco, Lucent, IBM, Hitachi, Nortel, Ericsson and Nokia. The global fibre optic links will be owned by companies like Global Crossing. The main software systems and IT services will be provided by the leading companies based in the advanced economies, such as Microsoft, Oracle,

SAP, and ADP. The main Internet companies through which people communicate with the world-wide web will be based in the advanced economies, including companies such as Goo (NTT), Yahoo!, Lycos, and Excite. The main entertainment companies that provide services through the telecoms service companies will be firms that are based in the advanced economies, such as Disney, Time Warner, News Corp, Viacom, and CBS. There are large opportunities for small and medium-sized firms in the IT sector based in developing countries to participate in the lower reaches of the global IT value chain, as outsourced providers of a wide array of products in software, hardware and services. However, there are very few, if any, firms based in developing countries that have the capability to compete directly with the global giants in this fast-consolidating industry. The 'global playing field' is hugely uneven.

Competitive capability of firms based in developing countries. In most areas of IT, companies based in developing countries have hardly begun to develop. In the telecoms service sector the enormous size and business capabilities of the leading service providers, mean that local players would find it extremely difficult to compete on the global level playing field. Most of the remaining powerful telecoms companies in developing countries are almost all either state-owned or strongly protected by government legislation.

In the hardware segment, there are few significant challengers in the developing world to the established giants of the advanced economies. Even the remaining 'national champions' in the telecoms services sector in developing countries have no alternative but to mainly buy equipment from the advanced economies.

The main area of potential competition is in software. India is much the most successful developing country in the software industry. India contains six of the world's top software development centres according to a study by the Carnegie Mellon Software Engineering Institute (*FT*, 25 October 1999). India's exports of software products and services has grown at high speed, reaching $3.9 billion in 1999, out of a total turnover of $5 billion (*FT*, 24 April 2000). The industry's 'phenomenal' growth has had a far-reaching impact, 'causing upheavals within corporate India, as owners of big corporations are finding that their tiny software subsidiaries are worth more than the parent company' (*FT*, 25 October 1999). Companies such as British Airways, Swissair, and GE Capital are setting up online back office, data processing and support centres in India. Two Indian information technology companies have listed on Nasdaq, 'a sign of the industry's growing confidence and international ambitions' (*FT*, 25 October 1999). By mid-1999 India had over 860 software exporting companies. Its share of the world market for software was reported to have reached 20 per cent. Two hundred and three companies out of the *Fortune* 500 have 'outsourced their software needs from Indian companies' (*FT*, 24 April 2000).

India's high quality elite-based scientific education has been an important factor in developing Indian firms' competitive advantage in this sector. A further crucial advantage compared to other developing countries has been the wide education among the Indian intellectual elite in the English language. However, there are still major shortcomings even in the Indian software industry compared to the global giants.

The industry has very limited domestic demand compared with exports. Domestic demand amounts to only one-fifth of total value of sales in the sector, reflecting the low income level and low level of access to information technology within India.

India's software exports are strongly oriented towards the lower value-added segments of the industry, in which competitive advantage relies principally on cost. A major boost to the industry has been undertaking contract work for the year 2000 problem for the multinationals. The industry relies very heavily on performing low-value-added outsourcing work for US-based multinationals. The industry's total annual sales amount to around $6 billion, including hardware, software and services (*FT*, 4 July 2000). This is in total only a small fraction of the revenues of a single one of the world's largest IT companies, such as IBM. The average revenue of the top 25 companies in the sector in 1999 was predicted to be only around $150 million (*FT*, 25 October 1999). The revenues of a single large US information company are typically many times greater than the revenue of the entire Indian software industry.

The market capitalization of the largest Indian software company, Wipro, in mid-1999 was $6.5 billion, compared to hundreds of billions of dollars for the industry's leading players. It is predicted that Indian software companies will start acquiring US-based companies. If Indian government regulations are relaxed, then it is predicted that Indian-based companies may be able to spend $3 billion in acquiring US-based companies in 1999/2000 (*FT*, 24 October 1999). Such sums are trivial besides the vast transactions that are re-shaping the entire industry. The total stock market capitalization of the Indian IT sector peaked at $104 billion in February 2000, still only a fraction of a single one of the world's leading firms in the sector. Moreover, by mid-year, the value had tumbled by more than one-half (*FT*, 4 July 2000), leaving the entire sector with a market capitalization only around one-tenth of that of Cisco Systems. The level of investment in R & D is minuscule compared to the world's leading companies in the sector.

The domestic Indian market is incredibly backward compared to that of the advanced economies, greatly weakening the domestic companies' international competitiveness. A crucial part of the success of the US-based firms is the virtuous circle of high incomes, high expenditure on information technology, massive outlays on R & D, huge institutional investment boosting stock market valuations, which provides the basis for further concentration and stock market appreciation. By contrast, developing countries have much more limited domestic purchasing power and a correspondingly more weakly-developed domestic information technology infrastructure (Table 11-6). The level of penetration of personal computers, mobile phones and the Internet is still trivial compared to the level of the advanced economies. Moreover, the international language of telecommunications is English and a large fraction of the population of developing countries cannot speak English. In India, for example, 'only one in twenty people has a

TABLE 11-6 **Selected Indicators of Information and Telecommunications Development, by Country Level, 1997**

| Country/ Country Group | TV Sets | Per 1000 People (1997) | | | Internet Hosts** 10 000 People Jan 1999 |
		Telephone Main Lines	Mobile Telephones	Personal Computers	
LIEs*	59	16	1	negl.	0.2
MIEs*	272	136	24	32	2.4
HIEs*	664	552	188	270	470
India	69	19	1	2.1	0.13
China	270	56	10	6.0	0.14
USA	847	644	206	407	1131.5

SOURCE: World Bank (2000: 226–7)

NOTES: * Excluding India and China
** Internet hosts are computers directly connected to the world-wide network. Many computer users can access the Internet through a single host.
LIEs: Low-Income Countries
MIEs: Middle-Income Countries
HIEs: High-Income Countries
negl = Negligible

sufficient command of the English language to participate in the new software meritocracy' (*FT*, 25 October 1999).

A major problem for the Indian software industry is that a large number of its software engineers have emigration as their main goal, with the USA as the main chosen destination. US software firms have already recruited a large number of software engineers from India, often going direct to Indian campuses to lure the best software engineers directly upon graduation (*FT*, 24 April 2000). Indians are reported to account for around 38 per cent of the total number of software engineers in the USA's Silicon Valley, as well as heading some of the most successful new ventures. The US government has lifted its visa quota for software engineers from 115 000 to nearly 200 000. Nearly half the current quota is taken up with Indians (*FT*, 24 April). The extent to which India's 'software migrants' will return to India is an open question. There are large gains for India in terms of remittances, ideas and incentives to acquire education, but the degree to which it is rational for the migrants to return to India to establish local software firms is uncertain.

There are obvious benefits for developing countries in opening their countries up to the world's most advanced information technology. Investments in this sector bring large positive externalities. This sector holds the key to economic progress in the early part of the next millennium. However, the brutal reality is that in all parts of the industry, from software through to services, the leading firms of the advanced capitalist economies have established an unassailable lead, in which there are already massive barriers to entry for firms based in developing countries. There are innumerable opportunities for firms based in developing countries to enter the lower end of the value chain. However, there are very limited possibilities for them to compete and win on the global level playing field against the leading systems integrators.

THE BATTLE FOR THE CHINESE MARKET

THE CHINA–US WTO AGREEMENT

China's decision to enter the WTO will have profound consequences for China's IT industry. Both the USA and the EU devoted enormous efforts to press the Chinese side to make large concessions on market access for its IT firms. The reason for this is simple. The advanced economies in general, and the US in particular, contain all the major players in the sector. This sector possesses immense opportunities for increased profits for the large corporations that occupy the leading positions in the industry. A central reason for the explosion in the stock price of the companies in this sector is the investors' belief that the leading firms in this sector will dominate the market across the world.

As we have seen, US-based IT firms are, by far, the most powerful. The US negotiators in the WTO talks put intense pressure on the Chinese side to make concessions in the IT sector. The outcome was an agreement to open up dramatically the Chinese industry to foreign competition. The White House's web site, which published the details of the US–China WTO agreement in April 2000, contained the following headline 'The US–China WTO accession deal: a clear win for US high technology, greater openness and US interests' (The White House, 2000).

The White House argues that access to the potentially vast China market for IT is 'vital to maintaining US global leadership in Information Technology'. Despite low levels of income, China's vast population and rapid economic growth is producing a market that is of great importance for the globally dominant US information technology firms. China is the world's fastest growing telecommunications market. Each year China instals enough phone lines to replace a network the size of Pacific Bell. By the end of 1999, China had around 40 million cellular subscribers. Only the US market is expected to be larger by the end of the year 2000. The US government believes that China will be the world's second largest personal computer market by the end of the year 2000, and third largest semiconductor market by 2001. It is predicted that there will be over 20 million Internet users by the end of 2000 (The White House, 2000).

US-based IT firms have already benefited greatly from rapidly growing Chinese demand for IT goods and services. Between 1990 and 1998, US high-technology exports to China increased more than fivefold, and exports of communications equipment grew over ninefold (The White House, 2000). These large increases were achieved despite substantial restrictions on access to the China market.

The terms of accession to which China has agreed open the possibility for far faster growth of US (and other foreign) business interests in the Chinese IT market than were achieved in the past. China's information technology tariffs in 1999 averaged 13 per cent. This added around $200 to the price of a $1500 computer, providing significant protection for indigenous manufacturers. After China's entry to the WTO, two-thirds of the tariffs will be eliminated by 2003 and the remainder by 2005. Immediately on entry to the WTO China's quotas on information technology products will be eliminated.

Up until 2000, the right to import and export, or to engage in distribution services, including wholesaling, retailing, repairing, warehousing or servicing, was restricted to a small number of firms with government authorization. After entry to the WTO, foreign firms will be allowed to import high technology products into any part of the country. Foreign firms will be allowed to establish, own and operate distribution services within three years of admission to the WTO. The US Government commented: 'This will allow our businesses to export to China from here at home, and to have their own distribution network in China, rather than being forced to set up factories there to sell products through Chinese partners' (The White House, 2000). After accession to the WTO, foreign IT firms will be able to distribute directly to customers, enabling them to tailor products to specific markets, and to provide direct, quality after-sales service and support.

Up until the year 2000, foreign investment in telecommunications was strictly prohibited. China's accession to the WTO will allow foreign investment in all telecommunication services.

For value-added services (including, for example, electronic mail, voice mail, Internet, on-line information and data base retrieval, and enhanced value-added facsimile services), China has agreed immediately on accession to allow 30 per cent foreign participation, rising to 49 per cent after one year and 50 per cent after two years. Foreign service suppliers may provide services in the key markets of Beijing, Guangzhou and Shanghai immediately upon accession, followed by 14 other major cities after one year, and nationwide after two years.

For mobile voice and data services (including all analogue/digital cellular and personal communication services), under the China–US Agreement, China agreed to allow a 25 per cent foreign equity share one year after accession, rising to 49 per cent five years after accession. Immediately on accession, foreign suppliers were to be allowed to provide services in the key cities of Beijing, Guangzhou and Shanghai, extending to 14 other major cities after three years and nationwide after five years. The EU–China agreement of May 2000 produced further concessions from the Chinese side. China agreed that immediately upon accession, multinational mobile phone companies would be allowed to take a 25 per cent stake in joint ventures, rising to 35 per cent after one year and 49 per cent after just two years (*FT*, 20 May 2000). These were major advances compared to the US–China Agreement, of great importance to the 'European champions' in the mobile phone sector.

For domestic and international services (including, for example, voice, facsimile, intra-company e-mail, voice and data services) foreign service suppliers will be allowed to hold a 25 per cent equity share three years after accession, 35 per cent after five years and 49 per cent after six years. Foreign service suppliers will have access to the Beijing, Guangzhou and Shanghai markets after three year, 14 other major cities after five years, and nation-wide after six years.

On accession to the WTO China will adopt WTO norms for telecoms regulation. China has agreed to implement 'the pro-competitive regulatory principles embodied in the WTO Basic Telecommunications Agreement' (The White House, 2000). These include 'access to the public telecom networks of incumbent suppliers (that is, interconnection rights) under non-discriminatory terms and at cost-oriented rates, as well as an independent regulatory authority'. This means that foreign telecom firms 'cannot be discriminated against in seeking to provide their services over the existing infrastructure of Chinese telecommunications providers'. China has also committed to technology-neutral scheduling, which means that any basic service may be provided through any means of technology (for example, cable, wireless, satellites).

China has agreed to 'eliminate practices that cost American jobs and technology'. Foreign IT firms that export to or invest in China will no longer be required to transfer their technology to China: 'This will better protect US competitiveness and the results of US research and development' (The White House, 2000). IT imports into China will no longer be conditional on performance criteria of any kind, including offset and technology requirements or the existence of a competing domestic producer: 'All this will make it significantly easier for American companies to export to China from the United States rather than having to set up in China in order to sell products there' (The White House, 2000).

China's state-owned electronics firms will be required to make purchases and sales 'solely on commercial terms' and 'will provide US firms the opportunity to compete on non-discriminatory terms' (The White House, 2000).

In sum, the conditions on which China has agreed to enter the WTO constitute a dissolution of China's right to implement an industrial policy in this sector. Immediately upon entry, if the terms to which China has signed are implemented, then the capacity to support the domestic IT industry will be dramatically weakened. The agreement means that within only a few years, there will be almost no capability at all to protect and support domestic firms in these sectors. Moreover, there is every incentive for multinational giants in these sectors to advance their actual behaviour beyond the formal regulations, in the expectation that these 'illegal' activities will be validated retrospectively, such as took place on a large scale under the China–China–Foreign arrangement (see below). If the Chinese government continues to use the standard instruments of industrial policy in this sector to support domestic firms, it will encounter fierce battles in the WTO, as these measures are contrary to the rules of the WTO, and contrary to the agreement to which China is a signatory. Such activity would cause immense difficulties in China's international relations.

The determination of the US (and EU) negotiators to push China towards rapid liberalization of its IT industry was not only motivated by economic considerations. A major explicit consideration also was the desire to overturn the Communist

Party and achieve the same political result in China as US policy under Reagan helped to achieve in the USSR. A further factor of great importance in evaluating the impact of the terms under which China's IT industry will be required to operate after China's entry to the WTO is the ideological purpose and consequences of the US and EU governments. As well as a business interest, there is also an explicit ideological objective to the China–US WTO agreement. A major objective is to greatly accelerate political change through undermining the control of the Chinese Communist Party: 'Opening China's Information Technology market will... increase the flow of information among Chinese and between China and the outside world, in ways and in such volumes that no amount of censorship or monitoring can totally control. *This cannot but promote the right kind of change in China*' (The White House, 2000, emphasis added).

A Chinese official at the State Commission for Restructuring the Economic System commented: 'This [WTO] agreement means that we will be dancing with wolves–hungry wolves' (Chinese official quoted in *FT*, 30 November 1999). The 'wolf' has well and truly arrived at the door of the Chinese IT industry.

CHINA'S COMPETITIVE CAPABILITY IN THE IT INDUSTRY

It is widely thought that, compared with other sectors, the IT sector offers a radically different prospect for indigenous Chinese firms. There is a widely-held view that there is a true 'global level playing field' in this new sphere of economic activity, in which 'everyone is starting at the ground floor' (Lau, 2000). The Internet is argued to be a 'democratic equalizer'. In the new information technology, it is argued, 'each firm pinches only a small piece of the action' (Lau, 2000). Competition in IT is argued to be 'all very open' (Lau, 2000). It is argued that these considerations mean that Chinese-based firms can compete and win. Most Chinese analysts believe that the IT sector offers China an opportunity to leapfrog the 'Second Industrial Revolution', which dominated the twentieth century, and rapidly become a leader in the new technologies of the Third Technological Revolution in the early twenty-first century. At the centre of this revolution are the new technologies of the IT industry. It is widely believed that this sector is still in its early stages of development and that new entrants can quickly become global leaders.

Such views are based on a naïve view of the structure of this industry. Within a few years, a process of industrial concentration and economic power has taken place which took many decades in other sectors. This process of concentration was strongly influenced by the fact that the main market for these firms was the USA, which has vastly higher incomes than China. Using this as the base, leading US firms have already consolidated almost global positions that are extremely hard for new entrants to attack.

Under the terms of China's accession to the WTO, the Chinese IT industry will find the competition with large global corporations, especially those based in the USA, extremely severe.

IT HARDWARE

China's leading IT hardware firms developed rapidly in the late 1990s. However, the prospects for even the most successful of these were highly uncertain if China strictly applied the WTO Agreement.

Personal Computers. By 1998, China's leading computer maker, Legend, had captured around 10.7 per cent of the total domestic PC market, ahead of IBM (7.5 per cent), Hewlett–Packard (6.5 per cent) and Compaq (4.6 per cent) (Legend, 1999: 14). By the middle of 1999, its share of the domestic PC market was reported to have exceeded one-fifth. It had established itself as much the most powerful indigenous PC maker, with a serious domestic brand, with a high quality manufacturing and marketing capability. However, Legend remained heavily reliant on several forms of protection. For example, it gained the sole distribution rights to Toshiba notebooks, which occupied 27.4 per cent of the Chinese domestic notebook market in 1997 (Legend, 1999: 18). It had a wide network of customers among China's state enterprises, to which it was extremely hard for multinational firms to gain access. Finally, it was heavily protected through a 15 per cent import tariff and a 17 per cent value-added tax. Like China's other leading IT hardware companies, Legend remains a minnow in international terms (Table 11-7). Their sales revenue, profits and R & D are tiny. In direct competition with the world's leading systems integrators in this field, it is hard to imagine that they could be successful. If the Chinese government applies the rules of the WTO Agreement strictly, the key competitive advantages of these firms in the domestic market will be eliminated.

TABLE 11-7 **China's Leading IT Hardware Firms in International Comparison, 1998**

Company	Revenue ($ billion)	Profits ($ million)	R & D spending ($ million)
Legend	1.0	(28)**	1*
TCL	1.3	(49)**	—
Huawei	0.7	(156)**	120
IBM	78.4	10 200	5100
Hitachi	71.8	2000	4400
Hewlett–Packard	45.3	4200	3200
Lucent	29.1	2500	4900

SOURCE: DTI (1999: 56–7); Legend (1999); China Reform Group (1999: 85, 248)

NOTES: *Legend's reported R & D spending in 1998 totalled 9.3 million Hong Kong dollars (Legend, 1999: 63); in 1998 Legend had 120 R & D engineers (Legend, 1999: 15)
    **Figures in brackets indicate pre-tax profits

Networking Equipment. Even before the conclusion of the WTO agreement, China's leading telecoms equipment manufacturers faced severe competition from the global leaders. Huawei is China's leading maker of networking equipment. Its business grew rapidly in the late 1990s as the telecoms revolution took hold in China. Huawei developed a high quality manufacturing capability and brand reputation. By the late 1990s it had established a domestic market share of one-fifth in 'network switches'. However, its development was crucially related to government support, especially, through restrictions on the import of networking equipment (China Reform Group, 1999: 63). At the end of the 1990s, despite rapid growth, Huawei still remained a small firm, with very limited R & D and tiny profits. Compared to the global giants in the field, such as Lucent, it stood little chance of winning in direct competition, without considerable state support.

Despite state support for selected domestic firms, the multinationals made rapid headway in the Chinese market for networking equipment in the 1990s. The leading multinationals frequently circumvented import restrictions by setting up production facilities in China, agreeing to transfer technology to joint venture partners as a condition for access to the domestic market. As in almost all countries, Cisco is the market leader in networking equipment. It sold more than $250 million worth of equipment to China Telecom in the late 1990s, mainly to upgrade the latter's fixed line network for Internet use, and will supply a further $200 million worth of Internet equipment to China Telecom's Guangdong subsidiary to build its Internet.

The lion's share of China's fibre optic transmission trunk, the backbone of China's telecoms system, built in the 1990s was constructed by a group of international industry leaders, namely Lucent, Alcatel, Nortel and Ericsson, with fierce competition for the large contracts. By 1998, Lucent had established six joint ventures in China, and had become the leading maker of fibre optics in the country, accounting for a reported 24 per cent of the domestic market (*China Economic Digest*, Spring 1998).

Some idea of the ubiquity of equipment from the global giants can be gained from the details of China Unicom's national network. Its long distance network consists of 23 circuit switches, all from Lucent. Its data and Internet Protocol networks consists of 90 asynchronous transfer mode switches, all from Lucent and routers and other Internet protocol equipment from Cisco (China Unicom, 2000: 73).

Wireless Hardware. In wireless communications equipment, the world's leading players, Nokia, Ericsson, and Motorola, together account for 80 per cent of the Chinese domestic market, produced mainly from local plants within China. Facing import restrictions, the global giants set up large-scale production facilities in China. For example, Motorola increased domestic output to 4.9 million phones in 1998, doubling in just one year, to a planned figure of 9.8 million in 1999 (*FT*, 3 November 1999). By 1998, Motorola had invested over one billion dollars in China, with plans to increase this to $2.5 billion by the year 2000.

Its production centre in Beijing had 10 000 employees by 1998 (*China Economic Digest*, Spring 1998). Its investments included construction of its largest wafer fabrication plant outside the USA. China is either the first or the second largest market for the world's three major producers of handsets.

Not only do the three global giants supply the handsets to China, but they supply also a large part of the base stations and switching equipment for the wireless network. In the late 1990s, NEC reportedly supplied 40 per cent of the total SDH microwave networks in use in China (*China Economic Digest*, Winter 1998). NEC's investment in China had already reached $1.5 billion by 1998.

Indigenous Chinese-owned suppliers have not been at all competitive so far, lacking the economies of scale or the technology of the global leaders in the most technically advanced, and high value-added, aspects of the industry. The leading domestic firms, such as Konka, face a severe battle in attempting to compete with such powerful companies. The Chinese state attempted to nurture domestic competitors through various measures of industrial policy. It set quotas on the import of telecoms equipment for each of the leading global firms in the sector. The size of the quota was linked to a company's performance in localizing production and transferring technology to Chinese companies (*FT*, 9 May 2000). In 1999, the government announced plans to impose production quotas as well as import restrictions on foreign manufacturers of mobile phones (*FT*, 3 November 1999). An official spokesman said: 'The government policy is to encourage development of the national mobile phone industry.' If China applies the rules of the WTO Agreement, such measures will have to be abandoned. It is already extremely difficult for the leading domestic firms to compete in this area, and after China joins the WTO, it will be much harder if the Agreement is observed strictly, since it prohibits the Chinese government from directing telecoms operators about the sourcing of their equipment. Moreover, there is great ambiguity about the meaning of 'local' firms, in this as in other sectors. In the telecommunications hardware industry the term 'local' has frequently been interpreted as including local production by multinationals.

In the not-too-distant future, China will introduce Third Generation (3G) mobile telephones, which will be a crucial aspect of the entire IT revolution. The established giants of the mobile phone industry have already invested huge amounts in becoming the global industry leaders in this technology. It will be very difficult indeed for China's fledgling indigenous manufacturers to compete as systems integrators in this field.

Set-top Boxes. China's low income level means that the penetration rate of PCs is very low compared to Western markets. China has just six PCs per thousand people, compared with over 400 per thousand in the USA (Table 11-6). The total number of PCs is 7 million, compared with 110 million in the USA alone. A major avenue for the development of the Chinese IT industry is through set-top boxes. China has 270 TV sets per thousand people, with a total of 335 million sets, meaning that most households have a set. Therefore, the most rapid way forward for the Internet in China is via the TV. However, this requires considerable investment in the technology of the 'set-top-box'. Microsoft has realized the enormous potential this provides for its technology. It has used its colossal R & D capability, with a total spending of almost $3 billion per annum, to develop rapidly this technology (called Venus) and is the market leader, having launched the product in March 1999.

IT SOFTWARE

It is extremely difficult for firms based in developing countries to compete directly with the industry leaders in this sector. They can have important roles as sub-contractors. It is this that largely accounts for the rapid growth of Indian software exports in recent years, as discussed above. While the number of India-based software firms has increased fast, few of them are able to challenge the global leaders in the higher value-added segment of the business. India is by far the most advanced of the low-income countries in the development of its software industry. Even India faces major difficulties in establishing large domestic firms that compete with the global giants of the industry. However, China still lags far behind India in the development of the software industry. The total output value of the entire Chinese software industry in 1999 was just $2.2 billion, only 0.42 per cent of the global industry (*CDBW*, 25 June 2000) and only around one-third of the size of the Indian industry.

TELECOMS SERVICES

Under state ownership, throughout the 1990s, China rapidly expanded its telecoms system, initially mainly through fixed lines, but increasingly through mobile communications. By the late 1990s, Chinese telecommunications were growing at high speed (Table 11-8), and the Chinese market had become a key part of the global development of telecommunications. The WTO Agreement presented a vista of greatly increased opportunities for the global telecoms giants.

Progress. In 1994, the Chinese government announced its intention to establish a group of globally competitive telecoms firms. Its goal was to establish more than one service provider in almost all sectors within the telecommunications industry. By the late 1990s, the Chinese government had broken up the monopoly of the former Ministry of Posts and Telecommunications, and established six major telecommunications carriers (Table 11-9). Much the most important of these were the two entities which emerged directly from the Ministry, namely, China Mobile and China Telecom. It was widely believed that the fixed line incumbent, China Telecom would be granted a licence in 2000 or 2001 to become the third mobile phone company. China Telecom is still wholly state-owned and commands a market share of almost 100 per cent in fixed-line

TABLE 11-8 Growth of China's Telecommunications Industry, 1997–9

	1997	1999	Average Annual Growth Rate (% 1997–9)
China's population (million)	1 236	1 259	0.9
GDP per capita (US$)	720	776	3.8
Fixed line subscribers (million)	70	109	24
Fixed line penetration rate (%)	5.7	8.6	
Cellular subscribers (million)	14	43	78
Cellular penetration rate (%)	1.1	3.4	
Paging subscribers (million)	47	74	25
Paging penetration rate (%)	3.8	5.9	
Internet users (million)	1.4	3.8	65
Internet penetration rate (%)	0.1	0.3	

SOURCE: China Unicom (2000: 54)

TABLE 11-9 Major Chinese Telecommunications Players in Each Sector, 2000

	Market Players	Market Share (%)
Local services	China Telecom, China Unicom	China Telecom: 99
Long-distance services (including Internet Protocol Phone)	China Telecom, China Unicom, China Jitong, China Netcom	China Telecom: 99
Mobile services	China Mobile, China Unicom	China Mobile: 88.6 China Unicom: 11.4
Paging services	Guoxin Paging, China Unicom, and 1600 other players	Guoxin: 59 Unicom paging: 5
Data communication services	China Telecom, China Unicom, China Jitong, China Netcom, China Mobile	

SOURCE: CICC (2000)

telecommunications (Table 11-9). In 1999 it had a total sales revenue of $19 billion, placing it roughly on a par with Telefónica and MCIWorldCom, in terms of revenue.

China Telecom (Hong Kong). The flagship of the process of commercialization was China Mobile. This was established as an independently incorporated company in 1999, consisting of the mobile phone segment of China Telecom. It was a state-owned entity, emerging from the Ministry, which developed the lion's share of China's mobile phone structure and services in the 1990s. In 1997, the Chinese government allowed China Mobile (then within China Telecom) to establish China Telecom (Hong Kong) (CTHK), with its mobile assets in the provinces of Guangdong and Zhejiang. In 1997, 25 per cent of the equity of CTHK was floated on international markets. The remaining 75 per cent was still held by the state-owned China Mobile. The IPO raised $4.5 billion, at that point a record in Asia for an IPO. CTHK raised a further $2.6 billion through an international share issue in 1999 (*FT*, 27 June 2000). This financed the acquisition of China Mobile's mobile phone assets in Fujian, Jiangsu, Henan and Hainan provinces. By the end of 1999, CTHK had a total of 15.6 million subscribers (CTHK, 2000). This represented 36 per cent of all mobile phone subscribers in mainland China. CTHK occupied an 87 per cent market share in the provinces in which it operated. These provinces had a total population of 320 million.

By late December 1999, CTHK had a market capitalization of over $92 billion (*FT*, 4 May 2000), ranking 51st in the *FT 500*. Its turnover in 1999 was $3.2 billion with pre-tax profits of $1.1 billion. In June 2000, CTHK announced plans to raise more funds from international capital markets with the objective of acquiring China Mobile's mobile phone assets in a further seven provinces and major cities – Beijing, Shanghai, Tianjin, Liaoning, Hebei, Shandong and Guangxi. It was intended to raise around $6 billion from international markets in order to contribute to the financing of these acquisitions, which would total around $24 billion (that is, international ownership would not exceed 25 per cent) (*FT*, 27 June 2000). In other words, CTHK appeared to be well on the way to becoming a serious player in global terms (Table 11-10). Market analysts drew favourable comparisons with Japan's DoCoMo.

China Unicom. China Unicom was established in 1993 as a state-owned entity intended to provide competition for the incumbent, China Telecom. It was licensed to operate in all segments of the telecoms industry. It rapidly developed its own nationwide fibre optic transmission network. By the late 1990s, it had developed into the largest paging company in China, with a market share of 59 per cent. It had rapidly increased its mobile phone business, with a total of 4.2 million subscribers at the end of 1999, and its market share stood at 14.2 per cent, compared with China Mobile's 85.8 per cent (China Unicom, 2000: 3). Its 1999 revenue was $2.1 billion, of which 33 per cent came from mobile phone business and 66 per cent from paging (China Unicom, 2000). Only a tiny amount of revenue was derived from fixed line telephony, which remained essentially a monopoly for China Telecom. In 1999, it was granted a licence to provide Internet services. China Unicom's growth was highly controversial. It received no direct investment from the central government, although it did receive large-scale loans. A major source of finance was through the 'China–China–Foreign' path, which involved two Chinese companies and one foreign company, to avoid direct investment by multinationals in the Chinese telecoms industry, which was illegal. This path was outlawed finally in late 1999. Simultaneously, the Chinese government gave China Unicom permission to float up to 25 per cent of its equity on international markets. Despite its relatively small size, the flotation attracted intense interest, and raised $4.9 billion. The flotation was seen as 'a play on

TABLE 11-10 **China Telecom, China Telecom (Hong Kong) and China Unicom Compared to Other Leading Telecoms Firms (billion Dollars), December 1999**

Company	Market Capitalization	Revenue	Pre-tax Profits
NTT Mobile	366	30	3.4
Vodafone (VAM)	291 (Apr. 2000)	26 (pro-forma)	3.0 (pro-forma)
NTT	275	94	12.6
Deutsche Telekom	210	37	5.1
AT&T	164	53	8.3
British Telecom	151	28	7.0
SBC	150	50	10.9
MCIWorldCom	141	18	(1.6)
France Telecom	131	25	3.7
Bell Atlantic	90	32	5.0
Bell South	84	25	5.5
Telefónica	81	18	2.5
TIM	71	6	2.3
Telecom Italia	70	24	4.9
Telstra	69	12	3.5
GTE	64	25	6.4
China Telecom	—	19	—
China Telecom (Hong Kong)	92	4.5	1.1
China Unicom	34	2.1	0.3

SOURCE: FT (4 May 2000, 8 September 2000); CTHK (2000); China Unicom (2000)

China's red-hot cellular industry' (*FT*, 13 June 2000). One analyst commented: 'There's a positive outlook on the cellular phone industry globally and China now accounts for one in every seven new subscribers world-wide' (quoted in *FT*, 13 June 2000).

PROBLEMS

The sector is of the greatest importance to the multinational corporations. It is the one that China fought longest and hardest over in its negotiations with the USA and the EU, since it is crucially related to the mass media and ideology. Superficially, China has been successful in establishing global giants in the telecoms sector. However, many difficulties await this sector.

Bureaucratic Struggle. Each of the main telecoms service providers, China Telecom, China Mobile, China Unicom, Jitong, and the newly established China Netcom Corporation, is under heavy bureaucratic control. China Telecom is a wholly state-owned enterprise which has evolved from the former Ministry of

Post and Telecommunications. Jitong is effectively under the control of the Ministry of Information Industries (MII). In October 1999 a new large telecoms provider, China Netcom Corp, was established, also under the control of a group of public institutions, including the Ministry of Railways and the Shanghai Government. China Unicom was established under the control of a group of ministries and leading state-owned companies. China Unicom's prospectus makes only passing mention of the majority owner of the company, China Unicom Group. This group has fifteen major stakeholders, all state-owned enterprises of one variety or another. They include the MII, the Ministry of Electric Power, and the Ministry of Railways, and some of China's largest SOEs, including CITIC, China Resources, China Huaneng and China Everbright (CICC, 1999).

This structure meant that China Unicom was unable to build a strong consensus among its mostly non-telecom stakeholders (CICC, 1999: 11). These difficulties are reflected in the fact that the chief executive of China Unicom was changed almost every year since the company started operation in 1994 (CICC, 1999: 11). The company has 'too many vested interests under a perplexing structure' (CICC, 1999: 11). The company's business strategy was heavily criticized for attempting to compete head-on with China Telecom in the fixed line market, rather than focus on the cellular market. This involved heavy investment, but could only produce highly uncertain and long-term revenues, while incurring a lot of debt (CICC, 1999: 14). China Unicom had no significant presence at all in the fixed line market despite its heavy investments.

There is intense bureaucratic in-fighting to attempt to capture the stream of rents stemming from the limited number of licences and the absence of multinational competition. A fierce, protracted struggle surrounded the separation of China Mobile from China Telecom. An equally ferocious bureaucratic struggle surrounds the decision over whether and when to grant a third mobile phone licence to China Telecom. The longer the decision can be delayed, the stronger the position of the dominant incumbent, China Mobile, and its interest groups. Intense bureaucratic struggle surrounded the decision to allow China Mobile and China Unicom to float part of their equity on international markets. China Unicom was fiercely attacked by China Telecom and, latterly, China Mobile, to deprive it of access to government funds to finance its expansion. For several years China Telecom used its dominant position to undermine China Unicom through long delays in providing interconnections as the latter tried to expand its network. China Telecom uses its near monopoly position in fixed lines to set the prices for Internet service providers in an aggressive way. The access charges for the ISPs (Internet Service Providers) amount to 80 per cent of total revenue compared to an average of just 6 per cent in the USA.

Where is the Firm? The IPOs of CTHK and China Unicom were highly successful in terms of raising funds from the flotations. However, in order to understand the way in which the multinationals will enter China after it joins the WTO and in order to understand the extent of the challenge to the global giants that these entities present, it is necessary to look more closely inside these 'firms'.

To what extent are they genuinely competitive autonomous firms in the sense that the global giants are?

Let us look more closely, for example, at China Telecom (Hong Kong) (CTHK). At first glance, CTHK is a 'firm'. It is a legal entity with shares that can be traded on the international market. However, it is not clear where the final control over the company resides. The company has six subsidiaries, consisting of the constituent provincial mobile telecoms firms. Each of the subsidiaries is an entity with its own ambitions and local responsibilities. The chairman, vice-chairman and chief financial officer of CTHK was each a senior official within the Chinese Posts and Telecommunications Bureau. The other six executive directors was each formerly also a senior official within the Posts and Telecommunications Bureau. Moreover, each is concurrently the chief executive officer of the respective provincial level mobile phone company (CTHK, 2000: 5–7). CTHK is still 75 per cent owned by China Mobile, which is, in turn, owned by the Ministry of Information Industries (MII), which is, in turn, the largest single shareholder in China Unicom, CTHK's main 'competitor'. The Chinese government is in the process of 'severing the MII's ties with the commercial interests', and allowing an autonomous and professional business structure to develop within China Mobile. The composition and background of the board of directors of CTHK casts considerable doubt as to how far this process has advanced.

In sum, it is not clear whether the 'firm' is CTHK, China Mobile, the provincial subsidiaries of China Mobile, or, the MII. Despite the successful flotations of both CTHK and China Unicom, the operational mechanism of these telecoms companies is far removed from that of the giants of the global telecoms industry, such as MCIWorldCom or Vodafone AirTouch Mannesmann (VAM). Their bureaucratic management methods and complex structure of ownership by different state interest groups, is far removed from even the partially privatized telecoms giants, such as France Telecom, NTT and Deutsche Telekom. Instead, they still have as a main goal the preservation of monopoly rents for their respective interest groups, both from other domestic entities, and, especially, from the multinational giants.

The operational mechanism of CTHK is quite different also from Telmex, arguably the most successful developing country telecom firm. Telmex was formerly Mexico's state telecoms monopoly. It was privatized in 1990. The company was sold to a single individual, Carlos Slim. In Mexico it is reported that Mr Slim's winning bid 'was a forgone conclusion, because he had promised Carlos Salinas de Gortari, then the country's president, an undisclosed stake in the company' (*FT*, 10 July 2000). Whatever the background, there is no doubt that the company is comprehensively controlled by Carlos Slim, with the strong support of the Mexican state. Mr Slim has fought to keep the multinationals out of the Mexican telecoms industry, to the intense chagrin of the global giants. Telmex still controls almost 100 per cent of the local telephone market, and newcomers rely on Telmex to route their incoming calls. Telmex has frequently refused outright to connect some competitors while the inter-connection agreements that have been reached are often heavily skewed in Telmex's favour. In the long-distance market there are similar problems for potential competitors, resulting in more than 200 court injunctions between competitors and Telmex, 'virtually paralyzing new investment and rendering the regulatory authorities powerless'. However, in the ten years since he took over, Carlos Slim 'has turned the once-rickety, state-run monopoly into Latin America's number-one blue-chip company, with a market capitalization of more than $50 billion' (*FT*, 10 July 2000).

Encirclement. Even if China is successful in delaying and restricting the access of the multinational telecoms firms, it faces serious medium-term challenges through 'encirclement' by giants that are far larger, and faster-growing than indigenous firms. At some point, it will have to directly confront this challenge. The incumbent telecoms giant, China Telecom, faces domestic 'encirclement', in the sense that the rate of growth of mobile telephony is far faster than the fixed line business (Table 11-8). Already it is facing the challenge of telephony provided through cable by cable TV companies (see below). However, the entire indigenously-owned industry faces a much deeper problem of encirclement from the global giants.

The global giants of Europe, the USA and Japan are building their companies on a truly international basis, while China's telecoms companies must prepare themselves for the coming battle using only their domestic market as the base for the competitive struggle, lacking the capability of directly competing in the international arena. On the one hand, there is an unprecedented process of merger and acquisition among the firms based in the advanced countries. It is certain that this process will continue. The last obstacle is the vestige of state ownership. This applies to such key players as BT, NTT, DoCoMo, Deutsche Telekom, France Telecom and Telefónica. These elements of state ownership are steadily being wound down. As this happens, so the possibility emerges for giant cross-border mergers among traditional telcos. Deutsche Telekom is already launching an aggressive battle to acquire the USA's Voicestream. It is quite imaginable that any of the major European giants could merge with each other. Further transatlantic mergers and acquisitions are highly likely.

Very rapidly, a group of super-giants is developing, that will soon dwarf even the present giant companies. Moreover, the global giants are fast moving into the developing countries. Already, almost the entire Latin American market is controlled by multinational operators. Only Mexico, in central America, has so far held out against the trend. However, the former incumbent, Telmex, is under incredible pressure from the US government to capitulate and accept the WTO rules to which Mexico is a signatory (*FT*, 16 May 2000, 10 July 2000). Furthermore, the telecoms business in the advanced economies is growing at high speed, with enormous income to be derived from the move into higher value-added services as broadband develops in the near future.

Fast as the Chinese market is growing, it is far smaller than that in which the global giants operate. Although China has a huge number of people within its still highly protected telecoms market, the size of the market is limited by the country's poverty. In 1998, China's average *per capita* income in the cities was the equivalent of just $650 and in the countryside was only $260 (SSB, ZTN,1999: 317). Even the top decile of income earners in the cities, who totalled around 40 million people, had an average *per capita* income the equivalent of just $1300 (SSB, ZTN,1999: 321). Some analysts believe that the rate of growth of China's telecoms market will slow down considerably. Moreover, the revenue per subscriber is low by international standards and falling. For example, the average annual usage fee per subscriber at CTHK fell from $396 in 1995 to $300 in 1999 (CTHK, 2000: 15). For China Unicom, the fall was even more severe, falling from $450 in 1997 to just $240 in 1999 (*FT*, 25 May 2000). In part, this is the successful result of competition. However, it is also related to the country's poverty: 'In a poor country like China, all those people who are financially capable have a mobile phone, so to really grow your subscriber base you have to move down the income ladder' (telecoms industry analyst, quoted in *FT*, 25 May 2000). This means especially, the pager market. China Unicom, for example, derives 63 per cent of its operating income from pagers (China Unicom, 2000: 36). The number of pagers in China grew from 47 million in 1997 to 74 million in 1999 (China Unicom, 2000: 11). Another market is for local mobile phones with no roaming capability, but which are much less expensive than cellular phones. China Unicom's revenue per subscriber for paging services is only $2 per month, compared with $20 for cellular phones (China Unicom, 2000: 11). However, revenue and profits per subscriber are far lower for such devices. Such business cannot form the basis of a competitive challenge to the global telecoms giants.

At some point, China's telecoms firms will have to face the global challenge. Under present policies, China will find it difficult to build domestic players that will be able to face the challenge once that has to be met on the global level playing field. One option is for the leading Chinese players themselves to try to become part of the international merger and acquisition process. However, this route also presents many challenges. China's main telecoms operator, China Telecom, is 100 per cent state-owned, and is likely to remain so for some time. As we have seen, China Mobile, through its subsidiary, CTHK, has grown at high speed, absorbed a great deal of international capital and achieved a market capitalization that compares favourably with some of the world's leading companies in the sector (Table 11-9). However, its revenue stream is far smaller than other firms with similar market capitalizations. It currently has annual revenues of less than $5 billion, Even if it took over the mobile phone operations in the seven other provinces planned for the near future, it is hard to imagine that its revenues could exceed $10 billion in the foreseeable future, far behind those of DoCoMo or VAM, which are directly comparable. Moreover, with 75 per cent state ownership, CTHK is limited in international expansion. Deutsche Telekom, DoCoMo and Singapore's Singtel, have all encountered serious barriers to international acquisitions due to their state ownership, since private telecoms firms do not wish to have any serious element of control in the hands of foreign governments. However, each of these operates in a relatively transparent way, with comprehensive autonomy for the management. China's telecoms firms have the difficulty of a much less transparent and more bureaucratic background than their international, majority state-owned competitors. In addition, China's telecoms firms have the huge obstacle that for many advanced economies, telecoms is still a highly sensitive sector from a national security perspective. It is most unlikely that the governments of high income countries, or even southeast countries, would allow a Chinese majority state-owned telecoms firm to merge with a domestic telecoms company.

Even China's fast-growing Internet sector may also face problems of 'encirclement' due to the relatively small size of the Chinese market. There are enormous prospects for market growth in China. It is thought that there are currently around 16–20 million Internet users in China. Predictions vary wildly. Some experts predict that by the year 2003 there will be around 33 million users, while other have predicted over 100 million for the same year. However, the reality is that today, access to the Internet is still extremely limited. In early 1999, China had just 0.14 Internet hosts per 10 000 people, compared with 470 per 10 000 in the high-income economies and 1131 per 10 000 in the USA (Table 11-6). We have already noted the tiny penetration of PC ownership in China compared with the high income economies. Moreover, as recently as 1996, only 3 per cent of the PCs were on a network. In early 2000, the proportion is still only around 20 per cent. Most PCs in China are used for routine office tasks, like typing, spreadsheets or making graphic presentations. Only a few employees in any given office have access to the Internet from work. Moreover, the low incomes of most Chinese people means that their capability to spend heavily on the diverse offerings available via broadband is relatively limited.

A deep constraint on the development of the Internet market, and the business capabilities of those indigenous firms trying to build Internet businesses, is the limited degree of connection with the global Internet. This results partly from the attempt to restrict access to global ideas that are unpalatable to the leadership. China has attempted to develop a 'Chinese-only' version of the Internet, walled off from the rest of the world. In its attempt to control the content that is transmitted through the Internet, and monitor the activities of dissident movements, such as the Falun Gong, the government has attempted to enforce tight controls over the use of encryption. It has forbidden the use of foreign encryption products, upon which so much of the Internet hardware and software depend.

A second constraint on Internet growth in China is the relatively low level of development of the international connections of Chinese Internet services. Despite rapid growth in capacity in recent months, China's total bandwidth for the five major ISPs connected with the rest of the world is only 355 Megabytes. By comparison, Taiwan, with one-fiftieth of China's mainland population, has a total international data communications bandwidth of 37 gigabytes, or one hundred times that of the mainland. The city of Hong Kong alone has 233 megabytes, while just one major multinational company, Intel, has 256 megabytes of bandwidth for international connectivity. A third problem for the development of the Internet is the high cost of Internet connections, reflecting the attempt by China's leading telecoms companies to use their monopoly position to extract monopoly rents from the connection to the Internet. Unlike in the USA, local calls in China are billed according to connection time rather than flat monthly fees.

Thus, despite the rapid growth of the Internet in China, the base from which domestic Internet companies are trying to build their businesses is much weaker than that which faces Internet companies in the advanced economies. Internet companies based in the advanced economies are starting the 'global race' with access to a vastly greater, more open and less regulated market than their erstwhile competitors in China. In an industry in which speed is crucial in building new global businesses, such a disadvantage is extremely important. The world leaders have already built global brands and a global business system that surrounds China.

In sum, China's aspiring globally competitive Internet companies will face extremely severe competition from the established global giants. These are rapidly changing their shape, and daily becoming more global and more powerful, developing their technical capabilities and their global brand name. In so far as East Asian companies have been able to compete with the US-based Internet giants, notably PCCW, they also will add to the challenge facing the mainland companies. Already, China's domestic companies lag far behind in this battle. There is a high incentive to use remaining monopoly controls to establish passive ownership positions in joint ventures with the global giants, rather than attempt to compete head-on with AOL, Time Warner, Yahoo!, Viacom, News Corp. or, even, PCCW. There is already a tremendous disparity in the basic elements of competitive edge in this sector between China's fledgling companies and the global giants.

Incentive to Establish Joint Ventures. If China applies the rules of the WTO Agreement, the competitive landscape of China's telecoms industry is likely to alter very rapidly indeed. The WTO Agreement provides a framework in which the doors are opened to joint ventures in the telecoms sector on a widespread basis from the moment that China joins. The global giants provide enormous attractions for different players in the Chinese telecoms industry. In the long-term, without an extremely clear-sighted government industrial policy, it is hard to imagine how any domestic telecoms company will compete with the global giants. However, while the market is in the process of liberalization, there are very strong financial incentives for the different players to enter joint ventures. Through access to international capital they can enhance their position in the domestic struggle. The different interest groups that are the ultimate owners of the wide variety of telecoms service providers, actual or potential, have powerful incentives to enter joint ventures. It is not necessary for the multinational telecoms companies to establish monopoly ownership of any individual joint venture in order to rapidly take control of the Chinese market. All that is necessary is application of the WTO Agreement which allows the multinationals at high speed to establish joint ventures across the whole spectrum of the telecoms businesses. Through a succession of minority or 50/50 joint ventures with a variety of different indigenous entities, the multinationals can develop national businesses that are far larger and more powerful than any individual Chinese joint venture partner. This is exactly the process that has happened in sector after sector, 'eating China piece by piece'.

As we have noted, there is currently one dominant fixed line incumbent operator, China Telecom. China Telecom is a massive institution, with 550 000 employees, but a revenue base that is only in the middle rank of world telecoms companies. It has a huge array of businesses in non-core areas. All but 11 of its 31 regional subsidiaries made losses in 1999 (*FT*, 8 September 2000). Already, there has been a massive switch of voice traffic to the mobile networks. In just two years, between 1997 and 1999, mobile phone subscribers increased from 20 per cent of the number of fixed line subscribers to 40 per cent (Table 11-8). In the late 1990s the heavily bureaucratic China Telecom could only promise to install a telephone within three months of receiving the customer's installation fee. In 1997, the average waiting time for telephone installation in Beijing was 36 days (Wang Xiaoqiang, 1998: 17). The incentive to get connected rapidly through alternative means is obvious. The potential challenge will not only come from mobile telephony. There is a serious danger that China Telecom will be by-passed by a wide variety of nimbler businesses that can offer numerous services as well as voice communication through broadband. China Telecom has announced that it intends to downsize employment and shed non-core businesses, reducing its staff by over 200 000. However, it has a long way to go before it can compete on an equal footing with the global giants. In the ferocious struggle with other domestic entities that team up with multinational giants after China's entry to the WTO, China Telecom at the national or local level may find it impossible to avoid 'partnership' with the global players if it is to survive. One expert concluded: 'China Telecom is much in need of assistance if it is to list successfully and achieve its goal of standing shoulder to shoulder with the world's largest telecoms operators within five years' (*FT*, 8 September 2000).

There are just two mobile phone licencees, China Unicom and China Mobile. It is possible that China Telecom will be added to that list. There will be intense pressure from different interest groups to establish more mobile phone licences. Joint ventures do not need to be only established with the central authority of each telecoms entity. Indeed, the typical pattern in other sectors is for the joint ventures to be established locally, albeit often requiring approval from the central bodies. It is logically possible that different subsidiaries within CTHK or the remaining provincial subsidiaries of China Mobile that are still outside CTHK, might establish separate joint ventures with the multinationals. There are innumerable such joint ventures with the state-owned parent company of Chinese firms floated on international markets. It is logically possible also for subsidiary segments of China Telecom and China Unicom to establish joint ventures.

It is highly uncertain what will happen to the licences for 3G mobile phones. There will be great pressure for different indigenous interest groups to form partnerships with multinational telecoms firms to bid for these licences. There are enormous benefits for individual indigenous interests to join with the global giants in bidding for 3G licences, not least their experience in developing 3G networks in other parts of the world.

There are currently seven major licensed Internet backbone providers in China. These are ChinaNet, Golden Bridge network, China Education and Research Network, China Science and Technology Network, China Unicom Network, China Netcom Network and China Mobile. Any of these could in principle team up in a joint venture with the global telecoms giants.

The share of Internet protocol (IP) voice traffic within total voice traffic is predicted to rise to one quarter by the year 2004. China has currently awarded five IP phone licences. These have been issued to China Telecom, China Unicom, Jitong, China Netcom and China Mobile. Any of these could establish joint ventures with the multinational telecoms giants.

China has a vast network of cable TV companies. By the year 2000 there were 1300 cable TV stations in China. In the urban areas almost every household was connected to cable TV. By the year 2000, more households had cable TV than had a telephone (*FT*, 12 August 2000). Most cable companies are independent legal entities, having been developed with local capital. A seminal paper on the Chinese telecoms industry warned: 'When China opens its telecom and cable TV market, it will have grave consequences for the survival and development of the Chinese telecoms industry if the telecoms or cable TV businesses are captured by the multinationals on a large scale. In the advanced economies, the cable network is beginning to form a critical path for the provision of broadband services, with voice telephony, entertainment and data all coming down a single cable. The cable TV industry is closely associated with the mass media and propaganda, and it ought not to be controlled by foreign companies' (Wang Xiaoqiang, 1998: 30).

Already there is, literally, warfare between the local cable companies, wishing to provide telephony services through their cable network, and the telecoms companies, wishing to provide non-telephony services through their fibre optic network, such as video and data services (*FT*, 12 August 2000). Despite a formal government prohibition, preventing cable TV and telephone companies from offering each others' services, in practice it has proved hard to stop the respective sectors using their networks to compete with the other sector. Shanghai has been formally exempted from this rule. This allowed Shanghai Cable, with three million subscribers, to experiment with pioneering broadband services, bundling together the Internet, education programmes, video-on-demand and telephone services. Shanghai Cable, and a separate company that runs the physical networks, are extending their reach beyond the city to nearby provinces, making a potential market of 21 million subscribers (*FT*, 12 August 2000). The cable company's pioneering experiment 'has provided a wake-up call for the local telephone monopoly, Shanghai Telecom (part of China Telecom), which in turn has begun offering video-on-demand services to some of its 6 million subscribers (*FT*, 12 August 2000). In the battle for the broadband market there is a high incentive for local players to link up with the multinational giants. At the moment only around 10 per cent of the national cable network is fully interactive offering two-way communication: 'Both camps will need substantial foreign capital and technology to upgrade their networks to make them fully interactive' (*FT*, 12 August 2000). The same battle is likely to be replicated across the length and breadth of China after China enters the WTO.

In addition, there are strong incentives for powerful entities outside the information technology industry to establish joint ventures with the multinational giants to devise paths into the industry. One has only to consider the ownership structure of China Unicom to realize how wide those interests in this potentially highly lucrative industry are (Table 11-11). Moreover, one can see from a partial list of China Unicom's 'China–China–Foreign' (CCF) how pervasive is the pattern of establishing local partnerships with the multinational giants even in this industry (Table 11-12). Around $1.4 billion is estimated to have been invested by multinationals under the now forbidden 'CCF' approach.

Once any entity establishes a joint venture with a leading multinational in this field, there is an unstoppable cumulative effect upon the incentives of other entities to do likewise. There are extremely powerful reasons for seeking a joint venture partner in the struggle for the domestic market. The global giants bring:

- huge capital resources to bid for telecoms licences, such as 3G mobile phones;
- access to the resources necessary to rapidly expand the network;
- powerful global brands;
- a global network of advertising revenue;
- rich content for multi-media, broadband provision;
- huge global procurement to leverage cost reduction and unique, customer-specific technologies;
- the ability to provide global services to global business customers;

TABLE **11-11 Shareholding Structure of China Unicom, 1999** (%)

Ministry of Information Industry,	13.4	China National Chemicals Import and Export Corp.,	6.0
Ministry of Electric Power,	7.5	China National Technology Import and Export Corp.,	6.0
Ministry of Railways,	7.1	Beijing CATCH Communications,	6.0
CITIC,	6.0	China Foreign Trade Centre Group (Fujian),	6.0
China Everbright,	6.0	Dalian Vastone Enterprise Development Co.,	6.0
China Resources,	6.0	Shanghai Science and Technology Investment Corp	6.0
China Merchant,	6.0	Guangzhou South-China Telecoms. Investment Corp.,	6.0
China Huaneng,	6.0		

SOURCE: CICC (1999: 13)

TABLE 11-12 A Partial List of China Unicom's CCF
Partners, 1999

Unicom's foreign partner	Place of investment
Ameritech	Shanxi
Asia America Telecom	Ningbo
Asia America Telecom	Chengdu, Chongqing
Bell Canada/AIG	Yantai, Jinan
Marubeni	Guangxi
Daewoo	Heilongjiang, Zhejiang
Siemens	Shenyang, Qingdao
France Telecom	Guangzhou
Korea Telecom	Anhui
NTT/Itochu	Hebei
Singapore Technologies	Chengdu, Chongqing
Sprint/Sumitomo	Tianjin
Telecom Italia	Jilin, Tianjin
Singapore Telecom	Suzhou

SOURCE: CICC (1999)

- management skills, especially those acquired through the development of broadband in other parts of the world.

An alliance with a global giant offers the possibility for large revenue streams as a passive partner, essentially deriving 'rentier' income from the business relationship. The main goal for the multinational giants will be in the high value-added markets of relatively affluent urban dwellers and international businesses in major cities: 'The focus is going to be on high value-added multinationals. I don't think people are interested in wiring villages in Hunan' (a telecoms consultant, quoted in *FT*, 30 November 1999).

CONCLUSION

The prevailing view among Chinese commentators is that the IT industry is new and unformed. In this environment, it is argued, China will be able successfully to compete on the 'global level playing field' in a way that it may be unable to do in the established industries of the 'Second Technological Revolution', such as aerospace, complex electrical equipment, pharmaceuticals, or automobiles. However, such a view is naïve. It ignores the fact that processes of concentration that took decades in other industries have been explosively telescoped into a matter of only a few years in this sector. In less than a decade a group of immensely powerful, mainly US-based, corporations have emerged to dominate and re-define the industry.

These industry giants have taken the lead through an explosive process of merger and acquisition across international boundaries, facilitated by the liberalization of international capital markets. They have established their lead through building a global business system. They have established global brands. They are able to invest billions of dollars in R & D in order to establish powerful leadership positions through proprietary technology. They have established themselves at the centre of a large global network of small and medium-sized firms, whose prosperity is dependent on their business relationship with the leading companies, whether as provider of new technologies or sub-contractors in content provision. They have rapidly developed huge market capitalizations, which provide the financial basis for further global expansion. They have rapidly developed their vertical integration, providing control over long stretches of the value chain.

By comparison with these companies, even the largest of China's domestic companies are fledglings. Moreover, they are deeply handicapped in the battle by the low level of income and low level of development of the domestic market. Despite its fast growth rate, it still provides a much weaker base for improving business capability than the global integrated market that confronts the firms based in the advanced economies. Moreover, Chinese indigenous IT firms still have extensive state ownership and bureaucratic intervention. Realizing the disparity in the struggle, domestic firms have strong incentives to use their remaining period of protection to reach deals with the global giants as passive joint venture partners rather than as challengers to the global leaders. If China does, indeed, strictly apply the terms of the WTO Agreement, there may be some examples of successful indigenous firms that emerge and challenge the global giants. However, the more general trend is likely to be comprehensive defeat for indigenous firms in the battle with the global giants on the newly-established 'level playing field'.

This could be perfectly consistent with many benefits for the Chinese economy, but the distribution of the gains would be highly uneven. Moreover, as will be argued later, there is a possibility that high-speed access of the global giants to the Chinese IT industries, especially to telecoms and media, could have a destabilizing impact on Chinese politics and society. This could have much wider implications for the security of property rights and the long-term growth of the Chinese economy.

12

The Challenges Facing China's Financial Services Industry

Wu Qing

The Judge Institute of Management Studies
University of Cambridge

Most J. P. Morgan employees have already accepted the inevitable: that to compete successfully in the global financial services industry, their firm now needs to become part of a more powerful entity. 'J. P. Morgan had to do something' was the common refrain as [J. P. Morgan's] employees streamed through the revolving doors that mark the pink and grey granite entrance to J. P. Morgan's headquarters at 60 Wall Street.
(Comments following take-over of J. P. Morgan by Chase Manhattan)
(FT, 14 September 2000)

In the past the United States has demanded that China dismantle most of its trade barriers and come into compliance with WTO standards as a precondition for membership. Given the weak condition of China's state-owned sector, especially its banking system, however, immediate dismantling of all trade barriers could cause a collapse of significant parts of the economy. China would be forced to absorb all the costs of restructuring in a compressed period of time, which is neither economically desirable nor politically feasible.
(Lardy, 1998)

INTRODUCTION

The winter of 1999 brought two events, which will deeply affect the Chinese financial services industry in the new millennium. One was the China–US WTO

Agreement, which the US government expects will 'dramatically expand' its access (as well as access for the EU and the other main players in the world economy) to 'a market of over a billion people'[1] (Clinton, 2000). The other was the newly enacted Financial Services Modernization Act of 1999 (Gramm–Leach–Bliley Act (GLB)), which will open the door to the creation of a 'financial supermarket'. Simultaneously, the USA abolished the Glass–Steagall Act that had influenced the financial services industry in the US and some other parts of the world for 65 years. The former means that the infant Chinese financial services industry has to face global competition in the context of internationally-determined rules of the game. The latter signals that the world's biggest financial services suppliers, the US financial institutions, are comprehensively deregulated. The dominant position of the financial giants from the advanced economies will be further enhanced. This will significantly alter the structure of the industry as well as the nature of financial services regulation across the world. In the new context of globalization, not only will the competitiveness of China's financial services industry be challenged, but the very safety of the financial system will be threatened.

NEW TRENDS IN FINANCIAL SERVICES

BACKGROUND OF DEREGULATION

Since the breakdown of the Bretton Woods System in the 1970s, financial liberalization has affected most countries. Following the winding up of the brokerage commissions and foreign exchange controls in the USA in the mid-1970s, many countries started gradually to reduce controls over interest rates and exchange rates, and international differences in tax rates were reduced.

Deregulation accelerated in the early 1980s after a surplus of capital was generated by the world oil crises of 1973–5 and 1979–82. In response to intense pressure from the domestic financial services industry, most Western governments decided to deregulate further their national financial markets. In the USA, government-imposed ceilings on interest rates were formally ended in 1983. The first major regulatory breaches of the rules governing the ability of financial institutions to start diversifying into other fields took place with the Garn–St Germain Depository Institutions Act of 1982 and the Supreme Court decision on regional banking in 1985. In the UK, the Big Bang took place in 1986. Fixed commission rates on bond and share transactions were abolished. The old distinction between jobbers and brokers was discarded and the Stock Exchange was opened up to full ownership of member firms by outside institutions. In sum, these changes constituted nothing less than a revolution in terms of the structure, speed and manner of conducting financial activity (Hamilton, 1986). They greatly increased the international mobility of capital and the volatility of international financial markets.

In the 1990s, financial deregulation went even deeper. In Europe and the USA, some of the main restrictions on cross-border and cross-sector financial transactions were removed completely. In the early 1990s, deregulation, such as the

Single Market Programme in the European Union in 1992[2], and the Riegle–Neal Act of 1994 in the USA, made cross-border M & A much easier and cheaper. According to the Bank for International Settlements (BIS), cross-border financial activities, including syndicated credits, securities issuance and M & A advice, increased sharply from 1992 to 1998. In the late 1990s, there began a 'campaign of financial modernization'. It included the Big Bang of 1998 in Japan and the Gramm–Leach–Bliley Act of 1999 in the USA. These far-reaching changes further liberalized the financial industry. They stimulated a new wave of M & A, based not only on cross-border transactions, but increasingly involving cross-sector transactions.

IMPACT ON THE INDUSTRY

The deregulation, together with explosive changes in information technology, are comprehensively transforming the financial services industry towards globalization, innovation, integration, concentration and Americanization.

GLOBALIZATION AND CROSS-BORDER TRANSACTIONS

The globalization of the world economy since the 1980s created a huge demand for world-wide financial services, and great opportunities for financial institutions to expand globally. Simultaneously, deregulation, particularly the erosion of the geographical entry restrictions, made it possible for aggressive financial institutions to become global.

Internal[3] expansion by financial institutions has not stopped. However, in the 1990s merger and acquisition became the major growth path for financial services firms. From 1989 to 1999, there were estimated to be 3844 mergers and acquisitions in the global banking industry, with the acquiring institutions purchasing more than $3 trillion in assets. Merger and acquisition among big banks increased drastically. In 1994 there were 444 banks involved in mergers, with only $99 million in assets (Table 12-1). By 1998, there were 406 banking institutions involved in mergers, with total assets of $1087 billion. Among these deals, many involved cross-border transactions. As a result of M & A among financial firms, the number of banks in most countries fell significantly (Table 12-2). In the late 1990s there was not only a large jump in US domestic M & A, but also a substantial increase in cross-border M & A (Berger *et al.*, 2000). In the mid-1990s, M & A activity among European financial institutions took off.[4]

During this wave of M & A, most of the big financial institutions, such as Citigroup, Bank of America, Chase Manhattan, Deutsche Bank, UBS, HSBC, Merrill Lynch, Morgan Stanley, ING, and AXA, achieved or enhanced their leading position in the global market. Today, about one-third of the world's largest financial institutions operate in three or more continents (*The Banker*, April 2000). Citigroup now has branches, subsidiaries or offices in more than 100 countries, while Merrill Lynch has 900 offices in 43 countries with a leading market position

TABLE 12-1 Global Banking Institution Mergers and
Acquisitions, 1989–99

Year	No. of banks	Bank assets ($ billion)	Bank deposits ($ billion)
1989	142	81.2	64.0
1990	170	36.4	31.0
1991	262	275.1	202.7
1992	319	104.8	90.3
1993	373	127.5	103.1
1994	444	100.0	79.7
1995	358	486.3	347.7
1996	364	188.7	155.4
1997	346	256.9	196.2
1998	406	108.9	656.9
1999*	81	87.1	59.6

SOURCE: Federal Reserve
NOTE: * Of 5 April

on all the key exchanges. AXA employs 140 000 people in 60 countries. HSBC is a striking example of growth from a leading regional position to a leading global position, through relentless cross-border acquisitions in the late 1980s and early 1990s. By the late 1990s, HSBC had become one of the biggest and most profitable banks in the world (Au *et al.*, 2000).

The banks that have led the globalization process argue that cross-border expansion is necessary in order to achieve economies of scale and scope in the global competition. A major motive is to be able to provide a global service to customers who themselves increasingly operate on a global basis, as well as acquiring new customers in other countries through international M & A. A further driving force is the need to distribute the risk internationally. The dramatic developments in IT radically increased the possibility of operating a bank on a global scale.

CONSOLIDATION: CROSS-SECTOR TRANSACTIONS

Traditionally, in most countries the financial services industry was divided into commercial banking, investment/merchant banking and insurance. The main exception was Germany, which operated with a universal banking system.

With the development of information technology and financial innovations (see below), especially securitization, the boundaries between different sectors (that is, commercial banking, investment banking and insurance) have become blurred. Traditional banks face severe challenges from other parts of the industry. Deregulation lowers the barriers to entry. Competition within the industry has greatly intensified. Some traditional commercial banks and insurance companies found themselves disadvantaged in the competition. In order to reduce costs and improve efficiency, many financial sector firms expanded their business not only in terms of size, but also in terms of scope, by moving into other sectors than that in which they had formerly operated. In the 1980s and early 1990s, some big European financial institutions diversified their business through M & A. These included Deutsche Bank's acquisition of the UK Merchant bank, Morgan Grenfell; Crédit Suisse's acquisition of the US investment bank First Boston; UBS's acquisition of the UK merchant bank Warburg; and ING's take over of the UK merchant bank Barings.

In the USA, the most important mergers and acquisitions took place either within the commercial banking sector (such as Bank of America/Nations Bank/ Barnet Bank, Chase Manhattan Bank/Chemical Bank, Bank One/First Chicago NBD) or within investment banking (such as Morgan Stanley/Dean Witter Discover, Salomon Brothers/Smith Barney). This was mainly because of the Glass–Steagall Act of 1933, which separated the banking, securities and insurance business. However, with the extensions of deregulation in the 1990s, the scope of major mergers widened. Some big banks tried to convert themselves into multi-business banks. For example, Citibank had dreamed of being a financial conglomerate since the 1980s (Hamilton, 1986). J. P. Morgan made great efforts to convert itself into an investment bank after 1989, when it became the first American commercial bank that was permitted to become involved in investment banking. After the late 1980s, the US Federal Reserve gradually loosened the limitation on the proportion of revenues from securities. This move stimulated further legislative reform. In 1998, the merger of Citicorp, a leading commercial bank, with Travelers, a big insurer with an investment banking subsidiary, Salomon Smith Barney, directly led to the enactment of the Financial Modernization Act of 1999 (Gramm–Leach–Bliley Act), which abolished the Glass–Steagall Act. This law created a new type of financial firm called a financial holding company (FHC), which is allowed to undertake almost any business in financial services. The Chairman and CEO of Chase Manhattan, Mr Harrison, commented: '[A]s we get into convergence, where traditional companies partner with dot.com companies, we'll be able to do a lot of things that will stretch the definition of banking and commerce' (Leuchter, 2000). Under the new law a FHC could own up to 100 per cent[5] of any of type of company (Financial Services Modernization Act 1999), so theoretically, a FHC could own any business 'from toothpaste to technology'. It is not expected that FHCs in the USA will become multi-industry conglomerates, or quickly convert into a US version of German universal banks.[6] However, it is more likely that highly integrated businesses (retail and wholesale financial services, banking and securities and insurance service) will be adopted by most of the FHCs.

The GLB Act has had a revolutionary impact on the global financial services industry. It meant that the biggest financial industry in the world, that of the USA, with the world's largest financial institutions, was liberalized completely. One of the most important results will be to permit even greater concentration in the global industry, dominated by US financial services firms (see below).

One of the important consequences of deregulation is financial innovation, which is spurred on by intensifying global competition. The financial engineers, a new generation of bankers, are creating a wide range of new financial products. The development of technology, particularly IT, has greatly accelerated the pace of innovation and made the innovations easier to deliver. From the 1980s, transactions in derivatives and securitized financial assets became key products in the financial market: '[T]here will no longer be clear dividing lines between raising money for corporations through commercial paper or through share issues, through long-term or through short-term instruments, depending on regulation and requirement. Instead debt will become interchangeable, an endless stream flowing one currency to another and from one type of paper to another without difficulty' (Hamilton, 1986). Since 1987, when Citibank and J. P. Morgan experienced debt problems in emerging markets, securitization has grown rapidly in the global market (Eng *et al.*, 1998). In addition, the separation between securitized mortgage loans, unit-based insurance contracts, and mutual funds has declined. Customers' demands for diversified financial assets have grown. In order to maintain their competitive advantage, big firms, especially the investment banks, needed to invest huge amounts in R & D. It is now commonplace for Wall Street investment banks to hire a large number of PhDs in Mathematics and Physics.

In the late 1990s, with the high-speed development of IT, e-commerce became a new way of doing business in every sector. Unsurprisingly, the financial services industry, especially the big firms, adopted it quickly and applied it widely to their business. Internet and Intranet information systems enable financial services firms to reduce dramatically their management and operation costs. IT has been a powerful instrument for developing competitive advantage and expanding market share for the successful financial services firms. It is the easiest, most cost-effective and rapid way to become a global operator. Some firms were even 'born global'. For instance, E*Trade created a global brand and established operations in 33 countries in only three years, while Merrill Lynch needed more than thirty years to achieve a similar coverage.

The development of IT along with lowered entry barriers makes it easier for non-financial industries, particularly retailers, to diversify their business and penetrate the financial services market. For example, Marks & Spencer, Tesco and Virgin have expanded into banking and financial services. The use of 'cash-back' from supermarkets has increased sharply. This has pushed the big financial institutions such as J. P. Morgan, Citigroup, and Chase Manhattan, to strengthen their online services. Recently, the top three investment banks, Merrill Lynch, Goldman Sachs and Morgan Stanley Dean Witter, launched an electronic bond trading system called BondBook. HSBC and Merrill Lynch invested $1 billion to set up an online joint venture, which is expected to share their customer network and technology (*FT*, 14 April 2000). Moreover, the innovation is not only in the instruments used, but also in the organization itself. In the last few years, many leading financial firms (such as Goldman Sachs and J. P. Morgan) radically changed their institutional structure to adapt to the changing world.

INTENSIFIED COMPETITION

Deregulation, especially the collapse of the 'wall' separating different financial sectors, removed the barriers preventing banks from entering the securities and insurance industry, as well as those preventing securities and insurance firms from entering other sectors. This means that there will be more players in each of the formerly separated sectors. Therefore, there will be more intense competition across the whole financial services industry. In the USA, only four months after the enactment of the GLB, 117 banks, large and small, applied for and received permission from the Federal Reserve to convert from bank holding companies to FHCs. They included both giant banks like Citigroup, Chase Manhattan, J. P. Morgan, Bank of America and HSBC, as well as small ones like Acadiania BancShares of Lafayette, LA, and Yarville National Bancorp of Hamilton, NJ. Under the umbrella of FHCs there are increasing numbers of financial institutions diversifying their business and supplying a wider range of financial services. It can be expected that there will be more and more financial firms moving from their current category of 'commercial and savings', or 'insurance', or 'securities' to the 'diversified financials' category in the *Fortune* 500 list.[7]

New entrants are not only coming from other branches of the financial services industry, but also from other industries. As we saw above, with the development of IT and the deregulation of financial services, the distribution channels for financial services are changing dramatically, and the barriers to entry are falling. Rival firms from the non-financial sectors, which are diversifying their businesses or converting themselves into firms focused on financial services, are penetrating the financial services market through their existing customers' network, or using their competitive advantage in brand, capital or technology. The most striking example is GE Capital, but other firms, such as GMAC, Tesco Finance and Virgin Money, have also followed this path. In addition, there are entirely new categories of financial services firms, such as the new e-bancasurances and online-financials.

Not only are there more threats from new entrants, but also the competition between existing rivals has intensified. Citigroup's successful business model has stimulated more and more cross-border and cross-sector M & A (see below). This has created intense competition between the giant financial conglomerates.

CONCENTRATION AND AMERICANIZATION

In today's intensive competition in global financial markets the mantra has become 'bigger is better' (Haddock, 2000). World-wide deregulation, especially the repeal of the Glass–Steagall Act, made it possible for the American financial

TABLE 12-2 Bank Restructuring: Number of Institutions and Size Concentration, 1980–97

| | No. of institutions[a] | | | Peak (since 1980) | | | Concentration top 5 (top 10) | | |
	(1980)[b]	(1990)	(1997)	(Number)	(Year)	(% change)[d]	(1980)[c]	(1990)	(1997)
	(Number)	(Number)					(% share in total assets)		
USA[e]	36 103	27 897	22 140	36 103	1980	−38.7	9 (14)	9 (15)	17 (26)
Japan	547	605	575	610	1988	−5.7	25 (40)	30 (49)	31 (51)
Euro area[f]	9 445	8 979	7 040	9 445	1985	−25.5	—	—	—
Austria	1 595	1 210	995	1 595	1980	−37.6	40 (63)	35 (54)	44 (57)
Belgium	176	157	136	176	1980	−22.7	53 (69)	48 (65)	57 (74)
Finland	631	498	341	31	1985	−46.0	63 (68)	65 (69)	77 (80)
France	1 033	786	567	1 033	1984	−45.1	56 (69)	52 (66)	57 (73)
Germany[g]	5 355	4 721	3 577	5 355	1980	−33.2	n.a.	n.a.	17 (28)
Italy	1 071	1 067	909	1 109	1987	−18.0	26 (42)	24 (39)	25 (38)
Netherlands	200	180	169	200	1980	−15.5	69 (81)	73 (84)	79 (88)

Portugal	17	33	39	39	—	1997	n.a.	n.a.	n.a.
Spain[h]	357	327	307	378	−18.8	1982	38 (58)	38 (58)	47 (62)
Norway	346	165	154	346	−55.5	1980	63 (74)	68 (79)	59 (71)
Sweden	598	498	124	598	−79.3	1980	64 (71)	70 (82)	90 (93)
Switzerland	478	499	394	499	−21.0	1990	45 (56)	45 (57)	49 (62)
United Kingdom	796	665	537	796	−32.5	1983	n.a.	49 (66)	47 (68)
Australia	812	481	344	812	−57.6	1980	62 (80)	65 (79)	69 (81)
Canada	1 671	1 307	942	1 671	−43.6	1984	n.a.	55 (78)	78 (93)

SOURCE: British Bankers' Association; Building Societies' Association; national data

NOTES: [a] Deposit-taking institutions, generally including commercial, savings and various types of mutual and co-operative banks

[b] For the euro area and Finland, 1985; for France and Canada, 1984; for the UK, 1983; for Portugal and Spain, 1981

[c] For France, 1986; for Italy, 1983; for Austria, Finland and the Netherlands, 1985; for Switzerland, 1987

[d] From peak to most recent observations where applicable

[e] Data including credit unions (commercial banks and thrifts only, 1997)

[f] Excluding Ireland and Luxembourg

[g] For 1980, Western Germany only

[h] Concentration data for commercial and savings banks only

giants, such as Citigroup and Chase Manhattan, to expand their cross-sector business. It also made it possible for those banks that have struggled for years to convert themselves into different types of firms, to achieve their objective. The consequence is increased industry concentration. Each of the world's top five banks in *The Banker*'s list of the world's top 1000 banks (*The Banker*, July 2000)[8] has been involved in mergers or acquisitions during the past three years. As well as innumerable take-overs of small financial institutions by large ones, most of the top banks have been involved in mergers with other giant banks. Since the late 1980s, the number of banks has fallen dramatically (Table 12-2). However, up until now, the biggest mergers and acquisitions have tended to be between financial institutions within the USA or within a given European country, rather than cross-border and cross-sector transactions.

With the accelerated deregulation and intensified competition in recent years, especially the enactment of the GLB Act, a new wave of M & A has started world-wide. In the first three quarters of the year 2000 alone, there was a wave of giant deals, most of which were cross-border and cross-sector transactions, undertaken by the global giants to enhance their global leadership position:

- In January, Citigroup through its subsidiary, Salomon Smith Barney, took over Schroders, the biggest UK merchant bank, to enhance its investment banking business in Europe.

- In April, following its acquisition of Hambrecht & Quist (a San Francisco-based boutique specialising in technology-related investment banking business) in December 1999, Chase Manhattan acquired Robert Fleming, one of the biggest (and almost the last) British merchant banks,[9] to build up its investment banking and assets management arm.

- In April, HSBC and Merrill Lynch established an online joint venture. It was predicted that they would merge the two companies fully.

- In May, HSBC acquired Commercial Crédit de France (CCF) to further enhance its European presence.

- In July, ING acquired the financial services and international operations units of Aetna, a US insurer; and shortly afterwards took over Charterhouse Securities, the investment banking arm of CCF.

- In July, UBS purchased Paine Webber, the number four US brokerage firm.

- In August, Crédit Suisse acquired the American investment bank DLJ to merge with its investment banking arm CS First Boston;

- In September, Citigroup purchased Associates First Capital Corp., the number one US consumer finance company, in order to boost its international reach and widen its already broad range of consumer products.

- In September, Chase Manhattan and J. P. Morgan, two of the biggest names in commercial and investment banking respectively, agreed to merge, with the goal of becoming one of a handful of firms that would emerge as 'end-game winners' in the financial services market (*FT*, 13 September 2000).

Today, as in many other sectors, a large proportion of the leading firms in financial services are US-based. There is a striking development of global business between leading financial services providers and globalizing large corporations. The top five M & A advisers are all US-based firms (Table 12-3). Four of the top five international equity bookrunners are US-based firms (Table 12-4). Three out of the top five firms in the issuance of international convertibles are US-based firms (Table 12-5). Three out of the top five syndicated credit arrangers

TABLE **12-3 World-Wide Completed M & A Advisers: Top Five Firms (January–June 2000)**

No.	Managing bank/ group	No. of issues	Total ($ billion)	Share (%)
1	Goldman Sachs (USA)	169	901.3	49.5
2	Morgan Stanley Dean Witter (USA)	197	808.2	44.4
3	Merrill Lynch (USA)	124	757.3	41.6
4	Crédit Suisse First Boston (Switzerland)	174	386.1	21.2
5	J. P. Morgan (USA)	107	359.3	19.7

SOURCE: Thomson Financial Securities; *International Finance Review* (Jan.–Jun. 2000)

TABLE **12-4 International Equities Bookrunners: Top Five Firms (January–June 2000)**

No.	Managing bank/group	No. of issues	Volume ($ billion)
1	Goldman Sachs (USA)	104	21.6
2	Morgan Stanley Dean Witter (USA)	49	13.6
3	Deutsche Bank (Germany)	44	10.4
4	Merrill Lynch (USA)	67	8.7
5	Salomon Smith Barney (USA)	70	8.4

SOURCE: Thomson Financial Securities; *International Finance Review* (Jan.–Jun. 2000)

TABLE **12-5 All International Convertibles: Top Five Firms (January-June 2000)**

No.	Managing bank/group	No. of issues	Total ($ billion)	Share (%)
1	Goldman Sachs (USA)	10	3.9	18.73
2	Salomon Smith Barney (USA)	7	2.9	13.97
3	Merrill Lynch (USA)	7	2.6	12.66
4	Deutsche Bank (Germany)	5	2.3	11.00
5	BNP Paribas (France)	3	1.9	9.18

SOURCE: Thomson Financial Securities; *International Finance Review* (Jan.–Jun. 2000)

TABLE 12-6 Syndicated Credit Arrangers: Top Five Firms (January–June 2000)

No.	Managing bank/group	Volume ($ billion)
1	Chase Manhattan (USA)	136.4
2	Bank of America (USA)	128.5
3	Citibank Salomon Smith Barney (USA)	113.8
4	Barclays (UK)	49.0
5	Deutsche Bank (Germany)	44.4

SOURCE: Thomson Financial Securities; *International Finance Review* (Jan.–Jun. 2000)

are US-based firms (Table 12-6). In terms of market share, from North to South America, from Europe to Asia, the ranks of the top firms in equities, bonds, syndicated loans and M & A, are dominated by US firms, such as Citigroup, Bank of America and Chase Manhattan in commercial banking, and Goldman Sachs, Merrill Lynch and Morgan Stanley Dean Witter in investment banking (*International Finance Review*, January–July 2000). Even in Japan, the top bookrunner in equities and the top advisers in M & A are US-based firms such as Citigroup and Merrill Lynch (*The Banker*, and *International Finance Review*, 2000). MSDW estimate that in the global equity business, the top three firms (namely, MSDW itself, Goldman Sachs and Merrill Lynch), which are all US-based, accounted for 36 per cent of the global equity market business in 1999, up from 31 per cent in 1998 (MSDW, 2000: 55). They estimate that these same firms accounted for between 34 per cent and 42 per cent of global M & A deals, compared with an estimated 27–40 per cent in 1998.

In the global *Fortune* 500 for the year 2000, 15 of the world's most profitable (total profits) firms are in the financial services sectors. Of these, nine are US-based firms. Four out of the top five are US-based firms (*Fortune*, 24 July 2000). Four of the top ten most profitable commercial banks are US-based. Out of the top five of securities firms by sales revenue, four are US-based. All of the six 'diversified financials' in the *Fortune* 500 are US-based companies. Within the financial services industry, only the global insurance market is not dominated by US institutions. However, analysts predict that even this will change in the near future: 'Most of the major insurance companies are European. But the big US investment banking houses will inevitably play a leading role in this sector. They have the financial muscle and the market strength' (an analyst from the International Securities Marketing Association quoted in *The Banker*, March 2000). The trend towards concentration is likely to intensify with the deregulation of US financial services. It can be expected that, in the future, a handful of US-based financial conglomerates will dominate the financial services industry and supply a full-range of products as 'one-stop-supermarkets' operating across the world.

There are hardly any developing country firms among the world's leading financial services companies: out of a total of 128 financial services firms in the *Fortune* 500, just six firms are from low and middle income countries (*Fortune*, 24 July 2000).

CHALLENGES FOR CHINA'S BANKS AFTER WTO ENTRY

The current strategy of China's financial reform, especially the policy of segregation of sectors, is focused on risk prevention rather than international competition and nurturing internationally competitive players in China's indigenous financial services industry. There is a serious risk that once China enters the WTO and opens the domestic financial market to foreign institutions, China's leading domestic financial institutions will find the competition extremely severe. Finance and telecoms are two of the cornerstones of China's political-economic stability. Firms in these sectors have been heavily protected from global competition. They will find the challenge of the global level playing field especially severe.

THE GLOBAL LEVEL PLAYING FIELD IN FINANCIAL SERVICES

Under the terms of the China–US Agreement of November 1999 on the terms of China's entry to the WTO, China agreed to liberalize drastically the environment in which its financial institutions would operate. Under the terms of the Agreement the global level playing field will soon arrive at the door of the Chinese financial services industry. The principal measures in the Agreement are the following (The White House, 2000):

- **Banking**. Currently, foreign banks are not allowed to undertake local currency business in China. Only a small number are allowed to engage in local currency business with their foreign clients. China also imposes strict geographical limitations on the establishment of foreign banks. China has agreed to allow full market access for foreign banks within five years. It has agreed to allow foreign banks to undertake local currency business with Chinese enterprises within two years of accession, and to allow local currency business with individuals from five years after accession. All geographic and customer restrictions will be removed within five years.

- **Insurance**. Currently, only four foreign insurance firms have been permitted to operate in China. These have been required to join a joint venture with a government-approved partner and their activities have been restricted to a narrow range of operations. Under the China–US WTO Agreement, China has agreed to award licences on a 'prudential' basis, with no economic needs test or quantitative limits on the number of licences issued. It has agreed progressively to eliminate geographical limitations within three years and permit internal branching consistent with the elimination of these restrictions. It has agreed to allow expansion over five years of the scope of activities for foreign insurers to include group, health, and pension lines of insurance. For non-life insurance, branch and joint-ventures at 51 per cent equity share for foreign firms are permitted on accession, and wholly-owned subsidiaries permitted within two years from date of accession. For life insurance, joint ventures are permitted with the partner of choice at 50 per cent equity share immediately upon accession.

CHALLENGES FOR THE INDUSTRY: INTERNATIONAL BENCHMARKING

The severe nature of the challenge that awaits China's financial institutions necessitates realistic benchmarking against the global giants that have emerged and grown at high speed since the 1980s.

Scale. The first problem is the simple gap in scale between domestic and global financial institutions, in terms of capital, assets and profitability. At the end of 1999, the equity capital and assets of the Industrial and Commercial Bank of China (ICBC), the biggest financial institution in China, were $21.9 billion and $42.8 billion respectively, while those of Citigroup were roughly double in respect to both indicators (Table 12-7). However, the revenue of Citigroup was four times greater than that of ICBC. In terms of profits, the gap is even more dramatic. In 1999, the profits of ICBC were $498 million, compared with $9.9 billion for Citigroup, 20 times those of ICBC. The scale of Bank of America was not far behind that of Citigroup (PBC, 1999; *Fortune*, 2 August 1999).

In the insurance sector, the gaps are even bigger (Table 12-8). In 1998, the equity capital, assets, revenue and profit of People's Insurance Company of China (PICC), the biggest firm in the sector and former monopolist, were $972 million, $5.4 billion, $3.9 billion and $101 million respectively, while those of ING were $34.1 billion, $46.4 billion, $5.6 billion and $2.9 billion respectively (PICC Website and *Fortune*, 2 August 1999). ING is not even one of the biggest insurance companies in the world. Other insurers (also financial conglomerates) such as AXA, and Allianz are even bigger than ING in terms of revenue and profit. The gap between them and PICC is even greater. Moreover, the rest of the insurance companies in China are much smaller than PICC. They are minnows in international terms.

In investment banking, the gap is simply vast (Table 12-9). In 1998, the total equity capital and assets of all 90 securities firms in China added together was about $4.0 billion and $45.0 billion respectively, while those of MSDW alone were $17.0 billion and $376.0 billion (about four times and eight times respectively those of the whole of China). The equity and assets of Guotai J & A (the newly merged and the biggest securities company in China), were only 2 per cent and 0.8 per cent of those of MSDW. The gap in revenue and profits is vast.

The relatively small scale of China's financial services sector means large competitive disadvantage with the global leaders in terms of unit costs, expenditure on R & D, IT systems and brand building, risk management, product development and diversification, and ability to attract the best staff and to provide services for global clients.

TABLE 12–7 Top Four Foreign and Domestic Commercial Banks, 1999

Rank	Institution	Revenues ($ million)	Profits ($ million)	Assets ($ billion)	Equity ($ million)	Employees	Profit per employee ($ 000)
G1	Citigroup (USA)*	82 005	9 867	716.9	49 700	176 900	55.8
G2	Deutsche Bank (Germany)	58 585	2 694	841.8	23 200	93 232	28.9
G3	Bank of America (USA)	51 392	7 882	632.6	44 432	155 906	50.6
G4	Crédit Suisse (Switzerland)	49 361	3 475	451.5	20 378	63 963	54.3
D1	ICBC	20 130	498	427.5	21 918	549 038	0.9
D2	BOC	17 632	534	350.7	17 921	208 792	2.6
D3	ABC	14 127	– 110	244.1	16 273	500 000	–0.2
D4	CCB	13 392	598	265.8	12 907	324 000	1.8

SOURCE: *Fortune* (31 July 2000)

NOTES: * The table puts Citigroup, which was grouped in diversified financials, in this group
   ICBC = Industrial and Commercial Bank of China
   BOC = Bank of China
   ABC = Agricultural Bank of China
   CCB = China Construction Bank

TABLE 12-8 **Top Three Foreign and Domestic Insurance Companies, 1998**

Rank	Institution	Revenues ($ million)	Profits ($ million)	Assets ($ billion)	Equity ($ million)	Employees	Profit per employee ($ 000)
G1	AXA (France)	87 645	2 155	508.6	16 395	92 008	23.4
G2	Nippon Life (Japan)	78 515	3 405	23.3	10 559	71 434	47.7
G3	Allianz (Germany)	74 178	2 382	383.7	28 854	113 584	21.0
D1	PICC*	3 858	101	5.3	972	84 657	1.2
D2	Pacific	2 832	19	2.0	366	9 690	2.0
D3	Ping An	2 409	42	3.4	446	110 595	0.4

SOURCE: *Fortune* (31 July 2000); PBC (1999)

NOTE: *PICC = People's Insurance Company of China

TABLE 12-9 **Top Four Foreign and Domestic Investment Banks, 1998***

Rank	Institution	Revenues ($ million)	Profits ($ million)	Assets ($ billion)	Equity ($ million)	Employees	Profit per employee ($ 000)
G1	Merrill Lynch (USA)	33 962	1 259	299.8	10 132	63 800	19.7
G2	MSDW	31 126	3 281	376.0	17 014	45 712	71.8
G3	Goldman Sachs	22 478	2 428	217.4	6 310	13 033	186.3
G4	J. P. Morgan*	18 110	2 055	260.9	11 439	15 512	132.5
D1	Guotai	325	75	1.5	192	2 800	26.7
D2	China South	288	10	1.9	171	2 500	4.0
D3	Shenyin Wanguo	258	44	2.1	265	3 000	14.7
D4	China Investment Bank	230	12	1.9	138	3 100	3.9

SOURCE: *Fortune* (July 2000); PBC (1999); Merrill Lynch, MSDW and Goldman Sachs Websites

NOTES: The table puts J. P. Morgan, normally regarded as a commercial but actually an investment bank now, in this group

* The data is based in 1999

Scope. The narrow business scope is becoming a more and more significant shortcoming of China's financial services industry. The newly enacted Chinese Securities Law of 1998 adopted the approach of the USA's Glass–Steagall Act, totally separating the securities, banking, insurance and trust businesses. In the year 2000 the separation was in the midst of being implemented. For example, the Big Four commercial banks and PICC, had transferred their securities arms from the bank-owned trust and investment companies to the Ministry of Finance, so as to form a new state-owned securities company.[10] All of the trust and investment companies owned by the Big Four and their branches had also become independent.

As we have seen, this is precisely the opposite direction from the global trends. Most of the EU countries traditionally did not have sectoral restrictions, and in recent years tended to apply the German universal banking model. The USA, as the inventor of the separation policy, and its follower, Japan, have repealed the laws separating business in the different sectors. We have seen that this has enabled the USA to produce giant financial conglomerates such as Citigroup and Chase Manhattan. By 1999, non-interest income (mainly from investment banking related business rather than conventional commercial banking) had become the largest single element in the revenue of the biggest American banks (*The Banker*, March 2000). Some big investment banks (such as Merrill Lynch) have established diversified financial services networks, and big insurance companies, both in Europe and the USA, have become multi-sector financial services suppliers.

While the financial giants are increasingly enjoying economies of scale and scope and becoming stronger, weak domestic Chinese firms are specializing and downsizing, and becoming weaker in terms of global competition. In the fast-moving world of IT, not only is the financial industry constantly innovating, but also the needs of its customers are growing and diversifying. The global financial conglomerates, which are able to provide 'one-stop shopping' for financial services, have big competitive advantages compared with China's narrowly-focused banks, brokers and insurers.

Productivity and Quality. As we have seen, not only is the scale of assets and capital of Chinese financial firms much lower than that of the leading global firms, but, crucially, their profits are much lower. The income and profit per employee in China's financial institutions is negligible compared with the global giants. In the year 2000, for the first time all of the Big Four Chinese state-owned commercial banks appeared in the *Fortune Global* 500, in which firms are ranked by sales revenue. In the commercial banking category, none of the Big Four ranks in the top ten. However, in terms of the number of employees, the Big Four Chinese banks are all in the global top four. Their level of productivity per employee is extremely low. For example, Industrial and Commercial Bank of China (ICBC) and Agricultural Bank of China (ABC), two of the biggest financial institutions in China, each had about 500 000 employees. In 1999 ICBC's profits per employee were about $900, while ABC had losses per employee of

$200.[11] In the sharpest contrast, Citigroup and Bank of America had 177 000 and 156 000 employees respectively, with profits per employee of $55 800 and $50 600 respectively (*Fortune*, 31 July 2000).

There is also a huge gap in the Return on Equity (ROE) and Return on Assets (ROA) between the domestic and global institutions. The fact that Chinese financial institutions have a huge number of employees, with low productivity and high costs, as well as large numbers of retired employees, and without a developed system of social and commercial insurance, intensifies their disadvantage compared with the global leaders. The productivity gap in the securities sector is somewhat less severe than that in the banking and insurance sectors (Tables 12-7, 12-8 and 12-9). However the scale of the leading domestic securities firms is far too small to be able to compete head-on with the global leaders. Moreover, most big securities firms have a problem of 'financial triangular debt' (*jinrong sanjiao zhai*) which needs a huge amount of provision and reduces profits significantly.

The quality of assets of Chinese banks has been a big problem for years.[12] The central or local governments have routinely interfered in the operation of China's banks, especially the Big Four, despite serious attempts to establish operational independence. Sometimes apparently commercial activities have been converted into 'political' or 'social ones', such as lending to the many State-owned enterprises that are on the edge of bankruptcy, recruiting redundant government employees and retired soldiers. The problem of 'quality' relates not only to their assets management and business operation, but also to their corporate governance and ownership.

THE CONSEQUENCES OF COMPETITION: CATCHING-UP OR BEING OVERTAKEN?

What will be the consequences for China's financial services industry of open competition on the global level playing field? Can Chinese financial institutions catch up with the global financial giants within the brief period of protection that has been agreed after China enters the WTO?

The Chinese financial services industry is unlikely to be simply wiped out. The Big Four banks have 139 000 branches nation-wide. They have long term commercial and social relationships with their customers. It will be difficult for multinationals to replace them in the local retail market, as well as in government-supported infrastructure projects. Some of the largest firms, such as Bank of China (BOC) and China International Trust and Investment Corporation (CITIC), which have a relatively long international experience, qualified staff and diversified business activity, may be able to make the transition to globally successful firms. As the most profitable bank of the Big Four, BOC has the largest share of revenue generated internationally, and it has established its investment banking arm in Hong Kong and London, where most of its employees have had experience in the leading investment banks. CITIC is already a financial conglomerate, which comprises both commercial and investment banking with nation-wide branches. It also has a trust and investment company, a leasing company and a wide range of financial products. In addition, some of the new mid-size institutions, such as Shenzhen-based China Merchant Bank, which have a clear strategy and a good record of product innovation, may survive and prosper as successful niche players in local markets. A major problem for indigenous Chinese financial services firms is that their competitive edge is strongest in those segments of domestic markets that tend to have lower quality customers, with less opportunity to earn high margins and generate large profits.

We have seen that there is an enormous gap in business capability between the global leaders and the leading Chinese financial services sector firms. There are certain to be major changes in the competitive landscape in the Chinese industry under the WTO Agreement. China's indigenous financial services sector firms will suffer loss of market share and loss of high quality customers. Currently, the domestic banks dominate the retail and wholesale banking market (for example, domestic banks have 99.4 per cent of deposits) (Xie Ping, 2000). Under the agreement of WTO entry, most of the restrictions on business scope and geographic expansion will be removed. Given the massive competitive advantages that the world's leading financial services firms enjoy in terms of global brand and network, IT systems, quality of service and capability for product innovation, foreign financial firms will significantly increase their market share in China. They have a huge competitive edge in generating business with global firms operating in China. This is likely to be a fast-growing part of their revenue. The global financial giants will be able to attract a large share of the best human resources in China in this sector. The salaries, training opportunities, working environment, and possibilities for career advancement within the global firm, are so much greater than those available within the domestic industry, that it is hard to foresee any other result. The haemorrhage of domestic talent to the global players is likely to further undermine the capability of the domestic firms in this sector to acquire and retain high quality customers, especially global firms. This still further undermines the domestic firms' capability to generate profitable business.

The greatest degree of market share loss is likely to take place in the insurance sector. The country's insurance income amounted to 124.2 billion yuan in 1998, nearly 200-fold greater than the 642 million yuan income generated in 1980 (*International Insurance Monitor*; Fourth Quarter 1999). However, the potential of the market is huge. China's insurance market is very underdeveloped, with an 'insurance density'[13] of only 1.46 per cent compared with 8.5 per cent in the USA, 11.9 per cent in Japan and 11.2 per cent in the UK (Qin Yuexing, 2000). Given the large concessions agreed by the Chinese government in this sector under the WTO Agreement,[14] foreign firms should be able to acquire a great large part of the increase in future revenue in this market.

While the relative competitive strength of China's financial services firms may be especially weak in the insurance sector, the challenges that indigenous firms will confront will be very severe in most parts of the industry. As we have seen, indigenous firms are at a serious competitive disadvantage in many key respects.

It is unrealistic to imagine that China's financial institutions will be able to catch up with the global financial conglomerates. It will be impossible for China's leading financial institutions to compete with them in the world market in the foreseeable future, due to the vastly superior scale, scope, R & D, innovative capabilities, human resources, operational mechanism and ownership structure of the world's leading firms in this sector.

CHALLENGES TO THE EXISTING REGULATORY REGIME: SYSTEM SAFETY AND CONSUMER PROTECTION

China's entry to the WTO will bring serious challenges to the stability of China's financial system. This will place great demands upon the financial system's regulators.

Observing the International Rules of the Game. After China enters the WTO, the first challenge faced by the financial regulators (also by most departments of the Chinese government) will be to meet international standards and trends in regulation, that is, deregulation and further liberalization of the financial services industry. These include lowering or removing barriers to entry, liberalizing interest rates and foreign exchange rate control, changing the methods of supervising, monitoring and regulating, and reducing government intervention to a minimum. Even if changing the rules could be achieved overnight, it would not be easy to change patterns of organizational behaviour which have been evolved over decades. Currently, the People's Bank of China (PBC) has joined the Bank for International Settlements (BIS) and started to use the Basle Accord to regulate banks, such as through capital adequacy and risk assets management. The State Securities Regulation Commission (SCRC) also actively participates in the activities of the International Organization of Securities Commissions (IOSCO). However, constraints still exist. They arise not only from different legislation and administration frameworks, weak jurisdiction, and a lack of qualified regulators, but also from the fundamental economic system, the ownership structure of enterprises and financial institutions, and the process and consequences of government reform.

Maintaining Systemic Safety. When China enters the WTO, a major issue for policy makers is the degree to which indigenous financial institutions can survive in the greatly intensified competitive environment. However, the most immediate and anxious concern for the Chinese government is whether it can avoid the onset of a disastrous financial crisis, such as happened in South East Asia in 1997–8. Huge international capital movements were major direct contributors to the Mexican financial crisis of 1994–5 and to the Asian–Russian Crisis of 1997–8. It is obvious that in a completely liberalized financial market, the contagion effect can easily spread from country to country. Recent research by the US Federal Reserve has confirmed what most observers already knew. It concluded that the main reason why China was able to escape the Asian Financial Crisis was the isolation of its domestic financial sector, the key factor being that the currency was not freely convertible (Federal Reserve Website). In fact, the fundamental economic situation in China is no better (and, in some aspects, even worse) than that in Thailand, Korea, Indonesia and Malaysia in terms of productivity, return on investment, government intervention in the economy and the ratio of non-performing loans (BIS, 2000).

Once the Chinese capital market and the money market is open completely to foreign investors, especially to financial institutions and institutional investors such as Soros' Quanta Fund, speculators can easily manipulate the prices of financial assets, since the Chinese financial market is still relatively small and the investors are very vulnerable. While the effects of large-scale financial speculation upon a large market may be likened to 'an elephant jumping into the ocean', the effects upon a relatively small market are analogous to 'an elephant jumping into a bath'.[15] Furthermore, the consequences of a financial crisis in China would be even more disastrous, because of the huge size of its population and the low *per capita* income, high levels of poverty, high levels of unemployment, lack of social security and absence of deposit insurance and investment compensation schemes.

Monitoring Multinationals' Cross-border Transactions. In the epoch of globalization, cross-border transactions are much more important than ever before. On the one hand, cross-border transactions bring huge amounts of money to finance economic growth and supply liquidity to financial markets. On the other hand, they are a channel for contagion effects and frequently are a primary source of financial instability. To monitor and supervise cross-border transactions requires not only regulatory expertise and technology, but also a sound legislative and enforcement system. Financial regulation is based on law that is based on the sovereignty of each country. The different legal system in China and the lack of relevant commercial and private laws will be an obstacle to regulating cross-border transactions. Moreover, to monitor cross-border transactions in financial markets is more difficult than in commodity markets because of the speed, size and intangible nature of the transactions.

In the era of high-speed developments in IT, especially the rapid development of e-commerce and m-commerce, financial regulation is becoming much more difficult. Online trading is not only intangible and fast, but also has absolutely no border at all. The e-banks, online brokers, or Internet insurers can easily access any country's market. Therefore, as research by the Centre for the Study of Financial Innovation (CSFI) pointed out, regulating internet finance activities is like 'embracing smoke' (Benjamin and Sabalot, 1999). In such circumstances, conventional regulatory instruments, such as geographical restriction and on-site-examination, become weak or even useless. China's Commercial Bank Law (1995), Insurance Law (1995) and Securities Law (1998) all require that financial institutions must conduct business according to their authorized geographical and sectoral scope. The Agreement on China's entry to the WTO also defines the step-by-step widening of the permitted scope within which foreign companies can legally operate. However, in reality, it is difficult to control unauthorized business, which can take place via the Internet, telephone or other modern delivery channels. In other words, financial regulation and telecommunications reform are intimately inter-connected. Together with the explosion of technological progress in the IT sector, they pose a deep challenge for China within the WTO.

Supervising Cross-sector Transactions of Giant Financial Conglomerates. With the recent increase in cross-sector mega-mergers resulting from deregulation, more financial conglomerates have been created, and the trend of consolidation continues. Most financial conglomerates have a presence in China. For instance, Citigroup has established seven branches and offices in the key cities (including Beijing, Shanghai, Shenzhen and Guangzhou) of China, and its investment banking arm Salomon Smith Barney (and former Schroders) have participated in the H-share and B-share securities markets. ING has built branches and offices in China in every sector of its businesses, including insurance, banking and securities. MSDW has established its joint venture, China International Capital Corporation (CICC), which has actively participated both in domestic and regional capital markets. After China enters the WTO, it can be expected that more conglomerates will enter the domestic market, not only through setting up branches but also through acquiring domestic institutions. This is likely to create new regulatory problems.

First, when foreign conglomerates or financial institutions which are focused on a single sector establish their branches or purchase domestic financial institutions, they will inevitably cross sectoral boundaries, and may create regulatory contradictions. For example, when a financial conglomerate acquires an insurance company or a securities firm, or a foreign insurance company buys a commercial bank or vice-versa, the regulator will face a serious dilemma. If the deal were permitted, it would violate the existing Securities Law (1998), which requires that China's banking, securities and insurance firms are separated completely. If the deal were prohibited, it would mean that the door was not truly open for most of the global financial institutions, which have already diversified their home businesses and become FHCs in the USA or their equivalent in other countries.

Secondly, as more financial conglomerates enter the Chinese market, they will use their one-stop-shopping services, global reputation, low cost, sophisticated IT systems, high quality human resources, and high levels of technical expertise to penetrate the Chinese market. With the increase in their market power, they may give Chinese customers inappropriate advice when cross-selling products, or may sell inappropriate packages of products, or focus more on serving bigger corporate customers while ignoring small retail ones. Most of these problems have already been encountered in the USA (Berger *et al.*, 2000). It is even more likely that these sorts of problems are likely to be encountered in the very near future in a poor, developing country such as China. China's financial market is still very small. In an underdeveloped market such as China's, which is dominated by less experienced and undereducated small depositors, investors and policyholders, consumers particularly need to be protected. For instance, the total tradeable stock market capitalization of the Shenzhen and Shanghai stock exchanges was only about $90 billion by the end of 1999 (Chinese Securities Regulation Commission (CSRC) Website), while the assets managed by Deutsche Bank amounted to $842 billion, Citigroup $717 billion, AXA $508 billion, Morgan Stanley $366 billion, Merrill Lynch $328 billion (*Fortune*, 31 July 2000). Speculative short-term funds controlled by institutional investors in 1995 had already reached $20 trillion (World Bank, 2000). Even if just 0.1 per cent of this 'hot money' flowed into the Chinese stock market, it would be enough to manipulate the whole market. Therefore, regulators have a heavy responsibility to protect the consumer in the new global context of financial services markets in which China will operate within the WTO.

Thirdly, as cross-sector transactions bring pooled products and services to the customers, and sophisticated derivatives come to the market, the process supplies new instruments of investment and risk management. However, it also creates high risks to the institutions and to the market. If even one part of a conglomerate failed, it could influence other parts of the firm. More seriously, problems in one sector could be contagious to other sectors through the channel of the financial conglomerate and could cause systemic crisis. Thus the task of prudential regulation will be much harder in the arena of cross-border and cross-sector financial services.

Implementing Regulation. The problem of constructing an appropriate legal structure for China's financial system is a massive task. However, finding a way to implement financial regulation effectively and efficiently is an even bigger task. The first problem of implementation is how to define the appropriate jurisdiction for cross-border transactions in the fast changing IT world. This should involve deep international co-operation, for which the regulators need to have sufficient international experience and knowledge. The second implementation problem is how to define the appropriate jurisdiction for cross-sector transactions. This needs both domestic and international co-ordination among different regulators. Even within the country, co-ordination is still far from simple. For example, multinational conglomerates need to be regulated by the PBC and/or the CSRC and/or the CIRC (Chinese Insurance Regulatory Commission). To implement prudential regulation or consumer protection regulation, it is necessary that they are closely co-ordinated and that overlap is avoided. Co-ordination is necessary not only at the national level, but also at the local level. Under the current regulatory regime, the PBC has nine regional branches, 326 central branches and 1827 county-level branches, while the CSRC has 15 regional branches and 30 province-level offices. The CIRC has no branches and delegates some of its functions to selected branches of the PBC (PBC Website, and CSRC Website). Consequently, co-ordination can be quite complicated, confusing and costly.

CONCLUSION

Financial deregulation, along with the development of technology, has caused great changes through globalization and convergence in the financial services industry. The boundaries of geography and product sectors are disappearing at high speed.

In the era of globalization, China can no longer be isolated from the world. After accession to the WTO, China's infant financial industry, which emerged from the old planned economic system, will encounter far more serious challenges than it has faced previously. When competing with the multinational financial conglomerates, the Chinese financial services industry will face serious disadvantages in scale, scope and productivity. For the financial regulators, the challenges will be especially severe. They have to consider not only the competitiveness of indigenous firms in this industry. They must also consider the safety of the entire financial system and the interests of the mass of uneducated consumers in a completely new environment.

The critical question is how to combine an industrial policy for this sector together with financial regulation to ensure overall system stability. The previous twenty years of financial reform succeeded in building a new system that was very different from that of the planned economy. However, China lacked a clear industrial policy for developing the international competitive capability of firms in the financial services industry. China's leading indigenous firms in this industry do not yet have the necessary capability to compete with the global financial conglomerates on the global level playing field. It is not enough to simply focus on 'regulation' or 'de-regulation'. Although there is no simple solution, China needs to re-examine and rebuild its strategy of financial services reform.

13

The Response

If China wants to join the WTO, and wants to be integrated into the international community, it must play by the rules of the game. China cannot do that without making concessions ... Backed by the achievements of the past two decades' reform and opening, Chinese enterprises will be able to withstand any impact.
(Premier Zhu Rongji, quoted in *Beijing Review*, 42 (19), 10 May 1999)

No WTO accession agreement has ever contained stronger measures to strengthen guarantees of fair trade and to address practices that distort trade and investment.
(Charlene Barshefsky, 2000a)

Our reforms failed and the US is partly to blame for interfering unnecessarily in Russian development. But we should also blame ourselves that their stupid advice was accepted.
(Sergei Karaganov, chairman, Council for Foreign and Defence Policy, quoted in FT, 3 June 2000)

INTRODUCTION

The case studies presented in the main body of this book have analyzed the ways in which in different sectors China's policy makers and managers have attempted to build large firms that can challenge the global giants. In the course of two decades of struggle, China's large enterprises have changed substantially, gradually undertaking evolutionary institutional change in key aspects of their business organization (Nolan and Wang, 1998). During the same period, the world's leading businesses have undergone high-speed revolutionary transformation. As the epoch of the 'global level playing field' moves ever closer, it becomes increasingly necessary for China's reforming large enterprises to benchmark themselves realistically against the global giants. The historic agreement of 15 November 1999 between the USA and China on China's accession to the WTO, makes that task even more urgent.

The nature of China's industrial policy is brought into the sharpest focus raising a sequence of fundamental questions. Are China's large enterprises able to compete with the global giants of the big business revolution? Is it possible to bridge that gap within the WTO? Is it possible for China to have an 'industrial policy' within the rules of the WTO? Does the agreement mark the end of an historic epoch in which large firms were able to catch-up in successful latecomer countries through different forms of government support? Are there more subtle ways than those used in the past to support the rise of indigenous large Chinese firms, which are compatible with WTO membership? Does it matter in the epoch of explosive internationalization of ownership and production whether China has indigenously-based large firms?

The large Chinese firms analyzed in this study have advanced their business capability in numerous ways. However, many deep issues remain to be resolved if these firms are to compete successfully with the world's leading firms in the twenty-first century.

KEY ISSUES IN THE CONSTRUCTION OF LARGE, INTERNATIONALLY COMPETITIVE FIRMS IN CHINA

WHERE IS THE FIRM?

China's reform path from the early 1980s onwards centred on the attempt to expand enterprise autonomy while cautiously and incrementally changing ownership structures. The central drive of policy was to increase the autonomy of the operational unit, the plant or 'enterprise', from the central authorities charged with administrative authority over it. The central drive of China's 'enterprise' reform was to enhance the autonomy of entities that in the world's largest corporations were essentially business units within a multi-plant company.

In the public sector restructuring in Western countries in the 1980s and 1990s, the fundamental unit of enhanced enterprise autonomy and, ultimately of privatization, has been the multi-plant company. This typically constituted the bulk of the state's assets within any given sector. This was the case in the steel sector (for example, Usinor, British Steel), in telecoms (for example, British Telecom, Telecom Italia, Deutsche Telekom, France Telecom, Telefónica), in aerospace (for example, Aérospatiale, Rolls-Royce, Casa and British Aerospace), in the auto sector (for example, Renault) and in oil and petrochemicals (for example, British Petroleum, Elf Aquitaine, ENI, Repsol). Each of these entities contained numerous subordinate operating units. However, the chosen level at which to enhance enterprise autonomy and, ultimately, the vehicle for privatization, was the large-scale, multi-plant entity which would be able directly to challenge existing private sector global giants in terms of their assets, revenues, R & D, and market share. At the time of their privatization, most of the firms were already large companies with the capability to compete on the global level playing field, provided management was given genuine autonomy.

The path chosen to experiment with China's reforms was to take its firms along a very different path for state enterprise restructuring than that followed in the West. It has left a legacy of many related unresolved issues in China' emerging business structure.

China's reform process has thrown up a group of powerful, visionary, industrial entrepreneurs who have led large-scale transformations of the businesses under their control. Among those firms analyzed in these studies, such leaders include Zhou Guanwu at Shougang, Ding Guiming at Daqing, Wu Yixin at Shanghai Petrochemical Corporation, Ye Qing at Shenhua, Zhu Yuli at AVIC, Zhao Xinxian at Sanjiu and Wang Jianming at Yuchai. In other countries, a key aspect of the transformation of failing state-owned enterprises or the successful operation of newly-established state-owned enterprises has been the appointment of powerful chief executive officers. They have been given comprehensive autonomy to manage and undertake capital market operations, including merger and acquisitions at home and abroad, disposal of unwanted businesses, downsizing and changes in remuneration systems. They have frequently undertaken comprehensive restructuring of the enterprises under their management. Such managers include Louis Schweitzer at Renault, Francis Mer at Usinor, Franco Bernabe at ENI, and Ian MacGregor at the British National Coal Board and then at British Steel. Comparable leaders in China's large enterprises have rarely been given consistent long-term support by the Chinese central authorities. Strong leaders at the enterprise level have frequently been dismissed by the central authorities who are fearful of the enterprise leaders' intense struggle to develop autonomous enterprises freed from central control. Often, the dismissal of strong enterprise leaders has been permitted because they have lost powerful patrons in the central government.

During the reform period, many of China's large state-owned enterprises developed a strong sense of corporate ambition. The initial key to their ambition was the contract system of the 1980s which allowed the retention of a large fraction of enterprise profits. This was reinforced by the establishment of 'legal person' rights at the level of the enterprise or operating unit. Subsequently, the 'enterprise' became the main unit through which domestic and international stock market flotations were made. It was also the main entity through which joint ventures were established. Numerous benefits could flow for both employees and the local community from successful growth. The majority of the enterprises examined in this study developed intense ambitions. Over and over again the senior managers spoke of their ambition to make their enterprise number one in China and eventually to become a world leader in their chosen field. In pursuit of this aim a group of large state enterprises responded to the growing impact of market forces in the context of a fast-growing domestic market through the pursuit of organic growth via different paths. They reinvested heavily, improved product quality and product mix, developed their marketing skills, developed their brand, reduced costs of production, invested in R & D, and acquired technology through joint ventures.

Ambitious large state-owned enterprises encountered major difficulties in attempting to expand within their core business. Large-scale projects involving organic growth outside the home territory typically require approval by central authorities, whether in the relevant ministry, its successor department or in the State Council. It was common for key projects that enterprises wished to undertake to be refused permission by superior authorities for a variety of reasons. For example, Shougang's strategy under Zhou Guanwu was based around the intention to build a second major steel plant at Qilu in Shandong province, following a similar expansion path, in this respect, as South Korea's Posco, now the world's largest steel company. After a tortuous bureaucratic wrangle, the Qilu project was eventually turned down by the central government, leaving Shougang's strategy in tatters, rendering many of its acquisitions useless. A second example is Daqing's persistent wish to be allowed to use its vast financial reserves to expand into the former Soviet Union. However, such expansion was over-ruled by Daqing's superior authorities in the central government.

A substantial group of Chinese state-owned enterprises is now floated on international stock markets. However, there are strict limits on the enterprises which are permitted to float and on the extent of the flotations. Many ambitious large enterprises that wished to float were not permitted to do so, with superior authorities that were fearful of the independence that this would provide for the enterprises through this independent source of capital. Daqing, for example, persistently requested permission to float internationally but was not allowed to do so by its superior authorities. Those that did float were typically subject to strict controls on the extent to which they issued shares, with stringent limitations on the degree of dilution of state ownership. Even domestic flotation was under tight bureaucratic control. Bribery of officials to obtain approval for listing has been openly reported. For example, in late 1999 it was publicly reported that top managers at Daqing had been arrested for bribing officials in order to allow the domestic listing, in 1997, of Daqing Lianyi Oil refineries, part of the Daqing Oilfield complex (*FT*, 27 November 1999).

A major path through which ambitious state-owned enterprises wished to expand was through merger and acquisition in their core business within China. A persistent theme is their stated wish to expand through merging 'through the markets' with other strong businesses in the same sector or by taking them over. It is easy to take over loss-making enterprises in the same sector, since this can take a poorly-performing business off the hands of the relevant central or local authorities. However, attempts by strong state-owned enterprises to merge with other strong state-owned enterprises were persistently thwarted by the superior authorities. Daqing tried repeatedly to merge with strong refineries. SPC tried to merge with other strong petrochemical companies and even held talks with Daqing about merger to become a vertically integrated oil and petrochemical firm. Harbin Power Equipment Company tried to merge with a group of powerful northeastern electrical companies. Yuchai tried to merge with other strong engine companies and with strong vehicle makers. Each of these attempts to build a powerful company through large-scale merger within the relevant core business was prevented by the enterprises' superior authorities, or by resistance from other local authorities within whose jurisdiction one of the enterprises lay. Frequently, when asked about the reason for the absence of a merger with a relevant firm within China, the large state-owned enterprise replied that there was no point in even pursuing the matter, since the chance of success was so low. In striking contrast to the massive boom in mergers and acquisitions between 'strong and strong' in the West since the early 1980s, China has not had any examples of merger of a strong state-owned company with another strong company within the same sector.

The inability of large, ambitious state-owned enterprises to be allowed to merge with and acquire other large state enterprises in the same sector has had a powerful effect on the nature of industrial reform in China. The reform process stimulated a significant growth of enterprise ambition and wish for autonomy from the superior authorities, but severely restricted the extent to which that autonomy could be exercised. The powerful group of enterprises analyzed in these studies were each prevented from expanding in a way comparable to that employed by large Western firms in the capitalist big business revolution of the 1990s. This pushed them into other forms of business behaviour, especially large-scale diversification.

In the late 1990s, there were signs that the central policy makers had realized the negative consequences of this path. The dramatic growth of globally powerful firms based around core business, achieved through massive mergers, became a more and more striking object lesson for the Chinese leaders. The attempt to construct two huge vertically integrated companies in the shape of Sinopec and CNPC represented a belated attempt to support the growth of a different type of firm. Instead of allowing increased autonomy to the enterprise, this represented an attempt to construct a unified multi-plant firm that spanned many production units. However, the subordinate enterprises had gained so much autonomy and developed such intense corporate ambitions, that it proved difficult to reintegrate them. Having been through two decades of 'enterprise' reform based around enhanced 'enterprise autonomy', it unsurprisingly proved difficult to re-centralize power within a multi-plant firm embracing a large part of any given sector. Not only were there strong controls on the expansion of ambitious enterprises through mergers with strong domestic firms. There were, additionally, serious barriers to their growth caused by mergers imposed by higher-level bureaucrats on unwilling, ambitious firms. Shougang was forced to take over a group of heavily loss-making 'Third Front' military factories. Shenhua was forced to take over the loss-making 'Five Western District Mines'. The leadership of CNPC and Sinopec were each forced to take over a substantial group of small-scale loss-making refineries, formerly under the Ministry of Chemical Industries, on their restructuring in 1998. SPC came close to being forced into an unwanted merger with a massive local diversified chemicals conglomerate, producing everything from washing powder to rubber tyres.

SPECIAL DIFFICULTIES OF BUILDING SUCCESSFUL LARGE, COMPETITIVE FIRMS
BASED IN A DEVELOPING COUNTRY

The environment in which large Chinese firms are attempting to construct
globally competitive companies is very different from that of the global giant
corporations.

Battle with domestic small and medium-sized enterprises. A large fraction of
the sales revenue of powerful multinational companies consists of high value-
added goods and services sold in high income countries. In a huge, poor, developing country such as China there is still a high degree of market segmentation
by product type and quality. A large fraction of demand is still for low quality,
low price products. Moreover, markets tend to be much less well-integrated, separated to a greater degree than in advanced economies by the isolation of geographical distance, and poorly developed transport and information systems. An
important part of the struggle for sales faced by large indigenous firms is with
domestic small and medium-scale producers. Large indigenous firms typically
have to pay a much higher wage than small local competitors. Also, they must
shoulder the burden of welfare payments. They typically have a commitment to
lifetime employment, unlike the flexible, non-unionized workforce of small
enterprises. Many of the products produced by large enterprises for these markets
are unbranded goods, with little benefit from R & D input.

We have seen many examples of the ferocious nature of the struggle between
aspiring global giants and the myriad small and medium enterprises with which
they must compete in domestic markets. For example, Shougang's main products
are low value-added building steel. In this sector they face a fierce battle with
township and village enterprises producing large quantities of low-quality steel
for China's housing construction industry. Shenhua is engaged in ferocious competition with surrounding township and village mining enterprises. The small
coal mining enterprises have virtually zero opportunity cost of labour and bear
little of the costs of pollution. They are strongly supported by local governments
for which they provide crucial local employment and income tax. They grew at
high speed during the reform period to seriously challenge the dominance of the
large state coal mines. Sanjiu faces a constant battle with the thousands of small
and medium traditional Chinese pharmaceutical companies. The township and
village enterprises typically have low start-up costs in this sector, require little
R & D and produce goods for which there are typically no patents. Major oil and
petrochemical companies such as CNPC and Sinopec, face intense competition
from small-scale enterprises in the refining and retail market. Such enterprises
have low entry costs, can often evade legal control over their safety requirements
and sell inferior, polluting products at a relatively low price in a market which
typically is in a state of shortage.

In so far as China's aspiring large global firms are forced into diversified production, they almost always produce with low economies of scale, little focused
R & D, little brand development and limited marketing capability. Each of the

firms studied faces intense competition in its myriad 'diversified undertakings' with a sea of small and medium enterprises. For example, on the one hand, Xian Aircraft Corporation is vying with leading Japanese corporations as a global sub-contractor for advanced aerospace components. On the other hand, it is battling with hundreds of Chinese township and village enterprises in the market for aluminium beams for building construction.

Downsizing and restructuring is more difficult than in an advanced economy. The restructuring of the leading state-owned firms in the advanced economies took place in economies with sophisticated welfare systems and relatively large savings within employees' families. Prior to restructuring, the number of employees was well below that of present-day China's large state enterprises. In China over 100 000 employees at a single production location is not uncommon. Indeed, the number of employees at a Chinese firm can frequently total many hundreds of thousands of people, or as much as a million or more in some cases, such as CNPC and Sinopec. We have seen that using the levels of employment per unit of output found in leading global corporations would produce downsizing that far exceeded that in the West in the 1990s. For example, using the manning levels of the global giants, the entire aerospace division of AVIC might employ less than 10 000 people. Much more than in the West, employees in China's large enterprises constituted a privileged elite amidst a sea of underdevelopment and poverty. Downsizing substantially is an even more complex political task than in the advanced economies of Western Europe or in Japan, due to the dramatic change in both status and income that might confront a large body of the workforce, especially older and less well-trained employees.

Weak supplier network compared with the multinational giants. The quality of the supplier network around large Chinese firms is radically different from that which surrounds a global giant based in the advanced economies. For example, globally competitive companies manufacturing large complex machinery are rapidly moving towards a closely integrated network of global suppliers. In sharp contrast, the manufacturers of complex machinery analyzed in these studies each operates with a network of predominantly local suppliers. For example, Harbin Power Equipment Company has a large network of suppliers in the northeast of China, mostly themselves producing on a small scale, with limited R & D capability. The same is true for Yuchai and many of the branches of AVIC. This means that China is able to produce relatively cheap final products, such as Xifei's Y-7 turbo-prop passenger plane, Yuchai's medium-duty truck engines, and Harbin's electric power plants. However, their products' operating costs are often much above comparable global leaders' products, and their performance in terms of key criteria such as energy efficiency, pollution, reliability and functional capability, are often far below those of the products of global leaders. Global corporations increasingly purchase huge volumes of inputs through central global procurement. This gives them enormous cost advantages over Chinese large-scale competitors which buy from small-scale local suppliers or in much smaller quantities from global suppliers. The sophisticated procurement system of the global giants dealing predominantly with other global companies as suppliers enables more timely delivery of inputs, with consequent cost-savings. Boeing or Airbus are able to achieve more timely delivery of a piece of a tailplane sub-contracted from China to Seattle or Toulouse than Xian Aircraft Corporation is able to achieve for a sub-contracted component of the Y-7 from a domestic Chinese supplier within AVIC.

Spatial distribution of industrial assets. Many of China's large enterprises are located in areas far from China's major markets. They were established because of the need to be self-sufficient during the long period of isolation from the world economy, especially after the split with the USSR in 1960. Many of China's natural resources were developed in order to ensure the country was self-sufficient in time of war rather than to achieve maximum economic efficiency. A significant fraction of China's industrial assets was established in remote areas designed to enable China to survive a nuclear war. By the late 1970s around two-thirds of China's industrial fixed assets were located away from the coastal areas (Nolan, 1995). A large fraction of China's aerospace, power equipment, coal mining, automobile, oil and petrochemical industries, is located far inland. This imposes a large transport cost burden upon China's aspiring global giants.

THE DRIVE TO DIVERSIFY

A central feature of the capitalist big business revolution of the 1990s has been the remorseless drive to focus on core business. China's emerging large firms have demonstrated a very different tendency. In common with many other East Asian businesses China's large firms have demonstrated a powerful tendency to diversify into non-core businesses or 'diversified undertakings' (*duozhong jingying*). In the extreme case of AVIC, China's 'national champion' aircraft maker, as much as two-thirds of total revenue comes from non-core business in a vast array of different industries. Even China's largest, most focused and internationally competitive steel company, Baogang, is in the process of diversifying into a wide range of businesses. China's largest single entity in the oil and petrochemicals sector, Daqing oilfield, has a huge array of over 1000 companies engaged in 'diversified undertakings'. The world's leading pharmaceutical corporations have steadily shed non-core business to focus exclusively on their core products. Alongside its rise to become one of China's top two pharmaceutical companies, Sanjiu acquired a bewildering array of businesses, from large-scale construction and autos to beer, wine and hotels.

There are many reasons for this pronounced trend. These include the following:

- **Need to provide for huge workforces**. Innumerable studies have investigated the extent of 'over-manning' in China's industrial enterprises. Multinational corporations in China with only a small fraction of the number of employees have typically produced similar or greater output than comparable Chinese companies. However, Chinese state-owned enterprises are not only units of production. They are also social entities, providing cradle-to-grave care for the employees and their families. A central aspect of the reform process has been to separate the 'productive' from the 'unproductive' aspects of enterprise activity. However, state-run welfare systems are still rudimentary and the enterprise still feels a strong commitment to assisting the 'downsized' workers to find employment. A central motivation for diversification has been an attempt to provide employment for the large surplus workforces that exist in most of the large state enterprises.

- **Imperfect markets with high transaction costs**. China is still a poor country with a poorly developed transport system, including massive railway bottlenecks. Information flows are moving faster and faster, but still are far behind the sophisticated IT of most global leader firms. Furthermore, a large part of the output of China's large-scale enterprises is competing in the relatively low value-added part of the relevant markets, in which the need for, and the proportion of, high quality, cutting-edge technology components is relatively small. These pressures increase the incentive to produce in a far more vertically integrated fashion than international competitor firms. The tendency to 'large and complete' stems in part from a rational response to the environment faced by the large Chinese firm. Whereas the leading international giant company integrates the 'external firm' across the value chain, a large Chinese firm is often trying to reduce transaction costs by internalizing a high share of the components and equipment necessary for the final product. This was a major reason for the diversification at Shougang into iron ore, steel machinery, and construction. The same tendency exists to a greater or lesser degree in each of the other companies analyzed in the case studies. However, on the global level playing field, such firms are at a severe disadvantage compared with their competitor firms, which purchase a large fraction of their inputs of goods and services from specialist firms that in turn benefit from economies of scale and scope.

- **Barriers to mergers and acquisition within the core business**. We have seen repeatedly that the efforts by increasingly autonomous firms to merge with other strong firms have been blocked. Merger of a majority state-owned firm requires the agreement of the superior authority. The central ministry or holding company has frequently opposed such mergers as the resulting powerful entities might undermine their authority: 'If two strong companies, X and Y, merge and expand their autonomy, who are we?' Merger of one large firm with another also typically requires the agreement of the local authorities within whose jurisdiction the enterprises are situated. Just as European governments have resisted the merger of national champions with other countries' national champions, so too do China's local authorities often resist such mergers. Each local authority fears that 'their' enterprise will be the one to suffer the bulk of redundancies or will be allocated the less attractive parts of any business expansion.

Even highly rational mergers which could bring large savings in costs, and which are not opposed by higher level authorities, can be resisted for mainly personal reasons. In Western companies, many large mergers do not take place because the chief executive of the weaker company fears s/he will lose their job or be demoted after the merger. However, shareholders get some chance to express their opinion by selling shares in the company. Moreover, there is always the possibility of a hostile take-over. In China, neither of these paths is possible. We have seen examples in these studies of apparently rational merger successfully resisted by an unwilling chief executive officer. For example, the attempt to form a large northeast China power equipment company, involving merger of Harbin Power Equipment Company with several other strong companies in related sectors, appeared to founder mainly due to the strong opposition of the chief executive officer of the most important potential company that might have joined such an entity. We have seen also that the attempt to merge Yuchai Diesel Engine Company with Erqi Motor Corporation, and, separately, to form a single large diesel engine company, merging with other entities in the sector, foundered for reasons that were at least partially personality related.

- **Constraints on organic growth**. Not only is growth through merger and acquisition limited mainly to take-overs of relatively weaker and small-scale businesses. In addition, as we have noted above, large-scale organic growth away from the main production site often faces substantial constraints. Major investments in new capacity can frequently be opposed successfully. Such opposition can be due to fears by central ministries or holding companies that the expansion will threaten their control by allowing autonomous growth of the technically subordinate entity. It can also be due to protectionism by the local authority within which the planned new venture is to be situated. A major new production facility might prove unwished-for competition for the 'local firm' in the same sector.

- **Weakness in competing on world markets**. Despite many major improvements in management and technology and substantial increases in scale, most of China's large firms are unable to directly compete on the global level playing field outside China. To be able to directly compete in global markets with firms making complex and high technology products, such as Nippon Steel, Usinor or British Steel in high quality steel, Siemens, GE or ABB–Alstom in power equipment, Boeing, Airbus, BAe and Lockheed Martin in aircraft, Cummins Diesel in diesel engines, Pfizer or Merck in pharmaceuticals, or with Exxon/Mobil, Shell and BP Amoco in oil, gasoline and petrochemicals, would require a massive leap in capability. It is questionable how rational it is for a large Chinese company to undertake large-scale investment in new technology which would still leave the firm far short of the technical capability of the global leader. In a comparable Western firm, the management would probably decide to exit the business rather than invest in a vain attempt to catch-up with the market leader. In the often-repeated phrase: 'if you're not number one, two or three in the world, you should leave the business'. In export markets, China's aspiring global giant corporation must content themselves mainly with selling lower-end sophisticated products (for example, power stations, steel mills, fighter planes) mainly to other developing countries. China's aspiring indigenous global giant firms have mainly to confine themselves to the domestic market. They must leave export markets mainly to indigenous large firms producing relatively simple products at the lower end of the Second Industrial Revolution, such as white goods, bicycles and motorbikes and to small-scale firms, including massive domestic sub-contracting for multi-national giant companies.

Faced with such limitations on international core business expansion, China's aspiring global champions have to confine themselves mainly to domestic markets. Here, their growth is limited also. They are constrained by the absence of a developed capital market which would allow them to merge with and/or acquire other large domestic firms, linking 'strong with strong' in the way that is happening at high speed within the advanced economies.

Faced with these constraints on expansion of their core business in domestic and international markets, there is a strong incentive for China's large enterprises to use their investment resources to develop diversified operations alongside organic growth. The contrast with the global big business revolution could hardly be stronger. The rapid collapse of international barriers on capital flows, the virtual disappearance of the concept of a national strategic industry, and the massive opening up through privatization of huge areas of business activity to the free flow of capital, have combined to produce an epoch of unprecedented freedom of inter-national, trans-national and transcontinental merger, facilitating the dynamic advance of core businesses. China still remains deeply limited in the freedom to merge, acquire and dispose of large businesses freely. The result has been a vicious circle of a tendency to diversify.

Complex forms of property rights have developed under China's reforms. The core company can be the full owner of diversified undertakings. It may have a majority stake, a minority holding, a joint venture or even act simply as a bank to business activities being set up by employees. Typically a large enterprise will have a wide range of business investments of all different types, with little knowledge of the business it has invested in. The drive to diversify also allows a cascade of investments from the mother company through a succession of layers of 'children', 'grandchildren' and 'great-grandchildren'. Such property rights arrangements can bring large problems of evaluating the quality of investments and monitoring the investments once undertaken. These problems were dramatically revealed when international accountants undertook extensive investigations of bankrupt red chip companies in Hong Kong with large mainland interests. They revealed a catalogue of poor project evaluation and monitoring, and multi-million dollar theft.

One consequence of the trend to diversify is the illusion of scale. Within an apparently huge business, employing a vast number of people and sometimes with large revenues, there was in fact a small core business and a sea of

small-scale businesses, often far below the economically efficient scale necessary for survival and prosperity on the global level playing field. After two
decades of reform, apparently huge firms often contain a myriad of businesses
without any significant R & D capability, without a marketing capability or a
meaningful brand. In their core business, they often are relatively small scale.

CONCLUSION

China began liberalizing the post-Mao economy in the late 1970s. The early versions of the contract system in industry were introduced in 1979, of which that at
Shougang was the most important and symbolic. Therefore, one can say that
China's industrial policy has been in operation for two decades. A consistently
stated goal has been to construct globally powerful companies that can compete
on the global level playing field.

During a similar period in Japan's development, from the 1950s to the 1970s,
Japan's industrial planners supported the growth of a series of globally powerful
companies. After two decades of industrial policy in Japan, the country possessed a whole corps of globally competitive companies. By the late 1980s, it
had twenty of the largest one hundred corporations in the *Fortune* 500 list,
including Toyota, Hitachi, Matsushita, Nissan, Toshiba, Honda, Sony, NEC,
Fujitsu, Mitsubishi Electric, Mitsubishi Motors, Nippon Steel, Mitsubishi Heavy
Industries, Mazda, Nippon Oil, Idemitsu Kosan, Canon, NKK, Bridgestone, and
Sumitomo Metal. These companies developed through extensive support from
state industrial policy, including tariff and non-tariff barriers, restrictions on
foreign direct investment, preferential purchase policy by state-owned utilities,
government defence procurement contracts, government-subsidized R & D,
government-sponsored rationalizations of different industries, and intentional
government support through a 'flexible' competition policy for the growth of
oligopolistic competition.

China's GDP has grown at an officially reported rate of 10.2 per cent per
annum from 1980 to 1990, and 11.1 per cent from 1990 to 1998. (See Table 13-1
for China's growth rate relative to other countries and regions.) Industrial value-
added grew at an officially reported rate of 11.1 per cent in the 1980s and
15.4 per cent from 1980 to 1998 (World Bank, 1999: 250–1). By 1998, China
was the world's seventh largest economy in terms of gross domestic product valued at the official rate of exchange and the second largest valued in purchasing
power parity dollars (World Bank, 1999: 230–1). After twenty years of industrial
policy in China, employing many similar measures to those used by Japan, and
with a similar explicit policy goal, major changes have taken place in China's
large, state-owned enterprises. The leading enterprises have grown rapidly in
terms of value of sales. They have absorbed a great deal of modern technology,
learned how to compete in the market-place, substantially upgraded the technical level of their employees, learned wide-ranging new managerial skills, gained
substantial understanding of international financial markets, and become sought-
after partners for multinational companies.

TABLE **13-1 Regional Differences in Economic Growth, 1980–98**

Country/ Group of Countries	Population		Growth of GDP (% p.a.)		Growth of Industrial value-added (% p.a.)	
	Total (million) 1998	Growth Rate, 1990–98 (% p.a.)	1980–90	1990–8	1980–90	1990–8
Low-/middle-income*	3641	1.8	3.5	3.3	3.7	4.2
Sub-Saharan Africa	628	3.0	1.8	2.2	0.9	1.2
East Asia/ Pacific	1817	1.5	8.0	8.1	9.5	11.5
South Asia	1305	2.1	5.7	5.7	6.8	6.5
Europe/ Central Asia	473	0.2	—	−4.3	—	−5.5
Middle East/ North Africa	285	2.6	2.0	3.0	0.6	2.2
Latin Am/ Caribbean	502	1.9	1.6	3.7	1.2	3.7
India	980	2.0	5.8	6.1	7.0	6.7
China	1239	1.2	10.2	11.1	11.0	15.4
High-income	885	0.7	3.1	2.1	—	1.5

SOURCE: World Bank (1999: Selected World Development Indicators)

NOTE: * Including India and China

Despite important progress, none of China's leading enterprises has become a globally competitive giant corporation, with a global market, a global brand, and a global procurement system. Mainland China has just five companies in the *Fortune* 500 (*Fortune*, 2 August 1999). China does not have one company in the world's top 300 companies by R & D expenditure (DTI, 1999). Mainland China does not have a single company in the *FT* 500 companies ranked by market capitalization (*FT*, 28 January 1999). Nor does it have any representatives in MSDW's list of the world's top 250 'competitive-edge' companies (MSDW, 1999).

The case studies examined in the China Big Business Programme (CBBP) show that the competitive capability of China's large firms after two decades of reform is still very weak in relation to the global giants. This is extremely marked in the high-technology sectors, such as aerospace, complex equipment such as power plants, pharmaceuticals, and in 'mid-technology' sectors such as integrated oil and petrochemicals and auto components. However, even in sectors with apparently less advanced technology, such as steel and coal, there is a significant gap with leading global companies in the high value-added segments of the market.

In these senses, China's industrial policy of the past two decades must be judged a failure. The reasons for the failure of China's industrial policy are partially internal and partially external.

Internal Problems. On the internal front, China's industrial policy encountered a number of peculiar problems which substantially differentiate the Chinese environment from that which faced Japan and Korea during their comparable period of catch-up at the firm level:

- First, China's industrial policy suffered from a lack of consistency in identification of the 'firm'. A great deal of China's economic reform process focused on increasing the autonomy of large 'enterprises', ultimately granting them rights as legal persons. This path of reform viewed the large plant as the core of enterprise reform. Based on the foundations of the contract system, the reform period witnessed an evolving struggle by former state-owned enterprises to increase their autonomy from the central authorities in Beijing. They did this through independently using their retained profits to modernize and grow, struggling to become joint venture partners of the major multinationals and acquire modern technology, struggling to list on international markets and raise capital for modernization and taking over or investing in second and third tier enterprises. This path of reform led to a situation in which it was almost impossible for strong state-owned enterprises to merge with other strong enterprises. Whereas in the world outside China, 'strong' were merging with 'strong' at high speed, in China, the strong enterprises remained substantially independent of each other. When the state turned its attention towards attempting to merge large strong enterprises into large multi-plant companies, it proved extremely difficult to rebuild central control over the large subordinate companies.

- Second, China's attempts to construct large modern firms took place within the confines of a still extremely poor economy. China's income level and level of urbanization was far below that of Japan in the 1950s or 1960s, or Korea in the 1970s and 1980s, during the comparable periods of their industrial policy. A large fraction of domestic demand is still for relatively simple, low value-added products. In this market, China's aspiring large firms had to confront a sea of domestic small and medium-sized competitors, competing on price, often protected by local government policy and by a poorly developed transport system. In the relatively small market for high-value-added products, China's aspiring large firms increasingly had to confront severe competition from imports and local production by multinationals. China's aspiring global giants were basically unable to compete in global markets, and remained confined to producing for the domestic market, caught in a vicious circle of limited scale in high value-added production, further restricting their capability to invest and grow in these areas of the market.

- Third, China's huge size and strong traditions of relatively autonomous local government created a strong basis of regional support for emerging large firms. This is advantageous for firm growth in some senses. However, in an epoch of explosive globalization, it is not feasible for a single country, even one of China's size, to support several major players in each sector. In Europe, the governments of France, Italy and Germany have been extremely reluctant to allow the process of cross-border merger to grow rapidly. However, it has been hard for them to resist this process where the government does not have an ownership share. A major fear has been the possibility that a given country may be the main loser in downsizing and rationalization. This issue is even more acute in China, given the massive over-manning. Consequently, local governments have strongly resisted the merger of large local firms with large firms based elsewhere in the country.

- Fourth, China's reforms began from an existing body of large-scale state-owned enterprises, with large numbers of employees. As in the former USSR, the core of China's industry was a small number of large-scale plants. Under the Maoist system, and possibly influenced also by a distinctive East Asian cultural approach, China's large firms were constructed as a 'large family', with cradle-to-grave social support, and a deep sense of social commitment to employees and their families. Only after two decades of reform were China's large enterprises seriously attempting to downsize their workforce. The retention of such a large number of employees on the payroll not only affected costs. It also drastically affected the possibility of creating a modern, competitive system of labour organization. A combination of government policy and the huge numbers of employees placed severe constraints on the growth of real wages. Moreover, the surrounding sea of poverty has meant that it is politically extremely difficult to implement such remuneration measures as stock options. Instead, the most successful large enterprises have allocated a large fraction of their disposable income to expanding welfare facilities which are provided reasonably equally for all employees, rather than reinforcing material incentive-based remuneration. A large number of highly qualified personnel have left large state enterprises to work in better-rewarded jobs. The exit of highly qualified personnel was influenced also by the uncertainty of the future path for large enterprises. The central government's industrial policy was widely perceived to be inconsistent and lacking a clear direction.

- Fifth, the constraints on mergers and acquisitions among large firms combined with the commitment to the 'large family', as well as the high transaction costs consequent upon the undeveloped nature of the infrastructure, created a powerful incentive for diversification into unrelated businesses in order to provide channels for growth, profits, and employment. This approach was legitimated by the central government's support for the idea of a 'business group' with a core firm at its centre. In an even more extreme way than in Korea or Japan, the typical large Chinese firm constructed a wide network of diversified second and third tier businesses in which it invested. Only a small fraction of these were able to benefit from economies of scale.

- Sixth, the bureaucratic apparatus with which China was attempting to implement industrial policy was very different from that in Japan or South Korea. They relied on relatively small professional civil services. These were powerfully imbued with a commitment to achieve economic advance in the face of massive military defeat in the one case and serious international threat in the other. China's bureaucracy was vastly greater absolutely and larger even in relative terms. It lacked the intense commitment to national development of its neighbours in northeast Asia. Despite great advances in its technical capabilities and important successes in aspects of industrial policy, it was unable truly to separate itself from the operations of the leading enterprises. Even after twenty years of reform, the Party remained deeply imbued with corruption, which seriously inhibited its efforts to implement a consistent, effective industrial policy.

- Seventh, in sharp contrast with Japan and South Korea, China's policy-makers remained committed throughout to maintaining the commanding heights of large-scale industry in state ownership. Large state enterprises were allowed gradually to expand the absorption of capital from non-state sources, including Sino–foreign joint ventures, and flotation on domestic and international stock markets. However, even after two decades of enterprise reform, the government remained committed to substantial public ownership of large enterprises, providing a continued channel for bureaucratic intervention in large firms' management, despite persistent attempts to 'separate ownership from management'. This was strikingly different to Japan and South Korea during their catch-up. It also ran counter to the trend in the advanced economies in which a string of global leading firms evolved out of privatized state enterprises. These included Usinor, Arbed, Corus (formerly British Steel), Posco and China Steel (Taiwan) in the steel sector, Elf Aquitaine, ENI, Repsol/YPF and BP Amoco in oil and petrochemicals, Rolls-Royce, British Aerospace and Aerospatiale-Matra in aerospace, VW and Renault in autos, and British Telecom, Deutsche Telekom, France Telecom, and Telecom Italia in telecoms.

By the year 2000, not one of the world's top 300 firms by R & D spending, and only a tiny handful of the world's top 500 companies by value of sales, was in the public sector. Whereas Japan and South Korea had a relatively simple non-ideological goal of building globally competitive giant corporations, China's industrial policy remained suffused with ideology intertwined with the objective of building global giant corporations. The ideological objective provided a justification for central bureaucratic intervention to limit the expansion of ambitious and increasingly autonomous large enterprises such as Shougang, SPC and Daqing, and for the persistence of bureaucratic interference in the management of technically autonomous large enterprises.

External Problems. At least as important as the special difficulties that confronted China on the internal front in implementing a successful industrial policy, is the fact that China's attempt to build large globally competitive firms coincided with the most revolutionary epoch in world business history, possibly even including the Industrial Revolution. The period during which Japan and South Korea were putting into place their industrial policy to build global giant corporations was a much less dynamic one, albeit that the international economy grew strongly. China's efforts to support the growth of competitive global corporations has taken place at a time of unprecedented change in the international business system and in technical progress. This had a number of aspects:

- First, the period since the late 1980s has witnessed for the first time the opening up of a truly global market-place in goods, services, capital and skilled labour. The only market which still remains bound firmly by nationality is the vast sea of unskilled labour. The integration of the global market-place has been facilitated by the dramatic transformation in information technology. It has been facilitated also by the comprehensive change in the impact of the international institutions. It is no longer practically feasible to benefit fully from trade with, and investment from, the developed countries without agreeing to extensive economic liberalization of international economic relations.

- Secondly, this period has witnessed by far the world's most explosive period of mergers and acquisitions. This process seems to be far from over, and already massively exceeds in real terms and in terms of its significance, previous merger booms. The advanced economies' business structures have been revolutionized, comprehensively transforming the previous structure of national champions and conglomerates. In almost every sector, from soft drinks and beer, to telecoms and aeroplanes, a small number of focused global producers dominates the world market. Not only have the core businesses experienced this explosive process of concentration, the deepening interaction between core companies and supplier companies has created an explosive 'cascade' effect that is rapidly leading to concentration and focus among the first tier suppliers and spilling over even into second and third tier suppliers.

- Thirdly, the epoch has seen a revolutionary growth in the real business capabilities of the leading firms in each sector. The leading firms are able to benefit from large expenditures on focused R & D. The resulting technical progress has been comprehensively dominated by the global giant corporations. In 1998, the world's top 300 corporations spent around $250 billion on R & D, providing an explosive propulsion to the world's stock of applicable knowledge: 'MNCs are the world's chief repositories of economically useful knowledge and skills. All the screaming in the world will not change this' (Martin Wolf, *FT*, 17 November 1999). The leading firms are able to benefit from massive expenditure on marketing and brand-building, of which advertising is just one component. They are able to benefit also from massive cost savings consequent upon global procurement systems and large benefits from deep, constant interaction with supplier companies, facilitated by the revolution in information technology.

A veritable *'external firm'* of global dimensions is being created in sector after sector. Increasingly, leading firms in all sectors are being distinguished by their capability to undertake *systems integration* stretching across the value chain. The most dramatic recent illustration of this process is the announcement by Ford, GM and Daimler–Chrysler that they are to establish a joint internet procurement network (*FT*, 27 March 2000). A large fraction of the world's auto components procurement will therefore flow through this unified system. The world's total auto components procurement amounts to almost $1800 billion. The central co-ordination of a large fraction of the world's auto components makers through a single system represents a highly significant step in the growth of the 'external firm' that stretches across the entire value chain.

The Dilemma for Industrial Policy in China. If China had not opened itself to the international economy through trade and foreign investment after the 1970s, the progress in its large enterprises would not have been anything like as great as has been achieved. However, the pace of change in global big business has massively outpaced that of China's large enterprises. As the global level playing field is further and further established within China after it enters the WTO, few Chinese enterprises are in a position to compete with the world's leading companies in each sector. No other latecomer countries have had to confront such an external environment in which, for the first time, in sector after sector, a small number of truly global corporations accounts for a large fraction of total world sales. China is joining the global level playing field at the point at which the degree of unevenness of business capability has never been greater.

The differential rate of change in business structures and technological capability between China and the outside world presented a massive challenge to China's industrial policy makers. Would a further ten years using the same measures as in the past two decades be able to ensure that China's large firms caught up with the global leaders? Is it possible that after a further 10 years China's large firms might be even further behind than they are today? In the face of such ferocious competition, is there any set of industrial policies that could enable China to establish a large group of globally competitive firms?

It is extremely difficult for many people in China to confront such possibilities. However, the blunt reality is that it may no longer be possible for industrial policy to build powerful competitive large firms based in even the largest and most powerful of the developing countries. If this were, indeed, to be the case, then it would require immensely subtle international relations to accommodate this new reality. It would require a radical re-drawing of the ambitions of large developing countries, especially, but not only, China. It would require separating the goal of catch-up at the firm level from the goal of catch-up by means of advancing national output, structural change, wage employment and the standard of living.

Even for advanced European countries, it is very difficult to accept that former 'national champions' may be unable to compete on the global level playing field as individual players. Whereas individual European countries may have to accept the demise of their national champions, the continent as a whole is breeding a group of regional champions and transatlantic champions. For China, a huge civilization with a proud economic and political history, it is very difficult to accept that it may be unable to emulate Britain, the USA, Japan and Korea in building national champions through industrial policy. However, for there to be an alternative, there has to be a coherent and realistic strategy. It is a great challenge for Chinese policy makers to identify what such a strategy could be in the face of the incredible pace of global change in the nature and business capability of large firms. It is better to 'seek truth from facts' than to live with illusions. It can be argued that there is no point in trying to fight a battle that cannot be won. It may be the case that the heroic age of building national champions through state-supported industrial policy is over. If this is, indeed, the case, the idea will not have been defeated by the triumph of small-scale perfectly competitive firms. Rather, it will have been defeated by the full flowering of global oligopolistic capitalism.

STRENGTHENING CHINA'S INDUSTRIAL POLICY?

Faced with the dramatic widening of the gap between the business capability of China's leading firms compared with the global giant companies, China faced a hugely important turning point in the late 1990s. Reflecting on the failures of industrial policy over the previous decade and a half, China's policy makers could have chosen to learn from the past failures and attempt to strengthen and improve their industrial policy. This would have been consistent with China's approach towards experimentation in its reform programme, with the incremental transition towards a market economy and with gradual, controlled integration with world economy.

China's strategic options for restructuring its large state enterprises had been narrowed by the late 1990s. Although the room for manoeuvre had been greatly reduced, there still were choices that planners could have made that might have enabled a group of large, globally competitive Chinese firms to emerge. China's aspiring global corporations faced a far more difficult international business environment than that which confronted Japan and the Four Little Tigers during a comparable stage in their catch-up efforts. However, China has the potential advantages of a huge, unified, ancient culture. It contains over one-fifth of the total world population. This is a mighty political force capable of being mobilized in support of such an endeavour. In addition, it has a domestic market that already is one of the world's largest and most dynamic, and that is potentially the largest of any country. These factors provided great potential 'leverage', if China's policy-makers were willing and able to use them in pursuit of a reinvigorated industrial policy.

STATE-ORCHESTRATED MERGERS

One option was to merge the domestic 'giant' companies into just one or two giant firms within each sector.

Japan pursued this route in the 1930s by state-led mergers of several leading steel firms to produce Japan Steel, which had a virtual monopoly over the domestic steel market prior to 1939. The state also encouraged the growth of just two giant auto firms in the 1930s, Toyota and Nissan, which accounted for 85 per cent of total production by the late 1930s. The Korean government allowed Posco to develop in a massively protected domestic market without any significant competition for a long period.

In early 2000 the Brazilian state allowed the formation of the giant domestic beverage company, Ambev, produced by a merger of the two leading domestic brewers, Brahma and Antarctica: 'The prospect of creating a Brazilian beverages multinational helped win regulatory approval for the merger, despite the fact that the new group will have about 65 per cent of the beer market. In a country with few internationally-known national champions, the national champion argument drowned out potential threats to competition in the domestic market' (*FT*, 10 April 2000).

In the 1960s Britain merged many different steel, aerospace and automobile firms to form, respectively, British Steel, British Aerospace and British Leyland. In the former two cases these were to form the basis for highly successful private enterprises. It is almost certain that they would not have become successful without the initial merger imposed by the British government. Other Western European countries followed similar industrial policies (for example, France's Usinor Steel Company was formed in this fashion).

This approach was a logical option for the Chinese government to pursue. Many of Europe's leading private or quasi-private companies of the 1990s emerged from similar structures. As we have seen, until the late-1990s in China there was not one merger of a large domestic firm with another. In 1998/99 there appeared signs of a new government approach to mergers and acquisitions. The bureaucratically-directed restructuring of CNPC and Sinopec, and the merger of

China Telecom (Hong Kong) with Jiangsu, Fujian and Henan Mobile Phone Companies provided examples of this policy. These were heavily criticized as being 'directed by the state' rather than occurring 'through the market'. As in other countries that pursued this strategy, this path opens up the possibility of domestic monopoly and requires skilful regulation to prevent low levels of efficiency. Due to the relatively small size of the domestic market, such mergers can still result in entities that are relatively small by world standards, given the massive growth in size of the world's leading system integrators. Such mergers do not directly address the problem of poor corporate governance. Nor do they solve the problem of backward technology. However, they provided a more realistic foundation for competition with the global giants than did the previously fragmented industrial structure.

INCREASED AUTONOMY FOR POWERFUL EMERGING CORPORATIONS

In Europe in the 1980s and 1990s, a succession of former state-owned 'national champions' were transformed into autonomous, competitive transnational corporations. These included ENI, Repsol, BP, and Elf Aquitaine in oil and petrochemicals, Usinor and British Steel in the steel industry, Volkswagen and Renault in the auto industry, and Aerospatiale, Rolls-Royce and BAe in the aerospace industry. The typical pattern was for the appointment of a strong, market-oriented chief executive officer who was subject to strict performance criteria. The CEO was authorized to change business practices radically, gradually privatize ownership rights, and develop an international capability, especially through mergers and acquisitions.

We have seen in the course of this study that in China in the 1990s, there emerged numerous powerful enterprises, with ambitious and effective chief executive officers. These included Shougang under Zhou Guanwu, AVIC under Zhu Yuli, Shanghai Petrochemical Corporation under Wu Yixin, Daqing under Ding Guiming, Shenhua under Ye Qing, Yuchai under Wang Jianming, and Sanjiu under Zhao Xinxian. Each of these leaders had a clear understanding of the nature of global competition. Each of them was ambitious to turn their firm into a true global competitive business. However, the enterprises' superior authorities were nervous at the loss of power that might result from these enterprises taking an increasingly independent path. The degree to which these enterprises were allowed to reduce the state's ownership share was tightly controlled. Not all of them were permitted to raise funds from the stock market and none was permitted to reduce the state's share below 50 per cent. Each of them had severe bureaucratic barriers placed in the path of their domestic expansion, and more than one had severe bureaucratic constraints on their international expansion. They each faced serious bureaucratic constraints on large-scale domestic mergers and acquisitions.

If the central government was willing to provide strong support for emerging autonomous enterprises, then the respective corporations would be much better able to raise funds from domestic and international stock markets. Instead of the disappointments of China's international flotations, China's leading corporations might be able to enjoy strong stock market performance, which facilitates further international expansion. It would also demonstrate the benefits of improved corporate governance to aspiring large corporations. The Argentinean oil and petrochemical company YPF and the Brazilian aerospace company Embraer both demonstrate that possibilities do exist for selected firms based in developing countries to absorb international capital and begin to grow in international markets.

GOVERNMENT PROCUREMENT CONTRACTS

To this day, state procurement contracts remain an important and highly controversial instrument of industrial policy in advanced capitalist economies. State procurement contracts were an important mechanism of state support for the emerging national champions in aerospace, telecoms equipment and power equipment. China's use of this instrument was relatively limited, and weakened significantly as the influence of market forces grew stronger over the course of the reforms. In the aerospace sector, the central authorities were able to do almost nothing to support the growth of a domestic aircraft industry by ordering domestic airlines to purchase short-haul jet aircraft from the McDonnell Douglas/Boeing or AE-100 ventures. In the power equipment sector, the state's ability or desire to influence the purchases made by power stations declined substantially over the course of the reforms. Increased use of this instrument still remained a logical policy choice for China's leaders at the end of the 1990s.

USING GLOBAL COMPETITION

We have seen that China was a major location for multinational investment by large global corporations. These were mainly in joint ventures. However, the very intensity of global competition between giant corporations threw up possibilities for a different strategy that might have been pursued by Chinese industrial planners. In the 1990s intense global oligopolistic competition in each sector produced firms based in the advanced economies that were technically strong, and which had a strong modern management system, but which fell behind in the global oligopoly race. They lacked the global scale necessary to compete. Such companies included:

- Westinghouse and Mitsubishi Electric in the power equipment sector;
- Fokker and Bombardier in the aerospace sector;
- Sumitomo, Pirelli and Continental in the tyre sector;
- Volvo, Nissan, Mitsubishi, Daewoo and even Fiat in the auto sector;

- Scania, Volvo, MAN and Paccar in the truck sector;
- Detroit Diesel in the diesel engine sector;
- Bethlehem Steel, YKK and Cockerill Sambrell in the steel sector;
- Astra, Rhône-Poulenc and Hoechst in the pharmaceuticals sector;
- Repsol, Arco and ENI in the oil and petrochemical sector;
- Alcatel and Marconi in the IT hardware sector.

In addition, there were a few thrusting new players from other developing countries which lacked the scale to grow into global giants on their own. Such firms included:

- Embraer (Brazil) in the aerospace industry;
- Hong Kong Telecom and Singapore Telecoms in the telecoms sector;
- YPF (Argentina), Reliance (India) and Petrobras (Brazil) in the oil and petrochemical sector.

If the Chinese government had been sufficiently purposive about industrial planning, in the way that Japan or South Korea had been, then it is logically possible for a full-scale merger to have been negotiated between selected large Chinese companies and the respective global partner. Without such a merger, the foreign partner anyway faced the prospect of extinction through bankruptcy or merger with another capitalist giant company. The terms of the merger with the Chinese company could have been constructed in such a way to provide better earning prospects for the foreign shareholders through access to the huge and fast-growing Chinese market. It would have provided the vista of secure long-term rentier income for the foreign shareholders.

The weak multinational would have been offered a minority share in the new entity, but would be ceded full management control. The Chinese partner's equity share would come from a combination of bank loans, stock market flotation and asset contribution. It would have been given privileged access to the Chinese market for a specified period of time, and various supportive policies. For example, in aerospace, a certain proportion of Chinese airliners would be allocated to the new firm established between the Chinese and the multinational. After which point protection would be steadily reduced, and it would have to sink or swim in open competition. The foreign management would be ceded full management authority to run the business in order to make a profit for the Chinese and foreign shareholders.

Thus in the aerospace industry, Xifei might have partnered Fokker, and Chengfei have partnered Embraer. In the auto industry, Yiqi might have partnered Daewoo, and Erqi have partnered Mitsubishi. In the auto components industry Yuchai might have partnered Detroit Diesel. In the pharmaceutical industry, Sanjiu might have partnered Astra and Huabei have partnered Rhône–Poulenc.

In the steel industry, Shougang might have partnered Cockerill Sambrell, Angang partnered YKK, and Wugang partnered Bethlehem Steel. In the oil and petrochemical sector, Daqing might have partnered ENI, SPC partnered YPF and Yanshan partnered Arco. In the telecoms industry, Guangdong Telecom might have partnered Hong Kong Telecom. In the IT hardware industry, Huawei might have partnered Alcatel or Marconi. Numerous such options still existed at the end of the 1990s.

The key purpose of such international mergers would be 'to liberate the large state enterprises from bureaucratic control, using the management methods of large global corporations' (Wang Xiaoqiang, personal communication).

SUPPORTING NON-SOE NATIONAL CHAMPIONS

A small group of relatively strong domestic non-SOE firms emerged in the late 1990s. Leading examples of such firms included Haier and Meidi in consumer electronics, Legend in personal computers, Huawei in IT hardware, Baiyunshan in pharmaceuticals, and Jianlibao in soft drinks. These firms were typically led by charismatic CEOs, such as Liu Chuanzhi at Legend and Zhang Ruiming at Haier. They emerged typically in relatively low technology sectors and were able to establish a degree of domestic brand recognition, and in some cases began to penetrate the lower value-added segments of international markets. They employed modern methods of business management. They raised funds from the stock market. They used stock options to stimulate employee enthusiasm. They established genuinely autonomous businesses free from detailed interference from the state. They competed ferociously with the multinational corporations.

These companies often received favourable treatment in the international press. They were sometimes written about by international business schools. For example, the Harvard Business School produced a much-read case study on Haier. They were lauded by the populist neo-classical economists within China as examples of the achievements that Chinese firms could make if left to compete on their own on the global level playing field, unaided by state intervention. They were held up as examples of the new shoots that could burst into life once the old world of the state-owned enterprises was destroyed.

However, a closer look at these firms reveals that they typically benefited from a protected domestic market, and from state support through soft loans, state procurement, and protected marketing channels. Despite their enormous achievements, without exception these firms were far behind the global leaders in terms of revenue, R & D expenditure, marketing expenditure and global market share. They were all anticipating serious competitive challenges after China's accession to the WTO. Without continued state support, they were most unlikely to be able to build on their considerable entrepreneurial achievements, and mount a serious challenge to the global giants in the respective sectors. Nurturing such already demonstrated 'green shoots' through industrial policy measures was an obvious path to pursue. Such measures included continued protection, continued soft loans, state support for their R & D, and state support for them in their efforts to expand through merger and acquisition.

The mythology surrounding these companies attributes their relative success to their 'success in market-place competition' not to government support (China Reform Group, 1999). The blunt reality is that, in most cases, relative success required both high entrepreneurial achievements as well as state support. Private discussion with the strategic officers of some of the leading non-state firms reveals great concern about the challenges that await them if China applies fully the WTO Agreement. The leaders of these firms are only too aware of the difficulty they will face in genuinely open competition with such firms as Cisco and Lucent, Coca-Cola and PepsiCo, Whirlpool and Electrolux, IBM and Dell.

STATE SUPPORT FOR TECHNOLOGICAL UPGRADING

The most successful examples of high-speed technical upgrading in developing countries have taken place through powerful direct and indirect state support. Taiwan provides a vivid example of this form of partnership in a developing country. To this day, almost two-fifths of US technical progress takes place through direct state support for R & D, funded by US tax-payers. In 1994, this totalled no less than \$62 billion (see Table 1-1), around the same size as the entire national product of Malaysia. One can only wonder at the impact on China's technical progress of such a vast infusion of state support for R & D.

In the early days of the reforms, China's central planners enacted a highly successful programme of technical transfer, including a large-scale programme in the power equipment industry. At that point it appeared as if the central planners might mimic the role of MITI in Japan. In fact, as the size of the Chinese market in aerospace, power equipment, autos, pharmaceuticals, high quality steel, oil and petrochemicals, and telecoms equipment grew ever larger, so the degree of state intervention to ensure technical transfer as a condition of access to the Chinese market became weaker. Instead of a centrally co-ordinated activity, linking procurement, market access and ownership, in a rational, explicit and transparent fashion, the technology transfer requirements from multinational companies became increasingly decentralized and unco-ordinated. There is no reason in principle why state-co-ordinated technical transfers should not be revived and greatly strengthened, 'trading market for technology' on a large scale.

CONCLUSION

A key aspect of following such a path was the necessity to create a credible threat of international competition that was sufficient to stimulate change, but not to create competition that was so severe as to prevent any realistic chance of competing with the global giants. Joining the WTO on terms that paid due recognition to the reality of China's developing country and impoverished status was one such possibility. A long transition period to accepting the full impact of WTO rules would have been one part of such a Programme. Following such a path of substantially reorganized industrial policy alongside the credible threat of incremental reduction in protection for Chinese large firms would have constituted a coherent path for industrial policy to follow. It would not have involved rejection of the importance of market competition. It would have involved further experimentation and learning from previous policy mistakes. It would have been realistic about the magnitude of the task facing China.

CHINA JOINS THE WTO: ABANDONING INDUSTRIAL POLICY?

There took place intense policy debates in China on these issues in the late 1990s. A hugely important shift in strategic direction took place. In November 1999 China decided to join the WTO on terms that involved comprehensive, high-speed, formal dismantling of China's long-pursued industrial policy. This was not only a decision of great importance for China, but also for the whole developing world, and, indeed, for the development of global capitalism. It is hard not to interpret the decision as a recognition that the gap between China's leading firms and those of the advanced economies had widened beyond the point of realistic catch-up. Through this decision China was bowing before the extraordinary force of global oligopolistic capitalism.

In November 1999, China and the USA signed the historic agreement under which China would be permitted to join the WTO. Under the terms of the Agreement (White House, 2000). China agreed to dismantle almost the entire range of mechanisms that has formed the core of industrial policy in the past 200 years as a succession of countries has supported the growth of domestic large corporations. China has accepted that there will be enormous changes in its dealings with the global market-place. It will become harder and harder within the WTO for China to limit access to its domestic market. China's agreement with the US on the terms under which China joins the WTO is of great historic significance. The agreement is 250 pages long, with a detailed account of the steps that China agrees to take in order to implement the WTO rules. This is not just an 'agreement on paper'. The minute details will be taken very seriously by the USA and Europe. The US–China WTO agreement in itself constitutes a massive programme of economic system reform. The US–China Agreement was followed after months of negotiations, by an agreement between the EU and China, signed on 20 May 2000. In certain areas this obtained important concessions from the Chinese side beyond even those agreed between China and the US, the most striking being in the retail sector.

The US–China Agreement is the most detailed agreement yet signed by any country on its entry to the WTO. No fewer than 900 Chinese laws will need to be changed and/or adapted for China to enter the WTO. The US is providing 'extensive legal and technical assistance' with a view to 'helping China in making its laws comply with WTO obligations in an effort to ensure that Beijing lives up to its obligations' (*FT*, 28 April 2000). China has been granted only a five year adjustment period before it must implement in full the rules of the WTO. Many important changes will have effect from the day that China joins the organization. Most of the significant changes will have been completed within only three years of China's entry. Moreover, there will be strong incentives for multinational businesses to push their participation in the Chinese economy beyond that which is permitted legally in anticipation of a future more liberal regime which will retrospectively sanction the quasi-illegal advances they have made. This has already been widely observed in the shape of the large-scale illegal entry of foreign capital into the Chinese telecoms industry through the 'China-China-foreign' formula.

For almost two decades the Chinese government experimentally charted its own internally-directed reform programme. With the entry to the WTO under such detailed, internationally-set conditions, China has voluntarily given up its autonomy in charting the complex path of economic reform. A recent careful evaluation of the impact of China's joining the WTO concluded: 'There should be no illusions that there will be a smooth ride over the next decade' (Cooper, 2000).

GENERAL MEASURES

The following are some of the key general measures to which China has agreed:

- **Tariffs**. China will reduce the average level of industrial tariffs from 24.6 per cent to an average of 9.4 per cent by 2005, with a wide range of detailed commitments to lower tariffs on other products. China will make substantial tariff cuts immediately upon accession, with further cuts phased in, two-thirds of which will be completed within three years and almost all of which will have been completed within five years. On US priority items, industrial tariffs will fall to 7.1 per cent, 'a figure comparable to those of most other major US trading partners' (Barshefsky, 2000a: 7).

- **Non-tariff barriers and conditions on foreign investment**. WTO rules prohibit quotas and other quantitative restrictions. Frequently, the Chinese government requires a variety of conditions to be fulfilled in order for foreign investment or imports to be approved. It has agreed that immediately upon entry to the WTO it will observe the WTO's rules on Trade-Related Investment Measures (TRIMS). China has agreed that the government (at central, provincial and local levels) will not condition import licences, quotas, tariff-rate quotas, or any other means of approval of importation, of the right to import or invest upon any kind of agreement as to whether a Chinese company is able to supply the given product, or on any kind of performance criterion. It has agreed that it will not enforce existing contracts that impose these requirements. Specifically, the Chinese government has agreed to the following:

  – **Quotas**. Quotas currently apply to a wide range of products. Most quotas will be eliminated immediately upon China's accession to the WTO.

Most of the remainder will be eliminated by 2003, and they will be entirely phased out by 2005.

– **Local content**. China has agreed to eliminate local content requirements for foreign investment and imports immediately upon entry to the WTO.

– **Technology transfer**. China has agreed to eliminate technology transfer requirements and offsets as a condition for investment or importation immediately upon entry. These include requirements to conduct R & D within China. The terms and conditions of the contract are to be agreed only between the respective business entities, without any government involvement. China has agreed to increase the guarantees of protection for any intellectual property that is transferred, and to eliminate requirements mandating that the Chinese partner in a joint venture gains ownership of trade secrets after a certain number of years.

– **Trade performance requirements**. China has agreed to eliminate export performance and trade balancing requirements as conditions for foreign investment immediately upon entry to the WTO.

- **Intellectual property rights**. China has agreed to implement the TRIPs agreement of the WTO immediately upon accession to the WTO.

- **Rights to import and establish distribution networks**. China has agreed to eliminate over a three year period the current tight restrictions on the right of foreign firms to import and operate independent distribution networks for either imported or domestically-produced goods. China's distribution commitment is comprehensive. It covers commission agents' services, wholesaling, retailing, franchising, sales away from a fixed location, as well as related activities, such as inventory management, repair and maintenance services. These rights are critical restrictions on the competitive capability of foreign firms operating in China: 'As in the case of trading rights, the rights to distribute our products is critical to our ability to export success-fully to China' (Barshefsky, 2000a: 6).

- **Support for state-owned and state-invested enterprises**. China has agreed to apply WTO rules to state-owned enterprises and to extend these rules to state-invested enterprises, that is, companies in which the state has an equity interest. Under these commitments, China's state-owned and state-invested enterprises are required to buy and sell based on commercial con-sideration, such as quality and price. China has agreed to provide foreign firms with the opportunity to sell products to state-owned and state-invested enterprises. China has agreed that purchases and sales of goods by state-owned enterprises, for commercial re-sale or for use in the production of goods for commercial sale, must not be considered for government procure-ment and are to subject to WTO rules. China has agreed that the US can determine whether government benefits to a given sector, such as equity injections or soft loans, have been provided using market-based criteria rather than Chinese government benchmarks (White House, 2000).

Some key aspects of the Agreement in relation to sectors analyzed in this study are as follows (The White House, 2000):

- **Autos**. China's tariffs on autos currently stand at 80–100 per cent, depending on the category of vehicle. China has agreed that by the year 2003 they will have fallen to 38–43 per cent, and will continue to fall to 25 per cent by the year 2006. Tariffs on auto parts will fall from an average of 23 per cent to 10 per cent. Quotas will be phased out by 2005, with an initial level of $6 billion (above the actual level of imports in 1999), growing by 15 per cent per annum until their final elimination. China has agreed that former tight restrictions on distribution of autos and parts within China will be eliminated three years after accession to the WTO. Foreign firms will be allowed to engage in a full range of auto-related services within three years of joining the WTO. Upon accession non-bank financial institutions will be allowed to provide finance for buying autos without any market access or national treatment limitation. China has agreed to end equity injections or soft loans to the auto sector using anything other than market-based criteria. China has agreed to end all local content rules after it enters the WTO, and not to enforce existing agreements in this regard. It has agreed that it will not condition imports or investment approvals in the auto sector upon technology transfer or on conducting R & D in China.

- **Oil and petrochemicals**. Tariffs on chemical imports will fall from 15 per cent to 7 per cent by 2005. Quotas will be virtually eliminated immediately upon accession. China has agreed that within three years of its accession any entity will be allowed to import chemicals (except chemical fertilizers) into any part of China. Foreign firms will be allowed to engage freely in the full range of distribution services. Importation or foreign investment approval in the chemicals sector will no longer be conditional on export performance, local content or similar requirements. For crude oil and petroleum products, China will allow foreigners to provide wholesale services within five years from the date of admission. For processed petroleum products, retail services will be permitted within three years from the date of accession. Crude oil will not be excepted from China's retail commitment, so it will be treated as any other product. If they are strictly applied, these conditions will involve a major challenge to the privileged position in the domestic market currently enjoyed by CNPC, Sinopec and CNOOC.

- **Civil Aircraft**. Currently, the right to import civil aircraft is restricted to a small number of entities with government approval. China has agreed that within three years, any entity can import civil aircraft into any part of China. Within three years also, foreign firms will be allowed to engage in the full range of distribution services for civil aircraft in any part of China. The Chinese government has agreed to eliminate equity injection or soft loans to the aircraft industry. It has agreed to end local content requirements, domestic R & D requirements and technology transfer requirements for the import of civil aircraft or for investment approvals in the civil aircraft industry. Importation of aircraft or investment in the sector will no longer be conditional on offset arrangements.

- **Pharmaceuticals**. China has agreed to reduce the average tariff on pharmaceuticals from 10 per cent to 4 per cent, commencing with the date of accession, to be completed by 2003. China's agreement to implement the TRIPs agreement on intellectual property rights immediately upon accession is of special importance for the pharmaceuticals sector, in which the profits of multinational firms are intimately related to the ability to enforce intellectual property rights. Other developing countries, notably India, have been much more cautious about the degree to which they agree to implement the TRIPs agreement on entry to the WTO. Rights to import and distribute pharmaceuticals are currently tightly controlled by government approvals, constituting an important source of protection for China's fledgling pharmaceuticals firms. China has agreed to phase in the elimination of these requirements over three years. After this period foreign pharmaceuticals firms will be able to import and distribute their imported products freely to any part of the country, including both wholesale and retail distribution.

- **Steel**. China has agreed to reduce its tariffs on steel and steel products from the current level of 10.3 per cent to 6.1 per cent by the end of 2002. The right to import steel is still restricted to a small number of entities that have been approved by the government. Over a period of three years from the date of China's accession to the WTO these restrictions on the import of steel are to be eliminated. Over the same period restrictions on the right to distribute steel within the domestic economy will also be phased out. Steel is of special importance in relation to so-called 'dumping'. China has agreed that for 12 years after China's accession to the WTO, the US should be able to retain legislation which prohibits 'import surges' in steel. Moreover, it has agreed that the USA's legislation known as Section 201 should remain in place to control surges in the import of steel and other products from China. The Chinese government has agreed to give up the right allocate equity injections or provide soft loans to the steel industry.

We have already seen that in the telecommunications and financial services service sectors, there will be rapid and large-scale opening of the Chinese market. In addition, the following important market access arrangements are contained in the US–China Agreement:

- **Agriculture**. China has agreed to reduce its agricultural tariffs from 31 per cent to 14 per cent for priority US farm exports over a maximum of four years. These include beef (falling from 45 per cent to 12 per cent), citrus fruits (40 per cent to 12 per cent), apples (30 per cent to 10 per cent), cheese (50 per cent to 12 per cent), wine (65 per cent to 20 per cent) and beer (70 per cent to 0 per cent). For grains, China has agreed to increase the import quotas for corn, wheat and rice together, from 2.6 million tons to 22 million tons in 2004. For imports within the quota, tariffs will be only around 1–2 per cent. China has agreed to eliminate export subsidies entirely.

- **Audiovisual**. Under current regulations, the distribution of books, magazines, movies, sound recordings, and videos is highly restricted. For example, foreign firms are not allowed to participate at all in the sound recordings industry. Under the China–US Agreement, China has agreed to allow 49 per cent foreign equity for the distribution of video and sound record-ings. It has agreed to allow majority ownership within three years for the construction and ownership and operation of cinemas. It will allow 20 films per year to be imported on a revenue-sharing basis immediately upon accession.

- **Travel and tourism**. Currently, the activities of foreign firms are highly restricted in this sector. China has agreed to allow unrestricted access to the China market for foreign hotel operators. Majority foreign ownership will be permitted immediately upon accession, and 100 per cent foreign ownership will be phased in within three years.

- **Retailing services**. Under the US–China Agreement, the retail sector is opened up to greater foreign participation. Within three years of accession, there are to be no limitations at all on the equity share of the multinational companies, or on their geographical location. However, the Agreement does limit multinationals to minority participation in stores of greater than 20 000 square metres, or where the multinational operates more than 30 stores in China. Under the EU-China Agreement, China agrees to lift the equity restriction on multinational retail chains and to remove the limi- tations on floor space, allowing them to establish wholly-owned retail chains throughout the country, 'representing unprecedented opportunities to department stores and chain stores in the world's most populous country' (*FT*, 20 May 2000).

SPEED OF IMPLEMENTATION

The integration of China into the full application of WTO rules will be rapid: 'On accession to the WTO, China will begin opening its market from day one in virtually every sector. The phase-in of further concessions will be limited to five years in almost all cases, and in many cases one to three years' (Barshefsky, 2000a: 6). Even a leading US economist, who is generally strongly supportive of the Agreement, Harvard University's Richard Cooper, cautioned that he was 'very uncomfortable' with the high speed of implementation required under the Agreement (Cooper, 2000).

ENFORCEMENT OF THE AGREEMENT

The Agreement that China has signed is going to be taken very seriously indeed by the advanced economies and the businesses based in those countries. In early May 2000, the US initiated a series of enforcement proceedings at the WTO against five countries for violations of WTO rules (*FT*, 2 May 2000). These included Brazil for alleged violations on textiles and patents, Romania on clothing, poultry and distilled spirits, India on requirements for the automotive industry, the Philippines on local content requirements for motorcycles, cars and commercial vehicles, and Argentina on patents.

The seriousness with which the USA takes the Agreement on China's entry to the WTO is indicated by the fact that the US President has requested special resources from the national budget to support what will be 'the largest monitoring and enforcement effort for any agreement ever' (Barshefsky, 2000a: 13–4). In April 2000 it was reported that the administration was asking Congress to provide $22 million for new enforcement resources for the Commerce, Agriculture, and State Departments, as well as the US trade representative's office. This would represent a tripling of resources dedicated to China's trade compliance (*FT*, 28 April 2000). There is no doubt that the US will be in the lead in attempting to enforce the WTO Agreement.

The fact that China will be within the WTO means that the full weight of international pressure can be brought to bear on it to observe the Agreement to which it has signed, rather than individual countries contending with China: 'Within the WTO, [the US] will be able to work with 134 other members, many of whom will be concerned about the same issues we raise and all of whom will have the legal right to enforce China's commitments' (Barshefsky, 2000a:13). The capability to enforce the Agreement is greatly increased by the fact that it is highly detailed, with 'highly specific commitments in all areas, clear time-tables for implementation, and firm end-dates for full compliance'. These will allow the USA to 'carefully monitor China's compliance and present evidence of failure to comply' (Barshefsky, 2000a: 6).

IMPACT OF THE AGREEMENT ON TRADE AND INVESTMENT

The economic impact of China joining the WTO will be wide-ranging with effects that extend beyond the scope of this study. The impact on the Chinese farm sector is of great importance, since there are almost 400 million farmers in China. A professional analysis of the likely impact of the WTO Agreement on this crucial sector is beyond the scope of this study. However, this is perhaps the most important area of potential impact, of greater significance even than the issues analyzed in this study.

Trade. Prior to the WTO Agreement, China already had relatively open access to the US and EU economies. It is not clear that the only way to maintain this access was to enter the WTO at all, let alone under the terms that were agreed. Under the existing conditions of market access, China was able to increase its exports more rapidly than virtually any other developing country. Its exports increased from $24 billion in 1980 to over $207 billion in 1997, and its share of world exports tripled from 1.03 per cent in 1980 to 3.01 per cent in 1997 (World Bank, 1999: 258–9). Its export growth rate from 1980 to 1990 was 11.5 per cent compared with 2.7 per cent for all low income countries (excluding India and China) and in 1990–98 its export growth rate was 14.9 per cent per annum compared with 7.0 per cent for low income countries (excluding India and China) (World Bank, 1999: 258–9). Under the existing trade rules, China already produced one-third of the world's export of suitcases and handbags, a quarter of the world's toys, and one-eighth of the clothing. China is 'hard to beat in low margin, quick-to-market manufactures' (*The Economist*, 20 November 1999).

Despite rapid growth of its exports, the base from which China's export growth started was very small. Consequently, by 1997, its export total was still smaller even than that of the Netherlands, and far behind that of the eight richest countries in the world. China's exports in 1997 were only one-fifth of those of the USA (World Bank, 1999: 258–9). The possibility of widespread restrictions on China's exports to the advanced economies was small.

In sum, the main impact of the WTO on China's trade is likely to be a large increase in China's imports rather than an increase in exports, reducing China's large current account surplus, especially that with the USA. The USA made no market-opening concessions at all to China in the Agreement. The increased market access was entirely on the Chinese side. The USA will be the principal beneficiary from the opening of China's markets through the Agreement. China is the USA's fifth largest trading partner and growing fast. The World Bank estimates that China needs over $750 billion in new infrastructure over the next decade, including power generation, transportation equipment, aircraft, environmental controls, and telecommunications networks (US–China Trade Council, 1999). The USA is in the prime position to be the major beneficiary from the opening of the China market through selling large quantities of these goods and services to China in the coming period. In addition to industrial products, the USA will be the main beneficiary from the opening of the Chinese market for farm products:

> The American Farm Bureau has called China the 'most important growth market for American agriculture into the 21st century'. It is already our sixth largest agricultural export market and a major purchaser of US wheat, grains, meat, chicken, pork, cotton and soyabeans. By 2030 it is forecast that China's

annual wheat imports could reach 90 million tons, half of today's total world grain exports. In the 21st century, USDA projects that Asia will account for 75 per cent of the growth of US farm exports, of which 50 per cent will be in China. (US–China Trade Council, 1999)

A major objective for the USA in negotiating the WTO Agreement is to reduce the trade deficit with China through high-speed growth of US exports:

> WTO membership would result in an unprecedented opening of China's market, creating opportunities for US companies and driving down the deficit in a beneficial way. Whatever happens in bilateral trade flows, China's WTO market-opening can only help the overall US trade balance. The US stands to gain unprecedented access to China's markets. We are giving up nothing, since the US market is already open. Getting rid of Chinese barriers will open markets for leading US exports, such as high technology, capital goods, services and agriculture. (US–China Trade Council, 1999)

Based on a Goldman-Sachs study, the Congressional Research Service estimates that a WTO agreement would boost US exports to China by between $12.7 billion and $13.9 billion per annum by the year 2005 (US–China Trade Council, December 1999).

Foreign Investment. China's membership of the WTO is likely to provide a stimulus to foreign direct investment, by ensuring a much more secure framework of international law within which multinationals' investment can be conducted. The elimination of the severe controls on distribution within China is likely to have a substantial effect on the incentive to conduct business in China. However, the effects are complex.

China's entry to the WTO may have a substantial impact on the incentive structure that confronts multinational companies. We have already seen that it will eliminate the requirement for multinationals to establish production bases within China in order to supply the Chinese market, enabling them instead to import from other production locations. The Agreement may even reduce the incentive to invest in China for many types of business. New options will become available, such as exporting cars to China from close at hand production sites, such as Thailand and South Korea in preference to production facilities in China. The incentive to export from close at hand rather than to produce within China will be increased to the degree that the multinationals have doubts about China's political stability.

A further major consequence of the liberalization of investment requirements, taken together with the liberalization of marketing channels, is a great reduction in the incentive to establish joint ventures. India's liberalization process is progressing more slowly than China's. However, even India's much slower liberalization has had major effects on the incentive structure facing multinational firms. One respected commentator concluded recently: '*I can see the writing on the wall. Joint ventures are gone. They are history*' (Omkar Goswami, chief economist at the Confederation of Indian Industry, quoted in *FT*, 19 November 1999 emphasis added). The landmark decision that woke India up was the decision of Honda to set up a wholly-owned subsidiary to produce scooters and bikes in direct competition with its joint venture, Hero Honda. Greater transparency and reduced state intervention in the distribution process has diminished the value of having a local partner. Foreign companies are becoming keen to nurture their intellectual property and brands rather than piggy-back on a local name: 'After a decade of reform, multinationals may at last be prepared to invest more in India, in high-value activities, more closely related to their global goals. However, local investors may not see many of the gains' (*FT*, 19 November 1999).

NON-ECONOMIC OBJECTIVES OF THE AGREEMENT

Chinese Side. It has long been recognized that state-directed industrial policy provides wide opportunities for corruption permitted by the existence of economic rents derived from control over non-market methods of resource allocation. Indeed, Adam Smith's *Wealth of Nations*, written at the end of the eighteenth century contained a sustained critique of the corrupt British state that intervened heavily in controlling imports and subsidizing exports. There is a large modern literature on rent seeking associated with state intervention (see Chang, 1994, for an evaluation of this literature).

China's highly-developed system of 'connections' is closely related to the huge web of state interventions in the economy. This system closely parallels that found in many developing countries with extensive state interventions to support industrial policies, such as the 'licence Raj' that is slowly being unwound in India. The extent of corruption associated with the Chinese system of state intervention in the economy is enormous, and impossible to measure. One-party rule combined with extensive channels for state intervention in the economy provides an environment in which corruption can flourish. Most observers believe that the extent of corruption increased in the 1990s (see, for example, Zhang, 2000: Ch. 14). There are innumerable channels available for officials to benefit from corrupt practices in the gradually-reforming economy.

Large-scale purchases by state-owned enterprises provide wide opportunities for bribery to steer contracts in particular directions. Large-scale state allocation of financial resources through state-owned banks and other quasi-state financial institutions such as the Industrial and Investment Trusts (ITICs) provides large opportunities for corrupt allocation of loans. The collapse of one 'ITIC' and the near collapse of a major 'Red Chip' company registered in Hong Kong in 1998/99, resulted in close involvement of international auditors. They revealed fraud and straightforward theft on a huge scale. State-owned enterprises, with little monitoring from shareholders, have developed hugely complex investments in 'children', 'grandchildren', and 'great-grandchildren' companies, with a cascade of virtually unmonitored investments. Local protectionism provides a huge arena for further official corruption. A mass of local official licence and unofficial approvals are required before investment by other Chinese entities is permitted in a given locality. A wide array of local 'non-tariff barriers' operates. All of these provide opportunities for bribery of officials.

Foreign exchange controls provide a wide range of possibilities to benefit from bribing corrupt officials. Continued state involvement in the distribution system, including remaining price controls, provides extensive opportunities for officials to benefit from their privileged access to allocative rights. Extensive state intervention in international trade provided large opportunities for smuggling. Huge profits can be earned from smuggling goods in the most highly protected sectors such as autos and tobacco. Many officials in powerful institutions, especially the People's Liberation Army, have been proved to be heavily involved in smuggling. Granting foreign trade rights to a small number of state-approved entities provides a large incentive to seek personal profit from using these rights.

The channels available for official corruption in dealing with foreign business in the 1990s included extraction of payments for the right to import goods, for the right to set up a business or establish a joint venture in China, for the right to have access to distribution channels from which foreign businesses were officially excluded, or for support in hastening a bureaucratic decision. The more important the deal, the higher the level of official involved.

A deep problem for China, as for other developing countries, is the relatively slow growth of the technical capability and ethical standards of the supervisory and legal system. Corruption of the police force has been a major source of public resentment. Those who are entrusted with the task of enforcing the regular anti-corruption drives are themselves often corrupt. In one such nation-wide drive in 1998, 756 prosecutors were themselves punished for corruption and mishandling of cases (Zhang, 2000: 137).

There has been huge and growing public anger at the deep extent of corruption associated with the 'network' society. One recent evaluation of the extent of corruption in China concluded: 'Corruption in China today has reached dangerous proportions, and involves collusion among officials, legal professionals, businessmen and even state institutions such as government agencies and banks. This trend of institutional corruption has undermined the integrity and reliability of the state apparatus and, if unchecked, may trigger serious and disruptive political repercussions' (Zhang, 2000: 139).

China's leaders have repeatedly warned of the growing dangers to the fabric of China's society of the large extent of corruption. A major anti-corruption drive in 1999–2000 resulted in some high-profile public prosecutions. In March 2000, the former deputy governor of Jiangxi province was executed for corruption. Just a few months later, Cheng Kejie, one of nineteen deputy chairmen of the National People's Congress, was sentenced to death for corruption. He was accused of amassing $4.7 billion in kickbacks from land deals and in return for granting development contracts. One controversial domestic critic commented on the recent death sentences: 'The problem can't be solved by just punishing some people, because this system itself breeds corruption' (Ms He Qinglian, quoted in the *IHT*, 1 August 2000). Many people within China believe that fundamental reform of the economic system is necessary in order to end corruption. They believe that application of WTO rules will greatly help to achieve this result, by greatly reducing both international and domestic state interventions through which officials can derive rents.

US Side. The US negotiators were explicit about their non-economic objectives. The language and objectives are strongly reminiscent of the US government discussions of their policy goals in the former Soviet Union in the late 1980s and early 1990s. A key part of this is the characterization of the debate within China in black and white terms. The US public is informed that there are only two groups, 'reformers', who are 'good', and 'hardliners', who are 'bad'. The goal of US policy is to support the people who are 'good' and seek for the overthrow of the people who are 'bad': 'These commitments are a remarkable victory for the economic reformers in China ... Altogether, this will give China's people more access to information, and weaken the ability of hardliners to isolate China's public from outside influence and ideas' (Barshefsky, 2000a: 5). There is, indeed, an extreme group of 'hardliners', the 'new left wing', which is deeply suspicious of further integration with the world economy. At the other extreme, there is a significant group of people, the extreme free marketeers, who favour high-speed liberalization and immediate 'close' integration with the world economic system. However, in between is a broad spectrum of opinion. This includes a wide range of people who totally support the move towards a market economy and closer integration with the world economic system, but who believe that China needs to proceed cautiously. They are deeply concerned at the potential destabilizing effect of ultra-rapid integration, given the immense power of the global oligopolies, and the weakness of China's domestic 'national champions'.

The US policy makers have made a strong linkage between the Agreement and the transformation of China's political system. The US government regards China's accession to the WTO under the agreed terms as having 'potential beyond economics and trade' (Barshefsky, 2000a: 5). It is viewed as 'a means to advance the rule of law in China', and 'a precedent for willingness to accept international standards of behaviour in other fields': 'That is why many Hong Kong and Chinese activists for democracy and human rights – Martin Lee, the leader of the Hong Kong Democratic Party; Ren Wanding, a dissident who has spent twenty years of his life in prison – see WTO accession as China's most important step toward reform in twenty years' (Barshefsky, 2000a: 5). The US government's support for the WTO 'rests on a long-term commitment to human rights and freedoms, as well as new opportunities and strengthened guarantees of fairness for Americans' (Barshefsky, 2000a: 5).

The US government explicitly links the destruction of China's large state enterprises with transformation of China's political system: 'Opening markets will put enormous competitive pressures on China's beleaguered state-owned industries – bulwarks of political conservatism and socialist economics.

In contrast a WTO Agreement will unleash China's entrepreneurial sector, which supports increased economic and political freedom' (US–China Trade Council, 1999).

CAN LARGE CHINESE FIRMS COMPETE ON THE GLOBAL LEVEL PLAYING FIELD?

The main issue that concerns us in this study is the implications of China's membership of the WTO under the terms it has agreed with the US, for the capability of China's gradually reforming large state-owned enterprises to compete with the global giant corporations: has restructuring progressed sufficiently far for China's large enterprises to be able to compete on the global level playing field?

Many commentators believe that entering the WTO will invigorate Chinese large-scale industry. One US business leader at a Sino–foreign meeting convened in Spring 2000 to analyze the impact of the WTO on China concluded: 'Competition from abroad will help the Chinese to raise their level of efficiency, just like the US auto industry did in the 1980s in the face of Japanese competition.'

Rather than make general statements about the competitive capability of Chinese businesses, this study has attempted to penetrate more deeply through micro-level case studies into the state of readiness of China's large corporations to face the forthcoming global competition. The case studies in the CBBP cover a wide range of industries. They reveal widespread progress in business management, technology and understanding of the market. However, they also reveal a wide-ranging set of shortcomings in relation to the global giant corporations in the respective sectors. As we have seen in Chapter 2, the global giants have been comprehensively transformed since the 1980s, with massively enhanced competitive capabilities for those corporations that now have powerful positions in almost every sector. As has been emphasized throughout this study, China's reforming large enterprises are chasing a fast-moving target, making the catch-up task for them more difficult than that which confronted the aspiring global giants in former latecomer countries such as Japan and the Four Little Tigers.

AVIC

In the 1970s there was a wide gap between China's aerospace industry and the world's leading companies. It is undoubtedly the case that in this, the most 'strategic' of all Chinese industries, the gap between China's 'national champion' and the global giant companies has widened drastically since the 1970s. The extent of the gap is revealed by the fact that the entire Chinese civilian aircraft fleet, with the exception of a small number of domestically-made turbo-props, is imported. China's attempt to build its own indigenous large aircraft, the Y-10, failed. China's attempt to partner the multinationals in co-designing and building a large civilian aircraft failed. China's sub-contracting for the multinational giants remains at a pathetically low level compared to the levels of Japan or South Korea. Even China's domestically-made turbo-prop is only able to make a few export sales through the use of key imported components, reflecting the backward nature of its aero-engine and avionics industry.

At least as revealing about the failure to make any inroads on the world's leading corporations is the fact that the Chinese military has been forced to rely more and more heavily on imports and domestic production under licence of fighter planes from the former USSR. China's airforce is now almost wholly dependent for advanced fighters on Su27s bought from the former USSR. The number either already produced or on order is now well over one hundred, and rising. Moreover, China is negotiating for the purchase of the even more advanced Su30s.

The core aerospace business of AVIC in the late 1990s was extremely small (Table 13-2), on a par with a medium-sized company such as Vickers (UK). Moreover, AVIC contained the full range of aerospace activities, including engines and avionics as well as airframes. AVIC had been turned into a vast empire of diversified businesses, totally unable to compete directly with the global giants in aerospace.

The 'reform' of AVIC in 1999 had no immediately comprehensible rationale. Instead of one huge diversified conglomerate with no capability to compete with the multinationals, it created two smaller, and even less internationally competitive conglomerates. The reform could have separated the vast civilian from the aerospace business, but was unable to do so because this would have provoked much opposition from the subordinate entities who stood to lose many of their most profitable activities. It could have separated engines and avionics from the airframe business, but it didn't. It could have separated military from civilian aerospace, but it didn't. If its main goal was to develop its capability as a sub-contractor, then it might have allowed strong subordinate production units such as Xian, Chengdu and Shenyang to become independent companies that could compete for business with the multinationals, but it didn't. In sum, the prospects for AVIC on the global level playing field are bleak.

TABLE **13-2 Selected Indicators of the Competitive Capability of Leading Chinese Companies Compared with the Global Giants: Aerospace, 1997**

Company	Revenues ($ billion)	Post-tax Profits ($ million)	Employees (000)	R & D ($ million)
Boeing (1997)	45.8	(178)	239	1830
Lockheed-Martin (1997)	28.1	1300	190	1060
BAe (1997)	10.4	681	44	690
AVIC (1997)	3.1	72	560	n.a.
of which: aerospace	0.7	—	—	—

SOURCES: *Nolan, P., Case Studies China Big Business Programme, 1996–99; Annual Reports*

NOTE: Figures in brackets indicate losses

Alongside the halting, uncertain reforms in the Chinese aerospace industry has gone the most revolutionary epoch in the history of the world industry. By the late 1990s, after an unprecedented epoch of merger and acquisition, only a tiny handful of firms dominated the entire world industry in both civilian and military aircraft. The epoch of 'national champions' had vanished, to be replaced by 'regional' European champions contesting with the massive US-based firms for the entire world's market. Moreover, the process was becoming even more internationalized by the beginning of a possible revolutionary period of massive transatlantic mergers and acquisitions, affecting even the formerly sacrosanct military aerospace sector. These changes placed China's halting efforts at industrial policy at an even greater disadvantage on the global stage.

The WTO Agreement means that China would be unable to use its huge imports of aircraft to require multinational companies to transfer technology to China's aircraft and components industry, to set up joint ventures with them, or to provide sub-contracting work for China's ailing aerospace enterprises. It will be unable to provide soft loans to the industry to help build business capability in key parts of the industry that might have a hope of becoming globally competitive, such as second or third tier suppliers in the aerospace components industry. China's rumored attempt to support the development of a 70–80 seat commercial aircraft along the lines of Embraer or Bombardier could not be supported by government soft loans or by procurement requirements from domestic airlines without running the risk of prosecution by the WTO.

Some indication of the possible consequences of such a path was provided by the case of the Brazilian aircraft manufacturer, Embraer. In April 2000 the WTO ruled on the case of alleged illegal Brazilian government support for Embraer, the Brazilian national champion in the aircraft industry. Canada filed the complaint, alleging that Brazil had granted subsidies worth $3.7 billion to Embraer in the form of export financing from Proex for the export of 900 aircraft already contracted for delivery. This unfairly disadvantaged the Canadian-based firm, Bombardier, which is Embraer's main competitor. Embraer argued that the subsidies were merely in order to equalize domestic and international interest rates for export finance. However, the WTO panel ruled that the subsidies went far beyond this 'legitimate' purpose. The WTO decision was regarded as 'a heavy blow for Embraer, which has become one of Brazil's most successful companies since it was privatized in 1994' and made record profits in 1999 (*FT*, 29 April 2000). Once the panel ruling is adopted, Canada will be entitled to negotiate compensation from Brazil or ask the WTO for authorization to impose retaliatory trade tariffs on trade equivalent to the losses from Brazil's 'illegal actions'.

SANJIU

Sanjiu is exceptionally interesting from the point of view of industrial policy and catch-up, since it had the backing of the People's Liberation Army. This provided many difficulties, but also conferred some important advantages, such as access to markets and the possibility of taking over other enterprises in the sector. Sanjiu developed a genuinely modern business system. It had the benefit of a powerful leadership team, and an outstanding chief executive officer. Sanjiu developed a powerful brand within China. It had an acute sense of the importance of product quality and modern production systems. It had a highly professional management team, with a deep awareness of global trends in the pharmaceutical industry. It was one of the earliest Chinese firms to develop a genuinely modern marketing system.

However, despite these great strengths and business achievements, Sanjiu faces enormous difficulties in competing directly with the multinationals (Table 13-3). China's pharmaceuticals industry is highly fragmented. China has thousands of small-scale pharmaceuticals producers that will face large difficulties on the global level playing field. The largest companies, such as Sanjiu, occupy only a tiny fraction of the national market. Even the leading pharmaceuticals companies, such as Sanjiu, are tiny in scale compared to the global giants. R & D is crucial to the ability to compete with the multinational giants. Even one of China's leading pharmaceutical companies, such as Sanjiu, has a minuscule research capability compared to the global leaders. Zhao Xinxian, Sanjiu's chief executive officer recognizes explicitly that his company cannot contemplate direct competition. The alternative routes within the pharmaceuticals sector are, firstly, to produce out-of-patent, low value-added medicines, with low rates of profit. Several of China's large state-owned enterprises have a considerable capability in this area. However, none of the global giant companies relies on this as their path to growth and high levels of profits.

The second path, and that which Sanjiu has chosen, is to focus on traditional Chinese medicines. Sanjiu's chosen route is especially interesting as it raises the issue of the degree to which Chinese firms can compete with multinationals without engaging in head-to-head competition. This path enabled Sanjiu to expand rapidly within China, rising quickly to become one of the top two pharmaceutical companies. However, Sanjiu has found it very difficult to grow in China apart from its main product, *Sanjiu Weitai*, the stomach medicine. On international markets, despite passing FDA health requirements, it is also

TABLE **13-3 Selected Indicators of the Competitive capability of Leading Chinese Companies Compared with the Global Giants: Pharmaceuticals, 1997**

Company	Revenues ($ billion)	Post-tax Profits ($ million)	Employees (00)	R & D ($ million)
Merck (1997)	26.03	8069	54	2760
Novartis (1997)	22.34	6166	87	2620
Glaxo Wellcome (1997)	17.38	4626	53	1870
Sanjiu (1997)	0.67	98*	13	n.a.

SOURCE: Nolan, P., *Case Studies China Big Business Programme, 1996–99; Annual Reports*

NOTE: *Pre-tax profits

difficult for it to grow. The overseas Chinese community is not sufficiently large to provide for sustained long-term growth. The extent of prescription by Western doctors is still small. Moreover, lacking a patent, there is nothing to stop Western pharmaceutical companies producing the product and using their massive marketing structure to sell traditional Chinese medicines such as *Sanjiu Weitai*, should they find the market growing more rapidly than at present. Sanjiu would find it hard, or simply impossible, to compete with such a strategy. Moreover, there is nothing to prevent the multinationals from adopting such a strategy even within China, if they find the profit margin sufficiently attractive.

Therefore, Sanjiu's ability to compete directly with the multinationals is virtually non-existent. It is a highly successful business that has performed extremely well in an important niche market, which is essentially a branch of the food industry, rather than a true medicine. However, this market, which avoids head-on competition with the multinational giants, has only limited long-term growth prospects. This fact explains to a large degree, Sanjiu's decision to enter a wide range of businesses other than pharmaceuticals. At one point it had a huge range of largely unrelated businesses, including even automobile production. Even after it had drastically reduced its portfolio's range, it still had a wide range of activities. However, these were mainly in food and drink, which are reasonably closely related to Chinese medicine. Sanjiu's main assets are now its high quality managerial personnel, its brand and its marketing skills. These may enable the company to remain a reasonably successful food and drinks conglomerate for a reasonable period of time. However, they do not in any degree suggest that Sanjiu will be able to compete with the multinational giants of the pharmaceuticals industry.

The 1990s saw a revolutionary change in the structure of the world pharmaceuticals industry. The global industry was massively transformed by a sequence of massive de-mergers and mergers. One after the other, the global giants of the chemical industry de-merged their pharmaceuticals businesses. These de-mergers were followed by a sequence of multi-billion dollar mergers. By the late 1990s, a small group of massive pharmaceuticals companies had emerged. They undertook vast, multi-billion dollar R & D expenditure. They developed a huge capability to develop drugs through clinical trials and to market their portfolio of drugs through common channels. They also had the financial resources to withstand the failure of a large fraction of their R & D investment and the possible disasters of drugs that turned out to be harmful to health. This global revolution made the emerging Chinese 'national champions' appear even more puny by comparison.

Under the terms of China's entry to the WTO the Chinese government could not try to nurture a group of 'national champions' through 'non-market' mechanisms. China's aspiring global giants in this sector cannot hope to grow through cloning Western patented drugs. The Agreement means that the protection provided for domestic producers through restrictions on access to the domestic distribution system will disappear. It means that global pharmaceuticals firms will be able to advertise freely in China and establish their own distribution systems.

It means that it will be illegal to require joint ventures to transfer pharmaceuticals technology and/or agree to transfer pharmaceuticals patents within a certain period of time. It means that the global giants will be able freely to import their products, drastically reducing the incentive to produce locally.

HARBIN POWER EQUIPMENT COMPANY (HPEC)

Compared with other developing countries, at the end of the 1970s China had a relatively advanced power equipment industry. It had three major producing units, with around three-quarters of the domestic market between them. At the beginning of the reform process, these three entities were under a single central source of control. Under reform, these enterprises faced two decades of rapidly growing demand, providing an important opportunity for catch-up. Under these circumstances, China's leading producers made considerable progress. Harbin benefited greatly from a government-orchestrated programme of technical transfer, enabling it to upgrade its technical capability significantly. If the three main Chinese producers had been able to effect a merger, they would have formed a genuinely large-scale entity, even in global terms. Not only was the Chinese market one of the world's fastest-growing, but also, a large fraction of Chinese equipment is coal-fired, so that China might have built a considerable capability in this branch of the industry.

However, China's industrial policy did not follow this path. Instead, China's policies of enhancing the independence of subordinate operational units allowed the separate units to become increasingly autonomous. Both Dongfang and Shanghai Electrical Corporation were allowed to establish joint ventures with multinational companies. In addition, many smaller Sino–foreign joint ventures were established. Harbin's own attempt to form a northeast China electrical company, uniting its interests with those of neighbouring electrical equipment producers foundered on the separate ambitions of the electrical equipment manufacturers. Moreover, even Harbin itself did not constitute a unified modern corporation. It consists of three main separate entities each with their own strong traditions. The 'unification' to form Harbin Power Equipment Company (HPEC), was principally as a vehicle to gain permission for flotation. Even after flotation, the separate entities within HPEC had a wide range of independent functions.

The increasing independence of the power generation sector from the equipment manufacturing sector already sharply changed the competitive landscape of the Chinese power equipment industry from the mid-1990s onwards. Foreign-invested and wholly domestically owned power stations increasingly looked towards buying equipment with the lowest costs, including costs of maintenance, with high levels of reliability and the ability to meet increasingly stringent anti-pollution regulations, irrespective of country of origin of the manufacturer. In this sector, China still has significant industrial policy measures, including restrictions on foreign investment in both the equipment and the generation sector, limitations on the size of power plant imported, and domestic content requirements. Even with these measures, the share of multinational companies, through import and domestic production in joint ventures, rose sharply, reaching around one-half of annual installed capacity by the mid-1990s. Most significantly, the entire first tranche of equipment for the massive Three Gorges Project, comprising 14 700 MW units, was awarded to multinational companies.

Despite considerable progress, China's domestic industry in the late 1990s remained institutionally fragmented. The fragmentation even penetrated its leading companies, including the separate sub-units within HPEC. Alongside the growth of autonomy at the enterprise level within China, the global 'battle of the giants' was reaching the endgame, with just three giant companies dominating the world market, emerging from the former diverse structure of separate national champions within each advanced country. As a separate entity, it would be extremely hard for HPEC, China's leading firm, to compete even within China with the global giants on the global level playing field (Table 13-4). China's main producers other than HPEC were increasingly being integrated into the global sub-contracting system of the multinational giant companies. Despite the considerable progress, even in this sector, the institutional and technical gap between China's leading companies and the world leaders has enlarged during the reform period.

Multinational firms already have developed strong positions in the Chinese market. Under the terms of the WTO Agreement, the key instruments of industrial policy in this sector would be illegal. Low interest loans to support technical modernization at Harbin would be illegal. Using the Three Gorges turbine purchases from multinationals to require sub-contracting of components from domestic firms and technical transfer to domestic firms would be illegal. Using government procurement contracts to purchase from domestic firms in 'unfair' competition with multinationals would be illegal. Using rights to establish a joint venture as a condition of technical transfer, such as at Shanghai Electrical Company, would be illegal.

TABLE 13-4 Selected Indicators of the Competitive Capability of Leading Chinese Companies Compared with the Global Giants: Power Equipment, 1998

Company	Revenues ($ billion)	Post-tax Profits ($ million)	Employees (000)	R & D ($ million)
Siemens	57.95	990	376	5008
: power division	6.39	n.a.	n.a.	n.a.
ABB	29.72	2500	208	2368
General Electric	100.47	9296	293	1930
: power division	8.47	1306	n.a.	n.a.
Harbin (HPEC)	0.35	9	27	3

SOURCE: Nolan, P., *Case Studies China Big Business Programme, 1996–99; Annual Reports*

CNPC AND SINOPEC

The Chinese oil, gas and petrochemical industry is highly important in a global perspective. China has risen to become a major player in the world energy economy. During the reform years the Chinese industry has made major technical advances. Large institutional changes have taken place. The industry has absorbed modern management techniques. It has raised substantial capital on international markets through a series of H-share flotations. A sequence of huge, multi-billion dollar international joint ventures has been agreed. With greatly increased autonomy for the production units, real competition began to develop among domestic producers.

However, despite these very significant advances, important difficulties remained unresolved for the industry, rendering it at a considerable disadvantage in the global competition. At the institutional level, the industry remained torn by the tension between trying to create powerful, autonomous enterprises and trying to construct globally competitive, giant multi-plant firms. For most of the reform period, production units gained increasing autonomy. However, the central authorities within the industry placed limits on that degree of autonomy. Powerful subordinate enterprises, such as Daqing and Shanghai Petrochemical Company, were not allowed to undertake large-scale mergers with other domestic enterprises, lest they challenge the authority of the ministry and/or holding company. Belatedly, in the late 1990s, the central government undertook a comprehensive change of direction. They attempted complete reorganization of the industry, integrating the upstream and downstream components of the sector, with the aim of greatly enhancing the authority of the central bodies so as to create two truly integrated, globally competitive firms. This is a huge task, since the embedded vested interests at the level of the production enterprises are very large. It will require a major struggle to truly centralize control within the sector.

Apart from the institutional issue, major technical problems still exist for the industry. China's reserves have not proved as prolific nor as well-located as was once hoped. Offshore oil reserves have proved disappointingly small and are typically located at considerable depths. China's onshore oil reserves are mainly located in relatively distant areas in China's central Asian republics, notably Xinjiang. These are of uncertain amount and typically are at great depth. Both the costs of raising and transporting the products are high. In the downstream part of the industry, China's major companies have a proliferation of high-cost, small-scale refineries. They have only a relatively small share of petrochemical output from high value-added, high profit margin products. The downstream distribution system is extremely backward compared to the global giants, lacking high value-added products, such as environmentally-friendly varieties of petrol, lacking modern logistics systems and without a high quality global brand.

The Chinese industry is still highly protected through tight restrictions on foreign direct investment, with projects typically requiring many years of negotiation before obtaining approval, major restrictions on the openness of bidding for major oil and gas exploration and development projects, and through labyrinthine controls on the distribution system for oil and petrochemical products. Under the terms of the WTO Agreement, all these forms of protection will become increasingly problematic. Alongside China's halting, uncertain reforms has gone a revolution in the world's oil and petrochemical industry.

A handful of companies in the advanced economies now occupy the commanding heights of the industry (Table 13-5). They possess large, high quality reserves, distributed around the globe. They have integrated oil refineries and petrochemical plants. They have high levels of R & D, and a portfolio of globally leading, high value-added, products in the petrochemical and oil products sectors. They have a sophisticated logistics system and global brand names. China's partially reformed national champions, CNPC and Sinopec are still far from the completion of a massive process of institutional restructuring. The weakness of the Chinese industry on the global level playing field was sharply revealed by the withdrawal of CNOOC's hoped-for $2.5 billion IPO in October 1999. Although there were disadvantageous short-term factors, at least part of the reason for the failure of the offering was the investors' perception of the institutional weakness of China's oil and petrochemical companies in the global competition. In April 2000, PetroChina's IPO raised just $2.9 billion, compared with the original intention to raise $10 billion (*FT*, 1 April 2000).

Under the terms of the WTO Agreement, multinationals will no longer be barred from the most lucrative downstream markets, the area in which their competitive advantage and the weakness of the Chinese companies is most marked. It will no longer be possible for multinationals to be required to enter joint ventures as a condition for operating in China. Any joint ventures in which they participate cannot any longer be made conditional on a transfer of technology to the Chinese partner. The multinationals will be able freely to procure their equipment from wherever they wish. They will be allowed to source their raw materials from wherever is most economically advantageous to them. The Chinese government will no longer be allowed to provide soft loans to help the

TABLE **13-5 Selected Indicators of the Competitive Capability of Leading Chinese Companies Compared with the Global Giants: Oil and Petrochemicals, 1997–8**

Company	Revenues ($ billion)	Post-tax Profits ($ million)	Employees (000)	R & D ($ million)
Exxon/Mobil (1997)*	182.36	11730	123	720
Royal Dutch/Shell (1997)	128.14	7760	105	770
BP Amoco (1997)	123.30	8540	123	390
CNPC (1998)	32.6	107**	1540	n.a.
Sinopec (1998)	34.0	194**	1190	n.a.

SOURCES: Nolan, P., *Case Studies China Big Business Programme, 1996–99*; *Annual Reports*

NOTE: * Pro-forma

      ** Pre-tax profits

domestic firms to modernize. The multinationals will be able freely to import oil, gas, oil products and petrochemicals from wherever is most efficient.

Yuchai

China entered the reform period with a highly fragmented automobile industry. The degree of fragmentation increased in the early years of reform as a large number of domestic new entrants entered the fast-growing industry, which was protected from international competition and had a high degree of local protection. In this, as in other sectors, the government built its industrial policy around the attempt to allow the growth of a small number of domestic producers, who were encouraged to compete with each other in the fast-growing domestic market. Three powerful production units within the old planned economy were selected to form the core of the reformed industry, namely Shanghai Auto, Yiqi (Number One Auto) and Erqi (Number Two Auto). Large-scale foreign direct investment in auto assembly was closely guided to these plants. The auto components sector was even more fragmented than the auto assembly sector. In the late 1980s there were more than 1600 components makers, and more than 200 enterprises manufacturing internal combustion engines. In this sector also the government tried to support the growth of a small number of powerful enterprises that could compete with the global giant companies.

Yuchai began as one of the large number of state engine manufacturers. It grew at high speed, stimulated by the rapid growth in the market for medium-duty trucks. Its growth was due to a number of astute management decisions. These included the purchase of second-hand equipment from abroad, clever product choice and development, a keen sense of the importance of brand and advertising, including a deep understanding of the importance of product reliability and product guarantees, and early development of a sophisticated, national marketing system. Yuchai was a pioneer in all these developments and reaped the benefits of first mover advantage. Yuchai's ambition was to form a pillar of the development of the Chinese components industry. Its chief executive officer hoped to develop Yuchai into a Chinese version of the giant US companies Detroit Diesel or Cummins Diesel Engine, both large-scale global diesel engine makers (Table 13-6).

In order to accomplish this goal, Yuchai needed to be able to develop the engine business by taking over other powerful diesel engine makers, and securing a long-term market with the main truck makers, namely Yiqi and Erqi, which between them occupy 90 per cent of the Chinese medium-duty truck market. The chief executive officer of Yuchai persistently lobbied the central government to support Yuchai as China's 'national champion' in the diesel engine sector, having already demonstrated its managerial and technical capabilities. However, Yuchai's main consumers, Yiqi and Erqi decided that they would prefer to retain their own engine making capability within the company, and internalize the profits from the diesel engine business. They were able to lobby the central government successfully to

TABLE 13-6 Selected Indicators of the Competitive Capability of Leading Chinese Companies Compared with the Global Giants: Auto Components, 1998

Company	Revenues ($ billion)	Post-tax Profits ($ million)	Employees (000)	R & D ($ million)
Bosch (1998)	28.61	446	n.a.	2020
Denso (1998)	13.76	461	57	1350
Caterpillar (1998)	20.98	1513	86	838
Cummins Diesel Engine (1998)	6.27	(21)	28	255
Detroit Diesel (1998)	2.16	30	7	98
Yuchai (1998)	0.14	15*	9	n.a.

SOURCES: Nolan, P., *Case Studies China Big Business Programme, 1996–99*; *Annual Reports*

NOTES: Figures in brackets indicate losses
    * Pre-tax profits

allow them to retain their independent capability in diesel engines. Indeed, Erqi had established a major joint venture with Cummins Diesel to develop its technical capability. By the late 1990s, despite having demonstrated immense entrepreneurial capability, Yuchai faced a bleak market prospect.

Despite rapid growth and institutional change, the Chinese auto industry remained at a severe disadvantage compared to the global giants at the end of the 1990s (Table 13-7). In the auto assembly sector, even its leading producers remained small-scale compared to the global giants. For example, Shanghai Auto, in the late 1990s, the country's largest auto company, with around 60 per cent of the national market, produced only around 200 000 vehicles per year. This compared with over 5 million vehicles for GM, almost 4 million for Ford and 3.5 million for Toyota. The company's domestic success was entirely due to its joint venture with VW. Shanghai Auto is closely integrated within the VW global system.

The global auto assembly industry is in the process of high-speed concentration, with large-scale mergers, including the Daimler–Chrysler path-breaking merger. In the auto components industry also, the late 1990s saw an explosion of mergers and concentration, as well as the de-merger of the auto component giants Delphi (from GM in 1999) and Visteon (from Ford, in 2000). Alongside the continued explosive growth through merger and acquisition of the leading tyre companies (Bridgestone, Goodyear and Michelin) other specialist components makers are merging at high speed in order to meet the globalizing needs of the world's biggest auto assemblers. The world's leading auto components companies, such as Cummins Diesel Engine, have already entered China in force, incorporating local joint venture partners into their global system. The capability even of the most successful of China's independent first tier auto components makers, such as Yuchai, to compete on the global level playing field is very limited

TABLE 13-7 **Selected Indicators of the Competitive Capability of Leading Chinese Companies Compared with the Global Giants: Autos, 1998**

Company	Revenues ($ billion)	Post-tax Profits ($ million)	Employees (000)	R & D ($ million)
GM (1998)	161.3	2960	600	7800
Ford (1998)	171.2	23160	364	7500
Daimler-Chrysler (1998)	154.6	5660	300	5800
Yiqi (1998)	4.4	21*	156	n.a.
Erqi (1998)	2.6	(5)	134	n.a.
Shanghai (1998)	4.8	594*	60	n.a.

SOURCES: Nolan, P., *Case Studies China Big Business Programme, 1996–99*; *Annual Reports*

NOTES: Figures in brackets indicate losses
    * Pre-tax profits

indeed. Had the central government supported Yuchai's bid to be the core national champion for China's diesel engine sector, then there might have been a serious possibility of challenging the global giant diesel engine companies.

The terms of the WTO Agreement would have a large effect on this industry, on both the assemblers and the components suppliers. Multinationals would no longer be required to participate in joint ventures in the assembly and components industry if they did not wish to do so. They would no longer be required to transfer technology as a condition for establishing a joint venture. China's high tariffs would be eliminated. The leading multinationals that do not yet have large production bases in China might well choose to export to China from their bases elsewhere in Asia, such as Thailand, South Korea and Japan, rather than expand production directly in China. China's government departments and state enterprises would no longer be able to procure their fleets of saloon cars and trucks 'unfairly' from domestic firms such as Yiqi and Erqi. Multinationals would be legally able to capture market share through ownership or franchised operation of dealerships and provision of finance for vehicle purchase.

SHOUGANG

China's steel industry boomed during the economic reforms. During this period, Shougang rapidly increased its output. It undertook a wide-ranging programme of modernization, technical upgrading, and diversification into activities that might support its further expansion. It developed a significant export capability in both steel and steel plant construction. Its computerization skills developed sufficiently for it to win an important competitive contract to design and install the control systems for a leading US steel maker. Both Shougang's plans for expansion and its management style bore a close resemblance to those of South Korea's Posco steel company.

Despite these important advances in Shougang's institutional and technical capability, Shougang faced severe limitations on its capability to compete on the global level playing field (Table 13-8). In the first place, although its output grew rapidly, a large part of the growth was in low-value-added, low-quality steel, such as construction steel. In the late 1990s, after two decades of rapid growth, high quality steel still accounted for only 15 per cent of its total output. Shougang's sales value in 1997 amounted to $2.2 billion, compared with $11 billion for British Steel, $12 billion for Usinor and $25 billion for Nippon Steel. All four of China's top producers together, namely Shougang, Angang, Baogang and Wugang, had a sales revenue of $9.0 billion, still well below that of the main European and East Asian producers, reflecting, to a considerable degree, their high proportion of low quality, low value-added products. Shougang found it hard to extricate itself from a vicious circle. The fact that it principally produced low quality steel meant that it was mainly in competition with small-scale local producers contesting with them for local markets. The low-value-added produced low profit margins, which in turn limited Shougang's capacity to modernize through investment in R & D and new products. In the late 1990s Shougang was extremely anxious to develop joint ventures with leading Western companies in order to acquire technology in high quality steels, such as those for large-scale modern buildings.

Shougang's plans to double its capacity by building a completely new steel plant at Qilu in Shandong province were overturned by the central government after the retirement in 1995 of its chief executive officer, Zhou Guanwu. At a stroke, this bureaucratic decision rendered irrational a large part of Shougang's diversified expansion, since many of its acquisitions had been intended to support the construction of Qilu. Without Qilu, these served little purpose for Shougang. Using the modern Kaiser Steel Plant, which Shougang had bought cheaply in California, Shougang might well have been able to make a high level of profits in a new plant with much lower manning levels than at the main site.

TABLE 13-8 Selected Indicators of the Competitive Capability of Leading Chinese Companies Compared with the Global Giants: Steel, 1998

Company	Revenues ($ billion)	Post-tax Profits ($ million)	Employees (000)	R & D ($ million)
Nippon Steel 1998)	21.59	90	28 (1995)	n.a.
Posco (1998)	9.72	680	23 (1994)	n.a.
NKK (1998)	14.15	849	18 (1995)	190
Usinor (1998)	10.65	373	58 (1995)	180
Shougang (1998)	2.16	25*	218 (1997)	n.a.
Baogang (1998)	3.12	265*	35 (1997)	n.a.

SOURCES: Nolan, P., *Case Studies China Big Business Programme, 1996–99*; Annual Reports
NOTE: *Pre-tax profits

This might have formed the basis for a serious challenge to the multinational giant companies.

Alongside the blockage placed on Shougang's expansion, the global industry began to enter a period of large-scale institutional and technical change. In the USA, a new form of large steel firm based around mini-mills began to develop, of which Nucor is the leading example. A truly global steel company, Ispat, based in London, with a collection of steel plants across the world, rapidly came to prominence. Within Europe a series of large-scale cross-border mergers transformed the industry. By the year 2000, a small group of 'European champions' had emerged in the industry, led by Arbed, Thyssen–Krupp, Usinor and Corus (the merger of British Steel and Hoogovens). Each of these firms had global reach, with plants across the world, and a high capability in specialist, high quality, high value-added steel. They were able to supply the global needs of large firms in such industries as packaging, automobiles, complex machinery, high quality construction, and white goods. The leading companies established close ties with their customers in order to met their global needs for high quality steel.

Baogang (Shanghai) is the only large Chinese steel company that, by the late 1990s, had established a capability to compete on the global level playing field with the world's fast-transforming steel companies. Its greenfield site, strongly supported by the local Shanghai government, without a large body of existing employees and with the benefit of a booming local market for high quality steels, had developed into a potentially competitive firm able to compete on the global level playing field. In contrast, other leading steel firms in China remained heavily dominated by low quality products. As import controls were reduced in the 1990s, China's imports of steel rose substantially. These principally consisted of high quality products, reflecting the weakness of domestic firms in these areas. For example, in 1996, China still imported one-half of its consumption of car sheets, 70 per cent of its tin sheets, and 80 per cent of its cold rolled stainless steel sheets.

China's leading steel firms may well be able to compete at the low value-added end of the market. However, the steel market is becoming increasingly segmented. In the high value-added and high profit part of the industry, which is closely linked with the needs of globalizing large firms, only Baogang can feel some degree of confidence that it is able to directly compete with the emerging global giants of Europe and the established giants of Asia in Japan and Korea. Shougang, like other large traditional Chinese steel firms, will find it difficult to compete directly on the global level playing field in high quality steel. Moreover, as China's international markets for steel are further liberalized, Shougang will face intensified competition from other countries' producers of low value-added steel, such as the former USSR.

China's entry to the WTO on the terms agreed would have a substantial effect on the steel industry. Despite the large fall in tariffs on steel imports, China still has extensive non-tariff barriers (NTBs) in this industry. These would no longer be legal. China's large steel producers all, with the partial exception of Baogang, have substantial technical weaknesses in high value-added steels. The Chinese government recently announced a major package of assistance through low interest loans to upgrade the technical quality of some of the key enterprises. Under the terms of China's entry to the WTO this would be illegal. Several of them have already established or are trying to establish major joint ventures with the multinational leaders. A major purpose is to upgrade technology through required technical transfer. Such requirements would be illegal. Several of the leading multinational firms have had protracted and often unsatisfactory negotiations to establish joint ventures in order to gain access to the Chinese market. They now would be legally entitled to establish independent, wholly-owned production facilities in China if they wished. They would also be able legally to take over Chinese steel firms, replicating the extensive take-overs of the most productive facilities in Eastern Europe by the world's leading steel producers. Chinese steel producers would no longer be able legally to prevent the multinational steel producers establishing their own distribution systems and making direct contact with their customers.

SHENHUA

In the midst of a vast sea of coal producers, the Chinese government has strongly supported the construction of a potentially globally competitive large coal company. The government has used powerful measures of industrial policy to help support the growth of a large modern 'high-quality coal company'. A primary objective is that this company can supply Chinese power stations with high quality coal that can reduce the environmental damage of burning coal to generate electricity. A subsidiary, but also important, goal is to create a firm that can compete with the global giant corporations in this sector, especially in supplying the fast-growing markets of northeast Asia, but also in supplying large modern coal-fired power stations on the Chinese coast. It has supported Shenhua's development through the grant of property rights to the vast coal reserves under the Ordos Plateau, as well as through the direction of large preferential loans. Following closely the model of the world's leading coal producers, Shenhua is building a dedicated railway line to ship coal 800 kilometres from Shenhua to a dedicated port facility on the coast. Starting from scratch, Shenhua has very low manning levels compared to old-established state-owned mines, which gives it a large advantage compared to domestic competitors in relation to wage costs, welfare burden and ability to organize a highly qualified and highly motivated workforce.

Despite these extremely positive aspects of Shenhua's development, it confronts many difficulties in battling with the global giant companies. Shenhua's property rights over the associated railway and port facilities are ambiguous. It is uncertain how secure will be Shenhua's long-term right to use the facilities exclusively. Nor is it clear how the long-term charge for using the facilities will be set. Shenhua operates in a fundamentally different environment from that of the multinational coal companies. The main source of domestic and international competition for the latter is other modern coal companies. However, Shenhua faces a fierce battle with other domestic producers as well as an increasing battle with the multinationals. Shenhua must compete with small-scale local producers that pay subsistence wages to workers in conditions that have not been seen for over 100 years in the advanced economies. The small producers are heavily supported by their local governments in their battle for survival with the large coal companies. Shenhua must compete also with heavily subsidized state-owned enterprises. Not only does Shenhua face severe domestic competition it has also had to accept a major reorganization of its business structure, being forcibly merged by the central government with five large state-owned enterprises. This drastically altered Shenhua's character. Three of the mines are in a terminal state of decline and heavily loss-making. Instead of being a company with 7000 employees, Shenhua overnight became a company with 80 000 employees.

Alongside the rise of the Chinese coal industry has gone a powerful re-shaping of the coal industry in the outside world. The world coal industry is becoming rapidly segmented. A large part of the industry is still producing with traditional methods within developing countries. In Europe, the industry has rapidly declined, as power stations have shifted heavily to oil and gas. However, a powerful group of modern, high quality coal companies has emerged. They are supplying the modern coal-fired power stations in the USA and East Asia. Increasingly, they are supplying the power stations of developing countries, as the power generation industry is privatized, and operators seek the lowest-cost source of high quality coal. The emerging global giants, such as RWE, Billiton, BHP and Rio Tinto, are able to compete successfully in these markets by benefiting from having large deposits of high quality, mainly open-cast mines, through the provision of coal that is washed and graded, through centrally purchasing large amounts of modern large-scale equipment, and through supplying coal reliably through a tightly integrated transport system. Shenhua's capability to compete with these companies is weakened greatly by the problems it faces in domestic competition and by the enforced merger with the five state-owned mines.

The terms of the WTO Agreement would have large implications for the Chinese mining industry. The world's leading international mining corporations have already developed large markets in East Asia and are deeply anxious to increase their access to China's huge potential market. In the coal industry, which has grown at high-speed, the leading international firms would now be able legally to bid to supply high quality coal to China's fast-growing modern power plants. It would be illegal for the contracts for these to be awarded on other than commercial criteria. The leading coal companies have been involved in protracted negotiations to establish joint ventures with China's leading coal companies. So far, none has been established on a permanent basis. Under the terms under which China has entered the WTO, the multinational coal companies could no longer be forced into joint ventures if they did not wish to be. China's aspiring global leaders, such as Shenhua, have received large-scale state support in the shape of low interest loans and other assistance, such as access to rail transport and internal port facilities at prices that are far below international transport prices. Much of this is illegal in terms of WTO rules. Moreover, a large fraction of the industry only survives thanks to low interest loans from state banks, especially the Construction Bank. Such subsidies to state enterprises are technically illegal under the terms of China's entry to the WTO.

CONCLUSION (i): CHINA OBSERVES THE AGREEMENT

LARGE STRUCTURAL CHANGE WILL BE NECESSARY

If China does, indeed, observe the conditions of the Agreement to which it is signatory, then it is impossible to avoid the conclusion that its entry to the WTO will have dramatic effects upon China's large-scale industry. This is readily acknowledged by US policy makers:

> In the short-term, WTO membership means painful short-term adjustments. Decrepit state-owned enterprises need massive overhaul to become internationally competitive. They will be forced to restructure by cutting costs, adopting modern production methods, and eliminating excess employment and overheads. Some will fail or go bankrupt. Such adjustments explain why state-owned enterprises and political conservatives oppose a WTO Agreement. The future of continued economic reform may ride on the WTO. (US–China Trade Council, 1999)

The Chinese leadership, by contrast, has emphasized the capability for China's large enterprises to be transformed and compete under pressure from the 'global level playing field'.

In the advanced economies, a succession of under-performing state-owned enterprises dramatically turned around their performance, and released enormous amounts of shareholder value. However, there are important differences between these enterprises and those of the Chinese 'commanding heights'. When the state enterprises of the advanced economies were privatized, they were already much more competitive than China's large state enterprises today. France's Renault, France Telecom, Alcatel, Elf Aquitaine, Aérospatiale, and Usinor, the UK's BAe, Rolls-Royce, British Steel, British Petroleum, and BT, Italy's ENI and Finnemecanica, Spain's Telefónica, and Repsol, and Germany's Deutsche Telekom and Volkswagen Group, were all much more powerful and business-oriented as state-owned enterprises than are China's state-owned industries today. Moreover, China's large state-owned enterprises are far behind the global first movers in the privatization and globalization race. Former state-owned companies and powerful private firms have already established powerful positions in sector after sector. China's potential global giants corporations are now entering the globalization race with the best positions already occupied by incumbent giant corporations.

There is no question that China's large state-owned enterprises would be required to undergo massive 'restructuring'. However, it is impossible to imagine that many, if any, of China's 'commanding heights' businesses would be able to build themselves into global leaders on the 'global level playing field' that is shortly to be introduced at high speed, under the close surveillance of the US government. Their only hope would be a renovated and much more effective industrial policy.

THE PROBLEM OF FINDING EMPLOYMENT FOR DISPLACED WORKERS

A key issue for the restructuring effort that will be necessary is the pace at which alternative employment opportunities grow for the large number of employees who are likely to lose their jobs if China fully applies the conditions to which the government has signed. There are several inter-connected issues that affect the answer to this issue:

- **SME employment**. The first issue is the pace at which employment opportunities for displaced workers in the large enterprise sector grow in the small- and medium-sized enterprise sector to take up the employment which is lost from the inevitable massive restructuring of the large state enterprise sector. We have already noted that even before the Agreement, China enjoyed one of the fastest rates of export growth, and its exports to the USA in particular grew at high speed. A large fraction of these exports came from small and medium enterprises, generating rapidly increased employment. It is hard to see how the Agreement can do much to accelerate this already rapid growth of exports from the SME sector. In addition the SME sector is itself likely to undergo a sharp increase in competitive pressure due to the opening of China markets, due to a reduction in subsidies available to the sector from local governments, and due to intense pressures to operate more efficiently on the global level playing field through advances in the use of IT. In other words, it is difficult to be optimistic that employment absorption in this sector will increase rapidly beyond the already high level of around 120 million people, even if output in the sector continues to advance rapidly. Indeed, employment might easily decline in this sector alongside rising sales revenue.

- **Growth of working-age population**. The issue of availability of alternative employment for workers in the disintegrating large enterprises has also to be considered in relation to the potential growth of other new entrants to the labour market in the non-farm sector. China's population and workforce are still growing at a significant, if much-reduced, pace compared to the 1970s. Between 1980 and 1998, the total working age population rose by no fewer than 286 million, at an annual average rate of 2.9 per cent (SSB, ZTN, 1999: 134). In the 1990s, the growth rate dropped considerably, as a result of the impact of the one-child policy. However, there still was an increase of almost 70 million in the working age population between 1990 and 1998, with a growth rate of 1.2 per cent per annum. If this rate of growth were sustained, China would add more than 140 million people to the working age population by the year 2020.

- **Restructuring in the farm sector**. The farm sector employs around 330 million people (SSB, ZTN, 1999: 138). There is no agreed estimate of rural 'surplus' labour, indeed it is extremely elusive empirically, but all estimates agree that the proportion is large. Recent Chinese estimates suggest that the number grew from 95 million in 1984 to 170 million in 1990, rising to 200 million in 1994 (Li, 1996; Ji and Shao, 1995). Most predictions suggest that, independently of China joining the WTO, the absolute number will continue to rise for some years. The farm sector has already felt considerable pressure from changes in farm technology and concentration of holdings that have led to increasing output per worker. It is thought that around 100–120 million semi-permanent migrants already work outside the farm sector. This issue has caused immense socio-economic problems. Coping with these has been a major headache for the leadership. The WTO Agreement is likely to have an independent and large impact on the demand for labour in the farm sector. Importing significant and steadily increasing quantities of farm produce from the US and other advanced economies is likely to have a substantial effect on the demand for labour in China's farm sector. It can be expected to substantially increase the flow of labour to the cities looking for employment in the non-farm sector, and competing for jobs with the displaced workers from the state-owned enterprises.

- **Regional distribution of new employment**. A large fraction of the decline in employment in state enterprises is likely to occur in North and Northeast China. A large fraction of any increase in employment in the non-farm sector is likely to occur in South China (including Shanghai). Inter-regional migration is a highly disruptive process, causing great stresses on public transport, public infrastructure, welfare demands and housing stock, let alone the personal stresses on family life.

If the Agreement allowed a long period of transition, then many of these stresses might be dealt with adequately, albeit that they amount to a massive structural change. However, it will be extremely difficult to cope with them at the high speed of integration that is envisaged by the US–China Agreement. The Agreement seems to have been designed with the interests of US business given complete priority over those of the adjustment problems of China's socio–economic system.

PSYCHOLOGICAL PROBLEMS OF ADJUSTMENT

Even for advanced European countries, it has very difficult to accept that 'national champions' may be unable to compete on the global level playing field as individual players. However, whereas individual European countries may have to accept the demise of their national champions, the continent as a whole is breeding a group of regional champions and transatlantic champions. For China, a huge civilization with a proud economic and political history, it is very difficult to accept that it may be unable to emulate Britain, the US, Japan and Korea in building national champions through industrial policy. The brutal reality is that US firms are by far the most powerful force in the global business revolution. Nowhere is their dominance more pronounced than in the industries of the Third Industrial Revolution. The US bombing of the Chinese embassy in Belgrade produced a massive outpouring of anti-American sentiment in China. This book argues that the USA's central position in the business revolution will enable its firms to take the lead in the defeat of China's large corporations. It is possible that Chinese people will simply applaud this result. However, a more likely result is considerable uneasiness among a wide range of Chinese people, including many of those who are positive about the benefits that capitalism might bring to China. It is impossible to predict in what form this might manifest itself politically, but it is possible that the response could be large-scale and even highly de-stabilizing to international relations.

CONCLUSION (ii): IMPLICATIONS FOR INTERNATIONAL RELATIONS OF CHINA'S FAILURE TO OBSERVE THE AGREEMENT

The US government put enormous effort into convincing the US public that the Agreement is in the interest of the US people. It had to cope with great opposition from human rights groups and from organized labour, convinced that US jobs will be lost by an even faster growth of Chinese imports than in the past two decades. The US people and especially, the relevant lobby groups, were barraged with arguments about the 'fairness' and ethical desirability of China joining the WTO. They were reassured at great length that China could be trusted and would, indeed, observe the rules to which it had signed agreement. We have seen that the US has put into place more comprehensive monitoring arrangements than exist for any other member of the WTO. It is significant that one of the major speeches delivered by Ambassador Barshefsky on the implications of the Agreement was delivered at the United States Military Academy, where she explicitly linked the issue of the Agreement with the US's national security interest: 'Trade and American National Security: The Case of China's WTO Accession' (12 April 2000). She commented: 'This Spring as Congress considers China's accession to the World Trade Organization and permanent normal trade relations, we face a decision which illustrates, as clearly as any in the past 50 years, the links between trade policy and national security' (Barshefsky, 2000b).

Within China, there are powerful forces that are dismayed by the Agreement. They will do all they can to slow down the implementation of the Agreement. It is unknown either in what ways the composition of the Chinese leadership might alter. A variety of possible factors, could lead to a shift in the leadership's position significantly towards foot-dragging on the Agreement. Among the most obvious such factors might be if the impact on China's large enterprises was greater than the leadership had anticipated. If there is widespread flouting of the terms of the Agreement, then there will be great difficulties for international relations, especially between the US and China. USA business and public opinion will be united in their indignation that the long-negotiated Agreement had not been treated seriously. There will be widespread feelings of anger at the 'unfairness' and 'non-ethical' nature of such behaviour. Such a background provides a fertile soil for escalation of conflict in ways that cannot today be predicted.

14
The Long-Term View

*The bourgeoisie, by the rapid development of all instruments of production,
by the immensely facilitated means of communication, draws all, even the
most barbarian, nations into civilization. The cheap prices of its commodities are the heavy artillery with which it batters down all Chinese walls,
with which it forces the barbarians' intensely obstinate hatred of foreigners
to capitulate. It compels all nations, on pain of extinction, to adopt the
bourgeois mode of production; it compels them to introduce what it calls
civilization into their midst, that is, to become bourgeois themselves. In
one word it creates a world after its own image ... The bourgeoisie has
through its exploitation of the world market given a cosmopolitan character
to production and consumption. To the great chagrin of Reactionists it has
drawn from under the feet of industry the national ground on which it stood.
All old-established national industries have been destroyed or are daily
being destroyed ... In place of the old local and national seclusion and
self-sufficiency, we have intercourse in every direction, universal interdepen-
dence of nations. As in material, so also in intellectual production. The
intellectual creations of individual nations become common property.
National one-sidedness and narrow-mindedness become more and
more impossible, and from the numerous national and local literatures,
there arises a world literature.*
(Karl Marx, The Manifesto of the Communist Party, 1848)

*In our world today economic competition between nations is in fact between
each nation's large enterprises and enterprise groups. A nation's economic
might is concentrated and manifested in the economic power and international competitiveness of its large enterprises and groups. International
economic confrontations in reality show that if a country has several large*

> *enterprises or groups it will be able to maintain a certain market share and hold an assured position in the world economic order. America, for example, relies on General Motors, Boeing, Du Pont and a batch of other multinational companies. Japan relies on six large enterprise groups and Korea relies on ten large commercial enterprise groupings. In the same way now and in the next century our nation's position in the international economic order will be to a large extent determined by the position of our nation's large enterprises and groups.*
>
> (Wu Bangguo, member of the Chinese State Council, quoted in *Economic Daily*, 1 August 1998)

> *If you outnumber the enemy by ten to one, surround them; by five to one, attack them; by two to one, divide them. If you are equally matched, be good and skillful in battle. If the enemy forces outnumber yours, retreat.*
>
> (Sun Wu, 1996)

THE PAST

It is impossible to appreciate the nature of the intense debates within China about large firms and China's entry to the WTO without understanding the long historical perspective against which the debates are conducted. China's political leaders almost always make reference to this background in discussing these issues. For example, in June 2000 Jiang Zemin held long talks with Lee Kuan Yew, former Prime Minister of Singapore, in the Great Hall of the People. The main topic was globalization. However, in discussing this issue, Jiang talked at great length about China's economic achievements prior to the European Industrial Revolution and about the achievements of China's ancient philosophers. China's enterprise managers and even young, commercially-oriented Chinese people typically use this background as a frame of reference. Despite the explosive growth of international business and ideas, the nation remains an immensely important and enduring frame of reference.

CHINA'S LONG SUPERIORITY

In 1997, *Life* magazine commissioned dozens of editors and experts to compile a list of the 100 most important people of the millennium for its September 1997 issue. It concluded: 'Westerners ... have done a disproportionate amount of global moving and shaking ... All but 17 [of the 100] are of European extraction; only 10 are women. This reflects not the biases of *Life*'s editors and expert advisors but the socio–political realities of the past thousand years' (quoted in Frank, 1998: 12). The overwhelmingly predominant view among Western scholars is that Europe began to significantly overtake Asia in the late Middle Ages in terms of social organization and economic development, and that this process led inexorably to the Industrial Revolution. The pioneering work of Joseph Needham in the field of technical progress (Needham, 1954–) and the research of numerous Chinese scholars in the sphere of economic history (see especially Li Bozhong, 1986, and Xu Dixin and Wu Chengming, 2000), demonstrate that the reality was quite different.

For long periods, the Chinese state was able to unite the vast territory of China into a single integrated market. In the eighteenth century, Father Du Halde, the Belgian Jesuit priest wrote:

> [T]he particular riches of every province, and the ability of transporting mer-
> chandise by means of rivers and canals, have rendered the empire always very
> flourishing ... The trade carried on within China is so great, that all of Europe
> cannot be compared therewith. (Quoted in Ho Ping-ti, 1959: 199)

The state provided a framework of law and order and necessary property rights within which powerful long-term economic development took place and was matched by corresponding technical progress.

Joseph Needham's pioneering research has documented the enormous techni-cal advances made in medieval China. From the tenth to the thirteenth century, China set out along the path of the 'Second Industrial Revolution' well before Europe. The list of technical innovations independently developed in China includes such items as the windmill, canal lock gates, mechanical clockwork, power transmission by driving belt, water-powered metallurgical blowing engines, and hemp-spinning machines, gear wheels, numerous naval inventions (for example, the stern-post rudder, watertight compartments), and water-pow-ered trip hammers for forges (Needham, 1965: 222–4). A key feature of industrial advance in the European Middle Ages was the crank: '[T]he powers of the crank were widely used and appreciated throughout the Chinese Middle Ages. For 3–400 years before the time of Marco Polo it was employed in textile machinery for silk-reeling and hemp-spinning, in agriculture for rotary winnowing and water-powered flour-sifting, in metallurgy for the hydraulic blowing-engine, and in such humble uses as the well-windlass' (Needham, 1965: 224). Although the pace of technical progress slowed down after China's medieval 'industrial revo-lution', a steady stream of significant technical advances was made thereafter through until the nineteenth century (Xu Dixin and Wu Chengming, 2000), without making the leap to a full-fledged modern 'Industrial Revolution'.

These technological developments were stimulated by powerful long-term growth of both domestic and international trade. Far from Europe dominating the long-term development of the world economy from the late Middle Ages onwards, Europe had little to sell that Chinese people wished to buy until well into the nineteenth century. The persistent pattern of international exchange over many centuries, right up to the early nineteenth century, was Chinese export of manufactured goods in return for specie, especially silver.

For around 1000 years, China constituted the centre of the world economy (Frank, 1998). In the late eighteenth China alone produced around one-third of global industrial output, and South Asia around one-quarter (Table 14-1). The period from the mid-nineteenth to the late twentieth can be viewed as a relatively

TABLE **14-1 Share of World Manufacturing Output, 1750–1998** (%)

Region/Country	1750	1900	1953	1980	1998
West	18.2	77.4	74.6	57.8	57.9
China	32.8	6.2	2.3	5.0	6.8
Japan	3.8	2.4	2.9	9.1	16.4
India/Pakistan	24.5	1.7	1.7	2.3	1.5
Others	20.7	12.3	18.5	25.8	17.4
Total	100.0	100.0	100.0	100.0	100.0

SOURCES: Huntington (1996: 86); World Bank (World Bank, 2000: 252–3)

brief intermission in the long-term position of China and, to a lesser extent, South Asia, as the centre of the world economy.

The textile industry was much the most important in traditional China, as it was in early modern Europe. Towards the end of the Ming dynasty (1368–1644), cotton replaced hemp and silk as the principal fabric for daily wear. The spinning and weaving of cloth became the largest handicraft industry (Xu Dixin and Wu Chengming, 2000: 213). By the early nineteenth century, there were around 60–70 million peasant households engaged in the occupation as a subsidiary activity to farming (Xu Dixin and Wu Chengming, 2000: 217). Around one-half of the cloth was for self-consumption and one-half for sale on the market. Of the marketed cloth, it is estimated that around 15 per cent entered long-distance trade.

By the early Qing (1644–1911), in the late seventeenth and early eighteenth century, there were many examples of large-scale businesses. Many of these were in the metallurgical industries. In the iron industry many large-scale private enterprises emerged as the market economy expanded. One of the largest was the Guangdong merchant, Ho Xi. In the early eighteenth century, he was recorded as owning 64 iron mines employing 130 000 workers (Xu Dixin and Wu Chengming, 2000: 251). In the manufacture of iron from iron ore, there were several examples of large iron works that employed two or three thousand workers (Xu Dixin and Wu Chengming, 2000: 250). Large copper mines also often employed several thousand workers (Xu Dixin and Wu Chengming, 2000: 267). One report even records a copper mine in which as many as 700 000 were employed (Xu Dixin and Wu Chengming, 2000: 280). Although this is thought to have been somewhat exaggerated, there are many reliable reports from the early Qing, of copper mines with many thousands of employees. In the coal industry, there are frequent references to large mines with many hundreds or even several thousand employees (Xu Dixin and Wu Chengming, 2000: 289–92, 298). However, examples of large-scale businesses were not confined to the metals and mining sector.

In the porcelain industry in the sixteenth century, Jingdezhen was reported to have up to 50 000 people employed in the different branches of the industry. Most of these were employed in private kilns, with around 100–200 employees per kiln (Xu Dixin and Wu Chengming, 2000: 314). In the salt fields of Sichuan there were many large businesses. Reliable evidence from the early nineteenth century records that in the large saltworks at Fushun and Jianwei, there were 'several hundred thousand' employees and in the smaller ones, 'several tens of thousands' (Xu Dixin and Wu Chengming, 2000: 338). In the late eighteenth century, there were reported to be about 5000 seagoing ships in the ports of Shanghai and Zhapu, with a total weight estimated at around 550 000 tons. Large merchants were reported to own fleets of more than 100 ships employing over 2000 people (Xu Dixin and Wu Chengming, 2000: 364).

Jiangnan was much the most developed area of China in the late Ming and early Qing. This is the Delta Region of the Yangtze River. In 1815 it had a population of around 26 million (Li Bozhong, 1986), out of a total Chinese population of around 330 million (McEvedy and Jones, 1978: 167). This compares with a European population in 1820 of around 190 million, including 31 million in France, 25 million in Germany, and 14 million in Great Britain (Cipolla, 1973b: 747). By the end of the seventeenth century Jiangnan was the world's biggest exporter of textiles and fibres and was more highly commercialized and urbanized than any other part of the world (Li Bozhong, 1986). Over many centuries Jiangnan's agriculture became steadily more intensified, with improvements in yields per crop, increases in multiple-cropping and rising real value of output per unit of farmland (Li Bozhong, 1986: 4–16).

By the late sixteenth century textiles had become the largest single part of the Jiangnan industrial economy. Nanjing was the centre of the silk industry. In the 1840s there were nearly 200 000 people engaged in the industry, with more than 35 000 looms (Li Bozhong, 1986: 21). Songjiang prefecture was the most highly developed part of China in terms of the production of cotton cloth for the market, and Suzhou, the country's most important commercial centre, 'teemed with cloth merchants and was also a dyeing centre' (Xu Dixin and Wu Chengming, 2000: 171). During the Qing about 90 per cent of the marketed cotton cloth produced in Jiangnan was exported to other parts of China or abroad. In the eighteenth century, the fastest growth rates of exports were to Europe: between 1786 and 1798, the export of 'Nankeens' (cloth woven in Nanjing and other places in Jiangnan) to Western Europe and the Americas increased almost fivefold (Li Bozhong, 1986: 27).

The level of urbanization in Jiangnan in the late eighteenth century may have been as high as 35–45 per cent, if the residents of small towns are included (Li Bozhong, 1986: 51). Around 5000 sea-going ships were based in Jiangnan, with a tonnage that was 2.8 times that of British ships of all kinds in 1700 (Li Bozhong, 1986: 53). The proportion of people who obtained some kind of education was 'very high by pre-modern standards', with a relatively high fraction of ordinary workers educated to a basic level. Jiangnan's farmers and craftsmen, were 'full of commercial awareness', and 'organized their production with an eye to the changing markets'. Its entrepreneurs 'organized their business activities in order to maximize profits' (Li Bozhong, 1986: 58).

Until the full flowering of the European Industrial Revolution, China remained the world's most powerful industrial and commercial region. The famous reply of the Emperor Qian Long to George III's request in 1793 to open China to free trade was based on the reality of China's long-term position at the centre of global civilization:

> I do not forget the lonely remoteness of your island cut off from the world by intervening wastes of sea ... My capital is the hub and centre about which all quarters of the globe revolve ... Our Celestial Empire possesses all things in prolific abundance and lacks no products within its own borders. There was therefore no need to import the manufactures of outside barbarians in exchange for our own produce. But as the tea, silk, and porcelain which the Celestial Empire produces are absolute necessities to European nations and to yourselves, we have permitted as a mark of favour, that foreign *hongs* should be established at Canton, so that your wants be supplied and your country thus participates in our beneficence. (Quoted in Schurmann and Schell, 1967: 103–4).

Within only a few decades of this proud response, China was to begin a dramatic process of political and economic decline, and humiliation before the world. The end of each Chinese dynasty had typically coincided with a prolonged period of civil disorder and serious economic downturn. However, few previous collapses had been so prolonged as this one. Moreover, this time the collapse took place alongside the explosive growth of economic and military power of Europe, followed by the USA, and then Japan, on China's very doorstep. China's relative position deteriorated at high speed. In the late eighteenth century China had produced around one-third of global industrial output. By the mid-twentieth century, its share had shrunk to only one-fiftieth of the global total (Table 14-1).

CHINA'S HUMILIATION

The Opium Wars. Much the most significant episode in China's turbulent history from the mid-nineteenth to the mid-twentieth century was the initial penetration of China by the Western powers through the Opium Wars. The immediate cause of the war was the destruction of opium stores by the Chinese government in January 1841, which was attempting to eradicate the import of large quantities of opium by British merchants. The prosecution of a war to defend the opium trade caused great controversy in Britain. W. E. Gladstone commented: 'A war more unjust in its origin, a war more calculated to cover this country with permanent disgrace, I do not know and have not read of' (quoted in Rodzinski, 1984: 181). The hostilities lasted a year and were concluded with the signing of the famous Treaty of Nanjing. The Treaty forced the Chinese government to agree to open up five ports to British trade and residence, and to cede Hong Kong to the British. It also required the Chinese government to cede control over the tariff system to the British. This effectively entailed the loss of tariff autonomy for almost a century. There was no mention in the treaty of the principal direct cause of the war, namely the opium question. The opium trade with Hong Kong as its base 'flourished splendidly in the decades following the Nanking Treaty' (Rodzinski, 1984: 184). The terms extracted from the Chinese at Nanjing were extended by the Treaty of Bogues in 1843. The treaty called for the application of the 'most-favoured-nation' principle. One commentator has described this as 'a device by which every nation thereafter could secure for itself any privilege which had been extorted by some other power from China by force, or tricked from her by fraud, without having to assume the moral responsibility for the method by which the concession had been obtained' (quoted in Rodzinski, 1984: 184). The First Opium War was followed by a second 'Opium War' from 1856 to 1860, which culminated in the conclusion of the Treaty of Tianjin. This resulted in the Chinese government agreeing to open up a further 11 ports to international trade.

The significance of the Unequal Treaties was far-reaching. They ushered in 'a century of degradation and ignominious humiliation, bitterly resented by the Chinese to the present' (Rodzinski, 1984: 184). They led the way to China's transformation into a semi-colony. China's humiliation and its inability to respond to the 'challenge' of the West led to anguished reflection among China's intellectuals and policy makers that lasts to this day. Having defeated the Chinese government, the Western powers now turned to support them, assisting China's rulers to defeat the massive Taiping Rebellion, which lasted from 1856 to 1864. The Manchu rulers were 'well on the way to becoming subservient tools to be employed for the extension of foreign control, thus obviating the necessity for direct rule' (Rodzinski, 1984: 206). The Taiping Rebellion caused a net loss of life of more than 30 million people (Ho Ping-ti, 1959: 275). China's population is estimated to have declined from 433 million in 1851 to just 349 million in 1871, a decline of over 80 million people (Perkins, 1968: 212).

The Sino–Japanese War. Following abortive efforts by the government to instigate a 'self-strengthening' movement in the 1870s and 1880s, foreign penetration took a step further in the 1890s. The immediate catalyst was the Sino–Japanese war, fought in 1894–95. The war concluded with the Treaty of Shimonoseki. The main provision was the right of Japanese to engage in manufacturing operations in the Treaty Ports. This right automatically accrued to the other nations under the terms of the 'most-favoured-nation' arrangements. It also resulted in the ceding of significant pieces of territory to Japan, including Taiwan and the Liaotong Peninsula, as well as allowing *de facto* Japanese control of Korea. The defeat by Japan was deeply humiliating. While Japan had responded to the Western 'challenge' with rapid state-led modernization, China had failed to modernize, and was now militarily weaker than the former offshore island: 'It had finally revealed the total bankruptcy of policies, followed for the preceding thirty years, of limited modernization and subservience to the foreign powers. It also showed how deeply the rot had set in throughout the entire Ch'ing administration, including its armed forces, thus rendering the country's defence almost impossible' (Rodzinski, 1984: 227–8). In the late 1890s each of the main imperialist powers developed their own 'concessions' and 'spheres of influence' in different regions, including rights to build railways, to develop mines, and leasing significant pieces of territory in that region, within which foreign investment from the respective country would be concentrated.

The Boxer Rebellion. The national humiliation led to the formation in 1899 of the *Yi He Tuan*, the 'Group of Righteous and Harmonious Fists' (Boxers), who led a fast-growing movement to 'Extirpate the Foreigners', and occupied Beijing in June 1900. A powerful expeditionary force marched on Beijing, and defeated the ill-armed Boxer rebels, indulging in 'many days of looting and rapine' (Rodzinski, 1984: 245). There followed several months of 'pacification' of North China, 'turning much of it into a foodless wasteland and causing the death of countless Chinese, thousandfolds more than the 242 foreigners who had been slain in the summer of 1900' (Rodzinski, 1984: 245).

The 1911 Revolution and Warlordism. The Qing dynasty collapsed in 1911. After a brief attempt to establish a democratic regime, power was seized by Yuan Shikai's military dictatorship, which lasted until his death in 1916. This was in turn followed by a period of political anarchy, the so-called 'Warlord' period. Japan used the outbreak of the First World War as the excuse to demand further concessions from the new Chinese government, the so-called Twenty-One Demands of January 1915. Japan demanded that China grant them the right to the German concessions in Shandong province, and extend the concessions already granted to them in Manchuria and Inner Mongolia. Their demand included also the appointment of Japanese 'advisors' in the Chinese government in political, financial and military matters, joint Sino–Japanese control of the police force, and the establishment of a mutually owned arms industry: 'The aim was transparently obvious, the transformation of China first into a protectorate, and then into an exclusively Japanese colony, along the pattern which the Japanese imperialists had followed in Korea' (Rodzinski, 1984: 267). Yuan Shikai accepted the demands within the forty-eight hours deadline demanded by Japan. On the conclusion of the First World War, the Versailles Treaty confirmed Japanese 'rights' in China, won through the Twenty-One Demands. This provoked tremendous anger within China. There were widespread demonstrations throughout urban areas on 4 May, giving birth to a much wider movement for China's cultural re-birth, the 'May Fourth Movement'.

The 1927 Revolution. China's collapse into warlordism continued unabated for a full decade after the death of Yuan Shikai. The 1920s saw the birth of the Chinese Communist Party (CCP) (1921) and the Kuomintang (KMT) (1924), both of which initially declared themselves to be socialist parties, and initially cooperated with each other. The period 1925–7 witnessed a growing intensity of anti-foreign feeling and a sharply increasing militancy among the urban workforce. On 19 June 1925 a workers' demonstration in Canton was machine-gunned by British and French troops, killing over 50 people and wounding hundreds more, inflaming anti-foreign sentiment (Rodzinski, 1986: 296). The foreign powers increased their military strength in China. By 1927 there were 45 foreign naval vessels and 30000 troops in Shanghai (Rodzinski, 1986: 310). In April 1927 antiforeign riots in Nanjing instigated bombardment of the city by British and American warships. In 1926/7 three different attempts at a mass uprising were instigated by the CCP in Shanghai, culminating in a massive uprising in 1927 which took control of the entire city. Emboldened by the powerful foreign military presence, the KMT turned on its former allies and massacred large numbers of workers and CCP members, initially in Shanghai, but spreading to other major cities. The CCP was forced to retreat to its base areas in the countryside. There followed an intense period of military struggle between the CCP and KMT, with immense loss of life, culminating in the virtual defeat of the CCP in 1934.

Japanese Invasion of China. In September 1931, Japan put into effect carefully laid plans to conquer Northeastern China. Within a few days, the Japanese army had conquered the whole of the vast territory of 'Manchuria', constituting the entire northeast of China. The KMT appealed to the League of Nations to oppose Japan's action, but the League simply recommended that Manchuria, a large part of Chinese territory, should be allowed 'autonomous' status. This amounted to *de facto* recognition of Japan's occupation of Manchuria. Japanese plans to incorporate China into the 'Greater East Asian Co-Prosperity Sphere' were taken a step further in 1937 with a full-scale invasion of the remainder of China. A bloody war followed including the notorious 'Rape of Nanjing', in which casualties are estimated to have been as high as 300000 deaths (Rodzinski, 1986: 347). By the end of 1938, Japan had consolidated its control of over most of China's major cities and main lines of communication. The Western powers did nothing to aid China against the Japanese invasion. Despite fierce resistance from the CCP, which grew rapidly again during the anti-Japanese struggle, Japan remained in control of China until its defeat in 1945. It is estimated that at least 20 million people died in the Sino–Japanese war of 1937–45 (Ho Ping-ti, 1959: 252).

Civil War. As the Second World War drew to a close, the CCP tried to establish good relations with the USA. In January 1945 Mao Zedong wrote to President Roosevelt requesting that he meet with himself and Zhou Enlai. The request was rejected and the USA began a sustained period of intervention in China's internal affairs. Upon the defeat of Japan, the US began a programme of large-scale financial and logistical support for the KMT in the civil war that began shortly after Japan's defeat. Immediately on the conclusion of war, the USA airlifted large numbers of KMT soldiers into key positions. By the end of 1945, the USA had over 100000 troops stationed in China, only withdrawing finally in April 1946. The USA provided around $4 billion worth of aid to the KMT in 1945–6 (Rodzinski, 1986: 382), a calculation which does not include the cost of US-provided transport for the KMT troops or the large US missions that trained huge numbers of KMT troops. By April 1948 a further $2 billion had been provided to the KMT to aid it in the civil war (Rodzinski, 1986: 386).

From 1945 to 1949 there took place a ferocious civil war, with huge loss of life on both sides and among the civilian population. Despite massive US support for the KMT, in 1949 the Chinese Communist Party emerged victorious, and the KMT fled to the island of Taiwan.

China in 1949. The century from the 1840s to the 1940s was one of immense suffering and humiliation for the Chinese people. Their country was wracked with internal military and political struggle. The country was turned into a semi-colony for many decades. A large part of the country was a part of the Japanese empire for a decade and a half, and the whole of it (apart from the base areas held by the resisting forces) was part of the Japanese empire for a decade. The Western powers intervened militarily in China on numerous occasions but failed to oppose Japan's invasion of China. China suffered huge losses of life in the anti-Japanese war, in civil war and through regular famines.

Over the whole period from the Opium Wars through to 1949, the Chinese economy grew at a snail's pace, estimated at only around 0.4 per cent per annum (Swamy, 1979: 31). For a brief period in the twentieth century, the Treaty Ports provided a relatively safe haven for both Chinese and foreign capital. Modern industrial output in these restricted areas grew quite rapidly from 1911 to the early 1930s. However, even in this period the overall performance of the Chinese economy was weighed down by the dominant position of agriculture and the traditional non-farm economy. The most reliable estimates of *per capita* average annual growth from 1911 to 1933 range from only 0.5 per cent (Perkins, 1969: 36) to a maximum of around 1.0–1.4 per cent (Rawski, 1989: 330). This performance placed China among the ranks of the slowest-growing countries in the world.

In 1933, after 100 years of opening up to the outside world China remained a backward and deeply impoverished country. Unlike the optimistic scenario predicted by Marx, China's forcible opening up to the global economy was not followed by rapid growth and economic development. Rather, one hundred years later, two-thirds of China's national income was generated by agriculture (Feuerwerker, 1968: 9). The industrial sector produced less than one-tenth of national output, and three-quarters of industrial output came from the traditional handicraft sector; 79 per cent of total employment was in the farm sector, working almost entirely in a non-mechanized fashion, hardly changed for hundreds of years (Feuerwerker, 1968: 7). J. L. Buck's study of the Chinese farm economy in the early 1930s found that death rates were 27 per thousand, compared with 10–12 per thousand in the advanced economies (Buck, 1968: 388). Buck estimated that infant mortality rates were around 190 per 1000 live births, and that less than 60 per cent of the persons born alive survived their tenth year. This 'terrific mortality rate' in the early years was 'largely due to the ravages of contagious and infectious diseases' which continued 'virtually unchecked' (Buck, 1968: 392).

Not only had China achieved insignificant economic and social progress, but the Western powers had grown explosively. First Britain had industrialized, then the Continental countries and the USA. By 1900, the West had increased its share of world industrial output from less than one-fifth in the eighteenth century to almost three-fifths by the early twentieth century. China had shrunk to a mere minnow in terms of global economic and political power, its share of global industrial output shrinking to a mere 2–3 per cent in the early 1950s (Table 14–1). China's total industrial output in the 1930s placed it on a par with a small European country, but with a vastly larger population. In *per capita* terms it was one of the world's least developed countries.

CHAIRMAN MAO: CHINA STANDS UP

On the establishment of the People's Republic of China in 1949, Chairman Mao made his famous speech, ushering in a new era in China's history which he hoped would restore China to its rightful place at the centre of world history:

> The Chinese have always been a great courageous and industrious nation; it is only in modern times that they have fallen behind. And that was entirely due to oppression and exploitation by foreign imperialism and domestic reactionary governments ... Ours will no longer be a nation subject to insult and humiliation. We have stood up. (Mao Zedong, 1949: 16–17)

After two decades of economic planning, dramatic progress was made towards Chairman Mao's goal. China's industrial growth rate was one of the fastest among developing countries and by the late 1970s, China's economic structure had been completely transformed. Agriculture's share of national product had fallen to just 31 per cent (World Bank, 1981a: 138). Death rates had fallen to an officially reported figure of under 7 per thousand and infant mortality had fallen to only 56 per thousand (World Bank, 1981a: 168). Life expectancy had reached 64 years (World Bank, 1981a: 174). These were remarkable achievements in comparison with most developing countries. Moreover, these achievements had been made despite deep hostility from the USSR after 1960, hostility from the advanced capitalist countries for much of the period, and deep hostility from the USA in particular for most of the period.

However, deep problems remained. China's highly centralized political system permitted Chairman Mao to put into effect his highly idealistic policies for social transformation during the Great Leap Forward and the Cultural Revolution. Each of these had serious detrimental effects on the economy. The damage to Chinese agriculture caused by the Great Leap led to as many as 25–30 million deaths through famine. The administrative planning system caused the growth process to be extremely wasteful, based around high rates of accumulation and a vicious circle of unbalanced development with high priority for heavy industry. The rise in China's incremental capital output ratio was 'unusually steep' (World Bank, 1981b: 50). The long-run growth rate of real *per capita* consumption was 'barely above the average for other low-income countries', and 'well below the middle-income countries' average' (World Bank, 1981b: 52). At the end of the Maoist period, the World Bank estimates that there were 260 million people below the poverty line (World Bank, 1992: 140), which was almost certainly above the number in the mid-1950s. The gap in China's technical level with the advanced economies had widened considerably since the 1950s, due to the extremely low level of foreign trade (amounting to less than 1 per cent of the world total in the late 1970s) (World Bank, 1981a: 148), the total absence of foreign investment, the absence of incentives in the planned economy at the enterprise level to invest in useful technical progress and the serious damage done to the higher educational system during the Cultural Revolution.

Chairman Mao's legacy was an ambiguous one. On the one hand China had truly regained its national pride and hugely advanced the mass of the population's 'human capital'. It was greatly admired by many developing countries for its health and educational achievements, and for the seriousness of its intentions to eliminate inequality in life chances. On the other hand, the period deepened China's isolation from the world, left it still very far behind the advanced economies, and caused deep social scars from the immense socio-economic upheavals and the associated suffering.

THE RUSSIAN DISASTER

The reform of the Communist system of political economy followed fundamentally different paths in the former USSR and China.[1] Russia's recent history provides a mirror image to China's, and a constant warning of the dire possibilities that might face China if incorrect policies are chosen.

A crucial part of the different path was the influence on Gorbachev of the 'New Thinking'. The ideas of the New Thinking were strongly influenced by the fast-growing transatlantic contacts that developed in the late 1980s, with a stream of leading policy advisors spending time at major US institutions. They absorbed mainstream US ideas in the social sciences and translated these into policy initiatives that deeply influenced the path that Soviet reform took. These ideas were based around deep hostility to the state.

At the heart of this process was the conception that the Soviet system needed comprehensive political reform, amounting to nothing less than the destruction of the old state apparatus. This was the essence of *perestroika*. Miller's meticulous study of Gorbachev concludes: 'The prima facie evidence is compelling, that he deliberately made trouble for the Party: that he criticized it, encouraged opposition to it, weakened it and then cast it aside' (Miller, 1993: 127). This political revolution, led from above, was almost universally applauded in the West: 'The mono-organizational Party has been broken and there seems little chance of such a power being reimposed ... This surely was Gorbachev's finest achievement' (Miller, 1993: 240).

In the economic sphere, the concept of a 'Third Way' was increasingly ridiculed, with China held up as an example of the bankruptcy of this approach. The Soviet authors of a radical plan for a 'big bang' argued: ' The time for gradual transformations has turned out to have been missed, and the ineffectiveness of partial reforms has been proved by the experiences of Hungary, Yugoslavia, Poland and China' (quoted in Åslund, 1991: 207). Even at the end of the Gorbachev period, the IMF and the World Bank had begun to have a powerful impact on Russia's policy making processes. Their combined report in 1990 strongly influenced the thinking of Gorbachev's policy advisors (IMF/World Bank, 1990). The report considered 'carefully' the case for a gradual system, but came down firmly on the side of radical reform:

> The prospect of a sharp fall in output and rapid increase in prices in the early stage of a radical reform is daunting. In advocating the more radical approach, we are well aware of the concerns of those who recommend caution ... A recovery of output should be able to get under way within two years or so ... Further strong growth of output could be expected for the remainder of the decade and beyond (IMF/World Bank, 1990: 18–19).

Following the disintegration of the USSR, the new Russian government, led by Yeltsin, and closely advised by the IMF and the World Bank, eventually was able to put into place the programme of rapid and comprehensive economic system reform.

Comprehensive price reform was put into effect on 1 January 1992. Introducing the programme, President Yeltsin commented: 'The time has come for resolute, strict, unhesitating action ... The one-time transition to market prices is a difficult, forced, but necessary measure ... Things will be worse for about half a year ... But the economy will stabilize and the standard of living will gradually improve by the autumn of 1992.' (quoted in Nolan, 1995: 269). At the same time, Russia's import regime was almost completely liberalized. Quantitative restrictions were abolished and tariffs slashed to only 5-15 per cent for most products (Nolan, 1995: 270).

Over a period of just two years, a process of mass privatization took place, at the end of which around 70 per cent of state assets had been transferred to the private sector. This was trumpeted by British economist Richard Layard as 'the fastest privatization in human history' (quoted in Nolan, 1995: 276). President Yeltsin expressed the hope that the privatization would 'create hundreds of millions of owners, not hundreds of millionaires' (quoted in Nolan, 1995: 275). This populist sentiment echoed that of the Shatalin 500 Day programme of 1990: 'The [privatisation] programme gives equal chances to everybody ... [P]ractically everyone, even if he doesn't have any considerable initial capital, will have an opportunity to get his share of the national wealth' (quoted in Nolan, 1995: 78–9). Mass privatization took place in the midst of an economic collapse, without any preparation, with completely inadequate legal institutions and with entrenched 'insiders' able to control the whole process. The result was a process of 'legalized theft' which recalled the epoch of 'primitive capitalist accumulation' in early modern Europe. The resulting massively unequal class structure will form the 'unique genetic code' of Russian capitalism for decades to come.

Instead of the hoped-for brief period of economic decline to be followed by rapid recovery and sustained growth, the disintegration of the Russian state, pursued as an explicit policy objective by the Western governments, combined with the destruction of the economic system through 'shock therapy', produced a disastrous environment of 'state desertion', insecure property rights and collapsed investment. The result was a vicious circle of economic collapse, that is still not exhausted. Between 1990 and 1998, Russia's gross domestic investment fell by an average of almost 15 per cent per annum (World Bank, 2000: 251). Cumulative inflows of foreign direct investment into Russia between 1993 and 1998 totalled a mere $15 billion, compared with $90 billion in China in the same period (UNCTAD, 1999: 479–80). From 1990 to 1998, Russian GDP fell by around one-half (EBRD, 1998: 225). By the late 1990s, its level of GNP *per capita* had fallen to around the level of the Philippines, Egypt and Jamaica, only around one-half of that of Mexico or Brazil (World Bank, 2000: 230–1). Russia was now truly in the Third World. Alongside the collapse of the economy went a collapse of the social fabric, resembling that in China in the late nineteenth and early twentieth century. Now it was Russia's turn to experience deep national humiliation. It also experienced deep pain. The extent of poverty hugely increased in the 1990s (Nolan, 1995: 296). The mortality situation worsened dramatically. Between 1991 and 1993, the crude death rate rose by 26 per cent, an unprecedented phenomenon in peacetime in the modern world.

Instead of the replacement of a corrupt bureaucracy with a transparent, open and democratic government, the collapse of Communism in Russia was followed by the establishment of a far more corrupt and incompetent government than that which it replaced. The tiny group of powerful businessmen who benefited massively from the 'wild capitalism' of Russia's privatization rapidly consolidated their economic and political position (Freeland, 2000). So strong had their control of the political process become that they were able effortlessly to propel a virtually unknown politician, Vladimir Putin, into the position of President. The 'democratic' right to a vote had been rendered meaningless, since no candidate was able to offer any realistic hope of resolving Russia's now intractable problems. For the mass of Russians, the sense of powerlessness, the massive increase in poverty, the deep decline in living standards, the greatly increased insecurity and the colossal decline in national power, produced a deep psychological crisis. One group of researchers concluded: 'The crisis which the country is in, is not only economic and political, but also socio-psychological. Such psychological phenomena are no less precise indicators of the crisis than inflation and the fall in production' (quoted in Nolan, 1995: 297).

Deng Xiaoping: Opening Up and Advancing

When Russian Premier Gorbachev visited China in the Spring of 1989, during the Tiananmen demonstration, the almost universal view outside China, and a widespread view inside China, was that China's leaders ought to follow the

Russian model. Gorbachev was hailed by the demonstrators as showing the correct way for China to reform its system of political economy. He was regarded as having identified the correct 'sequence' of system reform: first tackle the problem of the political system and then put into place rapid economic reform. Thousands of Chinese protesting students dropped 'little bottles' ('*xiaoping*', or 'little bottles', is a play on Deng Xiaoping's name) indicating their judgement that their leadership was incompetent compared with that of the USSR.

Under Deng's leadership, China's reforms followed a fundamentally different approach from that in the former USSR (Nolan, 1995). On the political side, despite growing pressure from inside and outside China, the leadership resisted demands for radical reform. Absolute priority was given to the maintenance of political stability. This was manifested in a succession of campaigns to counter 'spiritual pollution' and enforce inner-party discipline, and most notably in the bloody suppression of the student occupation of Tiananmen Square in 1989. Memories of China's national humiliations, of political disintegration in the late nineteenth and early twentieth century, and the anarchy of the Cultural Revolution, were deeply embedded in the minds of the leadership. In his key speech of 1979, Deng Xiaoping set the tone for the coming period:

> Talk about democracy in the abstract will inevitably lead to the unchecked spread of ultra-democracy and anarchism. To the complete disruption of political stability and unity, and to the total failure of our modernization programme. If this happens then the decade of struggle against Lin Biao and the Gang of Four will have been in vain. China will once again be plunged into chaos, division, retrogression and darkness, and the Chinese people will be deprived of all hope. (Quoted in Nolan, 1995: 164)

Deng Xiaoping recognized that bureaucracy was a 'major and widespread problem' in the political life of both the CCP and the state. Under his leadership China put into effect a massive programme of technical upgrading and slimming down of the bureaucracy. Despite this, corruption remained a deep-rooted problem, which the leadership struggled to overcome throughout the reform period.

China's economic reforms comprehensively eschewed the orthodox path advocated by the international institutions, by most foreign scholars and by an increasingly vocal group of neo-liberal domestic policy advisors. The international economy was only gradually liberalized. Even at the end of the 1990s, China's indigenous firms remained heavily protected through tariffs and non-tariff barriers. China gradually liberalized the restrictions on foreign direct investment. Through a variety of policies, the government strongly encouraged exports, in the classic 'mercantilist' fashion, just as Britain did during the Industrial Revolution, and the East Asian Newly Industrializing Countries did in the 1970s and 1980s. In every sector, China's reforms were experimental and cautious, beginning with agriculture, extending to the rural non-farm enterprises, then turning to the state-owned industrial enterprises and the financial system. The essence of the reform was gradually to allow the unfolding of market forces and competition. China's cautious, experimental approach to system reform was widely criticized and even held up to ridicule by 'transition experts' such as Jan Prybyla. Writing in 1990 he commented:

> The sad chronicle of China's post-Mao attempt to introduce a modern eco-nomic system contains a useful lesson which others, notably the East Europeans are taking to heart. The lesson is that to address the economic prob-lem in a modern way in the context of a low calibre, inefficient, slothful, wasteful, cronified socialist system, one must go all the way to the market sys-tem, do it quickly, and not stop anywhere on the way. To go part of the way slowly, "crossing the river while groping for stones" as the Dengists put it, is to end up the creek to nowhere. (Quoted in Nolan, 1995: 76)

This cautious, incremental approach to economic reform, combined with absolute priority for political stability produced a result that confounded the orthodox opin-ion. Under Deng Xiaoping, China enjoyed the most successful period of growth in its modern history. It was able to enter an extraordinary period in which there took place a 'virtuous circle' of growth, with high rates of savings and investment, high rates of growth of consumption and final demand, and powerful improve-ments in economic efficiency. China's gross domestic investment grew by 13.4 per cent per annum from 1980 to 1998 (World Bank, 2000: 250–1). China was by far the largest recipient of Foreign Direct Investment among developing and for-mer Communist countries, with 11.1 per cent of the world's total amount by 1997 (UNCTAD, 1999: 477). China's annual average inflow of FDI between 1993 and 1998 was $38 billion, compared with $11 billion for Brazil and just $2.5 billion into Russia (UNCTAD, 1999: 477–80).

By the late 1990s, the state-owned industrial sector had drastically shrunk in terms of its overall relative size, as other institutional forms were allowed to grow and compete. In 1998 the state-owned industrial sector had already declined to just 28 per cent of total industrial output value (SSB, ZTN, 1999: 421–8). The collective sector accounted for 38 per cent, but much of the collective sector was *de facto* private enterprise. Other forms of industrial enterprises, of which for-eign-funded enterprises were the most important, accounted for 34 per cent of total industrial output value. Overall, the private sector (*de facto* and *de jure*) accounted for considerably more than one-half of total industrial output value, a striking testimony to the distance that China's incremental reforms had already travelled.

Between 1980 and 1990, China achieved a growth rate of GDP of 10.2 per cent per annum and a growth rate of industrial output of 11.1 per cent per annum. Between 1990 and 1997, the growth rates increased to 11.1 per cent and 15.4 per cent respectively. Over these two decades, China achieved more rapid growth than any other economy (World Bank, 2000: 250–1). China's export performance in this period was remarkable, with a growth rate of 12 per cent per annum in the 1980s, rising to 15 per cent per annum in the 1990s (Table 14-2). China's share of world exports rose from just one per cent in 1980 to 3 per cent in 1997.

TABLE **14-2 Growth of the Chinese Economy, 1980–97 (% per annum)**

Item	1980–90	1990–7
GDP	10.2	11.1
Industrial value-added	11.1	15.4
Agricultural value-added	5.9	4.3
Export of goods and services	11.5	14.9

SOURCE: World Bank (2000: *World Development Indicators*)

TABLE **14-3 China's World Ranking in the Production of Selected Products, 1949–98**

Item	1949	1957	1978	1998
Cereals	—	—	2	1
Meat	3	—	3	1
Cotton	4	—	3	1
Fruit	—	—	10 (1980)	1
Crude steel	26	9	5	1
Coal	9	5	3	1
Electricity	25	13	7	2
Cement	—	8	4	1
Chemical fibres	—	26	7	2
TV sets	—	—	8	1

SOURCE: SSB, ZTN (1999: 987–9)

TABLE **14-4 China's National Output Compared to the USA and the World, 1998**

Item	Absolute Amount	% of World	% of USA
GNP ($ billion)	923	3.2	11.7
($ PPP billion)	3 984	10.9	50.3
GNP per person ($)	7 50	15.3	2.6
($ PPP)	3 220	51.9	11.0

SOURCE: World Bank (2000: 230–1)

By the late 1990s, China national output in a range of key commodities had surpassed that of all other countries (Table 14-3). Conventional data which convert national product at the official rate of exchange have many well-known problems, such as the departure of the official rate of exchange from a market-determined rate, the large international differences in the prices of non-traded goods and government intervention to determine prices. The World Bank has re-worked conventional estimates of national product by means of 'Purchasing Power Parity' conversion factors, which aim to convert each country's national product using a common set of prices. These revised data suggest that China has risen to become the world's second largest economy (Table 14-4), with a GNP in

1998 that was 10.9 per cent of the global total and over one-half of that of the USA. Measured in PPP dollars, China's national output in 1998 was 36 per cent greater than that of Japan, and 2.3 times larger than that of Germany (World Bank, 2000: 230–1). On this basis, at current growth rates, China could expect to overtake the US as the world's largest economy before 2020.

However, the re-working of national output data with the aim of producing meaningful international comparisons of national product has its own set of problems. These include such well-known difficulties as identifying a meaningful common set of prices for services and the huge differences in output quality between rich and poor countries. The seriousness of these difficulties is sharply revealed by the data on energy efficiency. At the official rate of exchange, China is one of the world's most inefficient users of primary energy, requiring 1.19 kilograms to produce a dollar of national output, which is 4.4 times that of the USA, and five times that of Japan (Table 14-5). However, if energy efficiency is measured in terms of energy required per PPP dollar of national output, the position is completely altered. China instead becomes as energy efficient as the USA and is shown to use only 80 per cent of the energy required to generate a unit of national product in Japan. As one commentator noted: 'The rate [of energy efficiency] based on the estimated real GNP is patently unrealistic: if China would be using the essential input into its economy with efficiency 40 per cent higher than Japan and 50 per cent higher than France and Germany, there would be no

TABLE 14-5 **Comparison of China's Energy Intensity, Using Two Different Methods of Calculation, 1998 (% in brackets)**

| Country | Energy Used per Unit of GDP (Kilograms of Oil Equivalent) | |
	Per Dollar at Official Rate of Exchange	Per PPP dollar
China	1.19 (100)	0.28 (100)
India	1.07 (111)	0.27 (104)
USA	0.27 (441)	0.27 (104)
Japan	0.24 (496)	0.34 (82)

SOURCE: Derived from World Bank (2000: 230–1, 248–9[2])

TABLE 14-6 **Changes in the Welfare of Chinese People, 1980 and 1997**

Item	1980	1997
Private consumption (index)	100	350
Infant mortality (no./1000)	42	32
Child mortality (under 5) (no./1000)	65	39
Life expectancy	68	71
Absolute poverty (million people)	262 (1978)	74 (1996)

SOURCES: World Bank (2000: *World Development Indicators*); World Bank (1992: 140)

need for fundamental reforms!' (Smil, 1993: 72). Unfortunately, estimates based on PPP conversion factors greatly overstate China's national product just as clearly as those based on the official rate of exchange understate it.

Of much greater significance than the growth performance achieved during the Deng Xiaoping era was the resulting improvement in mass welfare (Table 14–6). Real average *per capita* incomes more than tripled in the two decades after Chairman Mao's death. Already low rates of infant and child mortality fell sharply, and already high life expectancy rose even further. One of the most remarkable results of this period of experimental reform, with gradual development of the impact of market reforms, was the massive decline in poverty. It cannot be emphasized sufficiently strongly, that this extraordinary growth performance and enormous improvement in popular welfare was achieved alongside economic policies and with a political structure that were totally different from those that had been advocated by almost the entire body of expert opinion in the international institutions, among international scholars and among many Chinese policy advisors. They stand in the sharpest contrast with the orthodox transition policies pursued in the former USSR, which were followed by dire results in every respect.

Despite the enormous progress made in the senses outlined above, China's huge population and the meagre base from which the modern epoch of accelerated growth began, mean that in *per capita* terms China is still a poor country. Even using PPP data, China's average output per person is still just $3220, only one-half of the world average and a mere 11 per cent of that of the USA (Table 14-4). At the official exchange rate China's output per person is just $750 per person, less than 3 per cent of that of the USA. In 1998, the average income of China's top decile of urban income earners, which totalled around 40 million people, was only $1300 at the official rate of exchange (SSB, ZTN, 1999: 329). Even if one makes a rough re-calculation at PPP dollars of this group, their income *per capita* is still less than $6000. The absolute number of China's population that is living in conditions approaching those of advanced economies is still very small indeed. This reality of poverty is reflected in the relatively low levels of consumption of high-priced consumer goods such as automobiles and personal computers.

By the time of Deng Xiaoping's death in 1997, China had made enormous strides towards resuming its role at the centre of the world economy and polity. It had prospered while the former USSR had disintegrated. It had achieved on a vast scale the same advances that had earlier propelled forward several of its much smaller East Asian neighbours. Its development strategy was distinctively Chinese, not following the universal advice of the international institutions and scholars. China's masses had achieved huge advances in their 'human rights' to live a decent and fulfilled life. China could once again be proud of its role in world affairs. Few world leaders could look back with such pride in their achievements as Deng Xiaoping could do as he approached death.

China's economic growth has been through a number of cycles since the reforms began. In the late 1990s, the average annual growth rate of GNP slowed down. From a peak of over 12 per cent per annum in the mid-1990s, the growth rate declined significantly in the late 1990s, to under 8 per cent per annum (SSB, ZTN, 1999: 57). However, this needs to be put into perspective. The period around the Tiananmen protests in the late 1980s saw an even more severe downturn in the growth rate, only to be followed by the most powerful period of growth that modern China has seen. The growth rate of national product is still high compared to most developing countries. China has avoided the switchback of growth performance that most developing countries have encountered. Moreover, although the late 1990s saw a decline in the growth rate of real average *per capita* consumption, the growth rate was still in the order of 4–5 per cent per annum (SSB, ZTN, 1999: 72), well above the average for other developing countries. Furthermore, China was able to survive the Asian crisis without serious damage to its economic performance. The decline in China's growth rate coincided with the worst crisis that the region as a whole had experienced in modern times. This was a testament to the robust nature of the institutional changes achieved by the Chinese reforms and to the fact that the economy was still only partially integrated with the world economy.

At the end of the 1990s, there were many deep economic problems to be overcome, including further advances in the reform of state-owned enterprises, improvements in the fiscal system and major reforms in the banking system, and measures to tackle the deeply-embedded corruption. However, when Deng Xiaoping died, he did not leave behind him a country with an economic or political crisis. There was no pressing reason for China to depart dramatically from the experimental reform path that it had followed for the previous two decades either in economics or politics. There was no need for China to 'take a gamble' with its whole strategy in the way that was urged upon it by a chorus of advisors. Their advice was closely reminiscent of that given to the leadership of the former USSR in the late 1980s, which led to such disastrous results. This chorus of voices also strongly recalled the views of many internal and external advisors to the Chinese government in the late 1980s, which were resisted after long struggles.

CHINA ENTERS THE WTO: THE SHOCK OF DEFEAT?

THE 'OPTIMISTIC' VIEW

Few commentators dispute that the terms under which China has agreed to enter the WTO will produce great difficulties for China's large enterprises. MSDW's China analyst, Andy Xie, believes that China is likely to experience 'considerable pain during the adjustment period' (Xie, 2000: 6). The former Prime Minister of Singapore, Lee Kuan Yew, believes that China joining the WTO will lead to 'creative destruction of out-dated industrial plants' (Lee Kuan Yew, 2000). Almost all commentators outside China, and many inside the country, welcome this likelihood. They believe that through joining the WTO, the destruction of China's 'value-destroying' large enterprises will liberate capital to infuse the small and medium-sized enterprise sector. Through this process, they believe that China will become 'one of the most important players in the global exchange of goods, services, capital, talent and ideas in the 21st century' (Lee Kuan Yew, 2000).

Many commentators and policy makers outside China, including the US president, as well as many within it, explicitly welcome the possibility of political turmoil stemming from China's entry to the WTO. They hope that through the resulting turbulence, the Chinese Communist Party will be overthrown promoting the 'right kind of political change'. They hope that China will experience the kind of dramatic system change that the former USSR went through in the late 1980s and early 1990s. They believe that only through system collapse can a 'clean sheet' be established for thoroughgoing system reform, including mass privatization. This approach has strong resonances with the debate about reform in the former USSR in the late 1980s and early 1990s. The tone is similarly populist in its promise of huge gains for the mass of the country's citizens from the proposed system change.

The same tone of approval of the destructive effects of international competition invades the language of those involved in the discussions. In the late 1980s and early 1990s it was axiomatic among commentators to talk of the desirability of compressing all the 'pain' of transition into a short period:

- 'If the only cure for a person is to cut off his leg, it is still more humane to perform a single amputation with the necessary anesthesia than to schedule a long-lasting operation and cut off a thin slice every week or month'. (Kornai, 1990: 159–60)

- 'The Polish economy clearly needs a surgical operation to remove the outdated and inefficient industries'. (Gomulka, 1989: 5)

Leading international commentators with a significant input into Chinese policymaking currently echo these slogans. Professor Laurence Lau, of Stanford University, argued: 'It is better to suffer pain for a short period than to drag the pain out over a long period of time' (Lau, 2000).

A major part of the discussion about the impact of the WTO on China has focused on the effect new information technology will have on the economy. At high-level meetings in China in 2000 to evaluate the impact of joining the WTO upon China,[3] there was immense optimism both from many Chinese participants as well as from almost all the non-Chinese participants about the positive impact of the WTO through the rapid penetration of new information technology into China. A wide range of commentators argued that the IT revolution will result in the democratization of economic life and hugely enhanced global opportunities for small firms. The promise is of everyone in China becoming rich through the internet which will expand at high speed after China enters the WTO. There will be a happy marriage of US business interests in information technology with the interests of the mass of Chinese people.

At the meeting of the 21st Century Forum in Beijing in June 2000, Klaus Schwab, President of the World Economic Forum, argued: 'we are witnessing the democratizing [effect] of the information revolution'. Capabilities that 'in the past were possessed only by large and powerful organizations' can now be 'obtained by individuals and small organizations in all walks of life' (Schwab, 2000). He is in no doubt that the net impact on employment in China will be strongly positive: 'These technologies and services can generate many new and rewarding employment opportunities for every nation's citizens'. Experience around the world 'demonstrates beyond any doubt that over time, new information and communications technologies increase the overall level and quality of employment' (Schwab, 2000).

Similar sentiments were expressed at the same meeting by Laurence Lau. He argued that the IT revolution will lead to 'existing demands for goods and services [being] increasingly supplied by new entrants, most of them small and medium-sized start-up firms'. He believes that the IT revolution will cause widespread 'creative destruction' in which 'new firms take away business from the old firms'. Lau believes that in developing countries such as China, there will be 'creation without destruction': 'Developing countries have the ability to leapfrog. There are no vested interests to protect; no existing businesses to be cannibalized; there can be creation without destruction' (Lau, 2000).

In this view, given its massive labour force, with a high level of literacy compared to other developing countries, China can become 'sub-contractor to the world'. There are argued to be huge opportunities for Chinese SMEs to become outsourced suppliers to the world leading systems integrators in almost every sector. Until now, the fastest-growing activities have been in 'old industries', such as garments, plastic products, luggage, sports goods, assembly of electrical goods, and furniture. However, there are opportunities for Chinese SMEs to provide sub-contracting for global systems integrators in a wide range of 'new technology industries', including components and sub-systems for aircraft, heavy electrical equipment, IT hardware and auto components firms, biotechnology research and drugs testing for global pharmaceutical firms, software services for software firms, and local music, TV programmes, advertising and movies for global media companies.

It can even be argued that as this process evolves, so China's myriad SME firms may form a steadily expanding part of the global corporations' 'external firm'. Over time, Chinese people may form a growing proportion of the managers, scientists, engineers and senior officials of globalizing systems integrator firms. Chinese financial institutions may gradually increase their ownership of 'Western' corporations as Chinese income levels rise and pension funds expand their operation. In the long-term, China's weight of population, the high and rising quality of its human resources, and the growing fraction of global output that is produced in China, may cause the gradual 'Sinification' of the world's business system. As China gradually re-assumes its position at the core of the world economy Chinese businesses and employees may transform global capitalism from the 'inside', within the global corporation, and within the 'external firm' that is co-ordinated by the global corporation. In time China may well return to the position at the heart of the business system that it occupied for one thousand years.

In fact, the difficulties of adjustment to the WTO under the terms agreed, may be much greater than such 'optimistic' views, with their populist undertones, suggest. Moreover, the impact on the socio–political environment could be highly de-stabilizing with a potential negative impact on the entire economy.

'CONVENTIONAL' STRUCTURAL ADJUSTMENT

A Painful Adjustment. When China enters the WTO, there will be intense pressure from the high-income countries to apply the rules to which it has agreed. The USA is already strongly pursuing other countries, including Japan, Brazil, India and Mexico, to apply the WTO rules fully, and has made clear its intention forcefully to push China to apply them to the full. China's leaders and negotiators have repeatedly emphasized that they intend carefully to observe the rules by which they have agreed to play. If China did, indeed, apply the rules to which it has signed up, then, as this book has demonstrated, it is very likely that a large fraction of its large-scale industry would not survive the resulting intense competition (Table 14-7).

The revolution in the nature of the global corporation is not only radically changing the nature of the opportunities for Chinese firms, but also the challenges they face. Across a wide range of sectors, from aerospace, complex engineering, pharmaceuticals, oil and petrochemicals, automobiles, IT hardware and software, and telecoms services through to production and retail of the simplest consumer goods, it has become almost impossible to compete directly on the global level playing field with the world's leading 'systems integrators' based in the advanced economies. Moreover, it is extremely difficult to compete head-on

TABLE **14-7 China's Employment Structure, 1998 (million)**

Sector	Employment
Total	699.6
Agriculture	332.3
Mining	7.2
Manufacturing	83.2
Construction	33.3
Wholesale/retail	46.5
Government	11.0
State owned enterprises	88.1
Mining	6.0
Manufacturing	18.8
Wholesale/retail	6.9
Financial services	2.1
Education/culture/media	14.1
Government/party organizations	10.8
Transport/post and telecommunications	5.8

SOURCE: SSB, ZTN (1999: 142–3)

even with the leading globalizing first-tier supplier companies, including such diverse goods and services as aero-engines, avionics systems, auto brake systems, car heating systems, metal cans, plastic bottles, investment banks, insurance, hotels, IT hardware and software, and advertising agencies. On the global 'level playing field', not only China's 'commanding heights' of large state-owned firms, but a wide range of first tier suppliers of goods and services would also find it impossible to compete.

Privatization would do little, if anything, to improve the competitive capability of China's 'national champion' firms in direct competition with the world's leading corporations. The situation that faces China's aspiring 'national champions' is different from that which faced the leading European state-owned firms at the time of their privatization. Even under state ownership, companies like Volkswagen, Repsol, Renault, Aérospatiale, Usinor, Alcatel, Finnemecanica, ENI, BP, Rolls-Royce, British Aerospace, and British Steel, were far more powerful, with much greater technical capabilities, a much more sophisticated portfolio of products, and much greater management skills than are possessed by the commanding heights of the Chinese economy today. Their capability to be rapidly turned into global leaders through radically changed management methods was far greater than is the case for China's 'national champions'. Moreover, the challenges they had to face in the early stages of globalization were far less severe than those that confront Chinese firms now that the global business revolution is well under way.

Instead of being turned into global leaders, like most of the powerful privatized state-owned enterprises in Europe in the 1980s and 1990s, a large fraction of China's 'national champions' face the prospect of, at best, take-over by the multinationals, followed by drastic downsizing and absorption into the production system of the global firm. Many of them will face bankruptcy. There are almost 90 million people employed in China's state-owned enterprises (Table 14-7). It is an open question how many of these will lose their jobs if China's state-owned enterprises are forced to compete rapidly on the global level playing field. It is hard to imagine that the number will be small. We have seen also that there are great uncertainties about the rate at which employment will grow outside the state sector, as well as problems concerning the location and nature of new employment. Moreover, large-scale structural adjustment will certainly be required also in the small and medium-sized sector as well as in agriculture. Coping with these huge structural adjustment issues simultaneously will be extremely difficult. Already, in the late 1990s there were numerous reports of strikes and violence as China's state-owned enterprises begin to downsize.

Some idea of the extent of the structural adjustment that will be required on the global level playing field can be derived from a consideration of the mining industry. China's mining industry employs over seven million people, of which around five million are employed in the coal sector. A large fraction of these work in arduous and dangerous conditions, using only the most primitive equipment. At China's large, modern coal mining company, Shenhua, it is planned that output will rise to over 100 million tons, with no more than 5000 employees.

Under the intense pressure that the WTO will bring, it is technically possible that as mine modernization proceeds, China could eventually produce all of its current coal output, of around 1 billion tons, with just 50 000 miners, instead of the present figure of around 5 million. Lest this be thought too fantastic an idea, it should be borne in mind that the South African mining industry has shed huge amounts of labour as the industry has introduced at high speed the most highly mechanized methods of production. This has been a major factor in the huge increase in unemployment in South Africa in recent years, which is causing a great challenge for political stability in that country (personal communication from Dr Morley Nkosi). In the UK the number of miners declined from 718 000 in 1947 to 230 000 in 1980, and fell to just 13 000 in 1999 (*FT*, 18 April 2000). Output per worker rose from 280 tons in 1947 to 550 tons in 1980 and 2800 tons in 1999 (*FT*, 18 April 2000). The scale of the potential adjustment problems in China's mining industry vastly exceeds those of either South Africa or the UK. The pace at which such adjustment may be required in China is likely to be extremely fast due to the pressure that will be exerted by China's membership of the WTO under the rapid transition to which it has agreed.

China's welfare system is still in its infancy. It is impossible to imagine how the Chinese state can provide suitable welfare provisions for the large number of people who may need assistance. One consequence of the magnitude of the task that may face the Chinese government, is accelerated pressure to privatize the most valuable assets in the state's portfolio. These include most obviously, China's telecoms assets and urban land and public housing. It is thought that these could raise $300–400 billion and $200–250 billion respectively for the Chinese government (Xie, 2000: 6), which 'appear to be sufficient for dealing with the pain of restructuring' (Xie, 2000: 6). These numbers are, however, highly speculative. They need to be treated with great caution.

To some degree, the poorly developed state of China's infrastructure may insulate inland areas from the full impact of structural adjustment, especially in the light industrial sectors. However, in most branches of the capital goods industries, including telecoms equipment, aerospace, automobiles and components, oil and petrochemicals, and power generating equipment, poorly developed infrastructure will provide no relief from intensified competition. Moreover, even in 'basic' capital goods such as steel, as well as in food and fast-moving consumer goods, in services, such as the mass media, retailing, financial services, and hotels, there will be sharply intensified competition in the high value-added parts of the industry. This competition will be greatest in the more highly developed coastal areas, where the bulk of China's higher income earners live. The low value-added 'commodity' parts of these businesses in the hinterland are of little interest to the global giants. They do not provide the basis on which Chinese indigenous firms could generate high profits and challenge the global giants.

IT and the Adjustment Process. Several cautionary points need to be made about the highly optimistic views concerning the impact of the IT revolution on China in the period immediately ahead.

- The IT revolution is already taking place in China. It is fallacious directly to associate this with the terms under which China has agreed to enter the WTO. For example, China had already become the world's largest market for mobile phones, with huge associated infrastructure needs, independently of whether and under what terms, China joined the WTO. Joining the WTO on the terms agreed, could even slow down the rate of progress of the IT revolution in China, since it reduces the incentive for multinationals to manufacture IT products within China as opposed to importing them.

- A major consequence of the IT revolution in China is to provide a potentially vast new frontier for the world's leading IT hardware, software and service firms, almost all of which are headquartered in the advanced economies. The potential benefits to US- and EU-based corporations from the Chinese IT revolution are enormous, with major implications for the stock price, wealth and pensions of US and EU citizens.

- The IT revolution is inseparable from the revolution in the global media industry. There is no doubt that the WTO Agreement has major implications for the telecoms and media industry in China. Dominance by US-based firms of the global media revolution has enormous implications for the way in which a global culture is being produced, dominated by US values and language. If China applies fully the terms of the WTO Agreement, then the combined impact of these two revolutions upon China's society and politics would be profound.

- Infrastructure over much of China is still too poorly developed to easily allow SMEs to integrate with the global value chain. An apocryphal story was circulating in China in the year 2000 about an old man who grew garlic in a remote part of China. In this story the old man passes an internet café (sic) and goes inside to investigate. The owner of the café helps him to surf the net and find a buyer for his garlic in the USA. The moral of the story is that even Chinese farmers can get rich on the internet, and that there is just one big, inter-connected, win–win world in the internet age. The story does not explain how the farmer was able to transport his garlic to the supermarket in the USA from a remote part of China.

- As we have seen, China's exports from SMEs have been the fastest-growing part of the Chinese economy during the reform period. It is questionable whether China's entry to the WTO and possible increased access to B2B business could significantly raise the growth rate of output value from China's SME sector much beyond the very high rates of growth already achieved. Thus, the rate of growth of new jobs in the SME sector consequent upon increased exports of goods from Chinese-based SMEs connected by new information technology to the global value chain of large corporations is highly uncertain.

- A major countervailing impact of the IT revolution is the dramatic reduction in administrative work undertaken directly by people that is made possible by the new technologies. The Chinese economy is ripe for large-scale replacement of the huge number of employees in SOEs who are engaged in routine administrative tasks. A sector in which employment levels are likely to be especially heavily affected by the rapid growth of information technology is the distribution system. At the end of the 1990s there were over 50 million people working in China's wholesale, retail and distribution systems. As global businesses and their 'external firms' expand in China, so they will increasingly replace the vast labour-intensive structure with a more reliable, modern logistics system co-ordinated by state-of-the-art information technology. This will have large implications for employment levels in the distribution sector.

- As we have seen, an important part of the change in the nature of the global firm in the business revolution has involved the 'cascade' effect, flowing down from global systems integrators to first, second and third tier suppliers. This places great pressure for consolidation and associated cost reduction and technical progress upon the whole supply chain. It is highly uncertain how far the IT revolution will lead to the emergence of local production among relatively large, capital-intensive firms in China as opposed to myriads of SME firms. The associated impact on employment is, correspondingly, highly uncertain. It cannot be assumed to be positive.

SOCIO–POLITICAL CONSEQUENCES OF THE SHOCK

If China strictly observes the terms of the WTO Agreement, as well as the conventional structural adjustment problems, it will face large-scale psychological and political adjustment problems. In almost all cases, successful late-industrializing countries established a group of indigenous large corporations that could compete on the global level playing field. This was true even for small countries like Sweden, Holland and Switzerland. If China were to continue to grow rapidly in the coming decades, then it would develop a unique form of capitalism among successful 'latecomer' countries. This would be one that had few internationally competitive corporations, and the commanding heights of whose business system were controlled mainly by international corporations based in the advanced countries.

This result would be likely to cause intense difficulties for the Chinese national psyche. We have seen that China has a long and proud economic history, combined with an acute sensitivity to its international humiliations from the 1840s onwards. The difficulties of accepting that the catch-up process is dominated by foreign corporations would be made all the more challenging by the fact that these corporations would be perceived as the instrument causing massive disruption within the state-owned sector. The challenge would be made even greater by the fact that the most powerful force of businesses within this process will be US-based large firms. It would undoubtedly be argued by many in China that

Chinese jobs were being sacrificed in the interests of American shareholders. Moreover, almost everyone recognizes that the gains from joining the WTO within China are likely to be highly unevenly distributed (see, for example Lee Kuan Yew, 2000). Many highly educated Chinese people would find employment within the global corporations or within the 'external firm' working indirectly for the global corporations. However, this number would de dwarfed by the number who were excluded from this magic circle. Indeed, China is entering the WTO at the time of the most intense pressure on employment within the global corporation and its surrounding 'external firm'. This pressure is being greatly intensified by the potentially large labour-displacing effects of new information technology.

The shock arising from the destruction of China's 'national champions' might not be confined to China. It might well have a deep impact on international relations. The most potent source of potential international conflict is in relations with the USA. We have already analyzed the USA's dominance of the global business revolution. This dominance is most marked in the most sensitive of sectors, information technology, which is laying the foundation for the global economy of the twenty-first century. Already, there is powerful anti-US sentiment in China. Many people who are totally supportive of China's move towards a market economy feel dismayed by the potential dominance of US-based multinational firms within the Chinese economy after China enters the WTO. It symbolizes a further national humiliation after more than one hundred years of humiliation.

As a result of the recent revolutionary process of international merger and acquisition within the advanced capitalist economies, former 'national champions' have become truly international corporations. However, they still remain headquartered within the advanced economies. The vast bulk of their shareholders are institutions or citizens based within the advanced economies. There is, consequently, still a strong possibility that the impending acceleration in the rate of growth in investment within China by multinational firms will be perceived as a highly unequal relationship of dominance by advanced cultures, within which the USA is pre-eminent, over the ancient culture of China. It is certain that many people in China will raise the cry of a 'Second Opium War'.

The forthcoming changes in the Chinese mass media will be a major element in the process of structural adjustment that awaits China within the WTO. It is highly uncertain how far the Chinese government will be able to control access to the global mass media once global corporations start to play an increased role in Chinese telecoms and mass media systems. There will be tremendous pressure to provide ubiquity of access to the global mass media. This pressure will arise from Chinese consumers, from Chinese equity partners, from Chinese firms in the industry, and from within the government itself to raise revenue from telecoms and media services. There will be constant pressure to push back the frontiers of access.

This will have at least two important and contradictory effects. On the one hand, the potential explosive increase in access to the global mass media will tend to lead to the fast growth of 'internet opium'. For private consumers of the global mass media, far from being a personally liberating, inter-active, learning medium, the evidence so far is that the principal activities that the global internet is used for by private consumers are, in descending order of revenues, pornography, sports and cartoons. To some degree this might tend to reinforce, not reduce, political stability. However, rapid penetration of China by the global media might make it much more difficult for the Chinese government to control political dissent. Moreover, much of the content of the global mass media, while not being explicitly political, could have a socially de-stabilizing effect through its corrosive impact on China's value system, especially among young people.

It is possible that the political and social instability that might result from full implementation of the WTO Agreement in China might increase the degree of central political control rather than reduce it. Only in this way might China be able to survive the coming period politically and avoid the nightmare of a Soviet-style collapse of the state.

CHINA ENTERS THE WTO: AN ALTERNATIVE OUTCOME?

If China does, indeed, stick closely to the agreed terms of entry to the WTO, then China's leaders would have to deal simultaneously with several shocks:

- the shock of 'normal' restructuring due to high-speed intensified competition consequent upon the terms under which China has entered the WTO;
- the shock of having to compete on the global level playing field with a global business system that has never been so concentrated;
- the shock of the impact of the IT revolution upon employment;
- the shock of the drastic impact of the global media revolution upon Chinese culture;
- the shock for Chinese people's self-esteem of the country's failure to establish a group of powerful indigenous corporations;
- the shock of dealing with the dominance of US-based corporations.

However, one logical possibility is that the very prospect of such shocks might lead to intense pressure to reinvigorate China's industrial policy. A number of factors could facilitate such a development:

- **Deep-seated Chinese ambitions**. A persistent theme of this book has been the intense ambitions within Chinese politics and society at large to construct large, globally competitive businesses that can take their place on the global stage alongside the world's leading corporations. The intense national ambitions are reflected in daily discussion with Chinese people, from ordinary citizens to leading business people and politicians. These powerful nationalist sentiments are reflected in forms such as the best-selling book, *China Can Say No?* (Song Qiang *et al.*, 1996) as well as other popular books, such as *The Foreign Armies Grab China* (Chen Fang, 1999) and *Robbing China* (Cun Fu, 1998). They are reflected also in the passionate and deeply-researched onslaught on China's decision to join the WTO in Han Deqiang's book, *The Globalisation Trap and China's Realistic Choices*:

> Even though the competitive strength of China's banking, insurance, automobile, communications, chemical industry, textiles and agriculture are still very weak, and even though these sectors have a fundamental importance to the Chinese economy, and although they could become completely controlled by foreign companies, China, with a thick head still wants free market competition, calling itself a fervent disciple of the free market economy (Han Deqiang, 2000).

China's decision to join the WTO under the terms agreed with the USA and EU respectively has prompted intense debate within the country about China's development path. Unsurprisingly, the degree of explicit public discussion among senior policy makers is limited. Beneath the surface there is deep, passionate argument. In wider circles, unconstrained by the burdens of political leadership, there is open public debate. These forces combine to produce intense pressure on China's leaders to demonstrate that they are defending China's perceived national interests.

- **High-quality, ambitious Chinese large enterprise managers**. Throughout this book there have been many examples of the deeply-felt ambitions of the managers of China's large enterprises. These entrepreneurs are now far more aware of the nature of the competition that awaits them on the global level playing field. Despite high levels of corruption, there are also deeply-held ambitions among China's bureaucrats to build a powerful 'national team' of large corporations. The China Big Business Programme itself, which formed the basis of this book, was initiated precisely by such a combination of bureaucrats and business leaders, who hoped through the Programme to advance their understanding of how China could construct globally competitive large firms. China has no shortage of entrepreneurs who are able to lead the growth of China's large firms if they are given the appropriate environment in which to do so. There is deep ambition within the Chinese large-scale enterprises to become genuine global players, despite the enormous difficulties that they face.

- **Increased East Asian co-operation in response to the Asian crisis**. There are strong feelings of resentment within the East Asian nations at the way in which the Asian crisis was perceived to be primarily an 'internal' problem of poor governance and lack of transparency in business institutions. There is also deep resentment in the region at the perceived crudeness of the IMF response, and the subsequent failure of the international financial institutions to implement substantial reforms that could prevent such a crisis occurring again. In June 2000 in Beijing, the Chinese People's Political Consultative Conference organized a high level meeting on globalization, with leaders of many of the world's multinational firms, several former national leaders, including Lee Kuan Yew, and a few scholars. At this meeting, the former Deputy Prime Minister of Thailand commented on the impact of the Asian crisis:

> In the 1990s capital flowed into the emerging economies like water into the lower basin after the floodgates are lifted. After a while, the whole basin becomes heavily flooded. All the farms, building and cattle are submerged under water. When everything is destroyed, the water is quickly drained out, and the whole area dries up completely. Then we are blamed that we are cronies, imprudent, inefficient, over-investors, have weak financial institutions, a poor supervision system, the wrong exchange rate regime, and a poor auditing system. After accepting the IMF's bail-out funds, we were forced to accept a ready-made formula prescription that forced our economies to contract drastically so that the lenders could recover their money as rapidly as possible... There has been a demand from the emerging countries that the world financial order should be reviewed. Globalization of capital movements can be destructive and destabilize the world economy. In the long-run it may not benefit anyone except the speculators, financial brokers, investment bankers and fund managers. The short-term gains of these groups of people will be a great obstacle in allowing the world to reach a high level of welfare. The gains will be concentrated only in a group of the world's financial centres... The credibility of the IMF has completely gone, at least in East Asia. They listen but they never hear (Virabongsa Ramangkura, 2000).

By the time Dr Ramangkura came to deliver his speech on the final day of the 21st Century Forum, most of the representatives of the multinational companies and many of those from the international institutions, had left the Forum for more important tasks.

The widespread feelings of resentment and humiliation among the East Asian countries began to take a concrete form later in the year 2000. In July the annual meeting of the 10 Asean (Association of Southeast Asian Nations) countries was marked by the first formal meeting of the foreign ministers from Asean with those of China, Japan and Korea, 'in a further manifestation of their intensifying co-operation' (*FT*, 21 July 2000). The meeting attracted special interest because some people believe that 'this group could eventually transform Asia's relationship with the rest of the world and alter the balance of global economic policy-making by creating a new regional bloc' (*FT*, 21 July 2000). The new group has been nicknamed 'Asean plus three' since it started to have regular meetings during the Asian crisis. For outsiders the new spirit of Asian co-operation is 'unnerving', since it seems to 'hark back to the East Asian Economic Caucus (EAEC) proposed in the mid-1990s by Mahathir Mohammad, Malaysia's Prime Minister'. That upset the USA, because it was specifically excluded from the arrangement.

It was the Asian economic crisis that drove the group towards closer economic co-operation. This includes an agreement in May 2000 to set up a network of bilateral currency swaps to help protect them against currency speculation. A key factor has been China's willingness to participate. The new institutional forum is important as a sign of improvement in China's 'prickly relationship with Japan' (*FT*, 21 July 2000). Asean is putting the finishing touches to its own free trade area and bilateral free trade negotiations are starting to proliferate, for example, between Japan and South Korea and Japan and Singapore. If these developments were the signal for more extended co-operation on matters of industrial policy, including significant cross-border mergers and acquisitions within the region, then it could herald a substantial shift in the balance of power in global business. A more deeply integrated East Asia, with regionally-based large corporations that spanned boundaries within the East Asia region, including both Japan and China, would be the basis for a powerful challenge to the emergence of large corporations based within the EU and the USA.

In August 2000 a highly significant development in East Asian business was announced. This was the agreement to deepen the partnership between Posco and Nippon Steel, to form 'one of the most high-profile alliances between a Japanese and a Korean company in decades' (*FT*, 3 August 2000). These were already the world's two largest steel producers. Their combined output totals around 50 million tons. They have a joint global market share of around 7 per cent, and significantly above this in high value-added steels. The groups agreed to broaden a strategic alliance to cut costs and increase their defences against a hostile takeover. The groups agreed to deepen their cross-ownership to around 3 per cent in each direction. They agreed to pool their resources in research and development, in information technology and to co-operate in overseas joint ventures. They are discussing the possibility of pooling their procurement and distribution.

- **Uncertainties over the US economy**. Despite the seeming invulnerability of the US economy and US large corporations, there are important uncertainties surrounding the US economy. Most obviously, it is still uncertain how the long boom of the US stock market will develop. In 1999, the 'old economy' stocks marked time. The year 2000 saw a large downturn in the value of dot.com companies. The gloss wore off the high technology sector. It remains to be seen if the US economy will achieve a 'soft landing' from the long stock market boom of the 1990s. Much of the US economic and stock market boom depended on the perception of the unlimited opportunities offered to US big business by the liberalization of the global economy. However, the future of the WTO is far from certain. The institution is dominated numerically by members from the developing countries. There is tremendous pressure from them to resist the US's wish to impose global standards on investment rules, on labour regulations and environmental conditions. If China and the main developing country members were to work together to attempt to push the institution to serve their own ends rather than those of the advanced economies, it could have profound results, with substantial implications for US business. Even the very survival of the WTO is uncertain.

- **Central role for East Asian people in US high technology**. A further important uncertainty in the development of the US business structure is the long-term role played by Chinese and Indian scientists and engineers in the growth of the 'brain' of the US economy, in the shape of the leading edge of research in the high technology industries. We have seen that there is a severe shortage of capable indigenous US citizens able to meet the technical challenges of these occupations. Consequently, a large and fast-growing fraction of the leading edge of US technological progress is being undertaken by Asian people. It is extremely uncertain what the implications of this will be. A highly important issue surrounds the degree to which these people will return to their native lands, either physically or in terms of business development. The scarcest resource by far in the information revolution is high quality human resources. In this sense, the Asian nations already are moving into the driving seat of the world economy in the early 21st century.

- **Intense competition produces opportunities as well as challenges**. The very intensity of global competition is producing many opportunities for Chinese firms to catch-up. In every sector in the advanced economies there are powerful players that cannot maintain the pace of competition with the leading players. They may possess strong technologies, global markets and global brands. If they were given the choice, they might prefer, in the long-run interests of their shareholders, to join forces with a major Chinese player, rather than being merged with another large corporation based in the advanced economies. This may be especially true within East Asia and in developing countries generally. The automobile, oil and petrochemical, steel, aerospace, telecoms services, IT hardware, media and fast-moving consumer goods sectors, all have obvious examples that spring to mind.

- **Renewed East Asian business confidence**. Despite the great severity of the East Asian crisis, and the deep problems it revealed in the institutional structure of the East Asian conglomerate, the region began quickly to regain its confidence. The number of Japanese companies in the *Fortune* 500 (ranked by sales) sharply dropped from 126 in 1997 to 100 in 1999, before starting to rise again to reach 107 in the year 2000. The number of companies from Japan in the *FT* 500 (ranked by market capitalization) collapsed from 110 in 1996 to just 46 in 1998, but in 1999, the number recovered quickly to reached 77. The number from the Four Little Tigers in the *FT* 500 collapsed from 21 in 1996 to just 11, but had recovered to 20 in 1998. Despite radical restructuring in Asian-based large firms, the Asian model of using state industrial policy to support the growth of indigenous big business was far from dead.

- **The role model of global oligopoly**. The global business revolution made it more and more clear that the neo-classical interpretation of capitalism was based on a deep misrepresentation of the real nature of the system it was analyzing. Chinese popular newspapers, for example, were at least as interested in the global merger and acquisition boom as the Western media. China's agreement with the USA in 1999 on entry to the WTO coincided with the value of global mergers and acquisitions considerably exceeding three trillion US dollars, of which the USA alone accounted for $1.9 trillion and Europe for $1.5 trillion. By comparison, mergers and acquisition within Non-Japan Asia were just $150 billion. In Greater China they stood at only $41 billion. The total of mergers and acquisitions in China in 1999 stood at a mere $15 billion.

It has become abundantly clear that the barriers to entry for Chinese firms were getting larger and larger. On the one hand, this produced feelings of despair at the possibility of industrial policy in China allowing Chinese firms to catch-up. On the other hand it made it increasingly clear that if Chinese firms wished to catch-up with the global leaders they could only do so on the basis of powerful large corporations. This meant that large internal mergers and acquisitions were crucial, whether they were through the market mechanism or were state-led. It meant also, that Chinese firms needed to think even more carefully than before about the need to realistically benchmark themselves against the global giant corporations, and allow modern corporate managers the autonomy to run their business in a competitive fashion. It meant that Chinese firms needed to think even more realistically about the need to expand into global markets for both products and for businesses. No globally competitive player can rely purely on the 'home market' any longer, even if that market is the USA or the EU, let alone China.

These factors combine to produce many dynamic possibilities. They provide an environment in which it is possible to imagine a combination of forces that could produce a different response from Chinese policy makers than simply administering the WTO rules as agreed with the USA and the EU. Indeed, as China enters the 21st century there are already contradictory signs in respect to industrial policy. On the one hand, the giant AVIC aerospace corporation was broken into two separate pieces. Separately they stood even less chance of global success than as a united entity. In the financial sector, China's policy makers were enacting the very polices which the USA had so recently rejected, of strictly separating the different sectors of business in order to maintain 'greater competition' among domestic financial institutions and help to prevent financial system instability. In sector after sector, as we have seen, there was a complete failure to achieve mergers across regions due to local protectionism.

On the other hand, there were signs that the prospect of intense competition within a very short period of time from the global giants, was focusing the minds of China's policy makers. There was a quickly-growing awareness of the great weakness of China's large firms, as the need to benchmark them realistically against the global giants greatly intensified. Indeed, this was a major reason that the final negotiations on China's entry were so prolonged. As this book went to press in Spring 2001, it seemed unlikely that China would join the WTO before Autumn 2001. It was no longer possible to think vaguely about the possible competition from ill-defined future competitors. The benchmark now had suddenly become the world's leading firms in each sector. There were some indications that this was leading to a shift in central policy makers' view of the degree of urgency of the task of creating genuinely competitive large firms. Faced with the extreme severity of the challenge, it is possible that the bureaucratic forces that previously prevented the necessary mergers and acquisitions, and the necessary appointment of high-quality managers with the authority to manage and improve enterprise performance, might be overcome. There were several indications that this might be the case.

Between 1998 and 2000 the central government led a massive restructuring and international flotation of CNPC and Sinopec. This process was widely criticized as an example of 'bureaucratic-led restructuring' as opposed to 'restructuring through the market'. The flotation of CNPC's PetroChina in the year 2000 was highly disappointing in terms of the total funds raised. It is possible that the flotation of Sinopec later in 2000 will also be disappointing in terms of the revenues raised. However, despite all the criticisms and shortcomings, the state-led restructuring and international flotation of CNPC and Sinopec, signalled a very different pattern of advance for Chinese industrial policy faced with the challenge of globalization. These were highly significant events for China as it entered the 21st century. They provided a very different signal from the break-up of AVIC into two separate 'competitive' firms.

In 1998 China Telecom (Hong Kong) merged with the Jiangsu Mobile Phone Company in a $2.9 billion deal, and in 1999, it merged again with Fujian and Henan Mobile Phone companies in a deal worth $6.9 billion. This increased the number of subscribers from nine million to almost sixteen million. By April 2000, the market capitalization of China Telecom (Hong Kong) had risen to $99 billion, so that the company was now a serious player in international markets (*FT*, 4 May 2000). At that point, China Telecom (Hong Kong) had a market capitalization almost equal to that of British Telecom and MCI WorldCom, and considerably greater even than that of Telefónica (Spain). This could form the basis for significant expansion outside China. A further indication of the capital-raising possibilities of China's potential global giants was provided by the IPO of the state-backed China Unicom, China's second-largest telecoms company, in June 2000. The listing raised almost $5 billion.

In July 2000, two important announcements provided a further signal that there might be a significant shift in policy under way. The first was the announcement that Chinese airlines were to be reorganized into three big groups, based around China Southern Airlines, China Eastern Airlines and Air China (*FT*, 24 July 2000). A few days later it was announced that Huaneng Power International and Shandong Huaneng Power Development Company were to merge (*FT*, 24 July 2000). This was much the largest merger of two foreign-listed Chinese companies. The merged companies will have a total installed capacity of

TABLE 14-8 Stock-Market Development in China and Other Countries/
Regions, 1998

Country/Region	Stock Market Capitalization	GNP	
	($ billion)	($ billion)	(%)
China	231	929	24.9
Hong Kong	413	158	261.4
USA	11 309	7 921	142.8
Low-income countries	387	1 844	21.0
Middle-income countries	1 405	4 420	31.8
High-income countries	21 749	22 599	96.2

SOURCE: World Bank, (2000: 230–1, 260–1)

10 814 MW. The new entity will be China's largest independent power producer. One enthusiastic analyst commented: 'It is the biggest meanest fish in the pond. It will be the McDonald's of power in China' (quoted in *FT*, 24 July 2000).

It is still far from certain that such a strategic shift has been made. However, should it, indeed, prove to be the case, then it is highly likely that the capital markets would respond to provide the needed capital for the radically restructured large Chinese firms. Despite rapid growth since the 1980s, China's domestic stock markets are still very immature. By 1998 China had almost 800 domestically-listed companies. Their total stock market capitalization was just $231 billion, amounting to around one-quarter of China's national product. This was not much above the average for low income countries and far below that of the mature, stock-market based economies (Table 14-8). China's overseas listings in 1999 had a market capitalization of only around $60 billion, far below the total domestic listings. Around 70 per cent of the total equity of China's enterprises was held by the Chinese state (Li Xiaoxue, 1999).

However, there is a relatively large volume of savings held by Chinese people. In 1998, funds held in Chinese savings deposits totalled over $640 billion. Therefore, even within China, there is considerable scope for China's potential global giant corporations to raise capital through the stock market and through the commercial banking system. This possibility is dwarfed by the potential of global financial markets. If China were to establish a credible industrial policy for building globally powerful commercially-oriented large firms, then there are almost unlimited opportunities to raise capital from international markets, through stock markets, bond markets and/or from bank loans. Passive privatization of China's large enterprises in the face of the impending challenge from global giants, would not produce this outcome since it is becoming increasingly obvious that on the 'global level playing field' few of China's large firms could survive in direct competition with the global giants. In order to raise capital in a sustained and large-scale fashion for China's large enterprises, China's government would need to demonstrate that it had entered a new era of industrial restructuring. This would involve demonstrating that strong domestic firms were able to merge with other strong domestic firms, whether through the market or through the bureaucracy, that they had genuinely independent and strong management, that they were able to pursue international mergers and acquisitions, and that they were supported by a coherent set of government industrial policies.

It is conceivable that China's industrial policies might be given fresh life with a renewed focus and sense of urgency due to the impending shock of joining the WTO under the terms agreed. Despite the enormous challenges presented by the global business revolution, it is possible to imagine a strategy that might lead to the growth of competitive large firms based in China. In this case, China's large corporations might assume an important place among the world's giant corporations and Chinese-based firms might themselves begin to directly assume the functions of 'global systems integrators'. Such a large shift in industrial policy would involve tense and complicated issues in China's international relations, especially in relation to the USA, since it would involve a *de facto* re-negotiation of the terms under which China enters the WTO.

History is far from dead. The uncertainties are great. The prospects are highly dynamic.

Afterword

On 27 Monday March 2000 I went to the Great Hall of the People in Beijing. There I was part of a group from the China Development Forum, organised by the Chinese State Council, that met with Chinese Premier Zhu Rongji. The group included the CEOs of many global corporations, such as the American International Group, Michelin, Shell, Rio Tinto and BP Amoco. He shook hands with each of us. He welcomed us. Then he invited us to ask him questions. He encouraged us to ask any questions at all: 'I am happy to deal with any questions you might wish to ask'.

On Tuesday 13 June 2000 I was part of a group from the 21st Century Forum that met for an hour and a half with the Chinese Head of State, Jiang Zemin. The group included Singapore's former Prime Minister, Lee Kuan Yew, Australia's former Prime Minister, Sir Malcolm Fraser, Dr. Klaus Schwab, President of the World Economic Forum, Richard Li, CEO, Pacific Century Cyberworks, Mickey Cantor, former Secretary of Commerce of the USA, Dr Lars Ramquist, CEO, Ericsson Group, Stephen Roach, of MSDW and Professor Laurence Lau, of Stanford University. The foreign participants remarked on how relaxed Jiang Zemin appeared. He talked easily and fluently about China's historical achievements, about China's ancient philosophy and its similarities with and differences from ancient European philosophy. He spoke of the differences between the Greek philosophers, Plato, Aristotle and Socrates. He enquired into the reasons for the huge rise in the US stock market, and wished to know the causes of the 'bubble' and whether it was about to end. Throughout the meeting he smiled confidently.

On Thursday 30 June I walked along the Great Wall at Jiankou with Wang Xiaoqiang and Wang Lixiong, author of *Yellow Peril*, a futuristic novel that chronicles the disintegration of China. Jiankou is a remote place where the Great Wall makes a bow-shaped turn over a series of mountainous peaks. On the wall are inscribed the following words: 'Here the terrain is so treacherous that even the hawks hesitate to fly overhead.'

Notes

Preface

1. See, e.g., Wang (1998a). Wang and Nolan (1998) contains several of Dr Wang's papers on Chinese enterprise reform as well as one long paper of my own.

Chapter 1

1. My own contributions to that debate, especially in relation to China, were published in various places (Nolan, 1990, 1993a,b, 1994, 1995).

2. The Pennsylvania Railroad employed 110000 people by 1891, probably the world's then largest business (Schmitz, 1993: 19).

Chapter 2

1. For example, between 1992 and 1997, revenues rose by 59 per cent at GE, 53 per cent at Ford, 33 per cent at Shell and 34 per cent at GM. Employment in these giant firms rose by just 19 per cent at GE, 12 per cent at Ford, and fell by 17 per cent at Shell and 19 per cent at GM (UNCTAD, 1995, 1999).

Chapter 3

1. These 100 enterprises were chosen in November 1994. Of these 28 were classified as super-large, 67 large and five medium-sized enterprises. They employed over 1.5 million people and most were members of large enterprise groups in their own right (Huang, Wu and Yao, 1998: 35) with an average of 20 members per trial enterprise group (Zou and Zhang, 1991).

2. These measures, shrouded in greater secrecy than those related to business group development, orient around closer relationships between the banking sector and the chosen LMEs. The 512 LMEs in this 'vanguard' were among the largest in the state sector. Although they constituted just 1 per cent of all state firms they accounted for 55 per cent of assets, 60 per cent of sales and 80 per cent of taxes of the state industrial sector (*CDBW*, 14 January 1998).

3. It is not clear to what extent the 512 'focal' (*zhongdian*) LMEs are integrated within the 120 business groups. Wu Bangguo in a speech referred to the LMEs as 'belonging to'

the trial groups (Sun, 1998: 4). Elsewhere it has been suggested 'the central government has chosen 512 enterprises to form the basis of these enterprise groups' (Smyth, 2000: 722). However, many of the LMEs appear to remain independent and there is no mention in the most important policies related to the trial business group development of the role the 512 LMEs play. Nonetheless, at least 70 of the LMEs are core enterprises in the 120 trial business groups (see Table 3-2 for provincial spread and Table 3-5 in Appendix 1, p. 101 for enterprise examples). Yuchai, a large diesel engine manufacturer, is but one example of a trial LME that is not part of the trial business groups.

4. AVIC and CNMEG. Sinopec was not included in the national team.

5. In particular, publicity has been attached to six groups (Baoshan, Haier, Founder, Changhong, North China Pharmaceutical and Jiangnan groups) which have been granted annual injections of no less than 20 million yuan to help them enter the ranks of the *Fortune* 500. However, this is not part of a wider parcel of measures specifically aimed at these six groups but instead part of the 'Ninth Five Year Plan state guide on key technological developments'. This plan has also chosen 166 key technology projects to be funded with state backing. These projects are related to the businesses of the 120 trial business groups and 512 preferred LMEs (CASS, ZGFB, 1998: 120).

6. By 2000 the number of trial groups had fallen below 120 because of a few strong/strong mergers between the trial groups, such as the formation in chemicals of the Donglian Group (Table 3-5 in Appendix 1). In total there are 203 enterprise groups registered at the national level with the State Industrial and Commercial Bureau. By the middle of 1998 there were also a further 1311 with ongoing applications (SCDRC, ZJN, 1998: 705).

7. The Association for the Promotion of China's Business Groups, established in April 1994 with members from 74 groups, including most of the 57 groups in the first batch of trials. It now has representatives from over 100 of the trial business groups permanently posted at its headquarters in Beijing. These representatives have all held important posts and are familiar with the problems facing their business groups. The forum for discussion between groups facilitates the introduction of policies that can be beneficially applied across all the groups. The evidence and descriptions presented here are based upon visits to several of China's largest business groups in 1998 and 1999 and interviews at the Association for the Promotion of China's Business Groups.

8. A further two groups were later added to the first batch, increasing the total to 57.

9. There were only 7199 large enterprises in China in 1997 (Table 3-2). Given that enterprise groups are usually based on a large-scale enterprise this would imply that at least a third of all large enterprises were in fact core members of provincially or nationally supported enterprise groups.

10. These data imply that even within the large-scale sector there are large size disparities but that the national team players are amongst the largest. A 1997 study into 1254 large enterprises found only 23 had sales over 10 billion yuan, accounting for only 2 per cent of the enterprises but over 30 per cent of sales and 55 per cent of the profits of these enterprises (CASS, ZGFB, 1998: 115). Table 3-5 in Appendix 1 also describes how the trial business groups in the national team are among the largest in China.

11. See CRES, ZJTGN for yearly updates on provincial- and city-level efforts at nurturing groups. Lower levels of governments have also initiated their own trials with the modern corporate system, there now being over 2500 provincial level groups undergoing trials.

12. According to Jiang Qiangui, vice-minister of the State Economic and Trade Commission (SETC) (*CDBW*, 17 January 2000).

13. The five mainland companies were: China National Petrochemical Corporation (Sinopec), Industrial and Commercial Bank of China, Bank of China, China National Chemical Import and Export Corporation (Sinochem) and China National Cereals, Oils and Foodstuff Import and Export Corporation (COFCO). The last two are included in the national team and Sinopec is experimenting as a national holding company.

14. In 1999, 435 LMEs were closed, 78 SOEs were involved in debt–equity swaps involving $10.9 billion and 11 million workers were laid-off (*CDBW*, 26 January 2000).

15. The term 'enterprise' is used in this chapter even though it is unclear just when autonomous 'enterprises' started to emerge from the centrally planned system. 'Plant' may in fact be more accurate as many production units were still bound to the planning apparatus and governmental control. Building enterprises out of state plants and departments has been a key objective of enterprise reform.

16. During the early and mid-1980s the policy of 'three no changes' (*san bu bian*) held back enterprise reorganisation.

17. This document is published in CRES, ZJTGN (1988: 9–17).

18. It was also at this time that the first articles on business groups began to be published in Chinese academia.

19. LMEs are defined by industry on standard criteria specified by the State Statistical Bureau (SSB).

20. Of these 431 groups 261 are reported as having large-scale enterprises at their core and 27 had assets exceeding one billion yuan (CRES, ZJTGN, 1992: 308).

21. They had also grown quickly. In the period 1991–6 the four trial steel groups increased their total capital by 295 per cent, and sales by 146 per cent. In chemicals the same respective figures were 314 per cent and 131 per cent (SCDRC, ZJN 1998: 708).

22. Although not all of the groups are industrial enterprises, at least 19 are classified as trade or agricultural groups (Table 3-3), the majority are in fact based around industrial enterprises or have industrial enterprises as members of the groups. The trade groups, for example, appear to possess their own manufacturing facilities.

23. It was at about this time that the policy of 'three no changes' (*san bu bian*) started to be relaxed.

24. Zhang Qi, Head of the Ministry of Electronics (*Far Eastern Economic Review*, 2 May 1998).

25. Among the first 57 groups there were 46 industrial groups, two foreign trade groups and five in transportation. In the second batch there were 39 industrial groups, six in foreign trade, eight in domestic trade and transportation, four other groups (investment, regional development) and five in agriculture. In total there were therefore 85 industrial groups.

26. Members of The Association for the Promotion of China's Business Groups have undertaken trips to Japan to discuss industrial policy with leading academics and policy makers and also are great admirers of South Korea's development model, which they claim to have tried to imitate (interview, Beijing: April 1999).

27. These documents are published in CRES, ZJTGN (1992: 67–71; 1998: 159–62).

28. The groups had established 30 trade companies.

29. Ten of these were listed on foreign stock markets.

30. In 1997 it is reported there were 209 A-share issues, 79 of which were affiliated to the 120 enterprise groups and 100 enterprises experimenting with the modern enterprise system (SCDRC, ZJN, 1998: 709).

Chapter 4

1. All references in the following two sections are taken from these sources. For example, the BAe 146's engines are imported from Allied Signal in the USA.

2. For example, British Aerospace is converting early generation Airbuses to freighters, and anticipates that the aircraft's total working life may then be as long as forty or more years.

3. I am grateful to Paul Heffernan for drawing my attention to the earlier development and operation of the De Havilland Comet.

4. The consortium consisted of BAe (at that time BAC), Messerschmitt–Bolkow–Blohm and Aeritalia.

5. For a few years the Ministry also included the production of rockets (extra-atmospheric), but in 1993 these were again cut away from the rest of the aviation industry, and placed into a separately organized rocket company.

6. National defence expenditure stood at 9.1 per cent of the total budget in 1986–90 and 9.5 per cent in 1991–5 (SSB, ZTN, 1997: 243).

7. It must be emphasized that these estimates are extremely rough.

8. The figure '2' refers to the fact that this was the second time that China and Russia had been 'close brothers', the first time being in the 1950s.

9. China is reported to have ordered four AWACs from Israel in 1997, using converted Il-76 aircraft as the platform (IISS, 1998: 171). The delivery date is not known.

10. These are derivations from a variety of other figures, as no complete series of sales or output was available to the author. It must be emphasized that these are only the roughest of estimates. For example, the total sales value is itself a derived figure, and the price index used is the general index of industrial prices rather than the index of prices of aerospace products.

11. The price deflator used is simply the general index of industrial prices, so the estimate of 'real' growth is only a rough estimate.

12. These were: Jincheng, Nanfang, Changhe and Hafei.

13. These included the main landing gear and nose landing gear doors, the aft service door jamb, aft service door, avionics access door and the cargo door.

14. One proposal involved a partnership with a South Korean company and included building two production lines, one in China and one in South Korea.

15. A rough approximation derived from other sources of information.

16. It appears to operate with separate financial responsibility and a separate budget.

17. A rough guess, assuming approximately one-third of total sales revenue generated by each of the branches.

Chapter 5

1. Report of the Centre for Medicines Research quoted in *FT* (24 April 1997) and *Observer* (8 February 1998).

2. In 1997, prior to the take-over of Unilever's downstream chemical business, ICI employed 663 chemical engineers, compared to 647 at British Petroleum, 356 at Kvaerner John Brown and 335 at Shell (*FT*, 3 April 1997).

3. See Yeung (1995) for an analysis of the PLA's commercial activities from the 'entrepreneurial state' perspective.

4. The PLA maintains direct ownership and control of defence firms.

5. In 1992, over 90 per cent of the value of output from the defence electronics industry consisted of civilian goods (Frankenstein and Gill, 1996: 417).

6. According to the SSB, 81 per cent of weapons ammunition producers were loss-making in mid-1994 (Frankenstein and Gill, 1996: 396).

7. Mr Wang Jun was the former head of the arms trader Polytechnologies under the China Poly Group.

8. To avoid the tedious and time-consuming procedures necessary for forming a public company, China Poly Group acquired Continental Mariner as a vehicle to generate capital in the Hong Kong stock market, a form of 'back-door listing' (Yeung, 1995: 164).

9. The authors are extremely grateful to Zhao Xinxian, the President and Chief Executive Officer of Sanjiu Group, for allowing us to carry out research at the Company in 1995–6, on which this paper is based.

10. In 1984 they had 8993 and 7086 employees, respectively (SSB, ZGJTZ, 1985: 294). The next largest plants were Beijing Pharmaceuticals, Shanghai No. 4 and Shanghai No. 6, each with under 3000 employees (SSB, ZGJTZ, 1985: 294).

11. It was registered in November 1986.

12. Similar advertisements are prominently displayed on the control towers at several of China's airports.

13. The cost of the sign was estimated to be $240 000–300 000 per year (Stuart Eniott, *New York Times*, 1 May 1995).

14. At seminars we have given on the paper that is the basis of this chapter, there are always members of the audience who assert confidently that this must be the 'real' explanation for Sanjiu's explosive growth.

15. Curiously, in 1992 it was ranked 73rd by sales volume and Nanfang was ranked 74th within the top 100 firms in China (DRC, 1994: 3).

16. Nanfang thereafter paid land rent to both the *wujing* and the Shenzhen City Government.

17. Li Zoukeng and Li Cunhou (1995: 64).

18. Nanfang's main plant has been visited by General Liu Huaqing and General Zhang Zhen, both Vice-Chairmen of the Central Committee of the PLA; Chi Haotian, Chinese National Defence Minister; General Fu Quanyu, Minister of the General Logistics Department of the PLA; Zhou Keyu, Party Leader of the General Logistics Department of the PLA; General Zhang Aiping, former Chinese Defence Minister.

19. Regarding the business ban, an official of the Sanjiu pharmaceutical factory said: 'We are waiting for an official notice ... Whatever is the order we will follow' (*SCMP*, 24 July 1998).

20. Between 1985 and 1993, output had risen from 3250 tons to 11 650 tons, and exports had risen from 1840 tons to 8490 tons.

21. China's trademark law was promulgated in 1982.

22. Neither the price nor the method of purchase was disclosed to us.

23. In 1995 the ratio for state-owned enterprises in Shenzhen was 76 per cent.

24. There are nine Party Committees, 36 Party branches with 428 Party members, totalling 14 per cent of the permanent employees in the Group.

25. The minimum wage necessary to survive in Shenzhen is thought to have been around 400 yuan in 1995.

26. Shenzhen's wage levels are far above those elsewhere in China, partially owing to the fact that Shenzhen's labour market is not fully integrated with the rest of China. Moreover, it was becoming more and more integrated with that of Hong Kong over the course of the reform years, with the impact of Hong Kong forcing up the real value of incomes here compared to elsewhere (Yeung, 1996). However, to a considerable degree, the higher monetary value of earnings in Shenzhen reflects the much higher costs of living in the zone. The average *monthly* family income in the zone in 1995 was reported to be around 3700 yuan (Yeung, 1996: 19).

27. The average annual wage of China's staff and workers in 1993 was around 290 yuan per month (SSB, ZTN, 1995: 113).

28. See below, n. 30.

29. The *xian* is to the West of Beijing, around 75 kilometres from downtown Beijing.

30. Under this scheme, the General Manager of any affiliated enterprise who turns over profits in excess of 50 million yuan will be promoted to be a Special Assistant General Manager within the Group. One who turns over profits in excess of 100 million yuan will be promoted to be Group Assistant General Manager (SJB, 8 April 1998b: 1).

31. Like many Western firms, Nanfang was reluctant to disclose the amount it spent on advertising.

Chapter 6

1. In July 1992 Westinghouse began an alliance with Rolls-Royce in order to improve its gas turbine technology (*FT*, 3 June 1996). Rolls-Royce agreed to transfer aero-engine technology for incorporation into existing and future industrial combustion turbine designs for Westinghouse and its other alliance partners, Mitsubishi Heavy Industry and Fiat Avio. In return Westinghouse agreed to transfer selected steam turbine, combustion turbine and combined cycle technologies to Rolls-Royce. Westinghouse agreed to join with Rolls-Royce in marketing its 50 MW industrial Trent engine in the USA, and Rolls-Royce agreed to work with Westinghouse in marketing Westinghouse's turbine in India (*FT*, 16 May 1996).

2. In its new range of turbines, Siemens uses Pratt and Whitney's advanced aerodynamics, materials, and thermal barrier coating technology. Siemens could have developed this technology independently, but it would have taken much longer (*FT*, 16 May 1995).

3. An interesting speculation in early 1998 was the possibility that Rolls-Royce aero-engines might merge with GEC–Alsthom: 'New GEC is thought to be keen to emulate General Electric of the US which owns power and aero-engine manufacturers' (*FT*, 28 February 1998).

4. The Asian crisis has reduced somewhat the medium-term predictions for the whole of Asia, but this has been compensated for by a faster than expected growth in demand from Latin America. Moreover, the long-term forecasts for Asia are still strong, with 49 per cent of new orders predicted to come from the region between 1998 and 2002 (*FT*, 4 June 1998).

5. The proportion will increase much further with its acquisition of Westinghouse's non-nuclear business.

6. For example, the French government was unwilling to allow Framatome to merge with GEC–Alsthom for fear of allowing control to pass out of French hands. Westinghouse suddenly and unexpectedly withdrew the nuclear part of the power equipment business from consideration for purchase by Siemens in 1997. This was widely thought to be due to pressure from the US government (*FT*, 17 November 1997)

7. The steam turbine business that Rolls-Royce was putting up for sale comprised two segments, International Combustion and Parsons engineering. Ironically, Sir Charles Parsons, who founded Parsons engineering, patented the modern steam turbine in 1884: 'Sir Charles' turbines laid the basis of the modern electricity industry, making it possible to build efficient large modern power stations' (*FT*, 29 July 1996). Parsons did not fully capitalize on the invention, and by the 1930s had been overtaken by rival manufacturers, notably Siemens of Germany, and General Electric and Westinghouse in the USA. After the Second World War the nationalization of the electricity industry created a captive market in the UK for domestic equipment producers. By the mid-1960s, Parsons had expanded to employ 12 000 people, flourishing on orders from the state-run Electricity Generating Board. In 1968 it merged with Reyrolle, a neighbouring maker of electrical switchgear, to form Reyrolle Parsons. At around the same time the British General Electric Company (GEC) was formed by the merger between English Electric and AEI. By the early 1970s, Britain had two turbine makers, GEC and Reyrolle Parsons, and two boiler makers, Clarke Chapman and Babcock International. The government wanted a four-way merger that would create a national champion, but the proposals foundered on local and corporate rivalries, including Reyrolle Parsons' fear of being swallowed by GEC. Instead, Reyrolle Parsons merged with Clarke Chapman to form Northern Engineering (NEI) in 1977, in order to try to compete with the 'giants' of the industry. By the 1980s it was obvious that the effort had failed, and the break-up of the Central Electricity Generating Board (CEGB) made it clear that the old world in which it had operated was over. In 1989, NEI agreed to be taken over by Rolls-Royce (see *FT*, 20 July 1996).

8. In 1980, reported GDP per kilogram of energy used (oil-equivalent) was just $0.5. In almost all developing countries for which there are data, the figure was above 1 dollar, and in most was considerably higher, for example, Egypt = $1.5, Pakistan = $2.0, Indonesia = $3.1, Brazil = $3.3, Bangladesh = $4.6 (World Bank, 1996: 202–3). It must be stressed that these data are of the roughest order of magnitude.

9. In 1994, China's total energy consumption was 770 million metric tons (oil equivalent), compared to 222 million tons in India, 110 million tons in Brazil, 140 million tons in Mexico, and 133 million tons in Korea, and 75 million tons in Indonesia (World Bank, 1996: 202–3).

10. This move attempted to end some of the ambiguity surrounding the ownership of power generating assets. In the past, state funding mainly came in the shape of loans to the local state generator. This meant that the local partner could claim that the central authorities investment in the plant was merely debt rather than equity (BZW, 1996: 31).

11. The Three Gorges Project provides a good example of the diversified approach to funding China's immense power-generating needs (*CDBW*, 7 September 1997). The total requirements for the whole project are estimated to be around $24 billion, the bulk of which would come from domestic sources (*CDBW*, 2 November 1997). In the first phase of the project (1992–7), The State Development Bank will provide $3.6 billion in loans over a 10 year period. The Gezhouba Power Station will provide $96.4 million annually from its profits from selling power. The Chinese government is levying a special electricity fee that will provide $481 million per annum. The China Three Gorges Project Company raised $120 million through the issuance of a domestic bond. Foreign funds from commercial loans and export credits will provide around $1.1 billion.

12. For example, the prospectus for Shandong Huaneng Power states on the one hand that tariffs will be set so as to achieve a predetermined payout ratio, but on the other hand it states quite clearly: '[I]n approving tariff increases ... the Shandong Price Bureau may take account of the ability of consumers to absorb tariff increases. If the proposed tariff increases exceed the Shandong Price Bureau's estimate of the tariffs that consumers are able to absorb, or if the tariffs would result in yearly increases that are considered too great, the Shandong Price Bureau may revise the tariffs accordingly' (CSFB,1994: 41).

13. For example, at Shandong Huaneng's Dezhou plant around one-half of the coal was bought from such mines at spot prices on a month-by-month basis (CSFB, 1994: 40).

14. ABB, for example, thought that it was unlikely that the Chinese government would allow a rate of return above around 15 per cent. At this rate of return it had reservations about committing ABB to heavy investment in Build–Operate–Transfer investments. Goran Lindahl, ABB's chief executive, warned: 'We have some requirements on rate of return. Common practice is plus or minus 20 per cent, depending on whether you are operating in a predictable environment'. He felt that China was 'predictable', but that its laws and regulations for BOT-type projects were still incomplete (quoted in *FT*, 6 January 1997).

15. This was the estimated cost of the Yangcheng Power Plant, with a total capacity of 2100 MW (*FT*, 23 August 1996).

16. The other owners are Lineng Hydropower Development Company, Yichang Three Gorges Project Duoneng Company and Beijing Three Gorges Yangtze Hydropower Technological Development Centre (*CDBW*, 30 November 1997).

17. Shandong Huaneng Power in turn owns 100 per cent of the Dezhou Power Plant, 75 per cent of the Jining Plant, and 60 per cent of the Weihai Plant, all in Shandong Province (CSFB, 1994: 9). It also owns 25 per cent of another plant, the Rizhao Plant, also in Shandong Province. The three wholly-owned or majority owned plants were set to expand from an installed capacity of 1325 MW in 1993 to 1750 MW in 1998. The Rizhao Plant is a greenfield site, with a planned installed capacity of 2500 MW by 1998, and a project cost of around $300 million, and plans for further expansion beyond that date.

18. As one potential investor expressed it: 'With such a high level of uncertainty about the regulatory environment, one would need a 30 per cent predicted return on equity

rather than the 15 per cent available on a comparable investment in the US, and that is far beyond what the Chinese government is willing to allow.'

19. The institutions were France's Banque Nationale de Paris and Société Générale, Britain's Hong Kong and Shanghai Banking Corporation, Germany's Dresdner Bank and Canada's Export Development Corporation (*CDBW*, 31 August 1997).

20. After intense, prolonged competition to win the orders to supply the power units, the Chinese government officially named the suppliers in August 1997. One consortium, consisting of GEC–Alsthom and ABB, received contracts for eight units, with the hydraulic design undertaken by Kvaerner. A second consortium, consisting of Voith, Siemens and GE (Canada), won the contract to supply the other six units (*CDBW*, 31 August 1997). Not only were the turbines of large size, but there were also large technical difficulties associated with the fact that the water level behind the dam will rise almost 100 metres between the first operation of the project in 2002 and its completion in 2009. In order to win the contract, competing companies needed to investigate the technical problems for around a decade. The bidding contest resulted in large progress in world hydro technology. Paul Chan, Vice-President of ABB China, says that success will 'provide a world-wide entry ticket for the next two decades to large-scale hydro-power projects' (quoted in *FT*, 17 February 1997).

21. For the third phase of the Qinshan project, Atomic Energy of Canada will supply two 700 MW heavy water reactors, at a total cost of $4 billion, of which $1.5 billion will be financed by a loan from the Canadian Government's Export Development Corporation (*China: Economic Digest*, Winter 1996–7: 41).

22. The Guangdong No. 2 nuclear power plant will be co-designed by Framatome and domestic Chinese firms. Framatome will co-operate with domestic firms in producing large-scale equipment for the project (*FT*, 18 July 1996).

23. The former USSR had considerable capability in nuclear engineering, Chernobyl notwithstanding. In 1997, China signed an agreement with Russian companies to design and build two 1000 MW nuclear reactors for a new power plant in Jiangsu Province on China's eastern seaboard. Construction was due to start in 1999, and the plants were planned to become operational in 2004–5 (*FT*, 30 December 1997).

24. Li Donghui, deputy Director General of the China National Nuclear Corporation said that 'localization is a strategic priority in China's long-term nuclear power development' (quoted in *China: Economic Digest*, Summer 1997: 16).

25. Westinghouse submitted successful tenders for around 14 power plant contracts in 1994–5.

26. In 1995, the average coal consumption rate at the four thermal plants was 325 grams of coal per kWh of net electricity generation, around the same level as the OECD average of 350 grams/kWh, compared to a Chinese national average of 411 grams (BZW, 1996: 94).

27. Moreover, all the generators were to be equipped with advanced imported sub-critical pressure turbines, reheating boilers and electrostatic precipitators.

28. This was the first 'trust' to be formed in the Machine Building Ministry.

29. As well as the other plants, typically over 200 for a single complete unit.

30. In 1992 the sales value of the four main plants in HPECG was around 1600 million yuan, compared to around 1700 million yuan in the three main plants in the Liaoning's Northeast China Transformer Group (DRC, 1994: 296–7, 300–1).

31. Only three foreign institutional investors own more than 10 per cent of the Company's shares, and these together amount to just 20 per cent of the total number of Company shares (HPEC, 1998: 27). Among the foreign shareholders subscribing to the initial offering, three institutions acquired substantial holdings: Hongkong and Shanghai Bank held around 34 per cent of the shares issued in Hong Kong, Chase Manhattan held around 18 per cent, Standard Chartered held around 16 per cent and ABB held around 4–5 per cent. After the listing, the maximum overseas ownership share in the total company, therefore, was the 13.3 per cent held by the Hongkong and Shanghai Banking Corporation.

32. In 1995 it received around 25.8 million yuan in dividends from its share ownership.

33. In 1995, HPEC paid 21.3 million yuan in taxation.

34. In 1995, HPEC paid 35.8 million yuan in pension and 93.6 million yuan in service fees to HPEGC.

35. The Harbin Cigarette Company generates more profits than HPEC, but it is not under the jurisdiction of the City authorities.

36. These are: Acheng Relay Works, Harbin Insulation Material Plant, Liancai, Number Two Rolled Steel Plant, and Harbin Sanlian 'Development' Company (*Shiye kaifa gongsi*). (The Chinese characters are indistinct in the source being used for the name 'Liancai', so this might not be the accurate name of this plant.)

37. These include the Lanzhou Fayang Electric Power Company, Jiangyang Special Steel Company, Shenzhen Kaiye'er Service Company, Hong Kong Zhonglian Power Materials Company, Beijing Quansantui Power Engineering Company, and Shanghai Xinhua Control Technology Group Company.

38. Thirty-six of these are considered to be of sufficient importance to be listed formally in the printed chart of the firm's organisational structure. Eleven of these are in Harbin, and nine in Shenyang, including the constituent plants in the former *Dongdian*.

39. This sum vastly exceeded the annual profits in the 1990s. In 1995, for example, the post-tax profits of HPEC were 122 million yuan, of which 41.6 million yuan was allocated as dividends.

40. The executive directors in 1997 were:

> *Tian Yushi*. Joined HPEC directly from graduation in 1964. Deputy general manager of the Boiler Works, vice-chairman of HPEGC since 1991 and vice-chairman of the Company HPEC since December 1996.
> *Wang Wenxiang*. Joined HPEGC in 1966 immediately after graduating from Qinghua University. Head of the Generator Works from 1990 to 1994, and became general manager of HPEC in October 1996.
> *Hu Jianqing*. Joined HPEGC in 1954. Chief engineer of the generator Works, and appointed general manager of the Engineering Company of HPEGC in 1993.
> *Wang Cunna*. Joined HPEGC in 1954. Chief accountant of the Boiler Works and from 1994 to 1997 was general manager of the HPEC.
> *Xu Damao*. Joined HPEGC after graduating from Qinghua University in 1961. Chief engineer at the Turbine Works. Deputy general manager of HPEC from 1994 to 1997.
> *Yuan Qihong*. Joined HPEGC immediately after graduating in 1982. Chief production controller at the Boiler Works. Appointed deputy general manager of HPEC in 1994.

Geng Lei. Joined HPEGC in 1968. Director and secretary of the Communist Party in the Boiler Works. Appointed chairman of HPEC in 1994.

Lao Daqian. Joined HPEGC in 1954 immediately after graduation. Deputy head of the generator Works.

Liu Jie. Joined HPEGC in 1962, immediately after graduating. Became general manager and chairman of the Turbine Works. In 1994 appointed deputy general manager of HPEC.

41. The non-executive directors in 1997 were:

Hong Qipeng. A turbine expert who worked in Harbin No. 1 Workshop from 1961 to 1985. Transferred to become vice-mayor of Harbin City and assistant director of Harbin City's Economic Commission, responsible for Harbin's industrial, technological and economic development. In 1993 transferred to the Harbin Municipal People's Congress.

Liang Weiyan. Joined HPEGC in 1951 immediately after graduating and rose to be chief engineer, initially of the Generator Works, and subsequently, of the whole of HPEGC. In 1992 transferred to become head of the Consultative Committee of HPEGC. Simultaneously became assistant director of the Three Gorges Project Equipment Office under the Ministry of Machinery. This position is strategically important for HPEC, since an important part of its prospects are linked to the possible orders it may derive from the Three Gorges Project.

Zhang Zhuoyuan. Director of the Industry and Economics Research Institute of the Chinese Academy of Social Sciences.

Lu Yansun. Joined HPEGC on graduating in 1954, and rose to become head of the Boiler Works in 1983. Transferred to the central government in Beijing in 1984, rising to become deputy head of the former Ministry of Machinery and Electronics 1989 to 1994. Since then has been a member of the Financial Committee of the National People's Congress, and chairman of the PRC's Association of Power Generation Equipment Manufacturing Industry. Has been a powerful public advocate of the need for government policy to support China's indigenous power equipment manufacturers.

Zhang Yichen. Studied at the Harbin Institute of Technology and then in the USA at MIT. Appointed director of the Asia–Pacific Region for the Merrill Lynch Group in 1996. He is also a consultant to the Ministry of Finance, and a member of the Harbin Municipal Government's Political Consultative Committee.

42. Moreover, there had been many internal problems arising also from the listing of the Electric Machine segment of Dongfang Power Equipment Company (Sichuan).

43. In its own company history (Harbin Boiler Works, 1994), prior to the 1980s almost all significant decisions affecting the company's development are prefaced by the statement 'according to the "disposition" (*bushu*) "notice" (*tongzhi*) "ratification" (*pizhun*) and so on of the No. 1 Ministry of Machinery'.

44. Much of the equipment is still functioning today, being used alongside state-of-the-art modern machines. The Leningrad Power Equipment Plant was the principal partner for HPEC. During the first phase of construction from 1954 to 1957, HBW alone had a total budgetary allocation of 80.4 million yuan. Following the withdrawal of Soviet assistance, and the disruption caused by the Great Leap Forward, HPEC began its second phase of construction in 1961 under the plans laid down by the First Ministry of Machine Building.

45. For example, by 1960 HBW was able to build power station boilers ranging from 35 tons/hour to 280 tons/hour. By the late 1960s–early 1970s it was able to build high-pressure power station boilers of between 220 and 410 tons/hour, and super-high-pressure power station boilers of 670 tons/hour.

46. For HBW alone it allocated 25.7 million yuan of investment to help achieve this goal.

47. Altogether, HBW supplied around 300 pieces of equipment, and sent 1200 staff and workers to construct the new plant.

48. In fact, the technical transfer deal was brought about through the activities of the China National Import–Export Corporation, which negotiated with the major multinational power generation equipment companies.

49. Circulation fluidized bed boilers offer potential advantages both for their environmental and operating efficiency in comparison with conventional boilers. They represent a major avenue of technical progress for boilers in the future.

50. For example, in 1996 HTC had 2651 'engineers and technicians', including 358 senior engineers. Over 200 of its engineers had been abroad for training. In 1996 HEC had 1800 'technicians' of whom 450 had 'high-level' scientific qualifications.

51. The advanced imports of machine tools include a German-made DH 2200/80 numerical-control lathe and a USA-made numerical-control side-entry slotting miller, both for processing steam turbine rotors, a PAG-224 numerical-control horizontal milling and boring machine from Italy, and a 20-10 FP500 numerical-control double-column milling machine from Germany, both for processing steam chambers. In addition, HTC has purchased a German-made 320 ton high speed dynamic balancing machine (8.5 metres high and 26 metres long), for final assembly and testing. Among the advanced machine tools that HEC has imported are a German-made high-speed 6 K numerical-control rotor milling machine, for processing generator rotors, a German-made HU2-500 automatic high-speed punching machine for processing iron core laminations, and a German-made high-speed numerical-control 5-coordinates blade milling machine, for processing hydro-turbine blades.

52. These include Narrow Gap welding machines from Sweden and Italy, an MIG arc welding machine from Japan, an X-ray industrial monitor for inspecting weld seams from Japan and an MPM automatic welding production line from Japan, for manufacturing heavy walls.

53. For example, HTC has bought a large numerically-controlled double-column milling machine from Beijing No. 1 Machine Tool Company, produced in a joint venture with the German company Waldrich Coburg. The frame is made by the Beijing plant and the main engine and control system are made by the German partner. It has also purchased a large new numerically-controlled machine tool from a joint venture between Waldrich Siegen (Germany) and Qiqihar Heavy Engineering.

54. These were being installed while we were at the plant by a team of Romanian technicians.

55. We were unable to obtain the exact purchase price for the second hand machinery.

56. Its main source of control systems is the Fulaerji Plant near Qiqihar, also in Heilongjiang Province.

57. Other areas in which it is pursuing technological advance in the immediate period ahead are integrated coal gasification combined cycle systems, and 500 MW Francis-type power generator sets suitable for the Sichuan Ertan power station; as well as a variety of

smaller projects, such as 50 MW or above circulation fluidized bed boilers, large capacity combined cycle fluidized bed boilers, 200 MW low temperature nuclear heat supply systems and large-scale pressurized petrochemical vessels.

58. For example, in 1996 it invested 101 million yuan ($12 million) and used a further 138 million yuan ($17 million) from the proceeds of the listing, to modernize its facilities. These included continuing the work of upgrading valve production, completing a test centre for large-scale generators and turbines, and installing a five-axle numerical-control horizontal boring and milling machine (HPEC, 1997: 16).

59. In 1995 HPEC as a whole paid a total of 93.6 million yuan to HPEGC's service companies, including 16 million yuan in medical fees, 10 million yuan in hospital costs, 19 million yuan in education fees, and 20.4 million yuan in heating fees.

60. HPEC agreed to pay 15 per cent of the aggregate wages into a pension fund run by HPEGC, with the balance of pensions payments being met by HPEGC.

61. Under this scheme, HPEC would pay 10 per cent of the wage bill to the City as a contribution to the City's medical insurance and 5 per cent for the City's housing fund. If the reforms are implemented, then HPEC will hand over altogether, from the retirement pension and other social service contributions, around 38 per cent of the total wage bill, compared to around 33 per cent under the previous arrangement. However, the HPEC workers are opposed to this as they think the standard of service will fall. Also the workers in the service companies, such as teachers and doctors are opposed as they think it likely that their income will fall. Thus, by 1996–7 the service activities had still not 'gone to society'.

62. These stipulate that 22 per cent of the wage bill should be paid into the Harbin City pension fund, which means an 'extra 15 million yuan per annum' from 1996.

63. The average price of steel surged from 2600 yuan in January 1993 to a peak of 3800 yuan per ton in June 1993, and then fell to 2500 yuan at the end of 1994. At the then current rate of exchange the average world steel price was around 3000 yuan per ton (Nolan, 1996).

64. Even if one made the heroic assumption that all of the 1500 staff involved in R & D at HPEC ought to be re-valued at the average wage levels of US scientific personnel, then the total expenditure on R & D at HPEC would still be a maximum of around $70 million. Properly adjusted for technical levels, it may well be substantially less than this.

65. For example, in 1995 HPEC experienced large difficulties, with a fall of almost 15 per cent in total installed capacity and 31 per cent in pre-tax profits (HPEC, 1995: 6). This was mainly owing to the shortage of funding in the industry, which caused two of their main customers to put their orders on hold.

66. For example, there still are local content regulations in both the USA and the EC for such products as motor vehicles, electronics, and integrated circuits (Ruigrok and van Tulder, 1995: 228–9).

67. In developing countries, political factors generally play an even greater role in the allocation of power contracts. For example, India has a policy of giving strong preference to domestic manufacturers in awarding contracts for power plants. The Iranian government requires that around 65–70 per cent of the value of any given power plant project must be supplied by domestic manufacturers.

68. The US government investigation of the proposed Siemens take-over of Westinghouse's non-nuclear division is the exception that proves the rule, and even this may be much more related to international politics than to narrowly economic issues.

Chapter 8

1. MITI skillfully played off one firm against another by promoting the fear that if they did not sell-out now the Japanese would simply buy from another foreign firm (Nester, 1991: 104).

2. From 1973 to 1980 Japan's global market share rose from 18 per cent to 30 per cent. By 1996, Japanese producers occupied 24 per cent of the US market for automobiles and light trucks.

3. In the 1970s, bought-in components accounted for 46 per cent of General Motors' material costs and 60 per cent of Ford's (Prais, 1981: 147).

4. For example, Bosch is able to produce anti-lock braking systems equipment in the USA at a wage rate of about $20 an hour compared with around $44 an hour from GM's internal brake business (*FT*, 26 June 1996).

5. 'The car-makers' search for economies of scale has led them to promote ratio-nalisation among suppliers, the process will inevitably make them more dependent on their suppliers' (*FT*, 28 October 1996).

6. In VW's new plant at Mlada Bolesaw, north of Prague, six important component suppliers have been allocated special zones adjacent to the production line to pre-assem-ble parts just before they are required by the new Octava saloon (*FT*, 4 November 1996).

7. In 1994, 'almost all' the government's funds for the auto industry were allocat-ed to three projects, Shanghai Volkswagen, Erqi's joint venture with Citroen, and Tianjin's joint venture for the production of Charades (Huang Wei, 1995).

8. For example, in 1997, Tianjin Engine Works agreed a joint venture with Varity–Perkins to manufacture diesel engines. The share held by the foreign partner was reported to be 60 per cent (*China: Economic Digest*, Summer 1997: 44).

9. The products of the different joint ventures are:
   Ninguo: rubber seals and parts; hydraulic jacks;
   NYC: diesel engine fuel injection systems;
   Danling: gears;
   Langfang: brake parts, air brake compressors and castings;
   BYC: diesel engine fuel injection systems;
   Harbin: ignition coils, horns, relays and other electrical parts;
   HSE: starter motors, alternators and mini-motors;
   Shanghai: wheels and wheel rims;
   CYPR: piston rings;
   Delphi sub-JV: alternators;
   CR sub-JV: oil seals;
   Shanxi: engine castings;
   CAC: brake pads and linings; clutch facings.

10. The main equipment for the new production line was manufactured at the Dalian Machine Tool Plant.

11. In fact the price was around $20 million after taking into account the transport costs.

12. The terms 'loose' and 'tight' are routinely used to describe the relationship between the core firm and their subsidiary 'second-' and 'third-'tier enterprises.

13. For accounts of the evolution of Dongfeng see Byrd (1992); Marukawa (1995).

14. Nanchong was a small plant in the mid-1990s, the main product of which was a 102 mm bore engine, principally the four cylinder 4102 series.

15. In fact, despite being selected by the Chinese government as an eligible firm, by late 1997 Dongfeng had not yet been floated on international stock markets.

16. Personal communication from Tim Clissold (Asimco).

17. In 1991, average *per capita* consumption stood at just 72 per cent of the national average, and only 60 per cent of that in China's richest province, Guangdong (SSB, ZTN, 1992: 277–8).

18. In fact, the rise in profits was so rapid, that Yuchai seems to have agreed to a premature re-negotiation of the contract in 1988.

19. The others are Liem Sioe Liong, Robert Kuok, Lim Goh Tong and Ting Pek Khiing.

20. Derived from the stated figure for total dividends, of 99.3 million yuan, and the total reported share ownership of the State Holding Company, of 22.1 per cent in Yuchai Machinery Company (Bear, Stearns, 1994: 10; Peat Marwick Huazhen, 1995: 16).

21. The original hope with the New York listing was to obtain $15 per share, but they had to settle for $10 per share. The listing obtained $75 million gross and $64 million net, after the deduction of costs.

22. The intended foundry was in Shanxi. This was a colossal plant, part of the 'Third Front' investment programme. It had originally been owned by the People's Liberation Army, producing castings for tanks. The plant was bought by CITIC from the Army, along with six other military plants. Asimco purchased a 57 per cent ownership share, with Caterpillar (USA) purchasing 27 per cent, and CITIC owning the balance. A main goal of the joint venture is to supply engine castings to Yuchai. Caterpillar are intended to make an important technology input in order to upgrade the quality of the products.

23. It is hard to see that the arrival of Hong Leong as the foreign partner in a Sino–foreign joint venture played any negative role in Yuchai's development.

Chapter 9

1. I have been unable to locate a reliable long-term series for the growth of real value of global steel output.

2. These figures were given for Ispat's Mexican subsidiary, Ispat Mexicana.

3. Including the privately-owned companies in Kazakhstan and Indonesia. Excluding these companies, Ispat's annual output will be around 16 million tons (*FT*, 19 March 1998).

4. For example, Japan's rise to world dominance in the steel industry in the 1960s and 1970s owed a great deal to huge investment in R & D. Great advances occurred in an inter-related set of technologies – the Basic Oxygen Furnace (BOF) technology, continuous casting and computerizing the production process: '[T]he adoption of the BOF led to the successive adoption of the innovations in the integrated production system and made Japanese industry the most efficient and productive in the world' (Yonekura, 1994: 222). Nippon Steel's central research institute alone had over 2000 engineers in the mid-1980s (Yonekura, 1994: 255).

5. In fact, the industry was already far from being an 'infant' and the removal of protection had no noticeable effect (Lake, 1988: 159).

6. Between 1887 and 1890 Britain, without tariff protection, accepted around 52 per cent of all US exports, yet the US market was highly protected against British exports. The proportion only fell slightly between 1891 and 1897 (Lake, 1988: Ch. 3).

7. Still in 1969 it produced 31.5 million tons of crude steel, compared to 19.8 million tons produced by Bethlehem Steel, its closest domestic competitor (Cockerill, 1974: 57). At that point, US Steel still accounted for one-quarter of total US steel output (Cockerill, 1974: 57).

8. In the 1950s, almost half of Japanese steel industry investment was from borrowings (Yonekura, 1994: 226).

9. Thirty per cent is owned by the government directly, 40 per cent by the Korea Development Bank (government-owned) and 30 per cent by private commercial banks, themselves government-controlled (Amsden, 1989: 315).

10. Krupps–Hoesch and Usinor–Sacilor together had around one-third of the world market between them in the mid-1990s (*FT*, 14 March 1996).

11. In fact, the bid was subsequently raised to $490 million in the face of competition from Allegheny Teledyne (*FT*, 6 January 1998). Bethlehem Steel disposed of its loss-making structural products division (makes structural steel shapes for construction industry), BethForge (makes large steel parts), Centec (makes parts for rolling mills) and BethShip (ship repair yard) in 1996. It is focusing on its core operation of flat-rolled steel business (*FT*, 31 October 1996).

12. Bethlehem Steel will sell the unprofitable but highly capital-intensive stainless steel unit from Lukens as the imports of stainless steel are surging in recent years. After the restructuring, Bethlehem Steel will have the broadest range of steel plate products in the industry, for example, used in shipbuilding, construction and mining (*FT*, 16 December 1997).

13. By the late 1970s the largest single steel plant in the USA was at Inland Steel, Indiana, with an annual capacity of 8.5 million tons. The largest Japanese plant was 17.6 million tons, more than twice the size (Yonekura, 1994: 7). Japan had no fewer than nine plants with an annual capacity larger than 8 million tons, four of which belonged to New Japan Steel (Yonekura, 1994: 7).

14. Faced with an adverse macroeconomic environment and rampant smuggling, a joint order from the SBMI and the State Development Planning Commission banned the dumping of steel by domestic enterprises from 1 October 1998. The ban covered steel rods, hot-rolled steel and threading steel. Under the new regulations, the SBMI would publish the average prices (based on the production costs, management fees, financial fees, marketing costs and sales taxes of the 35 major steel-makers) of steel products 20 days after the end of each quarter. Offenders who persistently sold steel below the guidance price floor were to be forbidden to have access to commercial bank loans and were to have their manufacturing permits rescinded (*Hong Kong Standard*, 26, 30 September 1998).

15. This is a rough approximation converting the total investment to US dollars at the 1996 exchange rate.

16. Defined as less than 10 million yuan.

17. A further six enterprises gave no data on profits.

18. Baogang has been able to shed about 2000 workers every year since its establishment by using two strategies. First, some workers are relocated into other subsidiaries

of Baogang. Second, some of its subsidiaries are 'spun-off' from the head company and become legal entities with their own managerial and financial autonomy (*CDBW*, 5–11 January 1997).

19. For a different interpretation of the Shougang story, see Steinfeld (1998).

20. Zhou Beifang was charged with having committed 'economic crimes'.

21. In the advanced economies, very little steel is now produced with the open hearth technique (Table 9-3). Compared to oxygen converter furnaces, open hearth furnaces produce steel more slowly and consume large amounts of energy (WCFL, 1993: 41).

22. Continuous-casting has the advantage over ingot casting that billets produced by this method do not require primary rolling, resulting in lower energy costs, higher yield of billets and shorter production time (WCFL, 1993: 42).

23. Over 5 per cent of Shougang's steel was produced with electric furnaces, compared with less than 1–3 per cent in most other large integrated steel plants.

24. Steinfeld (1998: 169–70) comments: 'Over the years, there have been a number of allegations levelled at the Beijing steel company, allegations that when taken together constitute a sort of "myth of Shougang". The overriding element of this myth is that Shougang's achievement throughout the 1980s and early 1990s were the product of a "sweetheart" deal with Beijing in the sense that the firm's profit contract granted a position in which failure would be absolutely impossible.'

25. In the initial contract in 1981, Shougang was to deliver to the state an amount that rose by 6 per cent each year on the initial base year figure. In 1983, the company volunteered to raise the annual increase to 7.2 per cent.

26. From 1980 to 1993, the average annual increase in the retail price index was 6.8 per cent (SSB, ZTN, 1994: 231).

27. The gross value of industrial output grew by just 4 per cent in real terms in 1981, the lowest figure in the whole period from 1978 to 1994, and even in 1982 the real growth was just 8 per cent, compared to 12 per cent per annum over the whole period 1978–94 (SSB, ZTN, 1995: 32, 377).

28. The retail price index rose from 100 in 1978 to 310 in 1994 (SSB, ZTN, 1995: 233).

29. Company officials at Shougang once fought through red tape to get 400 yuan to buy a 7.5 kilowatt electric motor. Under the existing rules, motors of any size were deemed to be a part of the enterprise's fixed assets and, as such, their replacement had to be approved by higher authorities (*CDBW*, 17 February 1984).

30. While he was head of Shougang, Zhou lived in a six–seven room two-storey house allocated to him by the MMI.

31. In 1994, it consumed 115 million tons of coal, 65 million tons of coke, and 1.7 million tons of crude oil (SSB, ZTN, 1995: 204–5).

32. In 1996, Shougang's coke output was only 55 per cent of that of Baogang, and 40 per cent of that of Angang (ISIC, 1997: 128).

33. For example, the iron ore content of Shougang's domestic iron ore is 25 per cent compared to a national average of 30 per cent, but China's best iron ore mines reach as high as 51 per cent (ISIC, 1997: 169–70).

34. Shougang's markets are nation-wide, with around 60–70 per cent of its sales located north of the Yangtze River and 30–40 per cent in Southern China.

35. In 1992, the official price for reinforced steels was about 1200–1400 yuan, but on the free market, especially in the densely populated coastal areas, the price was as high as 3000–3100 yuan (*Metal Bulletin Monday*, 23 November 1992).

36. For example, in 1988 Shougang's planned steel output was 2.1 million tons. Shougang was allowed to sell 15 per cent of this output (that is, 350 000 tons) at the market price. Shougang also produced 1.5 million tons above the plan. According to the contract, Shougang could sell all of this 1.5 million tons of steel at market prices. This meant that around 1.8 million tons or around 51 per cent of the total output (by weight) in 1988 was sold to the free market. Moreover, the 'within-plan' requirements for different products were based on a physical output figure set in tons. This produced a very clear incentive to raise the quality (and hence the unit price) of extra-plan output.

37. For example, its contract with Beijing Steel Company (*Beijing gantie gongsi*) estimated its planned profits for 1995 to be 5 billion yuan. The contract with Shougang stipulated that 3.7 billion yuan be handed over to the headquarters, and the remaining profits were to be distributed in the proportion of 4:3:3 (development funds, collective welfare funds, and workers' bonuses, respectively).

38. For example, in 1990 Shougang merged with three factories employing around 10 000 people. It attempted to develop their capability to make electronic equipment. The venture was unsuccessful, and Shougang simply returned them to their original administrative authority.

39. These include a 6000 ton hydropress, 100 ton vacuum smelting furnace and 15 metre well-annealing furnace that can process comprehensive heavy machinery for the metallurgical, mining and power industries. The annual hot-working capacity is 35 000 tons and the cold-working capacity is 30 000 tons.

40. The attempts to solve the problems of these factories also involved administrative co-ordination with the state at a local level. For example, in Gansu province, Shougang closed down two of the factories and moved them and their workers to the site of a third of the merged military factories in Lanzhou, the capital of Gansu. Shougang and the state together invested in restructuring the equipment so that the plant shifted to producing ball bearings. A major issue in attempting to salvage loss-making military enterprises was the housing costs of re-locating the workers. Both Shougang and the state contributed towards the cost of re-housing them.

41. It was common for enterprises that failed to meet their profit targets to continue to pay welfare and bonuses to workers as if they had met their targets, so that the enterprises were unable to pay over their stipulated profits and/or reduced reinvestment out of retained profits. See for example the detailed account of the Nanning Silk and Ramie Factory (Byrd, 1992: 296). This factory was one of the early experimenters with the profit retention contract. As profits fell in the early 1980s, the factory sharply reduced profits handed over to the state, and even more drastically reduced the share of retained profits allocated to investment. The proportion of retained profits allocated to workers' welfare and bonuses rose from 42 per cent in 1979 to over 86 per cent in 1982.

42. It is beyond the scope of this chapter to investigate the precise details of the level at which the decision was taken for Zhou Guanwu to go into retirement.

43. By the late 1990s, some of the keypoint plants were lagging considerably in their average wages. For example, in 1996 the average wage at the 33 keypoint plants was 10 500 yuan. Six plants had a less than 7000 yuan average wage, and one had less than 5000 yuan. Average wages at that plant, Shuicheng Iron and Steel Group stood at just 45 per cent of

the national average for keypoint plants and a mere 19 per cent of the average wage at Baogang, with the highest wage level among the keypoint plants (ISIC, 1997: 122–3).

44. Byrd makes the same point forcefully in his analysis of Erqi (Byrd, 1992).

45. From 1979 to 1986, it is estimated that 44 per cent of Shougang's profits was attributable to improved product quality, 16 per cent to reducing costs of production and 40 per cent to increased sales.

46. Two generators manufactured by Siemens in the 1920s were still in use. Siemens offered to replace them with new ones free of charge because they wanted to use the old ones to advertise the company's 'sixty years' of quality production' (*Beijing Review*, 13–19 January 1992: 18). Some boilers and steam turbines, which had been imported in 1918, when the company was first established, were still in use (*CDBW*, 6 November 1982).

47. State investment in Shougang fell from 150 million yuan in 1978, to 70 million yuan in 1979, 50 million yuan in 1980 and 10 million yuan in 1981, falling to zero in 1982 (*CDBW*, 10 November 1982).

48. The former Belgian owner of the machine visited Shougang in February 1990. When he was told the daily production capacity of the machine, he was doubtful. However, after he checked the speed of the rolled steel coming out of the machine, he said: 'You've done better than we did' (*Beijing Review*, 27 January–2 February 1992: 23–4).

49. For example, in May 1989, one of the iron plants missed the total monthly output by 1000 tons. The resulting penalty was not merely exacted from those directly responsible. Instead none of the 1500 workers in the plant was given a bonus (which amounted to more than 25 per cent of their take-home pay) (Xu and Liu, 1992a: 202). In October 1989, the Corporation failed to fulfil its monthly growth target due to a big accident at the No. 3 Blast Furnace. This stopped production for five days and the Corporation lost the equivalent of $11 million as a result. In that month, no-one in the whole Corporation was given their monthly bonus (*CDBW*, 6 December 1989).

50. Shougang's approach, which combined relatively high remuneration for regular employees in the core firm with tight discipline, is similar to that at Posco.

51. The trade unions, which are responsible for monitoring the service systems, distributed more than 4000 questionnaires each month to investigate whether the workers were satisfied with the service systems. The company ruled that, for example, canteen staff could only obtain their full bonuses if the ratio of satisfied answers was over 89 per cent (Hao, 1992: 159). This pressure contributed to a rise in the quality of service in the canteens, with the proportion of Shougang employees who ate there rising from around 50 per cent before 1980 to 98 per cent in 1990.

52. From 1979 to 1990, around 20000 families moved into new apartments, and around 11000 families added to their living space. Basically all the workers at the main site in Beijing were in Corporation housing.

53. The proportion of people with infectious disease fell from 28 per cent before the reform to 7 per cent in 1990. Absence due to illness fell from 3.8 per cent to 1.7 per cent over the same period.

54. It was the biggest joint venture deal in Beijing in that year (*CDBW*, 29 July 1990). The joint venture was scheduled to last for 20 years, with a 60 per cent controlling share ownership in the hands of Shougang. Shougang chose the chairman of the Board of Directors and NEC chose the General Manager.

55. The new production line was scheduled to begin mass production of 4-megabit D-Rams in November 1996. The number of chips manufactured was planned to rise to 6.7 million units in 1997. NEC was also schedules to manufacture advanced 16-megabit D-Rams from July (*FT*, 24 January 1996).

56. The $4.12 million leveller, which was designed by Mesta and manufactured by Shougang, was the first piece of metallurgical equipment exported by China to a developed country (*Beijing Review*, 4–10 October 1993: 19).

57. Angang has taken a 40 per cent holding in the Koolyanobing Mine in Western Australia, and China Metallurgical Import and Export Corporation has also taken a 40 per cent holding in CRA Hammersley Iron's new mine in Western Australia. In each case 100 per cent of the iron ore output from the mine was purchased by the Chinese partner (*FT*, 2 February 1995)

58. At the end of 1985, the reported prices of Shougang shipping to China the second-hand equipment it had bought in Belgium was $115–120 per ton. It purchased 50 000 tons of equipment and so was required to pay $6 million in shipping costs, equivalent to over one-half of the amount that Shougang had paid to purchase the equipment in the first place.

59. Diversification into shipping is not unusual among large steel firms. For example, in the late 1950s, Japan's leading steel firms, co-ordinated by MITI, also vertically integrated into the shipping business. They together formed a separate company and, with loans from the government, bought a fleet of large, specialised iron-ore transporting ships (Yonekura, 1994: 218).

60. Four months later, Shougang bought a 25.12 per cent interest in Eastern Century Holdings, which produces and trades in manganese ore and manganese ferrous-alloys, an essential raw material for steel production (*SCMP*, 27 February 1993). In 1992, Eastern Century expanded into the production of manganese ferrous-alloys within China by setting up the domestic firms of Xinyu Far East Ferro Manganese and Shanghai Shenjia Ferro-alloys (*SCMP*, 25 February 1993). By July 1993, Shougang joined forces with Li Kashing jointly to establish the Kader Investment Group (*SCMP*, 19 May 1993) and Santai Manufacturing, which is in the steel and electronic-related manufacturing industries (*SCMP*, 8 July 1993).

61. 1996 sales for the three companies were $4.4 billion for Shougang, compared with $4.7 billion for Hutchison Whampoa and $5.1 billion for Singapore Airlines (UNCTAD, 1998: 48).

62. Indeed, Byrd's (1992) meticulous account of Erqi specifically discounts this as the main explanation of Erqi's rapid growth and modernization.

63. Such as the British Monopolies and Mergers Commission (MMC) and the European Commission.

64. A recent dramatic example of government-mediated merger is the business revolution in the US defence industry in the 1990s. Under the close guidance of the Pentagon the number of defence equipment companies was reduced from over 20 to just four (Boeing–McDonnell Douglas, Lockheed–Martin, Northrop Grumman and Raytheon) (Nolan and Wang, 1997).

65. This is a highly sensitive issue, which it is not possible to investigate directly. It involves also complex psychological issues.

66. Indeed, it appeared to be the case that after 1995, the City government and Shougang simply manipulated the accounting procedures in order to produce the desired

outcome in terms of total hand-overs to the City government. Under the new turnover tax system, Shougang, with the agreement of the government would simply place under the heading of 'costs', many items that formerly were included in 'profits'. The main 'flexible' item is depreciation, which can be altered 'more or less at the Corporation's discretion'. Under the contract system Shougang 'raised' their reported profits by having a 'low' depreciation figure and under the new system they are increasing the reported depreciation rate, thereby lowering reported profits. Shougang's reported post-tax profits plummeted with the ending of the contract system. Shougang's reported post-tax profits in 1993 were 3.0 billion yuan (MMI, 1994: 411) and in 1995 were 3.1 billion yuan, declining to 183 million yuan in 1996 and 209 million yuan in 1997 (CMISI, 1997: 170, 288).

67. It was initially planned to do this in 1998, but, for obvious reasons, the listing was postponed.

68. These data are ambiguous. Another source lists Shougang's total overseas assets in 1997 as only $0.73 billion, amounting to 12 per cent of the Group's total assets (Luo Bingsheng, 1998).

69. In 1997 the profit rate on sales revenue was 3.1 per cent for Krupps, 6.9 per cent for British Steel, 7.3 per cent for Usinor and 9.2 per cent for Thyssen (DTI, 1998: 22, 62–3).

70. The approach to merger and acquisition taken by the Chinese government is likely to be strongly influenced by the pace of merger and acquisition in the international steel industry. If this continues at the present high speed it is more likely that central government will encourage large mergers across regions.

Chapter 10

1. The international price of coal rose by 11 per cent from 1980 to 1995 (i.e. it fell substantially in real terms), compared to a 29 per cent fall in the price of natural gas, and a 53 per cent fall in the price of oil (MGB, ZMGN, 1997: 332–3).

2. These kinds of international comparisons of energy-efficiency are fraught with huge conceptual difficulties. Smil (1993: 72–3) has vividly illustrated this. Using official exchange rates to convert national product, China is one of the world's most energy-*ine*fficient large economies. Using purchasing power parity (PPP) measures of national product, 'China's position is completely reversed', and it becomes 'the world's most energy-efficient large economy'.

3. It is, of course, of much lower quality than washed coal from large coal mines.

4. The 14 fees' are: goods yard rental fee (3.5 yuan), vehicle dispatching fee (1.5 yuan), coal handling fee (2.0 yuan), coal loading fee (2.2 yuan), coal weighing fee (1 yuan), inlet monitoring and keeping fee (0.4 yuan), special railway usage fee (1 yuan), goods yard storage fee (0.35 yuan), labour and service fee (0.75 yuan), site cleaning fee (0.25 yuan), coal pushing and coal way opening fee (2.55 yuan), security fee (0.10 yuan), self-coal train car management fee (2 yuan) and 'agreement to transport' fee (6 yuan) (China Coal Consultancy, 1998).

5. Prices are for Australian steam coal to Japan.

6. Chinese coal prices are for cities in non-mining areas, and the range reflects different transport costs. The US coal prices are for power utilities (low) and industry (high), and vary depending on quality. The spot market price is for Australian exports.

7. The information in this paragraph is based on an interview with Ye Qing, conducted in June 2000, by my PhD student, Ms Rui Huaichuan.

8. For a pioneering study of the informal sector in India, see Breman, 1997. There is nothing remotely comparable for China. A vast array of human activity takes place virtually unrecorded.

Chapter 12

1. Noted by the author.

2. In fact, the passage was in 1987, but implementation was from 1992.

3. Internal expansion here refers to establishing branches and subsidiaries directly rather than through M & A.

4. Berger *et al.* (2000) found that, from 1986 to 1998, about three-quarters of the value of the intra-EU M & A was generated by the same EU nation. But the truly domestic M & As have declined as a fraction of total EU merger activity since the mid-1990s.

5. Before the passage of the new act, the Bank Holding Companies (BHCs) could own up to only 5 per cent of non-financial companies.

6. In fact, with the globalization of German universal banks, giants like Deutsche and Dresdner are restructuring to build more focused businesses. (See *FT*, May and July 2000.)

7. According to the industry categories of *Fortune*, the financial services industry is divided into 'commercial and savings banks', 'diversified financials', 'insurance-life & heath', 'insurance-P & C', and 'securities'.

8. They are Citigroup, Bank of America, HSBC, Bank of Tokyo– Mitsubishi and Chase Manhattan.

9. Following the acquisition of Morgan Grenfell by Deutsche Bank, the acquisition of Warburgs by UBS, Kleinwort Benson by Dresdner, Barings by ING, Schroders by Salomon Smith Barney, and the Rothschild alliance with ABN Amro, Fleming (now Chase Fleming) was almost the only big merchant bank that remained in British hands.

10. In August, the new securities company, named China Galaxy Securities Co., was established, as the only securities company wholly owned by the central government.

11. In fact, it is not the year of ABC's most severe losses in recent years.

12. See especially, Lardy (1998) for an extended discussion.

13. Insurance density = Insurance premium/GDP.

14. See <www.chinapntr.gov>, and EU and White House Website.

15. Wang Xiaoqiang, personal communication.

Chapter 14

1. See Nolan (1995) for a comprehensive account.

2. This table updates a similar table in Smil (1993). I am indebted to Smil for this simple and vivid illustration of the deficiencies of both approaches to measuring national product.

3. These included the China Development Forum, organized by the Development Research Centre of the Chinese State Council, and the 21st Century Forum, organized by the Chinese People's Political Consultative Conference.

Bibliography

ABN–AMRO. *Yanzhou Coal Mining Co Ltd* (Hong Kong: ABN–AMRO, 1998).

AI FENG. 'Shougang's Enlightenment', in Editorial Commission of *Reform in Shougang*, 1 (1992), 188–98 (in Chinese).

AMSDEN, A. A. *Asia's Next Giant: South Korea and Late Industrialization* (New York and Oxford: Oxford University Press, 1989).

AMSDEN, A. and T. HIKINO. 'Project execution capability, organizational know-how and conglomerate corporate growth in late industrialization', *Industrial and Corporate Change*, 3(1) (1994), 111–47.

AMSDEN, A. and A. SINGH. 'The optimal degree of competition and dynamic efficiency in Japan and Korea', *European Economic Review*, 38 (1994), 941–51.

ANDREWS-SPEED, C. P. and S. DOW. 'Reform of China's electric power industry: challenges facing the government' (1999) (mimeo).

ANDREWS-SPEED, C. P. and GAO ZHIGUO. 'China's petroleum legal regime foreign participation in upstream operations: the foreign oil company's view', *Journal of Energy and Natural Resources Law* (1996), 161–78.

AOKI, M. 'The Japanese firm in transition', in Yammamura and Yasuba (1987).

AOKI, M. 'The Japanese firm as a system of attributes: a survey and research agenda', in Aoki and Dore (1994).

AOKI, M. and R. DORE (eds). *The Japanese Firm: the Sources of Competitive Advantage* (London: Oxford University Press, 1994).

AOKI, M., B. GUSTAFFSON and O. WILLIAMSON (eds). *The Firm as a Nexus of Treaties* (London: Sage, 1990).

ARNETT, E. 'Beyond the threat perception: assessing military capacity and reducing the risk of war in Southern Asia', in Arnett (1997).

ARNETT, E. (ed.). *Military Capacity and the Risk of War: China, India, Pakistan and Iran* (Oxford: Oxford University Press, 1997).

Asimco. *Asimco*, Asimco publicity brochure (1997).

ÅSLUND, A. *Gorbachev's Struggle for Economic Reform* (London: Pinter, 1991).

AU SHUN, EBISAKI MIYUKI, HUNG MAY and WU QING. *Has HSBC's Acquisition of Midland Bank Created Value?* (Judge Institute of Management Studies, University of Cambridge, 2000) (unpublished report).

AVIC. *Aviation Industries of China* (Beijing: AVIC, 1998).

Bank for International Settlements (BIS). *70th Annual Report* (2000).

Baosteel, *Baosteel Marching toward one of the Larger Modernised Integrated Complexes in the World* (1998) (mimeo).

BARSHEFSKY, C. 'China's WTO accession: American interests, values and strategy', Testimony before the House Committee on Ways and Means <www.ustr.gov> (2000a).

BARSHEFSKY, C. 'Trade and American national security: the case of China's WTO accession', Speech at the United States Military Academy, <www. Chinapntr.gov/speeches/barshefsky> (2000b).

BAUMOL, W., R. NELSON and E. N. WOLFF (eds). *Convergence of Productivity: Cross-National Studies and Historical Evidence* (New York: Oxford University Press, 1994).

Bear, Stearns. *China Yuchai International Limited*, Prospectus (New York, 1994).

Bear, Stearns. *Yanzhou Coal Mining Company Limited*, Prospectus (Hong Kong, 1998).

BENEWICK, R. and P. WINGROVE (eds). *China in the 1990s* (London: Macmillan, 1995).

BENJAMIN, J. and D. SABALOT. *Embracing Smoke: The Internet and Financial Services Regulation* (Centre for the Study of Financial Innovation, 1999).

BERGER, A., R. YOUNG, H. GENAY and H. UDELL. *Globalization of Financial Institutions: Evidence from Cross-Border Banking Performance* (Washington, DC: Federal Reserve, 2000).

BERNSTEIN R. and R. H. MUNRO. *The Coming Conflict with China* (New York, Random House, 1998).

BEST, M. *The New Competition* (Cambridge: Polity Press, 1990).

BLANCHARD, O., M. BOYCKO, M. DABROWSKI, R. LAYARD and A. SHLIEFER. *Post-Communist Reform* (Cambridge, MA: MIT Press, 1993).

BOLTHO, A. *Japan: An Economic Survey, 1953–7* (Oxford: Oxford University Press, 1975).

BOSERUP, E. *Population and Technology* (Oxford: Blackwell, 1981).

BREMAN, J. *Footloose Labour* (Cambridge: Cambridge University Press, 1997).

British Petroleum (BP). *BP Statistical Review of World Energy* (1996).

British Petroleum (BP). *BP Statistical Review of World Energy* (1997).

British Petroleum (BP). *BP Statistical Review of World Energy* (1998).

BP Amoco. 'BP Amoco targets faster delivery of $2 billion savings', BP Amoco press release, 17 February 1999 <www.BPAmoco.com/scripts/pressrelease.asp?PressReleaseID=174> (1999a).

BP Amoco. 'BP Amoco–ARCO announcement' <www.BPAmoco.com/ums> (1999b).

BP Amoco. *Annual Report & Accounts, 1998* (1999c).

BP Amoco. *Presentation to the Financial Community, 15/16 July 1999* (1999d).

BUCK, J. L. *Land Utilisation in China* (New York: Paragon Reprint, 1968) (originally published 1937).

BYRD, W. A. 'The Second Motor Vehicle Manufacturing Plant', in Byrd (1992).

BYRD, W. A. (ed.). *Chinese Industrial Firms under Reform* (Washington, DC: Oxford University Press, 1992).

BZW. *Power Asia* (London: BZW, 1996).

CAMPBELL, J. L., J. R. HOLLINGSWORTH and L. N. LINDBERG (eds). *Governance of the American Economy* (Cambridge: Cambridge University Press, 1991).

CAO, Y. Z., Y. Y. QIAN and B. R. WEINGAST. 'From federalism, Chinese style to privatization, Chinese style', *Economics of Transition,* 7 (1999), 103–31.

Centre for Medicines Research International (CMR). *World-wide Pharmaceuticals R&D Expenditure 1986–1996* (Internet Edition, 1998).

CHAI, JOSEPH C. H. *CHINA Transition to a Market Economy* (New York: Oxford University Press, 1997).

CHANDLER, A. *Scale and Scope: The Dynamics of Industrial Capitalism* (Cambridge, MA: Harvard University Press, 1990).

CHANDLER, A., F. AMATORI and T. HIKINO (eds). *Big Business and the Wealth of Nations* (Cambridge: Cambridge University Press, 1997).

CHANDLER, A. and T. HIKINO. 'The large industrial enterprise and the dynamics of modern economic growth', in Chandler et al. (1997).

CHANG HA-JOON. *The Political Economy of Industrial Policy* (New York: St Martin's Press, 1994).

CHEN FANG. *The Foreign Armies Grab China (Haiwai bingtuan qianggou zhongguo)* (Beijing: *Zhongguo shehui chubanshe*, 1999).

CHEN QIAOSHENG. *'Erqi jituan jihua danlie de huiti huigu he qishi'*, *Zhongguo Jingji Yanjiu,* 8 (1992), 63–9.

CHEN QIAOSHENG. *'Fazhan qiye jituan tuijin guoyou jingji zhanlue chongzu'*, *Contemporary Finance and Economics (Dangdai Caijing),* 4 (1998), 18–25.

CHEN ZHUN et al. *Restructuring the Assets of the Chinese Oil and Petrochemical Industry* (Beijing: *Jingji kexue chubanshe,* 1998).

CHIANG KAISHEK. *China's Destiny* (London: Dennis Dobson, 1947).

CHIANG, P. K. *A Window on Taiwan's Economic Development Experience* (Taiwan, ROC: Council for Economic Planning and Development, 1999).

China Chemical Information Centre. *China Chemical Industry Yearbook* (Beijing: China National Chemical Information Centre, 1997).

China Coal Consultancy (Technology Consulting Committee of the Ministry of Coal Industry, China Technical Economic Consulting Centre of the Coal Industry). Research Materials on the Chinese Coal industry (mimeos of unpublished documents) (1998).

China International Capital Corporation (CICC). *China Telecom Hong Kong: Embracing a Competitive Era* (Beijing: CICC, 1999).

China International Capital Corporation (CICC). *China Unicom: Approaching Our Near Term Target* (Beijing: CICC, 2000).

China Metallurgical Information and Standardization Institute (CMISI). *China Steel Statistics 1997* (Beijing: The Developing and Planning Department, Ministry of Metallurgical Industry, 1997).

China National Petroleum Corporation (CNPC). *Chinese Oil and Natural Gas Industry Yearbook (Zhongguo shiyou tianranqi gongye ninajian)* (ZSTGN) (Beijing: *Shiyou gongye chubanshe,* various years).

China National Petroleum Corporation (CNPC). *China Petroleum Corporation, Annual Report, 1998* (1999).

China Petrochemical Corporation (Sinopec). *Annual Report, 1994* (1995).

China Petrochemical Corporation (Sinopec). *Annual Report, 1995* (1996).

China Petrochemical Corporation (Sinopec). *Annual Report, 1998* (1999).

China Petrochemical Corporation (Sinopec). *China Petrochemical Corporation Yearbook 1994 (Zhongguo shiyou gongye gongsi nianjian)* (ZSGGN) (Beijing: Sinopec, 1995).

China Petrochemical Corporation (Sinopec). *China Petrochemical Corporation Yearbook 1997 (Zhongguo shiyou gongye gongsi nianjian)* (ZSGGN) (Beijing: Sinopec, 1998).

China Pharmaceutical Yearbook 1997 (CPY). (Beijing: China Pharmaceutical Technology Publication, 1997) (in Chinese).

China Reform and Development Report Expert Group (China Reform Group). *'Growing up to Maturity': Case Studies of China's Outstanding Large Enterprises (Zhongguo jiyou da qiye anli yanjiu)* (Shanghai: Far East Publishing Company, 1999).

China Telecom (Hong Kong) (CTHK). *Annual Report, 1999* (2000).

China Unicom. *Prospectus, 2000.*

Chinese Academy of Social Sciences (CASS). Industrial Economics Research Department, *China's Industrial Development Report (Zhongguo gongye fazhan baogao)* (ZGFB) (Beijing: *Jingji guanli chubanshe*,1996–8).

Chinese Auto Technology Research Centre (*Zhongguo qiche jishu yanjiu zhongxin*) (ZQJYZ). *Chinese Auto Industry Yearbook (Zhongguo qiye gongye nianjian)* (ZQGN) (Beijing: Chinese Auto Technology Research Centre, 1999).

CHOUNG, E. and D. TERRESON. *China's Emerging Energy Landscape: A Bird's Eye View* (Hong Kong: MSDW, 1998).

CIPOLLA, C. (ed). *The Fontana Economic History of Europe: The Industrial Revolution* (Glasgow: Collins, 1973a).

CIPOLLA, C. (ed). *The Fontana Economic History of Europe: The Emergence of Industrial Societies (2)* (Glasgow: Collins,1973b).

CIPOLLA, C. (ed). *The Fontana Economic History of Europe: Contemporary Economies* (Glasgow: Collins/Fontana, 1976).

CLARKE, R. A. *Soviet Economic Facts* (London: Macmillan, 1983).

CLINTON, W. *The Clinton Administration Statement on PNTR for China: A Strong Deal in the Best Interest of America,* in White House Website (2000).

COASE, R. H. 'The nature of the firm', reprinted in Coase (1988) (originally published 1937).

COASE, R. H. *The Firm, the Market and the Law* (Chicago: University of Chicago Press, 1988).

Coca-Cola. *Annual Report, 1995* (1996).

Coca-Cola. *Annual Report, 1998* (1999).

COCKERILL, A. *The Steel Industry* (Cambridge: Cambridge University Press, 1974).

Commission for the Reform of the Economic System (CRES). *China Economic System Reform Yearbook (Zhongguo jingji tizhi gaige nianjian)* (ZJTGN) (Beijing: *Zhongguo gaige chubanshe,* various years).

Commission for the Reform of the Economic System (CRES Research Group). *Guoyou qiye gaige gongjian* (GQGG) (Beijing: *Gaige chubanshe*, 1998).

COOPER, R. Speech at China Development Forum (Beijing 2000).

Council for Economic Planning and Development (CEPD). *Taiwan Statistical Data Yearbook* (Taipei: CEPD, 1998).

Crédit Suisse First Boston (CSFB). *Shandong Huaneng Power Development Co. Ltd.* (CSFB, 1994).

CUN FU, *Robbing China (Qiangtan Zhongguo)* (Beijing: *Zhongguo minhang chubanshe*, 1998).

CUSUMANO, M. A. *The Japanese Automobile Industry* (Cambridge, MA: Harvard University Press, 1985).

Daimler–Chrysler. *Annual Report, 1998* (1999).

DENG XIAOPING. *Selected Works of Deng Xiaoping (1975–1982)* (Beijing: Foreign Languages Press, 1984).

DENG XIAOPING. 'Speech [1977] at a plenary meeting of the military commission of the Central Committee of the CPC', in Deng Xiaoping (1984).

DENG YINGTAO. *A New Mode of Development and China's Future (Xin fazhan moshi yu zhongguo de weilai)* (Beijing: *Zhongxin chubanshe*, 1991).

Denso. *Annual Report, 1999* (2000).

Department of Trade and Industry (DTI). *The UK R&D Scoreboard 1994* (Edinburgh: DTI, 1994).

Department of Trade and Industry (DTI). *The UK R&D Scoreboard 1995* (Edinburgh: DTI, 1995).

Department of Trade and Industry (DTI). *The UK R&D Scoreboard 1996* (Edinburgh: DTI, 1996).

Department of Trade and Industry (DTI). *The UK R&D Scoreboard 1998* (Edinburgh: DTI, 1998).

Department of Trade and Industry (DTI). *The UK R&D Scoreboard 1999* (Edinburgh: DTI, 1999).

Detroit Diesel. *Annual Report, 1998* (1999).

Development Research Centre of the State Council (DRC). Listings of China's Largest Enterprises, 1993 (*Zhongguo daxing qiye paixu*) (ZDQP) (Beijing: Management World, 1994).

DICKEN, P. *Global Shift* (London: Paul Chapman, 1992).

DICKEN, P. *Global Shift,* 2nd edn (London: Paul Chapman, 1998).

DICKSON, I. 'China's steel imports: an outline of recent trade barriers', *Chinese Economy Research Unit Working Paper,* 96/6 (Adelaide: University of Adelaide, 1996).

DING, ARTHUR S. 'China defence finance: content, process and administration', *The China Quarterly,* 146 (1996), 428–42.

Economic Co-ordination Bureau, Metallurgy Ministry (ECB). 'Analysis of the economic performance of the metallurgy industry in 1994', *Metallurgy Economic Study* 4 (1995), 1–10 (in Chinese).

Editorial Commission of *Reform in Shougang* (Beijing 1992) (in Chinese).

ENG, M., F. LEES and L. MAUER. *Global Finance* (New York: Addison-Wesley, 1998).

European Bank for Reconstruction and Development (EBRD). *Transition Report, 1998* (London: EBRD, 1998).

Exxon. *Annual Report, 1997* (1998).

Exxon. *Annual Report, 1998* (1999).

FEUERWERKER, A. *The Chinese Economy, 1912–1949* (Ann Arbor, Michigan: University of Michigan, 1968).

Financial Times. Survey: Power Generation Equipment (London: *FT*, 19 June 1997).

FINDLAY, R. 'Trade development and the state', in Ranis and Schultz (1988).

Fortune. The Fortune Global 500, 138 (3) (3 August 1998).

Fortune. 1999 Fortune 500 (1999) <cgi.pathfinder.com/fortune/fortune500/>.

FRANK, A. G. *ReOrient* (Berkeley: University of California Press, 1998).

FRANKENSTEIN, J. and B. GILL. 'Current and future challenges facing Chinese defence industries', *The China Quarterly*, 146 (June 1996).

FRANSMAN, M. 'Is industrial policy obsolete?', *Cambridge Journal of Economics,* Vol. 19 (1995).

FREELAND, C. *Sale of the Century: The Inside Story of the Second Russian Revolution* (London: Little Brown, 2000).

FRIEDMAN, M. *Capitalism and Freedom* (Chicago: University of Chicago Press, 1962).

FRIEDMAN, W. 'Arms procurement in China: poorly understood processes and unclear results', in Arnett (1997).

GALBRAITH, J. K. *The New Industrial State* (Harmondsworth: Penguin, 1967).

GE. *Annual Report, 1998* (1999).

GERLACH, M. L. *Alliance Capitalism: The Social Organization of Japanese Business* (Berkeley: University of California Press, 1992).

Glaxo Wellcome. *Annual Report, 1999* (2000).

GODWIN, P. H. B. 'Military technology and doctrine in Chinese military planning: compensating for weakness', in Arnett (1997).

GOMULKA, S. 'Shock needed for the Polish economy', *The Guardian,* 19 August 1989.

GROOMRIDGE, M. A. and C. E. BARFIELD. *Tiger by the Tail: China and the World Trade Organization* (Washington, DC: American Enterprise Institute, 1999).

GURTOV, M. 'Swords into market shares: China's conversion of military industry into civilian products', *The China Quarterly*, 134 (June 1993).

HADDOCK, F. 'A tough act to follow', *Global Finance* (January 2000).

HAKANSON, H. *Corporate Technological Behaviour: Co-operation and Networks* (London: Routledge, 1989).

HAMILTON, A. *The Financial Revolution – The Big Bang World-Wide* (Harmondsworth: Penguin, 1986).

HAN DEQIANG. *The Globalisation Trap and China's Realistic Choices (Quznqiuhua xianjing yu zhongguo xianshi xuanze)* (Beijing: *Jingji guanli chubanshe*, 2000).

HAO ZHEN. 'Innovation: the path for the socialist firm with Chinese characteristics', in Editorial Commission of *Reform in Shougang,* 1. (Beijing: Beijing Press, 1992), 153–62 (in Chinese).

Harbin Boiler Works. *Harbin Boiler : Forty Years, 1954–1994 (Harbin guolu chang: sishi nian)* (Harbin: Harbin Boiler Works, 1994).

Harbin Power Equipment Company (HPEC). *Annual Report, 1994* (1995).

Harbin Power Equipment Company (HPEC). *Annual Report, 1995* (1996).

Harbin Power Equipment Company (HPEC). *Annual Report, 1996* (1997).

Harbin Power Equipment Company (HPEC). *Interim Report, 1997* (1998).

Harbin Power Equipment Company (HPEC). *Annual Report, 1998* (1999).

HASHIMOTO, M. and J. RAISIAN. 'Employment tenure and earnings profiles in Japan and the United States', *American Economic Review*, 75(4) (1985), 721–35.

HASSARD, J. *et al. The Contract Responsibility System at the Shougang Steel Works, Beijing: A Review of the System and Recent Developments* (Keele: Department of Management, Keele University, 1992) (mimeo).

HIKINO, T. and A. AMSDEN. 'Staying behind, stumbling back, sneaking up, soaring ahead: late industrialization in historical perspective', in Baumol *et al.* (1994).

HIRST, P. and G. THOMPSON. *Globalization in Question* (London: Routledge, 1995).

HO PING-TI. *Studies on the Population of China, 1368–1953* (Cambridge, MA: Harvard University Press, 1959).

HOGAN, W. T. *Steel in the 21st Century* (New York: Lexington Books, 1994).

HOLSCHUH, L. J. *Short and Medium Term Outlook for Steel Demand – Annual Report of the Secretary General*, Presentation to the 32nd Annual Conference of the International Iron and Steel Institute, Taipei, Taiwan (5 October 1998).

HUA DI. 'Threat perception and military planning in China: domestic instability and the importance of prestige', in Arnett (1997).

HUANG LANGHUI, WU ZHONGHUA, and YAO YUMIN. *'Bai hu shidian zhidu chuangxin chengxiao xianzhu'*, *Modern Enterprise Herald*, 1 (1998), 35–9.

HUANG WEI. 'Auto industry faces challenge and opportunities', *Beijing Review*, 38, (45) (6 November 1995).

HUNTINGTON, S. P. *The Clash of Civilizations and the Remaking of the World Order* (New York: Simon & Schuster, 1996).

HYMER, S. 'The multinational corporation and the law of uneven development' (1975), reprinted in Radice (1975).

IBM. *Annual Report, 2000* (2000).

IMF World Bank, OECD and EBRD. *The Economy of the USSR: Summary and Recommendations* (Washington DC: World Bank, 1990).

ING–Barings. *Angang New Steel Company (New Issue and Placing)* (Hong Kong: ING–Barings, 1997).

International Energy Agency. *Coal Information* (1998 Edition).

International Institute for Strategic Studies (IISS). *Military Balance, 1998/99* (London: IISS, 1998).

International Institute for Strategic Studies (IISS). *Military Balance, 1999/2000* (London: IISS, 1999).

Iron and Steel Industry of China (ISIC). *The Yearbook of Iron and Steel Industry of China 1997* (Beijing: The Editorial Board of the Yearbook of Iron and Steel Industry of China, 1997) (in Chinese).

JANELLI, R. *Making Capitalism* (Stanford: Stanford University Press, 1993).

Jane's Combat Aircraft (Glasgow: Collins, 1995).

Jane's Civil Aircraft (Glasgow: Collins, 1996).

JI D. and Q. SHAO (eds). *The Situation and Management of China's Population Movement* (Beijing, 1995).

JOHNSON, C. *MITI and the Japanese Miracle* (Stanford: Stanford University Press, 1982).

Joint Research Group. 'New changes in the employees after Shougang's reform', in Editorial Commission of *Reform in Shougang* (Beijing: Beijing Press, 1992), 89–109 (in Chinese).

KANTER, R. M. 'Transcending business boundaries: 12 000 world managers view change', *Harvard Business Review*, 69 (3) (1991), 151–64.

KAO, A. 'China: electric utilities', *Morgan Stanley Dean Witter, Asia/Pacific Investment Research* (23 March 1998).

KEISTER, L. 'Engineering growth: business group structure and firm performance in China's transition economy', *American Journal of Sociology,* 104 (1998), 404–40.

KOIKE, K. 'Human resources development and labour-management relations', in Yammamura and Yasuba (1987).

KORNAI, J. *The Road to a Free Economy* (New York: Norton, 1990).

KRUGMAN, P. R. 'New thinking about trade policy', in Krugman (1987).

KRUGMAN, P. R. (ed.). *Strategic Trade Policy* (Cambridge, MA: MIT Press, 1987).

LAKE, D. A. *Power, Protection and Free Trade* (Ithaca: Cornell University Press, 1988).

LARDY, N. *China's Unfinished Revolution* (Washington, DC: Brookings Institution, 1998).

LAU, L. Speech at meeting held to discuss China's impending entry to the WTO, organized by the State Council's Development Research Centre, Beijing (February 2000).

LAU, L. 'Economic globalization and the information technology revolution', paper presented to the 21st Century Forum, Beijing (14–16 June 2000).

LEE KUAN YEW. Speech to the 21st Century Forum, Beijing (14–16 June 2000).

Legend Holdings. *Annual Report, 1999* (2000).

LEUCHTER, M. 'Getting rich with merchant banking', *US Banker* (April 2000).

LI BOZHONG. *The Development of Agriculture and Industry in Jiangnan, 1644–1850: Trends and Prospects* (Hangzhou: Zhejiang Academy of Social Sciences, 1986).

LI BOZHONG. *Agricultural Development Jiangnan, 1620–1850* (London: Macmillan, 1998).

LI JIAJIE, ZHAI HUISHENG, and LIU LUSHA. 'The model of enterprise technological advance', in Editorial Commission of *Reform in Shougang* (Beijing: Beijing Press 1992), 223–6 (in Chinese).

LI R. 'Some considerations on the floating population in Contemporary China' (*Renkou yu jingji*), *Population and Economics*, 94 (1996).

LI XIAOXUE. Speech at China Big Business Programme, Cambridge (17 October 1999).

LI YIXUE. '*Zhongguo chanye jishu jinbu de wentie he duice*', *Management World*, 1 (1999), 139–43.

LI ZUOKENG and LI CUNHOU (eds). *Exploring Sanjiu* (*Sanjiu tansuo*) (Guangzhou: Guangdong renmin chubanshe, 1995).

LICHTENBERG, F. R. and G. M. PUSHNER. 'Ownership structures and corporate performance in Japan', *NBER Working Papers Series*, 4092 (Princeton: National Bureau of Economic Research, 1992).

LILLEY, S. 'Technological progress and the Industrial Revolution 1700–1914', in Cipolla (1973a).

LIN, JUSTIN Y. F., FANG CAI and ZHOU LI. *The China Miracle* (Hong Kong: Chinese University Press, 1996).

LINDBERG, L. N. and J. L. CAMPBELL. 'The state and the organisation of economic activity', in Campbell *et al.* (1991).

LIPSEY, R. *An Introduction to Positive Economics* (London: Wiedenfeld & Nicolson, 1963).

LIU JINGHAI. 'Resources and promoting competitiveness of steel industry', in *Metallurgy Economic Study* 23, 24 (1994) (in Chinese).

LIU LI, JIANG DONGSHENG, and SHANG ZENGJIAN. '*Jingji fazhan, tizhi zhuanji, dui wai kaifang yu Zhongguo daxing gong qiye de chengchang*', *Management World*, 5 (1999), 118–31.

LIU X., H. SONG, and P. ROMILLY. 'Stock returns and volatility: an empirical study of Chinese stock markets', *International Review of Applied Economics*, 12 (1998), 129–39.

LIU ZHIYONG, LIU LEI, and GAN XIAOQING. 'An Empirical Study on Transnationalisation of Shougang Corporation', in *Shougang Research and Development*, 3 (1994), 61–5 (in Chinese).

LO DIC. *Market and Institutional Regulation in Chinese Industrialization, 1978–94* (London: Macmillan, 1997).

LO DIC. 'Re-appraising the performance of China's state-owned industrial enterprises, 1980–1996', *Cambridge Journal of Economics*, 23 (1999), 693–718.

LO DIC and T. CHAN. 'Machinery and China's nexus of foreign trade and economic growth', *Journal of International Development*, 10 (1998), 733–49.

LU YANSUN. 'Outlook for China's power industry', in Lu Yansun (1997).

LU YANSUN (ed.). *China Power and Electrical Equipment* (Beijing: Chinese Power and Electrical Equipment Association, 1997).

LUO BINGSHENG. 'Reform of the Shougang Group for the twenty-first century' (1998) (mimeo).

MA WEIJIE and MA WEIGANG. *Shijie jingji 500 qiang* (Guangdong: Guangdong luyou chubanshe, 1998).

MADDISON, A. 'Explaining the economic performance of nations, 1820–1989', in Baumol *et al.* (1994).

MALONE, T. W. and R. L. LAUBACHER. 'The dawn of the e-Lance economy', *Harvard Business Review*, September–October (1998).

MARKHAM, J. W. 'Survey of evidence and findings on mergers', *NBER Working Papers* (*Business Concentration and Price Policy*) (Princeton: National Bureau of Economic Research, 1955).

MARSHALL, A. *Principles of Economics* (London: Macmillan, 1920; 1st edn, 1890).

MARUKAWA, T. 'Industrial groups and division of labour in China's automobile industry', *The Developing Economies*, 33, (3) (1995), 330–55.

MARX, K., *Capital*, 1, (1867) (New York: International Publishers, 1967 edn).

MARX, K. *The Communist Manifesto* (1888) English edn, reprinted in *Karl Marx and Frederick Engels, Selected Works*, (London: Lawrence & Wishart, 1968).

MAO ZEDONG. 'The Chinese people have stood up' (1949), in Mao Zedong (1977).

MAO ZEDONG. *Selected Works of Mao Zedong* (Beijing: Foreign Languages Press, 1977).

McEVEDY, C. and R. JONES. *Atlas of Population History* (Harmondsworth: Penguin, 1978).

Merck. *Annual Report, 1998* (1999).

MILLER, J. *Mikhail Gorbachev and the End of Soviet Power* (London: Macmillan, 1993).

MIN CHEN. *Asian Management Systems* (London: Routledge, 1995).

MINCER, J. and Y. HIGUCHI. 'Wage structures and labour turnover in the United States and Japan', *Journal of the Japanese and International Economies*, 2, (2) (1988) 97–133.

Ministry of Coal Industry *(Meitan gongye bu)* (MGB). *Yearbook of China's Coal Industry* (*Zhongguo meitan gongye nianjian*) (ZMGN) (Beijing: *Meitan gongye chubanshe*, 1997).

Ministry of Electric Power. *Annual Report, 1997* (1998).

Ministry of Machine Building (MMB). *Chinese Automobile Industry Yearbook* (*Zhongguo qiche gongye nianjian*) (ZQGN) (Beijing: Chinese Automobile Industry Publishing House, 1996, 1998).

Ministry of Metallurgy Industry (MMI). *Statistics on China's Iron and Steel* (Beijing: Ministry of Metallurgy Industry, 1994) (in Chinese).

MITCHELL, B. 'Statistical Appendix', in Cipolla (1976).

Mobil. *Annual Report, 1998* (1999).

Morgan Stanley Asia. *China Eastern Airlines Prospectus* (Hong Kong: Morgan Stanley Asia, 1997a).

Morgan Stanley Asia. *Beijing Datang Power Generation Company* (Hong Kong: Morgan Stanley Asia, 1997b).

Morgan Stanley Dean Witter (MSDW). *The Competitive Edge* (New York and London: MSDW, 1997)

Morgan Stanley Dean Witter (MSDW). *The Competitive Edge*. 14 January 1998, (New York: MSDW, 1998a)

Morgan Stanley Dean Witter (MSDW). *The Competitive Edge: April Update* (New York: MSDW, 1998b).

Morgan Stanley Dean Witter (MSDW). *The Asian Edge: A Closer Look:* 29 May 1998 (New York: MSDW, 1998c).

Morgan Stanley Dean Witter (MSDW). *The Competitive Edge:* 16 July 1998 (New York: MSDW, 1998d).

Morgan Stanley Dean Witter (MSDW). *Yanzhou Coal Mining Company Ltd: A Natural Advantage* (Hong Kong: MSDW, 1998e).

Morgan Stanley Dean Witter (MSDW). *The Competitive Edge* (New York and London, 1999).

Morgan Stanley Dean Witter (MSDW). *The Competitive Edge: April Update* (New York and London, 2000).

MUKHERJEE, A. and T. SASTRY. 'Automotive industry in emerging economies', *Economic and Political Weekly* (30 November 1996).

Nanfang Pharmaceutical Factory, *Collection about Nanfang Pharmaceutical Factory, 1987–1995* (*Guanyu Nanfang zhiyao Chang Xuanji*) (Shenzhen, 1996)

NAUGHTON, B. 'The third front: defence industrialisation in the Chinese interior', *The China Quarterly*, 115 (September 1988).

NAUGHTON, B. *Growing Out of the Plan : Chinese Economic Reform, 1978–1993* (Cambridge: Cambridge University Press, 1995).

NEEDHAM, J. *Science and Civilization in China* (Cambridge: Cambridge University Press, 1954-).

NEEDHAM. J. *Science and Civilization in China, Vol. 4, Part 2: Mechanical Engineering* (Cambridge: Cambridge University Press, 1965).

NEEDHAM, J. 'Iron and steel production in ancient and medieval China', in Needham (1970).

NEEDHAM, J. *Clerks and craftsmen in China and the West* (Cambridge, Cambridge University Press, 1970).

NESTER, W. R. *Japanese Industrial Targeting* (London: Macmillan, 1991).

New Star Press. *Selected Documents of the 15th CPC National Congress* (Beijing: New Star Publishers, 1997).

NOLAN, P. 'China's new development path', in Nolan and Dong Fureng (1990).

NOLAN, P. *State and Market in the Chinese Economy* (London: Macmillan, 1993a).

NOLAN, P. 'Political economy and the reform of Stalinism: the Chinese puzzle', *Contributions to Political Economy*, 12 (1993b).

NOLAN, P. 'Democratisation, human rights and economic reform: the case of China', *Democratisation*, 1 (1) (1994).

NOLAN, P. *China's Rise, Russia's Fall* (London: Macmillan, 1995).

NOLAN, P. 'Large firms and industrial reform in former planned economies: the case of China', *Cambridge Journal of Economics,* 20 (1996), 1–29.

NOLAN, P. *Indigenous Large Firms in China's Economic Reforms: the Case of Shougang Iron and Steel Corporation* (London: Contemporary China Institute, 1998).

NOLAN, P. *Coca-Cola and the Global Business Revolution: A Study with Special Reference to the EU* (Cambridge: Polity Press, 1999).

NOLAN, P. and DONG FURENG (eds). *The Chinese Economy and its Future* (Cambridge: Polity Press, 1990).

NOLAN, P. and WANG XIAOQIANG. 'Enlightenment from US military restructuring for Chinese industrial adjustment', *Strategy and Management,* 6 (1997), 60–7 (in Chinese).

NOLAN, P. and WANG XIAOQIANG. 'Beyond privatization: institutional innovation and growth in China's large state-owned enterprises', *World Development,* 27 (1) (1998), 169–200.

NOLAN, P. Case Studies China Big Business Programme, 1996–99.

NYE, J. and W. A. OWENS. 'America's information edge', *Foreign Affairs,* March–April 1996.

OHMAE, KENICHI (ed.). *The Evolving Global Economy – Making Sense of the New World Order* (Boston: Harvard Business School Publishing, 1995).

OKIMOTO, D. I. *Between the MITI and the Market* (Stanford: Stanford University Press, 1989).

Peat Marwick Huazhen. *Guangxi Machinery Company Limited: Statutory Accounts of the Company* (Beijing: Peat Marwick Huazhen, 1995).

PENROSE, E. *The Theory of the Growth of the Firm* (Oxford: Oxford University Press, 1995).

People's Bank of China (PBC). *Almanac of China's Finance and Banking, 1999* (Beijing: PBC, 1999).

Peregrine Capital Limited. *Consolidated Electric Power Asia Limited* (Hong Kong: Peregrine Capital Limited, 1993a)

Peregrine Capital Limited. *Denway Investment Limited* Prospectus (Hong Kong: Peregrine Capital Limited, 1993b)

PERKINS, D. H. *Agricultural development in China, 1368-1968* (Edinburgh: Edinburgh University Press, 1968)

PIORE, M. and C. SABEL. *The Second Industrial Divide: Possibilities for Prosperity* (New York: Basic Books, 1984)

PORTER, M. *The Competitive Advantage of Nations* (London: Macmillan, 1990)

PRAIS, S. J. *Productivity and Industrial Structure* (Cambridge: Cambridge University Press, 1981)

PRATTEN, C. F. *Economics of Scale in Manufacturing Industry* (Cambridge: Cambridge University Press, 1971).

QIN YUEXING. 'Opportunities and Challenges – the Impact on Chinese Insurance from WTO entry', *International Financial Research* (*Guo ji jin rong yan jiu*) Vol. 2 (2000).

RADICE, H., ed. *International Firms and Modern Imperialism* (Harmondsworth: Penguin, 1975).

RAMANGKURA, VIRABONGSA. 'Financial globalisation and globalism', Speech at the 21st Century Forum, Beijing, 14–16 June 2000

RANIS, G. and T. P. SCHULTZ, eds. *The State of Development Economics* (Oxford: Basil Blackwell, 1988).

RAWSKI, T. G. *Economic Growth in Pre-War China* (Berkeley: University of California Press, 1989).

REICH, R. 'Who is them?' in Kenichi Ohmae (1995).

Research Centre of Metallurgy Economic Development (RCMED). 'The summary of investment efficiency of fixed assets in eight largest steel complexes in the periods of the Sixth and Seventh Five-Year Plans' in Editorial Commission of *Reform in Shougang*, Vol. 2 (Beijing: Beijing Press, 1992), 134–43 (in Chinese).

Research Centre of Metallurgy Economic Development (RCMED). 'Total steel demand in the World will be 720 million tons in 2000', in *Reference for Enterprise Decision Making*, 26 (1994) 13–14 (in Chinese).

RHYS, G. 'Smaller car firms – Will they survive?', *Long Range Planning*, Vol. 22 (1989) 107–35.

Rio Tinto. *Annual Report, 1997* (1998).

ROBERTSON, D. H. *The Control of Industry* (Cambridge: Cambridge University Press, 1923).

ROBINSON, A. 'Energy policy', in Nolan and Dong Fureng (1990).

RODZINSKI, W. *The Walled Kingdom* (London: Fontana, 1984).

Rolls-Royce. *Annual Report, 1997.*

RUIGROK, W. and R. VAN TULDER. *The Logic of International Restructuring* (London and New York: Routledge, 1995).

Salomon Brothers. *Shougang Concord International – A Multifaceted China play* (Hong Kong: Salomon Brothers, 1994).

Sanjiu Enterprise Group (SEG). *Unpublished report* (1997) (in Chinese).

Sanjiu Enterprise Group (SEG). *Report Submitted to the General Logistics Department by Zhao Xinxian* (1998) (internal document, in Chinese).

Sanjiu Jituan Bao (SJB). 'Establish risk monitor mechanism', 8 (231), 25 Feb. 1998 (in Chinese)

Sanjiu Jituan Bao (SJB). 'New mechanism for promotion', 14 (237) (8 April 1998 (in Chinese).

Sanjiu Jituan Bao (SJB). 'Ya'an Pharmaceuticals: can it be the second "Nanfang"?' 15 (233) (15 April 1998). (in Chinese).

Sanjiu Jituan Bao (SJB). 'Stock-ownership Reform', 16, (239), (22 April 1998) (in Chinese).

Sanjiu Jituan Bao (SJB). 'Sanjiu Mechanism and the development of Sanjiu', 18 (241) (6 May 1998) (in Chinese).

SCHERER, F. M. and D. ROSS. *Industrial Market Structure and Economic Performance*, 3rd edn (Boston: Houghton Mifflin, 1990).

SCHERER, F. M. *Industry, structure, strategy and public policy* (New York: Harper Collins, 1996).

SCHMITZ, C. J. *The Growth of Big Business in the United States and Western Europe, 1850–1939* (London Macmillan, 1993).

SCHURMANN, F. and O. SCHELL (eds.) *Imperial China* (Harmondsworth: Penguin, 1967).

SCHWAB, K. Speech at the 21st Century Forum, Beijing (14–16 June 2000).

Sciences and Technology Department, the Ministry of Metallurgical Industry (STD), *Research in the Technological Innovation Strategy in the Iron and Steel Industry: Final Report* (December 1997) (mimeo).

Shanghai Petrochemical Company (SPC). *Interim Report for 1997* (1998).

Shanghai Petrochemical Company (SPC). *Report to the US Securities and Exchange Commission for 1998* (1999).

Shanghai Turbine Company. *Annual Report, 1999* (1999).

SHAO JIANYUN. '*Zhongguo qiye goubing shichang de fazhan yu zhengce jianyi'*, *Management World*, 4 (1997) 83–92.

Shell. *Royal Dutch Petroleum Company: Summary Annual Report 1998* (1999a).

Shell. *The Shell Report 1999: People, Planet & Profits* (1999b).

Shell. *Shell Financial and Operational Information 1994–98* (1999c).

Shenhua Group. *Annual Report, 1997* (1998).

Shougang Group (SG). *Shougang Corporation* (Beijing: Shougang Assiqi Advertising Company, 1995).

Shougang Group (SG). *The Reform Agendas of the Shougang Group* (30 June 1998) (internal document).

Sidel. *Annual Report, 1998* (1999).

Siemens. *Annual Report, 1998* (1999).

SLATER, J. '*What does the 21st century hold for the coal industry?*' Website: World Coal Institute (1998).

SMIL, V. *China's Environmental Crisis* (London: M.E. Sharpe, 1993).

SMITH, A. *The Wealth of Nations* (1776) (Chicago: University of Chicago Press, 1976 edn).

SMYTHE, D. J. *Technological Change, Competitive Capital Markets, and the Turn of the Century Merger Movement* (1995) (mimeo).

SMYTH, R. 'Should China be promoting large-scale enterprises and enterprise groups?', *World Development*, 28 (2000), 721–37.

SONG QIANG et al. *China Can Say No? (Zhongguo keyi shuo bu?)* (Beijing: *Zhongguo wenlian chubanshe*, 1996).

State Bureau of Metallurgical Industry (SBMI). *Chinese Steel Industry into the 21st Century* (1998) (mimeo).

State Capital Management Bureau (SCMB). *China State Capital Yearbook (Zhongguo guoyou zichan nianjian* (ZGZN) (Beijing: *Jingji kexue chubanshe*, 1993).

State Council Development Research Centre (SCDRC), *China Economic Yearbook (Zhongguo jingji nianjian)* (ZJN) (Beijing: *Zhongguo jingji nianjian chubanshe*, various years).

State Planning Commission (SPC). *China Energy Report (Zhongguo nengyuan)* (Beijing: China Prices Publishing House, 1997).

State Statistical Bureau (SSB). *Statistical Yearbook of China* (SYC) (English language edn) (Hong Kong: Economic Information and Agency, 1981).

State Statistical Bureau (SSB). *Chinese Industrial Economy Statistical Materials (Zhongguo gongye jingji tongji ziliao)* (ZGJTZ) (Beijing: *Tongji chubanshe*, various years).

State Statistical Bureau (SSB). *A Guide to Industrial Statistics (Xinbian gongye tongji gongzuo zhinan)* (XGTGZ) (Beijing: *Zhongguo tongji chubanshe*, 1999).

State Statistical Bureau (SSB). *Chinese Large and Medium-Sized Enterprises Yearbook (Zhongguo daxing qiye nianjian)* (ZDQN) (Beijing: *Tongji chubanshe*, various years).

State Statistical Bureau (SSB). *Chinese Industrial Economy Statistical Yearbook (Zhongguo gongye jingji tongji nianjian)* (ZGJTN)) (Beijing: *Tongji chubanshe*, various years).

State Statistical Bureau (SSB). *China Statistical Yearbook (Zhongguo tongji nianjian)* (ZTN) (Beijing: *Zhongguo tongji chubanshe*, various years).

State Statistical Bureau (SSB). *Guangdong Statistical Yearbook (Guangdong tongji nianjian)* (GTN) (Guangzhou: *Zhongguo tongji chubanshe*, various years).

Steinfeld, E. *Forging Reform in China* (Cambridge: Cambridge University Press, 1998).

STOKES, E. *The English Utilitarians* (Oxford: Clarendon Press, 1959).

SUN RUIHUA. *'Jiakuai da qiye jituan fazhan bufa'*, *Modern Enterprise Herald* (1998) 4–7.

SUN WU. *The Essentials of Warfare* (Beijing: New World Press, 1996).

SUZUKI, Y. *Japanese Management Structures, 1920–80* (London: Macmillan, 1991).

SWAMY, S. 'The response to economic challenge: a comparative economic history of China and India, 1870–1952', *Quarterly Journal of Economics*, (February 1979), 25–46.

TAN CHENGDONG. 'Optimising the structure is the main target of developing the steel and iron industry at socialist market economic system' *Metallurgy Economic Study*, 3 (1994). 1–16 (in Chinese).

Tasman Asia Pacific. *Australia's Black Coal Industry: The Scope for Productivity Improvement* (Canberra: Tasman Asia Pacific, 1993).

THOMPSON, E. 'Reforming China's coal industry', *The China Quarterly*, 147 (1996) 726–50.

Thomson Financial Data Services Website www.fds.com.

THUROW., C. *Japan: the Challenge of Producer Economics*, Marshall Lecture, Cambridge University (1991) (mimeo).

UNCTAD (United Nations Conference on Trade and Development). *World Investment Report 1994: Transnational Corporations, Employment and the Workplace* (Geneva: UN Publications, 1994).

UNCTAD (United Nations Conference on Trade and Development). *World Investment Report 1995: Transnational Corporations and Competitiveness* (Geneva: UN Publications, 1995).

UNCTAD (United Nations Conference on Trade and Development). *World Investment Report 1996: Investment, Trade and International Policy Arrangements* (Geneva: UN Publications, 1996).

UNCTAD (United Nations Conference on Trade and Development). *World Investment Report 1997: Transnational Corporations, Market Structure and Competition Policy* (Geneva: UN Publications, 1997).

UNCTAD (United Nations Conference on Trade and Development). *World Investment Report 1998: Trends and Determinants* (Geneva: UN Publications, 1998).

UNCTAD (United Nations Conference on Trade and Development). *World Investment Report 1999: Foreign Direct Investment and the Challenge of Development* (Geneva: UN Publications, 1999).

UNDP (United Nations Development Programme) *Human Development Report* (New York: Oxford University Press, 1999).

United States Energy Information Agency, *Country Analysis Brief: China* (1998).

US–China Trade Council, 'Questions and answers: US–China WTO Agreement', 1 December, The White House (1999).

Usinor. *Annual Report, 1997* (1998).

Valeo. *Annual Report, 1997* (1998).

Valeo. *Annual Report, 1998* (1999).

VOGEL, E. *The Four Little Dragons* (Cambridge, MA: Harvard University Press, 1991).

WADE, R. *Governing the Market: Economic Theory and the Role of Government in East Asian industrialization* (Princeton: Princeton University Press, 1990).

WAGNER, D. *The Traditional Iron and Steel Industry and its Modern Fate* (Richmond: Curzon Press, 1997)

WANG WEIJUN. 'The market-oriented management system in HPEC' (1996) (mimeo).

WANG XIAOQIANG. *China's Price and Ownership Reform* (London: Macmillan, 1998)

WANG XIAOQIANG. *Development strategies for China's telecommunications industry* (Cambridge: China Big Business Programme, 1998.).

WANG XIAOQIANG and P. NOLAN, *Strategic Restructuring (Zhanlue chongzu)* (Shanghai: *Wenhui chubanshe,* 1998) (in Chinese).

WANG ZONGREN. *Zhou Guanwu and Shougang – Record of Reform in Shougang* (Tianjin: Hundred Flowers Art Press, 1993) (in Chinese).

Warburg Securities. *Harbin Power Equipment Company Limited,* (Hong Kong: Warburg, 1994).

Warburg Securities. *Yizheng Chemical Fibre Company* (Hong Kong: Warburg, 1991).

Wardley Corporate Finance Limited (WCFL). *Maanshan Iron and Steel Company Limited* (Hong Kong: WCFL, 1993).

White House, the US government web site on the China–US WTO accession agreement <www.chinapntr.gov> (2000).

World Bank. *China: Macroeconomic Stability in a Decentralised Economy,* (Washington, DC: World Bank, 1995).

World Bank. *China: Reform of State-owned Enterprises* (Washington, DC: World Bank, 1996a).

World Bank. *Clear Water, Blue Skies* (Washington, DC: World Bank, 1997a).

World Bank. *China 2020* (Washington, DC: World Bank, 1997b).

World Bank. *World Development Report* (New York: Oxford University Press, 1981a).

World Bank. *World Development Report* (New York: Oxford University Press, 1990).

World Bank. *World Development Report* (New York: Oxford University Press, 1991).

World Bank. *World Development Report* (New York: Oxford University Press, 1992).

World Bank. *World Development Report* (New York: Oxford University Press, 1996).

World Bank. *World Development Report* (New York: Oxford University Press, 1998).

World Bank. *World Development Report, 1999/2000: Entering the 21st Century* (New York: Oxford University Press, 2000).

World Bank. *China: Socialist Development*, (Washington, DC: World Bank, 1981b).

XIE, A. 'From quantity to quality growth', *MSDW Asia/Pacific, China Monthly, Investment Review* (26 May 2000).

XIE PING. 'WTO and the Financial Reform of China', *Forum of Innovation and Risk Management in Securities Brokerage* (2000).

XU DIXIN and WU CHENGMING (eds). *Capitalism in China 1644–1840* (London: Macmillan, 2000) C. Curwen (ed), (English en).

XU RENZHONG and LIU PUQUAN. 'Contract system in Shougang: inducing public ownership in everyone', in Editorial Commission of *Reform in Shougang*, 1 (Beijing: Beijing Press, 1992), 199–204 (in Chinese).

XU RENZHONG and LIU PUQUAN. 'Breaking the big pot to establish true equality', in Editorial Commission of *Reform in Shougang*, 1 (Beijing: Beijing Press, 1992b), 213–17 (in Chinese).

YAMMAMURA, K. and Y. YASUBA (eds). *The political economy of Japan, Vol. 1* (Stanford: Stanford University Press, 1987).

YATSKO, P. 'The bigger, the better', *Far Eastern Economic Review,* 161 (21) (1998), 10–13.

YERGIN, D. *The Prize* (London: Simon & Schuster, 1991).

YEUNG, G. 'The People's Liberation Army and the market economy', in Benewick and Wingrove (1995).

YEUNG, G. 'The political economy of Hong Kong–Shenzhen integration with special reference to corporate structure' (Cambridge: Department of Land Economy, 1996) (mimeo).

YIN WENRU, YUAN JIALU, and ZANG YAORU. '*Mianxiang 21 shijie de qiye jituan fazhan zhanlue*', *Management World,* 5 (1999), 132–45.

YING WENQUAN. '*Wo guo qiye jituan fazhan zhong de zhengfu jiaose dingwei*', *Zhongguo gongye jingji (Chinese Industrial Economics)*, 6 (1999), 34–8.

YONEKURA SEIICHIRO. *The Japanese Iron and Steel Industry, 1850–1990* (London: Macmillan, 1994).

YU JIANMING. '*Shenhua daxing qiye jituan shidian tuijin liang ge genbenxing zhuanji*', *Hongguan jingji guanli (Macro Economics Management),* 8 (1997).

ZHOU PINGJUN. '*Bai hu xiandai qiye zhidu shidian de xiaoguo yu jingyan*', *Zhongguo gongye jingji (Chinese Industrial Economics)*, 7 (1997) 60–7.

ZHANG SHOURONG. 'Trend of international steel and iron industry development' *Metallurgy Economic Study,* 1 (1994), 26–32 (in Chinese).

ZHANG WUCHANG. 'China and the WTO' (2000) (mimeo).

ZHONG CHANGYUAN and HUANG JIAN. *Drilling and Gas Recovery Technology in Ancient China* (London: Shell, 1997).

ZOU DONGYAO and ZHANG XIAOWEN. '*30 jia xiandai qiye zhidu shidian qiye de diaocha yu fenxi*', *Management World,* 1 (1991), 154–61.

Index

ABB (Switzerland/Sweden), 59, 336, 398
  'close relationship' with HPEC, 382
  'expands aggressively in PRC', 362–3
  involvement in Three Gorges Project,
    945(n20)
  joint tenders with HPEC, 387
  joint venture with 'HEC' (1996–), 371
  merger with GEC-Alsthom (1999), 338
  'national champion' (Sweden/Switzerland),
    396
  operations in PRC, 391
  origins, 336
  R&D expenditure, 329
  rate of return in PRC, 944(n14)
  re-location of manufacturing base, 333
  revenues, profits, employees, R&D (1998),
    882
  servicing, 394
  shareholder in HPEC Limited, 946(n31)
  size (late 1990s), 330
  supply network, 384
  technology transfer (nuclear) to PRC, 358
ABB-Alstom, 59, 848
  ancillary equipment, 365
  'European' credentials, 338
  globalization, 335
  market share worldwide (power generation
    equipment, 1993–8), 337
  merger of ABB and GEC-Alsthom (1999),
    338, 339
  one of the top three, 339
  size (late 1990s), 330
  source of profits, 333
ABB China, 945(n20)
Abbott (pharmaceuticals), 249, 250
Abu Dhabi National Oil Company: output
  (1996), 409
AC/DC motors, 371, 394
Acadiania BancShares (Lafayette, LA), 819
'accelerator' principle, 714
accounting, 70, 282, 849
Acer Computer (Taiwan), 21
Aceralia (Arbed Group), 602n

Acesita (Brazil): investment by Usinor, 611
Acheng Relay Works (Harbin), 363–4, 365
  main statistics (1992), 364
  part of HPEGC, 365
  wholly-owned subsidiary of HPEGC, [367,]
    946(n36)
acid
  acetic, 423
  nitric, 466
  phthalic acid, 466
  sulphuric, 466
  see also pollution/acid rain
acknowledgements, xxiv-xxvi
  to Zhao Xinxian, 941(n9)
acrylics, 452, 456, 472
acrylonite technology, 423
ADP, 786
advanced economies (incorporating 'high-
  income countries'), 848–9, 854, 855, 892
  big business, 62–4
  differences from developing countries, 844
  dominance of firms based in, 46, 47
  dominant position of large firm, 13–14
  economic growth (1980–98), 851
  expenditure on health, 767
  financial services, 814
  GNP (1998), 932
  internet hosts per 1,000 people (1997), 789
  internet-users, 805
  IT development (1997), 789
  IT firms, 770, 788, 790
  oil and petrochemicals, 884
  per capita energy use (1994), 341
  personal computers per 1,000 people (1997),
    789
  pollution, 703
  public health expenditure (1900–7), 243
  steel, 592
  stock market capitalization (1998), 932
  strict view of PRC undertakings (WTO
    accession), 870
  tariff barriers, 28
  telecommunications development (1997), 789

advanced economies (incorporating 'high-
  income countries') – *continued*
  telephone main lines per 1,000 people
    (1997), 789
  TV sets per 1,000 people (1997), 789
  wages, 891
  wireless telephones per 1,000 people (1997),
    789
  see also global business revolution; OECD
    countries
Advanced Micro Devices (AMD), 768–9
advertising, 9, 11, 34, 856
  economies of scale (automobile industry),
    503, 510
  global market share, 37
  internet companies, 780
  mass media, 781
  minimum economy of scale (auto industry),
    503
  Nanfang, 298–9, 321, 323, 943(n31)
  pharmaceutical sector, 251
  Sanjiu hotel chain, 313–14
  television (PRC), 557
  tyres, 526
  Yuchai, 557, 885
advertising companies, 781
AEI, 943(n7)
Aeoleus, *see* Dongfeng Group
Aeritalia, 940(n4)
aero-engines (general), 145, 171–3, 329–30,
    332, 398, 942(n1)
  AVIC, 186, 199, 227, 229, 877
  BMW, 173
  barriers to entry, 64, 171, 173
  design, 43
  global triopoly, 141
  Harbin Aero-engine Company, 205
  high-thrust, 173
  jet, 142, 171, 177, 180–1
  joint ventures, 216–17
  Mitsubishi, 173
  Pratt and Whitney, 142, 172, 180, 204, 205
  PRC, 175, 200, 222, 877
  technology useful in power generation
    equipment sector, 329–30, 942(n1)
  Trent series (Rolls Royce), 172, 174–5, 177
  Volvo, 173
aero-engines (specific)
  CF34–8C, 177
  F120 engine, 164
  GE-90, 172
  JT3D, 202
  JT8D, 217
  PW400, 172
  RB-211, 174–5
  RB211–535, 179
  Rolls Royce Spey, 190
  SNECMA, 173
  Trent 500, 175
  Trent 600, 175

Trent 900, 177
V2500, 172, 208
see also CEC
Aeroflot, 179
aerospace industry (global), 3, 12, 141–240,
    615, 844–5, 854, 859, 860, 861, 863,
    876–8, 929
  aero-engines, 171–3
  barriers to entry, 63–4, 173–6
  conclusion, 231–40
  consolidation in USA, 152–6
  consolidation in 'Europe', 156–70
  demand, 149–52
  drivers of international change, 141–52
  engine makers, 39
  example of Brazil, 180–3
  example of Japan, 176–8
  example of USSR, 178–80
  general difficulties for 'Europe', 170–1
  importance of scale, 142
  internal systems integration capabilities,
    147–9
  international trends, 141–84
  oligopoly, 37, 39, 40
  on-line procurement networks, 45
  options facing developing countries, 183–4
  PRC, 184–240
  privatization (general), 32
  process of aerospace consolidation, 152–73
  research and development, 49, 596
  Samsung, 53
  South Korea, 54
  Soviet bloc, 149
  strategic choices for developing countries,
    173–84
  suppliers, 39
  supply, 142–7
  technological gap (facing Third World), 184
  transatlantic option, 162–5, 235, 236, 338
aerospace industry (PRC): 184–240, 921
  AVIC, 184–7
  barriers to entry, 195–6
  building a modern jet airliner, 206–13
  catch-up, 188, 195–6, 240
  'children' and 'grandchildren', 221–6
  civilian aircraft, 202–21
  competitive capability (1997), 877
  conclusion, 231–40
  cooperation with Russian Federation, 233
  declining military orders, 187–95
  end of holding company experiment, 226–31
  first batch of trial business groups, 109
  importance of 'indigenous' industry, 240
  institutional change, 221–31
  institutional re-structuring, 226–31
  joint ventures, 217–21
  leading companies, 200
  lessons for PRC from Brazil, 238–40
  lessons for PRC from Euro-American
    relations, 234–6

aerospace industry (PRC) – *continued*
  lessons for PRC from 'Europe', 232–4
  lessons for PRC from Japan, 236–7
  lessons for PRC from USA, 231–2
  lessons for PRC from USSR, 237–8
  market prospects, 202–3, 234
  military aircraft, 187–96
  modern jet airliner, 206–13
  national team, 76, 84, 85, 112–13
  need for 'indigenous' aircraft industry, 240
  non-aviation production, 196–202, 222
  policy change, 196–7
  production, 197, 940(n10)
  production of military aircraft (1974–94),
    189–90
  restructuring, 500
  sub-contract/subsystem joint ventures,
    213–17
  sub-contracts, 217–21
  Xian Aircraft Company, 199–202
  Yun-10 (Y-10), 203–5
  Yun-7 (Y-7), 205–6
  see also AVIC; Xian Aircraft Company
aerospace machinery: competitive advantage, 36
Aérospatiale (France), 499, 840, 920
  dwarfed, 146
  grants sub-contracts in PRC, 209, 214
  part-owner of Airbus Industrie, 167
  privatization, 859, 892
  and proposed EADC, 159–60
  research and development, 142, 143, 175,
    536
  size (1998), 166
  state-owned, 499
  turbo-prop feeder aircraft, 205–6
Aérospatiale–Matra (6.1999–), 160, 165,
    169–70, 235, 499, 854
  market capitalization (1999), 236
  merger with Dasa, 161
  still partly state-owned, 499
  see also EADS
Aetna (US insurer), 822
Affymax (USA), 255, 258
  acquired by Glaxo (1995), 253[–]8
Africa
  economic growth (sub-Sahara, 1980–98), 851
  electricity generation capacity (1990–2010),
    697
  lack of indigenous 'competitive edge'
    corporations, 63
  natural gas production and reserves (1997),
    405
  oil production (1987–97), 405
  PRC aircraft exports, 205
  production and sales of automobiles (1998),
    508
  projected demand for power equipment
    (1980–2010), 334
  share of world electricity generation
    (1995–2015), 335

Shougang expansion, 690
  steel production (1991–7), 589
  TotalFinaElf, 417
after-sales service, 512
afterword, 935
agribusiness, 261, 262
agricultural
  equipment (PRC national team), 76
  groups (PRC national team), 135
  machinery, 75, 104, 108, 346, 548
  productivity, 767
  technology (Sanjiu), 315–16
Agricultural Bank of China (ABC), 96
  key indicators, 1999 (global-leaders
    comparison), 827
  losses, 830–1, 958(n11)
  productivity, 830–1
agriculture, 316
  China (pre-1949), 901, 906
  employment (PRC 1998), 919
  growth (PRC 1980–97), 913
  migration (PRC), 894
  PRC, 926
  restructuring (PRC), 894
  share of national product (Mao era), 907
  WTO rules (PRC implementation), 868–9,
    870–1, 871–2
agro-chemicals, 252
Ahdab oilfield (Iraq), 441
Ahlstrom Group (USA), 378
AHP, *see* American Home Products
air brake compressions and castings, 950(n9)
air conditioners, 197, 198
air defence systems, 148
Air France, 149, 213
air intake systems, 520
Air New Zealand, 149
air pollution, 430
Air Touch, 778
air transport: PRC (1978–97), 432
airbags, 526
airborne warning and control (AWAC) system
    PRC, 191, 940(n9)
Airbus Industrie (1970–), 161, 162, 164, 165,
    171, 182, 203, 208, 239, 498, 848, 940(n2)
  civilian aircraft, 149
  corporate structure, 167
  creates difficulties for MD (1993), 209
  economies of scale (procurement), 846
  employees, 168
  fails to become a single company, 170
  formation 'owed to government intervention',
    498
  grants sub-contracts in PRC, 209, 216, 221
  importance of PRC market, 237
  joint venture with AVIC (scrapped), 211–13
  lessons for PRC, 232–4
  origins, 166
  owners, 167
  'plans to build 100–seater aircraft', 183, 211

Airbus Industrie (1970–) – *continued*
  and proposed EADC, 160
  restructuring, 168–71
  rivalry with Boeing 149–50, 155, 167–9, 184,
    220, 233
  role model for PRC, 206
  sales, 144, 167, 203
  structure, 230
  success story despite the textbook, 498–9
  suppliers, 145
  turnover, 168
  'uncertain future', 170, 233, 234, 235
Air Canada, 149
Air China, 80, 122, 213, 931
  national team player (first batch), 123
  talks with CSA, 123–4
air combat weapons (USA), 147
air conditioners (vehicles), 523, 524–5, 526,
    536, 546, 547
aircraft (general)
  attack, 189
  bombers, 168, 178, 179, 189, 190, 201
  civilian, 141, 149–50, 166–70, 175, 177, 179,
    202–21, 230, 236, 238, 867–8
  combat, 148
  commercial, 181, 182
  dual use, 174
  'Europe', 166–70
  fighters, 157–8, 178, 179, 188, 189, 190, 195,
    197, 199, 217, 233, 849, 877
  global duopoly, 141
  helicopters, 179
  jets, 144, 171, 175, 177, 180–1, 199, 203,
    206–13, 860
  mentioned, 15, 42, 43, 45, 848, 860, 855
  military, 150–66, 173, 175, 176, 178, 186,
    187–90, 193, 195–6, 210, 230, 237, 239
  modern jet airliner, 206–13
  operational timespan, 148, 940(n2)
  passenger airliner fleet (PRC), 202–3
  PRC, 871
  size (passenger capacity), 142
  small regional jets, 180–2
  supersonic, 199
  trainers, 189, 190, 197
  transporters, 179
  turbo-prop, 180, 205–6, 876–7
  USA, 154–6
  world demand (projected to 2017), 142, 149
  WTO rules (implementation by PRC), 867–8
  see also aircraft (specific); individual
    companies
aircraft (specific)
  AE-100 (Air Express 100; scrapped), 212,
    214, 216, 221, 237, 238, 860
  Airbus (general), [148], 166, 940(n2)
  Airbus A3XX, 143, 167, 212
  Airbus A300–600, 202
  Airbus A-310, 202
  Airbus A-318, 213

Airbus A-319, 167, 182, 209, 211, 216
Airbus A-320, 173, 179, 209, 213, 214, 216,
    221
Airbus A-321, 167, 209, 216
Airbus A330/340, 144
Airbus A-340, 173, 179–80
Airbus A-340–600, 173
Antonov 12, 202,
Antonov 24, 202, 205
ATR-42, 205–6, 209, 214
ATR-72, 209
ATR72–500, 206
Avro RJ (formerly BAe 146), 211
AWACs, 191, 193, 940(n9)
B-6 bomber (PRC), 101
B-52 (heavy bomber), 155
B-707 (1958–), 144, 155, 202, 204
  'world's most successful commercial
    jet', 155
B-717, 179, 183, 211, 212, 214, 219, 221
B-720s, 144
B-727, 144, 179
B-737, 144, 173, 182, 202, 208, 209, 211,
    213, 214, 215
B-747, 144, 155, 166, 173, 202, 214
B-757, 144, 202, 208, 213, 215, 216
B-767, 144, 178, 202
B-777, 144
BAC 1–11, 211
BAe 146 (regional jet), 144, 145, 183, 202,
    211, 214, 940(n1)
  re-named Avro RJ, 211
Bombardier 70–seater, 181
C-17 globemaster transport aircraft, 164
C-130J, 164
Canadair RJ-500, 181
Dash 8, 205, 214
De Havilland Comet (1952–), 155, 166,
    940(n3)
ERJ-135, 181
ERJ-145, 181
ERJ-170, 182, 183
ERJ-190, 239
ERJ-190–200, 182, 183
Eurofighter, 158–9, 161, 162, 170
F-1, 193
F-4 (fighter), 190
F-4 (McDonnell-Douglas), 193
F-5, 193
F-10 (PRC fighter), 193
F-15, 157, 193, 195
F-16 (Lockheed Martin fighter), 144, 152,
    158, 193, 195, 233
F-18, 195
F-22 (USA Air Force), 143, 144
Fokker 28, 211
Fokker 100, 202, 211
Grumman E-2 Hawkeye AWAC, 193
H-5 bomber, 189
H-6 bomber, 189

aircraft (specific) – *continued*
Harrier, 158, 163
Hawker Siddeley Trident, 166
HJ-5 trainer, 189
Il-76, 192, 940(n9)
Il-86, 179–80
Il-96, 180
J-7 fighter, 189, 190
J-8 fighter, 189, 190
J-11 fighter, 191
JJ-5 trainer, 189
JJ-6 trainer, 189
JJ-7 trainer, 189, 190
Joint Strike Fighter (JSF) (USA), 144, 152, 153, 157, 158, 159, 163, 164
KC135, 155
Lockheed Tristar, 144, 166, 174
McDonnell Douglas DC-9, 179
McDonnell Douglas DC-10, 166
MD-11, 202
MD-80, 206–8, 209, 216, 219, 221, 237
MD-82, 202, 208, 213
MD-82/83, 207
MD-90, 208–10, 213, 214, 216, 219, 221, 237
MD-95, 179, 183, 211, 219
Mikoyan-Gurevich (MiG) fighters, 178
Mirage, 157
Mirage-2000, 193
Mitsubishi FS-X (fighter), 233
Nimrod 2000, 163
Q-5 attack, 189, 190
Rafale fighter, 158–9
RAH-66 (US Army), 143
Saab fighters, 157, 159
Saab 200, 205
Short 360, 202
Soviet (old), 195
Su-27 ('Flanker', 1984–), 178, 191–2, 877
Su-30, 178, 192, 877
Su-35 ('Flanker'), 178
T-45 (Hawk), 163
Tornado, 157, 158, 159, 233
Tu-134, 144, 179
Tu-154, 144, 179, 202
Tu-204, 179, 180
Tupolev bombers, 178
Vickers VC 10, 166
YS-11, 177
YS-X, 177
Yun-7 or Y-7 (civilian aircraft), 197, 201, 202, 205–6, 215, 229, 239, 845, 846
Yun-10 or Y-10 (large jet airliner), 203–5, 206, 239, 876
aircraft carriers, 148, 191
Aircraft and Shipbuilding Industries Act (UK 1977), 498
airlines
approved trial groups (PRC), 77
competition, 149
first batch of trial groups (PRC 1991), 85
foreign ownership restrictions, 149
international alliances, 149–50
PRC, 77, 80
privatization, 32, 149, 150
state-owned, 203
airports, 126
Airtours (UK), 227
AIDS, 246, 319
Alaska, 404, 416
Alcatel (France), 861, 920
fibre optic transmission trunk (PRC), 795
merger (1989) with GEC (UK), 336
missed merger opportunity, 862
privatization, 892
Alcatel Alsthom, 396
Alcoa (Aluminium Company of America), 591
Alenia (Italy)
Eurofighter project (1983–), 158
grants sub-contracts in PRC, 209, 214
proposed EADC, 160
turbo-prop feeder aircraft, 205–6
Alenia Marconi Systems, 162
Algeria, 408, 416
Alison (helicopter engines company), 164, 181
Alitalia, 149
all international convertibles, 823
All Nippon Airways, 149
Allegheny Teledyne, 952(n11)
Allianz (Germany), 826, 828
Allied Signal (USA), 239, 940(n1)
merger with Honeywell (announced 6.1999), 146–7
sale of seatbelt business (1997), 526
size (1998), 166
supplier to Embraer, 181
top five global aerospace company, 146
alloy steel, 596
Almanac of China's Economy, 100
Alstom, 59, 398
origins, 336
see also ABB-Alstom; GEC-Alsthom
alternative energy sources, 426–7
alternators (automobile component), 547, 950(n9)
aluminium, 39, 45, 112, 590, 592
advantages, 590
alternative to steel, 590, 595
Hoogovens, 610
Rio Tinto, 708
Ambev (Brazil), 858
American Airlines, 149
American Eagle (airline), 181
American Eximbank, 174
American Farm Bureau, 871
American Home Products (AHP), 247, 250, 259, 262
abortive merger with Monsanto (1998), 266
buys American Cyanamid (1994), 259
market share, 267

American Home Products (AHP) – *continued*
  merger activity, 259
  research and development (1994–7), 248
American Insurance Group, 935
America Online (AOL), 780, 781
  market capitalization (2000), 764
  merger with Time Warner (2000), 782
  sales revenue (2000), 764
  targets PRC market, 781
America Online/Time Warner, 782–3, 806
  AOL TV, 783
  market capitalization, 782
Ameritech: CCF partner of China Unicom, 810
Amgen (USA), 301
ammonia, 490
ammunition producers (PRC), 941(n6)
Amoco: merger with BP (1998), 414–15
Amro-Fleming (Chase Fleming), 958(n9)
Andersen Consulting, 251
Angang, *see* Anshan Iron and Steel Corporation
Angang New Steel, 643
Angat Plant, 387
angina, 250
Anglo-Saxon business structure, 46, 52, 58
  influence in East Asia, 52
  literature on 'apparent disadvantages' of, 46
  'rise to dominance', 58
Angola, 404
Anhui, 307, 352, 391, 719, 810
Anhui Electric Power Company, 110
Anhui Hailuo Group, 128
Ansett Australia (airline), 149
Anshan Iron and Steel Corporation/Group
    (*Angang jituan*)
  coke output, 953(n32)
  continuous casting, 627, 629–30
  crude steel output (1996–7), 602
  debt, 684
  energy efficiency, 638
  holding in Koolyanobing Mine (WA),
    956(n57)
  joint-ventures sought, 629
  listed on the HK stock market, 640
  mentioned, 384, 464, 496, 638
  missed merger opportunity, 862
  national team player (first batch), 115, 116
  non-core businesses, 642
  output structure (1997), 646
  'over-manning', 640
  principal steel products (1997), 636
  product quality, 638
  production costs, 659
  productivity, 642, 659
  profitability, 638
  remuneration and labour productivity (1997),
    641
  reports directly to SBMI, 622
  return on investment (1980–90), 660
  rivalry from Shougang, 670
  sales (1997), 888

  steel production methods (1997), 597
  technological modernization, 629–30
  top ten steel producer (PRC 1997), 634
  wages, 658
  workforce, 639
  world rank (1996), 638
Anshan Passenger Car Works, 565
Antaibao mine, *see* Pingshuo
anti-aircraft missiles (AAM), 191
anti-dumping (AD) measures, 29, 607, 868
anti-lock braking systems equipment, 950(n4)
anti-lock brake systems (auto components), 544
anti-ship missile systems, 192
antibiotics, 283
Anyang Iron and Steel Group Company, 633,
    635
apples, 869
appliances, 592
Arbed (Luxembourg), 602, 602n, 609, 612–13,
    889
  acquisitions, 612–13
  crude steel output (1996–7), 602, 602n
  emerging European 'steel oligopoly', 609
  largest producer in Europe, 613
arbitrage activities, 275
Arch Coal (1997–), 710
Arch Mineral Corporation, 710
Arco, *see* Atlantic Richfield Company
Argentina, 47n, 409, 611, 870
  investment by Usinor, 611
  number of companies in *FT* 500 (1998), 47n
  oil sector, 409
  WTO enforcement proceedings, 870
Ariane, 171
Aristotle, 935
Aristrain, 602n
Armco Steel: Kawasaki investment in, 608
armoured personnel carriers, 156
arms trade, 151, 152, 157–8, 274
Army Police (PRC), 291, 941(n16)
army veterans, 382
Arnett, E., 189
Arrow Point (IT company), 774
arthritis, 247, 261, 267, 307
arts and crafts, 130
Arun LNG business (Indonesia), 416
Arvedi (Italy): investment by Usinor, 611
Arvin: exhaust systems and shock absorbers,
    525
Asahi Glass: reduction of workforce (1999), 56
Ascend Communications, 773
Asea (Sweden), 336
Ashland Coal, 710
Asia
  coal consumption (1986–96), 698
  coal output (1980–95), 698
  exporter of oil to PRC (1995–7), 434
  internet race, 780–1
  number of 'competitive edge' companies
    (outside Japan, 1997–8), 50

Asia – *continued*
  production and sales of automobiles (1998),
    508
  share of world electricity generation
    (1995–2015), 335, 943(n4)
  steel consumption *per capita*, 595
  steel production (1991–7), 589
Asia-Pacific
  coal reserves, 407
  coal as source of primary energy, 705
  electricity generation capacity (1990–2010),
    697
  Exxon Mobil's interests, 416
  largest companies, 23
  lorry sales (1995, 2005), 509
  natural gas production and reserves (1997),
    405
  oil production (1987–97), 405
  'poorly endowed' (hydrocarbons), 406–7
  population (including South Asia), 406–7
  primary energy consumption (1987–97), 402
  share in global electricity generation
    (1990–2010), 696
  shortage of natural gas, 705
  tyres, 526
Asia America Telecom, 810
Asia Cement (Taiwan), 718
Asian financial crisis (1997–), 23, 71, 72, 124,
    242
  effect on electricity demand, 334–5, 943(n4)
  effect on world coal price, 729, 759
  GM takeover of Isuzu (1999), 518
  hits Shanghai Petrochemical Corporation,
    455
  impact on demand for cars (PRC), 536
  impact on PRC flotation plans, 746
  impact on Sanjiu, 290, 318
  impetus to exports of steel from East Asia,
    595
  implications for Shenhua, 749
  Kia Motors bought by Hyundai, 506
  Posco and Nippon Steel share-swap (1999),
    613
  PRC immune, 833–4, 916
  prospects for car sales remain good, 526
  resentment, 926
  ridden by Posco, 604–5
  South-East Asia (1997–8), 833
  'worst may be over', 746
Asimco (Beijing), 545, 951(n22)
  investment company, 545
  joint ventures in PRC (1994–), 545, 553, 576,
    580, 950(n9)
  'major force' (PRC components industry),
    580
  specializes in auto components, 545
Aspin, Les, 152
aspirin: catch-up possibilities, 64
ASRAAM missile, 164
asset management companies (PRC), 71

Associates First Capital Corporation, 822
Association for Peaceful Use of Military
    Industrial Technology (PRC 1987–), 272
Association of Power Generation Equipment
    Manufacturing Industry, 947(n41)
Association for the Promotion of China's
    Business Groups (4.1994–), 138, 938(n7)
Association of South-East Asian Nations
    (ASEAN), 927–8
  'ASEAN Free Trade Area', 928
  'ASEAN plus three' (PRC, Japan, South
    Korea), 927–8
asthma and allergy drugs, 263, 268
Aston Martin (Ford), 515
Astra (Sweden), 59, 861
  best sellers (drugs), 250
  joint venture with Merck, 264
  merger with Zeneca, 264
  missed merger opportunity, 861
  research and development (1994–7), 249
AstraZeneca, 250, 262, 264–5, 267, 268
  best sellers (drugs), 250
  market share, 267
  R&D expenditure, 264
  sales, 264
A.T. Kearney management consultants, 146
AT&T (American Telephone and Telegraph),
    777, 782, 786
  'giant of broadband age', 782
  international comparison (12.1999), 800
  market capitalization (2000), 764, 800
  revenue, profits (12.1999), 800
  sales revenue (2000), 764
Athlon chips, 768–9
Atlantic Richfield Company (Arco), 861
  discussions with Shenhua (1995–), 750
  missed merger opportunity, 862
  sale of coal-mining interests (USA), 710
  takeover by BP Amoco (1999), 416
Atomic Energy of Canada, 945(n21)
audiovisual: WTO rules (implementation by
    PRC), 869
auditing, 226–7, 276
Australasia, 434, 589
Australia, 145
  bank restructuring (1980–97), 821
  BP-Solarex manufacturing facilities, 426
  coal, 710
  coal exports, 706, 728, 729, 957(n5–6)
  coal output (1980–95), 699
  comparatively-cheap open-cast mining, 710
  exports of iron ore to PRC, 640
  iron ore, 675
  iron ore costs (1997), 619
  IT companies (2000), 765
  labour productivity (coal-mining, 1996),
    711
  land rights, 709
  output per worker (coal), 751
  port charges (Queensland), 740

Australia – *continued*
  PRC and South Korean investment (coal industry), 718
  production and sales of automobiles (1998), 508
  strength of trade union movement, 711, 712
  top twenty steel-producing country (1991–8), 617
  transport costs (coal), 750
  wage costs (steel industry, 1997), 620
  wages (coal industry), 752
  working days lost (1992–6), 712
  world's leading coal exporter, 717
Austria: bank restructuring (1980–97), 820
Austrian Airlines, 149
Auto Industry, 524
Autolina, 513
Autoliv, 522, 525
automobile companies
  foreign assets, sales, employment (1997), 509
  role (1990s), 511
automobile design, 503, 511, 512, 521
automobile groups (PRC), 74
automobile industry (global), 6, 45, 501–86, 859, 861, 950–1
  alliances, 512–13
  aluminium prototypes, 590
  autos in the global business revolution, 507–12
  barriers to entry, 63, 64, 532–6
  brake systems, 39
  central to Japan's industrial rise, 57
  components, 519–32
  conclusions, 532–6, 581–5
  dealerships, 503, 887
  developing countries, 532–6
  drivers of industry change, 507–12
  economic determinants of industrial structure, 502–4
  extending the value chain beyond car manufacture, 512
  first batch of trial business groups, 109
  fuel-cell technology, 427
  global context, 502–36
  global market share, 37, 39
  global oligopoly, 40–1
  global production and sales (1998), 508
  globalization of outsourcing, 511–12
  impact of global competition on manufacturers' costs, 509–10
  industrial structure: autos, 512–17
  industrial structure: lorries, 517–19
  institutional structure and change, 506–7
  Japanese competition and the global industry, 510–11
  largest companies (foreign assets, 1997), 509
  lifetime expenditure, 512
  mergers and acquisitions, 514–18
  miscellaneous, 3, 43, 271, 346, 854, 860, 863, 929

  national team (various indicators, 1995), 78
  national team (PRC), 77
  non-aviation output of AVIC, 198
  privatization (general), 32
  PRC, 197, 536–86, 921, 926
  prospective mergers, 517
  research and development expenditure (1995, 1998), 49
  Sanjiu, 316, 317, 320, 321
  second batch of trial groups (1997), 86
  sectoral share of PRC national team (1991, 1997), 84
  size, 590
  smuggling, 275, 874
  South Korea, 19, 22, 53, 54, 604
  state intervention and industrial structure, 504–6
  state protection, 533, 534
  steel industry, 590–1
  suppliers, 39
  Sweden, 59
  tooling costs, 503
  top ten companies (1998), 533
  traditional industry, 502–7
  transatlantic corporations, 338
  tyres, 39
  world-beating corporations (Japan and South Korea), 176
  world lorry sales (1995, 2005), 509
  world market (project growth, 1995–2001), 507
  WTO rules (implementation by PRC), 867
  WTO enforcement proceedings, 870
  Yuchai, 548–86
automobile industry (PRC), 197, 536–86, 921, 926
  ability to compete on global level playing field, 885–7
  approved trial groups (PRC), 77, 87
  assembly plants, 538
  barriers to entry (components), 535
  car production (comparative), 534
  components, 537, 540, 543–8
  components industry investment companies, 545–6
  conclusion, 581–5
  decision-making autonomy (PRC 1986–), 91
  diesel engine producers (1995), 562
  diesel engine producers (1998), 559
  diesel engines, 529, 558–60
  economies of scale, 538
  failure to catch up, 541
  foreign investment (components), 545–6
  foreign investment (engines), 546–7
  four key enterprises (PRC), 463–4
  government funds, 950(n7)
  heavy duty trucks, 565–6
  imports, 536, 537
  institutional structure, 538–47
  Japanese example, 504–5, 532

automobile industry (PRC) – *continued*
  joint ventures, 538, 569
  leading car producers (1998), 556
  lessons from Brazil, 547
  lorries (output 1995–8), 551
  low product-development capability, 540
  main producers of light trucks (1998), 554
  market size, 537
  mergers, 80
  missed merger opportunities, 861
  national champions, 76, 101–3, 539
  nature of entrepreneurship, 585
  output growth, 536–9
  petrol engine production, 567–8
  plant size (1995), 539
  policy announcement (1994), 539
  production and imports (1978–98), 536
  production and sales of automobiles (1998),
    508
  road system, 541, 551, 566
  saloon car production (1998), 540
  South Korean example, 532
  tariffs, 536–7
  tyre sector, 526
  vehicles, 538–43
  Yuchai, 548–85
automobile lighting, 546
automotive
  electrical motors, 546
  electrical systems, 546
  electronic control components (automobile
    component), 546
  generators, 545
automotive industry
  WTO enforcement proceedings, 870
Aventis (1998/9–), 59, 256, 262–4
  best sellers (drugs), 250
  Hoechst, 262
  Rhône-Poulenc, 263
  market capitalization, 269
  sales, 269
Avery, Chris, 168
Aviation Industries of China (AVIC), 79, 112,
    184–7, 208–9, 221, 239, 841, 845, 859,
    938(n4)
  ability to compete on global level playing
    field, 876–8
  aerospace component, 227, 940(n17)
  auto and motorcycle components, 199
  'bleak prospects', 877
  bucks world trend towards merger, 230
  buses, 199, 210, 229
  business structure, 225–6
  catch-up difficulties, 233
  'children' and 'grandchildren' companies,
    221–6
  'competitive global supplier of components',
    214
  core business, 877
  diversification, 877

downsizing scope, 845
employment, 226, 227–9
'five thousand non-aviation products', 198
growth, 197–8
holding company experiment, ended, 226–31
institutional change, 221–26
joint venture with Airbus (scrapped), 211–13
micro-vans, 199
motorcycles, 198–9
non-aviation production, 196–202, 222, 227,
    229, 846
'now split into two', 79
'overall responsibility for domestic aircraft
    industry', 218
policy change, 196–7
'reform' (1999), 877
relative size (1997), 228–9
research and development budget (1997), 175
restructuring, 226–31
revenues, profits, employees, R&D (1997),
    877
sales, 227
'simply a minnow on the world stage', 227,
    230
size, 226
slump in military aircraft orders, 196–7
split into two (AVIC 1, AVIC 2), 112, 230,
    930, 931
state holding company (1996–), 186
structure, 185, 186, 198
sub-contracting work, 213–14
Vickers (UK) comparison, 877
see also CAC; CATIC; CEC; XAC
AVIC, *see* Aviation Industries of China
avionics, 144, 146, 148, 174, 175, 179, 180,
    181, 190, 191, 192, 193, 204, 205, 208,
    210, 220, 237, 238, 877
AVL (Austria), 553
Avon Products: competitive advantage, 35
AXA (France), 815, 816, 826, 828, 837

Babcock International (UK), 943(n7)
Babcock and Wilcox (USA), 368, 391
BAC, *see* British Aircraft Corporation
BAe, *see* British Aerospace
BAe – GEC Marconi, 60
BAe Matra Dynamics, 162
BAe Systems (1999–), 161, 163, 165, 235
  Avro-RJ, 182
  'legacy of distrust' with Dasa, 170
  market capitalization, 236
  state aid, 167
  twenty per cent stake in Airbus Industrie, 170
  see also mergers
Baiyun Hotel (Guangzhou Airport), 558
Baiyunshan (Guangzhou), 279, 298
  'dynamic new business', 291
  'largest pharmaceutical manufacturer' (PRC,
    late 1980s), 291
  listed company, 307

Baiyunshan (Guangzhou) – *continued*
  non-SOE national champion (PRC), 862
  'relies mainly on single product', 297
  sales (1992), 941(n15)
ball bearings, 954(n40)
Bangladesh, 943(n8)
Bank America (USA), 815, 817, 824
  conversion to FHC, 819
  global top five bank, [822], 958(n8)
  key indicators, 1999 (PRC comparison),
    827
  productivity and profits, 831
  top five firm (syndicated credit arrangements,
    2000), 824
Bank of China (BOC), 93, 96, 107, 831,
    939(n13)
  key indicators, 1999 (global-leaders
    comparison), 827
Bank Holding Companies, 819, 958(n5)
Bank for International Settlements (BIS), 815,
    833
Bank One, 817
Bank of Tokyo-Mitsubishi
  global top five bank, [822], 958(n8)
  The Banker, 822
banking, 501, 646
  Big Four (PRC), 827, 829, 830, 831
  doctors of mathematics and physics, 818
  financial engineering, 818–19
  global market share, 37
  Japanese, 56
  mergers (continental Europe), 58
  on-line, 782
  PRC, 68–9, 95, 937(n2 to ch3), 813, 926
  PRC-US Agreement (11.1999), 825
  productivity gap (PRC v global leaders), 831
  quality of assets (PRC), 831, 958(n12)
  regional (USA), 814
  restructuring (1980–97), 820–1
  shortcomings (PRC), 93
  state-run enterprises in Singapore, 23
  support for enterprise groups (PRC), 70, 95,
    96–8
  widening scope, 817
  see also financial services
bankruptcies (PRC), 97
banks, 351
  corruption (PRC), 874
  PRC, 70, 939(n13)
  re-nationalized (South Korea), 54
  'soft loans' (PRC), 349
  state-owned (PRC), 873
Banque Nationale de Paris, 945(n19)
Banque Paribas, 168
Baoan county, 315
Baoding, 137
baogan ('contract for hand-overs'), 440
Baogang, *see* Baoshan Iron and Steel
    Corporation; Shanghai Baoshan Iron and
    Steel Group

Baoshan Iron and Steel Corporation (Baogang
    1982–98), 464, 496
  approach to modernization, 661
  began production in 1982, 639
  capacity (1998), 639
  capital construction spending (1996), 639
  coke output, 953(n32)
  continuous casting, 627
  crude steel output (1996–7), 602
  downsizing, 952–3(n18)
  employees (1997), 888
  energy efficiency, 638
  external funding, 661–2
  high value-added steel, 639
  joint venture in Ningbo, 629
  local champion (Shanghai), 454
  mergers, 639
  'most advanced integrated steel producer',
    629
  no space constraints, 651
  principal steel products (1997), 636
  product quality, 638
  profitability, 638, 639, 643
  remuneration and labour productivity (1997),
    641
  renamed Shanghai Baoshan Iron and Steel
    Group (1998), 639
  reports directly to SBMI, 622
  research and development, 629
  return on investment (1980–90), 660
  revenues, profits (1998), 888
  sales (1997), 888
  sheet steel output, 636, 638
  Shenhua comparison, 749
  steel production methods (1997), 597
  technological modernization, 629
  top ten steel producer (PRC 1997), 634
  wages, 658
  welfare costs, 639
  workforce, 639
  world rank (1996), 638
  see also Shanghai Baoshan Iron and Steel
    Group
Baoshan Steel Group ('Baogang'), 384, 938(n5)
  'aims to become multi-national', 115
  assets, 77[–]79
  grooming for entry into *Fortune* 500, 115
  involved in mergers, 80, 114
  national team player (first batch), 115
  revenues, profits (1998), 888
  suggested merger with Wugang Group, 115
Baosteel Group International Trade
    Corporation, 639–40, 646
Baotou (coal-mine), 753–4
Baotou (place), 747, 755
Baotou Iron and Steel Company (Inner
    Mongolia), 753
  output structure (1997), 646
  possible merger with Shougang, 694
  principal steel products (1997), 636

Baotou Iron and Steel Company (Inner
    Mongolia) – *continued*
  productivity, 659
  purchases Kaiser Steel, 686
  remuneration and labour productivity (1997),
    641
  steel production methods (1997), 597
  top ten steel producer (PRC 1997), 634
Barclays Bank (UK), 824
Barfield, C.E., *see* Groomridge, M.A.
Barings (UK), 817, 958(n9)
Barnet Bank, 817
barriers to entry, 9, 63, 930
  aero-engines, 171, 173
  aerospace, 141, 148, 173–6, 195–6
  auto industry, 532–6
  'catch-22' problem, 148
  financial services, 816, 833
  impact of IT, 818
  internet, 780, 786–7
  IT sector, 762, 769, 786–7, 789–90, 793
  military aircraft, 195–6
  'normal path of capitalist development', 13
  pharmaceuticals, 267, 270–1
  power equipment, 332
  steel (developing countries), 618–22
  telecommunications, 770–1, 777, 786–7
  TRIPs Agreement (1994), 786–7
barriers to growth
  inadequate energy supply (PRC), 340
Barshefsky, Charlene, 607, 761, 786, 839, 895
Basel Accord, 833
BASF, 118, 249, 262, 454
basic oxygen furnace (BOF), 596, 597, 603,
    621, 645, 659, 672, 673, 951(n4), 953(n21)
batteries, 109
battlefield reconnaissance system, 164
Bayer (Germany), 248, 261, 262, 269, 307
Becker (car components manufacturer), 523
Beecham (UK)
  merged (1989) with SmithKline Beckman
    (USA), 254
beef, 868
beer, 314–15, 855, 869
Beijing, xxvi, 80, 123, 125, 224, 312, 935,
    938(n7)
  advertising by Yuchai, 557
  anti-pollution measures, 748
  average wages (manufacturing sector), 665
  Boxer Rebellion, 904
  Capital Iron and Steel Group, 115
  Citigroup office, 835
  coal consumption, 748
  employment provided by Shougang, 688
  foreign investment in telecommunications
    (post-WTO accession), 791–2
  geographical location of national team
    members, 82, 83
  Men Tou Gou coal-mine ('nearby'), 748
  Motorola production centre, 795–6

pharmaceuticals, 307
real estate, 688
Shangri La Hotel, 130
steel, 464
telephone installation (waiting time), 807
thermal coal price (7.1997), 729
Beijing Automotive Industry Corporation
  in-house engine production, 567
  joint venture with Chrysler (1984–), 539,
    540, 567
  sales, profits, employees, output (1998), 556
  saloon car production (1998), 540
  same as 'Beijing Jeep', 537, [539], 541
  second layer enterprises, 560
Beijing Aviation College
  Yuchai MBA Programme, 579
Beijing Boiler Works (Beiguo), 391
Beijing CATCH Communications, 809
Beijing Construction Group, 126
Beijing Datang Power Generation Company
    Limited, 110
  'fast-growing', 359
  floated on an international stock market, 349,
    359
  major pieces of equipment (1960–2002),
    360–1
  shareholders, 359
  subsidiary of North China Power Generating
    Group, 344, 359
Beijing gantie gongsi, *see* Beijing Steel
    Company
Beijing Group Company, 562
Beijing Heavy Electrical Generator Company,
    391
Beijing Heavy Machinery, 360
Beijing Heavy Machinery Factory, 656,
    954(n39)
Beijing Internal Combustion Engine Company
    ('Beinei'), 567–8
Beijing International Airport, 289
Beijing International Power Development and
    Investment Company (BIPDIC), 359, 361n
Beijing Light Vehicle Company, 554
Beijing Metallurgical Bureau, 654
Beijing Municipal Government, 125, 622,
    646–8, 650, 656, 657, 659, 683–4, 685,
    689, 690, 953(n25), 956–7(n66)
  see also Shougang Group
Beijing No. 1 Machine Tool Company,
    948(n53)
Beijing Pharmaceuticals, plant, 941(n10)
Beijing Quansantui Power Engineering
    Company, 946(n37)
Beijing Shougang (Group) Company Limited
    (BSGCL 1995–), 647, 685
  core company (1995–) of Shougang Group,
    685, 694
  previously (until 1995) known as 'Shougang
    Corporation', 685
  profits (1997), 692

Beijing Shougang Stock Holding Company Limited (planned)
    listing postponed, 685, 957(n67)
Beijing Steel Company, 954(n37)
Beijing Three Gorges Yangtze Hydropower Technological Development Centre, 944(n16)
Beijing University: Centre for Economic Research, 4
Beijing Yanshan Petrochemical [corporation], 469
Beilun Port (Ningbo), 640
Beinei, see Beijing Internal Combustion Engine Company
Belgium
    bank restructuring (1980–97), 820
    investment by Usinor, 611
    production of plastics (1989–96), 451
    purchase of missiles from USA, 158
    steel output (1974–96), 593
    top twenty steel-producing country (1991–8), 617
Bell Atlantic, 800
Bell Atlantic/GTE, 777
Bell Canada/AIG, 810
Bell South, 777, 800
Belridge (oil company), 411
Benelux; steel production, 594
Bengang, see Benxi Iron and Steel Group
Benxi Iron and Steel Group ('Bengang jituan')
    national team player (second batch), 115, 116
    output structure (1997), 646
    principal steel products (1997), 637
    productivity, 659
    remuneration and labour productivity (1997), 641
    return on investment (1980–90), 660
    steel production methods (1997), 597
    suggested merger with Anshan Steel Group, 115, 116
    top ten steel producer (PRC 1997), 634
benzene, 466
Berger, A., R. Young, H. Genay and H. Udell (2000), 958(n4)
Bernabe, Franco, 841
Bernstein, R. and R.H. Munro (1998), 435
Bestfoods: competitive advantage, 35
BethForge, 952(n11)
Bethlehem Steel (USA), 861
    acquisition of Lukens (1997–8), 613, 952(n11–12)
    crude steel output (1996–7), 602
    disposal of loss-making segments, 952(n11–12)
    industrial concentration, 613
    missed merger opportunity, 862
    output (1969), 951(n7)
    remuneration and labour productivity (1995), 641
BethShip, 952(n11)

beverages, 316–17, 318, 592, 858
    cans, 592
    lightweighting, 592
BHP (Australia), 602, 710, 755, 891
bicycles, 198, 849
big business, 242
    advanced economies, xxiv
    'anti-consumer tendencies', 16
    benefits, 61–2
    central to development of capitalism, 61
    continental European response, 58
    Four Little Tigers (1999), 21
    France, 18
    gap between advanced economies and developing countries, 62–4
    Germany, 18
    Hong Kong, 23
    Japan, 16–18
    market share, 38–9
    'merger frenzy', 38
    PRC, 24–5
    regional distribution, 46–51
    reinvigorated in Japan and Europe, 60
    Singapore, 23
    South Korea, 22
    Taiwan, 21
    UK, 15, 18
    unprecedented power (1990s), 64
    USA, 15–16
    Western, 462
Bilger, Pierre (CEO ABB-Alstom), 338
billing, 8
Billiton (mining corporation), 695, 891
bio-informatics, 246, 258
bio-technology, 246, 261, 325, 763
    mergers and acquisitions (1988–98), 769
    Sanjiu, 307
biomass energy, 426
BIPDIC, see Beijing International Power Development and Investment Company
Bischoff, Manfred, 160, 164, 169, 170
Blanchard, O., 2
blast furnaces, 598, 619–20, 621, 630
    cheaper alternatives, 598
    Shougang, 645, 659, 672, 676, 690
blood pressure, 250
Bloomberg, 781
Bluetooth (wireless linking technology), 782
BMG (music), 781
BMW, 173, 509, 513
BNP Paribas (France)
    top five firm (all international convertibles, 2000), 823
BOC, see Bank of China
body technology (cars), 522
Boeing (USA), 13, 164, 182, 183, 239, 848, 860, 897
    civil airliners, 154–5
    competition with Lockheed, 157
    competitive advantage, 173–4

Boeing (USA) – *continued*
  delivers 8,000 jet aircraft, 144
  divide and rule tactics (PRC v South Korea),
      suggested, 219
  dominates PRC market (pre-1997), 203
  economies of scale (procurement), 846
  employees, 168
  grants sub-contracts in PRC, 209, 214–15
  importance of PRC market, 237
  keiretsu, 145
  lessons drawn by PRC from, 71
  market capitalization, 236
  'massive, integrated defence and civilian
      company', 230
  mergers, 152
  military aircraft, 152–4
  relative size (1997), 228, 236
  research and development, 142, 143, 175,
      510, 535
  revenues, profits, employees, R&D (1997),
      877
  rivalry with Airbus, 149–50, 155, 167–9, 184,
      220, 233, 499
  sales, 144, 227
  size (1998), 166
  state aid for research and development, 176
  sub-contracts let to CAC, 216
  sub-contracts let to PRC, 213, 219–20, 221
  suppliers, 145–6
  turnover, 161, 168
  World War II, 154
  'world's largest aircraft company', 145
Boeing-McDonnell Douglas, 956(n64)
boiler-makers (UK), 943(n7)
boilers, 328–9, 368, 377, 378, 391, 948(n45,
    49)
  HPEC output (1959–98), 374
Bombardier (Canada), 180–4, 211, 239, 240,
    860
  turbo-prop feeder aircraft, 205
  WTO ruling (4.2000), 878
bombing, 163
  laser-guided, 163, 192
BondBook, 818
bonds, 540, 932
  CNPC, 440
  corporate, 37
  PRC, 944(n11
  Sinopec, 465
  Three Gorges Finance Company, 350
book of *Dao and De* (Lao Zi), 401, 501, 695
borrowing, 37
  Japanese steel industry, 603, 952(n8)
  keiretsu, 55
  PRC oil sector, 453, 471
Bosch, *see* Robert Bosch
Boserup, E., 763
BOT, *see* Build-Operate-Transfer projects
Botelho, Mauricio, 183
bottling (Coca-Cola), 530

bourgeoisie, 897
Bowden, John, 608
Boxer Rebellion, 904
Bozano Simonson, 180
BP, *see* British Petroleum
BP Amoco, 848, 854, 935
  business units, 424
  chemicals division, 423
  comparison with New CNPC and New
      Sinopec, 479
  cost-cutting, 414
  employees, 480
  ethylene crackers, 422
  exploration, 414
  financial indicators, 480
  Fortune 500 ranking, 414, 416
  headquarters staff, 424
  largest producer outside OPEC, 416
  merger with Arco (1999), 413
  new fuel technologies, 426
  oil and gas production, 481
  oil and gas reserves, 416
  performance monitoring, 424–5
  petrochemicals, 414
  production and exploration in 27 countries,
      481
  profitability, 414
  profits, 480
  refinery throughput, 421
  research and development, 423
  revenues, profits, employees, R&D
      (pro-forma, 1997), 884
  sale of assets in refining division, 426
  state-of-the-art integrated site, 422
  takeover of Atlantic Richfield (Arco), 416
  turnover, 480
  turnover ('revenues'), 414
  use of information technology, 425
  see also BP Amoco/Arco; British Petroleum
BP Amoco: Company Capital Approvals
    Committee, 425
BP Amoco/Arco (UK-USA)
  basic statistics, 418–20
  comparison with New CNPC and New
      Sinopec, 479
  30,000 petrol stations, 422
BP Solar, 426
BP-Solarex [takeover of Solarex by BP Solar],
    426
brakes, 521, 535, 950(n9)
brands, 9, 11, 24, 32, 42, 51, 61, 125, 873, 929
  absent, 844
  automobiles, 503, 509, 511
  barriers to entry, 64
  coal sector, 712
  competitive advantage, 34, 35
  cost of building an internet brand, 780
  diesel engines, 530
  Dongfeng, 563
  'dragon head' products, 75

brands – *continued*
  financial services, 826, 832
  GE (USA), 332
  global leaders, 856
  global giants (oil), 486
  global, 34, 37, 486, 856
  Huawei, 795
  internet companies, 779–80, 806
  IT sector, 769
  Legend (PRC), 794
  mass media, 781
  non-SOE national champions (PRC), 862
  oil, 420, 427–8, 486, 493, 883
  oil (PRC), 883
  pharmaceuticals, 246, 247, 251, 270, 286,
    298
  PRC, 75, 841, 850, 862, 880, 883
  Sanjiu (general), 314, 315, 319, 324
  Sanjiu, 880
  Sanjiu hotels, 313
  steel sector, 693
  tyre industry, 527
  Yuchai, 557, 558, 885
  see also competitive advantage; *Sanjiu Weitai*
Brazil, 20, 531, 858, 878
  aerospace industry, 180–3
  catch-up (steel), 621
  comparative advantage, 20
  'competitive edge' companies (1997–8), 62–3
  energy, 340, 943(n8–9)
  enforcement of WTO rules, 919
  ethylene crackers, 421
  exports of iron ore to PRC, 640
  FDI inflow, 31
  Fortune 500 (1998), 47n
  FT 500 (1998), 47n
  iron ore, 618, 619, 675
  job losses (steel), 606, 640, 688, 692
  labour cost per ton of coal, 620
  lessons for PRC, 238–40, 548
  major exporter of steel (mid-1990s), 606
  per capita energy use (1994), 341
  Posco iron-ore pellet-manufacturing facility,
    609
  privatization (steel), 606, 640, 688, 692
  production and sales of automobiles (1998),
    508
  share in *Fortune* Global 500 (1997), 50
  steel, 593, 606, 616, 620, 621, 640, 688, 692
  steel output (1974–96), 593
  Thyssen-Krupp willingness to produce in,
    612
  TNCs (1999), 21
  top ten steel-producing country (1991–8),
    616
  wage costs (steel industry, 1997), 620
  WTO enforcement proceedings, 870
breast cancer, 250
Breed (car components sector), 525
  '60 plants in 30 countries', 525

Bretton Woods System, 814
brewing, 37, 545
bribery, 842, 873–4
bridges, 126, 133
Bridgestone (Japan), 19, 527, 535, 850, 886
Briggs, Elizabeth, xxvi
Bristol-Myers Squibb, 249, 282
Britain, *see* United Kingdom
British Aerospace (BAe), xxvi, 840, 848, 854,
    920, 940(n2)
  acquires Siemens Plessey business (1997),
    147
  proposed EADC, 159–60
  dwarfed, 146
  Eurofighter project (1983–), 158–9
  formed through Act of Parliament (1977),
    498
  merger activity, 170
  merger with GEC (1999), 147
  offers sub-contracts in PRC, 214
  origins, 166
  overseas sales (1997), 174
  part-owner of Airbus Industrie, 167
  partnership with Boeing, 163, 164
  partnership with Lockheed-Martin, 163–4
  previously BAC, 940(n4)
  privatization, 169, 859, 892
  product of state-orchestrated merger (1960s),
    858
  production of 100–seater jets, 211
  Regional Jet, 144, 145, 940(n1)
  relative size (1997), 228
  research and development, 143, 175
  restructuring, 169
  revenues, profits, employees, R&D (1997),
    877
  sales, 227
  size (1998), 166
  state aid, 167, 174–5
  state-owned, 498, 499
  suppliers, 145, 146
  30% foreign-owned (1998), 163
  wings, 221
British Aircraft Corporation (BAC), 15, 163,
    498
British Airways, 149, 203, 787
British Leyland, 858
British Motor Corporation, 15
British Nuclear Industry Forum, 704
British Petroleum (BP), 65, 407, 410, 840, 892,
    920
  chemical engineers, 941(n2)
  corporate culture, 411
  cost-cutting (use of IT, 1996–), 422–3
  internationalization, 493
  job losses, 427
  joint venture with Mobil, 415
  joint venture with Shanghai Petrochemical
    Corporation, 454, 455, 472
  LNG project (Shenzhen), 717

British Petroleum (BP) – *continued*
  merger with Amoco (1998), 413, 414–15
  origins, 407
  output (1996), 409
  privatization (1987), 407, 493, 892
  purchase of oil supplies from outside the
    company, 411
  purchase of Sohio, 411
  sale of coal-mining interests (USA), 710
  sale of non-core businesses, 425–6
  transformation (SOE national champion into
    privatized TNC), 859
  US shareholders, 415
  see also BP Amoco
British Steel Corporation (1967–99), 15, 498,
    600, 609–10, 840, 841, 848, 920
  crude steel output (1996–7), 602
  efficient, 610
  emerging European 'steel oligopoly', 609
  exports, 610
  'largest loss in British corporate history'
    (1979), 609
  management (Shougang contrast), 671
  merger with Hoogovens (1999), 610
  origins, 609, 670
  privatization (1988–9), 498, 610, 859, 892
  product of state-orchestrated mergers
    (1960s), 858
  profitable (by 1985), 610
  profits (1997), 957(n69)
  remuneration and labour productivity (1995),
    641
  research and development, 595–6, 618, 694
  restructuring, 609–10
  sales (1997), 888
British Telecommunications (BT), 786, 803,
    840, 854
  international comparison (12.1999), 800
  market capitalization, revenue, profits
    (12.1999), 800
  market capitalization (4.2000), 931
  privatization, 892
Britoil, 411
broad spectrum penicillin, 250
broadband equipment, 771, 774–5
broadband services, 782–4, 803, 805, 808–9
broadcasting, 53, 761
Brown Boveri (Switzerland), 336
Browne, (Sir) John (CEO BP Amoco), 426, 703
'Brundtland' Report, 704
Brunner, 264
Brusch, Howard, 358
BSGCL, *see* Beijing Shougang (Group)
    Company Limited
BT, *see* British Telecommunications
BTI (Israel): Chinese sub-contractor (CEC),
    217
Buck, J.L., 906
Buicks, 103
Build-Operate-Transfer (BOT) projects

power plants (PRC), 345, 349, 352–3, 354,
    386, 944(n14), 944–5(n18)
building materials, 77, 118, 120, 133
Bureau of Metallurgical Statistics, 689
bureaucracy (PRC), 911
buses, 112, 199, 201, 210, 229, 513, 541–2, 551
  coaches, 513, 541
  minibuses, 546
  PRC, 112, 537, 565
  production and imports (PRC 1978–98), 536
bushu ('disposition'), 947(n43)
business
  activity ('meso' level), 8
  administration, 2, 10
  bureaucracies, 13
  history (textbook v reality), 13
  systems, xxiv
  see also trial business groups
BYC, 576
Byrd, W.A., 955(n44), 956(n62)

CAAC, *see* Civil Aviation Administration of
    China
cable companies, 781, 808
cable television, 783, 784
  fierce competition, 808
  internet, 782
  PRC network, 808
  security considerations (PRC), 808
  telephony via, 803
Cable and Wireless, 784
CAC, *see* Chengdu Aircraft Corporation
Cadbury Schweppes: competitive advantage, 35
CAIC, *see* China Auto Industrial Corporation
Caihong Group, 107–8
Caiyang Engine Plant (1995), 562
calicoes, 15
California Iron Industrial Company, 662
California Iron and Steel Company, 662
Caltex (1936–): Chevron-Texaco joint venture,
    417
Cambridge: Judge Institute of Management
    Studies, xxvi
Campbell, J.L., *see* Lindberg, L.N.
Canada, 878
  bank restructuring (1980–97), 821
  Hyundai plant, 506
  Ispat, 600
  IT companies (2000), 764–5
  labour productivity (coal-mining, 1997), 711
  land rights, 709
  production of ethylene (1989–96), 451
  steel output (1974–96), 593
  supplier of nuclear power units to PRC, 357,
    945(n21)
  top twenty steel-producing country (1991–8),
    617
Canadair, 214
Canadian Airlines, 149
cancer, 246, 307

cangu (mixed share ownership), 314
Canon, 19, 850
cans, 43, 45
Canton, *see* Guangzhou
Cantor, Mickey, 935
capital, 9
  accumulation, 1
  allocation (Japan), 54
  components sector (PRC), 545
  developing countries, 5–6
  enterprise groups (PRC), 75
  foreign (PRC), 90
  GE (USA), 334
  globalization, 855
  international, 860
  international flows, 849
  international mobility (UK), 814
  liberalization, 29–32
  'no nationality', 65
  Norwegian oil sector, 499
  oil sector, 421, 425
  power equipment companies, 331
  power generation (PRC), 348–9
  PRC, 68–9, 71, 73, 76, 92, 97, 133, 932,
    938(n5)
  raising (PRC), 96
  redistribution (PRC), 72
  service activities, 333
  Shanghai Petrochemical Corporation, 472
  Sinopec, 465,
  state-owned (PRC), 89, 93–4
  venture, 371
  working, 97
  working (HPEC subsidiaries), 370
Capital, Volume I (Marx 1867), 9
Capital Iron and Steel Corporation, 115
Capital Iron and Steel Group, 115–16
capital markets, 72, 129, 130, 282
  pharmaceutical sector (PRC), 282
  undeveloped (PRC), 72
  foreign, 130
capitalism
  advanced, 4, 37
  'competitive market system', 4
  'distortions', 4
  nature, 2
  tendency to concentration, 9, 13
  see also advanced economies; industrial
    concentration
car braking systems, 525, 535
carbon dioxide emissions, 430, 702–4
carbon steel, 596
Cargill Inc., 256, 265
Caribbean: economic growth (1980–98), 851
Carnegie, Andrew (1835–1919), 670, 678; cited,
  587
Carnegie Mellon Software Engineering
  Institute, 787
Carnegie Steel Company (1864–1900), 601,
  681–2

merged with Federal Steel, 601
cars, *see* automobiles
Casa (Spain), 840
  Eurofighter project (1983–), 158
  part-owner of Airbus Industrie, 167
  privatized, 161
  proposed EADC, 160
  taken over by Daimler-Chrysler, 161, 170
CASC, *see* Civil Aviation Supply Company
cascade effect, 38, 39, 923
  see also suppliers
cash-back, 818
Caspian Sea, 415, 416
Catalytic Partial Oxidation, 427
'catch-up' process, 14–24, 785, 848, 923
  dangers of 'catch-up' strategy, 240
  developing countries, 857
  first-tier Asian NICs, 785
  Four Little Tigers, 19–24, 858, 876
  influence of China, 24
  IT sector, 768
  Japan, 16–19, 24, 785, 850, 852, 854, 855,
    858, 876
  new entrants, 49, 241
  possibilities, 64, 618–22, 693, 929
  PRC, 852, 855, 857, 858, 876, 878, 929, 930
  South Korea, 852, 854, 855
  steel industry, 600, 618–22, 693
  West, 14–16, 24
catering, 8
Caterpillar, 529, 535, 559, 951(n22)
  acquisitions, 529
  joint venture in PRC, 105
  'largest producer of diesel engines', 529
  'major US exporter', 13
  sales, profits, employees, R&D (1998), 584,
    886
  Yuchai comparison, 583, 584
Cathay Investment Fund Ltd, 573, 575
Cathay Pacific, 149
Cathay Clement (HK), 306
CATIC, *see* China Aviation Technology
  Company
CATIC Shenzhen
  floated in Hong Kong, 226
  subsidiary of CATIC, 224, 225, 226
CBBP, *see* China Big Business Programme
CBS, 787
CCB, *see* China Construction Bank
CCF, *see* China-China-Foreign; Commercial
  Crédit de France
CCP, *see* Chinese Communist Party
CCP: Central Military Commission, 188
CCP: Organizations Department, 448
CDI amplifiers (automobile component), 547
CE, *see* Combustion Engineering (USA)
CEC, *see* Chengdu Aero-engine Company
Celanese, 263
cellular telephones: smuggling, 275
cement, 128, 590, 716, 913

Centec, 952(n11)
Central America, 434, 595
Central Asia, 441, 706, 851
Central China Electric Power Group, 110, 345
Central Committee for Economics and Finance
    (PRC), 137
Central and Eastern Europe: FDI inflow
    (1984–98), 30
Central Electricity Generating Board (UK),
    943(n7)
central government (PRC), 131, 275, 277, 346,
    842, 859–60
  aircraft purchase policy, 218
  ban on commercial activity by local PLA
    units (1993), 276
  blocks prospective joint ventures, 311
  closure of small-scale mining operations
    (1998–9), 759
  control of oil groups by headquarters, 488
  creation of Donglian, 466–7
  creation of national champions (oil sector),
    472
  creation of 'super-large' companies, 650, 654
  curbs on Shougang, 651, 686
  Dongfeng, 563, 564
  Erqi, 563, 885–6
  financial services, 830, 831, 958(n10)
  flotation of oil groups (1999), 471, 476
  funding for power sector investment, 349,
    944–5(n18)
  industrial policy 'lacking clear direction', 853
  injection of capital (Wugang), 629
  Laibin B power plant, 352–3
  lobbied by Wang Jianming (Yuchai), 568
  lorry-makers (PRC), 542
  oil sector, 444–5, 455, 488, 497–8, 883
  pharmaceutical sector, 286
  power station construction, 355
  powerful CEOs, 841, 842
  Qilu steel works vetoed, 842, 888
  rail network, 742
  Shenhua, 750, 757, 758, 759
  Shougang, 656, 657, 685
  vetoed steel plant at Qilu (1995), 671, 686
  Yiqi, 561, 885
  Yuchai, 885, 887
  see also national champions; state-owned
    enterprises; state intervention
Central Military Commission (CMC), PRC,
    272, 273, 276
central planning (PRC), 72, 939(n15)
Central Trade Development Company (CTDC),
    Taiwan, 387
Centre for the Study of Financial Innovation
    (CSFI), 834
CEOs, see chief executive officers
CEPA, see Consolidated Electric Power Asia
ceramics, 77, 131, 590
cereals: PRC world ranking (1949–98), 913
Cerent (IT company), 773

CESEC, see China Electronic Systems and
    Engineering Company
CEUPEC, 469
CFM: joint venture between SNECMA and GE,
    173
chaebol (South Korea), 22, 52–4, 604, 692
Chagra Steel (Indonesia), 676
Chai Tai Company (Thailand), 306
Chambers, John (CEO, Cisco Systems), 762,
    771
Chan, Paul (Vice-President, ABB China),
    945(n20)
Chandler, Alfred, 11–12, 84–5, 393, 551
Chandler, A. and T. Hikino (1997), 14
Changchun (Jilin province)
  FAW, 101
  Yiqi-VW joint venture, 539
Changhe (Jingdezhen) Aviation Industry
    Company, 199, 200, 940(n12)
Changhong Group, 97, 109, 938(n5)
Changjiang Computer Group, 107
Changjiang Shipping Group, 124
Changjiang United Economic Development
    Group, 86, 121
Changsha (Hunan Province), 353
Changsha Electrical Equipment Manufacturing
    Plant, 108
Changsha Medical Materials Company, 300
Changshu Special-Purpose Vehicle Works (HK),
    564
Chaoyang Diesel Engine Company, see
    Dongfeng
Charade mini-car (Tianjin-Daihatsu), 539, 540,
    546, 950(n7)
Charterhouse Securities, 822
Chase Manhattan Bank (USA), 815, 817, 818,
    822, 824, 830
  acquisitions, 822
  conversion to FHC, 819
  global top five bank, [822], 958(n8)
  shareholder in HPEC Limited, 946(n31)
  takeover of J.P. Morgan, 813, 822
  top five firm (syndicated credit arrangements,
    2000), 824
cheese, 869
Chemical Bank, 817
chemical businesses
  conglomerates, 252
  de-merged by pharmaceutical companies
    (1990s), 252
  diversification into pharmaceuticals, 244
chemical fertilizers, 133, 433, 450, 452, 458,
    466
chemical fibres, 113–14, 118, 433, 466, 913
Chemical Overseas Co-operation Centre (PRC),
    468
chemicals, 3, 11, 12 14, 107, 119, 262, 263,
    265, 452
  barriers to entry (1998), 63, 64
  import and export (PRC), 129

chemicals – *continued*
  Japanese leadership, 56
  national team (PRC), 77, 78, 117–18,
    939(n21)
  PRC, 77, 431[–]433, 926, 938(n6), 939(n21)
  research and development (1995, 1998), 49
  restructuring, 80
  second batch of trial groups (1997), 86
  South Korea, 22
  speciality, 64
  Taiwan, 20
  UK, 264
chemotherapy, 246
Cheng Kejie: death sentence, 874
chengbao wei ben ('the contract is the base'),
  668
Chengdu (Sichuan), 391
  aircraft manufacturing, 186
  China Unicom joint venture activity, 810
  pharmaceuticals, 283
  Zhufeng Hotel, 312–13
Chengdu Aero-engine Company/Corporation
  (CEC), 200, 216–17
  assigned to 'AVIC 2', 230
  investments, 222–3
  subsidiary companies, 222–3
  survival strategies, 222
Chengdu Aircraft Company (CAC), 208, 877,
  950(n9)
  assigned to 'AVIC 1' (no date, c.1999), 230
  competition with XAC, 215, [218–]219
  statistics, 200
  sub-contracting work, 209, 210, 214, 216,
    218
Chengdu Engine Company
  main product, output, profits, taxes (1995),
    562
Chengdu Engine Plant, 562
Chengdu Kaiwei Internal Combustion, 560
Chengfei: missed merger opportunity, 861
chengshi jianshe shui (city construction tax,
  PRC), 648
Cherepovets (Russian Federation): crude steel
  output (1996–7), 602
Chernobyl (1986), 402, 945(n23)
Cherokee (high quality vehicle), 567
Cheung Kong Holdings (HK), 351
Cheung Kong Infrastructure (HK), 351
Chevron, 411, 417, 418, 420, 481, 710
Chi Haotian, 941(n18)
Chiang Kaishek, 20
chicken, 871
child mortality: PRC (1980–97), 914, 915
children, 381
chief executive officers (CEOs), 841
  'Europe', 859
  power (PRC), 847–8, 859
China (pre-1949)
  Boxer Rebellion, 904
  centre of world economy, 899

civil war, 905–6
'concessions', 903
'early masterly development of steel-making'
  (Needham), 587, 628
humiliation, 902–7
industrial policy challenge, 65
intellectuals and policy-makers, 903
Japanese invasion, 905
long superiority, 897–902
long-term view, 897–33, 958
in 1949, 906–7
origins of oil industry, 433
past, 898–916
Revolution (1911) and warlordism, 904
Revolution (1927), 904–5
share of world manufacturing output
  (1750–1998), 900
single market, 899
Sino-Japanese warfare, 903–4, 905
'spheres of influence', 903
technological advance (mediaeval era), 899
textile industry, 15
trade, 899
wars with western powers (C19), 902–3
see also People's Republic of China
China (PRC investment bank), 829
China-China-Foreign (CCF) arrangement, 792,
  799, 809–10
China.com (HKSAR), 781
China Administrative Centre for New Drug
  Research and Development, 286
China Aerospace Automotive Industry Group,
  547
China Aircraft Industry Company, 562
China Auto Industrial Corporation (CAIC),
  103
China Aviation Technology Company for
  Import and Export of Aviation Products
  (CATIC 1979–), 186, 214, 215–16, 272,
  940(n16)
  AVIC subsidiary, 224 ('technically', 226)
  business structure, 224
  flotation of subsidiaries, 226
  place within AVIC structure, 225–6
China Big Business Programme (CBBP),
  xxv–xxvi, 851, 876, 926
China Can Say No? (Song Qiang *et al.*, 1996),
  925
China Coal Consultancy (CCC), 718, 723, 731
China Construction Bank (CCB), 96, 97, 128,
  827
China Development Forum, 935, 958(n3)
China Dongfeng Automotive Industry Export
  and Import Corporation, 565
China Eastern Airlines, 80, 122, 123, 207,
  931
China Eastern Power Group: national team
  player, 110
China Economic Daily, 435
China Economic Reform Yearbook, 100

China Education and Research Network (ISP), 808
China Electronic Systems and Engineering Company (CESEC), 272, 274
China Electronics Industry Corporation (Chinatron), 272, 273
China Everbright ('Guangda'), 574, 575, 809
  'essentially a Mainland institution', 574
  'red chip' company (HK), 574
  SOE, 801
China Everbright Holdings Company Ltd
  affiliate of China Everbright ('Guangda'), 574
  CYI Limited ownership structure, 575
  owns 47% of Diesel Machinery Limited, 574
China Galaxy Securities Company, 958(n10)
China General Purpose Airline Company, 123
China General Technology (Group) Holding Ltd, 129
China Great Wall Industry Corporation (GWIC), 272
China Hualu Group: national team player, 109
China Huaneng Group, 343, 350, 740, 809
  absorbs Huaneng Power Corporation (1988), 740
  assets, 740
  first batch, 109, 740
  SOE, 801
  subsidiary of State Power Corporation of China, 343–5
  twelve main subsidiaries, 350
  assets (1993), 350
  national team player (first batch), 350
China Huitong, 272, 274
China Instruments Import and Export Corporation, 129
China International Capital Corporation (CICC), 835
China International Trust and Investment Corporation (CITIC), xxvi, 274, 801, 809, 831–2, 951(n22)
China Jilin Chemical Industry, 117
China Jitong, 798, 800, 801, 808
China Light and Power (CLP), 351
  dominant electricity producer (HK), 351
China Lucky Film Group, 132–3
  national team player (first batch), 131–2
China Machinery Corporation, 129
China Merchant Bank (Shenzhen), 809, 832
China Metallurgical Import and Export Corporation, 956(n57)
China Minmetals, see China National Minerals and Metals Import and Export Corporation
China Miracle (Justin Yifu Lin et al. 1996), 4
China Mobile, 797
  high-speed growth, 804
  IP licensee, 808
  ISP, 808
  mobile phone licensee, 807

owned by MII, 802
partial flotation on international market (under discussion), 801
previously part of China Telecom, 798, 801
segments (telecommunications) and market share, 798
SOE, 799
see also CTHK
China National Aerospace Industries General Company, 231
China National Armaments General Company, 231
China National Cereals, Oils and Foodstuff Import and Export Corporation (COFCO), 130, 939(n13)
  included in national team, 939(n13)
  represented in Fortune 500, 130
China National Chemicals Import and Export Corporation (Sinochem), 444, 809, 939(n13)
  activities, 129
  included in national team, 939(n13)
  national team player (first batch), 129
China National Coal Import and Export Company (CNCIEC), 752
  'China National Coal Export Company', 718
China National Corporation for Overseas Economic Cooperation, 129
China National Crafts Import and Export Corporation, 130
China National Electricity Equipment Company, 377
China National Foreign Trade Transportation Group (Sinotrans), 122
China National Heavy Duty Truck Corporation, 541
  joint venture with Hino, 547
  joint venture with Volvo, 566
  produces Steyer trucks and engines, 566
  sales, profits, employees, output (1998), 556
  second-largest producer of heavy-duty lorries (PRC), 566
China National Import and Export Commission (CMEC), 387
China National Minerals and Metals Import and Export Corporation (China Minmetals), 129–30
China National New Building Materials Corporation (1984–), 127
China National New Building Materials Group (CNNBMG), 127–8
China National Non-Ferrous Metals Corporation, xxv, 655
China National Non-Metallic Minerals Enterprise Group (CNMEG 1983–), 79, 120, 938(n4)
China National Nuclear Corporation, 945(n24)
China National Nuclear Industries General Company, 231

China National Offshore Oil Corporation
    (CNOOC 1982–), 436, 456, 489–90, 500
  aborted flotation in HKSAR and New York
    (1999), 490
  containment of costs, 490
  contracts with multinationals, 489
  ENI comparison, 490
  foreign participation, 440
  IPO withdrawn (10.1999), 884
  joint venture with Shell at Huizhou, 454
  LNG project (Shenzhen), 717
  new role (mid-1990s), 464
  production, 489
  reserves (oil and gas), 490
  SOE, 489
  'uncertain prospects', 490
  vertical integration, 490
  workforce, 490
  WTO rules (implementation by PRC), 867
China National Petrochemical Corporation
    (Sinopec 1983–98), 436, 445
  assets value (1995), 446
  auditing, 465
  business operations, 465
  clash of interests with CNPC, 462
  'complementary to CNPC', 446
  corporate structure, 460–1, 465
  decision-making, 465
  distribution function, 457
  'downstream', 445–52
  employees, 480
  ethylene output (1995), 447
  experimenting as a national holding
    company, 79, 939(n13)
  financial indicators, 480
  financial autonomy, 448–9
  floatation of subsidiaries (1990s), 453
  functions, 464, 465
  government organ, 446–8
  holding company experiment, 464–6
  included in *Fortune* Global 500 (1999), [70],
    939(n13)
  independent rights to import crude oil
    (1997–), 457
  industrial association, 448
  investment, 465
  joint ventures, 453–4
  management of capital and property, 465
  'massively dominant', 452
  mergers and acquisitions, 454
  'Ministry-level enterprise', 445–6
  'not included in national team', 938(n4)
  oil products, 458
  oil refining, 446–7, 449–50, 457, 459, 883
  personnel arrangements, 465
  petrochemicals, 450–2
  petrol stations, 460
  production (1989–98), 450
  profits, 446, 449, 465, 480
  range of activity, 446

  refineries transferred to New CNPC, 478
  research and development, 465
  resource and product allocation, 449
  restructuring (1998), 453, 467, 468
  roles ('seriously conflicting'), 446–9
  selection of managers, 448, 465
  state holding company, 436, 448, 452
  subordinate enterprises, 446, 452–7
  subordinate enterprises (numbering 36),
    446
  turnover, 480
  vertical integration, 465–6
  see also New China National Petrochemical
    Group (New Sinopec, 1998–)
China National Petroleum Corporation (CNPC
    1988–98), 80, 436–45
  annual report, 439
  casts off 'ministerial' functions (1998), 437
  clash of interests with Sinopec, 462
  corporate structure, 460–1
  Daqing, 441–5
  employees, 480
  financial control, 439–41
  financial indicators, 480
  formerly the Ministry of Petroleum Industry
    (pre-1988), 436
  internal tensions, 437
  'limited authority over regional companies',
    440
  main production units, 437–9
  monopoly of onshore oil production, 436–7
  oil products, 458
  oil refining, 450
  output (1996), 409
  output, sales and pre-tax profit (1996), 442
  overseas investments, 441
  period of experimentation (1988–98), 437
  petrol, kerosene, diesel oil, lubricants, 450
  petrol stations, 460
  produces 89% of PRC's oil (1997), 436
  profits, 439, 442, 480
  refineries transferred to New CNPC, 477
  restructuring (1998), 467, 468
  right to import oil (1998–), 457
  state holding company, 436
  turnover, 480
  see also New China National Petroleum
    Corporation (New CNPC 1998–)
China National Shipbuilding General Company,
    231
China National Star Petroleum Resources
    (1996–), 468
China National Technology Import and Export
    Corporation, 809
China National Technology Import and Export
    Group (CNTIC), 81, 129
China National Textiles Import and Export
    Corporation (Chinatex), 130
China Netcom Corporation (10.1999–), 798,
    800, 801, 808

China North Industries Corporation
(NORINCO), 272–4, 275
China North Western Electric Group, 110
China Northeastern Pharmaceutical Group,
110
China Northern (airline), 123, 207
China Ocean Shipping Corporation (COSCO),
130
  debt-asset ratio, 121
  national team player (first batch), 121–2
  China Oil (New CNPC's newspaper), 478
China Poly Group (1984–), 272–4, 277,
941(n7–8)
  subsidiaries, 274
China Poly Investments Holdings, 274
China Ports Construction Group, 133
China Resources, 801, 809
China Science and Technology Network (ISP),
808
China Shareholding Enterprises Evaluation
Centre, 272
China Shenma Group, 113–14
China Shougang International Trading and
Engineering Corporation (CSITEC), 647,
690
China South (PRC investment bank), 829
China Southern Aero-equipment
Company/Corporation, 200, 230
China Southern Airlines (CSA), 80, 122–3,
123–4, 931
China State Construction Engineering
Corporation (CSCEC), 126
China State Construction Engineering Group,
75
China State Development and Investment
Corporation (SDIC), 133
China State Farms Agribusiness Group, 135
China Steel (Taiwan), 21, 600, 602, 641, 854
China Telecom (PRC)
  equipment supplied by Cisco, 795
  550,000 employees, 807
  fixed-line telecommunications, 797–8, 807
  international comparison (12.1999), 800
  internet protocol (IP) licensee, 808
  market capitalization, revenue, profits
    (12.1999), 800
  mentioned, 274
  partial flotation on international market
    (under discussion), 801, 807
  PRC's 'main telecoms operator', 804
  sales revenue (1999), 798
  segments (telecommunications) and market
    share, 798
  separation of China Mobile, 801
  wholly state-owned, 797, 800–1, 804
  see also CTHK; Shanghai Telecom
China Telecom (Hong Kong) (CTHK 1997–)
  DoCoMo comparison, 799, 804
  'encirclement', 803
  established by China Mobile (1997), 798–9

  floated 25% on international markets (1997),
    799
  high-speed growth, 804
  international comparison (12.1999), 800
  international share issue (1999), 799
  IPO, 799, 801
  joint ventures (possibility), 807
  market capitalization, 799, 800, 931
  market capitalization, revenue, profits
    (12.1999), 800
  mergers, 858–9, 931
  nature of 'firm', 802
  operational mechanism, 802
  six subsidiaries, 802
  SOE, 799
  still 75% owned by China Mobile, 802
  usage fee per subscriber, 804
  wireless telecommunications assets (various
    provinces), 799
China Textile Machinery Group Company
    (CTMC), 79, 104
  national team player (PRC), 104
China Unicom (PRC 1993–)
  bureaucratic struggle, 801
  CCF partners, 809, 810
  cellular phones, 804
  debt, 801
  equipment from Lucent and Cisco, 795
  fibre optic transmission network (PRC), 799
  flotation (25%) on international markets,
    799–800
  international comparison (12.1999), 800
  internet, 799, 808
  IPO (6.2000), 801, 931
  largest shareholder (MII PRC), 802
  market capitalization, revenue, profits
    (12.1999), 800
  mobile phone licensee, 807
  'mostly non-telecom stakeholders', 801, 809
  ownership structure, 809
  pager market, 804
  segments (telecommunications) and market
    share, 798
  SOE, 799
  sources of finance, 799
  started operations in 1994, 801
  usage fee per subscriber, 804
  wireless telecommunications, 799–800
  see also China Unicom Group
China Unicom Group: owner of China Unicom,
    801
China Xinjiang Construction Group, 121
China Xinxing Corporation (1989–), 272, 273,
    274, 277
China Yangtze Three Gorges Project
    Corporation (CYTGPC), 350, 944(n11)
  subsidiaries, 350
  under auspices of MOEP (latterly SPEC),
    350
China Yaohua Glass Group, 128

China Yuchai International Limited (CYI
1994–)
appoints most directors of Yuchai, 574
'Bermuda-based holding company', 573
failed to raise as much capital as hoped,
951(n21)
floated on Wall Street, 571n, 573, 585,
951(n21)
IPO (NY 1994), 581
main shareholder, 573
'majority owner of Yuchai', 571n
ownership structure, 574
prospectus, 575, 581
public shareholders, 574
see also Yuchai Diesel Engine Company
China Zhenhua Electronics Group, 106
ChinaNet (ISP), 808
Chinatex, see China National Textiles Import
and Export Corporation
Chinese Academy of Sciences: Computer
Institute, 107
Chinese characters, 732–3
Chinese Communist Party (CCP 1921–), 20,
188, 904, 917
discipline enforced, 911
14th Conference (11.1993), 138
15th Conference (1997), 70–1, 96
galvanizing tradition, 667
Geng Lei, 947[n40]
'imbued with corruption', 854
leadership, 71
Li Genshen, 372
military struggle with KMT (1927–34), 905
need global giants (oil sector), 476
'plays important role in Nanfang', 304, 323
resistance to Japan (WW2), 905
'rich legacy of motivational skills', 680
role in Sanjiu Enterprise Group, 316–17
Shougang, 643, 670
US and EU desire to overturn, 792–3
US hopes for overthrow of, 917
victory in civil war (1945–9), 905–6
Chinese Insurance Regulatory Commission
(CIRC), 836
Chinese language: internet sites, 780
Chinese Large and Medium-Sized Enterprises
Yearbook (1997), 100
Chinese National Foreign Trade Corporation,
377
Chinese People's Political Consultative
Conference (Beijing, 6.2000), 926–7,
958(n3)
Chinese State Pharmaceutical Corporation, 286
Chinese State Planning Commission
'drastically reorganized' (1998), 345
electricity generation needs, 342
power generation industry, 343
Chirac, Jacques (b 1932), 212
Chiron (USA), 261
chlorine, 252: catch-up possibilities, 64

cholesterol, 247, 250, 259, 260, 268
Chongqing, 391, 547, 810
Chongqing Iron and Steel Group
assets, 77[–]79
listed on HK stock market, 640
national team player (second batch), 116
profitability, 643
top twenty steel producer (PRC 1997), 635
Chromatis (IT company, Israel), 773
Chrysler, 101
interests in Mercosur, 508
joint venture with Beijing Automotive
Industry Corporation (1984–), 539
model of lean production, 514
saved by a US government loan guarantee
(1982), 510
twice nearly bankrupt, 514, 532
chuangjian jieduan ('developmental' stage), 80,
137
Chung Ju-Yung:
diversification of Hyundai Group (1938–87),
53
Ciba-Geigy (Switzerland)
demerges Ciba Speciality Chemicals (1996),
261
'life sciences', 261
merges with Sandoz to form 'Novartis'
(1996), 261
origins (1970), 261
cigarettes (smuggling), 275
cinemas, 44, 869
circuit design: TRIPs Agreement (1994), 785
Cisco Systems (USA), 771, 773–4, 786
acquisitions, 771, 773
'biggest player in data networking market',
773
internet, 773–4, 775
competition with Lucent, 773
equipment used by China Unicom, 795
hardware revenues, 772
Indian IT sector (comparison), 788
'largest corporation in world', 774
little to fear from PRC competition (post-
WTO accession), 863
market capitalization (2000), 764, 772
'market leader in networking equipment', 795
sales revenue (2000), 764
telecommunications hardware, 771
Citibank, 817, 818
Citibank Salomon Smith Barney (USA), 824
Citicorp (USA), 306, 817
Citigroup, 815, 818, 819, 822, 824, 826, 827,
830, 831, 835, 837, 958(n8)
citrus fruits, 869
civil aviation: PRC national team (1991, 1997),
84
Civil Aviation Administration of China
(CAAC), 203, 204, 205, 210, 212, 214,
215, 218, 237, 238, 239
'lets down' indigenous aviation industry, 213

Civil Aviation Supply Company (CASC, PRC), 203
civil transportation: PRC national team, 77
CITIC, *see* China International Trust and Investment Corporation
Clariant, 261, 262
Clarify (IT company), 774
Clarke Chapman (UK boiler-maker), 943(n7)
Clean Air Act (USA), 593
Clean Coal Corporation (PRC 1988), 740, 741
Clinton, William Jefferson (b 1946), 193, 607
Clissold, Tim, 951(n16)
clocks and watches, 198
clothing, 6, 133, 274, 311
CLP, *see* China Light and Power
clutches, 546, 526, 950(n9)
CMC, *see* Central Military Commission
CMEC, *see* China National Import and Export Commission
CNMEG, *see* China National Non-Metallic Minerals Enterprise Group
CNNBMG, *see* China National New Building Materials Group
CNOOC, *see* China National Offshore Oil Corporation
CNPC, *see* China National Petroleum Corporation
CNPC: Research Institute of Petroleum Exploration and Development, 439
CNTIC, *see* China National Technology Import and Export Group
coal (global), 695–760, 957–8
    bulk cargo, 705
    catch-up possibilities, 64
    catch-up (developing countries), 712–13
    consolidation, 707–12
    decline (in 'Europe'), 891
    demand, 695–706, 745
    diversified portfolio of global industry leaders, 712–13
    electricity generation (1990–2010), 696, 697
    employment, 706–7
    energy, 696–9
    energy demand, 695–6
    forecasts, 699, 705, 706
    global perspective, 695–713
    global warming, 702–5
    globalization, 707, 710
    international trade, 705–6, 713
    investment, 708, 709, 713
    'key issue in international relations', 705
    labour costs (1996), 710, 711
    labour productivity (1996), 711
    labour relations 'confrontational', 711–12
    low-sulphur (USA), 710
    management, 713
    mentioned, 119, 133, 596, 598, 618, 687
    mine development (initial costs), 708
    open-cast mining, 706
    output (1980–98), 341

output (1980–95), 699
output per worker, 706
output and energy use (PRC, Japan, USA 1992–5), 700
pollution, 699–702
power station input, 349, 944(n13)
PRC, 697, 698–9, 704, 705, 707, 713–60, 957–8
price, 697, 728–30, 732, 749, 957(n1, n5)
primary energy consumption (1986–96), 696
primary energy consumption (1996), 697
privatization, 32
reserves, 696, 706
share of world primary energy consumption (1987–97), 402
Shenhua Project, 731, 732–3, 734–60, 958(n7)
subsidies, 731–4
supply, 706–13
transportation costs, 355
USA, 405–6
varieties, 378
world consumption (1986–96), 698
world output, 404
world reserves v world population (1998), 406
coal (PRC): 355–6, 378, 619, 713–60, 957–8
    ability to compete on global level playing field, 890–2
    anthracite, 718
    assets, 727
    best-practice technology, 716
    bituminous, 718
    carbon dioxide emissions, 703, 746
    chemistry, 748–9
    coking, 619, 718, 753
    conclusions, 756–60
    consumption, 698, 716
    consumption per unit of power supply (PRC 1979–95), 355
    cost structure of different producers (1995), 722
    costs, 717, 720, 722–3
    demand, 713–18, 745
    depth, 718
    domestic demand, 713–17
    electricity generation (fuel type, 1996), 698
    employment, 707, 727, 749, 920
    employees (1991), 727
    employment (1980–95), 707
    employment (early 1990s), 749
    energy reserves, 716
    exports, 706, 717–18
    'fees', 723, 957(n4)
    forecasts, 714, 717, 734, 749
    foreign investment, 729, 750, 755
    importance, 714
    imports, 748
    industrial and domestic use, 748

coal (PRC) – *continued*
  institutional distribution of output (1979–97),
    721
  international demand, 717–18
  investment, 734
  keypoint state mines, 721, 723, 724, 725,
    729–31
  labour cost per ton of coal, 620
  labour unrest feared, 745
  liberalization of markets, 726, 728–9
  lignite, 718
  local taxation (1995), 722
  map, 732–3
  mine closures (issues surrounding), 726, 731,
    745
  mines, 714, 720–6, 729–31, 744, 745
  national team, 77, 80–1, 84
  open-cast, 718, 722, 736–7, 753
  output (1980–95), 698–9
  output (1980–98), 341
  output (1995), 725
  output (1995–2050), 714
  output and consumption (1996), 719
  output, reserves, mine depths (1996), 736
  policing, 725
  pollution, 429–31, 701–3
  prices, 723–4, 728–9, 759, 957(n6)
  prices (dual-track system), 728
  prices, profits and losses, 729–34
  primary energy consumption (1986–96),
    696
  primary energy consumption (1996), 697
  productivity, 620
  profit margins, 725
  profitability, 726
  profits (1991), 727
  quality, 718, 723, 737, 748, 752, 957(n3)
  recovery rate, 725
  redundancies, 726
  by region (1996), 719
  reserves, 706, 716, 718–20, 735, 741
  reserves *per capita*, 715
  safety (1995–6), 725
  share of PRC's energy requirements
    (1980–96), 354–5
  Shenhua Project, 731, 732–3, 734–60,
    958(n7)
  size distribution of output (1997), 721
  size structure (1991), 727
  small local mines, 720–7, 740–1, 758–9
  state-owned mines, 720–8, 741, 744, 745,
    753–5, 759
  strategic choices, 749, 759–60
  subsidies, 731
  sulphur content, 718, 737
  supply, 718–29
  taxation, 722, 723
  technology, 716
  thermal coal prices (7.1997), 729
  transport costs, 717, 720, 726

TVE mines, [720–]721, 722, 723, 724, 726,
    727, 745, 746–7, 753, 755, 759
  underground, 718, 737
  unlicensed mining, 724–5
  use in steel industry, 652, 953(n31)
  wages (1995), 722
  world ranking (1949–98), 913
  world's largest producer (1990), 429
  see also Shenhua Project
Coal Bureau (PRC), 731
coal companies: importance of size, 713
Coase, R.H., 7
'Coasian' terms, 563
Coca-Cola, 35, 65, 863
Cockerill-Sambrell (Belgium), 611, 861, 862
Cockerill Mechanical Industries (Belgium), 378
Coface (French government's credit agency),
    353
COFCO, *see* China National Cereals, Oils and
    Foodstuff Import and Export Corporation,
    130
COFCO Capital Corporation, 130
coke ovens, 593
coking coal, 598, 600, 652–3, 705
  use in steel industry (PRC), 652–3, 953(n31)
Cold War, 158, 761
Colgate, 259
Colgate Palmolive: competitive advantage, 35
Colombia, 706, 710, 711, 751
combinatorial chemistry, 246, 258
Combustion Engineering (USA), 351, 372, 377,
    397
command and control systems, 157, 192
command economy / planned economy
    (communist), 2, 3, 241, 283, 369, 385, 464
  coal, 729–30, 751
  'inefficient', 340, 943(n8)
  Maoist, 340
  'no concept of marketing', 557
  PRC, 67, 87, 91–2, 502, 554, 561, 563, 570,
    581, 622, 653, 657, 671, 680–1, 908
  transition (PRC) from, 72
  vehicle-makers (PRC), 544–5
  see also market economy
commanding heights (PRC), 892–3, 920
commerce, 121
Commercial Bank Law (PRC 1995), 834
Commercial Crédit de France (CCF), 822
commercial vehicles (PRC), 537
  WTO enforcement proceedings, 870
Commission for the Reform of the Economic
    System (CRES, PRC), xxiv, 74, 76, 136–8,
    364, 373, 572, 793, 947(n42)
Commission on Science, Technology and
    Industry for National Defence (COSTIND,
    PRC 1982–), 273, 276
commodities, 9
Commonwealth of Independent States (CIS)
  share of world electricity generation
    (1995–2015), 335

communications equipment, 107, 148
communism (collapse), 32, 910
communist countries, 32, 408, 507, 707
Communist Party of China (CCP), *see* Chinese
    Communist Party
Company Law (PRC 1994), 90, 437
Compaq, 768, 772, 794
comparative advantage, 1, 12
    Brazil, 20
    small firms, 4–6
    USA (information), 761
competition, 2–8
    defence industries (PRC), 231
    'driving force of concentration', 9
    new entrants, 6–7
    oligopolistic, 61
    power equipment, 384–92
    PRC, 73
    'Schumpeterian', 18
    threat to large firms, 6–7
competition authorities, 45
competitive advantage, 13, 33–7, 44
    ability to obtain loans, 354, 945(n19)
    aerospace, 142, 162, 173–4
    brands, 34
    core business, 33–4
    defence sector, 157
    diesel engines, 529, 531
    financial resources, 36–7
    financial services, 818, 830, 832–3
    GE (USA), 329
    HPEC, 386
    innovation and execution (IT sector), 775
    Indian software companies, 787–8
    IT expenditure, 36
    IT sector, 769
    mining, 708, 712–13
    oil sector, 426
    pharmaceutical industry (1998), 247
    pharmaceuticals, 267, 270
    research and development, 34–6
    Sanjiu, 320
    Shenhua, 739, 748, 749, 750–1, 752, 756–8,
        759
    Three Gorges Project, 353–4
    through investment in R&D, 64
    tyre industry, 526–7
    Yuchai, 557–8, 566
    see also competitive edge companies
competitive edge companies, 52
    aerospace ('big is beautiful'), 148
    IT sector, 766–7, 770
    Japanese steel industry, 621
    oil sector, 421
    pharmaceutical sector, 269
    by sector (2000), 767
    steel sector, 693
    US dominance (2000), 767, 770, 771–2,
        775
    see also brands; global business revolution

Competitive Edge studies (MSDW 1997–2000),
    49–51, 62–3
competitive markets, 28
competitiveness, 46, 51, 57, 72
complex capital goods, 43
complex equipment/machinery
    barriers to entry (1998), 63–4
    global oligopoly, 41
components, 45, 57, 145, 346, 199, 519–29,
        535–6, 856, 886, 950
    accelerated globalization of production, 520
    aerospace, 38, 142, 143, 184, 186, 229
    air conditioners, 524, 535
    airbags and seatbelts, 525
    aligned suppliers, 519
    auto, 38, 43
    auto industry (South Korea), 505
    automobile parts, 133
    automobile glass, 525
    car braking systems, 525, 535
    Caterpillar, 529
    concentration pressures, 38
    constant velocity joints, 524, 535
    Cummins, 530–1
    Detroit Diesel (DDC), 531
    economies of scale (automobile industry),
        504, 535
    exhaust systems and shock absorbers, 524,
        535
    global oligopoly, 41
    global value, 856
    growth of producers with cross-functional
        specializations, 525
    incorporating IT into components systems,
        522
    liberalization of global vehicles markets, 520
    'mega-suppliers', 519
    missed merger opportunities for PRC, 861
    modularization, 521
    non-aviation output of AVIC (auto), 198
    outsourcing, 520
    procurement capabilities, 522
    rapid evolution of 'global' vehicles, 520–1
    relentless pressure on prices, 523
    seats, 523, 535
    spinning off components makers from vehicle
        assembly, 520
    spiralling R&D costs, 521
    tyres, 526–9
    vehicle engines, 529–32
    wheels, 524
components (PRC)
    ability to compete on global level playing
        field, 885–7
    consolidation, 543–5
    domestic content requirement (PRC), 537,
        543
    economies of scale, 545
    Erqi, 544
    foreign investment, 543

components (PRC) – *continued*
  in-house manufacturing, 582
  institutional structure (PRC), 543–7
  investment companies, 544–5
  investments by multinationals, 545–7
  joint ventures, 544, 545
  lessons from Brazil, 547
  mentioned, 538, 921
  national team, 76
  sales (1995), 543
  size of manufacturers (1995), 543
  specialist-makers, 545
compressor discs, 145
computer-aided design (CAD), 214
computer industry
  mergers and acquisitions (1988–98), 769
  'year 2000 problem', 788
computer programming: TRIPs Agreement
    (1994), 785
computerization (steel industry), 603, 951(n4)
computers, 15
  allow greater efficiency (steel industry), 598
  invention of, 142
  USA, 761
  see also information technology
conclusions
  aerospace, 231–40
  autos and auto components, 532–6, 581–5
  coal, 756–60
  financial services, 837
  global business revolution, 61–5
  global business revolution (PRC response),
      850–2, 863–4, 892–6
  Harbin Power Equipment Company, 372–3
  large firms and economic development, 24–5
  oil and petrochemicals, 491–500
  pharmaceuticals, 320–6
  power equipment, 392–9
  Shougang Group, 678–83
  third technological revolution, 810–11
  Yuchai, 581–5
concrete: alternative to steel, 595
condenser (component), 581
Condit, Philip (head of Boeing), 212
conglomerates
  developing countries, 51–2
  'failing' (Asia), 72
  out of fashion (advanced economies), 855
  pharmaceutical sector, [251–]252
Congressional Research Service (USA), 872
'connections' (PRC), 873
Conoco (oil division of Du Pont), 265, 411
Consol, 710
Consolidated Electric Power Asia (CEPA), 351,
    353
constant velocity joints, 525, 536
Construction Bank (PRC), 440
construction industry
  alternatives to steel, 591, 595
  boom (PRC), 126

employment (PRC, 1998), 919
first batch of trial groups (PRC, 1991), 85
Japan, 603
mentioned, 116, 118, 119, 311, 847,
    952(n12)
national team (PRC), 77, 78, 84, 126–7
Samsung, 53
Sanjiu, 315, 318
second batch of trial groups (PRC, 1997), 86
South Korea, 54, 604
Three Gorges Dam, 315
construction machinery, 64
construction materials, 75, 84, 127–8, 198, 274
  national team players, 127–8
  non-aviation output of AVIC, 198
  PRC, 75
  sectoral share of PRC national team (1991,
      1997), 84
consultancy, 127
consumer appliances, 272
consumer confidence, 503
consumer electronics
  non-SOE national champions (PRC), 862
  South Korea, 53, 54
  world-beating corporations (Japan and South
      Korea), 176
consumer goods, 64, 86
  see also fast-moving consumer goods
consumers, 34
consumption, 64
  PRC (Deng era), 912
  Third Technological Revolution, 763
container fleet, 121
containers, 591–2
Continental (airline), 149
Continental (tyre-maker), 529, 860
Continental Express (US airline), 181
Continental Mariner (shipping company), 274,
    941(n8)
continuous casting (steel industry, 1997), 596,
    597, 603, 627, 628, 645, 674, 690, 951(n4)
contract system (PRC), 678, 852, 956(n62)
  see also Shougang Group
Cooper (drug distributor), 263
Cooper, Richard, 869–70
copper, 708, 900
copyright (TRIPs Agreement, 1994), 785
cord fabric, 113
core business, 8, 52, 58, 61, 81, 842, 843, 846,
    849, 855
  AVIC, 877
  competitive advantage, 33–4, 37
  keiretsu, 54
  market share, 39
  mining companies, 709
  pharmaceutical sector, 251–2
  Sanjiu, 296–309, 318–20
  South Korea, 54
core systems integrator, 42–5
core technology, 51

Cork, 614
Corporación de la Siderúrgica Integral (CSI), 613
corporate bond issues (PRC), 90, 114, 122, 130
corporations, 923
  attempt to construct (PRC), 69
  boundaries, 44
  challenges to US dominance, 37
  competitive modern, xxiv
  European champions, 59
  fast-growing, 33–4
  giant, xxiv
  global, xxv, 2
  global business revolution, 919
  Japanese, 54–8
  large, 4, 6–7, 14, 24
  'large modern industrial', 84–5
  life sciences, 767
  'less and less important', 8
  'most explosive change in history', 65
  multinational, 27
  national champions, 58, 65
  PRC, 24–5, 925
  R&D expenditure, 35–6
  state-owned (UK), 15
  'strategic industries', 338
  transatlantic giants, 59–60
  transatlantic, 338
  TRIPs Agreement (1994), 786
  US-owned, 31
  vertically-integrated, 44–5
corrosion, 590
corruption, 873–5
  death sentences, 874–5
  potential political repercussions (PRC), 874
  PRC, 911
  Russian Federation, 910
  WTO membership (possible solution), 875
Corus, 854, 899
COSCO, *see* China Ocean Shipping Corporation
COSCO Pacific, 122
cost-cutting
  auto industry, 512, 514, 515, 521, 523, 532, 535
  Bethlehem Steel, 613, 952(n11–12)
  British Steel Corporation, 600, 610
  coal-mining, 706, 708
  CSI, 613
  global leaders, 856
  impact of IT, 818
  Ispat, 614
  Japan (steel sector), 607
  mentioned, 58, 62
  multi-national corporations, 44
  oil sector, 412, 422
  Renault, 515, 519
  Shougang, 955(n45)
  SOEs (PRC), 892
  Thyssen-Krupp, 612

tyre industry, 526–8
use of IT, 422–3
  see also outsourcing
COSTIND, *see* Commission on Science, Technology and Industry for National Defence
COSTIND, *see* State Defence Industries Commission
cotton, 265, 871, 913
Cox Report, 193, 194
CRA, 707–8
CRA Hammersley Iron
  new iron-ore mine (WA), 956(n57)
credit, 54
credit control (South Korea), 54
Crédit Suisse, 817, 822, 827
Crédit Suisse First Boston (Switzerland), 823, 833
CRES, *see* PRC: Commission for the Reform of the Economic System
criminal activity, 275
Cromme, Gerhard, 612
cross-holdings (*keiretsu*), 54
Crossair (subsidiary of Swissair), 182
CSA, *see* China Southern Airlines
CSCEC, *see* China State Construction Engineering Corporation
CSN (largest steel producer in Brazil), 612
CSRC, 836
CST (Brazil): investment by Usinor, 611
CTHK, *see* China Telecom (Hong Kong)
CTMC, *see* China Textile Machinery Group
Cuba, 178
cultural chauvinism, 194
Cultural Revolution (PRC), 187, 376, 907, 911
Cummins Diesel Engine, 530–1, 535, 848, 886
  acquisitions, 530
  joint venture with Dongfeng, 583
  joint venture in PRC, 547, 548, 566, 567
  presence in PRC, 530, 531
  sales, profits, employees, R&D (1998), 584, 886
  Yuchai comparison, 584
Cummins Perkins Diesel, 559
cun (village), 727
currency (PRC), 717
currency swaps, 928
CYI, *see* China Yuchai International Limited
Cyprus (US coal company), 710
CYTGPC, *see* China Yangtze Three Gorges Project Corporation

da er quan, xiao er quan (large and complete, small and complete) problem (PRC), 72
Da La Te power station, 746–7, 755
Da Zhong (Japanese pharmaceutical company), 283
Dadong (big buses), 578
Daewoo Aviation Manufacturing Industry, 218

Daewoo Motor Corporation (South Korea), 23, 505, 506, 532, 860
  capacity, 506
  car-manufacturer, 54
  CCF partner of China Unicom, 810
  debts (1999), 54, 516
  interests in Eastern Europe, [508–]509
  interests in India, 508
  joint venture with GM, 506
  missed merger opportunity, 861
  negotiations with Daewoo (1999), 54
  outright bankruptcy, 532
  overseas operations, 506
  restructuring (1998), 54
DAF (Netherlands lorry company), 517, 534
Daihatsu, 103, 508, 539–40
  interests in Turkey, 508
  joint venture with Tianjin Auto (1988–), 539–40
Daimaru: reduction of workforce (1999), 56
Daimler-Benz
  foreign assets, sales, employment (1997), 509
Daimler-Benz Aerospace (Dasa)
  Eurofighter project (1983–), 158–9
Daimler-Benz-Chrysler, see Daimler-Chrysler
Daimler-Chrysler (Dasa), 160, 169
  aerospace division, 165
  candidate to merge with Fiat, 517
  comparative size (global, 1998), 561
  diesel engine purchases (1998), 531
  fuel-cell technology, 427
  internet procurement network, 856
  'legacy of distrust' with BAe Systems, 170
  language (English), 514
  management 'blood-letting' (9.1999), 497
  merger (1998), 514
  merger activity, 161, 164, 170
  on-line procurement networks, 45
  output (truck), sales, profits, employees (1998), 542
  output, turnover, profit, R&D (1998), 533
  part-owner of Airbus Industrie, 167
  Powertrain division, 532
  profits, 514
  and proposed EADC, 159–60
  research and development, 510
  revenues, profits, employees, R&D (1998), 887
  sales, profits, employees, R&D (1998), 561
  share of European bus market, 513
  takeover of DDC (7.2000), 531
  takeover of Casa (Spain), 161, 235
  workforce, 514
  world's leading lorry-maker, 518, 532, 535
  world's second largest company, 415
  world's third largest auto producer, 514
  see also EADS
Dalian, 444, 729
Dalian (engine-maker)
  'bulk of output supplied to Yiqi', 561, 566

capacity, 561
  competitive advantage, 565
  competitor to Yuchai, 552
  output, 561
  6110 series (engine), 561
  Yiqi takes full control (1995), 561
Dalian Machine Tool Plant, 950(n10)
Dalian Petrochemical Corporation, 469, 478
Dalian Vastone Enterprise Development Company, 809
Dalian West Pacific Petrochemical [enterprise] transferred to New CNPC by New Sinopec (1998), 469
Dana, 522, 535, 547
dangan ('file'), 318
Danling, 950(n9)
Daqing complex
  managed by New CNPC (1998–), 470
Daqing (General) Petrochemical Corporation transferred to New CNPC by New Sinopec (1998), 469, 478
Daqing Lianyi Oil refineries, 842
Daqing oilfield (Heilongjiang Province), 429, 433, 441–5
  comparative size, 437, 438, 486
  'diversified undertakings', 846
  local patriotism, 443
  population, 443
  price of Daqing crude oil, 457
  refinery (run by Sinopec, not CNPC), 486
Daqing Petroleum Administration, 441–5, 456, 470, 495, 497, 841, 842, 855, 883
  corporate ambition, 443–5, 474, 495, 496
  hopes for stock market flotation, 474[–]476
  joint ventures, 445
  merger philosophy, 444
  merger talks with Shanghai Petrochemicals, 842
  missed merger opportunity, 862
  most profitable enterprise in PRC, 442
  new role (mid-1990s), 464
  non-core business, 445
  not allowed to float internationally, 842
  output, sales and pre-tax profit (1996), 442
  place in New CNPC structure, 475
  profits, 439, 474
  restructuring (1998–9), 445
  struggle with New CNPC headquarters, 474[–]476, 497–8
  subsidiaries, 445
  wages, 443
  welfare system, 443
Darnell, Robert, 615
Dasa, see Daimler-Chrysler
Dassault, 159; and proposed EADC, 160
data processing (Samsung), 53
data systems, 43
Datong Mining Bureau (Shanxi)
  average mining depth, 737
  largest coal-mining company (PRC), 749

Datong Mining Bureau (Shanxi) – *continued*
  mine-mouth coal price (6.1994), 728
  national team player (second batch), 118
  output, reserves, mine depths (1996), 736
  quality of coal, 737
  transport costs, 720, 723
  workforce, 79
  alternative usage: 'Datong Group'; 'Datong
    Mine Group'
Daya Bay nuclear power plant (Guangdong
  Province 1993–), 351, 357, 358
Daye Steel (company), 640
DBB Fuel Cell Engines, 427
dealers: diesel engines, 529, 530, 531
dealerships (auto industry), 503, 887
Dean Witter, 817
death rates, 906, 907, 910
debt, 818
  Air China, 123
  COSCO, 121
  Monsanto, 266
  oil sector (PRC), 489
  PRC, 71, 136, 939(n14)
  Shanghai Petrochemical Corporation, 472
  TVEs, 133
defence
  barriers to entry (1998), 63–4
  industrial concentration (global), 141
  research and development expenditure (1995,
    1998), 49
defence budget
  NATO Europe, 156, 233
  post-Cold War, 150, 233
  PRC, 188, 194, 271, 940(n6)
  USA, 156
defence electronics, 147
defence equipment: privatization (general), 32
defence sector: global market share, 37
DeKalb Genetics (USA), 256, 265
Dell, 863
Delphi Automotive Systems, 535, 950(n9)
  de-merger from GM (1999), 886
  globalization, 521
  joint ventures (PRC), 545
  research and development, 535
  seat business acquired by Lear (1997), 524
  turnover, profit, R&D (1998), 522
  world's joint largest component-maker
    (1999), 521
  see also General Motors
Delta (airline, USA), 149
Delta (airline alliance), 149
Delta & Pine, 256, 265
Deng Xiaoping, 190, 274, 646
  approach to reform process, 911–12
  cited, 141, 195
  concentrates on economic construction, 195
  'most successful', 912, 915
  1977 speech, 188
  'opening up and advancing', 910–16

re-thinking of national priorities, 196
  visits Shougang (5.1992), 650
Deng Yingtao, 763
Denmark: purchase of missiles from USA, 158
dense wavelength division multiplexing
  (DWDM) equipment, 774
Denso, 19, 535
  air conditioners, 524, 535
  globalization, 521
  incorporating IT into components systems,
    522
  IPO (5.1999), 522n
  joint ventures (PRC), 546
  research and development, 522, 535–6
  revenues, profits, employees, R&D (1998),
    886
  turnover, profit, R&D (1998), 522
department stores, 132
deregulation: financial services, 814
derivatives, 818, 836
deserts (PRC), 438
design, 674–5
  auto industry, 521
  costs (lorries), 518
'designated key users' (PRC), 459
Desmarest, Thierry (chairman, TotalFina), 417
destroyers (Sovremenny), 192
Detroit Diesel (DDC), 529, 531, 559, 568,
  861
  growth and acquisitions, 531
  missed merger opportunity, 861
  'originally part of GM', 531
  profits, 567
  sales, profits, employees, R&D (1998), 584,
    886
  taken over by Daimler-Chrysler (7.2000),
    531
  Yuchai comparison, 585
Deutsche Bank (Germany), 815
  acquisition of Morgan Grenfell, 817, 958(n9)
  assets managed (1999), 837
  key indicators, 1999 (PRC comparison), 827
  retreat to core business, 958(n6)
  top five firm (all international convertibles,
    2000), 823
  top five firm (international equities
    bookrunners, 2000), 823
  top five firm (syndicated credit arrangements,
    2000), 824
Deutsche Telekom, 58, 786, 840, 854
  international comparison (12.1999), 800
  market capitalization, revenue, profits
    (12.1999), 800
  partially-privatized, 802, 803, 892
  state ownership (barriers to international
    acquisition), 804
developing countries, xxiii, 1, 5, 23, 46, 860,
  929
  'ability to leapfrog', 918
  aerospace, 173–84

developing countries – *continued*
  barriers to entry, 141, 231, 173–6, 195,
    270–1, 532, 535, 618–22
  big business, 62–4
  BOT, 352
  'capital-scarce, labour-abundant', 5
  catch-up (coal industry), 712–13
  co-finance of industrial development
    (aerospace), 174–5
  competitive capability, 787–90
  difficulty of building large firms, 844–6,
    857
  difficulty of competing, 62
  difficulty of framing industrial policy, 60
  energy demand, 695–6
  energy-intensive activities, 699
  entire GNP smaller than wealth of some
    multinational companies, 534
  example of Brazil (aerospace), 180–3
  example of Japan (aerospace), 176–8
  example of USSR (aerospace), 178–80
  export credit guarantees (aerospace), 174
  FDI inflow, 29–31
  financial services, 824
  foreign investment (benefits), 789
  growth rate, 916
  importance for drugs companies, 243
  industrial policy, 12, 64–5
  industrial structure, 6
  internet sector, 780
  Japanese investment (steel, 1990s), 608
  largest private industrial enterprises, 51–2
  leap forward strategy, 1
  liberalization, 507, 707
  loss of skilled labour, 33
  market capitalization, 51
  'massively disadvantaged', 46
  military procurement (aerospace), 174
  mini-mills inappropriate (steel industry),
    599–600
  'normal' sequence of development, 6
  oil sector, 421, 461
  options (aerospace), 183–4
  pollution, 701, 703, 704
  poverty, 704
  power equipment producers, 339
  power generation, 332, 943(n8)
  power stations, 891
  PRC achievements (Mao era), 907
  privatization, 32, 336, 413
  production by global car giants, 520
  protectionism, 28–9
  research and development, 48, 175–6
  scrap steel availability, 599
  share in *Fortune* 'Global 500', 46, 50, 62
  share in *FT* 500, 46
  shortage of 'competitive edge' companies
    (1997–8), 50, 62–3
  Shougang expansion, 690
  software sector, 787–8

  steel, 593, 594–5, 604, 605, 608
  strategic choices (aerospace), 173–84
  telecommunications, 779, 787
  Third Technological Revolution, 762
  TNCs (PRC comparison), 79
  trade policy, 13
  TRIPs Agreement (1994), 785–6
  vehicle industry, 536
  World Telecoms Agreement, 786
  see also Embraer
Development Bank of Singapore, 23
Dezhou plant (power generation), 944(n13, 17)
diabetes, 319
Diageo, 34, 35
Dictionary of National Biography (UK), 290
Diesel Engine Machinery (BVI) Limited
  CYI Limited ownership structure, 573
  'DML', 574
  'main shareholder of CYI', 573
  owned 53% by HLA, 574
  owners, 574
diesel engines, 848, 861
  manufacture (PRC), 938(n3)
diesel oil, 460: smuggling, 275
difang qiye (local firm), 367
  see also HPEC
Ding Guiming, 443, 445, 495, 841
Direct Digital Device (DDD), 782
directly-reduced iron (DRI), 598, 614
Disney (USA), 781, 787
distilled spirits, 870
distribution
  automobile industry, 511
  costs, 44
  networks (WTO rules), 866
  PRC, 923
diversification
  'defensive tactic for growth', 52
  European and US businesses, 51
  HPEC, 381–2
  illusion of scale (PRC), 849–50
  PRC, 846–50
dividends
  international comparison, 18
  Sinopec, 465
  Yuchai, 574, 951(n20)
division of labour, 7
  among countries, 12
  vehicle sector (PRC), 545
DLJ (US investment bank), 822
Dobb, Maurice, 7
DoCoMo, 799, 803, 804
doctors (PRC), 300
dogs, 291
domestic content requirements, 395–6,
  949(n67)
domestic trade/services (1991, 1997), 84
domestic workers, 33
Dongbei, 307[–]9
  plant at Shenyang, 283, 941(n10)

Dongbei – *continued*
  listed (pharmaceutical) company (1996–),
    282
Dongbei Dianli Shebei Tuoluosi (Northeast
  Power Equipment Trust), 946(n38)
  Dongdian for short, 364
  six plants, 383
  wound up in 1967, 364
Dongfang Boiler Works (Deyang, Sichuan,
    1971–), 376, 948(n47)
Dongfang Electric Power Group, 111
Dongfang Electric Corporation, 389
Dongfang Group, 93
Dongfang International Group, 130
Dongfang Power Equipment Company
    (Sichuan), 346, 356, 360–1, 371, 387,
    390–1, 398, 947(n42)
  boiler plant at Jiaxiang, 390
  first 600MW thermal power station (1998),
    377
  'floated its turbine generator plant' (HK stock
    market, 1994), 390
  joint ventures, 389, 390
  shareholders, 390
  technical ownership by local authority, 370
  Three Gorges Project, 356–7, 881
  unit production capability, 377
Dongfeng Automobile Company, 73, 74, 136,
    138, 223, 444, 464, 496, 539, 563–6, 885,
    887
  ability to compete on global level playing
    field, 885–7
  centred at Erqi, 557
  Chaoyang (diesel engine enterprise), 560
  comparative size (global, 1998), 561
  'core firm' of Dongfeng Group, 564
  customer preference for Yuchai engines,
    557
  decision-making autonomy (1986–), 91
  demand for diesel engines, 557
  deteriorating relations with Yuchai, 557
  diesel engine production (1998), 559
  engine guarantees, 557
  enhanced autonomy, [658], 955(n44)
  favoured enterprise (by PRC state), 563
  first internal finance company (7.1987), 92
  first-tier subsidiaries, 563
  formed Dongfeng with eight other vehicle
    enterprises (1981), 563
  'group' structure, 563
  in-house components production, 563
  in-house production (diesel engines), 582
  influence with central government, 563
  joint venture with Citroën (Hubei Province),
    539, 540, 950(n7)
  joint venture with Cummins, 547, 566, 567,
    568
  leading lorry-maker (PRC), 518, 534, 542,
    543, 554, 567
  lobbying power, 577

main product, output, profits, taxes (1995),
    562
  merger activity, 848
  middle-level player (global lorry output), 542
  minuscule (in international comparison), 534,
    538
  missed merger opportunity, 861
  output of light trucks (1998), 554
  output (truck), sales, profits, employees
    (1998), 542
  purchases of engines from Yuchai (1995),
    554
  revenues, profits, employees, R&D (1998),
    887
  sales, profits, employees, output (1998), 562
  sales, profits, employees, R&D (1998), 561
  saloon car production (1998), 540
  second-tier subsidiaries, 563
  Second Automobile Manufacturing Factory,
    136
  'Shougang' contract system, 678, 956(n62)
  'terrible year' (1996–7), 549
  state capital management rights (1990–),
    93–4, 137
  super-large plant (Wuhan), 102
  third largest automobile firm (PRC), 556
  vertical integration, 544
  and Yuchai, 551, 554, 557, 569, 567–8,
    577–8
  alternative usage 'Dongfeng'; 'Erqi'; 'Erqi
    Motor Corporation'; 'Number Two
    Auto'; 'No 2 Automobile Works'
Dongfeng Automobile Industry Finance
    Company
  directly-controlled subsidiary of Dongfeng
    Group, 564
Dongfeng Automobile Trade Corporation
  directly-controlled subsidiary of Dongfeng
    Group, 564
Dongfeng Chaoyang Diesel Engine Company
  4102 diesel engine, 565
  6102 diesel engine, 565
  6105 diesel engine, 565
  changes of ownership, 565
  diesel engine production (1998), 559
  engines not as powerful as those produced by
    other PRC engine-makers, 565
  leaves Yiqi system (1993), 565
  main product, output, profits, taxes (1995),
    562
  quality problems, 565
  'second layer' enterprise (Dongfeng Group),
    564
  supplier to Yiqi, 563, 565
  taken over by Dongfeng Group (1994), 565
  technology transfer by Cummins, 565, 567
Dongfeng Group (Aeoleus), 74, 75, 80, 87, 102,
    127
  Chinese name, 102
  decision-making autonomy (1986–), 91

Dongfeng Group (Aeoleus) – *continued*
  first internal finance company (7.1987), 92
  state capital management rights (1990–),
    93–4, 137
  super-large plant (Wuhan), 102
Dongfeng Group Corporation (1981–)
  capital participation, 565
  components suppliers, 563
  components plants, 563
  diesel engine manufacture, 559[–]566, 568
  division of labour, 563
  Erqi 'core firm', 563
  evolution, 950(n13)
  factories, 563
  first layer enterprises (directly controlled),
    564, 565, 566
  four layers (1990s), 564
  fourth layer enterprises, 564, 565
  headquarters, 563
  investments, 563
  joint ventures with foreign companies, 565
  long-term ambition, 566
  losses (1996), 576
  majority-controlled subsidiaries, 564
  managerial autonomy, 563
  one of PRC's earliest 'enterprise groups'
    (1981–), 563
  prospectus for New York flotation, 567–8,
    951(n15)
  raised to status of Ministry (1987), 563
  research centres and schools, 564
  responsible for 300 enterprises (by 1989),
    563
  second layer enterprises, 561, 564, 565, 566
  structure of ownership and capital (1992),
    564
  third layer enterprises, 564, 565
  Xiangfan engine plant, 565, 566
  and Yuchai, 566–7
Dongfeng Group Nanchong Engine Plant
  main product, output, profits, taxes (1995),
    562
Dongfeng Hangzhou Automobile Corporation,
    542, 565, 577
  majority owned by Dongfeng, 554
  purchases of engines from Yuchai (1995),
    554
  'second layer' enterprise (Dongfeng), 564
  Yuchai sales, 554, 555
Dongfeng Hangzhou Heavy Machinery Plant
  'second layer' enterprise (Dongfeng), 564
Dongfeng Joint Management Company, 73, 74,
    136
  preferential planning status, 74
Dongfeng Lianying Company, 542
Dongfeng Liuzhou Auto Company, 542, 577
  majority owned by Dongfeng, 554
  purchase of engines from Yuchai (1995), 555
  Yuchai sales, 554, 555
Dongfeng Liuzhou Automobile Works

'second layer' enterprise (Dongfeng), 564
Dongfeng Nanchong
  diesel engine production (1998), 559
Dongfeng Nanjing Auto Company, 542
  'Nanjing (Special Automobile Plant)',
    554[–]557
  'Nanjing Dongfeng Special Automobile', 554
  part of 'Dongfeng system', 554[–]7
  purchases of engines from Yuchai (1995),
    555
  Yuchai sales, 554, 555
Dongfeng Sichuan: diesel engine production
    (1998), 560
Dongfeng system, 557
Dongfeng Xinjiang, 577
Dongfeng Yunnan, 554, 555, 577
Dongfeng-Thomson (joint venture), 565
Dongguan Power Plant, 352
Donglian Petrochemical Group (Nanjing
    1997–), 80, 117, 464, 938(n6)
  commences operations (1998–), 466
  experiment (1997–), 466–7
  international joint ventures, 466
  merger of four companies, 117, 454, 466
  origins, 117
  super-group, 80
  wishes (1997) to issue new shares, 466
Dongsheng mining company (PRC), 735
Dou He Plant, 360, 362
Dow Chemical/s, 262, 454
downsizing, 61, 64
  aviation industry (PRC), 220–1
  avoidance (by Shougang), 657, 688, 692, 694
  BAe, 169
  HPEC, 381–2, 385
  Japan, 56
  mining sector (PRC), 920–1
  mining sector (UK), 921
  political considerations (PRC), 845
  PRC, 71, 640–2, 845, 920–1, 939(n14)
  steel industry (PRC), 640–2
  strikes and violence (PRC, late 1990s), 920
  Yuchai, 581
  see also unemployment
downstream capability
  iron and steel (Shougang), 655
  oil, 460, 461–2, 464, 471, 472, 485, 490,
    495, 883
  oil (PRC), 883
  Shougang (diversification), 673, 682, 692
  steel, 609, 611
  Thyssen-Krupp, 612
  TotalFinaElf, 417
  WTO rules, 884
Dr Reddy's Laboratories (Hyderabad), 245
Dresdner Bank (Germany), 945(n19),
    958(n6, 9)
drivers of change
  aerospace, 141–52
  autos and auto components, 507–12

drivers of change – *continued*
  collapse of communism, 32
  global business revolution, 28–33
  information technology, 32
  migration, 32–3
  pharmaceutical sector, 242–52
  privatization, 32
  trade liberalization, 28–32
  tyre industry, 527
drugs (general)
  anti-depressant, 250, 268
  anti-herpes, 268
  anti-histamine, 250
  anti-infective, 268
  anti-obesity, 250
  anti-ulcer, 268
  top ten world-wide (1998), 250
  products selling over US$500 per annum
    (1998), 250
drugs (specific)
  Augmentin (SKB), 250
  Ceftriaxon, 306
  Celebrex (Monsanto), 247
  Claritin (Schering-Plough), 250
  ENU (Amgen), 301
  EPO (Amgen), 301
  Examethasene (Upjohn), 301
  Flixotide (Glaxo Wellcome), 247
  Lipitor (Warner-Lambert), 247, 250, 259, 260
  Locekin, 306
  Losec (Astra), 250, 264
  Novasc (Pfizer), 250
  Premarin (American Home Products), 247,
    259
  Prozac (Eli-Lilly), 247, 250
  Renitec (Merck), 250
  Seroxat/Paxil (SKB), 247, 250
  statin group (Merck), 268
  Vasotec (Merck), 247
  Viagra (Pfizer), 247, 251, 259
  Zantac (Glaxo), 247
  Zocor (Pfizer), 250
  Zoloft (Pfizer), 250
Du Halde, Father, 899
Du Pont, 265, 897
  acquisitions, 256, 265
  advantages, 265
  joint venture (coal) with RWE (Germany),
    710
  joint ventures in PRC, 118
  lessons drawn by PRC from, 71
  'life sciences', 261, 265
  oil division (Conoco), 265
  products, 265
  purchase of Conoco, 411
  purchases ICI Titanium Dioxide business,
    265
  sale of coal-mining interests (USA), 710
duli hesuan faren ('child' companies
  independent legal persons), 475

Dunlop, 527
duo zhong jing ying ('diversified business'), 496
  duozhong jingying ('diversified production'),
    475, 846
DVDs, 108
dyes, 502, 503
Dystar (industrial dyes), 263

e-commerce, *see* electronic commerce
E-Systems (defence electronics company), 147
E*Trade, 818
EADC, *see* European Aerospace and Defence
  Company
EADS, *see* European Aircraft, Defence and
  Space Company
EADS-Casa, 170
earth-moving equipment, 43
East Africa: immigration (pre-World War I),
  32–3
East Asia
  arms deliveries (1987–98), 151, 152
  business revolution, 51–8
  catch-up strategy for big business, 51
  coal supplies, 717–18
  diversification, 51
  'diversified conglomerates', 290, 316, 323,
    324
  economic growth (1980–98), 851
  energy demand, 695–6
  influence of List, 12
  'limited wars', 196
  pharmaceuticals market, 243
  privately-owned businesses, 51
  rapid growth rates (1990s), 507
  rapid industrialization, 699
  renewed business confidence, 929
  steel output (1974–96), 593, 594
  strategic re-thinking, 51
  success of 'latecomers', 46
East Asian crisis, *see* Asian financial crisis
East Asian Economic Caucus (EAEC), 927
'East Asian miracle': neo-classical view, 4
East Asian model
  crisis, 51–8
  USA absorbs lessons, 48
East China (regional electricity grid), 345
East Germany, 699n
Eastern Century Holdings (HK), 956(n60)
Eastern China Electric Group, 391
Eastern Europe (communist era), 2, 37, 178
Eastern Europe (post-communist), 506
  approach to industrial reform, 3
  arms deliveries, 152
  automobile industry, 508–9
  Daewoo operations, 506
  economic growth, 2
  electricity generation capacity (1990–2010),
    697
  lack of indigenous 'competitive edge'
    corporations, 63

Eastern Europe (post-communist) – *continued*
  lorry sales (1995, 2005), 509
  power equipment, 337
  production sector, 2
  production and sales of automobiles (1998),
      508
  projected demand for power equipment
      (1980–2010), 334
  share of world electricity generation
      (1995–2015), 335
  size of firms, 2
  steel, 588
  steel production (1991–7), 589
Eastman Kodak: competitive advantage, 35
Ebay, 780
Echeng Iron and Steel (company), 640
Echlin, 548
economics: free market orthodoxy, 2
economies of scale
  aerospace, 143–4, 146, 152, 167, 233, 239
  ATR 42, 206
  auto industry (general), 502, 503, 506,
      509–10, 512
  auto industry (Japan), 505, 510
  auto industry (PRC), 538, 560
  Boeing v Airbus, 168, 184, 232
  components, 535, 547
  components (PRC), 544, 559
  dedicated rail lines, 739–40
  defence sector, 157
  engines, 529
  fighters, 158–9
  financial services, 830
  Ford Motor Company, 506
  general, 13
  global giants (procurement), 845–6
  helicopters, 157
  HPEC, 393
  international trade, 12–13
  internet, 779
  IT sector, 775, 796
  Japan, 17
  lacking (PRC), 854
  low, 53
  modern industrial enterprise, 14
  oil refineries, 412, 484–5
  oil sector, 421, 427, 464, 484–5, 492
  pharmaceutical sector, 253, 270–1, 286
  power generation equipment, 328–34, 338
  PRC, 72, 74, 76, 80, 81, 84, 87
  Shenhua, 751
  Shougang (tertiary sector), 668, 692
  South Korea, 22
  steel industry, 600, 618, 621, 658, 694
  suppliers (car industry), 511, 521, 522,
      950(n5)
  Taiwan, 21
  telecommunications, 777
  Volvo (auto division) unable to compete, 515
  see also industrial concentration; oligopoly

economies of scope
  components, 535
  diesel engines, 531
  HPEC, 393
  pharmaceutical sector, 246, 270–1, 286, 300
  power generation equipment, 328–34
  PRC, 76
  steel industry, 600
  Yuchai, 551
  see also synergies
Edison Electric, 704
EDS, 146, 772
education, 196, 381, 949(n59)
Egypt, 943(n8)
  arms purchases, 193
  Daewoo operations, 506
  GNP no more than Ford's global
      procurement (1998), 535
  IBM comparison (annual revenues), 772
  per capita energy use (1994), 341
Egyptair, 213
elasticity
  demand, 86, 98
  electricity (PRC), 340
  energy (PRC), 340
electric
  fans, 272
  generating equipment (PRC), 75
  generator capability, 377
  motors (PRC), energy savings (potential), 716
  power generation, 119
electric arc furnaces, 596, 598
  PRC, 628
  Shougang, 645, 953(n23)
  steel production method (1997), 597
Electric Power Law (PRC 1996), 345–6
electrical
  equipment (Mitsubishi Electric), 55
  goods (Xinfei), 573
  parts, 950(n9)
  products, 11, 108
  systems (auto components), 545
Electricité de France, 351, 353
electricity, 329, 397, 890
  cost of anti-pollution measures, 701–2, 703
  demand (1990–2010), 696
  demand (PRC 1998–9), 725
  essential, 327
  global consumption (1980–94), 334
  global output (1980–98), 341
  grids, 345–6, 349
  installed generating capacity (1991–7), 359
  installed capacity and output (PRC
      1980–2010), 342
  PRC, 340, 341, 713, 714
  steel industry, 600
  structure of output (PRC 1980–2010), 354
  tariffs (PRC), 346, 349, 944(n12)
  Tibet, 345
  world ranking (PRC 1949–98), 913

electricity companies, 336
electricity generation
  anti-pollution regulations (PRC), 746
  capacity (1990–2010), 697
  coal-fired, 429
  cost, 697
  de-regulation, 697–8
  fuel type, 696, 698
  greenhouse gases, 702–5
  international implications of coal use, 705
  mentioned, 133
  national grid (PRC), 746
  national team (PRC), 77, 84
  PRC, 77, 703, 714, 715, 746
  privatization, 697, 706
  six trial groups (PRC), 77
  subsidized by coal industry (PRC), 728
  substitution of coal for oil, 433
  Taiwan, 20
  water shortage (NW China), 747
Electricity Generating Board (UK), 943(n7)
electro-optics, 148
Electrolux, 59, 863
electronic commerce (e-commerce), 818, 834
electronic control, 673
electronic data-processing technologies, 12
electronic mail (e-mail), 791
electronic products, 129
  non-aviation output of AVIC, 198
electronics, 12, 15, 116, 133, 191, 941(n5)
  'fastest growing industrial sector' (PRC), 86
  'high income elasticity of demand', 86
  mergers (PRC), 80
  national team (PRC), 76, 77, 78, 106–9
  PRC, 75, 97
  research and development (1995, 1998), 49
  Samsung, 53
  second batch of trial groups (1997), 86
  sectoral share of PRC national team (1991, 1997), 84
  South Korea, 22, 604
  US recovery of global dominance (late 1990s), 48
electronics systems, 523
Elf Aquitaine (France), 58, 408, 500, 840, 854
  basic statistics (1997), 418
  comparison with New CNPC and New Sinopec, 479
  employees, 480
  financial indicators, 480
  merger with TotalFina (1998–9), 416–17, 493
  'national champion' (France), 408
  privatization, 408, 493, 500, 859, 892
  profits, 480
  and Saga Petroleum (1999), 413
  turnover, 480
Eli-Lilly, 247, 249, 250, 269, 283
Embraer (Brazil), 180–4, 211, 239–40, 860, 861
  missed merger opportunity, 861
  rise 'highly significant event', 183

  suppliers, 181
  WTO ruling (4.2000), 878
EMC: software, 775
emergency signal sending, 523
emerging markets, 50, 507
EMI, 781
empennage, 214, 216
employees, 13, 43, 45, 937(n2 to ch1)
  Japanese, 18
  largest number in any one capitalist firm (GM), 44
  Nissan, 58
  PRC, 939(n14)
  reduction of numbers, 36, 61
  South Korea, 21
  Taiwan, 21
  see also labour
employment
  auto industry, 507
  China Xinxing Corporation, 274
  Daqing, 443
  General Electric (USA), 333
  impact of information technology (PRC), 918
  modern corporate system (PRC), 937(n1 to ch3)
  national team (PRC), 77
  New CNPC, 479
  New Sinopec, 479
  oil refineries (PRC), 485
  over-manning (PRC), 920
  PRC, 72, 196, 271, 919, 923
  PRC steel industry, 640–2
  restructuring (PRC), 893–4
  Third Technological Revolution, 763
  threatened by WTO entry (PRC), 924, 925
  Xinjiang Construction Group, 86
energy, 340, 943(n8–9)
  demand, 695–6
  national team (PRC), 77
  national team (various indicators, 1995), 78
  on-line procurement networks, 45
  output (global), 341
  per capita use (global), 341
  sources, 696
  strategic issues (PRC), 717, 720, 729, 749
energy efficiency, 329, 704, 715
energy intensity (PRC), 715, 957(n2)
energy supply
  sectoral share of PRC national team (1991, 1997), 84
engine block: key component, 581
engine management systems (EMS), 546
engines
  castings, 950(n9)
  cooling systems, 526
  diesel, 223, 513, 529–32, 536, 537, 544, 547–8, 552, 557, 558, 566
  efficiency, 532
  foreign investment (PRC), 546–7
  guarantees, 558–9

engines – *continued*
    high profit margin (diesel engines, PRC), 567
    importance of fuel pump, 580
    lorries, 517
    petrol, 529–30, 532, 552, 557, 558, 568–9
    spiralling R&D costs (cars), 521
    vehicles, 529–32
    see also aero-engines, Dalian, Wuxi, Yuchai
engineering, 48, 49
engineers: computer software, 221
English language, 787, 788–9
ENI, 407–8, 499, 840, 841, 854, 861, 920
    basic statistics (1997), 418
    comparison with New CNPC and New
        Sinopec, 479
    employees, 480
    financial indicators, 480
    flotation, 500
    job losses, 427
    missed merger opportunity, 862
    oil and gas production, 481
    possible merger, 417, 420
    privatization (1995–), 407, 413, 493, 892
    profits, 480, 484
    transformation (SOE national champion into
        privatized TNC), 859
    turnover, 480
    upstream activity, 408
enterprise: problems of definition (PRC),
    939(n15)
enterprise reorganization barriers, 72, 939(n16)
enterprise groups (PRC) *see* national team; trial
    business groups
enterprises (PRC)
    departmental relations, 94
    financial relations, 94
    ownership rights, 94
'enterprises' (PRC), 461
entertainment, 53, 782
entertainment companies, 781
entrepreneurship (PRC), 242
environment, 412, 423, 427, 435, 436, 485, 487,
    758, 883, 890
    aerospace, 182, 183
    automobile design, 511
    blast furnaces, 619–20
    controls (PRC), 871
    emission standards (diesel engines), 530, 531
    gas-fired power stations, 339
    large-scale mining operations, 709
    legislation/regulation, 510, 619–20, 699, 709,
        710, 746, 871
    mining companies, 709, 713
    Mitsubishi engine, 558
    PRC, 429–31, 746
    pressure groups, 757
    6112 engine, 553
    USA, 699, 709, 710
    see also pollution

environmental protection equipment, 198
erci chuangye ('Second Enterprise
    Establishment') policy, 309
equipment, *see* machinery
Ericsson (Sweden), 59, 786, 935
    fibre optic transmission trunk (PRC), 795
    market capitalization (2000), 764
    sales, 774
    sales revenue (2000), 764
    share of PRC market, 795
    third generation, 774–5
    wireless handsets, 774
erji gongsi, 654
    'second tier of one hundred enterprises'
        (Sanjiu), 318
Erqi Motor Corporation, *see* Dongfeng
    Automobile Company
erzi gongsi ('child' company), 221–6, 476, 478
ethanol, 422
ethyl acetate, 422
ethylene, 252
    catch-up possibilities, 64
    Donglian, 466
    at Huizhou, 454, 490
    'need to expand supply' (PRC), 487
    New Sinopec, 447, 448, 450, 452, 454, 472
    PRC production, 450, 451, 452, 470, 486–7
    Shanghai Petrochemical Corporation, 454–5,
        472
    world production (1989–96), 451
ethylene crackers, 421–2
EU, *see* European Union
'Euro-Oil', 417
euro [currency] area: bank restructuring
    (1980–97), 820–1
Eurofighter project (1983–), 158–9, 161, 162,
    170
'Europe'
    aerospace, 149, 156–70
    arms trade with USA, 156–7
    automobile market, 537
    coal consumption (1986–96), 698
    consolidation (steel sector), 609–13
    'continental Europe', 58–60
    copies Japan, 57
    defence sector (industrial concentration),
        141
    defence spending (post-Cold War), 150
    economic growth (1980–98), 851
    emerging 'steel oligopoly', 609
    employment in coal industry, 706
    general difficulties, 170–1
    global business revolution, 58–60
    iron ore costs (1997), 619
    Japanese penetrate (automobile market), 510
    Japanese production capability in, 511
    lessons for PRC (aerospace), 232–4
    military aircraft procurement, 174
    multinational corporations, 27
    national champions, 58

'Europe' – *continued*
  natural gas production and reserves (1997),
    405
  number of 'competitive edge' companies
    (1997–8), 50
  oil production (1987–97), 405
  primary energy consumption (1987–97), 402
  privatization, 32
  privatization of oil companies, 413
  productivity (coal), 620
  railways (C19), 13
  Renault, 515
  research and development expenditure
    (1997), 48
  share in *Fortune* Global 500 (1997), 50, 60
  South Korean expansion in, 23
  state ownership (steel industry), 605
  state protection (car industry), 533
  steel industry (consolidation), 598–9
  TotalFinaElf, 417
  transatlantic giants, 59–60
  wage costs (steel industry, 1997), 620
  see also Eastern Europe; European Union;
    Western Europe; individual countries
European Aerospace and Defence Company
    (EADC), 159–62, 163, 164, 233, 234–5
European Aircraft, Defence and Space Company
    (EADS), 59, 60, 161–2, 169, 171
  merger between Dasa and Aérospatiale-
    Matra, 161, 170
European champions, 59, 857, 895
  Airbus, 498
  aerospace, 878
  oil sector, 493
  power engineering, 338
  steel, 609, 889
European Commission, 956(n63)
European Future Large Aircraft, 164
European Union (EU), 922, 930
  aerospace, 165, 234–5, 237, 238
  agreement with PRC (telecommunications,
    5.2000), 791
  BOF method (steel production), 596
  coal as source of primary energy, 705
  continuous casting (steel industry), 596
  cooperation with USA (aerospace), 233
  defence procurement, 156–7
  defence forces, 162
  defence restructuring, 192
  electricity generation (fuel type, 1996), 698
  financial services (sectoral restrictions), 830
  industrial concentration (banking), 815,
    958(n4)
  market access (PRC IT sector), 790
  net importer of steel (1998), 607
  'plummeting profits' (steel, 1998), 607
  PRC accession to the WTO, 864
  relative size of US and EU aerospace
    companies (1998), 166
  'relatively open' to PRC exports, 871

  Single Market (effective 1992–), 814,
    958(n2)
  steel, 588, 595, 606
  voluntary export restraints (steel), 601
  see also 'Europe'
European Union-PRC Agreement (5.2000)
  WTO-accession, 864, 869
Everbright Group (HK), 306
Excel Switching, 773
exchange rate control, 833
exchange rates, 814
Excite, 787
exhausts (cars), 522, 525, 530, 536
experimental, developmental position, xxiii
exploitation, vii, 907
export
  credit guarantees, 97, 174, 178, 181–2
  credits, 353–4, 387
  earnings (arms sales), 152
  industries (South Korea), 54
  markets (for PRC), 86, 98
  restraints (voluntary), 395
  rights (PRC), 70
  subsidies (WTO rules, PRC implementation),
    869
Export-Import Bank of China, 97
  'Eximbank' (PRC), 387
Export Development Corporation (Canada),
    945(n19, n21)
exports
  drive world boom (1945–), 31
  growth (PRC 1980–97), 913
  HPEC, 386–7
  national team (various indicators, 1995), 78
  PRC (Deng era), 912
  PRC to USA, 893
  USA, 31
'external firm', 39–45, 61, 145, 523
  auto sector, 512
  Boeing, 145
  Coca-Cola, 530
  diesel engines, 530
  external firm, 847, 856
  IT sector, 769
  PRC, 923, 924
  sphere of co-ordination and planning, 39
  see also firm; outsourcing; sub-contracting
Exxon, 414
  merger with Mobil (1998), 413, 415
  not state-owned (1996), 410
  output (1996), 409
  production and exploration in 30 countries,
    481
  refinery and chemicals operations, 422
  refinery throughput, 421
  research and development, 423
  sale of coal-mining interests (USA), 710
  unit operating expenses (1993–7), 411
Exxon Mobil (USA), 415–16, 848
  basic statistics, 418–20

Exxon Mobil (USA) – _continued_
  comparison with New CNPC and New
    Sinopec, 479, 500
  employees, 480
  financial indicators, 480
  fuel-cell technology, 426–7
  job losses, 427
  natural gas, 416
  oil and gas production, 481
  oil reserves, 415
  profitability, 414, 420
  profits, 480
  revenues, profits, employees, R&D (1997
    pro-forma), 884
  size, 415, 500
  turnover, 480
  world's third largest company, 415

FAA, _see_ USA: Federal Aviation Authority
facsimile service, 791
fair market value, 227
Falun Gong, 805
famine, 907
fangquan (flats), 381
fans and pumps (PRC): energy savings
    (potential), 716
Far East
  dependence on Middle Eastern oil supplies,
    405
  industrial concentration, 613
  projected demand for power equipment
    (1980–2010), 334
farm equipment, 3
  barriers to entry (1998), 64
  global market share, 37
Farnborough Air Show, 150, 212
fast-moving consumer goods (FMCG), 45, 113,
    921, 929
  global oligopoly, 41–2
  core systems integration, 42, 43, 44
  packaging, 43
  see also consumer goods
FAW (First Automobile Works), _see_ Yiqi
FDA, _see_ USA: Food and Drugs Administration
FDI, _see_ foreign direct investment
Federation of Korean Industries (FKI), 517
fenliu ('main company'), 472
ferrous metals: PRC (national team), 77
FEV (Germany), 553
Fiat (Italy), 311, 504, 860
  collaboration with Peugeot, 513
  foreign assets, sales, employment (1997),
    509
  interests in Eastern Europe (post-1989), 508
  interests in India, 508
  interests in Mercosur, 508
  interests in Turkey, 508
  output, turnover, profit, R&D (1998), 533
  prospective merger, 517, 533
  state subsidies, 504

technology and marketing agreement with
    Westinghouse and MHI, 336
Fiat Avio, 942(n1)
fibre optics, 774, 786, 795
fibres, 265
film stars: used in advertising (PRC), 298
films, 131
filters (cars), 530
finance, 42, 121, 124
  access to foreign (PRC), 88
  aviation industry (PRC), 219, 237
  minimum economy of scale (auto industry),
    503
  power generation industry (PRC), 343,
    348–54, 358–9, 362, 375
finance companies (PRC), 70, 88, 110, 138, 139
financial
  assets ('securitized'), 818
  discipline (PRC), 71
  information, 781
  innovation, 31
  institutions, 815, 831, 958(n3)
  markets, 31
  regulation, 834, 835
  resources, 36–7
  sector, 640
  strength (power equipment), 329
financial holding company (FHC), 817, 819,
    835
financial services (global), 813–37, 958
  concentration and Americanization, 819–24
  conclusion, 837
  consolidation, 816–17
  cross-border transactions, 815–16, 819
  cross-sector transactions, 816–17, 819
  deregulation, 814–15, 837
  e-banking, 818–19
  financial engineering, 818–19
  globalization, 815–16
  innovation, 818–19
  intensified competition, 819
  mergers and acquisitions (1989–99), 816
  new trends, 814–24
  non-interest income (US banks), 830
  PRC, 813–14, 825–37
  problems (USA), 835
  sectors (according to _Fortune_ 500), 958(n7)
  separation of sectors (USA), 816, 830
  US dominance, 823–4
  see also Glass-Steagall Act (USA 1933)
financial services (PRC), 813–14, 825–37, 921,
    958
  banking, 825
  challenges after WTO entry, 813–14, 825–36
  conclusion, 837
  consequences of competition, 831–3
  consumer-protection, 835–6, 837
  cross-border transactions, 834–5, 836
  cross-sector transactions, 835–6
  employment (PRC 1998), 919

financial services (PRC) – *continued*
　global level playing field, 825–6, 831
　human resources, 832
　implementing regulation, 836
　infant, 814
　insurance, 825–6
　international benchmarking, 826–31
　international rules, 814, 833
　productivity and quality, 830–1, 837
　reform strategy, 825
　regulatory regime, 833–6, 837
　return on assets, 831
　return on equity, 831
　scale, 826–9, 837
　scope, 830, 837
　separation of sectors (PRC), 830
　systemic safety, 833–4, 837
　top four foreign and domestic commercial
　　banks (1999), 827
　top four foreign and domestic investment
　　banks (1998), 829
　top three foreign and domestic insurance
　　companies (1998), 828
　WTO rules (implementation by PRC), 868
Financial Services Modernization Act (USA
　1999), 814
Financial Times, 159, 164–5, 272, 336
Financial Times 500 (ranked by market
　capitalization), 19, 46, 47, 50
　CTHK, 799
　dominance of IT companies (early 2000),
　　771
　Four Little Tiger share (1996–8), 929
　Japanese share (1996–9), 929
　life sciences, 767
　no PRC representation (1999), 851
Findlay, Ronald, 19
Finland, 764, 775, 820
Finnair, 149
Finnemecanica, 892, 920
Firestone: purchased by Bridgestone (1988),
　528
firm
　changing nature, 762
　'lack of consistency in identification' (PRC),
　　852
　small v large, 1
　theory, 605, 679
　see also 'external firm'
First Automobile Works (FAW), *see* Yiqi
First Chicago NBD, 817
First Heavy Machinery Group (PRC): national
　team player (PRC), 104
First Industrial Revolution, 13
'First Ministry of Machine Building', 376,
　947(n44), 948(n46)
'first movers'
　Carnegie Steel Company, 601
　institutional, 680–1
　Yuchai, 885

First Tractor and Construction Machinery
　Group, 104
Fisons Pharmaceuticals (UK), 255, 263, 264
Fitzgerald, Niall, 34
Five Western District mines (Inner Mongolia),
　749, 753–6, 759, [843, 891]
Five Year Plans (PRC)
　first (1953–7), 363, 368, 391
　sixth (1980–5), 659, 667
　seventh (1985–90), 373, 659
　ninth (1996–2000), 342, 349, 353, 357, 358,
　　447–8, 734, 938(n5)
Fleetguard (company), 530
fluidized-bed combustion, 338
Flying Horse (brand-name), 197–8
FMCG, *see* fast-moving consumer goods
Foden (UK lorry company), 518
Fokker, 183, 205–6, 211, 212, 860, 861
food, 14, 132, 316–17, 318, 921
foodstuff packaging machinery, 198
Ford, Henry (1863–1947), 678
Ford Motor Company (1903–), 101, 176, 264,
　506
　acquires Volvo's auto business (1999), 515
　assets, 79
　brought-in components (1970s), 950(n3)
　candidate to merge with Fiat, 517
　co-operation with Honda and Peugeot, 513
　comparison with Shanghai Auto, 886
　diesel engines, 513
　foreign assets, sales, employment (1997),
　　509
　fuel-cell technology, 513
　global procurement, 515, 535
　global oligopoly in the business revolution,
　　40
　interests in India, Mercosur, Thailand, 508
　internet procurement network, 856
　Japanese operations, 505
　joint venture with Volkswagen (Latin
　　America and Portugal), 513
　negotiations with Daewoo (1999), 54
　number of employees (1992–7), 937(n1 to
　　ch2)
　on-line procurement networks, 45
　one of the three largest TNCs, 79
　output (PRC comparison), 533
　outsourcing, 511
　potential bidder for Daewoo (1999), 516
　purchase of Kwik-Fit (UK), 512
　research and development, 510
　revenues (1992–7), 937(n1 to ch2)
　revenues, profits, employees, R&D (1998),
　　887
　sale of Visteon (announced 9.1997), 521
　sales, 79
　stake in Mazda, 513
　transformation to 'consumer-service
　　company', 512
　workforce, 79

Ford-Volvo
  comparative size (global, 1998), 561
  matches entire GNP of Thailand, 534
  output, turnover, profit, R&D (1998), 534
  sales, profits, employees, R&D (1998), 561
Ford Foundation, 4
Fordism, 8, 44, 519
  see also vertical integration
Foreign Armies Grab China (Chen Fang, 1999),
    926, 961
foreign direct investment (FDI), xxiii, 29–30,
    520, 904
  auto assembly (PRC), 885
  Brazil (1993–8), 912
  coal industry (PRC), 729
  developed countries (inflow, 1984–98), 30,
    31
  East Asian steel companies, 608–9
  'grows much faster than trade' (1990s), 31
  impact of US-PRC Agreement (11.1999),
    872–3
  iron and steel industry (PRC), 640
  Japanese (in USA), 601
  offshore oil (PRC), 489
  oil sector (PRC), 457
  oilfields (PRC), 440
  pharmaceutical sector (PRC), 282
  PRC, 30, 31, 463, 860, 908, 910, 912
  rate of return (in PRC), 349, 353, 944(n14),
    944–5(n18)
  restrictions (PRC), 881, 883
  Russian Federation (1993–8), 910, 912
  Singapore, 23
  steel, 587, 595
  telecommunications sector (PRC), 791
  US-based companies (mid-1980s-), 48–9
  WTO rules (PRC implementation), 872–3
  see also investment
foreign exchange, 31, 86, 501
foreign trade, 78, 84, 87, 88, 501
foreign travel, 304
forestry and forests, 7, 77, 84, 134–5, 763
Forgeard, Noel, 150, 168, 212
'Former USSR', 401, 406, 433, 488, 842, 917
  coal, 698, 699, 707 718
  energy demand, 695
  example for PRC, 462–3
  fighter aircraft sales to PRC, 877
  hydrocarbon exports to PRC, 407
  Ispat, 614, 615
  natural gas production and reserves (1997),
    405
  oil, 403, 405, 434, 435
  primary energy, 696, 697
  steel, 589, 593, 594, 595, 596, 597, 608, 615,
    889
  see also Kazakhstan; Russian Federation;
    USSR
Formosa Chemicals, 21
Formosa Plastics (Taiwan), 21, 718

Fortune, 146, 608
Fortune 'Global 500' (ranked by sales revenue),
    18–19, 44, 46, 67, 95
  attempt by PRC to gain entrants into, 108,
    109, 115, 119, 126, 938(n5)
  auto firms, 507
  BP Amoco, 414, 416
  companies ranked by number of employees,
    44
  component-makers (vehicles), 521
  Continental Europe, 60
  'diversified financials', 819, 824, 958(n7)
  financial services, 824
  IT sector, 785
  Japan, 850, 929
  life sciences, 785
  New CNPC, 479
  New Sinopec, 479
  oil sector, 414–17
  pharmaceutical sector, 269, 785
  PRC/HKSAR representation, 70, 130, 830,
    851, 854, 939(n13)
  profit margins (1998), 245
  'return on revenues', 785
  research and development, 95
  sales value (1998), 47, 49
  Shougang's aspirations, 643
  software outsourcing to Indian companies,
    787
  South Korean representation (2000), 23
  telecommunications sector, 785
  TotalFinaElf, 416
  Wal-Mart, 479
fossil fuel power-generation, 339
Founder Group, 108, 109, 938(n5)
foundry operations, 513
Four Little Tigers, 6, 858
  'catch-up' process, 19–24
  companies in *FT* 500 (1996–8), 929
  comparative advantage, 6
  economic growth, 24
  'labour-intensive structures', 6
  neo-classical view, 19
  role of state, 19
Framatome, 358, 391, 396, 943(n6), 945(n22)
France
  air force, 157
  auto industry, 504
  bank restructuring (1980–97), 820
  central government, 943(n6)
  concentration of manufacturing output
    (1909–63), 14
  cross-border mergers, 853
  defence spending, 157
  energy efficiency (PRC comparison), 914
  German occupation, 504
  global business revolution (1990s), 58
  industrial concentration (steel), 605
  industrial concentration (auto industry), 507
  IT companies (2000), 764

France – *continued*
   'national champion' (oil sector), 416
   number of auto manufacturers (1920), 506
   oil and petrochemicals, 408
   pharmaceutical corporations, 248
   primary energy consumption, 401, 696, 697
   production of plastics (1989–96), 451
   production of ethylene (1989–96), 451
   protection of Elf, 493
   remuneration and labour productivity (steel
      industry, 1995), 641
   royalty and licensing fees (paid), 785
   share in *Fortune* Global 500 (1997), 50
   state aid for research and development
      (aerospace), 175–6
   state-owned airline, 203
   steel output (1974–96), 593
   steel production, 594
   supplier of nuclear power units to PRC, 357,
      945
   top twenty steel-producing country (1991–8),
      617
France Telecom, 786, 840, 854
   CCF partner of China Unicom, 810
   international comparison (12.1999), 800
   market capitalization, revenue, profits
      (12.1999), 800
   privatization, 892 (partial, 802)
   vestige of state ownership, 803
franchise stores, 132
Frankenstein, J. and B. Gill (1996), 189–90
Fraser, Sir Malcolm, 935
free markets, xxiii, 20, 150, 762, 926
free trade, 15, 51
   ASEAN Free Trade Area, 927–8
   Hong Kong and Singapore, 19
   Japan and Singapore, 928
   Japan and South Korea, 928
   Krugman's critique, 13
   List's critique, 12
   UK (1840s), 15
freight transportation, 77, 432
Freightliner (USA), 519, 535, 567
Freund (Japan) pilling machine, 303
Friedman, Milton, 3, 13, 14
fruit: world ranking (PRC 1949–98), 913
Fryna (Switzerland) ointment composer, 303
FT8 ('gas turbine non-aviation engine'), 217
Fu Quanyu, General, 941(n18)
fuel-cell technology, 426–7, 513
fuel consumption, 590
fuel injection, 521, 545, 950(n9)
fuel pumps, 576, 580
Fuji: competitive advantage, 35
Fuji Film, 19
Fuji Steel, 603
   see also New Japan Steel
Fujian
   coal production and consumption (1996), 719
   'grasping the large', 83

mobile phone company, 931
   wireless telecommunications, 799
'Fujian Five', 573, 951(n19)
Fujian Province
   new power station, 352
   nuclear power (planned), 357
   provincial electricity grid, 345
Fujitsu, 19, 764, 772, 850
Fulaerji Plant (Heilongjiang Province),
   948(n56)
furnaces, 596
furniture-making, 311
Fushun (Liaoning), 730–1, 901
Fushun Electro-magnetic Plant, 365
Fushun Petrochemical [enterprise], 469
fuwu gongsi ('technical service companies'),
   475
fuwu yewu ('non-core' business), 476
Fuxin (Liaoning): loss-making coal mines,
   730–1
Fuyo *keiretsu*, 53, 54, 56–7

Gallon, Louis, 212
GalvaSud, 612
gambling, 782
gandalei (mud houses), 443
'Gang of Four', 204, 911
Ganmaoqing (medicine for common cold), 297
Ganmaoling (likewise), 298
ganqing (feelings), 380
Gansler, Jacques, 150, 155–6, 165
Gansu (province), 656, 954(n40)
   electricity tariff, 346
   geographical location of national team
      members, 82, 83
   petrol stations, 470
Gansu Electric Power Company, 110
Garn-St Germain Depository Institutions Act
   (USA 1982), 814
Garnier, Jean-Pierre, 258, 269
gas, *see* natural gas
gas stations, *see* petrol stations
gasoline, *see* petrol
GATT, 28–9
   restrictions on protectionism, 507
   Uruguay Round (1985–93), 28, 784–5
   see also World Trade Organization
GDP, *see* Gross Domestic Product
GE, *see* General Electric (USA)
GE (Canada), 357, 378, 390, 945(n20)
GE Capital, 57, 331–2, 362, 787, 819
gears, 950(n9)
GEC-Alsthom, 398
   involvement in Three Gorges Project,
      945(n20)
   merger with Framatome (blocked), 843(n6)
   operations in PRC, 351, 353, 391
   origins, 336
   possible merger with Rolls-Royce (1998
      speculation), 943(n3)

GEC-Alsthom – *continued*
  R&D expenditure, 329
  servicing, 394
  size (late 1990s), 330
  supplier to SHP, 362
  see also Alstom
GEC-Marconi, 160
  acquires Tracor, 146
  merger with BAe (1999), 147–8, 161, 170
  see also BAe Systems
Gelsenkirchen, 426
Genay, H., *see* Berger, A.
gene therapy, 261
General Administration of Customs (PRC), 275
General Allocation Plan (GAP): coal sector
  (PRC), 726
General Armaments Department (PRC), 276
General Dynamic/s, 147, 165, 231
General Electric (USA), 164, 172–3, 178, 180,
  181, 239, 336, 398, 848
  aero-engine technology, 329, 331, 943(n3)
  ancillary equipment, 365
  assets, 79
  considering merger with Lockheed Martin
    (late 1998), 164
  dealings with HPEC, 372
  employment, 333
  F-class gas turbine, 329, 331
  global oligopoly in the business revolution,
    40, 42
  government procurement contracts, 396
  H-series combined cycle turbines, 329
  involvement in PRC power generation
    industry, 362, 386
  joint tenders with HPEC, 387
  'major beneficiary' of ABB merger with
    GEC-Alsthom, 338–9
  market leader (in USA), 338, 339
  market share worldwide (power generation
    equipment, 1993–8), 337
  number of employees (1992–7), 937(n1 to
    ch2)
  one of the three largest TNCs, 79, 339
  research and development, 143, 175, 329
  revenues (1992–7), 937(n1 to ch2)
  revenues, profits, employees, R&D (1998),
    882
  sales, 79
  servicing, 332–3, 394
  Six Sigma (systems management)
    programme, 334
  size, 330, 393
  source of profits, 333
  steam turbine manufacture, 943(n7)
  supplier to SHP, 362
  supply network, 384
  technical lead in turbine technology, 329
  workforce, 79
General Electric Company (UK), 336, 943(n7)
General Instruments, 771

General Motors (GM), 101, 103, 147, 176, 506,
  897
  adopts lean production system, 511
  alliance with Isuzu, 513
  anti-lock braking systems equipment,
    950(n4)
  'broad cooperation' with Sony (under
    discussion), 783
  brought-in components (1970s), 950(n3)
  candidate to merge with Fiat, 517
  co-operation with Honda, 513
  comparative size (global, 1998), 561
  comparison with Shanghai Auto, 886
  employment, 226
  engine supply, 513
  foreign assets, sales, employment (1997),
    509
  global oligopoly in the business revolution,
    40
  interests in Eastern Europe (post-1989), 508
  interests in India, 508
  interests in Mercosur, 508
  interests in Thailand, 508
  internet procurement network, 856
  Japanese operations, 505
  joint venture with Daewoo, 506
  joint venture with Shanghai Automotive
    Works (1997–), 539
  joint ventures with Toyota and Suzuki, 513
  largest capitalist employer world-wide, 44
  lessons drawn by PRC from, 71
  matches entire GNP of Turkey, 534
  number of employees (1992–7), 937(n1 to
    ch2)
  on-line procurement networks, 45
  output (PRC comparison), 538
  output, turnover, profit, R&D (1998), 533
  production line sold to Beinei, 567–8
  research and development, 507
  research and development, 510
  revenues (1992–7), 937(n1 to ch2)
  revenues, profits, employees, R&D (1998),
    887
  sale of Delphi (component-making)
    subsidiary (1999), 520
  sales, profits, employees, R&D (1998), 561
  takeover of Isuzu (1999), 518, 534
  world's largest company, 415
  see also Detroit Diesel (DDC)
General Motors/Isuzu: leading lorry-maker,
  518–19
genetic engineering, 265, 306
Genetic Therapy, 261
genetically-modified
  crops, 268
  seeds and associated chemicals, 266
Geneva Steel Works, 673
Geng Lei, 947[n40]
genomics, 246, 258
GeoCorp (IT company), 773

Germany, 262, 663
  air force (Luftwaffe), 157, 158, 159
  auto industry, 504
  bank restructuring (1980–97), 820
  banking sector, 816
  coal, 699, 706, 707, 732
  cross-border mergers, 853
  domestic manufacturing output produced by
      foreign-owned firms (1986–95), 31
  economies of scale needed (defence
      equipment), 158
  electric furnace (steel industry), 596
  energy efficiency (PRC comparison), 914
  enmity with UK abandoned, 233
  Eurofighter, 158–9
  Fortune Global 500 (1997), 50
  global business revolution (1990s), 58
  globalization, 514
  high cost of underground coal-mining, 710
  Hitler government, 504
  industrial concentration (auto industry), 506
  industrial concentration (steel), 605
  Ispat, 600
  IT companies (2000), 764
  joint venture (printing) in PRC, 311
  labour productivity (coal-mining, 1996), 711
  mentioned, 676
  national output in PPP dollars (PRC
      comparison, 1998), 914
  output per worker (coal), 706, 751
  pharmaceutical corporations, 248–9
  power equipment (exports to PRC), 379,
      948(n51)
  primary energy consumption (1986–96), 696
  primary energy consumption (1996), 697
  production of ethylene (1989–96), 451
  production of plastics (1989–96), 451
  protectionism, 396
  remuneration and labour productivity (steel
      industry, 1995), 641
  research and development (locale), 95
  royalty and licensing fees (paid), 785
  Sanjiu Germany Pharmaceutical Co Ltd, 308
  Sanjiu sales offices, 300
  state aid for research and development
      (aerospace), 175–6
  steel output (1951–60), 623
  steel output (1974–96), 593
  steel production, 594
  steel production methods (1997), 597
  state-owned airline, 203
  subsidies (coal industry), 731–3
  top ten steel-producing country (1991–8),
      616
  'universal banks', 818, 830, 958(n6)
getihu (private business), 315
Gezhouba Group
  hydroelectric dam construction, 85
Gezhouba Hydro-Power Plant (company), 350
Gezhouba Power Station, 944(n11)

hydro-power, 350
Gezhouba Water Resources and Hydropower
      Engineering Corporation, 127, 344
  national team player (first batch), 127
Ghosn, Carlos (CEO Nissan), 57, 516, 519
Gilbertson, Brian (Chairman, Billiton), 695
Gilbira, Samir, 527
Gill, B., *see* Frankenstein, J.
Gillette: competitive advantage, 35
GKN, 522, 525, 536
Gladstone, W.E., 903
glass, 77, 128, 525, 591
Glass-Steagall Act (USA 1933)
  repealed (1999), 814, 817, 819
  followed in PRC (1998), 830
Glaxo (USA), 247, 255
  market share (1994), 267
  merger (1995) with Wellcome (UK), 255
Glaxo Wellcome (1995–2000), 247, 253[–]8,
      255, 257n
  aborted merger with SKB (1998), 256, 258
  best sellers (drugs), 250
  market capitalization, 269
  marketing expenditure, 251
  merges with SKB (2000), 251, 257, 260, 262,
      268, 269
  products, 268
  research and development expenditure
      (1994–7), 248
  revenues, profits, employees, R&D (1997),
      879
Glaxo Wellcome/SKB (2000–), 253, 258, 269
  joint venture in Chengdu, 283
  'market share 1999', 268
  marketing, 270
  operational headquarters, 269
global
  capability, 52
  capital markets: revolution in, 32
  economy, 49, 51
  financial system, 31
  market share, 37
  markets (opening up of), 51
  procurement offices, 42
  production networks, 29
global business revolution (general 1990s), xxiv,
      8, 25, 27–65, 269, 898, 933
  advanced economies, 919, 924, 929
  autos, 507–12, 533, 536
  benefits, 61–2
  big business central to development of
      capitalism, 61
  brand, 34
  co-ordination and planning, 39–45
  coal industry, 695–713
  collapse of communism, 32
  competitive advantage, 33–7
  conclusion, 61–5
  continental Europe, 58–60
  core business, 33–4

global business revolution (general 1990s) – *continued*
  crisis for the East Asian model, 51–8
  dominance of firms based in advanced economies, 46, 47
  drivers, 28–33
  European champions, 59
  external firm, 39–45
  financial resources, 36–7
  financial services, 813–24
  gap between advanced economies and developing countries, 62–4
  industrial concentration, 37–9
  information technology, 32, 761–90
  iron and steel, 587, 588–622, 693, 694
  IT expenditure, 36
  IT hardware, 770
  Japan, 54–8
  liberalization of capital flows, 29–32
  market share, 38–9
  mass media, 781
  merger frenzy, 38
  migration, 32–3
  national champions, 58
  national industrial policy undermined, 60
  policy challenge, 64–5
  potential threats from the WTO, 928–9
  PRC response, 839–96
  privatization, 32
  regional distribution of firms, 46–51
  reinvigorated big business in Japan and Europe?, 60
  research and development, 34–6
  revolutionary change in business systems outside USA, 51–60
  South Korea, 52–4
  telecommunications, 761–2, 777
  trade liberalization, 28–9
  transatlantic giants, 59–60
  US dominance, 46–51, 775, 924, 925
  see also globalization; industrial concentration; mergers
global business revolution (PRC response), 839–96
  barriers to mergers and acquisitions, 847–8
  battle with domestic SMEs, 844–5
  central argument, 895
  conclusions, 850–2, 863–4, 892–6
  constraints on organic growth, 848
  construction of internationally-competitive firms, 840–57
  developing countries: special difficulties, 844–6
  downsizing and restructuring, 845
  drive to diversify, 846–50
  employment for displaced workers, 893–4
  external problems, 855–6
  general measures, 865–6
  global level playing field (PRC ability to compete), 876–92

government procurement contracts, 860
impact on trade and investment (WTO Agreement), 870–3
imperfect markets with high transaction costs, 847
increased autonomy for emerging corporations, 859–60
industrial policy 856–7, 857–64, 864–76
internal problems, 852–5
joining WTO, 864–76
need to provide for huge workforces, 846–7
non-economic objectives of WTO Agreement, 873–6
psychological problems of adjustment, 894–5
spacial distribution of industrial assets, 846
speed of implementation, 869–70
state support for technological upgrading, 863
state-orchestrated mergers, 858–9
structural change necessary, 892–3
supplier network, 845–6
supporting non-SOE national champions, 862–3
terms of WTO agreement in specific sectors, 867–9
using global competition, 860–2
weakness in competing on world markets, 848–9
where is the firm?, 840–52
WTO Agreement: enforcement, 870
WTO Agreement: 'not observed by PRC' (scenario), 895–6
WTO Agreement: 'observed by PRC' (scenario), 892–5
Global Crossing, 786
global level playing field, *see* mantras
global warming, 430, 702–5, 714
Globalisation Trap and China's Realistic Choices (Han Deqiang, 2000), 926, 965
globalization, xxiii, 2, 46, 48–9, 51, 58, 61, 64, 162, 242, 920, 926–7, 931
  automobile industry, 512, 516
  barriers to entry, 63
  benefits, 61–2
  coal industry, 695–713
  components, 520, 521, 523–4
  continental European response, 58
  impact on costs (automobile manufacturing), 509–10
  impact in Sweden, 59
  Japanese lean production, 511
  limits, 395–6, 949(n66–7)
  lorries, 519
  oil sector, 401–28, 441, 491–2, 494–5
  patented drugs, 243, 258
  pharmaceuticals, 262, 263, 266–7, 269
  policy debate (PRC), 463
  power equipment companies, 335, 336–9, 389
  shift to the Far East, 65

globalization – *continued*
  steel, 608–17, 621, 693, 694
  suppliers, 511–12
  vehicle industry, 520
  see also global business revolution; industrial
    concentration
GM, *see* General Motors
GMAC, 819
GMP, *see* Good Manufacturing Procedures
GNP, *see* Gross National Product
gold, 708
Golden Bridge (ISP), 808
Golden Palace (hotel chain), 313
Goldman Sachs (USA), 54, 818, 819, 824, 872
  key indicators, 1998 (PRC comparison), 829
  top five firm (all international convertibles,
    2000), 823
  top five firm (international equities
    bookrunners, 2000), 823
  top five firm (M&A Advisers, 2000), 823
Golf (car), 591
gongshang shui (industrial and commercial tax,
    PRC), 648
Good Manufacturing Procedures (GMP)
  pharmaceutical companies, 301–3, 323
goods: globalization, 855
goods and services, 7, 33, 62, 92, 918
Goodyear Tyre and Rubber (USA), 57, 535,
    886
  'Impact' technology, 527
  industry leader (tyres), 528–9
  research and development, 526
  takeover of Sumitomo, 526, 528–9
  turnover, profit, R&D (1998), 522
Gorbachev, Mikhail (b 1931), 908–9, 910–11
Goswami, Omkar, 873
government
  employment (PRC 1998), 919
  Japan, 54, 505, 603
  procurement, 4, 505
  resistance to trans-national mergers, 512
  support, 794, 795
grain, 705, 869, 871
Gramm-Leach-Bliley (GLB) Act (USA 1999),
    814, 815, 817, 819, 822, 958(n5)
Grangemouth, 422
'Great Leap Forward' (1958–9), 633, 907,
    947(n44)
Great Wall of China, 935
Great Wall Group: national team player, 106
Greater East Asian Co-Prosperity Sphere, 905
Greece, 158
greenhouse gases, 339, 406, 407, 430–1, 702–5,
    743, 890
grocery chains, 44
Groeningen (natural gas field), 416
Groomridge, M.A. and C.E. Barfield (1999)
    cited, 241
'groping for stones', 70
Gross Domestic Product (GDP)

expenditure on health (low-income
    countries), 243
  growth (PRC), 623–4, 713, 798, 850, 913
  mentioned, 29
Gross National Product (GNP)
  Austria v top five IT companies, 768
  Brazil v 57 hardware corporations (1997),
    766
  Chile v IBM, 768
  Egypt v IBM, 768
  forty-six developing countries v IBM's R&D
    expenditure (1998), 768
  Malaysia v US tax-funded R&D expenditure,
    863
  mentioned, 47
  per capita (various countries), 910
  PRC, 340, 913–14, 932
  Thailand v Ford-Volvo, 534
  upper-middle-income countries v top ten IT
    companies, 765
  various countries (1998), 932
Groupement d'intérêt économique, 167, 168,
    232
Gruma: competitive advantage, 35
GS Capital Partners, 573, 575
GSD, *see* PLA: General Staff Department
GTE, 800
gua paizi ('hanging signs'), 76
Guangdong (province), 24, 125
  geographical location of national team
    members, 82, 83
  'grasping the large', 83
  No 2 (nuclear power plant), 945(n22)
  nuclear power (planned), 357
  nuclear plant at Daya Bay, 351, 357
  nuclear power, 391
  pharmaceutical sector, 283
  power plant capacity, 350
  provincial government, 120
  rail network, 124
  richest province (PRC), 951(n17)
  Shajiao 'B' and 'C' power plants, 351
  wireless telecommunications, 799
Guangdong Capital, xxvi
Guangdong Ceramics Group, 131
Guangdong Nuclear Electric Group, 110
Guangdong Nuclear Power Group, 85
Guangdong Telecom, 862
Guangxi (province), 82, 83, 501, 573, 810
  China Unicom joint venture activity, 810
  geographical location of national team
    members, 82, 83
  Laibin B power plant (BOT project), 352–3
  'poor region', 569, 951(n17)
  power station construction (CEPA letters of
    intent), 353
  provincial government, 572, 580, 582
  see also Yuchai
Guangxi Economic Management College, 579
Guangxi Guitang Group, 86, 131

Guangxi Liufa Joint Stock Company, 562
Guangxi Yuchai Joint Stock Company, 562
Guangxi Yuchai Machinery Company
    (7.1992–), 575n
Guangzhou (Canton), 224
    advertising by Yuchai, 558
    China Unicom joint venture activity, 810
    Citigroup office, 835
    foreign investment in telecommunications
        (post-WTO accession), 791–2
    GLD-owned hotel, 311
    massacre of workers by British and French
        (19 June 1925), 904
    mine-mouth coal price (6.1994), 728
    Peugeot joint venture (1993–7), 539
    pharmaceutical sector, 283
    thermal coal price (7.1997), 729
Guangzhou Army Hospital, 290–1, 297, 303,
    323
    continues to receive proportion of Nanfang
        profits, 294
    develops a skin ointment, *Piyanping*, 298
    establishes Nanfang (1986), 290, 321–2
    sole shareholder in Nanfang, 291
    stomach medicine, 297
Guangzhou Auto
    joint venture with Peugeot (1985–), 539
Guangzhou military region, 276
Guangzhou Rail Group, 124
Guangzhou South-China Telecommunications
    Investment Corporation, 809
gufen gongsi ('joint-stock company'), 475, 476
guided weapons systems, 144
Guixi County (Jiangxi Province), 655
Guizhou Aero Industry Group, 113, 197
Guizhou Automobile Works
    'third layer' enterprise (Dongfeng), 565
Guizhou Province, 82, 83, 138, 186
Guizhou Shuangyang Aircraft and Plane
    [company], 200
Gulf of Mexico, 416
Gulf Oil, 411
Gulf War, 162, 192, 435
    impact on PRC military thinking, 190–1, 194
Guotai (PRC insurance company), 829
Guotai J&A (PRC insurance company), 826
Guoxin Paging, 798
GWIC, *see* China Great Wall Industry
    Corporation

Hafei: subsidiary of AVIC, 940(n12)
'Haguo people', 368
'Haguo spirit', 368
Haguoren ('Haguo people'), 368
Haibowan (coal-mine), 753–4
Haier Group (PRC), 862, 938(n5)
Haihua Group, *see* Shandong Haiyanghua
    Group
Haikou Pharmaceutical Company, 299, 321
    Baodao trademark, 299

Haikou Weitai, 299
Hainan
    electricity tariff, 346
    local government, 299, 321
    provincial electricity grid, 345
    rail network, 124
    wireless telecommunications, 799
Hambrecht & Quist, 822
Hamburg, 167, 427
Hamilton, Alexander (1757–1804), 15
Hamilton (USA) propellers, 205
Hammersley Iron (Australia)
    building a reputation, 752
    iron ore operations, 708
    railway to coast, 708, 739–40
Hamre, John, 157, 164
Han Deqiang, 926
Handan Iron and Steel (PRC), 633, 634
handbags: PRC exports, 871
Hangang: continuous casting, 627
Hangzhou (Zhejiang), 134, 283, 391
Hangzhou Automobile Engine Plant, 547, 559,
    562
Hangzhou vehicle assembly plant, 564
Hanjiang (Hangzhong), 199
Hanyang Special-Purpose Vehicle Works
    'fourth layer' enterprise (Dongfeng), 564
Harbin Aero-engine Company, 205
Harbin Aircraft Corporation
    assigned to 'AVIC 2', 230
    statistics, 200
Harbin Automatic Control Equipment
    Company, 367
Harbin Aviation Company
    AVIC subsidiary, 199
    'largest producer of micro-vans', 199
Harbin Boiler Company (1994–)
    limited liability company (1994–), 366, 369,
        371, 378
    plant and equipment (1994 valuation), 379
    power equipment imports, 379
Harbin Boiler Works (HBW 1954–94), 363,
    365, 368, 375, 376, 377, 948(n45–7)
    cooperation with Pyropower Corporation,
        378
    main statistics (1992), 364
    part of HPEGC, 365
Harbin Cigarette Company, 946(n35)
Harbin City (Heilongjiang Province), 104, 363,
    371, 950(n9)
    aircraft manufacturing, 186, 662
    city government, 364, 391, 393, 398
    'city of power generation equipment', 111,
        363
    relies on HPEC for revenue, 367, 385,
        946(n32)
    social services, 381, 949(n61)
    thermal coal price (7.1997), 729
Harbin City Petroleum Company, 486
Harbin Control Machinery Company, 367

Harbin dianzhan chengtao gongsi, see HPE
Harbin Dongan Aero-engine Corporation, 230
Harbin Dongan Engine Corporation, 200
Harbin Electric Cable Plant
    excluded from the HPEGC, 365
    main statistics (1992), 364
Harbin Electrical Generator Plant (HEC
        1951–94), 363, 365, 377–8, 379
    main statistics (1992), 364
    part of HPEGC, 365
    Soviet aid project, 368
    second hand machinery, 379
Harbin Electrical Instrument Company, 367
Harbin Electrical Machinery Company, 365
    'HEC' (post-1994 references), 371, 378, 379,
        381, 948(n50–1)
    housing, 381
    limited liability company (1994–), 366
    plant and equipment (1994 valuation), 379
    second hand machinery, 379
Harbin Engineering Company
    limited liability company (1994–), 366
Harbin Fenghua Machinery Company, 367
Harbin guolu jingshen ('Haguo spirit'), 368
Harbin Heavy Machinery Company, 367
Harbin Insulating Materials Plant
    part of HPEGC, 365
Harbin Insulation Material Plant
    wholly-owned subsidiary of HPEGC, [367,]
        946(n36)
Harbin Pharmaceutical Group, 126
Harbin Power Equipment Company (HPEC
        1980–), Limited (10.1994–), 328, 343,
        355, 357, 363–92, 398
    ability to compete on global level playing
        field, 881–2
    Annual Report (1995), 369
    basic company data (1995), 367
    competitive mechanism, 384–5
    competitors, 359, 376, 387–91
    conclusions, 372–3
    control, 371–2
    dividends, 367, 946(n39)
    downsizing/diversification, 381–2, 385
    employment (core and non-core), 380–1
    engineering services, 394
    equipment, 360, 362, 378–9, 394
    exports, 386–7, 388
    floated on HK stock market (10.1994–),
        366–7, 370–1, 375, 881, 946(n31, 39)
    four subsidiaries, 366, 369
    government-orchestrated merger, 397–9
    growth, 373–5
    housing, 381
    installed capacity (1991–8), 390, 949(n65)
    'investment holding company', 369, 371
    joint tenders with multinational companies,
        387
    joint ventures, 391
    labour organization, 380–3, 949

lessons from advanced economies, 395–6
manufacturer of power equipment, 346, 356
marketing, 386
merger activity, 842, 848
modernization, 375–80, 948–9
national champion, 391–2, 395
national team player (first batch), 111, 364
new ownership structure, 365–8
output (1959–98), 374
ownership and control, 363–73
ownership by local authority, 370
pension and service fees, 367, 946(n34)
personnel management ethos, 380
plans, 379–80
plant and equipment (1994 valuation), 379
policy choices, 395
PRC power equipment production (1991–6),
    389
prices, 383–4, 385–6
profits, 375, 380, 882, 946(n39), 949(n65)
remuneration, 382–3
revenues, profits, employees, R&D (1998), 882
restructuring (10.1994–), 366, 372
scope, 363–5, 945(n29)
size, 330, 392–4
SOE, 501
Soviet aid, 375, 378, 947(n44)
state factory to competitive firm, 392
sub-contracting work, 391, 392
suppliers, 367, 373, 383–4, 845
taxation, 367, 375, 946(n33)
technical capabilities, 376, 380, 386,
    948(n45)
technical upgrading (self-organized), 377–8
technology transfer, 376–7, 394, 397
Three Gorges Project, 356–7
'three main separate entities', 881
turnover (1996), 394
see also Harbin Power Engineering Group
    Company
Harbin Power Engineering Group Company
    (HPEGC)
    constituent companies, 365
    executive directors, 372, 946–7(n40)
    four wholly-owned subsidiaries, 367,
        946(n36)
    integrating the merged companies, 368–71
    internal power struggles, 373
    jointly-managed companies, 367, 946(n38)
    listed overseas, 365–6
    motive for formation, 365
    nature, 365
    non-controlling ownership in other
        companies, 367, 946(n37)
    one of the preferred LMEs, 392
    'owns 62pc of HPEC share capital', 366
    profits, 369
    receives pension and service fees from
        HPEC, 367, 946(n34)

Harbin Power Engineering Group Company
    (HPEGC) – *continued*
  restructured (10.1994), 366, 369
  sales, 945(n30)
  services, 383
  state holding company, 366, 369, 392
  see also Harbin Power Equipment Company
Harbin Power Station Engineering Company
    (HPE), 383–4
Harbin Research Institute of Large Electrical
    Machinery (1958–), 378
Harbin Sanlian 'Development' Company
  wholly-owned subsidiary of HPEGC, [367],
    946(n36)
Harbin State Assets Management Bureau, 366
Harbin Steam Turbine Plant (HTC 1956–94),
    363, 365, 368, 371
  main statistics (1992), 364
  part of HPEGC, 365
  purchase of second-hand machine tools
    (1980s), 379
Harbin Turbine Company (HTC 1994–)
  housing, 381
  limited liability company, 366, 371
  milling machine, 948(n53)
  numerical-control systems, 379, 948(n56)
  plant and equipment (1994 valuation), 379
  power equipment imports, 379, 948(n51)
  research workers (1996), 948(n50)
hardware (IT), 107, 765, 766, 770–5, 794–7,
    861
  competitive advantage, 769
  missed merger opportunities for PRC, 862
  networking equipment, 795
  non-SOE national champions (PRC), 862
  personal computers, 794
  research and development, 766
  sales revenue, 766
  set-top boxes, 796–7
  wireless communications, 795–6
Harrison, Mr (Chairman of Chase Manhattan),
    817
Harvard Business School, 862
Hassan, Fred, 246, 266
Hawaii: Holiday Inn, 313
Hawker Siddeley Dynamics, 498
Hayes Wheels, 525
HCIC, 361n
He Ping, Major-General, 274
health, 767
  damaged by pollution (PRC), 430
  damaged in small-scale mining, 758, 759
  oil sector, 427
  PRC, 196
  public expenditure, 243
health care, 261
heart failure, 260
heart valve defects, 250
heating costs, 381, 949(n59)
heavy asphalt, 466

Heavy Electrical, 176
heavy engineering, 176
Heavy Truck
  sales, profits, employees, output (1998), 542
Heavy Vehicle Group (HVG), 74, 77, 93, 102,
    136
heavy walls, 379, 948(n52)
Hebei (province), 80
  agricultural science park, 321
  China Unicom joint venture activity, 810
  coal production and consumption (1996), 719
  depth of coal mines, 737
  economic development zone, 315
  new power station, 352
  pharmaceuticals, 307
  transport costs (coal), 720
Hebei Power Company, 110
Hebei Provincial Government, 137, 653, 742
Hebei Provincial Investment Company (HPIC),
    359
Hefei (Anhui Province), 391
Heffernan, Paul, 940(n3)
Heilongjiang
  China Unicom joint venture activity, 810
  coal production and consumption (1996), 719
  cost structure (TVE coal-mine, 1995), 722
  loss-makers, 730
  petrol stations, 470
Heilongjiang Anling Forestry Group, 135
Heilongjiang Forest Industry Group, 135
Heilongjiang Passenger Car Works, 564
Heilongjiang Province: provincial government,
    364, 371
Heineken: competitive advantage, 35
Heinz, H.J., 35
helicopter and aircraft companies, 156
helicopters
  AH-64D (USA), 157
  CH-47D (USA), 157
  EH-101 (Anglo-Italian), 157
  Kiowa Warrior, 164
  Mi-17, 192
  Ka-28, 192
  Shmel, 192
Henan [mobile phone company], 931
Henan (province), 353, 686, 719, 799
Henan Electric Power Company, 110
Hengyang (Hunan Province), 553
herbicides, 265
Hero Honda (joint venture), 873
Hewlett-Packard (USA), 764, 772, 794
Hiep Phuoc Plant, 387
high-income countries, *see* advanced economies
high-technology plant equipment, 129
high-technology sector
  barriers to entry (1998), 64
  PRC, 97
  Singapore, 23
  South Korea, 22
  Taiwan, 20

high-technology sector – *continued*
  US dominance, 48, 51
  see also information technology
high blood pressure, 261, 267, 268
highways (PRC network), 541, 551, 566
Hikino, T., *see* Chandler, A.
Hino (affiliate of Toyota), 547
Hitachi, 19, 360, 377, 378, 786
  global top hundred company, 850
  joint venture with Dongfang, 390
  profits (1998), 794
  reduction of workforce (1999), 56
  research and development (1998), 768, 794
  sale of unprofitable businesses, 56
  turnover (1998), 794
HK, *see* Hong Kong (pre-7.1997)
HKM, 602n
HKSAR, *see* Hong Kong Special
  Administrative Region (7.1997–)
HLA, *see* Hong Leong Asia (HLA) Holdings
  (Singapore)
Ho Xi (Guangdong merchant), 900
Hoechst, 59, 248, 256, 261, 262, 861
  see also Aventis
Hoechst Marion Roussel (HMR), 255, 262
Hoesch (German steel-maker), 611
holding companies
  AVIC (1996–), 186
  PRC, 68, 138
  state, 109
  Sinopec, 448–9
Holiday Inn (hotel group), 313
Holliday, Chad (Du Pont), 265
Holschuh, Lernhard, 588
Holset (company), 530
home shopping, 782
Honda, 19
  alliance with Rover (UK), 513
  co-operation with Ford and GM, 513
  engine supply, 513
  foreign assets, sales, employment (1997), 509
  fuel-cell technology, 513
  global top hundred company, 850
  interests in India, 508
  interests in Mercosur, 508
  interests in Thailand, 508
  interests in Turkey, 508
  joint venture in India (Hero Honda), 873
  output, turnover, profit, R&D (1998), 533
  share of foreign production (1989–94), 510
  wholly-owned subsidiary in India, 873
Honeywell, 146–7, 179, 181, 205, 239
Hong Kong (HK; pre-7.1997), 123, 565
  advertising by Sanjiu, 289
  big business, 23
  ceded to UK (1842), 902
  coal imports from PRC (1997), 718
  'conforms to principle of comparative
    advantage', 4–5
  consumption of construction steels, 676

degree of state intervention, 19
demand for pharmaceuticals (per capita
  1996), 277
flotation of PRC oil groups, 453, 471, 490
influence on PRC advertising, 298
joint venture (printing) in PRC, 311
location, 23
neo-classical view, 23
'politically-trusted companies', 351
power generation, 351
proximity, advantage to Shenzhen SEZ, 321
Sanjiu processing factory, 300, 308
Shenzhen's integration with, 942(n26)
Shougang's operations, 643
state expenditure on education, health,
  housing, 19
stock market (1996), 282
see also Hong Kong Special Administrative
  Region (7.1997–)
Hong Kong Democratic Party, 875
Hong Kong Special Administrative Region
  (HKSAR, 7.1997–), 691
  advocates of PRC membership of WTO
    (political reasons), 875
  bankrupt red chip companies, 849
  BOC investment banking arm, 831
  coal imports from PRC (1997), 718
  companies in *FT* 500 (1998), 47n
  GNP (1998), 932
  impending (1999) flotation of New CNPC
    and New Sinopec, 479
  internet, 780–1, 805
  IT companies (2000), 764–5
  'red chip' companies, 873
  stock market capitalization (1998), 932
  stock market collapse, 746
  taken over by PRC (1997–), 275
  telecommunications companies, 779
  see also Hong Kong (pre-7.1997)
Hong Kong Telecom (HKT), 784, 861, 862
Hong Kong Zhonglian Power Materials
  Company, 946(n37)
Hong Leong Asia (HLA) Holdings (Singapore),
  573, 575, 577, 581, 582–3, 951(n23)
  'appears to have real control over Yuchai',
    575–6
  appoints six of eleven directors of CYI, 575
  appreciation of Wang Jianming, 577
  interests, 573
  joint ventures, 573–4, 586
  owns 53% of Diesel [Engine] Machinery
    Limited (DML), 574
  'Special Share' in CYI, 575
Hong Qipeng, 947(n41)
Hongda Shipping Company (HK), 676
Hongdou Group (Red Bean Group), 133
Hongkong and Shanghai Banking Corporation
  (HSBC, UK), 815, 816, 945(n19)
  conversion to FHC (USA), 819
  global top five bank, [822], 958(n8)

Hongkong and Shanghai Banking Corporation
    (HSBC, UK) – *continued*
  joint venture (online) with Merrill Lynch,
    818, 822
  shareholder in HPEC Limited, 946(n31)
Hongkong Shanghai Hotels Group, 274
Hoogovens: merger with British Steel (1999), 610
  see also Corus
Hopewell Holdings (HK), 351
horizontal economic linkages, 136
horizontal integration (PRC), 72
horns, 950(n9)
hospitals, 53, 282, 381, 949(n59)
hotels, 126, 311–14, 316–17, 573, 921
Hou Dejian (Taiwanese film star), 298
household appliances, 59, 198
housing, 229, 304, 306, 314, 315, 321,
    954(n40)
  construction industry (PRC), 844
  Daqing, 443
  employee-purchase, 381
  HPEC, 381
  management-level (Shougang), 651, 953(n30)
  PRC, 921
  rents, 381
  Shougang, 668, 688
  Yuchai, 580
HPE, *see* Harbin Power Station Engineering
    Company
HPEC, *see* Harbin Power Equipment Company
HPEGC, *see* Harbin Power Engineering Group
    Company
HPI, *see* Huaneng Power International Inc.
HPIC, *see* Hebei Provincial Investment
    Company
HR Vet (animal health), 263
HSBC, *see* Hongkong and Shanghai Banking
    Corporation
HSE, 950(n9)
Hsinchu Science Park (Taiwan), 20
Hu Jianqing, 946(n40)
Hua Xia: bank owned by Shougang Group, 647,
    650
Huabei (pharmaceuticals)
  missed merger opportunity, 861
  plant at Shijiazhuang, 283, 941(n10)
Huaibei Mining Bureau, Anhui (coal producer),
    720
Huaneng Group, 75, 81, 109
Huaneng (China Power) Power Corporation
    (1985–), 109, 349–50, 748
  assets, 740
  capacity, 740
  'electricity-generation company', 741
  joined China Huaneng Group (1988), 350
  origins of Shenhua Project, 740
    (responsibility lost, 741)
  projects, 740
  sets up two new subsidiaries, HPI and SHP
    (1994), 350

  shareholder in Shandong Huaneng Power
    Development Company Limited, 350
  subsidiary of MOEP, 350
  subsumed into China Huaneng Group (1988),
    740
  takes over Clean Coal Corporation (1988),
    740
  tasks, 350
Huaneng Power International Inc. (HPI 1994–),
    96, 344, 931
  floated on an international stock market, 349,
    350
  subsidiary of Huaneng Power Corporation,
    350
  see also Shandong Huaneng Power
    Development Company Limited (SHP
    1994–2000)
Huanghua Port, 733, [890]
  capacity, 740
  further construction, 740, 742
  investment, 742
  map, 732–3
  newly-constructed, 739, 740
  rail links, 738–9
Huawei
  leading manufacturer of networking
    equipment (PRC), 795
  missed merger opportunity, 862
  non-SOE national champion (PRC), 862
  profits (1998), 794
  research and development expenditure
    (1998), 794
  turnover (1998), 794
Huayi Group (Shanghai 1996–), 118, 456
Huayin County (Shanxi Province), 655
Hubei (province), 546, 555, 564
Hubei Automobile Body Works
  'third layer' enterprise (Dongfeng), 564
Hubei Electric Power Company, 110
Hubei Special Vehicle Company, 542, 555
Hubei University, 302
Hughes (defence electronics business), 147, 164
Huizhou ethylene and petrochemicals complex,
    454, 490
Hull, 422
human resources, 9, 762, 775, 779
  appropriation of best, 42
  Hong Kong and Singapore, 19
  oil sector, 427
human rights, 501, 875, 895
  abuses, 194
  economic well-being, 915
Hunan (province), 124, 352, 357, 553, 810
Hunan Dongli Group, 560
Hunan Electric Power Company, 110
Hunan Engine Plant, 562
Hungary, 909
Huo Shuoping, 311–14
Hutchison Whampoa (HKSAR), 677, 765,
    956(n61)

Huttl, Adolf (Siemens), 337
hydraulic equipment, 198
Hydro (oil company, Norway), 499
hydro-electric power
  dam construction, 85
  electricity generation (fuel type, 1990–2010), 696
  electricity generation (PRC), 715
  fuel for electricity generation, 698
  fuel for electricity generation (1996), 698
  HPEC output (1959–98), 374
  facilities, 127
  plant, 111
  plant capacity (1980–2010), 335
  PRC, 354, 356–7, 391
  reserves (PRC 1997), 716
  reserves *per capita* (PRC), 715
  share of PRC's energy requirements (1980–96), 354
  share in primary energy consumption (1996), 697
  share of world primary energy consumption (1987–97), 402
hydro-electric power generation equipment
  Alstom, 338
  HEC, 368, 377
  HPEC, 377, 392
  'Kaplan-type', 378
  market share worldwide (1993–8), 337
  turbines, 378
hydrogen filling station, 427
Hymer, S., [1–]2, 27
hypertension, 260, 268
Hyundai Group (South Korea), 54, 176, 214, 221
  acquisitions, 53
  aspirations, 506
  diversification (1938–87), 53
  interests in India, Turkey, 508
  plans for overseas plants, 506
  restructuring, 54
  semiconductor manufacturing, 54
  stake owned by Mitsubishi, 515
  '13th largest auto producer' (1994), 505–6
  unable to rescue Daewoo (1999), 517
  vehicle exports (1986), 505

Iberia (airline), 149
IBM (International Business Machines), 772–3, 786
  acquisitions (1999), 772
  hardware revenues, 772
  joint ventures in PRC, 106
  little to fear from PRC competition (post-WTO accession), 863
  market capitalization (2000), 764, 772
  outsourcing, 772
  profits (1998), 794; (1999), 772
  research and development expenditure (1998), 768, 794; (1999), 772

sales revenue, 764, 788
  share of PRC market (1998), 794
  software, 775
  software revenues, 772
  turnover (1998), 794
ICBC, *see* Industrial and Commercial Bank of China
Idemitsu Kosan: global top hundred company, 850
ignition coils (automobile component), 547, 950(n9)
Ikea, 576
ILVA LP, 602n
Ilyushin, 179
imperfect competition, 13
Imperial Chemical Industries (ICI)
  de-merger of Zeneca (1993), 59, 264
  largest employer of chemical engineers (UK), 264, 941(n2)
  'life sciences', 261
imperialism, vii, 907
import-export corporations, 129
import-substitution
  Brazil, 20, 180
  South Korea, 22
  Taiwan, 20, 22
import licences
  WTO rules (implementation by PRC), 865, 866, 867–8
impotence, 247
independent power producers (IPPs), 337, 350–2
India, 145, 506
  BP-Solarex manufacturing facilities, 426
  brain drain (software sector), 789
  car production (comparative), 534
  caution *re* TRIPs, 868
  coal output (1980–95), 699
  'copies Western medicines', 244
  costs per ton of steel, 620–1
  'deluge' of foreign vehicle investment, 508
  economic growth (1980–98), 851
  energy, 340, 428, 914, 943(n9)
  enforcement of WTO rules, 870, 919
  exports, 871
  ethylene crackers, 421
  free trade (early nineteenth century), 5
  human capital, 762
  informal sector, 958(n8)
  internet hosts per 1,000 people (1997), 789
  'inward-looking', 24
  iron ore costs, 618, 619
  IT development (1997), 789
  labour cost per ton of coal, 620
  liberalization, 508, 872–3
  'licence Raj', 873
  mass media market, 781
  'most successful developing country' (software), 787–8, 797 (shortcomings, 788)
  number of companies in *FT* 500 (1998), 47n

India – *continued*
  number of companies in *Fortune* 500 (1998),
    47n
  patent laws, 244
  per capita energy use (1994), 341
  personal computers per 1,000 people (1997),
    789
  pharmaceutical sector, 270
  pharmaceuticals market (1995), 277
  production and sales of automobiles (1998),
    508
  productivity (coal), 620
  protectionism, 949(n67)
  share of world manufacturing output
    (1750–1998), 900
  Siemens' plants, 338
  software exports, 762, 787–8, 797
  steel output (1974–96), 593
  tariffs on steel products (1997), 619
  telecommunications development (1997), 789
  telephone main lines per 1,000 people
    (1997), 789
  textile industry, 15
  TNCs, 21, 23
  top ten steel-producing country (1991–8),
    616
  TV sets per 1,000 people (1997), 789
  value of English-language education, 787
  wage costs (steel industry, 1997), 620
  war, 5
  wireless telephones per 1,000 people (1997),
    789
individualism, 1
Indonesia, 145
  arms deliveries (1987–98), 151
  coal, 710
  coal exports, 706
  difficulty of framing industrial policy, 60
  energy consumption *per capita*, 428
  energy, 340, 943(n8–9)
  ethylene crackers, 421
  'fundamental economic situation', 834
  Ispat's interests (steel), 614
  oil producer, 413
  per capita energy use (1994), 341
  pharmaceuticals market (1995), 277
  political turmoil, 413
  Posco plant, 609
  PRC and South Korean investment (coal
    industry), 718
  steel, 600, 951(n3)
  tariffs on steel products (1997), 619
  TNCs based (1999) in, 21. 23
industrial
  associations, 448
  boilers (PRC), 716
  co-finance (aerospace), 174–5
  development (aerospace), 174–5
  gas turbines (AVIC), 198
  policy, 3, 60, 83–6, 240

  reform, 2
  sector (Deng era), 912
  sector (transition literature), 2–3
  structure, 5–6
  structure (Taiwan), 21
Industrial and Commercial Bank of China
    (ICBC), 96–7, 826, 939(n13)
  key indicators, 1999 (global-leaders
    comparison), 827
  productivity, 830–1
  scale (Citigroup comparison), 826
  zero-interest-rate loans to PRC coal industry,
    731
industrial concentration, 14, 37–9, 50, 61
  aerospace, 141, 142, 148, 152–73, 240
  automobiles, 506–7, 514–18, 532–6
  banking, 815, 820–1
  coal, 707–12
  components (vehicles), 519–29, 535–6,
    543–6
  financial services, 817, 819–24
  global business revolution, 37–8
  information technology, 762, 768, 769–70,
    793, 810
  internet, 779
  lorry-makers, 518, 534
  pharmaceuticals, 266, 286
  power generation equipment, 327–8, 335–9,
    397–8
  PRC, 71, 107, 939(n14)
  steel, 605, 608–17
  see also global business revolution; mergers;
    trial business groups
Industrial and Investment Trusts (ITICs), PRC,
    873
'industrial planning', 37, 42
Industrial Revolution, 1, 15, 898
industrialization
  central importance of steel, 588
  need for protection, 19–20
  western countries, 906–7
industry, 27
  China (pre-1949), 899–902, 906
  PRC (1980–97), 913
infant mortality, 906, 907, 914, 915
infants (PRC), 277
inflation, 189
information technology (IT) (global)
  'architecture', 775
  companies, 764–5
  competitive advantage, 36
  cost savings (oil sector), 422
  developing countries, 787
  development (1997), 789
  driver of big business revolution, 32
  expenditure, 36
  hardware, 35, 49, 787, 929
  human resources, 775
  impact on financial services, 816, 818–19,
    830, 832, 834, 836

information technology (IT) (global) – *continued*
  incorporation into vehicle components
    systems, 523
  India, 23, 787
  mentioned, 8, 61, 246, 501, 763–7
  monitoring of performance within firms, 45
  oligopoly, 40
  outsourcing, 146
  product specification, 43
  research and development, 49, 510, 766
  revolution, 48, 492, 761, 925
  scarcity of high-quality human resources, 929
  services, 775–90
  state-of-the-art, 42
  super-normal profits, 768
  systems integration (supplier network), 543
  US dominance, 48
  use in oil sector, 411–12, 425, 427
  use in outsourcing (auto industry), 511
  used to monitor product performance, 43
  WTO adjustment process (PRC), 921–3
  see also hardware; software; Third
    Technological Revolution
information technology (PRC), 115, 789,
    790–811, 847, 924
  battle for PRC market, 790–811
  bureaucratic struggle, 800–1
  China-China-Foreign (CCF) arrangement,
    792, 799, 809–10
  competitive capability, 793–7
  conclusion, 810–11
  encirclement, 803–6
  hardware, 794–7
  impact on economy, 917–18, 925
  joint ventures, 806–10
  leading IT hardware firms (1998), 794
  networking equipment, 795
  personal computers, 794
  political considerations, 792–3
  problems, 800–10
  set-top boxes, 796–7
  Shougang, 687–8
  software, 797
  telecommunication services, 797–800
  US exports to PRC (1990–8), 790
  where is the firm?, 801–3
  wireless hardware, 795–6
  'wolf at the door', 793
  WTO Agreement (PRC-USA), 790–3
Infosys (IT firm, India), 23
infra-red sensors, 148
infrastructure (PRC), 89, 348, 921, 922
ING, 815, 817, 826, 835, 958(n9)
Initial Public Offerings (IPO), 160
  Aérospatiale-Matra (1999), 160
  China.com (HKSAR), 781
  China Unicom (6.2000), 801, 931
  CNOOC (withdrawn 10.1999), 884
  CTHK, 799, 801
  New CNPC, 474

oil sector (PRC), 500
PetroChina (4.2000), 489, 884
Inland Steel (Indiana, USA), 613, 614, 615,
    952(n13)
inland waterways, 124
Inner Mongolia (China/PRC)
  coal-mining region, 717, 723
  coal production and consumption (1996), 719
  cost structure (TVE coal-mine, 1995), 722
  depth of coal mines, 737
  Five Western District mines, 749, 753–6
  Japanese demands (1915), 904
  loss-makers, 730
  mentioned, 687
  open-cast potentialities, 718
  petrol stations, 470
  pithead price of coal, 723
  problem of outward transport of coal, 739
  see also Shenfu Dongsheng Coalfield
Inner Mongolia Cashmere Group, 113
Inner Mongolia Electricity Company, 361n
Inner Mongolia Forest Industry Group, 135
Inner Mongolia Power Company, 110
innovation, 12, 13
institutional investors, 32, 37, 61, 414
institutions (international investors in PRC),
    349
insurance, 37, 819, 825–6, 926
  global market share, 37
  PRC, 926
  PRC-US Agreement (11.1999), 825–6
  USA, 817
insurance companies, 816–17, 824, 830
  market share (implications of PRC WTO-
    entry), 832, 958(n14)
  productivity gap (PRC v global leaders), 831
insurance density, 832, 958(n13)
Insurance Law (PRC 1995), 834
integrated circuits (IC), 687
Intel (USA)
  internet bandwidth, 805
  joint venture in PRC, 106
  market capitalization (2000), 764
  Pentium III microprocessor (10.1999–),
    768–9
  sales revenue (2000), 764
intellectual property, 243–4, 270, 319, 785, 811,
    866, 868, 873
Inter-Continental Ballistic Missiles (ICBM),
    195
interest rates, 37, 814
internal finance companies, 76, 87, 92–3, 98–9
international
  competition (PRC attempts to meet challenge
    of), 70
  competitiveness, 17
  competition, 14–15, 16
  economy, 4
  market place, 91
  market share, 17

international – *continued*
  markets, 89, 90
  relations, 46, 463
  trade, 4, 5, 12, 13, 29, 31
International Aero Engines, 172
International Combustion (Rolls Royce),
    943(n7)
international equities bookrunners, 823
International Institute for Strategic Studies, 150
International Iron and Steel Institute, 588
International Lease Finance Corporation, 213
International Monetary Fund (IMF), 2, 608, 909
  East Asian resentment, 926–7
International Organization of Securities
    Commissions (IOSCO), 833
internet, 511, 523, 769, 773, 773–4, 775–6, 778,
    779–84, 834–5, 917
  bandwidth, 805
  Chinese language, 780
  competitive advantage, 769, 775
  'democratic equalizer', 793
  encryption, 805
  financial services, 818
  global procurement network (auto
    components), 856
  industrial consolidation, 779
  penetration (developing countries), 788
  PRC, 790, 791, 795, 796–7, 798, 799, 805–6,
    922
  race into Asia, 780–1
  Shanghai Cable, 808
  users (PRC), 790, 798, 805
'Internet Christmas' (USA 1999), 779–80
internet companies, 786–7
internet hosts per 1,000 people (global 1997),
    789
  definition, 789n
'internet opium', 924–5
  pornography, sports, cartoons, 925
Internet Protocol (IP) traffic, 808
Internet Protocol Infrastructure, 771
internet switching equipment, 774
Interpublic, 781
Intertechnique (France), 181
intranet: financial services, 818
investment, 61
  CNPC, 440
  funds, 13, 88, 98
  Japan, 17
  Japanese, 56
  mining, 707
  New CNPC, 471
  New Sinopec, 471
  oil sector (PRC), 436, 453, 471
  patent medicines, 244
  power generation equipment, 329
  PRC (Deng era), 912
  PRC, 77, 90, 348
  Sinopec, 465
  South Korea, 22

technical progress (aerospace), 142–3
  see also foreign direct investment
IPO, *see* Initial Public Offerings
Iran
  arms purchases, 193
  Daewoo operations, 506
  export market for HPEC, 388
  foreign investment (oil sector), 413
  nationalization of oil assets (1951), 408, 411
  oil reserves and production (1997), 403
  protectionism, 949(n67)
  proven oil reserves, 404
Iraq
  contracts with international consortia, 413
  nationalization of oil and gas (1972), 408,
    411
  oil reserves and production (1997), 403
  proven oil reserves, 404
Ireland: Ispat, 600, 614
iron: average price (PRC 1980–93), 655
iron ore, 596, 598, 618, 640, 653, 675, 847,
    953(n33)
  bulk cargo, 705
  PRC, 618–19, 675, 956(n57)
  PRC import requirements, 675
  PRC's foreign investments, 956(n57)
  rail transport (Australia), 708, 739–40
  Rio Tinto, 708
iron and steel
  eight trial groups (PRC), 77
  industrial concentration, 114
  national team (PRC), 77, 84, 114–16
Ispat International, 598, 600, 613, 670
  acquisitions, 613–15
  annual output, 600, 951(n3)
  based in London, 598, 889
  cost-cutting, 614
  'fastest growing international steel company',
    600, 951(n3)
  floated in NY and Amsterdam (1997), 614
  global steel corporation, 613–15
  interests in Indonesia, 614, 615, 951(n3)
  interests in Kazakhstan, 614, 951(n3)
  mini-mills, 614
  privately-owned companies in Kazakhstan
    and Indonesia, 951(n3)
  purchase of Sicartsa complex (Mexico), 614
  takeover of Inland Steel (1998), 613, 614
Ispat Mexicana, 614, 951(n2)
ISPs (Internet Service Providers), 801, 808
Israel, 191, 192–3, 218, 219, 773, 940(n9)
Isuzu, 506, 513, 518
IT, *see* information technology
Italy
  air force, 157, 158
  auto industry, 504
  bank restructuring (1980–97), 820
  cross-border mergers, 853
  Eurofighter, 158–9
  global business revolution (1990s), 58

Italy – *continued*
  industrial concentration (auto industry), 507
  industrial concentration (steel), 605
  IT companies (2000), 764–5
  number of auto manufacturers (1920), 506
  oil and petrochemicals, 407–8
  power equipment (exports to PRC), 948(n51)
  primary energy consumption, 401
  purchase of missiles from USA, 158
  steel output (1974–96), 593
  top ten steel-producing country (1991–8),
      616
  welding machines (exports to PRC),
      948(n52)
Itochu Corporation (Japan), 455, 810
ITT, 545
ITT Automotive Pacific, 545
ITT Electrical Systems, 526
Iveco (Fiat), 103, 518
IWKA (Germany) injector-seamer, 303
Izvestiya, 191

J.C. Penny (department store, USA), 311
J.P. Morgan (US bank), 813, 817, 818, 819
  conversion to FHC, 819
  key indicators, 1998 (PRC comparison), 829,
      829n
  merger with Chase Manhattan, 813, 822
  top five firm (M&A Advisers, 2000), 823
J&A Securities (Shenzhen), 276
JAA, *see* Joint Aviation Authority
Jacobs Ranch coal-mine (USA), 710
Jaguar (Ford), 515, 533
Janelli, R., 669–70
Jannsen (Belgian pharmaceutical company)
  joint venture in Xian, 282–3
Japan
  acquisitions by foreign corporations, 57
  aerospace, 175, 176–8, 845, 877
  Air Force, 193
  anti-trust legislation, 16–17
  arms deliveries (1987–98), 151
  'ASEAN plus three' forum, 927–8
  attitude to competition, 669
  automobiles, 505, 506, 507, 508, 510–11,
      515, 538, 887, 950(n2)
  bank restructuring (1980–97), 820
  Big Bang (1998), 815
  business organization, 510
  business strategy, 18
  coal, 119, 620, 718
  'competitive edge' companies (1997–8), 50
  competitiveness problems, 55
  corporations (by value of sales, 1998), 56
  cross-ownership, 17
  currency appreciation (1980s), 608
  demand for pharmaceuticals (per capita), 277
  difficulties (1990s), 18–19
  dwarfing of companies, 55–6
  economic effects of WW2, 37

electric furnace (steel industry), 596
employment practices, 18
energy, 428, 914
enforcement of WTO rules, 919
enterprise groups, 897–8
environmentally-friendly power stations, 705
ethylene (1989–96), 451
European protectionism, 504
example for PRC, 71, 462
example for rest of world, 24
export-oriented firms, 54
exporter of oil to PRC (1995–7), 434
FDI (in USA), 601
'fierce domestic competition', 18
foreign-owned firms (1986–95), 31
global business revolution, 54–8
globally-competitive companies (created
      1950s-70s), 850
GMP (pharmaceuticals), [301–]302
government support for auto industry, 505,
      510
industrial concentration, 506, 605
'insurance density', 832
internet, 780–1
investment rates, 18
iron ore costs (1997), 619
IT companies (2000), 764–5
lessons for PRC (aerospace), 236–7
market capitalization, 51, 56
military metaphor (in management style),
      669
miscellaneous, xxiv, 68, 145, 311, 676, 854
multinational corporations, 27
national output (PPP dollars, 1998), 914
oil sector, 421
oligopoly, 17, 86, 939(n26)
outflow of FDI, 49
pharmaceuticals market (1995), 277
plants, 952(n13)
plastics, 451
poverty (PRC comparison), 852
PRC comparison, 70, 99
primary energy consumption, 402, 696, 697
protectionism (auto industry), 505, 510
reduction of workforce (1999), 56
research and development, 48, 95
role of government, 54
royalty and licensing fees (paid), 785
savings, 18
sectors (financial services), 830
share of world manufacturing output
      (1750–1998), 900
share in *Fortune* Global 500 (1997), 50, 60
state-orchestrated mergers (1930s), 858
steel, 593, 594, 596, 597, 600, 601, 602–4,
      605, 606, 616, 620–1, 623, 641, 677,
      889, 951(n4), 952(n13), 956(n59)
structure of output (1992), 700
sub-contractors (civil aviation), 218, 219, 220
synthetic fibres, 451

Japan – *continued*
  third generation handsets, 775
  urbanization (PRC comparison), 852
  US dominance (financial services), 824
  US military presence, 193
  use of profits, 18
  vehicle output, 505
  wars with China, 903–4, 905
  welding machines (exports to PRC),
    948(n52)
Japan: Ministry of International Trade and
    Industry (MITI), 16, 17, 57, 505, 863,
    950(n1), 956(n59)
  creation of New Japan Steel (1970), 603
  Renault takeover of Nissan, 516
Japan Airlines: reduction of workforce (1999),
    56
Japan Leasing, 57
Japan Steel (1934–), 602–3, 858
Java (programming language), 776
jewellery, 130
Jialing Motorbikes, 103
jian bing (government administrative merger),
    314
Jiang, Dr Simon, xxvi
Jiang Qiangui, [70], 939(n12)
Jiang Zemin, President (b 1926), 70–1, 96, 781,
    898, 935
  chairman of the CMC, 276
  speech to military leaders (22.7.1998), 275,
    276–7
Jiangnan, 901
Jiangnan group, 938(n5)
Jiangsu, 24, 105, 109
  coal production and consumption (1996),
    719, 720
  geographical location of national team
    members, 82, 83
  'grasping the large', 83
  nuclear power plant (under construction,
    1997–), 945(n23)
  power station construction (CEPA letters of
    intent), 353
  transport costs (coal), 720
  wireless telecommunications, 799
Jiangsu Electric Power Company, 110
Jiangsu Mobile Phone Company, 931
Jiangsu Provincial Government, 466
Jiangxi (province)
  coal production and consumption (1996), 719
  execution of former deputy governor, 874
  pharmaceuticals, 307
  nuclear power (planned), 357
Jiangxi Electric Power Company, 110
Jiangyang Special Steel Company, 946(n37)
Jianlibao: non-SOE national champion (PRC),
    862
Jianwei: salt, 901
Jiaxiang (Zhejiang Province), 390
Jiefang (Liberation), 74, 136

jiegu ('sacked'), 382
jihua danlie ('plan list'), 370
Jilin, 83, 109, 470, 730, 810
Jilin Chemical Fibre Group, 80
Jilin Province Development Group, 135
Jilin Senlin Group, 134
Jinan (manufacturer of small trucks), 578
Jinan (Shandong): China Unicom joint venture
    activity, 810
Jinan Iron and Steel Group Company, 635
Jincheng: Shanghai subsidiary of AVIC, 198,
    940(n12)
Jincheng Mining Bureau, Shanxi, 720, 736, 737
Jingdezhen, 900
jingyingzhi (managers), 295
Jini (intelligent networking technology), 776
Jining coal field (Shandong), 119
Jining Plant (power generation), 944(n17)
Jinling Petrochemicals, 117
Jinling Petrochemical company (Nanjing), 466
jinrong sanjiao zhai ('financial triangular
    debt'), 831
Jinzhou Petrochemical Corporation, 469
jituan gongsi ('mother' company), 475, 476,
    478–9
jituanhua (transformation) process, 77
Jiuquan Iron and Steel Company, 635
Jiuxin pharmaceutical plant, 306
Jiuxing Printing and Packaging (Sanjiu), 311
Jixi (Heilongjiang): loss-making coal mines,
    730–1
Johansson, Leif, 515, 520
Johnson Controls (USA), 522, 524, 536
Johnson & Johnson
  joint ventures in PRC, 282
  research and development expenditure
    (1994–7), 248
Joint Aviation Authority (JAA, 'Europe'), 205
joint stock companies, 10
Joint Strike Fighter (JSF) (USA), 144, 152, 153,
    157, 158, 159, 163, 164
joint ventures (general), 103, 105, 106, 108,
    109, 118, 122, 132, 178, 222, 273, 841,
    874
  aero-engines, 216–17
  auto components, 886
  auto industry (Japan 1950s), 505
  auto industry (PRC), 539–40, 541
  buses, 210
  coal, 710, 729
  components sector (PRC), 544, 546–8, 559
  domestic content requirements, 328, 347
  Eastern Europe (automobile industry),
    [508–]509
  engine manufacture (PRC), 544, 547–8,
    950(n8)
  European aerospace, 162, 170, 171, 173
  insurance sector (PRC), 825–6
  India, 508, 872–3
  machine tool plants, 379, 948(n53)

joint ventures (general) – *continued*
  means of technology transfer, 842
  means of access to PRC market, 389–90
  mobile telephone companies, 791
  oil and petrochemicals, 883
  oil sector, 453–4, 461, 471, 496, 497
  people's car (in negotiation), 316
  pharmaceutical sector, 246
  pharmaceuticals, 282, 297, 300, 304, 320
  power equipment industry (PRC), 347, 358,
    362, 363, 881, 882
  PRC, 398, 852
  PRC aviation industry, 213–17 (significance,
    217–21, 940:n15)
  PRC power equipment companies and
    multinational corporations, 334, 391
  rarity (mining sector), 750
  reduced incentive to establish, 872–3
  Sino-foreign, 197, 665, 687, 746, 854, 860,
    881
  Sino-foreign (electricity generation), 746
  telecommunications sector (PRC), 806–10
    (advantages, 809–10)
  traditional Chinese medicines, 310
  tyres, 526, 528
  Vitamin C, 296
  WTO rules, 884
joint ventures (specific)
  ABB and PRC concerns, 362, 371
  Airbus-AVIC, 211–12, 940(n14)
  Chevron-Texaco (= Caltex), 417
  China Huitong and Hongkong Shanghai
    Hotels Group, 274
  Dongfang and GE (Canada), 390
  Dongfang and Hitachi, 390
  Dongfeng and Citroën, 102
  Du Pont and Merck, 256, 265
  HSBC and Merrill Lynch (online), 818, 822
  Lucent (in PRC), 795
  merger of ABB and GEC-Alsthom (1999),
    338
  MSDW (in PRC), 835
  Phoenix (News Corporation and Liu
    Changle), 784
  Shenhua Railway Company, 742
  Sinopec, 465
  SNECMA and GE, 173
  Star TV and Hong Kong Telecom (HKT),
    784
  US Steel and Kobe Steel, 601
  US Steel and Posco, 601
  Vivendi and Vodafone, 784
  XAC-Volvo, 201–2
  Yahoo! and Softbank, 780
Jones and Laughlin (US steel-maker), 611
Jordan, Michael (chairman, Westinghouse), 358
jun zhuan min (military into civilian) policy,
  197
'just-in-time' delivery, 510, 521, 524, 538
juste retour principle, 167, 168

JV, *see* joint ventures

Kader Investment Group, 956(n60)
Kaifeng Combine Harvester Plant, 655
Kaifeng Heavy Machinery Company, 686
Kailuan Mining Bureau, Hebei
  average mining depth, 737
  output, reserves, mine depths (1996), 736
  quality of coal, 737
  transport costs (1997), 720
Kaiser Steel (California), 662, 686, 888–9
kanban ('just-in-time') inventories (Japan), 510
Kanematsu (Japan): power generation company,
  351
Kang Dian, Mr, xxvi
Kaoru Yosano (MITI), 516
Karaganov, Sergei, 839
Karamay oilfield (Jungar Basin, Xinjiang), 438
Kawasaki (Japanese steel-maker), 603, 679
  crude steel output (1996–7), 602
  investment in Armco Steel, 608
  remuneration and labour productivity (1995),
    641
Kawasaki Heavy Industries, 177
Kazakhstan, 441, 600, 614, 951(n3)
Keidanren, 56
Keiner (car components manufacturer), 524
keiretsu (industrial groups), 17, 54, 516
  Boeing, 145
  reform (1999), 56–8
Kellogg: competitive advantage, 35
Kelong (TVE), 223
Kennecott Energy (USA), 710
Kenworth Truck Company, 518
Kerr McGee (USA), 710
Kia Motors (South Korea), 505, 506, 508, 517
Kilian (Germany) RX55AM tablet-expresser,
  303
Kim Dae Jung, President (South Korea), 718
King (UK) plastic container packing machine,
  303
Kingsun (PRC software company), 107
Kleinwort Benson: taken over by Dresdner,
  958(n9)
KLM (Netherlands), 149
Kloekner Werke (Germany), 612
KMT, *see* Kuomintang
Kobe Steel: joint venture with US Steel, 601
Kodak, 132
Kombinat (East German 'combine'), 363
konggu gongsi
  'controlling company', 478
  'holding company', 345
kongzhi gufen (controlling share ownership
  stake), 314
Konka (PRC), 97, 796
Koolyanobing [iron-ore] Mine (WA), 956(n57)
Korea, Republic of ('South Korea')
  aerospace, 176, 877
  Air Force, 193

Korea, Republic of ('South Korea') – *continued*
  arms deliveries (1987–98), 151
  'ASEAN plus three' forum, 927–8
  automobiles, 505–6, 508, 533, 887
  catch-up, 21–3, 236, 533
  coal imports from PRC (1997), 718
  'conform to principle of comparative
      advantage', 4–5
  degree of state intervention, 19, 21
  economies of scale, 22
  energy, 340, 943(n8–9)
  energy consumption *per capita*, 428
  enterprise groups, 898
  environmentally-friendly advanced power
      stations, 705
  example for PRC, 462
  exports, 22
  'fundamental economic situation', 834
  heavy industry, 19, 22
  industrial concentration, 22–3
  internet, 780
  iron ore costs (1997), 619
  IT sector, 770
  Japanese control *de facto* (1895–1945), 903
  lessons drawn by PRC from, 71, 72, 99
  market for steel in South-East Asia, 677
  mentioned, 68, 145, 854
  military metaphor (in management style),
      669
  mini-mills (steel), 599
  number of companies in *Fortune* 500 (1998),
      47n
  number of companies in *FT* 500 (1998), 47n
  oligopoly, 22, 86, 939(n26)
  potential car exports to PRC, 872
  poverty (PRC comparison), 852
  PRC comparison, 70
  production of ethylene (1989–96), 451
  production of plastics (1989–96), 451
  production of synthetic fibre (1989–96), 451
  proposed joint venture with AVIC, 940(n14)
  protection, 19
  securities, 54
  share in *Fortune* Global 500 (1997), 50
  state banks, 53
  steel, 593, 594, 596, 597, 600, 606, 616, 619,
      620, 623, 641, 889
  sub-contractors (civil aviation), 218, 219
  TNCs, 21, 23
  urbanization (PRC comparison), 852
  US military presence, 193
Korea Development Bank, 952(n9)
Korea Telecom: CCF partner of China Unicom,
    810
Koromo ('Toyota City', Japan), 510
Kosovo, 163, 191, 194, 895
Kotri Plant, 387
Kowloon (HKSAR), 351
Krakatau Steel, 615
Krugman, Paul, 12–13

Krupp, 599, 611
  hostile takeover of Hoesch (early 1990s), 611
  remuneration and productivity (1995), 641
Krupp-Hoesch, 611–12, 952(n10)
  cost-cutting, 612
  hostile bid for Thyssen (1997), 612
  profits (1997), 957(n69)
  stainless steel, 615
Kunming Iron and Steel Corporation, 635
Kuok, Robert, 951(n19)
Kuomintang (KMT 1924–), 20, 904, 905–6
Kuss (company), 530
Kuwait
  arms purchases, 193
  nationalization of oil and gas (1975), 408,
      411
  oil reserves and production (1997), 403
  proven oil reserves, 404
  service agreements with Western companies,
      413
Kuwait Petroleum Corporation: output (1996),
    409
Kvaerner, 391, 945(n20)
Kvaerner Brug A/S (Norway), 377–8
Kvaerner John Brown: chemical engineers,
    941(n2)
Kyoto agreement (1997), 430–1, 702–5
  developing countries 'not signatory', 703,
      704

L Electronics (South Korea), 23
L'Oréal: competitive advantage, 35
labour, 129
  developing countries, 5–6
  discriminatory legislation (UK) against, 15
  Eastern Europe (transitional), 2
  globalization, 855
  Japan, 510
  'no world market' for, 33
  oil sector (PRC), 492
  PRC (national team), 79
  price of, 15
  productivity, 9
  skilled, 33, 302, 855
  tyre industry, 528
  unskilled, 33, 855
  Yuchai, 578–81
  see also employees
labour organization (HPEC), 380–3, 949
labour unions (Japan), 18
labour unrest, 711, 712, 745
Lagardère, 160, 161
Lagardère, Jean-Luc, 169
laissez-faire, 15, 20
Laiwu Iron and Steel, 635
Lan Chile (airline), 149
Lancashire, 159
land rights, 709
Langfang, 950(n9)
Lanzhou (capital of Gansu), 954(n40)

Lanzhou Chemical Company, 454, 469
Lanzhou Fayang Electric Power Company,
    946(n37)
Lao Daqian, 947[n40]
Lao Zi: cited, 401, 501, 695
Laos: national airline, 205
Lardy, N., 813, 958(n12)
large firms (general)
    'catch-up' process, 14–24
    competition, 2–8
    conclusion, 24–5
    disintegration, 7–8
    dominant position in advanced capitalism,
        13–14
    economic development, 1–25
    economies of scale, 9, 10, 11, 14
    forces leading to emergence of, 9
    four little tigers, 19–24
    Hong Kong, 23–4
    Japan, 16–19
    limits to size and stability, 6–7
    neo-classical view, 2–8
    'no theoretical limits to size', 11
    outsourcing, 7–8
    power, 14
    rise and fall, 6–7
    role of state, 14–24
    Singapore, 23
    small firms, 2–8
    South Korea, 21–3
    stability, 10–11
    state and trade policy, 12–13
    Taiwan, 20–1
    technical progress, 11–12
    tendency to concentration, 9
    United Kingdom, 15
    unorthodox view, 8–24
    USA (nineteenth century), 15–16
    the West, 14–16
    see also advanced economies
large firms (PRC)
    attempts to build, 839
    competitive capability, 851
    creation (China, late 1970s-), 27
    difficulties of building (PRC), 844–6
    impact of PRC-USA Agreement (1999), 896
    mentioned, 69, 926, 932, 933
    weaknesses (PRC), 850
    see also large and medium enterprises
        (LMEs); national champions
large and medium enterprises (LMEs)
    China Textile Machinery Group, 79
    concentration, 71, 939(n14)
    definition, 75, 939(n19)
    512 preferred, 68, 76, 88, 96–7, 108, 116,
        119, 124, 131, 139, 937(n2 to ch3),
        938(n5)
    introduction of modern corporate system, 68,
        96, 131, 937(n1 to ch3)
    number, 938(n9)

PRC, 67, 68, 70, 117, 937–8(n1–4, 9–10)
    'produce over 10pc of China's GDP', 70
    provincial distribution (1997), 82–3
    research institutions, 94
    research and development, 94–5
    stock exchange listings, 96, 940(n30)
    workforce (1995), 77
'latecomer' industrializing countries, 46, 65,
        176. 768, 923
    automobiles, 533
    steel, 621
    see also barriers to entry; catch-up
Latin America
    'competitive edge' companies (1997–8),
        62–3
    economic growth (1980–98), 851
    internet sector, 780
    privatization (steel), 606
    projected demand for power equipment
        (1980–2010), 334, 335
    share of world electricity generation
        (1995–2015), 335, 943(n4)
    telecommunications, 779, 802–3
Lau, Professor Laurence, 917, 918
Lavi programme (Israel), 193
law
    amendments required post-WTO accession
        (PRC), 864–5
    on BOT-type projects (PRC) 'incomplete',
        944(n14)
    domestic (PRC) and international, 319
    patents, 244
Layard, Richard, 909
League of Nations, 905
lean production, 48, 145, 510, 511, 514, 520–1
Lear (USA), 522, 524, 536
'learning journeys' xxv
Lee, Martin, 875
Lee Byung-Chul, 52
Lee Kuan Yew (b 1923), 898, 916, 927, 935
Lee Yong-keun, 517
legal institutions (PRC), 86
legal persons
    'child' company, 478
    CNPC subsidiaries, 487
    Daqing, 476
    importance of status, 488
    incorporated, 437
    large enterprises (PRC), 852
    New CNPC, 488
    oil sector (PRC), 495
    Shanghai Petrochemical Corporation, 454,
        472
    Shenhua Huanghua Port Company Limited,
        742
    Shougang Group and subsidiaries, 684–5
    Sinopec and subsidiaries, 448–9, 487
legal system
    PRC, 874
    Russian Federation, 909

Legend (PRC 1984–)
  advantages, 794
  international minnow, 794
  leading computer-maker (PRC), 794
  national team player (second batch), 107
  non-SOE national champion (PRC), 862
  profits (1998), 794
  research and development engineers (1998),
      794n
  research and development expenditure
      (1998), 794
  share of PRC market (1998), 794
  size, 107
  turnover (1998), 794
Leningrad Electrical Equipment Plant, 368
Leningrad Power Equipment Plant, 947(n44)
Lester, W., 5
Levin, Gerald (CEO Time Warner), 781
Leyland (UK lorry company), 517, 534
LG
  restructuring (1998), 54
  semiconductor manufacturing, 54
Lhasa (Tibet), 204
Li, Richard, 784, 935
Li Bozhong, 898
Li Donghui, 945(n24)
Li Genshen, Dr (Chairman, HPEC/HPEGC,
      1994–), 369, 371–2
Li Ka-shing, 351, 784, 956(n60)
Li Moran (actor), 298–9
Li Peng, 392
Li Yizhong, 466, 469
Li Yongwu, 468
liabilities, 72
Liang Weiyan, 947(n41)
lianying, 'jointly-managed' (companies), 367
lianying qiye (supplying firms), 384
Lianyungang (PRC): coal port, 720
Liaohe complex; managed by New CNPC
      (1998–), 470
Liaohe Petroleum Administration, 438
  output, sales and pre-tax profit (1996), 442
Liaoning (province), 112, 115, 116, 368
  'grasping the large', 83
  loss-makers, 730
  petrol stations, 470
  power equipment production, 111, 364, 365
  provincial government, 365
Liaoning Electrical Engineering Plant, 365
Liaotong Peninsula, 903
liberalization
  developing countries, 243, 270
  foreign equity involvement (PRC), 351
  former Communist countries, 243, 245, 270
  global vehicle markets, 520
  India, 872–3
  markets for mining products, 709
  mentioned, 2
  PRC, 279–82, 282–3, 297, 875
  steel (PRC), 385, 622–3

telecommunications, 786
Libya, 178, 411
Libya National Oil Corporation, 409
LIC/LIE, *see* low-income countries/economies
Liem Sioe Liong, 951(n19)
Life, 898
life expectancy (PRC), 277, 907, 914, 915
life sciences, 48, 244, 252, 260–6, 271, 763,
      767
lifetime employment, 56, 321
light industry, 119, 130, 131
lighting (cars): spiralling R&D costs, 522
lightweighting, 590–1, 595
Lim Goh Tong, 951(n19)
limestone, 596
Lin, Justin Yifu, 1, 4, 19
Lin Biao (1908–71), 911
Linatron 4 Mev linear accelerator, 379
Lindahl, Goran (CEO ABB), 363, 944(n14)
Lindberg, L.N. and J.L. Campbell (1991), 154
Lineng Hydropower Development Company,
      944(n16)
ling qi dian ('start from scratch every day'),
      549, 579
liquefied natural gas (LNG), 416, 490, 717
  project in Guangdong Province (announced
      1999), 717
  projects, 490
lishihui ('Board of Directors'), 657
List, Friedrich (1789–1846), 12
Liu, Henry (hotel manager), 313–14
Liu Changle, 784
Liu Huaqing, General, 194, 941(n18)
Liu Jie, 947[n40]
Liu Shaoqi, 363
Liu Xingli, Mr, xxv
Liu Yan, Dr, xxiv
Liuyuan Hydraulic Company, 226
Liuzhou (Guangxi Province), 686
Liuzhou Automobile Plant, 554, 555, 564, 576
Liuzhou Diesel Plant, 562
Liuzhou Steel plant, 651
Lizhu (Zhuhai), 298
LMEs, *see* large and medium enterprises
LMN (UK): crude steel output (1996–7), 602
LNG, *see* liquefied natural gas
loans
  aerospace (UK), 175
  CNPC, 440
  commercial, 354, 945(n19)
  components sector (PRC), 543
  foreign exchange (PRC), 392
  foreign, for railway construction in PRC, 742
  HPEC subsidiaries, 370
  to Legend, 107
  mentioned, 932
  PRC, 89, 94, 95, 97, 348, 373, 392
  Shanghai Petrochemical Corporation, 455
  soft, 440, 866–8, 878, 884–5
lobbying, 428, 463

local content, 866, 870, 881–2
local government (PRC)
  coal supplies, 724
  and local refineries, 485, 891
  and local SMEs, 844
  mentioned, 349
  oil refining, 450
  required to take over PLA enterprises (1994), 276
  resistance to takeover of local champions, 847
  responsible for keypoint coal mines (10.1998–), 731
  revenue from small local coal mines, 724–5
  taxation of diesel-engine-makers, 563
localization (PRC), 357–8, 945(n24)
Lockheed, 144, 155
  internal systems integration, 147
  purchases Martin Marietta (1995), 147
Lockheed-Martin
  competition with Boeing, 157
  competitive advantage, 173–4
  considering merger with GEC USA (late 1998), 164
  'mainly defence producer', 230
  market capitalization, 236
  merger with Northrop-Grumman vetoed, 164
  military aircraft, 152–4
  miscellaneous, 144, 147, 155, 160, 161, 165, 184, 235, 848, 956(n64)
  out of business in civil airliner production, 167
  relative size (1997), 228, 236
  research and development, 143, 175, 877
  revenues, profits, employees, R&D (1997), 877
  sales, 227, 877
  size (1998), 166
London: BOC investment banking arm, 831
Long Beach, 207, 208, 209
Long-Term Development Plan (PRC), 734
Loral, 147, 153
Lorraine-Escaut (steel-maker), 611
lorries
  Daimler-Benz, 514
  demand (PRC), 551, 552
  global market share, 37
  heavy-duty, 565–6
  heavy-duty (PRC), 568
  industrial structure, 518–19
  leading manufacturers (1995–2005), 518
  medium-duty (PRC), 568
  miscellaneous, 102, 271, 507, 861
  output (PRC), 536, 551, 552
  PRC (Yiqi and Dongfeng), 534, 542
  PRC output (1998), 559
  production and imports (PRC 1978–98), 536
Los Angeles, 274
loss-makers
  Agricultural Bank of China (ABC), 830–1, 958(n11)

airlines, 124
  among top 500 PRC enterprises, 730
  Angang auxiliary units, 642
  to be avoided as take-over targets (by Sanjiu), 319
  BAe 146, 211
  Brazilian steel industry (pre-1994), 606
  British Steel Corporation, 609
  car industry (PRC), 540
  China Telecom subsidiaries, 807
  CNPC (excluding Daqing), 439
  coal sector, 713, 729–31, 749, 753
  Cummins, 584
  Daewoo, 516
  Dongfeng and Yiqi (early 1996), 576
  ENI, 408
  Five Western District Mines, 843, [891]
  foisted on CNPC, 843
  foisted on Sinopec, 843
  'Hierro' iron mine (Peru), 691
  MD-90 project (PRC), 208–10
  military enterprises (PRC), 656
  military-controlled businesses (PRC), 274–5, 294, 311
  miscellaneous, 71, 88–9, 98, 106, 295, 842
  Nissan, 516
  pharmaceuticals (Chinese traditional), 297
  Qian'an iron ore mines, 653
  Sanjiu subsidiaries, 314–15, 320, 322, 324
  Shenhua subsidiaries, 843, [891]
  Shougang subsidiaries, 654, 682, 686–7, 692, 843, 954(n38)
  steel, 114, 633
  Universal Machine Works (PRC), 656
  Xiangfan Iron and Steel Group, 640
  Yuchai (pre-Wang Jianming), 576
Loughborough University, 302
low-income countries (LIC/LIE)
  economic growth (1980–98), 851
  expenditure on health, 767
  exports, 871
  GNP (1998), 932
  internet hosts per 1,000 people (1997), 789
  IT development (1997), 789
  mentioned, 47
  per capita energy use (1994), 341
  personal computers per 1,000 people (1997), 789
  public health expenditure (1900–7), 243
  stock market capitalization (1998), 932
  telecommunications development (1997), 789
  telephone main lines per 1,000 people (1997), 789
  TV sets per 1,000 people (1997), 789
  wireless telephones per 1,000 people (1997), 789
low technology, 53
lower middle-income countries
  health expenditure, 243, 767
Lower Saxony Government, 504

LTV (US steel-maker), 641
Lu Yansun, Mr, xxv, 327, 947(n41)
Lu Yiping, 455
Luan Mining Bureau, Shanxi (coal producer)
    transport costs (1997), 720
Lucas: car braking systems, 525, 535
Lucas-Varity, 525, 547
    joint venture in PRC, 547
    purchased by TRW (1999), 525
Lucas Aerospace, 181, 239
Lucent Technologies (1996–), 773, 786
    acquisitions (1.1999–4.2000), 771, 773
    competition with Cisco and Nortel, 773
    fibre optic transmission trunk (PRC), 795
    hardware revenues, 772
    Huawei contrast, 795
    IT spending (1998), 773
    joint ventures in PRC, 795
    little to fear from PRC competition (post-
        WTO accession), 863
    market capitalization (late 1999), 773;
        (2000), 764, 772
    profits (1998), 794
    research and development expenditure
        (1998), 768, 794
    sales (1998), 773
    sales revenue (2000), 764
    spun-off from AT&T (1996), 773
    telecommunications hardware, 771, 773
    turnover (1998), 794
Lufthansa (Germany), 149, 213
Lukens (US steel-maker), 613, 952(n11)
Lukoil: output (1996), 409
Luoyang, 132, 137
Luoyang Auto Company, 542
Luoyang Bearing Group, 105
Luoyang Chundu Group, 132
Luoyang Floating Glass Group, 128
Luoyang Vehicle Company
    main product, output, profits, taxes (1995),
        562
Luxembourg, 676
LVMH, 35
Lycos, 787
Lycra, 265

m-commerce [thus], 834
Ma Fucai, 470, 476
Ma Hong (head of SCDRC), 74, 75, 136
Ma Weijie and Ma Weigang (1998), 67
Ma Yue (head of Dongfeng), 568
Maanshan Iron and Steel Company Limited
    ('Magang'), 634, 640
    continuous casting, 627
    output structure (1997), 646
    principal steel products (1997), 636
    production costs, 659
    productivity, 659
    profitability, 643

remuneration and labour productivity (1997),
    641
return on investment (1980–90), 660
steel production methods (1997), 597
McDonalds: competitive advantage, 35
McDonnell-Douglas, 144, 184, 860
    competition from Airbus, 209
    grants sub-contracts in PRC, 209, 213, 216
    improves market share in PRC (1986–93),
        207–8
    MD 80/90 series of planes, 206–10
    merged (1967), 155
    out of business in civil airliner production,
        167
    research and development, 142, 143
    rivalry with Boeing, 207, 208, 209
    state aid for research and development, 176
    see also aircraft (specific)
MacGregor, Sir Ian, 498, 609–10, 841
machine building, 118
machine tools, 64, 198
machinery/equipment, 116, 119, 129, 346
    ancillary, 365, 383–4, 387, 394, 398
    complex, 32, 36, 845, 889
    heavy equipment, 346
    Japan, 603
    national team (PRC), 77
    national team (various indicators, 1995), 78
    'ordinary', 105
    second batch of trial groups (1997), 86
    sectoral share of PRC national team (1991,
        1997), 84
    special purpose, 104
McKinsey Telecoms Group, 761
Macmillan, Neil, 786
Maeda, Katsunosuke, 56
Magang, see Maanshan Iron and Steel
    Company Limited
magnetos (automobile component), 546
Mahathir bin Mohamad, Datuk Seri Dr
    (b 1925), 927
maize, 869
MaK Motors (Germany), 530
Malaysia
    arms deliveries (1987–98), 151
    demand for pharmaceuticals (per capita), 277
    energy consumption per capita, 428
    'fundamental economic situation', 834
    GNP, 863
    HPEC tenders (1996), 387
    increased supply of oil (post-1973), 404
    mentioned, 927
    natural gas, 416
    number of companies in Fortune 500 (1998),
        47n
    pharmaceuticals market (1995), 277
    Sanjiu processing factory, 300, 308
    tariffs on steel products (1997), 619
    TNCs (1999), 21
MAN, 861

management
  BAe, 169
  'best practice' (global transfer), 711
  'by regulations and laws', 380
  coal sector, 708, 711, 713
  components (global giants), 547
  components (PRC), 544
  Dongfeng, 563
  corporate governance (PRC), 859, 860
  empowerment (PRC), 98–9
  hotel, 311–12
  integrated system, 89
  mentioned, 9
  oil sector, 412
  oil sector (PRC), 448, 461, 487–9, 497
    ('poor', 489, 492)
  pharmaceuticals (PRC), 283, 290, 303–5,
    310, 320, 942(n30)
  PRC, 73, 74, 926, 876
  remote-area factories (PRC), 275
  Sanjiu, 880
  Shougang, 650–1, 654, 657, 663–71
  Soviet model, 650, 953(n29)
  value chain, 512
  Wanxiang Group, 134
  western pharmaceutical companies, 297
  Yuchai, 569, 579, 885
  see also privatization
'managerial economies', 10
managers (Japanese), 17–18
'Manchuria', 904, 905
manganese, 956(n60)
Mannesmann (Germany), 311, 778
  links with Wugang, 629
  market capitalization (2000), 764
  moving into IT sector, 765
  sales revenue (2000), 764
mantras
  'allow plenty of water in order for fish to
    grow' (*fangshui, yangyu*), 222
  'bigger is better', 819
  'consumer should decide', 347
  'crossing river while groping for stones', 912
  'employ the able', 311
  'floating boats on water', 324
  'following guidance of market', 493–7
  'get close to market', 297
  'global level playing field', 14–15, 28, 46,
    52, 54, 62, 158, 195, 244, 270–1, 310,
    325, 328, 348, 393, 398, 417, 492–3,
    533, 536, 717, 758, 766, 784–90
    ('hugely uneven', 787), 793, 804,
    810–11, 825–6, 831, 839, 848, 850, 856,
    862, 876–94, 920, 925, 932
  'growing through the market', 472
  'grasp large, let go small', 69, 75, 76, 77, 83,
    87, 98, 99, 463, 638–40
  'grasp strong, let go weak', 760
  'hard and arduous struggle', 303
  'I have and you have too', 327

'if an asset can't pay its way, we sell it' (BP
    Amoco), 425
'if you are not 1, 2, 3 in the world, you
    shouldn't stay in the business', 34, 848
'if you want to be mayor, go for
    pharmaceuticals', 279
'learning by doing' (Shougang), 663
ling qi dian ('start every day from zero'), 579
'no mistake, no demotion', 665
'parched by years of planning' (World Bank
    1997), 67, 68
'production first, life later', 303
ren wei ben ('people are the foundation'),
    579
'resources limited, human creativity
    unlimited' (Posco), 668
'seek truth from facts', 857
'size matters greatly' (aerospace), 231
'take action only when useful to do so' (Sun
    Wu), 65
'trading market for technology', 356, 358,
    863
'we can't pull the sapling upward in the hope
    they will grow', 67, 95, 99
zheng di yi ('strive to be number one'), 579
manufacturing, 11, 28, 939(n22)
  Eastern Europe (transitional), 2
  global, 31
  Taiwan, 21
  employment (PRC 1998), 919
  see also industrial concentration
mao (one-tenth of a *yuan*), 669
Mao Zedong (1893–1976), 199, 203, 275, 905
  achievement assessed, 907–8
  austerity, 442
  'Chinese people have stood up', vii, 907
  Daqing Petroleum Administration, 442
  disastrous impact (military technology),
    187–8
Maoism, 376, 387, 392, 630, 643, 682, 720, 758
Marathon Oil, 411
  acquired by US Steel (1980s), 601
Marconi, 861, 862
Marion Labs, 262
Marion Merrell Dow (MMD), 262
market
  functioning of, 1
  understanding (PRC) of, 876
market capitalization, 50
  firms based in high-income countries (1997),
    47
  aerospace industry, 235–6
  IBM v entire PRC stock market (1.2000),
    772
  Japan, 51, 56
  pharmaceutical corporations, 269
  Pharmacia Upjohn, 266
  ranking of TNCs by, 46
  Sony, 56
  Telmex, 803

market capitalization – *continued*
    TotalFina, 415
market economy
    pharmaceuticals, 282
    PRC, 197, 630, 670, 680–1, 684
    transition (general), 2–3
    transition (PRC), 275, 343, 346, 369, 387
    transition (Russian Federation), 909
market forces, 14
    coal sector (PRC), 726
    oil sector (PRC), 453
    oil sector, 458
    PRC, 544, 582
    Yuchai, 569, 577, 581, 582
market mechanism (PRC), 87, 91, 98–9
market reform (PRC), 67, 283
market share, 17, 71, 841
    competitive advantage, 37
    global, 49
    industrial concentration, 38–9
    pharmaceuticals, 266–8
market size: pharmaceuticals (PRC), 277–9
marketing
    automobiles, 511, 521, 533
    crude oil (PRC), 457–8
    delays (pharmaceutical industrial), 245–6
    diesel engines, 531
    economies of scale (automobile industry),
        503
    expenditure (pharmaceutical sector), 251
    Ford-Volvo, 515
    General Electric (USA), 333
    globalization, 512
    high-volume, 14
    HPEC, 386
    Legend (PRC), 794
    lorries, 543
    marketing, 9, 11, 34, 37
    mentioned, 856, 872
    Microsoft, 776
    oil sector, 420, 422, 423, 426
    oil products (PRC), 458
    oil sector (PRC), 459–60, 493
    petrochemical products (PRC), 458–9
    pharmaceutical sector, 251, 270–1, 286, 323
    PRC, 841
    Sanjiu, 290, 300, 307, 314, 318, 324, 880
    Shenhua, 750
    steel industry, 600, 694
    tyre industry, 527
    wholesale and retail (oil sector, PRC),
        459–60
    Yuchai, 557–8
marketing systems, 61
markets
    autos and auto components, 507–9
    globalization (steel industry), 621
    'imperfectly competitive', 12
Marks & Spencer, 818
Marshall, Alfred (1842–1924), 7, 9–10

Martin Marietta, 147
Marubeni (Japan), 352, 810
Marx, Karl (1818–83), 9, 897, 906
mass media, 781, 811, 925, 929
    global market share, 37
    PRC, 921, 922, 924–5, 930
    US dominance, 781
Matra, 160
Matra BAe Dynamics, 144, 164, 170, 171
Matra Marconi Space, 162
Matsushita, 19, 850
Mattel: competitive advantage, 35
Maxus Energy (USA), 494
May Fourth Movement (China 1919–), 904
Mazda, 508, 513, 850
MCA-Polygram, 781
MCI, *see* Ministry of Chemical Industry (PRC)
MCI [US telecommunications giant], 786
MCIWorldCom, 777, 798
    corporate culture (PRC contrast), 802
    international comparison (12.1999), 800
    market capitalization (4.2000), 931
    market capitalization, revenue, profits
        (12.1999), 800
meat, 871, 913
Media One, 782
medical equipment
    non-aviation output of AVIC, 198
    Samsung, 53
medical fees, 381, 949(n59)
medicines
    Chinese traditional, 125, 279, 288–9, 290–1,
        296, 297, 300–1, 309–10, 318, 319, 325,
        879
    development timespan, 247, 941(n1)
    generic, 296, 299
    non-patented, 283, 289
    out-of-patent, 244
    patented, 242–5, 245, 246, 268, 270, 283,
        286, 288–9, 296–7, 310, 324, 325
    traditional, 243
    western, 288–9, 296, 306, 310–11
medium income countries, 47
MEG requirements (Yizheng), 466
Meggitt: acquires Whittaker Corporation
        (6.1999), 147
mei dai you ('substituting coal for oil') policy
        (PRC), 714, 742, 748–9
    US government financial support, 749
Meidi: non-SOE national champion (PRC),
        862
meiyou banfa de banfa ('path to follow when
        there is no other solution'), 649
Memorandum on Market Access
    PRC-USA (1992), 623
Mer, Francis 498, 611, 841
mercantilism, 911
Mercedes-Benz
    abortive joint venture with Yuchai, 568
    interests in India, 508

Mercedes-Benz – *continued*
  joint venture with South China Motor
    Corporation, 546
  joint venture with Yangzhou Motor (buses),
    541–2
  lorries, 532
  modern technology, 583
  self-sufficient in heavy-duty engines, 566
merchant banks, 822, 958(n9); *see also* named
    banks
Merck & Co., 247, 256, 258, 260, 263, 264,
    848
  aborted joint venture with Sanjiu, 294, 307,
    310
  Annual Report (1998), 244
  best sellers (drugs), 250
  buys (1993) Medco (USA), 254, 260
  market share (1994–9), 267, 268
  marketing, 270
  marketing expenditure (1998), 251
  plant at Hangzhou, 283
  research and development expenditure
    (1994–7), 248, 310
  revenues, profits, employees, R&D (1997),
    879
  size, 266
  successes and new pressures, 260
Mercosur, 508
mergers (general)
  aerospace, 59
  auto industry, 512, 514–18
  components sector, 523–4, 525
  continental Europe, 58
  decline of 'national champion' concept, 533
  European banking, 58
  European, 49
  in PRC 'tiny in international comparison', 81
  Japanese capability, 56
  Japanese banking (1999), 56
  life sciences, 59
  missed opportunities (PRC), 861
  national champions (Europe), 58
  oil sector, 411, 412–17, 492, 497
  pharmaceuticals, 59, 246, 251, 271
  postponed by 'alliances', 513
  power equipment, 59
  PRC, 79–81, 96, 97–8, 136, 137
  prospective, 60, 417, 517
  second-tier suppliers (aerospace), 146
  state-orchestrated, 858–9
  steel, 59
  strong with strong, 80, 756
  strong with weak (PRC), 753–6
  suggested (power generation, PRC), 397–9
  transatlantic, 59–60, 165, 414, 493, 514–15,
    778, 784, 857, 895
  USA (1998), 81
mergers (specific)
  ABB and GEC-Alsthom (1999), 263, 338
  ABB and Alstom, 59

ABN and Rothschild, 958(n9)
Aérospatiale and Matra (1998–9), 160, 58, 170
Aérospatiale-Matra-Dasa (= European
    Aircraft, Defence and Space Company),
    59
AHP and Pfizer, 268
Allied Signal and Honeywell, 146–7
Amoco and BP, 55
AOL and Time Warner (2000), 781, 782–3
Asea (Sweden) and Brown Boveri
    (Switzerland), 336
Asea and Brown Boveri (late 1980s,
    = ABB), 59
Ashland Coal and Arch Mineral Corporation
    (1997), 710
Astra and Zeneca, 59, 263, 264–5, 268
AT&T and TCI (6.1998), 782
AT&T/TCI and Media One Group (6.2000),
    782
BAe and GEC-Marconi (1999), 147–8, 161,
    170, 236
BAe and GEC Marconi's defence arm, 58
BP and Amoco, 60, 414–15, 460, 467, 493
BP Amoco and Arco, 416, 493
British Steel and Hoogovens (= Corus,
    1999), 59, 610, 889
Chase Manhattan and J.P. Morgan (9.2000),
    813, 822
China Telecom (Hong Kong) and Jiangsu
    Mobile Phone Company (1998), 931
China Telecom (Hong Kong) with Fujian and
    Henan mobile phone companies (1999),
    931
Ciba-Geigy and Sandoz (= Novartis, 1996),
    55, 58, 261, 268
Citicorp and Travelers, 817
Daimler-Benz and Chrysler (1998), 55, 60,
    415, 514–15, 519, 528, 533, 534, 886
Daimler-Chrysler (Dasa) and Casa, 161, 170
Dasa and Aérospatiale-Matra, 161, 170, 263
Deutsche Bank and Bankers Trust, 60
Deutsche Bank and Morgan Grenfell,
    958(n9)
Dresdner and Kleinwort Benson, 958(n9)
Exxon and Mobil, 55, 415, 460
Ford and Volvo, 515, 533
Fuji Bank, Industrial Bank of Japan, and Dai-
    Ichi Kangyo, 56
GEC (UK) and Alcatel (France) (= Alstom),
    59, 336
Glaxo Wellcome and SKB (2000), 251, 257,
    260, 262, 268, 269
GM and Daewoo, 516
Goodyear and Sumitomo (1999), 527, 528–9
Hayes Wheels and Motor Schools, 524
Hoechst and Rhône-Poulenc (= Aventis), 59,
    262–4, 268, 269
Huaneng Power International and Shandong
    Huaneng Power Development Company
    (announced 7.2000), 931

mergers (specific) – *continued*
  ING and Barings, 958(n9)
  Krupp takeover of Hoesch, 611
  Krupp and Thyssen (steel interests), 599
  Krupp-Hoesch and Thyssen (1997–8), 612
  Krupps and Thyssen, 58
  McDonnell-Douglas and Boeing, 142, 149,
      152–2, 155, 168, 210, 216, 235
  Meggitt and Whittaker Corporation, 147
  Morgan Stanley and Dean Witter, 817
  Pfizer and Warner-Lambert, 259, 260, 262
  Pharmacia Upjohn and Monsanto, 265–6,
      268
  Renault and Nissan, 515–16, 533
  Rio Tinto and CRA (1995), 707–8
  Salomon Brothers and Smith Barney, 817
  Salomon Smith Barney (USA) and Schroders
      (UK), 822, 958(n9)
  Sanofi and Synthelabo, 269
  Seagram and Polygram (1998), 783
  Seagram and Vivendi (2000), 784
  Shenfu and Dongsheng mining companies
      (PRC), 735
  Shouang and Tangshan Steel, 80
  Telecom Italia and Olivetti, 58
  Total and PetroFina (= TotalFina), 415
  TotalFina and Elf Aquitaine (= TotalFinaElf),
      416–17, 493
  UBS and Warburg, 958(n9)
  Usinor and Cockerill Sambrell, 59
  Usinor and Hoogovens, 263
  Usinor + Wendel-Sidelor + Sacilor, 611
  Vodafone and Air Touch, 60
  Vodafone and Mannesmann, 263
  Volvo and Saab, 58, 518
  Volvo and Scania, 534
  WPP/Young and Rubicam, 781
  Yanshan and Tianjin Hangu (= Yanhua), 454
  Yawata and Fuji (= New Japan Steel, 1970),
      603
  see also EADC; industrial concentration
mergers and acquisitions, 34, 37, 50–1, 64, 930,
    932
  advisers (top five firms, 2000), 823
  aerospace industry (USA), 152–3
  automobile industry (PRC), 540
  banking sector (USA), 817, 822
  biotechnology industry (1988–98), 769
  chronology (global pharmaceutical sector,
      1989–2000), 254–7
  coal sector, 707, 710
  computer industry (1988–98), 769
  cross-border, 815–16, 822
  cross-sector, 815, 816–17, 822
  financial services, 815, 816, 822, 958(n3–4)
  frenzy, 38
  global, 855
  impact on number of employees, 44
  initiated by Nanfang, 314–15
  IT sector, 769–70

Japan, 17–18
  means of technology acquisition, 771, 772,
      773–4, 775
  pharmaceutical companies, 251, 252–3
  pharmaceutical sector (PRC), 286
  PRC, 81, 97–8, 842–3
  Sanjiu, 290, 295, 319, 324
  steel, 587
  strong PRC companies, 495–7
  telecommunications, 769, 777–8
  UK (1919–), 15
  US dominance, 50–1
  USA (1890s), 16
Merrill Lynch (USA), 57, 815–16, 818, 824
  assets managed (1999), 837
  diversified financial services networks, 830
  joint venture (online) with HSBC, 818, 822
  key indicators, 1998 (PRC comparison), 829
  top five firm (all international convertibles,
      2000), 823
  top five firm (international equities
      bookrunners, 2000), 823
  top five firm (M&A Advisers, 2000), 823
Messer (industrial gases), 263
Messerchmitt-Bolkow-Blohm, 940(n4)
Messier, Jean-Marie (Head of Vivendi), 784
Mesta Engineering Company (Pittsburgh,
    1888–)
  bolt plate leveller, 674, 956(n56)
  purchased by Shougang Corporation
      (7.1988), 674–5
Mesta International [Shougang Group], 647,
    673
metal
  cans, 38
  goods (fabricated), 106
metallurgy, 77, 78, 118, 900
metals, primary, 11
Mexico
  energy, 340, 943(n8–9)
  enforcement of WTO rules, 919
  expanded production of oil (post-1973), 404
  FDI inflow, 31
  financial crisis (1994–5), 833
  Ispat, 600
  nationalization (oil sector), 409
  number of companies in *Fortune* 500 (1998),
      47n
  number of companies in *FT* 500 (1998),
      47n
  number of 'competitive edge' companies
      (1997–8), 62–3
  oil production, 355
  per capita energy use (1994), 341
  resistance to global telecommunication
      giants, 802, 803
  steel output (1974–96), 593
  Thyssen-Krupp willingness to produce in,
      612
  TNCs based (1999) in, 21, 23

Mexico – *continued*
  top twenty steel-producing country (1991–8), 617
  wage costs (steel industry, 1997), 620
MHI, *see* Mitsubishi Heavy Industries
Michelin (France), 522, 527, 528, 536, 576, 886, 935
micro-electronics, 673
micro-vans, 199
Microsoft (USA), 776, 786
  market capitalization (2000), 764, 772, 776
  overtaken by Cisco (market capitalization, 5.2000), 774
  profits (1999), 772
  research and development, 776, 797
  sales revenue (2000), 764
  software revenues, 772
  'Venus' system, [796–]797
Microsoft Office, 776
Microsoft Windows, 776
middle-income countries (MIC)
  economic growth (1980–98), 851
  GNP (1998), 932
  internet hosts per 1,000 people (1997), 789
  IT development (1997), 789
  per capita energy use (1994), 341
  personal computers per 1,000 people (1997), 789
  stock market capitalization (1998), 932
  telecommunications development (1997), 789
  telephone main lines per 1,000 people (1997), 789
  TV sets per 1,000 people (1997), 789
  wireless telephones per 1,000 people (1997), 789
middle-income countries (upper)
  energy consumption *per capita*, 428
Middle Ages (Europe), 898
Middle East
  arms deliveries (1987–98), 151, 152
  economic growth (1980–98), 851
  electricity generation capacity (1990–2010), 697
  exporter of oil to PRC (1995–7), 434, 435
  hydrocarbon exports to PRC, 407
  investments by CNPC, 441
  lack of indigenous 'competitive edge' corporations, 63
  military aircraft procurement, 174
  national champions (oil and petrochemicals), 408
  natural gas production and reserves (1997), 405
  oil reserves and production (1997), 403
  oil supplies to the UK, 407
  oil supply, 410
  production and sales of automobiles (1998), 508
  projected demand for power equipment (1980–2010), 334

proven oil reserves, 404–5
Sanjiu sales offices, 300
share of world electricity generation (1995–2015), 335
SOEs, 410
steel production (1991–7), 589
TotalFinaElf, 417
US strategic interest, 406
midi-mills: 'overlarge mini-mills', 599
MIE (middle-income economies)
  see middle-income countries
MII, *see* Ministry of Information Industries (PRC)
Mikoyan-Gurevich, 179
military
  enterprises, 656
  intelligence, 163
  strategy (Sun Wu), 241
  technology transfer, 190
military-industrial construction and maintenance, 188
'Military Industries', head of, 656
Miller, J., 908
Milton Friedman Foundation, 4
minerals, 120, 708
mines, 904
Ming Dynasty (1368–1644), 900
mini-mills, 604, 605, 619, 662, 889
  consolidation of sector (USA), 600, 613
  Ispat, 614
  'long steel products', 598
  non-unionized labour, 598, 599
  Posco, 609
  PRC, 599, 631, 633
  steel industry, 598–600
  thin-slab casting, 598
  Usinor, 611
  see also steel mills
mini-motors, 950(n9)
mining, 675 920, 952(n12)
  'capital intensive', 708
  employment (PRC 1998), 919, 920
  global market share, 37
  national team players, 118–20
  open-cast, 708, 891
  PRC (national team), 79
  second batch of trial groups (1997), 86
mining commodities, 709
mining companies (coal), 707
Ministry of Aviation Industry (PRC), 184[–]186, 196, 940(n5)
  non-aerospace sales, 197, 940(n11)
  'three-step take-off plan', 206 ('in tatters', 213)
  Y-10 project, 204
Ministry of Chemical Industry/Industries (MCI, PRC)
  abolished (1998), 467, 468
  mentioned, 843
  refineries transferred to New CNPC, 477, 485

Ministry of Chemical Industry/Industries (MCI, PRC) – *continued*
  refineries transferred to New Sinopec, 483–4, 485
  transfer of assets to New CNPC and New Sinopec (1998), 469
Ministry of Coal Industry (PRC), 652, 731
  abolished (1998), 467, 468
  succeeded by the Coal Bureau, 731
Ministry of Communications (PRC), 122
Ministry of Electronics (PRC), 107
Ministry of Electric Power (MOEP, PRC), 343, 347, 348, 359, 399, 801, 809
  abolished (1998), 346
  function, 343
  'key task', 346
  'subsequently the SP', 346
  see also Huaneng (China Power) Power Corporation
Ministry of Electricity Industry (PRC), 753
Ministry of Finance (PRC), 830, 958(n10)
  'handovers' of profits by oil sector, 471, 474
  subsidies to coal industry, 731
Ministry of Geology and Mineral Resources (MGMR, PRC), 467, 468
Ministry of Information Industries (MII, PRC), 801
  largest single shareholder in China Unicom, 802, 809
  owner of China Mobile, 802
Ministry of Land and Natural Resources (PRC 1998–), 467, 468
Ministry of Machine Building (MMB, PRC), 101, 343, 364, 369, 370, 376, 540, 570, 572, 671, 945(n28), 951(n18), 968
  abolished (1998), 346
  'downgraded', 346
  and HPEGC, 365, 371
  role, 347
  see also 'First Ministry of Machine Building'; 'Ministry of Machinery'
'Ministry of Machinery' (PRC), 369, 373, 386, 391, 544, 569, 576, 656, 947(n43)
  see also Ministry of Machine Building
Ministry of Metallurgical Industry/Industries (MMI, PRC), 467, 622, 651, 657, 689, 968
  'Ministry of Metallurgy', 622
  see also Bureau of Metallurgical Statistics
Ministry of Petroleum Industry (MPI, PRC)
  transformed from a ministry into a holding company (1988), 436
Ministry of Posts and Telecommunications (PRC), 797, 800–1
  'Post and Telecommunications Bureau' (PRC), 802
Ministry of Power Industry (PRC), 340, 699
  abolished (1998), 468
Ministry of Public Health (PRC), 299
Ministry of Railways (PRC), 801, 809

  joint venture partner in Shenhua Railway Company, 742
  represented on Shenhua board, 741
Ministry of Textiles (PRC), 452
Ministry of Transport (PRC), 652
Ministry of Transportation (PRC)
  represented on Shenhua board, 741
Minmetals Development, 129–30
missile companies, 156
missiles, 191
  AMRAAM, 158
  anti-aircraft, 191
  ASRAAM, 164
  ballistic, 157, 187
  Dongfeng-31 (ICBM), 195
  Dongfeng-41 (ICBM), 195
  air-to-air (PRC), 199
  anti-radar, 192
MITI, *see* Japan: Ministry of International Trade and Industry
Mitsubishi, 176, 181, 860
  candidate to merge with Fiat, 517
  engines more expensive than those of Yuchai, 558
  interests in Thailand, 508
  joint venture with China Aerospace Automotive Industry Group (Shenyang), 547
  joint venture with Shenyang Construction Investment, 547
  missed merger opportunity, 861
  output, turnover, profit, R&D (1998), 533
  supplier to SHP, 362
Mitsubishi Chemical, 56
Mitsubishi Electric, 55, 396, 850, 860
Mitsubishi Heavy Industries (MHI), 177, 379, 942(n1)
  ancillary equipment, 365
  global top hundred company, 850
  joint ventures (aero-engines), 173
  market share worldwide (power generation equipment, 1993–8), 337
  one of the top four power equipment companies, 339
  technology and marketing agreement with Westinghouse, 336
Mitsubishi Motors, 514–15, 850
Mittal, Lakshmi, 670
Mittelstand engineering firms (Germany), 535
Mlada Bolesaw (Prague): Volkswagen plant, 950(n6)
MMI, *see* Ministry of Machine Building Industries (PRC)
Mobil, 415, 710
mobile phones, *see* wireless telephones
modern corporate system
  PRC, 90, 96, 105, 114, 119, 131, 139, 940(n30)
modern industrial enterprise
  characteristic features, 14

MOEP, *see* Ministry of Electric Power (PRC)
Mond, 264
Monitoring Committee (Shougang), 647, 685–6
Monkey King: national team player (PRC), 106
monomers, 417, 422
monopolies, 3, 17, 802, 956(n63)
Monopolies and Mergers Commission (UK), 956(n63)
Monroe Equipment (subsidiary of Tenneco), 525
Monsanto, 247, 259
    abortive merger with AHP (1998), 266
    'life sciences', 261
    merger with Pharmacia Upjohn announced (12.1999), 257, 266
    mergers and acquisitions, 256–7, 265–6
    research and development (1994–7), 248
Monti, Roberto, 494
Moody-Stuart, (Sir) Mark (b 1940), 414
moon landings: computer power (comparative), 523
Morgan Grenfell (UK), 817, 958(n9)
Morgan Stanley, 815, 817
    merger with Dean Witter, 817
Morgan Stanley Dean Witter (MSDW, USA), 49, 62–4, 824, 916
    assets managed (1999), 837
    BondBook, 818
    competitive edge companies, 142, 173–4, 766–7, 770, 851
    evaluation of (hypothetical) Nippon Steel merger with Posco, 613
    evaluation of pharmaceutical industry (1998), 247, 269
    interests in PRC, 835
    investment philosophy (aerospace), 148
    key indicators, 1998 (PRC comparison), 829
    oil sector, 421
    rating of Posco, 605
    scale (Guotai J&A comparison), 826
    survey of mining industry, 709
    top five firm (international equities bookrunners, 2000), 823
    top five firm (M&A Advisers, 2000), 823
Morgan Steel Mills Inc., 674
Morton, 526
'most-favoured nation' principle, 903
mother company (PRC), 87, 90, 99, 100, 112, 127, 138, 476, 849
    first, second, third-tier subsidiaries, 849
    mother/son company system, 87, 94, 114, 478–9
    son companies, 124
motorcycles, 103, 198–9, 272, 849, 873
    components, 199
    non-aviation output of AVIC, 198–9
    PRC 197
    second layer enterprises (PRC), 561
    WTO enforcement proceedings, 870
'Motorman' Robotics, 687

Motorola (USA)
    acquisitions (1.1999–4.2000), 771
    investment in PRC, 795–6
    market capitalization (2000), 764
    sales, 764, 774
    share of PRC market, 795
    wireless handsets, 774
motorways, 444
Motor Wheels, 525
MPI, *see* Ministry of Petroleum Industry (PRC), 436
MSDW, *see* Morgan Stanley Dean Witter
mugongsi ('mother' [company]), 478
multi-national corporations, *see* trans-national corporations
Munich, 159
munitions: precision-guided, 163
Munro, R.H., *see* Bernstein, R.
Murdoch, Rupert (b 1931), 784

NAFTA, *see* North American Free Trade Agreement
Nanchang: aircraft manufacturing, 186
Nanchang Aircraft Company, 200
Nanchong Diesel Engine Company, 564, 565
Nanfang Aero-engine Company (Dongli), 199, 940(n12)
Nanfang Pharmaceutical Company (1986–)
    advertising, 298–9
    automation, 302–3, 304
    'bulk of workforce civilians', 304
    'core enterprise' in Sanjiu Group, 295
    debt-assets ratio, 303, 319
    established by Guangzhou Army Hospital (1986), 290
    employment structure, 304–6, 319
    financial indicators (1987–97), 292
    GMP, 301–3
    human capital, 320
    later Sanjiu, 290, 318
    mergers and take-overs, 314–15
    modern business organization, 322–4
    output and profits (1992–7), 301
    placed under the GLD of the PLA (1992), 294, 311
    'premises governed by army regulations', 304
    product choice, 297
    production equipment, 303
    profitability, 291
    profits, 292, 306, 309, 319
    role of CCP, 304, 942(n22)
    sales (1992), 941(n15)
    sales network, 300
    share in Sanjiu's output value (1992–7), 318
    sources of growth, 320–2
    specialized pharmaceutical firm, 290
    stomach medicine (*Sanjiu Weitai*), 297–8
    struggle for autonomy, 322–3

Nanfang Pharmaceutical Company (1986–) –
    continued
  takes over GLD's loss-making enterprises
      (1992), 295
  trademark battle, 299
  VIP visitors, 294, 941(n18)
  wage system, 294, 305–6
  wholly-owned subsidiary of Sanjiu
      (2.1998–), 307
  workforce, 301, 304, 305, 320, 321
  see also Sanjiu Enterprise Group
Nanguang Group, 226
Nanhai Jinagnan Power Plant, 352
Nanhai Power Plant, 352
Nanjing, 546, 729, 901, 905
Nanjing Aero Motive Machinery Group, 112
Nanjing Air Industry Group, 113
Nanjing Chemical Fibre Company, 117
Nanjing Chemical Group, 117, 466
Nanjing Dongfeng Special-Purpose Vehicle
    Works
  'second layer' enterprise with Dongfeng
      capital participation, 565
Nanjing Gear
  diesel engine production (1998), 559
Nanjing Special Vehicle Company, 577
Nanning (Guangxi Province), 502
Nanning Airport, 575
Nanning Silk and Ramie Factory, 954(n41)
Nanya Plastics, 21
Nanyue Fuel Pump Company (Hengyang), 553,
    576, 580
naphtha, 466
NASA, 176
NASDAQ: Indian listings, 787
Nasser, Jacques (CEO Ford), 512
nation-state epoch: 'not over', 234
National Bureau of Commerce and Industry,
    299
National Bureau of Land Resources (PRC), 741
national champions (global)
  auto industry (Europe), 504
  auto industry (Japan), 505
  Brazil, 858
  decline of concept (auto sector), 533
  disappearance (advanced economies), 849,
      853, 855, 857, 878
  'Europe', 58, 847, 857, 859, 894–5
  Japan, 895
  Mannesmann, 778
  non-SOE, 862–3
  oil and petrochemicals, 407–8, 416
  power generation equipment, 335–6, 339
  power generation equipment (UK failure),
      943(n7)
  PRC, 67–139, 876–8, 937–40
  South Korea, 895
  steel, 587, 595, 606, 609
  steel industry (UK, France), 498
  telecommunications sector, 787

USA, 895
see also European champions
national champions (PRC), 65, 67–139, 846,
    857, 862–3, 875, 876–8, 880, 885, 887,
    895, 920, 924, 930, 937–40
  appendices, 100–39
  auto industry (PRC), 539
  conclusion, 98–9
  direct support measures, 95–8
  empowerment of business groups, 93–4
  enterprise groups, 75–6
  geographical location, 81–3
  'grasp the large', 69–72, 75, 76, 77, 83, 87,
      98, 99
  group expansion and diversification, 79–81
  industrial policy evolution, 83–6
  internal finance companies, 92–3
  national team, 76–83
  national team: origins, 72–6
  pillar industries, 83–6, 98, 99
  policies to build, 67–139
  policies promoting institutional change, 87–91
  policy implementation, 91–5
  preferential planning status, 91–2
  right to manage state capital, 93–4
  scale, 76–9
  State Council Directive: first (12.1991), 69,
      87–90, 95, 98, 938(n8), 940(n27)
  State Council Directive: second (4.1997), 69,
      90–1, 94, 95, 98, 940(n27)
  stock market listings, 96, 940(n30)
  strategy and policy, 69–72
  support from banking sector, 96–8
  technology centres, 94–5
  trial business groups, 85–6, 87–91
  trial business groups: chronology (1980–98),
      136–9
  trial business groups: list and description,
      100–35
  see also 'national team' (PRC)
National Coal Board (UK), 841
National Enterprise Contracting Meeting
    (6.1986), 136
National Enterprise Group Convention (1997),
    139
National Exchange Meeting, 138
National Iranian Oil Company: output (1996),
    409
National People's Congress (PRC)
  corruption, 874
  ninth (3.1998), 467
  1999 session, 430, 702
National Power (UK), 352
national security, 85, 805
National State Capital Management Office
    (1989–), 137
National Steel (USA), 678
'national team' (PRC enterprise groups), xxiv,
    2, 67–139, 926, 938(n10)
  assets, 79

'national team' (PRC enterprise groups) –
  continued
  composition, 68
  disparities, 77, 78
  first batch (1991), 69, 84, 85, 87,
    101–35(column 4), 138, 939(n25)
  geographical location, 81–3
  group expansion and diversification, 79–81
  holding companies, 68
  industrial policy evolution, 83–6
  industrial sectors, 84
  loss-makers (few), 77
  120 largest emerging enterprise groups, 68,
    69–70, 76, 83, 98, 938(n8), 940(n30)
  origins, 72–6
  pillar industries, 83–6
  sales, 79
  scale, 76–9
  second batch (1997), 69, 84, 85–6, 87,
    101–35(column 4), 139, 939(n25)
  'small by comparison with largest TNCs', 79
  various economic indicators, 78
  workforce, 79
  see also trial business groups
National Textile Council, 466
nationalism, 463
nationalization
  mining properties (developing countries), 707
  oil sector, 408–9
  South Korea, 54
Nations Bank, 817
NATO, 158, 178
  arms deliveries (1987–98), 151
  defence spending (post-Cold War), 150
  eastward expansion, 194
NATO Europe, 156
natural gas
  exports from Russia to PRC, 192
  Exxon Mobil, 416
  fuel for electricity generation, 696, 698
  increasing US dependence on, 405
  power stations switch to, 891
  PRC, 192, 354, 429, 715, 716
  price, 697, 957(n1)
  research and development (1995, 1998), 49
  reserves, 421, 696–7, 707
  reserves (PRC), 715, 716
  share of PRC's energy requirements
    (1980–96), 354
  share in primary energy consumption (1996),
    697
  share of world primary energy consumption
    (1987–97), 402
  substitute for coal, 705
  turbines, 335, 337, 338–9
  world distribution, 404–7
  world reserves v world population (1998),
    406
  world reserves and production (1997), 403
  see also liquefied natural gas (LNG)

Navistar, 518–19, 535, 543
NEC (Japan)
  global top hundred company, 850
  investment in PRC, 796
  joint venture with Shougang (1990–), 673,
    955(n55)
  mentioned, 19
  microwave networks (PRC market), 796
  reduction of workforce (1999), 56
Needham, Joseph (1900–95), 587, 898, 899
Nelson Industries, 530
neo-classical economics, 2–8, 28, 679, 862,
  929–30
Nescafé, 311
Nestlé, 35, 311
Netherlands
  bank restructuring (1980–97), 820
  exports 1997 (PRC comparison), 871
  industrialization, 923
  national energy security, 441
  production of plastics (1989–96), 451
  purchase of missiles from USA, 158
  royalty and licensing fees (paid), 785
networking equipment, 795
New China National Petrochemical Group
  (New Sinopec, 1998–), 467, 468
  ability to compete on global level playing
    field, 883–5
  activities largely confined to one country, 481
  ambition to create a truly integrated
    company, 473
  assets, 471, 479
  bureaucratic restructuring, 858
  central control, 488–9
  comparison with global giants, 479–89
  comparison with New CNPC, 471
  competition from SMEs, 844
  economies of scale, 484–5
  employment, 480, 845
  ethylene capacity, 471
  ethylene crackers, 485
  financial indicators, 480
  financial performance, 481[–]484
  forced to take on loss-makers, 843
  Fortune Global 500, 479
  gas production, 481
  global competition, 491, 493, 494–5
  holding company, 473
  imports of crude oil, 488
  integration of operations, 485–6
  interests, 469
  international flotation, 931
  national champion, 481
  natural gas output, 471
  need to increase 'deep processing' capacity,
    487
  oil output, 471
  oil production, 481
  oilfields, 471
  organizational structure, 487–9

New China National Petrochemical Group
    (New Sinopec, 1998–) – *continued*
  output, 479
  petrochemical plants, 471
  petrol stations, 470
  polyethylene (PE) capacity, 471
  polypropylene (PP) capacity, 471
  primary oil processing, 471
  product mix, 486–7
  profits, 480, 484
  re-organized along geographical lines, 468–9
  refineries, 482–4, 484–5
  refineries formerly under Sinopec, 482
  refineries transferred by CNPC, 482–3
  refineries transferred by MCI, 483–4
  research and development, 487
  research institutions, 488
  reserves, 479[–]481
  restructuring, 931
  restructuring through administrative means,
    499–500
  restructuring (1999) for flotation in HKSAR,
    471–4, 479, 488–9
  revenues, profits, employees, R&D (1998), 884
  sales, 471, 479
  sales companies, 471
  size, 479
  statistics, 469
  'still essentially government organ', 498
  structure, 469
  subsidiaries, 469
  synthetic resin capacity, 471
  ten listed subsidiaries, 472
  transfer of assets by Ministry of Chemical
    Industry (1998), 469
  transferred 19 enterprises to New CNPC
    (1998), 469
  turnover, 480
  twelve enterprises transferred by New CNPC
    (1998), 469
  wholesale and retail of petroleum products,
    486
  WTO rules, 867
  see also China National Petrochemical
    Corporation (Sinopec 1983–98);
    Shanghai Petrochemical Corporation
New China National Petroleum Corporation
    Group (New CNPC, 1998–), 467, 468,
    470, 931
  ability to compete on global level playing
    field, 883–5
  activities largely confined to one country, 481
  assets, 470, 471, 479
  bureaucratic restructuring, 858
  central control, 488–9
  comparison with global giants, 479–89
  comparison with New Sinopec, 471
  competition from SMEs, 844
  dangers of exposure to global competition
    (post-PRC WTO entry), 491, 493, 494–5

economies of scale, 484–5
employees, 480
employment, 845
ethylene capacity, 471
ethylene crackers, 485
financial indicators, 480
financial performance, 481[–]484
forced to take on loss-makers, 843
Fortune Global 500, 479
gas production, 481
headquarters (real location), 476, 478–9
integration of operations, 485–6
interests, 470
international flotation, 931
international joint ventures, 488
IPO, 474
listed portion (2000) re-named 'PetroChina',
    489
national champion, 481
natural gas output, 471
need to increase 'deep processing' capacity,
    487
nineteen enterprises transferred by New
    Sinopec (1998), 469
oil output, 471
oil production, 481
oilfields, 471
organizational structure, 487–9
output, 479
petrochemical plants, 471
petrol stations, 470
polyethylene (PE) capacity, 471
polypropylene (PP) capacity, 471
primary oil processing, 471
product mix, 486–7
profitability, 474
profits, 480, 484
re-organized along geographical lines, 468–9
refineries, 477–8, 484–5
research and development, 487
reserves, 479[–]481
restructuring, 931
restructuring through administrative means,
    499–500
restructuring (1999) for flotation in HKSAR,
    471, 474, 476, 479, 488–9
revenues, profits, employees, R&D (1998),
    884
sales, 479, 471
sales companies, 471
size, 479
'still essentially government organ', 498
structure prior to flotation, 475
struggle with Daqing, 474, 476
synthetic resin capacity, 471
transfer of assets by Ministry of Chemical
    Industry (1998), 469
transferred 12 enterprises to New Sinopec
    (1998), 469
turnover, 480

New China National Petroleum Corporation
Group (New CNPC, 1998–) – *continued*
wholesale and retail of petroleum products,
486
WTO rules (implementation by PRC), 867
see also China National Petroleum
Corporation (CNPC 1988–98)
New Japan Steel (Nippon Steel, 1970–), 19,
176, 601, 602–4, 611, 640, 848, 951(n4)
creation (1970), 603
crude steel output (1996–7), 602
deepening partnership with Posco (8.2000–),
928
diversification, 604, 673, 678
employees (1995), 888
global top hundred company, 850
goal, 670
joint venture (1997–) with Usiminas (Brazil),
608
joint ventures in Thailand (early 1990s), 608
management (Shougang comparison), 671
plants, 952(n13)
remuneration and labour productivity (1995),
641
revenues, profits (1998), 888
sales (1997), 888
share-swap with Posco (1999), 613
workforce halved (1985–95), 607
New Mexico: coal, 710
New Seekers (1971), 27
'New Thinking', 908
'New Trade Theory' (1980s), 13
New US Steel, 678
New York, 123, 289
New York stock market
China Yuchai International (CYI), 571n, 574,
576–7, 951(n21)
Dongfeng prospectus, 567–8, 951(n15)
Yuchai listing, 549, 553, 573–4, 574–6, 582
Yuchai prospectus, 576–7, 582
New Zealand, 582
Newly-Industrializing Countries (NICs), 19,
911
news companies, 781
News Corporation, 784, 787, 806
Nigeria, 355, 411
Nigerian National Petroleum Corporation, 409
Nikkei 300, 54
Nikko Securities, 57
Ningbo (PRC), 640
Baogang joint venture, 629
China Unicom joint venture activity, 810
thermal coal price (7.1997), 729
Ningbo Medical Materials Company, 300
ningjuli jituan ('cohesive groups'), 76
Ninguo, 950(n9)
Ningxia: petrol stations, 470
Ningxia Autonomous Region, 656
Ningxia Electric Power Company, 110
Nippon Life, 828

Nippon Oil: global top hundred company, 850
Nippon Steel, *see* New Japan Steel
Nishiyama Yataro, 679
Nissan Motors, 55, 176, 506, 858, 860
dealers, 58
domestic market share, 505
factory closures, 57–8
foreign assets, sales, employment (1997), 509
global top hundred company, 850
interests in Thailand, 508
'national disgrace/betrayal', 57, 516
near-bankruptcy, 532
restructuring (1999), 516
share of foreign production (1989–94), 510
suppliers, 516
take-over by Renault, 57, 515–16, 533
workforce, 58
zaibatsu (1937), 54
NKK (Japan)
crude steel output (1996–7), 602
employees (1995), 888
global top hundred company, 850
investment in an integrated mill with
National Steel, 608
mentioned, 603
reduction of workforce (1999), 56
remuneration and labour productivity (1995),
641
research and development, 595–6, 618
revenues, profits, R&D (1998), 888
Nobel, 264
Nobel Prize winners: General Electric (USA)
research division, 329, 396
Nobuyuki Idei (Sony president), 783
Nokia (Finland), 764, 772, 774–5, 786, 795
Nolan, Peter, 937
non-core business, 8, 34, 39, 61
Aventis, 263
China Telecom, 807
Daqing, 445
Goodyear, 528
oil sector, 425, 427
non-ferrous metals, 77, 120
non-price competition, 11
non-tariff barriers (NTBs), 28–9, 328, 396, 874
auto industry (Japan), 505
power generation (PRC), 881–2
steel, 618, 623, 889
Taiwan, 19
WTO rules (implementation by PRC), 865
Nordic countries, 58
NORINCO, *see* China North Industries
Corporation
Nortel Networks (Canada), 774, 786
acquisitions (1.1999–4.2000), 771, 774
advanced Internet transmission equipment,
774
competition with Cisco and Lucent, 773, 774
fibre optic transmission trunk (PRC), 795
hardware revenues, 772

Nortel Networks (Canada) – *continued*
  market capitalization (2000), 764
  research and development expenditure, 768,
    774
  sales revenue (2000), 764
North Africa, 151, 434, 851
North America
  automobile market (project growth,
    1995–2001), 507
  coal as source of primary energy, 705
  'competitive edge' companies (1997–8), 50
  electricity generation capacity (1990–2010),
    697
  FT 500 (market capitalization, 1999), 50
  Fortune Global 500 (1997–8), 49, 50
  Nissan, 515
  output per worker (coal), 751
  research and development expenditure
    (1997), 48
  steel production (1991–7), 589
North American Free Trade Agreement
    (NAFTA)
  lorry sales (1995, 2005), 509
  production and sales of automobiles (1998),
    508
  projected demand for power equipment
    (1980–2010), 334
  share of world electricity generation
    (1995–2015), 335
  steel consumption *per capita*, 594
North China Pharmaceutical group, 938(n5)
North China Plain, 738
North China Power Generating Group, 359, 361
  national team player (second largest), 110
  SPC subsidiary, 344, 359
North Korea, 178
North Sea
  natural gas (UK), 698
  new source of oil (post-1973), 404
  Norwegian oil interests, 408
  TotalFina, 415
  UK sector, 416
Northeast Asia, 193
  coal supplies, 717–18
Northeast China (regional electricity grid), 345
Northeast China Electrical Equipment
    Company, 365
  floated on the HK stock market, 365
Northeast China Transformer Group, 398,
    945(n30)
Northeast Electric Transmission and
    Transformation Equipment Group
  national team player (first batch), 112
Northeast Power Equipment Company, 394
Northeast Power Equipment Group (Dongbei
    Group), 111
Northern Electrical Industries, 331
Northern Engineering (UK), 943(n7)
Northern Pharmaceutical Group (PRC)
  grooming for *Fortune* 500 entry, 126

investment funds (preferential treatment), 126
  national team player (first batch), 126
Northrop-Grumman, 147, 152–4, 956(n64)
  dwarfed, 146
  relative size (1997), 228
  sales, 227
  size (1998), 166
  'sub-contractor for the two giants', 152
  takeover target, 164, 165
Northwest Airlines (USA), 149
Northwest China Electricity Bureau, 345, 747
Norway, 158, 408, 426, 499, 821
Norway: State Direct Financial Interest, 408
Notable World Figures and their Achievements,
    290
Novartis (1996–), 58, 261–2
  best sellers (drugs), 250
  formed by merger of Ciba-Geigy and Sandoz
    (1996), 255, 261, 268
  joint ventures in PRC, 282
  market capitalization, 269
  market share, 267
  research and development expenditure, 248,
    261, 263
  revenues, profits, employees, R&D (1997),
    879
  sales, 263
  share prices, 262
  workforce, 261–2
NTT
  CCF partner of China Unicom, 810
  international comparison (12.1999), 800
  market capitalization, revenue, profits
    (12.1999), 800
  mentioned, 787
  partially-privatized, 802
  vestige of state ownership, 803
NTT Mobile, 800
nuclear energy, 85, 380, 396, 715
  barriers to use, 406
  fuel for electricity generation, 696, 698
  Guangdong No 2 nuclear power plant, 391
  industrial concentration, 339
  national champions, 336, 943(n6)
  power plant capacity (1980–2010), 335
  PRC, 204, 351, 354, 357–8
  problem of waste disposal, 715
  reduction of greenhouse gas emissions, 704
  safety fears, 402, 704–5
  share in primary energy consumption (1996),
    402, 697
nuclear war, 846
nuclear weapons, 187, 195
Nucor (USA), 599–600, 602, 620, 889
Number One Automobile Group, *see* Yiqi
Number Two Auto, *see* Dongfeng Automobile
    Company
numerical-control systems, 379, 948(n56),
    949(n58)
nutrition, 261

NYC, 950(n9)
Nye, J., and W.A. Owens (1996), cited, 761
nylon, 265; catch-up possibilities, 64

Occar, 157
Occidental, 729
Oceania, 33, 508, 595
OECD countries, 29, 193, 242
   coal consumption rate, 945(n26)
   primary energy efficiency, 355
   steel output (1974–96), 593
   see also advanced economies
Office of Experimental Areas for Agricultural
      Reform (PRC), 316
oil, 848, 854, 859, 860
   asset reorganization, 425–6
   demand, 402
   electricity generation (fuel type, 1990–2010),
      696
   exploration, 252
   exports from Russia to PRC, 192
   fuel for electricity generation (1996), 698
   global market share, 37
   power plant capacity (1980–2010), 335
   power stations switch to, 891
   PRC and global output (1980–98), 341
   price, 697, 957(n1)
   price trend (1970s-), 404
   privatization (general), 32
   production (PRC 1978–94), 355
   production by region (1987–97), 405
   research and development expenditure (1995,
      1998), 49
   reserves, 421, 696–7, 707
   share in primary energy consumption (1996),
      697
   share of world primary energy consumption
      (1987–97), 402
   substitute for coal, 705
   supply, 404
   transportation problems (PRC), 438–9
   world distribution, 404–7
   world production (1997), 403
   world reserves (1997), 403
   world reserves v world population (1998),
      406
oil companies, 44
   alternative energy source, 426–7
   capital control and asset reorganization,
      425–6
   centralized procurement, 422–3
   competitive capability, 417–21
   diversification (temporary) into coal, 707
   economies of scale, 421
   ethylene crackers, 421
   global brand, 427–8
   human resources, 427
   integrated, 413
   integration of refining and marketing, 422
   integration of operations, 421–2

large integrated sites, 421–2
   oil and gas reserves, 421
   organizational structure, 423–5
   product mix, 423
   refineries, 421
   size, 417–21
   super-majors, 417–21, 492, 494
   top 15 (by output, 1996), 409
   see also named individual companies
oil and petrochemicals (global), 401–500, 861,
      929
   alternative energy sources, 426–7
   battle for change, 462–4
   capital control and asset reorganization,
      425–6
   centrality of oil and gas in primary energy
      supplies, 402–4
   centrality of oil and gas in global political
      economy, 401–7
   centralized procurement, 422–3
   conclusion, 491–500
   creation of super giants, 407–28
   'disintegration' of world oil and
      petrochemical industry, 407–10
   economies of scale, 421
   geographical distribution of world oil and
      gas, 404–7
   global brand, 427–8
   global setting, 401–28
   growth of primary energy consumption,
      401–2
   human resources, 427
   integration of operations, 421–2
   internal management systems, 412
   major oil and gas deals (1997–9), 413
   mergers, 411, 412–17
   modern IT, 411–12
   oil industry restructuring (1980s, 1990s),
      410–12
   organization structure, 423–5
   PRC, 428–500
   product mix, 423
   reduced reliance on internally-generated
      crude oil, 410–11
   revolution in oil and gas (global), 407–28
   share of world energy consumption
      (1980–95), 428
   technical progress in exploration and
      development, 411
oil and petrochemicals (PRC), 428–500, 714,
      863, 921
   building strong firms through administrative
      means, 497–500
   carbon dioxide emissions, 430
   China National Offshore Oil Corporation
      (CNOOC), 489–90
   choices facing policy makers, 493–500
   CNPC, 436–41, 474
   comparison with global giants, 479–81
   competitive capability (1997–8), 884

oil and petrochemicals (PRC) – *continued*
  conclusion, 491–500
  corporate structure, 460–1
  Daqing, 441–5, 474–9
  decisive shift in government policy, 497
  direction of PRC government policy, 500
  Donglian experiment, 466–7
  downstream, 445–52
  economies of scale, 484–5
  financial performance, 481–4
  flexibility for future restructuring, 499–500
  flotations, 453, 461, 465, 883
  'following the guidance of the market',
      493–7
  gas reserves, 429, 479[–]481, 706
  global level playing field, 492–3, 883–5
  holding company experiment, 464–6
  increased supply of oil (post-1973), 404
  industrial structure, 461–2
  institutional change, 436–62, 462–89
  integration of operations, 485–6
  international competition and restructuring,
      491
  international trade, 433–5
  joint ventures, 883
  marketing and distribution, 457–60
  merger and acquisition, 495–7
  missed merger opportunities, 862
  national energy security, 441
  natural gas reserves, 407, 491
  obstacles to domestic mergers (PRC), 883
  oil exploration, 436, 440, 706
  oil imports, 433–5
  oil production, 434, 436
  oil reserves, 407, 429, 438–9, 479[–]481,
      491, 492, 706, 715, 716
  oilfields, 437–9
  operational methods, 410
  organizational structure, 487–9
  partially reformed structure, 436–62
      (problems, 460–2)
  population, 406, 407
  primary energy, 402, 428–9
  privatization, 410, 493–5
  product mix, 486–7
  production of ethylene (1989–96), 451
  production of plastics (1989–96), 451
  production of synthetic fibre (1989–96), 451
  reforms of 1998, 462–89
  regional rivalries, 496
  restructuring, 467–71, 493, 883
  revolution in oil and gas, 428–90
  Shanghai Petrochemical Corporation, 454–7
  share of PRC's energy requirements
      (1980–96), 354–5
  Sinopec, 445–52, 464–6, 472–4
  structure of primary energy use, 429–33
  struggle to centralize power, 497–8
  struggle between Daqing and CNPC
      headquarters, 474–9
  subordinate enterprises, 452–7
  supply and demand (oil and gas), 428–35
  upstream, 436–45
  use in steel industry (PRC), 953(n31)
  weaknesses (oil sector), 492–3
  WTO rules (implementation by PRC), 867,
      884
oil price
  collapse (1997–8) and sharp rise (1999), 459
  future uncertainty, 749
  long decline (1980s-), 410, 412, 748
  PRC, 448, 453, 457–8, 748
  rise (1992–4) and fall (1994–7), 459
  shocks (1970s), 401, 402, 405, 410, 706, 707,
      748, 814
oil products
  'in-plan high price' (PRC), 458
  'in-plan low price' (PRC), 458
oil refining, 421, 422
  Caltex, 417
  New CNPC (1998–), 470
  PRC, 444
  Sinopec, 446–7, 449–50
  South Korea, 22
  Taiwan, 20
  TotalFinaElf, 417
oil seals, 950(n9)
oil tanker fleets, 486
oligopoly, 4, 11, 15–16, 17
  auto industry (Japan), 505, 510
  coal sector, 713
  commercial seeds (1998), 768
  computers (1998), 768
  diesel engines (PRC), 567
  EU, 234
  form of warfare, 670
  global, 40–2, 61, 62, 857, 860, 875, 929–30
  iron ore sector, 713
  IT, 767–70
  Japan, 17, 60, 176, 236, 463
  job of investment banker, 27
  'normal path', 13, 61
  oil sector (PRC), 468
  pesticides (1998), 768
  pharmaceutical industry, 245
  pharmaceuticals (1998), 768
  power equipment business, 338, 395
  promotion (PRC), 86
  South Korea, 22, 176, 236, 463
  sub-categories of markets, 40–2, 61
  telecommunications (1998), 768
  Triad group of countries, 60
  USA, 35, 60, 154, 232
  veterinary medicines (1998), 768
  Western Europe, 60
  see also industrial concentration
Olivetti, 786
Omnicom, 781
Oneworld (airline alliance), 149
online trading, 834

OPEC, 415
open hearth furnace, 596, 597, 628, 953(n21)
    energy inefficient, 953(n21)
    steel production method (1997), 597
opium, 902–3
oppression, vii, 907
Oracle (USA), 764, 772, 776, 786
Orange (telecommunications company), 786
Ordos Plateau (PRC), 734, 890
organ transplants, 246
Ortel, 773
outsourcing, 7–8, 51, 61, 145, 159, 918
    aerospace, 144
    components, 333–4, 520–1
    globalization (automobile industry), 511,
        950(n3)
    IBM, 772
    IT companies, 775
    IT systems, 146
    lessons learnt by US and Europe, 51
    pharmaceutical sector, 246
    power equipment, 337
    service contracts, 332
    software, 787–8
    'Toyotist', 48
    Yiqi bucks trend (1995), 561
    Yuchai, 580
    see also 'external firm'; sub-contracting
Overseas Chinese, 291, 300–1, 310, 573, 880
Owens, W.A., *see* Nye, J.
ownership reform, xxiii
oxides of nitrogen (NOx), 700

Paccar, 861
    acquisitions, 535
    leading lorry-maker, 517
    origins, 517
    output, sales, profits, employees (1998), 542
    price of lorry (average), 534
Pacific (PRC insurance company), 828
Pacific Century Cyberworks (PCCW), 784, 806,
    935
packaging, 34, 42, 43, 311, 318
Paine Webber, 822
Pakistan, 378, 388, 619, 900, 943(n8)
Paloma Partners (USA), 306
Panda Group (national team player), 108
Pangang, *see* Panzhihua Iron and Steel Group
Panzihua Iron and Steel Group (*'Pangang
    jituan'*)
    continuous casting, 627
    national team player (first batch), 114
    output structure (1997), 646
    principal steel products (1997), 637
    production methods (1997), 597
    productivity, 659
    remuneration and productivity (1997), 641
    return on investment (1980–90), 660
    top ten steel producer (PRC 1997), 634
paper, 53, 56

paraxylene, 416
'Pareto optimal' solution, 3
Paris, 212
Paris Air Show (6.1999), 182
Park Chung Hee, President, 21–2
Parson, Sir Charles, 943(n7)
Parsons engineering, 943(n7)
passenger transport: PRC (1978–97), 432
patents
    absence, 844
    dominance of high-income countries, 785
    IBM, 772–3
    pharmaceuticals, 879, 880
    royalty and licensing fees, 785
    TRIPs Agreement (1994), 785
    WTO enforcement proceedings, 870
Peabody (USA), 709, 710, 735–6
'Peace Programme', 190
Peirson, Jean, 155
Pemex, 409
Peng, Li (b 1928), 212
Peninsular and Oriental Steam Navigation
    Company (P&O): joint venture with
    Shougang, 687
Pennsylvania Railroad, 937(n2 to ch1)
Penrose, Edith, 10–11
pension funds, 180, 381, 918, 949(n60, 62)
pensions, 271, 315, 321, 367, 383, 922
Pentagon (USA), 144, 147, 150, 152–3, 154,
    155, 157, 162, 165
    promotion of mergers, [682], 956(n64)
People's Armed Police (PAP, PRC), 273, 276–7
People's Bank of China (PBC), 833, 836
People's Insurance Company of China (PICC),
    826, 828, 830, 958(n10)
People's Liberation Army (PLA), 188, 192,
    194, 201, 951(n22)
    commercial activities v military goals, 274–7
    commercialization, 271–7, 941(n3–6, 9)
    direct ownership of defence firms, 941(n4)
    fraud, 276
    galvanizing tradition, 667
    involvement in smuggling, 275
    military enterprises converted to civilian
        production, 272
    military modernization 'undermined', 276
    'most powerful institution in PRC', 241–2,
        277
    new businesses, 272[–]4
    owner of Sanjiu Group (until 1998), 241–2
    pilots, 191
    professionalization programme, 276
    reform proposals *re* commercial activities
        (1998), 242, 324–5
    'rich legacy of motivational skills', 680
    smuggling, 874
    'technological backwardness', 194, 195
    Tibet, 312
    'transition to civilian ownership', 277
    see also Sanjiu

People's Republic of China (PRC, 1949–)
  ability to compete globally, 839, 840
  administration, 923
  agrees to join WTO (1999), 4–5, 25
  air force, 189–90
  air traffic, 202
  anti-US sentiment, 924
  arms deliveries (1987–98), 151, 152
  'ASEAN plus three' forum, 927–8
  aspiring global champions, 849
  automobile and vehicle components industry
      (PRC), 536–85
  aviation industry, 184–240
  business groups, 76
  central administration (1998 reforms), 346–7
  changes in ideology, 328
  city government (PRC), 69, 70, 938(n11)
  co-operation agreements (PRC), 73
  coal, 619, 713–60, 957–8
  collective enterprises, 73
  communications, 926
  comparative advantage, 6
  demand for pharmaceuticals (per capita), 277
  destabilizing forces, 811
  drive to diversify, 846–50
  economic growth, xxiii, 339, 340, 428, 536,
      623–4, 649, 713, 851, 907, 912, 913,
      915–16, 953(n27)
  electronics (impact on trade balance), 86
  elevation in status of business leaders, 92
  energy, 339–42, 348, 354, 428, 715, 716,
      943(n9)
  enterprise law (1994), 138
  EU/US access to markets, 813–14
  experiments in enterprise reform, 68
  export markets, 848–9
  fifth largest oil producer in world (1994), 355
  fifth-largest trading partner of USA, 871
  fiscal difficulties, 649
  forecasts, 871–2, 914
  'foreign medicines' (market share), 283
  foreign trade rights, 874
  'fundamental economic situation', 834
  geographical distribution of aviation industry,
      187
  ground forces, 192
  'hardliners' and 'reformers', 875
  high transaction costs, 847
  holding companies, 847
  human capital, 762
  imperfect markets, 847
  import-substitution industries, 623
  importance of electronics to trade balance,
      106
  industrial policy, 4, 24–5, 27–8, 65, 74,
      186–7, 241, 840, 853, 854, 856–7,
      857–64, 864–76, 932–3
  inflation, 650, 953(n28)
  influence of mainstream neo-classical ideas,
      25

infrastructure investment, 643
institutions, 87, 98–9
'insurance density', 832
international relations, 2
internet hosts per 1,000 people (1997), 789
'inward-looking', 24
large SOEs, 853
legal system, 298, 834
'macroeconomic adjustment capabilities', 88
maritime claims, 196
mass media market, 781
mentioned, 145
military-industrial complex, 272, 273
military technology, 187–8
ministries, 847
models for economic development
    (post-Mao), 24
national champions, 67–139
national defence industries, 231
naval forces, 192
net importer of oil, 706, 714
'new left wing', 875
non-mainstream economic theory, 8
non-signatory to World Telecoms Agreement,
    786
nuclear capability, 195
number of companies in *Fortune* 500 (1998),
    47n
offshore oil reserves, 883
120 largest emerging enterprise groups, 68,
    69–70, 83, 98, 938(n8), 940(n30)
onshore oil reserves, 883
'outstanding economic progress' (1978–95),
    67
'over-manning', 846–7, 853, 892, 893–4
passenger airliner fleet (1985–96), 202
People's Republic of China (PRC 1949–)
per capita energy use (1994), 341
personal computers per 1,000 people (1997),
    789
pharmaceutical companies, 284–5, 286
pharmaceuticals, 270, 277–89, 289–320
police corruption, 874
policy debates (1980s–), xxiii-xxiv, 4, 6, 25,
    937(ch1,n1)
political considerations affecting commercial
    decisions, 212, 218
political stability considerations, 872, 875
poorer regions, 86, 113
potential consequences of a financial crisis
    (post-WTO entry), 834
poverty, 196, 803–4, 852
power equipment needs, 342–3
power generation equipment, 327–8, 339–99
primary energy efficiency, 355
priority given to economic modernization,
    196
prosecution of prosecutors (corruption cases),
    874
rapid industrialization, 699

People's Republic of China (PRC, 1949–) –
    continued
    reform process, 841, 843, 850, 851 ('failure',
        852, 857), 852–6, 857
    regional and departmental barriers, 88, 92
    regions, 74
    restructuring, 813
    role of imports (military technology), 190–5
    'second largest economy' (PPP), 850, 913–14
    sense of vulnerability (defence), 193, 194–5
    'seventh largest economy' (1998), 850
    share of world exports (1980–97), 871
    'six unifications' policy, 89, 137
    state equity holdings, 932
    steel, 587–8, 593, 594, 615, 616, 619,
        622–94, 889, 952–7
    stock market capitalization (1998), 932
    structure of output (1995), 700
    'technologically backward', 95, 194, 195
    telecommunications development (1997), 789
    telecommunications (effect of WTO
        accession), 777
    telecommunication statistics, 798
    telephone main lines (1997), 789
    television sets per 1,000 people (1997), 789
    theory of the firm (lessons from Posco), 605
    trade surplus with USA, 872, 893
    urbanization, 852
    US 'threat', 194
    wages, 313, 942(n27)
    weakening of planning system, 328
    wireless telephones, 778, 789
    workers 'nominally the masters', 665
    working-age population, 893–4
    see also China (pre-1949); global business
        revolution (PRC response); individual
        sectors of economy
People's Republic of China (PRC, 1949–):
        long-term view, 897–33, 958
    centralized political system, 907
    China in 1949, 906–7
    'conventional' structural adjustment, 919–23
    'distinctively Chinese' development strategy,
        915
    employment structure (1998), 919
    energy intensity (1998), 914, 958(n2)
    opening up and advancing (Deng era),
        910–16
    output of key commodities (1998), 913
    past, 898–916
    political destabilization fears, 919
    prospects: 'optimistic' view, 916–19
    resuming role as 'core of world economy',
        899, 901–2, 918
    Russian disaster (avoided by PRC), 908–10,
        915
    shock of defeat, 916–25
    spiritual pollution countered, 911
    stands up (Mao), 907–8
    technology gap, 908

    world ranking (selected products, 1949–98),
        913
    world's largest economy, prediction (by
        2020), 914
    WTO entry, 898, 916–25, 925–33, 958(n3)
PepsiCo, 35, 863
Peregrine (HK-based investment bank), 545
perestroika, 908
perfect competition, 3–4, 13, 19, 149, 232, 670,
        857
Perkins Diesel Engine (UK), 530, 547–8
personal computers, 106–7, 108, 272, 769
    global (per 1,000 people, 1997), 789
    Microsoft, 776
    non-SOE national champions (PRC), 862
    penetration (developing countries), 788
    PRC, 790, 794, 796
Pertamina (Indonesia): output (1996), 409
Peru, 646, 690
    copper and nickel, 691
    exports of iron ore to PRC, 640
    investments by CNPC, 441
    purchase of 'Hierro' iron mine by Shougang
        (11.1992), 675, 691
    Shougang Hierro (Peru) SA, 647, 672n
pesticides, 265, 456
Peterbilt (lorry company), 518
Petrobas (Brazil), 409, 494, 861
Petrobas de Venezuela (PDVSA), 409, 418
petrochemicals, 355, 368, 458–9, 848, 854, 859,
        860
    BP Amoco, 414
    Donglian, 466–7
    Exxon, 415
    global 'disintegration', 407–10
    global market share, 37
    global oligopoly, 41
    Huizhou, 454, 490
    imports (into PRC), 452
    'one of least protected sectors' (PRC), 453
    PRC, 433, 436, 444, 446, 448, 449, 450–2,
        453, 485, 487, 715
    privatization (general), 32
    restructuring, 80
    Samsung, 53
    Sinopec, 449, 450–2
    South Korea, 54
    TotalFinaElf, 417
PetroChina (2000–), 80, 931
    IPO (disappointing yield, 4.2000), 884
    listed portion of New CNPC, 489
    super-group, 80
    'wake-up call for PRC', 489
PetroFina (Belgium), 415, 493
petrol, 458, 485, 848, 883
petrol stations, 44, 416, 422, 444, 459, 486,
        494
petroleum, 265
petroleum refining, 11
Petronas (Malaysia), 410

Peugeot
    collaboration with Fiat, 513
    diesel engines, 513
    foreign assets, sales, employment (1997), 509
    Guangzhou joint venture (1993–7), 537
    interests in India, 508
    joint venture with Guangzhou Auto (1985–), 539
    output, turnover, profit, R&D (1998), 533
    partnership with Ford, 513
    suppliers, 519
Pfizer, 247, 259, 848
    best sellers (drugs), 250, 269
    takeover of Warner-Lambert (2000), 259, 260, 262
    R&D, 259
Pfizer/Warner-Lambert (2000–), 257, 258–60
pharmaceutical companies
    global oligopoly, 245
    global top twenty by R&D expenditure (1994–7), 248–9
    manufacturing procedures, 301
    PRC, 283[–]286, 287
    profit margins (1998), 245
    research and development necessary, 247
    response to change, 252–66
    restructuring, 252
    traditional, 243–4, 253–60
    see also Sanjiu Enterprise Group
pharmaceuticals (global), 241–326, 848, 861, 863
    assets, 80
    barriers to entry, 63–4, 270–1
    brand and marketing, 251
    commercialization of the PLA, 271–7
    conclusion, 320–6
    consolidation, 80
    consumer goods, 86
    consumption (selected countries), 278
    de-mergers and mergers, 252–3
    demand, 242–5, 277, 283
    drivers of change, 242–71
    global changes, 242–71
    global market share, 37
    global oligopoly, 40
    liberalization (international), 282–3
    life sciences, 260–6
    market share (global), 266–8
    PRC, 277–320
    profits, 283
    research and development, 49, 245–51
    stock market pressure, 251–2
    Sweden, 59
    traditional pharmaceutical companies, 253–60
    transatlantic corporations, 338
    TRIPs Agreement (1994), 785
    US dominance, 269
    Western, 288–9
pharmaceuticals (PRC), 277–320

ability to compete on global level playing field, 878–81
    basic data (1996), 280–1, 284–5, 287–8
    competitive capability (1997), 879
    conclusion, 320–6
    distribution, 299–300
    industrial structure, 283–9
    liberalization, 279–82
    market size, 277–9
    missed merger opportunities, 861
    national team, 77, 78, 125–6
    non-SOE national champions, 862
    production (1980–96), 279
    Sanjiu Group, 289–320
    sectoral share of national team (1991–7), 84
    traditional (Chinese), 242, 282, 288–9
    WTO rules (implementation by PRC), 868
    see also Sanjiu Enterprise Group
Pharmacia and Upjohn, 246, 249, 257, 266
Pharmacia Upjohn/Monsanto, 265–6
pharmacies (PRC), 300
Philadelphia, 269
Philip Morris: competitive advantage, 35
Philippines
    demand for pharmaceuticals (per capita), 277
    difficulty of framing industrial policy, 60
    export market for HPEC, 388
    HPEC tenders (1996), 387
    pharmaceuticals market (1995), 277
    tariffs on steel products (1997), 619
    WTO enforcement proceedings, 870
Phillips Petroleum Corporation (USA), 454, 455, 472
Phoenix (Chinese-language TV station), 784
pig iron, 603, 626
Pilkington Automotive Division, 525
pillar industries, 83–6, 98, 99, 241, 316, 318, 320, 520, 537, 540, 545
Ping An (PRC insurance company), 828
Pingdangshan Mining Company, 720
pingpang touzi ('investment salad'), 347
Pingshuo (coalfield, PRC), 718
Pingshuo Coal Company (Shanxi), 718, 720, 736, 737
    Antaibao mine, 729
Pioneer (components-manufacturer), 522
Pioneer Hi-Bred (Iowa), 265
pioneering provinces (PRC), 69
pipelines: oil, 441
Pirelli, 522, 527, 529, 860
Pirelli Optical systems (IT company), 773
Pittsburgh (USA), 609
Piyanping (skin ointment), 298
pizhun ('ratification'), 947(n43)
PLA, *see* People's Liberation Army
PLA: General Logistics Department (GLD), 272, 273, 276, 306, 311, 314, 318
    creams off Sanjiu's profits, 294, 296, 322, 323
    new meeting hall in Beijing, 295, 322

PLA: General Logistics Department (GLD) –
    continued
  occupancy rights (Hebei province), 315–16
  owner of Nanfang/Sanjiu Group (1986–),
      242, 290–1, 294, 321–3
  runs Guangzhou Army Hospital, 291
  sets up 35 enterprises in Shenzhen (by 1992),
      294, 311, 319, 324
PLA: General Staff Department (GSD), 272,
    273, 274, 276
planned economy, *see* command economy
Plant Breeding International Cambridge Ltd,
    265
plants, 73, 74, 76, 91, 95, 98, 109, 126, 187
  Liaoning, 111
  micro-vans, 199
  nuclear power, 85
  pharmaceuticals, 283, 941(n10)
  pharmaceutical (PRC), 279, 283, 307
  problems of definition, 939(n15)
  Shenzhen, 291
  size, 3
  Wuhan, 102
plastics
  alternative to steel, 590, 591, 595
  bottles, 39, 43, 416
  mentioned, 252
  packaging, 455
  PRC, 433, 450, 451, 452, 472, 487
  Shanghai Petrochemical Corporation, 472
  Sinopec, 450, 452
  Taiwan, 20
  world production (1989–96), 451
Plato, 935
Poland, 909, 917
  coal output (1980–95), 699
  coal-sector employment, 706, 707
  deaths in coal-mining accidents (1994), 725
  labour productivity (coal-mining, 1996),
      711
  output per worker (coal), 751
  wages (coal industry), 752
pollution, 127, 590, 653, 689–90, 691
  acid rain, 700, 701
  Beijing, 748
  coal-burning, 699–702
  control (PRC), 546, 740
  government action required, 700–1
  household use of coal (PRC), 748
  minimization, 338
  oil refineries (PRC), 485
  power stations (PRC), 355, 881
  PRC, 429–31, 460, 845
  small oil refineries (PRC), 485
  SMEs (PRC), 844
  steel industry, 593, 598, 628, 629, 631
  urban air (PRC), 748
  see also environment
polycrystalline silicon, 426
polyester, 452, 466

polyethylene, 262, 416, 417, 423, 455, 470
polymers, 265, 417, 422, 487
polypropylene, 417, 423, 470
polystyrene, 417
Polytechnologies, 941(n7)
Pondimin (anti-obesity drug), 250
population, 47, 851
  Asia-Pacific (including South Asia), 406–7
  China (early C19), 901
  China (Taiping Rebellion), 903
  PRC, 438, 703, 798, 851, 893–4
porcelain, 130, 900
pork, 871
ports, 119
Portugal, 513, 821
Posco (South Korea, 1968–), 176, 599, 600,
    611, 640, 842, 854, 858, 887
  'big family', 669
  capacity, 604
  catch-up (steel industry), 604–5, 621
  crude steel output (1996–7), 602
  debt-control, 604–5
  deepening partnership with New Japan Steel
      (8.2000–), 928
  employees (1994), 888
  eschews diversification, 692
  four plants in PRC, 609
  goal, 670
  Japanese reparations, 604
  joint venture with US Steel, 601
  key slogan, 668
  management (Shougang comparison), 671
  military discipline, 669
  mini-mills, 609
  'most successful steel company', 604, 605,
      692
  overseas operations (1990s), 609
  privatization process, 605
  remuneration and labour productivity (1994),
      641
  revenues, profits (1998), 888
  role model for Shougang, 668, 669
  share-swap with Nippon Steel (1999), 613
  state-owned, 604, 605, 952(n9)
  subsidiary in Pittsburgh (USA), 609
  tight discipline and high remuneration,
      955(n50)
  workforce reduced (1992–7), 605
postal services, 32
pottery, 130
poultry, 870
poverty
  absolute (PRC 1978–96), 914, 915
  income deciles, 915
  output per capita (PRC), 913, 915
  PRC, 196
  Russian Federation, 910
power equipment (global), 327–99, 848, 860,
    942–9
  barriers to entry (1998), 63–4

power equipment (global) – *continued*
  biggest single market (PRC), 342–3
  conclusion, 392–9
  demand, 334–5
  financing PRC's power industry, 348–54
  gas-fired, 337, 339
  global market share, 37
  global oligopoly, 42
  Harbin Power Equipment Company, 328,
    363–92
  hydro, 356–7, 394
  industrial concentration, 335–9
  main features of industry worldwide, 328–39
  marketing, 942(n1)
  multinational giants as suppliers (PRC),
    358–63
  power equipment markets, 354–8
  PRC, 327–8, 339–99
  'quintessential capital good', 327
  size of leading firms (late 1990s), 330
  technical progress, 329–31
power equipment (PRC), 327–8, 339–99, 848,
    921
  Build-Operate-Transfer (BOT), 352–3
  command economy era, 3
  commercial loans, 354
  competitive capability (1998), 882
  equity participation, 350–2
  export credit, 353–4
  exports (by HPEC), 387
  Fifteen Year Programme for Technical
    Transfer (1981–96), 376–7
  finance, 348–54
  500 MW Francis-type power generator sets,
    948(n57)
  flotation, 349
  Harbin Power Equipment Company, 328,
    363–92, 948(n57)
  hydro power, 356–7
  imports, 347
  integrated coal gasification combined cycle
    systems, 948–9(n57)
  involvement of multinational corporations,
    358–63
  local finance, 350
  markets, 354–8, 863
  national team, 76, 111–12
  new investment institutions, 349–50
  nuclear power, 357–8, 380
  power generation and distribution, 343–6
  price (PRC), 385–6
  role of multinational giants, 358–63
  price determination, 345
  rate of return, 349, 944(n14)
  regulation, 343–8
  state procurement, 860
  steam/gas combined cycle, 380
  sub-contracting, 347
  technology transfer, 347
  thermal power stations, 354–6, 380, 394

  WTO accession, 882
power equipment companies
  Asea and Brown Boveri merger (late 1980s),
    59
  concentration, 335–9
  economies of scale and scope, 328–34
  financial strength, 331–2
  flotation, 349
  job losses, 337, 338
  low-cost supply base, 333–4
  market share worldwide (power generation
    equipment, 1993–8), 337
  PRC, 349
  service capability, 332–3
  source of profits, 333
power generation
  nation team players (PRC), 109–10
  PRC, 871
  PRC (national team), 76, 81
  privatization (general), 32
  South Korea, 54
power generation equipment, *see* power
    equipment
power stations, 43, 109, 119, 126, 328, 329,
    849, 860, 881
  BOT ('Build-Operate-Transfer'), 331, 352–3
  coal supplies (PRC), 723
  coal-driven, 339, 350, 380
  coal-fired (PRC), 714, 716
  construction and finance (PRC), 345
  conversion to coal-fired (PRC), 740
  cost of construction, 349, 944(n15)
  developing countries, 891
  East Asia, 891
  energy savings (potential) (PRC), 716
  environmentally-friendly, 705
  'Europe', 891
  fossil-fuels, 339
  fuel type, 335
  gas-fired, 337, 339
  global market, 334
  hydro, 390
  large, modern (PRC), 714
  low-emission coal (PRC), 734
  market for Shenhua, 746–8
  oil-fired, 350, 740
  pit-head (PRC), 715, 747, 753
  pollution control, 700
  PRC, 192, 713, 714–15, 740, 890
  security of supply 'crucial', 757
  Shenhua Project, 735, 738, 743n
  Shougang, 672
  size (PRC), 714–15
  small-scale (PRC), 724
  steam, 390
  tax (possible) on emissions (PRC), 714–15
  thermal efficiency, 329
  thermal, 350, 380, 386
  USA, 891
Prague, 950(n6)

Pratt and Whitney, 142, 172, 178, 180, 204, 205
    alliance with Siemens (1990) 330, 942(n2)
    Chinese sub-contractor (CEC), 217
PRC, *see* People's Republic of China
precision machinery (Samsung), 53
precision tools (AVIC), 198
preferential planning (PRC), 70, 74–5, 89,
        91–2, 120
    phased out, 92
    single-track, 98–9
PREVI, 180
price deflator, 940(n11)
price mechanism, 7
price reform, xxiii
    Russian Federation (1992–), 909
price regime
    'in-plan high price' (PRC), 458
    'in-plan low price' (PRC), 458
    international (oil), 458
    liberalization, 457, 458, 459
    New Policy (1994), 457–8
    oil sector (PRC), 457, 462
    petrochemical products (PRC), 458–9
    State Low Price (crude oil, PRC), 457
    State High Price (crude oil, PRC), 457
prices, 3, 7, 13, 44, 64
    attained by suppliers, 42
    competition, 11, 62
    controls, 604, 874
    cutting, 61
    market-determined, 1, 5
    PRC (domestic), 435
    primary commodity, 709
    stabilization (Japan), 17
primary energy
    centrality of oil and gas, 402–4
    consumption (1996), 697
    demand (PRC), 428–9
    global consumption, 401–2
    use (PRC), 429–33
primary metals, 14
Prince (car components manufacturer), 523
Principles of Economics (Marshall 1920), 7
print machinery, 38
printing and packaging, 311
Prior, Charles (Westinghouse), 357
private consumption (PRC index, 1980–97),
        914
private sector
    PRC (Deng era), 912
    Taiwan and South Korea, 19
privatization, 3, 498, 707, 840–1, 849, 917
    advanced economies, 892
    aerospace, 163, 180
    airlines (Europe), 149
    Brazil, 180, 688
    driver of big business revolution, 32
    electricity generation, 336, 397, 697
    Embraer, 181–2
    'Europe', 920

former Communist countries, 32
    not essential for growth, 682
    oil and petrochemicals (global), 407–8, 413,
        436, 492
    oil sector (PRC), 496
    Peru, 691
    power plants (advanced economies), 331
    PRC, 69, 96, 496, 920, 921
    Rolls-Royce (1989), 173, 331
    Russian Federation, 909
    steel industry, 587, 600, 605, 606, 609
    telecommunications, 779
    Volkswagen, 504
Procter and Gamble, 34, 35
procurement, 45, 863, 395–6
    aerospace (USA), 170, 231–2, 235
    auto industry, 523, 533, 535
    components, 398
    defence equipment, 156–8, 240
    diesel engines, 531
    GATT talks (Uruguay Round), 395
    global, 39, 851, 856
    global giants, 845–6
    government contracts, 860
    internet network (Ford, GM, Daimler-
        Chrysler), 856
    military (PRC), 276
    military aircraft, 150, 154, 174, 196–7, 201
    oil sector, 414, 422–3
    on-line networks, 45
    USSR/Russian Federation, 178
    weapons (PRC), 188, 196–7, 216, 217, 232
product development, 43, 600
product mix, 423, 436, 484, 487, 684, 841
production
    costs, 9, 10
    flows, 14
    inter-enterprise agreements (PRC), 73
    processes, 11
    'social value', 13
    Third Technological Revolution, 763
productivity, 11, 17, 72, 92, 127, 338
Proex (Brazil), 181–2, 878
profitability, 64
profits
    automobile sector (PRC), 442, 539
    CNPC, 439
    Daqing, 439–40
    miscellaneous, 61, 189
    Mobil (downstream), 415
    New CNPC (1998–), 468
    New Sinopec (1998–), 468
    oil sector, 419, 410, 480
    oil sector (PRC), 442, 459, 495
    patent medicines, 244
    pharmaceuticals (PRC), 279
    PRC, 73, 77, 92, 94, 98, 136, 938(n10)
    retained (PRC), 348
    right to retain, 437, 495
    Sinopec, 446, 449, 465

property, 107, 121, 124, 130
property management, 8
property rights, 137, 215, 274, 283, 290, 495
  insecure (developing countries), 757
  Shenhua, 890
  PRC, 72, 87, 88, 849
prostitution, 33, 275
protectionism
  Adam Smith's critique, 5
  anti-Chinese ('Europe', USA), 218
  auto components (PRC), 885
  auto industry (South Korea), 505
  auto industry (general), 533, 534
  calls for, EU and USA (steel, 1998), 607
  declining level (steel, 1990s), 607
  declining in oil sector (PRC), 458
  dismantling (PRC post-WTO accession),
    864–9
  East Asia (telecommunications), 779
  essential for 'green shoots' (PRC), 862–3
  French auto industry, 504
  Germany, 396
  IT sector (PRC), 791, 794 (undermined, 792)
  Italian auto industry, 504
  Japan, 17, 18
  Japanese auto industry, 505
  local (PRC), 874
  lorry industry (PRC), 535, 554
  mentioned, 4, 14, 15, 52
  Mexico (telecommunications), 779, 802–3
  non-SOE national champions (PRC), 862–3
  oil sector (PRC), 883
  power equipment (PRC), 347–8
  power generation (PRC), 881–2
  PRC, 4, 70, 463, 813, 911
  PRC car industry, 537–8
  PRC (telecommunications), 803
  'regional aid' (Europe), 533
  South Korea, 19, 22, 52–3
  South Korea (steel), 604, 858
  steel industry (developing countries), 605
  steel industry (general), 618
  steel industry (USA), 601, 951(n5)
  Taiwan, 19, 20
  telecommunications sector, 787
  UK, 15, 873
  USA, 15, 601, 952(n6)
  voluntary export restraints, 601
  wireless telecommunications (PRC), 796
  see also anti-dumping; World Trade
    Organization
protest movements: anti-GM seeds, 266
provinces
  distribution of China's preferred large-scale
    enterprises and groups (1997), 82
  PRC, 80
  R&D (PRC), 94
  teams of business groups, 70
provincial government (PRC), 69, 70, 349,
  938(n11)

Prybyla, Jan, 912
PTA technology (BP Amoco), 423
PTA (Yizheng), 466
Publicis (advertising sector), 781
public transport: privatization (general), 32
pulp and paper: global market share, 37
purchasing power parity (PPP), 850, 913–15,
  957(n2)
Putin, Vladimir, 910
PX (Paraxylene) technology (BP Amoco), 423
Pyropower Corporation, 378

Qantas, 149
Qatar: natural gas, 416
Qian Long, Emperor (r 1736–96), 901–2
  ignorance of proverb 'pride comes before
    fall', 902
Qian'an *xian* (Hebei Province)
  projected deep water port, 676
  Shougang iron ore mine (1960–), 653, 672n,
    675, 687
qiansanfei (severance payment), 315
Qilu (Shandong Province), 643
  plan (aborted) to build steel plant, 651–2,
    653, 662, 670, 671, 675, 679, 686–7,
    842, 888
Qilu Iron and Steel, 671
Qilu Petrochemical Corporation, 469, 472
Qin Xiao, Mr, xxvi
Qing Dynasty (1644–1911), 125, 900, 903, 904
Qingan Aerospace Equipment Corporation, 200
Qingdao (PRC)
  China Unicom joint venture activity, 810
  coal port, 720
  thermal coal price (7.1997), 729
Qinghai Electric Power Company, 110
Qinghuangdao (PRC), 720, 723, 739, 740
Qingling Auto Group Corporation
  diesel engine production (1998), 559
  output of light trucks (1998), 554
Qinhuangdao Tractor Component Plant, 655
Qinshan (Zhejiang Province) nuclear plant
    (1994–), 357, 945(n21)
  Atomic Energy of Canada, 945(n21)
  GE (Canada), 357
Qiqihar, 948(n56)
Qiqihar Heavy Engineering, 948(n53)
qiye jituan (enterprise groups), 364
Qtera (optical networking firm), 774
quality control
  pharmaceutical sector, 286, 298, 303, 310,
    323
  power equipment, 337
  see also GMP
Quanta Company (Taiwan), 21
Quanta Fund (Soros), 834
quanzi zigongsi (wholly-owned subsidiaries),
  563
Quek Leng Chan, 573, 951(n19)
quotas, 865–6, 867

radar, 148, 192, 193, 523
Rafale fighter, 158–9
rail transport (PRC, 1978–97), 432
railway stations, 126
railways, 13–14, 119, 124, 653, 904, 937(n2 to
        ch1)
    Baotou-Datong-Beijing, 739
    Beijing-Kowloon, 738
    boom (USA), 601
    coal transport (PRC), 723, 726, 738–40, 750,
        752
    Datong-Qinghuangdao, 739
    'fees', 723, 758, 957(n4)
    freight traffic (PRC), 738–9
    funding, 742, 743
    iron ore transport (Australia), 708, 739–40
    high-speed trains, 206
    map, 732–3
    network of power stations (PRC), 747
    PRC network, 738
    rolling stock (South Korea), 54
    'salaried professional managers', 14
    Shenfu Dongsheng Coalfield, 734, 738–40
    Shenmu-Baotou, 738, 739, 741–2
    Shenmu-Shuozhou-Huanghua, 733, 738–9,
        741–2, 743n, 747, 890
    subsidies (PRC), 739
Ramangkura, Dr Virabongsa, 927
Ramquist, Dr Lars, 935
'Rape of Nanjing', 905
rate of return, 349, 353, 944(n14)
Raytheon, 147, 160, 171, 235, 956(n64)
    'mainly defence producer', 230
    market capitalization (1999), 236
    relative size (1997), 228
    size (1998), 166
Reagan, Ronald (b 1911): downfall of USSR,
        793
real estate, 53, 127, 311, 315, 316, 317, 688,
        921
Redmond, Sumner (CEO Viacom), 781
redundancies, 313, 315, 321
Redux (anti-obesity drug), 250
reform process (PRC), xxiii, 841, 843, 850, 851
    external problems, 855–6
    'failure', 852
    internal problems, 852–5
    local autonomy, 853
refrigerators (PRC) 197
Regional Airlines (French airline), 182
regional groups (PRC): national team players,
        120–1
Reliance (India), 861
remote areas (PRC), 187, 196, 224, 227, 656,
        758, 846
    coal mines, 731
    military factories, 275, 309
    offshore oil reserves, 481, 489, 490
    oil reserves (PRC), 883
    onshore oil reserves, 438–9, 481

Shenfu Dongsheng Coalfield, 734
Yuchai, 582
    see also 'Third Front' movement; Yuchai
        Diesel Engine Company
Ren Wanding, 875
ren wei ben ('people are the foundation'), 579
Renault, 840, 841, 854, 920
    breakdown of alliance with Volvo, 513
    'controlling stake in Nissan Motors', 57
    foreign assets, sales, employment (1997), 509
    44% state-owned, 516
    interests in Eastern Europe (post-1989), 508
    interests in Mercosur, 508
    interests in Turkey, 508
    merger with Nissan (3.1999), 515
    nationalization, 504, 859
    privatization, 504, 892
    suppliers, 519
Renault-Nissan
    comparative size (global, 1998), 561
    output (PRC comparison), 538
    output, turnover, profit, R&D (1998), 533
    sales, profits, employees, R&D (1998), 561
renewable energy
    power plant capacity (1980–2010), 335
renmin wei ben ('the people are the base'), 668,
        681
renyuan taotaizhi (selection and competition)
        system, 295
Repsol (Spain), 408, 840, 861, 920
    hostile takeover of YPF (1999), 408, 413, 494
    privatization
    privatization, 408, 493, 494, 892
    transformation (SOE national champion into
        privatized TNC), 859
Repsol-YPF (Spain-Argentina 1999–), 854
    world's eighth largest oil group, 494
research and development
    ABB-Alstom, 338
    aerospace, 141, 142, 146, 148, 165, 173, 175
    automobiles, 503, 507, 510, 511, 512, 514,
        521, 533, 539
    CNPC subsidiaries, 487
    competitive advantage, 34–6, 37
    components (car industry), 522, 524, 535–6
    Continental Europe's share, 48, 60
    contracted out, 43
    costs (pharmaceutical companies), 245–51
    cross-industry comparison, 618
    Daimler-Chrysler, 518
    defence sector (USA, NATO Europe, EU),
        156, 192
    'determines competitive advantage', 13
    diesel engines, 530, 531–2
    expenditure (1997), 47
    financial services, 818
    GE (USA), 393
    high value-added sub-sectors, 64
    HPEC and subsidiaries, 371, 378, 380, 393,
        396, 948(n50), 949(n64)

research and development – *continued*
  independent capability (PRC power
    equipment), 363
  investment, 62
  India (pharmaceuticals), 245
  Japan, 19, 24, 48, 56, 60
  leading pharmaceutical corporations, 248–9
  Legend (PRC), 107
  'life sciences', 261
  lorries (PRC), 535, 543
  mentioned, 4, 8, 10, 11, 39, 42, 61, 840
  military (PRC), 195–6
  minimum economy of scale (auto industry),
    503
  mining sector, 712
  minuscule success rate (pharmaceuticals),
    245
  need for enforceable patent legislation, 244
  not needed by SMEs, 844
  oil, 420, 423
  pharmaceuticals, 243, 258, 266, 267, 269,
    270–1, 286, 310, 318, 319, 325, 880
  power equipment, 329, 331, 398
  PRC, 94–5, 108, 134, 188, 535, 539, 543,
    842
  risky investment, 331
  Russian Federation, 178
  Shanghai Petrochemical Corporation, 456–7
  share of developing countries in, 62
  Shougang, 659, 661, 681, 687, 694
  Sinopec, 465
  Sinopec subsidiaries, 487
  spiralling costs (auto industry), 522
  steel industry, 595–6, 600, 618, 694, 951(n4)
  Taiwan, 20
  top 300 companies, 48, 49
  tyre industry, 526–8, 529
  USA, 14
  Western firms, 674
  WTO rules (implementation by PRC), 867,
    868
research and development expenditure
  auto industry, 770
  concentrated in ten countries (1993), 785
  global leaders, 855–6
  IT sector, 763, 770, 785, 794
  key to success in IT sector, 767–8, 769, 775
  lack of PRC representation among top 300
    companies (1999), 851, 854
  life science companies, 763
  Microsoft, 776, 797
  'minuscule' (Indian IT sector), 788
  pharmaceutical sector, 770
  ranking of TNCs by, 46
  by sector (1995–8), 766
  software and IT services, 775
  telecommunications, 770
research institutes (PRC), 196
research and technology centres (PRC), 70
resource allocation, 39, 96, 99

respiratory medicines, 268
restaurants: quick-service, 44
restructuring
  Airbus, 168–71
  AVIC, 229
  Boeing, 168
  cement sector, 128
  chemical industry (PRC), 118
  defence (EU, USA), 192
  'European' aerospace industry, 229, 230
  international, 81
  pharmaceutical sector, 252
  PRC, 68, 80, 136
  PRC (post-WTO), 925
  role of stock market (PRC), 96
retail price index (PRC), 648, 650, 953(n26, 28)
retail sector, 44, 132, 459–60, 511, 864, 869,
  919, 921, 923
Reuter, 781
Reyrolle Parsons (1968–77), 943(n7)
Rhodia, 263
Rhône-Poulenc, 59, 263, 861
  'life sciences', 261
  merges with Hoechst to form Aventis
    (1998–9), 256
  merges with Rorer (USA 1990), 254
  missed merger opportunity, 861
  research and development expenditure
    (1994–7), 248
  takes over Rhône-Poulenc Rorer (USA
    1997), 255
Rhône-Poulenc Rorer (USA 1990–7), 263
  takes over Fisons Pharmaceuticals
    (UK 1995), 255
rice, 869
ride control systems, 525
Riegle-Neal Act (USA 1994), 814–15
Rio Tinto, 707, 891, 935
  coal output, 710
  'dwarfed' by Shenhua Group, 735–6
  merger with 'CRA' (1995), 707–8
  moves into the USA (1993), 710
  profits (coal division, 1997), 711–12
  role model for Shenhua, 735
  specialist mining company, 707–8
Riva (Italy), 602, 602n
Rizhao (PRC): coal port, 720
Rizhao Plant (power generation), 944(n17)
road transport (PRC, 1978–97), 432
Robbing China (Cun Fu, 1998), 926
Robert Bosch, 535
  anti-lock braking systems equipment,
    950(n4)
  car braking systems, 525, 535
  fuel injection components (Wuxi joint
    venture), 546
  globalization, 521
  joint ventures (PRC), 546
  multinational supplier firm, 57
  research and development, 535

Robert Bosch – *continued*
  revenues, profits, employees, R&D (1998),
    886
  spark plugs plant in Nanjing, 546
  turnover, profit, R&D (1998), 522
  world's joint-largest component-maker
    (1999), 520
Robert Fleming (UK merchant bank), 822
Robertson, D.H., 1
robotics, 246
Roche, 248, 250, 269
rocket vehicles (PRC), 203
rockets (PRC), 940(n5)
Rockwell, 105, 205, 239
Rockwell-Collins, 179, 180, 181
Rockwell International, 143, 175
rolling mills, 368
Rolls-Royce, 164, 177–8, 190, 239, 840,
  854, 920
  aero-engines, 172–3
  Chinese sub-contractor (CEC), 217
  50MW industrial Trent engine, 942(n1)
  foreign ownership, 163
  limitations, 398
  outsourcing (IT systems), 146
  possible merger with GEC-Alsthom (1998
    speculation), 943(n3)
  privatization, 163, 331, 859, 892
  relative size (1997), 228
  research and development, 142, 143, 175
  sales, 227
  sells steam turbine business, 330, 331, 337,
    338, 943(n7)
  size (1998), 166
  state aid, 174
  supplier to Embraer, 181
  suppliers, 144–5
  Trent aircraft engine, 331
  vulnerable to take-over, 172
  Westinghouse alliance, 330–1, 942(n1)
Romania, 379, 745, 870, 948(n54–55)
Roosevelt, President, 905
Rorer (USA), 263
Rothschild: alliance with ABN, 958(n9)
Roussel Uclaf (France), 262
Rover (UK), 513, 533
Royal Air Force (RAF), 157, 158, 159
Royal Dutch/Shell (Netherlands-UK), 409,
  418–20, 884
  see also Shell
Royal Navy, 158
rubber seals and parts, 950(n9)
Rubicam, 781
Rugby Group, 262
Ruhrkohle, 732
Rui Huaichuan, Ms, 958(n7)
rule of law, 875
Rural Development Group, xxiv
Russian Federation (1991–)
  aerospace, 178–80, 237–8

arms sales, 150–2, 191–2
collapse of social fabric, 910
cooperation with PRC (aerospace), 233
deaths in coal-mining accidents (1993), 725
disintegration, 910
financial crisis (1997–8), 833
'former USSR', 219, 237–8, 337, 357,
  945(n23)
GDP (1990–8), 910
liberalization, 909
mentioned, 165
non-signatory to World Telecoms Agreement,
  786
number of companies in *Fortune* 500 (1998),
  47n
oil fields, 416
oil producer, 413
political turmoil, 413
privatization, 909
'psychological crisis', 910
reform programme, 908–10
Sanjiu sales offices, 300
second-hand machine tools, 379
state aid (aerospace), 237–8
top ten steel-producing country (1991–8),
  616
'truly in Third World', 910
Russian Federation: Council for Foreign and
  Defence Policy, 839
RVI (Renault): leading lorry-maker, 518
RWE (Germany), 710, 891

Saab, 59, 157, 160, 162, 205
Sabena (Belgium), 149
SAC, *see* Shenyang Aircraft Corporation
safety
  oil sector, 427
  SMEs (PRC), 844
SAIL (India)
  crude steel output (1996–7), 602
salaries (PRC), 92
sales
  global 500, 95
  national team (various indicators, 1995), 78
  New Sinopec, 479
  New CNPC, 479
  oil sector (PRC), 459–60
  PRC, 70, 77, 98, 938(n10)
  ranking of TNCs by, 46
sales tax, 574
Salinas de Gortari, President Carlos (b 1948),
  802
Salomon Brothers, 817
Salomon Smith Barney (USA), 817
  interests in PRC, 835
  takeover of Schroders (UK), 822, 958(n9)
  top five firm (all international convertibles,
    2000), 823
  top five firm (international equities
    bookrunners, 2000), 823

saloon cars, 507, 536, 537, 538, 551, 556
salt, 433, 900–1
Samsung, 23, 52, 53–4, 176
sanatorium, 291
sanctions: UN on Iraq, 441
Sandoz (Switzerland), 261
Sanlian Service Company (HPEC), 381
Sangyong (South Korea), 23
Sanjiang Air Industry Group, 113
Sanjiu Automobile Company, 316
Sanjiu Enterprise Group (1992–), 241, 272,
    274, 283, 289–320, 841, 859,
    941(n11–14), 942(n19)
  ability to compete on global level playing
      field, 878–81
  advertising, 289, 298–9, 941(n12–13)
  agencies, 301
  agricultural technology, 315–16
  'apparent puzzle' (reason for growth), 290,
      941(n14)
  aspirations, 289
  biotechnology, 307
  business structure, 314, 318–20
  Chinese medicines, 296–309
  competition within pharmaceuticals, 296–7
  competition from TVEs, 844
  competition within Western medicines,
      310–11
  comprises 'Nanfang' and GLD's loss-making
      enterprises, 295
  conglomerate, 290
  construction, 315
  core business, 296–309, 318–20
  debt-assets ratio, 303
  diversification, 242, 290, 309–18, 880
  'diversified conglomerate', 125
  'East Asian diversified conglomerate', 324
  employee stock-holding scheme, 320
  employment structure, 304–6
  expansion of pharmaceutical business, 306–0
  financial indicators (1992–98), 293
  'getting close to market', 297–301
  good example of 'Modern Enterprise
      System', 294
  group structure (mid-1990s), 308, 316–18
  hotel chain, 311–14
  human capital, 324
  joint ventures, 294, 306–7, 311
  management, 294, 295–6, 303–4
  marketing system, 290, 300, 307
  meaning of 'Sanjiu', 295
  mergers and acquisitions, 290, 295, 307–9,
      311–14
  modernization, 301–3
  Nanfang 'core enterprise' (1992–), 295,
      314–15
  national team player (second batch), 125
  'new entrant', 241–2
  non-core businesses, 309–18, 846
  operational autonomy, 294

  options, 879
  organizational structure (1997), 317
  originally known as 'Nanfang' (1986–92),
      290
  output and profits (1992–7), 301
  PRC's 'largest pharmaceutical firm', 289
  principal businesses (mid-1990s), 308
  product choice, 297–8
  profits, 293, 294–5, 296, 306, 307, 309, 311,
      315, 318–19, 324, 325, 879
  prospects, 325–6
  real estate, 315
  reform (1998), 296, 942(n19)
  relationship with PLA, 290–6
  revenues, profits, employees, R&D (1997),
      879
  role of CCP, 304, 942(n22)
  sales force, 310
  sales network, 318, 320
  'Second Enterprise Establishment' policy,
      309
  selling methods, 299–301
  SOE, 290
  subsidiaries, 318
  Three Gorges Dam, 315
  trade-mark battle, 299
  traditional Chinese medicines, 309–10,
      879–80
  vehicles, 316
  workforce, 318, 321
  see also Nanfang Pharmaceutical Plant
Sanjiu Enterprise Group: Decision Management
    Committee, 316, 317
Sanjiu Enterprise Group: Strategic Decision
    'Think-tank' Committee, 316, 317
Sanjiu Pharmaceutical Company (1993–),
    306–7
'Sanjiu spirit', 304
Sanjiu Trading Company, 300, 942(n22)
Sanjiu Weitai (Sanjiu stomach medicine), 289,
    297–8, 309–10, 879
  marketed in USA (1994–), 301
  'most valuable indigenous brand name', 299,
      319
  packaging, 303
  trademark battle, 299
Sanofi, 269
Santai Manufacturing (company), 956(n60)
SAP, 786
Sara Lee: competitive advantage, 35
satellite navigation, 523
satellites (PRC), 203
Saudi Arabia: arms purchases, 193
Saudi Aramco, 403, 404, 408, 409, 413–14
savings, 18, 348, 912, 932
SBC, 800
SBC/Ameritech, 777
Scandinavian Airlines System, 149
Scania, 861
Scharmann, 379

Scherer, F.M., 503
Schering-Plough, 249, 250, 283, 310
schizophrenia, 261
Schmitz, C.J., 14
schools, 126
Schroders, 958(n9)
Schwab, Dr Klaus, 917, 935
Schweitzer, Louis, 504, 841
science, 9
scientific research centres (PRC), 120
scooters, 873
Scottish Aviation Corporation, 498
SDH microwave networks, 796
SDIC, *see* China State Development and
    Investment Corporation
Seagram (Canada), 783
Searle (Monsanto), 266
seatbelts, 525
seats (cars), 521, 523, 535
Seattle, 168, 846
'Second Enterprise Establishment' (*erci
    chuangye*) policy, 309
Second Heavy Machinery Group (PRC), 104
Second Industrial Revolution, 11, 56, 849, 452
securities business (USA), 817, 819
    productivity gap (PRC v global leaders), 831
Securities Law (PRC 1998), 830, 834, 835
security systems (vehicles), 526
segments (business), 267
semi-conductors, 15, 53, 54, 769
Seraing Works (Belgium), 662
service sector
    developing countries, 29
    industrialized countries, 29
    PRC, 724
services, 769
    competitive advantage, 769
    globalization, 855
    IT, 765
servicing
    components, 512, 535, 536
    diesel engines, 529, 530, 531
    lorries, 542
    power generation equipment, 332–3, 337,
        394
    Yuchai, 552, 557, 558–9
SETC, *see* State Economic and Trade
    Commission
SGEG, *see* Shanghai General Electronics Group
Shaanxi, 107, 687
    coal-mining region, 723
    coal production and consumption (1996), 719
    depth of coal mines, 737
    problem of outward transport of coal, 739
    see also Shenfu Dongsheng Coalfield
Shaanxi Aircraft Corporation, 200, 230
Shandong
    coal production and consumption (1996), 719
    geographical location of national team
        members, 82, 83

German concessions, 904
'grasping the large', 83
investments by Daqing, 445
Japanese demands (1915), 904
nuclear power (planned), 357
oilfield, 437
new power generation plant (commissioned
    1996), 351
power generation, 350, 944(n17)
power plant capacity, 350
power station construction (CEPA letters of
    intent), 353
provincial electricity grid, 345
provincial government, 118
Shandong Haiyanghua Group
    also known as Haihua Group, 118
    national team player (second batch), 118
Shandong Huaneng Power Development
    Company Limited (SHP 1994–2000), 344,
    350, 931, 944(n12)
    coal consumption rate, 945(n26)
    Dezhou plant, 944(n13, 17)
    five power plants (1996), 362
    floated on Wall Street (1994), 349, 350,
        359
    imported equipment, 362
    main shareholders, 350
    Jining Plant, 944(n17)
    Rizhao Plant, 944(n17)
    subsidiary of Huaneng Power Corporation,
        350
    taken over by Huaneng Power International
        (2000), 96
    Weihai Plant, 944(n17)
Shandong International Power Development
    Company, 349
Shandong International Trust and Investment
    Corporation (Shandong ITIC), 350
Shandong Mouping Engine Group Company,
    562
Shandong Power Company
    shareholder in Shandong Huaneng Power
        Development Company Limited, 350
    SOE, 350
Shandong Price Bureau, 944(n12)
Shandong Rizhao Power Station, 362, 945(n27)
Shandong Xinhua, 282
Shanghai, 80, 115, 123, 224, 226
    advertising by Yuchai, 557
    automobile industry, 464
    biscuit and chocolate manufacturing, 315
    cable television, 781
    CCP uprising (1927), 905
    Citigroup office, 835
    coal production and consumption (1996),
        719, 720
    coal prices (1994–7), 728
    foreign investment in telecommunications
        (post-WTO accession), 791–2
    foreign military presence (1927), 905

Shanghai – *continued*
  geographical location of national team
      members, 82, 83
  'grasping the large', 83
  mentioned, 894
  migration of entrepreneurs to Hong Kong
      (1949–), 23
  mine-mouth coal price (6.1994), 728
  municipal government, 117, 454, 456, 670,
      801
  pharmaceuticals, 282–3, 307, 941(n10)
  Pudong area, 134
  research and development, 134
  retailing, 132
  sea-going ships (C18), 901
  steel, 464
  stock market, 282, 836
  thermal coal price (7.1997), 729
  Y-10 programme (civil aviation), 204
Shanghai Aero Industry Group, 112
Shanghai Agricultural, industrial and
    Commercial Group, 135
Shanghai Aircraft Manufacturing Corporation
    (SAMC), 207, 210, 219, 940(n13)
Shanghai Aircraft Manufacturing Factory,
    204–5
Shanghai Automobile Company, 210
Shanghai Automobile Industrial Corporation
    (SAIC)
  ability to compete on global level playing
      field, 885–7
  Chinese name, 103
  comparative size (global, 1998), 560
  comparison with global giants, 886
  components (automobile), 546
  joint venture with Volkswagen (1985–), 524,
      534, 537, 538, 540–1, 544, 546, 567,
      886, 950(n7)
  member of the national team, 103
  mentioned, 950(n9)
  minuscule (in international comparison), 534,
      538
  'most successful auto manufacturer', 103
  output of cars (1995), 515
  revenues, profits, employees, R&D (1998),
      887
  sales, 103
  sales, profits, employees, R&D (1998), 561
  sales, profits, employees, output (1998),
      556
  second layer enterprises, 560
  SOE, 538
  workforce, 103
Shanghai Automobile Corporation Group, 442,
    454, 496
  local champion, 454
  profits, 442
Shanghai Automotive Works
  joint venture with GM (1997–), 540
Shanghai Aviation Research Institute, 208

Shanghai Baoshan Iron and Steel Group ([new]
    Baogang 1998–)
  ability to compete on global level playing
      field, 889
  ambitions, 639–40, 670
  assets, 639
  considering a HKSAR stock market listing,
      640
  diversification, 639–40, 846
  downsizing, 952–3(n18)
  merger activity expected, 639
  port construction, 640
  state-of-the-art, 692
  see also Baoshan Iron and Steel Corporation
Shanghai Cable, 808
Shanghai Chemical Industrial Group, 117
Shanghai Construction Group, 126
Shanghai Diesel Joint Stock Company, 562
Shanghai Electric Power Company, 110
Shanghai Electric Power Group, 111
Shanghai Electrical Company/Corporation
    (SEC), 389–90, 356–7, 371, 376–7, 387,
      398, 881, 882
  joint ventures, 389
  manufacturer of power equipment, 346
  output (mid/late 1990s), 390
  technical ownership by local authority, 370
  unit production capability, 376–7
  Westinghouse technology transfer, 389–90
Shanghai General Electronics Group (SGEG),
    109
  national team player, 109
Shanghai Heavy Machinery Plant, 662
Shanghai Hualian Group, 132
Shanghai Huchang Iron, 635
Shanghai Jincheng Group, 199
Shanghai Jinjiang Acrylic Fibre Plant, 456
Shanghai Meishan (Group), 115, 639
Shanghai Metallurgical Holdings (Group), 115,
    639
Shanghai No 1 Iron and Steel, 634
Shanghai Pacific Chemical Group, 118
Shanghai Petrochemical Corporation Limited,
    444, 448, 457, 469, 497, 841, 842, 855,
      883
  case study, 454–7
  constraints, 473
  corporate ambitions, 472, 495, 496, 497–8
  ethylene, 454–5
  floated (HK 1993), 449, 453, 455
  growing autonomy, 454–7
  growth strategy, 456–7
  human resources, 472
  joint ventures, 454, 455
  listed subsidiary of (New) Sinopec, 472
  local champion, 454, 456
  merger activity, 843
  mergers and acquisitions, 455–6, 473
  missed merger opportunity, 862
  new role (mid-1990s), 464

Shanghai Petrochemical Corporation Limited –
    continued
  (New) Sinopec subsidiary, 454, 473
  operational autonomy, 454–5
  ownership change, 455, 473
  planned joint venture with BP, 472
  price fluctuations, 459
  profits, 446, 454, 455, 473
  research and development, 456–7
  size, 454
  SOE, 501
  subsidiary of New Sinopec (1998–), 469
  wage policy, 473
Shanghai Pharmaceutical Administration, 117
Shanghai Pharmaceutical Group, 118
Shanghai Power Bureau, 362
Shanghai Pudong Iron and Steel
  stainless steel JV with Krupp-Thyssen, 630
  technological modernization, 630
  top twenty steel producer (PRC 1997), 635
Shanghai Research Institute for Combustion
    Engines, 552
  'Shanghai Internal Combustion Engine
      Research Institute', 578
Shanghai Rubber Tyre Company, 528
Shanghai Science and Technology Investment
    Corporation, 809
Shanghai Shenjia Ferro-Alloys (company),
    956(n60)
Shanghai Telecom (part of China Telecom), 808
Shanghai Tianyuan Group, 117–18
Shanghai Tyre and Rubber Group, 118
Shanghai United Electric Corporation, 389
Shanghai Xinhua Automobile Works, 564
Shanghai Xinhua Control Technology Group
    Company, 946(n37)
Shangrao Passenger Car Works, 564
Shantou Chaoyuan Power Plant, 352
Shantou Chenghai Power Plant, 352
Shantou Tuopu Power Plant, 352
Shanxi (province), 116, 578, 715, 950(n9)
  China Unicom joint venture activity, 810
  coal mining, 118, 717, 719, 723, 737, 739,
      752
  coke supplies for Shougang, 653
  iron and steel, 116
  local government, 742
  Shenhua Railway Company, 742
Shanxi Power Company, 110
Shapiro, Bob, 265, 266
share
  issues (PRC), 97
  options, 651
  prices (aerospace sector), 235
  prices (pharmaceutical sector), 252
  values, 37, 64
shareholder pressure (oil sector), 492
shareholder value, 58, 264, 496
shareholders
  'activism' (oil sector), 414

advanced economies, 62, 924, 929
  chance to express opinion, 848
  enterprise group (PRC), 75
  institutional, 8
  oil sector, 414, 426, 428
  preference for large aerospace firms, 148
  railways, 13–14
  Shell, 426
  state (PRC), 96
  US, 924
shares
  A-shares, 472, 685
  B-share, 835
  H-shares, 282, 295, 453, 471, 472, 473, 479,
      835, 883
  pharmaceutical sector, 282, 300
Shatalin 500 Day Programme (1990), 909
Shell Oil (USA), 411
The "Shell" Transport and Trading Company
    plc (UK)
  acquisitions, 411
  assets, 79
  basic statistics, 418–20
  chemical engineers, 941(n2)
  chemical operations, 422, 426
  comparison with New CNPC and New
      Sinopec, 479
  environmental protection, 428
  50,000 petrol stations, 422
  fuel-cell technology, 427
  joint venture with CNOOC at Huizhou, 454,
      490
  LNG project (Shenzhen), 717
  mentioned, 414, 848, 935
  not state-owned (1996), 410
  number of employees (1992–7), 937(n1 to
      ch2)
  oil and gas production, 481
  oil reserves, 415
  one of the three largest TNCs, 79
  petrochemical plants (planned), 454
  profits, 420, 484
  renewables, 426
  research and development, 423
  revenues (1992–7), 937(n1 to ch2)
  rivalry of BP Amoco, 416
  root and branch reform, 424
  sale of coal-mining interests (USA), 710
  sales, 79
  'vast global empire', 424
  workforce, 79
Shenfu (Inner Mongolia Autonomous Region),
    741
Shenfu Dongsheng Coalfield, 750, 753, 757
  high-quality coal, 734, 735, 737–8, 740, 748
  location (Inner Mongolia/Shaanxi), 741
  map, 732–3
  mine depths (1996), 736, 736n
  output, 734, 736, 736n
  remote, 734

Shenfu Dongsheng Coalfield – *continued*
  reserves, 735, 736, 736n, 741
  'still in its infancy', 752
  see also Shenhua Project
Shenfu mining company (PRC), 735
Sheng Huaren (President, Sinopec), 454
Shengang Liming Aero-engine Corporation, 200
Shengli oilfield (Shandong), 437–8
Shengli Petroleum Administration, 437–8, 442
Shenhua Group Company
  ability to compete on global level playing field, 890–2
  activities, 85
  advantages of concentration of activity, 752, 757
  Baogang comparison, 749
  benefits from stricter environmental rules, 748
  board of directors, 741
  building a reputation, 752–3
  coal supplies to Beijing, 748
  competition from TVEs, 844, 891
  conclusions, 756–60
  Da Liu Ta mine, 744 (possible flotation, 746)
  diversification, 119–20
  electricity generation, 747
  employment, 749, 751, 755, 920
  established to run Shenhua Project, 741
  exports, 748, 752–3
  goal, 713
  holding company, 742
  international flotation plan, 735, 746
  joint venture partner in Shenhua Railway Company, 742, [747]
  loans, 742, 745
  main communication links, 732
  merger with 'Five Western District Mines', 749, 753–6, 759
  merger of Shenfu and Dongsheng mining companies, 735
  'millstone around neck', 759, 843, 891
  national team player (first batch), 119–20, 741
  nine mines, 741, 744
  output, 749, 920
  output per worker, 749, 751
  overall structure, 741
  position of strength (multinational joint venture negotiations), 750–1
  productivity, 751
  profitability, 745, 755
  profits, 741, 743
  prospects, 756–60
  proximity to international markets, 752
  reserves, 735–8, 741
  restructuring (8.1998), 745, 753–6
  source of funds, 744–5
  vertical integration (speculation), 747–8
  wages, 751–2

  wholly state-owned, 741
  workforce (flexible), 749
  see also Shenhua Project
Shenhua Huanghua Port Company Limited, 742
Shenhua Project (1985–), 119–20, 731, 732–3, 734–60, 841, 859, 958(n7)
  capital construction investment (1985–97), 743
  coal chemistry, 748–9
  competition, 735, 749–51
  competitive advantage, 756–8
  conclusions, 756–60
  costs, 735, 737
  debts, 743[–]745, 750
  depth, 736–7
  diversification, 735
  domestic market, 746–8
  employment, 735, 745
  exports, 735, 748, 750, 751–3
  facilities (1998), 744
  finance, 739, 742–6
  Huo Ji Tu Mine, 743, 744
  imported mining equipment, 743, 751
  industrial and domestic use of coal, 748
  investment, 734, 735, 741, 743
  Japanese loans, 743
  management, 735
  map, 732–3
  marketing, 750
  markets, 746–53
  mines, 741, 743
  origins, 734–5, 740–1
  output, reserves, mine depths (1996), 736
  pithead cost of coal, 723, 751
  port facilities, 740, 741–2, 743, 750
  power stations, 735, 747–8
  problems, 758–9
  profits, 743
  property rights, 740–2
  prospects, 743, 750–1, 756–60
  quality, 737–8, 748
  railways, 738–40, 741–2, 743, 747, 750
  reserves, 735–8, 741
  sales revenue (1997), 743
  scale, 734
  size, 735–6
  sources of investment funds (1985–97), 744
  strategic choices, 743[–]745, 749, 759–60
  strategic role in PRC economic development, 734–5
  transport, 738–40
  transport costs, 720, 751
Shenhua Railway Company
  Shuozhou-Huanghua line, 742
  shenhui ('society'), 475
Shenlong Automobile Limited
  Dongfeng-Citroën joint venture, 565
Shenyang, 111, 115
  aircraft manufacturing, 186
  China Unicom joint venture activity, 810

Shenyang – *continued*
　'Cradle of China's jet fighter industry', 199
　Dongbei plant, 283, 941(n10)
Shenyang Aircraft Corporation (SAC), 208,
　219, 877
　assigned to 'AVIC 1' (no date, *c.*1999), 230
　bus-producer, 199
　statistics, 200
　sub-contracting work, 209, 210
Shenyang Construction Investment, 547
Shenyang Electrical Cable Plant, 364, 365
Shenyang High Voltage Switch Plant, 364, 365
Shenyang Insulation Materials Plant, 364
Shenyang Low Voltage Switch Plant, 365
Shenyang Medical University, 319
Shenyang Transformer Plant (SYT), 112, 364,
　365
Shenyin Wanguo (PRC investment bank), 829
Shenzhen (Guangdong Province), 137, 224, 275
　Chinese traditional medicines (proposed
　　Sanjiu factory), 319
　Citigroup office, 835
　integration with Hong Kong, 942(n26)
　labour market, 302
　LNG project (announced 1999), 717
　pharmaceutical sector, 283
　real estate, 315
　site of Nanfang plant, 291
　stock market, 214, 282, 295, 836
　thermal coal price (7.1997), 729
　wage levels, 306, 314, 942(n25–26, 30)
　see also Nanfang; Sanjiu
Shenzhen: Cyber City, xxvi
Shenzhen: Great White Shark Fin Restaurant,
　315
Shenzhen: Nanhuan Motorway Project, 315
Shenzhen: Sanjiu Skyscraper, 315
Shenzhen City Government, 294, 307, 321,
　941(n16)
Shenzhen FIYTA Group, 226
Shenzhen Kaiye'er Service Company, 946(n37)
Shenzhen Nanguang Industrial Trading
　Company, 226
Shenzhen SEZ, 290, 302, 321, 351
Shenzhen Special Economic Zone Development
　Group (10.1981–), 86, 120–1
Shenzhen Tianma, 226
Sherman Act (USA 1890), 16
Shijiazhuang: Huabei plant, 283, 941(n10)
Shijiazhuang Beer Factory (Hebei province),
　314–15, 318, 322
shipbuilding, 952(n12)
　Japan, 56, 603
　PRC, 97
　Samsung, 53
　South Korea, 54, 604
　Taiwan, 20
shipping, 116, 121, 124, 129, 675–6, 956(n58)
ships (South Korea), 53
shipyards, 156

Shiyan Axle and Hub Works (Dongfeng), 564
shiye gongsi
　'business development companies', 472
　'service companies', 381, 949(n59)
shock absorbers, 524
'shock therapy', 70
shoes, 274
Shorts (Northern Ireland), 181
Shougang: Commission for Managing the
　Livelihood of Employees, 668
Shougang Concord International, 643
Shougang Construction Corporation, 647, 672
Shougang Electronics Corporation, 647, 673
Shougang Corporation
　'core company' of Shougang Group, 685
　member of Shougang Group, 635n
　productivity, 635n
　renamed 'Beijing Shougang (Group)
　　Company Limited' (1995), 685
　top ten steel producer (PRC 1997), 634, 635n
Shougang Group, 80, 116, 136, 464, 496, 588,
　635n, 638, 643–94, 841, 842, 855, 859,
　953–7
　ability to compete on global level playing
　　field, 887–90
　affiliates, 645
　ambitions, 676, 679, 690
　assets, 690, 691, 957(n68)
　autonomy within constraints, 650, 651–8,
　　682
　Beijing authorities, 622, 644n, 683–4
　Beijing origins, 643
　'big family', 669, 688
　bolt plate leveller, 674, 956(n56)
　bonuses, 650, 657, 658, 665–6, 666n,
　　954(n41), 955(n49)
　cadres, 665, 667, 686
　CCP and, 670
　civilian heavy machinery enterprises, 655–6
　coal supplies, 652, 687
　coke supplies, 652–3, 689–90, 953(n32)
　competition from TVEs, 844
　computerization, 661, 673, 689
　conclusions, 678–83
　considering a HKSAR stock market listing,
　　640
　construction capacity, 672–3
　construction enterprises, 655
　continuous casting, 627, 645
　contract system (1979–1995), 643–83, 693,
　　850, 953–6
　controls on expansion, 651–2
　corporate structure (1998), 647
　cost-cutting, 660, 955(n45)
　debt, 654, 656, 684, 691
　design capability, 674–5
　development funds, 657
　different interpretation, 953(n19)
　diversification, 645, 651, 655–6, 677–8,
　　679–80, 682, 691–2, 694, 956(n59)

Shougang Group – *continued*
  diversification, 847
  downsizing, controls on, 657, 688, 692, 694
  electricity supplies, 652
  electronic control capability, 673
  employment, 672, 694, 888
  energy efficiency, 638
  export capability, 676–7
  first piece of metallurgical equipment
    exported by PRC to a developed country
    (1993), 956(n56)
  flotation plans, 693
  foreign trade, 650, 676–7
  full mobilization, 667–8
  further development in overseas business,
    690–1
  gaining autonomy, 646[–]648
  good luck: 'industrial flea market', 661–3
  growth, 644–6, 657, 678–9, 680, 681,
    953(n24)
  growth begets growth, 658–9
  housing, 651, 668–9, 688, 955(n52)
  identity (state factory or modern
    corporation?), 681–2
  imports, 661
  industrial entrepreneurship, 678
  input and output co-ordination, 652–4
  institutional first-movers, 680–1
  integrated development of IT, 687–8
  integrated diversification, 679–80
  interests in Hong Kong, 676, 691, 956(n60)
  investment, 648, 650, 657, 659–60, 692,
    955(n47)
  iron ore, 646, 653, 672n, 675, 953(n33)
  joint ventures, 644, 645, 650, 651, 673, 676,
    677, 687, 690, 955(n54)
  kindergartens, 669
  loss-makers, 686–7, 843
  machine-building capability, 671–2
  main products, 844
  main site (Beijing), 644, 651
  management, 650–1, 657, 663–71, 684–6
  marketing, 653–4, 689, 953–4(n34–6)
  medical services, 669, 955(n53)
  merger, diversification, transnationalization,
    671–8
  mergers, 654–8, 682–3, 694, 956(n65),
    957(n70)
  military approach to management, 661,
    669–71, 679
  military enterprises, 656, 954(n40)
  military-style organization, 663–71
  mining capability, 675
  missed merger opportunity, 862
  modernization, 654, 658–63, 664, 670, 679,
    682, 684–6
  'museum of metallurgical history', 659,
    955(n46)
  organizational capabilities, 680
  output (iron), 655

output (steel), 644, 653–4, 655, 694,
    954(n36)
output structure, 646, 655
over-manning, 640, 684
overseas businesses, 646, 672n, 674, 676–7,
    684, 690–1
oxygen converters, 645, 953(n21)
physical restraints, 651, 694
plants, 645
pollution, 653, 689–90
post-contract system, 683–92, 956–7
power stations, 652
principal steel products (1997), 636
product mix, 684, 689
product prices, 653, 954(n35–6)
product quality, 638, 657–8, 955(n45)
production costs, 659
production targets, 665, 955(n49)
productivity, 659
profit distribution (1978–92), 649
profitability, 638, 684
profit retention, 646–50, 657, 659
profits (1978–97), 644
profits, 649, 655, 659, 661, 663, 692, 888,
    955(n45)
prospects, 693–4
rear services, 668–9
reassessment of strategy, 684
relationship between steel and non-steel
    production, 691–2
remuneration and productivity (1997), 641
research and development, 659, 661, 674,
    681, 687, 694
restructuring, 684, 689–90, 691
revenue, 690, 888
sales, 650, 659, 690, 888, 955(n45), 956(n61)
second-hand equipment, 662–3, 956(n58)
selected statistics (1978–97), 644
shipping capability, 675–6, 687, 956(n58)
'Shougang first, China second, imports third',
    661
since contract system (1995–), 683–92, 693
'6:2:2' system, 648, 657, 668
slogans, 663, 668
Soviet aid, 644
state co-ordination, 651–8
steel enterprises, 654–5
Steel Mill No. 1 (1965–), 660
Steel Mill No. 2, 660, 689
Steel Mill No. 3, 689
steel production facilities (1993), 645
steel production methods, 597, 645
strategic control, 657–8
strategic re-assessment, 684
strict discipline, 664–7, 955(n49–50)
subsidiaries, 684, 685
subsidies, 658
summaries, 658, 677–8
'super enterprise' (1992–), 650
targets, 667

Shougang Group – *continued*
taxation, 648, 659, 683–4, 956–7(n66)
technological renovation, 659–61, 663–4, 684, 689–90
tertiary sector, 668, 684, 688–9
training, 667–8
turnover tax, 644n
unified command system, 664
wage grades (1986), 666
wage growth, 658
wage structure, 657, 658, 954–5(n43)
wages, 644, 648, 649, 665–7, 686, 955(n50)
welfare, 657, 668–9, 954(n41), 955(n51)
Wire Rod Plant, 660
wire rods, 658, 659, 663
workforce, 639, 644
world rank (1996), 638
see also Zhou Guanwu
Shougang Heavy Machinery Corporation, 647, 656, 671–2, 686–7
Shougang High Technology Development Office, 687
Shougang Holdings (Hong Kong), 647, 690
Shougang NEC, 673, 687, 955(n55)
Shougang Party Committee, 657
Shougang Real Estates Stock Holding Company, 688
Shougang Service Company, 688
Shougang Shipping and Ship Construction Company (1990–), 676, 956(n59)
Shougang Southeast Asia Holdings (Singapore, 1995–), 676
Shougang Special Steel Corporation, 647, 690, 692
shougou (outright purchase), 314
Showa depression (1930s), 602
SHP, *see* Shandong Huaneng Power
Shuicheng Iron and Steel Group, 954–5(n43)
Shunde (Pearl River Delta), 298
Sibavia (airline), 179
Sicartsa complex (Mexico), 614
Sichuan, 104
coal production and consumption (1996), 719
Chinese traditional medicines (proposed Sanjiu factory), 319
petrol stations, 470
pharmaceuticals, 307
provincial electricity grid, 345
salt wells, 433
Ya'an Pharmaceutical Plant, 308, 309
Sichuan Changhong Electric, 272
Sichuan complex
managed by New CNPC (1998–), 470
Sichuan Ertan power station, 948(n57)
Sichuan Vehicle Plant, 542
Siemens (Germany)
abortive joint venture with Dongfang, 390
acquisition of Westinghouse's non-nuclear business (1997), 337–8, 390, 398, 943(n5–6), 949(n68)

alliance with Pratt and Whitney, 330, 942(n2)
CCF partner of China Unicom, 810
cooperation with 'HEC', [377–]378
cost-cutting (1990s), 337, 338
'four main plants', 338
globalization, 335, 943(n5)
government procurement, 396
investment, 332
involvement in Three Gorges Project, 356, 945(n20)
joint ventures in PRC (1997), 390
market capitalization (2000), 764
market share worldwide (power generation equipment, 1993–8), 337
mentioned, 336, 848
moving into IT sector, 765
one of the top three, 339
plants (PRC), 338
R&D expenditure, 329
revenues, profits, employees, R&D (1998), 882
sales revenue (2000), 764
servicing, 394
'sixty years of quality production', 955(n46)
size (late 1990s), 330
source of profits, 333
steam turbine manufacture, 943(n7)
supplies five coal-fired plants (PRC), 362
Siemens Plessey, 147
Siemens Power Ventures (1994–), 362
Silicon Valley (USA), 789
silk, 15, 901
Singapore
arms deliveries (1987–98), 151
'conforms to principle of comparative advantage', 4–5
consortium involved in power generation projects (PRC), 352
degree of state intervention, 19, 23
ethylene crackers, 421
foreign investment, 23
genetic engineering, 306, 307
internet, 780
mentioned, 145
number of companies in *FT* 500 (1998), 47n
state expenditure on education, health, housing, 19
state-run enterprises, 23
TNCs based (1999) in, 21, 23
see also Hong Leong Holdings
Singapore Airlines, 23, 677, 956(n61)
Singapore Technologies, 212, 810
Singapore Telecom, 23, 804, 810, 861
Singapore University, 307
Sino-Soviet split (1960–), 186, 187, 442, 846
Sinochem, *see* China National Chemicals Import and Export Corporation
Sinochem International (1998–), 129
Sinopec, *see* China National Petrochemical Corporation

Sirocco (Egyptian leasing company), 179
SISTEL, 180
Sithe, 352
'six unifications' policy (PRC, 1991–), 89, 94, 137
SK (South Korean oil company)
    basic statistics (1997), 418
    name changed from Sunkyong from 1 January 1998, 418n
    restructuring (1998), 54
SKB, _see_ SmithKline Beecham
Skylark brand (mini-vans and engines), 197
Slim, Carlos, 802
small and medium-sized enterprises (SME), 2–6, 13, 28
    comparative advantage, 4–6
    competitors for PRC large SOEs, 852
    employment (PRC), 893
    exports from PRC to USA, 893
    Four Little Tigers, 19
    neo-classical theory, 3–4
    PRC, 67, 88–9, 916, 918, 922, 923
    research and development, 43
    SMEs, 844–5, 852
    suppliers, 62
    Taiwan, 20–1
    transitional economies, 2–3
    see also TVEs
small business groups (PRC), 76
smart cards, 776
SME, _see_ small and medium-sized enterprises
Smil, V., 701–2, 957(n2), 958(n2)
Smith, Adam (1723–90), 1, 5, 873
Smith Barney
    merger with Salomon Brothers, 817
SmithKline Beecham (SKB, 1989–2000), 247, 250, 253, 254, 256, 257, 257n, 259, 297
    best sellers (drugs), 250
    joint ventures in PRC, 282
    market capitalization, 269
    merges (2000) with Glaxo Wellcome (UK), 257
    research and development expenditure (1994–7), 249
smuggling
    oil/petrochemical products (PRC), 458, 459
    PRC, 275, 277, 321, 874
    vehicles (into PRC), 537
SNECMA, 142, 143, 172, 180
social
    benefits (Posco), 605
    dislocation (feared, PRC oil sector), 495
    stability (PRC), 72
    welfare, 229
Société Générale (France), 945(n19)
Socrates, 935
SOE, _see_ state-owned enterprises
soft drinks, 297, 615, 855
    aluminium suppliers, 39
    competitive advantage, 36

global market share of leading companies, 39
non-SOE national champions (PRC), 862
plastic bottles, 39
suppliers, 39
Softbank Corporation, 780
software (IT)
    competitive advantage, 769
    developing countries, 797
    IBM, 772
    Indian success, 787
    mentioned, 107, 108, 115, 765, 769, 775–90, 797
    research and development, 49, 766
    'sphere of influence', 775
solar energy, 426
Solarex (USA), 426
Solaris operating system, 776
Solutia: spun-off from Monsanto (1997–), 265
Sonatrach: output (1996), 409
Songhuajiang (micro-van brand, PRC), 199
Sony (Japan), 18, 176, 783
    Columbia Pictures, 783
    global top hundred company, 850
    market capitalization, 56, 764
    Memory Stick, 783
    moving into IT sector, 765
    PlayStation, 783
    sales revenue (2000), 764
    Vaieo computer, 783
Sony Music, 781
South Africa
    coal, 699, 706, 751
    exports of iron ore to PRC, 640
    immigration (pre-World War I), 32–3
    labour productivity (coal-mining, 1996), 711
    mining sector, 921
    Sanjiu sales offices, 300
    top twenty steel-producing country (1991–8), 617
    unemployment, 921
South America
    electricity generation capacity (1990–2010), 697
    exporter of oil to PRC (1997), 434
    lorry sales (1995, 2005), 509
    natural gas production and reserves (1997), 405
    oil production (1987–97), 405
    production and sales of automobiles (1998), 508
    Renault, 515
    Shougang expansion, 690
    steel consumption _per capita_, 595
    steel production (1991–7), 589
    Volkswagen-Ford joint venture, 513
South Asia
    economic growth (1980–98), 851
    tariffs, 28
South China (regional electricity grid), 345
South China Motor Corporation, 546

South China Sea, 193, 416, 435, 706
South Korea, *see* Korea, Republic of
Southeast Asia
  ABB manufacturing operations, 333
  automobile industry, 508
  ethylene crackers, 421
  financial crisis (1997–8), 833
  Hopewell Holdings (HK) infrastructure
      business, 351
  oil reserves, 435
  Sanjiu sales network, 300
  Shougang's interests, 676, 690
  steel production, 609
Southern Company (Atlanta, USA), 351
Soviet Union, *see* USSR
soya beans, 265, 871
SP/SPC, *see* State Power Corporation of China
SPC, *see* Shanghai Petrochemical Company;
      State Power Corporation of China
Spain
  bank restructuring (1980–97), 821
  BP-Solarex manufacturing facilities, 426
  defence spending, 157
  Eurofighter, 158–9
  investment by Usinor, 611
  IT companies (2000), 764
  joins Airbus project (1971), 166
  oil and petrochemicals, 408
  steel output (1974–96), 593
  top twenty steel-producing country (1991–8),
      617
spare parts, 150, 316
special vehicles, 102
sports entertainment: Samsung, 53
Spratly Islands, 193, 194, 435
Spring Festival (PRC), 665
Sprint, 786, 810
SSB, *see* State Statistical Bureau (PRC)
Stacey, Mike, 147
Stalinism, 643
Stallkamp, Tom (Chrysler), 511
Standard Chartered Bank, 946(n31)
Standard Oil of Ohio (Sohio), 411
Stanford University, 917
Star Alliance (airlines 10.1999–), 149
Star TV, 784
starter motors, 950(n9)
starters (automobile component), 546
state-owned enterprises (SOE)
  banks, 96
  barriers to mergers and acquisitions, 847,
      853–4, 859
  bureaucratic apparatus, 854–5, 859
  'business groups', 854
  coal (PRC), 891
  commanding heights, 854
  constraints on organic growth, 848
  Daqing Petroleum Administration, 441–5
  debt-assets ratio (Shenzhen), 942(n23)
  diversification, 854

domestic markets, 849, 852–3
downsizing, 845, 853
employment (PRC 1998), 919
first, second, third tier subsidiaries, 873–4
floated on international stock markets, 842
forestry, 134
HPEGC, 366
impact of WTO accession, 875–6
investment difficulties, 848
large, 71, 97
'large family', 853
loss-making, 71, 80
major changes, 850
merger activity, 683, 843
need for further reform (end 1990s), 916
oil companies, 407–10
operating costs, 845
performance, 845
pharmaceuticals (PRC), 279, 283
power equipment makers (PRC), 346
power generation companies (PRC), 350
PRC, 69, 71, 73, 81, 98, 117, 350, 489,
      501–2, 650, 681, 813, 841, 842, 853,
      873, 892, 912, 920, 923, 937–8(n2, n5),
      939(n14)
profits (1997), 77
reform, xxiv, 501
restructuring, 845, 857–8, 892–4
Shougang, 643, 663, 681
small, 69, 71
'social entities', 846–7, 853
transition to modern corporations, 681–2
wages, 853
weakness in competing on world markets,
      848–9, 850–1
workforce (1995), 77
working capital, 97
WTO rules (implementation by PRC), 866
State Administration of Building Materials
      (PRC), 128
'State Bureau of Building Materials
      Industry', 120
State Administration of Machine-Building
      Industry (PRC), 346
State Bureau of Metallurgical Industry (SBMI),
      622, 627, 952(n14)
State Bureau of Petroleum and Chemical
      Industry (SBPCI), PRC
  established in 1998, 467, 468
State Capital Management Office/Bureau
      (PRC), 89, 93, 94
State Coal Industry Bureau (PRC), 726
State Construction Bank (PRC), 742, 892
State Council (PRC), 68, 73, 74, 76, 120, 122,
      127, 133, 136, 137, 273, 276, 651–2, 841,
      935
  appoints chairman of Shenhua, 734
  AVIC 'directly responsible' to, 186
  AVIC restructuring (1999), 229–30
  civil aviation, 203, 223

State Council (PRC) – *continued*
  creation of Donglian (1997), 466
  direct support measures, 95, 97
  directives, 69–70, 87, 95, 938(n8), 940(n27)
  feasibility of Shenhua Project, 740–1
  first directive (12.1991), 69, 87–90, 95, 740,
      741, 938(n8), 940(n27)
  governmental reform (1998), 467–8
  'highest decision-making body', 68
  orders Shenhua to merge with 'Five Western
      District Mines', 753
  petrochemical industry (1.1997), 464–5
  power equipment industry, 376, 391
  research and development, 94–5
  second directive (4.1997), 69, 90–1, 94, 95,
      940(n27)
  and Shougang, 647, 650, 657, 685
  and Sinopec, 445, 448
  supervision of Sinopec, 445
State Council Development Research Centre
    (SCDRC, PRC), 74, 75, 136, 958(n3)
State Council Economic and Trade Office
    (PRC), 138
State Defence Industries Commission
    (COSTIND, PRC), 231
State Development Bank (PRC), 392, 440, 742,
    745, 944(n11)
State Development and Planning Commission,
    467, 471, 622, 952(n14)
State Direct Financial Interest (SDFI, Norway),
    499
State Economic and Trade Commission (SETC,
    PRC), 68, 71, 108, 120, 124, 137, 139,
    345, 346, 392, 467, 468, 471, 939(n12)
State Goods and Materials Department (PRC),
    133
State Holding Company (Yuchai Group
    Company, 7.1992–), 572, 573, 575n,
    579–80, 951(n20)
  CYI Limited ownership structure, 574
State Industrial and Commercial Bureau (PRC),
    938(n6)
state intervention
  aerospace, 152–3, 154–5, 170, 173, 175–6,
      237, 233
  Airbus, 166–7
  BAe, 174–5
  Bombardier and Embraer, 181–2
  Brazil, 180
  capitalist countries, 4
  direct preferential support measures (PRC),
      68, 937(n2 to ch3), 938(n5)
  East Asia, 52
  'Four Little Tigers', 19–24
  HPEC, 391
  importance, 14
  India, 873
  industrial restructuring (Europe), 498–9
  industrial structure (auto industry), 504–6
  Italy, 58
  Japan, 16–17
  large firms, 14–24
  mentioned, xxiii, 2, 6
  military aircraft purchases (USA, 'Europe'),
      150
  needed in power generation equipment
      industry (PRC), 328
  power equipment, 329
  PRC, 68, 69–70, 81, 873, 938(n5)
  research and development, 35–6, 175–6, 237
  Rolls-Royce, 174–5
  Russian Federation (aerospace), 237–8
  South Korea, 52–3
  support for indigenous corporations, 37
  technological upgrading, 863
  United Kingdom, 15, 873
  USA (C19), 15–16
  Y-10 project (PRC), 204–5
State Pharmaceutical Administration (PRC),
    286, 299, 320, 325
State Planning Commission (PRC), 74, 75, 92,
    137, 138, 364, 370, 449, 457, 471, 564,
    651, 735
  role, 92
State Power Corporation of China ('SP' or
    'SPC', 1997–), 109, 343–5, 359, 399,
    944(n10)
  functions, 343
  'holding company', 345
  'key task', 346
  structure, 344
  subsidiaries, 344, 359
State Price Control Bureau (PRC), 347, 385
State Securities Regulation Commission
    (SCRC, PRC), 833
  'State Securities Commission', 365
State Statistical Bureau (SSB, PRC), 939(n19),
    941(n6)
Statoil (Norway), 408, 499
steam
  engines, 391
  power plant capacity (1980–2010), 335
  turbines, 337, 338, 374, 377, 943(n7)
steel (global), 587–694, 952–7
  appliances, 592
  automobiles, 590–1
  barriers to entry, 63, 64, 618–22
  booming market, 618
  catch-up possibilities, 64
  central importance, 588
  changes in demand, 588[–]590
  changes in distribution (1974–96), 593
  competition from other products, 590–600
  consolidation, 608–17
  construction, 591
  containers, 591–2
  cycles, 588[–]590
  demand, 588–92
  downsizing, 595, 605–7
  employment, 595, 605–7

steel (global) – *continued*
  environmental considerations, 593
  European consolidation, 609–13
  Far East consolidation, 613
  global steel corporation (Ispat), 613–15
  globalization, 608–17
  growth rate, 590
  high carbon, 64
  high quality, 863, 889
  high value-added, 38
  industrial concentration, 615–17
  institutions, 595, 600–17
  international trade, 607–8
  Japan, 56, 176
  laser welding, 591
  mini-mills, 598–600
  miscellaneous, 3, 45, 384, 452, 523, 848,
      854, 859, 861, 929
  on-line procurement networks, 45
  PRC, 587–8, 615, 622–94, 887–90, 921,
      952–7
  privatization, 32, 595, 605–7
  process technology, 596[–]598
  product change, 595–600
  production (1991–7), 589
  production (changes in global distribution),
      590, 592–5
  production methods (1997), 597
  productivity, 591, 606
  prospects, 595
  protectionism, 595
  real value, 590, 951(n1)
  regulation, 595
  remuneration and productivity (1994–7), 641
  research and development (1995, 1998), 49
  scrap, 598, 599, 619
  segmentation of market, 889
  South Korea, 53, 176
  special, 621–2
  stainless, 64, 596, 612, 623, 624, 630
  substitutes, 587, 595, 605
  supply, 592–600
  tailored blanks, 591
  Taiwan, 20
  technical progress, 587, 590, 595
  top twenty companies (1996–7), 602
  transport costs, 618
  US consolidation, 613
steel industry (PRC), 587–8, 615, 622–94,
      887–90, 921, 952–7
  ability to compete on global level playing
      field, 887–90
  administrative control, 622
  ambitions, 588, 638–9, 670
  Anshan Iron and Steel (Angang), 622,
      629–30
  Baoshan Iron and Steel (Baogang), 622, 628
  capacity (1980–97), 631
  consolidation (PRC), 80
  consumption (1980–97), 630

consumption of selected steel products
      (1996–2005), 624
continuous casting, 627, 628, 629–30
contract system, 588
customers, 623
debt, 642
demand, 623–4, 658–9
domestic liberalization, 622–3
downsizing, 640–2
dumping, 952(n14)
electric arc furnaces, 628
employment, 631, 632, 640–2
energy consumption, 629
energy savings (potential), 716
environmental regulation, 622
exports (1957–97), 626
first batch of trial business groups (PRC),
      109
fixed assets, 632, 633
forecasts, 624, 625
fuel, 652, 953(n31)
giants, 464
grasp the large, let go of the small, 638–40
high value-added products, 624, 626–7, 628,
      629, 639, 689, 690, 694
imports, 625–6, 629, 642, 643
industrial concentration, 630–40
international capital, 640
international comparison (size of enterprise),
      638
investment, 625, 628, 630, 952(n15)
joint ventures, 640
keypoint enterprises, 631, 632, 633–8, 658,
      665
large number of very small plants, 630–3
local plants, 631, 632, 633, 637
machine-building, 671–2
major products (1980–97), 631
mergers and acquisitions, 622 (possibilities,
      694, 862)
mini-mills, 599, 631, 633
modernization, 628–9
national team (PRC), 77, 939(n21)
number of enterprises (1991), 632
'non-system' plants, 632, 633, 637
open-hearth furnaces, 628
output (1980–97), 630, 632
output growth, 625–6
'overmanned', 640
pollution, 628, 629
Posco plants (four), 609
price of iron, steel, rolled bar (1980–93), 655
prices, 622, 655, 952(n14)
product mix, 623, 636–7
product quality and structure, 626–7, 636–7
productivity, 631, 638
profitability, 622, 638, 642–3, 952(n14)
profits, 631, 632, 633, 638, 639, 643,
      952(n15)
prospects, 588

steel industry (PRC) – *continued*
protection, 622, 623
raw materials, 652, 953(n31)
remuneration and productivity (1997), 641
return on investment (1980–90), 660
sales, 630, 633
second batch of trial groups (PRC 1997), 86
selected statistics (1980–97), 630–1
self-sufficiency ratio (1957–97), 626
self-sufficiency (steel products, 1996), 627
Shanghai Pudong Iron and Steel, 630
Shougang, 622, 643–94, 953–7
silicon steel sheets, 629
small-scale plants, 630–3, 638, 658
smuggling, 643, 952(n14)
Soviet aid, 628
state and market, 622–3
'still an infant industry', 623
supply, 625–42
technology, 628–30
top twenty producers (1997), 634–5
value-added (1980–97), 630
wages (Shougang, 1986), 666
wholly owned foreign enterprises, 640
world ranking (PRC 1949–98), 913
world's largest steel-making country (1996–),
    625
WTO rules (implementation by PRC), 868
Wuhan Iron and Steel (Wugang), 622, 629,
    640
steel machinery, 847
steel mills, 598–9, 619–21, 849
British Steel, 600
coal supplies (PRC), 723
computer technology, 599
lower productivity, 659
lower wage costs (developing countries), 620
pulverized coal injection (PCI), 599
reduction of workforce, 599
Shougang, 691–2, 645, 953(n23)
see also mini-mills
steel prices, 385, 949(n64)
Steinfeld, E., 953(n24)
Steyer trucks and engines, 566
Stigler, George, 13, 14
Stock Exchange (UK), 814
stock market listings
AVIC subsidiaries, 226
China Poly Investments Holdings, 274
Continental Mariner (shipping company),
    274, 941(n8)
domestic, 349
Harbin Power Equipment Company (1994),
    366
HK, 274, 282, 295, 941(n8)
international, [88], 349, 366, 940(n29)
pharmaceutical companies (Shenzhen,
    Shanghai, HK), 282
PRC, 88, 90, 95, 96, 101–35(column 6)
PRC power companies, 349

PRC steel companies (HK 1993–), 640
Sanjiu (aborted), 295
Sichuan Changhong Electric, 272
XAC International, 214
stock markets
absent (PRC 1970s), 436
capitalization: various countries (1998), 932
dominance of firms based in advanced
    economies (1997), 46, 47
flotation (PRC SOEs), 854
foreign listings for PRC corporations, 852,
    860
Hong Kong, 24
importance for raising funds, 320
Japan, 55–6
not essential for growth, 682
pharmaceutical companies, 251–2, 260
potential effect of a crash in the USA, 60
PRC, 96, 97–8, 836, 940(n29–30)
preferential listings (PRC), 69
pressure (pharmaceutical sector), 251–2,
    260
rise in value, 414
shift to East Asia, 65
systematic introduction of listings (PRC), 70
uncertainties (USA 2000), 928
Western, 36–7
stock prices, 922
stomach medicine (Sanjiu), 289, 941(n12)
Stonecipher, Harry, 150
storage tanks (oil), 486
strategic industries, 13
oil and petrochemicals, 407, 463, 495
steel, 605
'strategic trade theory', 12
strikes (Japan), 18
sub-contracting
aero-engine joint ventures, 216–17
aerospace, 177, 206–10, 213–21, 237, 877,
    878
aircraft industry survival (PRC), 220–1
by Boeing, 207
European aerospace companies to US giants,
    163–4
fragmented, internally-competitive market
    (PRC), 218–19
growth, 213–14
international competition, 219
mechanism for developing independent
    manufacturing capability (PRC), 219–20
power equipment, 882
PRC, 206–10, 237, 849, 877, 878, 918
significance, 217–21
size of contracts, 217–18
undertaken in PRC (aerospace), 197
way forward for PRC aerospace?, 230
XAC, 214–16
see also 'external firm'; outsourcing
Sub-Council of the Chemical Industry (PRC),
    468

sub-systems
 aero-engines, 173
 components suppliers, 511
 joint ventures (PRC aviation industry),
  213–21)
 mentioned, 397
 military, 193
 role of developing countries, 184
submarines, 192
subsidiaries, 122, 132
subsidies (PRC), 869, 891–2, 893
Sudan: investments by CNPC, 441
sugar, 53, 86, 131
suitcases: PRC exports, 871
Sukhoi, 178
sulphur dioxide, 430, 700–2
Sumitomo (Japan), 527, 528–9, 602, 810, 860
Sumitomo Metal, 850
Sumitomo Rubber, 57
Sun Microsystems (USA), 764, 775, 776
Sun Wu, 65, 241, 898
Sun Yuan BVI, 573, 575
Sunkyong Group (South Korea), 23
 see also SK (South Korean oil company)
sunzi ('grandchildren') companies, 221–6
super giants (oil sector)
 alternative energy sources, 426–7
 asset reorganization, 425–6
 capital control, 425
 centralized procurement, 422–3
 economies of scale, 421
 global brand, 427–8
 human resources, 427
 integration of operations, 421–2
 organizational structure, 423–5
 product mix, 423
 size, 417–21
supermarkets, 132
suppliers, 37–8, 39, 42–3, 61, 147, 855, 856
 aerospace, 511
 'aligned', 37, 512
 bargaining power, 521, 950(n5)
 to Bombardier, 181
 to BP, 423
 concentration pressures, 37–8, 39
 Daimler-Chrysler, 514
 to Embraer, 181
 first tier, 38, 39, 42–3, 45, 57, 61–2, 145,
  511, 512, 519, 521, 535, 536, 855, 920,
  923
 Japan, 57
 multinational, 57
 Nissan, 516
 pharmaceuticals (PRC), 279
 PRC, 845
 pressure exerted by automobile giants, 583
 prices, 42
 second tier, [38], 39, 57, 62, 146, 496, 511,
  512, 535, 536, 855, 923, 950(n12)
 sub-system (aerospace), 143, 146

third tier, 39, 57, 511, 535, 536, 855, 923,
  950(n12)
Toyota, 510
US companies, to Japan (1999), 57
 see also cascade effect
supply
 aerospace industry (global), 142–7
 oil and gas (PRC), 428–35
 Samsung, 53
 sources of, 11
supply chain
 aerospace, 144–7
supply demand
 'simple concepts', 12
Supreme Court (USA), 814
surface-to-air missiles (SAM), 192
surveying, 126
suspension (cars): spiralling R&D costs, 521
Sutherland, Dylan, xxv
Suzhou, 283, 391, 810
Suzuki: ranks sixteenth (world car-makers), 534
Sweden
 air force, 157
 bank restructuring (1980–97), 821
 defence spending, 157
 division to Ford, 515, 533
 force of globalization (sale of Volvo's auto
  industrial concentration (auto industry),
  507
 industrialization, 923
 IT companies (2000), 764
 pharmaceutical corporations, 249
 welding machines (exports to PRC),
  948(n52)
Swissair, 149, 182, 787
Switzerland, 262
 bank restructuring (1980–97), 821
 industrialization, 923
 pharmaceutical corporations, 248
syndicated credit arrangements
 top five firms (2000), 824
synergies, 373, 415, 456
 diesel engines, 531
 Rio Tinto and 'CRA' (1995–), 707–8
 Shougang, 678
 tyres, 529
Syngenta (agribusiness), 262
Synthelabo, 269
synthetic detergents (PRC, 1980–97), 433
synthetic fibres, 252, 450, 451, 452, 487
synthetic resin, 470
synthetic rubber, 452, 487
Syria, 178
system costs, 61
system integration, 37–8, 42–3
 aero-engines, 170
 Bombardier, 181
 competitive advantage, 44
 Embraer, 181
System Reform Commission (PRC), 365

System Reform Institute, xxiv
systems capability, 785
systems control, 107
systems integration, 693, 769, 918, 919, 933
systems integrators, 146, 172, 236
SYT, *see* Shenyang Transformer Plant

Taigang, *see* Taiyuan Iron and Steel Group
Taiping Rebellion (1856–1864), 903
Taiwan
    arms deliveries (1987–98), 151, 152
    arms purchases, 193
    big business, 21
    catch-up, 20–1, 621
    coal imports from PRC (1997), 718
    comparative advantage, 6
    'conforms to principle of comparative
        advantage', 4–5
    degree of state intervention, 19, 20
    demand for pharmaceuticals (per capita), 277
    environmentally-friendly advanced power
        stations, 705
    exports, 20
    heavy industry, 19, 20
    industrial structure, 6
    internet, 780, 805
    iron ore costs (1997), 619
    IT sector, 770
    mentioned, 903
    number of companies in *Fortune* 500 (1998),
        47n
    number of companies in *FT* 500 (1998), 47n
    privatisation, 20
    production of plastics (1989–96), 451
    production of synthetic fibre (1989–96), 451
    proposed joint venture with BAe
        (abandoned), 211
    protectionism, 19, 20
    remuneration and labour productivity (steel
        industry, 1996), 641
    small firms, 20–1
    steel output (1974–96), 593, 594
    tariffs on steel products (1997), 619
    technological upgrading, 863
    top twenty steel-producing country (1991–8),
        617
    wage costs (steel industry, 1997), 620
Taiwan Semi-Conductor, 21
Taiyuan Iron and Steel Group (*Taigang jituan*),
    116, 635, 660, 694
Takeda (Japanese pharmaceutical company),
    310
Takeda, Mr (President of New Japan Steel), 604
takeovers, 72–3, 79–80, 96, 848
    see also mergers
Tangguh (natural gas field, Indonesia), 416
Tangshan, 131
Tangshan Ceramics Group, 131
Tangshan Iron and Steel Group, 635, 694
tanks, 156, 518, 951(n22)

tariffs, 28–9
    Brazil (steel sector), 606
    China (C19), 902
    coal imports (PRC), 728
    diesel engines (PRC), 537
    imports of motor vehicles (Japan), 505
    IT sector (PRC), 794
    petrochemical sector (PRC), 453, 458
    power equipment (PRC), 348
    PRC, 70
    steel industry (South Korea), 604
    tariffs, 28–9
    USA (steel sector), 601, 951(n5)
    on vehicles, 520, 536–7
    WTO rules (implementation by PRC), 865,
        867, 868–9
    see also protectionism; taxation
Tarim Basin (Xinjiang), 438–9, 441
Tarim (Talimu) complex, 470
Tarim Petroleum Exploration and Development
    Headquarters, 438–9
Tata Iron and Steel (TISCO, India), 600
tax benefits (Taiwan), 20
tax exemptions (PRC), 540
taxation
    customs duties (PRC), 275
    income tax, 367, 569, 571, 573
    international differences narrowed, 814
    losses through smuggling (PRC), 275
    national team (various indicators, 1995), 78
    PRC, 70, 77, 88, 98, 138
    value-added tax, 367, 574, 731
taxi renting, 311
Taylorist monitoring, not used, 667
TCI (US cable television company), 782
TCL (PRC hardware firm), 794
technical progress, 11–12, 61, 62, 64
    'most essential characteristic of economic
        growth', 11
    pace (steel industry), 618
technological revolutions
    first (8000–2500BC), 763
    second ('Middle Ages' to late C20), 763, 810
    third (information technology age, late
        C20–), 761–811
technological upgrading
    PRC, 863
    USA, 863
technology, 129
    combined cycle, 329, 335, 356, 380,
        950(n57)
    metallurgical, 510
    oil sector, 421, 448
    PRC, 448, 876
    revolutionary change, xxiv
technology centres, 88, 91, 94–5, 131
    PRC (1997–), 88, 94–5
technology projects (PRC), 89
technology transfer
    hydro power, 356

technology transfer – *continued*
  imported (power equipment), 355
  to Japanese auto industry (1950s), 505
  nuclear power, 358
  power equipment, 328, 347, 350, 369, 377–8, 380, 882
  to PRC, 207–8, 559, 852, 863
  US keenness to avoid, 792
  Westinghouse, 389–90
  WTO rules (implementation by PRC), 866, 882
Telecom Italia, 786, 800, 810, 854
telecommunications (global)
  barriers to entry (1998), 63
  competitive advantage, 769
  consolidation (USA 1996–), 777–8
  development (1997), 789
  East Asia, 779
  'international language' (English), 788
  internet, 776
  markets, 779
  mentioned 272, 769, 854, 855, 861, 863, 929
  mergers and acquisitions (1988–98), 769
  privatization (general), 32
  protectionism, 779
  Samsung, 53
  services, 776–9
  state-run enterprises in Singapore, 23
  Sweden, 59
  Vodafone-Mannesmann, 778
  wireless telephones, 776
  see also Third Technological Revolution
telecommunications (PRC), 797–800
  bureaucratic struggle, 800–1
  China Telecom (HKSAR), 798–9
  China Unicom (1993–), 799–800
  encirclement, 803–6
  EU-PRC agreement (5.2000), 791
  growth (1997–9), 798
  joint ventures, 806–10
  leading firms (1999–2000), 798, 800
  mentioned, 825, 871, 921, 924
  missed merger opportunities, 862
  problems, 800–10
  progress, 797–8
  nature of firm, 801–3
  seaborne telecommunications monitoring capability (PRC), 204
  World Telecoms Agreement, 786–7
  WTO rules (implementation by PRC), 868
Telecommunications Act (USA 1996), 777
telecommunications companies
  globalization, 761–2
  market capitalization, 777
  mergers and acquisitions, 777–8
  privatization, 776
  profit margins (1998), 245
  USA, 761
telecommunications equipment, 54, 771, 773
telecommunications services, 49

Telefónica, 798, 800, 803, 840, 892, 931
telephones
  main lines per 1,000 people (global 1997), 789
  PRC, 808
  see also wireless telephones
television, 107–8, 109
  advertising of prescription drugs (USA), 251
  colour, 272
  internet access, 796–7
  PRC, 796
  set-top boxes, 796–7
  sets per 1,000 people (global 1997), 789
  sets: PRC's world ranking (1949–98), 913
Telmex, 779, 802–3
Telstra, 800
Tenneco Automotive, 524, 525, 535, 547
Tesco, 818
Tesco Finance, 819
Texaco (USA)
  basic statistics (1997), 418
  comparison with New CNPC and New Sinopec, 479
  employees, 480
  financial indicators, 480
  oil and gas production, 481
  possible merger with Chevron, 417, 420
  profits, 480
  turnover, 480
Texas Instruments, 147
textile dyes, 262
textile machinery, 197, 198
textiles, 15, 118, 130
  China (pre-1949), 900–1
  national team players, 113–114
  PRC, 926
  sectoral share of PRC national team (1991, 1997), 84
  Taiwan, 20
  woollens, 53
  WTO enforcement proceedings, 870
Textron, 231
Thai Airways, 149
Thailand, 927
  arms deliveries (1987–98), 151
  automobile exports to PRC (WTO rules), 887
  automobile industry, 508
  energy consumption *per capita*, 428
  ethylene crackers, 421
  'fundamental economic situation', 834
  GM matches entire GNP of, 534
  natural gas, 416
  pharmaceuticals market (1995), 277
  Posco plant, 609
  potential car exports to PRC, 872
  tariffs on steel products (1997), 619
Thainox (Thailand), 611
thalidomide, 250
Theatre Missile Defence System, 194

Theory of the Growth of the Firm (Penrose 1959), 10
thermal plants, 945(n26)
thermal power, 118, 354–5, 358, 374
thermal power station equipment, 363
'Third Front' movement (PRC), 187, 197, 275, 376, 656, 843, 846, 951(n22)
Third Industrial Revolution, 12
Third Technological Revolution, 33, 761–811
  advanced economy oligopoly, 767–70
  barriers to entry, 762, 769
  battle for Chinese market, 790–811
  'brain' activities, 762, 765, 766, 770
  broadband and convergence, 782–4
  central position of knowledge-intensive industries, 763–70
  competitive capability (developing-country firms), 787–90
  competitive-edge companies (IT 2000), 767
  conclusion, 810–11
  global level playing field, 766, 784–90
  global market share (top ten companies in knowledge-intensive industries, 1998), 768
  information and telecommunications development (selected indicators, 1997), 789
  information technology, 763–7
  internet, 779–80
  IT companies (2000), 764–5
  IT hardware, 770–5
  life sciences, 767
  media, 781
  mergers and acquisitions (1998–9), 769
  obstacles for firms based in developing countries, 763–90
  PRC, 790–811
  research and development (1995–8), 766
  software and IT services, 775–90
  telecoms services, 776–9
  US consolidation (telecommunications, 1996–), 776–7
  US dominance (2000), 767, 770, 771–2, 775
'Third Way', 908
Third World: pharmaceutical companies, 310
Thompson CSF, 165
Thomson Marconi Sonar, 162
Three Gorges Dam: Shenhua comparison, 734
Three Gorges Finance Company, 350, 944(n16)
Three Gorges Project (1995–), 343, 353–4, 356–7, 368, 371, 375, 378, 380, 392, 882
  foreign suppliers, 356, 945(n20)
  funding, 944(n11)
  HEC, 368
  'largest hydroelectric scheme in world', 356
Three Mile Island (1979), 402
'three no changes' policy (*san bu bian*), 137
  defined, 94
  'held back enterprise reorganization' (PRC), 939(n16)

'relaxed', 939(n23)
'three sisters' (oil giants), 417
Thurow, C., 669
Thyssen, 612
  merger with Krupp-Hoesch (1997–8), 612
  profits (1997), 957(n69)
  remuneration and labour productivity (1995), 641
Thyssen-Krupp (Germany), 889
  crude steel output (1996–7), 602, 602n
  emerging European 'steel oligopoly', 609
  industrial concentration, 611–12
  joint ventures, 612, 630
  joint venture in Shanghai, 612
  overseas operations, 612
  research and development, 595–6, 618
  stainless steel, 612, 615
Tian Yushi, 946(n40)
Tiananmen Square, 190
  demonstration (1989), 910
  massacre (1989), 911, 916
Tianjin, 80, 282–3, 391, 464, 546, 729, 810
  automobile component manufacture, 546
  automobile industry, 464
  China Unicom joint venture activity, 810
  Denso plant, 546
  pharmaceuticals, 282–3
  power equipment company in, 391
  thermal coal price (7.1997), 729
Tianjin Auto Industrial Corporation
  Chinese name, 103
  joint venture with Daihatsu (1988–), 539–40, 546, 950(n7)
  joint venture with Toyota, 546
  petrol engine capability, 567
  sales, profits, employees, output (1998), 556
  saloon car production (1998), 540
  second layer enterprises, 560
Tianjin Bohai, 117
Tianjin Engine Works, 547
Tianjin Hangu Petrochemical Plant, 454
Tianjin Petrochemical Company/Corporation, 454, 469
Tianjin SmithKline Beecham, 283
tiaojie shui (adjustment tax, PRC), 648
Tibet, 312, 345
TIM, 800
Time Warner (USA), 787
  'global leader', 781
  market capitalization (2000), 764
  merger with AOL (2000), 781, 782
  recorded music, 781
  sales revenue (2000), 764
Ting Pek Khiing, 951(n19)
tingxing linzhi ('keeping the post but receiving no wages'), 382
tinplate, 591
titanium dioxide, 265
TNC, *see* trans-national corporations

Toaster, John, 426
tobacco smuggling (PRC), 874
Tongrentang Group (1992–), 125
tongwang, tongzhi, tongjia
  'unified network, unified quality, unified
    price' (electricity, PRC), 345
tongzhi ('notice'), 947(n43)
Toshiba, 176, 794, 850
Total (France)
  LNG project (Shenzhen), 717
  merger with PetroFina (1998), 413, 415
TotalFina (Franco-Belgian), 415
  basic statistics, 418
  merger with Elf Aquitaine (1998–9), 416–17
TotalFinaElf, 416–17, 420, 499
  comparison with New CNPC and New
    Sinopec, 479
  oil and gas production, 481
  rivals BP Amoco/Arco, 417
Toulouse, 167, 846
tourism, 121, 124, 127, 311, 316–17, 640
township and village enterprises (TVEs), 6, 222
  coal-mining, [720–]721, 722, 723, 724, 726,
    727, 736, 745, 759
  competitors for larger corporations, 844–5
  demand for electricity, 746
  employment (in mines), 724
  lower-priced coal, 746–7, 753
  national team players, 133–4, 139
  second batch of trial groups (1997), 85–6, 91
  sectoral share of PRC national team (1991,
    1997), 84
  small oil refineries, 485
  source of revenue to local governments, 724
Toyota, 19, 103, 176, 505, 506, 858
  comparative size (global, 1998), 561
  comparison with Shanghai Auto, 886
  domestic market share, 505
  foreign assets, sales, employment (1997), 509
  global top hundred company, 850
  interests in Mercosur, Turkey, 508
  joint venture with Tianjin Auto, 546
  'lean production', 510, 520
  output (PRC comparison), 538
  output, turnover, profit, R&D (1998), 533
  research and development, 510
  sales, profits, employees, R&D (1998), 561
  share of foreign production (1989–94), 510
'Toyotism', 512
toys (PRC exports), 871
TRACER land system, 163–4
Tracor, 146
trade, 121, 124, 311
  'increase in PRC imports rather than PRC
    exports', 871
  WTO rules (PRC implementation), 871–2
Trade-Related Intellectual Property Rights
    (TRIPs) Agreement (1994), 244, 245, 270,
    785–6
  control of technology transfer, 785

implementation by PRC, 866, 868
  Indian caution, 868
Trade-Related Investment Measures (TRIMs),
    865
trade barriers, *see* protectionism
trade companies (PRC), 70, 81, 940(n28)
trade groups
  first batch of trial groups (1991), 86
  second batch of trial groups (1997), 86
  national team players, 129–30
trade performance requirements
  WTO rules (implementation by PRC), 866
trade policy, 12
trade rights (PRC), 90–1
trade secrets: TRIPs Agreement (1994), 785
trade unions, 512
  absence (mini-mills), 598, 599
  'Europe', 706
  monitoring of service systems (PRC),
    955(n51)
  resist trans-national mergers, 512
trademark law (PRC 1982), 942(n21)
trademarks
  Sanjiu, 314, 319
  TRIPs Agreement (1994), 785
trans-national corporations
  Asia-Pacific region, 24
  development planning, 44, 45
  established in Singapore, 23
  evolution, 1–2
  Four Little Tigers (1999), 21
  Japanese, 18
  managers, 62
  mining sector, 750, 755
  number of employees, 44
  operational autonomy, 45
  overseas assets, 44
  power equipment, 328, 358–63, 384
  South Korean, 23
  three largest (Ford, GE, Shell), 79
  vertical integration, 44–5
transgenic crops: TRIPs Agreement (1994), 785
'transition orthodoxy', 2
transplanted organs, 261, 267
transport and transportation
  barriers to entry (1998), 64
  costs, 9, 846, 883
  employment (PRC 1998), 919
  equipment, 11, 14, 64, 871
  national team, 78, 121–4
  PRC, 84, 348, 431, 432, 538, 871
  sectoral share of PRC national team (1991,
    1997), 84
  state-run enterprises in Singapore, 23
travel agents, 43
travel and tourism, 869
Travelers ('a big insurer'), 817
Travellers (corporation), 57
Treaty of Bogues (1843), 903
Treaty of Nanjing (1842), 902–3

Treaty of Shimonoseki (1895), 903
Treaty of Tianjin (1858), 903
Treaty of Versailles (1919), 904
treaty ports, 902–3, 906
trial business groups (PRC), 68, 85–6, 87–91,
    137, 854, 897–8, 937–8(n1–3, 5), 939
    (n18, 21)
  applicants (mid-1998), 938(n6)
  assets, 101–35(column 3), 939(n20–1)
  attempt to build (PRC), 69
  car industry, 540, 563
  chronology (1980–98), 136–9
  city-level, 75, 83, 93, 938(n11)
  conclusion, 98–9
  decision-making autonomy (1986–), 91–2
  definition, 75–6
  'developmental' stage (*chuangjian jieduan*),
    80, 137
  direct support measures, 95–8
  first policy document (12.1987), 73–4, 137,
    939(n17)
  first (1991) or second (1997) batch,
    101–35(column 4)
  geographical distribution (1997), 82
  gestation period, 73
  international competition, 897
  list and description, 100–35
  lower-level, 70, 75, 83, 938(n11)
  'majority based around industrial
    enterprises', 939(n22)
  membership of Association for the Promotion
    of China's Business Groups (4.1994–),
    938(n7)
  mergers, 938(n6)
  miscellaneous, 938(n9–10)
  names, 101–35 (column 1)
  need for, 71–2
  number of enterprises within group, 79,
    101–35 (column 5)
  120 of largest (PRC), 68, 69, 70, 83, 96,
    938(n6), 940(n30)
  policies promoting institutional change,
    87–91 (implementation, 91–5)
  profits (1997), 77
  provincial, 70, 75, 83, 93, 94, 938(n11)
  sales, 77, 101–35(column 2), 939(n21)
  stock exchange listings, 96, 101–35 (column
    6)
  taxes paid (1997), 77
  '203 registered at national level', 938(n6)
  truck sector, 560
  workforce (1995), 77
  see also global business revolution; national
    team
trial cities, 68
trial enterprise groups, *see* trial business groups
TRIMs, *see* Trade-Related Investment Measures
Trinidad and Tobago: Ispat, 600
TRIPs, *see* Trade-Related Intellectual Property
  Rights

trucks, *see* lorries
trust, 42
TRW (USA), 166, 522, 526, 536
Tu-Ha Basin, 438
Tung Wing Iron and Steel Limited (HK), 676
tuoluosi ('trusts'), 363
Tupolev, 144, 178, 179
turbine blade construction, 329
turbine disks (LM2500), 214
turbine technology, 942(n1)
turbines, 328–9, 380, 391
  gas turbines, 331
  hydro, 378
  nuclear power steam, 380
  size, 329
  Three Gorges Project, 945(n20)
turbocharge technology, 530
Turkey, 506
  Ford matches entire GNP of, 534
  liberalization (1990s), 508
  purchase of missiles from USA, 158
  steel output (1974–96), 593
  top twenty steel-producing country (1991–8),
    617
Tutor Pharmaceutical (USA), 306
TVEs *see* township and village enterprises
TWA, 213
Twenty-First Century Forum (Beijing, 6.2000),
  917, 926–7, 935, 958(n3)
Twenty-One Demands (1915), 904
tyres, 57, 64, 456, 521, 526–9, 535, 860

UBS, 815, 817, 822, 958(n9)
UCH Plant (Pakistan), 387
Udell, H., *see* Berger, A.
UK, *see* United Kingdom
UK: Department of Trade and Industry, xxvi
UK: Foreign and Commonwealth Office, xxvi
UK: Ministry of Defence, 160
Ukraine, 616
ulcers, 250, 267–8
unemployment
  'Europe', 706
  PRC, 920–1
  South Africa, 920–1
  see also downsizing
Unilever, 34, 35, 264, 265
Union Bay Sportswear (Sanjiu), 289
Union Carbide, 455
Union of Soviet Socialist Republics (USSR,
  1922–91), 24, 165, 371
  aerospace, 144, 175, 178–80, 190
  aid to PRC, 95, 360, 375, 628, 644, 753,
    947(n44)
  approach to industrial reform, 3
  arms sales (1987–98), 151, 152, 178–9
  catch-up (steel), 594
  collapse, xxiii, 190, 910
  'disaster', 908–9
  disintegration, 909

Union of Soviet Socialist Republics (USSR, 1922–91) – *continued*
  downfall, 793
  economic effects of WW2, 37
  industrial reform policies, 2
  lack of indigenous 'competitive edge' corporations, 63
  large plants, 3
  large-scale plants 'core of industry', 853
  lessons for PRC (aerospace), 237–8
  nuclear accident (1986), 402
  oil production (1987–97), 405
  power generation plant (supplied to PRC), 360, 375, 947(n44)
  steel, 587, 588
  see also 'Former Soviet Union'; Russian Federation
unionization, 520–1
Uniroyal Goodrich (USA), 528
United Airlines (USA), 149
United Kingdom (UK)
  aircraft manufacturers (1950s), 166
  banking, 817, 821
  Big Bang (1986), 814
  'catch-up' process, 15
  coal, 698–9, 706, 707, 710, 711, 725, 733–4, 751, 752, 921
  corruption (C18), 873
  defence spending, 157
  demand for pharmaceuticals (per capita), 277
  economies of scale needed (defence equipment), 158
  enmity with Germany abandoned, 233
  Eurofighter, 158–9
  'first industrial nation', 15
  Fortune Global 500 (1997), 50
  globally-successful firms, 51
  home of free trade (1840s), 15
  industrial concentration, 14, 506
  'insurance density', 832
  iron ore costs (1997), 619
  Industrial Revolution, 15
  IT companies (2000), 764
  joins Airbus project (1979), 166
  market share of leading firms (1919–45), 15
  mentioned, 676, 952(n6)
  national energy security, 441
  number of auto manufacturers (1920), 506
  oil and gas reserves, 416
  oil and petrochemicals, 407
  pharmaceutical corporations, 248–9
  power industry, 733–4
  primary energy consumption, 401, 696, 697
  protectionism, 5
  royalty and licensing fees (paid), 785
  state intervention, 15, 858
  steel, 593, 594, 606, 617, 620, 641
  wages, 620, 752
United Security Company, 640
United States of America
  absorbs lessons of East Asian model, 48
  aerospace, 152–6, 233, 878
  agriculture, 5, 871–2
  anti-trust legislation, 15, 16
  armed forces (integration), 162
  arms trade, 151, 152, 157–8, 193
  automobiles, 506, 510–11, 538
  banking, 815, 817, 820
  BP-Solarex manufacturing facilities, 426
  'bull' market (equities), 48, 51
  carbon dioxide emissions, 430, 702
  civil airliners, 154–6
  coal, 698–9, 706, 707, 709–10, 718, 725
  competition among small firms, 3
  competitiveness, 48
  concentration of manufacturing output (1909–63), 14
  defence, 141, 150, 156, 157, 162, 192
  demand for pharmaceuticals (per capita), 277
  demand for energy (relative to PRC), 341
  dependence on Chinese and Indian 'brains', 929
  domestic manufacturing output produced by foreign-owned firms (1986–95), 31
  'dominant military power' in Asia, 195
  domination of IT sector, 48, 770, 771–2, 775, 790, 793, 810–11
  economic model for rest of world, 27
  economic uncertainties, 928–9
  electricity generation (fuel type, 1996), 698
  energy intensity (1998), 914
  energy reserves (1997), 716
  enforcement of WTO rules, 919
  enmity with Japan abandoned, 233
  enterprise groups, 897
  environmental regulation, 699, 701, 709
  ethylene crackers, 421
  exporter of oil to PRC (1995–7), 434
  exports 1997 (PRC comparison), 871
  FDI inflow, 31
  fear of exclusion from East Asia, 927
  global super-power, 2
  globally-successful firms, 51
  GNP (1998), 932
  government funding of aerospace industry, 141
  government procurement, 15–16
  independent diesel engine makers, 559
  industrial concentration, 37, 506, 710, 815
  industrialisation, 15
  influence of policy debates in PRC, 25
  information technology, 762, 764–5, 789, 928
  'insurance density', 832
  interest rates, 814
  internet, 789, 805
  Japan, 57, 233, 510–11, 950(n2)
  labour productivity (coal-mining, 1996), 711
  leadership of global business revolution, 46–51
  lessons for PRC (aerospace), 231–2

United States of America – *continued*
  market access (PRC IT sector), 790
  market leader (aerospace), 237–8
  mentioned, 922, 930
  'merger frenzy', 38
  military aircraft, 152–4, 174
  'most important market' (pharmaceuticals),
      269
  multinational corporations, 27
  national energy security, 441
  national security, 895
  natural gas production and reserves (1997),
      405
  nuclear accident (1979), 402
  number of auto manufacturers (1920), 506
  oil, 405, 406, 435
  oligopoly, 4, 11, 15–16, 35
  open society, 761
  output per worker (coal), 706
  personal computers per 1,000 people (1997),
      789
  petrol stations, 414
  pharmaceutical corporations, 248–9
  potential effect of anti-pollution measures on
      electricity prices, 703
  power (through leadership of IT revolution),
      761
  PRC entry into the WTO, xxiii
  PRC inter-action with, 2
  PRC rivalry for title of world's largest
      economy (1998–2020), 914
  primary energy, 401–2, 696, 697
  production of automobiles (1998), 508
  production of ethylene (1989–96), 451, 452
  production of plastics (1989–96), 451, 452
  production of synthetic fibre (1989–96),
      451
  protectionism, 15
  railways (C19), 13, 937(n2 to ch1)
  relative size of US and EU aerospace
      companies (1998), 166
  'relatively open' to PRC exports, 871
  reliance on hydrocarbon imports, 405
  research and development, 14, 35–6, 48, 95
  royalty and licensing fees (received), 785
  Sanjiu sales offices, 300
  Section 201 (anti-dumping), 868
  separation of sectors (financial services), 816,
      830
  sources of prosperity, 13
  space-based surveillance, 761
  state aid for research and development
      (aerospace), 175–6
  state protection (car industry), 533
  stock market, 48, 51, 414, 932, 935
  structure of output (1993), 700
  technological superiority to EU (aerospace),
      162–3
  telecommunications, 761, 789
  television sets per 1,000 people (1997), 789

  trade deficit with PRC, 872
  trade policy, 13
  wages (coal industry), 752
  world's largest defence market, 163
United States of America: steel industry
  alternatives to steel (construction industry),
      591
  appliances, 592
  automobiles (use of steel, 1976–88), 590
  BOF method, 596
  continuous casting, 596
  costs per ton of steel, 620–1
  electric furnace, 596
  fragmentation, 598
  'free riding on free trade' with the UK, 601,
      952(n6)
  imports (steel), 607
  industrial concentration (steel), 605
  iron ore costs (1997), 619
  Ispat, 600
  Japanese investment (1980s), 608
  labour cost per ton of coal, 620
  mentioned, 588, 676
  midi-mills, 599
  mini-mills, 598–600
  output (1933–40), 623
  output (1974–96), 593
  'plummeting profits' (steel, 1998), 607
  pollution (coke ovens), 593
  production, 594
  production methods (1997), 597
  productivity (coal), 620
  remuneration and productivity (1996), 641
  rise, 600
  Thyssen-Krupp willingness to produce in,
      612
  top ten steel-producing country (1991–8),
      616
  use of plastics (alternative to steel), 591
  wage costs (1997), 620
United Technologies, 239
  research and development, 142, 143
  size (1998), 166
  top five global aerospace company, 146
Universal Machine Works (UMW), 656, 672
  incorporated into Shougang Heavy
      Machinery Corporation, 672
  taken over by Shougang (3.1992), 656
Universal Music Group (1998–), 783
Universal Silencer (company), 530
Universal Studies, 783
universities (PRC), 94, 120
Unlogo Company (Italy), 303
unmanned aerial vehicles (UAVs), 157
Upjohn (USA), 255, 301
upper-middle-income countries
  expenditure on health, 767
  GNP (global top ten IT companies
      compared), 765
  public health expenditure (1900–7), 243

upstream capability, 460, 461–2, 464, 471, 485, 495, 609, 883
uranium, 715
urban areas: economic reform (PRC), 73
urbanization, 901
urea, 450, 490
US Air Force, 154, 155, 157
US-China Trade Council, 327
US Hydro-Carbon Corporation, 749
US Navy, 195
US Steel (1900–nd), 601–2, 613, 614, 670, 681–2
    challenge from Japan, 601
    diversification, 601
    joint ventures, 601
    management (Shougang contrast), 671
    output (1969), 951(n7)
    purchase of Marathon, 411
    saved from bankruptcy, 601
    see also USX
US Trade Representative, 779
USA: Defence Department, 153–4
USA: Environmental Protection Agency (EPA), 585n, 701
USA: Federal Aviation Authority (FAA), 204, 205, 207
USA: Federal Reserve, 817, 819, 833–4
USA: Food and Drugs Administration (FDA), 250, 301, 310, 319, 879
USDA, 872
Usiminas (Brazil), 600, 608
Usinor Steel Company (France), 498, 610–11, 840, 841, 848, 854, 889, 920
    crude steel output (1996–7), 602
    emerging European 'steel oligopoly', 609
    employees (1995), 888
    international investment and growth, 611
    national champion, 611, 859
    privatization (1995), 611, 859, 892
    product of state-orchestrated mergers, 858
    profits (1997), 957(n69)
    research and development, 595–6, 618, 694
    restructuring, 611
    revenues, profits, R&D (1998), 888
    sales (1997), 888
    stainless steel, 615
    takes over Cockerill-Sambrell (1998), 611
Usinor-Sacilor, 641, 952(n10)
USSR, *see* Union of Soviet Socialist Republics
USX (nd-)
    crude steel output (1996–7), 602
    diversification into oil, 678
    'previously US Steel', 673
    remuneration and labour productivity (1995), 641
utilities, 85, 336

vaccines, 268
Valeo, 519, 535

acquisition of ITT's Electrical Systems (1998), 525
air conditioners, 524, 535
'500 patents' (1997), 521
globalization, 521
joint ventures (PRC), 546
multinational supplier firm, 57
research and development, 535
'3,000 research scientists', 521
turnover, profit, R&D (1998), 522
value chain, 42, 43, 45, 48, 171–2, 847, 856
    automobile industry, 511, 512
    extending beyond car manufacture, 512
    global IT, 787
    information technology, 779
    oil sector (PRC), 484
VAM, *see* Vodafone AirTouch Mannesmann
Varig (airline), 149
vehicle
    components, 519, 536
    engines, 529, 536
    refitting, 539
    repair, 512
vehicles, 274
    environmentally-friendly, 510
    institutional structure (PRC), 538–42
    research and development, 596
    Sanjiu, 316
    second layer enterprises (PRC), 560
Venezuela
    ethylene crackers, 421
    GNP no more than Ford's global procurement (1998), 534
    investments by CNPC, 441
    number of companies in *Fortune* 500 (1998), 47n
    oil, 355, 416, 421
    receptive to foreign investment (oil sector), 413
Venus (Microsoft 'set-on-box' technology, 1999–), 797
vertical integration, 14, 44, 147
    CNPC, 843
    Daqing Petroleum Administration, 444
    keiretsu, 57
    Nissan, 516
    oil sector (PRC), 471
    PRC, 72, 847
    Shenhua Project, 747–8
    Sichuan Changhong Electric, 272
    Sinopec, 843
    steel industry, 600, 956(n59)
    vehicle-makers (PRC), 544–5
    vertical integration
    Yiqi, 561
Viacom (USA), 781, 787, 806
vicious circle
    Russian Federation, 910
    Shougang, 888
    tendency to diversify (PRC), 849

Vickers (UK), 181, 227, 228
video, 782, 783, 784, 808
video conferencing, 106
video links, 332
Vietnam, 178, 387, 388, 506, 609, 619
vinyl acetate, 422
Virgin, 818
Virgin Mary, 409
Virgin Money, 819
virtuous circles
    aerospace, 148–9, 162, 239
    IT firms (USA), 788
    Shougang, 663
Visteon, 57, 520, 886
    see also Ford Motor Company
vitamins, 282, 283
    catch-up possibilities, 64
    multivitamins, 282
    Vitamin C, 64, 296, 942(n20)
Vivazzi (6.2000–), 784
Vivendi (France), 784
    merger with Seagram (6.2000), 784
Vivendi/Seagram, 783–4
Vnukovo (airline), 179
Vodafone: merger with AirTouch (USA), 778
Vodafone AirTouch (UK)
    market capitalization (2000), 764
    merger with Mannesmann (Germany), 778
    sales revenue (2000), 764
Vodafone AirTouch Mannesmann (VAM
    2000–), 784, 786
    corporate culture (PRC contrast), 802
    CTHK comparison, 804
    international comparison (12.1999), 800
    market capitalization, revenue, profits
        (12.1999), 800
    statistics, 778
    'wireless data platform', 778
Voest-Alpine furnaces, 662
voice mail, 791
Voicestream (USA), 803
Voith, 356, 945(n20)
Volkswagen (VW), 854, 920
    commercial aluminium car (Audi 80), 590–1
    comparative size (global, 1998), 561
    entirely state-owned (until 1960), 504
    foreign assets, sales, employment (1997), 509
    German national champion (1937–), 504
    interests in Mercosur, 508
    interests in Eastern Europe (post-1989), 508
    joint ventures, 101, 513, 534, 546, 886
    Octava saloon car, 950(n6)
    output (PRC comparison), 538
    output, turnover, profit, R&D (1998), 533
    overtaken by Daimler-Chrysler, 514
    partially state-owned (1990), 504
    plant at Mlada Bolesaw, 950(n6)
    privatization, 892
    research and development, 510
    sales, profits, employees, R&D (1998), 561

transformation (SOE national champion into
        privatized TNC), 859
Volvo, 59, 860, 861
    aero-engines, 173
    auto business acquired by Ford (1999), 515,
        518
    breakdown of alliance with Renault, 513
    buses, 201, 229
    concentrates on lorries, 515, 518
    joint ventures in PRC, 201–2, 540–1, 566
    merger with Saab, 518
    merger with Scania, 534
    saloon vehicle branch purchased by Ford,
        264
    self-sufficient in heavy-duty engines, 566
    suppliers, 519
    taken over by larger firm, 533
Volvo-Scania, 518, 532, 583
VW, see Volkswagen

Wacker (chemicals), 263
wages, 223
    coal sector, 711
    components, 520–1
    Guangxi, 580
    Posco, 605
    PRC, 306, 313, 942(n25–7)
    TVEs, 891
    Yuchai, 579
Wal-Mart, 226, 479
Waldrich Coburg (German company), 948(n53)
Waldrich Siegen (Germany), 948(n53)
Walker Manufacturing (subsidiary of Tenneco),
    524
Walters, J.P., 411
Wang Cunna, 946(n40)
Wang Jianming (CEO Yuchai), 548–9, 551, 553,
    567, 575, 576–7, 582, 583, 841, 859
    'Big Yuchai' plan, 576–7
    biography, 575–6
    cited, 501
    'dynamic', 501–2, 568, 585
    explicit goal, 558
    labour relations, 578–9
    lobbying efforts, 568
    relations with Dongfeng and Yiqi, 557–8, 568
    rise and fall, 501–2
    'risk-taking entrepreneur type', 585
Wang Jun, 274
Wang Lixiong, 935
Wang Wenxiang, 946(n40)
Wang Xiaoqiang, Dr, xxiv-xxv, 935, 937
Wang Xuejia, xxiv-xxv
Wang Zhen, 274
Wang Zuxun, General, 194
Wanjie Group: national team player, 133
Wanli (coal-mine), 753–4, 755
Wanxiang Group, 134
Warburg (UK), 817; taken over by UBS,
    958(n9)

warfare, 142, 762
Warner-Lambert, 247, 250, 257, 258–9, 260
washing machines, 198, 272
'Washington Consensus', 2–3, 4
watchmaking (Samsung), 53
water heaters, 108
water transport (PRC, 1978–97), 432
Watson Pharmaceuticals, 262
Waxicun Power Station (Hebei Province), 367
Wealth of Nations (Smith, 1776), 873
websites, 774, 780, 790
Wei Maohe, 726
Weifang Diesel Plant, 562
Weihai Plant (power generation), 944(n17)
weituoren, '[right to sign] contracts', 684–5
Welch, Jack (CEO GE), 392
welding, 329, 379, 380, 948(n52)
welfare
    PRC, 914, 915, 921
    Yuchai, 579–80
Wendt, Gary (CEO, GE Capital), 332
West: share of world manufacturing output
    (1750–1998), 900
West Africa, 415, 434
Western Europe
    arms sales (1987–98), 151, 152
    automobile market (projected growth,
        1995–2001), 507
    challenged by East Asia, 507
    economic effects of WW2, 37
    electricity generation capacity (1990–2010),
        697
    exporter of oil to PRC (1995–7), 434
    lorry sales (1995, 2005), 509
    production and sales of automobiles (1998),
        508
    projected demand for power equipment
        (1980–2010), 334
    share of world electricity generation
        (1995–2015), 335
    steel production (1991–7), 589
    see also advanced economies; European
        Union
Western Star (Canadian lorry-maker), 535
Westfälische Drahtindustrie (Germany), 615
Westinghouse, 336, 860
    alliance with Rolls-Royce, 330–1, 942(n1)
    ancillary equipment, 365
    co-operation with HPEC, 377, 397
    dealings with HPEC, 372
    involvement in PRC power equipment
        industry, 358, 945(n25)
    joint tenders with HPEC, 387
    joint venture in Shanghai, 358, 375
    limits, 398
    links with Wugang, 629
    losses (power equipment branch, 1995–6),
        337
    market share worldwide (power generation
        equipment, 1993–8), 337

marketing in India, 942(n1)
    sale of non-nuclear business to Siemens
        (1997), 337–8, 390, 398, 943(n5–6),
        949(n68)
    servicing, 394
    size (late 1990s), 330
    steam turbine manufacture, 943(n7)
    technology and marketing agreement with
        MHI, 336
    technology transfer (nuclear) to PRC, 358
    technology transfer to SEC, 389–90
Weston, John (CEO, BAe), xxvi, 165, 236
wheat, 869, 871, 872
wheels, 522, 525, 950(n9)
Whirlpool: little to fear from PRC competition
    (post-WTO accession), 863
'white goods', 849
White House, 153
Whittaker Corporation, 147
wholesale sector, 919, 923
Wilkinson, Bill, 704
wind power, 697
windscreens, 522
wine, 316, 869
Wings (airline alliance), 149
Wipro (India), 23, 788
wireless telephones, 776, 777, 795–6, 931
    European lead (threatened by USA), 777
    hardware, 795–6
    internet communication, 776, 778
    penetration (developing countries), 788
    per 1,000 people (global 1997), 789
    PRC, 790, 798, 799–800, 807, 922
    third generation, 774, 778, 782, 796, 801,
        807–8
wood (as energy source), 426
Woodard, Ron, 155
world
    automobile market (projected growth,
        1995–2001), 507
    coal consumption (1986–96), 698
    coal output (1980–95), 699
    coal reserves, 718
    distribution of steel production, 592–5
    economy, xxiii, 5
    electricity generation (fuel type, 1990–2010),
        696
    electricity generation capacity (1990–2010),
        697
    energy demand, 695–6
    energy reserves (1997), 716
    lorry sales (1995, 2005), 509
    manufacturing output (1750–1998), 900
    natural gas production and reserves (1997),
        405
    number of 'competitive edge' companies
        (1997–8), 50
    oil production (1987–97), 405
    political economy (twenty-first century), xxiii
    primary energy consumption (1986–96), 696

world – *continued*
primary energy consumption (1987–97), 402
primary energy consumption (1996), 697
production and sales of automobiles (1998), 508
regional differences in economic growth (1980–98), 851
steel (long-term changes in regional distribution, 1974–96), 593
steel industry, 587–622
steel output (1974–96), 593
steel production (1991–7), 589
steel production (1991–8), 616–17
steel production methods (1997), 597
top ten automobile companies (1998), 533
World Bank, 2, 4, 909, 913
advice to South Korea (ignored), 604
Chinese economy (1997), 67
energy efficiency (PRC), 715
interpretation of PRC economic success (1970s-), 3
PRC infrastructure requirements, 871
World Coal Institute, 698
WorldCom, 786
World Economic Forum, 917, 935
World Health Organization, 748
World Telecoms Agreement (2.1997), 761, 779, 785, 786–7
PRC accession, 792
Russia non-signatory, 786
'triumph for American way', 761, 786
world trade
liberalization, 28–9
rise of East Asia, 507
steel crisis (1998–9), 607–8
warning of general trade war (1.1999), 608
World Trade Organization (WTO), xxiii, 29, 244:   application of rules (implications for PRC), 790–2, 793, 794, 796, 806, [808–]809, 811
application of rules (Mexican resistance), 803
Bombardier and Embraer, 181–2, 878
challenges faced by PRC on entry (autos and auto components sector), 501, 517, 543
China agrees to join (1999), 4–5, 25
competition issues, 491
conditions for PRC entry, 813
developing country resistance, 928–9
environmental conditions, 431
impending PRC entry, 497
implications for PRC (financial services), 825, 831–7
implications for PRC (political stability), 825
international economic relations, 784–5
internet sector, 781, 784
investment issues, 491
local content regulations, 395, 949(n66)
lower tariffs (PRC steel industry), 623
negotiations with PRC, 800
pharmaceuticals, 325

power equipment tariffs, 348
restrictions on protectionism, 507
retail sector (PRC), 460
rules, 930
telecommunications (challenge facing PRC), 777–8, 801–2
telecommunications (Mexico), 779
terms agreed for China's entry (11.1999), 28
threat to PRC oil corporations, 489, 491, 494, 494–5, 496
uncertain future, 928–9
USA's 'best tool for opening PRC market', 401
see also TRIPs; World Telecoms Agreement
World Trade Organization (PRC accession), 69, 70, 72, 101, 104, 112, 125, 327, 537–8, 856, 863–4, 916–33
alternative outcome, 925–33
Asian crisis (response), 926–8
central role for East Asian people in US high technology, 929
'dancing with wolves', 762, 793
deep-seated Chinese ambitions, 925–6
fears for PRC competitiveness, 862–3
five-year adjustment period (for PRC), 864–5
high-quality, ambitious Chinese large enterprise managers, 926
impact on PRC industrial policy, 864–76
increased East Asian co-operation, 926–8
intellectual framework, 898
intense competition produces opportunities, 929
'internet opium', 924–5
IT and adjustment process, 921–23
painful adjustment, 919–21
potential impact on international relations, 896, 924
PRC observance of rules (scenario), 923, 925
PRC's ability to compete, 876–92
pressure on PRC to apply rules, 919
prospects, 933
renewed East Asian business confidence, 929
role model of global oligopoly, 929–33
socio-political consequences, 923–5
shocks, 925
uncertainties over US economy, 928–9
US debates, 762, 785
US economic imperialism, 924
World Trade Organization (PRC-US Agreement, 11.1999), xxvi, 790–3, 813, 825, 835, 840, 864–70, 930
automobiles, 887
coal, 891–2
contracts (commercial criteria), 878, 882, 891
distribution networks (PRC), 866, 890
enforcement (PRC), 870
farm products, 871
foreign investment (PRC), 865, 872–3
foreign production facilities (in PRC), 890
general measures (agreed by PRC), 865–6

World Trade Organization (PRC-US
    Agreement, 11.1999) – *continued*
  impact on trade and investment (PRC), 870–3
  intellectual property rights (PRC), 866
  joint ventures, 878, 881, 884, 887, 890, 891
  local content (PRC), 866
  monitoring, 870, 895
  non-economic objectives, 873–6, 917
  non-tariff barriers (PRC), 865–6
  opposition within PRC, 895
  patents, 881
  potential political repercussions, 895–6
  PRC trade surplus with USA put at risk, 872
  PRC (non-economic objectives), 873–5
  'priority of US business interests', 894
  procurement, 884
  quotas (PRC), 865–6
  raw materials, 884–5
  right to export to PRC, 866, 872, 887
  soft loans, 884–5, 891–2
  speed of implementation (PRC), 869–70
  steel, 889
  strict PRC observation (scenario), 923
  sub-contracting work, 878
  subsidies, 891–2
  support for SOEs (PRC), 866
  tariffs (PRC), 865
  technology transfer (PRC), 866, 878, 884,
    887, 890
  trade performance requirements (PRC), 866
  USA (non-economic objectives), 875–6
  USA 'principal beneficiary', 871
World War I, 904
World War II, 518
  China-Japan, 905
  economic effects, 37
  Japan Steel, 603
  Volkswagen, 504
woven products, 130
WPP/Young, 781
WTO, *see* World Trade Organization
Wu, Gordon, 351
Wu Bangguo, 71, 81, 897–8, 937–8(n4)
Wu Chengming, 898
Wu Qing, xxv
Wu Yixin, 455, 473, 495, 841
Wu Zhao, Mr, 272
Wuda (coal-mine), 753–4
Wugang, *see* Wuhan Iron and Steel Group
Wuhan, 360, 564, 642
Wuhan Iron and Steel Group (Wugang)
  debt, 684
  energy efficiency, 638
  mentioned, 384
  mergers, 640
  missed merger opportunity, 862
  national team player (first batch), 114
  No 3 Steel Plant, 629
  output structure (1997), 646
  principal steel products (1997), 636

  product quality, 638
  productivity, 659
  profitability, 638, 643
  remuneration and labour productivity (1997),
    641
  reports directly to SBMI, 622
  return on investment (1980–90), 660
  rumours (1998) of merger with Baogang, 640
  sales (1997), 888
  social responsibilities, 642
  steel production methods (1997), 597
  technological modernization, 629
  top ten steel producer (PRC 1997), 634
  wages, 658
wujing (Army Police), 291, 941(n16)
Wuxi (engine-maker)
  capacity, 561
  competitive advantage, 565
  competitor to Yuchai, 552
  diesel engine fuel injection components
    (Bosch joint venture), 546
  output, 561
  6110 series (engine), 561
  Yiqi takes full control (1995), 561
Wuxi Pharmaceutical Company, 300

XAC, *see* Xian Aircraft Company/Corporation
XAC Aluminium Company, 201–2, 214, 217,
    226
XAC International, 214, 226
Xenical (anti-obesity drug), 250
xi wu ju (Five Western District) mines, 749,
    753–6
Xiamen
  CATIC subsidiary, 224
  mine-mouth coal price (6.1994), 728
  thermal coal price (7.1997), 729
Xiamen Jinlong United Automotive Industry
    Ltd (HK), 565
xian (county) level
  pharmaceutical distribution (PRC), 299
Xian
  aircraft manufacturing, 186, 662
  pharmaceuticals, 282
Xian: Holiday Inn, 313
Xian Aero-Engine Company/Corporation, 190,
    200
Xian Aircraft Company/Corporation (XAC)
  AE-100, 212, 860
  assigned to 'AVIC 1' (no date, *c*.1999), 230
  bus-producer, 199
  competition with CAC, 215, [218–]219
  competitors (two types), 844–5
  disappointed aspirations, 215, 216
  joint venture with McDonnell-Douglas,
    208–10
  joint venture with Volvo (bus production,
    1994–), 541–2
  miscellaneous, 190, 846, 877
  national team player (first batch), 199[–]201

Xian Aircraft Company/Corporation (XAC) –
continued
 non-aviation production, 201, 229
 statistics, 200
 sub-contracting work (1980–), 214–16,
  217–18
 subsidiary of AVIC, 199
 Yun-7 turbo-prop plane, 205–6
 see also aircraft
Xian Aircraft Group, 112
Xian Jannsen, 283
Xian Power Generation Machinery
 Manufacturing Group, 111
Xian Volvo Bus Company, 201–2, 217–18
xiang (township), 727
Xiangfan engine plant (Dongfeng Group), 564,
 566
Xiangfan Iron and Steel Group, 640
xiao er quan ('small and complete'), 371, 464
Xiaofeng Technology and Equipment
 Corporation, 273, 276
xiaoping ('little bottles'), 911
Xie, Andy, 916
Xifei, 861, 845
Xinfei (Henan), 573
Xinjiang (province)
 electricity grid, 345
 geographical location of national team
  members, 82, 83
 oil pipeline from Kazakhstan ('shelved'), 441
 oil reserves, 883
 oilfields, 438
 regional development, 121
Xinjiang Automobile Works (Dongfeng), 564, 565
Xinjiang complex: managed by New CNPC
 (1998–), 470
Xinjiang Construction Group, 75, 86
Xinjiang Electric Power Company, 110
Xinjiang Petroleum Administration (XJPA),
 438, 442
Xinjiang Production and Construction Corps
 (1954–), 121
Xinjiang Textiles Group, 86, 113
Xinwen Mining Bureau, Shandong (coal
 producer), 720
Xinyu Far East Ferro Manganese (company),
 956(n60)
Xishan Mining Bureau, Shanxi (coal producer)
 average mining depth, 737
 output, reserves, mine depths (1996), 736
 quality of coal, 737
 transport costs (1997), 720
XJPA, see Xinjiang Petroleum Administration
Xu Damao, 946(n40)
Xu Dixin, 898
Xuzhou Construction Machinery Group, 105
Xuzhou Mining Bureau, Jiangsu, 720

Ya'an Pharmaceutical Plant (Sichuan), 308, 309
 acquired by Sanjiu (1995), 309

Ya'an Sanjiu Pharmaceutical Co. Ltd, 309
Yahoo! (USA), 764, 780, 787, 806
Yamaichi Securities, 57
Yamamoto, Mr (of Fuji Bank), 56
Yancheng (Shanxi Province), 715
Yang Ying (Jenny), xxiv-xxv
Yangchen (PRC): Kia joint venture, 506
Yangcheng Power Plant, 349, 944(n15)
Yangquan Mining Bureau (Shanxi), 720, 737
Yangtze River, 901
 hydroelectric plants, 357
 see also Three Gorges Project
Yangwei chongji (medicine), 310
Yangzhou Motor
 joint venture with Mercedes (buses), 541
 purchases of engines from Yuchai (1995),
  555
Yangzhou Passenger Car Works
 'second layer' enterprise with Dongfeng
  capital participation, 564
Yangzi Petrochemical Company/Corporation
 (Nanjing), 117, 466, 469
 joint venture with BASF, 454
 listed subsidiary ('A-share') of (New)
  Sinopec, 472
Yanhua Corporation
 floated (HK 1997), 453
 listed subsidiary of (New) Sinopec, 472
 result of Yanshan merger with Tianjin Hangu
  (1997), 454
Yankuang Group (1996–), 119
Yanshan Oil (Beijing), 444, 446, 464, 862
 merger with Tianjin Hangu Petrochemical
  Plant (1997), 454
 see also Yanhua Corporation
Yantai, 547, 810
Yantian (port), 315
Yanzhou (Shandong): mining, 119
Yanzhou Coal Company, Shandong, 720, 736,
 737
Yanzhou Diesel Engine, 560
Yanzhou Group: workforce, 79
Yarville National Bancorp (Hamilton, NJ), 819
Yawata Steel (post-war), 603
 merger with Fuji (1970), 603
 see also New Japan Steel
Yawata Steelworks (1896–1934), 602–3
Ye Qing, 734–5, 749, 841, 859, 958(n7)
Yellow Peril (Wang Lixiong), 935
Yellow River, 747
Yeltsin, Boris (b 1931), 909
Yeung, Dr Godfrey, xxv
Yi He Tuan ('Group of Righteous and
 Harmonious Fists'), 904
yibashou (company head), 315
Yichang Three Gorges Project Duoneng
 Company, 944(n16)
Yiqi (First Automobile Works), 438, 444, 464, 496
 ability to compete on global level playing
  field, 885–7

Yiqi (First Automobile Works) – *continued*
  comparative size (global, 1998), 561
  customer preference for Yuchai engines, 557
  Dalian (engine-maker), 552
  demand for diesel engines, 557
  deteriorating relations with Yuchai, 557–8
  diesel engine production (1998), 559
  diesel engine capability, 567
  'diversified output structure', 560
  and Dongfeng, 567
  engine guarantees, 558
  favoured enterprise (by PRC state), 560
  'Fordist' path, 561
  'group' structure, 560
  in-house production (diesel engines), 582
  influence with central government, 568
  joint venture with VW, 539, 540, 547
  largest automobile plant (PRC), 560
  leading lorry-maker (PRC), 518, 534, 541,
      542, 553, 561
  local champion, 566
  losses (1996), 576
  middle-level player (global lorry output), 542
  minuscule (in international comparison), 534,
      538
  missed merger opportunity, 861
  No 1 Automobile Plant, 560–3
  output of light trucks (1998), 554
  output (truck), sales, profits, employees
      (1998), 542
  petrol engine capability, 567
  'potential market' for Yuchai, 561
  relationship with suppliers, 561, 950(n12)
  relationship with Chaoyang Diesel, 565
  revenues, profits, employees, R&D (1998),
      887
  sales, profits, employees, output (1998), 556
  sales, profits, employees, R&D (1998), 561
  saloon car production, 541, 560
  second layer enterprises, 560
  strained relations with Yuchai, 568, 577
  takes full ownership of Dalian and Wuxi
      Diesel Plants (1995), 561
  vertical integration, 561
  Wuxi (engine-maker), 552
  and Yuchai, 568, 577
  alternative usage: 'FAW'; 'Number One
      Auto[mobile Group]'; 'Yiqi Auto
      Corporation'
Yiqi Group (First Automobile Works Group),
      80, 97, 138
  Dalian Diesel Plant, 561
  description, 101
  name in Chinese, 101
  sales, 77
  workforce, 77
  Wuxi Diesel Plant, 561
Yizheng: listed subsidiary of (New) Sinopec,
      472
Yizheng Chemical Fibre Company, 117, 466

Yizheng Group, 97, 117
YKK, 861, 862
Yonekura, Seiichiro, 678
Young, R., *see* Berger, A.
YPF (Argentina), 408, 409, 413, 494, 860, 861
  links with Petrobas (Brazil), 494
  missed merger opportunity, 862
  national champion, 494
  privatized in 1993, 408, 409, 494
  see also Repsol
Yuan Qihong (HPEC Company Secretary), 372,
      946(n40)
Yuan Shikai, 904
Yuchai
  'China Yuchai International' (CYI), 571n
  'Guangxi Machinery Company', 571n
  'Guangxi Yuchai Machinery Company
      Limited', 549
  'Yuchai Diesel Engine Company', 501
  'Yulin Diesel Engine Company', 571n
Yuchai Diesel Engine Company (Yulin City,
      Guangxi Province), 501, 543, 548–85,
      841, 845, 859
  ability to compete on global level playing
      field, 885–7
  accounting procedures, 573
  Big Yuchai, 569, 576–7, 951(n22)
  business strategy, 566, 568–69
  capacity, 548–49
  collapse, 550, 580–3
  comparative size, 584
  competitors, 558–68
  conclusion, 581–5
  consolidated profit and loss account
      (1991–5), 549
  customers, 553–8
  development of a heavy-duty truck engine,
      553
  diesel engine production (1998), 559
  directors, 574
  downsizing, 580
  employees, 550
  engine castings, 951(n22)
  ethos, 577–8
  expansion plans, 568
  foreign flotation, 571
  foundry (needed), 576, 581, 951(n22)
  global giants (in comparison, 1998), 584
  'greater caution' advisable, 566
  growth (1975–98), 550
  growth, 548–50
  guarantees, 557–8
  heavy-duty trucks, 565–6
  and Hong Leong Holdings (HLA), 568,
      572–5, 585
  housing, 579
  improving quality of fuel pump injection,
      553
  independence of provincial government
      control, 571

Yuchai Diesel Engine Company (Yulin City, Guangxi Province) – *continued*
institutional change, 569–77
international comparison, 583, 584
joint stock company (5.1993–), 573–4
joint venture route, 568, 572, 577, 582
labour organization, 577–80
market growth and structure, 551–3
market-oriented firm to Sino-foreign joint venture, 571–3
marketing, 557–8
markets, 551–8
merger activity, 842–3, 848
missed merger opportunity, 861
New York listing, 548, 552, 573–4, 574–7, 951(n21)
ominous developments (mid-1990s), 565
output of medium-duty diesel engines (1988–91), 571
output, sales, profits, employees (1975–98), 550
overseas partners, 572
peak year (1995), 549
product choice and development, 552–3
production line, 548, 553, 567, 571, 578, 585, 950(n11)
profit handover/retention, 569, 570, 951(n18)
profits, 549, 550, 552, 556, 567, 569, 575, 951(n18)
recruitment, 578
relationship with Dongfeng, 554–9, 566–7, 568, 576
remuneration, 579
research and development, 567
revenues, profits, employees, R&D (1998), 886
rise and fall, 548–50, 581–5
sales (1995), 555
sales, profits (1970–93), 570
sales, profits, employees, R&D (1998), 584
second-hand equipment, 885
service network, 552, 567
shareholders, 573
6105 engine, 550, 552, 553, 558, 562, 567, 569, 572, 585
6108 engine, 552–3, 569, 572
6112 engine, 549, 553, 571, 573, 581
specialist engine-maker, 546
strained relations with Erqi and Yiqi, 568
supplier relationships, 580–1
technology gap, 583
traditional SOE to market-oriented firm, 569–71
training, 578–9
'trial LME, not part of trial business groups', 938(n3)
upgrading the 6105 engine, 552, 572, 585, 950(n10)
wage costs, 567

Wang Jianming, 568, 575–6
welfare benefits, 579–80
and Yiqi, 568
Yuchai International Holdings Company Limited
CYI Limited ownership structure, 574
Yuchai Machinery Company Limited, 573, 951(n20)
CYI Limited ownership structure, 574
partly state-owned, 573
Yuchai Revolutionary Committee, 575
'Yuchai spirit', 577–8
Yuejin, 103
Yuejin Auto Group Corporation, 554, 559
Yuejin Group Company, 562
Yuejin Group Nanjing Shandong Engine Plant, 562
Yugoslavia, 150, 435, 909
bombing of PRC embassy (Belgrade), 194, 895
war, 162–3, 194
Yulin City (Guangxi Province), 502, 571, 578
'essentially a huge, poor village', 502
labour force 'poor quality', 577
'rough, backward', 577
see also Yuchai Diesel Engine Company
Yulin City Asset Management Bureau, 573
Yulin Diesel
later Yuchai, 571, 575n
restructured (7.1992), 575n
machinery business transferred to Guangxi Yuchai Machinery Business, 575n
transferred to State Holding Company (except machinery business), 575n
Yunnan
geographical location of national team members, 82, 83
FAW (Yiqi), 101
Yunnan Automobile Works (Dongfeng), 563, 564
Yunnan Engine Plant
main product, output, profits, taxes (1995), 562
Yunnan Internal Combustion
diesel engine production (1998), 559

zaibatsu, 16–17, 54
Zeneca, 249, 264
Zhang Aiping, General, 941(n18)
Zhang Jin, Ms, xxv
Zhang Qi, 939(n24).
Zhang Wuchang: cited, 501
Zhang Xinchuan, Professor, xxv
Zhang Yichen, 947(n41)
Zhang Zhen, General, 941(n18)
Zhang Zhuoyuan, 947(n41)
Zhao Wangqi, 294
Zhao Xinxian, Professor, 841, 859, 879
advertising strategy, 298
CEO Sanjiu, 289–90, 310–12, 316, 941(n9)

Zhao Xinxian, Professor – *continued*
  General Manager, Nanfang, 294, 296, 303,
    305
  'leading researcher' at Guangzhou Army
    Hospital, 291, 322
  options, 296–7
  Party Secretary of Nanfang, 304
  'powerful motivator', 304
  Sanjiu's 'legal person', 294
  wages, 306
Zhapu: sea-going ships (C18), 901
Zhejiang (province)
  China Unicom joint venture activity, 810
  coal, 719, 720
  Dongfang boiler plant, 390
  nuclear plant at Qinshan, 357
  nuclear power (planned), 357
  Tongrentang Group, 125
  wireless telecommunications, 799
Zhejiang Acrylic Fibre Plant, 456
Zhejiang Electric Power Company, 110
Zhejiang Goods and Materials Group, 132
Zhejiang Juhua Group, 118
zheng di yi ('strive to be number one'), 579
Zheng Xiaoyu, 286
Zhengda (Thai investment firm), 310
Zhengzhou Bus Company, 577
Zhenhai Refinery
  listed subsidiary of (New) Sinopec, 449, 472
Zhenjiang Shipbuilding Plant, 655
Zhenjiang Shipping company, 676
zhongdian ('focal' LMEs), 937–8(n4)
Zhongguo ('Chinese nation'), 368
Zhongguoren ('Chinese people'), 368
Zhonglian Automotive Electronics Company
  (Shanghai), 545

Zhongshui Group, 135
Zhongyang maoyi kaifa gongsi (Central Trade
  Development Company, Taiwan), 387
Zhongyuan Petrochemical, 469
Zhou Beifang, 643, 646, 953(n20)
Zhou Enlai, Premier (1898–1975), 203, 905
Zhou Guanwu, 588, 646, 650–1, 652, 663–4,
  676, 678–9, 680, 682, 684–5, 841, 842,
  859, 888, 953(n30)
  anti-Japanese guerrilla leader, 669
  monthly earnings, 666n
  retirement (2.1995), 643, 657, 953(n42)
  strategy, 670
  see also Shougang
Zhou Keyu, 941(n18)
Zhou Yinong, 473
Zhou Zouming, 365
Zhoulu *xian* (Hebei province), 315, 942(n29)
Zhoushan islands (near Shanghai), 640
Zhu Guiming, 859
Zhu Rongji, 71, 430, 702, 839, 935
Zhu Yuli (head of AVIC), 212, 230, 841
zhua da, fang xiao ('gasping the large and
  letting go the small'), 639
Zhuang Gu Guan Jie (pills), 303
Zhufeng Hotel (Chengdu), 312–13
zhugan yewu ('core business'), 476
Zhuhai Power Plant, 352
Zhunge'er (coal-mine), 753–5
  Heidaigou No 1, 753–5
  Heidaigou No 2, 753–5
  Haerwusu, 753–5
Zigong area (Sichuan), 433
Zimbabwe, 690, 710
ziyuanfei (natural resource fees), 653